£14
set

Aigun

Ussuri

HEILUNGKIANG

Sungari

Harbin

Changchun

KIRIN

Tumen

NINGHSIA-HUI
tonomous Region

Autonomous

Region

Mukden
(Shenyang)

LIAONING

Yalu

Port Arthur-Dairen

Mongolian

Huhehot

Great Wall

WU-T'AI

Peking
Tientsin

HOPEH

Paoting

Yinchwan

T'AI-HANG

Taiyuan

Tsinan

Tsingtao

chow

Wu-ch'i
Yenan

SHANSI

SHANTUNG

Hui-ning

Sian

Hwang Ho

(Yellow)

Chengchow

Grand Canal

KIANGSU

La-tzu-t'ou

SHENSI

HONAN

Hwai

Hofei

Nanking

Shanghai

ourth Front
Army

HUPEH

TA-PIEH

ANHWEI

SZECHWAN

Yangtze

Wuhan

Hangchow

Chengtu

Tung-t'ing

CHEKIANG

Chungking

P'o-yang

Changsha

Nanchang

CHINGKANGSHAN

Tsun-i

KIANGSI

Kweiyang

First Front Army

HUNAN

Juichin

FUKIEN

Foochow

KWEICHOW

Amoy

TAIWAN

KWANGSI-CHUANG
Aut Region

KWANGTUNG

Canton

Swatow

Nanning

Macao

HONG KONG

VUNI

Biographic Dictionary
of Chinese Communism
1921–1965

VOLUME II: Lo Jui-ch'ing–Yun Tai-ying

Donald W. Klein / *Anne B. Clark*

Harvard University Press   Cambridge, Massachusetts   1971

Contents

ABBREVIATIONS

CB	*Current Background*
CCP	Chinese Communist Party
CPPCC	Chinese People's Political Consultative Conference
ECMM	*Extracts from China Mainland Magazines*
JMJP	*Jen-min Jih-pao* (*The People's Daily*)
KMT	Kuomintang (i.e., the Chinese Nationalists' political party)
NPC	National People's Congress
PLA	People's Liberation Army
PRC	People's Republic of China
SCMM	*Selections from China Mainland Magazines*
SCMP	*Survey of China Mainland Press*

Lo Jui-ch'ing

(c.1906–   ; Nan-ch'ung, Szechwan). Former
minister of Public Security; member, CCP Secretariat and Central Committee.

Lo Jui-ch'ing, one of the earliest members of
the Red Army, was a top staff and political
officer during the Sino-Japanese War and the
civil war against the Nationalists in the late forties. He was elected an alternate member of the
Party Central Committee in 1945 and a full
member in 1956. He is best known for his role
as minister of Public Security during the first
decade of the PRC.

Lo was reportedly born into a landlord family. Japanese sources assert that he came from
Liang-shan (Liang-p'ing) in east Szechwan, but
it is more likely that he comes from Nan-ch'ung,
formerly known as Shunking (Shun-ch'ing), an
important regional center in the Chia-ling river
basin in central Szechwan. He received some vo-
cational training in a Nan-ch'ung school run by
Chang Lan, the well-known head of the China
Democratic League until his death in 1955. He
then went to Canton where he was enrolled in
the fifth class of the Whampoa Military Academy. The fifth class matriculated from February
to November 1926, but because the Northern
Expedition began in mid-1926, many of the
cadets left the classrooms for the battlefronts
and then returned to a more normal training
program at the northern branch of the academy
in Wuhan after the Northern Expeditionary
Forces captured that city in the fall of 1926.
It appears that Lo followed this pattern. Like a
large number of his fellow cadets, he also joined
the CCP at approximately this time.

Lo took part in the Communist uprising at
Nanchang on August 1, 1927 (see under Yeh
T'ing), an event in which many ex-Whampoa
students participated. However, his role at Nanchang must have been minor, because there is
no record of the nature of his activities. After the
failure at Nanchang, the Communists moved
south to Kwangtung, and after sustaining further
defeats, many of them made their way to the
Hunan-Kiangsi border base at Chingkangshan.
In any case, Lo was at Chingkangshan in 1928,
serving there in the Fourth Red Army, led by
Chu Te and Mao Tse-tung. Lo remained with
the Chu-Mao forces, which underwent a major
reorganization in mid-1930 in west Fukien. At
that time the First Army Corps was established,
composed of the Third, Fourth, 12th, and 21st
Red Armies. Lo was assigned to the Fourth Red
Army, led by Lin Piao and Lo Jung-huan, serving as political commissar of the 11th Division.
In this capacity he took part in the brief but
savage Second Annihilation Campaign waged by
the Nationalists against the Red Army in east-
central Kiangsi during the last two weeks of
May 1931.[1]

In the spring of 1932 Lo was severely wounded
in a battle against Nationalist troops. There are
unconfirmed reports that he then went to the
Soviet Union where in the next two years he received training in security and intelligence work.
In any event he was back in the Kiangsi area in
1934 when he was elected a member of the
Chinese Soviet Republic's Central Executive
Committee at the Second All-China Congress of
Soviets (January–February). In the same year
he became director of the Political Security
Bureau for Lin Piao's First Army Corps; in this
post he was probably subordinate to Teng Fa
(q.v.), the over-all security chief for the Communists.

Lo made the Long March, which brought the
Communists from Kiangsi to Shensi. Little is
known about the part he took in the long trek,
but to judge from an article by a Long March
participant it appears that Lo was a relatively
important staff officer in the First Front Army,
which included Mao, Lin Piao, and Nieh Jung-
chen (qq.v.).[2] When the march was completed
in the autumn of 1935, Lo became Political Department director of the First Column of a unit
known as the Shensi-Kansu Detachment, which
was under Lin Piao's First Army Corps. He was
a graduate in 1936 of the Red Army Military
Academy, which the Communists reopened in
north Shensi several months after the marchers
arrived there. The school was moved to Yenan
in early 1937 and renamed the Anti-Japanese
Military and Political Academy (K'ang-ta). Lo
was assigned to the school, initially serving as
dean of studies (*chiao-yü chang*).[3] He later became vice-president (by 1938) under President
Lin Piao, as well as political commissar. He was
the acting head of the academy after Lin Piao led
units of the Eighth Route Army into Shansi in
the early stages of the Sino-Japanese War, which
began in mid-1937. Lo wrote a brief but useful
description of K'ang-ta for the 48th issue of the
Communist journal *Chieh-fang* (Liberation),
published on August 8, 1938. Not long afterwards, in 1939, a Communist publishing house
brought out a book-length work by Lo entitled
K'ang-Jih chün-tui chung te cheng-chih kung-tso
(Political work in the anti-Japanese military
forces); Lo's preface was written at K'ang-ta and
was dated November 10, 1938. This has been
described in a bibliography dealing with Chinese
Communist military affairs as "probably the
most comprehensive work on political organization and indoctrination in the Communist
forces."[4]

Lo's wartime record is not well documented.
From 1939 to the end of the war in 1945 he
seems to have divided his time between Yenan
and the front line headquarters of the Communists' Eighth Route Army in the T'ai-hang Mountains in Shansi province. In regard to his work
in Shansi, he reportedly served from 1940 to
1945 as director of the Field Headquarters' Political Department under the over-all direction

of the Eighth Route Army, and during approximately these same years he was also a member of the CCP's North China Bureau. According to a Communist account dealing with the middle war years, Lo worked closely with Eighth Route Army Deputy-Commander P'eng Te-huai and Deputy Chief-of-Staff Tso Ch'üan (qq.v.). When the latter was killed in southeast Shansi in June 1942, Lo presided over the memorial services.[5] He was back in Yenan in the late summer of 1944, and he may have remained there until the Party held its Seventh Congress in Yenan (April–June 1945), when he was elected an alternate member of the Central Committee. In 1946 he became deputy political commissar of the Shansi-Chahar-Hopeh Military Region where he served for a brief time under Nieh Jung-chen, the region's commander and political commissar.

From early 1946 to early 1947, holding the simulated rank of lieutenant general, Lo served under Yeh Chien-ying (q.v.), who headed the Communist delegation at the Peking Executive Headquarters. There, under the auspices of the Marshall Mission, negotiations were conducted for a year in an attempt to arbitrate CCP-KMT differences and to prevent the outbreak of civil war, which had in fact already erupted by the time the Executive Headquarters was formally disbanded in early 1947. During this period Lo was chief-of-staff of the Communist group attached to the Executive Headquarters, the top post under Yeh Chien-ying. When the negotiations completely collapsed in early 1947, Lo went back to his work in the Shansi-Chahar-Hopeh Military Region where the North China PLA under Nieh Jung-chen was in charge of operations.

As a top political officer in north China, Lo took an active part in a series of campaigns, mainly in Hopeh, from the fall of 1947 to January 1949. During this period he was associated with PLA commanders Yang Ch'eng-wu, Yang Te-chih, and Keng Piao (qq.v.). Lo was then director of the Political Department of the North China PLA and political commissar of the 19th Army Group. The operations in which he participated were carried out in coordination with Lin Piao, who was moving his troops from Manchuria into north China by late 1948; these campaigns culminated in the capture of Tientsin and Peking in January 1949. Soon after this Lo was transferred to become deputy political commissar in the army that Hsu Hsiang-ch'ien (q.v.) was moving toward Taiyuan, the Shansi capital. Yen Hsi-shan, the famed Shansi warlord, fled Taiyuan in March 1949, and in the following month it was captured by the Communists. Hsu was immediately placed in charge of the Taiyuan Military Control Commission, and Lo was made vice-chairman.

Lo's term of office in Taiyuan was of brief duration, because a few weeks after the fall of that city he was transferred to Peking where, in a short time, he was to assume important assignments in the national government. First, however, in June 1949 he was named to the Preparatory Committee of the China New Legal Research Society, and in the same month (representing P'eng Te-huai who was still fighting in the northwest) he served on a special committee that was charged with drafting the Common Program, the document that served as the equivalent of a constitution in the formative years of the PRC. This committee assignment was given to Lo by the CPPCC Preparatory Committee, headed by Mao Tse-tung. The work of the Preparatory Committee was completed by September 1949 when the CPPCC held its inaugural session to form the national government. Representing the First Field Army, Lo attended the session and served on the *ad hoc* committee that prepared the final draft of the Common Program, which was formally adopted at this time.

Under the new national administration Lo was given several top appointments, the most important being the portfolio for the Public Security Ministry. In addition, he became a member of: Chou En-lai's Government Administration Council (GAC; the cabinet), the GAC's Political and Legal Affairs Committee, the Supreme People's Procuratorate, and the People's Revolutionary Military Council (PRMC). Moreover, under the PRMC he also served as a member of the National Defense Research Council. In brief, during the formative years of the PRC, Lo was one of the leading Communist officials in the fields of security, law enforcement, and the interpretation of legal matters. Although specific documentation is lacking, he probably worked directly under Politburo member P'eng Chen (q.v.). Lo continued to hold all these posts until they were abolished in 1954—excepting only the Ministry of Public Security where he remained as the minister until the fall of 1959.

Lo's tasks in the early years of the PRC were not concerned solely with the central government. In the fall of 1949 he was also named to membership on the Peking Municipal People's Government Council as well as director of the Peking Public Security Bureau; he held the former position until February 1955 but it is not known how long he retained the municipal security post. In addition, he was chief procurator for the Peking city government from November 1951 to the mid-1950's. Like many key CCP personnel, Lo held a seat on the Executive Board of the Sino-Soviet Friendship Association from 1949 until 1954 when it was among the most active of the "mass" organizations. From its establishment under the presidency of P'eng Chen in July 1951 to at least mid-1954, Lo was also a member of the Administrative Committee of the Central Political and Legal Cadres' Academy.

One of Lo's earliest assignments for the new government was to preside over the First National Public Security Work Conference in October–November 1949. Because the conference was attended by virtually every important security official at the national and provincial level, it is plausible to assume that it laid the groundwork for the nationwide security network—a task that was doubtless given high priority at this eary stage of Communist control. Over the next decade Lo was almost always the featured speaker at similar conferences, and it was usually he who made the official reports on security work before government bodies. Lo's numerous reports, as well as his articles in the Communist press, normally referred to security matters in terms of "suppressing counterrevolutionaries," and punishment was usually described in terms of "reform through labor." It also fell to Lo to announce executions carried out by the PRC; writing for the October 11, 1951, issue of the *JMJP*, for example, he candidly admitted that persons had been executed "in order to appease the rightful indignation of the people." He was particularly prominent in the early fifties during the three- and five-anti movements—nationwide campaigns directed against both CCP members and businessmen for "crimes" regarded as inimical to the interests of the PRC (e.g., graft).

As chief administrator of nationwide security programs, Lo normally acted in the name of the Public Security Ministry. He received a closely related post by 1950 when he was identified as commander of the PLA's Public Security Forces, and by 1953 he was identified as the political commissar. He held both posts until 1959 or possibly later, after which Hsieh Fu-chih (q.v.) replaced him. In November 1952 he was promoted from membership to a vice-chairmanship on the GAC's Political and Legal Affairs Committee, and four months later he accompanied Chou En-lai to Moscow to attend Stalin's funeral. Immediately before this trip he served as a member (January–February 1953) of a special committee to draft the national election law. As a result of the elections, Lo was selected as a deputy from Hopeh to the First NPC, which convened in September 1954 to inaugurate the PRC constitutional government.

Under the reorganized central government formed in September 1954, Lo retained the Public Security portfolio. In addition, he was made a member of the newly established National Defense Council and, in the following month, he was concurrently named to head the new First Staff Office of the State Council, an office that had the task of coordinating the work of the various ministries, commissions, and bureaus concerned with security and legal matters. A year later (November 1955) he was given still another assignment in security work when he was appointed president of the Central People's Institute of Public Security, a post held until January 1959 when he relinquished it to Wang Chao (q.v.). When PLA ranks were inaugurated

in September 1955, Lo was made a senior general, the equivalent of a four-star U.S. Army general and next only to the highest rank of marshal. At the same time he was given the three newly established awards for military service covering the period from 1927 to 1950—the Orders of August First, Independence and Freedom, and Liberation.

Lo's long military-political career was given recognition at the Party's Eighth National Congress in September 1956 when he was promoted from alternate to full membership on the Central Committee, and during the Congress he addressed the delegates on the subject of public security. Lo continued to be the dominant Communist official in matters of security throughout the middle and late fifties, but beginning with the initial session of the Second NPC in April 1959 (which Lo attended as a deputy from his native Szechwan), he began to play a more significant role in the national government and, soon afterwards, in the PLA. At the close of the 1959 NPC session he was appointed one of the four new State Council vice-premiers and was reappointed a member of the National Defense Council, as well as minister of Public Security. Then, in September 1959, following the political downfall of National Defense Minister P'eng Te-huai and PLA Chief-of-Staff Huang K'o-ch'eng (qq.v.), Lo was appointed the ranking vice-minister of Defense under the new Defense minister, Lin Piao. In addition, he replaced Huang as chief-of-staff. Because of these new key assignments, he turned over the directorship of both the Public Security Ministry and the State Council's First Staff Office (now known as the Political and Legal Affairs Office) to Hsieh Fu-chih. Considering all the critical personnel changes made in the power elite in 1959, few if any Communist officials rose in stature as quickly as Lo. And within a little more than a year (1961), he was also identified as a member and secretary-general of the most powerful military organ—the Party Central Committee's Military Affairs Committee. Equally if not more important, at the CCP's 10th Plenum in September 1962, Lo was added as a new member of the Party's Central Secretariat, the organ responsible for carrying out Politburo policies. In effect, Lo replaced the two military representatives on the Secretariat: former Chief-of-Staff Huang K'o-ch'eng and National Defense Vice-Minister T'an Cheng (q.v.).

Although Lo has not played a major role in foreign affairs, after becoming PLA chief-of-staff in 1959 he was somewhat more active in this field. In October–November 1960 he was deputy leader of a military delegation led by Ho Lung to North Korea, and in January of the next year he accompanied Chou En-lai to Burma on a goodwill visit. In addition, he frequently participated in negotiations in Peking with prominent visitors, as in July 1961 when he took part in the talks between Chou En-lai and Korean leader Kim Il-sung, which led to the signing of the Sino-Korean Treaty of Friendship, Cooperation, and Mutual Assistance. But Lo's role in foreign affairs remained subsidiary to his participation in domestic military affairs, as demonstrated, for example, by the fact that he was a featured speaker at three important PLA "political work conferences" held between 1961 and 1964. In addition, as chief-of-staff it usually fell to Lo to serve as host for celebrations and ceremonies connected with the PLA, e.g., the annual August First receptions, marking the birth of the Red Army.

In the fall of 1964 Lo was again elected a deputy to the NPC, this time representing the PLA Headquarters. He was among the speakers at the first session of the Third NPC, held in December 1964–January 1965, and at the close of the meetings he was promoted from member to vice-chairman of the National Defense Council. Lo continued to be very active until the end of November 1965 when he suddenly disappeared from the public scene. In the following summer, during the early phases of the Great Proletarian Cultural Revolution, he was replaced as PLA chief-of-staff by Yang Ch'eng-wu, and within a short time he was among the major targets of the Cultural Revolution.

Lo's numerous articles and speeches form an important body of source material for the study of public security work in China. Among the most important are his speech at the Eighth Party Congress and a review of the "struggle between revolution and counterrevolution," which he wrote to commemorate the 10th anniversary of the PRC. The latter article was published in a collection entitled *Ten Glorious Years* (Peking, 1960). Other important articles or speeches have appeared in *Cheng-fa yen-chiu* (Political and legal studies), especially the third and fourth issues of 1958 and the third issue of 1959.

1. *JMJP*, July 22, 1961.
2. *Stories of the Long March* (Peking, 1958), p. 8.
3. *Chinese Literature*, no. 1:84 (1966).
4. Edward J. M. Rhoads, ed., *The Chinese Red Army, 1927–1963: An Annotated Bibliography* (Cambridge, Mass., 1964), p. 155.
5. *Hung-ch'i p'iao-p'iao* (Red flag fluttering; Peking, 1957), V, 147.

Lo Jung-huan

(1902–1963; Heng-shan hsien, Hunan). Veteran Red Army political officer; PLA marshal; member, CCP Politburo.

From the formation of the Red Army until his death in 1963, Lo Jung-huan was one of its most important political officers. He participated in practically all the landmark events of the

Maoist military forces, including the Long March. He played a key role in both the Sino-Japanese War and the conquest of the Nationalists in the late forties. After the formation of the PRC in 1949 he was the top political officer in the PLA until his death. He was elected to the Party Central Committee in 1945 and to the Politburo in 1956.

Lo was born in 1902 in Nan-wan village in Heng-shan hsien, a community about 80 miles south of Changsha, the Hunan capital. His father was a grocer. After Lo graduated from a Changsha middle school he attended San Yat-sen University in Canton, then the revolutionary center of China. Active in the student movement, he joined the Communist Youth League and the CCP in 1927 when he was 25. In the summer of that year he took part in the famed Nanchang Uprising (August 1, 1927; see under Yeh T'ing), which marked the final break between the Communists and the Nationalists and which is generally described as the birth of the Red Army.

Escaping from Nanchang, Lo was sent by the CCP to southern Hupeh to organize and incite peasant rebellions, a campaign usually described as the Autumn Harvest Uprisings. Lo I-nung (q.v.) was the leading Party official in the area where Lo worked, and in neighboring Hunan Mao Tse-tung was similarly occupied. When the uprisings failed in both provinces, Mao and a small band of followers went to the Chingkang Mountains on the Hunan-Kiangsi border. En route to Chingkangshan Mao's battered units paused and reorganized their forces at San-wan village in Yung-hsin hsien (a few miles from Chingkangshan). In a commemorative article by Lo regarding his early association with Mao, he wrote that the "San-wan reorganization was in essence the rebirth of our army, for it was there that the Communist Party firmly established its leadership over the revolutionary armed forces."[1] Lo was still with Mao in the spring of 1928 when the latter was joined by the forces of Chu Te. He remained with the Chu-Mao army when it retreated from Chingkangshan in early 1929, moving with it across Kiangsi into Fukien. Lo was also a participant in the important Ku-t'ien Conference in December 1929 (see under Mao Tse-tung). By this period Lo had advanced from company to battalion level, and finally, in January 1930, he became political commissar of the Second Column of the Chu-Mao Fourth Red Army.[2]

The Chu-Mao forces settled down on the Kiangsi-Fukien border, making their headquarters in Juichin until the Long March began in 1934. The army was constantly on the defensive in these years and was savagely attacked by the Nationalists in a series of "annihilation" campaigns. Forced to regroup following these attacks, the Communist army nonetheless grew in size as it brought together other guerilla units that were operating in the areas over which it fought. In the span of a few years the army was frequently reorganized and redesignated, but it continued to be the force commanded by Chu Te and Mao and had on its staff a number of young officers who later became top Chinese Communist military leaders. Known as the Fourth Red Army after Chu and Mao merged their forces in 1928, it was expanded into the First Army Corps in June 1930 and the First Front Army in August, retaining this name up to and during the Long March. At approximately the time of the June 1930 reorganization, Lo became the political commissar of Lin Piao's Fourth Army, and from that time the two men worked in close cooperation for many years. When Lin's Fourth Army was expanded into the First Army Corps, Lo was made director of the Corps' Political Department, and for a period in the early 1930's he was also commander of the Kiangsi Military District.

Lo played an important role in Party work within the Red Army prior to the Long March, but he apparently took a less active part in the political life outside the army. In November 1931 the Communists established the Chinese Soviet Republic as the principal governmental authority over the widely separated areas under their control. The capital was at Juichin, and the governing body was known as the Central Executive Committee (CEC). In January–February 1934, the Second Congress elected a new and much larger CEC. Lo was elected an alternate CEC member; apparently this was his only non-military post in this period. Not long before this, in 1933, Lo had been transferred from Lin Piao's First Army Corps to become head of the Eighth Army Corps' Political Department. There is little information about the Eighth Corps, which, with the First, Third, Fifth, and Ninth Army Corps, was one of the units under the Chu-Mao First Front Army, which evacuated Kiangsi in October 1934 to make the Long March. Maoist historians may have neglected the Eighth Corps for the simple reason that it was virtually wiped out in November 1934 as it was crossing southern Hunan. Lo apparently joined other elements of the Chu-Mao forces, because he is known to have arrived in north Shensi in the fall of 1935.

After making the Long March with the First Front Army, Lo was a political instructor by 1937 at the Anti-Japanese Military and Political Academy (K'ang-ta) where Lin Piao was the president. Concurrently, Lo was director of the Political Department for the Garrison Corps at the Communist capital in Yenan. In September 1937 Lin led the Eighth Route Army's 115th Division from Shensi into the mountainous region along the northern and central border of Shansi and Hopeh. This area, centered at Wu-t'ai, came to be the most highly developed of all the Red military bases behind Japanese lines. It served as the center for the Shansi-Chahar-Hopeh Border Region Government (see under Sung Shao-wen) and was the headquarters for Party activity among the local population. Because Lin Piao spent little time at the Wu-t'ai base, Nieh Jung-chen (q.v.) became the acting commander there, and Lo, the number three officer in the 115th Division, became in fact the number two. He was director of the division's Political Department in 1937, serving under Nieh Jung-chen, who was the political commissar. It is not clear how long Lo retained the Political Department post, but he probably only held it at the start of the war, for at some time in 1938 Nieh Jung-chen took over the division's headquarters as the acting commander, and Lo was promoted to become the division's political commissar.

Though he was attached to the 115th Division headquarters at the Wu-t'ai base in Shansi, in March 1939 Lo was put in charge of the division's operations in Shantung where he spent a large part of the war period. From the start of the war a number of separate anti-Japanese resistance forces operated in Shantung, some of them infiltrated by Communist Party cadres. In August–September 1938 elements from the Eighth Route Army began entering Shantung when Ch'en Keng's (q.v.) 386th Brigade (a part of Liu Po-ch'eng's 129th Division) infiltrated into northern Shantung. These actions brought forth savage retaliations from the Japanese. The Communists, in turn, decided in late 1938 to send further aid to the Shantung guerrillas, especially those in northwest Shantung in the Liao-ch'eng area. Hence, in the spring of 1939 the 115th Division headquarters at Wu-t'ai dispatched the 343rd Brigade through Hopeh to Shantung. The Brigade was commanded by Ch'en Kuang (not to be confused with Ch'en Keng). Attached to the 343rd Brigade was Hsiao Hua (q.v.), who was to become one of Lo's principal commanders in Shantung. By the late spring of 1939 the Brigade had made contact with the local resistance at Yun-ch'eng, south of the Yellow River from Liao-ch'eng.[3] Probably about the time Ch'en Kuang's brigade was pushing toward Shantung, Lo was made commander and political commissar of the Shantung Military District, positions he held until 1944 or 1945. By 1943 he was also secretary of the CCP Shantung Sub-Bureau, thus combining the Party leadership and the military command for the province under his authority. During the later war years an important part of the military operations of the 115th Division were conducted by Lo's forces in Shantung. This was reflected in the military assignments that Lo held at the time. Dating from some time in 1943 or early 1944 he was acting commander of the 115th Division (in charge of its forces in Shantung), in addition to holding the posts mentioned above. In Shantung Lo was aided by Hsiao Hua, who first commanded the West Shantung Military District and later took charge of the political work in the same area (and possibly in some of the border territory in Hopeh and Honan).

In April–June 1945, when the Party held its Seventh Congress in Yenan, Lo was elected to the Central Committee. Soon after the war ended in 1945 he was sent to Manchuria to take part in the establishment of the Northeast Democratic Allied Army (NEDAA) under Lin Piao. An important segment of the NEDAA consisted of the troops Lo had previously commanded in Shantung. From 1946 to 1948 he was director of the NEDAA's Political Department and deputy political commissar (under P'eng Chen) of both the NEDAA and the Northeast Military Region. Although he was mainly concerned with military affairs in these years, he was one of the speakers at the Sixth Labor Congress held by the Communists in Harbin in August 1948. He was also identified at this time as a deputy secretary of the Party's Northeast Bureau. By the same year, as the Communists prepared for the final battles in Manchuria, Lo succeeded P'eng Chen as political commissar of the Northeast PLA (the new designation for the NEDAA) and retained this post when Lin Piao's troops were redesignated the Fourth Field Army in the winter of 1948–49. Lo was with Lin in January 1949 during the military takeover of Tientsin and the negotiations for the surrender of Peking. During these important but short-lived operations he was political commissar of the Peking-Tientsin Field Headquarters.[4]

Lo remained with Lin's forces when they left the Peking-Tientsin area and moved southward in a drive which culminated in the capture of Hainan Island in the spring of 1950. However, he returned to Peking for a brief time in September 1949 to participate in the establishment of the national government at the inaugural session of the CPPCC in September. Lo attended these meetings as the ranking delegate from the Fourth Field Army; he served on the CPPCC presidium (in charge of managing the meetings) as well as the *ad hoc* committee that drafted the Common Program, the equivalent of the PRC constitution until one was adopted in 1954. With the formal establishment of the central government in October 1949, Lo received three major assignments. First, he was made a member of the Central People's Government Council, the most important government body from then until 1954. Second, he was made chief procurator of the Supreme People's Procuratorate, the approximate equivalent of the United States Attorney General. Finally, under the Government Administration Council (the cabinet), Lo was made a member of the Political and Legal Affairs Committee. He was also a member of the First Ex-

ecutive Board of the Sino-Soviet Friendship Association from 1949 to 1954, the same years during which he held the three above-mentioned governmental positions.

Following the establishment of the government in Peking, Lo returned to Lin Piao's Fourth Field Army, participating in its campaigns of late 1949 and early 1950. With their victories consolidated, the Communists established the Central-South Military Region, with Lin as the commander and Lo as political commissar. He was also second secretary (again under Lin Piao) of the Party's Central-South Bureau, which controlled the six provinces of Honan, Hupeh, Hunan, Kiangsi, Kwangtung, and Kwangsi. In early 1950 he became political commissar of the PLA Central-South Military and Political Academy. However, all his positions in the central-south region were essentially nominal by the early summer of 1950, for by that time he had returned to Peking where he worked for most of the remainder of his career. Lo's political tasks with the PLA in central-south China were assumed by T'an Cheng, and his work with the Party's Central-South Bureau fell mainly to Teng Tzu-hui (qq.v.).

Lo attended the second session of the First CPPCC in Peking in June 1950 when the important land reform law was adopted, and soon after he was identified as the director of the General Political Department, then subordinate to the People's Revolutionary Military Council (PRMC). In this capacity he made most of his relatively few public appearances between 1950 and 1954. For example, he addressed the National People's Armed Forces Work Conference in Peking in October 1950 on behalf of the Political Department. In 1950 he also assumed the directorship of the PRMC's General Cadres' (personnel) Department, thus being placed in charge of two key posts in the military establishment. Then in June 1954 he was appointed a vice-chairman of the PRMC, although he only held this post until September 1954 when the PRMC was abolished.

There are reports that Lo served as political commissar of the Chinese forces in Korea—the Chinese People's Volunteers (CPV)—during the Korean War. It is noteworthy that he was not reported in Peking after the CPV entered the war in October 1950. Moreover, units from the Fourth Field Army (to which Lo was still officially attached) bore the brunt of the fighting in the early days of the war. However, his presence in Korea cannot be confirmed, and in any event Lo was again reported regularly in the Communist press from October 1951 in connection with his various duties in Peking.

In preparation for the convocation of the First NPC, deputies to this legislative body were elected in mid-1954. Lo was chosen to represent the Northeast Military Region. At the inaugural session of the NPC in September 1954, when the national constitution was adopted and the central government reorganized, Lo relinquished his post as chief procurator to Chang Ting-ch'eng. Lo in turn became a member of the NPC Standing Committee and a vice-chairman of the National Defense Council, the less powerful successor to the PRMC. The General Political Department and the General Cadres' Department were transferred from the now defunct PRMC to the PLA Headquarters; Lo was formally reappointed to head both departments in November 1954. Less than a year later, in September 1955, he was one of only 10 PLA officers given the rank of marshal, and at the same time he was awarded the newly created Orders of August First, Independence and Freedom, and Liberation, which were given for service in the Red Armies from 1927 to 1950.

When the CCP held its Eighth Party Congress in September 1956, Lo was again elected to the Central Committee. Immediately after, at the First Plenum of the new Central Committee, he was elevated to membership in the Politburo, which then consisted of 17 full and six alternate members. Then in December 1956 Lo was relieved of his top military commands, being succeeded as head of the Political Department by T'an Cheng and in the Cadres' Department by Hsiao Hua. Both men had been associates of Lo for a number of years. However, it appears that Lo returned to the Political Department as the *de facto* director after about 1960–61, from which time T'an Cheng (q.v.), then in political difficulties, seems to have been divorced from the duties of this important department. The thought that Lo was reassigned to the Political Department is further buttressed by the fact that he took a prominent part in several Political Department-sponsored conferences, particularly in 1961. Moreover, the Canton *Nan-fang jih-pao* (Southern Daily) of December 16, 1963, noted that he headed the department at the time of his death (although this was not indicated in the more authoritative *JMJP* dispatches in connection with his death).

Lo continued as a prominent figure in the late fifties and early sixties. He served in the Second NPC from its convocation in April 1959 (representing the Shenyang Military Region) and was again elected to the NPC Standing Committee, a position he held until his death. But his work in connection with the legislature was clearly less important than his military duties. He was among those who spoke at the conference of the Party Central Committee's Military Affairs Committee (MAC) held from May to July 1958, a period coinciding with the crisis in the Middle East (when the United States landed forces in Lebanon and the British in Jordan). His membership on the MAC probably dated from at least that time, but by the spring of 1961 he was

specifically identified as one of the members of the MAC's Standing Committee, probably the most elite military group in China.

As might be expected of the long-time chief political officer in the PLA, Lo's public statements constantly emphasized the primacy of politics within the PLA, including the necessity for the PLA to maintain its close ties with the "masses." Two random but typical examples that stress these themes are found in Lo's articles commemorating Red Army Day (August 1), which appeared in the *JMJP* of August 1, 1955, and *Peking Review* (no. 31, August 3, 1962).

Lo died at age 61 in Peking on December 16, 1963. For the next few days the national press carried a number of dispatches in connection with the elaborate memorial ceremonies, as well as several commemorative articles by former colleagues. His funeral committee was headed by Liu Shao-ch'i and the funeral oration was delivered by Teng Hsiao-p'ing, but his place in the Chinese Communist hierarchy was perhaps best summarized by the accolade reserved for the select few: "close comrade-in-arms of Mao Tse-tung."

Lo married Lin Yueh-ch'in in the spring of 1937 in Yenan. She had previously been married to a political worker in the Fourth Front Army of Chang Kuo-t'ao and Hsu Hsiang-ch'ien (qq.v.). At the time of his death Lo had at least one son and a daughter. His wife has been a member of the Executive Committee of the National Women's Federation since 1957 and a PLA deputy to the Third NPC since 1964. She wrote a commemorative article about her husband, which appeared in the December 25, 1963, issue of the *JMJP*.

1. *SCMM* 328, pp. 10–15.
2. *Ibid.*; *JMJP*, June 23, 1961, and December 20, 1963.
3. Chalmers A. Johnson, *Peasant Nationalism and Communist Power* (Stanford, Calif., 1962), p. 112.
4. A. Doak Barnett, *China on the Eve of Communist Takeover* (New York, 1963), pp. 327–332.

Lo Kuei-po

(c.1911–   Kwangtung?). Diplomat; alternate member, CCP Central Committee.

A veteran Red Army political officer, Lo Kuei-po has been a senior member of the Chinese diplomatic service since the mid-1950's. He was probably born in Kwangtung (although some sources say 1915 in Hunan). Most of the information on Lo's early career comes from journalist Harrison Forman, who interviewed Lo in 1944.[1] He told Forman that he left his family to join the Nationalist armies when he was 15 (about 1926) and that when he was 16 he joined the Communists, not long after the KMT–CCP split in mid-1927. He later became a Red guerrilla fighter in the rural parts of Kiangsi province. About 1932 he was a deputy commander of a military unit numbering some 5,000 men, and in the 1933–34 period he was a deputy commandant of the Red Army Academy in the Juichin (Kiangsi) area. Lo made the Long March (1934–35) to north Shensi as head of a detachment of political workers.

After his arrival in the northwest Lo was assigned to Ho Lung's 120th Division of the Eighth Route Army, the division which maintained a base in the Shansi-Suiyuan area throughout the Sino-Japanese War. Lo was a political commissar during most of the war, although he also assumed military commands for brief periods. By 1938 he had become propaganda director of the Political Department of the 120th Division, as well as propaganda director of the Party's sub-bureau for Shansi and Suiyuan. In 1939 Lo was also serving as political commissar of the 120th Division's 358th Brigade with Commander P'eng Shao-hui (q.v.). From the earliest part of the war the Communist armies in northwest Shansi had been cooperating against the Japanese with guerrilla units of the so-called "Shansi New Army," a military force which consisted mainly of Communist-infiltrated "dare-to-die" corps. The "New Army" was commanded by KMT member Hsu Fan-t'ing and was ostensibly under the control of Shansi warlord Yen Hsi-shan. This three-cornered arrangement had been satisfactory to the beleaguered Yen in the early war years when he believed that cooperation with the Communists and Communist-infiltrated organizations was the only feasible means to hold off the Japanese Army. However, by 1939 Yen's fear of the growing strength of the Communists in Shansi caused him to take a series of political and military steps which led to the defection in December 1939 of Hsu Fan-t'ing. Hsu took some 3,000 of his men and joined the Communist forces.

Lo is credited with an important part in Hsu's defection, and when the "New Army" was re-organized under the Communists, Hsu was appointed commander of the provisional headquarters and Lo was made his political commissar.[2] These developments paved the way for the formation in 1940–41 of the Communists' Shansi-Suiyuan Liberated Region (see under Lin Feng).

Lo apparently continued to conduct guerrilla operations in the northwest Shansi area, and when Forman visited the headquarters of the 120th Division in Shansi-Suiyuan in 1944, Lo was political commissar of the eighth sub-region of the Shansi-Suiyuan Military Region. He remained in the area after the cessation of hostilities in August 1945 and by 1948 was serving both as the military commander and as the Party official in charge of an area which was formerly under the jurisdiction of the Shansi-Suiyuan base. At that time he was secretary of the Shansi-Suiyuan Sub-bureau of the CCP Northwest Bureau and commander and political commissar of a newly organized military district in central Shansi.

Communist armies took Taiyuan, the capital of Shansi, in April 1949 and immediately established a military control commission, upon which Lo served as a member. Among his fellow members were Hsu Hsiang-ch'ien, Lo Jui-ch'ing, Lai Jo-yü, and Chou Shih-ti (qq.v.). Following this appointment were four years of obscurity, though at some time between 1950 and 1953 he moved to Peking. There he was assigned to the leading PRC military body, the People's Revolutionary Military Council (PRMC), until its dissolution in September 1954 when the constitutional government was established. A 1953 report identified Lo as a political commissar with the air defense command of the PRMC. He was also identified as the "former" director of the PRMC Staff Office in August 1954 when he was appointed ambassador to North Vietnam. These identifications are somewhat puzzling because the post with the Staff Office was also held by other men between 1952 and 1954. There are reports that Lo was a member of the Chinese delegation to the Geneva Conference of 1954, which led to the partition of French Indochina. However, his participation in Chou En-lai's delegation to Geneva cannot be established. It is possible that he was initially named to the delegation but did not go.

Lo presented his credentials in Hanoi to Ho Chi Minh on September 1, 1954. China and North Vietnam had recognized each other in early 1950, and the Vietnamese had sent a "delegate" with ambassadorial rank to Peking in 1951. However, prior to Lo's arrival in Hanoi there had been no report of Chinese diplomatic representation in Vietnam. During the next three years he was an active member of the diplomatic set in Hanoi. He twice accompanied Ho on visits to China: in June–July 1955 when the latter went to Peking to sign an agreement by which China promised aid to North Vietnam and in July 1957 when the Vietnamese leader was en route to North Korea and satellite nations of East Europe. Lo was also on hand in Hanoi when Chou En-lai visited there in November 1956, an important occasion because the Chinese premier was making a tour of Southeast Asia to visit Communist and non-Communist leaders there in the wake of the Communist revolt in Hungary.

In September 1956 Lo was elected *in absentia* as an alternate member of the Central Committee by the Eighth National CCP Congress. The following year he was called back to Peking.

Appointed vice-minister of Foreign Affairs in October 1957, he left Hanoi on December 2 and was officially replaced a few days later by Ho Wei (q.v.). The only position he has received since that time was given to him in late 1964 when he was named as a representative of "organizations for peaceful and friendly relations with foreign countries" to the Fourth National Committee of the CPPCC. (The Fourth Committee held its initial session in December 1964–January 1965.)

Since returning to Peking Lo has been seen frequently at diplomatic and semi-official gatherings for foreign visitors, though the functions he attends are not those of the highest importance. In mid-July 1959 he made a 10-day visit to Iraq to attend the celebrations marking the first anniversary of Iraqi National Day. Apparently Lo's most important activity in Peking since his return there was in June 1961 when he participated in the talks between premiers Chou En-lai and Pham Van Dong of Vietnam during the latter's visit to China.

1. Harrison Forman, *Report from Red China* (New York, 1945), pp. 228–229.

2. *JMJP*, May 22, 1962; *Hung-ch'i p'iao-p'iao* (Red flag fluttering; Peking, 1957), V, 235–251.

Lo Mai, see **Li Wei-han**

Lo Ming

Early Party leader.

Aside from Lo Ming's involvement in a controversy which bears his name, almost nothing is known about him except that he was a CCP operative in west Fukien from the beginning of the Communists' penetration there in the late 1920's.[1] Lo later headed the Fukien Party Committee and was the focal point in a protracted intra-Party dispute regarding the appropriate strategy to resist the efforts by the KMT armies to wipe out the Communist base on the Kiangsi-Fukien border in the early thirties. In late 1930 Chiang Kai-shek's armies launched the First Annihilation Campaign to destroy the Communists. In the four successive campaigns, the Communists were initially able to hold off Chiang's armies, but steady inroads were made in Kiangsi and Fukien during the Fourth Campaign begun in mid-1932. In the meantime, at the CCP's Fourth Plenum in January 1931, a new group of leaders had taken control of the Party. These men, the so-called Russian-returned students (or "28 Bolsheviks"), were headed by Ch'en Shao-yü, Ch'in Pang-hsien, and Chang Wen-t'ien (qq.v.), and they were strongly influenced by their Comintern mentors.

The new leaders were well versed in Party theory, but had little experience in building Communist bases. Asserting that the Nationalists were on the verge of collapse, they wanted to intensify the revolutionary struggle in China. They advocated engaging the enemy in positional warfare, trying to capture cities, and clearly defining class status.[2] These policies became known as the "forward and offensive line." After the Comintern's 12th Executive Committee Plenum in September 1932, at which Communists throughout the world were urged to step up the revolutionary pace, the returned-student leadership advocated a broad-scale political and economic mobilization, as well as an expansion of the Red Army.

Lo Ming, the acting secretary of the Fukien Party Committee in 1933, became the symbol of this conflict between the reality of Nationalist attacks and the policies of the returned-student leadership to thwart them. According to the accusations made about him when the campaign against the "Lo Ming line" was begun in February 1933, Lo felt that the peasants were too war-weary and apathetic to be aroused to a successful fight against the Nationalists. Instead, he favored moderating the revolutionary effort and using guerrilla tactics until the Communist position could be strengthened. To demonstrate Lo's "incorrect" viewpoint, Ch'in Pang-hsien quoted Lo as saying: "I don't think we can thoroughly change the mood of the masses even if we ask our best leader Chairman Mao or Chairman Hsiang Ying (of the Military Council), Comrade Chou En-lai, Comrade Jen Pi-shih, or go to the Soviet Union to ask Comrade Stalin or bring Lenin back to life and ask them all to . . . address the masses three days and nights to step up political propaganda."[3] Chang Wen-t'ien dated Lo's mistakes from the Fourth Plenum of 1931, criticizing him for separating military mobilization from political mobilization, for divorcing the Party from the masses, and for insisting on the use of guerrilla warfare.

Accoding to a February 15, 1933, decision of the Party's Central Bureau, Lo's policies were "opportunistic," and they were supported by a group of his associates who were "filled with pessimism and despair, inclined toward retreat and escape, isolated from the masses, and addicted openly to liquidationism." Such "faulty" leadership, it was asserted, had been detrimental to the peasants' understanding of their role in repulsing the Nationalist attacks. Those who were not directly threatened by the Nationalists tended to minimize the seriousness of the attacks, resulting in complacency and pacifism. Those directly threatened had panicked, resulting in despair and defeatism. The peasants in general considered the "forward and offensive" policy to be the Red Army's problem, not theirs.[4] The campaign against the "Lo Ming line" was designed to counter these attitudes.

Lo himself was removed as head of the Fukien Party Committee in February 1933 when the attacks against him began. But the campaign against his alleged followers continued for many months and, according to the returned-student leadership, the suppression of the Lo Ming policies enabled the Communists to repulse the Nationalists' Fourth Annihilation Campaign in 1933. Most accounts stress that those criticized were close to Mao Tse-tung, but few versions have emphasized that the critics included many leaders who were not members of the returned-student leadership. For example, both Chou En-lai and Jen Pi-shih (qq.v.) wrote blistering attacks against the Lo Ming group. The men who were censured during the campaign included such notables as T'an Chen-lin, Ch'en T'an-ch'iu, Teng Tzu-hui, Teng Hsiao-p'ing, Hsiao Ching-kuang (qq.v.), and Mao's younger brother, Mao Tse-t'an. It should be noted, however, that with the exception of Mao Tse-t'an (who was killed in 1935 by the Nationalists) all these men went on to have highly significant careers in later years.

With the Nationalists' successful Fifth Annihilation Campaign, which resulted in the Communists' abandonment of their base and the subsequent Long March (October 1934), the controversy was set aside. Based on the available record, the Lo Ming dispute lay dormant for over a decade. Then, on the eve of the CCP Seventh National Congress, the Party adopted the famous "Resolution on Certain Questions in the History of Our Party" (April 1945). This resolution, the definitive Maoist interpretation of Party history, charged that the returned students had incorrectly espoused the "third Left line" and had "wrongly opposed" the Lo Ming line.[5] The annotators of Mao's *Selected Works* further argued that Lo had been "attacked by the 'Leftists' because he held that as the Party was confronted with a rather difficult situation in Shanghang, Yungting and other outlying parts of western Fukien, its policy there should be different from that in the stable base areas. The 'Leftists' wrongly and exaggeratedly represented his views as 'a line of opportunist-liquidationist flight and retreat, due to pessimism and despair about the revolution,' and, organizationally, waged the so-called 'struggle against the Lo Ming line.' "[6]

In response to the difficulties in Fukien, an interim Party committee, which included Liu Hsiao (q.v.) among its members, was established to take over Lo Ming's responsibilities. Nothing further, however, is known of Lo Ming himself.

1. Tso-liang Hsiao, *Power Relations within the Chinese Communist Movement, 1930–1934* (Seattle, Wash., 1961), pp. 230–247.

2. *Ibid.*, pp. 160–161.

3. *Ibid.*, p. 234.

4. *Ibid.*, p. 217.

5. *Selected Works of Mao Tse-tung* (Peking, 1965), III, 204.

6. *Ibid.*, p. 224.

Lo Ping-hui

(1897–1946; I-liang, Yunnan). Military leader.

Lo Ping-hui was an important Red military leader from the early 1930's until his death in 1946. He had had considerable military experience when he became a Communist in 1929, but his reputation rests upon his exploits in some of the military operations that are now ranked among the landmarks of the Chinese Communist Movement. Lo came from I-liang near Kunming in Yunnan province. His family were said to have been of peasant stock; he had little formal education and received most of his military training from practical experience. In 1915, when he was 18, Lo ran away from home to join the garrison force at nearby Kunming, which was part of the army of Yunnan's military governor, T'ang Chi-yao. At this time T'ang's army supported the provincial separatist movement in Yunnan,[1] and the army offered ample opportunity for advancement to Lo. He soon began attending daily lectures on military affairs. He did so well that he came to T'ang's attention and was put on his headquarters staff. Lo held responsible positions in T'ang's army for the next several years. Then, when T'ang had to escape Yunnan after being defeated by other local militarists, Lo accompanied him to Hong Kong as his purchasing agent. In Hong Kong he lived in T'ang's household for eight months (1920) until he began to tire of a life of luxury.

In 1921 he returned home by way of Indochina only to find that his previous connections with T'ang Chi-yao made him unpopular with T'ang's rival warlords; they had Lo arrested and imprisoned. Released after two weeks through the aid of former military colleagues, he made his way via Kweichow into Kwangsi where he joined the army of Chu P'ei-te, a military supporter of Sun Yat-sen. By this time Lo had made something of a reputation as a talented young officer, and he was able to win Chu's confidence as quickly as he had earlier won T'ang's. Chu first entrusted Lo with a special mission to Kwangtung to gather intelligence on provincial military leaders whom he suspected of supporting southern military leader Ch'en Chiung-ming, then opposing Sun Yat-sen. When he had completed this mission, Lo rejoined Chu in Canton and was allied with him during the 1922 campaigns fought against Ch'en Chiung-ming in Kwangtung. Advancing from the rank of captain in the Canton arsenal guards to acting battalion commander, Lo was next sent north with the arsenal guards to engage forces allied to Wu P'ei-fu and opposed to Sun Yat-sen. Lo became a full battalion commander in 1926 at the start of the Northern Expedition. Between July 1926 and August 1927 his battalion fought from Kwangtung to Hunan and from there to

Kiangsi as part of Chu P'ei-te's Third Nationalist Army. By mid-1927 Lo was stationed near Nanchang, the Kiangsi capital. It was during the Northern Expedition that he began to use the revolutionary alias Lo Ping-hui. It was probably also at this time that he joined the KMT. He was involved in some intensive fighting during the northern military campaign, was twice wounded, and managed to reach Nanchang with only 80 survivors from his original unit of about 400.

When the Nanchang Uprising took place on August 1, 1927, Communist-led troops that took over the city disarmed the Chu P'ei-te troops, with which Lo was serving. Lo had already met Communist leader Chu Te, but when Chu asked him to join the CCP at the time of the uprising, he refused, he said, partly because at the time he did not have any good friends who were Communists. Hence, when the Communists were forced to flee from the city (August 5, 1927), Lo remained with Chu P'ei-te's army. Later he was sent into Fukien and Kiangsi as a "bandit suppression" commander. As head of a "peace preservation corps" in the river port city of Chi-an (Kian) in 1929, he first fought against Chu Te's army, which was operating in the Kiangsi countryside near Chi-an. But as peace preservation corps commander, Lo's sympathies had come to be with the workers and peasants, so he finally joined the CCP in July 1929 after he had received several invitations from members of the Kiangsi Provincial Party Committee.

After joining the Party, Lo remained for a time in Chi-an, but in the latter part of 1929 he defected with a small number of troops. Then, after making contact with Red Army troops south of Chi-an in early 1930, he was made commander of the Second Column in Huang Kung-lueh's (q.v.) Third Army. He campaigned in Kiangsi during the early months of 1930 with troops led by Chu Te, P'eng Te-huai, and Huang, after which he was transferred to west Fukien where, in July 1930, he was placed in command of the 12th Red Army. A few years later, about 1933, he was commander of the 22nd Red Army. In the meantime, however, while still heading the 12th Red Army, the major Red Army units in the Kiangsi-Fukien area were ordered to move north into central china by the impetuous young Party leader Li Li-san (q.v.), whose influence was then paramount at the CCP headquarters and who planned a major military campaign to take over the Yangtze industrial cities. Lo was a member of the force led by Chu Te and Mao Tse-tung which began an assault on Nanchang in August 1930 as part of this strategy. At the same time that the Chu-Mao army was attacking Nanchang in Kiangsi, P'eng Te-huai was making an attack upon Changsha, the Hunan capital. Both attacks failed in short order. Then the

retreating Communist armies met to reconnoiter and prepare for a second attack to be made jointly upon Changsha. This opened on September 1 and was as unsuccessful as the first. After the second Changsha defeat, Lo accompanied Chu Te's troops eastward into Kiangsi. They attacked and entered Chi-an on October 5, 1930, to establish a short-lived Communist government there. The attack on Chi-an was spearheaded by Lo's 12th Red Army, Lo receiving cooperation from some of his former colleagues with whom he had worked a year earlier in the peace preservation corps.

From 1930 to 1934 Lo's troops were almost continually engaged in action against encircling Nationalist armies conducting the five Annihilation Campaigns to eliminate the Communists from central-south China. (In 1930 Lo's 12th Army was absorbed into Chu Te's First Army Corps.) After surviving the first three campaigns, Lo's army was sent on a mission to decoy the Nationalists in central Kiangsi to the north in hopes of breaking the blockade that was beginning to menace the Communists. In fighting near Lo-an in central Kiangsi in 1931, he was successful for a time. His army participated in another drive for Nanchang in 1933 when the forces of Chu Te, K'ung Ho-ch'ung, and Fang Chih-min attempted to take the city. Then, when the Communists were finally driven off, they called a military conference to review their campaign and to plan their next moves. At this conference, which occurred in the spring of 1933, it was decided to create two new army corps, the Ninth and the Seventh.[2] Lo was put in charge of the former, which apparently absorbed his former 22nd Army troops into the new unit. Ts'ai Shu-fan (q.v.) was political commissar of the Ninth Army Corps. In the interim, Lo had been elected to the Central Executive Committee (CEC) of the Chinese Soviet Republic, established in November 1931 at the All-China Congress of Soviets held in Juichin in southeast Kiangsi. He was re-elected at the second congress held in January–February 1934. During the summer of 1934, at the height of the Nationalist campaigns against the Communists, Lo was sent on a mission to Fukien, apparently with the intent of decoying Nationalist troops from the Communist capital in Kiangsi. Thus, in July 1934 he started from Kuei-hua (Ming-ch'i) in western Fukien and marched in a northeasterly direction to the Min River, and then traveled down river to Shui-k'ou. From there Lo's force covered the coastal area of northeast Fukien from the vicinity of Fu-ting to Lien-chiang just above Foochow, occupying briefly the towns of Hsia-p'u, Fu-an, Ning-te, Lo-yuan, and Lien-chiang. The maneuver forced the Nationalists to come to the defense of Foochow and meanwhile the Communists plundered the countryside for supplies. While thus engaged, Lo dispatched a part of his army north to join Fang Chih-min, who had at the same time been sent on a similar decoying expedition from northeast Kiangsi (see under Fang Chih-min). When this unit reached Fang's 10th Army, it formed part of the so-called "Resist Japan Vanguards," with which Fang fought until he was captured by the Nationalists in early 1935.[3] Lo himself, however, found it necessary before long to pull back into Kiangsi, and when his troops suffered heavy losses at Kuang-ch'ang in east Kiangsi north of Juichin, he was again forced to withdraw.

Lo embarked upon the Long March in the fall of 1934 as commander of the Ninth Army Corps with Ho Ch'ang-kung (q.v.) as his political commissar. When Mao's army reached west Szechwan in mid-1935 and rendezvoused with the Fourth Front Army of Chang Kuo-t'ao, Lo was with Mao. But after the two leaders had separated, with Mao going north to Shensi while Chang turned west into the then Sikang province, Lo's Ninth Corps went with Chang and spent the winter of 1935–36 at his headquarters in the Tibetan-peopled area near Kantzu. Ho Ch'ang-kung, Lo's political commissar, also made this move. In the spring of 1936 Chang's army was joined by the Second Front Army, commanded by Ho Lung and Jen Pi-shih, and Lo made the next lap of the march north to rejoin Mao with Ho's army. By December 1936 he had arrived at Huan-hsien in eastern Kansu. Lo's Ninth Army Corps was subordinate to Chang Kuo-t'ao's army, which did not follow Ho Lung from Kansu to Shensi but remained in Kansu by order of Chang. After crossing the Yellow River at Ching-yuan they met with disaster in the Kansu corridor at the hands of generals Hu Tsung-nan and Ma Pu-fang and had to flee into the Ch'i-lien Mountains of Tsinghai. Only some 500 soldiers from the Ninth Corps survived and these were brought to north Shensi in the spring of 1937 (see under T'eng Tai-yuan and Wang Shu-sheng). However, it is very doubtful that Lo accompanied his Ninth Army Corps on the Kansu-Tsinghai Expedition, because at some point in the year he was known to have had his headquarters in the small town of Yü-wang-pao in southern Ninghsia. Lo was in north China in mid-1937 when the American authoress Nym Wales interviewed him. The information she obtained from him, in addition to a semi-official Communist biography of Lo, provides most of the data for his early career.[4]

When the Sino-Japanese War broke out in July 1937, Lo became director of the Wuhan office of the Communist Eighth Route Army. In the following year he joined the New Fourth Army as deputy commander of the Army's First Detachment headed by Ch'en I (q.v.).[5] This was the army the Communists put into operation in

east-central China early in 1938. It was commanded by Yeh T'ing and drew together the scattered Communist guerrilla forces that had been operating in central and east China since before the outbreak of the war. By April 1938 Yeh had organized four detachments of New Fourth Army troops, and the first three detachments soon moved south of the Yangtze into the southern portions of Kiangsu and Anhwei provinces. The detachments occupied an area extending from Tan-yang in southwest Kiangsu to Fan-ch'ang southwest of the river port city of Wu-hu in Anhwei, in territory bounded by the Yangtze stretching south toward the Chekiang border to She-hsien.[6] By 1940 Yeh's headquarters were only some 50 miles south of Wu-hu, near the county seat of Ching-hsien. In this territory Lo was deputy commander of the Second Detachment, which made its headquarters in early 1939 at Chin-t'an, south Kiangsu.[7]

During the next two years most of the New Fourth Army troops moved north of the Yangtze. Part of Lo's Second Detachment was one of the first units to make the move. In the first quarter of 1939 Lo led a small force from Chin-t'an across the Yangtze and west to Lu-chiang at the edge of the Ta-pieh Mountains in Anhwei where in May they joined forces with about 1,000 men from the Fourth Detachment (which had remained north of the Yangtze the whole time), and together the two units formed the Fifth Detachment of the New Fourth Army. Lo, commander of the new unit, then moved it eastward toward the border of Anhwei and Kiangsu. By July 1939, when it was operating near Lai-an and Liu-ho, the Fifth Detachment had grown to about 5,000 men. By the end of the year it had again moved to the east, settling in an area on the Anhwei shores of Lake Kaoyu. It fought against the Nationalists late in 1939 and was then badly depleted in battles with the Japanese in the late summer of 1940. By the end of 1940 Lo and his detachment were operating in T'ien-ch'ang (now Ping-hui) hsien, Anhwei, on the western shore of Lake Kao-yu.[8]

To return to Lo's operations in the fall of 1939: he was then under attack from Nationalist-allied local military forces, commanded by Han Te-ch'in, which were based near Hsu-i on the Kiangsu-Anhwei border. Han's troops were blocking the Communists' entrance into Kiangsu, but despite serious losses Lo succeeded in defeating some of Han's forces and in capturing a large amount of equipment. Following this, Lo was able to retire to the shores of Lake Kao-yu and await reinforcements. These came to him from two sources, the largest force from a Communist unit that had been operating in the coastal area under the command of Kuan Wen-wei (presently a vice-governor of Kiangsu).[9]

Kuan's units made contact with Lo early in 1940. At about the same time he received aid from an advance detachment numbering about 1,000 men from the Fifth or Eighth Column of the Eighth Route Army (see under Huang K'o-ch'eng). Huang's column was sent to the aid of the New Fourth Army in 1940, and in January of that year this advance unit, which had moved south through Shantung, joined Lo's headquarters near Lake Kao-yu. Hence, despite serious losses to the Japanese, Lo's Fifth Detachment was able to regain its strength in 1940 from the addition of the above-mentioned forces and from local recruitment.

From October 1940 to February 1941 the New Fourth Army Troops were engaged in battles with both the Nationalists and the Japanese. This was a period when all but the headquarters staff of the Army was fighting north of the Yangtze. Ch'en I, who had brought his First Detachment north of the river in June 1940, became the commander of a reorganized North Yangtze Command (see under Ch'en I) and the Third Detachment commanded by T'an Chen-lin (q.v.), the Fourth Detachment under Tai Chi-ying, Lo's Fifth Detachment, and the Sixth Detachment under P'eng Hsueh-feng (q.v.) were all fighting along the Yangtze in Anhwei and Kiangsu provinces.

Then in January 1941, as the New Fourth Army's headquarters staff was attempting to move across the Yangtze, they came into conflict with Nationalist troops and were badly routed in the famous New Fourth Army Incident (see under Yeh T'ing). The CCP headquarters in Yenan immediately assigned Liu Shao-ch'i to be the New Fourth Army's political commissar. In Liu's subsequent reorganization of the army the former six detachments, plus one semi-independent unit under Li Hsien-nien, were the nucleus of seven new divisions. Ch'en I now became acting commander of the entire army, while Lo's Fifth Detachment was reformed into the Second Division. It was initially led by Chang Yun-i (q.v.), who was also a deputy commander of the New Fourth Army. In 1941 Lo was deputy commander and political commissar of the Second Division, but in 1942 he succeeded Chang as commander and held two posts concurrently. The Second Division operated in the Communists' South Huai Military District for the remainder of the war. The boundaries of this critical area in north Anhwei and Kiangsu, which was traversed by the important rail line to Nanking, are described in the biography of Chang Yun-i.

Soon after the war ended in August 1945, Ch'en I's army began to move northward into southern Shantung. Lo made this move with his division, but illness soon forced him to retire from active command. In April 1946, perhaps as a gesture to a dying colleague, Lo was appointed a deputy commander of both the New Fourth Army and the Shantung Military District. Two months later, on June 21, 1946, he died of heart trouble at Lan-ling. Although he never held a significant Party post, his impressive military record was given recognition by the Communists when they renamed T'ien-ch'ang hsien (near Lake Kao-yu in east Anhwei) as Ping-hui hsien.

1. Li Chien-nung, *The Political History of China, 1840–1928* (New York, 1956), p. 329.

2. Jerome Ch'en, *Mao and the Chinese Revolution* (London, 1965), p. 178.

3. Anthony Garavente, "The Long March," *The China Quarterly,* no. 22:99–101 (April–June 1965).

4. Nym Wales, *Red Dust* (Stanford, Calif., 1952), pp. 113–130; *Hung-ch'i p'iao-p'iao* (Red flag fluttering; Peking, 1957), V, 180–224.

5. *Hung-ch'i p'iao-p'iao,* V, 209.

6. Chalmers A. Johnson, *Peasant Nationalism and Communist Power* (Stanford, Calif., 1962), p. 124.

7. *Ibid.,* p. 127.

8. *Ibid.*

9. *Ibid.,* p. 134.

Lo Teng-hsien

(1904–1933; Kwangtung). Labor leader; member, CCP Politburo.

Lo Teng-hsien is one of the very few Communist leaders of genuine proletarian origin who achieved high Party status. He is best known for his role in the Canton–Hong Kong strike in the mid-twenties and his leadership of the anti-Japanese resistance movement in Manchuria in the early thirties. Orphaned at an early age, Lo went to live with a sister in Hong Kong where, about 1915, he began to work in the Butterfield and Swire dockyards. The first highlight of Lo's career was in connection with the famous Canton–Hong Kong strike (see under Su Chao-cheng). The strike started in June 1925 in response to the May 30th Movement, which began in Shanghai and had the support of Chinese from many walks of life. Directing the 16-month-long strike was a special "strike committee" composed of 13 men headed by Su Chao-cheng. Lo was a member of the "strike committee," nine of whom were from Hong Kong and four from Shameen (Sha-mien), the foreign concession in Canton.[1] Lo had joined the CCP in 1925 after the strike began, and by the next year he was a member of the Standing Committee of the Party's Hong Kong Committee.

Lo participated in the Canton Uprising in December 1927 (see under Chang T'ai-lei), and he is credited with having set up a "fighting unit" of workers to assist the regular Communist troops. After that debacle he remained in the south, briefly working for the Party's Kwangtung Committee, then headed by Teng Chung-hsia. By the spring of 1928 Lo was in Shanghai, where he led demonstrations protesting Japan's occupation of Tsinan, Shantung. Shortly afterward, the CCP convened its Sixth National Congress in Moscow (June–July). It is not known if he attended, but his biographers K'ang Sheng (q.v.), who worked with Lo in the Shanghai underground, and Feng Chung-yun, who knew him in Manchuria, assert that Lo was elected to the CCP Politburo.[2] At this same time he was also appointed secretary of the important CCP Kiangsu Committee, headquartered in Shanghai. Lo probably replaced Hsiang Ying (q.v.) in this assignment. After working for the Kiangsu Committee for two years, Lo was transferred in 1930 to the Party's Secretariat (Shu-chi ch'u), also in Shanghai. Until the fall of 1930 Li Li-san (q.v.) had been the de facto head of the Party, but it is not known if Lo was tainted with the stigma of having followed the famed "Li Li-san line."

In addition to his post with the Party Secretariat, Lo was also appointed in 1930 as secretary of the Party Corps (Tang t'ang) of the Communist-led underground All-China Federation of Labor. Hsiang Ying had chaired the Labor Federation since its secretly held Fifth Congress in late 1929, but in the latter part of 1930 this position was assumed by Lo Chang-lung. During the last few months of 1930 and the early part of 1931, the CCP was rent by extremely serious factional struggles. The three major factions were led by Li Li-san, labor leader Lo Chang-lung and his colleagues, and the Russian-returned student group led by Ch'in Pang-hsien and Ch'en Shao-yü (who had strong backing from Comintern representative Pavel Mif). At the Party's Fourth Plenum in January 1931, the Russian-returned group emerged the victor. This new leadership element apparently looked with favor upon Lo Teng-hsien, because after the Plenum he was named to succeed Lo Chang-lung as chairman of the Labor Federation.

Lo's leadership of the Labor Federation was short-lived, because after the Japanese invasion of Manchuria in September 1931, he was assigned there as the representative of the Party Center and as secretary of the CCP's Manchurian Provincial Committee (Man-chou sheng-wei). Using the alias Ta P'ing,[3] he traveled from Harbin, the headquarters of the CCP Committee, to various parts of Manchuria in an effort to coordinate the Party's activities with local resistance leaders and to assist in the formation of new guerrilla units. K'ang Sheng's biography of Lo asserts that he worked among the coal miners at Fushun and that he "laid the foundation" for the ultimate establishment of the First Army. The First Army was one of six armies set up in 1933–34 by Chinese and Korean Communists

in Manchuria. (The details are discussed in the biography of Chou Pao-chung who, like Lo, was sent by the CCP to Manchuria in 1931.)

The Manchurian assignment was clearly one of the Party's most dangerous, and in fact Lo narrowly escaped arrest on a number of occasions. Therefore, fearing for his safety, the Party Center ordered him back to Shanghai in December 1932. In the meantime, in November 1931 Lo had been elected *in absentia* to membership on the Central Executive Committee of the Chinese Soviet Republic. The Republic had been established at the First All-China Congress of Soviets in Juichin, Kiangsi, the headquarters of the armed forces led by Chu Te and Mao Tsetung. Upon his return to Shanghai at the end of 1932, Lo was made secretary of the Shanghai Executive Bureau (*chih-hsing chü*) of the All-China Federation of Labor, which, in effect, was one of the various posts that collectively made up the Party underground in Shanghai. In early 1933 he was attempting to organize a strike on the rail line from Hangchow, Chekiang, to Nanchang, Kiangsi, in order to disrupt Nationalist supply lines during one of their major Annihilation Campaigns against the Central Soviet in Kiangsi. During the course of this work he was arrested by the International Settlement police in Shanghai on March 28, 1933. Three days later he, Liao Ch'eng-chih, and Ch'en Keng (qq.v.) were tried and convicted in the settlement. Despite an appeal to the authorities by Mme. Sun Yat-sen, all three were turned over to the Nationalist authorities.[4] Ch'en Keng escaped from prison and Liao was released, but Lo was executed in Nanking in July. Lo's colleague Teng Chung-hsia was also arrested and executed at approximately the same time.

1. Jean Chesneaux, *Le Mouvement ouvrier chinois de 1919 à 1927* (Paris, 1962), p. 412.

2. *Lieh-shih chuan* (Biographies of martyrs; USSR [Moscow?], 1936), pp. 154–161; Hua Ying-shen, ed., *Chung-kuo Kung-ch'an tang lieh-shih chuan* (Biographies of Chinese Communist Party martyrs; Hong Kong, 1949), pp. 277–280.

3. *Hung-ch'i p'iao-p'iao* (Red flag fluttering; Peking, 1957), I, 93.

4. *SCMM* 281, pp. 1–11.

Lü Cheng-ts'ao

(c.1904–   ; Hai-ch'eng, Liaoning). Minister of Railways; member, CCP Central Committee.

Manchurian-born Lü Cheng-ts'ao is one of Communist China's foremost railroad and transportation specialists. After serving for many years with warlord armies in Manchuria, he became commander of the Central Hopeh District, which was dominated by the Communists during the Sino-Japanese War. He served briefly in the early 1940's as commander of the Shansi-Suiyuan Border Region and then went to Manchuria when the war ended. Lü was called to Peking in 1949 where he began his long career as a vice-minister in the Ministry of Railways. He was elected a full member of the Party Central Committee in 1956 and in 1965 was promoted to be minister of Railways.

Much of the information about Lü's early life and activity before the end of the Sino-Japanese War in 1945 comes from three interviews which he granted to Haldore Hanson (1938), Evans Carlson (1938), and Harrison Forman (1944).[1] He was born in the Manchurian province of Liaoning into a poor peasant family. His birthplace was either Hai-ch'eng, a city about midway on the rail line running from Mukden (Shen-yang) to Dairen, or Liao-yang hsien, slightly north of Hai-ch'eng on the same rail line. After receiving a primary school education, Lü, in his late teens or early twenties, joined warlord Chang Tso-lin's forces in Manchuria, working his way up through the ranks to become a platoon leader. He then attended the Northeast Military Academy in the early 1920's, apparently returning afterwards to active duty with Chang's army and remaining with it after Chang's death when his son Chang Hsueh-liang took over its command in 1928.

In 1931, when the Japanese invaded Manchuria, much of Chang Hsueh-liang's army retreated into north China in accordance with a policy of non-resistance adopted by Chiang Kai-shek, with whom Chang was then cooperating. Lü was apparently with this force, because in 1932 he was a regimental commander in Wan Fu-lin's 53rd Army, which had been part of Chang's army before it was reorganized and put under Chiang Kai-shek's command. Lü was still serving in this capacity after the Sino-Japanese War began, when Japanese troops pushed down the Peking-Hankow railroad line forcing the evacuation of Paoting, Hopeh, in September 1937. As the 53rd Army retreated, Lü's regiment (variously identified as the 683rd and the 691st) was separated from the main force. By early October it had reached Chao-hsien, Hopeh, about 200 miles south of Peking, where it was surrounded by Japanese troops. Lü told Carlson that in the action his regiment was reduced to battalion size.[2] Afterwards he decided to remain with his surviving troops in Hopeh to wage guerrilla warfare.

Other groups were also forming guerrilla bands in Hopeh. Among them were Communist guerrillas that had infiltrated the central Hopeh plains under the command of Nieh Jung-chen's 115th Division, which was headquartered in northeast Shansi near the Hopeh border. These men, who operated north of Lü in the areas around Kao-yang, Li-hsien, and Jen-ch'iu, made contact with Lü's units and were quickly able to

place them under their control. In January 1938 the various anti-Japanese elements that were generally dominated by the Communists met in Fou-p'ing (in west Hopeh near the Shansi border), where they inaugurated the Shansi-Chahar-Hopeh (Chin-Ch'a-Chi) Border Region Government. The political head of the government was Sung Shao-wen (q.v.); Lü was a member of the nine-member committee, not all of whom were Communists, which ran the government.[3]

By at least June 1938, and possibly as early as the fall of 1937, Lü was head of the Chin-Ch'a-Chi Region's Central Hopeh Military District (with Ch'eng Tzu-hua as his political commissar) and concurrently commander of the Eighth Route Army's Third Column.[4] His headquarters was near Jen-ch'iu. It appears that by mid-1938 Lü had formally joined the CCP. Few Communist commanders faced more serious difficulties than Lü during the early years of the war. Many of his problems are graphically described in George E. Taylor's account of anti-Japanese resistance in north China,[5] and Lü himself explained his difficulties to U.S. Naval Observer Evans Carlson. One of the chief problems was the flat terrain of central Hopeh, which offered no natural protection, thus forcing his men to depend on rivers, foliage, and darkness. Furthermore, the area's nearness to Peking and Tientsin, where the Japanese had large garrisons, as well as the importance of the communications route that traversed it subjected it to frequent Japanese attacks. In September 1939, for instance, An-kuo hsien was occupied by the Japanese, forcing Lü's troops to withdraw until the Japanese left in late 1940. Relations with the KMT posed another serious problem. In mid-1938 General Lu Chung-lin was sent to central Hopeh by the Nationalists to organize armed units. Initially, Lu and Lü cooperated, but soon political rivalry drove them to open hostility, which continued throughout 1939 until Lü Cheng-ts'ao won the upper hand.

As the war continued and the Communist gains in north China became better consolidated, the CCP formed a Joint Defense Headquarters at Yenan, unifying the command for the Shansi-Suiyuan and Shensi-Kansu-Ninghsia Border Regions. Sometime in the year 1942–43 Ho Lung was transferred from the Shansi-Suiyuan Border Region to Yenan to take charge of the new Headquarters. Lü replaced Ho as commander of the Shansi-Suiyuan Border Region in October 1943. Ch'en Man-yuan (q.v.), who had been working in west Hopeh, was his chief-of-staff. Lü remained in the Border Region for about a year and a half.

At the Seventh National CCP Congress, which met in Yenan in April–June 1945, Lü was elected an alternate member of the Central Committee. After the Japanese surrender, he accompanied Lin Piao and the large Communist force, which was sent from north China into the Jehol-Liaoning area of southern Manchuria. Lü became one of three deputy commanders of the Northeast Democratic Allied Army, which was established in January 1946 under Lin Piao's command. As the Communists expanded their control over Manchuria Lü became increasingly involved with communications and railways, which were vitally important for military control and economic development. In the summer of 1946 the Northeast Administrative Committee was created by the Communists to govern those parts of Manchuria which they controlled. Lü became a member under Chairman Lin Feng (q.v.) and was also named director of the Committee's Communications Department. Concurrently, Lü was commander of the Liaotung Military District.

In the late 1940's Lü also assumed the deputy directorship of the Railway Department of the Chinese Communist People's Revolutionary Military Council (PRMC), the top military policy making body of that period. T'eng Tai-yuan (q.v.) headed the department, which was abolished in late 1949. In May 1949, after north China was in Communist hands, the PRMC created the PLA Railway Corps, which was composed of a portion of Lin Piao's Fourth Field Army's Railway Column. T'eng became its commander and Lü again served as his deputy. Lü apparently left Manchuria when he took this post, for by the early summer of 1949 he was active in Peking trying to reorganize the nation's battered transportation network. In July he spoke at the All-China Railway Workers' Provisional Conference and at the close of the meetings was elected to the Preparatory Committee for the All-China Railway Workers' Trade Union. (When the union was formally inaugurated in February 1950, he was named to its Standing Committee.)

In September 1949 Lü was a representative of the PLA Headquarters to the First CPPCC, which inaugurated the PRC (October 1). He was named as a CCP representative to the Second (1954–1959), Third (1959–1964) and Fourth (1964–   ) CPPCC's, serving on the Standing Committee of the Second and Third CPPCC's, and on the National Committee of the Fourth. Immediately after the central government was established in October 1949, Lü was appointed as the senior vice-minister, once more under T'eng Tai-yuan, in the Ministry of Railways, and in early 1950 he became director of the ministry's Engineering Bureau. Since the earliest days of the PRC Lü has devoted his time almost entirely to the field of communications and railroads. For example, in January 1950 he gave a report on railway building at the National Railway Construction Conference. In March 1951 he signed the Sino-Soviet Agreement on Through Railway Traffic, and in September of

that year he spoke at a conference for railway "labor models."

In September 1954 the constitutional government was inaugurated by the First NPC (1954–1959). Lü served as a delegate from the southern Manchurian city of Penki (Pen-ch'i), which was then a special municipality with its own delegates to the Congress. He was re-elected to the Second NPC (1959–1964), this time as a deputy from his native Liaoning province (which had absorbed the Penki constituency). Lü also represented Liaoning in the Third NPC, which opened in December 1964.

Although Lü has been chiefly occupied with railways and communications problems since 1949, he has received recognition for his former military service. He has been a member of the National Defense Council since its creation in September 1954. This is largely an honorary post because the Council seldom meets and has little power. In September 1955, when national military honors were bestowed on military veterans, Lü received the Orders of Independence and Freedom and of Liberation for service between 1937 and 1950. A year later, at the Eighth Party Congress (September 1956), he was promoted to full membership on the CCP Central Committee.

In the late 1950's Railway Minister T'eng Tai-yuan's political activity declined, and by August 1960 Lü began to serve as the acting minister. He was designated as such (except for one identification of T'eng as minister in September 1962) until January 1965 when, after having been a vice-minister for 15 years, he was promoted to the post of minister at the first session of the Third NPC. Because of his importance in the ministry, Lü has appeared fairly regularly at functions in Peking concerned with railways and has also attended several international conferences dealing with the field. In December 1954 he was the chief Chinese negotiator for talks with the North Vietnamese in Peking, which resulted in a protocol to assist Vietnam in the restoration of its railways. In June–July of the following year Lü led a delegation to a meeting of the Communist bloc's "International Railway Passenger and Freight Traffic Agreement" held in East Berlin, and in January 1956 he presided over ceremonies in Peking marking the opening of the through-railway between Outer Mongolia and China. In addition, Lü led the Chinese delegations to the Sixth, Eighth, Ninth, and Tenth Conferences of Railway Ministers of Socialist Countries (Budapest, July 1961; Warsaw, May 1963; Moscow, June 1964; Hanoi, March 1965).

Although Lü had not been mentioned in a specific military assignment for many years, in March 1964 he was identified as a PLA colonel general, a rank equivalent to a three-star general in the U.S. Army. This may indicate that he holds some little publicized post (probably in logistics because of his experience in transportation and communications), which is subordinate to the Party's powerful Military Affairs Committee.

Little is known about Lü's personal life. When Hanson saw him in 1938 he commented that he was "a small man" who "breathed dignity and quiet confidence."[6] Carlson said he was "a quiet, self-effacing man" and "had the erect bearing and self-assurance of the trained officer, and yet there was a thoughtfulness about him, a respect for the dignity of the human being, which inspired confidence."[7]

1. Haldore Hanson, *"Humane Endeavour"* (New York, 1939), pp. 220–221; Evans Fordyce Carlson, *Twin Stars of China* (New York, 1940), pp. 243–247; Harrison Forman, *Report From Red China* (New York, 1945), pp. 200, 223.

2. Carlson, p. 245.

3. *K'ang-chan chung-te Chung-kuo cheng-chih* (Chinese politics during the war of resistance; Yenan, 1940), p. 454.

4. Chalmers A. Johnson, *Peasant Nationalism and Communist Power* (Stanford, Calif., 1962), p. 35.

5. George E. Taylor, *The Struggle for North China* (New York, 1940), pp. 102–104.

6. Hanson, p. 220.

7. Carlson, pp. 243–244.

Lu Hsu-chang

(c.1911–   ; Shanghai). Specialist in trade with non-Communist nations; vice-minister, Ministry of Foreign Trade.

Lu Hsu-chang is generally regarded as Peking's leading official in the conduct of trade with non-Communist nations. He is a graduate of the College of Commerce in Shanghai. He worked for a number of years in insurance and trading companies and by 1946 was the shipping department manager in a large export firm in Shanghai. By the next year Lu was general manager of the China National Trade Company, a concern that imported American medicines and exported Chinese drugs and pharmaceuticals. In the postwar period he was also reported to have managed Communist-sponsored foreign trade and insurance companies in Hong Kong. Presumably he was a CCP member by this time, but in any event Lu had joined the Communist government in Shanghai after the fall of that city in May 1949, becoming by the latter part of the year a deputy director of the East China Finance and Economics Committee, an interim body established in September under Ch'en I's East China Military Region. To administer the coastal provinces, the Communists established in early 1950 the East China Military and Administrative Committee (ECMAC), and in February Lu was appointed to membership on the ECMAC's Finance and Economics Committee and as deputy director of its Trade Department. He served in the latter post until September 1951 and continued to sit on the Finance and Economics Committee under Chairman Tseng Shan until September 1952, but by this date he had already been transferred to Peking.

Lu was transferred from Shanghai to Peking by early 1952, and in April of that year journeyed to Moscow to participate in the First International Economic Conference (see under Nan Han-ch'en, the Chinese delegation leader). The main purpose of the conference was to break through the trade embargo imposed on the Communist bloc by the Western powers as a consequence of the Korean War. The Chinese delegation concluded a number of preliminary agreements in Moscow with business and industrial circles from several non-Communist nations, and to exploit these agreements Lu was sent to East Berlin where in June he signed trade contracts with English firms in his capacity as manager of the China National Import and Export Corporation, a position he held from 1950 to about 1954. In the meantime, in May 1952, Lu was named to membership on the China Committee for the Promotion of International Trade (CCPIT), established in hopes of further exploiting the trade contacts made at the Moscow meetings. In practice, the CCPIT has been an unofficial arm of the Foreign Trade Ministry and is used principally to trade with nations not having diplomatic relations with Peking. Four years later, in April 1956, Lu was made a member of the CCPIT's Foreign Trade Arbitration Committee, set up to secure "speedy and equitable settlements" of disputes that might arise.

In September 1953 Lu was made director of the Foreign Trade Ministry's Third Bureau, responsible for trade with the West. He quickly won promotions in the ministry, advancing to assistant-minister in June 1955 and to vice-minister in October 1956, a position he still retains. In the meantime, he had made two further trips abroad, visiting Japan from March to May 1955 as a deputy leader of a trade delegation and leading another such group to Ulan Bator, where he remained from March to August 1956, finally signing an agreement providing for Chinese economic and technical aid to Mongolia. Over the ensuing years Lu's record of foreign travels has been as impressive as that of any foreign trade official in the PRC. On two occasions he journeyed to Communist nations, the first of these from January to March 1958 when he signed trade agreements in Yugoslavia and Albania. The second trip took him in July–August 1960 to Cuba where he signed long-term trade and payments and scientific-technical agreements.

These trips to Communist areas, however,

have been the exceptions in Lu's work, which has been almost entirely concerned with non-Communist nations. Perhaps his two most significant trips abroad took place in 1961 and 1964, in both cases to Africa where he signed trade agreements or conferred with officials about future trade prospects, in addition to representing the PRC at various official functions. The first of these trips was a four-month tour from January to May 1961 that took Lu to the United Arab Republic, Mali, Guinea, Ghana, Nigeria, Sierra Leone, and Morocco. He devoted himself to trade relations in each nation, excepting Sierra Leone, which he visited as the official PRC representative to independence ceremonies. This trip was one of the first made by a Chinese Communist official to Black Africa. He was again in Africa on a seven-nation tour, described as a government goodwill mission, lasting from July to September 1964. Once more he spent most of his time talking with economic administrators on his visits to Mali, the Congo (Brazzaville), Niger, Nigeria, Dahomey, Cameroun, and the Central African Republic. While in Brazzaville, he represented the PRC at celebrations marking both the first anniversary of the "August Revolution" and the Congolese national day. Lu has been on the African continent on two other occasions, the first from October to December 1958 when he negotiated a trade and payments agreement in Cairo (in addition to a side trip in December 1958–January 1959 to Iraq where he signed a similar agreement). His other visit to Africa occurred in December 1964 when he spent three weeks in Kenya working out the details of an economic and technical cooperation protocol, in addition to attending the first anniversary celebrations of the republic. In brief, few Chinese officials have spent as much time in Africa as Lu.

Apart from his extensive tours of Africa, Lu has been abroad on still other occasions. In May–June 1959 he conducted trade talks in Helsinki and Stockholm, and then in March 1963 he arrived in London on what was described as the first visit by a Chinese of ministerial rank as an official guest of the British government. The visit came at a time when the Chinese were reorienting their trade away from overdependence upon the Communist bloc; the British, realizing this, were anxious to gain their share of the China trade. Lu spent three weeks in England conferring with top government and industrial leaders, and during the course of the visit his group displayed particular interest in purchases of fertilizers and chemical plants. Then he went for brief but official visits to Switzerland and the Netherlands, after which he spent a week in mid-May on a "private" visit in Hong Kong, one of Peking's major trading partners.

Summarizing the record, in the 1952–1964 period, Lu has visited 27 nations (some of them twice), all but six of them non-Communist countries. The emphasis on his dealings with the non-Communist world becomes all the more strikingly apparent from a review of the negotiations he has conducted in Peking. In the same 1952–1964 period, he signed one or more agreements or protocols with representatives from 13 countries, each of them non-Communist. He has also participated in trade negotiations on numerous other occasions in which some other Chinese official was the signatory, and in the overwhelming majority of cases these talks were held with officials from non-Communist countries. Peking's massive importations of food grains that began in the early sixties, mainly from Australia and Canada, have never been publicly acknowledged in the Chinese Communist press, presumably because it would embarrass the PRC to admit reliance upon foreign sources. As a logical result of his extensive knowledge of Western trading practices and potentials, Lu has been one of the key Chinese participants in these negotiations.

Lu is regarded by Western business and government officials who have dealt with him as a man of considerable intelligence, and one completely in control of the facts. He is said to be aided in his work by an affable personality and a casual manner, and he gives the impression of being fully entrusted by his superiors to make firm decisions and commitments in the name of the PRC.[1] Lu's career since 1949 suggests that his talents as a highly trained specialist are appreciated by higher authorities. Unlike many other PRC officials he has devoted virtually no time to extracurricular activities (e.g., engaging in ideological campaigns). He has been a Central Committee member since April 1955 of the China Democratic National Construction Association (ostensibly a non-Communist political party), and in December 1956 he was elected to the Standing Committee of the All-China Federation of Industry and Commerce. Membership in such organizations could be regarded as a nominal assignment in the case of many PRC officials, but as both organizations consist largely of leading business and commercial figures, Lu's association with these men is doubtless beneficial to his work in the promotion of foreign trade.

1. Interviews conducted in Hong Kong with Western businessmen and government officials, July 1963, May 1964, and August 1964.

Lu P'ing

(c.1910–   ; Hopeh?). Former president, Peking University.

A member of Communist-led youth organizations in the mid-1930's, Lu P'ing was among the top youth leaders in the early years of the PRC. He was subsequently in charge of the Harbin Railway Administration, and from 1954 to 1957 he was a vice-minister of Railways. From 1957 to 1960 he was vice-president of Peking University, and from 1960 until he fell victim to the Cultural Revolution in 1966, he was president of this famed school.

Judging from the date of his student days in Peking, Lu P'ing was probably born in 1910 or soon thereafter, and a former professor at Peking University believes that he is a native of Hopeh.[1] He apparently had his first contact with the left-wing, and ultimately the Communists, when he was a student in the mid-1930's at China's foremost academic institution, Peking University (Peita). He was almost certainly a participant in the December Ninth Movement, the name given to a series of student demonstrations that began on December 9, 1935, in response to Japanese incursions into north China (see under Li Ch'ang). At first the demonstrations were motivated principally by nationalism, but soon the Communists became active organizers. One of the outgrowths of this patriotic activity was the National Liberation Vanguard of China (NLVC), a student group formed in early 1936, mainly from students in Peking and Tientsin. By no later than the spring of 1936 Lu was deeply involved in the affairs of the NLVC. Although the students were united in their opposition to the Japanese, they were splintered into a number of student organizations, and thus the NLVC was engaged in internal battles for the allegiance of the students within the various north China universities. According to a Communist account of 1961, Lu took part in a series of debates in the spring of 1936, in which the students argued the appropriate tactics to follow to arouse the nation to action against Japan.[2] The NLVC had been established in February 1936, but it did not hold its first congress until the next February. Although it is not known if Lu attended, he was elected one of the 39 members of the NLVC Executive Committee. A former faculty member at Peita believes that Lu went to Communist-held areas in the northwest to engage in guerrilla warfare after the Japanese attacked in mid-1937.

A number of young students like Lu fled to the northwest in the late 1930's, and because of their youth, most of them did not receive much public attention in those war years. But a large number of these young men emerged after the end of the Sino-Japanese War to positions of authority. Only fragmentary information is available on Lu, but apparently he worked briefly in 1945 as a propagandist for the CCP in Shanghai, and then from 1946 was in Hong Kong serving as secretary of the Kowloon Branch Office of the CCP South China Bureau (Kowloon being a major sub-division of the Crown Colony of Hong Kong). Lu next emerged on the public scene back on the mainland in 1948. In August of that year the Communists held the Sixth

Labor Congress in Harbin, Manchuria, out of which grew the All-China Federation of Labor (ACFL). Lu was named in May 1949 as a deputy director of the ACFL Youth Labor Department (under Feng Wen-pin, then a senior youth leader), a post he held until about 1952. He became even more deeply involved in youth affairs with the convocation of two youth congresses in the spring of 1949. Out of one of these congresses grew the New Democratic Youth League (NDYL), China's most important youth organization, constitutionally linked to the CCP. Lu was elected to the Central Committee and named to the Standing Committee, then consisting of only nine members. He was also given three other tasks with the Laegue: from 1949 to about 1952 he was head of the NDYL Young Workers Department, secretary of the League's "Railway Work Committee," and a committee member of the North China branch of the NDYL. A few days after the NDYL was established (April 1949), another youth congress met (May 1949) and formed the All-China Federation of Democratic Youth (ACFDY). Lu served on the preparatory committee for the congress (representing the North China "liberated areas") and was subsequently named to the ACFDY First National Committee. Both of these youth organizations held congresses in mid-1953, at which time Lu (already transferred to other work) was dropped from all his positions within both the League and Federation.

Aside from youth work in the first few years of the PRC, Lu P'ing also participated in the formation of the central government in 1949 as well as the formation of the Sino-Soviet Friendship Association and the All-China Railways Workers' Trade Union. He was a delegate of the Youth League to the first session of the CPPCC in September 1949, at which time the central government was formed. During the session he served as a member of the committee which drafted the Organic Law of the CPPCC, one of the key documents adopted at that time. In October 1949 he was selected for membership on the Executive Board of the newly formed Sino-Soviet Friendship Association (remaining on the board until December 1954 when the Second Executive Board was formed), and late in 1949 he was named to the Preparatory Committee of the All-China Railways Workers Trade Union; when the union was brought into existence in February 1950, Lu was elected a vice-chairman under Li Chieh-po (later a Party Central Committee alternate). He remained as a vice-chairman of the union until the second congress was held in April 1954. Closely associated with his work in the railway trade union was his activity within the Ministry of Railways. From 1950 to about 1952 he was head of the ministry's Political Department, and in September 1951 he served on the presidium (steering committee) for a nationwide conference of "model" railway workers.

From the end of 1952 to October 1954, Lu was in Harbin serving as director of the Harbin Railway Administration, an organization directly subordinate to the Ministry of Railways. Apparently his work was viewed with favor, for in October 1954 he was brought to Peking and made a vice-minister of Railways under Minister T'eng Tai-yuan. Despite the importance of this post, nothing was heard of Lu until October 1957 when he was transferred from his position as a vice-minister to a vice-presidency of his alma mater, Peking University. The Peita president at that time was Ma Yin-ch'u, a non-Communist and one of China's most famed economists. Within a few months of becoming vice-president, Lu was identified as secretary of the CCP Committee at Peita; politically, therefore, Lu was the ranking university official by early 1958. Two years later, in March 1960, Lu succeeded to Ma's post as president. Ma had been strongly attacked in the Party press for three years prior to his removal for his open disagreement with various Party-sponsored economic policies. Apart from the presidency of Peita, Lu has held still another post within the school from at least March 1959 when he was identified as chairman of the university "political course pedagogical research office."

In 1958, Lu assumed two new posts, one in a "friendship" association and the other in the legislative arm of government. In September 1958 the China-Rumania Friendship Association was formed; Lu was named as a vice-president and then in 1960 succeeded to the presidency. Normally, such posts are not particularly taxing on the time of the officials involved; in this instance, however, the increasingly close Sino-Rumanian ties, dating from the winter of 1963–64, have meant that Lu has had to be fairly active in entertaining the frequent visitors from Rumania. Also in 1958, he was elected as a deputy from Heilungkiang to the Second NPC; after serving during the term of the Second NPC (1959–1964) he was re-elected to the Third NPC (which first met in December 1964–January 1965), but on this occasion he was elected as a deputy from Peking. In 1960 he became involved with another friendship association when he was named to council membership on the newly formed (March 1960) China-Latin America Friendship Association. Three months later (June 1960), Lu attended a national conference of "advanced" workers in the fields of culture and education.

From the mid-1950's Lu has been often reported in the national press, most frequently in connection with Peita. To cite a random but typical example, he spoke on the achievements of Albania on November 25, 1962, at a meeting at the university held to mark the 50th anniversary of Albanian independence. On occasion he has written articles on educational matters. He wrote one on the achievements of Peita for the university journal in 1959[3] and another on teacher training for the Peking *Kuang-ming jih-pao* of September 12, 1963;[4] in the latter he urged that teachers have more time for research and discussed the need for technical proficiency among teachers (apart from ideological considerations).

Lu is known to have suffered from high blood pressure from at least the late 1950's,[5] but to judge from his frequent public appearances this does not seem to have impaired his capacity for work. In fact, a former Peita student who was acquainted with Lu asserts that he is a large, robust, and very energetic man. This same person further described him as a very confident personality, a believer in hard work, and a person who tended to be patronizing toward intellectuals.

Lu continued to enjoy an active political career until the late spring of 1966 when, in one of the opening phases of the Great Proletarian Cultural Revolution, he was severely denounced and removed from the presidency of Peita. He has subsequently been the object of innumerable attacks in the official press and the famed Red Guard wall posters and periodicals.

1. Interview in San Francisco with former professor at Peking University, 1962.

2. Li Ch'ang *et al., "I-erh-chiu" hui-i-lu* (Reminiscences of "December Ninth"; Peking, 1961), p. 21.

3. "Peking University's Colossal Achievements during the Past Decade and Its Current Work," *Pei-ching Ta-hsueh hsueh-pao* (Peking University journal), no. 4, 1959; translated in *SCMM* 207.

4. Translated in *SCMP* 3078.

5. Interview, see note 1; interview in Cambridge, Mass., with a former Peita student, May 1966.

Lu Ting-i

(c.1901–　　　; Wu-hsi, Kiangsu). Propagandist; alternate member, CCP Politburo.

Lu Ting-i, a Youth League leader in the twenties, has devoted most of his career to propaganda work for the Red Army and later the CCP. For the better part of two decades after 1945 he headed the Party's Propaganda Department and wrote a large number of authoritative articles delineating Party policies in cultural and educational fields. He has also been a frequent spokesman for international policies advocated by the Chinese Communists, particularly in connection with the United States and the Soviet Union. Elected to the Party Central Committee in 1945, he was elevated to alternate membership on the Politburo in 1956. However, a decade later he was one of the victims of the Great Proletarian Cultural Revolution.

Lu was born in Wu-hsi (Wusih), Kiangsu, where his father was a small landowner and the operator of a textile factory. He graduated from Nan-yang (South Seas) University in Shanghai (later known as Chiao-t'ung or "Communications" University) and while there participated in the May Fourth Movement (1919). He joined the Socialist (later Communist) Youth League in the early twenties and was also said to have been employed by the Canton-Kowloon Railway. Various Japanese sources claim that he studied in the United States, but other details known about his career suggest that these reports are erroneous. In 1924 Lu joined the CCP and the editorial board of *Nan-yang* (published at the Nan-yang school in Shanghai), a journal that promoted patriotism and social reform.[1] During these years of the mid-twenties, he apparently worked closely with Party leader Jen Pi-shih (q.v.), whom, after the latter's death, Lu described as his "leader, comrade, and teacher."[2] In 1927 Lu became head of the Propaganda Department of the Youth League, then led by Jen. In the same year he also became editor of *Chung-kuo ch'ing-nien* (China youth), the organ of the Youth League, but within a year or so he had been replaced by Li Ch'iu-shih (q.v.).

Partly because of the dangers of holding Party meetings in China, the CCP convened its Sixth National Congress in Moscow in mid-1928. Lu attended and was also the chief Communist Youth League (CYL) delegate to an international Communist youth conference in Moscow. He remained there as a student; according to some sources he studied at the Sun Yat-sen University. Returning home in 1929 he worked in the Propaganda Department of the CCP headquarters in Shanghai. Like many prominent CCP and CYL leaders, Lu left Shanghai for the Kiangsi Soviet by 1931, and from that year to 1934 he headed the CYL Propaganda Department, then headquartered in Juichin. During a part of this period he was concurrently editor of *Hung-se Chung-hua* (Red China), then one of the most important Party newspapers. In addition, he was identified in 1933 as a member of the Propaganda Department of the Red Army's General Political Department, continuing in this capacity during the Long March (1934–35).

When Edgar Snow was in north Shensi in 1936 he identified Lu as a member of the CYL Central Committee, then headed by Feng Wen-pin (q.v.). Snow saw a good deal of Lu during his visit, and records that Lu requested (presumably in jest) that the American writer "buy, equip, and man an air fleet" on the proceeds of

his sales of photographs of the Communists.[3] Authoress Nym Wales also saw Lu during her visit to Yenan in 1937, noting that he spoke "excellent English."[4] During the period from 1936 to 1937, Lu headed the Propaganda Department of the Red Army's General Political Department and in 1937 was also identified as director of the Propaganda Department of the First Front Army, the force that Mao had led from Kiangsi on the Long March. When the Eighth Route Army was activated immediately after the outbreak of war in mid-1937, Lu became deputy director of its Propaganda Department, a post he presumably held throughout the war against Japan.

By the time of the Party's Seventh Party Congress, held in Yenan from April to June 1945, Lu could be regarded as one of the CCP's top propagandists. He addressed the meetings and at the close of the Congress was one of only 44 full members elected to the Central Committee. That same year he succeeded Ch'in Pang-hsien as director of the Party's Propaganda Department, a post he was to hold for most of the next two decades (see below). In 1946, when the Communists last participated in the national government's Political Consultative Conference in Chungking, Lu attended as one of the CCP representatives. He was also among the chief Party negotiators in the discussions held between the CCP, the KMT, and the Americans following the cease-fire agreement (January 1946) worked out by U.S. Special Envoy George C. Marshall (see under Chou En-lai, the top CCP negotiator).

In the early days of January 1947, when all hopes for any reconciliation between the KMT and the CCP were collapsing, Lu delivered a strong statement denouncing the KMT and the United States. In this "memorandum" dealing with the postwar international situation, Lu called for a "world-wide united front against . . . American imperialism" and support for the Soviet Union.[5] His statement was the logical extension of Mao's international policies, outlined in the latter's famous "On New Democracy" of 1940, and a precursor of Mao's 1949 statement that China was "leaning to one side" (i.e., the Soviet Union).[6] Lu closed his January 1947 statement with the prophecy: "It may be forecast categorically that the face of China and the world will be vastly different after three to five more years." Within a few weeks after this statement, KMT forces captured Yenan. The top command of the CCP broke up into two sections (see under Hsu Kuang-ta); Lu joined Mao, Chou En-lai, and his old colleague Jen Pi-shih in a circuitous march through the barren hills of north Shensi in an effort to avoid pursuing Nationalist forces. To lead this small band of key Communists, a special unit known as the Third Detachment was formed, with Jen as the commander and Lu as political commissar.[7]

The period in the "wilderness" ended in early 1949 when Mao, Lu, and the others went to Peking, which had been surrendered to the Communists in January 1949. Like most of the leading Communists, Lu spent the remainder of the year engaged in preparations for the inauguration of the new central government and many of the "mass" organizations. For example, he spoke at two major conferences in July 1949, one of literary and artistic workers and another of social science workers, and in September he was named as a vice-chairman of the China New Political Science Research Association's Preparatory Committee. In the last part of September, as a representative of the CCP, Lu attended the First CPPCC, the organization that brought the new government into existence (October 1). When assignments were made in the central government in October, Lu was appointed as a vice-chairman of the Culture and Education Committee (CEC) under Chou En-lai's Government Administration Council (the cabinet). Kuo Mo-jo was the chairman of the CEC, but the real political authority was obviously held by Vice-Chairmen Lu and Ch'en Po-ta (q.v.), Lu's deputy in the Propaganda Department. The CEC, in fact, could be regarded as the government counterpart of the Propaganda Department and under its authority. In addition to his government assignment, Lu received three others during October 1949 in "mass" or professional organizations: member, Executive Board, Sino-Soviet Friendship Association (to date); member, National Committee, China Peace Committee (to 1958); and Council member, Association for Reforming the Chinese Written Language (to 1954).

From the earliest days of the PRC Lu made some of the most authoritative statements pertaining to the field of propaganda, journalism, arts and letters, and education. In fact, the basic CCP policies in these fields during the first 15 years of the Communist government can be traced by an examination of Lu's numerous speeches and articles, as is readily revealed in the writings of scholars who have dealt with Chinese Communist cultural and educational programs.[8] One of his earliest essays, which echoed Mao's theories about art and literature, was published in the Cominform journal *For a Lasting Peace, For a People's Democracy!* (Bucharest, March 31, 1950) and reprinted in authoritative CCP publications. Lu summarized the new government's educational philosophy and stressed that art and literature must be regarded as "major weapons" in "ideological education." In a section dealing with the "reformation of intellectuals" he noted that the Communists had already given more than 200,000 intellectuals short courses to "build up a revolutionary outlook on life and an ideology of dialectical materialism and historical materialism."

Although Lu has written most frequently about domestic questions, he authored an important article on the 30th anniversary of the CCP (July 1, 1951) entitled "The World Significance of the Chinese Revolution." This was published in *Hsueh-hsi* (Study), then the Party's leading journal, and also in *For a Lasting Peace, for a People's Democracy!* One authority has written of this: "Probably the high-water mark of propaganda for the Chinese revolutionary model occurred on July 1, 1951 [when Lu] described the Chinese revolution as the 'greatest event in world history since the October Revolution' and as the 'prototype of the revolutions in colonial and semi-colonial countries.' This and other strident claims evoked a Soviet denial that the Chinese revolution could serve as a 'stereotype' for the rest of Asia. During 1952, in view of this Soviet attitude, the need for Soviet support because of the growing tension in Korea, and the failure of the Communist insurrections in Southeast Asia except in Vietnam, the [CCP] dropped its calls to 'armed struggle' against 'imperialism' in Asia and moderated its claims for its own revolutionary model."[9] In many respects Lu's article followed the call issued less than two years earlier by Liu Shao-ch'i for "Chinese style" revolutions (see under Liu). The fact that little was heard of Lu for the next two years, suggests that he may have been offered as the scapegoat for having made a policy statement opposed by the Soviets. If true, it is ironic that his "re-emergence" in 1953 was marked by a eulogistic article on Stalin's writings, published in the *JMJP* (November 23, 1953). Lu also ran afoul of domestic Party policies in 1952, and in April of that year made a "self-confession," apparently in connection with the "correct" manner of dealing with China's bourgeois capitalists.[10] A more substantive sign of his temporary decline in power is the fact that by mid-1953 Hsi Chung-hsun (q.v.) replaced Lu as director of the Propaganda Department, holding the post for about a year and a half. Hsi was a veteran associate of Politburo member Kao Kang (q.v.), often regarded as a "pro-Soviet" element within the CCP. During the 1953–54 period Lu served as a deputy to Hsi. However, by October 1954 Lu was back as the director, retaining the post for more than a decade, during which he once again made some of the regime's most important pronouncements.

In 1954 Lu was elected to represent his native Kiangsu in the First NPC, the organization that inaugurated the constitutional government at its initial session in September 1954. At this time Lu was made a member of the NPC Standing Committee, retaining the post until the Second NPC opened in April 1959. In 1956 he received the following related posts: vice-chairman, Committee for the Popularization of the Common Spoken Language (*p'u-t'ung-hua*); member,

National Association for the Elimination of Illiteracy; and member, Committee for the Examination and Formulation of the Plan for the Phoneticization of the Han Language. (The language reform programs are described in the biography of Wu Yü-chang.) But these assignments were far overshadowed by Lu's speech of May 25, 1956—one of the most famous and important speeches in the history of the PRC. Entitled "Let Flowers of Many Kinds Bloom, Let Diverse Schools of Thought Contend," it was delivered before a meeting of Party members, scientists, and men of letters. This was an elaboration of an unpublished speech earlier in the month by Mao, as well as of a talk given earlier in the year by Chou En-lai. Collectively, these speeches were an attempt by the Party to encourage the intellectuals to have greater independence of thought and creativity. In particular, encouragement was given for work in scholarship and the arts, although it was made clear that the advocacy of "counterrevolutionary" political ideas would be crushed. In the words of one writer, the campaign "seemed designed to encourage the intelligentsia to believe that the regime should be viewed as authoritarian but not totalitarian."[11] In fact, however, the movement was slow in gathering force—probably because the intellectuals had learned to be cautious in light of previous campaigns directed against them. Although the Hundred Flowers or "blooming and contending" period is often dated from Lu's May 1956 speech, it was not until a year later that, under further encouragement, the intellectuals expressed themselves with extraordinary candor. The CCP, suddenly finding itself under a sweeping attack, moved swiftly to end the movement, launching a counterattack known as the "anti-rightist" campaign. It was under these circumstances that Lu, a major initiator of the "liberal" program, was now cast in the opposite role, that of articulating the Party's demand to silence the critics of the CCP. This new "rectification" campaign directed against "rightists" was a major theme of the third session of the First NPC in June–July 1957. Lu's speech, a major document in the Party's *volte-face,* was entitled "Where We Differ from the Rightists." Its sharp attack on the "rightists" and its staunch defense of the CCP ("without the Communist Party there is no New China") set the tone for a campaign against dissident elements, including many within the Party, which lasted through the spring of 1958.

In the meantime, at the Party's Eighth Congress in September 1956, Lu was re-elected a member of the Central Committee. A day later, at the First Plenum of the new Central Committee, Lu made a significant advance in the Party hierarchy when he was elected for the first time as an alternate Politburo member. Fourteen

months later, in November 1957, he was among the large group of key Party leaders who accompanied Mao Tse-tung to Moscow for the celebrations marking the 40th anniversary of the Russian Revolution.

In late 1957 the Party decided to inaugurate two important and closely related educational measures, the "part-work, part-study" concept and a nationwide system of agricultural middle schools. Lu has been specifically cited as the man who proposed these programs, which were in keeping with the spirit of the Great Leap Forward and the "people's communes," inaugurated in 1958. These new educational measures were the subject of a major article by Lu, which appeared in the new Party journal *Hung-ch'i* (Red flag; no. 7, September 1, 1958). Emphasizing the necessity of political guidance in the educational system, he claimed that by mid-1958 1,240 hsien had "universal primary education" and that 68,000 middle schools had been set up and were being managed "by the people themselves." Writing in March 1959 on the first anniversary of the establishment of the agricultural middle schools, Lu claimed that there were already 37 million students enrolled. A year later, in *Jenmin chiao-yü* (People's education, February 1960), Lu summarized some of the developments in the new educational endeavors, stressing the relationship of the programs to the need for technically trained cadres for China's rural areas. Two months later he again spoke on these and other educational questions in an important address before the Second NPC. These educational innovations and Lu's role in them are discussed in detail in a monograph by Robert D. Barendsen.[12]

Serving again as a deputy from Kiangsu, Lu attended the first session of the Second NPC in April 1959. Although not re-elected to the NPC Standing Committee, he was named one of four new vice-premiers in Chou En-lai's State Council. In February 1960 Lu was chairman of the preparatory committee for a national conference of "advanced workers" in cultural and educational fields. The conference was held in June, and with over 6,000 persons in attendance it was one of the largest meetings in the history of the PRC. Lu gave a brief inaugural address, but the keynote speech was delivered by Lin Feng (q.v.).

In 1960 Lu returned to the forefront as a spokesman for the Chinese viewpoint in the Sino-Soviet ideological dispute, which was becoming increasingly public. The Chinese used the month of April (the 90th anniversary of Lenin's birth) as the occasion for major articles in *Hung-ch'i* (Red flag) and the *JMJP,* as well as a major speech by Lu, to attack and reject the Soviet position on crucial issues—"peaceful co-existence, the non-inevitability of war, and the possibility of peaceful roads to power in non-

Communist countries."[13] The issues were the subject of further discussions in November–December 1960 when Liu Shao-ch'i led a top-level delegation (including Lu) to Moscow. The ostensible purpose was to attend the 43rd anniversary of the Russian Revolution, but far more important was the "Moscow Meeting of Representatives of Communist and Workers' Parties." In later years Communist media revealed that this landmark "summit" meeting of world Communist leaders was the scene of bitter Sino-Soviet disputes.

The next major event in Lu's career took place in September 1962 when the CCP held its 10th Plenum. Lu, K'ang Sheng, and Lo Jui-ch'ing became new members of the Central Secretariat, and Huang K'o-ch'eng and T'an Cheng (qq.v.) were removed. Headed by Teng Hsiao-p'ing, the Secretariat is responsible for implementing the policies of the Party Politburo. As of the 10th Plenum, Lu was one of only six men concurrently a member of both the Politburo and the Secretariat. In 1964 he was elected from Kiangsu to the Third NPC, and at the close of its inaugural session in January 1965 he replaced Shen Yen-ping as minister of Culture. Throughout the early and mid-sixties Lu continued to play an extremely prominent role in educational and propaganda activities and frequently appeared in public with the CCP's top leaders, including Mao Tse-tung. However, he was one of the first and most important victims of the Great Proletarian Cultural Revolution, and by mid-1966 he had been replaced as director of the CCP Propaganda Department by T'ao Chu (q.v.).

Lu's first wife, by whom he had two children, was executed by the Nationalists in 1928. He remarried in 1941 and by 1947 he and his second wife had three children.

1. Chow Tse-tung, *Research Guide to the May Fourth Movement* (Cambridge, Mass., 1963), p. 56.

2. *CB* 26.

3. Edgar Snow, *Random Notes on Red China, 1936–1945* (Cambridge, Mass., 1957), p. 52; Edgar Snow, *Red Star over China* (New York, 1938), p. 367.

4. Nym Wales, *Inside Red China* (New York, 1939), pp. 26–27.

5. *United States Relations with China, with Special Reference to the Period 1944–1949* (Washington, D.C., 1949), pp. 710–719.

6. Tang Tsou, *America's Failure in China, 1941–50* (Chicago, Ill., 1963), p. 349; Stuart Schram, *Mao Tse-tung* (New York, 1966), p. 207.

7. *Hung-ch'i p'iao-p'iao* (Red flag fluttering; Peking, 1957), III, 345.

8. E.g., Stewart Fraser, ed., *Chinese Communist Education* (New York, 1965); Frederick T. C. Yu, *Mass Persuasion in Communist China* (New York, 1964).

9. Harold C. Hinton, *Communist China in World Politics* (Boston, Mass., 1966), p. 70.

10. Arthur A. Cohen, *The Communism of Mao Tse-tung* (Chicago, Ill., 1964), p. 18.

11. *Ibid.,* p. 150.

12. Robert D. Barendsen, *Half-Work Half-Study Schools in Communist China* (Washington, D.C., 1964).

13. Donald S. Zagoria, *The Sino-Soviet Conflict, 1956–1961* (Princeton, N.J., 1962), pp. 299ff.

Lü Tung

Minister of Metallurgical Industry.

Lü Tung has devoted almost his entire career to the field of heavy industry. He was first reported, according to Japanese sources, as director of the "first sub-office" of the "Central Shansi Administrative Office" in 1945. In using the term "administrative office" at that time the Communists referred to government as opposed to Party or military offices. In the summer and fall of 1945, thousands of Communist soldiers and cadre moved into Manchuria from north and northwest China. Lü was probably among this group, for in the postwar period he was reported (again by Japanese sources) as head of the Finance and Economics Office for those portions of Liaotung province controlled by the Communists.

By 1949 Lü was serving as deputy director of the Industry Department of the Northeast Administrative Committee, the organ of governmental rule for all of Manchuria, a post he retained when this committee was transformed into the Northeast People's Government in August 1949. (For a period in 1949 this department was known as the Heavy Industry Department.) Lü's superior in the Industry Department was Wang Ho-shou (q.v.), under whom he was to serve for most of the next 15 years. Another post that Lü held for a brief time in 1949 under the Northeast People's Government was membership on the Finance and Economics Committee.

Although Lü did not hold high rank in 1950, he was with the highest ranking Party officers in January 1950 when he accompanied Chou En-lai to Moscow, where Chou joined Mao Tse-tung for the negotiations that led to the signing of the Sino-Soviet Treaty of Alliance on February 14, 1950. In addition to this key treaty, lesser agreements were signed at the same time, including an agreement on the joint use of the Chinese Changchun Railway in Manchuria and another concerning credit to China amounting to U.S. $300,000,000. In view of Lü's background, it seems probable that his assignment on this mission had to do with these technical agreements rather than the political-military treaty of alliance.

In August 1952, economic specialist Li Fu-ch'un relinquished his position as minister of Heavy Industry to Wang Ho-shou, Lü's mentor in Manchuria. Simultaneously, Lü also transferred to Peking, becoming a vice-minister under Wang. Lü made a report on the ministry before the Government Administration Council (the cabinet) on June 6, 1953, and at an October–November 1954 forum in Peking on metal–research work, Lü spoke on metallurgical work. Otherwise, his activity was not frequently mentioned in the national press in the early 1950's.

In May 1956, during a partial government reorganization, the Ministry of Heavy Industry was divided into three ministries: Chemical Industry, Building Materials Industry, and Metallurgical Industry. Lü joined the last-named, to which he was officially appointed a vice-minister in January 1957, once again under Minister Wang Ho-shou. From that time until he replaced Wang in mid-1964, Lü was the senior vice-minister in this important industry. He was rather active in the mid-1950's, serving as a host to foreign visitors concerned with the metallurgical industry, and was often reported speaking at conferences, conducting inspections, or attending ceremonies in connection with iron and steel plants. In February 1960, Lü made an official report before a meeting of the NPC Standing Committee on the work of his ministry in 1959 and the plans for 1960. Then for unexplained reasons he was out of the news for four years. He continued to be listed on official rosters as the senior vice-minister, so perhaps his absence was due to ill-health.

Then, in July 1964, Lü was appointed to replace Wang Ho-shou as Minister of Metallurgical Industry. Later in the year he was named to membership on the Fourth National Committee of the CPPCC as a representative of the China Scientific and Technical Association; the Fourth Committee held its first session in December 1964–January 1965. At the same time the CPPCC was meeting, the Third NPC was holding its first session. At these meetings Lü was reappointed to his ministerial post and spoke on the metallurgical industry, claiming that new strides had been made by China in both the variety and quality of metallurgical products manufactured in recent years.

Ma Hsi-wu

(1898–1962; Pao-an hsien, Shensi). Vice-President, Supreme People's Court.

Ma Hsi-wu worked as a revolutionary in the northwest for over two decades and is credited with a major role in evolving a new system of legal procedures. From his transfer to Peking in 1954 to his death eight years later he was a vice-president of the Supreme People's Court. Ma was born in Pao-an hsien, Shensi, which was later renamed Chih-tan hsien in honor of Liu chih-tan (q.v.). Ma was a Hui, one of the several Moslem nationality groups living in China. His family, which may have originally come from Kansu, were poor peasants and Ma received only a primary school education. In the words of his obituary, he "started his revolutionary career" in 1930. He joined the CCP in 1935, the same year that Mao Tse-tung's Long Marchers arrived in Shensi. Ma's obituary states that under the leadership of the Party he "carried out the work of the soldiers' movement among the KMT troops" and that he took part in "organizing Red armed forces." The exact meaning of this is not clear, but it probably refers to the continuing efforts made by the Communists in Shensi to entice KMT troops in the northwest into joining the Communists, particularly troops under the command of Yang Hu-ch'eng.

Ma is officially credited with having a role in the development of the Shensi-Kansu-Ninghsia (Shen-Kan-Ning) Border Region Government, established in 1937. He held a number of posts under this administration. In the government's early days these included: director of the Shensi-Kansu Grain Department, director of the Shensi-Kansu National Economic Department, and chairman of the Shensi-Kansu Soviet. At a later date (probably midway in the Sino-Japanese War), Ma was vice-commissioner and then commissioner for Ch'ing-huan and Lung-tung administrative districts under the Shen-Kan-Ning government. Information on Ch'ing-huan is lacking, but Lung-tung, centered about 100 miles west of Yenan, was one of the five subdivisions into which the Shen-Kan-Ning Border Region was divided.

During the war Ma gained a reputation for his work in the field of law, although he was not known to have had any legal training. He allegedly originated a special method of getting evidence directly from the local populace for presentation in court. This work was commended by Border Region Chairman Lin Po-ch'ü (q.v.) at a meeting of the government in January 1944. Reviewing the steps required to improve judicial work in the border region, Lin stated that "Legal procedures must be simple and easy. The method of trial invested by Ma . . . should be promoted to educate the people. The verdict must be written in simple, popular language, not in the same old way as used by the old courts."[1] Lin Po-ch'ü also noted that in 1943 a change had been made in the judiciary whereby one man would be both district commissioner and the head of the local court, adding the comment that the "separation of the judicial from the executive organs is entirely meaningless."[2] It is interesting that by 1945 Ma Hsi-wu was serving in this dual capacity, that is, as chief of the branch court and the commissioner (executive head) of the Kuan-chung district under the Shen-Kan-Ning government. (Kuan-chung was another of the Shen-Kan-Ning sub-divisions, situated about 100 miles southwest of Yenan.) He held these two positions until 1946. Ma's work came to the attention of journalist Gunther Stein, who visited the Shen-Kan-Ning area in mid-1944. Stein asserted that the "mass movement which propagandizes mediation has given rise to another popular figure, the Mediation Labor Hero Ma Hsi-wu."[3] Anna Louise Strong, who spent considerable time in Yenan during 1946, was struck by his combination of outer simplicity and inner intelligence. "In outer appearance Judge Ma was the shabbiest official who came to my Yenan cave. He wore the usual suit of dark blue cotton, but the material had been badly dyed and had faded to a streaked and dingy gray. A cap of darker gray was stuck a bit askew above his big horn spectacles. Warm, white woolly socks flowered up from his dusty cotton shoes; these were a concession to his age . . . He was as easygoing as his own old shoes. Yet seldom have I seen a face that so combined intelligence, kindly humor, and authority as the countenance of old Judge Ma."[4]

In the meantime, Ma was elected to serve as a delegate to the Shan-Kan-Ning Assembly, a legislative body with powers broadly similar to those of the NPC, inaugurated in 1954. Delegates from the various hsien within the Shen-Kan-Ning area sat in this assembly; Ma was named from Ch'ü-tzu hsien (Kansu) and in this capacity attended the first session of the Second Shen-Kan-Ning Assembly in Yenan in November 1941. He attended the second session of the Second Assembly in December 1944, and was re-elected to the Third Assembly, which met from 1946 until the Border Region was dissolved in 1949. At the first session of the Third Assembly (April 1946), Ma was named to the presidency of the Higher Court for the Shen-Kan-Ning Border Region Government, holding the position for the remaining years of the Shen-Kan-Ning era.

In addition to the tasks already noted, Ma held at least two more posts in the Shen-Kan-Ning government in the late 1940's, both related to his work in the judicial field. He was head of the border region's prison and was a member of the People's Supervision Committee for the border region government.

With the Communist conquest of the mainland in 1949, the Shen-Kan-Ning border area was absorbed by the newly created government organ known as the Northwest Military and Administrative Committee (NWMAC; changed to Northwest Administrative Committee, NWAC, in early 1953, and dissolved in mid-1954). As under the Shen-Kan-Ning government, Ma held several posts with the NWMAC/NWAC, positions having an emphasis on judicial work. These were: member, Land Reform Committee, 1950–1954; member, Political and Legal Affairs Committee, 1952–53; member, NWAC, 1953–54; and director, Election Work Committee, 1953–54 (the committee established to prepare for the elections to the First NPC in 1954). During these same years (1950–1954), Ma also served as a member of the Kansu Provincial People's Government Council. Perhaps the most important post held by Ma in the early 1950's was as chief justice of the Northwest Branch Court under the Supreme People's Court. It was in this capacity, for example, that he was named by the Northwest Party Bureau in December 1953 as the "responsible person" for conducting a region-wide "study campaign" to examine the tasks of judicial work in the northwest.

When the constitutional government was inaugurated in 1954, Ma was transferred to Peking and named as a vice-president of the Supreme People's Court, serving first under Politburo member Tung Pi-wu and then under Hsieh Chueh-tsai, another Party veteran. Ma held this post until his death in April 1962. Like many senior government officials, Ma was relatively active in receiving foreign visitors in Peking; quite naturally he was mainly involved with visiting juridical delegations, and he continued in this extracurricular activity until ill health apparently incapacitated him about a year before his death.

Although his work on the Supreme People's Court was easily his most important assignment after 1954, Ma was also engaged in other official and quasi-official activities. From its inauguration in April 1953 until his death nine years later, he served on the National Council of the Political Science and Law Association of China, then headed by Tung Pi-wu; he was a member of the presidium (steering committee) for the inaugural meeting of the association in 1953. From 1954 to 1959 he was a deputy to the First NPC from Kansu, and from April 1959 to his death he was a "specially invited personage" on the Third National Committee of the CPPCC.

Among Ma's writings is an article in *Cheng-fa yen-chiu* (Political and legal research; no. 1, February 2, 1955), which reviews judicial work in the Shen-Kan-Ning Border Region during the Yenan period. He also wrote an article for *Hung-ch'i* (Red flag, October 15, 1959) commemorating the changes during the first ten years of the PRC.

Ma made his last public appearance in April 1961. One year later, on April 10, 1962, he died in Peking at the age of 64. The men on his funeral committee reflected both his association with legal work and his northwest China background and included the president of the Supreme Peoples Court, Hsieh Chueh-tsai, and the past president, Tung Pi-wu. In the ensuing days both Hsieh and Tung wrote commemorative articles in the *JMJP* (April 11 and 16) about Ma. Nothing is known of Ma's personal life apart from the fact that some of his relatives attended a memorial service for him on April 15.

1. Stuart Gelder, *The Chinese Communists* (London, 1946), p. 138.
2. *Ibid.,* p. 137.
3. Gunther Stein, *The Challenge of Red China* (New York, 1945), p .389.
4. Anna Louise Strong, *The Chinese Conquer China* (New York, 1949), pp. 177–178.

Ma Ming-fang

(1904–   ; Mi-chih, Shensi). Third secretary, CCP Northeast Bureau; member, CCP Central Committee.

A veteran Party leader from the northwest, Ma Ming-fang is one of the few Communist leaders of the present generation who has seen little military service in the Red armies. His early career, spent mainly in the northwest, was interrupted from 1942 to 1946 by imprisonment in Sinkiang. After serving as one of the top CCP leaders in the northwest during the early years of the PRC, Ma was transferred in 1954 to Peking where he spent the next six years as a leading official in the Party Center and the NPC. Since 1961 he has been a senior official in Manchuria where he serves as third secretary of the Party's Northeast Bureau.

Ma, who has been known by the names Ma Ju-chou and Ma Chi-min, was born in the same year and place that Liu Lan-t'ao (q.v.) was born. He studied at a normal school in nearby Sui-te and may also have studied at Yü-lin Normal School, an institute attended by such Party stalwarts as Kao Kang, Liu Chih-tan, and P'an Tzu-li (qq.v.), all contemporaries in age. (A discussion of the modernizing influences in northern Shensi, and especially Yü-lin, during the twenties is contained in the biography of Chia T'o-fu, another important Communist from Shensi.) In 1925, when Ma was 21, he joined the CCP and began to participate in revolutionary activities, possibly in association with Kao Kang and, after about 1928, with Liu Chih-tan. Ma worked in the Party's North Shensi Special Committee after it was established by Kao and Liu in 1928. The Special Committee was first led by Liu Chih-tan, but about 1931 Ma assumed the secretaryship and retained it until 1938. On one occasion in 1932, when the Special Committee was meeting in Chia-hsien (about 25 miles northeast of Mi-chih), Ma and a colleague named Ma Wen-jui (q.v.) narrowly avoided arrest by the authorities, who had been informed of the meeting through the "treachery of a renegade" from the CCP.[1]

In January 1935, when the First North Shensi Soviet Congress was held in An-ting hsien, the Shensi-Kansu Provisional Soviet Government was set up. Ma became its chairman and concurrently head of the Propaganda Department of its Northwest Work Committee. During the year he was involved in a dispute that led to the arrest of Liu Chih-tan and Kao Kang (see under Liu Chih-tan).[2] However, Ma was on hand with other senior local leaders to greet Mao Tse-tung when he arrived in north Shensi in October 1935 at the end of the Long March.[3] During the mid-thirties Ma was also chairman of the North Shensi Soviet Government and secretary of the CCP Shensi Party Committee.

In 1937, by which time the Communist position in the northwest was fairly well consolidated, the Shensi-Kansu-Ninghsia (Shen-Kan-Ning) Border Region Government was established. Ma was named to head the Civil Affairs Department, but in the following year he was sent to the Soviet Union for medical treatment and further study. (While there he is reported to have used the name Malov.) In 1939 he returned to China from the USSR, traveling via Sinkiang, then under the control of the semi-independent warlord Sheng Shih-ts'ai. At this time a number of prominent Communists were in Tihua (Urumchi), some returning from and others en route to the Soviet Union. According to a Communist account, Sheng would neither permit them to proceed to Yenan nor to the Soviet Union.[4]

Ma's whereabouts for the next two to three years are not clear. He apparently made his way back to the Soviet Union, for a Communist account describes his second arrival in Sinkiang from the USSR in January 1941.[5] In the next year, following the rupture of relations between the Communists at Yenan and Sheng Shih-ts'ai in Sinkiang (see under Ch'en T'an-ch'iu), Ma was imprisoned in Urumchi. Unlike some of his fellow Communist prisoners who were executed (e.g., Ch'en T'an-ch'iu and Mao Tse-min), Ma survived the four-year imprisonment and was finally released in mid-1946. According to a Communist newspaper of that time, he was one of 129 Party members who had been in prison[6] to return from Sinkiang. In the meantime, before and during his years of imprisonment, Ma was given new appointments in the Shen-Kan-Ning Government and the CCP. Presumably in anticipation of his return from Sinkiang to Yenan, he was named in 1941 as a deputy from his native Mi-chih to the second Border Region Assembly, and when the Assembly met in November he was appointed a member of the Shen-Kan-Ning Border Region Government (the cabinet). Far more important, however, was the election of Ma as an alternate member (and Ch'en T'an-ch'iu as a full member) of the Party Central Committee at the Seventh Party Congress held in Yenan from April to June 1945. The Communists at Yenan were apparently completely out of contact with their jailed comrades in Sinkiang when the Seventh Congress met—although Ma lived to serve on the Seventh Central Committee, Ch'en T'an-ch'iu had been executed by Sheng Shih-ts'ai almost two years before. The distinction of having been placed on the Seventh Central Committee while in prison is also shared by Liao Ch'eng-chih (q.v.).

Ma's activities in the northwest are not well documented in the postwar years. By 1948, however, he had become the deputy secretary of the Party's Northwest Bureau, serving under Secretary Hsi Chung-hsun (q.v.). Ma continued to hold the subordinate post until the winter of 1952–53 when Hsi transferred to Peking, after which Ma became the senior Party official in the northwest. (At various times in the period from 1948 to 1954, Ma was known as deputy secretary, second secretary, and third secretary—but in effect he was Hsi's senior deputy until early 1953 and the head of the Bureau thereafter.) In 1949 Ma also became president of the Northwest People's Revolutionary University, but it is not known how long he held this post.

Ma was in Peking in September 1949 to take part in the establishment of the central government at the first session of the CPPCC. Attending as a representative of the "Northwest Liberated Areas," he served on the presidium (steering committee) of the first session as well as the *ad hoc* committee to draft the Organic Law of the CPPCC, one of the most important documents adopted at that time. When the session closed in late September, he was named to membership on the CPPCC's First National Committee, holding this post until December 1954 when the Second CPPCC was formed. In October 1949 Ma was appointed to the Executive Board of the Sino-Soviet Friendship Association (holding the post to December 1954), after which he returned to the northwest to resume his duties. For the next five years he worked in Shensi, where from December 1949 to November 1952 he was the governor (being replaced by Chou Shou-shan, q.v.). Ma was concurrently named in March 1950 to head the Shensi Finance and Economics Committee, a post he probably held until he relinquished the governorship in late 1952. In January 1950 the Communists inaugurated the regional government for the northwest; known as the Northwest Military and Administrative Committee (NWMAC) and headquartered in Sian, it had jurisdiction over Shensi, Kansu, Ninghsia, Tsinghai, and Sinkiang provinces. Ma was a member of the NWMAC and in October 1952 was promoted to a vice-chairmanship. He continued as a vice-chairman when the NWMAC was reorganized into the Northwest Administrative Committee

(NWAC) in January 1953, holding this position until the regional governments were abolished in the latter half of 1954. P'eng Te-huai was the chairman of both the NWMAC and the NWAC, but because he spent most of the early years in Korea as head of the Chinese army there, the *de facto* chairmanship fell to Hsi Chung-hsun, a vice-chairman of the NWMAC–NWAC. Then, with Hsi's departure for Peking in the winter of 1952–53, Ma became, in effect, the acting chairman. Under both the NWMAC and the NWAC, he was also a member of the Finance and Economics Committee.

As described above, Ma was the Shensi governor from 1949 to 1952. It is probable, though not fully documented, that he was the senior Party secretary in Shensi for this same period. (He was listed by the American Consulate General [Hong Kong] as the probable secretary in late 1951 and mid-1952.[7]) In any event, he was succeeded by P'an Tzu-li (q.v.) in this post in the latter half of 1952. Particularly after he became a vice-chairman of the NWMAC in October 1952 (at the same time as the transfer of Hsi Chung-hsun to Peking), Ma's duties seemed to have been principally concerned with the work of the NWMAC and NWAC. He gave most of the important reports before these bodies, as in December 1953 when he spoke before the NWAC on the work completed in 1953 and the tasks ahead for 1954.

Following the abolition of the regional administrations in 1954, Ma was transferred to Peking. There, as a deputy from his native Shensi, he attended the first session of the First NPC held in September 1954, and since that time has been one of the more important leaders in the PRC legislative branch. At the close of the NPC session he was elected a member of the NPC Standing Committee as well as chairman of the NPC Credentials Committee. He served in a similar capacity during the term of the Second NPC (1959–1964). More important, however, not long after the initial NPC session closed, he was identified (early 1955) as a deputy secretary-general of the Party Central Committee, a post that made him directly subordinate to Secretary-General Teng Hsiao-p'ing (q.v.). Ma retained this post until the Party Center underwent a reorganization at the close of the Eighth Party Congress in September 1956. To manage the affairs of the Congress, three *ad hoc* bodies were established: a presidium (steering committee), secretariat, and credentials committee. Ma and only six others (Liu Lant'ao, T'an Cheng, T'an Chen-lin, Li Hsueh-feng, Lin Feng, and Sung Jen-ch'iung) served on all three bodies. At the close of the Congress he was promoted from alternate to full membership on the Central Committee. Furthermore, when the new Central Committee held its first plenum (the day after the Congress closed), he was elected as a member of the Party's Central Control Commission, in charge of internal Party discipline and inspection. Before the next two years had passed, he was to receive other posts in key Party Center organs. By late 1956 he was identified as a deputy director of the Organization Department (although he has not since been identified), and by June 1958 he was director of the apparently newly established Finance and Trade Department. Thus, with this impressive array of posts (none of which receive much publicity in the Party press), Ma could be regarded as one of the CCP's top organization men by the mid-fifties.

Although Ma's public appearances have been infrequent, the nature of his activities in the late fifties and early sixties suggested that he was playing an important role, particularly in connection with finance and trade. He frequently traveled in the provinces, as in June 1958 when he spoke before a finance and trade conference in Kwangtung, which stressed the need to improve management techniques. Similarly, he spoke at a symposium on industry and commerce in rural areas held in Harbin in August 1959. Ma also appeared at a number of conferences in Peking, as in May 1960 when he attended the National Demonstration Conference of Finance and Trade Departments; speaking before the 5,000-odd "technical innovators," he emphasized the urgency of improvements in agrotechnical techniques. In the same month he wrote an article on trade and finance for the Party's top journal, Hung-ch'i (Red flag, issue of May 16, 1960). His last appearance in Peking in his capacity as director of the Party's Finance and Trade Department was in October 1960. Not long afterwards he was transferred to Manchuria (see below). Although Ma has been principally occupied with domestic problems since the PRC was established, he did make one trip abroad in March 1958 when he accompanied alternate Politburo member Ulanfu to Ulan Bator for the 13th Congress of the Mongolian People's Revolutionary (Communist) Party.

After more than six years of work in Peking, Ma was transferred to Manchuria in 1961, a transfer occasioned by the re-creation of the regional Party bureaus, which were set up in accordance with the decision of the Party's Ninth Plenum (January 1961). By July of that year he was identified as the Third Secretary of the Northeast Bureau headed by First Secretary Sung Jen-ch'iung (q.v.). Ma's assignment to the northeast was a reversal of the pattern of the mid-fifties to transfer many of the Party's top leaders to Peking. But then, in response to the serious shortcomings of the Great Leap Forward (1958–1960), a number of key leaders —many of them, like Ma, specialists in Party organization as it pertains to economic matters—

were transferred back to the outlying provinces. Hence, although he has presumably been relieved of some of his tasks in the Party Center, Ma's transfer to Manchuria, the heartland of Chinese industry, probably attests to the trust placed in him by the Party's most senior leaders.

Largely because of the paucity of information available from the provinces since the Great Leap Forward, little is known of Ma's work in Manchuria. His publicized appearances are mostly ceremonial, for example, attendance at May Day or National Day rallies. Similarly, he is occasionally mentioned in the press when a top Chinese leader or an important foreign visitor travels to Shenyang, where Ma works at the regional Party headquarters. His transfer to Manchuria has also resulted in changes in his participation in the NPC. In the First and Second NPC's (1954–1964) he had been a deputy from Shensi, but he was switched to the Kirin constituency in 1964 for the Third NPC. Although he was re-elected to head the Credentials Committee at the close of the first session of the Third NPC (January 1965), he was not re-elected to the NPC Standing Committee, which meets regularly in Peking.

1. JMJP, August 2, 1957.

2. Mark Selden, "The Guerrilla Movement in Northwest China: The Origins of the Shensi-Kansu-Ninghsia Border Region," The China Quarterly, no. 29:70–71 (January–March 1967).

3. Ch'en Ch'ang-feng, On the Long March with Chairman Mao (Peking, 1959), p. 70.

4. Hung-ch'i p'iao-p'iao (Red flag fluttering; Peking, 1957), V, 150.

5. Ibid., X, 125.

6. Chi-Je-Liao jih-pao (Hopeh-Jehol-Liaoning daily), July 16, 1946.

7. CB 137, p. 12; CB 192, p. 12.

Ma Wen-jui

(1909–   ; Sui-te, Shensi). Minister of Labor; alternate member, CCP Central Committee.

Ma Wen-jui was a member of the CCP apparatus in Shensi in the early thirties, and in the late forties and early fifties he was a top official in the Party's Northwest Bureau. He was transferred to Peking in 1954 to head the Ministry of Labor, and since 1956 he has been an alternate member of the CCP Central Committee. Ma was born in Sui-te, a small city not far north of the Communists' wartime capital of Yenan. By 1932, when he was 23, Ma was a member of the Special Party Committee for north Shensi, then headed by Ma Ming-fang (q.v.). In that same year the two Ma's narrowly escaped arrest in Chia-hsien (some 25 miles northeast of Mi-chih) when a Party "renegade" informed the local authorities of a meeting of the Special Party Committee.[1] Other prominent Communists working in this region during this period include Liu Chih-tan, Liu Lan-t'ao, Chia T'o-fu, Wang Shih-t'ai, and Yen Hung-yen (qq.v.).

It is likely that Ma remained in the Shensi area throughout the 1930's, because by 1941 he was working with the Shensi-Kansu-Ninghsia (Shen-Kan-Ning) Border Region Government, which had been created in 1937. Though not particularly prominent then, he was a member of the assemblies for the Shen-Kan-Ning Government, and in the early 1940's also took part in Party affairs in Kansu. He attended the First Session of the Second Shen-Kan-Ning Border Region Assembly of November 1941 as a deputy from Ch'ing-yang hsien in Kansu. He also attended the next session of the Second Assembly in 1944, and in April 1946, when the First Session of the Third Border Region Assembly met, he served as a representative of Tzu-chou hsien in Shensi. About this time he also became a member of the People's Supervision Committee under the Shen-Kan-Ning Government. In 1942, coinciding with his term as a Kansu representative in the Border Region Assembly, he was also identified as secretary of the East Kansu District Committee of the CCP organization for the Shen-Kan-Ning area. By at least 1947 Ma had been elevated to the directorship of the Organization Department under the Northwest Party Bureau.[2]

From the beginning of the Communist occupation of the mainland in 1949 until the establishment of the constitutional government in 1954, Ma continued to serve with the Northwest Party Bureau, as well as the government administration controlling the northwest provinces, known as the Northwest Military and Administrative Committee (NWMAC). In the Party structure he continued to head the Organization Department of the Northwest Party Bureau until 1954; he concurrently served as secretary of the Women's Work Committee from 1949 to about 1952, and in 1949 (and probably until 1953) he was also a member of the Northwest Bureau. In the period from 1953 to 1954 he was a deputy secretary of the bureau, and then by April 1954 was promoted to third deputy secretary. All these posts were held under Party Secretary Hsi Chung-hsun (q.v.), also a native of Shensi. In this same period (1950–1953) he was a member of the NWMAC, which was reorganized into the Northwest Administrative Committee (NWAC) early in 1953 (with Ma continuing to serve on the Committee). He also belonged to two other organizations which were part of the NWMAC and its successor, the NWAC. From March 1950 he was chairman of the People's Supervision Committee, and from May 1952 he was a member of the Political and Legal Affairs Committee.

Ma's work in the northwest ended in September 1954 when he was transferred to Peking to replace the famed Li Li-san (q.v.) as head of the Ministry of Labor. Li had been a favorite target for Maoist ideologues for many years, but he had an intimate familiarity with the Chinese labor movement, which reached back to the early 1920's. In contrast, Ma's previous experience had been with the Party bureaucracy and government administrations in the northwest. Since his arrival in Peking, the Ministry of Labor has been Ma's principal post, and his work there has received a fair amount of press attention. In addition, he has served on the quasi-legislative CPPCC from December 1954 when the Second National Committee was inaugurated. Under the Second (1954–1959) and Third (1959–1964) National Committees of the CPPCC, Ma represented the CCP, but when the Fourth National Committee first met in December 1964, Ma attended as a "specially invited personage." In the interim, he was elected an alternate member of the CCP Central Committee at the Eighth Party Congress in September 1956.

As minister of Labor Ma addressed the Third Session of the First NPC in June 1956 on the "defects of the existing wage system." At the same time he called for better living conditions for workers. This was one of several speeches he has given on labor matters before the NPC and the State Council. In 1956 and 1959 he served on the preparatory committees for the National Conferences of Advanced Workers, and when they were held in April 1956 and October 1959 he was a member of the conference presidiums.

In June 1959 Ma made his only trip outside China when he led a group to Poland for the opening ceremonies of the 28th international fair at Poznan. In returning to China the delegation visited in the USSR and had an interview with Premier Khrushchev on June 25.

Two of Ma's more significant writings appeared in the *JMJP* of September 25, 1959, and in *Hung-ch'i* (Red flag) of March 1, 1961.[3] Both articles dealt with labor problems.

---

1. *JMJP*, August 2, 1957.

2. *Wei ch'un-chieh tang-te tsu-chih erh tou-cheng* (Struggle to purify the Party organization; Hong Kong, 1948), p. 66.

3. *CB* 606 and *SCMM* 253.

Ma Yü-huai

(1917–   ; Jen-ch'iu hsien, Hopeh). National minority leader; vice-chairman, Ninghsia-Hui Autonomous Region.

Ma Yü-huai was born in Jen-ch'iu hsien, some 30 miles east of Paoting in Hopeh province, of Hui (Muslim) parents. He has risen within the Chinese Communist hierarchy to become one of the most influential of the national minority leaders, presently serving as one of the ranking officials in Ninghsia. After graduation from the T'ung-jen Middle School in Paoting in the mid-1930's, he joined in the nationwide movement to resist the Japanese and, presumably, joined the Communist Party. As war with Japan approached, a number of patriotic "national salvation" organizations emerged throughout China, especially in the north where the Japanese were the most aggressive. By 1938 Ma was the head of the "Hui People's Anti-Japanese Salvation Association" for both the Central Hopeh District and for the Shansi-Chahar-Hopeh (Chin-Ch'a-Chi) Border Region, the latter being a Communist-inspired government established in January 1938. Ma held two military posts in these same areas during the war with Japan; he was political commissar of the "Hui People's Detachment" and deputy political commissar of the Ninth Military Sub-district of the Central Hopeh Military District. Though Ma may not have come into contact with the highly important Shansi-Chahar-Hopeh Military Region commander Nieh Jung-chen, it is likely that he had close contacts with Lü Cheng-ts'ao, commander of the Central Hopeh Military District from 1938 to 1943 and later a Party Central Committee member. The District Military Headquarters was located in a village near Ma's native Jen-ch'iu, an area where the Communists had been especially active soon after the war with Japan began. His early career suggests that he was among the first of the young men of central Hopeh to be enlisted in the Communist cause.

The record fades out on Ma during the postwar years, but he probably remained in North China as a guerrilla fighter. He was in Peking in 1949 after its capture and was to remain there for nine years until his transfer to Ninghsia in 1958. Ma's assignment in the early years of the regime was to represent the Hui people in the central government and in the Peking city government. His first specific assignment was as chairman of the Hui People's Work Committee, established under the Peking city government in 1949, presumably to mobilize the Huis (a minority of significant size in Peking) to participate in the new government. In the fall of 1949, Ma received posts under both the national and city governments. In the former he was named as a member of the Nationalities Affairs Commission, and within the municipal government he was appointed as deputy director of the Civil Affairs Bureau; in 1954 he was promoted to be the director. He was elected in February 1951 as a member of the Peking Municipal People's Government and throughout the early and mid-1950's was rather active in the work of the city government. To cite but one of several examples: he served as a member of the Peking Election Committee, formed in May 1953 in preparation for the elections to the NPC in 1954. His principal activity, however, centered on the question of minority groups. He was known to have been the president of the "Hui People's Institute" in Peking in the early 1950's, but the work of this institute is not clear. In 1953 the Communists established two nationwide organizations involving Muslim groups. The first was the China Islamic Association, formed in May 1953. Ma, who had served from July 1952 as the secretary-general of the preparatory committee, was selected as a vice-president, a position he still retains under Burhan (q.v.). The other organization was the China Association for the Promotion of Hui People's Culture, also formed in May 1953 under Chairman Liu Ko-p'ing, China's leading Hui and later a Party Central Committee member. Ma was named as a member of this association; for reasons that are not clear this organization was disbanded in October 1958, just a few days after the formation of the Ninghsia-Hui Autonomous Region (see below).

As already noted, Ma took part in the preparations for the elections to the NPC. When these were held in 1954 he was elected as a Peking deputy to the First NPC (1954–1959). From 1949 he had served on the Nationalities Affairs Commission, an organ of the executive branch of government; now, at the first session of the NPC in September 1954, he was transferred to the Nationalities Committee, subordinate to the NPC, the legislative branch. He was re-elected to this committee in April 1959 and January 1965 during the initial sessions of the Second and Third NPC's, in which he served as a deputy from Ninghsia.

In April 1955, Ma was named as president of the Institute of Islamic Theology in Peking. He spoke at the inauguration of the institute in November of that year and retained the post until about 1958 (the date of his transfer to Ninghsia). It was also at this time in the mid-1950's that the Chinese Communists were slowly emerging from the international isolation imposed on them by the Korean War. This emergence was most effectively dramatized by the Bandung Conference in Indonesia where the Chinese delegation made a strong and generally favorable impression. Chief Chinese delegate Chou En-lai invited Indonesian President Sukarno, at the close of the conference, to visit China. Sukarno accepted, and on June 1, 1955, at the time of his visit, the Chinese established the China-Indonesia Friendship Association, naming Ma as one of the vice-chairmen, another post he still retains. One month later, in July 1955, he was also named to the Board of Directors of the Chinese People's Institute of Foreign Affairs, one of the most important of the mass organizations. Ma's appointment was probably due to his Hui nationality, because at this point the Communists were beginning to make their first moves to gain influence in the Islamic world. On the very day of his selection to this organization (July 19, 1955), Ma left for his first trip abroad—significantly, to the heart of the Islamic world: Mecca, in Saudi Arabia. Although ostensibly subordinate to Ta P'u-sheng (q.v.), the delegation leader and a much respected Moslem, Ma's stature within the CCP suggests that he may have been the actual leader of the group. Within the next few years, he made several more important trips abroad for the PRC. In February 1956 he set out as a deputy leader under Burhan on one of the longest journeys abroad made by any Chinese delegation. Described as a culture and art delegation, the group spent lengthy periods in Egypt, the Sudan, Ethiopia, Syria, and Lebanon between February and June 1956. (In July Ma left for home, taking most of the delegation with him, but Burhan continued his visit in the region for a few more weeks.) It is noteworthy that when this journey began not a single nation in the Middle East or Africa recognized Peking and, indeed, few Chinese Communists had even visited the area. However, by the time the group returned to China, Egypt and Syria had granted diplomatic recognition to Peking. Ma's four other trips abroad can be summarized briefly: he led a 71-member art ensemble to Pakistan and Ceylon from November 1957 to February 1958; he headed a small Moslem delegation to Indonesia in December 1962–January 1963 to attend the 24th Congress of the Moslem Scholars Association of Indonesia; in May–June 1964 he was again in Indonesia leading a delegation to the fourth national conference of the Indonesia-China Friendship Association; and in March 1965 he was once more in Indonesia as head of an Islamic delegation to the Afro-Asian Islamic Conference in Bandung, where he delivered a speech stressing the need for Afro-Asian unity in the face of "American imperialism." Like so many leaders who journey abroad on behalf of the PRC, Ma was named to the Standing Committee of the Chinese People's Association for Cultural Relations with Foreign Countries (December 1956), but he relinquished the post in 1959 when the association was slightly reorganized.

During the 1957–58 "rectification" (*cheng-feng*) campaign, he took part in accusations against fellow Hui. He denounced Ma Sung-t'ing at a meeting of the now defunct China Association for the Promotion of Hui People's Culture in August 1957, asserting that Ma, a vice-chairman of this association, was guilty of "anti-Communist and anti-socialist utterances and deeds." A year later (August–September 1958), at a forum held in Yin-ch'uan, the Ninghsia capital, Ma Yü-huai took part in "exposing and criticizing" another Muslim leader, Ma Chen-wu, an alleged "ultra-rightist."

A new chapter in Ma's career began in 1958 with the inauguration of the Ninghsia-Hui Autonomous Region (NHAR). The province of Ninghsia had been abolished by the Communists in 1954, but then the province was re-created in an apparent bid to mollify Hui opinion. Ma was named to a vice-chairmanship of the NHAR Preparatory Committee in June 1958, and when the region was formally inaugurated that October he was named as a vice-chairman under Liu Ko-p'ing (and, after 1960, Yang Ching-jen, q.v.). Not long after, in February 1959, Ma was identified as a secretary of the NHAR Party Committee, serving under First Secretary Wang Feng until 1961 when Yang Ching-jen replaced Wang. After Wang Feng's transfer in 1961, Ma can be regarded as the second-ranking official in Ninghsia, being outranked only by Yang Ching-jen, a fellow Hui. Since Ma's transfer to Ninghsia in 1958 he has spent most of his time there, although he usually goes to the capital for NPC meetings and, as described, has led several rather important delegations abroad. His activities in Ninghsia appear to be those normally associated with a person of his rank; thus he speaks at conferences of "advanced" workers, makes periodic visits to military units posted in Ninghsia, and gives reports before organs of the Ninghsia government. The only national-level position he has received since going to Ninghsia in 1958 (apart from re-election to the NPC) occurred in April 1960 when he was named to the Council of the newly formed China-Africa People's Friendship Association, an appointment that may have been meant to take advantage of contacts he probably made on his 1956 trip to Africa. Ma has described the life of the Hui people in an article for the April 1964 issue of the English-language monthly *China Reconstructs*.

Mao Tse-min

Mao Tse-min (1895–1943; Hsiang-t'an hsien, Hunan). Early Party leader; younger brother of Mao Tse-tung.

Mao Tse-min, the most prominent of Mao Tse-tung's siblings, played a moderately important role in the Chinese Communist Movement. An adviser to his brother in the Kiangsi Soviet period, he worked in financial affairs in the early thirties and led a transportation unit during the Long March. In north Shensi he headed the Department of National Economy in the Communist government. Mao was sent to Sinkiang in 1938 as a special envoy from Yenan to the government of Sheng Shih-ts'ai. When Sheng broke with the Communists, Mao was accused of plotting against Sheng's administration. He was arrested in 1942 and executed in September 1943.

Mao Tse-min was born at the family homestead in Shao-shan village, located about 30 miles west of the hsien seat of Hsiang-t'an in eastern Hunan. Shao-shan was connected with the provincial capital of Changsha by steamer down the Hsiang-t'an River. The only one of Mao Tse-tung's siblings to live into his late forties, Mao Tse-min spent his entire life as a revolutionary but his career is so far overshadowed by his famous brother that little is known of his youth aside from those events in which the two brothers are connected. Both spent their middle school years in Changsha, where Mao Tse-min belonged to the small nucleus of radical students who attended Mao Tse-tung's alma mater, the Hunan First Normal School. He may have belonged to the *Hsin-min hsueh-hui* (New people's study society), which his brother and Ts'ai Ho-sen (q.v.) established in 1918.

In July 1921 Mao Tse-tung and Ho Shu-heng (q.v.) attended the founding congress of the CCP in Shanghai as delegates from Hunan. In the next month, following their return to Changsha, they established the Self-Education College (Tzu-hsiu ta-hsueh). Mao Tse-min and such other latter-day Communists as Hsia Hsi (q.v.) were among the first students.[1] The ostensible purpose of the school was to attract students who wanted to study China's problems and do research on ways of strengthening the nation, but in fact it served as a CCP recruiting and training center. To start the college the Party had used buildings and funds collected by Hunanese literati in the early days of the Chinese Republic for study of the works of the Ming scholar Wang Fu-chih, whose writings were popular among the Chinese "patriot-reformers" at the close of the Manchu dynasty. Housed in the same building as the Self-Education College was the Hunan Students' Union. Mao Tse-min headed the Union's business department.[2]

In 1922 Mao Tse-min joined the CCP. His older brother was then both secretary of the Hunan CCP Committee and head of the Changsha branch of the Chinese Labor Unions' Secretariat. As such, Mao Tse-min's responsibilities included Party and labor activities on the rail line running east from Changsha into the important An-yuan and P'ing-hsiang coal mining districts in western Kiangsi. Mao Tse-tung sent his brother to this area to work in the labor movement in which Li Li-san (q.v.) and others had been active for several months. In the fall of 1922 these Communist activists reorganized a workers' club *(chi-lo-pu)* under the overall direction of Li Li-san. Mao served as a director of the Miners' Cooperative (subordinate to the club) for the Anyuan Coal Mines. He also enrolled in a workers' night school where he could propagate Marxist ideology at first hand.[3]

Mao continued to work in the Hunan-Kiangsi labor movement until 1925 when he was transferred to the Party headquarters in Shanghai. There he assumed the direction of the Central Committee's Publications Department *(ch'u-pan pu)*.[4] For the next three years he spent most of his time publishing and distributing Communist literature, a task that frequently took him to such centers of Communist activity as Wuhan and Changsha. In this capacity he maintained close connections with the Shanghai Book Store (Shang-hai shu-tien), which was established under CCP auspices in 1923. When it was closed

down by the Shanghai authorities in late 1926 Mao was transferred to Wuhan to establish the Yangtze River Book Store (Ch'ang-chiang shu-tien).[5] Mao interrupted his work in the publications field for a brief time in late 1925, when he enrolled as one of 133 students in the fifth class of the Peasant Movement Training Institute in Canton. This had been founded under joint KMT-CCP auspices the year before and its first classes were recruited mainly from Kwangtung. However, probably under the encouragement of the Mao brothers, the number of students from Hunan suddenly jumped to over 35 per cent of the fifth class held from October to December 1925.[6]

In 1927 Mao was managing the *Min-kuo jih-pao* (Republic daily) in Wuhan, but he was forced to relinquish this post in mid-1927 when the Communists and the left-KMT severed all relations. He remained in Wuhan in the Communist underground, where he continued his publications work. However, he was soon forced to leave the city and made his way to Hunan. Attempting to go from Hunan to Kiangsi to join the Communist insurgents, he was arrested by the Nationalists. He succeeded in concealing his identity and was therefore able to proceed to Kiangsi where he joined his brother in the Ching-kang Mountains. In the spring of 1928 he took part in the negotiations that brought together the Red armies of Mao Tse-tung and Chu Te. The two forces had been drawing closer together for several months before they actually met, and it was Mao Tse-min who was sent from Ching-kangshan to meet Chu's troops and make the final arrangements for their uniting.[7]

By no later than 1930 Mao had returned to the Party headquarters in Shanghai, which was now underground. In that year he was arrested again, but once more he gained his release by concealing his identity. In 1931 he was sent to the Communists' Fukien-Kwangtung-Kiangsi base where he became director of the General Affairs Department *(ching-li pu)*, an assignment principally concerned with logistics work for the three-province military region. But he was soon transferred to Juichin to join his brother in the southeast Kiangsi base. Mao Tse-min took part in the preparations for the First All-China Congress of Soviets, which established the Chinese Soviet Republic in November 1931 under the chairmanship of Mao Tse-tung. Immediately after the Congress he was made a member of the Republic's Finance Committee,[8] and in the next year he was appointed director of the State Bank *(kuo-chia yin-hang)*. In this connection he was in charge of raising funds and purchasing supplies for military operations and of regulating tax revenues. A report by Mao based on an inspection he made of financial work in Kiangsi appeared in the important newspaper *Hung-se Chung-hua* (Red China) on March 2, 1932.

During the Long March, which began in 1934, Mao led a transportation unit that was responsible for the "revolutionary assets carried by the troops," with which the Communists made their purchases.[9] In November 1935, after the Communists arrived in north Shensi, he was appointed director of the Department of National Economy. The April 24, 1936, issue of a Communist journal published in Shensi carried an article by Mao on economic work in Shensi and Kansu, but little else is known of his work during this period.[10] After spending a year or two in Yenan, Mao went to Moscow for medical treatment. In 1938, after his brother had appointed him as one of his special envoys to the government of Sheng Shih-ts'ai in Sinkiang, Mao Tse-min went from the Soviet Union to Tihwa,[11] arriving at approximately the same time as Ch'en T'an-ch'iu, Yenan's chief representative in Sinkiang.

Ch'en's and Mao's arrival in Sinkiang coincided with increasingly close ties between Sheng's government and both the Moscow and Yenan Communists. By 1938 a large number of Chinese Communists had arrived in Sinkiang, at Sheng's request, to serve as technical experts.[12] Mao Tse-min, for example, was made director of the Finance Office of the Sinkiang government, a post he held until 1942, and his wife was in charge of a middle school for girls. Mao was known in those years by the name Chou Pin.[13]

Sheng Shih-ts'ai's autobiography presents a bizarre story of the plots and counter-plots in Sinkiang after the arrival of the Chinese Communists, intrigues in which Ch'en T'an-ch'iu and Mao were chief actors. It also contains an alleged confession by Mao, dated June 25, 1942, that implicates both Ch'en and Mao in the death of Sheng's brother in the spring of that year. Though Sheng's version must be treated with caution, it is a fact that he turned on the Communists immediately after his brother's death. Ch'en and Mao were among the many Communists placed under detention; they were formally imprisoned in September and a year later, on September 27, 1943, they were executed. The Communists in Yenan apparently did not learn of their colleagues' deaths in Sinkiang until mid-1946, when a number of the survivors of the Sinkiang imprisonment were allowed to return to Yenan (see under Ch'en T'an-ch'iu). Mao and his associates were buried in a cemetery near the Sinkiang capital.

Mao was survived by his wife, Chu Tan-hua, who had a child while she was in prison in Tihwa. Since the early 1950's she has been active in cultural and educational work in Kiangsi. When Chu led a women's delegation to the Mongolian People's Republic in March 1960, she was identified as chairman of the Kiangsi Women's Federation. She has been a member of the Executive Committee of the National Women's Federation since 1957, and in 1964 she was chosen to represent the Federation on the Fourth National Committee of the CPPCC.

Mao Tse-tung's youngest brother, Mao Tse-t'an, was also a revolutionist. Like his two brothers he was born in Hsiang-t'an (1905). He worked in the labor movement with Mao Tse-min in the early twenties in Hunan and Kiangsi and was probably then already a Party member. He participated in both the labor and peasant movements in Kwangtung when Mao Tse-tung was there in the mid-twenties and then accompanied him to Chingkangshan in the winter of 1927. On one occasion when Mao Tse-tung's forces were badly in need of supplies, Tse-t'an was sent to contact P'eng P'ai's (q.v.) peasant guerrillas in the Hai-lu-feng area of eastern Kwangtung. After two months he rejoined his brother[14] and remained in the Kiangsi-Fukien area for the rest of his life. In the early 1930's he was associated with the so-called Lo Ming (q.v.) line. Lo, then acting secretary of the Fukien Party Committee, was severely criticized by the "28 Bolsheviks" leadership of the CCP for being a "defeatist" and for allowing the Party to suffer losses during the Nationalists' Annihilation Campaigns against the Communists from the early to the mid-thirties. In this connection Mao Tse-t'an was censured for his association with the Lo Ming line.[15]

Mao Tse-t'an, never especially prominent aside from the fact that he was a brother of Mao Tse-tung, was left behind when the Long March began in October 1934. He remained with the small group of Communist guerrillas led by Hsiang Ying (q.v.) and others who fought rear guard actions in the territory of the old Chinese Soviet Republic. Ch'ü Ch'iu-pai (q.v.) was also among the group. By February 1935 the pressures from Nationalist forces became so great that the Communists were forced to seek refuge in the mountains along the Kiangsi-Fukien border. Toward the end of March 1935 Mao was with Ch'ü in the vicinity of Shang-hang in southwest Fukien when the Communists were surrounded by Nationalist troops, and in the fighting Mao was killed and Ch'ü was taken prisoner. Tse-t'an's wife, who engaged in revolutionary work in Hunan, stayed in Hsiang-t'an to carry on her efforts there and did not go to other areas with her husband. In mid-1930, when the Communists attacked Changsha, the Mao family land was taken over by the Nationalists, and at this time she was arrested along with Mao Tse-tung's first wife and his younger sister. The latter two were executed, but the wife of Mao Tse-t'an was released.[16] Nothing further is known about her.

---

1. Chow Tse-tsung, *Research Guide to the May Fourth Movement* (Cambridge, Mass., 1963), pp. 121–122.

2. *Ibid.*, p. 111.

3. Liu Li-k'ai and Wang Chen, *I-chiu-i-chiu chih i-chiu-erh-ch'i te Chung-kuo kung-jen yun-tung* (The Chinese workers' movement from 1919 to 1927; Peking, 1954), p. 22; *Chung-kuo kung-ch'an-tang tsai chung-nan-ti-ch'ü ling-tao ko-ming tou-cheng te li-shih tzu-liao* (Historical materials on the revolutionary struggles led by the CCP in central-south China; Wuhan, 1951), I, 59; *SCMP* 158, pp. 24–25.

4. Li Jui, *Mao Tse-tung t'ung-chih ti ch'u-ch'i ko-ming huo-tung* (Comrade Mao Tse-tung's early revolutionary activities; Peking, 1957), p. 181.

5. Chang Ching-lu, ed., *Chung-kuo hsien-tai ch'u-pan shih-liao* (Historical materials on contemporary Chinese publishing; Peking, 1954), pp. 64–65.

6. Stuart Schram, *Mao Tse-tung* (New York, 1966), p. 76; *Chung-kuo nung-min* (Chinese peasants; Canton), no. 2:204 (February 1, 1926).

7. Edgar Snow, *Red Star over China* (New York, 1938), p. 352.

8. *Hung-se Chung-hua* (Red China), December 18, 1931.

9. *SCMP* 158; *Hung-ch'i p'iao-p'iao* (Red flag fluttering; Peking, 1957), V, 152–155.

10. Snow, p. 245.

11. *Min-tsu t'uan-chieh* (Nationalities unity), September 1963, pp. 6–8.

12. Allen S. Whiting and Sheng Shih-ts'ai, *Sinkiang: Pawn or Pivot?* (East Lansing, Mich., 1958), p. 60.

13. *Kuang-ming jih-pao*, December 28, 1960.

14. Robert Payne, *Mao Tse-tung* (New York, 1950), p. 102.

15. Tso-liang Hsiao, *Power Relations within the Chinese Communist Movement, 1930–1934* (Seattle, Wash., 1961), pp. 239–244.

16. Snow, p. 160.

Mao Tse-tung

(1893–   ; Hsiang-t'an hsien, Hunan). Leader of the Chinese Communist Party.

Mao Tse-tung, one of the historic figures of the twentieth century, was among the founders of the CCP. He played a major role in the establishment of the Red Army and the development of a viable base in Kiangsi during the late 1920's and early 1930's. Mao consolidated his rule over the Party in the years after the Long March, after which he directed the grand strategy during the Sino-Japanese War and the civil war with the Nationalists. His realization of the role of the peasantry and of the military as political forces in the revolution were vital elements in his triumph over Chiang Kai-shek. Mao gained world-wide eminence after the establishment of the PRC in 1949.

Mao was born on December 26, 1893, in Shao-shan, a village in Hsiang-t'an hsien, not far from the Hunan capital of Changsha. His father, a man with only two years education, and his mother, who was illiterate and a devout Buddhist, were of peasant stock. By Mao's teenage years his family had achieved what in his own words was the status of rich peasants. He worked on the land from his childhood, and during these same years he was constantly at odds with his stern father, which some authors feel was a root cause for his later revolutionary career. However, before becoming a revolutionist, Mao received, from his eighth year, a traditional education in the classics at a primary school. Five years later his father removed him from school and put him to work on the family fields, but Mao continued to study on his own. Three years later, having run away from home, he began a year of study at a modern higher primary school in Hsiang-hsiang hsien, only a few miles south of Hsiang-t'an. His political horizons were broadened there, and like so many youths of his generation, he was deeply influenced by the reformist writings of K'ang Yu-wei and Liang Ch'i-ch'ao.

In 1911 Mao went to Changsha where he was to spend most of the next decade. He was there to witness the overthrow of the Manchu dynasty authorities in the province in the fall, and as a consequence joined the revolutionary army as a common soldier. There was little to distinguish his first encounter with military life, and in the spring of 1912 he left the army to return to school. Just prior to his half-year military service, and for a year afterwards, he attended various Changsha schools and studied independently at a library in the city. Finally, in the spring of 1913, in his 19th year, he entered the Hunan Fourth Normal School to embark on a career in teaching. In the fall the school merged with another one, and from then to his graduation in 1918, Mao studied at the Hunan First Normal School.

Mao's years at the normal school had a profound effect upon both his personal and professional life. Changsha in general and the normal school in particular were alive with intellectual and political ferment during the May Fourth period. He and his friends frequently gathered to discuss political issues, and they were deeply influenced by the demands for sweeping changes in China found in the pages of Ch'en Tu-hsiu's (q.v.) *Hsin ch'ing-nien* (New youth). Mao later became a political enemy of Ch'en, but he nonetheless acknowledged his intellectual indebtedness to him. The students often extended their activities beyond the school doors, as in 1917 when they founded a night school for illiterate workers. In 1917–18 Mao and his close friend Ts'ai Ho-sen (q.v.) were prime movers in establishing the *Hsin-min hsueh-hui* (New people's study society). The organization was involved in a number of endeavors to encourage students to further their participation in public affairs, one of which was a work-and-study scheme under which many Hunanese students went to France (see under Ts'ai Ho-sen). The *Hsin-min hsueh-hui* was comparable in many ways to similar organizations set up by Yun Tai-ying (q.v.) in Wuhan and by Chou En-lai (q.v.) in Tientsin, and like them it became one of the nuclei of the CCP when it was established in 1921. In addition to Mao, Ts'ai, Li Wei-han, and Hsia Hsi (qq.v.), other members of the society (who were all killed during the early years of the Communist movement) included Chang K'un-ti, Lo Hsueh-tsan, and Ch'en Chang-fu (also known as Ch'en Ch'ang). Apart from his fellow students at the normal school, Mao was also close to and influenced by several of his professors, including Hsu T'e-li (q.v.) and his future father-in-law, Yang Ch'ang-chi.

Mao finished his schooling in the spring of 1918, and in the fall went to Peking where he got a minor post in the library of Peking University. He quickly came into contact with the group of young radicals who were disciples of Li Ta-chao (q.v.). Mao was then 25, but he had not settled on a single political belief, though he had gained some knowledge of and was attracted in varying degrees to liberalism, democracy, utopian socialism, anarchy, and socialism. Equally if not more important, he was a profound nationalist, proud of being a Hunanese, and still deeply influenced by many of China's legendary heroes. In early 1919 Mao left Peking for Shanghai, but after a brief time he returned to Changsha, arriving there soon after the May Fourth Incident. In June Mao took part in forming a provincial student organization, and a month later he founded and edited the *Hsiang-chiang p'ing-lun* (The Hsiang River review). This journal, which attempted to politicize the students, was closed down a month later. He then edited another student paper, *Hsin Hu-nan* (New Hunan). This too was suppressed, and after Mao took an active part in organizing a student strike in December 1919, directed against the provincial governor, he was forced to leave the province. He spent the next half year in Peking and Shanghai. His talks in Shanghai with Ch'en Tu-hsiu led him further along the road to Marxism, and by the summer of 1920, in his own words, he "had become, in theory and to some extent in action, a Marxist."[1]

The ouster of the governor, who had driven Mao from Hunan, allowed him to return there in the summer of 1920. He won a post as head of the primary school attached to his alma mater and not long afterwards married Yang K'ai-hui. In the same year the Comintern took one of its first steps toward contacting Marxist groups in China by sending Gregory Voitinsky to China. As described in the biography of Yang Ming-

chai, Voitinsky was put in touch with Li Ta-chao and Ch'en Tu-hsiu, and during the next few months Communist cells were established in a few cities. In addition, the nucleus of the Socialist (later Communist) Youth League was formed in Shanghai in August. Mao soon learned of these activities and, with the assistance of his *Hsin-min hsueh-hui* colleagues in Changsha, proceeded to establish a Communist cell in the fall and a Youth League branch at the end of the year. Not long before, in July, he had set up a bookstore to disseminate radical literature, which was similar to (and had business dealings with) a store set up a bit earlier in Wuhan by Yun Tai-ying. These various endeavors were meshed in the next year when Mao and others met in Shanghai to establish the CCP.

In July 1921 Mao was among the dozen-odd men who gathered in Shanghai to establish the CCP, a meeting now described as the First Congress. Another participant, Ch'en T'an-ch'iu (q.v.), claims that Mao served as one of the two congress secretaries. Afterwards Mao returned to Changsha as secretary of the newly created CCP Hunan Committee, which also had jurisdiction over Party activities in an area of western Kiangsi where the important An-yuan mines are located. The Party founders also established the Secretariat of the Chinese Labor Unions, the forerunner of the All-China Federation of Labor (see under Teng Chung-hsia). Thus, in addition to his Party post Mao was also head of the Secretariat's Hunan branch. In fact, the posts can be regarded as virtually one and the same; the CCP consisted of only 60-odd members throughout China, and there were probably no more than 10 or so in Hunan when Mao assumed his posts there.

In the two years following the founding congress, Mao was occupied in a variety of Party, labor, and educational endeavors. Among the more significant was the establishment with Ho Shu-heng of the Self-Education College in Changsha, a small school which trained a number of latter-day Communists (see under Mao Tse-min). He also met with some success in organizing labor, especially in An-yuan where two assistants, Li Li-san and Liu Shao-ch'i (qq.v.), were the major figures in the successful strike of September 1922. In November this work led to the formation of the Hunan Federation of Trade Unions. Mao was the general executive (*tsung-kan-shih*), but in 1923, when he left the province, he relinquished the post to Kuo Liang, a close colleague in the labor movement. These periods in Changsha provided Mao with useful experience in organizing the two groups which were the major contributors to the ranks of the Party in its early days: students and labor union members.

In June 1923 Mao was in Canton for the Third CCP Congress, which discussed the then emerging policy of a united front with the KMT against an imposing array of north China warlords. Mao was elected for the first time to membership on the Party Central Committee, which consisted of only nine full and five alternate members. Moreover, he replaced Chang Kuo-t'ao as head of the Party's Organization Department, and to assume this post he took up residence in Shanghai where the CCP maintained its headquarters. KMT–CCP cooperation reached a new level of importance in January 1924 when many Communists participated in the First Congress of the KMT in Canton. Mao attended as a member of the nine-man Hunan delegation. While the congress was in session he was one of the three Communists who served on a 19-member committee to examine the new KMT Constitution, and he also expressed himself on the floor of the congress in support of Sun Yat-sen's principles. Only three CCP members won seats on the 24-member Central Executive Committee (CEC), but seven Communists, including Mao, were placed on the list of 17 alternate CEC members. On the day after the congress, at a meeting presided over by Sun Yat-sen, further assignments were made. Mao was named an alternate member of the Shanghai Executive Committee, which was headed by the important KMT leader Hu Han-min. Mao gained further stature and authority within the KMT a month later at the first meeting of its Shanghai branch when he was made secretary of the Organization Department, which was also chaired by Hu Han-min.

Mao's intensive work for the KMT in Shanghai gave rise to accusations within the CCP that he was sacrificing the independence of the Communist Party on the altar of excessive cooperation with the KMT. Among his critics was Li Li-san, who sarcastically characterized Mao as "Hu Han-min's secretary." Mao apparently spent most of 1924 in Shanghai, but he was reported on a visit to An-yuan in the late spring[2] and in August he spoke on rural problems at the Peasant Movement Training Institute in Canton (see under P'eng P'ai).[3] This seems to have been one of the first occasions when Mao addressed himself specifically to rural questions, although it was not until after the May 30th Incident (1925) that, in his own words, he "realized the degree" of revolutionary potential "among the peasantry."[4] Because of illness, Mao had left Shanghai late in 1924 for his native hsien. After recovering he spent a few months investigating conditions in the countryside. In his autobiography, Mao makes rather grand claims regarding his work in organizing peasant associations, but a detailed study of this period suggests these claims were greatly exaggerated.[5]

In the fall of 1925 Mao's work in the Hunan countryside was brought to a halt by the provincial governor, and he was forced to flee to Canton. There was then much that united the KMT and the CCP, but in the period after Sun Yat-sen's death in March 1925 factionalism was on the increase in the KMT. One of the key issues dividing the left- and right-wing KMT groups was the question of how much reliance (if any) should be placed on the policy of cooperating with the CCP. The Communists were also divided on the united front issue, but Comintern discipline prevailed in favor of a continuation of the alliance. Whatever Mao's attitude regarding this question may have been, during the next year and a half he played a rather significant role within the KMT apparatus. In November he and two Communist colleagues were able to gain the dominant voice on the credentials committee for the forthcoming Second KMT Congress.[6] At approximately the same time he became de facto head of the KMT Propaganda Department. In this capacity, Mao delivered a report on propaganda at the Second KMT Congress in January 1926, in which he stressed the need for the KMT to center its work on the peasantry. Mao was again elected an alternate member of the KMT's CEC and he continued to serve as acting head of the Propaganda Department. In the next month Mao received still another KMT post as a member of the Peasant Movement Committee. This nine-member committee (more than half of whom were Communists) was apparently intended as a device by which the CCP hoped to gain control of KMT organizations which dealt with peasant questions.[7]

The influence of Mao and his many Communist colleagues working within the KMT (see under Lin Po-ch'ü) received a severe blow in the wake of the Chung-shan Incident of March 1926 (see under Chou En-lai). Chiang Kai-shek quickly moved to curtail Communist power, and he was able to accomplish much in this direction at the Second Plenum of the KMT CEC in May 1926. Mao was removed from his Propaganda Department post, and most of his fellow Communists were stripped of their key positions in name if not in fact. In his conversations a decade later with Edgar Snow, Mao attempted to give the impression that he dissociated himself from the KMT after the Chung-shan Incident, and Maoist historians continue to maintain this fiction. In fact, at almost the same moment that he lost his propaganda post, Mao assumed direction of the sixth class of the Peasant Movement Training Institute. The institute, though under KMT jurisdiction, had been a stronghold of the CCP since the school was established two years earlier.

While Mao headed the Peasant Institute, he altered the curriculum toward a more Marxist orientation and arranged for a number of top Communist leaders to teach or give lectures. In the late summer of 1926 he took the class on a field trip to Hai-feng hsien where P'eng P'ai had been active in peasant organization work for several years. One authority believes that Mao's tenure as institute director was a turning point in convincing him that the peasants were the pivotal element in the revolution.[8] Mao remained with the school until the sixth class ended in the early fall, and he was still in Canton toward the end of October. The next half year of Mao's career was a reflection of the turbulent situation which prevailed throughout China after the launching of the Northern Expedition in July 1926. It appears that he went to Shanghai for a brief time in his capacity as secretary of the newly established CCP Central Peasants' Committee[9] and he also made a brief inspection tour of rural areas in Kiangsu and Chekiang. He was then in Changsha in December where he gave the keynote speech to the First Hunan Peasants' Association Congress, stressing the critical importance of the peasantry to the revolution.

For a month in early 1927 Mao made an investigation of rural conditions in five hsien near Changsha (including his native Hsiang-t'an). The celebrated report which resulted from his survey has been commented upon by many writers. Mao failed "to mention the leading role of the proletariat," but as Schram notes, the "importance of the report lies not in its Marxist ideological content, which is primitive, but in the revolutionary passion which animates it and in the historic movement it records."[10] Mao anticipated massive rural uprisings in which the peasantry would overthrow the landed classes. Unfortunately, from Mao's viewpoint, there were numerous forces within the revolution which strongly resisted such radicalism. Many officers of the National Revolutionary Army were from landed classes, and the attitudes of Stalin and the Comintern were predicated upon reliance on this army. Even within the CCP there was hostility to Mao's report (see under Ch'ü Ch'iu-pai). In March, immediately after Mao completed his report, he actively defended his policies at the Third Plenum of the KMT held in Wuhan, and then in early April he was made one of the five members of the KMT's Central Land Committee to hold further discussions about peasant questions. This body held the first of several meetings on April 19, but a week earlier Chiang Kai-shek had already engineered his anti-Communist coup in Shanghai. CCP ties with Chiang's right-KMT were now totally severed, but Mao and his Communist colleagues continued their alliance with the left-KMT in Wuhan, an alliance which would also collapse within three months. With each passing day the left-KMT leaders displayed greater hostility toward and anxiety about Mao's radical proposals as they sought to maintain the support of military units which, as already noted, had many officers from landed families.

In late April and early May 1927, with the political situation growing increasingly precarious, the Communists held their Fifth National Congress. Mao attended the opening session, but discouraged over the conservatism of his colleagues regarding the peasant movement, he stopped attending, claiming illness. The standard Maoist histories of the Fifth Congress depict Party leader Ch'en Tu-hsiu (q.v.) as an opportunistic leader who failed to appreciate the latent force of the peasantry, and these same accounts blame Ch'en for not allowing Mao to give full voice to his opinions. Mao's vexation was no doubt aggravated further by the fact that he was elected only an alternate member of the Party Central Committee.

In April 1927, the same month that the Fifth Congress opened, Mao had been named to the five-man Standing Committee of the Provisional Executive Committee of the All-China Peasants' Association. In this capacity, during the weeks following the congress, he was placed in the awkward position of having to take steps to restrain the excesses of the peasants. This course of action was in accord with directives from Stalin, notwithstanding the fact that generals nominally loyal to the left-KMT were already beginning to repress peasant associations in an extremely brutal fashion. Such an anomalous situation, of course, could not long survive; in late June and early July the CCP alliance with the left-KMT finally collapsed. In Schram's apt phrase, Mao was now about to embark on his "years in the wilderness."

The dramatic Communist response to these events was the Nanchang Uprising of August 1, 1927, now celebrated as the birth of the Red Army (see under Yeh T'ing). Many of the CCP's top leaders took part in the uprising, and most of those who did not attended the famous August 7 "Emergency Conference" in Hankow (or Kiukiang). Mao was among the latter. The conference deposed the Ch'en Tu-hsiu leadership and established a provisional Politburo under the direction of Ch'ü Ch'iu-pai. Mao was made an alternate member of the Politburo. A series of rural uprisings was planned along the Yangtze and its tributaries—principally in Hupeh, Kiangsi, and Hunan provinces—with the ultimate goal of surrounding and capturing the major Yangtze Valley urban centers. To carry out this grand scheme, now known as the Autumn Harvest Uprisings, key leaders were assigned to various areas. Mao was sent to his native Hunan to lead uprisings which he began in early September. This chapter of Mao's career has been covered in numerous sources, including the detailed account by Roy Hofheinz.[11] In the narrowest view, the Mao-led uprising was a marked failure, but in a larger "sense its echoes have still not died. For out of the survivors Mao put together a little guerrilla army which he led up into the Chingkangshan, the first stop on the road to Peking."[12] Adopting the narrow view, the Party high command, in November 1927, chastised Mao and his colleagues for their alleged "military adventurism." Mao was stripped of his membership on the CCP Hunan Committee and his position of alternate membership on the provisional Politburo. The fortunes of the Party were at a low ebb. The survivors of the Nanchang Uprising had marched south to Swatow in Kwangtung where they were totally crushed, and soon after Mao was chastised, the Canton Commune (see under Chang T'ai-lei) met with a similar disaster. Most of those who survived these misadventures went into hiding or left for Moscow. Only a handful, of whom Mao was the most prominent, had begun the arduous task of creating secure bases and developing armed guerrilla units.

Mao and his ragtail band of guerrillas encountered numerous difficulties at Chingkangshan, but its relative remoteness offered a refuge of sorts. In addition, the mountain fastness was astride the border of Kiangsi and Hunan, approximately equidistant from the provincial capitals of both provinces. This fact, in an era of rampant warlordism, proved to be of importance, because many provincial warlords were willing to allow a degree of banditry or Communist-sponsored organizational work so long as it was conducted in areas removed from their centers of power. The selection of Chingkangshan may have been more accident than design, but the use of "border regions" (as they were more graphically labeled in later years) emerged as a hallmark of Communist strategy.

The first order of business at Chingkangshan was the organization of peasant uprisings against landlords and the recruiting of peasants into the "workers' and peasants'" army. Draconian measures were often resorted to, as Mao himself has written. However, owing in part to poor communications, Mao soon found himself at odds with higher authorities in Moscow, CCP headquarters, and within Hunan. He was, in a technical sense, out of power during various periods in 1928, and it was not until late that year that he became in name as well as fact the most powerful Communist figure in Hunan. In the meantime, in the spring of 1928, Chu Te and Mao met and merged their troops into the Fourth Red Army (see under Chu), a force of about 10,000 poorly equipped soldiers to whom the concepts of Communism were at best remote. Chu was commander of the Fourth Army and Mao the Party representative (a title changed to political commissar at the turn of the year 1929–30). The Chu–Mao army was reinforced in late 1928 by the arrival of P'eng Te-huai (q.v.) and a band of soldiers who had revolted against their KMT army during the previous summer. P'eng's arrival was quickly followed by KMT assaults on Chingkangshan which necessitated the abandonment of the base. The Chu–Mao army moved eastward across Kiangsi, and during the next half year fought a series of battles against the KMT in south Kiangsi, west Fukien, and north Kwangtung. Because of the severity of the campaigns, they made little headway in augmenting the troop strength of the Fourth Army, but they were able to establish a viable base in the area around Juichin in southeast Kiangsi, which became their headquarters and later the capital of the Chinese Soviet Republic.

Chu and Mao made much greater progress in the last half of 1929, but Mao was still dissatisfied with the political training of his men. He moved to correct this situation in December at the Ninth Party Congress of the Fourth Army (better known as the Ku-t'ien Conference). Mao laid down a program of intensive political education to improve discipline and to bring the typical soldier and Party cadre into closer contact with the populace. Several decades later, Maoist ideologues were still citing the Ku-t'ien Conference as the basic model for politicizing a military force. In the meantime, Mao had been involved in a number of controversies over guerrilla tactics and land policies with the CCP headquarters in Shanghai. Both Mao and Li Li-san (q.v.) had been elected to the Central Committee at the Sixth CCP Congress held in Moscow in mid-1928, but Li, with Moscow's blessings, quickly emerged as the strong man of the Party following his return to Shanghai. Li and his colleagues in Shanghai had already attempted, with little success, to impose their authority on Mao. From Li's viewpoint, this became imperative in the early months of 1930 as he began to unfold his grand scheme to assault the major cities of central China—known to history as the "Li Li-san line." Several Red Army units were to be involved in this futile plan, but its endorsement by Mao and Chu was of vital importance because they controlled the largest military force. Ultimately but reluctantly, Chu and Mao finally agreed, and in June 1930 their armies were reorganized into the First Army Corps, with Chu as commander and Mao as political commissar. At the same time P'eng Te-huai's forces were organized into the Third Army Corps.

In mid-summer 1930 P'eng Te-huai captured Changsha, the Hunan capital, and held it for a few days. Simultaneously, Mao and Chu made an abortive attempt to capture Nanchang. The two retreating armies immediately afterwards met and reorganized their forces into the First Front Red Army. Chu continued as the commander and Mao as political commissar. In addition, Mao became secretary of the General Front Committee. As described in Chu's biography, a second attempt was made on Changsha in September. Then, in direct defiance of Li Li-san, Chu and Mao suspended the attack and retreated to their base in Kiangsi. The net effect of this action was the death of the Li Li-san line. Li weathered the attacks on his policies at the Party's stormy Third Plenum later in September, but he was soon deposed and "exiled" to Moscow for the next decade and a half.

From the Third Plenum in September through the Fourth Plenum in January 1931, the leaders in the Party headquarters fought a savage battle among themselves. The Li Li-san element, as noted, was routed in late 1930, and then in early 1931 the Russian-returned student faction led by Ch'en Shao-yü (with powerful backing from Comintern agent Pavel Mif) triumphed over a labor faction headed by Lo Chang-lung and Ho Meng-hsiung (qq.v.). Neither Mao, Chu, nor any other major Red Army commander attended these meetings. But as history was to demonstrate, the power of the Communists had already gravitated to the rural strongholds, of which the Chu–Mao base in Kiangsi was the strongest. Chu, Mao, and P'eng had retreated to their base with their forces relatively intact. In December 1930 Mao successfully met a severe challenge to his leadership (the Fu-t'ien Incident, see under P'eng Te-huai), and in the closing days of the year the Red Army was subjected to the first of Chiang Kai-shek's Annihilation Campaigns. This was successfully repulsed, as were the second and third campaigns in the spring and summer of 1931.

By the end of 1931 most of the key figures in Shanghai had gone to the Juichin base, and there in November the First All-China Congress of Soviets established the Chinese Soviet Republic. Mao emerged with two of the highest posts: chairman of the Central Executive Committee (head of state) and chairman of the Council of People's Commissars (the cabinet). In addition, he became one of the 15 members of the Central Revolutionary Military Council, headed by Chu Te. But his position within the Party apparatus was considerably less imposing, and over the next half year his policies—especially regarding military strategy—came under constant attack from the returned student faction and Chou En-lai. By mid-1932, as described in Chou's biography, Chou had succeeded Mao as the chief political officer of the Red Army. At approximately the same time Mao purportedly took ill and had to be hospitalized for several months. In terms of the Kiangsi soviet period, 1932 was a turning point for Mao; nonetheless, according to an official biography (published in 1951) it was in that year that he was elected to the Politburo.[13]

With much less authority in the military sphere, Mao devoted the last two years of the Kiangsi period mainly to civil affairs. In 1933 he once again was the object of an intensive, though indirect, attack on his authority (see under Lo Ming). When the CCP held its Fifth Plenum in January 1934, Mao played little or no role in the proceedings. In later years he bitterly attacked the policies adopted then, which from his viewpoint played a major role in the collapse of the Kiangsi soviet. Later in the same month, at the Second All-China Congress of Soviets, Mao retained the chairmanship of the Central Executive Committee, but he was succeeded by Chang Wen-t'ien (q.v.) of the returned student group as chairman of the Council of People's Commissars. Then, in October 1934, Mao and his colleagues set out on the Long March, which would bring them to north Shensi a year later.

Mao's authority at the beginning of the Long March is a matter of uncertainty. Although the Red Army was successful in breaking through the KMT blockade, the initial phase of the march was disastrous in terms of personnel and equipment losses. This fact may have played into Mao's hand, since he was not formulating the military strategy. In any event, at the famed Tsun-i Conference in Kweichow, Mao was apparently able to gain control of the Party apparatus. In the scores of later Maoist accounts of Tsun-i, the standard practice is to skirt the exact post which Mao held then (in preference to vague words such as "leader"), but one 1958 Peking source does state that he became secretary of the Central Secretariat.[14] In the numerous analyses of the Chinese Communist movement, much attention has been devoted to Mao's rise to mastery of the CCP, and it is often maintained that this process took several years. Yet there are few disagreements that Tsun-i was a notable turning-point in Mao's career. (See also under Chou En-lai, who in effect gave way to Mao in terms of political authority in the Red Army.)

From Tsun-i the Long March columns pushed northwestward to the Szechwan-Sikang border, and there in mid-1935 they rendezvoused with the military forces led by Chang Kuo-t'ao. A critical dispute arose between Mao and Chang over the destination of the Red Army (see under Chang). As a consequence, the army was divided into two columns; one, led by Mao, Chou En-lai, P'eng Te-huai, and Lin Piao moved north to Shensi; the other, led by Chang Kuo-t'ao and Chu Te, remained in the Szechwan-Sikang area for another year before it joined Mao's men in north Shensi. In a tactical sense, the Long March was a lengthy retreat marked by one disaster after another, with losses in personnel reaching to perhaps 90 percent of the initial force. Yet in a larger sense it was one of the great military epics of the century. Mao chose to view the march as a great psychological victory for communism; if his men could survive this, they could survive anything. The Long March became an instant legend, and from the leading core of its participants Mao built a cohesive leadership that survived largely intact for three decades.

In mid-1935, a few months before Mao's arrival in Shensi, he had been elected a member of the Executive Committee of the Comintern at the Seventh Comintern Congress in Moscow. More important, the decision of the Comintern to promote a world-wide front against fascism soon had important repercussions in China where Japanese incursions were becoming increasingly flagrant. Japanese militarism created a political atmosphere in which many vocal elements demanded a cessation of internal warfare in favor of measures to resist Japan. Given the relative weakness of the Communist forces, it was to Mao's advantage to push for a "broad national revolutionary united front," the phrase he employed at the important Wa-yao-pao Conference of December 1935. Exactly a year later, Chiang Kai-shek was kidnapped by two dissident generals, and from this famed Sian Incident (see under Chou En-lai) there soon developed an increased willingness on both sides to join in a united front against Japan. The issue was settled in July 1937 with the outbreak of the Sino-Japanese War, and in the early years of the war there was considerable cooperation between the CCP and the KMT. Whatever Mao may have felt about the long-range wisdom of the new united front, in the early war years he often articulated before his Party colleagues and the general public the primacy of cooperation to defeat Japan. Not surprisingly, his more glowing comments about the KMT and even Chiang Kai-shek were later expunged from his *Selected Works*.

Mao had braved many dangers in the pre-Yenan period, but during the war years he spent almost all his time in the relative safety of Yenan and its environs. Generals Chu Te, P'eng Te-huai, Lin Piao, Ho Lung, Liu Po-ch'eng (qq.v.), and others did the front-line fighting, and Chou En-lai and his coterie took care of the day-to-day problems of KMT–CCP cooperation in the national capital. Similarly, other men, such as Kao Kang and Lin Po-ch'ü (qq.v.) played leading roles in everyday Party affairs and in the new government apparatus, known as the Shensi-Kansu-Ninghsia (Shen-Kan-Ning) Border Region. The early war years also saw Mao further consolidate his leadership in the hierarchy. If in fact Chang Kuo-t'ao posed a threat to Mao's leadership, he was decisively beaten, after which he defected in 1938. Ch'en Shao-yü, the long-time CCP delegate to the Comintern, is also suggested in some works as a serious rival for Mao's mantle. If so, he was no more successful than Chang. In this connection, it is noteworthy that the standard encyclopedia in Moscow described Mao, in 1938, as the *vozhd* of the CCP—that is, "leader," in the absolute sense conveyed by the German word *Führer*.

The exigencies of war naturally required Mao's attention to questions of grand military and political strategy. The massive and almost totally victorious Japanese offensives during the first year and a half of warfare had compelled the Nationalists and Communists to cooperate. But after the end of 1938 the Japanese confined themselves largely to holding operations and occasional mopping-up forays. With the immediate pressures thus relieved the two Chinese sides became increasingly concerned with consolidating their power in the areas they controlled, and because no clear lines of jurisdiction had been laid out, a number of incidents and skirmishes took place between Nationalist and Communist troops. Chiang Kai-shek attempted to impose his will on Yenan by a blockade of the Shen-Kan-Ning Border Region, and then in January 1941 a serious armed clash in south Anhwei (the New Fourth Army Incident—see under Yeh T'ing) ripped apart what little remained of the façade of the united front. Mao responded to the blockade and the resulting economic hardships by a pragmatic program of "self-reliance" (which, two decades later, he was to refurbish in another period of economic crisis). Mao and other top leaders spoke before various conferences of model workers on the necessity to increase production, and the army, when not engaging the enemy, was called upon to produce its own food (see under Wang Chen). The concept of self-reliance had another facet which was an important part of the experience gained during the Yenan years. In addition to the Shen-Kan-Ning region, the Communists controlled a number of other areas, many of them of huge size and dense population. All these areas received general direction from Yenan, but for the most part they were dependent upon their own resources, and as a consequence many leaders gained experience in dealing with local problems which proved invaluable in the post-1949 years.

Freed from many of the mundane tasks which occupied him in earlier years, Mao was able to devote a good portion of the Yenan years to a serious study of Marxist–Leninist works and to his own writing. These years, in fact, were his most prolific as a writer, and many of his more important pieces date from this period. Singling out the 1938–1940 period, Schram notes that Mao's works fall into two categories, "the first concerned primarily with the military aspects of the . . . war, and the second with political questions. The military writings . . . constitute a trilogy analyzing the war at various levels. Characteristically, Mao began with a small volume . . . dealing in concrete terms with the day-to-day conduct of guerrilla warfare. He then proceeded to discuss the place of guerrilla warfare in the anti-Japanese struggle, and only afterward the strategy of the war as a whole." Schram continues: "The main content of political work both within the army and among the population was to preach national revival, to stimulate national consciousness, and to publicize Japanese atrocities, in order to strengthen 'the resolve to fight to the death to kill the enemy.' "[15] A bit later in the war, during the *cheng-feng* movement (see below), Mao took up the issue of the role of creative writers. Literature, he stated, must be placed in the service of politics and must not only convey basic Party policies, but also be written in a form comprehensible to a mass audience.

If any doubts existed about Mao's primacy in the CCP, they were dispelled during the *cheng-feng* (rectification) movement of 1942–1944. In the scores of meetings and conferences during this period, the basic Maoist idea of combining theory and practice was hammered home. Dogmatism of all varieties was attacked, particularly when, in Mao's view, the dogma had little pertinence to the problems of China. In the words of one authority on this period, Mao's "idea of a real theoretician . . . was one who had done as much organizing as he had reading."[16] This theme in the *cheng-feng* movement is widely regarded as an attack on the returned student faction which, though far less potent than in earlier years, still had considerable power. It seems significant that (according to an official 1951 biography of Mao) he was first elected chairman of the Politburo and Central Committee in 1943.[17] This same source, without elaboration, also states that he was re-elected to these posts in the next year.

In April 1945, on the eve of the Seventh Party Congress, a famous resolution on Party history was adopted by the Central Committee. Clearly Mao's handiwork, it deals with the numerous errors of the "right" and "left" by Mao's political opponents—notably Ch'en Tu-hsiu, Li Li-san, Lo Chang-lung, Ch'en Shao-yü, Ch'in Pang-hsien, and Chang Kuo-t'ao (qq.v.). It was only after Tsun-i, the argument continues, that the CCP grew in strength and vigor under Mao's "correct leadership." The document is now sanctified by its inclusion in Mao's *Selected Works*. At the Seventh Congress, held from April to June, Mao delivered as the keynote address his well-known "On Coalition Government." Although Mao temporarily softened his demands for an end to the "one-party KMT dictatorship" later in 1945 when he conferred with Chiang Kai-shek, the tone of "On Coalition Government" made it plain that he was prepared for

an all-out struggle for control of China once Japan had been defeated.

At the close of the Seventh Congress, Mao was re-elected chairman of the Central Committee and the Revolutionary Military Council. (He had assumed the latter post during or soon after the Long March.) He also continued to head the Central Secretariat, a small body, probably of five men, which was a kind of inner-Politburo. At the urgings of senior American diplomats, Mao flew to Chungking in late August 1945, immediately after the war ended, to confer with Chiang Kai-shek on a number of outstanding issues between the two sides. The talks lasted for six weeks, after which Mao returned to Yenan in October. Some tentative agreements were reached, and Chou En-lai (who had assisted Mao in the talks) remained in Chungking to continue the negotiations. This led to the convocation, with CCP representation, of the Political Consultative Conference on January 10, 1946, the same day that a cease-fire agreement was signed. The failure to maintain the cease-fire agreement is described in Chou's biography.

In the fall of 1945, while Mao and Chiang were talking, their armies were marching. Both sides sought to gain control of north China and, particularly, of Manchuria. For the KMT, whose power rested in central and southwest China, this meant long lines of communications. On the other hand, the Communists had been operating in north China for many years, and the movement of Lin Piao's army into neighboring Manchuria was accomplished with relative ease. Chiang's firepower was then vastly superior to Mao's, and the number of men in his armies was also several times larger. Chiang concentrated on holding the cities and the rail lines; Mao concentrated on building his strength by organizing peasant armies in the countryside. The often recounted story of Mao's success and Chiang's failure is described in the biographies of Mao's generals—the familiar cast of P'eng Te-huai, Lin Piao, Liu Po-ch'eng, Ho Lung, Nieh Jung-chen, and Ch'en I. For the first year of the civil war Mao directed the grand strategy from Yenan, where he remained until just before the city was captured by the Nationalists in March 1947. The uncontested departure from Yenan symbolized Mao's strategy—he was still willing to trade cities for the time to organize even stronger forces from the countryside.

A year and a half after Mao's flight from Yenan he was to proclaim the inauguration of the PRC from the Gate of Heavenly Peace in Peking. In the meantime, he undertook what might be called a miniature Long March. Accompanied by Chou En-lai and Jen Pi-shih, Mao moved from place to place in northern Shensi for a year and, because of the inherent dangers of the situation, he used the name Li

Te-sheng. During this year the continued prosecution of the war was the paramount issue, but as the tide began to turn in favor of the Communists in the last half of 1947 and early 1948, increased attention was given to developing land policies in "liberated areas." The lessons learned from this period probably played a major role in the manner in which the Communists moved on the critical land question after 1949. In the spring of 1948 Mao went to P'ing-shan hsien in west Hopeh, which for the next year was the *de facto* Communist capital. There, in March 1949, Mao delivered another major report when the Seventh Central Committee held its Second Plenum. With nationwide victory now in the offing (and Peking already in Communist hands), Mao turned his attention to the question of shifting the focus of power from the countryside to the cities. Sensing this would be a formidable task, he cautioned against arrogance in managing the large coastal cities which the PLA was now conquering in rapid succession. Later in the month the Central Committee and PLA Headquarters were transferred to Peking.

With the PLA moving swiftly southward, Mao was able to lay plans for a new government in comparative leisure. On June 30, 1949, to commemorate the 28th anniversary of the Party, he published his well-known "On the People's Democratic Dictatorship," declaring his administration would "lean to one side," the side of the Soviet Union. In domestic affairs he indicated a willingness to ally the peasants and workers with the petty and national bourgeoisie as the four groups which would constitute the "people's democratic dictatorship." The "enemy," the landlord class, would be "transformed" or, failing that, crushed. Earlier in the month Mao had chaired the preparatory meeting of the CPPCC, and three months later this organization met in full session to establish the new government. Amidst great fanfare, Mao declared the PRC to be in existence on October 1, and he took for himself the senior government posts as chairman of the CPPCC, the Central People's Government Council, and the People's Revolutionary Military Council. Chou En-lai headed the cabinet and Chu Te continued as PLA commander.

By the end of 1949 the PLA had wiped out all but the last vestiges of KMT military strength on the mainland. Under these circumstances, and as ruler now of the number two Communist power, Mao arrived in Moscow on December 16, in time for Stalin's birthday five days later. The two men had been dealing with one another indirectly for a quarter of a century, and Mao, better than most Communists, knew how dearly the CCP had paid for Stalin's monumental blunders in the 1920's. Yet, with a larger sense of history, he admired Stalin's accomplishments in turning Russia into a modern industrial state. Details have not been released regarding their extended negotiations. Mao was in Moscow for a month before Chou En-lai arrived to assist in the talks which, on February 14, culminated in the Sino-Soviet Treaty of Friendship, Alliance, and Mutual Assistance. The details concerning the treaty are contained in Chou's biography. In brief, Mao won Stalin's assurance of military support in the event China was attacked, and Stalin in turn gained some important economic privileges within Chinese borders and rights to use certain Chinese military facilities.

In the spring and summer of 1950 Mao turned to important social and economic issues. On April 30 (as he had done two decades earlier in Kiangsi) he promulgated a new marriage law, and two months later the new agrarian reform law. The latter had been a major topic at both the Party's Third Plenum in early June and the second session of the CPPCC a few days later. Speaking at the Party meeting, Mao listed the completion of agrarian reform first in his three-point program to accomplish a "fundamental turn for the better in the financial and economic situation in China." The other two points were a "readjustment" of existing industry and commerce and the large-scale reduction in government expenditures. He estimated that it would take three years to carry out this program, and in general he outlined a relatively gradual approach. (For further details on the important land law, see under Liu Shao-ch'i, who also made a major speech on the subject.) Mao also called for a partial demobilization of the PLA, but a dramatically new situation unfolded later in the month with the outbreak of the Korean War.

In the early stages of the Korean War Mao stayed in the background and let his subordinates, like Foreign Minister Chou En-lai, make the pronouncements indicating that China would aid North Korea if its very existence seemed threatened. The threat became a near-reality in October with the crumbling of the North Korean army before an American–South Korean offensive which reached the Yalu River on the Manchurian border. Late in the month Peking intervened, its army known as the Chinese People's Volunteers (see under CPV commander P'eng Te-huai). Just one month later Mao learned that his son, An-ying, had been killed in action.[18] In the next summer the truce talks began in Korea, but it was two more years before a settlement was reached.

Despite the great demands of the Korean War on China's limited resources, Mao proceeded with his program of national reconstruction and rehabilitation. He addressed himself to this theme at the third session of the CPPCC in October 1951. His remarks on "ideological remolding" set the tone for two of the more wide-ranging campaigns of the early 1950's, the famous "three-anti" and "five-anti" movements. The first, directed internally at the CCP and the state apparatus, was designed to root out corruption, waste, and bureaucracy; the second, an assault on the bourgeoisie, was aimed at eliminating bribery, tax evasion, fraud, theft of government property, and theft of state economic secrets. Mao moved on these campaigns only after eliminating what were termed "counterrevolutionaries" in the first half of 1951, a program that took the lives of well over 100,000 people (figures derived from official Chinese Communist, not hostile, statistics).[19] In the same year, on the 30th anniversary of the CCP, ideologue Hu Ch'iao-mu (q.v.) published the most Maoist of the Maoist histories (*Thirty Years of the Communist Party of China*). At the same time a special body under the Central Committee began to issue the texts of what is now known as the *Selected Works of Mao Tse-tung*. There had been earlier versions, but the new edition was bowdlerized "so as to remove both youthful errors and any points of fact or doctrine which did not suit the current orthodoxy."[20] The growing "cult of the thought of Mao Tse-tung" thus received a new impetus, though at this stage it was still considerably less intense than a similar campaign to deify Stalin in his last years.

In early 1953 the first formal steps were taken to establish a national legislative body. Mao himself assumed the chairmanship of a special committee to draft the constitution, which was adopted a year and a half later at the First NPC (see below). In the meantime, the harmony at the higher reaches of the CCP was disrupted by the most serious purge since Mao eliminated earlier rivals in the late 1930's and early 1940's. Mao took the initiative in the celebrated Kao Kang case by a call to strengthen Party unity at a Politburo meeting in December 1953. Two months later, at the Central Committee's Fourth Plenum, Liu Shao-ch'i warned that "certain high-ranking cadres" were attempting to build "independent kingdoms." Mao missed the plenum, the official explanation being that he was "away on holiday." In any event, Kao and his alleged accomplice Jao Shu-shih were publicly purged a year later. (The details are contained in the biographies of these two men.)

At the First NPC session, held in September 1954, the constitution was adopted. In the reorganized government, Mao continued as head of state, officially styled chairman of the PRC. As such, he was commander-in-chief of the armed forces and ex-officio chairman of the National Defense Council. The chairman was also authorized to convene a special body known as the Supreme State Conference; this was done occasionally by Mao and his successor Liu Shao-ch'i in succeeding years, but there

is little to suggest that the body was of any special significance. Immediately after the NPC meetings, Nikita Khrushchev, the new Soviet leader, arrived for celebrations marking the fifth anniversary of the PRC. The talks resulted in a fundamental reordering of the Sino-Soviet alliance. Some cooperative ventures were launched (see under Chou En-lai, who officially led the Chinese side in the negotiations), but arrangements were made to liquidate various Soviet privileges within Chinese borders.

The First Five-Year Plan was launched in 1953, but it received little attention in the press until Li Fu-ch'un (q.v.) made a major speech on the subject at the second session of the NPC in July 1955. Many outside observers were struck then by the relatively moderate pace outlined in regard to most phases of industry and agriculture. However, only one day after the meeting adjourned, Mao spoke at a meeting of Party secretaries of provincial, municipal, and area committees. He took cognizance of the goals for collectivization which had just been spelled out at the NPC session but suggested in almost bland fashion that the pace of establishing the famous agriculture producers' cooperatives could be speeded up considerably. Within a matter of days the press carried reports of the rapid formation of cooperatives, and by the end of the year most of rural China had been collectivized. Given such speed it is not surprising that many problems arose, but, if only in contrast to the blood-letting which characterized Stalin's parallel program of the early 1930's, China's collectivization under Mao was conducted with relatively little disruption and a minimum of physical force. Possibly emboldened by this success, Mao then socialized industry and commerce in another campaign during the following winter.

In September 1956 the CCP convened the Eighth Party Congress, the first held in 11 years. Under the terms of the revised constitution, Mao retained the Party chairmanship. He was also elected to the newly established Standing Committee which, in effect, replaced the former Secretariat as the "inner-Politburo." The Standing Committee then consisted of Mao, Liu Shao-ch'i, Chou En-lai, Chu Te, Ch'en Yun, and Teng Hsiao-p'ing, and a year and a half later Lin Piao was added to the group. Mao delivered only a perfunctory speech at the congress, but in many ways it was his finest hour: there was peace throughout a land of 600 million people, the Party seemed to be in full control, industry and agriculture were moving ahead, and Peking's international relations were steadily expanding. However, events were soon to show that the optimistic mood which characterized the Eighth Congress was, if not mistaken, at least premature. In February 1957 Mao delivered a speech on the "correct handling of contradictions among the people." This gave a new impetus to the lagging Hundred Flowers campaign launched a year earlier (see under Lu Ting-i), which was designed to stimulate thought and creativity, especially among intellectuals. Yet it was understood, or so Mao thought, that discussions of various Chinese problems would be held within the framework of socialist tenets. However, it soon became clear during the peak of the Hundred Flowers discussions in the spring of 1957 that many persons were challenging the unchallengeable: the rule of China by the CCP. Mao quickly changed course; the relative freedom of expression turned overnight in the late spring into an "anti-rightist" campaign. It was only then, on June 10, that Mao's "contradictions" speech was published—in revised form.

The "anti-rightist" campaign was waged with growing ferocity for many months. There were a number of victims within the ranks of the CCP (see, for example, P'an Fu-sheng), but many more were singled out from among the eight non-Communist political parties such as the China Democratic League. In February 1958, at an NPC session, many of these men lost posts of considerable stature if only nominal authority in the government apparatus. However, it is suggestive of the peculiar style of Maoist rule that the overwhelming majority of those who fell from political grace in 1957–58 returned to the political scene, usually after two or three years in a kind of political limbo. Not surprisingly, most of these men—both Party and non-Party figures—did not regain their previous eminence, although there were even some exceptions to this general pattern.

The shift to a more militant stance regarding dissident or potentially dissident elements was almost certainly related to similar readjustments in other spheres. In a single phrase—"The east wind prevails over the west wind"—Mao turned away from the then famed "five principles of peaceful coexistence" which had characterized Chinese foreign policy from the Geneva and Bandung Conferences of 1954 and 1955. This was not, of course, a whimsical phrase. It was coined by Mao during his visit to Moscow in November 1957. He had gone there for the ostensible purpose of attending celebrations marking the 40th anniversary of the Russian Revolution, but it was clear from the number (over 150) and importance of the men who accompanied him that he was intent upon a major review of Sino-Soviet relations. Mao's delegation included Peking's top military leaders (see under P'eng Te-huai) and its leading scientists (see under Kuo Mo-jo). He also participated in the important summit meeting of leaders from other Communist nations at which a joint statement was agreed upon. However, as described in the biography of Teng Hsiao-p'ing, the Chinese had serious reservations about Moscow's hopes for a *détente* with the "west," which in Mao's imagery meant the United States.

On the domestic scene, the movement toward a more militant posture apparently crystallized at the Third Plenum held in September–October 1957, just prior to Mao's departure for Moscow. In somewhat oversimplified terms, the decision was made about then to turn from material incentives to programs propelled by a massive mobilization of human resources. Within a few months this came to be known as the Great Leap Forward (see under Liu Shao-ch'i), which received Mao's imprimatur at the second session of the Eighth Party Congress in May 1958. This grand scheme to modernize China at breakneck speed has been discussed by every author who has written about China in the late 1950's and early 1960's. There are many disputes about its short- and long-range significance, but there is little debate regarding the economic dislocations which followed in the 1959–1961 period. The failures, initially ascribed to faulty local leadership and disastrous weather conditions, were in later years embellished by claims that additional major factors were the abrupt departure of thousands of Soviet technicians (in 1960) and the failure of Moscow to send machinery for which the Chinese had contracted.

In late 1958, Mao announced his intention to retire as chief of state. Some authors (usually hostile ones) have asserted that he was forced into this step by the faltering Great Leap Forward. Whatever the truth, he did step down in April 1959 at the inaugural session of the Second NPC, being replaced as PRC chairman by Liu Shao-ch'i. (Earlier, in December 1954, Mao had relinquished to Chou En-lai the chairmanship of the CPPCC, but by then this body was already of minor consequence.) Thus, as of 1959, Mao's only official post in the government was as a deputy from Peking to the NPC. He did, of course, retain his senior Party post, not to mention his still immense if somewhat tarnished prestige. Not long afterwards, despite the embarrassment of having to admit a sharp cutback in economic goals (an onerous task performed by Chou En-lai and others), Mao was fully equal to the challenge to his policies by Defense Minister P'eng Te-huai, whose biography describes his downfall in the summer of 1959.

In the years after 1959, the image of Mao's activities in domestic affairs became blurred. To a large extent this was true of most of the senior Peking leaders and is doubtless a result of the fact that texts of articles and speeches were less frequently released than in previous years. Moreover, those released were often so vague in detail or exhortative in nature that they seemed to have been written in committee fashion. For example, Mao presided over the important Ninth and Tenth Plenums of the Central Committee in January 1961 and September 1962, respectively, but no texts of speeches were issued. The first of these meetings put the stamp of approval on the policy of subordinating industry to agriculture, and, to strengthen the Party apparatus, regional bureaus (which had been abolished in the mid-1950's) were re-created. At the September 1962 Plenum, another step to tighten Party control was taken by the expansion of the size of the Central Control Commission. In addition, the Plenum communiqué suggested that Mao was becoming increasingly dissatisfied with what he felt to be a lagging revolutionary fervor. Accordingly, he outlined a policy for what came to be called in the next few years the "socialist education" movement. This movement was intended to touch all strata of society, but it seemed to focus on the youth of China. Within the next few years a number of young model heroes were unveiled (more often posthumously than not) whose greatest inspiration was invariably drawn from the "thought of Mao Tse-tung." Another aspect of the socialist education campaign was its obvious ties to the PLA. Lin Piao had succeeded P'eng Te-huai in 1959, and in the ensuing years there was considerable emphasis on "learning from the PLA." By 1964–65 the socialist education campaign was centered on the alleged shortcomings of the Party leadership, which Mao apparently believed was in the process of becoming a bourgeois "new class." The failure of this campaign was a major factor in the initiation of the Great Proletarian Cultural Revolution of 1966.

While Mao was resorting more and more to campaigns to glorify and indeed almost deify himself, his colleagues were attempting with considerable success to put the economy back in shape. This was accomplished in the early and middle 1960's, but Mao's attitudes toward the various tactics employed to restore the economy are at best ambiguous. However, there were no ambiguities regarding his views on foreign affairs. As the 1960's unfolded he became more involved in the duel with Moscow, whose leaders were labeled (at first indirectly and then openly) "modern revisionists" who were corrupting world communism. Some of the major chapters in this complex story are related in the biographies of K'ang Sheng, Liu Ning-i, P'eng Chen, Liu Shao-ch'i, and Teng Hsiao-p'ing, each of whom played key roles in trading charges with their Moscow counterparts. Many of the issues came to a head in mid-1963 when Teng held fruitless talks in Moscow. Mao was pointedly present at the airport to see off and to welcome back Teng from his trip. At the same time the Chinese began to issue a series of "letters" to Moscow. The language and style were so similar to Mao's that their authorship was widely attributed to him; in any case it is clear from their importance that Mao at least authorized them. The letters contained endless charges against the Soviet Union and presented arguments, often characterized by pungent wit and keen logic, that China's sponsorship of continuing revolutionary activity in the "third world" was the only hope for sustaining the international Communist movement. Soviet responses indicated their sensitivity on a number of issues, but Mao's goal of turning Soviet policies around were, in large part, a failure as of the middle 1960's. It was at this point that Mao turned to domestic affairs once again with the launching of the Cultural Revolution, and within the space of a few months purged scores of senior leaders, many of whom had been colleagues for three and four decades.

Mao's role in history is firmly in place, regardless of the paths he takes in his last years. As the builder of a revolutionary movement, he is perhaps without a peer in the twentieth century, and in this regard his influence reached far beyond the shores of China—however distorted his "thought" may have become in its passage from one country to another. He also consolidated his rule over a continental-size nation and earned respect for China from friends and foes alike. Those who judge him in the future will have to come to grips with the troubles which beset China after the late 1950's, but even the most negative interpretation must accept the fact that Mao ruled over the largest population in history.

Many biographies in this volume have pointed to the personal losses suffered by so many leaders of the Communist movement. In this regard, and even accounting for the most extravagant claims of Peking polemicists, few Chinese leaders have endured more than Mao. Both of his brothers, Tse-min and Tse-t'an, died by violence in the revolution (see under Mao Tse-min). His only other sibling, a younger sister, and his wife Yang K'ai-hui were executed in Changsha by the KMT in 1930. And, as noted, his son An-ying, born in 1922 and educated during the war years in the Soviet Union, was killed in Korea in 1950. Mao was more fortunate with his two later wives. Ho Tzu-chen, reportedly a normal school graduate and a Party member from 1927, married Mao about 1930. She bore Mao five children. Ho was one of the few women to make the Long March;[21] she left for the Soviet Union in 1937 for medical treatment. Mao then set up housekeeping with Chiang Ch'ing, who as an actress had used the name Lan P'ing. Chiang had two daughters by Mao, both of whom were living at home in 1957.[22] According to a former classmate, one of the girls was a third-year student in the history department of Peking University in 1959 but left school in the same year.[23] Chiang Ch'ing played almost no role in public life until 1966, when during the earliest period of the Cultural Revolution she emerged as a powerful spokesman for her husband and was soon given several high posts.

There is far more literature both in Chinese and English on Mao than on any other Chinese Communist. The best of the biographies, Stuart Schram's *Mao Tse-tung,* is the major source for this sketch. Unlike many other biographers, Schram has exploited contemporary sources for Mao's early career and has thus sorted out the facts from the fables. Schram has also authored *The Political Thought of Mao Tse-tung* (New York, 1969), an indispensable guide to many of Mao's writings. The bibliography in the latter book deals with the various works by and about Mao.

1. Edgar Snow, *Red Star over China* (New York, 1938), p. 139.
2. *Hung-ch'i p'iao-p'iao* (Red flag fluttering; Peking, 1959), XII, 150–152.
3. Li Yun-han, *Tsung jung kung tao ch'ing tang* (From the admission of the Communists to the purification of the [Nationalist] Party; Taipei, 1966), p. 275.
4. Snow, p. 143.
5. Roy Hofheinz, "The Peasant Movement and Rural Revolution: Chinese Communists in the Countryside (1923–7)," Ph.D. diss., Harvard University, 1966, pp. 232–234.
6. Li Yun-han, p. 463.
7. Hofheinz, pp. 21–23.
8. *Ibid.,* pp. 46–50.
9. *Ibid.,* pp. 26–27; Miao Min, *Fang Chih-min chan-tou te i-sheng* (A life of Warrior Fang Chih-min; Peking, 1958), p. 38.
10. Stuart Schram, *Mao Tse-tung* (New York, 1966), p. 85.
11. Roy Hofheinz, Jr., "The Autumn Harvest Insurrection," *The China Quarterly* (October–December 1967), no. 32:37–87.
12. Schram, p. 104.
13. *People's China,* July 1, 1951, p. 27.
14. *Stories of the Long March* (Peking, 1958), p. v.
15. Schram, pp. 94–95.
16. Boyd Compton, *Mao's China* (Seattle, Wash., 1952), p. xxxviii.
17. *People's China.*
18. *ECMM* 175, p. 13.
19. Schram, p. 247.
20. *Ibid.,* p. 251.
21. Nym Wales, *Inside Red China* (New York, 1939), pp. 169, 178.
22. *ECMM* 172, p. 43.
23. Interview with former Peking University student, Cambridge, Mass., April 1966.

Mao Tun, see **Shen Yen-ping**

Mei I

(c. 1910–   ; Swatow, Kwantung). Journalist; director, Broadcasting Affairs Administrative Bureau, State Council.

Mei I has become one of the most politically important journalists in Communist China. On the eve of the Sino-Japanese War in 1937, Mei was working as a newsman in Shanghai where, utilizing his knowledge of Russian, he also engaged in translation work for a small news service which translated Russian materials into Chinese. It may be that he was persuaded to join the Communist cause in the course of this work with Soviet documents. In any case, Japanese sources claim that during the Sino-Japanese War Mei remained in and around Shanghai as a Communist Party underground worker.

Not long after the war ended, Mei was working in Nanking (spring 1946) for Chou En-lai, then head of the Communist delegation to the Nationalist-convened Political Consultative Conference in Nanking. Eric Chou, a former journalist for the Communist *Ta-kung pao,* has stated that Mei was among a group of ranking Communists (which included foreign affairs specialist Ch'iao Kuan-hua, q.v.) who were attempting to influence Chinese newsmen covering the sessions of the Political Consultative Conference.[1]

When the Communists withdrew their missions from Nanking and elsewhere because of the renewal of the civil war in 1946–47, Mei apparently went to Yenan where he was a New China News Agency (NCNA) staff member and director of its Broadcasting Department. From that time onward, his chief task for the Chinese Communist movement has been within the field of radio journalism. He was in Peking in 1949 to take part in the formation of mass organizations and the central government. Mei served on the preparatory committee for the All-China Youth Congress, and when this met in May 1949 he was elected a member of the National Committee of the All-China Federation of Democratic Youth (ACFDY) under Chairman Liao Ch'eng-chih, who, as head of the NCNA in the late 1940's, was doubtless familiar with Mei. (When the ACFDY elected its second national committee in 1953, Mei was not re-elected.) In July 1949 he also participated in the establishment of the All-China Journalists' Association (ACJA). An ACJA preparatory committee was formed at that time with Mei as one of the members; when it was established on a permanent basis in September 1954 Mei was elected as a vice-president, serving under Teng T'o (q.v.) and, after March 1960, under *Jen-min jih-pao* Editor-in-chief Wu Leng-hsi (q.v.).

As a delegate from the Youth Federation, Mei attended the first session of the CPPCC in September 1949, at which time the central government was organized. Several *ad hoc* committees were set up during the session; Mei served as a member of a special committee to draft the declaration outlining the results of the first CPPCC meetings, a committee headed by Kuo Mo-jo. In the weeks after the CPPCC meetings, a large number of appointments were made to staff the various government posts. In December of 1949 Mei was named as a deputy director of the Broadcasting Affairs Bureau, serving under Director Li Ch'iang (q.v.). In September 1952 Mei was appointed to succeed Li Ch'iang as head of the Broadcasting Bureau. He has remained in this post from that time (although the name was slightly altered in November 1954 to "Broadcasting Affairs Administrative Bureau"). Although Mei's bureau is not well known, it is the organization in charge of the internationally famous Radio Peking.

In September 1952 Mei led a delegation to a meeting of the Communist-sponsored International Broadcasting Organization (IBO) in Hungary, as well as to a meeting of its technical commission. In the next spring he was again abroad, this time in Prague, Czechoslovakia, for another meeting of the IBO in late April 1953. Mei was elected as IBO chairman and in this capacity presided over still another IBO meeting in Peking in September–October 1953. At the close of these sessions, he was elected an IBO vice-chairman for the year 1954. These two trips abroad were but the first of nine such journeys which took Mei to 13 different nations from 1952 through 1964, most of them directly in connection with journalism. In November 1957 he was a member of a cultural delegation to Moscow for the 40th anniversary of the Russian Revolution; in April 1959 he led a journalists' group to Warsaw, and in December 1961–January 1962 he took another such group to Cuba where he also attended a session of the Communist International Organization of Journalists. From Cuba Mei took his delegation to Ecuador, Chile, and Brazil (February–March 1962), thereby becoming one of the extremely few Chinese Communist leaders to have visited these Latin American nations. Mei then returned home in April 1962 after a brief visit in London at the invitation of the managing director of the British Commonwealth International Newsfilm Agency.

Mei's other trips abroad were to Indonesia (April–May 1963), North Korea (May–June 1964), North Vietnam (August–September 1964), and to Albania (November–December 1964). The journeys to North Korea and North Vietnam were routine journalistic visits, and the one to Albania was to attend the 20th anniversary of the Albanian "liberation" from the Nazis. However, the visit to Indonesia in the spring of 1963 was one of the more interesting

and provocative trips made by a Chinese leader in recent years. This was to take part in the first Asian-African Journalists' Conference. By 1963 the Sino-Soviet ideological rift was very much in the open, and the Chinese used this occasion to chastise the Soviets. Press reports from Jakarta[2] claimed that the Chinese deliberately thwarted Soviet efforts to gain admission to the conference. Not long after, in the famous Soviet "open letter" to the Chinese of July 13, 1963, the Russians charged that the Chinese had prevented Soviet participation on the grounds that the Soviet Union was not an Asian nation.[3]

Either during the trips abroad described above, or in Peking, Mei signed 15 agreements involving radio broadcasting or television between 1953 and 1964. Except where noted, these agreements were signed in Peking, and 13 of the 15 were with Communist nations: Czechoslovakia, Prague, May 1953; Bulgaria, October 1953; Hungary, October 1953 and January 1964; Poland, October 1953; Rumania, October 1953; Albania, September 1955; Poland, Warsaw, April 1959; Mongolia, May 1960; the USSR, May 1961; Cuba, Havana, January 1962; Indonesia, November 1962; Mali, August 1963; North Korea, May 1964 and December 1964. Mei, in brief, has signed almost all the international agreements concluded by the PRC with regard to cooperation in radio and television work.

Mei's work in radio and television journalism has naturally brought him into the realm of foreign affairs, as his many visits abroad suggest. This has been given organizational expression in a number of ways, mainly through the complex network of "people's" or "mass" organizations which the PRC has established as auxiliary arms in the execution of foreign policy. For example, Mei is a ranking member in four different "friendship associations" with foreign countries (or continents) from the dates of their formation: China-Rumania Friendship Association, September 1958; China-Latin America FA, March 1960; China-Africa People's FA, April 1960; and, China-Cuba FA, December 1962. He is a vice-chairman of the China-Rumania FA and a member of the Standing Committee of the other three. Earlier, in May 1954, he was named to the Board of Directors of the Chinese People's Association for Cultural Relations with Foreign Countries, a position he probably continues to hold. In February 1958, the PRC created a governmental counterpart to this organization known as the Commission for Cultural Relations with Foreign Countries, with Mei being appointed to membership on the Commission in March 1958.

He has held a number of other positions of an official or semi-official nature. In May 1954 he was identified as a deputy editor-in-chief of the *Jen-min jih-pao,* the organ of the Party

Central Committee, but the lack of later identification suggests that he no longer holds this position. From 1954 he has been a deputy to the NPC. He was a deputy to the First NPC (1954–1959) from his native Kwangtung, but then switched to Yunnan for the Second NPC (1959–1964). However, he was again elected from Kwangtung to the Third NPC, which held its first session in December 1964–January 1965. In February 1956 Mei was named to membership on the "Central Work Committee for the Popularization of Standard Spoken Chinese" (*p'u-t'ung-hua*), a committee subordinate to the State Council and headed by Vice-Premier Ch'en I. However, nothing further has been heard of Mei's activity on this committee. In August 1960, at the close of a major conference of literary figures, Mei was selected as member of the third National Committee of the All-China Federation of Literary and Art Circles, a position he continues to hold. He also served briefly in about 1960–61 as a vice-chairman of the Preparatory Committee of the China Electronics Society.

As might be expected, Mei makes frequent appearances in Peking when foreign visitors are being entertained, particularly those having connections with radio or television broadcasting. And as head of the Broadcasting Bureau, he also makes appearances at domestic conferences dealing with this work. A typical example of this occurred in July 1959 when he went to Huhehot, the capital of Inner Mongolia, to speak at a conference on broadcasting in national minority areas.

1. Eric Chou, *A Man Must Choose* (London, 1963), p. 14.
2. Hong Kong *Tiger Standard,* April 29, 1963.
3. *Peking Review,* July 26, 1963.

Meng Yung-ch'ien

(c. 1910–   ; Peking?). Specialist in industrial cooperatives; director, International Relations Research Institute, Academy of Sciences.

Meng Yung-ch'ien, well known to many Americans during the Sino-Japanese War, became prominent during the war as a senior official in the Chinese Industrial Cooperatives (better known by its abbreviated name of Indusco). After spending 10 postwar years in the cooperative movement, he was transferred to other fields in about 1955. Since the early 1950's he has also devoted much time to the field of international relations and is today regarded as something of an expert on the American economy.

Although little is known of Meng's early training, he speaks English well and is regarded by Americans who have known him as an efficient person with leadership qualities. His con-

nections with the cooperative movement began in the late thirties. Indusco was formed in August 1938 in Hankow as a means of stimulating the small-scale industry that was so vital to China following the loss of most of her industrial centers to Japan early in the war. It was informally sponsored by the Nationalist Government (which also contributed a share of the finances), as well as by contributions from charitable and labor organizations from all over the world. Such prominent persons as H. H. Kung and Sung Ch'ing-ling (Mme. Sun Yat-sen) were among the backers of the organization. Indusco reached its peak in 1941, at which time it had over 1,800 member societies with more than 29,000 members in areas held by both the Nationalists and Communists. By that same year Meng was director of the Indusco office in Loyang, Honan. Journalist Graham Peck, who was in Loyang in the fall of 1941, records that Meng was so harassed by the KMT secret police that he was forced to flee to Chungking.[1]

In order to revitalize the organization, an Association for the Advancement of Indusco was established in June 1943, with H. H. Kung as president and a three-member committee in charge of the actual work. Meng was one of the three members,[2] and from this year he also served as director of the Kweilin (Kwangsi) Office. During the last stages of the war Meng went to Chungking where he worked briefly for the U.S. Office of War Information (OWI). Eric Chou, a former correspondent for the Hong Kong *Ta-kung pao* (Communist), claims that a friend of his, then employed by OWI in Chungking, had managed to bring a number of Communists into U.S. agencies in China. He specifically mentioned Meng as among these Communists.[3] In view of Meng's later record with the Communists, it is probable that he was, in fact, a secret member of the CCP during the Sino-Japanese War. In 1945 Meng transferred to the United States Information Service and worked until 1946 in Peking and Mukden. Then, late in 1946, he went to the Communist-held areas.

Meng next emerged in 1949 as the chairman of the Supply and Consumer Cooperatives Commission under the jurisdiction of the North China People's Government (NCPG). By the time Meng assumed this post (March 1949) the NCPG had moved from Shih-chia-chuang (Hopeh) to Peking, which the Communists had occupied in late January. In the summer of 1949 he participated in the formation of the China New Economic Research Association, being named to the Standing Committee when it was formed in July 1949. However, little was heard of this organization in later years. As in the case of most NCPG officials, Meng was given an assignment under the central government following its establishment in October 1949. In accordance with his past experience, he was named as director of the Central Cooperatives Enterprise Administration (CCEA), one of the subordinate units of the most important economic organ of the new cabinet, the Finance and Economics Committee. In October 1950 Ch'eng Tzu-hua (q.v.) became director of the CCEA. Meng, in turn, was dropped back to the post of deputy director, thus giving way to a far more senior Party member. He retained his post as deputy director until the Cooperatives Administration was abolished in September 1952. At the same time that he held his post in the CCEA, Meng was also a member of the government's Finance and Economics Committee, a post he held from October 1949 until the central government was reorganized in the early fall of 1954.

As part of a series of efforts to pressure the United Nations into recognition of the legitimacy of the PRC as a U.N. member, the Chinese Communists made a number of appointments to the United Nations and its constituent agencies. In 1950 Premier Chou En-lai appointed Meng to two U.N. posts; in May, he informed the United Nations that Meng had been appointed as Peking's delegate to the Trusteeship Council, and in August he named Meng as a member of the Chinese delegation to the United Nations led by Chang Wen-t'ien, a top specialist in foreign affairs. These efforts, of course, were futile, and Meng continued with his work in the cooperatives movement. Already a senior official in the government effort to promote cooperatives, Meng received parallel assignments in 1950–1952 in the counterpart "people's" organization established in July 1950. In that month the Chinese formed the All-China Federation of Cooperatives (ACFC), with Meng as a member of the provisional Board of Directors. A few weeks later he gave an official report (September 15) before the Government Administration Council (the cabinet) on the results of the conference that established the ACFC. And, when the provisional Board of the ACFC held its first major meeting in November, Meng delivered the keynote address, a report that was reprinted in the semi-official gazette.[4] At the close of the meeting, his position in the cooperatives movement was reaffirmed when he was named to the ACFC Standing Committee as well as to one of the deputy directorships, a post that placed him under Po I-po, a top economic leader. The ACFC also established a number of subordinate organs in 1951–52. In addition to his ACFC deputy directorship Meng also served as the director of both the Trade Bureau (1951–c.1952) and the Supply Bureau (c.1952–1954).

When the ACFC was permanently established in July 1952, Meng retained his post as a deputy director. The Federation underwent a major reorganization and was renamed the All-China Federation of Supply and Marketing Cooperatives in July 1954; Meng was once again elected a deputy director. However, he was phased out of the organization in about 1955 and since that time has had no direct connections with it. Before breaking off his relations with the Federation, however, Meng led two delegations of the organization abroad. The first was to Budapest for the Third National Congress of the Hungarian Farm Products Marketing Cooperative Society in April 1954 and the second was to Moscow in June 1954 to attend the Soviet Consumer Cooperative Congress.

In the interim, beginning in 1952, Meng was engaged in further endeavors, both foreign and domestic, to promote China's economy. In an attempt to break through the economic blockade of the Communist bloc (imposed by Western nations in response to the Korean War), the Communists organized a large "international economic conference" in Moscow. Meng was named as a member of the Chinese delegation to this conference, held in Moscow in April 1952. The delegation was led by Nan Han-ch'en (q.v.), then the director of the People's Bank of China. Immediately upon the return of the group to Peking, a permanent organization was formed in China. Entitled the China Committee for the Promotion of International Trade, it was formally inaugurated with Nan Han-ch'en as its chairman on May 4, 1952, with "its objective the implementation of the Moscow International Economic Conference and the promotion of foreign trade." In practice, however, the Committee has been mainly used as the organization to promote economic ties with nations not having diplomatic relations with Peking. Since its formation in 1952, Meng has been one of its members, representing the Federation of Cooperatives.

The other activity that engaged Meng in 1952 was the formation of the All-China Federation of Industry and Commerce (ACFIC). In 1951–52, a nationwide campaign (the "five-anti" movement) was conducted against bribery, tax evasion, fraud, theft of government property, and the theft of state economic secrets. The movement, in effect, was directed against the nation's businessmen and industrialists. In June 1952, just after the peak of this campaign, the regime established the Preparatory Committee of the ACFIC; Meng was named as one of the vice-chairmen, ostensibly serving under non-Communist Ch'en Shu-t'ung, a prominent businessman and publisher from pre-Communist days. However, it appears that the guiding force of the ACFIC was Hsu Ti-hsin (q.v.), a deputy director of the Party's United Front Work Department. In the following year (October–November 1953), at the first congress of the Federation of Industry and Commerce, Meng was again named a vice-chairman of the now permanently organized Federation, a position he held until the next congress in December 1956.

Until 1952, Meng's work for the PRC had centered almost exclusively on economic matters. Since that year, however, he was engaged in a rather wide variety of other activities, most of them related to international relations. In December 1952 he attended the Communist-backed World Peace Congress in Vienna and in November 1953 he was once again in Vienna for a meeting of the permanent World Peace Council (WPC). It was also in 1953 that he first became a member of the WPC, a position he may still retain. He was abroad once more in connection with the WPC in May 1959 when he traveled to Stockholm for meetings marking the 10th anniversary of the "world peace movement" and in March 1961 when he journeyed to New Delhi for a WPC meeting. Closely related to his work with the WPC was his participation in the efforts of the PRC to improve relations with Asian and African nations. The first of the major Chinese efforts in this direction occurred in April 1955 when a delegation was sent to New Delhi for the "Asian Countries Conference," a meeting that was partially Communist-dominated and one intended to set the tone for the more famous Bandung Conference held later that month. Meng went to New Delhi as a member of a large delegation led by Kuo Mo-jo. From this conference came the series of "Afro-Asian Conferences," the first of which was held in Cairo in December 1957–January 1958. Meng did not attend this conference, but he did attend the Second Afro-Asian Conference held in Conakry, Guinea, in April 1960.

As a logical outgrowth of these activities, Meng received a series of appointments between 1954 and 1965, each related to international relations. In December 1954 he was elected to the Second Council of the Sino-Soviet Friendship Association (and re-elected in May 1959). In November 1956 he was named as the director of the newly created International Relations Research Institute (*Kuo-chi kuan-hsi yen-chiu so*) under the Academy of Sciences—not to be confused with the International Relations Institute (*Wai-chiao hsueh-yuan*), which has been headed by Foreign Minister Ch'en I since 1961. Meng was also named to the Standing Committee of the reorganized and expanded China Peace Committee in July 1958 and was identified by August 1961 as a Council member of the Chinese People's Institute of Foreign Affairs. He became a member of the Council of the newly formed Asia-Africa Society of China in April 1962, and when the various subordinate bodies of the Fourth National Committee of the CPPCC were staffed in early 1965, Meng was appointed as a deputy director of the International Problems Section.

Although Meng's activities since the mid-1950's have centered on the development of international relations, he has received a few other assignments that relate mainly to domestic affairs. From May 1957 to November 1958 he served as a member of the State Council's Scientific Planning Commission and in 1964 he was named as a representative of social science organizations to membership on the Fourth National Committee of the CPPCC, which opened its initial session in December 1964. Also, from the mid-1950's (presumably to date) he has served as a member of the Editorial Board of *Ching-chi yen-chiu* (Economic research), Peking's leading economic journal.

It appears that Meng is regarded as one of Peking's top specialists on the state of the American economy in particular and on the United States in general. He has, at any rate, written a number of articles dealing with the alleged crises in the American economic scene. Three of his articles have appeared in China's top journal, *Hung-ch'i* (issues of July 16, 1958, April 1, 1959, and April 25, 1962). However distorted these may be as interpretive articles, they do indicate that he has at his disposal a considerable amount of technical data on the United States. In a similar vein, Meng is used from time to time as a spokesman to denounce American policies. An example occurred in January 1962 when he castigated the United States (in an interview with NCNA) for its alleged persecution of the U.S. Communist Party.

1. Graham Peck, *Two Kinds of Time* (Boston, Mass., 1967), pp. 322–323.
2. Nym Wales, *The Chinese Labor Movement* (New York, 1945), pp. 124–135.
3. Eric Chou, *A Man Must Choose* (London, 1963), p. 140.
4. *Hsin-hua pan-yueh-k'an* (New China semimonthly), pp. 624–626 (January 25, 1951).

Nan Han-ch'en

(c.1892–   ; Chao-ch'eng hsien, Shansi). Leading trade official; chairman, China Committee for the Promotion of International Trade.

Nan Han-ch'en is one of the PRC's most important finance, trade, and banking figures, beginning his career in these fields during the war years in Yenan. From 1949 to 1954 he headed the People's Bank of China, and since 1949 he has been chairman of the Bank of China, the financial institution in charge of overseas banking. Since its establishment in 1952 Nan has headed the China Committee for the Promotion of International Trade, and in this capacity he has negotiated both in Peking and abroad a number of trade agreements, mainly with non-Communist organizations and governments.

Nan was born into a peasant family about

1892 in Chao-ch'eng, located in southern Shansi province on the Fen River about 25 miles north of Lin-fen. Despite the humble economic status of the family, Nan was able to attend Shansi University, presumably in the early years of the Chinese Republic. It was apparently during these student days that he had his first contact with revolutionary activities, and as a consequence of his participation in a student movement he was expelled from the university. According to unconfirmed Japanese accounts, Nan graduated from Peking University, but in any event he seems to have spent most of his early adulthood in his native Shansi. There, from about 1926, he began to work in the famous "Nationalist Army" (Kuo-min chün) led by Feng Yü-hsiang, the well-known "Christian general." Feng carried on a long flirtation with Russian Communists (see under Teng Hsiao-p'ing), and it may have been through such contacts that Nan became involved with Communism. Over the turn of the year 1926–27 he went to the Soviet Union as a member of a delegation led by Lu Chung-lin, one of Feng Yü-hsiang's top lieutenants. The group returned to China via Outer Mongolia in early 1927, after which Nan reportedly became a secret member of the CCP.

At some time after the 1927 KMT–CCP split, Nan is said to have fled to Japan. He was back in China by 1932, again working under Feng. Then, during the period from 1933 to 1936, he engaged in CCP underground work in the Tientsin area, together with such important Party members as Ch'en Po-ta and K'o Ch'ing-shih (qq.v.).[1] In late 1936, presumably under CCP orders, Nan was working as secretary-general to warlord Yang Hu-ch'eng, one of the major figures in the famed kidnapping of Chiang Kai-shek in December 1936 (the Sian Incident; see under Chou En-lai). After the outbreak of the Sino-Japanese War in mid-1937, Nan worked behind enemy lines in Shansi; from this time until 1940 he has been variously described as director of both the Political Department and the Organization Department under the Mobilization Committee in Shansi. The Mobilization Committee was subordinate to the Second War Zone, commanded by Shansi Governor Yen Hsi-shan. During the early stages of the war in particular, the Communists' Eighth Route Army fought against the Japanese in Shansi in rather close cooperation with Yen Hsi-shan's units, and a significant number of Communists and covert Communists were also collaborating with Governor Yen in a variety of civil and quasi-military functions (see under Po I-po).

During the winter of 1939–40 a large number of troops nominally under Yen Hsi-shan's control defected to the Communists. Thereafter, although Communist troops remained in Shansi, relations between Yen and the Communists were severely strained. These factors may have been the cause for Nan's transfer in 1940 to Yenan where he made public his CCP membership. By this time, if not earlier,[2] Nan was already a deputy director of the Party's United Front Work Department. In this capacity, he served under Director Ch'en Shao-yü; another deputy director, K'o Ch'ing-shih, had been Nan's colleague in the underground several years earlier. In addition to being the nerve center of the Communist movement throughout China, Yenan was also the capital of the Shensi-Kansu-Ninghsia (Shen-Kan-Ning) Border Region Government. Nan was elected to the Second Assembly of the government in November 1941 as a representative of troops stationed in the Yenan area. In spite of the fact that he represented the military forces, his major assignment seems to have been in financial matters—a task in which he has been involved since that time. Nan presented the official financial report before the Assembly and was elected as secretary-general of the Second Assembly (1941–1946), chaired by Kao Kang (q.v.). At the close of the meetings he was elected a member of the Border Region Government (the executive branch).[3] In view of his speech on financial matters, it is probable that he was already the head of the Government Finance Department; by 1942 he was specifically identified in this post. During his years in Yenan he seems to have been mainly involved in financial work for the Border Region Government, but, as noted, he was also a deputy director of the Party's United Front Work Department. Such an assignment was probably intended to take advantage of Nan's contacts with dissident elements who had worked under Feng Yü-hsiang or Yang Hu-ch'eng. In the wartime atmosphere the Communists muted their more extreme policies in favor of placing stress on nationalistic themes (e.g., "save the nation," "resist Japan") and were able to draw much talent to Yenan, particularly after many intellectuals became disenchanted with the efforts of the KMT to resist the Japanese. Aside from the fact that Nan attended the second session of the Second Shen-Kan-Ning Assembly in December 1944, little else is known of his work during the late war years.

After spending some six years in the Shen-Kan-Ning Border Region, Nan was transferred in 1946 to another of the major Communist governmental units in north China—the Chin-Ch'a-Chi (Shansi-Chahar-Hopeh) Border Region Government, which had its capital at Kalgan (Changchia-k'ou). There, as previously in Shen-Kan-Ning, he served as head of the Finance Department; Communist author Anna Louise Strong identified him in this position when she interviewed him in Kalgan in 1946.[4] Nan worked under the jurisdiction of the Chin-Ch'a-Chi Government until it was merged with the Chin-Chi-Lu-Yü (Shansi-Hopeh-Shantung-Honan) Border Region Government in August 1948 to form the North China People's Government (NCPG). Under the NCPG, which existed until it was absorbed by the central government in October 1949, Nan was a member of the Government Council as well as the NCPG's Finance and Economics Committee. From 1948 he had also been manager of the North China Bank, and when this was merged with two other banks in December 1948, he became general manager of the People's Bank of China, as it was now called.

Nan worked in Shih-chia-chuang, Hopeh, where the capital of the NCPG was located, until sometime after the Communists took Peking in January 1949. Like many important Communists, he participated in the preparatory work that led to the formation of the "mass" organizations and of the new central government. Thus, in June 1949 he attended the conference that established the China New Legal Research Society's Preparatory Committee (of which he was named a member), and in July he was one of the conveners of a large conference of social science "workers." When the central government was formed in October, Nan was given two assignments in his field of economics. First, he was named to membership on the Finance and Economics Committee (FEC), a post similar to the one he had held in the North China Government. The FEC was one of the four major committees subordinate to Chou En-lai's Government Administration Council (the cabinet). The other post was as director-general of the People's Bank of China. This position, in effect, was a continuation of his past work, but now on a nationwide basis. Nan's primacy in the field of banking was emphasized in May 1950 when he was named as chairman of the Bank of China, the organ of the People's Bank that controlled Chinese Communist banking abroad (including banks in Hong Kong and several Southeast Asian cities). On the same day he was also named to the Board of the Bank of Communications. The major portion of Nan's time in the early fifties was devoted to these endeavors, as is reflected by the fact that he made a number of official reports on banking activities before the Government Administration Council. He still heads the Bank of China, but he relinquished his post in the Communications Bank in 1954, and in November of that same year he was succeeded as director-general of the People's Bank by Ts'ao Chü-ju (q.v.), another veteran specialist in banking. Representing the People's Bank, Nan was named in July 1950 to membership on the Provisional Board of Directors of the important All-China Federation of Cooperatives (see under Ch'eng Tzu-hua), and when the provisional Board was made into a permanent organization in July 1952, he was reappointed. serving there until mid-1954.

It is not possible to credit Nan specifically with a major role in curbing the runaway inflation that gripped the China mainland at the time of the Communist takeover. At the policy level this credit probably belongs mainly to Ch'en Yun (q.v.), Peking's top economic specialist during the first decade of the PRC. However, as the chief official in the Chinese banking world, Nan almost certainly played a key role in implementing the fiscal policies that in a remarkably brief period brought a halt to the disastrous inflation that is generally described as one of the major causes of the collapse of the KMT Government.

As head of both domestic and foreign banking, Nan was a logical choice to lead the Chinese delegation to the International Economic Conference in Moscow during early April 1952. The conference had been convened in an attempt by the Communists to circumvent the embargoes imposed on them by the West as a result of the Korean War. According to Chinese claims, Nan's large delegation in Moscow was able to negotiate contracts providing for exports and imports valued at over U.S. $200,000,000. Immediately after his group returned to Peking the Chinese established the China Committee for the Promotion of International Trade (CCPIT), with Nan as chairman, a position he still retains. Ostensibly non-governmental, the CCPIT has been utilized principally to conduct trade relations with nations not having diplomatic relations with Peking (e.g., Japan, West Germany). And because so much Chinese trade has been conducted outside the Communist bloc, the CCPIT is one of the most important "unofficial" organizations in China. Nan's frequent trips abroad (see below) have almost always been made as the CCPIT chairman. Presumably to coordinate all aspects of foreign trade, the International Economic Affairs Bureau was established in August 1952 under the Finance and Economics Committee; Nan served as the Bureau director until the fall of 1954.

Although Nan was to become increasingly identified with foreign trade and related overseas activities, he has also been affiliated with domestic organizations connected with the business world. From 1951 to 1955 he was a Standing Committee member of the China Democratic National Construction Association, one of the eight non-Communist political parties, which consists mainly of non-Communist industrialists and commercial figures who remained on the mainland. Since 1955 he has been one of the Association's vice-chairmen. Similarly, he has been connected with the All-China Federation of Industry and Commerce (ACFIC), a sort of Communist-style chamber of commerce. He was named to a special "preparatory office" in late 1951, and then served as a vice-chairman of the ACFIC Preparatory Committee from June 1952 until November 1953 when he was named as a vice-chairman of the permanent organization, continuing in this position until the next congress of the Federation was held in late 1953. Nan has also been affiliated with the NPC since its establishment in 1954. He was a deputy from his native Shansi to the First NPC (1954–1959), the Second NPC (1959–1964), and again to the Third NPC, which held its initial session in December 1964–January 1965. In each term of the Congress he has also been a member of the permanent Standing Committee.

As already indicated, Nan's principal activities have been related to foreign affairs. Exploiting the atmosphere of the 1955 Bandung Conference, the Communists established the Asian Solidarity Committee of China in February 1956 (known as the Afro-Asian Solidarity Committee since 1958). Nan was named as a member and nine years later (June 1965) was elevated to a vice-chairmanship. Also in February 1956 Nan led a delegation to the annual Leipzig International Industrial Fair in East Germany, after which his group made an extended tour in Poland, Czechoslovakia, and Hungary. While abroad, the Chinese Communists had established (April) the Foreign Trade Arbitration Committee under the CCPIT; Nan was named as a member and still retains this position. He went abroad again in late November 1958 as head of the Chinese delegation to the Afro-Asian Economic Conference held in Cairo in December. He then took his group to India, returning to Peking in early January 1959. Soon afterwards, he accompanied Hsi Chung-hsun (q.v.) to the 1959 Leipzig Fair, which opened in late February. In December of the same year he went to Damascus (then a part of the United Arab Republic) to attend a conference of the Consultative Committee of the Afro-Asian Organization for Economic Cooperation, an organization born as a result of the above-mentioned 1958 Cairo conference. In April–May 1960 he represented China in Cairo at the Second Afro-Asian Economic Conference. He made his first trip to Latin America in 1961 when he was head of a delegation sent to Havana to hold an exhibition of China's achievements in "economic construction." After spending more than a month in Cuba, Nan led a small commercial mission to Rio de Janeiro, arriving there in late April 1961. During his month in Brazil he conferred with some of the nation's leading officials (including the president and vice-president) and gained the agreement of the Brazilians to establish a "trade mission of a non-official character." He proceeded to Chile where he spent a week talking with industrialists and businessmen and then went to Argentina for similar talks in early June 1961. Nan is one of the relatively few Chinese Communists to have visited these three South American nations.

Having led the Chinese delegations to the first and second Afro-Asian Economic Conferences, Nan was again given the assignment of heading the Chinese delegation to Karachi for the fourth conference in December 1963. Later in that month he traveled from Pakistan to Mali to inaugurate another exhibition to display China's "economic construction," remaining there until early January 1964. Three months later he was again abroad, this time in Japan where he remained for six weeks as head of an "economic and friendship" delegation. In June–July 1964 he was in North Korea to attend the Second Asian Economic Seminar. By this time the Sino-Soviet dispute was of such intensity that mutual recriminations at international meetings had become commonplace. Nan attacked Soviet aid practices in underdeveloped nations and was in turn attacked by the Soviet press, with the Russians chiding the Chinese for their alleged failure to fulfill aid commitments. Nan was once again on the attack against the Soviets (as well as the Western nations) in Algeria in February–March 1965 when he led a Chinese delegation to the Afro-Asian Economic Seminar. In June 1965 he spent six days in Kuwait where he discussed trade matters with leading Kuwait officials. He was back in Japan again in July–August 1965 as a deputy leader (under Liu Ning-i, q.v.) of the Chinese delegation to the 11th annual World Conference against Atomic and Hydrogen Bombs.

Nan's global travels have been matched by a series of appointments to organizations involved in foreign affairs. He was given leading positions in the following "friendship" associations when they were established: vice-chairman, China-Africa People's FA, April 1960; member, Standing Committee, China-Cuba FA, December 1962; vice-chairman, China-Japan FA, October 1963. In addition, as already described, he was elevated to a vice-chairmanship of the Afro-Asian Solidarity Committee of China in June 1965. Although Nan has dealt with nations throughout the world, he seems to specialize in Sino-Japanese relations. In addition to his two trips to Japan, he has negotiated and signed several agreements with Japanese traders in Peking and has served as a host for scores of Japanese delegations, particularly after the mid-fifties. Also, as the ranking official in the Bank of China, Nan has usually been the Chinese official to issue public denunciations when foreign governments have taken actions adverse to the interests of the overseas branches of the Bank, as in January 1959 when he denounced the decision of the Malayan government to close the branch in Kuala Lumpur, or in November 1962 when he issued similar denunciations regarding the closure of Bank of China branches in Calcutta and Bombay, actions taken by the Indians at the time of the Sino-Indian border war.

In private life, Nan is married to Wang Yu-lan, who was identified when she traveled to Japan with her husband in 1964 as deputy director of the Administrative Office of the CCPIT. To judge from photos of Wang, she appears to be contemporary in age to Nan. In 1942 Nan was said to have 12 children, but it is not known if Wang is the mother of these children.

1. *Hung-ch'i p'iao-p'iao* (Red flag fluttering; Peking, 1957), V, 68.
2. Lyman P. Van Slyke, *Enemies and Friends: The United Front in Chinese Communist History* (Stanford, Calif., 1967), p. 117.
3. *Shen-Kan-Ning pien-ch'ü ts'an-i-hui wen-hsien hui-chi* (Collection of documents of the Shensi-Kansu-Ninghsia Border Region Assembly; Peking, 1958), pp. 73, 74, 169, 268.
4. Anna Louise Strong, *Tomorrow's China* (New York, 1948), pp. 62–63.

Nieh Jung-chen

(1899–   ; Chiang-ching, Szechwan). PLA marshal; vice-premier; chairman, Scientific and Technological Commission; member, CCP Central Committee.

Nieh Jung-chen, one of China's most experienced military officers, has been a member of the CCP since 1923. Trained in France, Belgium, and the Soviet Union, he played a major role in many of the landmark events of Chinese Communist history, including the Long March. During the Sino-Japanese War he was the top Communist military and political official in the Shansi-Chahar-Hopeh Border Region. In the early years of the PRC Nieh was acting chief-of-staff of the PLA and since the mid-1950's he has been China's leading official in the field of scientific and technological development. He has been a member of the Party Central Committee since 1945.

Nieh is from a landlord family in Chiang-ching, Szechwan, a small Yangtze River port about 25 miles southwest of Chungking. He graduated from a middle school in Chungking, and while there he participated in the May Fourth Movement (1919). Toward the end of that year he left for France to take part in the work-and-study program (see under Ts'ai Ho-sen). Of the 1,600-odd students who took advantage of this scheme in the 1919–20 period, Szechwan was second only to Hunan in the number of participants. Fellow Szechwanese included Ch'en I and Teng Hsiao-p'ing (qq.v.).

Like many of his student colleagues, Nieh arrived in France with unformed political ideas, aside from the broad notion that he must work for the independence and modernization of China. Also like many of them, he had been influenced by Ch'en Tu-hsiu (q.v.) and his famous journal *Hsin ch'ing-nien* (New youth). But unlike many of the worker-students who spent more time in political activities than in educational pursuits, Nieh concentrated on work and study. His student life consisted of a year or so in Grenoble

and Paris, and about two years in Charleroi in Belgium where he studied chemical or electrical engineering at the Université de Travail under the financial sponsorship of the Belgian Socialist Party. During this period he held jobs with the Schneider-Creusot arms factories, the Renault auto works, and the Thomson Electric Company.[1] He was also moving toward an allegiance to Marxism. Nieh began reading Marxian literature, and he and Li Fu-ch'un (q.v.), another of the worker-students, were reportedly taught both French and Marxism by the same teacher. As a result of his new commitment, Nieh joined the Youth League in 1922 and the CCP in 1923. Edgar Snow reports that Nieh and Li spent some time in Germany in 1923, and while there Nieh helped to organize students.[2] Snow writes that Nieh spoke German, French, and some English, and, because of his period of study in the Soviet Union (see below), he presumably has some knowledge of Russian.

Nieh was among the many students in France who went to Moscow in 1924. There he studied at the Communist University of the Toilers of the East for six months, and at the Red Army Academy for a year. Returning home in the fall of 1925, Nieh went directly to Canton, then the revolutionary center of China. He went to work under Chou En-lai in the Military Committee of the CCP Kwangtung Regional Committee, and at the same time he was a political instructor for the fourth and fifth classes (beginning, respectively, in October 1925 and February 1926) at Whampoa Military Academy, as well as secretary-general of the academy's Political Department.

After Chiang Kai-shek forced many of the Communists to leave Whampoa in the early spring of 1926, Nieh left the academy. Soon after this, in mid-1926, the Northern Expedition began. Serving as a representative of the CCP Military Committee, Nieh was with the army of Kwangtung General Chang Fa-k'uei, which moved north from Kwangtung to Wuhan in the summer and fall. By mid-1927 Chang's Second Front Army was headquartered at Kiukiang (Chiu-chiang), an important Yangtze port in north Kiangsi. At this juncture the uneasy alliance between the CCP and the "Left" KMT was rapidly deteriorating, and its inevitable collapse became apparent in mid-July 1927. On July 26, one of Chang Fa-k'uei's major units, the 24th Division led by CCP member Yeh T'ing (q.v.), arrived at Nanchang, not far south of Kiukiang. Then, on August 1, Yeh, Chou En-lai, Ho Lung, and Chu Te staged the famed Nanchang Uprising. Nieh, who had helped plan the revolt, also took part in it, and on the same day he was sent north to the area near Kiukiang where Chou Shih-ti (q.v.) had his 73rd Regiment (subordinate to another of Chang Fa-k'uei's divisions). Nieh and Chou immediately staged an uprising there, and after reportedly wiping out 500–600 of Chang Fa-k'uei's men, they returned south with the 73rd Regiment to rejoin their colleagues-in-revolt at Nanchang.[3]

Under the new Communist order of battle, Nieh was made the chief political officer (*tang tai-piao*) in Yeh T'ing's 11th Army. After a few days the Communists were driven from Nanchang. Moving south to Kwangtung, they captured Swatow in late September, but once again they were quickly routed. After this serious defeat Yeh and Nieh made their way to the nearby Hailu-feng Soviet (see under P'eng P'ai), and from there they took a ship to Hong Kong. In early December Yeh and Nieh went to Canton to participate in the Communist-led uprising there (see under Chang T'ai-lei), but this was just as unsuccessful as the debacles at Nanchang and Swatow.

Official Communist biographies of Nieh are silent about the next three years of his career. However, according to what Edgar Snow and Nym Wales learned from their interviews with top Communist leaders in 1936–37, Nieh fled from Canton to Hong Kong where he remained until 1930, and from Hong Kong he went to north China where he was engaged in Party organizational work in Peking, Tientsin, and the mines around the city of T'ang-shan.[4] In 1931 he went to Shanghai where he worked for the Party Central Committee's "military advisory committee." In the same year he went to Kiangsi where Mao Tsetung and Chu Te had been building a major revolutionary base. Nieh was assigned to the Red Army Headquarters as a deputy director of the General Political Department. However, he was not in this post for long, because by no later than January 1932 he had joined Lin Piao to become political commissar of Lin's First Army Corps, one of the major components of the Chu-Mao First Front Army. For the next two and a half years Nieh remained with Lin for most of the time, although on the eve of the Long March he was serving as political commissar with Ch'en I's (q.v.) troops in the vicinity of Hsing-kuo hsien in central-south Kiangsi.[5]

In January–February 1934, at the Second All-China Congress of Soviets, Nieh was elected a member of the Central Executive Committee, the chief political organ of the Chinese Soviet Republic. Then, on the Long March that began from Kiangsi in October 1934, Nieh was again Lin Piao's chief political officer. Nieh's active participation in several of the heroic exploits which characterized this epic, year-long march to Shensi has been described in many Long March accounts.[6] Lin and Nieh arrived with Mao in north Shensi in October 1935, and after a brief period for rest and reorganization the Red Army mounted a major "eastward campaign" across the Yellow River into Shansi in February 1936. Among the participants were such leading figures as Mao Tse-tung, Lin Piao, Liu Chih-tan, and Nieh Jung-chen.[7] This expedition, described in greater detail in the biography of Liu Chih-tan,

was designed to gain food, supplies, and recruits for the Communist forces. After some partial successes, the Communists were driven back into Shensi in the spring of 1936. In the late summer of that year, Nieh and Tso Ch'üan were ordered to move a large force into east Kansu to assist the Second and Fourth Front Armies (under Ho Lung and Chang Kuo-t'ao), which were then completing the last stage of their portion of the Long March (see under Tso Ch'üan).[8]

Immediately after the outbreak of the Sino-Japanese War in July 1937 the Communists reorganized their units and established the Eighth Route Army. It had three divisions, one of which, the 115th, was commanded by Lin Piao. Nieh was made deputy commander and political commissar. In September Lin and Nieh led their division into northeast Shansi where, in cooperation with Nationalist units, they won a much heralded battle against the Japanese at P'ing-hsing Pass. After this victory Lin took most of the division south to aid in the defense of Taiyuan, but Nieh was ordered in late October to move to the Wut'ai Mountain area south of the P'ing-hsing Pass, where he was to set up the Communists' first guerrilla base behind enemy lines. His small force of one regiment, one cavalry battalion, and portions of two companies, totaled only 2,000 men.[9] Soon afterwards, on November 7, the Shansi-Chahar-Hopeh (Chin-Ch'a-Chi) Military Region was established, with Nieh as the commander and political commissar. Not long after these events, Lin Piao returned to Yenan, and for most of the remaining war years Nieh was acting commander of the 115th Division. As the top Communist official in the Wu-t'ai area, one of Nieh's first acts was to make contact with local provincial officials, most notably Wu-t'ai hsien magistrate Sung Shao-wen (q.v.), and also with Lü Cheng-ts'ao (q.v.), a military leader across the border in Hopeh who had previously served in the Nationalist Army.

Through the efforts of Nieh, Sung, Lü, and other local civil and military leaders who were eager to join the common effort against the Japanese, a conference was convened in January 1938 in Fu-p'ing hsien, located in west Hopeh not far from Wu-t'ai hsien. In the spirit of the united front which characterized the early stages of the war, Nieh emphasized in his speech to the conference the need to unite "all parties, factions, and classes" and de-emphasized a "Soviet type of administration," which, he declared, would be "madness to seek to establish." [10] The Fu-p'ing Conference created the Chin-Ch'a-Chi Border Region under the chairmanship of Sung Shaowen. Sung, Nieh, and Lü were all members of the nine-member Administrative Committee, which was the highest organ of authority. In addition to these responsibilities, Nieh was also head of a military training school at Fu-p'ing (a branch of the Communists' military academy in Yenan) and a member of the CCP Committee in the border region. Because of the steady Japanese harassments, Nieh's headquarters were seldom in one place for any length of time, but for most of the war years it was located in one or another rural village between Fu-p'ing and Wu-t'ai.

The territory under the jurisdiction of the border region varied during the war. From its earliest period it consisted of two well-defined areas, the Wu-t'ai base in the mountains of northeast Shansi and western Hopeh, and the central Hopeh plain where Lü Cheng-ts'ao operated. Its boundaries were formed, in rough outline, by four important rail lines: the Peking-Suiyuan line on the north, the Peking-Hankow line on the east, the Shih-chia-chuang–Taiyuan line on the south, and the Ta-t'ung–Taiyuan line on the west.[11] The military forces under Nieh's command also varied sharply throughout the war. Some of the fluctuations resulted from transfers, as in 1939 when units from the Wu-t'ai base were dispatched to Shantung province where they were under the command of Lo Jung-huan (q.v.), one of Nieh's most important subordinate officers. Toward the end of the war the United States War Department placed Nieh's fighting strength at 64,000 men, armed with 21,000 weapons.[12] (For further details on the border region, see under Sung Shao-wen.)

Nieh participated in the first congress of the Chin-Ch'a-Chi Border Region Government in January 1943. Then, in the late summer of that year, he was ordered to lead some of his troops to the Shansi-Shensi border, and by the early fall of 1943 Nieh was in Yenan, reportedly to attend "important conferences." [13] At approximately this time Lo Jung-huan took over as acting commander of the 115th Division, and Nieh stayed in Yenan for the remainder of the war.[14] At the Party's Seventh National Congress, held in Yenan from April to June 1945, Nieh was one of the speakers, and at the close of the meetings he was elected a member of the Party Central Committee. Nieh was back at his base in the closing days of the war when he and other top commanders in north China were ordered to move north toward Inner Mongolia and Manchuria.[15] Within a few days after the end of the war Nieh's troops were in the Kalgan region (then the capital of Chahar), and it was approximately at this time that the border region capital and military headquarters were moved to that city. Kalgan proved to be of considerable importance to the Communists, because it was through this general area that Lin Piao was able to move tens of thousands of troops from north China into Manchuria.

In the fall of 1947 Nieh took five columns southward in a 10-week campaign which culminated in the capture of Shih-chia-chuang in mid-November.[16] This city was of particular strategic importance because it controlled rail traffic running south from Peking, as well as the rail lines connecting west Hopeh and Shansi. The fall of Shih-chia-chuang led to the merger of Nieh's Chin-Ch'a-Chi area with the Shansi-Hopeh-Shantung-Honan (Chin-Chi-Lu-Yü) Border Region to the south. In May 1948, as a result of this merger, the Communists established the North China Military Region. Nieh was named commander of the region, as well as of the Communist armies which operated in the area. At this same time the CCP organizations for the two border regions were amalgamated into the North China Bureau; Nieh was appointed second secretary under First Secretary Po I-po (then a top political figure in the Chin-Chi-Lu-Yü Border Region). The next major step taken by the Communists to formalize their rule in north China took place in August 1948 at a congress to which Nieh delivered a report on the North China Military Region. He was elected a member of the newly created North China People's Government, which was headed by Party veteran Tung Pi-wu (q.v.). The government by this time controlled a population of about 50 million in some 280 hsien covering most of Hopeh and Shansi, and parts of Suiyuan, Chahar, Jehol, Honan, and Shantung provinces.

After the August 1948 congress Nieh moved north of Peking and in mid-November his forces captured Ch'eng-te, the capital of Jehol province. By this time the Nationalist position in north China was growing increasingly precarious, and when Lin Piao moved his powerful army out of Manchuria and into the Peking-Tientsin region in the winter of 1948–49, the KMT armies found themselves in a desperate situation. The combined Lin-Nieh armies began to close the net around Peking and Tientsin where KMT General Fu Tso-i had half a million troops. There was a brief battle for Tientsin in mid-January 1949, and after a series of intricate negotiations in which Nieh played a major role, Peking was peacefully surrendered at the end of the month.[17]

Nieh, one of the first of the top Communists to enter Peking, was immediately made commander of the Peking-Tientsin Garrison, a post he held until 1955. He continued to take part in the affairs of the North China People's Government, attending meetings held in February and April 1949. More important, however, he was one of the key Communist negotiators in meetings held with KMT delegations sent to Peking to discuss peace terms. The first of these KMT missions, ostensibly an unofficial group, arrived in Peking on February 14 and held talks with Nieh, Lin Piao, and other top military leaders, and a week later went to Shih-chia-chuang for talks with Mao and Chou En-Lai. This round of negotiations failed, but then on April 1 an official group led by the veteran KMT leader Chang Chih-chung arrived for further talks. The Communist delegation, led by Chou En-lai, consisted of Lin Po-ch'ü, Lin Piao, Yeh Chien-ying, Li Wei-han (qq.v.), and Nieh. They presented the KMT delegation with terms tantamount to surrender, and when these were rejected the civil war continued.

In June 1949 the Communists established a special committee chaired by Mao Tse-tung to prepare for the convocation in September of the CPPCC, the body which brought the PRC into existence on October 1. Nieh was made a member of this preparatory committee, but a few weeks later P'eng Te-huai's First Field Army ran into unexpected opposition from KMT General Hu Tsung-nan and his allied armies in the area west of Sian, the Shensi capital. Nieh was called upon to lead two armies to reinforce P'eng.[18] After this brief and successful campaign, Nieh returned to Peking where on September 8 he replaced Yeh Chien-ying as both mayor of Peking and chairman of the Peking Military Control Commission. Nieh thus had the distinction of being mayor of the city which three weeks later would become the capital of the PRC.

Nieh attended the inaugural session of the CPPCC in September 1949 as a representative of the PLA Headquarters, and during the meetings he served on the *ad hoc* committee which drafted the Organic Law of the CPPCC, one of the major documents adopted at that time. With the formation of the central government, he became a member of the Central People's Government Council, the singularly important body (chaired by Mao) which was vested with broad executive, legislative, and judicial functions and which from 1949 to 1954 passed on virtually all vital matters of state. He was also made a member of the People's Revolutionary Military Council and, subordinate to the council, he was made deputy chief-of-staff. However, because of the continuing absence of Chief-of-Staff Hsu Hsiang-ch'ien (q.v.), Nieh served for most of the 1949–1954 period as acting chief-of-staff. During this same period he was also a member of the Executive Board of the Sino-Soviet Friendship Association. In addition to these national and municipal positions, Nieh continued to be a top figure in the north China apparatus; he retained his post as second secretary of the North China Party Bureau until it was abolished in 1954 (although Chou Jung-hsin temporarily replaced him in 1950–51), and from the end of 1951 to 1954 he was also a member of the North China Administrative Committee.

In March 1950 Nieh was made vice-chairman of an *ad hoc* committee which was given broad powers to regulate, on a nationwide basis, the allocation of vital supplies and personnel (see under Po I-po, the chairman). More important, however, was his role as acting chief-of-staff. In this capacity, it was Nieh who gave one of the first "signals" that the Chinese intended to intervene in the Korean War, which had begun in June 1950. In late September, by which time the United Nations' forces were moving rapidly toward the Yalu River, Nieh informed Indian Am-

bassador K. M. Panikkar that China did not intend to "sit back with folded hands" as the Americans advanced to the Chinese border. Nieh continued: "We know what we are in for . . . The Americans can bomb us, they can destroy our industries, but they cannot defeat us on land." China could, he claimed, survive atomic attacks: "After all, China lives on the farms."[19] Within a month of this conversation with the Indian diplomat, PLA units—known as the Chinese People's Volunteers—had entered the Korean War.

In February 1951, not long after China had gone into the Korean conflict, Nieh relinquished his post of mayor of Peking to P'eng Chen (q.v.). However, he retained a seat on the Peking Municipal People's Government Council until early 1955. In February 1952 he led China's delegation to Ulan Bator to attend the funeral of Mongolia's top leader, Marshal Khorloin Choibalsan. In June 1954 Nieh was promoted from membership to a vice-chairmanship of the People's Revolutionary Military Council, but he lost this post in September 1954 when, at the inaugural session of the First NPC, the council was abolished. Nieh attended the First NPC as a deputy from the North China Military Region and he was appointed a member of the NPC Standing Committee, as well as a vice-chairman of the newly established National Defense Council. At approximately this time the Chinese were in the process of initiating steps to "professionalize" the PLA. In this connection, Nieh and Defense Minister P'eng Te-huai gave explanatory speeches before a meeting of the NPC Standing Committee in February 1955 on the new conscription law, which was finally adopted in July 1955. Another step was taken in September 1955 when personal military ranks were created and decorations awarded to PLA veterans. Nieh was made one of the 10 marshals, the highest rank, and he was also awarded the three top decorations—the Orders of August First, Independence and Freedom, and Liberation.

Aside from the above-mentioned trip to Mongolia in 1952, Nieh's work was confined to domestic affairs until 1955. Then in December of that year he left Peking with Chu Te to attend the Second Congress of the Rumanian Workers' (Communist) Party. From Bucharest, the group went to East Germany in early January 1956 to celebrate the 80th birthday of President Wilhelm Pieck. Nieh then visited Hungary, Czechoslovakia, and Poland. While in Prague he attended, as the official Chinese "observer," a meeting of the Political Consultative Committee of the Warsaw Treaty powers in late January. Chu Te and Nieh then went to Moscow; Chu remained there to attend the famous 20th CPSU Congress, which opened February 14, but on the next day Nieh left for home. Two months later he led the Chinese delegation to the Third Congress of the Korean Workers' (Communist) Party, and remained in Pyongyang long enough to attend May Day celebrations. In March 1957 Nieh was the official Chinese envoy to the independence celebrations in Ghana (formerly the Gold Coast) and was thus the first high-ranking Chinese Communist official to visit sub-Sahara Africa. En route there he stopped over in Moscow, and on his return home he traveled via London, Berne, and Prague. Nieh made his last trip abroad in October 1959 when he led a delegation to East Germany to take part in the 10th anniversary celebrations of the establishment of the German Democratic Republic.

In the meantime, Nieh had been re-elected a member of the CCP Central Committee at the Eighth National Party Congress in September 1956. Soon afterwards, in mid-November, he was made a vice-premier of the State Council, and because of this assignment in the executive branch (as it was officially explained), he was removed as a member of the NPC Standing Committee in July 1957. This appointment to a high State Council post coincided with a partial reorientation of Nieh's career—after three decades of devoting himself mainly to military affairs, he was about to become Peking's leading figure in the field of science and technology. One of the first suggestions of this change occurred in December 1956 when Nieh presided over a meeting of the State Council's Scientific Planning Commission. The commission had been created in March 1956, immediately after the decision had been made to adopt a 12-year plan for scientific development. Originally headed by Ch'en I, the commission chairmanship was assumed by Nieh in May 1957 when it was reorganized and considerably expanded in size. It underwent another reorganization in November 1958 when it was combined with the State Technological Commission and redesignated the Scientific and Technological Commission. It should also be noted that the establishment of the commission and the 12-year plan coincided with a dramatic rise in funds budgeted for science (from approximately US$15 million in 1955 to nearly US$100 million in 1956).[20] One authority has written that the commission is responsible for "organising scientific institutions and undertakings, collating and co-ordinating plans for scientific research in each area, integrating plans and activities in science with national plans and programmes, supervising the execution of all plans, controlling the use of research funds, establishing working standards and pay scales for scientists, developing training programmes, organising international exchanges and communications among scientists and promoting the recruitment of Chinese scientists abroad."[21]

In the absence of a science department subordinate to the Party Central Committee, it may be presumed that Nieh's commission is the leading policy-level scientific organization in China. One Western authority on Chinese military affairs carries this further with the suggestion that Nieh is the "co-ordinator" between the military and science fields.[22] In view of Nieh's technical training, his stature in the Party hierarchy, and his lengthy experience in the PLA, such a role would seem logical and fitting. In any case, he has delivered many of the major policy statements on science and technology since assuming the chairmanship of the commission. Over the years he has delivered scores of speeches and written a number of articles on science and technology, of which the following are only a representative selection. For the *JMJP* of August 2, 1958, he wrote "Let the Entire Party Take a Firm Hold on Scientific and Technological Work to Carry Out the Technological Revolution." For *Hung-ch'i* (Red flag; no. 9, October 1, 1958) he reviewed scientific work during the early phases of the Great Leap Forward and indicated that the above-mentioned 12-year science plan should be fulfilled five years ahead of schedule, and for the same journal (no. 8, April 16, 1960) he discussed the technological "revolution" in factories. His review of science written for the 10th anniversary of the PRC appeared in the *JMJP* on September 27, 1959, and was reprinted in *Ten Glorious Years* (Peking, 1960). A particularly useful policy statement on science and technology is contained in a speech Nieh delivered in October 1959 and published in a pamphlet entitled *The National Conference of Outstanding Groups and Workers in Socialist Construction* (Peking, 1960, pp. 112–131).

Nieh was one of the speakers at the meeting of the Party's Military Affairs Commission (MAC) held from late May to late July 1958. At that time the MAC membership was not known, nor was its importance fully appreciated. However, in 1963 the United States Government released issues for the year 1961 of a classified, intra-PLA journal known as the *Kung-tso t'ung-hsun* (Bulletin of activities). This publication revealed that by at least March 1961 Nieh was a vice-chairman of the MAC (the only others mentioned being Lin Piao and Ho Lung). Moreover, it also indicated that he was fairly active in the work of the MAC; he regularly received its reports on a variety of military issues, and on at least one occasion he made a trip to Amoy to inspect maritime defenses there.[23]

As noted above, Nieh served as a PLA deputy to the First NPC (1954–1958). However, in the Second and Third NPC's, which held their first sessions in April 1959 and December 1964–January 1965, respectively, he attended as a delegate from his native Szechwan. On each occasion he was reappointed a vice-premier, a vice-chairman of the National Defense Council, and chairman of the Scientific and Technological Commission. Then, in January 1967, during the early phase of the Great Proletarian Cultural Revolution, it was revealed that Nieh had been elevated to membership on the Party Politburo.

In addition to his speeches and articles on science, Nieh's writings and reports represent an important body of information on two other subjects: military affairs and the management of Peking in the takeover period after 1949. A wartime article on military affairs appeared in the Chungking-published Communist journal *Ch'ün-chung* (The masses; no. 17, October 16, 1940). In mid-1951, to commemorate the 30th anniversary of the CCP, he wrote a long article entitled "How the Chinese People Defeated the Japanese Fascist Aggressors." [24] Nieh's report on the draft act in 1955 provides a useful view of various aspects of the professionalization of the military establishment.[25] His detailed reports on the early days of Communist rule in Peking appear in *Hsin-hua yueh-pao* (New China monthly; no. 4, February 15, 1950, pp. 878–879; no. 6, April 15, 1950, pp. 1336–1338; no. 5, September 15, 1950, pp. 999–1003) and *People's China*, no. 3, February 1, 1951, pp. 8–9, 31.

Nieh made a strong impression on a number of Westerners who met him during the war and postwar years in north China. United States military observer Evans Carlson, who had extensive conversations with Nieh, characterized him as the "brains and driving force" behind the Chin-Ch'a-Chi Border Region government,[26] and journalist Haldore Hanson provided a vivid sketch of Nieh on the basis of his interviews in 1938.[27] In 1944 an American diplomat who met Nieh in Yenan described him as a man of "commanding presence, evident vigor and determination," [28] and a few years later United States Military Attaché Robert B. Rigg wrote that Nieh was an "exponent of mobility," who had built a reputation on "sudden attack and elusiveness." Rigg also reported that the Japanese had been sufficiently impressed with his skills to make a study of Nieh's guerrilla tactics.[29] American journalist Harrison Forman, who visited Communist-held areas in 1944, also stressed and described in some detail Nieh's adroit use of guerrilla tactics.[30]

Nieh is married to Chang Jui-hua, whom Edgar Snow met in 1936 in Kansu. She had just "slipped into the Soviet districts" from KMT-held areas and had not seen her husband for five years.[31] Evans Carlson met her two years later and reported that she had recently graduated from a military or political training school in Yenan and was on her way to the Wu-t'ai base where she was expected to work.[32] In 1938 the Niehs had two children.

---

1. Claire and William Band, *Two Years with the Chinese Communists* (New Haven, Conn., 1948), p. 98; information supplied by Dr. Conrad Brandt.

2. Edgar Snow, *Random Notes on Red China, 1936–1945* (Cambridge, Mass., 1957), pp. 136–137.

3. Wei Hung-yun, ed., *"Pa-i" ch'i-i* (The "August First" uprising; Wuhan, 1957), p. 14.

4. Snow, p. 137; Nym Wales, *Inside Red China* (New York, 1939), p. 308.

5. Agnes Smedley, *The Great Road* (New York, 1956), pp. 308–309.

6. *The Long March, Eyewitness Accounts* (Peking, 1963), pp. 75, 82–95; *Stories of the Long March* (Peking, 1958), pp. 11, 61–76.

7. *Shan-hsi ko-ming tou-cheng hui-i-lu* (Reminiscences of revolutionary struggles in Shansi; Taiyuan [?], 1961), p. 31.

8. *The Long March, Eyewitness Accounts*, pp. 222–223.

9. *K'ang-Jih chan-cheng shih-ch'i chieh-fang-ch'ü kai-k'uang* (A sketch of the liberated areas during the Anti-Japanese War; Peking, 1953), p. 26.

10. George E. Taylor, *The Struggle for North China* (New York, 1940), p. 36.

11. Chalmers A. Johnson, *Peasant Nationalism and Communist Power* (Stanford, Calif., 1962), p. 102.

12. Lyman P. Van Slyke, ed., *The Chinese Communist Movement: A Report of the United States War Department, July 1945* (Stanford, Calif., 1968), p. 180.

13. Band, pp. 182, 239.

14. *Ibid.*, pp. 265–266; *Foreign Relations of the United States; Diplomatic Papers, 1944,* vol. VI, *China* (Washington, D.C., 1967), pp. 602, 753.

15. *Selected Works of Mao Tse-tung* (Peking, 1961), IV, 30.

16. *Ibid.*, p. 216.

17. A. Doak Barnett, *China on the Eve of Communist Takeover* (New York, 1963), pp. 331–333; C. P. Fitzgerald, *The Birth of Communist China* (Baltimore, Md., 1964), pp. 114–115.

18. F. F. Liu, *A Military History of Modern China, 1924–1949* (Princeton, N.J., 1956), p. 269; Lionel Max Chassin, *The Communist Conquest of China* (Cambridge, Mass., 1965), p. 226.

19. K. M. Panikkar, *In Two Chinas* (London, 1955), p. 108.

20. John M. H. Lindbeck, "The Organisation and Development of Science," *The China Quarterly,* no. 6:105–106 (April–June 1961).

21. *Ibid.*, p. 117.

22. Alice Langley Hsieh, *Communist China's Strategy in the Nuclear Era* (Englewood Cliffs, N.J., 1962), p. 152.

23. J. Chester Cheng, ed., *The Politics of the Chinese Red Army* (Stanford, Calif., 1966), pp. 352, 437, 579, and 743.

24. *China's Revolutionary Wars* (Peking, 1951), pp. 13–32; also in *People's China*, no. 1:20–22, 27–31 (1951) and *CB* 100, pp. 5–14.

25. *CB* 314, pp. 9–16.

26. Evans Fordyce Carlson, *Twin Stars of China* (New York, 1940), p. 114.

27. Haldore Hanson, *"Humane Endeavour"* (New York, 1939), pp. 248–252.

28. *Foreign Relations of the United States; Diplomatic Papers, 1944,* vol. VI, *China* (Washington, D.C., 1967), p. 753.

29. Robert B. Rigg, *Red China's Fighting Hordes* (Harrisburg, Pa., 1952), pp. 35–36.

30. Harrison Forman, *Report from Red China* (New York, 1945), pp. 133–137.

31. Edgar Snow, *Red Star over China* (New York, 1939), p. 359.

32. Evans Fordyce Carlson, *Twin Stars of China* (New York, 1940), p. 105.

Ou Meng-chueh

(1903–   ; Kwangtung). Secretary, Kwangtung Provincial Party Committee; alternate member, CCP Central Committee.

Miss Ou Meng-chueh has the distinction of being one of the eight women who hold membership on the Eighth Party Central Committee. She has spent most of her career in Kwangtung serving in provincial Party and government posts. One of her major activities has been in the field of Party control and supervision work.

In 1923–24, while attending the K'un Wei Middle School for Girls in Canton, Ou probably made her first contact with Communism through one of her teachers, T'an T'ien-tu, who was then working for the Party. She married T'an, but they were later divorced. Like his former wife, T'an presently works under the Kwangtung Provincial CCP Committee as a deputy director of the United Front Work Department. In 1926 Ou joined the CCP while enrolled (1924–1926) at Kwangtung University, known after 1926 as Sun Yat-sen University. She engaged in Party work while a student there and a year later she accompanied Su Chao-cheng, P'eng P'ai, and Ch'en Yen-nien (all leading Party members in South China; qq.v.) to the Fifth National Party Congress held at Hankow in April–May 1927.[1] It is not clear whether Ou attended the Congress; if so, she was among the fewer than 100 Party members who were present. The Congress approved continued support for the "left" KMT Government, which had been established at Wuhan in late 1926. However, in mid-1927 a complete break occurred between the CCP and the KMT. By August Ou had returned to Canton to work with the Party underground, which was preparing for the Canton Commune (see under Chang T'ai-lei). The resulting coup which took place in December 1927 was a fiasco, costing the lives of some of the CCP's most important leaders and many of its members and followers. Miss Ou was among those who escaped.

Nothing is known of Ou's activities for the next two decades, but by the late 1940's she was apparently working in one of the Communist-held areas of north China. In any event, she was a member of the delegation led by Ts'ai Ch'ang (q.v.) to the Second Congress of the Communist-dominated Women's International Democratic Federation, held in Budapest in early December 1948. The delegation went to Hungary in November and returned to Peking on February 9, 1949, just a few days after the city had been surrendered to the Communists by the Nationalists. Immediately after her return, Ou went to work for the Preparatory Committee for the inaugural Congress of the All-China Federation of Democratic Women (ACFDW). At the close of the Congress, held in Peking in March–April 1949, she was elected a member of the First Executive Committee, which directs the work of the Federation between congresses. She held this seat for the term of the First Committee (1949–1953), serving also on the Committee's Standing Committee until sometime in early 1951. For a brief time in 1949 Ou was the ACFDW secretary-general, but she was soon succeeded by Teng Ying-ch'ao (q.v.), the wife of Chou En-lai. Ou served on the Presidium for the Second ACFDW Congress in April 1953 and was re-elected to the Second Executive Committee. The Third Congress of September 1957 elected her to the Third Executive Committee, upon which she still serves, but she has been less active in the Federation since 1957. Ou has also worked in the provincial and municipal branches of the women's movement, being chairman of the Kwangtung Women's Federation from February 1954 to 1957 and of the Canton Women's Federation from December 1955 to 1957.

Paralleling her work in the women's movement was Ou's activity in the Sino-Soviet Friendship Association (SSFA). When the Association was formed in October 1949, she became a member of its First Executive Board (1949–1954). She attended the Second SSFA Conference in December 1954 as a representative of the ACFDW but was not re-elected to any national post. On the provincial level, Ou was a member of the Kwangtung SSFA Branch as of November 1952 and was later twice identified as a vice-president, first in September 1957 and again in November 1960.

From its formation in October 1949 to its reorganization in October 1950, Ou was a member of the China Peace Committee. She was also identified in 1949 as director of the official New China News Agency's South China Branch. In January 1953 she was named a vice-chairman of the Kwangtung provincial committee for the implementation of the Marriage Law.

Aside from her semi-official tasks, Ou also helped establish and develop the provincial government machinery in Kwangtung. She was appointed a member of a Kwangtung Provincial People's Government Council in October 1949 and was re-elected to this post in February 1955.

Although she was active in the Kwangtung Government for the next several years, she was not re-elected to the Council by the Kwangtung Congress of December 1963. When the People's Supervision Committee for Kwangtung was set up in March 1951, Ou was named a vice-chairman; by mid-1953 she had become chairman, but the committee seems to have been abolished sometime in 1954. The committee was originally charged with "accepting complaints" about provincial government officials and overseeing their performance. In a similar capacity Ou served on the People's Supervision Committee of the Central-South Administrative Committee in 1953 and 1954.

Though Ou has worked principally in Kwangtung, she has also represented the provincial government in Peking. She attended the first session of the First CPPCC (September 1949), which inaugurated the PRC, as a representative from the "South China Liberated Area." During the session she served on the committee, headed by Chou En-lai, which drafted the Common Program; it served as a draft constitution until one was formally adopted in 1954. In April 1953 she was appointed to the Kwangtung Election Committee. Such committees were responsible for holding provincial elections to select delegates to the legislative body of the soon-to-be-created constitutional government. When the elections were held, Ou became a Kwangtung deputy for the term of the First NPC (1954–1959). Although she was not re-elected to the Second NPC (1959–1964), she was again elected from Kwangtung to the Third NPC, whose first session opened in December 1964. On the provincial level she was elected in December 1960 as chairman of the Second Kwangtung Committee of the CPPCC, replacing T'ao Chu (q.v.), then first secretary of the provincial CCP Committee; she was re-elected in December 1963 to chair the Third Kwangtung Committee, a post she continues to hold.

To date Ou's most important role has been in the Kwangtung Party Committee, and in the 1950's she was especially active in CCP organizational and control organs. In February 1952 she was identified as deputy director of the Organization Department of the CCP South China Sub-bureau, subordinate to the Central-South Bureau. She became director of the Organization Department and secretary of the sub-bureau's Women's Work Committee in 1954, holding these posts until the sub-bureau was abolished in July 1955. She then became prominently associated with the work of the Kwangtung Party Committee. By at least September 1955 and until sometime in 1958 she was director of the provincial Organization Department. In the aftermath of the purge of Party veterans Kao Kang and Jao Shu-shih (qq.v.) in 1954–55, national and provincial control commissions (whose establishment was provided for in the 1945 Party Constitution) were instituted to keep a close watch on intra-Party discipline. In September 1955 Ou became a member of the Party Control Commission for Kwangtung, a post she probably still holds.

In September 1956 Ou was elected by the Eighth National Party Congress in Peking to alternate membership on the CCP Central Committee. She was one of only eight women to receive this honor, the others being Ts'ai Ch'ang, Teng Ying-ch'ao, Ch'en Shao-min, Ch'ien Ying (full members), Chang Yun, Shuai Meng-ch'i, and Li Chien-chen (alternate members, qq.v.). Following this elevation at the national level, Ou was identified in January 1957 as a secretary of the Kwangtung Party Committee. She continues to hold this position, serving under First Secretary T'ao Chu until 1965 and since then under Chao Tzu-yang (q.v.).

In 1957–58 the political life of Communist China was disrupted by the nationwide "rectification" campaign, which led to the dismissal of many persons accused of being "rightists" or "local nationalists." Kwangtung, noted for its hostility to rule by northern Chinese, allegedly harbored many persons who opposed rule from Peking. The most important of these were Ku Ta-ts'un and Feng Pai-chü (qq.v.), alternate members of the Party Central Committee, who were also fellow secretaries of Ou on the Kwangtung Party Committee. Miss Ou, in an article entitled "What Have Been the Mistakes of Ku Ta-ts'un and Feng Pai-chü?," attacked the two men in a stinging denunciation written for the inaugural issue of a Kwangtung Party journal in 1958.[2] Her article indicated that the Kwangtung Party organization had been torn with factionalism for some time. Ku and Feng lost their posts as Kwangtung Party secretaries as a result of the accusations although they were not removed from the Party Central Committee.

The titles of other articles and speeches by Ou indicate her continuing involvement in supervisory aspects of Party work: "Kwangtung's Fight against Localism Ends in Victory," JMJP, June 6, 1958; and "The Great Victory for the Thought of Mao Tse-tung," Canton Nanfang jih-pao (Southern daily), October 4, 1960. In October 1963 Ou chaired a forum on ideological work and delivered a speech entitled "Strengthening the Ideological and Fighting Character of Literature and Art."

---

1. *Chung-kuo Kung-ch'an-tang tsai chung-nan-ti-ch'ü ling-tao ko-ming tou-cheng te li-shih tzu-liao* (Historical materials on the revolutionary struggles led by the CCP in central and south China; Wuhan, 1951), I, 182–184.
2. *Hsin-hua pan-yueh-k'an* (New China semi-monthly), October 10, 1958; translated in *SCMP* 1899, pp. 16–23.

Ou T'ang-liang

Secretary-general, China Peace Committee.

Miss Ou T'ang-liang is one of the most important women leaders in the Communist-backed peace movement in her capacity as secretary-general of the China Peace Committee. She first came to prominence prior to the establishment of the PRC (October 1949) when she spoke at a council meeting of the Communist International Union of Students in Paris in September 1948. At that time she was identified as an official of the "Liberated Areas Students' Union," presumably in Yenan in the northwest, or possibly in one of the Communist-held areas in Manchuria, then almost completely conquered by the Communists.

In the spring of 1949 Ou was given assignments in the two main youth organizations, the New Democratic Youth League and the All-China Federation of Democratic Youth. In the former she was elected an alternate member of the Central Committee; she became a Standing Committee member in 1951 and an alternate secretary in 1952. Also, from 1950 to about 1953 she was head of the League's International Liaison Department. Within the Federation of Democratic Youth, Ou was elected (in 1949) to the Standing Committee of the first National Committee. In the summer of 1953, both of these youth organizations held congresses. Within the Federation she was elected as a vice-chairman (one of four) and in the Youth League as a member of the Secretariat (one of nine). In each case she was the only woman elected to these key positions and thus in the mid-1950's appears to have been the ranking woman youth leader. Four years later (1957), having by then moved on to other work, Ou was only re-elected to the Central Committee within the League (and not elected to any post at the 1964 congress); she was not elected to any position in the Federation at its congress in 1958.

Ou's work in youth affairs in the 1950's was equaled by her activity in the peace movement. The China Peace Committee, established in 1949, was reorganized in October 1950, at which time Ou was elected to the National Committee. During another reorganization, in July 1958, she was elevated to the Standing Committee of the National Committee and, more important, was named as secretary-general to replace Liao Ch'eng-chih (a member of the CCP Central Committee). The Peace Committee, one of the most important and active of the Chinese Communist mass organizations, is headed by a chairman and several vice-chairmen of considerable stature and importance (e.g., Kuo Mo-jo and Liao Ch'eng-chih); the multiple responsibilities of these men probably means that they can only devote a small portion of their time to the day-by-day duties of the Peace Committee. Appar-

ently, therefore, since 1958 (when she became secretary-general) this has made her the principal agent in the execution of the policies of the Committee decided at a higher level.

Apart from work in the youth and peace movements, Ou has received several other official and semi-official positions in the early and mid-1950's. When the All-China Federation of Democratic Women (ACFDW) held its second congress in April 1953 she was elected to the Standing Committee, and four years later (1957) was re-elected to this same body (which was renamed the Presidium). She has retained this position within the National Women's Federation, as the ACFDW has been known since the September 1957 congress. In May 1954 she was named to the Standing Committee of the newly established Chinese People's Association for Cultural Relations with Foreign Countries, a post to which she was re-elected in April 1959. In December 1954 she was selected for membership on the national Council of the Sino-Soviet Friendship Association and was then renamed to the Council in 1959. At the official level, Miss Ou was elected a deputy from Kwangsi to the First NPC (1954–1959); she was re-elected to the Second NPC (1959–1964) and to the Third NPC, which held its first session in December 1964–January 1965; at the close of this session she was elevated to membership on the NPC Standing Committee. She has also made appearances at some of the many conferences held in China. To mention a random but typical example, she was a member of the presidium (steering committee) for a national conference of "young activists in building socialism" held in Peking in September 1955.

But Ou's most important work from the early 1950's has been as an international liaison official with emphasis on the Communist-backed peace movement. Organizationally, this has meant her active participation in the numerous meetings of the Communist World Peace Council. Her record of travels has been statistically impressive: including the above-mentioned trip to France in 1948, Ou made 13 trips abroad to 11 different nations between 1948 and 1963. Eight of these 14 trips were to meetings of the World Peace Council or one of its offshoots. These eight journeys took her to Czechoslovakia (April 1949), Austria (December 1952 and March 1962), Sweden (July 1958 and May 1959), the USSR (February 1959 and July 1962), and India (March 1961). Befitting her role as a youth leader in the late 1940's and 1950's, she attended the Third World Youth Congress in Rumania in mid-1953 and the Fifth World Youth and Students' Festival in Warsaw in mid-1955; in both instances she was a deputy leader of large delegations. (In 1954 she was identified as a council member of the Communist World Federation of Democratic Youth, but she has probably relinquished this post.) Miss Ou has also been a member of two of the more important delegations sent abroad in recent years. The first was from November 1956 to January 1957 when she accompanied Politburo member P'eng Chen on an extensive tour of the USSR and five of the East European satellite nations (Rumania, Czechoslovakia, Bulgaria, Albania, and Yugoslavia). Officially, this was a delegation representing the NPC, but in fact it was obviously an attempt to bolster "Socialist solidarity," coming as it did a few weeks after the Soviet image was badly tarnished by the Hungarian Rebellion (see under P'eng Chen). The other important mission occurred in June 1963 when Ou was a deputy leader under Yang Yun-yü to a "World Women's Congress" held in Moscow. At this juncture the Sino-Soviet dispute had broken into the open, with a resulting verbal brawl in Moscow between the Soviet and Chinese factions (see under Yang Yun-yü).

Between 1958 and 1962 Ou was given four new positions which, if not very important, were illustrative of her role as an official advocate of "peace and friendship." She was appointed to the expanded Afro-Asian Solidarity Committee of China in July 1958 and was then named to the national Councils (board of directors) of the China-Iraq Friendship Association (FA), the China-Africa People's FA, and the China-Cuba FA, formed, respectively, in September 1958, April 1960, and December 1962. (Within the structure of the China-Cuba FA she was also named to the Standing Committee). Ou continues to hold all these positions. In one or another of her numerous posts she is often on hand in Peking to host the huge number of peace and friendship delegations which constantly visit Peking. A typical example occurred in the fall of 1964 when she escorted "noted American Negro leader Robert Williams" and his wife around China and was present when Williams met with Party General Secretary Teng Hsiao-p'ing.

Ouyang Ch'in

(c.1907– ; Ning-hsiang hsien [?], Hunan). Second secretary Northeast Bureau, CCP; first secretary, Heilungkiang CCP Committee; member, CCP Central Committee.

Ouyang Ch'in, trained at the Whampoa Military Academy and a veteran of the Long March, has been in the Communist Movement since the early thirties. He has served as a senior Party official in Manchuria since the Communists came to power in 1949 and has been a member of the Party Central Committee since 1956. Ouyang is a native of Hunan where he was born about 1907. A Whampoa student directory listed his mailing address as Ning-hsiang hsien, which is probably also his place of birth. Ning-hsiang, not

far west of Changsha, is the native hsien of Liu Shao-ch'i, who was born about nine years before Ouyang. Ouyang was in the engineering section of the fourth class (October 1925–October 1926) at the Whampoa Academy in Canton. Lin Piao was among his classmates in the fourth class. Nothing is known of his career during the next few years, but by the early thirties he was serving in the Kiangsi area as head of the political department of a Red Army school and also as director of the Organization Department of the First Army Corps, the force led by Chu Te and Mao Tse-tung. He continued with this unit (then known as the First Front Army) during the Long March from Kiangsi to northern Shensi in 1934–35.

After his arrival in Yenan, Ouyang was apparently assigned to political work. In any event, he was not known to have held any military post during the Sino-Japanese War, and one report asserts that in 1938 he was serving as a member of the North China Bureau of the Party. Many of the members of this bureau were working underground behind Japanese lines. If he did work in this bureau, it is likely that he was associated with such senior Party leaders as Liu Shao-ch'i and P'eng Chen. Toward the close of the war with Japan, a number of top men were dispatched to Manchuria in a bold attempt to gain a foothold for the Communists in this strategic area. Ouyang, apparently, was among these men who, under the direction of the veteran military leader Lin Piao, developed a highly effective fighting force in Manchuria in the late 1940's. He was known to be serving in Lin's army in the fall of 1948 as a deputy political commissar of a column that participated in the last great battle with the Nationalists for Manchuria, known in Communist annals as the Liaohsi-Shenyang campaign.

The forces led by Lin Piao went on to capture Tientsin and Peking in early 1949 and then pushed southward in a sustained drive that consumed the remainder of the year and continued into the spring of 1950 with the capture of Hainan Island in southernmost China. It is not clear when Ouyang broke away from Lin's armies, but by September 1949 he had assumed the ranking secretaryship of the Party Committee for Port Arthur-Dairen, an area then jointly administered with Russian occupation forces (see under Han Kuang). Not long after assuming this post, Ouyang was named to a top-level delegation, led by Premier Chou En-lai, that went to Moscow in January 1950 to join Mao Tse-tung, who had been negotiating with the Russians from the previous month. In retrospect, Ouyang's presence in Moscow is easily understood. In addition to the historic treaty of alliance and mutual defense (signed on February 14, 1950), several other subordinate agreements were signed on the same day or soon thereafter.

One of these, a pact clarifying the status of the Soviet Union in Port Arthur-Dairen, provided for Chinese civil control over the area and for the joint use of the important naval facilities. These facilities were to be jointly utilized until the conclusion of a peace treaty with Japan, but not later than 1952 even if a treaty were not concluded. (As it developed, Soviet forces were given an extension in usage in 1952 and remained there until the spring of 1955.) The February 1950 agreement also provided for a joint Sino-Soviet military commission to be in charge of military affairs in Port Arthur and for another commission charged with the task of transferring Soviet-administered properties in Dairen to Chinese control. Although no specific information is available, it is reasonable to assume from Ouyang's stature in Port Arthur-Dairen that he was instrumental in the management of both joint commissions.

Ouyang returned to Port Arthur-Dairen in the spring of 1950 and remained there for the next four years. During this time he assumed three new posts. In June 1951 he was made a member of the Port Arthur-Dairen People's Government, and when Mayor Han Kuang (q.v.) was transferred in February 1953 he assumed Han's job. He also served as a deputy from Port Arthur-Dairen to the First NPC (1954–1959). However, at almost exactly the same moment that he was elected to the NPC from the Port Arthur-Dairen constituency, he was transferred to Manchuria's northernmost province, Heilungkiang. On August 1, 1954, he was the principal speaker at a meeting in Harbin marking the merger of the Heilungkiang and Sungkiang provinces into a "new" Heilungkiang. The reason for the sudden transfer was almost certainly due to the fact that the previous ranking secretary in Heilungkiang, Chao Te-tsun, had become implicated in the famous Kao Kang "plot" against the top elite in China. Although this cabal was not formally disclosed until early 1955, it is clear that the activities of Kao Kang (q.v.) and his accomplices were known to the Party center by at least mid-1954, thus necessitating changes in the Heilungkiang Party personnel. From that time onward Ouyang has been the ranking Party secretary in Heilungkiang, assuming the new title of first secretary by March 1956.

Apart from his Party post in Heilungkiang, Ouyang assumed other positions within the Heilungkiang hierarchy soon after his arrival there. In February 1955 he was elected a member of the Heilungkiang Provincial People's Government. He was elevated to the governorship in September 1956, replacing his long-time colleague Han Kuang. Ouyang was in turn replaced in September 1958 by Li Fan-wu (q.v.). Ouyang received still another post in 1955 when in April of that year he became chairman of the First Heilungkiang CPPCC; he was re-elected to the Second CPPCC in August 1959 and presumably still holds the position. In the other remaining channel of authority, the military establishment, he was serving as the political commissar of the provincial military district by December 1956, but was apparently replaced in the spring of 1958.

Ouyang's career reached a new peak at the Eighth National Party Congress in September 1956. The role he played at the Congress gave evidence of his growing importance in the Party. First, a 63-member presidium (steering committee) was chosen from among the 1,100-odd delegates. Ouyang was one of only 16 persons on the presidium who had not been a member of the Seventh Central Committee (elected in 1945), the then ruling elite of China. Further, he served on the rather exclusive Credentials Committee, acted as one of the executive chairmen for three of the sessions of the Congress, and gave one of the speeches (on conditions in Heilungkiang). At the close of the congress he was elected a full member of the 97-member Central Committee. He was one of only 33 men who had not been a member of the Seventh Central Committee.

In the first decade of Ouyang's tenure in Heilungkiang he has been exceedingly active in a wide array of activities, including inspections of industrial and agricultural enterprises, meetings of both provincial government and Party organizations, anniversaries of important Communist holidays (such as May Day), and entertainment for the rather large number of foreign visitors who go to Harbin, the Heilungkiang capital. In addition, he has served on various *ad hoc* organizations. For example, when the provincial Party Committee established a "rectification" committee in May 1957 (during the nationwide "rectification" campaign), he was named as chairman. In the following January he was appointed chairman of the Sungari River Basin Planning Committee. Ouyang received a new assignment in 1961 following the decision by the Ninth Plenum of the Central Committee (January 1961) to re-create the regional Party bureaus. By March 1961 he had become second secretary of the Northeast Bureau, the organization with jurisdiction over the three Manchurian provinces. Here he serves under a fellow Hunanese, Sung Jen-ch'iung (q.v.), a man about the same age as Ouyang but with greater seniority in the CCP. In this capacity he accompanied Sung on a visit to North Korea in October–November 1963. The purpose of the trip was never revealed, but it may have been related to Chinese efforts to gain support for their ideological dispute with the Soviet Union.

Befitting his role as an important Party leader, Ouyang Ch'in has been a rather regular contributor to the national press. Several of his articles, usually heavily political in content, have appeared in the *JMJP* (*e.g.,* issues of November 14, 1959, December 28, 1959, January 4, 1960, July 21, 1961, and July 11, 1964). He has also published in two of the most important Party journals, *Hsueh-hsi* (Study) and *Hung-ch'i* (Red flag). In the former, he wrote an article for the July 3, 1958, issue on the "mass line and socialist construction," and for April 1, 1960, issue of *Hung-ch'i* he wrote a lengthy article on agricultural mechanization (Heilungkiang being an area where agriculture is far more mechanized than in most provinces).

Pai Ju-ping

(Shensi). Specialist in handicraft cooperatives; governor of Shantung.

Pai Ju-ping, who once used the alias of Pai Shu-hsun, is a native of Shensi. As early as 1932 he was reported to be an active Communist Party member in Ch'ing-chien hsien in the northern part of his native Shensi. It was in this same period that Liu Chih-tan (q.v.), the major Communist figure in Shensi in the early 1930's, was organizing guerrilla forces in northern Shensi. Thus, although specific evidence is lacking, it is possible that Pai's career at this stage was linked with Liu Chih-tan.

By 1942, Pai was working in Shansi in the area under the military control of the 120th Division commanded by Ho Lung. The important Shansi-Suiyuan Border Region was divided into two major parts, the Ta-ch'ing Mountain District, which was mainly north of the Great Wall in Suiyuan and the Northwest Shansi District, most of which was south of the Wall. In October 1942, the provisional assembly of the Northwest Shansi District convened with 145 members in attendance. A 19-member Administrative Committee was elected as the executive organ of the District; Pai was elected a member, as was Commander Ho Lung.[1] The talents Pai brought to this body were apparently financial, for Japanese sources assert that he served as head of the Finance Office of the Northwest Shansi District. Some 20 years later Pai was extolled in the Communist press for the simple and industrious life he had led in Shansi. It was noted that he spent some of his time spinning cotton yarn and also engaged in farming.[2]

It seems almost certain that Pai remained in the northwest throughout the war with the Japanese, as well as the civil war with the Nationalists in the late 1940's, because when the Shensi-Kansu-Ninghsia and the Shansi-Suiyuan Border Regions were merged to form a Northwest Liberated Region in February 1949, he received two important posts with the new government. He was named to head the Finance Office and was appointed as a member of the Finance and Economics Committee under the direction of Ho Lung, an associate from at least 1942. By the end of 1949, the Northwest Liberated Region Government was dissolved in favor of the Northwest Military and Administrative Committee (NWMAC; known as the Northwest Administrative Committee, NWAC, from 1953 to 1954). Pai's positions with the new government were very similar to those he held earlier. He was named as a member of the NWMAC, as well as director of its Finance Department and a vice-chairman of the Finance and Economics Committee; he held the Finance Department position until March 1953 and the others until the NWAC was abolished in 1954. Another important position Pai held in the Northwest (from September 1950 to July 1951) was that of director of the Northwest Railway Trunkline Construction Bureau, although this bureau was directly subordinated to the Ministry of Railways in Peking rather than to the NWMAC.

Even the scanty information on Pai in the early 1950's suggests that he continued to specialize in financial matters. For example, he was selected to be a vice-chairman of a committee to promote the sale of 1954 construction bonds in the northwest, a committee established in Sian, the NWAC capital, in January 1954.

Pai was transferred to the national capital in 1954 and remained there for the next four years. His first nationwide post was as a member on the national committee of the All-China Federation of Supply and Marketing Cooperatives, one of the largest and most important of the "mass" organizations. He was named to the organization in July 1954. A few months later, during the governmental reorganizations in the fall of 1954, a Central Handicrafts Administrative Bureau was established as an organ directly subordinate to the State Council. Pai was named as director in November 1954, holding the post until March 1958 when the bureau was transferred to the jurisdiction of the Ministry of Light Industry. At a December 1954–January 1955 conference, just one month after the creation of the Handicrafts Bureau, a "mass" organization was created to parallel the governmental bureau—a fairly common practice of the Chinese Communists. At this inaugural conference a preparatory committee for the All-China Federation of Handicraft Cooperatives was established, with Pai as the committee chairman. Three years later, in December 1957, he was named as chairman (and member) of the board of directors of the Federation when it was established as a permanent organization at the first national congress of handicraft cooperatives in Peking.

One of the several categories of membership on the CPPCC is reserved for persons working with cooperatives. Given Pai's intensive involvement with cooperatives by 1954, it was appropriate that he should be a member of the Second National Committee as a representative of co-operatives from December 1954 when the committee was established until the third committee was inaugurated in April 1959.

Pai spoke at two important meetings in 1956 and 1957. The most important was the Eighth Party Congress, held in September 1956, where he delivered a speech entitled "New Questions about the Domestic and Foreign Relationships of the Handicraft Industry," a talk reproduced in the 1957 *Jen-min shou-ts'e* (People's Handbook). His speech in July 1957 before the National Conference of Handicraftsmen on the growth of the industrial arts in the post-1949 period was printed in the 1958 *Jen-min shou-ts'e*.

As already mentioned, the Central Handicrafts Bureau headed by Pai was transferred to the Ministry of Light Industry in March 1958. Presumably Pai was removed from the post at that time, for soon after he was transferred to Shantung, China's second most populous province (after Szechwan) and, to judge by the frequent turnover of personnel, one of the more difficult to administer. Pai was appointed by July 1958 as one of the secretaries of the Shantung Party Committee, a post he continues to hold. Because of this transfer, he surrendered his chairmanship of the All-China Federation of Handicraft Co-operatives to another person in mid-1958; however, he remained on the board of directors until the second national congress of the federation in October 1963. It was also in about 1958 that he was removed as a national committee member of the All-China Federation of Supply and Marketing Cooperatives.

In November of 1958, at a session of the Shantung Provincial Congress, Pai was elected as a vice-governor under Governor (and Party Central Committee alternate member) T'an Ch'i-lung. Five years later, at a December 1963 session of the congress, Pai succeeded T'an as Shantung governor. In January 1961, Pai had been named as a Shantung deputy to the Second NPC to replace a deceased delegate. In 1964 he was re-elected from Shantung to the Third NPC, which held its first session in December 1964–January 1965.

As might be expected for a provincial leader of his stature, Pai is regularly mentioned in the press; he has attended numerous Party and government meetings in Shantung (such as the sessions of the Shantung Provincial People's Council) and taken part in rallies commemorating Communist holidays. He has also been reported in the company of top Party leaders on inspections in Shantung; for example, he was with Mao Tse-tung in September 1959 and May 1960, and with Chu Te in May 1960. Among the articles written by Pai about Shantung are two which appeared in the *JMJP* (October 19, 1959, and February 3, 1960).

As already noted, Pai was cited for his frugal living habits when he was an official in Shansi in the early 1940's. This was mentioned in a New China News Agency dispatch of September 15, 1963, from the Shantung capital, which stated that Pai's son, Pai Ch'ing-sheng, was then a student at the Wu-ying-shan Primary School in Tsinan, Shantung, and had been inspired by his father's "simple living." This same dispatch also mentioned that Pai had a daughter, older than his son.

1. *K'ang-Jih chan-cheng shih-ch'i chieh-fang-ch'ü kai-k'uang* (A sketch of the liberated areas during the Anti-Japanese War; Peking, 1953), p. 103.

2. *SCMP* 3070.

P'an Fu-sheng

(1905–   ; Wen-teng hsien, Shantung). Chairman, All-China Federation of Supply and Marketing Cooperatives; alternate member, CCP Central Committee.

P'an Fu-sheng was a Party and government leader in Pingyuan and Honan provinces in the decade before 1958 and was elected an alternate member of the CCP Central Committee in 1956. In 1958 he was purged during the Great Leap Forward only to reappear in 1962 as head of the All-China Federation of Supply and Marketing Cooperatives.

P'an was born in Wen-teng hsien near the eastern tip of the Shantung peninsula. He was first identified in 1947 as deputy director of the Administrative Office of the Hopeh-Shantung-Honan Border Region. This area had been one of the Communist "liberated areas," which were, in effect, pockets of Communist control during the Sino-Japanese War. By 1949 P'an had been promoted to director, the Border Region by then having been placed under the North China People's Government (a short-lived administrative division lasting from August 1948 to October 1949). In 1949 the Communists made the region into a new province called Pingyuan, largely composed of parts of Honan and Shantung. P'an served from 1949 to 1952 as a member of the Pingyuan Provincial People's Government and as political commissar of the Pingyuan Military District. From 1950 to 1952 he was also a member of the provincial government's Finance and Economics Committee as well as a deputy secretary subordinate to Wu Te (q.v.), Pingyuan's ranking Party secretary.

In the meantime, P'an had also taken part in the formation of the national government in Peking in September 1949. When the First CPPCC met in that month to bring the central government into existence, P'an attended as a delegate from the "North China Liberated Area." During the meetings he served under

Chou En-lai on an *ad hoc* committee to draft the Common Program of the CPPCC, the document that served as the constitution until a formal constitution was adopted in 1954.

Pingyuan was dissolved in November 1952 and the former provincial boundaries were approximately restored. In 1953, not long afterwards, P'an was transferred to Honan where he held posts similar to those he had held in Pingyuan. He was identified as the ranking Honan Party secretary by early 1953. From 1953 to mid-1958 he was also political commissar of the Honan Military District. In February 1955 he became a vice-chairman of the First Honan Provincial Committee of the CPPCC and was promoted to the chairmanship at some time before mid-1958. Concurrently, from February 1955 he held a seat on the Honan Provincial People's Council.

At the Eighth National Congress of the CCP in September 1956, P'an was elected an alternate member of the Central Committee, apparently in reward for at least a decade of service in north-central China. However, less than two years later he was in serious political trouble, his career foundering on the rocks of the commune movement that was initiated in 1958.

Honan was the province where the first model commune was established in April 1958. Known as the "Weihsing" (Sputnik) Commune, its alleged success was said to have encouraged the top Party leaders to establish communes throughout China as a major ingredient in the Great Leap Forward. These developments did not take place without internal Party struggles and disagreements. In certain provinces those on the winning side made the names of the opposition public, and thus it was easier to determine the contestants than at the national level where reports of the controversy were more guarded. The troubles in Honan were aired at the second session of the Eighth National Party Congress in May 1958. From the moment the session's communiqué was published it was apparent that P'an was at the center of the trouble. Accusations brought against him made it seem that he had been in trouble almost from the time of his arrival in Honan in 1953. He was charged with having made the mistake of "right opportunism," and he was also identified as the "former first secretary of the Honan Party Committee," showing that punitive action had already been taken.

These charges were immediately followed by the convocation of the ninth enlarged session of the provincial Party committee in Honan, which met from June 9 to July 1, 1958. Wu Chih-p'u, a Honanese Communist who outranked P'an on the Central Committee (having been made a full committee member in 1956) and who was also the governor of Honan, presided as the new first secretary of the Honan Party Committee. In addition to P'an two other mem-

bers of the Honan CCP Committee were sharply criticized. These were Yang Chueh, a secretary of the Honan Party Secretariat, and Wang T'ing-tung, deputy secretary-general of the Committee. The three men, it was said, had worked together in Pingyuan before coming to Honan and had formed an "anti-Party faction" in Honan as soon as they arrived there. In one of the reports at the session it was asserted that, although P'an had come to Honan in 1953, he had been running the Party Committee for only about two years because he had taken a "rest cure" from the "summer of 1954 to the spring of 1957." The inference was that this was enforced inactivity because he had been in some political trouble. The comment is difficult to explain because P'an was not wholly inactive during the time, even by the facts of the report. It was during this very period (as already described) that he was elected an alternate member of the Party Central Committee, an honor not likely to be given to one then in political trouble. Furthermore, according to the criticisms made during the meeting, P'an had been actively opposed to the development of higher agricultural cooperatives in Honan from at least the winter of 1956 and possibly even earlier, another fact suggesting that he was not totally inactive in provincial politics at the time. It was alleged that he kept up his opposition all during 1957, even calling a fourth session of the provincial Party congress to try to impose his point of view. Apparently he felt that the province was too poor to support an acceleration in agricultural production and the peasants too apathetic toward collectivization to warrant pushing them into agricultural cooperatives so quickly. It was obvious from the charges that P'an must have been among those in Honan who favored a more conservative approach toward socialization. In addition, he was accused of having lived extravagantly, wanting to be too well dressed, and desiring the same of his subordinates—all bourgeois tastes denoting softness. The Honan Party session accepted the Central Committee's decision to oust P'an from the provincial Party committee and then proceeded to censure him. It relieved him of his duties as a member of the Honan CCP's Standing Committee and recommended that he also be removed as commissar of the Honan Military District and chairman of the provincial CPPCC. He and his two associates were then to be allowed to reflect upon their mistakes. It is noteworthy, however, that P'an was not forced to relinquish his post on the Central Committee. (The charges against P'an are conveniently assembled in *CB* 515.)

Nothing further was heard of P'an for almost five years. He suddenly reappeared in November 1962 when he welcomed a delegation of the Polish Peasants Mutual Aid Agricultural Cooperatives to Peking. He was identified as acting chairman of the All-China Federation of Supply and Marketing Cooperatives (ACFSMC), replacing Chang Ch'i-lung, a vice-chairman who had been *de facto* head of the organization since 1957 when Ch'eng Tzu-hua, the official chairman, had become otherwise occupied. The ACFSMC is the principal mass organization of the cooperative movement and is one of the most important of the so-called "people's" organizations. By July 1963 P'an formally replaced Ch'eng Tzu-hua as full chairman of the ACFSMC, indicating that he had regained political favor in Peking. In late 1964 P'an was given still another post when he was named as a representative of the cooperatives to the Fourth CPPCC, which held its first session in December 1964–January 1965. At the close of this session he was named to the governing body of the CPPCC, the Standing Committee.

P'an Tzu-li

(c.1900–   ; Shensi). Diplomat; alternate member, CCP Central Committee.

A veteran Red Army political officer, P'an Tzu-li was a leading Party official in Ninghsia and Shensi in the first five years of the PRC. He was transferred to the foreign service in 1954 and since then has served as ambassador in North Korea, India, Nepal, and the Soviet Union. He has been an alternate member of the Party Central Committee since 1956.

P'an comes from Shensi, and in the early 1920's attended a middle school in the north Shensi town of Yü-lin. About the time that the CCP was organized (1921), a group of young teachers went to Yü-lin from Peking University where they had been students of Li Ta-chao, one of the Party founders. It was in part through their influence that an interest in Marxism was brought to the Yü-lin Middle School (see under Liu Chih-tan). Liu Chih-tan, Kao Kang, and Ma Ming-fang (qq.v.) were among P'an's classmates in the early twenties. By the mid-twenties P'an had become a member of the CCP. In the fall of 1925 Liu Chih-tan, the most important of the early Shensi Communists, went to Canton where he studied at the Whampoa Military Academy. It appears that P'an also went to Whampoa about that time (because a decade later, during the Long March, he was identified as a former Whampoa student.)[1] Liu took part in the Northern Expedition (1926–27) and then returned to Shensi. P'an, on the other hand, seems to have remained in central-south China. He set out on the Long March in the fall of 1934 with the forces led by Chu Te and Mao Tse-tung. However, after mid-1935, when the Communists had reached the Szechwan-Sikang borderlands en route to north Shensi, P'an became a propaganda worker in the General Political Department of the Fourth Front Army

commanded by Chang Kuo-t'ao and Hsu Hsiang-ch'ien,[2] which separated from Mao and did not rejoin him in Shensi until the latter part of 1936 (see under Chang Kuo-t'ao).

After the Communists consolidated their position in the northwest they established the Shensi-Kansu-Ninghsia Border Region Government in 1937 with Yenan as the capital. Lin Po-ch'ü (q.v.) was the Border Region chairman; P'an served under him as secretary-general of the government, but in 1938 he was succeeded by Wu Hsiu-ch'üan (q.v.).[3] Nothing further is known of P'an's wartime activities, but it seems likely that he was a political officer in the Communists' Shansi-Chahar-Hopeh (Chin-Ch'a-Chi) base. In any case, by March 1946 he was a deputy director of the Chin-Ch'a-Chi Military Region's Political Department,[4] and two years later he was in charge of the Propaganda Department in the Northern Sub-bureau of the CCP's North China Bureau. In the latter part of 1949, as the civil war was drawing to a close, P'an was an army corps political commissar in P'eng Te-huai's (q.v.) First Field Army, which was then fighting against the Nationalists in northwest China.

In September 1949 the Communists captured Yinchuan, the capital of Ninghsia province. Before the year ended P'an had assumed the three key provincial posts, becoming the ranking secretary of the Ninghsia CCP Committee, political commissar of the Ninghsia Military District, and the provincial governor. Within the Ninghsia government he concurrently served from August 1950 to 1951 as chairman of the Finance and Economics Committee. In the early PRC years most key provincial leaders were concurrently assigned to the multi-provincial regional governments, and thus P'an was a member of the Northwest Military and Administrative Committee from 1950 to 1954 (known from 1953 until its abolition in 1954 as the Northwest Administrative Committee).

In about November 1951 P'an relinquished his posts in Ninghsia, and by the spring of 1952 had returned to his native Shensi. He spent the next two years there performing many of the same tasks he had performed in Ninghsia. From about May 1952 until September 1954 he served as the ranking secretary of the Shensi Party Committee, succeeding his old Yü-lin schoolmate, Ma Ming-fang. He was also a provincial vice-governor under Governor P'ei Li-sheng (q.v.). During these same years he was identified in two other posts: by August 1952 he was director of the Political Department of the Northwest Military Region, and in April 1953 he became chairman of the newly established provincial election committee, which was responsible for running the elections to the First NPC (1954–1959). P'an himself was elected one of the provincial deputies, but he could not have been very active in the Congress, because in the same month that the NPC held its first session (September 1954) he was transferred to the foreign service.

P'an's first diplomatic assignment was as the ambassador to North Korea. He has remained in the foreign service, and after serving in three important posts he ranks among Peking's leading diplomats. He presented his credentials in Pyongyang in January 1955. His brief tour there was relatively uneventful, perhaps owing to the fact that the Chinese diplomatic mission in Korea tended to be overshadowed by the presence of the large number of Chinese troops still there from the Korean War. One of the few times his name appeared in the press was in August 1955 when he was a member of Chu Te's delegation to the celebrations marking the 10th anniversary of the North Korean government.

After only 13 months in Korea, P'an was replaced in February 1956 by Ch'iao Hsiao-kuang. In the next month P'an was named to succeed Yuan Chung-hsien (deceased) as ambassador to India and Nepal. The six years he spent in India were critical ones in the history of Sino-Indian relations; it was during his tour that growing tensions erupted into border warfare along the Sino-Indian frontier. P'an presented his credentials in New Delhi to President Prasad on April 17, 1956. That same month he joined Ulanfu's (q.v.) delegation to the coronation of King Mahendra of Nepal, and while in Katmandu he presented his credentials as ambassador. The following September P'an was elected *in absentia* by the Eighth Party Congress to alternate membership on the Central Committee.

P'an resided in India while holding the two ambassadorial posts, but he went on a number of official visits to Nepal and also returned home on several occasions. In September 1956 he negotiated and signed in Katmandu the Sino-Nepalese Agreement on Friendship, Trade, and Communications between the Tibetan Region of China and Nepal. The agreement replaced one which had been in effect between Nepal and Tibet for a century. Later that month he accompanied Nepalese Prime Minister Prasad Acharya on a state visit to China. While in Peking P'an probably took part in the negotiations for the Sino-Nepalese Agreement on Economic Aid (signed October 7) and in the meeting which led to the Sino-Nepalese Exchange of Notes on Questions of Foreign Exchange. Back in New Delhi, on May 25, 1957, he signed the Sino-Indian Exchange of Notes on the Extension of the 1954 Trade Agreement and the Sino-Indian Exchange of Notes on the Promotion of Relations of the State Trade Companies for the Two Countries.

The International Red Cross held its 19th Conference in New Delhi in October–November 1957. The Chinese Red Cross delegation was led by Minister of Public Health Li Te-ch'üan (q.v.) and P'an headed another delegation representing the PRC Government. He disrupted the proceedings by walking out on November 5 after accusing the United States of trying to engineer a "two-China's plot." In June 1958 P'an was one of eight Chinese ambassadors called home during the crisis in Lebanon and Jordan when American and British troops were rushed to the Middle East. He was again in Peking in March 1960 accompanying Nepalese Premier Koirala on a visit to the Chinese capital. Koirala signed the Sino-Nepalese Boundary Agreement and another one that called for a grant of 100,000,000 Indian rupees from China. P'an returned to India the next month and was on hand for the visit of Premier Chou En-lai, who was in New Delhi to discuss a border agreement. Chou also visited Nepal and signed a treaty of friendship in April 1960. P'an presumably accompanied Chou to Nepal, but soon afterwards, in July 1960, Chang Shih-chieh was appointed to Katmandu as China's first resident ambassador in Nepal, while P'an continued as ambassador to India.

By the spring of 1962 the recurring border tensions between India and China began to increase seriously. The latent dispute, though muted during the early and mid-fifties, had been exacerbated by the flight of the Dalai Lama from Tibet to India in March 1959. P'an was called upon (May 1959) to express Chinese displeasure over the fact that India had given asylum to the Tibetan leader, although at that time it was clear that Peking was anxious to avoid a showdown. By 1962, however, the situation was far more serious. In what appeared to be a deliberate gesture by the Chinese, P'an left New Delhi for home on July 18. In the previous year the Indian ambassador to China had been recalled, and thus when P'an departed both embassies were left in the care of chargés d'affaires. The sporadic border clashes erupted into a brief war in the fall of 1962, which ended, in effect, on November 21, 1962, when the Chinese cease-fire and withdrawal went into effect. Two days later Peking announced P'an's formal removal as ambassador to New Delhi and his appointment as ambassador to Moscow where he replaced Liu Hsiao (q.v.). (The Chinese continued to maintain an embassy in India, but as of the mid-1960's no ambassador had been named to succeed P'an.)

P'an moved from one scene of international crisis to another. He arrived in Moscow on December 10, 1962, and presented his credentials five days later. The Sino-Soviet dispute was worsening even as P'an was being accredited. In the first two weeks of December, at congresses of the Italian and Czech Communist Parties, the Chinese position had been vigorously attacked (see under Wu Hsiu-ch'üan). Italian and Czech support for the Soviet view was commented upon in a *Pravda* article of December 9, officially revealing the Sino-Soviet conflict to the Russian public for the first time. After his arrival in Moscow P'an's activities received relatively little attention in the Chinese press—particularly in contrast to the 1950's when Chinese diplomats in Moscow were constantly in the news. Most of P'an's activity, in fact, seemed to center around the Sino-Soviet dispute. He served, for example, as a member of the important CCP delegation, led by Teng Hsiao-p'ing (q.v.), which unsuccessfully attempted to settle differences in a round of negotiations in Moscow in July 1963.

In 1964 P'an was elected a deputy from Kansu to the Third NPC, a somewhat unusual assignment for a person stationed abroad. As already noted, he had been a Shensi deputy to the First NPC, but he did not serve in the Second Congress (1959–1964).

P'an is married to Yao Shu-hsien, whose antecedents are unknown. They have a son born in 1958.

---

1. John E. Rue, *Mao Tse-tung in Opposition, 1927–1935* (Stanford, Calif., 1966), p. 269.

2. Sian, *Ch'ün-chung jih-pao* (The masses daily), August 2, 1950, reprinted in *Hsin-hua yueh-pao* (New China monthly), 2:5 (September 15, 1950).

3. Modern China Project, Columbia University, New York, Howard L. Boorman, director.

4. Kalgan, *Chin-Ch'a-Chi jih-pao* (Shansi-Chahar-Hopeh daily), March 1, 1946.

P'ei Li-sheng

(1897–   ; Shansi). Vice-president, Academy of Sciences.

P'ei Li-sheng was born in 1897 in Shansi, according to Japanese sources, which also credit him with a degree from Moscow University and, following his return to China, with underground work in his native Shansi and in Shanghai. The Japanese also assert that during the Yenan period P'ei was head of the "bureau of resistance against the enemy" under the Social Affairs Department of the Party Central Committee. Writing in December 1937, Agnes Smedley refers to an "enemy department" which interrogated Japanese prisoners of war.[1] It would be logical for these to be the same, because the Social Affairs Department was for many years the Communist term for the intelligence section within the Party structure.

Soon after the end of the Sino-Japanese War, P'ei was with the Red armies as a political commissar at the army corps level. He was probably working in north China; in any case, in March 1949, as the Communists were fighting their way through Shansi, they decided to merge the Central Shansi Administrative Office (a governmental organ) with the Taiyuan Municipal People's Government in order to unify and strengthen their leadership and to support the fighting front. P'ei was named as the Taiyuan mayor even though the Communists did not capture the city for another month (April 1949). He held this post only for a brief period, but from this time until his transfer to Peking in 1956, P'ei held a number of important positions within both the government and Party hierarchies in Shansi. The Shansi government was formally established over the winter of 1949–50, at which time P'ei was named to head the provincial Industry Department (until June 1952). More important, he was appointed as a vice-governor, serving first under Ch'eng Tzu-hua and (from February 1951) under Lai Jo-yü, both senior Party leaders. Still another post held by P'ei in the early fifties in the Shansi government was as a vice-chairman of the Finance and Economics Committee.

In late 1951 Governor Lai Jo-yü was transferred to Peking to work with the All-China Federation of Labor. Therefore, in December 1951, P'ei succeeded Lai as governor, retaining the post until April 1956 when he too was transferred to Peking. Within the Party structure in Shansi, P'ei rose from membership on the Shansi Party Standing Committee in 1953 to second deputy secretary in the same year, and then to second secretary from 1953 until transferred in 1956. Shansi was subordinated to the multi-provincial government organization known as the North China Administrative Committee; P'ei was a member of this body from January 1953, retaining membership until its dissolution in the late summer of 1954.

P'ei was mentioned in the press with the frequency generally accorded to an official of his stature—attending meetings of the Shansi Government Council, inspecting agricultural or industrial enterprises, greeting visitors to Taiyuan, and similar activities. For example, he gave the major report on the work of the government at a Shansi government congress held in February 1955. The year before he had headed the *ad hoc* committee formed in Shansi to discuss the draft constitution of the PRC, which was ultimately adopted in September 1954 at the First NPC.

In early 1956, in an attempt to quicken the pace of scientific development, the Communist government established the Scientific Planning Commission under the State Council, with P'ei as one of the members, a post he held until the commission was merged with another in November 1958. A more important but closely selated appointment was made by August 1956 when he was named as one of the secretaries-general of the Academy of Sciences. He remained in this position until August 1960 when he was elevated to a vice-presidency within the Academy, replacing T'ao Meng-ho, a distinguished scientist who died in April 1960. P'ei remains in this position, and as of 1965 was one of six vice-presidents.

From the time he came to the Academy in 1956, P'ei has been one of the senior Party functionaries working in scientific administration, being associated with other such science administrators as Chang Chin-fu, Fan Ch'ang-chiang, and Tu Jun-sheng (qq.v.). A vignette of P'ei has been provided by J. Tuzo Wilson, professor of geophysics at the University of Toronto, who visited China in 1958 where he encountered P'ei on several occasions. Wilson described him, perhaps with irony, as a "doctor" and as being "austere and commanding." He told of a banquet given by P'ei in his honor. Although there were a number of distinguished Chinese scientists present, P'ei was "far the most commanding personality present. He conducted himself with the greatest dignity, although the fact that he was an agriculturist suggested that he came from peasant stock. He spoke no English, and I do not think he knew the West."[2]

In April 1959 P'ei was named as a "specially invited delegate" to the Third National Committee of the CPPCC; soon afterward he was named a deputy chief of the Science and Technical Section of the CPPCC. (However, when the Fourth National Committee of the CPPCC was formed in December 1964–January 1965, P'ei was not again named to the national committee.) In November 1959, at the first stratigraphic conference, P'ei was named as a vice-chairman, although nothing in his background suggests that he is qualified to hold such a position in terms of technical competence. More frequently he is mentioned in the press in connection with work requiring political rather than scientific competence. For example, he served on the preparatory committee for a conference of "advanced units" in agriculture, and when the conference was convened in December 1958 he served on the presidium (steering committee). Similarly, P'ei is often on hand to welcome visiting scientific delegations from abroad and spends much time entertaining them during their stay in China.

In February 1960 P'ei led a five-member delegation of the Academy to Moscow where, on February 20, he signed an agreement of cooperation for 1960 between the Chinese and Soviet academies. While in Moscow he served concurrently as a member of the delegation led by Liu Ch'ang-sheng (a Central Committee member) to mark the 10th anniversary of the signing of the Sino-Soviet Treaty of Friendship, Alliance and Mutual Assistance, the accord which formed the cornerstone of relations during the 1950's (but the force of which was weakened with the Sino-Soviet rift of the early 1960's). Four years later, P'ei was the signatory to another agreement; on February 6, 1964, he signed a cooperation agreement between the academies in China and North Korea, as well as the cooperation plan

for 1964. Later in 1964 he was elected as a deputy from his native Shansi to the Third NPC, which held its first session in December 1964–January 1965.

1. Agnes Smedley, *China Fights Back* (London, 1938), p. 225.
2. J. Tuzo Wilson, *One Chinese Moon* (London, 1959), pp. 75, 77.

P'eng Chen

(c.1902–   ; Ch'ü-wu, Shansi). Mayor of Peking; member, CCP Politburo and Secretariat.

One of the major leaders of the CCP since the 1940's, P'eng Chen was among the earliest Communists in Shansi province. He spent six years in prison, but after his release in 1935 he quickly emerged as a key Communist operative in north China. He worked as a top political officer in the Shansi-Chahar-Hopeh Border Region during the early war years, after which he held important posts in the Party apparatus in Yenan. In the postwar years he worked both in the Border Region and in Manchuria, and for a decade and a half after the Communists won control of the mainland he was the ranking leader in the CCP Peking Committee. From the mid-1950's to the mid-1960's P'eng was the dominant figure in the NPC, and during this same period he was deeply involved in liaison with foreign Communist parties. He was one of the most prominent figures during the early 1960's in the ideological dispute with the Soviet Union. P'eng was elected to the Politburo in 1945 and to the Central Secretariat in 1956.

P'eng comes from Ch'ü-wu in southwest Shansi, where he was born into a poor peasant family. Rather little is known of his younger years, but he received a primary and middle school education in his native province, after which he joined the Socialist Youth League. According to a Soviet biography of P'eng, he became a CCP member in 1923 and took an active part in the creation of the Party organization in Shansi.[1] Party work in north China was then far less developed than in the south, and the difficulties in Shansi were compounded by the presence of the powerful warlord-governor Yen Hsi-shan. However, many of the youths in Shansi were strongly attracted to the anti-imperialist doctrines of both the KMT and the CCP. P'eng, for example, is said to have been a leader of student and labor movements in Taiyuan, the provincial capital, and in this capacity he organized a society in 1925 to boycott Japanese goods.

Both the KMT and the CCP gained considerable prestige in Shansi in the period after the Northern Expedition was launched from Kwangtung in mid-1926. Governor Yen Hsi-shan was under considerable pressure to join with the rapidly advancing Northern Expeditionary forces, but he was fearful of the radicalism among the youths in Shansi. During this period, according to a detailed study of Yen's career, P'eng was among the student leaders in Taiyuan who, in 1927, came to dominate the Taiyuan labor movement.[2] After the KMT-CCP split in mid-1927, little is known of P'eng's activities for the next decade. Reports are conflicting, but it appears that he was mainly engaged from 1927 to 1930 as a labor leader in Taiyuan and on the Cheng-t'ai (Taiyuan–Shih-chia-chuang) Railway, and that he worked as a Communist organizer in various north China cities, including Peking, Tientsin, and T'ang-shan. The Soviet biography of P'eng asserts that he was arrested three times by the "northern militarists" and the KMT, and that he spent a total of six years in prison before his release in 1935; a 1958 account published in Peking mentions his imprisonment, but neither the dates nor the locale is mentioned.[3]

After P'eng's release from jail he became one of the senior officials in the CCP North China Bureau. In the wake of the student-led December Ninth Movement (1935) in Peking (see under Li Ch'ang), a number of student organizations were formed in north China cities to agitate for more effective resistance against the steady Japanese incursions upon Chinese sovereignty. Among the more important of these organizations was the National Liberation Vanguards of China (NLVC). During the winter of 1936–37, P'eng was instructed to make direct contact with the NLVC, and it was allegedly under his personal guidance that the student organization held its inaugural congress in Peking in February 1937. Inferential evidence suggests that P'eng was working directly under Liu Shao-ch'i.

P'eng went to Yenan by May 1937, but when the Sino-Japanese War broke out in the middle of that year he accompanied the Communist armies into Shansi to engage the rapidly advancing Japanese forces. In the fall of that year he was in Taiyuan, which fell to the Japanese in November, but by early 1938 he had been assigned as a key political officer with those portions of the Communists' 115th Division which were stationed in and around Wu-t'ai hsien in northeast Shansi. The Wu-t'ai area became the center for the Shansi-Chahar-Hopeh (Chin-Ch'a-Chi) Border Region, which was set up in the early days of 1938. The history of this important base is contained in the biographies of Nieh Jung-chen, the top military commander, and Sung Shao-wen, the chairman of the Border Region. P'eng was a member of the Border Region Government Council from its establishment, and from that time or soon thereafter he was also the secretary of the CCP Chin-Ch'a-Chi Border Region Committee. U.S. military observer Evans Carlson visited Wu-t'ai in early 1938, where he interviewed P'eng, whom he described as director of the "People's Movement." The

Communists were particularly dependent in the early stages of the war upon the support of the populace, and from Carlson's interview it appears that P'eng's major task was to mobilize this support. As he explained to Carlson, this meant attempting to "develop the political consciousness of the people." Special rooms were set aside in each village and in each company of the army where the people gathered to "read, sing songs, and prepare dramas." Concerted efforts were made, according to P'eng, to eliminate graft among village and hsien officials. Army commanders were ordered to "aid the farmers in every way possible. Troops . . . [were] sent to aid in the planting of crops, and in the harvesting." The Communists also provided "seed for new crops" and a "few soil experts who [advised] the farmers what crops to plant." P'eng claimed that people had begun to respond by supplying intelligence information, taking part in partisan warfare against the Japanese, and providing some logistic support for Communist troops.[4]

Concurrently with his duties in the Chin-Ch'a-Chi Border Region, P'eng reportedly headed the Party's North China Bureau from 1938. Little else is known of his work in those years, but for the 55th issue of *Chieh-fang* (Liberation; October 31, 1938) he wrote an article on political affairs in the border region and a book published in 1939 in Kweilin carried an article by him dealing with alleged Trotskyite activities in the border region.[5] By 1941 he had been called back to Yenan. There, in 1941, he became vice-president of the important Central Party School,[6] then headed by Teng Fa (q.v.). In 1942 the school was one of the focal points for Mao Tse-tung's famous *cheng-feng* ("rectification") movement, and according to a 1961 Communist account, P'eng was one of the leading figures in organizing the movement within the school.[7] Teng Fa relinquished the presidency in 1943, and then when journalist Gunther Stein visited Yenan in the spring of 1944, he identified P'eng as the president.[8] Stein reported that the school had an enrollment of about 5,000.

In the previous year (1943), P'eng had already assumed the directorship of the Party's Organization Department, one of the key posts in the CCP hierarchy. Relatively little information is available on the Organization Department during those years, but it is a reasonable assumption that this post gave P'eng a major voice in Party personnel matters. When Gunther Stein interviewed him in 1944, he found it difficult to judge whether the "peasant or the intellectual element" was the "main characteristic of [P'eng's] personality." P'eng was not then a nationally known figure in China, but Stein came away with the impression from his "intellect and energy" that P'eng "may be one of [the Party's] most important men." This judgment was soon borne out.

When the CCP held its Seventh National Congress in Yenan from April to June 1945, P'eng was one of only 15 members of the congress presidium. He was elected a member of the Central Committee, and immediately afterwards, at the First Plenum of the new Central Committee, he was elected a member of the Politburo. The exact composition of the Politburo at that time is not known, but it appears that P'eng was the only member who had not spent the early years of his career in central-south China and who had not made the Long March. Moreover, according to an unconfirmed report, he was also elected an alternate member of the Party's Secretariat, then the most important CCP organ (serving as a kind of "inner" Politburo). In the period immediately after the Japanese surrender in August 1945, the Communists began to move thousands of troops and many key Party leaders into Manchuria. P'eng was among this group, which included Ch'en Yun, Kao Kang, Lin Piao, Li Fu-ch'un, Lo Jung-huan, and Lin Feng (qq.v.). Because Manchuria had been so completely dominated by the Japanese, these Communists leaders were virtually forced to start from scratch in building a viable Party structure and in recruiting more men for their armed forces. However, as they began their three-year test of strength with the Nationalists for this vital area, they were given a notable boost by the presence of the Communist-controlled Anti-Japanese Allied Army (see under Chou Pao-chung).

In those early postwar days in Manchuria, P'eng quickly emerged as the top Party leader and political officer. He was made the secretary of the CCP Northeast Bureau, and for a period in 1946 he was concurrently director of the Bureau's Organization Department. In the military hierarchy he was political commissar of both the newly formed Northeast Democratic Allied Army (commanded by Lin Piao) and the Northeast Military and Political Academy. Although full details are lacking, it appears that P'eng came into conflict with military officers and administrators from the Soviet Union who had moved into Manchuria in the closing days of World War II. The Soviets have charged that P'eng and Lin Feng were at the head of a group which "slandered" the USSR and the Soviet Army in Manchuria. These accusations (first published in 1964) and the Chinese response to them are discussed in detail in the biography of Lin Feng.

P'eng relinquished the senior Party post in Manchuria to Lin Piao in mid-1946, and for the balance of that year and a part of 1947 it appears that he shuttled back and forth between Manchuria and the neighboring Chin-Ch'a-Chi Border Region. However, in the period from the latter part of 1947 to the winter of 1948–49 he seems to have spent most of his time in the Chin-Ch'a-Chi Border Region. To judge from his writings of this period, he apparently devoted much

of his time to land reform measures, which the Communists were attempting to implement in areas long under their control, as well as those areas which they were capturing as the Nationalist armies were defeated in north China.

By the time P'eng had relinquished the top Party post in Manchuria to Lin Piao in mid-1946, he had also been replaced by An Tzu-wen (q.v.) as head of the CCP Organization Department. However, he reassumed the post about 1949 and continued to head the department until he in turn was replaced by Jao Shu-shih (q.v.) in 1952. In the meantime, in late January and early February 1949 the Communist armies marched into Peking, which had been surrendered to Lin Piao's troops by Nationalist General Fu Tso-i. P'eng was one of the first of the top Communists to arrive in the city, and he was immediately made the ranking secretary of the CCP Peking Committee. In September 1949 the Communists convened the CPPCC, the organization which set up the PRC. P'eng was elected a member of the First National Committee of the CPPCC and of the powerful Central People's Government Council (CPGC), both of which were chaired by Mao Tse-tung. In addition, under Chou En-lai's Government Administration Council (the cabinet), P'eng was made a vice-chairman of the Political and Legal Affairs Committee. Many of Peng's public appearances during the next five years were in this capacity; the committee was headed by the elderly Tung Pi-wu (q.v.), but it appears that P'eng was the dominant figure. Within the "mass" organizations P'eng was a member of the First Executive Board of the Sino-Soviet Friendship Association (1949–1954), as well as chairman of the association's Peking branch (1949–1958). In February 1950 he became chairman of the Peking Trade Union Council; in October 1950, when the China Peace Committee was reorganized, P'eng became one of the vice-chairmen (until July 1958), and in the next month he became a member of the committee's Peking chapter.

P'eng did not initially hold any posts of importance in the Peking municipal government, but then in November 1950 he was named chairman of its Finance and Economics Committee. More important, he succeeded Nieh Jung-chen (q.v.) as the mayor of Peking in February 1951. P'eng thus became the top man in both the CCP and governmental hierarchies in the national capital, a stature he was to enjoy for the next 15 years. Quite apart from the political responsibilities which he shouldered in this dual capacity, the requirements of protocol also necessitated countless public appearances, and this task was to become even more demanding in the mid-1950's when hundreds of foreign delegations began to visit Peking. Some of P'eng's subordinates were able to relieve him of many of his protocol duties, but the fact remains that during the first 15 years of the PRC few other major Party leaders made as many public appearances.

After an initial period of consolidation, the Communists began to control or suppress various elements within the society which they regarded as inimical to their interests. P'eng had a major role in these campaigns. For example, after hearing his report the CPGC in February 1951 approved regulations for the "punishment of counterrevolutionary activities." Similarly, he took an active part in the campaigns of 1951–52 to root out various forms of corruption within the CCP and the business community (the so-called three-anti and five-anti campaigns). In this connection, he was appointed a vice-chairman of an *ad hoc* committee in December 1951 to check up on the economy and to impose austerity measures and, as in the case of the alleged counterrevolutionaries, it was after hearing a report by P'eng that the CPCG adopted regulations in April 1952 on the punishment of corruption. His deep involvement in political and legal affairs was further illustrated in July 1951 when the Central Political and Legal Cadres' Academy was established. From then until November 1956 he served as the academy president. Relatively little is known about this school, but when P'eng spoke at graduation exercises for the second class in July 1954, the Communist press reported that the 1,000-odd graduates would be assigned as responsible officials in administrative and legal organs at the hsien level. He received still another post in December 1951 when he became a member of the newly established North China Administrative Committee (see under Liu Lan-t'ao), a position he held until the committee was abolished in 1954.

During the formative years of the PRC, P'eng was mainly involved with domestic issues, but not to the total exclusion of foreign affairs. For example, it fell to P'eng to deliver the major report in October 1951 before the CPPCC National Committee on the subject of the nationwide "Resist United States aggression, aid Korea" campaign, which had been in full swing since the Chinese entered the Korean War a year earlier. Also in connection with the Korean War, he was one of the key figures in the activities that led to the convocation in Peking of the Asian and Pacific Regions Peace Conference. P'eng was one of the two deputy leaders of the Chinese delegation to this large meeting in October 1952, which concentrated on attempts to prove the alleged use of bacteriological warfare by the United States in Korea (see under Liu Ning-i). At the close of the conference he was elected a member of the Peace Liaison Committee of the Asian and Pacific Regions.

In early 1953 the initial steps were taken toward the establishment of a constitutional government. In January P'eng was appointed a member of the committee to draft an election law, and in the following month he became a member of the Central Election Committee. A year later he was elected a deputy from Peking to the first NPC, and at its inaugural session in September 1954 (which adopted the national constitution), P'eng was elected one of the vice-chairmen of the NPC Standing Committee, the organ which controls NPC affairs between sessions of the congress. More important, he was also elected secretary-general of the Standing Committee, a position which apparently gave him day-to-day control of the work of this important body. Liu Shao-ch'i served as chairman of the First NPC (1954–1959), and Chu Te has been the chairman since the Second NPC, but in the decade after 1954 P'eng was clearly the most active of the top Party leaders in NPC affairs. During this period, for example, he made scores of reports before the full sessions of the congress (normally held once a year) and the many Standing Committee meetings. He continued as a vice-chairman during the Second and Third NPC's (elected in April 1959 and January 1965, respectively), but he relinquished the important post of secretary-general to Liu Ning-i (q.v.) in January 1965. Paralleling his NPC assignments, P'eng was elected a vice-chairman of the CPPCC in December 1954 and was re-elected in April 1959 and January 1965.

At the Party's Eighth National Congress, held in September 1956, P'eng was re-elected a member of the Central Committee, which, at its First Plenum, held the day after the congress closed, re-elected him to the Politburo. In addition, he was elected the second-ranking secretary (under Teng Hsiao-p'ing) of the Central Secretariat, which, under the terms of the newly revised Party Constitution, was given the task of implementing on a day-to-day basis the directives of the Politburo. The Secretariat, then regarded as one of the key organs of the CCP, initially consisted of only seven members, and only two of them—Teng and P'eng—were concurrently members of the Politburo. P'eng's prominence within the CCP elite was already evident in the years before 1956, but in the decade after the Eighth Congress he came to be regarded as one of the half-dozen most powerful men in China and was sometimes mentioned by Western analysts as a dark-horse contender to succeed Mao Tse-tung.

During the middle and late 1950's P'eng became increasingly involved in foreign affairs. In mid-1955 he was named to head a delegation to a meeting of the Inter-Parliamentary Union (IPU) in Helsinki, but the trip was canceled at the last moment when the IPU Executive Committee denied the PRC admission to this organization. A year later P'eng led a large NPC-Peking Municipal Government delegation, which visited the Soviet Union and five East European Communist nations (Czechoslovakia, Rumania, Bulgaria, Albania, and Yugoslavia). The trip lasted from mid-November 1956 to late January 1957, and because it came in the wake of the Hungarian Revolution, the major theme stressed by P'eng at the countless banquets and airport stops was that of Communist bloc solidarity. This long tour coincided in part with one made by Chou En-lai, and between them they conferred with virtually every leading Soviet and East European Communist official. In December 1956, while his group was in Czechoslovakia, P'eng left the delegation briefly to attend the Eighth Italian Communist Party Congress. As of that time he was one of the extremely few Chinese Communist officials to have visited Italy.

After the 20th CPSU Congress in 1956 and the subsequent erosion of solidarity within the Communist world, each of the major Communist nations began to play a far more active and direct role in inter-Party relations. In retrospect, it appears that P'eng's 1956–57 trip to Moscow, East Europe, and Italy was his initiation into a role in which he would become increasingly important—namely, as one of Peking's leading negotiators with foreign Communist party leaders. Others who were similarly engaged in these liaison functions in the late 1950's and early 1960's included such key CCP members as Liu Shao-ch'i, Teng Hsiao-p'ing, K'ang Sheng, Yang Shang-k'un, Liu Ning-i, and Wu Hsiu-ch'üan (qq.v.). P'eng received an important assignment in June 1960 when he led the Chinese delegation to the Third Congress of the Rumanian Workers' (Communist) Party in Bucharest. By this time Sino-Soviet relations had deteriorated rather markedly, particularly in regard to views held in Moscow and Peking about the appropriate strategy to deal with the non-Communist West. At the meetings in Bucharest the Russians purportedly circulated a letter sent to the CCP in which they "refuted" Chinese views; the situation was made all the more dramatic in view of the fact that Nikita Khrushchev was present for the CPSU. Khrushchev and P'eng engaged in a bitter verbal duel; the Soviet leader accused Mao of being another Stalin who was unrealistic and lacking in an understanding of the modern world. P'eng replied in acid terms that Khrushchev was confused on basic issues, that he could not be trusted to evaluate the world situation, and that he had deliberately set out to damage Chinese prestige.[9]

Following the Bucharest meetings there was a further deterioration in Sino-Soviet relations, as evidenced by the withdrawal of thousands of Soviet technicians from China in the late summer of 1960. Negotiations between the two giant Communist powers continued in Moscow in November 1960. The Chinese sent a top-flight delegation led by Liu Shao-ch'i and Teng Hsiao-p'ing, which also included P'eng, Li Ching-ch'üan, Lu Ting-i, and K'ang Sheng. The group ostensibly went to take part in the celebrations marking the 43rd anniversary of the October Revolution, but far more important was the convocation of a meeting of representatives from 81 Communist parties throughout the world. The Moscow negotiations failed to settle Sino-Soviet differences, and for the next few years Moscow and Peking dueled for the dominant position within the Communist world. P'eng was particularly active during this period, as the Chinese sought to maintain close ties with foreign Communist leaders. In July 1961 he was prepared to travel to Japan for the Eighth Congress of the Japanese Communist Party, but the trip was postponed when the Japanese government refused to allow the Chinese delegation to enter Japan. In October he was the ranking member of the delegation which Chou En-lai led to Moscow for the 22nd CPSU Congress. When Chou left for home before the Congress had ended (as a way of showing his displeasure over Soviet attacks on Albania), P'eng took over as acting head of the delegation.

In 1962 P'eng led delegations to Peking's two major Communist allies in Asia, North Korea, and North Vietnam. He was in Korea for 10 days in late April and early May as head of an NPC delegation. He conferred with Kim Il-sung and was given the National Flag Medal, Korea's highest order. P'eng spent almost two weeks in Vietnam in late September and early October, and there, as in Korea, he held talks with the top Vietnamese leaders, including Ho Chi Minh. In July 1963 P'eng was back in Moscow, this time as the deputy leader of the delegation led by Teng Hsiao-p'ing that was sent to hold further talks regarding CCP-CPSU relations. The talks ended in total failure, in the sense that neither side compromised its view on the means for dealing with the non-Communist world. In November 1964 P'eng was again slated to lead a CCP delegation to a congress of the Japan Communist Party, but once more the Japanese government refused to admit P'eng and his group.

Apart from his several trips abroad, P'eng was exceedingly active in the decade from the mid-1950's to the mid-1960's in negotiations with the many foreign Communist leaders who visited Peking. More specifically, from 1957 through 1964 P'eng is known to have held talks with nearly 100 different Communist party delegations. (Some parties, such as those in Japan, North Korea, and North Vietnam, sent several delegations to Peking during those years). It is doubtful if any other top CCP official saw more important Communist party leaders than P'eng during that period. As already indicated, during these same years he was also deeply occupied with the work of the NPC, and he continued to make scores of ceremonial appearances in his capacity as mayor of Peking. On the other hand, his previous heavy involvement with the legal apparatus tapered off sharply after the late 1950's. Although it is always difficult to assess the role of any CCP figure in the policy-making procedures, P'eng's seat on the Politburo and his frequent public appearances with the top Communist leaders, including Mao Tse-tung, provide strong inferential evidence that he had a powerful voice in deciding basic policies through the mid-1960's. In this regard, in September 1964 P'eng was described (apparently for the first time) as a "close comrade-in-arms of Mao Tse-tung," an accolade reserved for the select few. P'eng held his place as one of the top CCP leaders until the late spring of 1966 when he became the first Politburo-level victim of the Great Proletarian Cultural Revolution. The charges against him indicated that he had attempted to build an "empire" centering around the CCP Peking Committee.

P'eng is married to Chang Chieh-ch'ing. Nothing is known of her career until the latter part of 1956 when she accompanied her husband on his trip to Moscow and East Europe. In 1964 Chang was elected a deputy from Hopeh to the Third NPC, which opened its first session at the end of that year.

1. *Bol'shaya Sovetskaya Entsiklopedya* (Large Soviet Encyclopedia), XXXV, 393 (1955).

2. Donald G. Gillin, *Warlord Yen Hsi-shan in Shansi Province, 1911–1949* (Princeton, N.J., 1967), pp. 105–106.

3. *Hung-ch'i p'iao-p'iao* (Red flag fluttering; Peking, 1958), VI, 115.

4. Evans Fordyce Carlson, *Twin Stars of China* (New York, 1940), pp. 221–223.

5. Chün-tu Hsüeh, *The Chinese Communist Movement, 1937–1939* (Stanford, Calif., 1962), p. 59.

6. *Bol'shaya Sovetskaya Entsiklopedya.*

7. *Hsing-huo liao-yuan* (A single spark can start a prairie fire; Peking, 1961), VI, 104.

8. Gunther Stein, *The Challenge of Red China* (New York, 1945), p. 151.

9. Donald S. Zagoria, *The Sino-Soviet Conflict, 1956–1961* (Princeton, N.J., 1962), pp. 319, 325–326.

P'eng Hsueh-feng

(1905–1944; Nan-yang, Honan). Important commander of the New Fourth Army.

P'eng Hsueh-feng was a career Red Army officer, who joined the CCP in 1927, participated in the Long March with Mao Tse-tung's forces, and then worked in Shansi with the Eighth Route Army during the first part of the Sino-Japanese War. However, his greatest fame derived from his role in the New Fourth Army in east China. He was killed while fighting the Japanese in 1944.

P'eng, whose real name was P'eng Hsiu-tao, was born into a poor peasant family which lived in a small village in Nan-yang hsien, southwest

Honan. An uncle who had once served as secretary-general to the famous north China warlord Feng Yü-hsiang sent P'eng to a military school in Peking for the children of officials in Feng's Northwest Army. While a student there he joined the Communist Youth League and took an active part in the school's League branch. His first involvement in revolutionary activity, according to one of his biographers, took place at the time of the May 30 Incident (1925), which sparked a series of strikes throughout the nation. The role that P'eng played is not known but two years later, in September 1927, he joined the CCP in Peking. His admission into the Party took place only a few weeks after the final break in the KMT-CCP alliance, and thus by definition he became a part of the Party underground in north China.

P'eng was in Tientsin in 1929, but by 1930 he had gone to Shanghai, and in February of that year, because of his previous training in a military school, he was sent to command a unit in the Fifth Column of the Eighth Red Army. This assignment coincided with the period when the Li Li-san leadership was preparing for major assaults in the industrial cities in the Yangtze Valley area. By the summer of that year the Eighth Army had been placed under P'eng Te-huai's newly formed Third Army Corps, and then in July and again in September, the Eighth Army was one of the units which took part in the attacks on Changsha, the Hunan capital (see under P'eng Te-huai). The defeated Communist units retreated southward to their base on the Kiangsi-Fukien border, but by the end of 1930 they were faced with the first of the five KMT Annihilation Campaigns, which culminated in the evacuation of the base area and the Long March to Shensi.

P'eng presumably took part in all of the Annihilation Campaigns, but details are not available on his role (if any) in the first two. During the third campaign (mid-1931), he served as political commissar of the Second Division (of P'eng Te-huai's Third Army Corps) and fought in cooperation with Ch'en I's (q.v.) units in southeast Kiangsi. In the next campaign (mid-1932 to early 1933) he was political commissar of the Fourth Division, which fought around I-huang, Lo-an, and Lin-ch'uan in central Kiangsi. During the fifth and final campaign (late 1933–34), P'eng was back to his original post as political commissar of the Second Division, and he was concurrently political commissar of Ch'en I's Kiangsi Military District. During the course of these battles, P'eng was wounded, and on one occasion his division commander, Kuo Ping-sheng, defected to the Nationalists; P'eng led the remaining division troops to safety and was subsequently awarded a decoration for this act of loyalty. P'eng spent most of these years in the field with his troops, but for a period in 1933 he headed a section for high-level cadres in the Red Army Academy (Hung-chün ta-hsueh) on the outskirts of Juichin, the capital of the Chinese Soviet Republic.[1]

When the Long March began in October 1934, P'eng was placed in command of the Fifth Division under P'eng Te-huai's Third Army Corps. However, because of the heavy losses suffered in the early stages of the march, P'eng's division was lowered in designation to the 13th Regiment, which he commanded until the troops reached north Shensi in the fall of 1935. After the arrival of the Long March forces in Shensi, the Red Army underwent a reorganization; the First and Third Army Corps were merged and designated the First Army Corps. All of the units which had originally been under P'eng Te-huai's Third Army Corps were combined into the First Division under the new command structure; the exception was P'eng Hsueh-feng's 13th Regiment, which was redesignated the Fourth Division. P'eng became the division's political commissar, and in this capacity, in the early months of 1936, he participated in the Communists' thrust across the Yellow River into Shansi. Ostensibly an "eastward march" to engage Japanese troops in north China, the Communists in fact fought against the troops of the Shansi warlord-governor Yen Hsi-shan. However, after some initial successes (see under Liu Chih-tan), the Red Army was driven back across the Yellow River into Shensi. P'eng was then assigned for a brief period of study to the Red Army Academy, which had just re-opened (mid-1936) in north Shensi.

Sometime in the second half of 1936 the Party sent P'eng to Shansi to persuade Yen Hsi-shan to stop the civil war and to unite with the Communists in a common endeavor to resist the steady encroachments of the Japanese. Although details are not available on the success of P'eng's mission, it is noteworthy that it coincided with Yen's willingness to cooperate with a wide spectrum of political and military forces in north China to oppose the Japanese—notwithstanding the fact that the Communists had invaded a large portion of his province earlier in the year.[2] It is probable that P'eng was in contact with the many newly organized left-leaning and often Communist-infiltrated political and paramilitary organizations which were being formed with Yen's blessing (see under Po I-po). P'eng was in Taiyuan, the Shansi capital, at least until the end of 1936, and possibly as late as mid-1937 when the Sino-Japanese War began.

Immediately after war erupted, the Communists reorganized their units into the Eighth Route Army and moved eastward into Shansi to engage the Japanese. P'eng became head of the office (ts'an-mou-ch'u chang) directly subordinate to the Army's chief-of-staff, and concurrently head of the Eighth Route Army's Staff Office (pan-shih-ch'u chang) in Shansi. The latter was initially located in Taiyuan, but when it fell to the Japanese in November 1937, P'eng went south to Lin-fen where, under the auspices of the Staff Office, he established and became commandant of a training school. The school ran a nine-week course to instruct young cadres, both men and women, in the arts of guerrilla warfare. Sixty per cent of the instruction was devoted to military tactics and techniques, and the remainder to political subjects. U.S. military observer Evans Carlson visited the school at the end of 1937 and interviewed P'eng, whom he found to be "dynamic."[3]

On August 8, 1938, P'eng published an article in Chieh-fang (Liberation), the leading Party organ in Yenan, on work behind enemy lines. In the following month he was given an opportunity to put some of these principles into practice when he was placed in charge of a guerrilla detachment that moved from Shansi into T'ai-k'ang and Huai-yang hsien in east-central Honan to assist in the fighting against the Japanese. In Honan, P'eng's force was augmented by disaffected students and peasants as well as by former KMT troops who had been defeated by the Japanese at Kaifeng in mid-1938. Moving east during the next year, by June 1939 P'eng's unit became the Sixth Detachment of the New Fourth Army, whose forces were rapidly expanding. In 1940 the Sixth Detachment moved into northern Anhwei, establishing its headquarters at Ko-yang and increasing its size to about 6,400 men.[4] P'eng's work was praised by Mao Tse-tung, who in a May 1940 directive to the Southeast Party Bureau commented on the "determined struggle carried on by P'eng Hsueh-feng's detachment north of the Huai river."[5] Before mid-1940, when Ch'en I's New Fourth Army troops moved into north Kiangsu, P'eng's Sixth Detachment was the most powerful Communist unit north of the Yangtze. It was further strengthened in August 1940 when it linked up with another force (led by Huang K'o-ch'eng, q.v.), which had also originally been under the Eighth Route Army.

Following the reorganization of the New Fourth Army in early 1941 after the New Fourth Army Incident (see under Yeh T'ing), Ch'en I became acting commander of the entire army, while the army's six detachments plus Li Hsien-nien's (q.v.) guerrilla fighters were reorganized into seven divisions, all of them stationed in the Yangtze Plain north of the river. P'eng's Sixth Detachment now became the Fourth Division, controlling the Communists' North Huai Military District. The region was bounded by the Huai River on the south, by the Tientsin-Pukow Railroad on the west, by a line running from the Grand Canal to Hsu-chou, Kiangsu, on the north, and by the Grand Canal on the east.[6] P'eng was made the Fourth Division's commander and political commissar. During 1941 he relinquished the latter post to Teng Tzu-hui (q.v.), and about 1944 Chang Ai-p'ing (q.v.) took over as commander, probably to enable P'eng to take on heavier responsibilities in Honan and the Honan-Anhwei-Kiangsu border area, into which the Communist armies advanced, beginning in 1941. P'eng was largely responsible for expanding the Communist-held areas of Honan where he assumed duties in Party, military, and governmental affairs. In September 1944, after the KMT retreated before an offensive staged by General Hata Shunroku, head of the Japanese Expeditionary Forces in China, P'eng was killed resisting the Japanese in Honan.

P'eng was survived by his younger brother, P'eng Chih-chiu, who was studying medicine in Taiyuan in 1936 when his elder brother was there. Chih-chiu and former colleagues of P'eng Hsueh-feng (including Ch'en I), contributed essays on P'eng's career to biographies edited by Hua Ying-shen (*Chung-kuo kung-ch'an-tang lieh-shih chuan* [Biographies of CCP martyrs; Hong Kong, 1949], pp. 183–198). This source is richly supplemented by other sketches which appear in *Hung-ch'i p'iao-p'iao* (Red flag fluttering; Peking, 1957 [V, 156–171] and 1958 [IX, 65–75]).

1. *Hung-ch'i p'iao-p'iao* (Red flag fluttering; Peking, 1957), III, 46.
2. Donald G. Gillin, *Warlord Yen Hsi-shan in Shansi Province, 1911–1949* (Princeton, N.J., 1967), p. 253.
3. Evans Fordyce Carlson, *Twin Stars of China* (New York, 1940), pp. 62–64.
4. Chalmers A. Johnson, *Peasant Nationalism and Communist Power* (Stanford, Calif., 1962), pp. 127–128.
5. *Selected Works of Mao Tse-tung* (Peking, 1965), II, 434.
6. Johnson, p. 145.

P'eng P'ai

(1896–1929; Hai-feng hsien, Kwangtung). Founder, Hai-lu-feng Soviet; alternate member, CCP Politburo.

P'eng P'ai, one of the earliest members of the CCP, was the first Party leader of significance to devote himself to the organization of the peasantry. Working in his native province, he established a number of peasant organizations between 1923 and 1927. He was an important member of the KMT Peasants' Department and the first director of the department's Peasant Movement Training Institute when it was established in 1924. P'eng is best known as the founder of the earliest Chinese Soviet government, which he inaugurated in Hai-lu-feng, Kwangtung, in late 1927. He was elected to the Party Central Committee in 1927 and to the Politburo in the following year.

P'eng P'ai was born on October 22, 1896, into a leading landlord family of Hai-feng hsien on the Kwangtung coast. His family controlled the livelihood of about 1,500 peasants, whose lot was made all the more arduous by the unproductive soil they tilled. Hai-feng was also the home of the reformer-general Ch'en Chiung-ming, whose progressive rule permitted the tide of "new culture" to penetrate the region, and young P'eng soon emerged as a local revolutionary. Having begun a modern education he went to Tokyo in 1918 to spend the next three years as a student of political economy at Waseda University, where Li Ta-chao (q.v.) had also studied (1913–1916). Although P'eng came from a family of means, he apparently received some financial assistance from Ch'en Chiung-ming's government, which was then actively promoting study abroad.[1] During P'eng's years at Waseda the school was a hotbed of Japanese Socialist groups, which took a profound interest in agrarian problems. He reportedly became a socialist under their influence; he was a member of one group, the Kensetsu-sha Domei (Reformers' alliance), and was a close associate of one of its leaders, Takatsu Masamichi. The influence of the Waseda socialists, who gave priority to organizing agricultural cooperatives and peasant unions over organizing urban workers, probably shaped P'eng's subsequent career to a large extent.

After graduating in July 1921, P'eng returned to China, and he probably first went to Canton where he joined the CCP. Kwangtung province, still ruled by Ch'en Chiung-ming, was in many ways a comfortable locale for advocates of the political left. For example, Ch'en Chiung-ming had induced Ch'en Tu-hsiu (q.v.) to become commissioner of education in Kwangtung in late 1920, and early in the next year the latter had transferred his famous journal, *Hsin ch'ing-nien* (New youth) to Canton. Moreover, Ch'en Tu-hsiu quickly proceeded to establish small groups for the CCP and the Socialist Youth League. Ch'en departed Canton for Shanghai in August 1921 to assume the leadership of the newly founded CCP, but he left behind a core of young activists—some of whom were to be associated with P'eng P'ai in the stormy years ahead.

Returning to Hai-feng, P'eng immediately showed his radicalism in an article "Appealing to My Countrymen," published in September 1921 in the first issue of *Hsin Hai-feng* (New Hai-feng), the organ of the Hai-feng Students' Union, in which he called for the abolition of private property, law, government, and state. He rallied a group of outstanding student leaders in the district and formed the Society for the Study of Socialism, which may have been a cover for a unit of the Socialist Youth League.

P'eng soon became known to Governor Ch'en Chiung-ming, who on October 1 appointed him chief of the Bureau of Education in Hai-feng. Seizing this as an opportunity "to accomplish a social revolution through education," he directed his attention to organizing the students. On May 1, 1922, P'eng led the Hai-feng students in the district's first May Day parade. The local gentry regarded this as a "Red scare" and succeeded in pressuring Ch'en Chiung-ming to dismiss P'eng. On May 9 P'eng resigned from the Education Bureau, and in the same month he embarked on the bolder venture of agitating among the peasants. Rural China being generally on the edge of revolt, P'eng found a quick response, and on January 1, 1923, he inaugurated the Hai-feng Peasants' Association, with a membership of 20,000. It developed a variety of community services in education, arbitration, medical aid, and agricultural information.

Peasant associations spread to more and more districts as in one case after another they succeeded in forcing the landlords to reduce rent, so that by May 1923 the Kwangtung Peasants' Association was inaugurated, with P'eng P'ai as chairman of its Executive Committee. The local gentry and officials were uneasy, but they hesitated to suppress the movement because of the prestige of some of the leaders, many of whom came from fairly prominent families. However, in August 1923 the local gentry and officials struck at the peasant union in Hai-feng and arrested many of its leaders. P'eng then met with Ch'en Chiung-ming at Lao-lung in eastern Kwangtung to secure his support for rent reduction, the release of the arrested leaders, and the reorganization of the peasant union in Hai-feng. Ch'en, whose influence in Hai-feng was decisive although he had been expelled from Canton by Sun Yat-sen's allied forces, agreed to P'eng's petition in principle, wishing to benefit from P'eng's prestige among the Hai-feng peasants.

In March 1924 Ch'en Chiung-ming returned to Hai-feng, and was persuaded by local officials and the gentry to suppress the peasant union in view of its close relation to the Canton government of Sun Yat-sen, to which Ch'en himself was hostile. On March 17, 1924, Ch'en ordered the peasant union dissolved; P'eng P'ai and others left Hai-feng for Canton, leaving a few leaders to operate underground in Hai-feng, including P'eng's elder brother, P'eng Han-yuan. It should be noted that P'eng's activities in Hai-feng at that time appear to have been outside the main concern of the Party Center, and there is no evidence that he received assistance from the Party headquarters. The CCP was then focused chiefly on the labor movement, and it was not until later that intensive work was begun among the peasantry.

While these events were taking place, the KMT and the CCP were moving toward a period of close cooperation. In the process of working out a reorganization of the KMT under the guidance of Soviet adviser Michael Borodin, Sun Yat-sen had agreed to the organization of the peasantry as one source of support for the national revolution. Accordingly, immediately after the First KMT Congress, held in Canton in January 1924, the Peasants' Department was set up (February) under the KMT Central Executive Committee. The department was initially headed by the prominent Communist Lin Po-ch'ü (q.v.). When P'eng arrived a month later, he was made secretary of the department upon the recommendation of Lin. Writing many years later, Chiang Kai-shek asserted that despite many changes in the directorship of the department, it was P'eng who dominated it.[2]

One of the first acts of the Peasants' Department was to recommend the establishment of the Peasant Movement Training Institute. This was approved by the KMT Central Executive Committee on June 30, 1924, and a few days later the institute opened under P'eng's direction. From rather modest beginnings—P'eng's first class (July 3–August 21) had only 33 graduates—the institute expanded to a graduation class of 318 in the sixth and final term (May–October 1926), when Mao Tse-tung was the director. In total, the institute turned out 771 graduates; during the first three terms the students all came from Kwangtung, but later there were many Hunanese (presumably because of Mao's influence), and by the last term the institute was drawing students from all parts of China. The directorship of the institute passed from one Communist to another; from P'eng it went to Lo Ch'i-yuan, Juan Hsiao-hsien, T'an Chih-t'ang, Lo Ch'i-yuan (again), and finally to Mao. The faculty and guest lecturers read like a checklist of the early Communist elite and included Hsiao Ch'u-nü, Ch'ü Chiu-pai, Lin Po-ch'ü, Chang T'ai-lei, Teng Chung-hsia, Chou En-lai, Li Li-san, Wu Yü-chang, and Yun Tai-ying (qq.v.). Many of the graduates took part in the Northern Expedition as peasant organizers, and a number of them later became prominent members of the CCP, for example, Wang Shou-tao and Mao Tse-min (Mao Tse-tung's younger brother). Mainly because of Mao's association with the Peasant Institute, orthodox Communist historians have written about it frequently. In doing so, however, they have normally inflated Mao's role and underplayed P'eng's endeavors.

P'eng continued as the secretary of the KMT Peasants' Department until about November 1924, when he was replaced by another young Communist, Lo Ch'i-yuan. (A few years later, after P'eng's death in 1929, Lo succeeded P'eng as director of the CCP Peasants' Committee.) However, P'eng remained a key member of the department, along with two other Communists, Juan Hsiao-hsien and T'an Chih-t'ang, while the department was headed by Ch'en Kung-po (q.v.). Among other duties in the 1924–25 period, P'eng traveled from place to place in Kwangtung to help organize peasant associations, to supervise the work of special delegates sent out by the department to various peasant associations, and to train these special delegates. These endeavors proved to be of use in February 1925 when the KMT took the first step to secure its Kwangtung revolutionary base by sending the First Eastern Expedition against Ch'en Chiung-ming in the East River area. From Canton P'eng carried on secret communications with his underground comrades in Hai-feng, who helped mobilize peasant support for the KMT forces. (Three months later, in the course of a speech delivered in Canton, Chiang Kai-shek acknowledged the aid which P'eng's peasants had given to his army.[3]) P'eng arrived in Hai-feng on March 9, after Ch'en Chiung-ming had been expelled, and reassembled his friends to reorganize the peasant movement. The Hai-feng peasant association was re-established and its members put forward the demand for a 25 per cent rent reduction and organized a self-defense corps. The First Eastern Expedition was only partially successful; in June 1925, when the Canton government was preoccupied with the revolts of the Yunnan and Kwangsi generals, Sun Yat-sen's erstwhile allies, the landowners in Hai-feng and neighboring hsien (alarmed by the government's Bolshevik tendencies) struck back at the peasant unions, butchering more than 70 of their members. P'eng was probably busy there when the First Congress of the Kwangtung Peasants' Association opened in early May 1925, because there is no evidence of his being present at the congress.

In October 1925 the KMT launched the Second Eastern Expedition in the East River area. In mid-October they occupied Waichow (Hui-chou), Ch'en Chiung-ming's stronghold, and by early November they had reached Swatow via Hai-feng and Lu-feng (known collectively as Hai-lu-feng), incorporating the entire region into the area of the revolutionary government's jurisdiction. The peasant underground once again aided the KMT armies. On October 25 a peasant conference was held at Hai-feng; P'eng called for vengeance for the 70 slain peasant leaders and for an unprecedented reduction of rent. He remained there for most of the next year, and in his capacity as secretary of the CCP Hai-lu-feng District Committee, he stimulated the radicalism of the peasant associations. In May 1926, he attended the Second Congress of the Kwangtung Peasants' Association[4] and was named director of the association's office in the East River area. Two months later, when the Northern Expedition began, P'eng remained behind in Kwangtung, being in charge of the entire peasant movement in the province as head of the KMT Kwangtung Peasants' Department. He was concurrently a member of the CCP organization in Kwangtung, then headed by

Ch'en Yen-nien (q.v.). However, toward the end of 1926 he led a few hundred peasants from Kwangtung to Hankow to join Ho Lung's troops garrisoning the city.

P'eng was present in Wuhan for the historic Fifth CCP Congress in April–May 1927 (see under Ch'en Tu-hsiu), where he joined with Mao Tse-tung and Lo Ch'i-yuan in arguing (unsuccessfully) for a rather extreme policy in terms of the confiscation of land. At this same time he also became a member of the Provisional Executive Committee of the newly founded All-China Peasants' Association, which included members of the left wing of the KMT, as well as such prominent Communists as Mao Tse-tung. The congress and the formation of the peasant association followed by only a few days Chiang Kai-shek's coup against the Communists on April 12. The Communists in Wuhan were able to maintain their alliance with the left-wing KMT, but by mid-July this tenuous arrangement collapsed—thus setting the stage for the famous Nanchang Uprising on August 1 (see under Yeh T'ing). P'eng took part in planning the revolt, and immediately after its initial success he was named to the 25-member Revolutionary Committee, as well as a commissar of the Workers' and Peasants' Committee (ostensibly a cabinet post under the Revolutionary Committee).[5] However, the uprising was quickly crushed, and the Communist military units began a southward march into Kwangtung.

While these events were taking place in the Yangtze Valley in the spring and summer of 1927, the Nationalists had attacked the Communists in Canton on April 15, only three days after Chiang Kai-shek's anti-Communist coup in Shanghai. As a consequence, the Communists in Hai-lu-feng lost contact with the Kwangtung branch of the CCP Central Committee. The Hai-lu-feng Communists set up a special organ, the East River Special Committee (Tung-chiang t'e-pieh wei-yuan-hui), which organized a Workers' and Peasants' Party Relief Army. This force staged an uprising on May 1 and seized power in Hai-feng; they soon lost the town (May 9) to the KMT army but entrenched themselves in the surrounding villages. In mid-August, when the Hai-lu-feng Communists received news of the pending arrival of the Yeh T'ing–Ho Lung forces, which had been marching south from Nanchang, as well as the Party's instruction to stage an Autumn Harvest Uprising, they made a second bid for power on September 8 in Hai-lu-feng and set up a Workers' and Peasants' Dictatorship. But toward the end of the month anti-Communist troops again forced their withdrawal to the rural villages and almost simultaneously they received the news of the disastrous defeat of the Yeh-Ho forces at Swatow and Ch'ao-chou. The Hai-lu-feng Communists sent out patrols which were able to round up about 800 men from the remnants of the Yeh-Ho troops. These men were soon organized into the Second Division of the Workers' and Peasants' Revolutionary Army and preparations were begun for a new insurrection. On November 1, KMT troops were withdrawn from the Hai-lu-feng area because of the impending showdown between Li Chi-shen and Chang Fa-k'uei in Canton. The peasant corps quickly grasped this opportunity and seized the towns and villages in the area. In mid-November "soviet" governments were established in Hai-feng and Lu-feng, and although the term Hai-lu-feng Soviet is used in most histories, there was no government organ which officially embraced the two hsien. In fact, however, they were both controlled by the East River Special Committee of the CCP, whose secretary was P'eng P'ai and in whose hands political power was concentrated. The Special Committee carried out an extreme "left" policy of land confiscation and a reign of terror against the landlords, which the CCP Politburo ratified at its November 1927 meeting in Shanghai.

P'eng and his colleagues in Hai-lu-feng were just in the process of gaining control in Hai-lu-feng when they received a request from Chang T'ai-lei to send troops to take part in the uprising in Canton. The Canton Commune was established on December 11 but was too short-lived (less than three days) for P'eng to render assistance. He was, however, elected *in absentia* to be commissar of Land. Immediately after the failure in Canton, the remnant troops there, led by Yang Yin, Hsu Hsiang-ch'ien (qq.v.), and others, reorganized their men into the Fourth Division of the Red Army and marched to Hai-lu-feng. The 1,200 men of the Fourth Division were thus added to the 800 men in the Second Division in Hai-lu-feng. However, these combined units were unable to withstand a major attack in late February 1928, led by General Yü Han-mou. The Second and Fourth Divisions were virtually wiped out during the ensuing weeks, and thus the Hai-lu-feng Soviet came to an effective end as a governmental unit. However, scattered bands in the area later joined together and, during the Sino-Japanese War, were known as the East River Column (see under Ku Ta-ts'un).

After the suppression of the Hai-lu-feng Soviet, P'eng and Yang Yin fled to Shanghai. In the summer of 1928 the CCP held its Sixth Congress in Moscow, and though it appears that neither of them were there, they were both elected members of the Central Committee. P'eng was also made a member of the Politburo, and Yang was made an alternate member. In addition, P'eng became head of the newly created Peasants' Committee in the CCP national organization. At the local level he was made a member of the Kiangsu Provincial Committee and the secretary of its Peasants' Department. He is purported to have made a secret visit to Hai-feng in early 1929, but most of his time during this period was spent in the Shanghai underground. On August 24, 1929, having been betrayed by Pai Hsin, a turncoat Communist, P'eng was arrested with Yang Yin, Yen Ch'ang-i, and several others. A week later he was executed.

In the years that followed P'eng has been commemorated by the Communists as one of their greatest revolutionary "martyrs." To honor P'eng and Yang Yin, the "P'eng-Yang Infantry School" was established in the Central Soviet Region in Kiangsi where Mao Tse-tung and Chu Te had their headquarters in the early 1930's. In the 1950's and 1960's P'eng was often mentioned as a model for youths to follow: for example, in *Chung-kuo ch'ing-nien* (China youth, no. 7, April 1, 1963), he was praised for having led the peasantry against the "feudal landlords" even though he himself had been born to wealth and privilege. P'eng was married to Ts'ai Su-p'ing in 1912. She was arrested by the KMT soon after the defeat in Hai-lu-feng and executed a month later after giving birth to her third son. In 1923 P'eng took a student named Hsu Yü-ch'ing as his mistress. She later moved to Hai-feng and lived with P'eng and his wife. After P'eng's death, Hsu reportedly went to a secret soviet area near Swatow. In 1962, and twice in 1964, the Communist press reported that P'eng's mother had attended meetings in Canton in connection with commemorative meetings to honor "old revolutionaries."

There is a relative wealth of information on P'eng P'ai's life and career, including his own study, *Hai-lu-feng nung-min yun-tung chi* (The peasants' movement in Hai-lu-feng; Canton, 1926). Hou Feng is perhaps the most important Communist biographer of P'eng. His short sketch published in the fifth volume of *Hung-ch'i p'iao-p'iao* (Red flag fluttering; Peking, 1957) was expanded into a book entitled *P'eng P'ai lieh-shih chuan-lueh* (A brief biography of Martyr P'eng P'ai; Canton, 1959). This is usefully supplemented by Chung I-mou's *Hai-lu-feng nung-min yun-tung* (Peasant movements in Hai-lu-feng; Canton, 1957). The best study of the Hai-lu-feng Soviet, which is the major source for this biography, is Eto Shinkichi's two-part article in *The China Quarterly* entitled "Hai-lu-feng: The First Chinese Soviet Government" (nos. 8 and 9, October–December 1961 and January–March 1962). Eto's article draws upon the above-mentioned sources, as well as a host of other primary and secondary sources on both the Hai-lu-feng region and P'eng P'ai's career.

---

1. Winston Hsieh, "The Ideas and Ideals of a Warlord; Ch'en Chiung-ming (1878–1933)," *Papers on China,* from seminars at Harvard University (Cambridge, Mass., 1962), XVI, 210.

2. Chiang Chung-cheng (Chiang Kai-shek), *Soviet Russia in China: A Summing Up at Seventy* (New York, 1957), p. 31.

3. Stuart Schram, *Mao Tse-tung* (New York, 1966), p. 82.

4. Miao Min, *Fang Chih-min* (Peking, 1962), p. 42.

5. C. Martin Wilbur, "The Ashes of Defeat," *The China Quarterly*, no. 18:11, 48; Wei Hung-yun, ed., *"Pa-i" ch'i-i* (The "August First" uprising; Wuhan, 1957), pp. 9, 14–15.

P'eng Shao-hui

(1910–   ; Hunan). Early military leader; deputy chief-of-staff, PLA.

P'eng Shao-hui, a veteran military officer, took part in the Communist-led insurrection at P'ing-chiang, northeast Hunan, in July 1928. Led by P'eng Te-huai, T'eng Tai-yuan, and Huang Kung-lueh (qq.v.), the P'ing-chiang insurrectionists immediately established the Fifth Red Army (see under T'eng Tai-yuan). The Communists were not able to consolidate their gains in the P'ing-chiang area, and thus the major elements of the Fifth Army were driven south into the Ching-kang Mountains, where they joined forces with Mao Tse-tung and Chu Te. However, a small nucleus from the Fifth Army was left behind under the command of Huang Kung-lueh. P'eng Shao-hui, among those who remained behind, was made a company commander in Huang's forces.

In March 1929 P'eng was wounded during a skirmish in the Liu-yang area (not far south of P'ing-chiang) and had to retire from active military life for a time. By the early spring of 1933, while commanding the First Division of P'eng Te-huai's Third Army Corps, he was wounded again during an attack on Kuang-ch'ang in east Kiangsi. (A photograph of P'eng in the *JMJP*, August 26, 1966, shows him to be missing his left arm, a loss that may date back to his days in Kiangsi or Hunan.) In September 1934, he fought together with Hsiao Hua (q.v.) in operations in southeast Kiangsi led by P'eng Te-huai.[1] In the following month the Communist armies left Kiangsi on the Long March, and it is probable that P'eng Shao-hui, like the others mentioned above, joined in the year-long retreat to north Shensi.

When war with Japan broke out in mid-1937, P'eng was assigned to Ho Lung's 120th Division, one of the three major divisions of the Communists' Eighth Route Army activated at that time. Throughout the war the division maintained a base in the Shansi-Suiyuan border area; within this large region the division's 358th Brigade was headquartered in northwest Shansi under the command of Hsiao K'o (q.v.). However, when Hsiao moved eastward during the winter of 1938–39, P'eng remained behind to assume command of the 358th Brigade. Throughout this early war period, the Communist armies in Shansi had been working in cooperation against the Japanese with guerrilla units of the "Shansi New Army." The "New Army," though commanded by KMT member Hsu Fan-t'ing and ostensibly under the direct control of Shansi warlord Yen Hsi-shan, was heavily infiltrated with Communist officers. Yen tolerated this situation for a time, but by 1939 he began to fear the growing strength of the Communists in Shansi, and as a consequence he took a number of provocative political and military steps to diminish Communist control. As a consequence of these maneuvers, Hsu Fan-t'ing defected in December 1939 to the Communist side, taking some 3,000 of his men with him. P'eng, as well as his political commissar, Lo Kuei-po (q.v.), played an important role in inducing Fan to defect,[2] and this defection, in turn, led to the establishment of the Communists' Shansi-Suiyuan Liberated Region (see under Lin Feng). P'eng appears to have continued his guerrilla operations in Shansi for a few more years, but by 1943 he was identified as head of the seventh branch of the Anti-Japanese Military and Political Academy (K'ang-ta) located near Yenan in north Shensi.[3]

P'eng remained in the border area after hostilities ceased in August 1945 and participated in the Communist takeover in Shansi, which was largely carried out by Ho Lung's army. In 1946 P'eng's immediate superior was Wang Chen (q.v.), chief-of-staff of Ho's joint command over the territories of the Shansi-Suiyuan and the Shensi-Kansu-Ninghsia Military Regions. In late 1946 Wang and P'eng led attacks upon Yen Hsi-shan forces, which brought new territory under Communist control. Within a year or so, when Ho Lung began to move farther to the northwest, P'eng apparently came under the command of Hsu Hsiang-ch'ien, who from 1947 to 1948 was in charge of the Shansi-Hopeh-Shantung-Honan Military Region, which included the southern part of Shansi. Hsu, like P'eng, had belonged to Ho's staff throughout the Sino-Japanese War. In 1947, when Ho went west, the northern military commands were reorganized and Shansi was placed under Nieh Jung-chen's North China PLA. The reorganization brought Hsu Hsiang-ch'ien (and presumably P'eng) over to Nieh Jung-chen's staff. In the fall of 1948, when the Communists captured Taiyuan, the Shansi capital, P'eng was identified as the commander of the Seventh Column of forces under Hsu.

Although P'eng was a field commander of considerable stature when the PRC came into existence in 1949, he does not appear to have received any position of prominence at that time. Apparently, however, he remained in the north-northwest where he had campaigned for many years, and within half a decade had risen quite high within the PLA hierarchy. By 1952 P'eng was serving as chief-of-staff of both the Northwest Military Region (NWMR) and the First Field Army, headquartered in Lanchow, Kansu. He continued in these posts until 1954 when he was promoted to deputy commander of the NWMR, holding this post until the Region was abolished in 1955. In the interim, in January 1953, P'eng received his first civil position when he was named to membership on the Northwest Administrative Committee (NWAC). The NWAC, under the nominal leadership of P'eng Te-huai (then in Korea), was the governing organization for the five provinces of Shensi, Ninghsia, Kansu, Tsinghai and Sinkiang.

By 1954–55 the regional governments and military regions were disbanded, a move coinciding with the formation of the constitutional government at the First NPC in September 1954. Although P'eng remained in the northwest until early 1955, he received his first assignment at the national level when he was named to membership on the National Defense Council, the military advisory organ created at the close of the First NPC. He was renamed to this position in April 1959 and January 1965. A far more important assignment was given to P'eng following his transfer to the capital in 1955; by June of that year he was identified as a deputy chief-of-staff of the PLA. In this capacity he has served under three chiefs-of-staff, Su Yü, Huang K'o-ch'eng, and Lo Jui-ch'ing (qq.v.). Not long after receiving the staff appointment, the PRC awarded (September 1955) military orders and personal military ranks to the officers of the PLA. P'eng received all three of the top national military honors (the Orders of August First, Independence and Freedom, and Liberation), awarded for service from the founding of the Red Army in 1927 to the eve of the Korean War in 1950. At the same time he was made a colonel-general.

By late 1956 P'eng was holding three other positions within the PLA Headquarters, the most important of which was a deputy directorship of the General Training Department, where he served under Liu Po-ch'eng until November 1957 and under Hsiao K'o thereafter. Subordinate to the Training Department he also became (by November 1956) director of the Sub-department of Military Science and Regulations as well as deputy inspector-general of military training. He was identified in the latter two posts when he gave a talk on scientific advancements in military units on the eve of the National Conference of Activists in the Dissemination of Scientific Knowledge. P'eng's association with the General Training Department was apparently short-lived —he was last identified with this important department in early 1958.

In 1959 P'eng was elected as a PLA deputy to the Second NPC, and at the close of the first session (April 1959) was named to membership on the NPC Standing Committee, the committee responsible for the work of the NPC when not in full session. In 1964 he was again elected as a PLA deputy to the Third NPC and, at the close of the first session of the Third NPC in January 1965, was once more named to membership on the Standing Committee. P'eng first went abroad in September 1963 when he led a military delegation to Sweden for a two-week visit. While in Stockholm he conferred with the Swedish defense minister.

Since his transfer to Peking in 1955, P'eng has made frequent public appearances typical of top PLA generals. He is very often on hand for rallies marking important military holidays (such as the founding date of the PLA on August 1) or for receptions given by military attachés stationed in Peking. More important, he has taken part on occasion in talks with important visiting delegations, an instance of which occurred in November 1964 when he was an official participant in the talks with Malian President Modibo Keita. He has also participated in many military conferences, such as a militia political work conference in Peking (November 1964) at which P'eng spoke.

In private life P'eng is married to Chang Wei, but nothing is known of her antecedents.

———

1. *Kung-ch'ing-t'uan, wo-te mu-ch'in* (The youth corps, my mother; Peking, 1958), p. 10.
2. *Hung-ch'i p'iao-p'iao* (Red flag fluttering; Peking, 1957), V, 235–251.
3. *Chung-kuo ch'ing-nien pao* (China youth news), September 16, 1960.

P'eng T'ao

(1913–1961; P'o-yang, Kiangsi). Former north China youth and Party leader; former minister, Ministry of Chemical Industry; alternate member, CCP Central Committee.

P'eng T'ao was a youth and Party leader in north China in the thirties and forties. In the early years of the PRC he served as a Party official in southwest China, after which he became an important economic planner and administrator in Peking. He was born in P'o-yang on the eastern shore of Lake P'o-yang in north Kiangsi. According to his obituary, which is the source for most of the pre-1949 data on his career, he began his "patriotic activities" as a youth, joining the Communist Youth League in 1927 and the CCP in 1932. In the following year he was engaged in Youth League activities as the secretary of the League Work Committee in Chang-chia-k'ou (Kalgan), the capital of Chahar. During the next few years he organized revolutionary activities in Peking and Tientsin, work that brought him into association with Huang Ching (q.v.), one of the most important Communist operatives in those two cities in the early and mid-thirties. In an article written under the name P'eng Wen-lung, P'eng revealed that he had spent some time in jail in Shanghai during his younger years.[1]

Possibly under instructions from the CCP, P'eng was enrolled as a student in 1935 at Fu-jen (Catholic) University in Peking. On December 9, 1935, large-scale student demonstrations broke out in Peking in opposition to Nationalist policies vis-à-vis Japan, policies that the students felt had failed to halt Japanese encroachments into north China. These demonstrations marked the beginning of what Communist histories describe as the December Ninth Movement. At this time P'eng was associated with the Peking Students' Federation, which had been formed secretly in October 1935. It is uncertain whether he took part in the December Ninth demonstrations, but Communist accounts claim that he was involved in planning for even larger demonstrations staged one week later, planning work that included colleagues Huang Ching, Yao I-lin (q.v.), and Miss Kuo Ming-ch'iu (see under Lin Feng, her husband). According to the Communist account, after the second demonstrations (December 16), the dean of Peking Normal University was sent to negotiate with the Students' Federation. Together with Huang Ching and Yao I-lin, P'eng took part in these unsuccessful talks.[2] (For further information on the December Ninth Movement, see under Li Ch'ang.)

It is not clear if P'eng remained as a student in Peking after the events of late 1935, but by the beginning of the Sino-Japanese War (July 1937) he was assigned as a Party official in the Shansi-Hopeh border area, which was under the jurisdiction of Liu Po-ch'eng's (q.v.) 129th Division of the Communist Eighth Route Army. His first post was as secretary of the Party's West Hopeh Local Committee in the T'ai-hang Mountain area on the Shansi-Hopeh border where he was secretary of the Party's Wu-hsiang (hsien) Local Committee in east-central Shansi. His subsequent wartime posts included membership on the T'ai-hang Region Party Committee and the directorship of the Committee's Departments of Popular Movements (*min-yun*) and Propaganda. His obituary credits him with "distinguished contributions" to the mobilization of the masses, to anti-Japanese guerrilla warfare behind enemy lines, and to the establishment and consolidation of bases in areas largely controlled by the Japanese.

P'eng spent part of the war years in Yenan (c.1942–1945) where he was on close terms with Party elder Hsu T'e-li (q.v.). Hsu was then president of the Natural Sciences Institute (*Tzu-jan k'o-hsueh yuan*) and it appears that P'eng also worked there.[3] After hostilities ended in 1945 P'eng returned to the T'ai-hang Mountain area where he became political commissar of the Third Column in the forces led by Liu Po-ch'eng and Teng Hsiao-p'ing. The Liu-Teng forces pushed southward into central China in the late forties in a move coordinated with the Communist army in east China led by Ch'en I. During this southward drive P'eng served briefly (c.1948–49) as secretary of the Party's West Anhwei Committee. In the latter half of 1949 Liu's field army moved into southwest China, but at this juncture P'eng was detached from military service and sent to Peking to be deputy director of the Tax Bureau of the Peking municipal government.

After less than a year in Peking P'eng was reassigned in mid-1950 to Szechwan where he was to remain for the next four years. Szechwan was unique among Chinese provinces in that it was divided for administrative purposes (until August 1952) into four sectors—north, east, south, and west Szechwan. P'eng was assigned to South Szechwan where the government apparatus was known as the South Szechwan People's Administrative Office (SSPAO), with its capital at Lu-chou (Lu-hsien) on the Min River. He became a member of the SSPAO in July 1950 as well as head of its Finance and Economics Committee. From 1950 to 1952 he was also second secretary of the South Szechwan CCP Committee and the deputy political commissar of the South Szechwan Military District. P'eng was probably the second most important official in south Szechwan, politically outranked only by Li Ta-chang (q.v.), who was the head of the SSPAO, the political commissar, and probably the Party first secretary.

In addition to his assignments in south Szechwan, P'eng had responsibilities in the governmental administration for the entire southwest area—the Southwest Military and Administrative Committee (SWMAC). From the formation of the SWMAC under the chairmanship of Liu Po-ch'eng in July 1950, P'eng was a SWMAC member and in 1951 he was also appointed to membership on the SWMAC's Land Reform Committee, which was chaired by Chang Chi-ch'un (q.v.). P'eng continued in both posts following the reorganization of the SWMAC into the Southwest Administrative Committee in February 1953. Following the dissolution of the four administrative areas of Szechwan in August 1952, P'eng was transferred from Lu-chou to Chungking where the capital of the SWMAC–SWAC was located. There he became a member of the Chungking branch of the All-China Federation of Trade Unions (ACFTU) and from 1953 to 1954 he was also second secretary of the Chungking CCP Committee. In the latter post he served under Secretary Ts'ao Ti-ch'iu, who was also the Chungking mayor (and, in 1965, the Shanghai mayor).

In 1954 P'eng made his first trip abroad when he attended May Day celebrations in Moscow as a member of an ACFTU delegation. Not long afterward he was transferred to Peking where he became (October 1954) a vice-chairman of the State Planning Commission headed by Li Fu-ch'un, one of Peking's top economic specialists. During a partial government reorganization in May 1956 the Ministry of Heavy Industry was abolished, with its functions divided between three new ministries, one of them the Ministry of Chemical Industry. P'eng was appointed as the minister (and retained the post until his death in 1961), while at the same time continuing as a vice-chairman of the State Planning Commission.

Despite the importance of his positions in the national bureaucracy, P'eng was infrequently mentioned in the Chinese press in the late fifties. Nonetheless, at the Party's Eighth National Congress (second session) in May 1958, he was elected an alternate member of the Party Central Committee. The Party Congress endorsed the economic Great Leap Forward, which had been launched earlier in 1958. It was in the spirit of the Great Leap that P'eng wrote "We Want to Wrestle with All Capitalistic Countries in the Chemical Industry" for the *JMJP* of May 29, 1958, an article that appeared just six days after the Congress closed. He is also the author of an article entitled "Build Up Our Agro-chemical Industry" for the Party's leading journal, *Hung-ch'i* (Red flag, issue of February 1, 1959). In November–December 1958 P'eng was among the Central Committee members in Wuhan for the Sixth Party Plenum, at which the excesses of the Great Leap Forward were partially cut back. In the following year he was a member of the preparatory committee for a large national conference of "advanced" workers in industrial fields, and when the conference was held in October–November 1959 he served on the presidium (steering committee). A month before the conference was held, the central government underwent another reorganization; P'eng was dropped from his vice-chairmanship in the State Planning Commission, but just six months later (March 1960) he was reappointed. In November of 1960 he made his second trip abroad, leading a chemical industry delegation to Poland where his group remained for three weeks.

P'eng remained active until October 1961 when he made his last public appearance. One month later, on November 14, 1961, he died of lung cancer in Peking. At the time of his death he was the head of a major economic ministry, a vice-chairman in the PRC's most important economic planning body, and an alternate member of the Party Central Committee. P'eng was accorded the honors befitting a senior Party official. His funeral committee, headed by Chou En-lai, included a number of colleagues from his student days in Peking, and a lengthy eulogy was delivered at a memorial

service by Li Hsueh-feng, another veteran of the Party who had worked in north China in the thirties and forties.

1. *Hung-ch'i p'iao-p'iao* (Red flag fluttering; Peking, 1959), X, 28.
2. Chiang Nan-hsiang *et al., The Roar of a Nation* (Peking, 1963), pp. 135, 141.
3. *Hung-ch'i p'iao-p'iao,* X, 25–43.

P'eng Te-huai

(1898– ; Hsiang-t'an hsien, Hunan). Veteran Red Army commander; former minister of National Defense; member, CCP Politburo.

P'eng Te-huai is one of the greatest military figures in the history of the Chinese Communist movement. He led an uprising against the Nationalist Army in 1928 and soon after joined forces with Red Army units led by Chu Te and Mao Tse-tung. Building up his guerrilla forces during the next two years, P'eng captured and held Changsha for a few days in mid-1930. For the next four years he was among the key Red Army commanders who fought against the Nationalists' Annihilation Campaigns in Kiangsi, and in 1934–35 he took an equally important part in the Long March to Shensi. P'eng was deputy commander of the Eighth Route Army under Chu Te during the Sino-Japanese War, and during the ensuing civil war and the formative years of the PRC he continued to be the number two man under Chu in the PLA. P'eng commanded the Chinese forces which fought in the Korean War, and from 1954 until his political fall in 1959 he served as minister of National Defense.

P'eng was born in a village in Hsiang-t'an hsien, Hunan, the same hsien where Mao Tse-tung was born. According to an account of his early life which P'eng gave to Edgar Snow, he came from a family of rich peasants.[1] He began his education in his ninth year, but because of a family dispute he soon left home, and for the next few years he earned his living through a series of menial jobs. Penniless by his 16th year, he returned home, but he soon got into trouble for participating in the looting of the rice provisions of a rich merchant. For this act he was forced to flee, after which he joined the provincial army. Soon afterwards, in Snow's words, "he was to become a revolutionary." In his 18th year he became a platoon commander and was involved in an abortive plot to overthrow the Hunan governor. His involvement in still another plot against the next Hunan governor resulted in his arrest and imprisonment. He was soon released, and after visiting home again he re-enlisted in the army.

Upon rejoining the army, P'eng was given a commission and sent to a military school in

Hunan. After graduation he became a battalion commander in units led by Lu Ti-p'ing, who later became a prominent KMT officer. At this juncture, approximately at the same time as the May Fourth Movement of 1919, P'eng began to take an interest in the writings of the reformers Liang Ch'i-ch'ao and K'ang Yu-wei. He also read Ch'en Tu-hsiu's influential journal *Hsin ch'ing-nien* (New Youth) and became acquainted with Sun Yat-sen's famous "three people's principles," works by Kautsky, and the *Communist Manifesto*. In P'eng's words, as quoted by Snow, after "reading the *Communist Manifesto* I dropped my pessimism and began working with a new conviction that society could be changed." As a consequence, though he himself was not yet a CCP member, he enlisted the aid of young Communists in his troops, "began Marxist courses of political training, and organized soldiers' committees."

By the time the Northern Expedition began in mid-1926, P'eng was commanding the First Regiment of the Fifth Independent Division, one of the units in an army led by T'ang Sheng-chih. T'ang had enlisted his forces in the KMT armies just before the Northern Expedition began. At this time P'eng became acquainted with Huang Kung-lueh (q.v.), a graduate of the Whampoa Military Academy and, like P'eng, a native of Hsiang-t'an. In the latter part of 1926 and the year 1927, both men took part in the many campaigns conducted by T'ang Sheng-chih in central China, and during this period Huang joined the CCP. By the early part of 1928, now serving in Ho Chien's 35th Army, Huang and P'eng were posted in northern Hunan to the west of Tung-t'ing Lake. In April, with Huang as his sponsor, P'eng joined the CCP. At about that same time their unit was transferred to the region around P'ing-chiang and Liu-yang in northeast Hunan, the same area that had only recently witnessed some of the Communist-led Autumn Harvest Uprisings.

In late July 1928, allegedly in defiance of orders to suppress the local peasantry, P'eng and Huang, with an assist from CCP peasant organizer T'eng Tai-yuan (q.v.), staged a revolt known in Communist annals as the P'ing-chiang Uprising. They immediately set up the Fifth Red Army, with P'eng as the commander and T'eng as the Party representative. After some heavy fighting in the P'ing-chiang area, it was decided to leave Huang with a portion of the Fifth Army to continue the struggle, while P'eng and T'eng withdrew southward with the rest of the army. By the latter part of the year they had joined forces with Mao Tse-tung and Chu Te at Chingkangshan on the Hunan-Kiangsi border. This historic meeting brought together the two men who were to be the greatest Red Army commanders for the next quarter of a century and the man who would soon become the leader of the CCP. At that moment in history, however, P'eng's

Fifth Army and the Chu-Mao Fourth Army were no more than an ill-equipped band of a few thousand men, and a few weeks later, in early 1929 Chu and Mao began a retreat eastward. P'eng was left to guard the Chingkangshan stronghold, but soon afterwards he too was forced to evacuate the area. According to his own account, as related by author-journalist Agnes Smedley, his 6,000 men were quickly reduced to about 700 by KMT attacks on the Chingkangshan base.[2]

P'eng marched east from Chingkangshan to Juichin, located in southeast Kiangsi not far from the Fukien border. There he met again with Mao and Chu in the spring of 1929. At a strategy meeting it was decided that the Chu-Mao Fourth Army would concentrate on building a base embracing central and south Kiangsi and west Fukien, while P'eng would return to the Chingkangshan area and attempt to expand northward to encompass parts of Hunan and Hupeh. For much of the next year P'eng tried with some success to carry out this assignment. By the early months of 1930 Li Li-san (q.v.), then the dominant figure of the CCP, was preparing his grand scheme, which envisioned large-scale uprisings in the major cities in the Yangtze River Valley. Li, operating from the Party headquarters in Shanghai, arranged for CCP activists in Wuhan, Changsha, and the other great central China cities to organize support from workers, but he placed his major trust in the rural-based guerrilla armies which were to attack the cities.

By the early summer of 1930 P'eng's troops were arrayed along the borders of northwest Kiangsi and northeast Hunan. From Li Li-san's point of view, this was a propitious moment to launch his attacks; there was widespread turmoil throughout the nation and Chiang Kai-shek was then engaged in a divisive war against several powerful warlord armies. The general turmoil, for example, was reflected in reports from American diplomats who, during the year 1930, filed scores of dispatches about the disruptive activities of "bandits and Reds" in the Yangtze Valley. P'eng and his troops were mentioned on several occasions; one report of July 6 from the American minister noted that all Americans in Yueh-yang (Yochow), located in northeast Hunan on the Yangtze River, had been evacuated a few days earlier immediately preceding the "peaceful taking of that city by P'eng . . . , notorious Communist, and his soldiers and followers roughly numbering 6,000."[3] Shortly before this, in June, P'eng's Fifth Army had been reorganized into the Third Army Corps, and the Chu-Mao forces were redesignated the First Army Corps. These and similar reorganizations of other Red Army units were part of Li Li-san's plans for his wide-ranging attacks. The overall plan called for P'eng to occupy Changsha, the Hunan capital, and then to proceed north to assist in the assaults on the Wuhan cities. This was to be coordinated with a Chu-Mao attack on Nanchang, the Kiangsi capital.

Of the various assaults on cities launched under the Li Li-san leadership, only the one led by P'eng met with any measure of success. At the end of July 1930 P'eng's 10,000-odd troops captured Changsha with little resistance from Hunanese provincial troops who were poorly disciplined, demoralized, and weary from their recent battles with warlord troops from Kwangsi.[4] Exultant from this initial success, the Communists established a provisional government. This exuberance was matched by the Comintern, which proclaimed that a "new chapter" in the Chinese revolution was being unfolded.[5] On the scene in Changsha there were considerable looting and destruction of Chinese and foreign property by P'eng's troops, many of them untutored peasants. An American diplomat who visited Changsha in mid-August reported that "almost all Government buildings and foreign missions were either burned or demolished."[6] Orthodox Communist accounts do not mention this, but one participant, Wang Chen (q.v.), admitted to journalist Nym Wales that in "their enthusiasm, the peasants confiscated commodities from some of the reactionary shopkeepers." Wang said this was not a "good method" and blamed it on Li Li-san's leadership.[7]

P'eng's Third Corps held Changsha for about a week before being driven out. He then marched eastward to rendezvous with Chu and Mao, who had been thwarted in their attempt to capture Nanchang. At this juncture, in August 1930, P'eng's Third Army Corps was united with the Chu-Mao First Army Corps to form the First Front Army. Chu was made the overall commander, Mao the chief political officer, and P'eng retained command of his Third Corps. The combined force was reportedly 40,000-strong, but fewer than half had weapons.[8] In early September, still operating under directives from Li Li-san, a second assault on Changsha was begun. After mounting an attack for a week, it was called off. According to Chu Te's account, he, Mao, and P'eng had deep misgivings about this operation, principally because they did not believe that the Red Army was trained or equipped to fight positional warfare.[9] The second failure at Changsha was the death warrant for the Li Li-san leadership and, in broader terms, it represented the last effort by the Communists to capture major urban areas for the next two decades.

From Changsha the defeated Red Army troops moved in a southeast direction toward Chi-an (Kian) in central Kiangsi. At the same time, in late September, the CCP convened the Third Plenum at Lu-shan in north Kiangsi to review the situation and plan future strategy. Li Li-san still had the political strength to maintain a precarious hold on the reins of power, but over the next several weeks the combined pressures from contending CCP factions and the Comintern forced his "exile" to Moscow. The intra-Party struggles continued at the Fourth Plenum, held in Shanghai in January 1931, when the Comintern-backed Russian-returned Student leadership acceded to power (see under Ch'en Shao-yü). In a very important sense the intra-Party disputes which characterized the Third and Fourth Plenums ignored the emerging reality that the core of Communist power was rapidly gravitating to the rural areas where Mao, Chu, and P'eng (none of whom attended either plenum) were in command of military forces. Despite the failure at Changsha, the Mao-Chu-P'eng troops had the strength to capture Kian in central Kiangsi in October 1930. The city was held only a few weeks before the decision was taken to abandon it, but, according to one account, enemy documents were captured there and revealed that an "A-B" (Anti-Bolshevik) Corps was operating within the Red Army.[10] These disclosures, in turn, set the stage for the famous Fu-t'ien Incident of December 1930.

There are few episodes in CCP history which are more complex and for which there are more contradictory interpretations than the Fu-t'ien Incident.[11] In late November 1930, presumably on the basis of disclosures in the captured documents, Mao ordered the mass arrest of some 4,000 men in a Red Army unit in the Huang-p'o district of Yung-feng hsien, as well as officials of the Kiangsi Provincial Action Committee in Fu-t'ien. The Action Committee, in Mao's eyes, had been an opposition group and one that supported Li Li-san. In reply, during the first week of December, men from the "rebel" army stormed the prison at Fu-t'ien, rescued some of their colleagues, and retreated westward across the Kan River. There, at a conference, they called for Mao's overthrow, but at the same time declared their support for Chu Te, P'eng, and P'eng's colleague at the 1928 P'ing-chiang Uprising, Huang Kung-lueh. However, immediately afterwards, Chu, P'eng, and Huang declared their unequivocal support for Mao.

Several years later Mao pinpointed the gravity of the incident when he remarked to Edgar Snow that the "events produced a sensation, and to many it must have seemed that the fate of the revolution depended on the outcome of this struggle." Mao also exonerated P'eng, whose Third Army Corps was apparently in nominal control of the "rebels"; Mao equated the revolt with a lingering manifestation of "Li Li-sanism," and asserted that P'eng had "fought vigorously" against the attempt by the "rebels" to separate the Third Corps from the rest of the Red Army.[12] Mao's version of the Fu-t'ien Incident was greatly oversimplified, but his comment concerning the "fate of the revolution" was not pure hyperbole.

At the very time that the Fu-t'ien Incident was taking place, KMT troops were converging on the soviet strongholds in southeast Kiangsi for the first of the Annihilation Campaigns. Thus, for the moment, the Fu-t'ien rebels gained a breathing spell, and it was not until mid-1931 that Mao was able to crush them.

In October 1930, fresh from victories over several warlords, Chiang Kai-shek announced that he was turning in earnest to the extermination of the Communists. It was his expectation that the "country should be rid of all communist-bandits within three or six months at the most."[13] This set the stage for the First Annihilation Campaign, which lasted for only a few days in late 1930 and early 1931. Led by Lu Ti-p'ing, under whom P'eng had once served, the KMT forces were thrown back by Red Army units commanded by Mao, Chu, P'eng, Lin Piao, Huang Kung-lueh, and others. P'eng was again one of the most active of the Red Army front-line commanders in the spring and summer of 1931 when the Communists fended off two more KMT attacks upon their Kiangsi bases. In the meantime, according to some (but not all) sources,[14] P'eng had been appointed a member in January of the Party's Central Bureau of the Soviet Areas, which is described in the biography of Hsiang Ying.

In November 1931, at the First All-China Congress of Soviets held in Juichin, the Chinese Soviet Republic was established as the government for the areas under Communist control. P'eng was elected a member of the principal political organ of the Republic, the Central Executive Committee (CEC), of which Mao was chairman. In addition, P'eng and Wang Chia-hsiang (q.v.) were appointed vice-chairmen under Chu Te of the Central Revolutionary Military Council. A little over two years later, at the second congress in January–February 1934, P'eng was re-elected to the CEC. However, he was replaced by Chou En-lai as one of the two vice-chairmen of the Military Council. Nym Wales, after her visit to Yenan in 1937, listed P'eng as a member of the Council, and from the context of her material it appears that the organ was then subordinate to the Party rather than the government.[15] P'eng was once again a vice-chairman of the Council during the civil war period (1946–1949) when the organization was subordinate to the CCP.

In the spring of 1933 P'eng, then commanding his Third Army Corps in east Kiangsi, was one of the major figures in repelling the Nationalists' Fourth Annihilation Campaign. In the fall of that year the KMT launched still another campaign. P'eng was then leading his troops in west Fukien; according to one account he (or at least men under his authority) made contact with the dissident 19th Route Army.[16] This unit, led by Ch'en Ming-shu, Chiang Kuang-nai, and Ts'ai T'ing-k'ai, established a rebel government in Fukien in opposition to Chiang Kai-shek in November 1933 and began to make overtures to the Communists. The Fukien rebel government, as described in the biography of Kai Feng, was crushed by Chiang Kai-shek in early 1934. Chiang then continued his Fifth Annihilation Campaign, and finally, in October 1934, the Communists evacuated their base and began the historic Long March to Shensi. In the meantime, according to a biography published by the Russians in 1955,[17] P'eng was first elected to the CCP Central Committee in 1934 and to the Politburo in 1935. The 1934 date suggests that this took place at the Party's Fifth Plenum in January of that year; his election to the Politburo in the following year might have taken place at the famous Tsun-i Conference in Kweichow in January, when Mao Tse-tung seems to have gained control of the CCP, or perhaps in December of the same year when the Politburo held an important meeting at Wa-yao-pao in north Shensi. Commanding his Third Army Corps, one of the key components of the Long Marchers, P'eng and his troops were in the vanguard of the year-long trek from Kiangsi to north Shensi in 1934–35. P'eng's importance during the march is emphasized in the many accounts of the Long March, including one account[18] which was published in a Comintern journal in June 1935 when the Red Army troops had completed only about half the march.

As described in the biography of Chang Kuo-t'ao, important elements of the Long March remained in the Szechwan-Sikang border area from mid-1935 to 1936 and thus did not proceed directly to north Shansi in the fall of 1935 with Mao, P'eng, Lin Piao, and Chou En-lai. Therefore, because of the reduced size of the troop units in Shensi, Lin Piao's First Army Corps and P'eng's Third Army Corps were merged, and because Chu Te was among those who had remained in the Szechwan-Sikang area, P'eng became the commander-in-chief. This unit was initially known as the Shensi-Kansu Column, but by the time Edgar Snow visited Shensi in mid-1936 he identified P'eng as the commander of the First Front Army (Chu Te's old position). This situation prevailed until Chu Te's arrival in Shensi in the latter part of 1936; P'eng continued to command the First Front Army, but Chu was his superior as commander-in-chief of the Red Army. In the meantime, in early 1936, the Red Army troops in Shensi launched an attack across the Yellow River into Shansi, the stronghold of warlord-governor Yen Hsi-shan. Orthodox Communist histories describe this as an "eastern expedition" to confront the Japanese, who were then steadily encroaching on Chinese territory in north China. In fact, this foray led by P'eng in the early months of 1936 was intended to gain recruits and military supplies for the Red Army (see under Liu Chih-tan). Reinforced by troops sent by Chiang Kai-shek, Governor Yen was able to expel the Communists, who then returned to the Shensi-Kansu border to await the arrival of Chu Te and his troops from the south.

By 1936 there was considerable sentiment throughout China for a cessation of warfare between KMT and Communist armies. The Communists in Shensi encouraged such sentiments to gain time to fortify their new bases and to complete the move north to Shensi of the troops in the Szechwan-Sikang area which had not yet completed the Long March. In regard to the latter problem, in the late summer and early fall of 1936 troops from Shensi moved southward into Kansu to assist Chu Te in completing the last leg of the Long March (see under Tso Ch'üan). While these events were taking place, the Communists were beginning to make covert contacts with Chang Hsueh-liang and Yang Hu-ch'eng, two dissident KMT commanders whose troops were, in effect, blockading the Red Army units in Shensi. According to one account,[19] P'eng was among those who took part in these endeavors, which culminated in December 1936 when Chiang Kai-shek was kidnapped during the famous Sian Incident (see under Chou En-lai). As a consequence of the tacit truce worked out then, the Communists were able to proceed with less harassment from the Nationalists to further strengthen the Red Army during the first half of 1937.

A few weeks after war with Japan erupted in July 1937, the Communist forces in north and northwest China were reorganized into the Eighth Route Army, ostensibly as part of the national government forces. Chu Te served throughout the war as the commander and P'eng was his deputy. In September the Eighth Route Army crossed the Yellow River to engage the invading Japanese forces in Shansi. By late October P'eng was with the army headquarters in northeast Shansi, not far from the battle lines. Agnes Smedley, who saw P'eng several times during this period, prophetically asserted that he would become "one of the greatest military leaders of Asia."[20] She described him as a "strong, heavy-set fellow of boundless energy," and like many other Westerners who have met P'eng, she commented on his "puritanical" and "austere" manner. Miss Smedley also made the observation that he was "Chu Te's shadow and, some said, his military brains."[21]

By the end of 1937 the Eighth Route Army headquarters had been removed to the region around Lin-fen in southwest Shansi. P'eng was in that region at that time, but then in mid-January 1938 he and Chu Te went to Loyang in north Honan to confer with Chiang Kai-shek on war strategy.[22] Immediately afterwards P'eng went to Hankow, then the provisional national capital, and in February he held further talks with

Chiang. During this period of relatively close cooperation between the CCP and the KMT, P'eng was among the senior Communist leaders readmitted to the KMT.[23] However, his contacts with KMT officialdom were confined to strategy sessions such as those mentioned above.

Exact details are lacking, but scattered reports suggest that P'eng spent most of the early war years moving back and forth from the Communist capital at Yenan to battlefront areas in Shansi and Hopeh. Chu Te also spent considerable time near the front in the period through 1939, but afterwards he remained in Yenan and P'eng assumed a more important role as the top field commander. Among the numerous wartime battles with the Japanese, P'eng is probably best known in connection with the Hundred Regiments Offensive. This series of battles took place on a five-province front in north China from August to December 1940. Some 400,000 Eighth Route Army troops were committed in a major effort to sever Japanese rail communications and to destroy enemy strong points and blockhouses. Significant damages were inflicted on the Japanese, but they in turn responded in 1941–42 with a savage counterattack known as the "three-all" policy (kill all, burn all, destroy all). These actions resulted in severe losses for the Eighth Route Army and the Chinese populace; according to one estimate, Communist military forces were reduced from 400,000 to 300,000 and the population under Communist control was sharply reduced.[24] In 1943 P'eng discussed the Hundred Regiments Offensive and its aftermath in a piece which appears in Stuart Gelder's study of the Chinese Communist wartime effort.[25] In the meantime, in addition to his military posts, P'eng served concurrently from 1941 to 1943 as secretary of the CCP North China Bureau. Then, in 1943, he returned to Yenan where he remained for most of the last two years of the war.

When the CCP held its seventh National Congress in Yenan from April to June 1945, P'eng was one of only 15 members of the congress presidium. He also spoke before the congress, but the speech was not published. At the close of the meeting, he was re-elected to membership on the Central Committee. Immediately afterwards the new Central Committee held its first plenary session; the Communists did not publish a list of the Politburo elected at that time, but it appears that P'eng was re-elected a full member. In the early postwar period most of the field commanders returned to their armies as the Nationalists and Communists began their maneuverings, which would lead to full-scale civil war by mid-1946. However, Mao Tse-tung, Liu Shao-ch'i, Jen Pi-shih, Chu Te, and P'eng were among the senior figures who remained in Yenan to direct overall strategy. Then, in March 1947, Yenan fell to the Nationalists. The Communist armies had by this time been expanded considerably and reorganized into the PLA; Chu Te continued as the commander and P'eng as his deputy.

The Communists had anticipated the fall of Yenan and took steps to tie down the maximum number of Nationalist troops in north Shensi (see under Ho Lung). Mao and a few others began a year-long trek which would take them to Hopeh by the late spring of 1948, but P'eng remained in the northwest, and there, in conjunction with Ho Lung, Hsi Chung-hsun, and Chang Tsung-hsun (qq.v.), he led a series of campaigns which culminated with the recapture of Yenan in April 1948. Over the winter of 1948–49 the troops in the northwest were redesignated the First Field Army, with P'eng in command. In late May 1949 Sian, the capital of Shensi, was captured by P'eng and Ho Lung, and from there they pushed west. However, an unexpectedly strong stand near Sian by KMT General Hu Tsung-nan necessitated a reinforcement by two armies led by Nieh Jung-chen (q.v.). After this brief and successful campaign, P'eng continued westward toward Lanchow, the Kansu capital, which fell on August 26. On September 5 elements of the First Field Army captured Sining, the capital of Tsinghai, and on September 23, Yin-ch'uan, the Ninghsia capital, fell. A few days later key KMT officials in Sinkiang went over to the Communists; soon thereafter one of P'eng's subordinate commanders, Wang Chen (q.v.), advanced into Sinkiang and entered Tihwa (now Urumchi), the provincial capital, on October 20. Aside from mopping-up operations, this completed the conquest of the five-province northwest area.

There was a lull on most battlefronts during the summer and fall of 1949 as the Communists consolidated their conquests, and consequently many major field commanders went to Peking to take part in establishing the central government. But in the northwest there was fairly intensive campaigning, and thus P'eng was one of the few commanders who did not go to Peking. The preparations for the new government began to take concrete form when Mao convened the Preparatory Committee of the CPPCC in June 1949. Because of P'eng's stature in the PLA, he was one of the seven military representatives named to the committee. But his absence was highlighted when a special group was formed to draft the Common Program (the equivalent of a constitution); P'eng was named to this *ad hoc* body, but Lo Jui-ch'ing acted in his stead. Moreover, when the CPPCC met in September to establish the PRC, Ho Lung presented the official report on P'eng's First Field Army. Nonetheless, P'eng was given key assignments in the new central government. He was made a member of both the National Committee of the CPPCC and the highly important Central People's Government

Council, and he also became one of the five vice-chairmen of the People's Revolutionary Military Council. All three organizations were chaired by Mao. Finally, like so many of the top leaders, P'eng was elected a member of the First Executive Board of the Sino-Soviet Friendship Association when it was established in October 1949 (a post he held until December 1954).

In a major step toward the institutionalization of Communist rule in the northwest, the Northwest Military and Administrative Committee (NWMAC) was set up in late 1949. (The official appointments were made in December, but the NWMAC did not go into operation until January 1950). P'eng was appointed chairman. The NWMAC was headquartered in Sian, which was also the headquarters of the Northwest Military Region under P'eng's command. Some reports, including a Russian biography of P'eng,[26] assert that he was secretary of the Party's Northwest Bureau at this time, but for most if not all of this period Hsi Chung-hsun held this post. In December the Communists also established the Sinkiang Military District under the Northwest Military Region. P'eng was made Sinkiang commander and political commissar, but these were nominal posts, and Wang Chen, the senior CCP figure in Sinkiang, soon became the acting commander. P'eng was in Sinkiang briefly toward the end of the year, but in early January 1950 he went to Peking to deliver a progress report on conditions in the northwest. His report, which dealt principally with the military campaigns he had just fought, was published in the authoritative *Hsin-hua yueh-pao* (New China monthly). The next issue of this journal reprinted an article by P'eng on "present tasks and future work" in the northwest, and again in October 1950 it reprinted an article summarizing a year of Communist control in this area.[27]

P'eng was in Peking again in June 1950 to attend the second session of the First CPPCC when Liu Shao-ch'i presented his important report on the land reform law. P'eng's presence in Peking at that time suggests that he also attended the Party's Third Plenum (June 6–9). In mid-August he was named to succeed Chia T'o-fu as chairman of the NWMAC's Finance and Economics Committee. However, this and his several other posts in the northwest became nominal when the Chinese entered the Korean War soon afterwards. PLA troops—styled the Chinese People's Volunteers (CPV)—crossed the Yalu River under P'eng's command in late October 1950. Many secondary sources claim that Lin Piao, whose Fourth Field Army supplied most of the troops initially assigned to Korea, was the commander in the early days of Chinese participation in the war. However, as indicated in Lin's biography, there is little to support this assertion. Moreover, in Peking's official biographies of both men, issued in 1955 when they were made PLA marshals, it was specifically stated that P'eng led the CPV from October 1950, whereas no mention was made of the Korean War in Lin's biography.

P'eng remained in Korea for three years. The most dramatic and difficult period was the first eight months. Both North and South Korean forces had been badly mauled during the early months of the war, and thus the period from October 1950 to the initiation of truce talks in July 1951 witnessed raging battles up and down the narrow peninsula. These were fought mainly between American and Chinese armies. To make up for what they lacked in equipment and firepower, the Chinese rapidly introduced huge numbers of troops. There are wide variations in estimates of Chinese troop strength, but one careful study places the figure at an average of 700,000 from 1951 to 1954.[28] By July 1951 something of a stalemate existed along an east-west line approximating the 38th parallel (that is, the same parallel that divided North and South Korea before the war). In the same month truce talks began, first in the village of Kaesong and later at Panmunjom. Three weeks later, P'eng wrote a piece claiming victory for the Chinese-North Korean side. He conceded that the American troops had "good modern equipment and large quantities of airplanes, tanks, and artillery, while the CPV have no tanks and previously had no air force." The Volunteers had "only a small quantity of artillery and light infantry weapons."[29] P'eng did not mention the extremely heavy casualties suffered by the CPV in the months prior to the beginning of the truce talks.

The truce talks lasted for two years, and throughout this period heavy but inconclusive fighting continued along the 38th parallel. As the months wore on the North Korean armed forces were rebuilt and began to assume a much larger role in the fighting, and in the south a similar situation prevailed as the Republic of Korea forces grew in strength and and ability. At some time during this two-year period P'eng presumably returned to Peking, but this was not reflected in Chinese press media. In fact, he was seldom mentioned by name during this period even though there was a mammoth Resist America, Aid Korea campaign in China to mobilize political support and resources. On at least three occasions P'eng was decorated by the North Korean government for his efforts. During the same period he received two new posts. In November 1952 he was made one of the 15 members of the State Planning Commission, and in January 1953 he was appointed to membership on the Committee to Draft the Constitution (chaired by Mao Tse-tung). However, there is no indication that he was an active participant in these bodies until his return home.

P'eng was the only first-rank PLA veteran who participated in the Korean War. There were, however, many important second-echelon military figures who were there during or shortly after the war. They include Ch'en Keng, Kan Szu-ch'i, Li Ta, Li Chih-min, Sung Shih-lun, Yang Te-chih, Yang Yung, Wang P'ing, Hung Hsueh-chih, Han Hsien-ch'u, and Teng Hua (qq.v.). In late July 1953 the Korean Armistice Agreement was signed, whereupon Kim Il Sung and P'eng issued armistice orders to the Korean People's Army and the CPV, respectively. Two weeks later, on August 11, P'eng returned to a hero's welcome in Peking, and a month later he reported on the war before the 24th meeting of the Central People's Government Council (September 12)—once again claiming total victory. During the following months P'eng and Kim Il Sung had some exchanges of official letters with the United Nations' Command and the chairman of the Neutral Nations Repatriation Commission regarding the repatriation of prisoners-of-war. By this time, however, the major negotiating responsibilities for the Chinese had been turned over to Huang Hua (q.v.), a representative of the Ministry of Foreign Affairs. In short, P'eng's direct involvement in Korea ended with his departure in August 1953, even though he was not formally replaced as CPV commander until September 1954 when the above-mentioned Teng Hua assumed the post.

In January 1953, the NWMAC, which P'eng still nominally headed, was reorganized into the Northwest Administrative Committee. He was reappointed the chairman, but from his return to China until the committee was dissolved in November 1954 there is no indication that he returned to Sian to assume his position. Rather, he was regularly reported in Peking in connection with his posts in the central government (for example, the Committee to Draft the Constitution). In 1954 elections were held for deputies to the First NPC. Representation was principally by geographic areas, but there were two special categories, one for overseas Chinese and another for the PLA. P'eng, still technically the CPV commander, was elected a CPV deputy. (Four years later there were still large numbers of Chinese troops in Korea, and even though P'eng had long since relinquished his command he was returned as a CPV deputy to the Second NPC.) P'eng attended the first session of the First NPC, held in September 1954, which adopted the constitution and reorganized the central government. Under State Council Premier Chou En-lai, P'eng was appointed the third-ranking vice-premier after Ch'en Yun and Lin Piao. In the newly established National Defense Council, headed by Mao, P'eng was selected as the second-ranking vice-chairman after Chu Te. Finally and most important, P'eng was appointed minister of the newly created Ministry of National Defense.

As the new minister of Defense, P'eng was one of the delegates led by Chou En-lai who held talks with Soviet leader Nikita Khrushchev in late September and early October 1954. A series of important agreements were reached, including large-scale Soviet economic assistance and an arrangement providing for the withdrawal of Soviet troops from Port Arthur and the return of the naval base there to China. In February 1955 P'eng journeyed to Port Arthur to bid farewell to the Soviet troops, whose withdrawal was completed in May. In March 1955 he was among the Politburo members who attended a national conference of the CCP. This meeting passed on the First Five-Year Plan and heard a report on the purge of Kao Kang and Jao Shu-shih (qq.v.). P'eng was listed as one of those who gave "important speeches," but the text was not released. In the period prior to the Eighth Party Congress in 1956, the CCP never issued a formal roster of Politburo members. However, the manner in which the speakers were listed at the March 1955 conference suggested that they comprised the full Politburo membership as of that time. P'eng was listed last among the 11 Politburo members. Chu Te was the only other military man on this list, but a few days later military veteran Lin Piao was newly elected to the Politburo (in addition to CCP Secretary-General Teng Hsiao-p'ing).

In late 1954 Chang Wen-t'ien (q.v.), then Peking's ambassador to Moscow, attended the Preparatory Conference of the European Security Conference as an observer. This meeting paved the way for a treaty signed by the USSR and the East European Communist countries on May 14, 1955. The treaty, officially entitled "On Friendship, Cooperation, and Mutual Aid," is best known as the Warsaw Pact and is usually regarded as Moscow's reply to NATO. P'eng Te-huai, who had spent a few days in East Berlin in early May 1955 to attend celebrations marking the 10th anniversary of the defeat of Nazi Germany, arrived in Warsaw on May 10 for the inaugural meeting of the Warsaw Pact. P'eng attended only as an observer, but nonetheless pledged Peking's support of the pact. Afterwards, he toured Poland for several days and then spent a few days in Moscow where he held talks with top officials, including Khrushchev. He returned to Peking in early June.

In the meantime, in February 1955, P'eng and Nieh Jung-chen had given explanatory reports before the NPC Standng Committee on a military conscription law, which was one of the major items in a broad program to "professionalize" the PLA. After further discussions, P'eng gave a report on the proposed law to the State Council on July 4, 1955. Two weeks later, at the second session of the First NPC, he reported in detail on the need for the law which was adopted at that time. Another step in the professionalization process was taken in September 1955 when personal military ranks were created and decorations

awarded to PLA veterans. P'eng was made one of the 10 PLA marshals (a five-star rank) and was given the three top awards—the Orders of August First, Independence and Freedom, and Liberation—which covered service in the Red Army from its birth in 1927 to the eve of the Korean War in 1950.

At the Eighth National Congress of the CCP, held in September 1956, P'eng served as a member of the standing committee of the congress presidium. After hearing three keynote addresses on political and economic affairs by Liu Shao-ch'i, Teng Hsiao-p'ing, and Chou En-lai, P'eng spoke on military affairs. This oft-cited speech briefly reviewed the history of the PLA, Soviet military aid, the relationship between the PLA and national construction in China, and various aspects of the above-mentioned program to professionalize the PLA. P'eng spoke on behalf of the Party's Military Affairs Commission (MAC). Analysts of the Chinese military establishment had long suspected that the CCP had an organ specifically devoted to military affairs, but this was apparently the first occasion on which such a body was openly mentioned in Chinese press media. The chairmanship of the MAC is probably held by Mao Tse-tung, but P'eng was presumably the de facto MAC chief from this date until he was succeeded by Lin Piao in 1959. Little was known about the MAC during P'eng's tenure as its active head, but Western commentators have come to regard it as one of the principal politico-military institutions in China. One military historian, in comparing the MAC with American government agencies, has written that it "appears to combine most of the functions" of the Secretary of Defense and Joint Chiefs of Staff.[30]

At the close of the Eighth Congress, P'eng was re-elected to the Central Committee. On the next day, at the First Plenum of the new Central Committee, he was re-elected to the Politburo, which then consisted of 17 full and six alternate members. Up to this point in his career, P'eng had long been considered second only to Chu Te in the PLA. (In fact, a persuasive case can be made that after the Sino-Japanese War Chu was relegated to the honorific role of "grand old man" of the PLA, whereas P'eng was the most important active military leader.) The exact rankings of Politburo members cannot be regarded as an infallible guide to political and military authority in China, but it is noteworthy that four military men—Chu Te, Lin Piao, Lo Jung-huan, and Ch'en I—were listed ahead of P'eng, who was put in the 13th place. In contrast, on the eve of the congress, he had been listed 11th, and among the military figures only Chu Te was ahead of him. As of 1956, however, there was little to suggest that P'eng would be purged three years later. In fact, during the middle and late 1950's P'eng was constantly in the spotlight—speaking before various military conferences, addressing Army Day rallies, and, in particular, conferring with the many foreign military delegations which were constantly touring China during those years.

In early November 1957 P'eng went to Moscow with Mao Tse-tung's delegation to the celebrations commemorating the 40th anniversary of the Russian Revolution. In addition to membership on Mao's official delegation, P'eng headed a sub-delegation of military leaders which arrived in Moscow a few days later. This was probably the most important group of military figures sent abroad in the post-1949 period; it included Marshal Yeh Chien-ying, Chief-of-Staff Su Yü, General Political Department director T'an Cheng (qq.v.), as well as the heads of the PLA Air Force, Navy, Armored Corps, Artillery, and General Rear Services (logistics). In short, P'eng was accompanied by a group capable of conducting full-dress negotiations on Sino-Soviet military affairs and strategy. P'eng and his military colleagues had arrived in Moscow in the wake of Moscow's impressive display of its growing military power—the test of an intercontinental ballistic missile and the launching of the first sputnik. Moreover, according to later Chinese assertions (which were not denied by the Russians), the Soviet Union had agreed in October to supply China with a sample atomic weapon and technical data on its manufacture. Apart from the military discussions which obviously took place, the Chinese leaders also participated in a "summit" meeting of leaders from Communist nations. P'eng's military group then toured Soviet military installations before departing for China. En route home in late November and early December they visited Khabarovsk and Vladivostok. The visit to these cities, both of which have important military installations, was noteworthy if only because so few Chinese delegations have been there, despite their immediate proximity to Manchuria.

While in Moscow P'eng had made remarks which indicated that the Chinese expected considerable Soviet support for the modernization of the PLA. But several weeks later, back in China, a speech by P'eng suggested that the Moscow negotiations had been less than satisfactory to the Chinese and that China would have to rely more on its own industrial base as a "prerequisite for a strong defense."[31] This attitude toward self-reliance was a major theme in the Great Leap Forward, which was unfolding about the same time P'eng delivered his speech (January 22, 1958). Further differences between Moscow and Peking were suggested in mid-1958, immediately after a two-month-long meeting of the MAC, which P'eng addressed. At the time of the close of this meeting on July 22, the Chinese mounted an intensive propaganda campaign on the "liberation" of Taiwan. Apparently in response to what the Russians regarded as a potentially serious confrontation between the United States and China in the Taiwan Straits, Soviet leader Nikita Khrushchev, accompanied by Defense Minister R. Ia. Malinovsky, arrived in Peking. For four days, from July 31 to August 3, talks were held; P'eng was one of the five Chinese participants, who were led by Mao. The communiqué issued at the close of the talks was conspicuous by its failure to make any mention of Taiwan, thereby suggesting that the Chinese failed to win a promise of support in the event of a showdown with Washington. A few weeks later Peking began a bombardment of the Nationalist-held offshore island of Quemoy, but after further high-level maneuvering involving Washington, Taipei, Peking, and Moscow, P'eng ordered a one-week cessation of shelling on October 6. A week later the cessation was extended, but then on October 25 P'eng issued a statement to "compatriots" on Taiwan designed to divide Taipei and Washington; he advised those on Taiwan "not to depend too much on other people" (meaning the United States), and suggested that to "arrange things between our two parties is very easy." P'eng also announced that shelling would only be carried out every other day. It soon became apparent that little military damage was being inflicted and that the crisis had passed.

In April 1959 P'eng left Peking as head of a 12-member military delegation to East Europe. From April 24 to June 2 he visited Poland, East Germany, Czechoslovakia, Hungary, Rumania, Bulgaria, and Albania. P'eng spent about a week in each country, where he conferred with top political and military leaders. Chang Wen-t'ien (q.v.), who was later to be linked with P'eng when the two men were purged, arrived in Poland on the same day as P'eng for a foreign ministers' meeting of the Warsaw Pact nations. In early June P'eng went from Albania to Moscow, and after remaining there for a few days he spent a week in Mongolia before returning to Peking in mid-June. In late April, while P'eng was abroad, the first session of the Second NPC had concluded. P'eng was re-appointed minister of National Defense and the third-ranking vice-premier of the State Council. Furthermore, in the National Defense Council, which was now headed by Liu Shao-ch'i (after Mao retired as PRC chairman), P'eng was re-appointed as a vice-chairman. Previously, from 1954 to 1959, he had been the second-ranking vice-chairman, but when "old soldier" Chu Te stepped down from the senior vice-chairmanship at this time, the post was assumed by P'eng.

In view of P'eng's reappointment to his senior posts in the government, together with his lengthy tour of East Europe, his position in the Chinese hierarchy seemed assured in the early summer of 1959. However, in August, at the Party's Eighth Plenum (better known as the Lushan Plenum from its locale in Kiangsi), P'eng came into serious conflict with the Maoist leadership. The disputes seemed to have centered on the economic policies of the Great Leap Forward, which P'eng allegedly opposed, and on a variety of questions concerning military policies (see under Huang K'o-ch'eng).[32] The immediate upshot of the dispute was that in September P'eng was replaced as Defense minister by Lin Piao. Those who fell from political grace with P'eng included the aforementioned Chang Wen-t'ien, PLA Chief-of-Staff Huang K'o-ch'eng, General Rear Services Director Hung Hsueh-chih (who had served in Korea with P'eng), and Hunan provincial Party leader Chou Hsiao-chou. P'eng was not denounced at that time, but he was not reported in the press again until late May 1960 when he took part in ceremonies in connection with the death of Politburo member Lin Po-ch'ü (q.v.). That was Peng's last public appearance, and with this minor ceremonial occasion his three-decade career as a Red Army leader came to a halt.

Unlike others who have been purged (for example, Kao Kang), P'eng was not expunged from history. For example, he nominally retained his posts as vice-premier of the State Council and vice-chairman of the National Defense Council until a new governmental hierarchy was named at the close of the Third NPC in January 1965, and as late as the 1965 edition of the authoritative *Jen-min shou-ts'e* (People's handbook) he was still listed as a Politburo member. Even in so carefully edited a collection as Mao's *Selected Works,* a volume published in 1965 referred to P'eng as "comrade" in a context which was favorable to him. Nonetheless, there is abundant evidence to show that authors writing on the history of the Chinese Communist movement are not expected to mention him any more than necessary. One of many illustrations of this can be seen by comparing a 1957 Chinese language account of one of P'eng's military exploits (the aforementioned expedition into Shansi in 1936) with a 1963 translation into English which does not mention his name.[33]

Edgar Snow learned from P'eng that in 1926 he married a middle-school girl who was a member of the Communist Youth League, "but during the revolution they became separated" and P'eng had not seen her after 1928. During the Sino-Japanese War he married P'u An-hsiu, who was born about 1920 near Shanghai in Kiangsu province. P'u served in Yenan as a cultural worker during the war years. She does not seem to have been politically active in the post-1949 years, but from 1959 to 1964 she was a deputy to the Second NPC from Kiangsu. P'u has two prominent elder sisters, P'u Hsi-hsiu and P'u Chieh-hsiu. Hsi-hsiu, a newspaperwoman who worked for many years for the *Wen hui pao* in Shanghai and Peking, has been an alternate member of the China Democratic League since 1956. Like so many members of the non-Communist political parties, she was labeled a "rightist" during the 1957–58 "anti-rightist" campaign. In her case this may have been directly related to the fact that her husband, Lo Lung-chi, a key official in the Democratic League, was one of the major victims of this same campaign. In early 1958 Lo was stripped of his post as minister of Timber Industry, and he remained in political limbo until his death on December 7, 1965. P'eng's other sister-in-law, P'u Chieh-hsiu, has been active in industrial and commercial circles since the PRC was established. She was elected in 1955 to the Central Committee of the China Democratic National Construction Association, and in 1964 she was elected a deputy from Peking to the Third NPC.

1. Edgar Snow, *Red Star over China* (New York, 1938), pp. 267–272.

2. Agnes Smedley, *The Great Road* (New York, 1956), pp. 252–253.

3. *Foreign Relations of the United States, 1930* (Washington, D.C., 1945), II, 141–142.

4. *Ibid.,* p. 181.

5. Benjamin I. Schwartz, *Chinese Communism and the Rise of Mao* (Cambridge, Mass., 1951), p. 144.

6. *Foreign Relations of the United States, 1930,* p. 183.

7. Nym Wales, *Red Dust* (Stanford, Calif., 1952), p. 98.

8. *Foreign Relations of the United States, 1930,* p. 185.

9. Smedley, pp. 278–279.

10. *Ibid.,* p. 280.

11. Ronald S. Suleski, "The Fu-t'ien Incident, December 1930," in Ronald S. Suleski and Daniel H. Bays, *Early Communist China: Two Studies,* Michigan Papers in Chinese Studies, no. 4 (Ann Arbor, Mich., 1969), pp. 1–27.

12. Snow, pp. 162–163.

13. *Foreign Relations of the United States, 1930,* p. 51.

14. Shanti Swarup, *A Study of the Chinese Communist Movement* (London, 1966), p. 247; O. Edmund Clubb, *Communism in China: As Reported from Hankow in 1932* (New York, 1968), p. 91.

15. Nym Wales, *Inside Red China* (New York, 1939), p. 343.

16. Edgar Snow, *Random Notes on Red China, 1936–1945* (Cambridge, Mass., 1957), p. 28.

17. *Bol'shaya Sovetskaya Entsiklopedya* (Large Soviet encyclopedia; Moscow, 1955), XXXV, 392.

18. *The Communist International,* 12.12:549–558 (London, June 20, 1935).

19. Charles B. McLane, *Soviet Policy and the Chinese Communists, 1931–1946* (New York, 1958), p. 80.

20. Agnes Smedley, *China Fights Back* (London, 1938), p. 84.

21. Agnes Smedley, *Battle Hymn of China* (New York, 1943), pp. 159–160.

22. I. Epstein, *The People's War* (London, 1939), p. 142.

23. Lyman P. Van Slyke, ed., *The Chinese Communist Movement: A Report of the United States War Department, July 1945* (Stanford, Calif., 1968), p. 62.

24. Chalmers A. Johnson, *Peasant Nationalism and Communist Power* (Stanford, Calif., 1962), pp. 57–58.

25. Stuart Gelder, *The Chinese Communists* (London, 1946), pp. 162–166.

26. *Bol'shaya Sovetskaya Entsiklopedya*, p. 392.

27. *Hsin-hua yueh-pao* (New China monthly), 1.4:873–874 (February 15, 1950); 1.5:1124–1125 (March 15, 1950); 2.6:1233–1236 (October 15, 1950).

28. John Gittings, *The Role of the Chinese Army* (London, 1967), p. 75.

29. *CB* 208, pp. 6–8.

30. Ralph L. Powell, *Politico-Military Relationships in Communist China* (U.S. Department of State, Washington, D.C., 1963), p. 5.

31. Ellis Joffe, *Party and Army: Professionalism and Political Control in the Chinese Officer Corps, 1949–1964* (Cambridge, Mass., 1965), pp. 95–96.

32. Gittings, pp. 225–234; David A. Charles, "The Dismissal of Marshal P'eng Teh-huai," *The China Quarterly*, no. 8:63–76 (October–December 1961).

33. *Hung-ch'i p'iao-p'iao* (Red flag fluttering; Peking, 1957), III, 191; *The Long March: Eyewitness Accounts* (Peking, 1963), pp. 184–190.

P'ing Chieh-san

(Hopeh). Deputy-Director, United Front Work Department, CCP Central Committee.

P'ing Chieh-san, a native of Hopeh, is reportedly a graduate of both Peking University and Sun Yat-sen University in Moscow, but no dates are available to indicate when he was at either institution.

P'ing is first mentioned in Chinese Communist sources in April 1951 when he was identified as director of the United Front Work Department of the North China Bureau of the CCP. United front work has been his main activity since at least this date. P'ing assumed another post in the same bureau, that of executive officer, by April 1952; he held both positions until the Bureau was abolished in August 1954.

Parallel to the Party Bureau for North China was the government organ known as the North China Administrative Committee, which existed from December 1951 until 1954 when the regional administrations were dissolved. P'ing served as a member of this committee as well as chairman of its Nationalities Affairs Committee. The major emphasis of united front work under the CCP has been the Party's relations with non-Communist intellectuals, but a closely related aspect of this work has been the management of the Party's relations with the tens of millions of the minority peoples, most of whom are not Communist Party members. For example, the regime's most senior official in united front work, Li Wei-han, has also been deeply involved in national minority affairs. Thus it was not surprising for P'ing to be the senior Party united front official in North China and to work in the minorities field. His work among the minority groups has stretched over a number of years. In April 1953, for example, he led a delegation to visit minority areas in north China, and in 1959 and 1962 he was a host for Tibetan leaders then visiting Peking.

In October–December 1953, P'ing accompanied Politburo member Ho Lung to North Korea as a deputy-leader of a delegation sent to "comfort" Chinese troops remaining in Korea after the war there ended in July 1953. In the following year he was elected to the First NPC and served as a member of the NPC Credentials Committee. P'ing was not, however, returned to the Second NPC, which first met in 1959. In retrospect, it appears that he was given rather major responsibilities in the CPPCC by 1959 and was therefore relieved of somewhat parallel tasks in the NPC.

P'ing's contributions to united front work were rewarded by November 1955 when he was identified as a deputy director of the Party's United Front Work Department, a post he continues to hold. Since the formation of the NPC in 1954, the CPPCC has increasingly come to be an adjunct of the United Front Department. Thus it was natural that P'ing should have attended as an observer the second session of the second CPPCC in January–February 1956. From mere observer P'ing rose to prominence in the CPPCC within the next decade. As a CCP representative he served on the Standing Committee of the Third CPPCC (1959–1964), and when the Fourth CPPCC was formed at a December 1964–January 1965 meeting, P'ing was the secretary-general of the Presidium, charged with conducting the proceedings. At the end of this session, he was not renamed a member of the Standing Committee, but instead received an even more important assignment as the permanent secretary-general of the Standing Committee, replacing CCP Central Committee alternate member Hsu Ping (q.v.).

In the interim, P'ing was becoming more deeply involved in united front work. Although details of his work are limited, his frequent appearances at high-level meetings or campaigns suggest a role of considerable importance. He was especially active during the 1957–58 "rectification" movement when China's intellectuals came under vigorous attacks. In carrying out similar activities he also reported on united front work at the Third National Youth Congress, April 13, 1958; he spoke on February 3, 1960, before a large gathering of businessmen; he held talks on November 9, 1961, with senior members of the Chinese Taoist Association following a national conference of the Association; he received officials of the Chinese Buddhist Association on February 28, 1962, following a national Buddhist conference; and he was present on January 14, 1963, when Liu Shao-ch'i received members of "democratic" parties and "non-Party democrats."

Po I-po

(1907– ; Ting-hsiang, Shansi). Vice-premier; chairman, State Economic Commission; alternate member, CCP Politburo.

Po I-po was active in the Shansi branch of the CCP from the late 1920's and during the war years he was a key official in the Shansi-Hopeh-Shantung-Honan Border Region government. He was first elected to the Party Central Committee in 1945, and 11 years later he was promoted to alternate membership on the Politburo. In the years after 1949 Po quickly emerged as one of the PRC's top financial and economic specialists.

Po comes from the town of Ting-hsiang, about 50 miles northeast of Taiyuan, the Shansi capital. He attended the Kuo-min Normal School in Taiyuan and while there joined a Communist cell (about 1927). Among his schoolmates who also became Communists were Lei Jen-min and Jung Tzu-ho (qq.v.). Prior to this period Shansi had been virtually the private domain of warlord-governor Yen Hsi-shan, but with the rising tide of nationalism and particularly the launching of the Northern Expedition in mid-1926, the province witnessed in the middle and late twenties an increasing amount of political activity by both the KMT and the CCP. Po and his fellow students, probably working in cooperation with the important Communist and labor leader, P'eng Chen (q.v.), came to dominate the Taiyuan labor movement in the period prior to the KMT–CCP split in mid-1927 and the ensuing struggle between the "Left" and "Right" factions of the KMT.[1]

Graduating from the normal school about 1930, Po went to Peking with some of his classmates, including Lei Jen-min. Po reputedly attended Peking University, but he apparently did not graduate. When the Japanese moved into Manchuria in 1931, he immediately became involved in anti-Japanese demonstrations. Arrested in 1932 for "incitement to riot," he was imprisoned in Peking until 1936[2] when he was released after ostensibly renouncing Communism. Although only in his late twenties, Po played a rather important role in the dramatic events of north China during the next two years as Japanese encroachments grew increasingly blatant and war finally erupted in mid-1937. Many of these events turned on the actions of Yen Hsi-shan, who was growing increasingly apprehensive about the Japanese. During the year 1936 it appears that Po shuttled back and forth between the Communist headquarters in north Shensi and Yen's capital at Taiyuan, Shansi. By the middle of 1936 Yen was already holding talks with important Communist officials who were attempting to induce him to join in a "united front" against the Japanese (see under P'eng Hsueh-feng). Receptive to such overtures, Governor Yen established the League for National Salvation through Sacrifice (Hsi-sheng chiu-kuo t'ung-meng-hui), better known as the Sacrifice League, in September 1936 (on the fifth anniversary of the Mukden Incident). In an interview a decade later with American journalist Jack Belden, Po claimed that he was in Yenan toward the end of 1936 when he received an invitation from Yen, asking him to return to Taiyuan to help train students for the anti-Japanese resistance.[3] Elsewhere, Po gave a slightly different version, asserting that in October 1936 Yen promised to form a united front with the CCP if Po would return to Shansi and assume leadership of the Sacrifice League.[4] In any case, by the turn of the year 1936–37 Po was in Taiyuan where he worked under the CCP's North China Bureau[5] (a fact presumably unknown to the Yen Hsi-shan administration). In 1937 he was instrumental in having Yen release Wang Jo-fei (q.v.), a top Party leader who had been imprisoned for several years. Po wrote an article on Wang's release for the JMJP (August 14, 1962), which provides a useful description of the workings of the Party underground in north China at that time.

In the period just prior to the beginning of war in mid-1937, Po and his colleagues (several of them ex-classmates) became prime movers of the Sacrifice League. In the early days of the war, as the Japanese advanced swiftly toward Taiyuan, the League officials persuaded Yen to allow them to form a military force known as the "Dare-to-Die Corps" (Chueh-szu tui). By the end of 1937 the Corps had formed four columns (tsung-tui), consisting of about 20 regiments.[6] The Communist domination of the Corps was striking—Po and three classmates (all Communists) were the commanders and chief political officers of all four columns. Po headed the First Column, which was dispatched to southeast Shansi. Yen was also persuaded to turn over to the Sacrifice League many of the local political functions as Yen's provincial administration began to crumble before the Japanese invaders.

Thus, Po was made special commissioner of the Third Area,[7] which covered 10 hsien in the same region of southeast Shansi where his First Column was operating.

Soon after the arrival of Po's "Dare-to-Die" column in southeast Shansi, the Communists' Eighth Route Army sent its 129th Division into the same area. This powerful force of some 6,000 men was led by Liu Po-ch'eng, the commander, and Teng Hsiao-p'ing (qq.v.), the political commissar. The 129th Division proceeded to establish the T'ai-hang–T'ai-yueh military base, in co-operation with Po's men and other partisan units in the area. The base subsequently became an important part of the Shansi-Hopeh-Shantung-Honan (Chin-Chi-Lu-Yü) Border Region. Po's area soon experienced a shortage of currency, which was one of the major difficulties felt by all the guerrilla bases cut off from Nationalist banking sources by the Japanese. When it became necessary for southeast Shansi to issue its own bank notes early in 1938, a bank was set up by Po. Located initially at Ch'in-hsien, the bank circulated its notes within the districts under his jurisdiction, and they were "closely linked" with those circulated by the Communists' Shansi-Chahar-Hopeh (Chin-Ch'a-Chi) Border Region to the north.[8] Po's work in this financial endeavor was apparently his first experience in a career which would later deeply involve him in such activities.

In the early part of the war the Communists and Yen Hsi-shan persisted in their uneasy alliance, bound together for the most part by their desire to resist the Japanese. This fiction was nicely maintained in 1938 when U.S. military observer Evans Carlson visited Liu Po-ch'eng's headquarters in the T'ai-hang Mountains in 1938. Po told Carlson about his activities with the Dare-to-Die Corps and about those on behalf of Yen Hsi-shan's government, but he did not mention his work with the CCP.[9] However, the fiction was destroyed in late 1939 when Po and his Dare-to-Die colleagues in other parts of Shansi became involved in a complex dispute with Yen Hsi-shan (see under P'eng Shao-hui). The upshot of this situation was that the Dare-to-Die columns denounced their allegiance to Yen and openly joined the Eighth Route Army. The separation was given further organizational expression a year and a half later when, in July 1941, the Shansi-Hopeh-Shantung-Honan (Chin-Chi-Lu-Yü) Border Region Government was formally established. Yang Hsiu-feng (q.v.), a former Peking professor, was the chairman of the government; Po and his longtime colleague Jung Tzu-ho became the two vice-chairmen.[10]

In the late war years Po commanded a division under the military region and concurrently served as commander of the T'ai-yueh Military Sub-district, which covered the western sector of the larger military region. It is evident that his work gained the approval of the higher echelons of the CCP, because when the Party held its Seventh National Congress in Yenan from April to June 1945 he was elected a full member of the Central Committee. The overwhelming majority of the 44 members were Long March veterans who had held high Party posts from the 1920's, and thus Po's election was all the more noteworthy.

By early 1946 Po was a deputy political commissar of the Chin-Chi-Lu-Yü Region, and he was still a vice-chairman of the Border Region government. His two superiors continued to be Liu Po-ch'eng and Teng Hsiao-p'ing, but judging from the available evidence Liu and Teng were primarily concerned with military operations, whereas Po seems to have concentrated on civil affairs. From its modest beginnings in 1937, the region had grown to huge proportions. Official Communist figures for 1944 claimed a population of 25 million in a region of more than 100,000 square miles (about the size of Italy). Po and his colleagues were in control of most of the area bounded on the west by the rail line running south from Taiyuan to Lin-fen, on the south by the Yellow River and the Lunghai Railway, and on the north and east by the long arc-shaped rail line from Taiyuan to Hsu-chou (Kiangsu). In terms of logistics, the Communist military units were within striking distance of every north-south and two of the most important east-west rail lines in north China.

Po was in Yenan in the spring of 1946, but he was back at his base in late 1946 when American Communist journalist Anna Louise Strong saw him at the Military Region's headquarters, then located in a village near Han-tan, a city in south Hopeh on the Peking-Hankow Railway. Her interview with Po, and a subsequent one in 1947 with journalist Jack Belden,[11] provide two of the rather few detailed sketches of a military-political headquarters and a top Communist leader at work. Po, whom Miss Strong found to be a "large, efficient-looking man," told her that some 600 people "comprise the top leadership" for the "civil government, the army headquarters, and the voluntary associations, such as trade unions, peasants' union, women's and youth associations, the cooperatives, [and] the Communist Party." Po continued: "When any general problem comes up, such as land reform or the defense of the area, we hold a meeting of all top-flight leaders of army, government, and voluntary associations. Each system assumes its share of the work and carries it out all over the area. All our forces of army, government and voluntary associations can be brought into play at once from here." Po claimed there were 200 men in the military headquarters, "not counting sentries and orderlies. We include here our Operations, Intelligence, Departments of Discipline and Education, military administration and personnel and signal corps. We do not include here our rear services, *i.e.,* supplies, transport, medical department, weapons and ammunition. These departments need not even be in the same county. They are placed according to convenience and we reach them by messengers, telephone or radio." The telephone network, according to Po, consisted of 10,000 miles of line and 1,000 phones. He also emphasized the mobility of the military headquarters, asserting that the entire headquarters' equipment could be packed in half an hour and transported on two mules and the backs of a few men.

According to Miss Strong, the members of the general staff arose at six and spent the first two hours in individual study. Po continued: "I personally am studying Chairman Mao's recent instructions on land reform and also the reports that come from our villages. For theoretical study I am giving some time to Lenin's *Two Tactics.* Each of us has his individual program. At eight we all breakfast together on rice and two vegetables. Then we assemble here for three hours' joint work. After that the heads of departments [for example, intelligence] go to their own offices and direct the work of their subordinates. At four we have our second and last meal, which is wheat bread, two vegetables and tea. At five we take an hour's recreation. Evenings are for miscellaneous work. The city of Hantan [where the headquarters had previously been located] was a convenient place to work in. It had better housing and electric light. But there are advantages also in working in a village. There are fewer distractions. In a city one becomes inclined to bureaucracy. Here everything is quiet and we concentrate on our work."

Po provided Belden with further information about the border region, which the latter recorded in considerable detail in *China Shakes the World.* He claimed that the Red Army in his area had grown from 6,000 regulars to 300,000 in addition to 800,000 "militiamen." Assuming the accuracy of the 800,000 figure, this indicates that one of the major activities in the Chin-Chi-Lu-Yü region during the late war and postwar years was the recruitment and training of militia forces. Only three years earlier the official Communist figure for the militia was 400,000.[12] For administrative purposes the region was divided into five military and government districts, and the districts in turn were divided into 24 sub-districts, each with parallel military and government organizations. Po claimed that the border region consisted of 126 hsien, but he noted that the number under Communist control was constantly changing. (The official 1944 figure was 198, and in 1946 Miss Strong had been given the figure 193.) Po also gave Belden his view of the strategic importance of the border region, and statistics on population, cultivated land, and the growth of small-scale industry.

In 1948, following the merger of the Chin-Ch'a-Chi and the Chin-Chi-Lu-Yü Border Regions, the North China Military Region was created; Nieh Jung-chen was made the commander and Po the political commissar. Broadly paralleling the military region, the Communists established the North China People's Government (NCPG) in August 1948 to govern those portions of Hopeh, Shansi, Suiyuan, Chahar, and Pingyuan provinces under their control. Po attended the congress that inaugurated the NCPG and delivered a report on the administrative policies of the Party's North China Bureau (of which he was the secretary). He was made first vice-chairman of the NCPG and vice-chairman of its Finance and Economics Committee, serving in both instances directly under Tung Pi-wu. These positions occupied most of Po's time until the PRC was created (October 1949) and the NCPG was absorbed into its central administration, at which time he entered the national government.

From June 1949 he served as a CCP representative on the Preparatory Committee of the CPPCC; however, when the CPPCC convened in September 1949, Po attended as a representative of the North China Liberated Area. He served on the presidium (steering committee) for the September session and also spoke on North China affairs. When the central government was formally inaugurated in October, Po received several high-level appointments. He was made a member of the singularly important Central People's Government Council (CPGC), an organization that had legislative, executive, and judicial responsibilities and which, in 34 meetings between 1949 and 1954, passed on virtually all the vital national legislation adopted in these first critical years of the PRC. It consisted of a chairman (Mao Tse-tung), six vice-chairmen, and 56 Council members. He was also named to membership on the Government Administration Council (GAC; the cabinet), and, under the GAC, as a vice-chairman of the Finance and Economics Committee, the important committee charged with the task of coordinating the work of the ministries concerned with finance, industry, trade, food, railways, communications, water conservancy, agriculture, forestry, and labor, as well as the People's Bank of China. The other important post that Po was given in October 1949 was as minister of Finance, a position he held until September 1953 when he was replaced by his wartime colleague Teng Hsiao-p'ing.

In mid-December 1949 Po was appointed political commissar of the Suiyuan Military District. Fu Tso-i, the KMT general who had surrendered Peking in January 1949, was the commander. However, even though Suiyuan fell under the jurisdiction of the Party's North China Bureau which Po headed, there is little indication that he was active in the Suiyuan military post. In fact, he was fully engaged in Peking in the years after 1949 working in the national bureaucracy and concurrently directing the North China Party Bureau until it was abolished in August 1954. In the "mass" organizations, Po was a member of the First Executive Board of the Sino-Soviet Friendship Association (1949–1954), and, more important, he was a key figure in the establishment of the All-China Federation of Cooperatives (ACFC). The task of the federation is to promote agricultural and handicraft production to ensure the flow of commodities between the urban and rural areas. When the ACFC was established in 1950, Po was named chairman. However, Ch'eng Tzu-hua (q.v.) assumed the acting chairmanship in 1953 and thereafter Po, who had numerous other major responsibilities, played no active part in the federation.

At a March 3, 1950, GAC meeting, Po was made chairman of the National Organization Committee, which was established then under the GAC. The committee, although temporary in nature, was given broad powers to conduct a nationwide inventory on supplies and personnel. The GAC announcement that accompanied the formation of this body made it clear that the central government intended to crack down on falsified reports it had been receiving about available supplies and taxes, in addition to what they termed "padded" personnel rosters. (It should be noted that the Ministry of Personnel was not established until September 1950 under An Tzu-wen, q.v.) Moreover, the same GAC meeting also authorized Po's Ministry of Finance to establish stricter controls over the nation's financial network. In the ensuing years Po was frequently called upon to make reports before the top government bodies, to speak before a variety of conferences, and to serve on various *ad hoc* organizations. In almost every instance, these tasks were in connection with financial and economic questions. For example, in his capacity as minister of Finance, a post he held for the first four years of the PRC, he delivered the major budget reports.

At the end of 1951 Po was made chairman of a special "austerity examination committee." During the course of the next year the committee investigated and brought charges against a number of Party and state employees accused of corruption, waste, and bureaucraticism (the "three-anti" campaign) and against the bourgeois elements accused of bribery, tax evasion, fraud, theft of government property, and theft of state economic secrets (the "five-anti" campaign). Po spoke on these campaigns before the GAC on January 14 and May 30, 1952, and he summarized the results in an article in the *JMJP* of October 1, 1952.

In November 1952 Po was appointed a member of the newly established State Planning Commission. This had been formed on the eve of the inauguration of the First Five-Year Plan (January 1953); Po continued to serve on the commission until the constitutional government was set up in the fall of 1954. In preparation for this, the PRC established in early 1953 a committee to draft the constitution. This was chaired by Mao Tse-tung, and Po was one of its members; then in 1954 he was elected a deputy from Tientsin to the First NPC, which at its inaugural session in September 1954 adopted the new constitution. Po was also in the Second NPC (1959–1964) as a deputy from Hopeh (which had absorbed the Tientsin constituency). However, when the Third NPC met initially in late 1964, Po represented his native Shansi. When the central government was reorganized at the time of the First NPC meetings and immediately thereafter (September–October 1954), Po received two important posts, both related to the economic field in which he had been working for so many years. He was named director of the State Council's newly established Third Staff Office, which was charged with coordinating the work of the various commissions and ministries engaged in heavy industry and construction work. One of the commissions under the Third Staff Office, the State Construction Commission, was also placed under Po's direction. He gave up the latter post in May 1956 to Wang Ho-shou, another economic specialist. However, when he relinquished the post to Wang, he assumed the chairmanship of the State Economic Commission. This body directs annual economic planning, in contrast to the State Planning Commission, which is charged with the task of preparing the five-year plans. Po also served for a fairly short time (March 1956–May 1957) on the Scientific Planning Commission as a vice-chairman under Vice-premier Ch'en I, but he relinquished the position when the Scientific Commission was reorganized.

At the Eighth Party Congress in September 1956, Po was one of the featured speakers. His address, which stressed the necessity for China to accumulate capital resources, was entitled "The Relationship between Accumulation and Consumption in Socialist Construction." At the close of the Congress he was re-elected to the Party Central Committee. Of greater importance was his election at the First Plenum of the new Central Committee (held the day after the Congress closed) to alternate membership on the Party Politburo, thus elevating Po to the innermost elite of the CCP. As of the time of the Eighth Congress, he could probably be rated among the most important economic specialists together with such men as Ch'en Yun, Li Fu-ch'un, and Li Hsien-nien (each of whom was elected or re-elected to the Politburo at this time).

Shortly after the Eighth Congress, Po received still another promotion when he was appointed (November 1956) as an additional vice-premier of the State Council. His position in the government hierarchy was slightly altered in September

1959 when the State Council underwent another reorganization. The Third Staff Office, which Po had headed since its formation in 1954, was merged with the Fourth and Fifth Staff Offices to form a new Industry and Communications Office. In view of the fact that Po was politically outranked by his fellow economic specialist Li Fu-ch'un, the latter was named to head the new office and Po was named as his deputy. However, in April 1961, Po succeeded Li as the director of the office, and he continues to hold this post. Then, in October 1962, he was named as one of several new vice-chairmen of the State Planning Commission under Chairman Li Fu-ch'un. With this appointment, Po holds top posts in the organization in charge of long-range planning (the State Planning Commission) as well as annual planning (the State Economic Commission).

Po's service to the Party has been strongly oriented toward domestic problems. However, on at least two occasions he has been directly involved with international economic affairs. In May 1960 he spent about three weeks in Poland as head of a delegation invited there by the Polish United Workers' (Communist) Party. Though the Communist press mentioned that economic cooperation was a major subject of discussion, no known agreement of any kind was signed. In January 1961, he led the negotiations with Vietnamese officials in Peking regarding a Chinese loan to Vietnam and a protocol on technical aid and the supply of equipment, both of which Po signed on January 31, 1961.

Throughout the late 1950's and early 1960's, Po continued to play a key role in the economy. Unlike such key economic specialists as Ch'en Yun (q.v.), he apparently did not run into political difficulties during the Great Leap Forward or its aftermath. Throughout those economically difficult years Po was a regular participant in scores of conferences which dealt with one or another phase of economic development. Po's writings in the Great Leap Forward suggest that he favored relatively conservative economic policies. One Western observer noted that in an important article by Po in early 1961 he outlined future economic tasks which were, in effect, a "complete reversal of the Great Leap Forward approach to local initiative,"[13] that is, central economic planning was to be restored in place of reliance on such planning at the commune level. Po continued to be a major economic and political figure until mid-1966 when, during the early phase of the Great Proletarian Cultural Revolution, he was denounced and, presumably, stripped of his numerous posts.

In the period after 1949 Po was a regular contributor to the Party press, and his numerous articles and speeches constitute a major body of information about China's economy. In the *JMJP* of June 29, 1951 (translated in CB 100), Po wrote an important article on Party policies in rural China. His "Three Years of Historic Achievements," which appeared in *People's China* (no. 20, October 16, 1952), is a fact-laden survey of the period of "reconstruction and rehabilitation." In 1959 he wrote an important, policy-oriented piece on the application of technology to agriculture, which appeared in a collection of articles commemorating the 10th anniversary of the PRC entitled *Ten Gorious Years* (Peking, 1960). Five other articles on economic questions appeared in *Hung-ch'i* (Red flag), the Party's leading journal (no. 1, 1959; no. 10, 1960; nos. 3–4, 1961; no. 13, 1962; and no. 20, 1963). He also wrote an article for the *JMJP* of June 28, 1961, on the 30th anniversary of the "martyrdom" of Chang Chao-feng and Ku Hsiung-i, early Communists who were killed in 1930 and 1931, respectively. Neither Chang nor Ku was particularly important, but Po's article is one of the few available sources on the CCP organization, underground, and guerrilla operations in north China during the early history of the Communist movement.

Po is known to have been married (as of 1964) to Hu Ming, whose antecedents are unknown.

1. Donald G. Gillin, *Warlord Yen Hsi-shan in Shansi Province, 1911–1949* (Princeton, N.J., 1967), pp. 105–106.
2. Lyman P. Van Slyke, *Enemies and Friends* (Stanford, Calif., 1967), pp. 132–133; *JMJP*, August 14, 1962.
3. Jack Belden, *China Shakes the World* (New York, 1949), p. 51.
4. Gillin, pp. 231–232.
5. *JMJP*, August 14, 1962.
6. Van Slyke, pp. 135–136; *Kuang-ming jih-pao*, December 25, 1958.
7. Van Slyke, p. 136.
8. Hsu Yung-ying, *A Survey of the Shensi-Kansu-Ninghsia Border Region* (New York, 1945), pt. II, p. 15.
9. Evans Fordyce Carlson, *Twin Stars of China* (New York, 1940), pp. 91–92.
10. *K'ang-Jih chan-cheng shih-ch'i chieh-fang-ch'ü kai-k'uang* (A sketch of the liberated areas during the Anti-Japanese War; Peking, 1953), pp. 63–64.
11. Anna Louise Strong, *Tomorrow's China* (New York, 1948), pp. 74–76; Belden, pp. 46–48, 51–53, 70.
12. *K'ang-Jih chan-cheng shih-ch'i chieh-fang-ch'ü kai-k'uang*, p. 76.
13. Kenneth R. Walker, *Planning in Chinese Agriculture* (London, 1965), p. 86.

Po Ku, see **Ch'in Pang-hsien**

Saifudin

(c.1915–   ; Artush, Sinkiang). Chairman, Sinkiang-Uighur Autonomous Region; alternate member, CCP Central Committee.

Saifudin is the most important Uighur in the CCP and one of the very few non-Han Chinese to have attained membership on the CCP Central Committee. He has been a top official in Sinkiang since the Communists came to power in 1949, and since 1955 he has been chairman of the Sinkiang-Uighur Autonomous Region. The name Saifudin is a Chinese corruption of Saif-al-din Azia (or Seyfudin Azizov, the Russian variant), and it is transliterated into Chinese as Sai Fu-ting. The son of a businessman, he was born into a Uighur Muslim family in the small town of Artush (A-t'u-shih), located about 15 miles northwest of Kashgar, not far from the Russian border. Kashgar is the major city on the western edge of the vast Tarim Basin and the home of the agricultural Uighurs, a Turkic people. In times past the city was the scene of Muslim revolt against Chinese authority, and it continues to be a center of racial tensions. In August 1954 the Communists made Kashgar the seat of their first administration to govern the minorities of southern Sinkiang, which contains a large proportion of the Uighur population of Sinkiang. Known as the South Sinkiang Administrative Ch'ü, it has two sub-divisions, one of which governs another Turkic group, the nomadic Kirghiz, which is centered around Saifudin's native Artush.

Saifudin grew up in a central Asian society that was not Chinese. Because his Uighur Muslim family could afford to give him a good education, he learned Russian and Chinese, as well as his native Turkic language. Chinese is said to be his weakest language. He apparently graduated from a college in Sinkiang before seeking further education in the Soviet Union, where he is known to have spent some time at the Central Asian Political Institute in Tashkent,[1] a school that enrolled a number of students from Chinese Turkistan in the years before World War II. Saifudin joined the Russian Communist Party during these student days, and he probably continued his membership in the CPSU until 1950 when he joined the CCP.

In 1961 Saifudin wrote that "Beginning in 1933, the Party sent many outstanding Party members and cadres at different times to carry out revolutionary work in Sinkiang, thus sowing the seed of revolution on a broad front."[2] Well before this account was published there were Japanese reports that in 1932 Saifudin himself had participated in Turkic rebel movements in western Sinkiang, an indication that if sent by "the Party," he must have received his orders from the CPSU. In November 1933 the "Eastern Turkistan Republic" was established in Kashgar, some 1,000 road miles from the provincial capital at Tihwa (Urumchi). Saifudin was reported to have held office in the new government whose Turki leaders were in revolt against the Chinese authorities at Tihwa. The establish-ment of the "republic" took place just at the time when Sheng Shih-ts'ai was consolidating his authority in Tihwa. Sheng, a professional officer of Manchurian origin, had accomplished this feat with Soviet support, and it was also with Soviet backing that he was able to expand his power throughout Sinkiang and into the territory of the "Eastern Turkistan Republic." The Muslim leaders of the "Republic" received encouragement at different times from the British, the Russians, and the Japanese, all of whom had interests of their own in controlling the politics of Sinkiang. In the latter half of 1934, when Sheng Shih-ts'ai crushed the rebellion at Kashgar with Soviet aid, "Republic" President Khoja Niaz made a temporary alliance with Sheng, while Sabil Mullah, the former premier, made an unsuccessful visit to Tokyo (1935) seeking help from the Japanese. When the rebellion was finally put down Saifudin fled back to the USSR, where he spent some time before going to live in Afghanistan. According to one report he did not return to Sinkiang until about 1943.

The political scene in Sinkiang had turned full circle during Saifudin's long absence. Soviet influence was still present, but in 1942 Sheng Shih-ts'ai, who had previously allied himself with the Russians, made an abrupt change and came to terms with the Chinese Nationalists. The change did not please the national minorities, especially those in northern and western Sinkiang, and revolts broke out among the Kazakhs in the north in 1944. These soon spread to the Ili region close to the Soviet frontier in western Sinkiang. In the winter of 1944–45 a new "Eastern Turkistan Republic" was created with its capital at Kuldja (I-ning), a city in northwest Sinkiang close to the border of the Kazakh SSR. The second "republic" included the three districts of Ili, Tarbagatai, and Altai and existed for about a year under a government headed by a Uighur, a Kazakh, and a non-Soviet Russian who was resident in the area. One of its Turki leaders was a military man named Akhmedjan Kasimi, whom Saifudin was subsequently to replace in the political sphere. Saifudin, the republic's minister of education and youth corps director, was a Communist; the others mentioned were radical nationalists but probably not Communist Party members. The Kuldja rebellion soon spread into the Tarim Basin area to the south, and in September 1945 General Chang Chih-chung was sent by Chungking to Tihwa to negotiate peace with the rebels. With the help of the Russian consul general from Tihwa, who acted as mediator, the Kuldja rebels and the Nationalist representatives came to a series of agreements by June 1946. Among other things they provided for a reorganization of the provincial government and the Sinkiang armed forces. A new government was to be inaugurated, but only part of it appointed by Chungking. In addition to Chungking's appointees, there were to be 15 members of the provincial government nominated by Sinkiang delegates.[3] As of June 1946, Saifudin, already a provincial assemblyman, became commissioner of education in the new government. He presumably received the appointment by nomination of the delegates to the Sinkiang assembly.

Despite efforts to bring the two sides together, final agreement could not be reached. In May 1947 Chang Chih-chung relinquished the provincial chairmanship to Masud Sabri, a Uighur and KMT member. The elderly Sabri did not please the national minorities and on June 4, following his inauguration on May 31, 63 members of the provincial assembly out of the 90 present adopted a resolution opposing him. In July a group of 27 assemblymen left Tihwa for Kuldja, and they were joined soon after by 22 others who came from Saifudin's Kashgar region. Finally, in August, Akhmedjan Kasimi, also an assemblyman, left Tihwa for Kuldja, taking with him the remaining Kuldja delegates.[4] It is not known when Saifudin left, but it is clear that he must have been among the dissenters.

Throughout the year 1948 the situation between Tihwa and Kuldja remained deadlocked, with each area maintaining a government of its own. In August 1948 the Kuldja group established the Sinkiang League for the Protection of Peace and Democracy, a quasi-political party whose ostensible aim was to promote the nationalistic aspirations of the minorities in north and west Sinkiang. Akhmedjan headed the new organization, with Saifudin serving as editor of the league's official organ, *Ch'ien-chin jih-pao* (Advance daily). Then, following Akhmedjan's accidental death in 1949 (see below), Saifudin became acting chairman.

The Communists took over Sinkiang with little fighting. Burhan Shahidi (q.v.), the prominent Uighur whom the Nationalists had appointed to succeed Masud Sabri as governor in December 1948, defected to the Communists in September 1949, and at the same time Sinkiang Garrison Commander T'ao Chih-yueh also went over to the Communists. The effects of these changes in allegiance were not immediately disruptive to the Tihwa administration, for the Communists rewarded Burhan by retaining him as the provincial governor, and T'ao remained as deputy military commander of the Sinkiang Military District. On October 21, the first units of P'eng Te-huai's First Field Army, the forces responsible for the takeover in the northwest, reached Tihwa under the command of veteran CCP military leader Wang Chen (q.v.), who was the top Communist official in Sinkiang until 1952.

While a change of regimes was being effected in Sinkiang, the Communist central government was being installed in Peking at the inaugural session of the CPPCC in September 1949, which was attended by delegates from all parts of China. When the Sinkiang group arrived in Peking it numbered only three men (Saifudin among them); Akhmedjan and a group of his supporters were to have attended, but they were killed in an air crash en route to Peking. Saifudin took an active part in the CPPCC meetings, an indication that he was by then well known to the CCP, and perhaps also that it had plans in store for him. He served on the *ad hoc* committee to draft the Organic Law of the PRC and made a short speech in which he presented the Party view of the events that had transpired in Kuldja. The Kuldja rebellion, he explained, was not a movement against Chinese rule, but a "movement of liberation," a "liberation" that would only be complete when the Communists were victorious throughout the mainland. At the close of the meetings Saifudin was elected as a "specially invited personage" to membership on the CPPCC First National Committee, a position he retained until the Second CPPCC was formed in late 1954.

With the establishment of the central government in October 1949, Saifudin assumed a number of significant posts, the most important of which was membership on the Central People's Government Council (CPGC). Chaired by Mao Tse-tung, the CPGC had six vice-chairmen and 56 members, a number of whom were non-Communists. The significance of the CPGC can be judged in part from the fact that 27 of the 29 CCP members were concurrently members of the CCP Central Committee; only Liu Ko-p'ing (q.v.) and Saifudin among the Communists were not Central Committee members. He remained a CPGC member until it was dissolved in 1954, and during this same period he was also a vice-chairman of the Nationalities Affairs Commission and a member of the Political and Legal Affairs Committee, both of which were subordinate to the Government Administration Council (the cabinet).

After the central government was formed and staffed, Saifudin returned to Sinkiang where over the winter of 1949–50 he took part in the formation of both the Sinkiang Provincial Government and the regional government known as the Northwest Military and Administrative Committee (NWMAC). In the former he became a vice-governor (December) in an administration nominally headed by Burhan Shahidi (q.v.). At the same time Saifudin was appointed chairman of the Sinkiang Nationalities Affairs Committee, thus making him the top provincial authority over the minority problems so important to Sinkiang. The NWMAC was established in January 1950 with headquarters at Sian; as a NWMAC member Saifudin must have spent part of the time between 1950 and 1954 in Sian as well as Tihwa (later Urumchi) and Peking. When the NWMAC was reorganized into the Northwest Administrative Committee (NWAC) in January 1953, he was elevated to a vice-chairmanship, retaining this post until regional administrations were abolished in 1954 with the advent of the constitutional government. From 1950 to 1954 he was also a vice-chairman of the NWMAC–NWAC's Nationalities Affairs Committee and from 1952 to 1954 he also served as a member of the regional Political and Legal Affairs Committee.

In December 1949 Mao Tse-tung had gone to Moscow to engage in the critical negotiations that led to a series of key treaties and agreements in the early months of 1950. He was joined by Chou En-lai on January 20, 1950, and 10 days later Saifudin arrived in Moscow leading a Sinkiang government delegation to participate in "commercial negotiations." Immediately after the signing of the Sino-Soviet Treaty of Friendship, Alliance, and Mutual Assistance on February 14, Mao and Chou left for home, but a number of top officials, Saifudin among them, remained behind for further talks. He probably took part in negotiating two agreements (both signed March 27) related to Sinkiang, under which two joint stock companies were established in Sinkiang, one for the prospecting and refining of petroleum and the other for the exploitation of non-ferrous and rare metals. Both companies were jointly operated until the end of December 1954 when, in accordance with the agreements reached in Peking during the Khrushchev-Bulganin visit two months earlier, the Soviet shares were turned over to the Chinese. Saifudin was among the speakers in Urumchi on December 31 when the shares in the petroleum company were transferred to the Chinese.

Saifudin remained in Moscow until April 1950, and while he was there it was announced by the Chinese (February) that he had been admitted to the CCP. In June 1950, shortly after returning from Moscow, the Sinkiang League for the Protection of Peace and Democracy held a meeting with the announced goal of establishing a "democratic united front of the various nationalities of Sinkiang." The name was changed to the Sinkiang People's Democratic League, and Saifudin was made the chairman. The league was listed in the official 1951 *Jen-min shou-ts'e* (People's handbook) among the "democratic" political parties, placing it on par with the China Democratic League and the other better-known parties. However, nothing has been heard of the organization since that time; it seems probable that the Communists abolished it to preclude the league's becoming a focal point for separatist tendencies in Sinkiang.

In addition to his role in the Sinkiang government administration, Saifudin has also participated in the military command for the province as well as in the affairs of the CCP organization there. When the Sinkiang Military District was set up in December 1949, P'eng Te-huai was named as commander, with Wang Chen, T'ao Chih-yueh, and Saifudin as deputy commanders. However, P'eng spent practically no time in Sinkiang, and T'ao was a defector from the Nationalist armies. In practice, therefore, Wang was the real head of the Sinkiang military establishment and Saifudin was his leading deputy. Wang Chen was later replaced by Wang En-mao (q.v.), and until at least the early sixties Saifudin remained as the top deputy commander. He was first identified in November 1952 in an administrative post with the CCP organization for Sinkiang, the Sinkiang Party Sub-bureau, where he was serving as fourth secretary under First Secretary Wang En-mao. Just two months before this identification the Communists set up a preparatory committee to transform Sinkiang from a provincial administration into an "autonomous" region—the Sinkiang-Uighur Autonomous Region (SUAR). Burhan was the nominal chairman of the preparatory committee, but the real authority obviously rested with Saifudin (a vice-chairman) and Wang En-mao (a member). When the SUAR was finally inaugurated on October 1, 1955, with Politburo member Tung Pi-wu sent to the ceremonies as Peking's official representative, Saifudin replaced Burhan as the top government administrator in Sinkiang, that is, as chairman of the new SUAR, a post he still retains. A few weeks later Saifudin relinquished the chairmanship of the Sinkiang chapter of the CPPCC to Burhan (a position the former had held from February 1955), but in contrast to the early fifties when the CPPCC was an organization of considerable importance, by 1955 it had become a quasi-legislative body with little or no power. At the same time that these changes were being made, the Sinkiang Party Sub-bureau was reorganized into the SUAR Party Committee. Within the space of a few months Saifudin advanced from fourth to second Party secretary and finally in early 1956 to a full secretaryship, although he continues to serve under First Secretary Wang En-mao. In summary, Saifudin soon emerged as the top man in the Sinkiang government structure and as number two man to Wang En-mao in both the Party and the military establishment. Then, at the Party's Eighth National Congress in September 1956, he was elected an alternate member of the Party Central Committee. One of the youngest elected, he was among the very few non-Han Chinese and the only Uighur.

In early 1953 the first steps were taken both nationally and locally to prepare for the inauguration of the constitutional government in

Peking. In January 1953, under the chairmanship of Mao Tse-tung, a committee was established in Peking to draft the constitution. Saifudin was a member of the committee (1953–54) and concurrently served as chairman of the Sinkiang Provincial Election Committee. In September 1954 he attended the opening session of the First NPC as a Sinkiang deputy. He was elected a vice-chairman of the prominent NPC Standing Committee, which is in charge of legislative work between the annual congress sessions. He continued as vice-chairman throughout the terms of the First and Second NPC's (1954–1964) and was re-elected when the Third NPC was formed in December 1964–January 1965. Saifudin has frequently spoken before the annual NPC sessions, usually on affairs in Sinkiang. His work with this legislative body continues to be one of his principal assignments in the national government.

In September 1954, at the same time Saifudin became active in the NPC, he was also made a member of the newly created National Defense Council. He continues in this post, but Council membership seems to carry more prestige than authority. Exactly a year later, when military ranks were established and national military honors first awarded, he was made a lieutenant general (equal to a two-star U.S. Army general) and given one or more of the military orders. (The award was not specified, but in view of Saifudin's career it is probable that he received the Order of Liberation, the one given for service between 1945 and 1950.)

In the years since the mid-fifties, Saifudin has been almost as occupied by extracurricular activities as he has been by his particular fields of specialization. Two of his major activities outside his tasks within the Party and the government are the Communist-sponsored peace movement and the field of international relations as promoted by certain of the mass organizations known as "friendship associations." Identified in August 1955 as a Council member of the China-India Friendship Association, he may still retain the post, although the association has not been active since the outbreak of the border disputes between the two nations in the late fifties. In November 1956 he was selected for membership on the Council of the newly created China-Egypt Friendship Association, established in the wake of the international disturbances over the Suez Canal. In February 1958, following the merger of Egypt and Syria into the United Arab Republic, the name of the organization was changed to the China-UAR Friendship Association. Also in the field of international relations, when the Asian Solidarity Committee of China was formed in February 1956 Saifudin became a member, retaining his membership after May 1958 when it was renamed the Afro-

Asian Solidarity Committee. In all these organizations it is likely that his central Asian background and Muslim heritage are useful in developing relations with nations having large Muslim populations. As a representative of China's national minorities, he has also been useful in work with the Soviet Union which has its own problems with minorities and their integration into a Communist system. In 1950 Saifudin became a vice-chairman of the Sino-Soviet Friendship Association's (SSFA) Sinkiang branch. Technically he still retains this post, but the SSFA has become relatively inactive since relations between China and the USSR became openly hostile. At the Second National SSFA Conference in December 1954, he was elected a vice-chairman of the SSFA, and he was re-elected at the Third Conference in May 1959. Saifudin's connections with the peace movement go back to October 1949 when he became a member of the newly established national China Peace Committee; he retained his membership until the Committee was reorganized in July 1958. By 1953 he was also a vice-chairman of the Peace Committee's Sinkiang branch, a position he may still retain.

Since the Communists came to power in 1949, Saifudin has been sent on a number of missions abroad, but only twice outside the Communist bloc. After the above-mentioned trip to Moscow, his next journey took him to New Delhi in April 1955 as a member of Kuo Mo-jo's delegation to the Asian Countries' Conference. He was in Moscow in July–August 1957 for undisclosed purposes, and from Moscow he went directly to Finland (August) as head of a Chinese parliamentary delegation. He was again in Moscow in November 1957 for the celebrations commemorating the 40th anniversary of the Russian Revolution as a member of the large delegation led by Mao Tse-tung. While the delegation was there Czech President Antonin Zapotocky died; Saifudin was sent to Prague for the funeral as a member of a group led by Politburo member Li Hsien-nien. He was a member of another Chinese delegation to a funeral when East German President Wilhelm Pieck died in September 1960; and in September–October 1962 he was deputy leader under P'eng Chen of the NPC delegation to North Vietnam.

It is notable that Saifudin, the CCP's most prominent Uighur, is not serving on either of the two major government bodies concerned with minority affairs—the NPC Nationalities Committee and the State Council's Nationalities Affairs Commission. And in his native Sinkiang the most important administrative posts have always been held by Han Chinese, first Wang Chen and then Wang En-mao. Yet the published records indicate that he has been a willing spokesman for Party policies in regard to minority groups. Saifudin has made numerous speeches on minority questions (e.g., at NPC sessions), and he is the author of a number of articles on the subject that have appeared in the *JMJP* and *Min-tsu t'uan-chieh* (Nationalities unity), the leading journal on minority affairs. During the latter half of 1957, when the Party staged the *cheng feng* ("rectification") campaign to squelch the outspoken criticisms that the Hundred Flowers period had brought forth, Saifudin was in the forefront of the campaign in Sinkiang, serving with Wang En-mao as co-director of the Sinkiang *cheng feng* committe. In the summer of 1958 he was called upon to deliver an attack at a meeting of the SUAR Party Committee on "local nationalists" in Sinkiang, a number of whom were purged at that time, principally for resisting Han authority in the region. Since mid-1961 Saifudin has participated in a program to encourage the compilation of histories of China's numerous national minorities.

Although Saifudin is primarily a political figure, he has also had assignments in cultural and educational fields. In August 1960 he was elected a vice-chairman of the All-China Federation of Literary and Art Circles, though there is no indication that he has himself been a creative writer. Four years later he was appointed (June 1964) as president of Sinkiang University, founded in Urumchi in 1960.

Like so many CCP leaders, Saifudin has been drawn into the bitter hostilities with the Soviet Union, a fact all the more noteworthy in his case because of the difficulties that have arisen in the 1960's along the Sinkiang-Soviet border. Speaking before a session of the SUAR Congress in March 1964, he bluntly accused the Soviets of having carried out large-scale "subversive activities" against Sinkiang. In one of the most revealing admissions made by a Chinese official in the course of the extended Sino-Soviet dispute, he charged the Russians with "enticing and coercing several tens of thousands of Chinese citizens into crossing into Soviet territory." Saifudin further accused the Russians of having created "propaganda machines" in areas near Sinkiang to "create rumors and slanders, attack frantically the leadership of the CCP, distort the history of Sinkiang, and attempt to destroy the unity of the various nationalities" in China. He closed by warning his listeners to be "alert" to the Soviet "intrigues."[5] As a former CPSU member, Saifudin's speech must have had an ironic ring in Soviet ears.

In private life Saifudin is married to A-i-mu (Ahyimu), whose name suggests that she is of Uighur origin. He has a daughter, born about 1938, who knows Russian and was apparently reared in the Soviet Union, because when she enrolled in Peking University in the late fifties she was placed in a special department for students unfamiliar with Chinese. About the year 1960, after two years' study, she entered the university's Chinese Language Department.[6]

1. *New York Times,* September 25, 1949.
2. *SCMM* 302, p. 24.
3. Owen Lattimore, *Pivot of Asia* (Boston, Mass., 1950), p. 90.
4. *Ibid.,* pp. 96–98.
5. *SCMP* 3210, p. 14.
6. Interview with former Peking University student at Cambridge, Mass., June 1966.

Sang-chi-yueh-hsi

(Songgi Ish; Sans-rygas-ye-shes; 1917–   ; Tang-pa, Szechwan). Tibetan leader; vice-governor of Szechwan; alternate member, CCP Central Committee.

Most of Sang-chi-yueh-hsi's career has revolved around the fact that he is a Tibetan. He has been deeply involved in nationalities affairs, serving on the Nationality Affairs Committees of the Government Administration Council and the NPC and holding important Party and government posts in southwest China and particularly in Szechwan where there are large concentrations of Tibetans.

The name Sang-chi-yueh-hsi is derived from the Chinese pronunciation of a Tibetan name. His less frequently used Chinese name is T'ien Pao. He was born in the small town of Tang-pa on the Ta-chin River in north Szechwan, close to the border of the former province of Sikang. He and two brothers were said to have been Tibetan lamas and thus must have had some early education under Buddhist auspices.

Before the Long March the Chinese Communists had very little contact with Tibetans; it was not until the Red armies pushed through western China that they encountered Tibetan minorities living in Sikang, Szechwan, and Kansu. At that time a few Tibetans joined the Red armies, the most prominent of these being Sang-chi-yueh-hsi. Mao Tse-tung's First Front Army met Chang Kuo-t'ao's Fourth Front Army at Mao-kung, Szechwan, in June 1935. The armies then marched north through the Tang-pa area to Mao-erh-kai, which was a center for Tibetans living in northwest Szechwan. The Communists did not endear themselves to the Tibetans, because they were then very short of supplies and forced the Tibetans to surrender stores of food. They even broke into the local lamaseries for rice and flour. At Mao-erh-kai, Chang and Mao held a final conference, at which they were unable to agree on future strategy (see under Chang Kuo-t'ao). In August 1935 Mao proceeded north toward Shensi, while Chang remained temporarily in Szechwan and then turned west into Sikang, the home of other large Tibetan colonies. In September Chang's army passed through the Szechwan town of A-pa, which is now located in one of the provincial Tibetan autonomous chou. Returning to Mao-erh-kai, the Communists met Nationalist troops and were driven west into Sikang, again passing near Tang-pa before making their winter headquarters in the lamasery town of Kan-tzu on the upper reaches of the Ya-lung River.[1] Sang-chi-yueh-hsi, then about 18, joined Chang's Fourth Front Army as it moved through his home area.

In mid-1936 the Fourth Front Army was joined by the Second Front Army of Ho Lung and Jen Pi-shih (qq.v.), which had been forced to retreat from its base in western Hunan late in 1935. Li Hsien-nien (q.v.), serving in Chang's army, was responsible for promoting cooperation between the Communists and the Kan-tzu Tibetans, enabling the Communists to purchase food and eventually to establish a small Communist area, a "Tibetan People's Government" known as Po-pa-i-t'e-wa Soviet Government.[2] Sang-chi-yueh-hsi was director of the Youth Department of this government and belonged to a youth vanguard unit there. (His only other connection with youth work occurred in 1949 when he attended an important youth congress held in Peking.) Nationalist forces drove the Communist armies from Kan-tzu in May 1936, but they left Tibetan converts behind, many of whom were later given posts in a Tibetan autonomous chou established in Szechwan in November 1950.[3] The Communist armies which left Kan-tzu and Sikang included a newly formed independent division from the Po-pa Soviet, with Sang-chi-yueh-hsi serving as its political commissar. Thus, he was with Chang's armies when they joined Mao Tse-tung in north Shensi late in 1936.

By 1939 Sang-chi-yueh-hsi was a member of the First Assembly of the Shensi-Kansu-Ninghsia (Shen-Kan-Ning) Border Region Government, whose headquarters was in Yenan. However, he was not on the Second Assembly, which opened in November 1941. In 1944 he graduated with the first class of the Yenan Nationalities Institute, the Communist training school for national minority leaders, which was opened in 1941 with Kao K'o-lin as vice-president and Ulanfu (qq.v.) as head of the Education Department. At some time during the Sino-Japanese War (probably before he enrolled at the Institute) Sang-chi-yueh-hsi served in Liu Po-ch'eng's 129th Division of the Eighth Route Army and was wounded in action.

After the war ended in 1945 he fought in northwest China against a member of the famous Muslim Ma family, as well as the forces of General Hu Tsung-nan, the Nationalist Pacification Commissioner for Shensi from 1946 to 1949. In the postwar period and as late as 1949 he belonged to the Nationalities Affairs Committee of the Shen-Kan-Ning Border Region Government. He was also rather active in the establishment of the national government on October 1, 1949. In June 1949 a preparatory committee was formed to lay the groundwork for the convocation of the First CPPCC in September. Sang-chi-yueh-hsi was a member of this preparatory committee, which included some of the Party's top leaders. When the CPPCC was convened in September, several *ad hoc* committees were established, one of which was the Committee to Draft the Organic Law of the CPPCC, a key document adopted at that time. He served as a member of the committee and also spoke before the conference, urging all Tibetans to assist the PLA in the complete liberation of the mainland—comments made a year prior to the invasion of Tibet by the PLA in 1950. He also warned Indian Prime Minister Nehru against being used by the English and American "imperialists" who were "plotting an invasion" of Tibet.

At the close of the First CPPCC in September 1949, he was elected to membership on the First National Committee as a representative of the national minorities; in February 1953 (at the fourth session of the CPPCC) he was elevated to the Standing Committee, holding both these seats until the close of the First CPPCC in late 1954. In October 1949 he was also appointed a member of the Nationalities Affairs Commission under the Government Administration Council (the cabinet), a position subordinate to Party veteran Li Wei-han (q.v.).

After the central government was established, Sang-chi-yueh-hsi returned to his native southwest China where he played an even more active part in the formation of the government and Party organizations for the area. Apart from Tibet proper, all of the southwest was conquered by the PLA by early 1950. To govern the area, in July 1950 the Communists set up the Southwest Military and Administrative Committee (SWMAC), embracing the provinces of Szechwan, Sikang, Kweichow, and Yunnan, under the chairmanship of Liu Po-ch'eng who had led the Red armies into the southwest. Sang-chi-yueh-hsi was named to membership on the SWMAC and he was also appointed a vice-chairman of the SWMAC's Nationalities Affairs Committee; he retained both posts when the SWMAC was reorganized into the Southwest Administrative Committee (SWAC) in February 1953, continuing to serve there until it was dissolved in November 1954. However, his major assignment was as the chief Party representative in those sections of western Szechwan and Sikang, where there is a large Tibetan population and where the Communists have established two of their local autonomous Tibetan governments. From October 1950 to January 1955 he was a member of the Sikang Provincial People's Government; he was promoted to a vice-governorship in January 1955, holding this post until October 1955 when Sikang was abolished and most of the territory was incorporated into Szechwan. Concurrently, from its establishment in November 1950 he served as chairman of the Tibetan Autonomous District in Sikang province, which had its capital at K'angting, 50 miles west of the Sikang capital of Ya-an. The status of this district was elevated in 1955 to the Tibetan Autonomous Chou. Finally, when Sikang was absorbed by Szechwan in 1955, this area became the Kan-tzu Tibetan Autonomous Chou of Szechwan. By the time of the change in 1955 from district to chou status, the capital had been transferred from K'ang-ting to Kan-tzu hsien, 150 miles northwest of K'ang-ting. However, in about 1957 K'ang-tung was restored as the capital. Sang-chi-yueh-hsi was, of course, familiar with Kan-tzu because of his experience there in the mid-1930's. He served as the first secretary of the chou Party Committee from at least 1957, but was replaced by early 1963. He also became head of another autonomous area established in December 1952, the Tibetan Autonomous District of northwestern Szechwan, which included his native town of Tang-pa. In December 1956, following the inclusion of Sikang in Szechwan, this Tibetan area was renamed the A-pa Tibetan Autonomous Chou of Szechwan. The capital had originally been in Mao-hsien, but it was later changed to Shua-ching-szu, and finally (in the spring of 1958) to its present site at Ma-erh-k'ang.

As already described, Sang-chi-yueh-hsi served as a member of the Sikang Provincial People's Government from 1950 to 1955, and from January 1955 to October 1955 as a provincial vice-governor. Concurrently, in November 1952, he was named to membership on the Szechwan Provincial People's Government; the reason for this unusual duality derives from the fact that he was heading autonomous Tibetan districts in both provinces. Then, in December 1955, following the abolition of Sikang, he was made one of the Szechwan vice-governors, a post he continues to hold. He has also served as a member of the Standing Committee of the Szechwan Party Committee since mid-1958 and as chairman of the Szechwan Nationalities Affairs Committee since 1959.

Although Sang-chi-yueh-hsi's principal contributions to the CCP have been in the southwest where he spends most of his time, he has also continued to hold posts in the national government. As already noted, he was a member of the Nationalities Affairs Commission under the Government Administration Council (the executive branch) from 1949 to 1954. When the constitutional government came into being in 1954, he continued his work in this field, but now as a member of the Nationalities Committee under the NPC; he was elevated to a vice-chairmanship in June 1956. He has been a deputy from Szechwan to the First (1954–

1959), Second (1959–1964), and Third (1964–) NPC's.

Sang-chi-yueh-hsi's long career in the CCP was given official recognition at the Eighth National Party Congress in September 1956 when he was elected an alternate member of the Party Central Committee. Not only is he the first Tibetan to reach the Central Committee, but he is also one of the youngest members, having been elected at the age of 39.

Since 1949 Sang-chi-yueh-hsi, like most high-ranking Party members, has engaged in a number of extracurricular activities apart from his principal work in nationalities affairs. He was a member of the China Peace Committee from October 1949 to July 1958, of the Executive Committee of the Chinese People's Relief Administration from April 1950 to date, and of the Chinese People's Committee in Defense of Children from November 1951 to the present. In the latter two organizations, both headed by Sung Ch'ing-ling (Mme. Sun Yatsen), he specifically serves as a representative of the national minorities.

He has twice participated in Communist "comfort" (or inspection) missions. The first such assignment was in February 1954 when he was a deputy leader of the All-China People's Delegation, which visited PLA units throughout China. Then in November 1956 he was again a deputy leader of a central government "comfort" mission that visited various national minority groups. More important was his visit to Lhasa from April to June 1956 when he was one of eight deputy leaders of the large delegation sent by Peking under the leadership of Vice-premier Ch'en I for the inauguration of the preparatory committee that was to establish a permanent Communist government in Tibet.

Sang-chi-yueh-hsi's name does not appear with great regularity in the Chinese press, a fact explained by the absence of regional and local news on Tibet and Tibetans. However, in 1958 the leading Communist journal on nationality questions, *Min-tsu t'uan-chieh* (Nationalities unity), published an important article by him entitled "Plant Red Flags in Every Corner of the Tibetan and Yi Regions of Szechwan."[4]

---

1. Ling Nai-min, *Tibetan Sourcebook,* (Hong Kong, 1964), p. 448.

2. *Ibid.*

3. *Ibid.* and p. 485.

4. *Min-tsu t'uan-chieh* no. 9, September 6, 1958.

Sha Ch'ien-li

(1903–   ; Su-chou, Kiangsu). Non-Communist; government administrator; minister, Ministry of Food.

Sha Ch'ien-li, a non-Communist, has held many important administrative posts in the central government since the establishment of the PRC in 1949, having served as minister or vice-minister in five ministries: Trade, Commerce, Local Industry, Light Industry, and Food. Sha was born in Soochow (Su-chou), an important city in Kiangsu on the Grand Canal to the west of Shanghai, and was educated at the Shanghai Law College, after which he practiced law in that city. He was one of the leaders of the National Salvation Association (NSA), formed in Shanghai in May 1936 by non-Communist politicians and intellectuals who were ardent critics of KMT policies, which they regarded as ineffectual in resisting the steady encroachments by the Japanese on Chinese sovereignty. For their advocacy of a united front against the Japanese, Sha and other prominent NSA members were arrested in Shanghai in November 1936 and imprisoned at Soochow until a few weeks after the outbreak of the Sino-Japanese War in July 1937. The case of Sha and his six imprisoned colleagues, who were widely known as the "Seven Gentlemen," is described more fully in the biography of Shih Liang.

Sha's wartime activities are not well documented, but he is known to have spent these years in west China, and toward the end of the war in 1945 he became a member of the China Democratic League (CDL), a loosely-knit political party whose membership included many National Salvation Association leaders. From 1945 to 1947 Sha was back in Shanghai where he practiced law and continued his work for the CDL, but then he fled to Hong Kong after the League was banned by the KMT in October 1947. In the following year he went to Communist-held areas in Manchuria, and from there to Peking in late February 1949, just a few weeks after the city had fallen to the Communists. Although already in his mid-forties, Sha was elected a vice-chairman of the All-China Federation of Democratic Youth in May 1949; he retained this post until mid-1953, but there is little indication that he was active in this assignment.

When Shanghai fell to the Communists in May 1949, Sha was sent there, serving as a member of the Shanghai Preparatory Committee of the Youth Federation and as deputy secretary-general of the Shanghai government. But the Shanghai assignments were of brief duration and by the end of the summer he was back in Peking where he has since worked. Prior to the establishment of the central government in October, Sha received two appointments in the political-legal field, being named in June to membership on the China New Legal Research Society's Preparatory Committee, as well as to membership on the Standing Committee of the New Political Science Research Association, which was formed in September. Later that month he attended the inaugural session of the CPPCC as a delegate of the National Salvation Association, which, for purposes of representation in the CPPCC, was regarded as a political party. At the close of the CPPCC, the organization that brought the new government into existence, Sha was elected to the CPPCC's First National Committee, holding his seat until the Second CPPCC was formed in late 1954.

Sha is one of the very few non-Communists who has continuously held important cabinet posts since the establishment of the PRC in October 1949, the first of which was a vice-ministership in the Ministry of Trade, responsible for both domestic commerce and foreign trade. He has worked primarily in the domestic sector, his most notable venture in the foreign trade field occurring from November 1951 to April 1952 when he led a delegation to Moscow, which negotiated the Sino-Soviet trade protocol for the year 1952. Also in the foreign field, he has been a board member since early 1950 of the Bank of China, the institution responsible for the PRC's foreign banking. In domestic commerce he received two collateral assignments in 1950–51, the first of these in July 1950 when he was appointed to membership on the provisional Board of Supervisors of the All-China Federation of Cooperations (ACFC), serving under Board Director Yeh Chi-chuang (q.v.), who was also his superior in the Ministry of Trade. Sha remained an ACFC supervisor until mid-1954.

Sha's second assignment in connection with domestic commerce was with the All-China Federation of Industry and Commerce (ACFIC). The decision to organize China's industrialists and business leaders, most of them non-Communists, had been made at the third session of the CPPCC in October–November 1951. A special office was immediately established, with Sha as its secretary-general, to prepare for the convocation of a national conference of businessmen. The national meeting, originally scheduled for March 1952, was delayed, however, because of the "five-anti" movement, a nationwide campaign directed largely at practices that the CCP authorities regarded as inimical to the interests of the state. Finally, after having been castigated by the Party press for several months, the nation's business leaders met in June 1952 to form themselves into a national organization. Sha reported on the work of his special office and, at the close of the proceedings, was elected secretary-general of the ACFIC Preparatory Committee. A year and a half later, in the fall of 1953, the ACFIC was established on a permanent basis, with Sha continuing to serve as the secretary-general. He retained his secretary-generalship until the next ACFIC congress in December 1956, and since that date has been a vice-chairman. Sha was clearly among the most important non-Communists involved in the early organizational period of the Federation, although it is equally evident that he was subordinate to Hsu Ti-hsin (q.v.), the CCP's leading specialist in the control of the Chinese industrial and business community.

Like many government officials in the early years of the PRC, Sha was called upon to lend his name to "mass" organizations, which were being established in rapid succession in 1949. From 1949 to 1950 he was National Committee member of the China Peace Committee, and from 1949 to 1954 he served on the Sino-Soviet Friendship Association's Executive Board, but such assignments were clearly peripheral to his more important tasks in domestic commerce. For example, he received a more pertinent assignment in July 1952 when he was appointed to membership on the central government's Labor Employment Committee, established to deal with the chronic problems of unemployment. In the following month, reflecting the growing complexities of the central bureaucracy, the Ministry of Trade was divided into the ministries of Foreign Trade and Commerce. Sha was assigned to the latter, where he served under Commerce Minister Tseng Shan (q.v.), and continued in the post until the constitutional government was inaugurated at the first session of the First NPC in September 1954. At the close of the NPC meetings he received his first ministerial portfolio when he was named to head the newly established Ministry of Local Industry. Sha had attended the NPC as a deputy from his native Kiangsu, and he has subsequently served in the Second NPC (1954–1959), as well as the Third NPC, which opened in December 1964. In May 1956, when Sha's Ministry of Local Industry was abolished, he was transferred to the Ministry of Light Industry, where he replaced Chia T'o-fu (q.v.) as the minister. Less than two years later, in February 1958, Sha was once more transferred, this time to the Ministry of Food, where he replaced Chang Nai-ch'i, a non-Communist industrialist and banker who had been one of the chief victims of the 1957–58 "rectification" campaign. Sha's succeeding Chang in the Food Ministry was particularly ironic—both had been among the seven Salvation Association leaders imprisoned together two decades previously.

Sha has continued to head the Food Ministry and most of his public appearances are in this capacity. Random but typical examples of his activities occurred in July 1959 when he addressed a ministry-sponsored conference on the purchase, sale, transport, and storage of grain and edible oils, and in January 1965 when he spoke on the food situation before the opening session of the Third NPC. He has also traveled away from the capital on occasion to make inspections, as in January 1962 and April 1964 when he visited Fukien. Closely related to his work in the Food Ministry, as well as the other

economic ministries with which he has been associated, has been Sha's membership since December 1954 on the Board of Directors of the Bank of Communications, which, under the direction of the Ministry of Finance, handles the state's investments in the so-called joint state-private enterprises.

Less than two months after the PRC had been established in October 1949, Sha's National Salvation Association was abolished—its tasks, in the eyes of the CCP, having been accomplished with the formation of a Communist government. Most of the Association leaders were transferred, in effect, to one of the other "democratic" political parties. Sha, who had been a China Democratic League member from about 1945, was elevated to Central Committee membership in the League in December 1949, the same month that the Salvation Association was abolished. He continues to serve on the Democratic League's Central Committee, and from 1949 to about the mid-fifties he also headed the League's Industry and Commerce Committee. Since April 1955 he has also been a Central Committee member in another "democratic" political party, the China Democratic National Construction Association (CDNCA), whose membership closely parallels that of the Federation of Industry and Commerce, in which Sha has been so active. In February 1960 he advanced to Standing Committee membership in the CDNCA, another post he still retains.

Apart from his 1951–52 trip to Moscow, Sha has been abroad on two other occasions. In November 1952 he led a "people's delegation" to North Korea and in May 1955 he accompanied Politburo member P'eng Te-huai to East Berlin to attend the celebrations marking the 10th anniversary of the defeat of Nazi Germany.

Unlike many of his colleagues in the non-Communist political parties, Sha has apparently not been the object of CCP-directed criticisms in the many ideological campaigns staged since 1949. It is noteworthy, for example, that 10 of the 24 ministries and commissions in 1949 were headed by non-Communists, whereas in the mid-1960's only nine of the 46 ministers were non-Communists—Sha among them. Thus, as of January 1965 (when all cabinet members were appointed or reappointed), only Sha and the following eight men shared the distinction of being non-Communist heads of ministries: Hsu Te-heng, Aquatic Products; Li Szu-kuang, Geology; Li Chu-ch'en, Light Industry; Chang Hsi-jo (qq.v.), Cultural Relations with Foreign Countries; Liu Wen-hui, Forestry; Fu Tso-i, Water Conservancy and Electric Power; Chiang Kuang-nai, Textile Industry; and, Chu Hsueh-fan, Posts and Tele-communications.

Of the "Seven Gentlemen" imprisoned in 1936–37, only Sha and Shih Liang continued to be prominent mainland personalities in the mid-sixties. Two of his colleagues, Tsou T'ao-fen and Li Kung-p'u, died before the Communists came to power (Tsou of natural causes and Li by assassination), and two others, Chang Nai-ch'i and Wang Tsao-shih, fell victim to the Communists' 1957–58 "rectification" campaign. Shen Chün-ju, the most important of the "Seven Gentlemen," had an active career with the Communists until his death in 1963. In personal life Sha is the father of at least three daughters and a son. The eldest of his girls received a degree in chemistry from Shanghai's Futan University in 1947.

Sha Wen-han

Purged ex-Governor of Chekiang.

Sha Wen-han was one of the most senior leaders to fall from power during the wide-sweeping purges of 1957–58 resulting from the "rectification" (*cheng-feng*) movement. He was charged, *inter alia,* with anti-Party activities. Although virtually nothing is known of Sha prior to the Communist conquest in 1949, the manner in which the charges were brought against him in 1957 suggests that his Party membership dated back for a long period—probably to at least the 1930's. It is likely that he was active in the New Fourth Army, the main Communist force in east China from 1937 until it was redesignated as the East China PLA in 1948. In any event, when the central government was established in Peking at the first session of the CPPCC in September 1949, Sha attended as a representative of the East China Liberated Areas, areas that had formerly been the territory of the New Fourth Army. (He was identified at that time as having the pseudonym of Chang Teng.) Earlier in 1949 Sha had taken part in the occupation of Ningpo in Chekiang after it fell in May 1949 to the forces in east China under the over-all command of Ch'en I; Sha served in 1949 as a vice-chairman of the Ningpo Military Control Commission.

Until his purge in 1957, Sha, who was apparently considered a specialist in propaganda and education, was one of the more important officials in Chekiang, serving under such prominent leaders as T'an Chen-lin (later a Politburo member), T'an Ch'i-lung and Chiang Hua (qq.v.). In 1949–50 he served as head of the provincial Education Department; he was a vice-governor from 1951 to 1952; and from 1951 to an uncertain date he was chairman of the provincial People's Supervision Committee, the government organ with wide inspection and discipline responsibilities. These positions within the Chekiang government were climaxed in January 1955 when he replaced T'an Ch'i-lung (who had been transferred to Shantung) as the Chekiang governor. Aside from these government positions, Sha held a number of posts under the Chekiang Party Committee. In the

1950–51 period he headed the Party Propaganda Department and in 1951 he served concurrently as director of the United Front Work Department. And at the time of his purge in late 1957 he was serving as a member of the Party's Standing Committee. At the regional level, Sha was a member of the Culture and Education Committee of the East China Military and Administrative Committee (ECMAC) from 1950 (and after the ECMAC was changed to the East China Administrative Committee in 1953, he continued in the post until 1954). Still another position he held within the educational field was the presidency of Chekiang University, one of China's best schools, from 1952 to about 1957. He was also a deputy from Chekiang to the First NPC, which met initially in September 1954; however, owing to his purge he was removed as a deputy before the end of the First NPC in 1959.

In the mid-1950's Sha's career had all the suggestions of a man on the rise within the Communist hierarchy. As governor of Chekiang he was constantly in the news in these years—giving reports before the sessions of the Chekiang government, welcoming foreign visitors to Hangchow, and attending the numerous conferences convened by the government for a variety of purposes. Interestingly, news about him appeared regularly up to the time of his purge in December 1957. Then, however, he was suddenly attacked in press with a series of devastating articles detailing his alleged offenses. He was accused of leading a corrupt and immoral life, engaging in criminal activities, advocating a provincial and sectarian viewpoint, and a series of lesser charges. But probably most important was the charge that he had been guilty of "anti-Party" activities, one of the most serious charges in the Communist lexicon. It was also noted at this time that he had been warned of his errant ways as early as the fall of 1956. One more nail was driven into the coffin of Sha's political career at the Second Session of the Eighth Party Congress in May 1958. In the resolution of the session reviewing the campaign against the "rightists," Sha's name headed the list of those accused. Once again, semantics seemed to suggest the seriousness of the offense: one list of names referred to the accused by the title "comrade," but the others (including Sha) were cited by name alone. (Some of the "comrades" were later reinstated to rather high political posts, e.g., P'an Fu-sheng, q.v.) Yet, 10 months after the charges against Sha, he was named (October 1958) as a member of the Second Chekiang Committee of the CPPCC. This large committee (totaling 292 members) is of little significance and nothing further has been heard of him since. One of the characteristics of the CCP since the Long March in the mid-1930's has been that total purges are few and far between. A large number, such as Sha, have been stripped of important positions and authority, but many of them are later given posts of trivial significance.

In private life Sha is married to Ch'en Hsiu-liang, who was elected a member of the Second Executive Committee of the All-China Federation of Democratic Women in April 1953. In retrospect, it is interesting that she was not re-elected to the Third Committee, formed in September 1957, just three months prior to the formal charges made against her husband.

Shao Shih-p'ing

(1899–1965; I-yang hsien, Kiangsi). Former governor of Kiangsi; alternate member, CCP Central Committee.

Shao Shih-p'ing was a prominent guerrilla leader from the 1920's in northeast Kiangsi, his native area, where with Fang Chih-min he organized the 10th Red Army and established the Fukien-Chekiang-Kiangsi Soviet base. Shao made the Long March and during the Sino-Japanese War he was active in north China, principally in educational assignments. He worked in Manchuria during the postwar period, and from 1949 until his death he was the Kiangsi governor and a leading provincial CCP official.

Shao was born in 1899 in I-yang hsien, about 100 miles east of Nanchang, the Kiangsi capital. His long-time colleague Fang Chih-min (q.v.) was born in the same year and the same hsien. Shao is said to have come from a declining petty bourgeois family. From 1916 to 1918 he studied at the I-yang Higher Primary School, and it was there that he became a close friend of Fang. Both young men took part in student demonstrations against the Japanese in 1918, a period when Chinese students were keenly sensitive to Japan's mounting incursions on Chinese sovereignty. Nothing is known of his whereabouts or activities for the next few years, but then in 1923 he went to Peking where he enrolled in Peking Normal University. In 1925 he joined the Communist Youth League and then the CCP. It is probable, though undocumented, that Shao was one of the many young men enlisted into the Communist movement by Li Ta-chao, then the leading CCP figure in north China. Like many Communists during this period of cooperation with the KMT, Shao was also a member of the KMT in the mid-twenties. During his student days he was successively chairman of the university's Students' Union and secretary of the CCP branch within this organization.

In March 1926 Shao was among the participants in the demonstrations staged by Peking students, Communists, and left-wing KMT members to protest the "Taku Ultimatum" presented to the Chinese by the signatory powers of the Boxer Protocol (most notably the Japanese). The ultimatum demanded the immediate removal (within 48 hours) of Chinese artillery installations from Taku, the port city for Tientsin. In the subsequent protest demonstrations, a number of the demonstrators were killed and Li Ta-chao was wounded and barely escaped capture by the soldiers. Shao was forced to leave school for his part in the demonstrations, and like many Communists then in Peking, he left the city for fear of being arrested.

Returning to Kiangsi, Shao taught school for a brief time at the First Normal School in Nanchang. The province was then in a state of great turmoil resulting from the advance of Chiang Kai-shek's Northern Expeditionary forces, which captured Nanchang in November 1926. Before the year ended Shao was back in his native I-yang where he worked in the peasant movement, presumably for both the KMT and the CCP; both parties were then eagerly wooing the peasantry in an attempt to hasten the success of the Northern Expedition. Sometime toward the end of 1926 Shao became a member of the Standing Committee of the KMT Kiangsi branch, as well as the secretary-general. The first half of 1927 was a period of considerable tension in Kiangsi as the CCP and the KMT jockeyed for power, a contest for authority further complicated by an intra-KMT struggle in which the Communists actively supported the left-wing KMT against the right-wing faction. In early April, the left-wing faction temporarily gained the upper hand and was thus able to reorganize the KMT Kiangsi branch as well as the provincial government. As a result of this turn of events, Shao was immediately appointed as a special inspector (*t'e-p'ai yuan*) of the provincial peasant association. He immediately proceeded to Hsien-feng hsien (adjacent to his native I-yang hsien) where he deposed the local officials who were hostile to the CCP and the left-KMT. He replaced them with two CCP members native to the hsien; Tsou Hsiu-feng became head of the new government organization in Hsien-feng, and Wu Hsien-min became the Public Security Bureau chief. Shao was given still another post within the KMT when he was made a member of the provincial Supervisory Committee at a conference in April of the KMT Kiangsi branch. However, Shao and his colleagues Fang Chih-min and Huang Tao were able to exercise their authority on behalf of the left-KMT and the CCP for only a few weeks, because by the late spring and early summer of 1927 Chiang Kai-shek's right-wing faction was rapidly moving toward control of the province. The final blow to the Communists took place in June and July when the steadily deteriorating alliance between the CCP and the left-KMT finally collapsed.

For a short time just prior to the KMT-CCP split in the middle of 1927, Shao was the secretary for both the CCP Committee in Fou-liang hsien in northeast Kiangsi and the committee for the city of Ching-te-chen, situated in the hsien. In the period after the Nanchang Uprising on August 1, the Communists turned to the countryside where they made concerted efforts to organize peasant rebellions and to establish armed forces to combat the Nationalists. By the fall of 1927 Shao had gone from Ching-te-chen to Heng-feng hsien. In November, in neighboring I-yang hsien, he attended a conference convened by Fang Chih-min which brought together CCP members from I-yang, Hsien-feng, and three other nearby hsien in northeast Kiangsi. They resolved to foment armed uprisings in the countryside and elected a small work committee, of which Fang Chih-min was the secretary and Shao one of the members. It was to be the highest Party authority until a more formal structure could be worked out. At this time or soon afterwards, Shao became secretary of the Heng-feng CCP Committee and political commissar of the guerrilla units within the hsien. Several years later, when Mao Tse-tung described the early history of the CCP movement to journalist Edgar Snow, he singled out Fang and Shao as the two key figures in the development of the Communist base in northeast Kiangsi.[1]

In the early part of 1928 Fang, Shao, and Huang Tao merged their armed bands into the I-yang–Heng-feng Guerrilla District. By the middle of the year the Communists found themselves compressed into a small area in I-yang hsien. At an emergency meeting convened to decide upon a future course of action, Shao was placed in command of the guerrilla units. A good indication of the smallness of the guerrilla forces is provided by Miao Min, the biographer of Fang Chih-min. Writing about the last months of 1928, Miao described Shao's efforts to increase the size of the guerrilla units by winning over defectors from nearby KMT units. He was able to get 70 defectors who, by bringing their weapons with them, doubled the number of weapons available to the Red units.[2]

In December 1929 the first congress of workers, peasants, and soldiers was held, and this resulted in the formation of the Hsin-chiang Soviet Government (so named after the Hsin-chiang River, which traverses I-yang hsien). Fang Chih-min was elected the chairman, and its 33-member executive committee included Shao and Huang Tao. The development of the Communist base in northeast Kiangsi, which evolved into the Fukien-Chekiang-Kiangsi Soviet area in the early 1930's, is described in detail in the biography of Fang Chih-min. Although exact dates are not given, Shao's obituary reveals that in the period prior to May 1933 he held the following posts: chairman of the Fukien-Chekiang-Kiangsi Soviet, commander of the Fukien-Chekiang-Kiangsi Military Region, and political commissar and secretary of the Frontline Committee of the 10th

Red Army. Shao apparently held the first-named post for only a brief time, because for most of the period between 1930 and 1934 it was held by Fang Chih-min. Similarly, Fang became acting political commissar of the 10th Red Army in March 1931, and by the next year he was the political commissar.

In November 1931, when the First All-China Congress of Soviets was held in Juichin, southeast Kiangsi, Shao was elected a member of the Central Executive Committee (CEC) of the Chinese Soviet Republic established by the congress. Mao Tse-tung was chairman of the CEC. At the same time Shao was one of 15 men named to membership on the Central Revolutionary Military Council. This important organ was chaired by Chu Te, and Wang Chia-hsiang and P'eng Te-huai (qq.v.) served as the vice-chairmen. The composition of the council suggests an effort to give representation to the various Communist military bases, some of which were quite distant from Juichin. For example, Hsu Hsiang-ch'ien, the top military figure in the Oyüwan Soviet, was a council member. Significantly, Shao was the only Communist leader selected from the Fukien-Chekiang-Kiangsi Soviet.

Shao's obituary is again the source for posts he held after May 1933. He was chairman of the Fukien-Kiangsi Soviet, commander of the Fukien-Kiangsi Military Region, and a little later he was secretary of the Fukien-Kiangsi Provincial Party Committee. Very little is known about this soviet, which was situated directly south of the Fukien-Chekiang-Kiangsi Soviet. Nonetheless, when the Second All-China Congress of Soviets was held in January–February 1934, Shao's two-province soviet sent a separate delegation, two members of which, Ku Tso-lin and Chu Wei-yuan, were elected to the Second CEC. Shao was also elected to CEC membership, and at this juncture or soon thereafter, he was transferred to Juichin, the capital of the Chinese Soviet Republic. When the main elements of the Red Army left the area on the Long March in October 1934, Shao accompanied them. During the march he was chief-of-staff and director of the Political Department of the Second Column. His obituary also lists him as director of the Local Work Department (ti-fang kung-tso pu) during the long trek, but the nature of this assignment is not clear.

After arriving in Shensi Shao was assigned to educational work. In 1937 he was director of the Educational Department of the North Shensi Public School (Shen-pei Kung-hsueh), one of the most important training institutes in the Shensi-Kansu-Ninghsia Border Region. He was still connected with the school in the spring of 1938 when, for the May 6 issue of Chieh-fang (Liberation), he wrote an article entitled "Experience and Lessons in the National Defense Education Program in the North Shensi Academy" (Public School).[3] In the same year, he was transferred to the Shansi-Chahar-Hopeh (Chin-Ch'a-Chi) Border Region (see under Sung Shao-wen), which was then headquartered in the Wu-t'ai Mountain area in northeast Shansi. From that time until the end of the war he was a member of the Chin-Ch'a-Chi Border Region Government Council and vice-president of the second branch of the Anti-Japanese Military and Political Academy (K'ang-ta). In the latter part of 1944 he returned to Yenan to attend the Central Party School. He apparently remained in Yenan through the spring, because he was one of the delegates to the Seventh National CCP Congress, held from April to June 1945.

Like a number of important Communist leaders in north China, Shao was sent to Manchuria after the Japanese surrender in the late summer of 1945. He was initially assigned as deputy secretary of the Liaoning-Kirin Provincial Committee and concurrently a deputy political commissar of the Liaoning-Kirin Military Region, then commanded by Chou Pao-chung (q.v.). Shao was later transferred to Nunkiang province where he held identical posts. The Nunkiang capital was located at Tsitsihar, and the provincial governor in the postwar period was Yü I-fu (q.v.). He was also a vice-chairman of the West Manchurian Finance and Economics Committee. During the 1946–1949 period, the Communist government organization for all of Manchuria was known as the Northeast Administrative Committee (NEAC) and was headed by Lin Feng (q.v.). Subordinate to the NEAC, Shao served as director of the Industry Department, as well as vice-chairman of the Planning Committee under the NEAC's Finance and Economics Committee. In the spring and summer of 1948 he took part in the preparatory work for the Communists' Sixth National Labor Congress, which was held in Harbin in August.[4]

In 1949 Shao was with Liu Po-ch'eng's (q.v.) Second Field Army, which took over portions of central China before marching into the southwest. Nanchang, the Kiangsi capital, fell to the Communists on May 22, 1949, and two weeks later Shao and Ch'en Ch'i-han (q.v.) were appointed vice-chairmen of the municipal Military Control Commission, which was headed by Ch'en Cheng-jen (q.v.). All three men are natives of Kiangsi. In the same month, June, Shao became the provincial governor, his principal position until his death 16 years later. At the time of Shao's death, only one other man, Ulanfu (q.v.) in Inner Mongolia, had held the equivalent post for a longer period.

As a representative of the Central China Liberated Areas, Shao went to Peking to attend the First CPPCC in September 1949 when the central government was brought into existence. During the CPPCC meetings, he served on the *ad hoc* committee that drafted the Common Program of the new government, the document that served as the constitution until a formal constitution was adopted in 1954. After the CPPCC sessions, Shao returned to Kiangsi where from 1950 to 1954 he was a member of the regional administration that controlled the province, the Central-South Military and Administrative Committee (which was reorganized into the Central-South Administrative Committee in early 1953). During approximately these same years he was a member of the Central-South China Party Bureau. In 1954 he received his first post on the national level when he was elected a deputy from Kiangsi to the First NPC (1954–1959). He was re-elected to the Second NPC (1959–1964) and again to the Third NPC, which opened its first session in December 1964.

After 1949 Shao's activities centered in Kiangsi where he was the governor and an important official in the provincial Party Committee. He was made a vice-chairman of the Kiangsi branch of the Sino-Soviet Friendship Association in 1952; he was re-elected to this post in July 1959, but the Association was not particularly active after the split between China and the Soviet Union. In the fall of 1953 Shao made his only known trip abroad, going to North Korea as a deputy chief of a "comfort" and inspection delegation led by Ho Lung. By May 1955 Shao was identified as the second secretary of the Kiangsi Party Committee; the designation was changed to secretary in late 1956, but in both cases he was subordinate to First Secretary Yang Shang-k'uei (q.v.). Shao's subordination to Yang is rather unusual in view of the fact that Shao was elected an alternate member of the CCP Central Committee at the Eighth Party Congress in September 1956. Yang, however, is not a member of the Central Committee.

Shao became president of the Kiangsi branch of the Academy of Sciences when it was established in July 1958. That same month he assumed another post in the science field, becoming chairman of the Kiangsi Provincial Government's Science and Technical Work Committee. In 1961 the Party re-created the regional CCP bureaus in accordance with a decision taken at the Central Committee's Ninth Plenum in January 1961. When the regional bureaus had existed, in the period from 1949 to 1954–55, Kiangsi had come under the jurisdiction of the Central-South Bureau. However, as constituted after 1961, Kiangsi was placed under the East China Bureau, which was headed by K'o Ch'ing-shih. Shao was serving as a member of this Bureau at the time of his death.

As a senior provincial leader, Shao was a frequent contributor to the press. For the Nanchang *Yueh-chin* (Leap forward), which began publication on July 1, 1958, as a provincial version of *Hung-ch'i* (Red flag), he wrote an article on industry in Kiangsi. In 1960 he wrote three articles for the national press, two dealing with the economic development of the mountainous regions of Kiangsi and one on his early experiences in the 10th Red Army. These were written for the *JMJP* of February 17 and December 25, and for the English-language monthly *China Reconstructs* (November 1960).

Throughout the fifties and early sixties, Shao continued to be one of the most active Kiangsi officials. Just two months before his death he was named to a preparatory committee for the Second National Sports Meet, and a month later he was appointed to a committee given the task of preparing for a provincial congress of industrial and communications workers. Shao died in Nanchang on March 24, 1965, at the age of 65. The funeral committee appointed at that time was chaired by Politburo member K'o Ch'ing-shih and included such notables as Chou En-lai, Teng Hsiao-p'ing, and P'eng Chen.

Shortly after Shao died Fang Chih-ch'un became the acting governor of Kiangsi, and in September 1965 he was formally elected to that post. Fang, a cousin of Fang Chih-min, was also a founder of the 10th Red Army in the late 1920's and early 1930's, and after 1949 he was a vice-governor under Shao Shih-p'ing.

Because Shao and Fang Chih-min were so closely associated for such a long period, the sources for Shao's early career are, in general, the same as those for Fang. They are reviewed toward the end of Fang's biography. One other source of importance is an article by Shao on the early history of the peasant movement in northeast Kiangsi, which appeared in *Chung-kuo Kung-ch'an-tang tsai Chiang-hsi ti-ch'ü ling-tao ko-ming tou-cheng te li-shih tzu-liao* (Historical materials on the revolutionary struggle led by the CCP in Kiangsi district; Nanchang [?], 1958), I, 242–255.

---

1. Edgar Snow, *Red Star over China* (New York, 1938), p. 153.
2. Miao Min, *Fang Chih-min* (Peking, 1962), pp. 77–78.
3. Hsu Yung-ying, *A Survey of Shensi-Kansu-Ninghsia Border Region* (New York, 1945), pt. 2, p. 37.
4. Li Kuang, ed., *Ti-liu-tz'u ch'üan-kuo lao-tung ta-hui* (The Sixth National Labor Congress; Hong Kong, 1948), p. 7.

Shen Hung

(Shanghai). Vice-minister, First Ministry of Machine Building.

Shen Hung, a native of Shanghai, is exceptional in that he is a former "labor hero" who has risen to a position of rather considerable authority within the government of the PRC. He was born into humble surroundings and as a youth was apprenticed to a draper. Shen had an avid interest in mechanical things and through self-study managed to gain a rudimentary education. He was able to establish a small machine shop in Shanghai where he manufactured simple metal goods. When the Japanese attacked in mid-1937, Shen moved his small shop to Hankow (briefly the capital of China) and there came into contact with liaison officials of the Eighth Route Army. He was persuaded to go to north Shensi, headquarters of the Communists, to serve as director and chief engineer of a small arsenal that produced small arms and ammunition as well as light industrial equipment, which was so badly needed in the isolated Chinese northwest. This period of Shen's career was climaxed in 1944 when he was officially named as a labor model and hero and given the appellation "father of industry" of the Shensi-Kansu-Ninghsia Border Region.

At some time after 1944, Shen was transferred eastward to the Shansi-Chahar-Hopeh (Chin-Ch'a-Chi) Border Region where he served as a mechanical engineer in the Industry Bureau for the region. He was working in this capacity in August 1948 when, at the Sixth Labor Congress in Harbin, he was elected as a member of the Sixth Executive Committee of the All-China Federation of Labor. He was not, however, re-elected to the Seventh Committee at the next congress in 1953. In the same month that the labor congress was being held in Harbin, the North China People's Government (NCPG) was being formed, drawing many of its officials from the Shansi-Chahar-Hopeh Border Region. During the life of the NCPG (August 1948–October 1949), Shen served as an engineer in the State-operated Enterprises Department, a department headed by Huang Ching, an important Party leader and industrial specialist. In February 1949, almost immediately after the surrender of Peking to the Communists, the NCPG moved to the Communist capital-to-be. That summer the Communists staged a large conference attended by many of the top scientists and science administrators in China. At the close of this conference, Shen was named (July 1949) to the standing committee of a preparatory committee charged with the task of creating a nationwide scientific organization. Out of this work grew one of the most important professional organizations in China, the All-China Federation of Scientific Societies, formally established in August 1950. In September 1949 he had served as an alternate member of the Federation of Labor delegation to the first session of the CPPCC, at which time the PRC was established.

In January 1950 Shen was singled out for a distinction unusual for a man of his then rather modest background: he was included in Chou En-lai's entourage to Moscow where Mao Tse-tung was negotiating with the Russians. These talks ultimately led to the signing on February 14, 1950, of the basic Sino-Soviet Treaty of Friendship, Alliance, and Mutual Assistance, as well as a series of lesser agreements dealing with economic matters. After his return home he was appointed (June 1950) to head the Heavy Industry Planning Division of the Central Finance and Economic Planning Bureau under the central government. The Bureau was the precursor of the State Planning Commission formed in late 1952.

In August 1954 Shen was named a Standing Committee member of the China Mechanical Engineering Society, one of the constituent organizations of the All-China Federation of Scientific Societies, which he had helped establish in 1949–50. By 1960 he was serving as a vice-chairman of this professional society, a position he still retains. In April 1955 Shen was appointed as an assistant minister of the newly formed Third Ministry of Machine Building, charged with directing the work of machine and electrical engineering industries and headed by Chang Lin-chih (q.v.), who was elected a Central Committee alternate in 1956. In May 1956, during a partial government reorganization, this ministry was abolished, but its functions were transferred to a newly created Ministry of Power Equipment Industry, also headed by Chang Lin-chih. Shen was not immediately reappointed, but in January 1957 he was named as a vice-minister under Chang (a promotion in rank, because he had previously been an assistant minister).

In the mid-1950's the Chinese established a number of joint commissions with other Communist nations for the purpose of exchanging scientific and technical information. During the year 1957 Chinese relations with Yugoslavia were relatively harmonious and a joint commission was thus formed with the Yugoslavs. The initial meeting of the commission was in January 1957 in Peking where Shen signed a protocol to the first session of the Sino-Yugoslav Joint Commission for Scientific and Technical Cooperation. In November of the same year he led a group to Belgrade for the commission; following a month of negotiations he signed the protocol to the second session on December 27, 1957. Sino-Yugoslav relations seriously deteriorated in the spring of 1958; the joint commission was one of the casualties of the bad relations and Shen has therefore had no further dealings with the Yugoslavs.

At almost the same moment that he departed for Yugoslavia (November 1957), he was removed as vice-minister of Power Equipment Industry and transferred (with the same rank) to the Ministry of Coal Industry, once again serving under Chang Lin-chih, who had assumed the portfolio in September 1957. (Despite Shen's seemingly close connections with Chang in the

mid-1950's, there is nothing in the earlier careers of these men suggesting past ties.) Little was heard of Shen until another government reorganization in September 1959, at which time he was again transferred. On this occasion he was removed from the Coal Industry Ministry and transferred, still as a vice-minister, to the newly formed (August 1959) Ministry of Agricultural Machinery, the fourth different ministry in which he had served within a period of slightly over four years. His qualifications in this ministry, where he served under Central Committee member Ch'en Cheng-jen, reached back to the war period when he had helped produce cotton gins and other implements useful in rural areas.

In December 1961 Shen was transferred still another time. In this instance he was made a vice-minister in the First Ministry of Machine Building, a position he still retains. Also in 1961 he assumed the chairmanship of the Preparatory Committee for another professional organization, the China Agricultural Mechanization Society. When it was fully established in 1963, however, Shen was not given any major position within the society. As already described, Shen headed the Chinese side of a joint commission for technical cooperation with the Yugoslavs in 1957. In December 1962 he received a similar assignment in dealing with Hungary. He led the negotiations in Peking for the seventh session of the Sino-Hungarian Commission for Scientific and Technical Cooperation and on December 14 signed a protocol for the meetings. Exactly a year later he was in Budapest for the eighth session, signing the protocol there on December 11, 1963. In 1964 Shen was elected as a Heilungkiang deputy to the Third NPC, which held its first session in December 1964–January 1965.

Unlike many government leaders, Shen is not often called upon to partake in the burdensome tasks of feting the many visitors to China. Rather, it appears that his mechanical skills are used in a more utilitarian manner in one or another of the many technical ministries. He also serves as a useful Party symbol: his class origins are appropriately proletarian; he served actively in the resistance to Japan, and through "self-reliance" he learned a trade that proved useful to "the people" (and therefore to the Party).

Shen Tse-min

(1898–1934; T'ung-hsiang, Chekiang). Early Party leader; member, CCP Central Committee.

Shen Tse-min, one of the most important of the so-called Russian-returned student faction, was a key official in the Oyüwan Soviet in the early 1930's. He was born into a large gentry family. After attending a secondary school in Shanghai, he enrolled at the Hohai School of Engineering in Nanking. There he became close friends with another student, Chang Wen-t'ien (q.v.). They soon came under the influence of one of their teachers, Tso Shun-sheng, who probably started them on their revolutionary careers by recruiting them into the Nanking-Shanghai branch of the Young China Association (Shao-nien Chung-kuo hsueh-hui) in the winter of 1919–20. Like Chang, Shen contributed to early issues of the association's journal, *Shao-nien Chung-kuo* (Young China), which was founded in mid-1919 and for which Tso Shun-sheng served for a time as the editor.[1] About the time they joined the association, Chang and Shen were becoming more interested in literature than in science. To pursue this new inclination they returned to Shanghai where Shen's older brother, the well-known author Mao Tun (Shen Yen-ping [q.v.]), apparently helped them in getting positions in the Commercial Press, China's largest publishing house. In the fall of 1920 the two men went to Japan, where they remained for half a year. By 1923 Shen's friends in the Young China Association had become sharply divided to the political left and right; the split found Shen among the group that was oriented to the left. His associates in the radical wing included early Communist leaders Li Ta-chao, Yun Tai-ying, Teng Chung-hsia, and Mao Tse-tung, as well as his friend Chang Wen-t'ien[2] (who was not yet a CCP member). It may have been through these contacts that Shen turned from an active career as an editor, essayist, and translator[3] to political activism and eventually to Communism. Chang Kuo-t'ao, who knew Shen well, has stated that Shen was a member of the Socialist Youth League (and inferential evidence suggests that he joined about 1923–24).[4]

In 1926, with a number of other Chinese students, Shen went to Moscow and enrolled at the revolutionary Sun Yat-sen University, headed by Pavel Mif, an outstanding "China expert" of the early Stalinist era. Mif maintained close connections with members of the Chinese student body during his years at the university. Many of the Chinese became his protégés and are usually known as the "Russian-returned students" or the "28 Bolsheviks." Shen was among this group, which stoutly supported Stalinist policies of that period. He had already gained a good knowledge of English from his earlier student days, and during his years in Moscow he also became fluent in Russian. In mid-1928 Shen attended the Sixth CCP Congress (held in Moscow); he served as one of the interpreters at the Congress and was elected a member of the CCP Central Committee.

In the late spring or early summer of 1930, Pavel Mif was sent as the Comintern delegate to China to influence a situation that was troubling the Comintern. The CCP was then being led by the impetuous Li Li-san, who was following tactics which ran somewhat against those formulated by the Comintern. As a result, Mif and his student protégés, led by Ch'en Shao-yü, Ch'in Pang-

hsien (qq.v.), and Chang Wen-t'ien, returned to China to take an important part in Communist developments during the next few years. At the Third Party Plenum in September 1930 the Mif group was not yet in sufficient control to take over the leadership of the Party. But at the Plenum and during the ensuing months when various factions dueled for control of the Party (see under Ch'in Pang-hsien and Lo Chang-lung), Li Li-san's policies were attacked. Party documents of that period reveal that Shen was among the more vocal of the returned-student faction in its bid for power.[5] He and his colleagues finally succeeded to leadership at the Fourth Plenum in January 1931 when they were able to oust Li's followers. Shen was among those named to the reorganized Central Committee, and immediately afterwards he published in a Party journal a lengthy account of intra-Party struggle at the time of the Plenum.[6]

At the Fourth Plenum and the period that followed, the Russian-returned student faction took over most of the key posts at the Party headquarters in Shanghai. Shen was made director of the Propaganda Department, probably assuming this position from Li Ch'iu-shih (q.v.), a Li Li-san follower. However, his tenure in the propaganda post was of short duration, because at a meeting in the spring of 1931 it was decided to send a number of the top Communists still in Shanghai to the various hinterland bases. Chang Kuo-t'ao, who had just returned from Moscow, was sent to the base on the borders of Hupeh, Honan, and Anhwei (Oyüwan), where Hsu Hsiang-ch'ien (q.v.) and other military leaders had already made considerable headway in developing an effective military force. At this same time, or soon thereafter, Shen also went to Oyüwan, as did Ch'en Ch'ang-hao (q.v.), another important member of the Russian-returned group. Chang Kuo-t'ao was the top Communist official in Oyüwan, in his capacity as head of the Central Sub-bureau there, and Shen became one of his top deputies as head of the local provincial committee which was under the jurisdiction of the sub-bureau.

By the time Chang, Shen, and their colleagues arrived in the Oyüwan base, it was already the second largest of the soviet areas, second only in importance to the Central Soviet base at Juichin, southeast Kiangsi, where Mao Tse-tung, Chu Te, and their armies were headquartered. Oyüwan was tightly surrounded by Nationalist troops by 1931, making direct communication with Mao's Kiangsi headquarters extremely difficult. Therefore, it is not surprising that there were few (if any) Oyüwan delegates present for the First All-China Congress of Soviets, which opened at Juichin on November 7, 1931, to establish the Chinese Soviet Republic (of which Oyüwan was a constituent member). Nonetheless, Shen was elected (almost certainly *in absentia*) a member of the Central Executive Committee (CEC), the governing body of the republic. Among the prominent members of the returned-student faction, only Shen, Ch'en Shao-yü, and Wang Chia-hsiang were elected to the CEC.

Despite its obvious importance, the history of the Oyüwan base has been neglected by Maoist historians—in large part because it was headed by Chang Kuo-t'ao, who later became one of Mao's arch rivals. Nonetheless, it is fairly evident that Shen was among the top Oyüwan leaders, together with Chang Kuo-t'ao, Ch'en Ch'ang-hao, and Hsu Hsiang-ch'ien.[7] Because of its strategic location (in particular, its proximity to Wuhan), the Oyüwan base was under constant attack by Nationalist armies in the early 1930's. Consequently, in October 1932 Chang Kuo-t'ao and Hsu Hsiang-ch'ien led a retreat of the principal Oyüwan military forces to a base in Szechwan. However, some important military and political leaders remained behind (see under Hsu Hai-tung). According to Chang Kuo-t'ao, Shen was left behind because of poor health. He died in 1934, either from natural causes or because he fell to the Nationalist armies.

Chang Kuo-t'ao, the source for most of the personal information about Shen, describes him as a scholarly type unsuited to the rigors of life with the Red guerrilla forces. He further recalls that Shen was particularly fond of quoting Lenin and Stalin in their many political discussions.

1. Chow Tse-tsung, *Research Guide to the May Fourth Movement* (Cambridge, Mass., 1963), p. 45.

2. Chow Tse-tsung, *The May Fourth Movement* (Cambridge, Mass., 1960), p. 252.

3. Chang Ching-lu, ed., *Chung-kuo hsien-tai ch'u-pan shih-liao* (Historical materials on contemporary Chinese publishing; Peking, 1954), pp. 277–297.

4. Modern China Project, Columbia University, New York, Howard L. Boorman, director.

5. Tso-liang Hsiao, *Power Relations within the Chinese Communist Movement, 1930–1934* (Seattle, Wash., 1961), pp. 93–94, 134.

6. *Ibid.*, pp. 139–141.

7. *Ibid.*, p. 195.

Shen Yen-ping

(1896– ; T'ung-hsiang, Chekiang). Novelist; chairman, Union of Chinese Writers; former minister of Culture.

Shen Yen-ping, often known by his pen-name Mao Tun, is one of the great novelists of 20th-century China. He has been a major figure in the Chinese literary world since the May Fourth period. During the 1920's and 1930's Shen was one of the dominant figures in two important literary organizations, the Literary Research Society and the League of Left-Wing Writers. He

joined the Communist administration in 1949, serving until 1965 as minister of Culture. He has headed the Union of Chinese Writers since 1949.

Shen was born into a large gentry family on May 27, 1896, in T'ung-hsiang, Chekiang, about midway between Hangchow and Shanghai. His younger brother, Shen Tse-min (q.v.), was one of the more important members of the CCP during its early years. Shen Yen-ping received a classical education during his younger years and graduated about 1914 from a middle school in Hangchow. Like his brother, he studied the natural sciences at the Hohai School of Engineering in Nanking. He later attended preparatory classes at Peking University, but about 1918 financial difficulties forced him to end his formal education. Shen then became a proofreader for the famous Commercial Press in Shanghai. This position afforded him the opportunity to gain a wide familiarity with foreign literature, especially the works of European writers. Within a short time Shen became associated with a number of young intellectuals of the May Fourth period, including Chou Tso-jen (a brother of Lu Hsun) and Cheng Chen-to. Cheng became an important cultural and education official in the Communist administration after 1949. In November 1920 these men and a few others founded the important Wen-hsueh yen-chiu hui (Literary Research Society). This was established for the "express purpose of creating a new literature, appraising traditional literature, and introducing Western literature." Then, "to facilitate this task, they persuaded the Commercial Press . . . to give them editorial control over" *Hsiao-shuo yueh-pao* (Short story monthly). Shen edited this journal from January 1921, and it "immediately set a standard for later journals of literary importance."[1] Shen and his colleagues stressed "art for life's sake," a theme which was soon countered by the Creation Society (see under Kuo Mo-jo), which emphasized "art for art's sake." These two societies contested with each other during the 1920's, and though their disputes were never settled, specialists on Chinese intellectual history agree that both organizations were among the most important of their kind during those intellectually turbulent years.

Shen continued in the employ of the Commercial Press until 1925. However, he relinquished the editorship of *Hsiao-shuo yueh-pao* in late 1922, partly to play a more active role in politics and partly because the editorial board of the Commercial Press feared that Shen's militancy would damage the reputation of their prestigious press. He had by then already shown a considerable interest in the Communist movement and had been a regular contributor to Communist-dominated and left-wing publications. In 1922 Shen, as well as Liu Shao-ch'i, lectured at the P'ing-min nü-hsiao (Popular Girls' School), which was headed by Li Ta, one of the founders of the CCP in 1921. In 1923–24 Shen was among the teachers at Shanghai University (see under Ch'ü Ch'iu-pai). This institute, though ostensibly under joint KMT–CCP management, was dominated by the Communists; it proved to be an important training center for the CCP and Youth League, and its faculty included some of the most important early Communist leaders. By the end of 1925 Shen was in Canton, then the revolutionary heart of China, where the KMT and the CCP were working together in relative harmony. Both he and Mao Tse-tung worked in the KMT Propaganda Department. In January 1926, immediately after the Second KMT Congress, Shen was appointed secretary of the department.[2] The influential KMT leader Wang Ching-wei was the nominal head of the department, but because he was so heavily occupied with his many other assignments, Mao was in effect the departmental chief.

When the Northern Expedition got underway in mid-1926, Shen joined as a propagandist in the General Political Department of the National Revolutionary Army. After the capture of the Wuhan cities in the fall, Shen became editor of the *Min-kuo jih-pao* (Republic daily), apparently working with Mao Tse-tung's younger brother, Mao Tse-min (q.v.), who is known to have managed the paper for a period in 1927. Shen remained in Wuhan until the KMT–CCP split in 1927, after which he spent a brief time in Kuling, a Kiangsi resort town, recuperating from an illness. Later in the same year he went to Shanghai where he remained for most of the next decade. It was also in this year that he began to use the pen-name Mao Tun (literally, "contradictions"); this is only one of the scores of pen-names Shen used over the years, but it is the one best known to students of Chinese literature.

In Shanghai, living a relatively secluded life, Shen began to write a trilogy, *Shih* (The eclipse), based on his experiences during the period of the Northern Expedition. In the words of one observer, this work was of "such scope and honesty that it cast into utter insignificance the few novels" written by Shen's contemporaries, and while he was vacationing in Japan in the latter half of 1928 he "found himself acclaimed in China as the foremost novelist of his time."[3] However, CCP scribes of that period, as well as members of the Creation Society, attacked Shen's trilogy as essentially hostile to the proletarian spirit. Shen replied that each writer had his own vision of reality and that to write about the middle class did not mean an author shared its values. The dispute lingered on inconclusively for the next few years.

In February 1930, in conjunction with Lu Hsun, Ch'ü Ch'iu-pai, and others, Shen became a founding member of the League of Left-Wing Writers. The avowed purpose of the league was to "promote and engage in the production of proletarian art." But in the words of literary historian Tsi-an Hsia, "Art was not their sole, or even their major, concern. Their works were dedicated to class struggle, to the 'bloody,' 'death or victory' battle, to the 'complete liberation of mankind.' "[4] The league soon came to be dominated by the CCP (see under Chou Yang), and its influence grew as the Chinese populace came to understand the mounting menace of Japanese imperialism. The League members operated under the severe handicap of KMT censorship and repression (see under Ting Ling), which was one of the chief reasons why Shen used so many different pen-names during these years. One commentator on his career has written that "since the early thirties" he has "followed rather faithfully" the CCP line in criticism, "but until the outbreak of the Sino-Japanese War he still maintained his standing as a discerning critic of his contemporaries."[5] During this same period Shen published a number of novels, stories, and essays. The best known of these works is *Tzu-yeh* (sometimes translated Midnight, sometimes Twilight), published in 1933 and usually regarded as one of the major novels of 20th-century China. In the next year he and Lu Hsun established the journal *I-wen* (Translated literature), which according to one source, "seems to have been the first Chinese periodical exclusively devoted to foreign literature."[6]

During the mid-1930's China's left-wing writers were in ready agreement about their distaste for the KMT, and they were in complete accord in their hostility to Japan. Nonetheless, the league members and their followers were constantly beset by a variety of disputes, many of them petty and personal. The most serious of these took place in 1936 after the league was dissolved in the early part of the year. This dispute, wryly labeled the Battle of Two Slogans by Tsi-an Hsia, pitted CCP member Chou Yang against the more free-spirited Lu Hsun. Chou's slogan, "literature for national defense," was countered by Lu's "people's literature for the national revolutionary struggle"; Chou advocated strict Party discipline for all writers, and Lu argued that writers should maintain their creative independence while supporting the anti-Japanese resistance movement. The debate generated more heat than light, and it has confounded the many literary historians who have attempted to unravel the affiliations of the various participants. It appears that Shen Yen-ping initially leaned to Chou Yang's side, but after Chou suggested that dissenters would be regarded as traitors, he tended to support Lu Hsun. In any event, the bickering ended when the contenders agreed upon a compromise manifesto in October 1936.

After the war began Shen left Shanghai, and for the next two years he spent much of his time in Hankow, which in 1937–38 served as the provisional capital. There in March 1938 Shen,

Kuo Mo-jo, and 40-odd other literary figures established the All-China Resistance Association of Art and Literary Workers, which published anti-Japanese propaganda materials and sent writers to front line areas to report on the war effort. Shen was in Chungking for a while in 1938, but then in 1939 he went to Sinkiang where, until 1941, he was dean of the College of Arts and Letters at Sinkiang University.[7] During the first half of the Sino-Japanese War, Sinkiang warlord Sheng Shih-ts'ai had rather close ties with the Nationalists and the Chinese Communists, as well as the Russians (see under Teng Fa and Ch'en T'an-ch'iu). However, by the 1941–42 period Sheng came to have deep misgivings—apparently with considerable justification—about his ties with the Yenan Communists. In later years Sheng claimed that Shen and many others were attempting to subvert his rule.[8] Shen left Sinkiang in 1941 for Kweilin and then Chungking, only a year before a number of his colleagues were imprisoned by Sheng Shih-ts'ai.

In 1941, after his return to Chungking, Shen became a member of the Cultural Work Committee under the Political Training Department. The committee was headed by Kuo Mo-jo. In theory, this was a position of some influence, because the Training Department was subordinate to the government's important National Military Council. In fact, however, the KMT was deeply distrustful of the left-wing intellectuals; Shen's post, therefore, was essentially a sinecure. This distrust led in March 1945 to the dissolution of the Cultural Work Committee; according to the Communists, this action represented the KMT's reply to the persistent demands by the intellectuals for a "democratic coalition government."

After the war Shen returned to Shanghai where he edited a literary journal and contributed to the various "third force" publications, which became increasingly critical of the KMT. In 1946 he was invited to lecture on Chinese literature in the USSR, an invitation tendered by the Soviet Union's All-Union Society for Cultural Relations with Foreign Countries. He left Shanghai in late 1946 and returned there in early April 1947. By then the Nationalists were locked in their life-or-death struggle with the Communists, a fact which made the KMT increasingly less tolerant of criticisms from any quarter. The dissolution by the KMT of the China Democratic League in October 1947 served as a signal to the leftist intellectuals that it was no longer safe to remain on the mainland. As a consequence, in the final weeks of the year Shen and many others left for Hong Kong. There, for the next year, he edited still another literary journal and contributed to the Communist press.

Shen left Hong Kong in December 1948 for Manchuria, then almost completely under Communist control. Two months later, in February 1949, he arrived in Peking with a large group of intellectuals and dissident KMT generals and politicians. They were accorded an elaborate welcome by the Communist authorities, who were eager to gain their allegiance. In late March Shen took part in establishing a preparatory committee for the convocation of a nationwide conference of writers and artists. The three top spots on the committee went to Kuo Mo-jo, the chairman, and Shen and literary czar Chou Yang (q.v.), the two vice-chairmen. When the Congress of Literary and Art Workers was held in July, these three held identical posts on the congress presidium, and at the close of the meetings they were again given the three top posts in the newly formed All-China Federation of Literary and Art Circles (ACFLAC). During the congress Shen spoke on the literary movement in KMT-controlled areas over the previous decade.

Immediately after the congress, several organizations were set up under the ACFLAC (see under Kuo Mo-jo). The most important of these, the All-China Association of Literary Workers (known since 1953 as the Union of Chinese Writers) was established on July 23, 1949. Shen was elected the chairman, and he was re-elected at the Second All-China Congress of Writers in September–October 1953. He continues to hold this post, and since December 1956 he has also been first secretary of the Writers' Union Secretariat, which was set up at that time. The ACFLAC and the Writers' Union publish several of the most important literary journals in China, including *Jen-min wen-hsueh* (People's literature), *Wen I-pao* (Literary gazette), *Shih-k'an* (Poetry), *I-wen* (literally "translated literature," but often rendered "world literature"), *Wen-i hsueh-hsi* (Literary studies), as well as the English-language monthly *Chinese Literature*. Shen has contributed frequently to these and many other literary journals. Moreover, he has been editor of both *Chinese Literature* and *I-wen* since 1953, and from October 1949 through June 1953 (after which he was replaced by Shao Ch'üan-lin), he edited *Jen-min wen-hsueh*.

It was also in July 1949 that Shen was elected a member of the Preparatory Committee of the Sino-Soviet Friendship Association. In the previous month, at a meeting chaired by Mao Tse-tung, he had been made a member of a similar body to prepare for the convocation of the CPPCC. Representing the ACFLAC, Shen attended the inaugural session in September of the CPPCC, the organization which brought the central government into existence on October 1. He was made a member of the CPPCC's Standing Committee and the important Central People's Government Council, both of which were chaired by Mao. He was also made a vice-chairman under Kuo Mo-jo of the Culture and Education Committee, one of the four most important committees subordinate to Chou En-lai's

Government Administration Council (the cabinet). Finally, and most important in terms of his governmental duties, Shen was appointed minister of Culture. He was one of the very few government administrators who continuously headed the same ministry for the first 15 years of the PRC. Like most top government officials, Shen was also given assignments in various "mass" and professional organizations. From 1949 to 1950 he was a vice-chairman (again under Kuo) of the China Peace Committee (and since 1950 he has been a Standing Committee member). He was also named in 1949 to the Executive Board of the Sino-Soviet Friendship Association (and since 1954 he has been a vice-chairman), and to the Standing Committee of the Association for the Reform of the Chinese Written Language (to 1954).

During the first decade of the PRC, many eminent men of letters were utilized as spokesmen for the Soviet-backed "peace" movement. Few men were employed in this fashion more often than Kuo Mo-jo and Shen. In addition to authoring many articles on this subject for the press, both men were frequently sent abroad to meetings sponsored by the World Peace Council (WPC). Between 1950 and 1955, Shen attended no less than 11 such meetings in Warsaw (November 1950), Copenhagen (May 1951), Vienna (November 1951, December 1952, and November 1953), Oslo (March 1952), Stockholm (May 1953 and June 1954), Budapest (June 1953), East Berlin (May 1954), and Helsinki (June 1955). Shen led two of these delegations (Vienna in 1953 and Helsinki in 1955), but on seven of the other occasions he was a member of groups led by Kuo. (Kuo's biography describes in more detail the activities of the WPC in those years.) Shen attended the meetings after 1951 in his capacity as a WPC Executive Bureau member. One of the major focal points of the WPC was American involvement in the Korean War, and during 1952 in particular there were incessant allegations that the United States was engaged in germ warfare. This was the theme of the Asian and Pacific Regions Peace Conference, which Shen attended in Peking in October 1952 (see under Liu Ning-i). Shen's participation in these aspects of Chinese foreign affairs made him a logical candidate for membership on the Board of Directors of the Chinese People's Association for Cultural Relations with Foreign Countries when it was set up in May 1954. Less than two years later (February 1956) the Asian Solidarity Committee was formed. Shen was elected a vice-chairman, and in July 1958, not long after the name was changed to the Afro-Asian Solidarity Committee, he was re-elected to this post.

During these same formative years of the PRC, Shen was also involved in foreign relations in his capacity as minister of Culture. Thus, between July 1951 and December 1957, he signed 14 cultural cooperation agreements or executive plans to implement these pacts. In all instances, they were signed with Communist states, and with the exception of one signed in Warsaw in January 1953, all were negotiated in Peking.

In early 1953 the Communists took the first major organizational steps toward the convocation of a national congress and the adoption of a constitution. In January and February, respectively, Shen was named to membership on committees to draft a national constitution (chaired by Mao Tse-tung) and to arrange for nationwide elections (chaired by Liu Shao-ch'i). In the next year, when these tasks were completed, Shen was elected a deputy from Shantung to the First NPC, which held its inaugural session in September 1954. He was returned from Shantung to the next two congresses, which opened their first sessions in April 1959 and December 1964. Since June 1955 Shen has been a member of the Department of Philosophy and Social Sciences (headed by Kuo Mo-jo) under the Academy of Sciences, and from May 1957 to November 1958 he was a member of the State Council's Scientific Planning Commission. He was also involved in the program to reform the Chinese language, an activity which reached its peak in the mid-1950's. In January 1956 he was made a member of a committee to popularize standard spoken Chinese (p'u-t'ung-hua); in the following month he was named to membership on the National Association for the Elimination of Illiteracy and he was also made a member in October of another committee to examine a plan for a phonetic written language.

As already noted, Shen's involvement in foreign affairs during the early years of the PRC was primarily in relation to the activities of the World Peace Council. However, after the mid-1950's he was more frequently utilized in terms of his special competence as a literary figure. In this capacity he led a group of Chinese authors to the Conference of Asian Writers in New Delhi in December 1956. In November 1957 he accompanied Mao Tse-tung to Moscow as an official member of the delegation to the 40th anniversary celebrations of the Russian Revolution. Shen concurrently headed a sub-delegation of cultural figures, and while there his group negotiated and signed the plan for cultural cooperation during 1958. Shen was back in the Soviet Union in October 1958 heading a 21-member delegation to the Afro-Asian Writers' Conference held in Tashkent. At this meeting, which was a follow-up of the conference held two years earlier in India, it was decided that the delegations would form liaison bodies after returning home. This was done in Peking in April 1959 with the formation of the China Committee for Liaison with the Permanent Bureau of Afro-Asian writers (located in Colombo, Ceylon). Shen was elected chairman of the Chinese committee. He also led the Chinese delegation to the Second Afro-Asian Writers' Conference, held in Cairo in February 1962. In the meantime, in May 1959, Shen headed a delegation to Moscow for the Third Congress of Soviet Writers, and in August–September 1960 he led a cultural delegation to Poland. (Shen has chaired the China-Poland Friendship Association since its formation in September 1958). He took his last trip abroad in July 1962 when, in his 66th year, he led a delegation to the World Congress for General Disarmament and Peace in Moscow.

Because Shen is one of China's best-known writers and a top official in the cultural hierarchy, he has been, perforce, involved in the constant seesaw between literary orthodoxy and heterodoxy which has characterized the literary scene since 1949. In 1951, for example, he was criticized for his "subjectivism," but two years later the climate was such that Shen apparently felt he could advocate that writers bring more creativity to their work. Then, when the pendulum swung toward orthodoxy in 1955, he was among those who attacked the well-known writer Hu Feng (q.v.). A year later, however, during the Hundred Flowers movement, Shen echoed the thoughts of Hu Feng when he asserted that literary criticism based on "vulgar sociology" had "harmed . . . free, lively creative forces."[9] But when the Hundred Flowers movement gave way to the "anti-rightist" campaign in 1957, Shen, "always atune to shifts" in the Party line, was in the forefront of those who called for the ideological remolding of writers to prevent the spread of bourgeois ideology.[10] Most students of the post-1949 literary scene agree that Shen, a non-Communist, has been a far less important figure than such CCP stalwarts as Chou Yang and Liu Pai-yü in terms of dictating the courses of action as the Party line has shifted over the years.

Shen himself has written practically nothing of literary value since 1949, but he has produced a number of reports and essays summing up the contributions of other writers. Many of these pieces are of particular use to students of contemporary Chinese literature, as well as to those who study Chinese literary output as a means to measure the political climate. Random but typical examples of these articles have appeared in *People's China*, November 16, 1952; *Chinese Literature*, no. 1, 1954 (also in *CB* 282); *Jen-min wen-hsueh*, no. 6, June 1958; and *Wen-i pao*, nos. 4, 5, and 6, April 26, May 26, and June 26, 1961 (also in *CB* 663). Shen has also continued to maintain his interest in foreign literature; as noted above, he is editor of *I-wen*, which, according to Shen's introduction for the inaugural issue in 1953, was set up to "introduce the best works of the progressive literature of other

countries." A year later, in August 1954, he was one of the keynote speakers at a national conference on literary translation work.

Shen continued to be fairly active during the early and mid-1960's, although his public appearances declined in contrast to the 1950's. As noted above, he was a member of the Standing Committee of the First CPPCC from 1949 to 1954. He held the same position in the Second (1954–1959) and Third (1959–1964) CPPCC's, but during those years this organization was far less significant than it had been during the early PRC years. In early January 1965, Shen was elected a vice-chairman of the Fourth CPPCC. However, the importance of this ostensible promotion was sharply mitigated by the fact that he was at the same time replaced as minister of Culture by Lu Ting-i (q.v.). Shen was by then in his late sixties. His departure from the Culture Ministry roughly coincided with Party attacks on a film which had been based on a novel written by Shen, and this in turn gave rise to speculation that he had been purged. However, he continued to appear in public, and he seems to have survived the more rigorous periods of the Great Proletarian Cultural Revolution launched in 1966 which, ironically, witnessed the abrupt downfall of his successor, Lu Ting-i.

K'ung Te-chih, Shen's wife, was still living in 1965, but she has not been active politically in the post-1949 period. Shen's daughter, who studied at Yenan University during the war years, died toward the end of the war. He is known to have had at least two sons who had reportedly taken part in "revolutionary work," but nothing more is known about them.

A selected bibliography of Shen's writings is found in C. T. Hsia's *A History of Modern Chinese Fiction, 1917–1957* (New Haven, Conn., 1961), which also lists translations of his works. Hsia's work also assesses Shen's importance as a literary figure. Other conveniently available discussions of Shen's career are found in Merle Goldman's *Literary Dissent in Communist China* (Cambridge, Mass., 1967) and Tsi-an Hsia's *The Gate of Darkness* (Seattle, Wash., 1968).

---

1. C. T. Hsia, *A History of Modern Chinese Fiction, 1917–1957* (New Haven, Conn., 1961), p. 55.

2. Li Yun-han, *Tsung jung kung tao ch'ing tang* (From the admission of the Communists to the purification of the [Nationalist] Party; Taipei, 1966), pp. 473–474.

3. C. T. Hsia, p. 141.

4. Tsi-an Hsia, *The Gate of Darkness* (Seattle, Wash., 1968), p. 101.

5. C. T. Hsia, p. 161.

6. Wolfgang Bauer, *Western Literature and Translation Work in Communist China* (Frankfurt and Berlin, 1964), p. 3.

7. I. Epstein, *The People's War* (London, 1939), p. 371.

8. Allen S. Whiting and Sheng Shih-ts'ai, *Sinkiang: Pawn or Pivot?* (East Lansing, Mich., 1958), pp. 213, 228, 292.

9. Merle Goldman, *Literary Dissent in Communist China* (Cambridge, Mass., 1967), p. 163.

10. *Ibid.*, p. 186.

Shih Liang

(c.1907–   Ch'ang-chou, Kiangsu). Lawyer; former minister of Justice; vice-chairman, China Democratic League.

Miss Shih Liang is among the more important non-Communist leaders in Communist China, having served during the first decade of the PRC as minister of the Justice Ministry. She was one of the founders of the National Salvation Association in 1936 and since the mid-forties has been an office holder in the non-Communist China Democratic League. Shih was born in Ch'ang-chou (Wu-chin), an important Yangtze River port city in Kiangsu midway between Shanghai and Nanking. She attended a girls' school in her home town and then graduated from the Shanghai Law College in the mid-twenties. Shih joined the KMT and during the Northern Expedition of 1926–27 she headed the Personnel Training Section under the Revolutionary Army's General Political Department. She held several minor posts with the KMT in the late twenties in Kiangsu, but by the end of the decade she was practicing law in Shanghai. After the Japanese occupation of Manchuria in 1931, she became increasingly involved in political affairs in Shanghai, particularly those related to efforts to strengthen Chinese abilities to resist the steady encroachments of the Japanese. In these endeavors she came to be closely associated with prominent figures in Shanghai, a group that included journalist Tsou T'ao-fen, banker Chang Nai-ch'i, and fellow lawyer Shen Chün-ju.

With war against Japan on the horizon, Shih and her colleagues became increasingly critical of the KMT government's policies. In particular, they objected to the KMT policy of first annihilating the domestic threat of Communism before strengthening China's military forces to withstand Japanese incursions into China. Finally, in 1936, Shih and others organized the National Salvation Association, first in Shanghai and then on a nationwide basis. In cooperation with student organizations, they constantly agitated for immediate resistance to the Japanese, the cessation of the war against the Communists, and for the release of political prisoners. The KMT struck back in November 1936 by arresting in Shanghai seven NSA leaders: Shih, the above-mentioned Shen Chün-ju, Chang Nai-ch'i, and Tsou T'ao-fen, as well as editor Li Kung-p'u, the lawyer Sha Ch'ien-li and professor Wang Tsao-shih. The imprisonment in Soochow (Suchou) of Shih and her six colleagues became an immediate *cause célèbre* under the name of the "Seven Gentlemen" incident.

Both Chiang Kai-shek and Mao Tse-tung have written about the Salvation Association and its influential members—Chiang viewing them as knaves and dupes of the Communists, Mao as useful allies. Chiang, in fact, assigns to the association an important role in the events leading to the dramatic Sian Incident of December 1936, when he was kidnapped by dissident KMT Generals Chang Hsueh-liang and Yang Hu-ch'eng. In Chiang's account he asserts that Chang and Yang had shielded Communists and "front organizations" and as a result the Third Party (see under Chi Fang) and the Salvation Association had "openly engaged in . . . propaganda. Unless timely measures were taken," he wrote, "the situation could lead to a rebellion. Thereupon, I went to Sian in the hope that my presence would constitute a stabilizing factor."[1] Mao, in turn, was quick to capitalize on the nationwide sympathy engendered by the arrest of the "Seven Gentlemen," which took place only three weeks before the Sian Incident. Although Mao conceded that Chiang did not sign any specific agreement to gain his release from Sian, he claimed (in a statement of December 28, 1936) that Chiang tacitly agreed to a six-point program, one of which was to release the "patriotic leaders in Shanghai" (i.e., Shih and her colleagues).[2]

The arrest of Shih and the others, widely regarded as patriots, backfired on the KMT; according to one authority, it "so boosted the number of adherents and sympathizers that [the NSA] . . . actually became the third most powerful party, next to the Kuomintang and the Communist Party."[3] All of the "Seven Gentlemen" were released soon after war with Japan began in July 1937, and all were to have careers intimately linked to causes espoused by the CCP and five of them were to work for the Communists after they conquered the mainland in 1949. Li Kung-p'u was assassinated in 1946, and two years earlier, when Tsou T'ao-fen died, he was posthumously admitted to the CCP. After 1949 Wang Tsao-shih worked in the PRC as an education official in east China, and Chang Nai-ch'i held a number of important posts in the PRC central government, but both were purged during the 1957-58 "rectification" campaign. Ironically, Chang was replaced as head of the Food Ministry by one of his fellow "Seven Gentlemen," Sha Ch'ien-li (q.v.). Until his death in 1963, Shen Chün-ju held important posts, including the presidency of the Communists' Supreme Court from 1949 to 1954, and Sha Ch'ien-li has served from the inauguration of the Communist government as a cabinet official of considerable importance.

Shih spent the Sino-Japanese War years in Chungking working, like many Chinese of the political left, with both the KMT and the CCP. She headed a liaison committee of the Women's Advisory Committee under the KMT-sponsored New Life Movement Association in which Mme. Chiang Kai-shek was a prominent leader. She was also associated with Mme. Chiang's sister, Mme. Sun Yat-sen, in women's work, and toward the end of the war was among the organizers of the leftist-oriented China Women's Association (Fu-nü lien-i hui), which was placed under the All-China Federation of Democratic Women (see below) when the Communists took power in 1949. Continuing her political work, Shih took part in forming the China Democratic League (CDL) in 1944. In 1946 Shih returned to Shanghai, remaining there after the CDL was outlawed by the KMT government in the fall of 1947. She quickly advanced in the League hierarchy, becoming a Standing Committee member in 1948 and, after the Communists took power, she rose to a vice-chairmanship in 1953. Shih is the only woman vice-chairman of the CDL, which is generally regarded as one of the most important of the eight "democratic" political parties in China.

Any doubts concerning Shih's political future were dispelled in December 1948 when she was elected to alternate membership on the Board of Directors of the World Federation of Democratic Women (WFDW), a Communist front then dominated by the Soviet Union. In May 1949 she led a Chinese delegation to the Congress of the Women's Union of France on behalf of the All-China Federation of Democratic Women (ACFDW), a member of the WFDW. Shih was not then a national office holder in the ACFDW, but she was added to its Executive Committee in 1950 and has been a vice-chairman since April 1953. As the Communists set about establishing the "mass" organizations and the central government in mid-1949, Shih was among the most active participants, first in Shanghai and then in Peking. In Shanghai she headed the Democratic League's Provisional Work Committee for east China and was a member of the Preparatory Committee for the Shanghai branch of the Women's Federation. Then she transferred to Peking where, as a lawyer, she helped draft new laws under the jurisdiction of the CPPCC Preparatory Committee, established in June 1949 under Mao Tse-tung. In the same month she became a vice-chairman of the New Legal Research Society's Preparatory Committee. In July she was a keynote speaker at a large conference of social scientists, many of them non-Communists; in the same month she was named to Preparatory Committee membership on the Sino-Soviet Friendship Association (SSFA), and when the association was established in October, she was named to the Executive Board, a post she still retains.

Representing the Democratic League, Shih attended the initial session in September 1949 of the CPPCC, the organization that brought the new government into existence. She was elected to the CPPCC's First National Committee and has continued to represent the Democratic League on the Second, Third, and Fourth National Committees, which first met in 1954, 1959, and 1964, respectively; moreover, Shih has had a seat on the CPPCC's Standing Committee since 1953. When the central government was formed in October 1949, Shih was appointed to head the Ministry of Justice, a portfolio she held for nearly a decade. Her legal background also won her seats on the central government's two major legal bodies, the ministry-level Law Commission and the Political and Legal Affairs Committee, the latter being one of the four major committees under the Government Administration Council (the cabinet); Shih lost her seat in these two organizations when they were dissolved in 1954. With the exception of leading women Communists Ts'ai Ch'ang and Teng Ying-ch'ao and other prominent women like Mmes. Sun Yat-sen (qq.v.) and Liao Chung-k'ai (Ho Hsiang-ning), few women emerged with so many significant posts as Shih Liang in the early days of the PRC. However, it must be noted that the CCP was anxious to present a façade of national unity and to enlist the support of women; consequently, there is little doubt that Shih's actual authority in the councils of government was considerably less than her positions would at first glance suggest.

Already in possession of numerous positions within and outside the government, Shih was to receive still others in the early years of the PRC. She was elected to the National Committee of the China Peace Committee in October 1949 and advanced to the Standing Committee in mid-1958. On behalf of this organization she accompanied Mme. Sun Yat-sen to Vienna in December 1952 to attend the Communist-dominated World Peace Congress. In November 1951 she became a member of a child-care organization headed by Mme. Sun known as the Chinese People's Committee in Defense of Children, and in the next month she was appointed to the central government's Austerity Examination Committee, established to investigate the state of the nation's economy. She has also served on the Board of the Political Science and Law Association of China since its inauguration in April 1953, and during that same year she also became a vice-chairman of a special committee to "thoroughly implement" the PRC's Marriage Law, which had been promulgated in 1950. She also served under Politburo member P'eng Chen (q.v.) from at least July 1954 until November 1956 as a vice-president of the Central Political and Legal Cadres' Academy.

Shih has been a deputy from her native Kiangsu since the inauguration of the First NPC in September 1954, and when the Second NPC came into existence in April 1959, she was advanced to membership on the Standing Committee, the body in charge of NPC affairs between the annual sessions of the full congress. During the life of the Second NPC (1959–1964) she was a member of the permanent NPC Bills Committee, continuing in this post when the Third NPC opened in December 1964. When the Second NPC opened in April 1959, a number of personnel and organizational changes were made in the central government, among them the abolition of Shih's Ministry of Justice, whose functions were placed under the Supreme People's Court. To judge from the rather large number of reports Shih had made before central government bodies and to national conferences dealing with legal questions, she was among the most active women members of the government throughout the 1950's. Since losing her ministerial portfolio, however, Shih seems to have devoted most of her time to the Women's Federation, the China Democratic League, and to legal argumentation in support of the PRC in its disputes with foreign countries. In regard to the last-mentioned activity, for example, she wrote an article for the July 13, 1964, issue of the Peking *Ta-kung pao* denouncing the imprisonment of PRC officials (ostensibly members of a trade delegation and journalists) who had been imprisoned by Brazilian authorities on espionage charges.

In addition to the trips already described, Shih led five delegations abroad in the fifties, the first from April to July 1955 when she took a jurists' delegation to the Soviet Union. In the following June and July she was in Prague for the Czech National Women's Congress, and in December 1956–January 1957 she headed a women's delegation to India. In October 1957 Shih traveled to Syria to take part in preparatory work for the November meeting of the "International Jurists' Conference" in that nation, and finally, in February 1958, she led a women's delegation to the Afro-Asian Women's Conference in Colombo, Ceylon. In contrast to this active schedule, and approximately since the loss of her ministerial post in 1959, Shih has not been abroad since her trip to Ceylon.

Shih was married to a Shanghai lawyer named Lu Chao-hua, but they were separated prior to the Communist conquest of the city in 1949. She has since remarried, and when former French Premier Edgar Faure visited China in 1956, he described Shih as "very beautiful and very chic," noting that she "spoke only Chinese but was accompanied by a polyglot husband."[4] Faure's flattering comments stand in contrast to the wry remark of "third force" political leader Carsun Chang (Chang Chün-mai) that Miss Shih was the "Communist Portia."[5]

1. Chiang Kai-shek, *Soviet Russia in China* (New York, 1957), pp. 73–74.

2. *Selected Works of Mao Tse-tung* (London, 1954), I, 255, 364.

3. Ch'ien Tuan-sheng, *The Government and Politics of China* (Cambridge, Mass., 1961), p. 357.

4. Edgar Faure, *The Serpent and the Tortoise* (New York, 1958), p. 8.

5. Carsun Chang, *The Third Force in China* (New York, 1952), p. 80.

Shirob Jaltso

(1884–   ; Hsun-hua hsien, Tsinghai). Chairman, Chinese Buddhist Association.

Shirob Jaltso (Hsi-jao-chia-ts'o in Sinicized form) is a Tibetan. He is a Living Buddha and the senior Buddhist leader in Communist China. As a child he was a novice in a monastery in his native Tsinghai. In 1896 he entered the Drepung Monastery near Lhasa, receiving a Tibetan ecclesiastical degree in 1916. He is said to be a man of great learning. After earning his degree, he remained at Drepung where he spent a number of years collating a new edition of the Tibetan Tripitaka. It is reported that he fell into disfavor with the 13th Dalai Lama because of unauthorized emendations made in this new edition.

In the mid-thirties he went (via India) to China proper, where he lectured at National Central, Chung-shan, Peking, Tsinghua, and Wuhan universities. He apparently spent most of the war years in Chungking; by at least the early 1940's he was associated with two organizations headquartered in that city. One was the Association for the Promotion of Tibetan Culture, of which he was the president, and the other was the China Association for the Promotion of Border Culture. In the latter, Shirob served as one of the executive directors under President Ch'en Li-fu, a top KMT leader. Shirob Jaltso was one of the three representatives from Tibet to the National Government's Third People's Political Council, which first met in October 1942. In the following year he was assigned to Lhasa to improve Sino-Tibetan relations, but was evidently not permitted to enter Tibet. From May 1945 to 1949 he served as an alternate member of the Sixth Supervisory Committee of the Kuomintang, and from 1947 to 1949 as a vice-chairman of the Mongolian and Tibetan Affairs Commission of the Nationalist Government.

Already an elderly 65, Shirob Jaltso elected to remain on the mainland when the Chinese Communists came to power in 1949. For this he was rewarded with a number of nominal positions within the government. When the Northwest Military and Administrative Committee (NWMAC) and the Tsinghai provincial government were formed over the winter of 1949–50, he was made a member of the former and a vice-governor of the province; he continues to hold the latter post. In March 1950 he was concurrently appointed as a vice-chairman of the NWMAC Nationalities Affairs Committee, member of the NWMAC Culture and Education Committee, and chairman of the Tsinghai Culture and Education Committee. In 1951 he also assumed membership on the Tsinghai Land Reform Committee and in 1952 on the NWMAC Political and Legal Affairs Committee. Finally, when the NWMAC was reorganized into the Northwest Administrative Committee in January 1953, he was reappointed to membership and held it until the NWAC was abolished in 1954. Thus, ostensibly, Shirob Jaltso was a fairly senior official in the northwest in the early years of the PRC. During these same years in the early 1950's, the first steps were being taken toward the establishment of the Chinese Buddhist Association, although Shirob Jaltso apparently did not have any major role in this endeavor. He was, however, in Peking in June 1950 to attend the second session of the First CPPCC, and during that same summer he took part in a meeting in the capital, which initiated the first steps toward the establishment of the Buddhist Association. At that time the decision was made that the formation of an association would be premature. Two years later, however, at another meeting (November 1952) it was announced that the association would be formed. Shirob Jaltso and Chao P'u-ch'u (q.v.) jointly presided over this meeting. Finally, at a May–June 1953 meeting in Peking, the Chinese Buddhist Association was established with Shirob named as the first vice-chairman. The chairmanship went to Yuan-ying, a revered and conservative Han Chinese Buddhist monk who had been head of the (original) Chinese Buddhist Association from the time it was established in Shanghai in 1929 until the reformer T'ai-hsu won control over it in 1945. Already ill when he was elected, Yuan-ying died on September 20, 1953, and in the next month the association named Shirob Jaltso as the acting chairman. Then in August 1955 he was elevated to the chairmanship, a post he continues to hold.

In spite of his advanced age, he spends a large amount of time entertaining foreign Buddhist delegations, a great number of which have visited China since the mid-1950's, particularly from countries with large Buddhist populations such as Burma, Ceylon, and Japan. He has also led Buddhist delegations abroad on at least five occasions, in addition to serving as a member of a delegation to a meeting of the World Peace Council in Sweden in May 1959. Two of his five trips as head of Buddhist groups took him to Burma (April–May 1955 and December 1960–January 1961), and in June 1961 he took another such delegation to Ceylon. But clearly the most important of these trips were the ones he took in 1956 and 1961. In November 1956 he led a 15-member group to the Fourth Conference of the World Fellowship of Buddhists (WFB) in Nepal, where he was elected a vice-president of the WFB and was re-elected to it (*in absentia*) at the fifth conference in 1958. The other visit of importance took place in November 1961 when he attended the sixth WFB conference in Cambodia where he was elected as one of the religious advisers of the WFB. A person who attended this meeting in Cambodia stated that Shirob was in fact only the titular head of the Chinese delegation and that the real head was Chao P'u-ch'u (q.v.),[1] China's leading lay Buddhist, and very probably a Party member, who is in effective control of the Chinese Buddhist Association as its secretary-general. An illustration of this relationship between the two men is found in the fact that Chao has accompanied Shirob Jaltso on all five Buddhist delegations abroad, of which Shirob has been the ostensible leader. Chao speaks a little English whereas Shirob purports to know only Tibetan, and thus the former has been able to communicate more effectively when abroad.

In August 1955 the decision was taken to establish the Chinese Buddhist Theological Institute to train monks. At that time Shirob Jaltso was named as one of the 12 members of the preparatory committee for the Institute, and when it was formally established in September 1956 he was named as the president, another position he continues to hold. In February 1956 he was also named as the honorary editor-in-chief of the committee to prepare an encyclopedia of Chinese Buddhism and contribute to the international encyclopedia being compiled in Ceylon. Apart from his work in the field of Buddhism, Shirob Jaltso has also held a number of official and semi-official positions within the PRC. In 1954 he was elected a deputy from his native Tsinghai to the First NPC (1954–1959) and was then re-elected for the Second NPC (1959–1964); under both he also served as a member of the NPC Nationalities Committee. He was not, however, re-elected to the Third NPC, which opened its first session in late 1964. He also served as a religious delegate to the National Committee of the Second CPPCC (1954–1959), and in March 1957 was elevated to the Standing Committee; he was then re-elected to both posts under the Third CPPCC (1959–1964). Although he was re-elected as a delegate to the CPPCC in late 1964 when the Fourth National Committee was being formed, he was not re-elected to the Standing Committee. In both instances, his failure of re-election can probably be attributed to his advanced age.

At the semi-official level, he has been a member of the Asian Solidarity Committee of China from its formation in February 1956 (renamed Afro-Asian Solidarity Committee in 1958), and of the National Committee of the China Peace Committee from July 1958. When the Asia-Africa Society of China was formed in April 1962 as an organization to conduct research, he was named to membership on the council. On the occasions when the Chinese Communists have reorganized provinces into "autonomous regions" in an attempt to win favor among minority groups, they have always held large celebrations in the areas in question. Shirob Jaltso has attended two of these; he was in Sinkiang in October 1955 for the inauguration of the Sinkiang-Uighur Autonomous Region and in Kwangsi in March 1958 for the establishment of the Kwangsi-Chuang Autonomous Region. Similarly, he journeyed to Inner Mongolia for the May 1957 celebrations marking the 10th anniversary of that autonomous region.

When he was in Ceylon in mid-1961, the *New York Times*,[2] quoting material published by the Chinese embassy in Colombo, described him as a former teacher of the Dalai Lama, who fled from Tibet in March 1959 during the Tibetan Rebellion. (Shirob Jaltso was definitely not the Dalai Lama's teacher for any lengthy period. He may have taught the Dalai Lama for a brief period in 1954–55 when the Dalai Lama was in Peking and was thus qualified as a "teacher" of the Tibetan Lama.) Shirob Jaltso is also known to have made a number of speeches, always dealing with Buddhism or some phase of national minority questions. For example, he spoke on such subjects before the NPC in July 1955 and in June 1956, and his speech before the Sixth World Buddhist Congress in Cambodia in November 1961 was carried in *Hsien-tai Fo-hsueh* (Modern Buddhism), no. 6, December 26, 1961.

1. Interview, San Francisco, 1961.
2. *New York Times*, August 6, 1961.

Shu T'ung

(1906–   ; Tung-hsiang, Kiangsi). Former Red Army political officer; secretary, Shensi CCP Committee; member, CCP Central Committee.

Shu T'ung was born in Tung-hsiang, located about 50 miles to the southeast of Nanchang, the Kiangsi capital. He graduated from the Kiangsi Provincial First Normal School in 1927 and in the same year joined the CCP. It is possible that his first association with the Party resulted from the Nanchang Uprising staged in August 1927. In any event, he was serving in the Kiangsi Soviet by 1931, at which time he was head of the Propaganda Section of the Political Department, under the First Army Corps' Second Division. Later in that same year he was serving as the acting director of the Political Department of this same division. He advanced by 1932 to become chief secretary of the First Army Corps' Political Department and then made the Long March (1934–35) as head of the Propaganda Department of the same Political Department. The First Army Corps was at that time subordinate to the First Front Army commanded by Chu Te and Mao Tse-tung.

During the Long March Shu T'ung took part in several of the heroic feats that have now become almost legendary. In the early summer of 1935, as Mao's troops moved north across remote eastern portions of former Sikang province, they were forced to cross the Ta-tu River at Lu-ting over a perilously narrow bridge spanning the river gorge. The capture and crossing of this bridge are among the epics of the Long March. Led by Lin Piao, commander of the First Army Corps, the Red soldiers were successful in a surprise maneuver in which the Fourth Regiment, to which Shu belonged, played an important part. When the crossing of the Ta-tu was accomplished, Mao's army proceeded on for its rendezvous with the Fourth Front Red Army, led by Chang Kuo-t'ao and Hsu Hsiang-ch'ien (qq.v.), which was then in western Szechwan. The route of this army after it was driven from the Oyüwan Soviet in the border area of Hupeh, Honan, and Anhwei provinces is described in the biographies of Chang and Hsu. Although the full account is not available, Shu apparently acted briefly as a liaison official between the Mao and Chang armies and perhaps effected their subsequent meeting. Shu took charge of a seven-man vanguard dispatched by Mao across the Chia-chin Mountain on the boundary of Sikang and Szechwan to meet with Chang in Szechwan. Mao and Chang finally met in Mao-kung, west Szechwan, in mid-June.

The whereabouts of Shu after the Long March are not clear, but apparently he continued to serve as a political officer with the Red Armies. By 1939 he was known to be the director of the Political Department of the Shansi-Chahar-Hopeh (Chin-Ch'a-Chi) Border Region Military District, then commanded by Nieh Jung-chen. In the same year he was also identified as a member of the Chin-Ch'a-Chi Border Region Government, originally formed in 1938 (see under Sung Shao-wen). It appears that in the 1939 period Shu was operating around the western Hopeh portion of the border region. Apparently he had some association with Norman Bethune, a Canadian surgeon who ran a hospital for the Communists in western Hopeh until his death in November 1939. The Communists erected a statue to Bethune and Shu was one of those who wrote an inscription for it.[1] The Chin-Ch'a-Chi Border Region was divided into three sub-districts; the western portion was known as the Pei-yueh Sub-district. By 1943 Shu was the director of the Organization Department of the Party Committee for the Pei-yueh Sub-district.[2]

In 1946, as a consequence of the cease-fire agreement worked out by U.S. Special Envoy George C. Marshall between the Nationalists and the Communists, a series of field teams were established to supervise the truce. Shu was assigned to the team that operated out of Tsinan, the capital of Shantung. When the truce broke down completely later in 1946, he was assigned to the

New Fourth Army, and in 1946–47 he headed the Political Department for both the New Fourth Army and the Shantung Military District.

As did many men of the New Fourth Army, Shu remained in east China after the Communist victory over the Nationalists in 1949. From 1949 to about 1952 he served as the director of the Political Department for both the East China Military Region and its armed force, known as the Third Field Army and commanded by Ch'en I. Also, from 1949 to about 1951 he headed the East China People's Revolutionary University, located in Soochow (Su-chou), not far west of Shanghai. However, like most east China officials of prominence, Shu was stationed in Shanghai, the capital of the East China region, and it is unlikely that he devoted much time to this school. In Shanghai, Shu directed the municipal Party Propaganda Department from 1949 to 1953, and he also headed the Propaganda Department for the entire East China Party Bureau (encompassing the five provinces of Kiangsu, Chekiang, Anhwei, Fukien, and Shantung) from 1949 to 1954. During the 1953–54 period he was elevated to the Standing Committee of the East China Party Bureau.

If Shu had held only these military and Party posts he would easily have been one of the key east China officials, particularly in the propaganda field. In addition, however, he held a number of governmental positions in east China, as well as a long series of *ad hoc* posts during the early 1950's. He was a member of the East China Military and Administrative Committee (ECMAC) from January 1950 and continued to hold membership when the ECMAC was reorganized into the East China Administrative Committee (ECAC) in December 1952, a position held until the abolition of the ECAC in 1954. Under the ECMAC/ECAC he was also the chairman of the important Culture and Education Committee. Almost all his *ad hoc* positions were in some way related to the educational-propaganda field. For example, he was named as chairman for a special committee to "readjust departments of institutions of higher learning in east China" in August 1952, and in the next month he was also appointed to chair a "study" committee for cadres in the various departments under the East China Party Bureau. Though Shu was not particularly active in the "people's" organizations, he did serve as a vice-chairman of the East China branches of both the Sino-Soviet Friendship Association (from November 1951) and the China Peace Committee (from November 1952).

In 1954–55, the regional divisions within the government, military, and Party were all abolished. Because virtually all Shu's positions were at this level, he had to be reassigned. By 1955 it was evident that he had become the senior official in Shantung, China's second most populous province. His initial assignment in Shantung came in

1954 when he was selected as a deputy from that province to the First NPC (1954–1959); he was re-elected from Shantung to the Second NPC (1959–1964). Far more important, however, was his assignment in early January 1955 as the provincial Party first secretary, replacing the very important leader K'ang Sheng (q.v.), who had been the undisputed head of the province for several years. A month later he was elected a member of the provincial (governmental) People's Council.

Shu's work in east China and Shantung was rewarded at the Eighth National Party Congress in September 1956. He served on the congress Credentials Committee, and at the end of the meetings was elected a full member of the Party Central Committee. Shu was one of only 33 persons newly elected to full membership on the Party Central Committee, the remainder of the 97 having served on the Seventh Central Committee elected in 1945.

By the late summer of 1959, Shu was given another assignment in Shantung, which added to his already impressive array of critical positions in that province. He was made the political commissar of the Tsinan Military Region and at approximately the same time became the first secretary of the Party Committee for the region (which controls the province of Shantung). In the wake of the falterings of the Great Leap Forward (initiated in 1958), Shantung Governor Chao Chien-min came under serious attacks and was ultimately removed from his post. At a session of the Shantung Provincial People's Congress in October–November 1958, T'an Ch'i-lung (a Party secretary in Shantung) led the attack on Chao. This was followed by an even more severe attack in January 1959 by Shu at a session of the Shantung Party Congress. Shu repeated many of T'an's charges and added a host of others. Most important was one that indirectly linked Chao with Hsiang Ming (see under Chao Chien-min); Hsiang had been the Party second secretary in Shantung in the early 1950's. When Kao Kang and Jao Shu-shih were formally ousted in 1955, Hsiang was identified as a member of their "anti-Party" group in the most sensational purge in the Chinese Communist movement since the late 1930's.

In March–April 1960 Shu served as a member of the presidium (steering committee) for the second session of the Second NPC. After this, his activities in Shantung were reported in the press until October 1960, after which he fell from public attention. Then, in the next month (November 1960), Tseng Hsi-sheng (q.v.) was transferred from Anhwei to assume Shu's role as the Shantung Party first secretary.

After more than three years of silence about the activities of Shu, he was identified in Shensi in January 1964 as a secretary of the provincial Party Committee. He continues to hold this post,

serving under First Secretary Chang Te-sheng
(q.v.) until the latter's death in 1965. Shu's position as a secretary in Shensi must be viewed, in
political terms, as a demotion. In the first place,
the long gap in his career (1960–1963) suggests
that he had got into some political difficulties in
Shantung, possibly in the aftermath of the Great
Leap Forward. Second, his position in Shensi as
a Party secretary created the quite unusual situation of a full member of the Party Central Committee (Shu) being placed under an alternate
member (Chang Te-sheng). Since Shu's transfer
to Shensi, he has been frequently mentioned in
the press media, for example, he attended the
inauguration of the Sian Philosophy Society in
February 1964 and took part in the 1964 May
Day celebrations in Sian. He was also elected in
1964 as a Shensi deputy to the Third NPC,
which opened in December 1964. (Shu had been
a deputy from Shantung to the First and Second
NPC's.) In addition, in January 1965 he was
named to membership on the Preparatory Committee for the Second National Sports Meet,
which was held in September 1965.

Shu's writings include an article for *Hung-ch'i*
(February 1, 1959), entitled "Develop the Mass
Line and a Businesslike Style of Work," which
appeared at the peak of the Great Leap Forward.
He is also a contributor to a handbook entitled
Hsueh-hsi Mao Tse-tung szu-hsiang (Study the
thought of Mao Tse-tung).[3] Other contributors
included such important Party leaders as Li Fu-
ch'un and Ch'en Po-ta.

---

1. Stuart Gelder, *The Chinese Communists*
(London, 1946), p. 232.

2. *Chinese Literature*, no. 11 (1965), p. 89.

3. Cited in Chalmers Johnson, *Peasant Nationalism and Communist Power* (Stanford,
Calif., 1962), p. 238.

Shuai Meng-ch'i

(1907–   ; Hunan). Deputy director, Organization Department, CCP; member, Control Commission, CCP; alternate member, CCP Central
Committee.

Miss Shuai Meng-ch'i, a native of Hunan, is
one of the few women in Communist China to
hold important posts in the national administration of the CCP. She is a deputy director of the
Party's Organization Department, a member of
Tung Pi-wu's Central Control Commission, and
one of only eight women on the Party Central
Committee. Rather little is known of her career
before 1949, but she spent some time studying in
the Soviet Union, apparently about 1928.[1]

By 1931 Shuai was working with the laboring
class residents of Shanghai's western district.[2]
She belonged to the CCP at that time, and after
the Japanese took over Manchuria in the fall of
1931 she was associated with a Communist-

supported women's group in Shanghai that protested Japanese actions. By 1932 Shuai was director of the Women's Department of the Kiangsu
Party Committee, then an underground organization under constant KMT surveillance. In July
1932 various left-wing groups from Kiangsu held
a "masses representatives' conference" in Shanghai, which was broken up by the Nationalist
Government. Not long afterwards Shuai was arrested and imprisoned until the outbreak of the
Sino-Japanese War in 1937. According to several
Communist accounts, Shuai was tortured by the
Nationalists while in prison, but nothing could
break her "revolutionary will-power." Her experiences in prison are described in a pamphlet
written by Li Po-chao (the wife of Party leader
Yang Shang-k'un, q.v.). Entitled *Nü Kung-ch'an-
tang yuan* (A Woman of the Party), it was published in Peking in 1950.

No further details of her career are available
until the spring of 1949 when she was active in
the affairs of the mass women's organization, the
All-China Federation of Democratic Women
(ACFDW). Attending the Federation's founding
congress in March–April 1949, she was made a
member of both the Executive and Standing
Committees and was also appointed director of
the ACFDW Organization Department. The latter position gave her considerable influence over
administrative and organizational matters of the
Federation during its formative years. She held
all the above posts until the Federation met for
its second congress in April 1953. Although she
was a member of the 1953 Congress Presidium
(steering committee), she was re-elected only to
membership on the Federation's Executive Committee. At the third national ACFDW Congress
(September 1957), Shuai was re-elected to the
Executive Committee, and she retains this post
with the National Women's Federation, as the
ACFDW was renamed at that time.

In addition to her work with the women's
movement, Shuai has held various posts in the
national government. She was a delegate from
the ACFDW to the First CPPCC in September
1949, and attended the third session of the First
CPPCC (October–November 1951). From 1949
to 1954 she was a member of the People's Supervision Committee of the Government Administrative Council (the cabinet). And she was made
a member of the Central Austerity Examination
Committee, an *ad hoc* committee formed in December 1951 and staffed by high-ranking members of the elite. Since the inauguration of the
constitutional government in September 1954
Shuai has represented Hunan in the NPC, serving
on the First (1954–1959) and Second (1959–
1964) NPC's and then being re-elected to the
Third NPC, which held its first session in December 1964–January 1965. At the close of this
session she was elected to the NPC Standing
Committee, the organ charged with managing the

affairs of the NPC when full congress is not in session. In May 1956 Shuai led a six-member delegation to North Vietnam to attend the Second Congress of the Vietnam Women's Federation.

From the Eighth Party Congress in September 1956 Shuai began a new phase in her career. At this time she was one of the very few women to serve on the Congress Presidium (steering committee). The role she played from the time the Congress opened indicated that she had been chosen for Party executive work, because she was one of the executive chairmen of two of the daily Congress sessions and was then elected an alternate member of the CCP Central Committee. She was one of only eight women members of the new Central Committee, four serving as full members, and four as alternates. In the latter group Shuai received the largest number of votes among the female alternates. The day after the Congress closed, the First Plenum of the Eighth Congress elected a 17-member Central Control Commission headed by Party veteran Tung Pi-wu. Shuai and Ch'ien Ying, a full Central Committee member, were the only women elected to the Control Commission. In about 1961 the Commission was slightly reorganized and a Standing Committee of nine persons was formed, with Shuai as one of the members. In the interim she was identified in June 1957 as a deputy director of the Party Organization Department, the only woman of this rank in this important Party organ. As of 1965 she was the ranking deputy director in terms of seniority.

In recent years Shuai has been a member of the Presidium of the fifth session of the First NPC (1958) and of the first session of the Third NPC (1964–1965). She continues to hold all her Party posts, and though her name does not appear frequently in the press, this is probably because of the nature of her work in the Party's disciplinary and organizational branches, work seldom mentioned in the press. Shuai is clearly one of the most senior of the Communist women leaders.

1. *Hung-ch'i p'iao-p'iao* (Red flag fluttering, Peking, 1958), VII, 56.
2. *Ibid.*

Soong Ching Ling, see Sung Ch'ing-ling

Su Chao-cheng

(1885–1929; Hsiang-shan hsien, Kwangtung). Early labor leader; Politburo member.

Su Chao-cheng was a major labor leader in the first decade of the Chinese Communist Movement and is one of the few men of proletarian origins to achieve a senior position in the CCP. He was one of the organizers and leaders of both the 1922 Hong Kong seamen's strike and the 1925–26 Canton–Hong Kong strike. Su was a CCP Politburo member from 1927 until his death two years later.

Su came from a poor peasant family and early in his youth became a seaman, a career which lasted more than 20 years. In an interview with American authoress Anna Louise Strong in 1927, Su said he had "never had any schooling" but "bought books and learned by myself."[1] In 1908 he joined Sun Yat-sen's T'ung-meng hui and worked for his cause in Kwangtung about the time of the 1911 Revolution.

About 1914–15, Sun Yat-sen had made an attempt to cultivate the support of the seamen, many of whom became members of the KMT; he had organized them into the Seamen's Mutual Benefit Society (Hai-yuan kung-i she), led by his protégés Ch'en Ping-sheng and Lin Wei-min. The association rendered valuable assistance in purchasing and. shipping arms for his military operations in south China. Su Chao-cheng was a member of the committee running the association. By the end of the second decade of the century, a new type of organization able to agitate for better working conditions for the seamen was felt to be needed, and together with Lin Wei-min, Su organized in March 1921 the Chinese Seamen's Union (Chung-hua hai-yuan kung-yeh lien-ho tsung-hui), with its headquarters in Hong Kong. Toward the end of the year, the union made its debut by putting forward to the shipowners a series of demands for improved working conditions. Failing to receive a reply on three occasions, the union issued an ultimatum, threatening to strike if no response was forthcoming within 24 hours. Ch'en Ping-sheng was chairman of the union, and Su Chao-cheng was in charge of general affairs at the Strike Headquarters. Shortly afterwards, Ch'en vacated his post because of a law suit, and Su succeeded him as chairman of the Seamen's Union. Initially involving the 10,000 members of the union, the strike began on January 13, 1922, and quickly gained momentum. The dockers, fuel-men, and warehousemen joined in a sympathy strike, followed by the Porters' Guild and the Hotel Workers' Union. The 150-odd labor unions in Canton organized relief work for those striking workers who fled to the freer atmosphere in Canton, and Sun Yat-sen's government openly expressed its sympathy (and thus earned the hatred of the British). The strike wave spread to other urban centers; the Postal Employees' Union and workers of the British Tobacco Company in Shanghai, workers in Hankow, on the Peking-Hankow Railway, and in Tientsin and Macao, by one means or another expressed their solidarity with the Hong Kong seamen. By February 1, 166 ocean steamers with a tonnage of over 280,000 lay idle in the Hong Kong harbor. At its height, the strike involved some 100,000 workers and ended after two months in complete victory for the seamen. In the words of Communist historian Ho Kan-chih, it was the "Chinese people's first victory in a century of anti-imperialist struggle."[2] Su Chao-cheng's role in the strike marked his rise to prominence as a labor leader.

According to his own testimony, Su claimed that after the Hong Kong strike he tried in vain to contact Communists in Canton. Nonetheless, although it would be three more years before he joined the CCP, he declared his adherance to Marxism in an interview that appeared in a Hong Kong newspaper just as the strike ended. Despite his failure to make direct contacts with the Communists, Su and other leaders of the Seamen's Union did begin in 1922 to develop relations with the Communist-dominated Secretariat of the Chinese Labor Unions (see under Teng Chung-hsia).[3]

In July 1924 Su attended the Pacific Transport Workers' Conference in Canton, convened under Profintern sponsorship. Some 25 delegates from north and south China, from Indonesia and the Philippines met for six days. Gregory Voitinsky was present as the Comintern representative. One of the controversial issues debated at the conference was whether or not to support Sun Yat-sen's KMT. Su Chao-cheng's seamen delegation joined with the delegates from the Philippines in supporting the alliance with the KMT, and the railroad union delegates from China and Indonesia criticized the KMT for not being revolutionary enough.

In the spring of 1925 Su was in Peking representing the workers' organizations in Hong Kong and Kwangtung at a conference engineered by the CCP to voice support for Sun Yat-sen's call for a national assembly with broad representation from public bodies. While in Peking, Su joined the CCP, and for several months carried on trade union work in the northern railroad network and industrial centers.

In early May 1925 he attended the Second National Labor Congress in Canton, which was sponsored by four large labor unions: the National Railroad Workers' Union (Ch'üan-kuo t'ieh-lu tsung-kung hui), the Canton Workers' Delegates' Association (Kuang-chou kung-jen tai-piao hui), the Han-yeh-p'ing Workers' Union (Han-yeh-p'ing tsung-kung hui), and the Chinese Seamen's Union. The Congress established the All-China Federation of Labor (Chung-hua ch'üan-kuo tsung-kung hui), affiliated it to the Profintern, and set up as one of its principal tasks the unification of the workers' movement in Canton and Hong Kong. Su was elected to the ACFL Executive Committee, and Lin Wei-min was elected chairman.

The next high point in Su's career was his role in the Hong Kong–Canton strike and boycott that began on June 19, 1925, in response to the May 30th Incident in Shanghai. Working with other Communist leaders like Teng Chung-hsia and Yang Yin (qq.v.), Su rallied the workers' unions in Hong Kong and Canton to declare a strike simultaneously on June 19. A strike committee was organized; Su was elected chairman and concurrently headed its Finance Section. The strike committee, fast becoming a mainstay of the Canton government, had under it some 800 men, who met in conference periodically, and an armed detachment of about 2,300 with the special task of isolating Hong Kong from the mainland. It also ran law courts, jails, a legal bureau to punish traitors, community mess halls, community dormitories, schools for workers, a bureau for searching out contraband goods, and a bureau for issuing sailing permits to Chinese and foreign vessels.

The Chinese seamen held their First National Congress in Canton in January 1926 while the strike was still in progress. Su was elected chairman of the union. The Congress also organized the Hong Kong Transport Workers' General Union, with Su again named as chairman. Moreover, at the Third Congress of the ACFL, convened in Canton in May 1926, he was elected chairman (replacing Lin Wei-min), thus being elevated to the leading role in trade union activities in south China among leftist-oriented unions.

The Canton–Hong Kong strike ended in the fall of 1926, but Su appears to have remained in south China until the spring of 1927, engaged in ACFL work. In March 1927 Communists began to enter the National Government in Wuhan, and Su was made minister of Labor. He arrived in Wuhan in April, moving the headquarters of the ACFL with him. He attended the Fifth CCP Congress in April–May 1927, at which time he was elected an alternate member of the Politburo.

On May 20, 1927, the Profintern convened the Pan-Pacific Trade Union Congress at Wuhan; Su was a member of the presidium (steering committee) and was elected head of the secretariat of the congress, to be set up in Shanghai.

Following the break with the Wuhan government, Su went to Kiukiang (Chiu-chiang) to take part in the preparations for the Nanchang Uprising (see under Yeh T'ing). Later, he attended the August 7 Emergency Conference, at which Ch'ü Ch'iu-pai replaced Ch'en Tu-hsiu as Party chief and Su became a full member of the Politburo. He drafted the resolutions on the workers' movement which were passed by the conference. Because of his distinction as a labor leader, Su was accorded the honor of being made the chairman of the Canton Commune during the Canton Uprising in December 1927. In fact, however, Chang T'ai-lei (q.v.) acted on his behalf during his absence. In addition to Party work, he continued to work for the ACFL, and in February 1928 convened a secret conference, at which he is said to have introduced a new system of factory committees more suited to withstand the pressures of the KMT police.

In the spring of 1928 Su went to Moscow where he attended the Fourth Profintern Congress held in April and the Sixth Comintern Congress in July–September; at both Congresses he was a presidium (steering committee) member and he was elected to their Executive Committees. He also attended the Sixth CCP Congress in June–July 1928, which re-elected him to the Politburo. More honors came: he was elected vice-chairman of the Red International of Peasant Unions (Krestintern) and he attended the Eighth Congress of the All-Russia Trade Union Congress, where he delivered a report on the Chinese labor movement.

Su's health broke down while he was in Moscow, and he nearly died of an acute case of appendicitis. After some rest in southern Russia he was still not well enough to undergo an operation. In January 1929 he departed for home, but the arduous journey was more than he could stand, and he died soon after reaching Shanghai.

The best biographical sketch of Su was written in 1929 by Teng Chung-hsia and is contained in Hua Ying-shen's *Chung-kuo Kung-ch'an Tang lieh-shih chuan* (Biographies of Chinese Communist martyrs; Hong Kong, 1949). Su's wife remained with the Communists and in 1939 was in Sinkiang when a number of leading Communists were working there in cooperation with Sheng Shih-ts'ai (see under Ch'en T'an-ch'iu).[4] His daughter married Liu Ya-lou (q.v.), the chief of the Communist Air Force until his death in 1965.

1. Anna Louise Strong, *China's Millions* (Peking, 1965), p. 83.
2. Ho Kan-chih, *A History of the Modern Chinese Revolution* (Peking, 1960), p. 57.
3. Jean Chesneaux, *Le Mouvement ouvrier chinois de 1919 à 1927* (Paris, 1962), pp. 294, 319, 556.
4. *Hung-ch'i p'iao-p'iao* (Red flag fluttering; Peking, 1957), V, 150.

Su Chen-hua

(c.1909–   ; Hunan). Navy political commissar; alternate member, CCP Central Committee.

Su Chen-hua, an alternate member of the Party Central Committee since 1956, has spent his entire career in the Chinese Communist military establishment. He joined the CCP about 1927, and by the next year he was with the guerrilla forces led by Chu Te and Mao Tse-tung on the Kiangsi-Hunan border. Lin Piao and P'eng Te-huai were also with the Red Army from its earliest years, and Su worked under both men. At some time in the late 1920's or early 1930's he was a company commander under Lin Piao, but by 1933 he was political commissar

of the 13th Regiment, which was commanded by Huang Chen. The 13th Regiment was subordinate to the Fifth Division, part of P'eng Te-huai's Third Army Corps. In 1933 and 1934 Su fought in a series of battles on the Kiangsi-Fukien border; the mission of his regiment was to take part in the defense of the Communists' Central Soviet area. In describing the 13th Regiment, Su commented that it had once been a part of the Seventh Red Army established in the late 1920's in Kwangsi (see under Chang Yun-i) and that it had subsequently campaigned in Kweichow, Kwangtung, Fukien, and Kiangsi.[1]

Su made the Long March in 1934–35, and after arriving in north Shensi he enrolled at the Red Army Academy, the school first set up in Kiangsi, which was re-established in north Shensi soon after the Red Army reached the northwest. When the Sino-Japanese War began in mid-1937, Su became a brigade political commissar in Lin Piao's 115th Division, part of the Eighth Route Army. He remained in Lin's forces during the early war years, but later his unit was attached to Liu Po-ch'eng's 129th Division, also part of the Eighth Route Army, which was headquartered in southern Shansi.

There is little reporting on Su's wartime record, but it is clear that it closely paralleled those of Yang Te-chih and Yang Yung (qq.v.), both of whom were top officers in Lin Piao's 115th Division. At the start of the war the Division's 340th Brigade, of which Su was the political commissar, took part in the famous victory over the Japanese at P'ing-hsing-kuan in northeast Shansi. In the spring of 1938, Yang Te-chih and Su moved eastward into the Hopeh-Shantung-Honan border area as head of a unit known as the Second Column. In 1939, in collaboration with units led by Yang Yung, they established the Hopeh-Shantung-Honan (Chi-Lu-Yü) Military Region; Yang Te-chih was the commander, Yang Yung the deputy commander, and Su the political commissar. (By 1945 he was also director of the Region's Political Department.) The Chi-Lu-Yü area was later incorporated into the larger Shansi-Hopeh-Shantung-Honan (Chin-Chi-Lu-Yü) Border Region, which was established in mid-1941 (see under Yang Hsiu-feng). The border region served as a vital communications link between the Eighth Route Army forces in north and northwest China and the New Fourth Army troops stationed in east-central China.

Toward the end of the war Yang Te-chih and Su moved north from the Chi-Lu-Yü Border Region into Jehol and Chahar, a rather unsuccessful expedition that is described in Yang's biography. Later, by 1948, Su had returned to the Chi-Lu-Yü area where he was political commissar of a military sub-district. For the next few years his career was closely linked with Yang Yung (q.v.). By the winter of 1948–49,

Yang was commander and Su the political commissar of the Fifth Army Group, which was subordinate to Liu Po-ch'eng's Second Field Army. In the spring, summer, and fall of 1949, Liu's men swept through parts of central China and into the southwest. Kweiyang, the capital of Kweichow, fell on November 15, 1949. A few days later, Su was appointed chairman of the Kweiyang Military Control Commission, a post he held for about a year. When the Kweichow provincial government was established in the last days of 1949 and the first days of 1950, the principal posts went to Yang Yung and Su. Yang became governor of the province and commander of the Kweichow Military District, and Su became Military District political commissar and the ranking secretary of the provincial CCP Committee. Concurrently, he was a member of the regional administration controlling Kweichow, the Southwest Military and Administrative Committee (known after early 1953 as the Southwest Administrative Committee) and in 1951 was deputy political commissar of the Second Field Army.

By the spring of 1954 Yang Yung was a deputy commander of the Chinese People's Volunteers in Korea. By February of that year Su had already assumed Yang's post as Military District commander, which he held in addition to his other Kweichow posts. Then by mid-1954 Su was also transferred from Kweichow. He appeared in Peking in August 1954 and has been working there since. When the national government was reorganized in September 1954, Su was named to the newly created military advisory body, the National Defense Council, a post to which he was reappointed in April 1959 and January 1965. Also in mid-1954 Su was made a deputy political commissar of the Chinese Navy. He presumably relinquished his Party post in Kweichow at about this time, though the changeover there was not confirmed until February 1955 when Chou Lin (q.v.) was identified as Kweichow's ranking Party secretary.

When the PRC first awarded military decorations in September 1955, Su was given the Orders of Independence and Freedom and of Liberation, covering military service during the period from 1937 to 1950. At about the same time he was identified as an admiral (personal military ranks also having been first created in 1955), the equivalent of a three-star admiral in the U.S. Navy. In September 1956, at the CCP's Eighth National Congress, Su was elected an alternate member of the Central Committee, and by February 1957 he had been promoted to political commissar of the Navy.

As in the case of many military leaders, Su's activities are seldom reported in the press. But a few items indicate that he attends important military conferences and meetings, especially those concerned with political work in the armed services. For example, in February–March 1957 he addressed a conference of Navy CCP "activists" on the need to "oppose doctrinairism" in their work, and in July 1960 he was among a group of senior generals and admirals who were active in the Party's campaign to have all officers spend some time working directly among low-echelon soldiers and sailors.

1. *Hung-ch'i p'iao-p'iao* (Red flag fluttering; Peking, 1957), III, 96–119.

Su Yü

(c.1908–   ; Fukien). Veteran military leader; vice-minister of National Defense, member, CCP Central Committee.

Su Yü is a native of Fukien but he spent, at the least, his middle school years in Hunan, where most reports state that he attended the Second Normal School in Chang-te. (One report states that he graduated from the Normal School in Heng-yang.) He joined the Communist Youth League in 1926 when he was 18 and still a normal school student. When his involvement in radical student activities caused him to be dismissed from the school, he went to Wuchang where he became a member of the cadet detachment of Yeh T'ing's Independent Regiment of the Fourth Nationalist Army, later changed to the 24th Division of the 11th Army, a part of Chang Fa-k'uei's Second Front Army by mid-1927, when Yeh's division mutinied and joined the Communists. The history of the division, which numbered many young Communists among its officers, is contained in the biography of Yeh, who led the division at the time of the Nanchang Uprising of August 1927. This event sealed the break in relations between the CCP and the KMT, and by the time it occurred Su had become a platoon commander in Yeh's 24th Division and a member of the CCP. He presumably escaped with Yeh after the Communists failed to hold Nanchang, the Kiangsi capital, which they seized for a few days beginning on August 1. When Su's activities were next reported he had joined the army of Chu Te and Mao Tse-tung at Chingkangshan on the Kiangsi-Hunan border (1928).

From Chingkangshan Su apparently followed Chu and Mao into eastern Kiangsi and Fukien, remaining for a time with their Red Army. From about 1930 to 1932 he was commander of the Red 64th Division, a division which at first belonged to the 22nd Army of Ch'en I and was then transferred to the army of Lin Piao (q.v.). Sometime in the year 1932 to 1933 Su Yü was transferred to the forces that were stationed along the border of Kiangsi and Fukien and were commanded by Fang Chih-min (q.v.), who had been operating in the area since the late 1920's. At an uncertain date following an important Communist military conference in April 1933, the Communists created two new military units; one of these units, the Seventh Army Corps under Hsun Huai-chou, was to take charge of the Fukien side of Fang's border area base. Su then became Hsun's second in command.[1]

In the latter part of 1933 and early 1934 Hsun Huai-chou's Seventh Corps campaigned in Fukien, but later it moved back into southeast Kiangsi. At approximately this time Su was transferred to Fang Chih-min's 10th Army in northeast Kiangsi. In mid-1934 Fang's troops began to move north into southern Anhwei, and at the same time Hsun's Seventh Corps left southeast Kiangsi to rendezvous with Fang. These movements are described in orthodox Communist accounts as an attempt to engage the "Japanese aggressors" in north China (see under Fang Chih-min), but it is more likely that the Communists were attempting a breakthrough of Nationalist lines, which were beginning to be more closely drawn around the main Red Army troops in southeast Kiangsi. The merger of Hsun's and Fang's forces in the border area between Kiangsi and Anhwei took place in July 1934, and the new unit, known as the 10th Army Corps, was under the over-all command of Fang. Su was chief-of-staff of the new corps, which consisted of three divisions. The newly merged force fought its first battle at T'an-chia-ch'iao in southern Anhwei and in the ensuing fighting Hsun Huai-chou, who had become the commander of the 19th Division, lost his life. Su Yü, however, was soon separated from Fang, which accounts for the fact that he was not with the latter when he was captured by the Nationalists early in 1935. Su had been ordered by Fang to return south just before the latter was captured, but only after the Communists had suffered heavy losses at the hands of the Nationalists. Su, together with Liu Ying, who was director of the Political Department for Su's small force, turned back into Kiangsi. The force the two men commanded was only a remnant of the army that had gone into south Anhwei; it numbered only about 800 men.[2] With this small band Su returned to the vicinity of Fang's original base on the Kiangsi-Fukien-Chekiang border and remained there when the Communists under Chu Te and Mao Tse-tung were forced to leave Kiangsi and make the Long March.

In the years before the outbreak of the Sino-Japanese War, Su Yü had no permanent base, but he continued to engage in guerrilla operations in areas which the Communists partially controlled along the borders of Fukien, Kiangsi, and Chekiang provinces. At some time he made contact with and may have joined the forces of the larger Communist guerrilla group headed by Chang Ting-ch'eng and Teng Tzu-hui, who maintained Red bases farther to the south in Fukien along the province's western border. The description of the Southwest Fukien Military and Administrative Committee, the Communist government for the Fukien base, is contained in the biography of Chang Ting-ch'eng, who headed the organization. At some time in the 1930's, but more probably in the period before the Long March, Su was wounded and lost an arm.

When war broke out in the summer of 1937 the Chinese Communists began to unite their forces then fighting in separate small bases in central China. In the spring of 1938 they activated their New Fourth Army (with the sanction of the Nationalists) to operate in the Third War Zone, which was commanded by KMT General Ku Chu-t'ung. The Communist army was headed by Yeh T'ing and Hsiang Ying (qq.v.), and as part of its Second Detachment (under Chang Ting-ch'eng) the army incorporated Su's forces from the Chekiang-Fukien border area. However, at the outbreak of the war Su himself was probably in Yenan on a brief visit, for there are a number of reports that he had gone there in 1937. If true he may have taken part in the initial plans for the organization of the New Fourth Army. After the New Fourth Army came into being, Yeh T'ing and Hsiang Ying operated from a headquarters in the area south of the Yangtze. However, certain units of the army were operating north of the river and after 1940 these became the larger of the two commands into which the New Fourth Army was divided. The South Yangtze Command, to which Su Yü belonged, was spread from the northern tip of Kiangsi and Chekiang into south Kiangsu and Anhwei. In addition to the headquarters staff, three of the six detachments of the New Fourth Army were stationed initially in the area south of the Yangtze. Ch'en I headed the South Yangtze Command and the Army's First Detachment, and the Second Detachment was led by Chang Ting-ch'eng with Su Yü as the political commissar. A brief history of the Second Detachment is contained in the biography of Chang Ting-ch'eng, who maintained Second Detachment headquarters at Chin-t'an, a small town about 50 miles southeast of Nanking. The detachment operated in the area immediately south of the Yangtze which is roughly bounded by the triangular points made by the cities of Wu-hu, Nanking, and Wu-hsi and which extended from Tang-t'u hsien in Anhwei south of the Yangtze into south Kiangsu toward Wu-hsi. In 1938 Su Yü's Second Detachment fought the Japanese in the Tan-yang area of Kiangsu not far east of Nanking, but by 1939 troops from his detachment had begun to move north of the Yangtze. The move was begun early in the year when Lo Ping-hui (q.v.), the detachment's deputy commander, led about 1,000 men into Li-chiang, where in May 1939 they joined forces with some of the troops from the Fourth Detachment. The united forces became the Fifth Detachment of the New Fourth Army (based north of the Yangtze). By June 1940 Lo had been followed by Ch'en I, who brought his own First Detachment and the remainder of the forces from the Second Detachment across the river. Then, following the New Fourth Army Incident of January 1941 when Yeh T'ing tried unsuccessfully to move across the Yangtze with the headquarters staff (see under Yeh T'ing), the New Fourth Army was reorganized.

In the reorganization of the New Fourth Army Ch'en I became the acting commander to replace Yeh T'ing, who had been captured by the Nationalists, and Liu Shao-ch'i became the Army's political commissar. Seven new divisions replaced the former six detachments in the breakdown of army forces; Su was given command of the First Division as well as the Central Kiangsu Military District, which his division largely controlled. The district was in the strategic region (because of its proximity to Nanking) of east-central Kiangsu, bounded on the west by the Grand Canal, on the east by the Pacific Ocean, on the south by the Yangtze, and on the north by a segment of the line running from Huai-an to the coast. The Central Kiangsu Military District (Su-chung Chün-ch'ü) was the site of the New Fourth Army headquarters and the central China branch of K'ang-ta (the Red military training school), as well as the location of Su's First Division. This base, the most important one for the New Fourth Army, was the equivalent of the Wu-t'ai Mountain base in Shansi, where Lin Piao maintained the headquarters of the 115th Division of the Eighth Route Army. And, as in Lin's base, there was a high degree of coordination between operations of the army, government, and mass organizations that influenced the local population. The activities carried on in this area, many of them under the partial direction of Su's division, are extensively treated by Chalmers A. Johnson in his *Peasant Nationalism and Communist Power,* from which most of the information on Su's activities with the First Division is taken. As the war continued, units of Su's division moved into areas near the major cities of Shanghai, Nanking, and Hangchow, and by 1944 they had returned to the area of the division's original base on the Kiangsu-Chekiang border. Hence, in 1944, Su became commander of the Kiangsu-Chekiang Military District, holding this post along with that in the Central Kiangsu Military District until 1946. From 1943 to 1946 he also served as the political commissar of the First Division, in addition to being the division commander.

In view of Su's rising prominence as a military leader it is not surprising that he was elected an alternate member of the Party Central Committee at the Seventh National Party Congress held in Yenan from April to June 1945. He was raised to full committee membership at the Eighth Congress in 1956. Recognized by the end of hostilities in 1945 as one of the more capable younger generals, Su was considered a "darling of daring" and was said to have had a "reputation for producing troops out of his cap." He was thought to have "more than the ordinary" Red general's skill in handling artillery. In fact, the military reputation of Ch'en I, Su's superior officer, was said to have stemmed in part from Su's efforts as a staff officer and commander.[3] Thus by 1945 Su held a recognized place among the CCP military elite. In the civil war period that followed he continued to work with his New Fourth Army troops, moving them from the Kiangsu-Chekiang base into central Kiangsu where he fought seven battles with the Nationalists in mid-1946 as negotiations were breaking down between the KMT and the CCP.[4] By 1946, and continuing to the reorganization of the New Fourth Army in 1947 (see below), Su was elevated to the position of deputy commander of the entire New Fourth Army. After the battles in Kiangsu in 1946, although he was technically deputy commander of Central China Military Region (see under Chang Ting-ch'eng), he withdrew his forces into Shantung at the end of the year, and there he assisted Ch'en I in reorganizing the bulk of the New Fourth Army into the East China Field Army of the PLA; he became deputy commander early in 1948, as well as deputy commander of the East China Military Region. Ch'en and Su led the Communist troops that won important victories over the Nationalists in Shantung in August 1947.[5] Su controlled all the East China PLA forces in Shantung in the fall of 1947 when Ch'en I left for operations in the Kaifeng area of Honan. By November 1947 Su Yü had extended his army's control in Shantung to the borders of Anhwei and Kiangsu, and the Communists also held the port of Wei-hai-wei, from which Red troops were able to move into Manchuria. By the end of April 1948 all the Shantung peninsula, except for the port of Chefoo (Yen-t'ai), was in Communist hands. Subsequently, Su's forces made their way south from Shantung into Kiangsu where, during the year, they captured areas east of Nanking. From the spring of 1948 Su was with Ch'en's army in its expansion through Kiangsu, where it captured the major industrial cities. During the Huai-Hai Campaign (see under Liu Po-ch'eng), Su served on a small committee charged with the task of coordinating the activities of the Central China and East China Field Armies.[6] By the close of the Huai-Hai Campaign in early 1949, the East China Field Army had been redesignated the Third Field Army. Su continued to serve as the deputy commander under Commander Ch'en I, participating in the crossing of the Yangtze and the capture of Nanking in April 1949, operations that were carried out jointly by the Third Field Army and Liu Po-ch'eng's Second Field Army. In May Su also took part in the capture of Shanghai.

Immediately upon the arrival of the Communist forces in Shanghai in May 1949 the Shanghai Military Control Commission was established under the chairmanship of Ch'en I. Su was named as vice-chairman of the commission, but a few months later he was transferred to a comparable post in Nanking. Then, on November 1, the staff of the Nanking Military Control Commission was reorganized because of transfer of Liu Po-ch'eng to the southwest. Su replaced Liu as the chairman and remained in Nanking for two more years, serving also as a member of the Nanking Party Committee and as the chairman of the Nanking branches of the Sino-Soviet Friendship Association and the China Peace Committee.

In the meantime, Su had received important appointments in national organizations and in the central government. Just as Shanghai was falling to the Communists in May 1949, the All-China Federation of Democratic Youth was being formed at a youth congress in Peking. Su was named to the federation's National Committee, a post he held until the next congress in 1953. In September 1949 he attended the First CPPCC, the legislative body that brought the PRC into existence, as a deputy from the Third Field Army. During the course of the meetings Su served as a member of both the Presidium (steering committee) and the Credentials Committee and spoke briefly about the fighting in which the Third Field Army was still engaged in east China. At the close of the session he was named to membership on the First National Committee, a position he held until the Second Committee was formed in December 1954. The principal military organ of the new government, known as the People's Revolutionary Military Council (PRMC), was formed under the chairmanship of Mao Tse-tung in October 1949; Su was named as a member, retaining this position until the constitutional government was established in the fall of 1954. It was also in October 1949 that the Sino-Soviet Friendship Association was established; Su became a member of the First Executive Board but dropped his affiliation with the association when it was reorganized in December 1954.

As the Communists consolidated their military victories they formed regional governments in 1949–50 to administer the newly conquered areas. The East China Military and Administrative Committee (ECMAC) was established in January 1950 under the chairmanship of Jao Shu-shih. Su was appointed as one of the four vice-chairmen; he was again appointed as a vice-chairman in December 1952, when the ECMAC was reorganized into the East China Administrative Committee, and continued to hold this post until the regional administrations were abol-

ished in 1954. Although Su was occasionally in Peking in the 1950–51 period (as, for example, in June 1950 when he attended a session of the CPPCC), most of his time during this period was spent in east China. An article by Su carried in the English-language *People's China* (February 16, 1950) suggests that he may have been involved in the planning for the "liberation" of Taiwan—although, of course, the invasion was never carried out. Also, a November 1951 speech by Su before a meeting of the ECMAC suggests that he was active in the suppression of remnant KMT troops and bandits in east China in the early fifties.

Although Su nominally retained major posts in east China until 1954, he had been transferred to Peking by early 1952; in February of that year he was identified as a deputy chief-of-staff of the PRMC (being officially appointed in April 1952). At that time Hsu Hsiang-ch'ien was the nominal chief-of-staff, but for most of the early fifties Nieh Jung-chen served as the acting chief-of-staff. One of Su's first important assignments in this post was to accompany Chou En-lai to Moscow in August–September 1952 for negotiations that led to an agreement providing for the transfer of the Chinese Changchun Railway in Manchuria to Chinese control and for the extension of the joint use of the naval facilities at Port Arthur, an extension that was justified in Chinese eyes by the Korean War, then still in progress. (The railway transfer took place at the end of 1952, but the joint use of the Port Arthur facilities was not terminated until 1955—see under Ouyang Ch'in.)

In October 1953 the Chinese press noted that Su was unable to attend a meeting of the ECAC owing to illness. However, he was active once again in the fall of 1954 when the constitutional government was inaugurated. Su was elected as a deputy from the East China Military Region (ECMR) to the First NPC. At the close of the NPC session in September 1954, the old PRMC was abolished; to some degree it was replaced by the newly created National Defense Council (NDC), although the latter organization is far less significant than the defunct PRMC. Su was named to membership on the NDC, a position he still retains. More important, in November 1954, he was named as chief-of-staff of the PLA, in effect replacing Nieh Jung-chen.

In September 1955 the PRC awarded military decorations to its officer corps and also gave them personal military ranks. Su was given the three highest military awards, the Orders of August First, Independence and Freedom, and Liberation. At the same time he was made a senior general of the PLA, the equivalent of a four-star general in the U.S. Army, a rank only below that of the 10 marshals. From the spring of 1956 until early 1957, Su was not reported in the national press and during this period Ch'en Keng (q.v.)

served as the acting chief-of-staff of the PLA. However, during this same time he was elected a full member of the Party Central Committee at the Eighth Party Congress in September 1956 (having served, as already described, as an alternate member from the Seventh Congress in 1945).

By 1957 Su was once again prominently in the news—attending PLA conferences, making inspections of military units, and serving as a host for visiting military delegations from abroad. In November of that year he was a member of the military delegation led by P'eng Te-huai to Moscow to take part in the celebrations marking the 40th anniversary of the Russian Revolution. He was a member of an even more important delegation in February 1958 when he accompanied Chou En-lai to North Korea (as the ranking Chinese military figure) for negotiations that led to the withdrawal of the "Chinese People's Volunteers," the name for the Chinese troops that had been in Korea since their entry in the fall of 1950 during the Korean War. By the latter part of the year most of the troops had returned to China.

Although Su began the year 1958 as a key figure in the PLA hierarchy, before the year ended he had fallen to near political oblivion. The circumstances surrounding his fall from power cannot be described with certainty. One authority has argued that from 1954, and especially during the 1957–58 period, Su had become involved in an intra-Party dispute that pitted those in favor of "modernizing" or "professionalizing" the PLA against those who favored a major stress on political control ("man controls the machine, not vice versa").[7] According to this argument, Su favored the "professional" view, and if true, the decision came at an unfortunate time for him because the year 1958 saw the beginnings of the Great Leap Forward when "politics were in command." His decline might also have been related to the Quemoy crisis, which lasted from the late summer to the early fall of 1958, a venture in which the PLA made a rather poor showing.[8] In any case, during the closing stages of the Quemoy (or "offshore islands") crisis, Su was replaced as the PLA chief-of-staff by Huang K'o-ch'eng (q.v.), a veteran PLA political officer.

Whatever the reason for Su's removal as chief-of-staff, it is apparent that his importance among the elite has notably diminished since that time. When he was first appointed as a vice-minister of National Defense in September 1959 (at the time that Lin Piao replaced P'eng Te-huai as the minister), it appeared that he might be making a political comeback. However, his appearances since 1959 have been largely confined to attending festivities in connection with PLA holidays (such as August 1) or serving on funeral committees for PLA veterans (like Marshal Lo Jung-huan in December 1963 and Air Force Com-

mander Liu Ya-lou in May 1965). As already described, Su had served in the First NPC as a deputy from the East China Military Region. In July 1958 (three months before his removal as PLA chief-of-staff) he was elected to the Second NPC (1959–1964) from the Nanking Military Region (NMR). He was again elected to represent the NMR in October 1964 at the Third NPC and, at the close of its first session in January 1965, he was named to the NPC Standing Committee and was reappointed to the National Defense Council. In addition to these two posts, he continues to be officially listed as a vice-minister of National Defense as well as a member of the Party Central Committee. Despite the fact that he continues to hold important positions in the government and the Party, the lack of reporting about Su's activities since 1958–59 suggests that his importance among the elite—especially in the PLA—probably ended in the late fifties.

1. Jerome Ch'en, *Mao and the Chinese Revolution* (New York, 1965), p. 175.

2. Miao Min, *Fang Chih-min* (Peking, 1962), p. 106.

3. Robert B. Rigg, *Red China's Fighting Hordes* (Harrisburg, Pa., 1952), p. 33.

4. *Selected Works of Mao Tse-tung* (Peking, 1961), IV, 106.

5. *Ibid.,* p. 216.

6. *Ibid.,* p. 339.

7. Alice Langley Hsieh, *Communist China's Strategy in the Nuclear Era* (Englewood Cliffs, N.J., 1962), pp. 22, 23, 46.

8. *Ibid.,* p. 117.

Sun Chih-yuan

(c.1911–1966; Hopeh). Former minister, Third Ministry of Machine Building; alternate member, CCP Central Committee.

Sun Chih-yuan was a political officer and troop commander in north China during the Sino-Japanese War. He served in southwest China in the early years of the PRC, but from 1952 until his death 14 years later he worked in Peking, primarily in economic affairs. He is reported to have graduated from a "teachers' training college," possibly Peking Normal College. He joined the Communist Youth League in 1929, probably during his student days, and in the following year he was admitted to the CCP. Little is known about his career prior to the Sino-Japanese War aside from the brief statement in his obituary that he "worked in KMT-controlled areas prior to 1937." With the outbreak of war he worked with guerrilla forces near Paoting in central Hopeh, and then about 1938 he became director of the Political Department of the Communist Eighth Route Army forces in the Central Hopeh Military District under the command of Lü Cheng-ts'ao (q.v.). Lü, who had joined the Party in 1937, commanded guerrilla forces in the

Hopeh District from 1938 to 1943. Both men were members of the Chin-Ch'a-Chi (Shansi-Chahar-Hopeh) Border Region Administrative Committee from its formation in early 1938 (see under Sung Shao-wen, the chairman); Sun Chih-yuan retained this post until 1945. He moved his headquarters to the west sometime before the end of the war and became chief-of-staff and Political Department director of both the Shansi-Suiyuan Military Region and the Shansi-Suiyuan Field Army, posts he held until the close of hostilities in 1945.

Sun remained in the Suiyuan area after the war and in 1946 he was the Communist representative on the Peking Executive Headquarters' Field Team at Chi-ning (Tsining; presently in Inner Mongolia), one of the teams responsible for implementing the terms of the Cease-fire Agreement of January 1946, arranged under the auspices of U.S. Special Envoy George C. Marshall. Personal military ranks were not in use in the Communist army, but at Chi-ning Sun held the simulated rank of major-general. After the collapse of the mediation efforts to bring the Communists and Nationalists together, the officers assigned to the field teams returned to the battlefields. Sun served as a column political commissar and an army political department director in the period prior to the defeat of the Nationalists in 1949; during this time he was apparently associated with P'eng Te-huai's First Field Army in the northwest. As a representative of this Army he attended the First Plenary Session of the CPPCC in September 1949, immediately after which the central government was established (October 1). When the CPPCC meetings closed, Sun was assigned to the southwest where, in July 1950, the Communists established the Southwest Military and Administrative Committee (SWMAC), with control over the provinces of Sikang, Kweichow, Yunnan, and Szechwan, and with its capital at Chungking. From 1950 to 1952 Sun was active in this administration; appointed a member of the SWMAC in 1950, he served concurrently as its secretary-general, as a member of the SWMAC Land Reform Committee from September 1951, and as chairman of its Labor Employment Committee from August 1952. In May 1951 he was one of four signers of an agreement for the "peaceful liberation of Tibet," negotiated between Peking and Tibet. The other signers were: Li Wei-han, then director of the Party's United Front Work Department (the chief signer for Peking), Chang Ching-wu, then Peking's chief representative in Tibet, and Chang Kuo-hua, the military commander in Tibet.

In late 1952 Sun was released from his posts in the southwest and brought to Peking where he was made a deputy secretary-general of the Government Administration Council (the cabinet) on November 15, 1952. Shortly thereafter he was also named a vice-chairman of the Council's Labor Employment Committee, which had

been established in July. In 1954 Sun was elected as a deputy from Szechwan to the First NPC; he was more actively involved in NPC affairs than many deputies, serving on the *ad hoc* Motions Examination Committee for each of the five sessions held between 1954 and 1958. In October 1954, shortly after the close of the initial NPC meeting, Sun was appointed as a deputy director of the State Council's Third Staff Office, where he served under Director Po I-po (q.v.). This office, in charge of coordinating and supervising the work of ministries and commissions in the heavy industry and construction field, underwent a reorganization in September 1959, at which time Sun was removed.

Concurrent with his 1954 appointment to the Third Staff Office, Sun was made a vice-chairman of the State Construction Commission, but he was released in November 1956 to become a vice-chairman of the State Economic Commission, in charge of annual economic planning. In both organizations he again served under Po I-po. In September 1959 Sun was reappointed a vice-chairman of the Economic Commission and, in addition, he was also made a commission member. Then, in April 1961, he was removed as a vice-chairman, but he retained some influence in commission affairs by his retention of commission membership until June 1964. In the meantime, in March 1956, Sun was named to the newly formed National Association for the Elimination of Illiteracy, but little was heard of his role in this organization.

Sun was made an alternate member of the Party Central Committee at the Second Session of the Eighth Party Congress in May 1958. He served as a CCP representative on the Third National Committee of the CPPCC (1959–1964), and when it first met in April 1959 he was named to its governing body, the Standing Committee. He again represented the CCP on the Fourth National Committee but was not reappointed to the Standing Committee when the first session closed in January 1965.

In January 1961 he became minister of the Third Ministry of Machine Building, a post to which he was reappointed in January 1965. The fact that the machine building ministries are not often mentioned in the press probably explains why little was heard about Sun in the sixties. At the time of his reappointment to the Third Ministry in January 1965, Sun was also made a member of the National Defense Council. Though this organization is not regarded as particularly significant, it seems noteworthy that the ministers of the Fourth, Fifth, and Sixth Ministries of Machine Building were also added to the Defense Council at this time, suggesting closer liaison between industry and the military establishment.

Sun's only noted writing, an article entitled "The Establishment of Industries by People's Communes and Its Great Significance," appeared in the *JMJP* of October 26, 1959. He remained an active member of the central bureaucracy until his death in Peking on October 11, 1966, at the age of 55.

Sun Ta-kuang

Minister of Communications.

Although Sun Ta-kuang has risen to the cabinet level in Communist China, he was virtually unknown when the regime was formed in the fall of 1949. At that time he was serving as head of the Northeast General Bureau of Navigation. On January 2, 1951 in Harbin, Sun signed an agreement with the Soviet Union on construction and navigation along the Amur, Ussuri, and other rivers and lakes on the Manchurian-Soviet Far Eastern boundary. By no later than mid-1951 Sun had been removed from the navigation bureau.

In August 1951 he was appointed as president of the Northeast Marine Navigation College, a position he held officially until June 1954, but one which in fact he must have relinquished by mid-1953 when he was reported in Peking serving as director of the Planning Department of the Ministry of Communications. From this rather modest beginning with the ministry he rose in little over a decade to become the minister. In January 1955 he was appointed as assistant minister, in July 1958 as vice-minister, and in July 1964 as minister.

Sun made his first trip abroad for the PRC in May–June 1955, when he led a delegation to Schevenigen in the Netherlands, where he attended the International Congress of Experts on Coastlighting, one of the relatively few non-political international events in which the Chinese Communists had participated as of that time. Two years later, like so many of his Communist colleagues, Sun became involved in the "rectification" campaign. At a meeting of his ministry on July 8, 1957, Sun "exposed" his minister, Chang Po-chün, a non-CCP member and one of the leading targets of the "rectification" movement. Early in 1958, Chang was removed from his post as a "rightist."

In January 1959, Sun was added as an additional member of the China Council for the Promotion of International Trade, an organization devoted essentially to the promotion of trade with countries not having diplomatic relations with Peking. Later in the same month the Council created the Maritime Arbitration Commission as a subordinate organization. Sun was named as the chairman, a position he still retains, but one about which virtually nothing is ever reported. A little over a year later, in February 1960, the State Council created a special Committee for Receiving and Resettling Returned Overseas Chinese. This had been formed to accommodate a large number of Chinese who returned to mainland China from Indonesia, partly

because of restrictions placed by the Indonesian government on Chinese merchants. Because of the large number of repatriates (about 100,000), this resettlement presented major logistical problems, and it was presumably for this reason that Sun, a specialist in logistics, was named as a member of the special committee.

Since 1961 Sun has devoted considerable time and effort to the China-Albania Joint Stock Shipping Company, formed under the terms of an agreement he signed in Peking in December 1961 with a visiting Albanian vice-minister of Communications. This was in obvious response to the worsening Tirana-Moscow and Peking-Moscow relations in that it provided Albania, shorn of its allies in Europe, with an additional link abroad for purposes of trade and receiving aid from China. Not long after signing the agreement, Sun journeyed to Tirana where, from April 23 to May 7, 1962, the first meeting of the "administrative council" of the stock company was held to discuss management and related problems; on May 7 Sun signed the protocol to the meeting. He then flew to Cairo where he spent two weeks on a "friendly" visit to the United Arab Republic. The second meeting of the shipping company was held in April–May 1963 in Peking. Sun took part in the negotiations and once again signed the protocol to the meetings (May 2).

As noted above, Sun became minister of Communications in July 1964, replacing Party Central Committee member Wang Shou-tao, who was transferred to south China. In his new capacity, Sun signed an agreement on maritime transportation with the Congo (Brazzaville) in Peking on October 2, 1964. At this juncture, Peking was making a determined effort to bring about closer relations with the Congo, as was well illustrated by the fact that PRC Chairman Liu Shao-ch'i signed a treaty of friendship with the visiting president of the Congo on the same day that Sun signed the maritime agreement.

In late 1964 Sun was elected from Anhwei to the Third NPC; at its first session in December 1964–January 1965, he was named to the National Defense Council (and reappointed as minister of Communications). Although this military advisory body is not of great importance, it provides the only clue that Sun may have been a military figure of some prominence prior to 1949. An alternative interpretation is that a decision was made to bring more technical specialists into the organization, a role to which Sun would be well suited.

Sun Tso-pin

(Kansu?). Purged Party leader, Northwest China.

Sun Tso-pin is one of the most prominent leaders purged in early 1958 in the wake of the nationwide "rectification" campaigns of 1957–58. By that time he had risen to the governorship of

Tsinghai province. Virtually nothing is known of Sun's early life, but some information was revealed in the charges brought against him in 1958. He was a Communist Party member by 1934 and once belonged to the Lung-tung District Party Committee and to the East Kansu Local Party Committee. During the Sino-Japanese War, Lung-tung was one of the districts into which the Communist Shensi-Kansu-Ninghsia Border Region was divided, an area straddling southern Ninghsia and eastern Kansu. No dates were given for Sun's activities in Lung-tung but presumably these were carried on in wartimes. In any event, by the latter half of 1949 he had become one of the leading Party officials in Kansu, where he was to remain for the next four years.

The Communists established their political instruments of power in Kansu following their capture of Lanchow, the capital, in August 1949. Sun became a deputy secretary in the Kansu Party apparatus under ranking Secretary Chang Te-sheng, a veteran of the northwest Party organization from the early thirties. Sun also held two posts within the provincial government structure, established in Lanchow on January 8, 1950. He served as a member of the Kansu Provincial People's Government from January 1950 and two months later was named as chairman of this government's People's Supervision Committee. He also held related posts under the multi-provincial Party and government organs for Northwest China; in 1953–54 he was deputy director of the United Front Work Department of the Northwest Party Bureau (a department headed by minority nationalities specialist Wang Feng [q.v.]). During these same two years he was also a vice-chairman (again serving under Wang Feng) of the Nationalities Affairs Commission of the Northwest Administrative Committee, a government committee (like the Party bureau) having jurisdiction over Kansu, Ninghsia, Shensi, Tsinghai, and Sinkiang. These two posts are related because a major task of the United Front Department is to gain cooperation from the various national minority groups. The problems of united front work are particularly pertinent in the northwest where so many non-Han Chinese live. Sun's specialization in national minority matters was already evident by 1950 when he wrote an article on minority affairs in Kansu for the *Kansu jih-pao* (Kansu daily) of January 10, 1950, an article reprinted in the *Hsin-hua yueh-pao* (New China monthly) of February 15, 1950.

Although Sun was politically overshadowed in Kansu by Party leaders Chang Te-sheng and Wang Shih-t'ai (qq.v.), he was reported with some regularity in the early 1950's. For example, he was a vice-chairman of the preparatory committee established to mark the opening of the T'ien-shui–Lanchow Railway in August 1952, the important line that provided access by rail to Sian

in the east and Chengtu in the southwest. In the following month he was identified as the man in charge of "political study work" in all Kansu Party organizations, and in December 1953 Sun was named as the responsible person of the Northwest Party Bureau for the implementation of Party policies involving minority nationalities.

In early 1954, Sun was transferred from Kansu to neighboring Tsinghai, where he served in the provincial Party Committee briefly under Chang Chung-liang and then (from August 1954) under Kao Feng (qq.v.). Four years later, when charges were brought against Sun, it was asserted that he resisted this reassignment to Tsinghai, declaring it to be insignificant. It was further alleged that he was dissatisfied when he was not named as the Party first secretary—a suggestion that he may have had some friction with Chang Chung-liang and Kao Feng, his two superiors in the Tsinghai Party organization. At first Sun was given the position as second secretary in the Tsinghai Party committee, but by mid-1956 his post was redesignated as secretary (although he continued to be subordinate to ranking Secretary Kao Feng). In 1954 he received his first national post when he was elected as a deputy from Tsinghai to the First NPC. He attended the first session of the First NPC in Peking in September 1954 and then presented a report about the NPC meetings before a session of the Kansu Provincial Congress in December 1954. At this same time, he was elected as the Tsinghai governor, replacing Chang Chung-liang.

The 1958 disclosures made note of the fact that Sun had spent a year studying in Peking at the Higher Party School, which, as the name suggests, is the leading Communist Party School for higher level leaders and cadres. The exact year that Sun attended the Higher Party School was not mentioned, but it was probably in the last half of 1955 and the first part of 1956, during which time he did not appear in Tsinghai.

In his capacity as either the Tsinghai governor or as a provincial Party secretary, Sun Tso-pin was frequently in the news in the mid-1950's. Most frequently, he was reported in Tsinghai attending meetings of "advanced workers," making inspection tours, or delivering reports before provincial governmental or Party organizations. He also returned to Peking annually for the sessions of the NPC. In July 1957, Sun spoke before the fourth session of the First NPC; the title of his speech may be freely translated "If There Were No Communist Party There Would Be No Unity of Nationalities." Ironically, half a year later Sun was charged with a host of offenses, one of which was sabotaging Party leadership by advocating "local nationalism" (the standard Communist term to describe separatist tendencies leading toward greater local autonomy). Refining these charges, it was claimed that Sun had proposed the "doctrine of Kansu for the Kansu people," a strong suggestion that Sun is himself a native of that province. The broad catalogue of charges against Sun can only be briefly mentioned. During his tenure in Tsinghai he allegedly: opposed expenditures for the exploitation of the mineral-rich Tsaidam Basin, favoring the use of these funds for the development of pastoral areas; directed personnel work for the Tsinghai Party Committee but neglected this work; and displayed attitudes toward work and leisure which were declared to be those of a "bureaucrat of the Kuomintang type." Of particular interest is the charge that as long ago as 1934 Sun had claimed that there is a "Communist Party of the white areas" and a "Communist Party of the Soviet areas." Strikingly similar charges had been leveled against Kao Kang in 1955. The "white areas" referred to the Party organizations and personnel working in areas controlled by the Kuomintang or the Japanese. Such claims, of course, were viewed by the Party leaders to be divisive and therefore harmful. Sun was further accused of leading a corrupt life, of aiding and harboring anti-Communists, and opposing the crackdown on counterrevolutionaries. Finally, he was charged with being "anti-Party, anti-socialist, and anti-people." He was stripped of all his posts in Tsinghai (and the NPC) and expelled from the CCP. Expulsion from the Party can be taken as the "ultimate" punishment in contemporary Communist China. In this connection, it is noteworthy that Sun was mentioned again at the Second Session of the Eighth Party Congress in May 1958, just a few weeks after his expulsion from the Party ranks. Those mentioned were all declared to be "rightists," but with an important distinction: approximately half the group was described as "comrades," with no mention made of the loss of Party membership. Several such men (e.g., P'an Fu-sheng and Ku Ta-ts'un, qq.v.) have subsequently been reinstated to posts of moderate importance. The "rightists" of the second category, on the other hand, were not given the appellation "comrade" and apparently have been precluded from any further work in the Chinese Communist movement. Apart from Sun, the other man of considerable stature who lost his Party membership at this time was Sha Wenhan (q.v.), the purged former Chekiang governor.

Sun Yat-sen, Mme., see **Sung Ch'ing-ling**

Sung Ch'ing-ling

(Soong Ching Ling; 1890– ; Shanghai). Widow of Sun Yat-sen; vice-chairman, PRC.

Sung Ch'ing-ling, by virtue of her marriage to Sun Yat-sen, is the most famous woman in Communist China. Through blood and marital ties, the Sungs became the unrivaled political family of twentieth-century China. One son, T. V. Soong (Sung Tzu-wen), was a towering figure in the

Nationalist government. The eldest daughter, Ai-ling, married the famed financier and political figure H. H. Kung (K'ung Hsiang-hsi), and the youngest girl, Mei-ling, married Chiang Kai-shek. These three offspring and Sung Ch'ing-ling—the most famous four of the six Sung children—had widely varied careers, but they shared one thing in common: they received all their higher education in the United States. The two youngest boys, Tzu-liang and Tzu-an, were also public figures, but of much lesser stature than their older sisters and brother.

Cast in another fashion, Sung Ch'ing-ling's career can be seen as a half-century interaction with the three greatest Chinese of the twentieth century—her husband Sun Yat-sen, her brother-in-law and political enemy Chiang Kai-shek, and her ultimate political ally Mao Tse-tung. She began her revolutionary career in a rather unpretentious manner as personal secretary to Sun Yat-sen when his political fortunes were at a low ebb. Her second decade as a political figure began as Sun's famed widow who sided with the left wing of the KMT. This period carried through the late forties and was characterized by innumerable verbal assaults on the Chiang Kai-shek administration. The last period of her life began with the Communist conquest of the mainland in 1949 and the assumption by Sung of nominally important posts in an administration eager to enhance its legitimacy by ties with Sun Yat-sen's widow.

Sung was born into a well-to-do Christian family in Shanghai. Her father, Charles Jones Soong, was educated in the United States and was an early supporter of Sun Yat-sen. His second daughter, Ch'ing-ling, received her early education at the McTyeire School for Girls in Shanghai and was then sent to Wesleyan College for Women in Macon, Georgia, a school her elder sister Ai-ling had attended. She received her bachelor's degree in 1913 and then left for China. En route she stopped in Tokyo where she met Sun Yat-sen, about 25 years her senior and already married. As she related the story to Edgar Snow years later, she offered her services to Sun, then in exile. Soon after returning to Shanghai she received word from Sun that he needed her. There are conflicting reports about the date of their subsequent marriage and about the circumstances surrounding Sun's "divorce" from his first wife. The marriage dates range from 1914 to 1915, and the most immediate result was that Sung's father, who vigorously opposed the marriage and tried to have it annulled, withdrew his support from Sun.[1]

The young Ch'ing-ling immediately became involved in Sun's revolutionary activities in Japan, and in the words of one of his biographers, she "acted constantly as her husband's most trusted secretary."[2] She also served as his English interpreter and continued in these roles until Sun's death. During these years Sun was in and out of exile, and the couple lived in Japan, Shanghai, and Canton. Perhaps her most important work was an active participation in the negotiations with Soviet official Michael Borodin, who, in late 1923, held talks with Sun in Canton. These led to the reorganization of the KMT and a rather active alliance with the CCP. During these same years Sung also became closely associated with a number of important Communists in Canton, as well as with left-KMT leader Liao Chung-k'ai (assassinated in August 1925) and his wife Ho Hsiang-ning. Sung was with her husband when he died in Peking in March 1925. She then returned to Shanghai where she renewed her ties with Communists she had known earlier, and met still others, particularly those associated with CCP-dominated Shanghai University (see under Ch'ü Ch'iu-pai). After the May 30th Incident in Shanghai Sung became active in the student movement there. In the summer and again toward the end of the year she publicly attacked various elements of the KMT right wing. In short, by the time the KMT convened its Second Congress in 1926, Sung's orientation toward the left wing of the party was well established.

Sung was in Canton in January 1926 for the Second KMT Congress, which elected her a member of the KMT Second Central Executive Committee (CEC). The new CEC appointed her to head the Women's Department, but Sung indicated that she wanted to return to Shanghai, and thus that the position was given to her friend Ho Hsiang-ning.[3] It appears, however, that she remained in Canton, but in any case she was there in mid-1926 when the Northern Expedition was launched. When the Wuhan cities were captured by the Northern Expeditionary forces in October, she went there, and during the subsequent months she was very active in left-KMT circles, which were then dueling with Chiang Kai-shek for control of the KMT (see under Lin Po-ch'ü). In March 1927 the CEC convened its Third Plenum in Wuhan, a meeting which saw the left-KMT emerge with key positions in the KMT hierarchy and the national government. Sung was elected one of the 15 members of the KMT Political Council and one of the 28 members of the National Government Council.

Chiang Kai-shek reacted quickly to the leftist orientation of the March 1927 plenum, and on April 12 he engineered his famed anti-Communist coup in Shanghai and elsewhere. Moreover, the left-KMT group in Wuhan was beginning to have doubts about its tenuous alliance with the CCP. When the two sides split in July, Sung denounced the ascendancy of the "militarists" in the KMT and left for Shanghai—the first step toward her self-imposed exile. American correspondent Vincent Sheean has provided a particularly vivid, first-hand account of the final agonies of the alliance of the CCP with the left-KMT.

He saw Mme. Sun frequently in Wuhan, and again in Moscow in the fall. He was deeply impressed with her shyness, dignity, and commitment to her husband's revolutionary goals.[4]

Sung was still in Shanghai when the Communists staged the famous Nanchang Uprising on August 1, 1927 (see under Yeh T'ing). The rebels, maintaining the fiction that they represented the KMT, established a Revolutionary Committee of 25 members, Sung among them. In theory, the committee was led by a seven-member Presidium, of which Sung was also a member. The Presidium composition was designed to demonstrate a broad base of political support. Only two of the seven were Communists (Yun Tai-ying and T'an P'ing-shan), and another of the members, General Chang Fa-k'uei, was the same man who would drive the insurgents from the city a few days later. As these events were unfolding, Sung was making plans to leave China. In late August she departed for Vladivostok and arrived in Moscow the next month in the company of Eugene Ch'en (Ch'en Yu-jen), the foreign minister of the former Wuhan administration. For Sung, the final touch of bitter irony was added a few months later when her sister Mei-ling married the conqueror of the left-KMT, Chiang Kai-shek.

From 1927 to 1929 Sung resided in Europe, spending most of her time in Moscow and Berlin. She returned to China to attend the state burial of Sun Yat-sen in Nanking in June 1929, but was back in Europe in 1930–31. Sung became affiliated with various left-wing groups, the most important of which seems to have been the World Committee against Imperialist War (which sponsored a secretly convened anti-war congress in Shanghai in September 1933, which Sung addressed). Sung returned to Shanghai in 1931, and from then until 1937 she lived in the French Concession. These years coincided with Japan's steady incursions into China—from the Manchurian Incident in 1931 to full-scale war in 1937. Opposition to Japan was particularly virulent among the intellectuals in the coastal cities, and efforts to "resist Japan" and "save the nation," two typical and favorite slogans, took a number of forms. With the prestige of her husband's name, Sung was in a unique position to assist in many such causes. For precisely the same reason she was perhaps the only person in China who could openly oppose Chiang Kai-shek, a favorite target of the intellectuals, who felt that the KMT was not doing enough to resist the Japanese.

After the Mukden Incident in Manchuria in September 1931, Sung worked intensively. to organize hospital care for wounded soldiers, and she was engaged in like fashion in 1932 following Japan's attack on Shanghai. Also in 1932 she was one of the organizers and chairman of the China League for Civil Rights, an organization which sought, sometimes successfully, to win the release from the KMT of political prisoners (many of them Communists—see under Liao Ch'eng-chih and Lo Teng-hsien). The nature of Sung's ties with the CCP during these years has not been fully explored, and many ambiguities remain. For example, Sung, Ho Hsiang-ning, and many others published a six-point program to resist Japan in April 1934, a program broadly similar to one published by the Communist hierarchy in Kiangsi at the same time. In later years it became standard practice for Communist historians to claim that Sung's declaration was really a CCP program which had merely been "published over the signature" of Sung and others,[5] and in 1951 it was included in an important collection of documents on CCP history.[6] Sung's declaration quickly gave rise to still another organization, the Chinese People's Committee for Armed Self-Defense. Further Japanese incursions into north China in 1935–36 led to a proliferation of organizations such as Sung's, which in 1936 were grouped together into the National Salvation Association (or, in the more literal and graphic translation, the "Save-the-Nation" Association). The organization, of which Sung was an Executive Committee member, received a major boost when seven very prominent professional men and intellectuals were arrested in November 1936 and imprisoned for their persistent advocacy of stronger measures to resist Japan. The case of the "Seven Gentlemen," widely regarded as martyrs to a great cause, became an immediate *cause célèbre*, the details of which are discussed in the biography of Shih Liang. Characteristically, Sung joined the chorus of denunciations of the government's action against the seven.

Few of these activities, of course, were welcomed by the Chiang Kai-shek administration. Sung had been re-elected to the KMT Central Executive Committee at congresses held in 1929 and 1931, but in November 1935, perhaps to chastise or embarrass her, she was demoted to alternate membership. Nonetheless, she traveled to Nanking for the Third Plenum of the Executive Committee in February 1937. This took place not long after the "Seven Gentlemen" case and the even more famous Sian Incident of December 1936 (see under Chou En-lai) when, though the details are murky and much disputed, Chiang Kai-shek arrived at some sort of modus vivendi with the Communists to cooperate in resisting Japan. At the plenum Mme. Sun added insult to injury by delivering a blistering attack on Nationalist policies. She did not mention the Generalissimo by name, but she ridiculed his "antiquated theory that first we must suppress the Communists and then resist Japanese aggression!" Could China go to war "with one arm broken," she added rhetorically and sarcastically. Such disputes were swept aside five months later

when the Sino-Japanese War began; the foreign aggressors had immediately healed the old wounds between the KMT and the CCP. In this spirit Sung issued a statement in Shanghai in November 1937 entitled "On the Reconciliation," which closed on the note of the "final victory" for China. Prior to this Sung had already plunged herself into the war effort. She authored a number of articles and pamphlets on the theme of "resistance" and traveled to Canton in August and September to promote women's patriotic associations and to seek funds and support from overseas Chinese.

When the Shanghai area fell to the Japanese in November 1937, Sung went to Hong Kong. There, in June 1938, she established the China Defense League to promote the war effort. Because KMT-CCP cooperation was then still relatively good, the league's leadership included some prominent KMT officials, like her brother T. V. Soong. Mme. Sun made repeated efforts to collect funds from abroad, particularly from the China Aid Council in the United States; they were then used by her league and by Chinese Industrial Cooperatives (see under Meng Yung-ch'ien), with which she had close ties. During her four years in Hong Kong she was able to keep in steady contact with the CCP through the two children of her old friend and colleague Ho Hsiang-ning. Ho's son, Liao Ch'eng-chih (q.v.), was then the top Communist official in Hong Kong, and her daughter, Liao Meng-hsing (Cynthia Liao), was for many years one of Sung's private secretaries.

The Japanese attack on Pearl Harbor, as well as Hong Kong, in December 1941 forced Sung to flee to Chungking. The wife of Sun Yat-sen was, of course, welcomed to the beleaguered wartime capital, but by this time she had already renewed her criticisms of the Chiang government, often in the foreign press—both directly in articles and indirectly through foreign journalists. She continued her criticisms throughout the remaining war years, often addressing them in private to American diplomats. Sung's various encounters with KMT officialdom led the American ambassador to observe in March 1944 that there was "much private comment among independent Chinese and some minor officials" about the "increasing trend toward . . . repressive methods to stifle opposition, suspicion of all elements considered critical of the Kuomintang and centralization of power in the hands of the Central Government (that is, the Kuomintang)." He went on to comment that "no Chinese of any importance has dared to give voice publicly even by implication to the existence of such conditions except Madame Sun."[7] She repeated her charges about "undemocratic conditions" in China to American Vice-President Henry A. Wallace, who visited there in mid-1944 on a fact-finding mission.[8]

On paper, Sung's official positions in the post-war period suggested an allegiance to the Nationalists. For example, in 1945 she was reinstated to full membership on the KMT Central Executive Committee, and in the next year she was elevated to the Standing Committee. In 1946 she was also elected a KMT delegate to the National Assembly, and in 1947 she was appointed an adviser to the national government. In fact, however, her actions and public statements indicated a contrary position. In 1946 Sung returned to Shanghai where she issued appeals for a coalition government (which the CCP was then fostering) and urged the United States to halt its aid to Chiang Kai-shek on the grounds that it contributed to the civil war. In the same year she reorganized her China Defense League into the China Welfare Fund, which supported various Communist-oriented organizations. If any doubt remained about her sympathies, they were brought to rest in the latter part of 1947. On October 10 (the anniversary of the 1911 Revolution) dissident KMT general Li Chi-shen announced plans to convene a congress of the "democratic elements" within the KMT. This took place two days later (on Sun Yat-sen's birthday), and on January 1, 1948, in Hong Kong, the KMT Revolutionary Committee was organized as a political party—with Li as the chairman and Mme. Sun as the honorary chairman. While these events were taking place, Sung remained in Shanghai where, protected by her name and fame, she continued to live until the city fell to the Communists in late May 1949. Earlier in the year, in a situation tinged with irony, Sung had one final encounter with her erstwhile colleagues in the KMT. On the eve of the surrender of Peking, Chiang Kai-shek "retired" and was replaced by Vice-President Li Tsung-jen, an advocate of peace talks with the Communists. Li immediately organized a delegation, and one of his representatives solicited Sung's participation. She summarily turned down the request.[9]

Sung did not travel to Peking until late August 1949. Earlier, in April, she and her old friend Ho Hsiang-ning had been elected the honorary chairmen of the All-China Federation of Democratic Women, and in July she had been made chairman of the preparatory committee of the Sino-Soviet Friendship Association. Soon afterwards, Sung was selected as a "specially invited delegate" to the CPPCC, which, at its inaugural session in September, established the PRC. During the meetings she served as a member of the Standing Committee of the CPPCC presidium (steering committee), and at the close of the session she was elected a member of the First National Committee of the CPPCC.

In the new People's Republic, inaugurated on October 1, 1949, the Central People's Government Council (CPGC), the highest organ of state authority, was chaired by Mao. The six vice-chairmen were obviously selected to strike a balance between the CCP and the various other political elements with which it was cooperating. Three of them, Liu Shao-ch'i, Chu Te, and Kao Kang, were drawn from the inner elite of the Party, and two others, Chang Lan and Li Chi-shen, headed the two most important "democratic" (that is, non-Communist) parties, the China Democratic League and the KMT Revolutionary Committee. Mme. Sun, aside from the obvious status deriving from her husband's name, was regarded as a representative of the loosely defined group known as "democratic personages" or "non-partisans" (that is, neither a member of the CCP nor any of the handful of "democratic" parties). The 34 CPGC meetings held from 1949 to 1954 passed on virtually all the important measures adopted by the PRC in its formative years. Records of these meetings are not complete, but based on a good sampling it is evident that despite her frail health Sung attended them rather regularly, particularly those in 1953–54.

As already noted, Sung had headed the preparatory committee for the Sino-Soviet Friendship Association, but when the organization was formally inaugurated in early October 1949, Liu Shao-ch'i was elected chairman and Sung one of the vice-chairmen. However, five years later, in December 1954, she succeeded Liu as chairman and has since retained this post. The association was quite active in the first decade of the PRC, but most of the day-to-day tasks fell upon neither Liu nor Sung, but rather on Ch'ien Chün-jui (q.v.). In December 1949 Sung gave a lengthy address before the Asian Women's Conference, one of the first major international meetings held in Peking. She emphasized women's rights, often in economic terms, and the tone of her speech was relatively mild, if only in contrast to the revolutionary ardor expressed by Teng Ying-ch'ao, whose biography contains further details about this important meeting.

In April 1950 a conference was held in Peking to amalgamate the various organizations dealing with welfare and relief problems. A new Chinese People's Relief Administration (CPRA) was inaugurated to unify relief and welfare plans throughout the nation, and to control the allocation of personnel, funds, and materials according to these plans. Sung was elected chairman of the CPRA, a position she still holds. The administration is ostensibly a "mass" or "people's" organization, but later that year Sung acknowledged that it was under the auspices of the national government. Other important officials elected then include Tung Pi-wu, Hsieh Chueh-tsai, Li Te-ch'üan, and Wu Yun-fu, whose biographies provide additional information on this and related organizations. With large-scale relief problems (for example, floods and famines) now under the CPRA, Sung's China Welfare Institute (the new name for the China Welfare Fund) was reorganized in August 1950. Thereafter, emphasis was placed upon women and children, including a maternity, health, and child-care network, model nurseries, a children's theater, and the gathering of statistics about children. The Institute, located in Shanghai, is probably best known abroad as the sponsoring body for *China Reconstructs,* which began publication in January 1952 as a bi-monthly, and in January 1955 as a monthly. Later the magazine was also published in Spanish (April 1962), French (April 1963), Arabic (March 1964), and Russian (January 1966) editions. In another activity related to welfare work, Sung has served as chairman of the Chinese People's Committee in Defense of Children, established in November 1951 in response to a proposal from the Communist-backed Women's International Democratic Federation. In the next year she was a member of the international sponsoring committee for the International Conference in Defense of Children held in Vienna in April, but Sung herself did not attend.

Sung was not present at the Communist bloc's Second World Peace Congress in Warsaw in November 1950, but she was elected a member of the Bureau (to 1952) of the World Peace Council (WPC). Then, in April 1951 she was a recipient of an International Stalin Peace Prize for 1950, an award formally presented to her in Peking in September 1951 by Soviet writer Ilya Ehrenburg. Much of the energies of the WPC in that period centered on the Korean War, and in this connection the council sponsored the Asian and Pacific Regions Peace Conference in Peking in October 1952. Liu Ning-i (q.v.) was probably the most important Chinese Communist in terms of actual involvement with the meeting, but Sung served as titular leader of the Chinese delegation, and she was elected chairman of the Peace Liaison Committee for Asian and Pacific Regions, a regional offshoot of the WPC. A few weeks later, in December, Sung went abroad for the first time in many years when she led the Chinese delegation to Vienna for the Congress of Peoples for Peace (or "Partisans for Peace"), which once more concentrated on the Korean War. En route home in January 1953, Sung went through Moscow where she was received by Stalin only a few weeks before his death.

In early 1953 the PRC took its first major organizational steps toward holding nationwide elections and adopting a constitution. Three special committees were set up, and Sung was named a member of two of them—one to prepare for elections and another to draft the constitution. When these tasks were completed in 1954, Sung was elected a Shanghai deputy to the First NPC, which, at its first meeting in September, adopted the new constitution. In the reorganized central government she became a vice-chairman

under Chairman Liu Shao-ch'i of the NPC Standing Committee. Three months later, in December, she was elected a vice-chairman of the Second National Committee of the CPPCC, which, after the establishment of the NPC, became a consultative rather than a legislative body. In the same month she replaced Liu Shao-ch'i as chairman of the Sino-Soviet Friendship Association, a position she still holds.

In the mid-fifties, when the "spirit of Bandung" was a major ingredient in Chinese foreign policy, prominent figures were sent on a number of goodwill missions. Sung made one of the first of these trips in December 1955 when she led a delegation to India. She was accompanied by the important CCP leader Liao Ch'eng-chih. The group was received by Prime Minister Nehru, and after touring India they visited Burma and Pakistan before returning home in early February 1956. Half a year later she led a similar group to Indonesia at the invitation of President Sukarno. Mme. Sun, who has often suffered from ill health since 1949, was delayed in traveling to Jakarta by a month, but she finally arrived in mid-August 1956, after a three-day stopover in Burma. Her group returned to China at the end of the month. In September she attended the CCP's Eighth National Congress. Her brief speech was undistinguished, but her very appearance at the congress illustrated anew her unusual role in Communist China: she was the only non-Communist speaker.

Chinese media again referred to her ill health in June 1957, commenting that it had kept her "somewhat inactive recently." However, in November she was a member of Mao Tse-tung's historic delegation to Moscow for the 40th anniversary of the Russian Revolution. Sung was again a Shanghai deputy to the Second NPC, which first met in April 1959. It was then that Mao stepped down as PRC chairman and turned the post over to Liu Shao-ch'i. Chu Te had served under Mao as the vice-chairman, but now he was replaced by two vice-chairmen, Sung and Party "elder" Tung Pi-wu (q.v.). This gives her the privilege, exercised rather infrequently, of receiving the credentials of foreign diplomats in the absence of the chairman. In fact, however, like most of her other posts, Sung's vice-chairmanship of the PRC is only of nominal importance. At this same time, Sung relinquished the vice-chairmanship of both the NPC Standing Committee and the CPPCC. Later that year she wrote a short piece to commemorate the 10th anniversary of the PRC, which was published in 1960 in a collection of articles entitled *Ten Glorious Years.*

In July 1960 Mme. Sun turned down an invitation to attend the inauguration of the Republic of Ghana because of ill health, and in the same year her friend of many years standing, journalist Edgar Snow, was unable to see her for the same reason. Snow commented that Sung lived in her old home in Shanghai most of the time, and added that her illness had reached an "acute stage."[10] However, in the early and mid-sixties, she continued to appear in public from time to time. For example, in the fall of 1961 she presided over ceremonies in Peking to mark the 50th anniversary of the 1911 Revolution. During these years she also received some foreign dignitaries, usually in Shanghai, as in February 1963 when she was called on by Cambodian head of state Norodom Sihanouk and his wife. Mme. Sun's health had apparently taken a turn for the better by late February 1964 when she traveled to Ceylon at the invitation of Mrs. Sirimavo Bandaranaike, the premier. En route, in Dacca, she was joined by Premier Chou En-lai and Foreign Minister Ch'en I, who made the four-day visit with her to Ceylon.

Sung was again elected from Shanghai to the Third NPC, and at the close of its first session in early January 1965, she and Tung Pi-wu were re-elected vice-chairmen of the PRC. Then in her 75th year, she continued to personify the great span of years from Sun Yat-sen's initial abortive attempts to overthrow the Manchus to Mao's conquest and control of the mainland.

Throughout her career Sung Ch'ing-ling was a prodigious writer, especially from the 1920's to the 1940's. But most of her pieces were brief and polemical, and she never authored any major work. A selection of her articles and public speeches from 1927 to 1952 was published in English in 1953 under the title *The Struggle for New China*. The pre-1949 materials are particularly useful, in part because they are difficult to obtain elsewhere. The post-1949 selections, which constitute half the volume, are generally prosaic, except for a very long account of an inspection trip she made to Manchuria in 1951.

---

1. Edgar Snow, *Journey to the Beginning* (London, 1960), p. 88.
2. Lyon Sharman, *Sun Yat-sen* (Stanford, Calif., 1968), p. 183.
3. Li Yün-han, *Tsung jung kung tao ch'ing tang* (From the admission of the Communists to the purification of the [Nationalist] Party; Taipei, 1966), pp. 474, 519.
4. Vincent Sheean, *Personal History* (New York, 1934), chap. 6.
5. *Selected Works of Mao Tse-tung* (Peking, 1964), I, 174; Shanti Swarup, *A Study of the Chinese Communist Movement, 1927–1934* (London, 1966), pp. 198–199; Tso-liang Hsiao, *Power Relations within the Chinese Communist Movement, 1930–1934* (Seattle, Wash., 1961), pp. 226–227.
6. Hu Hua, ed., *Chung-kuo hsin min-chu-chu-i ko-ming shih ts'an-k'ao tzu-liao* (Reference materials on the history of China's new democratic revolution; Peking, 1951), pp. 261–262.
7. *Foreign Relations of the United States: Diplomatic Papers, 1944, China* (Washington, D.C., 1967), VI, 385–386.
8. *Ibid.*, pp. 241–242.
9. *China Digest,* Hong Kong, February 8, 1949, p. 23.
10. Edgar Snow, *The Other Side of the River* (London, 1963), p. 544.

Sung Jen-ch'iung

(1904–   ; Liu-yang, Hunan). Veteran Red Army political officer; first secretary, CCP Northeast Bureau; member, CCP Central Committee.

After joining the CCP in 1928 Sung Jen-ch'iung was an officer in the Communist armies until the conquest of the mainland was completed in 1950. He spent the early 1950's in the southwest where he was active in the Party, government, and military administrations and then transferred to Peking in 1954. He was elected to the Party Central Committee in 1956 and was appointed minister of the Third Ministry of Machine Building shortly thereafter. In 1961 he became first secretary of the Party's Northeast Bureau and has served in Manchuria since that time.

Sung was born in 1904 in Liu-yang, about 50 miles east of Changsha, the Hunan provincial capital. In the mid-1920's he went to Canton, then the revolutionary center of China, and enrolled at the newly opened Whampoa Military Academy, whose president was Chiang Kai-shek. Edgar Snow has described Sung as a "former Kuomintang officer,"[1] and although the dates are not available, it would appear to have been in the period between his graduation from Whampoa and 1928, the year he joined the Communist Party. He apparently soon went to the Kiangsi-Fukien area controlled by the Communists, because by 1930 he was a regimental political commissar in forces led by Lin Piao. In the next year he advanced to the post of a division political commissar in the Fifth Army Corps. This corps was established under the command of Tung Chen-t'ang and Chao Po-sheng in December 1931 after these two officers led a revolt in the Nationalists' 26th Route Army and joined the Communists. Sung later studied at the Red Army Academy, which opened in 1933 just outside Juichin, the capital of the Communist Chinese Soviet Republic. Then, during the Long March (1934–35), Sung and Ch'en Keng (q.v.) were political commissar and commander of the Red Cadres' Regiment, which consisted of cadets from Red Army military institutes in Kiangsi. This regiment was responsible for "protecting the leaders and organizations" of the Party

Central Committee, including Mao Tse-tung.[2]

In January 1936, soon after the first group of marchers reached north Shensi, Sung became political commissar of the 28th Red Army; he was with this force when it was ordered to cross the Yellow River into west Shansi in early 1936. This campaign is described in the biography of Liu Chih-tan, the 28th Army commander. When Liu was mortally wounded in the Shansi operation, Sung assumed command of the 28th Army[3] (presumably also continuing as its political commissar). The Communists reorganized their armies after the start of the Sino-Japanese War in mid-1937 and Sung's forces became part of Liu Po-ch'eng's 129th Division, one of three divisions making up the newly created Eighth Route Army. Sung was made director of the division's Political Department, serving directly under Political Commissar Teng Hsiao-p'ing (q.v.). Sung remained with Liu's forces for nearly two decades.

In early September 1937 the three divisions of the Eighth Route Army entered Shansi and dispersed into different sections of the province. Moving into eastern Shansi, the 129th division engaged the Japanese in October along the Cheng-t'ai Railroad (running from Shih-chia-chuang, Hopeh to Taiyuan, Shansi), and after the Japanese broke through the Communist lines, Liu's division established its major base in the T'ai-hang Mountains north of Ch'ang-chih in southeastern Shansi. As Liu expanded operations from his base (near Liao-hsien), part of his army moved into southern Hopeh where political and military units under his deputy commander Hsu Hsiang-ch'ien (q.v.) organized the South Hopeh Military District in the summer of 1938.[4] Sung took part in these moves, leading a cavalry regiment into south Hopeh in 1938 where he was active for the next five years. From 1938 he was the commander of the South Hopeh Military District.

In August 1938 Sung also became vice-chairman of the South Hopeh Administrative Office, the political organization paralleling the Military District.[5] Offices like this provided the governmental machinery for a Communist base and were distinct in function from the military command and from the Party organ established in every guerrilla area. However, the principal governmental personnel were often the same men who conducted the base's military and Party affairs. The chairman of the South Hopeh Administrative Office was Yang Hsiu-feng (q.v.), a former professor who joined the resistance at the outbreak of the war. Yang was not then a Party member, and Sung was thus the important Party official in his administration. Sometime in 1939 Sung replaced Yang as chairman in South Hopeh. In July 1941, when the Communists created the Shansi-Hopeh-Shantung-Honan (Chin-Chi-Lu-Yü) Border Region Government, the South Ho-

peh Administrative Office became part of it. Yang became the Border Government chairman, and Sung was made a member of the Chin-Chi-Lu-Yü Government Council.

In addition to his political work Sung was also active on the military front. In 1942 he organized and directed for a time a "dare-to-die" column of guerrillas in south Hopeh. Units of the so-called Dare-to-Die Corps were the military arm of the Sacrifice League, the leading mass patriotic association of the Shansi resistance, which had been organized in 1936 with Governor Yen Hsi-shan as its titular head. In the early war years, the League's membership grew quite large and many of its members later joined the CCP.[6]

Sung apparently left south Hopeh at least temporarily in 1943 when he went to Yenan to study at the Central Party School. At that time the Party was in the midst of conducting an intensive indoctrination movement known as the *cheng-feng* (rectification) campaign. Begun in 1942, it consisted of training in Communist doctrine with special emphasis on Mao Tse-tung's works and principles. Sung presumably took part in it during his stay in Yenan. Later, when the Party met in Yenan for its Seventh National Congress (April–June 1945), Sung was elected an alternate member of the CCP Central Committee.

From the end of the war with Japan in 1945 until 1954, Sung continued to serve with Liu Po-ch'eng's army. This army's advance from south Shansi into central and central-south China, and then into the southwest late in 1949 where it captured Yunnan province is described in Liu Po-ch'eng's biography. During 1945–46 Sung was commander of the Hopeh-Shantung-Honan Military Region, as well as the South Hopeh Military District, in which he had served since 1938. In 1947 he was also political commissar of the South Hopeh Military District and of the Second Column of Liu's forces. By 1949 Sung had become political commissar of the Fourth Army Corps in Liu's army, which was now called the Second Field Army. He also served as vice-chairman of the Nanking Military Control Commission from April to November 1949.

After Kunming, the Yunnan capital, was captured in February 1950, Sung was given key posts at the regional, provincial, and municipal levels. In the next month he became chairman of the Kunming Military Control Commission, and by this time he was also a deputy political commissar of the Southwest Military Region and director of the Second Field Army's Political Department. In July he was appointed a member of the overall regional government for the southwest, the Southwest Military and Administrative Committee (SWMAC), and shortly thereafter he was made a member of the Yunnan Provincial People's Government Council and chairman of its Finance and Economics Committee. From 1951 Sung was also the ranking Party secretary in

Yunnan. He was promoted to a vice-chairmanship of the SWMAC in August 1952 and he retained this post when the SWMAC was reorganized into the Southwest Administrative Committee in February 1953. Finally, by mid-1952 he was also first deputy secretary of the CCP Southwest Bureau, ranking third after Secretary Ho Lung and Second Secretary Liu Po-ch'eng. Because Ho was frequently in Peking and Liu was seldom in the southwest after 1951, much of the responsibility fell to Sung. Similarly, after 1952 Teng Hsiao-p'ing, the regional political commissar, spent most of his time in Peking, and thus from then until 1954 Sung was probably the key political officer in the area.

When the constitutional government came into being in September 1954 at the first session of the First NPC, Sung was transferred to Peking where he became a member of the newly created National Defense Council, a military advisory body with little power but considerable prestige. He was reappointed to the Council in April 1959 and again in January 1965. In December 1954 he attended the Second Congress of the Sino-Soviet Friendship Association as a PLA representative.

Since 1955 Sung's stature among the Communist elite has been steadily rising. When personal military ranks and decorations were first awarded in 1955 he was made a colonel-general (equivalent to a U.S. Army lieutenant-general) and was awarded the three top military awards. These decorations, the Orders of August First, Independence and Freedom, and Liberation, were given for military service from 1927 to 1950. He also assumed an important PLA staff post in 1955 as deputy director of the General Cadres Department under Lo Jung-huan. It is uncertain how long Sung held this post; he may have been dropped from the department around December 1956 when Hsiao Hua replaced Lo as the director.

In addition to his military posts, Sung was also identified in 1955 as a deputy secretary-general of the CCP Central Committee. In this capacity he worked under his long-time colleague, Secretary-General Teng Hsiao-p'ing, until the post was abolished when the Party Center was reorganized in September 1956 at the Eighth Party Congress. Sung took an active part in the Congress, serving as a member of its Presidium and Credentials Committee and as a secretary of its Secretariat. He also delivered a speech entitled "Experience in Collective Leadership." When the Congress elected the new Central Committee, Sung was promoted from alternate to full membership.

In November 1956 Sung received his first key appointment in the national government as minister of the Third Ministry of Machine Building, a ministry re-established after having been abolished the previous May. In February 1958 the ministry was renamed the Second Ministry of Machine Building, and the Third Ministry was again abolished. Sung continued to hold the portfolio in the new Second Ministry until September 1960. In May 1957 he was named to the State Council's Scientific Planning Commission. First established in March 1956, it was absorbed by the Scientific and Technological Commission in November 1958 at which time Sung was dropped. In 1958 he was elected a Yunnan delegate to the Second NPC, which opened in April 1959. During the term of the Second Congress (1959–1964) he was transferred from Peking to Liaoning, and when re-elected to the Third NPC (opening December 1964) it was as a Liaoning deputy.

In 1961 Sung left Peking for Manchuria. In January of that year the regional CCP bureaus were re-established, and in March Sung was identified as first secretary of the Northeast Bureau, which is headquartered in Shenyang (Mukden), the Liaoning capital. Since his arrival in Shenyang Sung has been quite active, attending a number of functions in his capacity as the top Party leader in Manchuria. In June 1963 he was on hand to welcome Korean President Choi Yong Kun to Shenyang when the latter arrived with Premier Chou En-lai for a visit to Manchuria. In October of that year Sung was in North Korea where he was identified among a group of Northeast CCP Bureau officials received by Kim Il Sung, chairman of the Korean Workers' (Communist) Party. Sung was presumably the leader of the Chinese delegation, but the purpose of the visit was not mentioned.

Although a top Party bureaucrat, Sung continues to work as a PLA political officer. In March 1964 he was identified as political commissar of the Shenyang Military Region, which is responsible for military affairs in the whole of Manchuria. At the close of the Fourth CPPCC in Peking in January 1965, Sung was also given the less important appointment as a CPPCC vice-chairman.

Sung has written two articles for *Hung-ch'i* (Red flag), the Party's most important journal. The first was entitled "The Basic Mass Movement Policy of the Proletarian Leadership of Industry" (January 16, 1960) and the second, "Promote the Revolutionary Perseverance of the Proletariat" (October 28, 1964).

1. Edgar Snow, *Red Star over China* (New York, 1938), p. 452.

2. *The Long March, Eyewitness Accounts* (Peking, 1963), pp. 47–60.

3. *Shan-hsi ko-ming tou-cheng hui-i-lu* (Reminiscences of revolutionary struggles in Shansi; Taiyuan [?], preface dated 1961), p. 28.

4. Chalmers A. Johnson, *Peasant Nationalism and Communist Power* (Stanford, Calif., 1962), pp. 95, 107–108.

5. *K'ang-Jih chan-cheng shih-ch'i chieh-fang-*

ch'ü kai-k'uang (A sketch of the liberated areas during the Anti-Japanese War; Peking, 1953), pp. 50–51.

6. Johnson, pp. 99–100; Donald G. Gillin, *Warlord Yen Hsi-shan in Shansi Province, 1911– 1949* (Princeton, N.J., 1967), *passim.*

Sung Shao-wen

(1910– ; T'un-liu hsien, Shansi). Former chairman, Shansi-Chahar-Hopeh Border Region; vice-chairman, State Planning Commission.

Sung Shao-wen was the wartime head of the Shansi-Chahar-Hopeh Border Region, and in the period since the establishment of the PRC in 1949 he has held a number of important posts in economic ministries and commissions. Sung is from T'un-liu in southeast Shansi. He studied the classics at an "old fashioned Confucian school" and then, during his middle school years, developed an interest in biology and mathematics. Still later, at Peking University, Sung studied history and political science. He was a student there when the Japanese occupied Manchuria (1931), after which he became deeply involved in the anti-Japanese student movement. Because of these activities he was arrested the day before his scheduled graduation in 1933; kept in prison for nearly a year, Sung was allowed to graduate in 1934. He then returned to Shansi and became a high school teacher in Taiyuan, the provincial capital.[1]

By the mid-1930's Yen Hsi-shan, the famous warlord-governor of Shansi, was becoming increasingly apprehensive of the steady incursions into north China by the Japanese. In early 1936, to strengthen his position in the province, Yen organized the Force for the Promotion of Justice (Chu-chang kung-tao t'uan; usually known as the Justice Force). This was conceived of as an anti-Communist mass organization, but by 1936 it had already been "infiltrated by younger and more liberal elements who would soon show how little they were in sympathy with its goals." Among the younger elements were Sung and Niu P'ei-tsung. (Niu, a 1932 graduate in economics from Tsinghua University in Peking, later became a vice-governor of Honan under the Communists, and since 1954 he has been a leading figure in economic affairs in the PRC). By the middle of 1936 Yen was reportedly engaged in secret negotiations with the Communists to ally together against the Japanese (see under P'eng Hsueh-feng and Po I-po), and according to Sung's account, Yen had actually worked out a truce with the Communists by June 1936.[2] As Japanese pressures continued, the younger elements of the Justice Force (presumably including Sung), persuaded Yen to form still another organization. This was the League for National Salvation through Sacrifice (Hsi-sheng chiu-kuo t'ung-meng-hui; best known by its short title,

Sacrifice League), which was formed in September 1936 on the fifth anniversary of the Japanese occupation of Manchuria.

Song was among the more active members of the Sacrifice League, and by approximately the outbreak of War in July 1937, he was also serving as chairman of the Civil and Military Training Committee and the Propaganda Section in Yen Hsi-shan's provincial administration. When the Japanese invaded Shansi in the earliest days of the war, Yen sent Sung to Wu-t'ai hsien (Yen's native district) to become the hsien magistrate. At this juncture, elements from the Communists' 115th Division led by Nieh Jung-chen (q.v.) were also in northeast Shansi. Nieh and Sung conferred about means to bring order out of the administrative chaos that was enveloping north Shansi. Sung then assumed the chairmanship of a preparatory committee which, with the approval of· Yen Hsi-shan, was to convene a conference to inaugurate a multi-provincial, emergency administration. This in turn led to the convocation of a conference at Fu-p'ing, located in west Hopeh, due east of Wu-t'ai. The famous Fu-p'ing Conference was held in mid-January 1938 and was attended by more than 140 delegates from 39 hsien in Shansi, Hopeh, and Chahar provinces; some were local magistrates, some military representatives of the Nationalist and Communist forces, but most were from the various mass organizations, especially the Sacrifice League and a wide variety of other local "salvation" organizations. Sung's inaugural address centered upon the theme of organizing all facets of society to resist the Japanese. He noted that, in contrast to the situation only two months earlier, there were already five military areas with "more than 20,000 armed people," and 60–70,000 "warriors who constantly attack the enemy."[3]

The conference established the Shansi-Chahar-Hopeh (Chin-Ch'a-Chi) Border Region and set up a nine-member administrative committee. Sung headed this committee, but it quickly became apparent that the dominant figure was the veteran Communist military leader Nieh Jung-chen. In speaking to a number of foreign visitors at this time and in the ensuing years, Sung and his colleagues were quick to note that the Communists did not hold a majority of seats on the administrative committee. Sung himself emphasized that he was not a Communist. (It is not known when he was admitted to the CCP, but he was definitely a member by the early 1950's, and probably long before that.) Of the other seven committee members, three later became members or alternates of the CCP Central Committee (Lü Cheng-ts'ao, Sun Chih-yuan, and Chang Su, qq.v.). Moreover, three of the remaining four members went on to hold positions of considerable significance after the Communists came to power in 1949. Hu Jen-k'uei worked for many years in the Foreign Trade Ministry, and in 1962 was appointed president of the Peking Forestry College. Li Chieh-yung was elected a vice-governor of Kiangsi in 1955, and Lou Ning-hsien has been a vice-mayor of Tientsin since 1958 and a vice-president of Nankai University since 1964. In brief, of the original nine members, only the KMT representative did not work for the Communists after 1949.

The formation of the Chin-Ch'a-Chi Border Region was a landmark event in the post-Long March history of the Communists. Not only was it the first behind-enemy-lines governmental administration dominated by the Communists, but it also grew to be the "most complex and highly developed of all the Communist rear-area strongholds set up during the war."[4] The area was visited by many Western journalists and military officials, and it has been described in considerable detail in a number of Western sources, most notably by George E. Taylor and by the authors of a United States War Department report.[5]

The new government was not able to remain for long at Fu-p'ing, because in March 1938 the Japanese moved into the city and destroyed it. Sung and his colleagues retreated to the Wu-t'ai area in northeast Shansi. It was moved again in late 1938, and three more times in the following year,[6] but for the balance of the war it remained in the general vicinity of Wu-t'ai hsien. At the time he was chairman of the government, Sung was also director of the Border Region's Finance Office for a portion of the war and postwar years. After the inaugural conference in 1938, it was not until January 1943 that the first full-fledged congress of the Border Region was held. This was also presided over by Sung, who continued to head the government. The Chin-Ch'a-Chi headquarters was transferred to Kalgan, the capital of Chahar, after the city was occupied by the Communists in August 1945, and it was through the Kalgan area that Lin Piao funneled tens of thousands of troops and cadres into Manchuria from north and northwest China. When the city fell to Nationalist troops in October 1946, Sung and his colleagues were forced to move their administrative headquarters to rural areas.

In August 1948, with victory in sight, the Communists convened the North China Provisional People's Congress. The Shansi-Hopeh-Shantung-Honan (Chin-Chi-Lu-Yü) Border Region to the south had already been militarily linked by the Communist armies to Sung's administration, and thus the congress was convened to establish a corresponding civil government. Sung served on the congress presidium (steering committee) and delivered a report covering the work of the Chin-Ch'a-Chi Border Region during the previous two years. At the close of the meetings, he was elected a member of the North

China People's Government (NCPG), which was headed by Party veteran Tung Pi-wu. In the following month, when the organs of government were set up, he was appointed director of the Agriculture Department and a member (also under Tung Pi-wu) of the Finance and Economics. The capital was located at Shih-chia-chuang (Southwest Hopeh), which had been captured by the Communists in November 1947. Only a few months before the NCPG was created, Mao Tse-tung had set up the Party headquarters in P'ing-shan hsien, only a few miles from Shih-chia-chuang.

Peking was surrendered to the Communists in late January 1949, and one month later the NCPG was moved there. Sung made this move too, and in April he was named to a five-man committee to deal with the question of changes in the government structure. At this juncture, in the absence of a central government, the NCPG served in many respects as a national administration. However, this became academic in October 1949 when the PRC was established in Peking and, within a few weeks, the central government absorbed the NCPG. As a delegate from the "North China Liberated Areas," Sung attended the inaugural session of the CPPCC, the body that inaugurated the national government on October 1. He was appointed a member of the Government Administration Council's (GAC) Finance and Economics Committee, which was headed by the top economic specialist of that period, Ch'en Yun (q.v.). Moreover, subordinate to this committee, Sung was made director of the Central Financial and Economics Planning Bureau. The bureau was abolished in August 1952, but at the same time that Sung lost this post he replaced Hsueh Mu-ch'iao (q.v.) as secretary-general of the Finance and Economics Committee.

In 1950 and 1952, Sung was named to three specialized bodies to deal with various pressing economic and administrative problems. In early 1950 he was secretary-general of a board charged with the task of conducting a nationwide inventory of commodities, finances, and personnel. Two years later he was also secretary-general (under Li Fu-ch'un) of a committee set up to improve the efficiency of government organizations, and in July 1952 he was made a member of a committee to deal with problems of unemployment. His involvement with tasks of this sort was illustrated in an article that appeared in *People's China* (no. 7, April 1, 1952) and that reviewed various steps taken to "increase production and practice economy."

In August 1952 Sung went abroad for the first time as a member of a delegation to Moscow led by Premier Chou En-lai, which included such key figures as Ch'en Yun, Li Fu-ch'un, PLA Deputy Chief-of-Staff Su Yü, Air Force Commander Liu Ya-lou, and Heavy Industry Minister

Wang Ho-shou (qq.v.). Over the next few weeks this top-flight delegation negotiated the return to China of the Chinese Changchun Railway and an extension for the joint use of the naval facilities at Port Arthur. Chou En-lai and most of the group then returned home, but Li Fu-ch'un and Sung remained in Moscow where they conducted further negotiations which led to the signing in March 1953 of a series of extremely important economic agreements (described in Li's biography).

Sung, who was still secretary-general of the GAC's Finance and Economics Committee, was given another important assignment in September 1953 when he was appointed a vice-minister of Light Industry. A year later, when the central government was reorganized, the Finance and Economics Committee was abolished, but Sung was reappointed (October 1954) to his vice-ministerial post. More important, he was appointed a deputy director of the State Council's Fourth Staff Office, which was responsible for coordinating the work of the various State Council organs involved in light industry and planning. As of that time Sung worked under economic administrator Chia T'o-fu (q.v.), who headed both the ministry of Light Industry and the Fourth Staff Office. In January 1955 Sung signed a protocol on science and technological cooperation with Hungary. He did this in his capacity as chairman of the Chinese side of the Sino-Hungarian Joint Committee on Scientific and Technological Cooperation, but when the committee held its next meeting in 1956 these responsibilities were assumed by another man. In March 1956 Sung received one of his few positions not involved in economic affairs when he was appointed a member of the newly established National Association for the Elimination of Illiteracy.

Like a number of colleagues in the major economic commissions and ministries, Sung shuffled from one post to another in the six-year period from 1956 to 1962. In November 1956 he was appointed a vice-chairman of the State Economic Commission, which is headed by Po I-po and which is in charge of annual planning (in contrast to the long-range planning done by the State Planning Commission). At approximately this time Sung was removed from his vice-ministerial post with the Ministry of Light Industry. In September 1958 he was appointed a vice-chairman of the newly created State Capital Construction Commission under Ch'en Yun. Exactly a year later he was reappointed to this post during a partial reorganization of the State Council, but at the same time he was dropped from both the Fourth Staff Office and the State Economic Commission.

In January 1961 the State Capital Construction Commission was abolished; Sung was the only one of the five vice-chairmen not given a comparable post in the State Planning Commission, which assumed the functions of the defunct Construction Commission. As a consequence, Sung was left with no known government post of significance. A year and a half passed before Sung was reported again, and then he received the anticlimactic post of deputy secretary-general of the Shanghai branch of the China Committee for the Promotion of International Trade (September 1962), the organization mainly responsible for foreign trade with nations not having diplomatic relations with Peking. Perhaps even more unusual, in October 1962 he was appointed as a vice-chairman of the State Planning Commission under Li Fu-ch'un. Most officials of this rank work in Peking, but Sung remained in Shanghai with the trade promotion organization through the mid-1960's. He was last reported in the mid-sixties in December 1964 when, as one of a group of "specially invited persons," he was named to membership on the Fourth National Committee of the CPPCC.

An Engish physicist who interviewed Sung in early 1943 reported that he had just married a mathematics graduate from Tsinghua University, but nothing further is known about her.

1. Claire and William Band, *Two Years with the Chinese Communists* (New Haven, Conn., 1948), pp. 137–138; Haldore Hanson, *"Humane Endeavour"* (New York, 1939), p. 244.
2. Lyman P. Van Slyke, *Enemies and Friends* (Stanford, Calif., 1967), p. 131; Hanson, p. 245.
3. George E. Taylor, *The Struggle for North China* (New York, 1940), pp. 35–36.
4. Chalmers A. Johnson, *Peasant Nationalism and Communist Power* (Stanford, Calif., 1962), p. 101.
5. Taylor, *passim;* Lyman P. Van Slyke, ed., *The Chinese Communist Movement, A Report of the United States War Department, July 1945* (Stanford, Calif., 1968), pp. 47–56, 168–171, 179–183.
6. Johnson, p. 101.

Sung Shih-lun

(c.1905– ; Hunan). Veteran PLA commander; alternate member, CCP Central Committee.

Sung Shih-lun is a career Red Army officer who joined the Communist movement after the Northern Expedition of 1926–27. He made the Long March in 1934–35, and throughout most of the Sino-Japanese War and the civil war with the Nationalists, he commanded troops in north China. During the Korean War Sung led one of the major elements of the Chinese People's Volunteers. He has served on the National Defense Council since its creation in 1954 and he became an alternate member of the Party Central Committee in 1956.

Sung attended a primary school in Li-ling hsien

in Hunan (c.1920–21),[1] and in the mid-twenties he attended the Whampoa Military Academy, which was opened in Canton by the KMT in 1924. Like many of the Whampoa cadets, he later joined the National Revolutionary Army and probably participated in the Northern Expedition. Still later, he deserted the Nationalists and joined the Communists, serving as chief-of-staff of the 20th Red Army in south Kiangsi. This unit gained a measure of fame when, in late 1930, one of its key officers revolted and imprisoned the army's commander. Known as the Fu-t'ien Incident, this revolt was directed against the leadership of Mao Tse-tung (see under P'eng Te-huai). However, Sung's role in the incident (if any), is not known.

In 1933 Sung attended the Red Army Academy in the Juichin area of Kiangsi, and afterwards he became a regimental chief-of-staff.[2] After making the Long March in 1934–35, he was assigned to Hsu Hai-tung's 15th Army Corps. When war broke out in mid-1937, Sung was assigned to Ho Lung's 120th Division, which moved into north Shansi. A year later, Sung and Teng Hua (q.v.), his political commissar, led a detachment said to number "several thousand" men into seven rural hsien in east Hopeh about midway between Peking and the Gulf of Pohai. There, on July 9, 1938, they set off a series of raids on Japanese garrisons and their logistic network, which had the support of the local peasantry and Communist organizers who had been in the area before the Sung-Teng detachment arrived. Communist accounts describe this in the cumbersome but graphic phrase, the "East Hopeh, seven-hsien, 20,000-man Great Uprising." Their guerrilla raids soon extended to 17 hsien, but by October the Japanese had wiped out the main force of the Sung-Teng unit.[3]

After suffering this severe defeat, Sung was barely able to hold together a small band of guerrillas. However, the situation improved somewhat in the first part of 1939 when the important Communist commander Hsiao K'o (q.v.) arrived in east Hopeh to assist Sung and Teng. They quickly decided that a major military campaign against the powerful Japanese forces was a hopeless venture, and thus the decision was made to concentrate on political work. For most of the war years Hsiao K'o was based in a mountainous area just west of Peking, but Sung remained to the east of the city where the Communists established a quasi-governmental body known as the East Hopeh Administrative District. This and other nearby pockets of Communist activity were known collectively as the Hopeh-Jehol-Liaoning base, which in turn was subordinate to the Shansi-Chahar-Hopeh Border Region under Nieh Jung-chen (q.v.). Sung's area of operation was of marginal value to the Communists during the war against Japan, but during the ensuing civil war with the Nationalists it was es-

pecially useful as one of the major gateways to Manchuria.

Sung remained in east Hopeh throughout the war, except for a period in about 1942 when he was sent back to Yenan to take part in the political "rectification" campaign being conducted in the Party School (see under Teng Fa). In the immediate postwar period, Sung collaborated with Hsiao K'o in moving his guerrilla units northward into Jehol province, and they were thus in a position to assist Lin Piao, who was then in the process of moving tens of thousands of troops from north China into Manchuria. In January 1946 the Nationalists and Communists signed a cease-fire agreement, and to implement this an Executive Headquarters was established in Peking (see under Yeh Chien-ying). Sung was assigned to the headquarters as director of operations for the Communist side. He remained with the headquarters until early 1947 when negotiations broke down; by that time the civil war was in full swing. Sung returned to the battlefield, this time to command the Po-hai Military District. The Po-hai area, adjacent to the Gulf of Pohai, consisted of a small section of southeast Hopeh and a rather large section of northwest Shantung. For administrative purposes, it was subordinate to the Communists' East China PLA under Ch'en I.

In 1948 Sung was commander of the 28th Army of the 10th Army Group and in the next year he became commander of the Ninth Army Group. Both units were subordinate to the East China PLA, which was redesignated the Third Field Army during the winter of 1948–49. From November 1948 to the early days of 1949, Sung took part in the critically important Huai-Hai Campaign, one of the last major battles fought by the Communists north of the Yangtze. After this notable success, the Communists moved southward, and when the Third Field Army captured Shanghai in May 1949, Sung was placed in command of the Shanghai-Woosung Garrison. After they consolidated their rule in the latter part of 1949, the East China Military and Administrative Committee (ECMAC) was established (January 1950). Sung was named to membership on the ECMAC and nominally retained this post until it was reorganized in December 1952. However, when the Chinese People's Volunteers (CPV) entered the Korean War in October 1950, Sung was in command of one of the major elements of the CPV to have engaged U.S. Marine units near the coast in northeast Korea.[4] He apparently remained in Korea throughout the war, because he was not reported in China again until February 1954 when he attended a PLA rally in Nanking; the news release was worded in such a way as to suggest that he headed one of the important infantry schools there. He was specifically identified as president of the Higher Infantry Academy by September

1954, and when a group of former Japanese military officers visited China in 1956, they again identified Sung as president. Also in September 1954, when the National Defense Council was created, Sung was named as a member. He was reappointed in April 1959 and January 1965.

Further military honors fell to Sung in 1955 when personal military ranks and awards were created. He was given the rank of colonel-general (equivalent to a three-star general in the U.S. Army) and received one or more of the top national military honors (although the specific award or awards were not mentioned). When the Eighth National CCP Congress met in Peking in September 1956, Sung was elected an alternate member of the Central Committee. In April 1958 he was identified as vice-president of the Naval Academy, but there has been no subsequent mention of this post.

Since 1958 Sung seems to have been stationed in Peking where the press has identified him at a number of official functions, especially those celebrating important military holidays or honoring visiting military delegations. In July 1962 he led a military delegation to Baghdad to celebrate the fourth anniversary of the founding of the Republic of Iraq. While there, Sung had interviews with top military leaders and the premier. Other than his alternate membership on the CCP Central Committee and his membership on the National Defense Council, Sung holds no top positions in the Party or the government, but his continuing presence in Peking suggests some high-level staff job in the PLA headquarters.

1. Interview in Hong Kong, July 1963, with a former resident of Li-ling.

2. *Kuang-ming jih-pao*, September 15, 1957.

3. *Kuang-jung te san-shih nien* (Thirty glorious years; Peking, 1957), p. 19; *K'ang-Jih chan-cheng shih-ch'i chieh-fang-ch'ü kai-k'uang* (A sketch of the liberated areas during the Anti-Japanese War; Peking, 1953), p. 27; Chalmers A. Johnson, *Peasant Nationalism and Communist Power* (Stanford, Calif., 1962), p. 114; George E. Taylor, *The Struggle for North China* (New York, 1940), p. 58.

4. Lynn Montross and Nicholas A. Canzona, *U.S. Marine Operations in Korea, 1950–1953* (Washington, D.C., 1957), p. 161.

Ta P'u-sheng

(1874–1965; Liu-ho hsien, Kiangsu). Former vice-chairman, China Islamic Association.

Sheikh Nur Mohammed Ta P'u-sheng, of Hui nationality, was one of the major figureheads connected with the continuing attempts by the Chinese Communists to gain support from Muslims, both domestic and foreign. According to a handbook published by the Nationalist Government in 1943,[1] he is said to prefer the name Haji Nur Mohammed Ta-pu-sun, the term "haji" signifying that he had made a pilgrimage to Mecca.

Nothing is known of Ta's early life, and it was not until he was almost 50 that he graduated (1923) from al-Azhar University in Cairo, the world's leading institute of Islamic studies. In the thirties and forties he was a fairly prominent official in the Nationalist Government, serving from 1938 as a counsellor to the National Military Council and from 1942 as a member of the People's Political Council. The purpose of the counsellors to the National Military Council, which exercised supreme command over all the armed forces, was to conduct research on non-military subjects and to give advice to the chairman of the National Military Council (Chiang Kai-shek).[2] Membership in the People's Political Council, a quasi-legislative body, was divided into four categories; the group to which Ta belonged was nominated by the Supreme National Defense Council (also headed by Chiang Kai-shek) and then appointed by the KMT Central Executive Committee.[3] Among Ta's colleagues in this category were such important Communists as Mao Tse-tung and Tung Pi-wu; however, this inclusion of the Communists was more nominal than real. Ta held his council seat in the Third and Fourth People's Political Councils, which held their first plenary sessions in October 1942 and July 1945, respectively.

Ta was an elderly 75 when the Communists took power in 1949. For the first three years he seems to have been ignored by the authorities. However, in about 1952, a decision was apparently made to organize various religious groups, notably the Buddhists and the Muslims. In mid-1952 a preparatory committee was formed to establish the China Islamic Association. Ta served as a vice-chairman under Burhan (q.v.), an important Muslim from Sinkiang, of both the preparatory committee and the fully established association when it was set up in May 1953. When the organization was established it was Ta who gave the official report on the work of the preparatory committee. He held his vice-chairmanship until his death in 1965, and although he was subsequently given a host of other positions, he probably devoted more of his time to the Islamic Association than any other organization. Under this association Ta was also a vice-president of the Institute of Islamic Theology from its establishment in November 1955. Ma Yü-huai (q.v.), another Hui leader, was the first president; however, he apparently relinquished the presidency to Ta in about 1958. In any event, at the time of Ta's death, it was stated in his obituary that he was the Institute president. The Institute, the most important of its kind in China, offers a four-year course, with instruction in the study of the Koran and other Islamic scriptures, as well as in the Arabic language.

In the same month that the Islamic Association was established (May 1953), a closely related organization known as the Chinese Association for the Promotion of Hui People's Culture was formed; its purpose was to study and develop the cultural and educational life of the Muslims. Ta was one of the founders of the association, but never held any leadership position. Rather little was heard of this organization, and in October 1958, having "completed its tasks," it was disbanded.

Although relatively little was heard about Ta in the early 1950's, he did serve as a member of the large delegation led by Mme. Sun Yat-sen (Sung Ch'ing-ling) to Vienna for the Communist-sponsored Congress of Peoples for Peace. Ta attended in his capacity as a vice-chairman of the Islamic Association's preparatory committee.

By the mid-1950's the Communists began to make concerted efforts to gain support from the Afro-Asian nations, among them such Muslim-dominated nations as Indonesia and Pakistan. The potential usefulness of a respected and elder Islamic figure like Ta P'u-sheng was naturally apparent to the Communist leadership. In consonance with this thought, Ta accompanied Premier Chou En-lai as an adviser to the Afro-Asian Conference in Indonesia, better known as the Bandung Conference. Almost immediately after the Bandung meeting, Indonesian Prime Minister Ali Sastroamidjojo made a state visit to China. To mark the occasion, the Chinese established the China-Indonesia Friendship Association, with Ta named as a member of the board of directors. Following up these contacts, Ta soon after led a group of Chinese pilgrims to Mecca (Saudi Arabia) in July 1955 and also made brief visits to Egypt, Afghanistan, Pakistan, India, and Indonesia en route. In the following years, Ta was very frequently on hand in Peking to serve as a host for the many Muslim groups that visited China. Further exploiting the gains made at Bandung, the Chinese created in February 1956 the Asian Solidarity Committee of China (known from 1958 as the Afro-Asian Solidarity Committee). Ta was named to membership in the new organization. In June 1956 he returned once again to Indonesia, leading a China-Indonesia Friendship Association delegation.

In the meantime, Ta had received several positions in the central government. In 1954 he was elected as a deputy from his native Kiangsu to the First NPC. He was re-elected from Kiangsu to the Second NPC (1959–1964) as well as the Third NPC, which first met in December 1964–January 1965. He was also elected as a representative of "religious circles" to membership on the Second National Committee of the CPPCC in December 1954; in April 1955, when several subordinate committees were formed under the auspices of the CPPCC, Ta was appointed to head the Religious Affairs Work Committee.

Then, in a by-election of February 1956, he was elevated to membership on the Standing Committee of the CPPCC, the body that runs the organization when the National Committee is not in session. He was re-elected to both the National and Standing Committees of the Third and Fourth CPPCC's, which first met, respectively, in April 1959 and December 1964–January 1965. However, probably because of his advanced age, Chao P'u-ch'u (q.v.), a leading lay Buddhist, was named to succeed him as head of the Religious Affairs Work Committee in early 1965. Ta has also held two other central government positions; in March 1958 he was named to membership on the State Council's Commission for Cultural Relations with Foreign Countries and in September 1959 he was appointed as a member of the Nationalities Affairs Commission, also subordinate to the State Council.

From his emergence on the public scene in the mid-fifties, Ta was named to a variety of other organizations or placed on *ad hoc* committees, each of which is self-explanatory in terms of Peking's attempts to curry favor abroad or in relation to the fact that Ta, an elderly and respected non-Han Chinese, is useful in this connection. Except where noted (or in the case of the *ad hoc* committees), he held all the following positions until his death: 1955: member, (*ad hoc*) Committee for the Signature Campaign Against the Use of Atomic Weapons, February; 1956: vice-president, China-Egypt Friendship Association (CEFA), November (he was also named as president of the China-Syria Friendship Association [CSFA] in September 1957, but when the CEFA and the CSFA were merged in February 1958—following the merger of Egypt and Syria—he became a vice-president of the new China–United Arab Republic Friendship Association); member of the presidium for the rally commemorating the 90th anniversary of the birth of Sun Yat-sen, November; member, Standing Committee, (*ad hoc*) Chinese People's Committee to Aid Egypt Against Aggression, November (formed at the time of the Anglo-French-Israeli attack on Egypt in the fall of 1956); member, Standing Committee, Chinese People's Association for Cultural Relations with Foreign Countries, December; 1958: member, National Committee, China Peace Committee, July; member, National Council, Political Science and Law Association of China, August; 1959: member, Preparatory Committee for Celebrating the 10th Anniversary of the PRC, September; 1960: member, Standing Committee, China-Africa People's Friendship Association, April; 1961: member, Preparatory Committee for Commemorating the 50th Anniversary of the 1911 Revolution, September.

Apparently Ta's last major service to the PRC occurred in December 1957–January 1958 when, at the age of about 84, he was a member of the large delegation led by Kuo Mo-jo sent to the first Afro-Asian Solidarity Conference held in Cairo. After that he made relatively few public appearances, most of them perfunctory. When he died in Peking on June 21, 1965, at the age of 91, a memorial service was held in his honor, a service attended by many state leaders and held under the auspices of his funeral committee, chaired by China's leading non-Han personality, Ulanfu. In the eulogy read at the service two days after his death, it was asserted that he had supported the nationality and religious policies of the CCP, including those related to "revolutionary and socialist reform in the Hui nationality areas," and had taken an "active part in political activities at home and abroad." His remains were then buried in the Muslim cemetery in the suburbs of Peking.

Although completely obscure in the early 1950's in terms of the Communist movement, in later years Ta was an active participant in the Communists' efforts to improve their relations with Islamic groups at home and abroad and to articulate the theory that religious liberties were upheld in China. For example, when he entertained former French Premier Edgar Faure in Peking in 1956, he claimed that religious liberty was widespread in China and denied contradictions between Communism and Islamic beliefs. Faure described Ta as "a refined and cultivated man" who "wore the black skull-cap of a priest and had a long, sparse Chinese beard."[4] With Ta's death in 1965 the Communists lost what was probably their most useful personal symbol of cooperation with the Muslims.

1. *China Handbook, 1937–1943* (New York, 1943), p. lvii.
2. *Ibid.*, p. 322.
3. *Ibid.*, p. 109.
4. Edgar Faure, *The Serpent and the Tortoise* (New York, 1958), pp. 144–145.

T'an Chen-lin

(1902–   ; Yu-hsien, Hunan). Vice-premier; director, Agriculture and Forestry Office, State Council; member, CCP Central Committee, Secretariat, and Politburo.

T'an Chen-lin, a top ranking Party member, has been a leading spokesman for China's agricultural policies since 1958, the same year he was elevated to a seat on the Politburo. He comes from Yu-hsien on the Yu River in eastern Hunan. The hsien seat is only a short distance northwest of the famous Chingkang Mountain retreat where Mao Tse-tung and Chu Te joined forces in 1928. The Communists were active in this part of eastern Hunan from soon after the Party's founding in 1921. Mao speaks of the retreat on the Hunan-Kiangsi border in his writings and he also mentions another base in the Kiulung (Chiu-

lung) Mountains, an area between Chingkang-shan and Yu-hsien. Both Kiulung and Yu-hsien sheltered groups friendly to the Communists.[1]

T'an's background is unquestionably that of a true proletarian. He speaks of his family having "neither land nor property" and of his father as being a "low-grade employee of a mine near Yu-hsien." In 1913, when the father lost his job, the sons among his eight children had to be sent to work. The eldest boy, then 16, went into a shop making joss-sticks. Another son (older than Chen-lin) went into a bean factory, and two more sons were adopted into other families. T'an seems to have been the student in the family (he speaks of having had three years in a private school) and he was sent to work in a bookstore dealing in old books. He was 12 when he entered the store in the fall of 1913. He states that he spent two years there; the work was hard and his only achievement was learning to master the abacus. He returned home when his employer died and the shop was closed and was sent to work in another bookstore in the town of Ch'a-ling, some 15 miles from his native Yu-hsien (Ch'a-ling bordered the Chingkangshan base). In his years in Ch'a-ling, T'an learned to print with wood blocks and to bind books, trades that were to occupy and support him until he became an active Communist. While working in the Ch'a-ling book store he began to read. He mentions among his favorite books the *San-kuo-chih yen-i* (*The Romance of the Three Kingdoms*) and the *Shui-hu-chuan* (*Water Margin*), the colorful tales of past dynasties that had long been read by Chinese schoolboys and upon which Mao also grew up. T'an commented also on his reading of a biography of Hung Hsiu-ch'üan, the leader of the Taiping Rebellion. After four years as an unpaid apprentice in book stores, T'an was able to earn a pittance and then to increase this small sum by meager amounts each year until, after about 10 years, the bookstore in Ch'a-ling also closed. This was in about 1925 when T'an was 23, and he returned to Yu-hsien to work as a book binder. In the Yu-hsien store in which he worked, he became friends with Yü Lei, a graduate of the Hunan First Normal School (the alma mater of Mao Tse-tung). Yü is described as "a responsible member" of the CCP. It was through Yü that T'an first learned about Communism and first heard of the Communist Revolution in Russia. In 1926, after many discussions with Yü, T'an joined the CCP.[2]

In September 1927 T'an participated in the Autumn Harvest Uprisings in Hunan, the peasant insurrections that were directed there by Mao Tse-tung. When they ended in defeat, Mao led a small band of his followers south through western Kiangsi to Chingkangshan where he made his headquarters. Chingkangshan was taken by the Communists in October, and nearby

Ch'a-ling in November of 1927. T'an remained with Mao's forces at Chingkangshan through the difficult winter of 1927–28, and Chu Te joined them in the spring of 1928. Although he had only belonged to the Communist Party for two years, T'an must have soon worked his way up to a responsible position with Mao's local Party group. By 1928 he was already taking part in the inner-Party struggle between Mao's group at the Chingkangshan base and the provincial Party Committee, which presumably took orders from the Party Central Committee, then under the leadership of Ch'ü Ch'iu-pai. The Hunan Committee first sent an emissary to see Mao in March 1928 when Mao was at Ning-kang on the northwestern border of the mountain base. This Party representative found Mao "leaning to the right" and saw to it that the Front Committee for the border area which Mao headed was abolished. In May Mao's group counterattacked; holding a congress of Party representatives from the Hunan-Kiangsi border region at Mao-p'ing in Ning-kang hsien, they elected the First Special Committee of the border area. This committee had 23 members; Mao was its secretary.[3] It was not long after the May meeting that an even more serious dispute occurred between Mao and the Hunan Provincial Party Committee over the military strategies to be followed at Chingkangshan. As the feud developed, Yang K'ai-ming from the Hunan Committee came to Chingkangshan (July) to replace Mao as the secretary of the newly formed Special Committee. But by September, when the Hunan Committee's advice had proven disastrous, Yang "fell ill and T'an Chen-lin took his place" as the secretary of the border region Special Committee.[4] In October Mao's army returned to Ning-kang to convene a Second Congress of the Party organization in the border area (October 4, 1928). Again they elected a Special Committee, this time with only 19 members. Mao was once more in charge of local Party affairs, with T'an Chen-lin again the secretary of the newly formed Special Committee. As such, T'an headed a five-member Standing Committee having Ch'en Cheng-jen (q.v.) under him as the deputy secretary. Mao Tsetung, Chu Te, and Ch'en I were also members of the new Special Committee.[5] On November 6, 1928, the Front Commitee was reactivated. Mao was again made chairman and given authority over both the second Special Committee and the newly created Army Committee, which was probably headed by Chu Te. According to Mao's writings, the Front Committee was now reorganized with five members designated by the Party headquarters in Shanghai: Mao himself, Chu Te, T'an (identified as the secretary of the local Party headquarters), Sung Ch'iao-sheng (a "worker comrade"), and Mao K'o-wen (a "peasant comrade"). The last two named are

unknown today. According to Mao, the Front Committee was now in charge of the work of the Special Committee, but it was still necessary to keep the latter going "because sometimes the Front Committee has to move with the troops."[6] In this same report, when Mao speaks of T'an as one of the five Standing Committee members of the Special Committee, he identifies him as a worker, in contrast to Ch'en Cheng-jen, an intellectual.

The life span of the second Special Committee at Chingkangshan was presumably very short, because by the end of 1928 the major part of the Chu-Mao force was obliged to leave the mountain retreat and move across Kiangsi to take up operations along the Kiangsi-Fukien border. Here they were engaged in combat for the next year and a half, until all the Red armies were called by Li Li-san, then the leading influence at the Party's headquarters, into a combined operation to take over the major industrial cities of central China. In the summer of 1930 T'an became attached to the Communists' 12th Army. The military command of this force was taken over in July 1930 (just before the Communists attacked Nanchang and Changsha) by Lo Ping-hui in whose biography the history of the army is described. At about the time Lo became 12th Red Army commander, T'an Chen-lin became its political commissar and T'an Cheng (q.v.) the director of the Army's Political Department. All three men have had an important career as leaders of the CCP; Lo died of illness near the battle front in June 1946.

The Communists do not detail T'an's activities in the period before the Long March, but he must have spent most of his time fighting along the Kiangsi-Fukien border and in other parts of Fukien. For some or most of this time he probably remained with Lo Ping-hui's army. In November 1931, when the Communists held their First All-China Congress of Soviets at Juichin, the capital of their base in southeast Kiangsi, T'an became a member of the 63-man Central Executive Committee (CEC), the governing organ of the Chinese Soviet Republic, which the Congress established. (However, as explained below, he was not re-elected to the CEC at the Second Congress held in January–February 1934.) In addition to his election to the CEC in 1931, T'an was also made a member of the CEC's Central Revolutionary Military Council, headed by Chu Te. During a part of the period when the Communists made their capital in Kiangsi, T'an was reported to have been associated with the Party's Central Political Security Bureau, but because he was active in Fukien in a military capacity for most of those years, it is likely that he carried out the work of the Bureau in Communist-held areas in Fukien. In 1931 he was identified as commander of the

Fukien Military District, and by October of that year he was stationed with Red forces fighting in the area of Ch'ang-t'ing, west Fukien. In 1932 he was still commander of the Fukien Military District.

In July 1933 an article criticizing T'an's work appeared in *Tou-cheng* (Struggle), the official organ of the CCP Central Bureau of the Soviet Areas published in Kiangsi. T'an, who was then in charge of Party work in the army in the military area in Fukien, was linked to the "Lo Ming line," which was then under strong attack from the Central Bureau of the Soviet Areas as well as by other elements in the Party (see under Teng Tzu-hui).[7] Teng Tzu-hui's association with the Lo Ming line was undoubtedly responsible for the former's demotion to alternate membership on the CEC of the Soviet Republic in 1934; similarly, the reason T'an was not re-elected to the CEC was related to the same inner-Party controversy over the so-called Lo Ming line.

When the armies commanded by Chu Te and Mao Tse-tung left Kiangsi on the Long March in October 1934, T'an was among the small group of important Party officials who remained behind. He was principally active in Fukien in the years before the Sino-Japanese War in association with Chang Ting-ch'eng, Ch'en I, Teng Tzu-hui, Ch'en T'an-ch'iu, and others, who continued to carry on guerrilla operations along the Kiangsi-Fukien border and to make further inroads into Fukien province. A description of these operations is contained in the biography of Chang Ting-ch'eng, the chairman of the Southwest Fukien Military and Administrative Committee, which existed from 1935 to the outbreak of war in 1937. T'an was the Committee's vice-chairman and also director of its Military Department in these years. When the war opened in mid-1937, the group on the Kiangsi-Fukien border organized their forces into a resistance army called the People's Anti-Japanese Volunteers (PAJV); T'an was especially active in the PAJV in southwest Fukien. At this time he was sometimes identified under the assumed name of Lin Chün.

In September 1937, after the Communists had activated their Eighth Route Army in north China, they entered into negotiations with the Nationalists for the creation of a second Communist army to operate along the lower Yangtze Valley, where Nationalist general Ku Chu-t'ung commanded the Third War Zone. Yeh T'ing, commander of this new Communist force (the New Fourth Army) set up his headquarters in Nanchang, the Kiangsi capital, early in 1938, but the army did not go into the field for a few more months. By the spring of 1938 Yeh had called into position all the scattered Red units operating in the area north and south of the river and launched operations along the Yangtze in Anhwei and Kiangsi. In the next three years

T'an conducted a number of operations behind the lines, where in addition to combat with the Japanese he also came into conflict with the local guerrilla forces under the leadership of Nationalist armies. When the New Fourth Army entered the field of battle in April 1938, it was composed of four detachments, three of them initially based south of the Yangtze. Yeh T'ing had initially made his headquarters in She-hsien, an area a little to the north of T'un-ch'i, a city in south Anhwei. At this time T'an's headquarters were somewhat to the northeast of his commander-in-chief, his forces being concentrated in Fan-ch'ang and Kuang-te hsien in an area partially bounded by a line stretching east from the Yangtze and south of the riverport city of Wu-hu to Nan-i Lake. Here T'an was serving as commander and political commissar of the New Fourth Army's Third Detachment.[8]

In April 1940 T'an Chen-lin (then known as Lin Chün) was dispatched by the New Fourth Army eastward into south Kiangsu to contact and reactivate the remnants of a local resistance force that had been operating there since the start of the Sino-Japanese War. This force had been badly decimated both in skirmishes with the Japanese and with local forces under partial Nationalist control. In April 1940 T'an joined this Kiangnan ("south of the Yangtze") force. By October of 1940 T'an had organized three guerrilla columns consisting of some 1,500–2,000 men and had helped establish a Communist-sponsored government for the area the troops controlled. This functioned in the rural parts of south Kiangsu around Chiang-yin, Ch'ang-shu, and Wu-hsi, towns near the Grand Canal and north of Soochow (Su-chou).[9] Small units of this force continued to harass the Japanese throughout the war. At about the same time that he conducted these operations, T'an also brought the rest of his Third Detachment north of the Yangtze. This was part of a general move to comply with Nationalist orders to evacuate the territory south of the river. Thus by September 1940 T'an's Third Detachment was located in an area on the southern bank of Lake Ch'ao in Wu-wei hsien, Anhwei. However, T'an's force did not long remain based in this area, and in the next year it again moved east into the region around T'ai Lake in south Kiangsu. By September 1941 it had re-entered the mountainous Kiangsu-Chekiang border area, by which time it had been renamed the Sixth Division of the New Fourth Army, a redesignation made in February 1941 when the New Fourth Army was reorganized following the disastrous defeat at the hands of the Nationalists as Yeh T'ing attempted to move his headquarters force north of the Yangtze in January 1941 (the New Fourth Army Incident; see under Yeh T'ing). Under the reorganization Ch'en I became the Army's acting commander, while T'an's former associates Chang

Ting-ch'eng and Teng Tzu-hui became, respectively, commander of the Seventh Division and head of the Political Department of the Headquarters staff. T'an was initially both commander and political commissar of the Sixth Division. He held the military command from 1941 to 1946, but at some time during these years Chiang Wei-ch'ing (q.v.) succeeded him as political commissar. Although T'an had brought his troops north of the Yangtze in September 1940 (as described above), after the 1941 reorganization of the New Fourth Army and the creation of seven new divisions, T'an's troops reentered the mountainous Kiangsu-Chekiang border area south of the Yangtze. This area was known as the South Kiangsu Military District; located around T'ai Lake, it commanded a strategic area because of its proximity to the important cities of Wu-hsi, Soochow, and Shanghai.

Although T'an was principally engaged in military operations during the war, he was also identified in 1942 as secretary of the CCP Kiangsu-Anhwei Border Region Committee. At the Seventh National Party Congress, held in Yenan from April to June 1945, T'an gained a place among the top echelons of Party leadership when he was elected (possibly *in absentia*) to membership on the Party Central Committee.

Like many members of the top command in the New Fourth Army, T'an remained with his troops once hostilities ended in August 1945, and helped conduct some of the major campaigns fought by the PLA as it began to expand over the China mainland when civil war erupted between the Communists and the Nationalists. From 1946 to 1947 he was the commander of the new Sixth Division of the East China PLA. The East China PLA, which absorbed most of the troops from the New Fourth Army, remained under the command of Ch'en I, whose territory the Communists called the East China Liberated Area. This comprised the areas in which they had long maintained bases in Shantung, Kiangsu, Chekiang, and Anhwei. Ch'en I's deputy commanders were Su Yü (also previously with the New Fourth Army) and T'an Chen-lin. According to Mao's military writings, from mid-July through August 1946, 18 regiments of the East China PLA commanded by Su, T'an, and others fought seven battles with Nationalist forces in central Kiangsu.[10] According to a Communist newspaper of this period, T'an also served as deputy political commissar of the Central China (Hua-chung) Military Region. His immediate superior was Political Commissar Teng Tzu-hui, and his military commander was Chang Ting-ch'eng.[11]

In 1947 the East China PLA began the conquest of Shantung and then pushed inland. The actions of Ch'en's army were coordinated with the army of Liu Po-ch'eng as it crossed the Yellow River and expanded through Honan to the border area of Hupeh, Honan, and Anhwei provinces, where the Communists had maintained their Oyüwan base in the period before the Long March. When Liu's army reached the boundaries of this area in mid-1947, they established a larger base known as the Central Plains Liberated Area; Liu's army was then known as the Central Plains PLA. Coordinating still with the East China PLA, late in 1948 and in the first part of 1949 the two armies captured the cities of Kaifeng, Hsu-chou (in north Kiangsu), and Nanking. There they separated, Liu's army moving to the southwest and Ch'en's taking over Shanghai and the coastal provinces. Early in 1949 Liu's army was renamed the Second Field Army and Ch'en's, the Third Field Army. T'an's particular operations during this period involved him first in the fighting in Shantung. From September to December 1947 three columns of the East China PLA commanded by Hsu Shih-yu (q.v.) fought in the eastern part of the province, where the Communists claim that they wiped out over 63,000 Nationalist troops.[12] During these operations T'an served as political commissar of the force led by Hsu. In September 1948 the two men led the attack upon Tsinan, the Shantung capital, which fell to the Communists on the 26th. Immediately after they took the city the Communists established the Tsinan Municipal Military Control Commission and made T'an the chairman. He held the post, at least on paper, for the year 1948–49. But in fact he could not have remained in Tsinan for long, because at this date the East China PLA (or Field Army) was moving rapidly, constantly expanding the territory under its control, and T'an was on active duty with the troops.

In order to coordinate the operations of the Central Plains and East China Field Armies, the Party's Revolutionary Military Committee (the military planning arm of the CCP), on November 16, 1948, decided to create a Front Committee to plan for the joint drive in the Huai-Hai area. Involved in the preparations for the forthcoming campaign were plans for capturing Hsu-chou, the important city at the junction of the railroads running north and south from Tientsin to Nanking and east and west from Sian to the coast. The Front Committee, established on the eve of the battle for Hsu-chou, was composed of T'an, Liu Po-ch'eng, Ch'en I, Su Yü, and Teng Hsiao-p'ing (the Committee's secretary).[13] The capture of Hsu-chou was the apex of the successful Huai-Hai campaign, which the Communists completed on January 12, 1949. The two field armies then moved into central China, capturing Nanking on April 23, 1949. Mao's writings list T'an among the top commanders of the Third Field Army who were partially responsible for the takeover of Nanking.[14] Other positions he held at this time included the deputy political commissarship of the Third Field Army and the deputy political commissarship of the East China Military Region, in which the Third Field Army was based. In both these positions T'an was subordinate to the important leader Jao Shu-shih (q.v.), who was to be involved in one of the CCP's major purges a few years later. In the military campaign for Hangchow in Chekiang it was the Seventh Army Group of the Third Field Army that conducted most of the operations which were successfully concluded on May 3, 1949. The Army Group was commanded by Wang Chien-an (a military leader who spent the war years in Shantung), with T'an as the chief political officer.

Immediately after the fall of Hangchow, the Communists established both the Municipal Military Control Commission and the Municipal People's Government. T'an became the chairman of the former and the mayor of the city government, but relinquished the latter post to Chiang Hua (q.v.) in August 1949. However, T'an's more important positions were at the Chekiang provincial level where from 1949 to 1952 he was the top Communist leader. When the Chekiang provincial government was formed in August 1949 he assumed the governorship, and soon afterward he was also identified as the ranking Party secretary and political commissar of the Chekiang Military District. Like most important Communist leaders in the early years of the PRC, T'an also held various positions in the "mass" organizations. Thus, from October 1949 to early 1950 he was a member of the preparatory committee of the Chekiang Federation of Trade Unions; from 1949 to 1952 he headed the Chekiang branch of the Sino-Soviet Friendship Association; and from 1951 to 1952 he was chairman of the Chekiang chapter of the China Peace Committee.

T'an also held posts in the regional government known as the East China Military and Administrative Committee (ECMAC), with jurisdiction over the five provinces of Shantung, Kiangsu, Anhwei, Chekiang, and Fukien. When the ECMAC was formally established in January 1950 under the chairmanship of Jao Shu-shih, T'an was named as a member, and in the following month he was appointed as chairman of the Land Reform Committee, one of the most important of the ECMAC's subordinate organs. In August 1952 he was elevated to a vice-chairmanship on the ECMAC, retaining this when the ECMAC was reorganized into the East China Administrative Committee (ECAC) in January 1953. During the period from 1952 to 1954 in particular, T'an regularly attended the meetings of (and meetings sponsored by) the ECMAC and the ECAC. In fact, with the exception of Ch'en I, T'an probably had a greater voice in the affairs of the regional government than any other east China official. Even more important

was T'an's role in the Party's East China Bureau, which, like the ECMAC–ECAC, was also headquartered in Shanghai. In the first part of 1952 he began to appear frequently in Shanghai where he was usually described as a "responsible member" of the East China Bureau. By the latter half of 1952 he was serving as Third Secretary of the Bureau, and in the frequent absence of Secretary Jao Shu-shih and Second Secretary Ch'en I (whose concurrent responsibilities regularly took them to Peking), T'an often served as acting secretary in 1953 and 1954.

In November 1952 T'an was transferred away from Chekiang; T'an Ch'i-lung (q.v.) assumed the more important posts that T'an Chen-lin had held, including the governorship and the secretaryship of the Chekiang Party Committee. T'an Chen-lin was transferred to Nanking to assume the governorship of Kiangsu province (November 1952). However, as already indicated, he was by this time spending much of his time in nearby Shanghai, and probably for this reason was not made head of the Kiangsu Party Committee, which operated from Nanking. The latter post was assumed by K'o Ch'ing-shih (q.v.), who was concurrently a Kiangsu vice-governor under T'an. Also in November 1952 T'an assumed still another assignment when he replaced Tseng Shan (q.v.) as director of the important Huai River Harnessing Commission—a seemingly appropriate assignment in view of T'an's extensive experience in the Huai River area. Some idea of the magnitude of the project can be gained from the fact that over 40,000 cadres were temporarily transferred to work on the huge enterprise over the winter of 1952–53.[15] As described above, T'an had been the deputy political commissar of both the Third Field Army and the East China Military Region from 1949. He continued in these posts until 1954, but there is little to indicate that he devoted much time to military affairs after 1949. Instead, as already suggested, his major responsibilities concerned east China governmental affairs and, in particular, the work of the Party's East China Bureau.

At approximately the time of the establishment of the constitutional government in September 1954 (at the First NPC), T'an seems to have transferred to Peking. Unlike most major Communist leaders, he did not receive any post in the central government at the close of the First NPC's initial session. He was, however, named in December 1954 as a CCP representative to the CPPCC's Second National Committee, as well as a member of its Standing Committee, but by that time the CPPCC was a relatively unimportant organization. He retained both posts until the Third CPPCC was formed in April 1959. In February 1955, shortly after his transfer to Peking, he was replaced as the Kiangsu governor by Hui Yü-yü (q.v.), although, as indicated above, he had apparently devoted little of his time to this post after assuming it in late 1952.

In view of T'an's stature within the CCP, it is probable that he was involved in more important matters than those of the relatively impotent CPPCC after his transfer to the national capital in 1954. In the light of later evidence, it seems likely that he assumed some position in the Party Center—possibly in connection with international liaison. The first suggestion of this occurred in January 1955 when he attended the Fourth National Congress of the Italian Communist Party in Rome. As of that date, extremely few Chinese Communists had visited Italy. Thirteen months later, in February 1956, T'an was a member of the delegation led by Chu Te to the historic 20th Congress of the CPSU in Moscow where Khrushchev delivered his famous "secret speech" denouncing Stalin. Chu did not return to Peking for several weeks, but T'an went directly back to Peking and in March was identified as a deputy secretary-general of the Party Central Committee, a post that placed him directly subordinate to Secretary-General Teng Hsiao-p'ing, who had only recently been made a Politburo member and who was then the fastest rising figure in the CCP elite. It is possible that T'an held this post from the end of 1954 or early 1955. He attended another congress in November–December 1959 when he led the CCP delegation to the Seventh Congress of the Hungarian Socialist (Communist) Workers' Party, which was also attended by Soviet leader Khrushchev.

T'an's stature within the CCP was reconfirmed at the Party's Eighth National Congress in September 1956. To manage the affairs of the Congress, three major *ad hoc* bodies were formed: a 63-member Presidium, a 13-member Secretariat, and a 29-member Credentials Committee. Although many Party leaders sat on two of these bodies, only T'an and six others (Li Hsueh-feng, Liu Lan-t'ao, Ma Ming-fang, Lin Feng, Sung Jen-ch'iung, and T'an Cheng) were members of all three. Moreover, only T'an and Liu Lan-t'ao were also vice-chairman of the Credentials Committee. T'an was re-elected to full membership on the Party Central Committee, and immediately afterwards, at the new Central Committee's First Plenum, he was named to membership on the newly organized Central Secretariat. As originally constituted, the Secretariat was composed of only seven full and three alternate members, with Teng Hsiao-p'ing as the senior member. This new structure, in effect, replaced the system under which Teng had been the secretary-general and T'an one of his several assistants (deputy secretaries-general). The task of the Secretariat is to carry out the policies decided upon by the Politburo.

About the year 1957 T'an began to take an active role in agricultural affairs and within a year had replaced Teng Tzu-hui (q.v.) as the top agricultural spokesman. There is a certain irony in this assignment, for T'an is one of the relatively few proletarians within the CCP elite and a man whose formative years were not spent on the land (unlike many of his colleagues). However, in the eyes of the CCP leadership, agrarian problems are solved first and foremost by organizational techniques rather than by technological skills. It may have been such reasoning that had led to his earlier assignment (1950–1954) as director of the ECMAC Land Reform Committee. In any case, one of the first indications of T'an's entry into the field of agriculture at the national level occurred in the spring of 1957 when he published an article on this subject in the *JMJP* (May 5, 1957). Not long afterwards, Chinese agricultural policies underwent a major change. The turning point occurred at approximately the time of the Party Central Committee's Third Plenum (September 20–October 9, 1957). At this time the more or less dormant 12-year (1956–1967) agricultural plan (first considered in early 1956) was resurrected and, in the words of the Plenum's final communiqué, it was to be presented to both the NPC and the next Party congress. Apparently at this junction T'an became major Party spokesman for a more "radical" as opposed to a "conservative" agricultural policy (advocated by Teng Tzu-hui). As events were to show, it was T'an who first presented the 12-year plan to the NPC Standing Committee (October 16, 1957, just one week after the Party Plenum). More important, he delivered the keynote address on agriculture at the second session of the Eighth Party Congress in May 1958. Because of this and later reports by T'an, one authority has described him as "one of the members of the radical group in the Politburo."[16] It was presumably T'an's espousal of more radical agricultural policies that led to his replacing Teng Tzu-hui, his colleague from the early thirties, as the Party's top agricultural spokesman, an informal position that he held at least through the Great Leap Forward (1958–1960). T'an's newly assumed leadership in the field of agriculture also probably accounted for his elevation to Politburo membership (together with K'o Ch'ing-shih and Li Ching-ch'üan) at a plenary session of the Central Committee held immediately after the May 1958 Party Congress. The addition of T'an, K'o, and Li brought the full membership of the Politburo to 20. (For further discussion of the change to more "radical" agricultural policies at this time, see under Teng Tzu-hui.)

T'an's continuing importance in agricultural affairs during the Great Leap period was illustrated in many ways. The titles of two articles for *Hung-ch'i* (Red flag, issues of August 16, 1958, and February 16, 1959), the Party's top journal, are indicative of his leadership in the radicalization of agriculture: "Strive for a Bountiful Life within Two to Three Years" and "Let's Have a Still Larger Harvest This Summer." Half a year after the publication of the second piece, the Party was forced to admit that the enormous claims for agricultural output in 1958 had been grossly exaggerated. Similarly, when a national conference of "advanced" agricultural workers opened in December 1958, T'an was listed first among the many presidium (steering committee) members. In a similar vein, T'an gave a report on the "pre-schedule realization" of the 12-year agricultural program before the second session of the Second NPC in April 1960.

In the meantime, in early October 1958, T'an was identified as a deputy director of the Party's top organ for controlling agriculture, the Rural Work Department, thus making him (on paper) a subordinate of Director Teng Tzu-hui. (However, since 1958 T'an has not again been identified in this post.) The approximate counterpart of the Rural Work Department in the central government is the State Council's Agriculture and Forestry Office. In October 1962 T'an replaced Teng Tzu-hui as the Office director, a post he still holds. It should be noted, however, that since the Party abandoned the Great Leap Forward in about 1961 (although, of course, it has never been officially abandoned), T'an's role in agriculture seems to have been somewhat muted. Yet he continues to receive foreign visitors who are concerned with agriculture and to speak before most domestic agricultural conferences. For example, he made "important" speeches at the National Agricultural Science and Technology Conference in February 1963 and at the National Conference on State Farms in February–March 1964.

Already a Politburo member, T'an received new positions within the central government in 1959 and later years. He was a deputy from Shanghai to the Second NPC, which opened in April 1959, and was re-elected to the Third NPC, which opened in December 1964. In April 1959 he was added as a vice-premier of the State Council, and in October 1962 (at the time he assumed the directorship of the Agriculture and Forestry Office) he became a vice-chairman of the important State Planning Commission. The Commission, headed by fellow Politburo member Li Fu-ch'un, is responsible for long-range (as opposed to annual) planning. During these same years since the late fifties, T'an has frequently been reported in the company of Mao Tse-tung —on inspection tours, while conferring with foreign visitors, and attending conferences.

T'an's career probably reached its peak during the Great Leap Forward, when he was the most vocal of the spokesmen for policies that presumably had the full backing of Mao Tse-tung. Although the "radical" policies espoused by T'an during the Great Leap were altered during the early sixties, he has continued to hold key posts within the CCP and the central government.

1. *Selected Works of Mao Tse-tung* (London, 1954), I, 84–87.
2. *SCMP* 2362, pp. 7–11.
3. *Selected Works of Mao Tse-tung*, I, 97.
4. *Ibid.*
5. *Ibid.*, p. 98.
6. *Ibid.*
7. Tso-liang Hsiao, *Power Relations within the Chinese Communist Movement, 1930–1934* (Seattle, Wash., 1961), pp. 239–240.
8. Chalmers A. Johnson, *Peasant Nationalism and Communist Power* (Stanford, Calif., 1962), pp. 124, 128.
9. *Ibid.*, p. 131.
10. *Selected Works of Mao Tse-tung* (Peking, 1961), IV, 106.
11. Chang-chia-k'ou, *Chin-Ch'a-Chi jih-pao* (Shansi-Chahar-Hopeh daily), March 4, 1946.
12. *Selected Works of Mao Tse-tung*, IV, 216.
13. *Ibid.*, p. 339.
14. *Ibid.*, p. 388.
15. *People's China*, no. 1:10 (January 1, 1953).
16. Franz Schurmann, *Ideology and Organization in Communist China* (Berkeley, Calif., 1966), p. 466.

T'an Cheng

(c.1903–   ; Liu-yang hsien?, Hunan). Veteran Red Army political officer; member, CCP Central Committee.

T'an Cheng served as a political officer in the Communist armies from the birth of the Red Army in 1927 and was an important officer from the time of the Long March until the early 1960's when he got into political difficulties. He was born about 1903 in Hunan; according to one report he comes from Liu-yang, a rural community in Hunan about 100 miles east of Changsha, which has produced such notable CCP leaders as Sung Jen-ch'iung, Wang Shao-tao, Wang Chen, Chang Ch'i-lung, and Yang Yung (qq.v.), all of whom are members of the Party Central Committee.

Very little is known about T'an Cheng before he became a Communist Party member in 1927. He graduated from a middle school (probably in Changsha, the provincial capital). T'an's career is better documented by the mid-1920's when he joined the Independent Regiment of Yeh T'ing. T'an was said to have joined the regiment in a clerical capacity. The history of this Independent Regiment is contained in the biography of Yeh T'ing, who was its commander when it left south China during the Northern Expedition; he continued to head this military force upon its arrival in the Wuhan area, when it was redesignated the 24th Division of

Chang Fa-k'uei's forces. Yeh's regiment was well staffed with Communist military cadets and by the time of the Nanchang Uprising in August 1927, when it mutinied and joined the Communists, it became a nucleus of the Communist military forces. T'an joined the CCP while he was with Yeh's troops, but it is not clear what role, if any, he may have played at Nanchang. After joining Yeh's regiment he is lost from sight until after the Nanchang Uprising, when, in October 1927, he was a member of Mao Tse-tung's military forces. This significant association with Mao is described in an article by T'an, in which he told of the meeting of Mao's loyal followers at San-wan village in Yung-hsin, in western Kiangsi very near to the Chingkang Mountain stronghold on the Kiangsi-Hunan border, which Mao was soon to make his headquarters.[1] The meeting at San-wan has now become a historic incident in Red Army annals because there Mao exerted his authority over the small band of guerrillas he had led from their recent defeat at P'ing-chiang during the campaigns of the Autumn Harvest Uprisings. It was also at San-wan that Mao succeeded in purging some of the less enthusiastic followers before making his way to Chingkangshan. T'an remained with Mao's forces when they reached Chingkangshan and may have been a special secretary to Mao for a time before he was dispatched to do political work with the Red Army.

There are few references to T'an's activities in the next decade, but those available place him among the Red forces that supported the Chinese Soviet Republic, which was formally established at Juichin, Kiangsi, in November 1931, and thus among the military group that followed Mao and Chu Te on the Long March in the fall of 1934. In 1930 T'an was identified as the director of the Political Department of the 12th Red Army, a military force commanded by Lo Ping-hui, whose biography contains a brief description of the army. It belonged to the military contingents that Li Li-san dispatched toward Nanchang in the summer of 1930 for the unsuccessful attack upon the Kiangsi capital. By 1932 T'an had risen to head the Political Department of the larger force, the First Army Corps, commanded by Lin Piao and Nieh Jung-chen. He probably made the Long March with this group in 1934–35.

Arriving in north Shensi in the fall of 1935, T'an continued to do political work with the Red Army. With the outbreak of the Sino-Japanese War in the summer of 1937 and the creation of the Communist Eighth Route Army in north China, he assumed more important posts. By 1938 he was identified as the deputy director of the Eighth Route Army's Political Department, serving under Wang Chia-hsiang (q.v.). T'an held this post until the end of hostilities in 1945, but because Wang, his superior, had to undergo medical treatment for wounds during these years, much of the work of the department probably fell to T'an. From 1943 to 1945 he also served as the deputy political commissar and concurrently as director of the Political Department of the joint military command, created about 1941 to combine the defenses of the Shansi-Suiyuan and the Shensi-Kansu-Ninghsia (Shen-Kan-Ning) Border Regions into one military headquarters. The joint command was headed by Ho Lung, but T'an's immediate superior in political work, Kao Kang, was political commissar for the command's military district and secretary of the Northwest Bureau of the CCP. (Kao's subsequent purge from the CCP is dealt with in his biography.) In April 1946, when the Third Assembly for the Shen-Kan-Ning Border Region Government met in Yenan, T'an attended as a deputy to the assembly representing the army. In the previous year, when the Party held its Seventh National Congress in Yenan, T'an had been elected an alternate member of the Central Committee, thus marking his rise into the highest ranks of the CCP.

The postwar period brought T'an further advancement. In 1946 he was in Manchuria as part of the staff brought there by Lin Piao soon after the Sino-Japanese War ended. In 1946 he was a Communist representative to the Northeast Truce Team, a unit ordered into the field by the Peking Executive Headquarters, which was attempting to implement the terms of the Cease-fire Agreement signed in January 1946. He was soon identified also as a member of the staff of the Northeast Democratic Allied Army (NEDAA), the Communist army that Lin Piao organized after merging his own troops with some of the Communist local resistance forces led by Chou Pao-chung (q.v.). It is not certain what post T'an held on Lin's staff, but presumably he continued to carry on the political work for which he had become known. By January 1948 he was identified as the deputy director of the Political Department of the NEDAA, serving there under a former associate from his days in Kiangsi, Lo Jung-huan, the Army's political commissar.

Over the winter of 1948–49, as Lin Piao's forces pushed southward from Manchuria into China proper, his army was redesignated the Fourth Field. Its first targets were the capture of the two key north China cities of Tientsin and Peking. After a brief fight, Tientsin fell in mid-January 1949. T'an was then named as the vice-chairman under Huang K'o-ch'eng (q.v.) of the Tientsin Military Control Commission to administer the city. However, when Peking surrendered just two weeks later, T'an was transferred to a comparable post there under Yeh Chien-ying, chairman of the Peking Military Control Commission. Lin Piao's forces continued to push southward and by mid-May 1949 had captured the key Yangtze River port of Wuhan; it is not clear if T'an was with Lin's forces during the spring drive southward, but within hours of the capture of Wuhan he had been named as chairman of the Wuhan Military Control Commission and at about the same time was also named as the director of the Central China Military District's Political Department.

Although Wuhan was the official capital of the Party, military, and government organizations of central-south China from 1949 to 1954, Canton was virtually an alternate capital. Thus, a number of top officials, such as T'an Cheng, divided their time in the 1949–1954 period between these two major cities. It appears that he spent the period from 1949 to 1952 in Wuhan, but most of the time from late 1952 to 1954 in Canton. Although he was an important Party and government official, T'an's major contribution in central-south China was as a political officer in the PLA. In 1949–50 he was deputy political commissar and director of the Political Department of the Fourth Field Army and held identical posts in the area controlled by this army, the Central-South Military Region (CSMR). In 1950 he relinquished the directorship of the Political Department to T'ao Chu (q.v.), to assume the more important post of third political commissar of the Fourth Field Army and the CSMR. His superiors at this time were Commander Lin Piao, First Political Commissar Lo Jung-huan, and Second Political Commissar Teng Tzu-hui. However, because Lin was ill for much of this period in the early fifties, because Lo was busy with important tasks in Peking, and because Teng devoted most of his time to economic problems, it appears that T'an was de facto head of political work in the region between 1949 and 1954, when the administrative areas were abolished. This was illustrated, for example, in September 1950 when it fell to T'an to deliver a major report before a government organization on the military situation in the central-south region. By mid-1952 (and until 1954), T'an's senior position in political work was formalized when he became political commissar for both the Fourth Field Army and the CSMR.

At the turn of the year 1949–50, the Communists established governmental organizations to provide civil rule for the areas now under their control. Thus, the Central-South Military and Administrative Committee (CSMAC) came into existence in February under the chairmanship of Lin Piao. T'an was named to membership on the CSMAC and was appointed one month later as chairman of one of its more important subordinate organs, the People's Supervision Committee. When the CSMAC was reorganized into the CSAC in January 1953, he retained his membership, but in May of that year he relinquished the chairmanship of the Supervisory Committee. In the early fifties T'an also held important Party posts in the central-south region. From 1951 to 1954 he was first deputy secretary of the Central-

South Party Bureau, a post that placed T'an below the following top leaders at one time or another in the period from 1951 to 1954: Secretary Lin Piao, Acting Secretary Yeh Chien-ying, and Second Secretaries Lo Jung-huan and Teng Tzu-hui (qq.v.).

In a situation unique to the central-south region, the Party also had a South China Subbureau, an organ responsible for the two provinces of Kwangtung and Kwangsi. Here T'an was the Third Secretary from late 1952, a position placing him (at varying periods) under Secretary Yeh Chien-ying, Acting Secretary T'ao Chu, and Second Secretary Chang Yun-i (qq.v.). Unlike the Central-South Bureau, which was abolished in November 1954, the South China Sub-bureau existed until July 1955, but by that date T'an had already been transferred to Peking.

Like so many regional leaders, T'an was transferred to Peking at the time the constitutional government was inaugurated at the initial session of the First NPC in September 1954. He was a deputy to the First NPC from the Central-South Military Region, and four years later was elected to represent the Canton Military Region to the Second NPC (1959–1964). He was not, however, re-elected to the Third NPC, which opened in late 1964, having by that time suffered a serious political decline (see below). He also served as an NPC Standing Committee member under the First NPC (1954–1958), but not under the Second NPC. At the close of the NPC session in September 1954, T'an was named to membership on the newly created National Defense Council, an organization with very limited power and authority, but one with considerable prestige. He continued to hold this post until the end of 1964. More important, in October 1954 he was appointed as one of the vice-ministers of National Defense under P'eng Te-huai until September 1959 and was thereafter subordinate to P'eng's successor, Defense Minister Lin Piao. It was also in the latter part of 1954 that T'an was identified as a deputy-director of the important PLA Political Department, working here under Director Lo Jung-huan.

In September 1955, when the PRC first awarded military decorations and personal military ranks, T'an received the three highest awards (the Orders of August First, Independence and Freedom, and Liberation) for his services in the Red armies from 1927 to 1950. At the same time he was made a senior general in the PLA, a rank subordinate only to the 10 marshals. Already an alternate Party Central Committee member, T'an was promoted to full membership at the Eighth Party Congress in September 1956. During the life of the Congress he served on both the Secretariat and the Credentials Committee, and also made a lengthy speech in which he stressed the need to subordinate the affairs of the PLA to political control. Finally, at the first plenum of the new Central Committee (held the day after the Congress closed), T'an was made a member of the Party's Secretariat, headed by Teng Hsiao-p'ing and charged with the task of carrying out Politburo policies on a day-to-day basis. As originally constituted, the Secretariat had seven full and three alternate members. Only two of the members were then connected with the PLA, T'an and another political officer, Huang K'o-ch'eng (q.v.).

T'an reached a new peak in his career in December 1956 when he was named to succeed Lo Jung-huan as head of the PLA Political Department, becoming, in effect, the political commissar of the PLA. A year later, in November–December 1957, T'an visited the Soviet Unon as a member of P'eng Te-huai's military delegation to the celebrations commemorating the 40th anniversary of the Russian Revolution. En route home the group visited Khabarovsk and Vladivostok in the Soviet Far East.

From the late 1950's through the first part of 1962 T'an made the type of public appearances usual for a political-military leader of his significance, particularly in connection with political conferences of the PLA. Then, without any forewarning, he was removed from membership on the Central Committee's Secretariat at the Party's 10th Plenum (September 1962). Huang K'o-ch'eng (q.v.), who had been implicated in the political downfall of former Defense Minister P'eng Te-huai (q.v.) in 1959, was also removed at this time. Beyond this coincidence of timing, however, there does not appear to have been any connection between Huang and T'an. Western specialists on PLA affairs have argued that T'an advocated strong Party control of the PLA, that he insisted Soviet military experience could not be "mechanically" copied by the Chinese and that the PLA must be guided by the Maoist tenet that men are more important than machines (i.e., political control takes precedence over modern weapons).[2] Consequently, it does not appear that T'an was on the "wrong side" of the dispute between PLA leaders who urged greater "professionalization" of the PLA (see under Su Yü), as opposed to those who felt that "politics must be in command" of the PLA. The best clue to T'an's downfall, therefore, may come from the information revealed in the Kung-tso t'ung-hsun (Bulletin of activities), the secret Chinese military journal. Issues of this journal for the year 1961, released by the U.S. Government in 1963, clearly reveal that political work in the PLA had seriously deteriorated in the late 1950's and into 1960—a period coinciding with the abortive Great Leap Forward and its aftermath. It would be logical to assume that T'an, as head of the PLA Political Department, was held directly responsible for this state of affairs.

It was not until September 1964 that political officer Hsiao Hua (q.v.) was named to replace T'an as the Political Department director, although it appears that T'an's erstwhile chief and former Director Lo Jung-huan (q.v.) may have reassumed the post, in effect, from about 1960–61 until his death in late 1963. In any case, since T'an's removal from the Party Secretariat in 1962, his appearances have been limited largely to attending celebrations of PLA holidays and serving on funeral committees for PLA leaders. Most important, however, in 1964–65 he was removed from three more positions. In 1964 he failed to be re-elected to the Third NPC, and at the close of the first session of the NPC in January 1965, he was one of a small handful of men not reappointed to the National Defense Council. Most telling of all was his removal in March 1965 as a vice-minister of National Defense. The net effect of these changes was to strip T'an of all his positions of authority in the PRC. Technically, T'an continues to be a member of the Party Central Committee, but the evidence cited above suggests that this membership has been largely *pro forma* since the early 1960's.

1. *JMJP*, July 14, 1951.
2. Ellis Joffe, *Party and Army: Professionalism and Political Control in the Chinese Officer Corps, 1949–1964* (Cambridge, Mass., 1965), pp. 43, 76–78; Alice Langley Hsieh, *Communist China's Strategy in the Nuclear Era* (Englewood Cliffs, N.J., 1962), pp. 45, 56.

T'an Ch'i-lung

(c.1911–   ; Kiangsi). First secretary, Shantung CCP Committee; alternate member, CCP Central Committee.

T'an Ch'i-lung is reported to be of peasant origin. By the start of the Sino-Japanese War in 1937 he was already a Party member, serving as political director of Communist guerrilla bands fighting in the border area of Hunan, Hupeh, and Kiangsi. He had been wounded in skirmishes with the Nationalist troops in this area just before war broke out, but his life was saved by the general amnesty brought about for a time between the Communists and the KMT by war with Japan. In the spring of 1943 he was identified as a political commissar with guerilla forces, known as the San-pei guerrillas, fighting in east Chekiang near Ningpo, an important coastal city. The Ningpo region was held by the Communists for much of the war, and by April 1945 it was claimed by official Communist sources as one of the 19 "liberated areas," in which the CCP was in control.

T'an's wartime career is obscure, but at some time in 1944 his San-pei Guerrillas were organized into the East Chekiang Column, a part of the Communist New Fourth Army of east-central China, with T'an remaining as the political commissar. By about September 1945 his column was moved from east Chekiang into Shantung, and in 1945 (but not necessarily connected with this move) T'an was identified as political commissar of the Eighth Division of the New Fourth Army, a division about which very little is known. (The Eighth Division is probably the same as the East Chekiang Column.) In addition, from 1945 to 1946 he was commanding officer of the East Kiangsu Military District, possibly the area over which the Eighth Division had control. T'an may have been transferred here from Shantung, or he may have been separated from his original guerrilla unit before it moved into Shantung in the fall of 1945.

From 1947 to 1948 T'an was secretary of the "South Chekiang Special Area Committee" of the CCP, a committee subordinate to the "Kiangnan" ("south of the river") CCP Bureau. Kiangnan was the area held by the Sixth Division of the New Fourth Army, the division under the command of T'an Chen-lin (q.v.), and was located in the delta plain of southern Kiangsu and northern Chekiang. Although specific evidence linking T'an Chen-lin and T'an Ch'i-lung at this time is lacking, they were closely associated in the early 1950's, a fact that may have added to T'an Ch'i-lung's rise in Party ranks, possibly as a protégé of T'an Chen-lin, a Politburo member since 1958.

In about 1948 or 1949, T'an was apparently transferred to Chang Ai-p'ing's Seventh Group Army, which had been operating in the Chekiang area from 1944. T'an was the political commissar of this group army, which was a part of the East China Liberation Army (later the Third Field Army), the force that conquered the east coast provinces of China. In April 1949, when Hangchow fell to the Communists, T'an was a member of the Third Field Army forces that occupied the city. In charge of these occupying forces was T'an Chen-lin, the man with whom T'an Ch'i-lung was to work so closely for the next few years.

By 1949 the Third Field Army gained control of the coastal provinces. To govern this area the Communists established in January 1950 a regional government known as the East China Military and Administrative Committee (EC-MAC), called the East China Administrative Committee (ECAC) after December 1952. In the early years of the PRC, T'an Ch'i-lung worked principally in Chekiang, but he also served in a minor capacity on the regional ECMAC–ECAC. Some idea of his rather rapid rise can be gathered from a brief résumé of his principal posts in the years from 1949 to 1954 when the constitutional government came into being and all regional administrations were abolished.

In 1949 T'an was vice-chairman of the Hangchow Military Control Commission, serving under T'an Chen-lin; political commissar of the Hangchow Garrison Headquarters; and secretary of the Chekiang Provincial Committee of the national New Democratic Youth League. He also served as deputy political commissar of the Chekiang Military District from the spring of 1949 until about August 1952, when he succeeded T'an Chen-lin as political commissar, holding the post until 1954. From 1950 to 1954 he was a member of T'an Chen-lin's Land Reform Committee under the ECMAC–ECAC. More important, however, were the Party and government positions he held first in Chekiang and later in Shantung. From the spring of 1949 until late 1952 or early 1953, he was a deputy secretary of the Chekiang CCP Committee, holding the post until he succeeded to the ranking secretaryship, which he took over from T'an Chen-lin. Similarly, he served under T'an from February 1951 to November 1952 as a vice-governor of Chekiang, succeeding him as governor in November 1952. In 1952 T'an Chen-lin was transferred from Chekiang to Kiangsu, thus ending the close association between the two men. From 1952 to 1954 T'an Ch'i-lung was the principal Party official in Chekiang, and then in about December 1954 he was transferred to Shantung.

Politburo member K'ang Sheng was the principal Party official in Shantung from 1949 to 1954, when he was assigned to more important responsibilities in Peking. T'an was transferred to Shantung in about December 1954, serving briefly as acting governor. The new governor, Chao Chien-min (q.v.), was appointed in March 1955 at which time T'an was made a member of the Shantung Provincial People's Government, a post he held until November 1958.

In Shantung T'an was given a succession of increasingly important assignments. From January 1955 to May 1961 he was known both as the second secretary and simply as secretary, but in fact both positions amounted to the number two post on the Shantung CCP Committee. During these six years he served under Shu T'ung and Tseng Hsi-sheng (qq.v.), the successive first secretaries during this period. Finally, in May 1961, he succeeded Tseng as the Shantung first secretary.

In 1958 the accelerated pace of the Great Leap was widely resisted in Shantung, with dissension reaching into the top ranks of the Party Committee. Governor Chao Chien-min (q.v.) was among those opposing the Leap, advancing the argument that Shantung lacked the agricultural resources to sustain the tremendously accelerated pace in production. At a Shantung Provincial People's Congress in October–November 1958, T'an devoted a long section of his report to a denunciation of Governor Chao's "errors." As a consequence, Chao was purged from the governorship on charges of being a "rightist," and T'an succeeded him as governor. T'an's strong advocacy of the Great Leap was made evident shortly before this Congress opened, when he published an article entitled "After All, Communalization Is a Good Thing" in the Party's leading journal, *Hung-ch'i* (Red flag, issue of October 1, 1958). At the same time that he succeeded to the governorship, T'an was also elected as a Shantung deputy to the Second NPC. When the NPC opened in April 1959, he spoke on the "great success of Shantung's industrial and agricultural production resulting from the proper execution of the Party's general line." T'an was re-elected from Shantung to the Third NPC in 1964, the first session of which opened in December 1964.

In addition to his positions on the Shantung Party Committee, T'an was elected chairman of the First Shantung CPPCC in January 1955 and re-elected to the Second provincial CPPCC in May 1959, a post he continues to hold. In September 1956, at the Party's Eighth National Congress, he was elected an alternate member of the Central Committee. He submitted a written speech to the Congress endorsing Party policy and stressing the importance of developing agricultural production in Shantung.

At the December 1963 session of the Shantung Provincial People's Congress, Pai Ju-ping (q.v.), an economic specialist, replaced T'an as governor. However, T'an continues to hold the chief Party post in Shantung and he continues to appear regularly in public. Aside from the above-mentioned article in *Hung-ch'i*, he is also the author of an important article for the October 5, 1963, issue of *Chung-kuo ch'ing-nien pao* (China youth daily), which dealt with the problems of youths in studying and training themselves and with the need to study the thought of Mao Tse-tung.[1]

---

1. *SCMP* 3091, pp. 11–14.

T'ang Liang

(c.1908–   ; Hunan). Political commissar, Nanking Military Region; alternate member, CCP Central Committee.

T'ang Liang has spent most of his life as a political officer in the Chinese Communist armies. In 1927 he was working as an apprentice in a firecracker factory in Liu-yang hsien, Hunan. He is apparently a man of humble origins, for at that time he was totally illiterate.[1] Liu-yang hsien was an area of considerable unrest in the 1927 period, and after the split in that year between the Communists and the Nationalists, Liu-yang became a center of recruitment for what the Communists have termed the Autumn Harvest Uprisings of 1927 (see under Mao Tse-tung). Liu-yang is also the native area of an impressive number of top Communist leaders, including Sung Jen-ch'iung, Wang Shou-tao, Wang Chen, and Yang Yung (qq.v.). It is probable (though undocumented) that T'ang came into contact with the CCP at approximately the time of the Autumn Harvest Uprisings. In any event, by 1930 he was active in southeast Kiangsi with Communist military units conducting guerrilla operations against the Nationalist government. He was secretary of the Party Committee in the Second Division of the Communist Eighth Army and a political commissar with a guerrilla division engaged in operations in the vicinity of Ning-tu in the winter of 1930. The Ning-tu area, not far from the border of Fukien, was the seat of Communist guerrilla actions in 1929, when troops commanded by Chu Te captured and recaptured the city several times. It continued to be a center of skirmishes between Communist and Nationalist forces throughout 1930 and 1931. In December 1931, after the conclusion of the Nationalists' third unsuccessful campaign to eradicate Communism from the Kiangsi-Hunan area, some 20,000 troops from former Nationalist armies switched allegiance to the Communists in what the latter have termed the "Ning-tu Uprising."

Sometime between the early 1930's and 1939, T'ang apparently received some schooling (probably in a Communist military institute), because by 1939 he was described as being literate.[2] In 1939 he was fighting in Liu Po-ch'eng's 129th Division (of the Eighth Route Army) in Shansi where the division headquarters were located; indirect evidence suggests that he was connected with the division's 386th Brigade commanded by Ch'en Keng (q.v.).[3] Apparently he was closely associated with Ch'en Keng until about 1948. By 1941 he had transferred to the Hopeh-Shantung-Honan Military Region, where he was director of the Political Department. T'ang was stationed in the same area at the close of the Sino-Japanese War, and in 1947 was a political commissar of an army corps in Shantung commanded by Ch'en Shih-ch'ü (q.v.). T'ang commanded troops under the general direction of Ch'en Keng, which captured Loyang (Honan) in mid-March 1948, lost it a few days later to the Nationalists, and then recaptured it in early April. In June he became director of the Political Department of the East China PLA, and from November 1948 to January 1949 he took part in the military campaign in the Huai-Hai area of north Kiangsu, one of the key battles of the civil war. This was carried out by the East China PLA, which was redesignated as the Third Field Army early in 1949. T'ang remained in the Huai-Hai area only until January 1949, but he continued as head of the Political Department of Ch'en I's Third Field Army until at least February 1954.

By the early fall of 1949, T'ang was in Nanking where he became a deputy secretary of the Party Committee, a vice-chairman of the Military Control Commission, and a vice-mayor of Nanking; by early 1950 he was a vice-chairman of the Nanking branch of the China Peace Committee. There is little evidence, however, that he held these posts for very long, presumably being more directly concerned with military affairs. At the national level, T'ang served on the preparatory committee (as a representative of the Third Field Army) of the All-China Athletic Federation from its formation in October 1949 until the Federation was formally established in June 1952.

Over the winter of 1949–50, the Communists established regional administrations governing large areas of China under which a number of provinces were grouped. The East China Military and Administrative Committee (ECMAC) was formed in January 1950, with T'ang as one of the members. These regional administrations were reorganized in early 1953, at which time the ECMAC was renamed the East China Administrative Committee, with T'ang remaining a member until its dissolution in 1954.

T'ang received little attention in the press in the early 1950's, the most notable report being in November 1951 in connection with the "First Model Hero Representatives Congress of the Third Field Army." He served on the congress presidium (steering committee), formally opened the congress, and gave a report before the congress a few days later.

In the 1953–54 period, T'ang assumed greater responsibilities in the East China Military Region, serving from early 1953 as director of the Political Department and as a deputy political commissar. In 1954 he was elected as a Shantung deputy to the First NPC (although he was not re-elected to the Second NPC, which opened in April 1959). When the constitutional government was formed at the first session of the First NPC (September 1954), he was named to the newly established National Defense Council, a post to which he was reappointed in April 1959 and January 1965. T'ang's position as a senior political officer in east China was reaffirmed in 1954–55 when the multi-provincial military regions underwent a nationwide reorganization. Like most regions, the East China Military Region was contracted in size; prior to 1954 it had embraced the provinces of Kiangsu, Chekiang, Anhwei, Fukien, and Shantung. Following the reorganization, T'ang was assigned as the political commissar of the Nanking Military Region, an area encompassing Kiangsu, Chekiang, and Anhwei. When Politburo member K'o Ch'ing-shih died in April 1965 he was identified as the "first" political commissar of the Nanking Military Region. K'o had evidently replaced T'ang as the senior political officer in the late 1950's or early 1960's. Nonetheless, the heavy demands on K'o's time suggest that this was largely a nominal appointment and that in fact T'ang has

served as the most important political officer in the Nanking Region since the mid-1950's.

In September 1955, the Communists created personal military honors for distinguished service covering the period between the civil war years of 1927 and the Korean War. At this time T'ang was made a colonel-general and given military awards, though it is not known which honors he received. He became an alternate member of the Central Committee when the CCP met for the Second Session of the Eighth Party Congress in May 1958. Since the announcement of his reappointment to the National Defense Council in 1959, T'ang's name has been mentioned infrequently in the press. One of the most significant times was in December 1963 when he attended a memorial service for Marshal Lo Jung-huan in Nanking, at which time he was identified as a senior commander in Nanking.

1. *Hung-ch'i p'iao-p'iao* (Red flag fluttering; Peking, 1958), VIII, 102–103.
2. *Ibid.*
3. *Ibid.*, p. 100.

T'ao Chu

(c.1906–   ; Hunan). Former senior Kwangtung Party official; member, CCP Central Committee.

A Party member from the mid-twenties, T'ao Chu was one of the leading Communist officials in Kwangtung in the early fifties. Within a few years he was also the most prominent political figure in all of central-south China and became first secretary of the Party's Central-South Bureau in 1961. He was elected to the Central Committee in 1956 and a decade later, during the early stages of the Great Proletarian Cultural Revolution, he was brought to Peking where he quickly emerged as one of China's top leaders. However, within a few months he himself fell victim to the purges which removed so many longtime Party leaders.

Like many youths of leftist persuasions, T'ao seems to have made his way by the mid-twenties to Kwangtung, then the center of revolutionary activity in China. It is rumored that he was a student at Whampoa, the KMT military institute, which opened in 1924, and that there he was a friend of Lin Piao's.[1] The rumor gains credence in the light of an autobiographical account written many years later by T'ao, who stated that "During the period of the Northern Expedition, I . . . worked in the KMT army";[2] these forces contained large numbers of Whampoa students and graduates. Moreover, a Communist history published in 1959 asserts that T'ao, as a regimental staff officer, participated in the abortive Canton Uprising of December 1927 (see under Chang T'ai-lei) and that after the Communist units were bady mauled in the uprising he was appointed as chief-of-staff of a reorganized Red Army regiment.[3] Many of the defeated Communist elements fled from Canton eastward to the Hai-lu-feng area (see under P'eng P'ai), and although there is no evidence to document this, T'ao's later career suggests that he may have been among those who followed this course. His activities are unreported for the next three years, but then in 1930 he was working as a Party official in Fukien, possibly in connection with the Communists in west Fukien, led by Chang Ting-ch'eng, Teng Tzu-hui, and T'an Chen-lin (qq.v.), who had set up a base there in the late twenties and early thirties.

In a speech made to Party cadres in the early fifties, T'ao claimed that he had made the Long March (1934–35),[4] but there does not seem to be any corroboration of this in the scores of historical articles the Communists have published about this famous trek. He is next mentioned in the latter half of 1938 as being in central Hupeh, where he was attempting to organize armed resistance to the Japanese and to build a Communist base. Among his colleagues there were Yang Hsueh-ch'eng (who died later in the war) and Miss Ch'ien Ying (q.v.), with whom he was later associated in central-south China after the PRC was established. The weakness of T'ao's minuscule guerrilla force is illustrated by the admission that they had "only eight rusty old guns."[5] His units were later incorporated into the far more significant guerrilla forces led by Li Hsien-nien (q.v.), which, in the early forties, became the nucleus of Li's Fifth Division, one of the major components of the Communists' New Fourth Army. Li's forces fought during the war in areas to the north and east of Wuhan, an area where T'ao was to work again a decade later.

T'ao's whereabouts and activities are undocumented for the latter war years and the immediate postwar period, but it appears that he was among the Communists sent to Manchuria after the Japanese surrender in 1945. In any event, when the Communists occupied Mukden in November 1948, he was named to membership on Ch'en Yun's Military Control Commission. However, he only remained briefly in Mukden, because a few weeks later he was among the key officers in Lin Piao's army, which was laying siege to Peking in the early days of 1949. With the KMT position in north China growing ever more hopeless, General Fu Tso-i, the Nationalist commander in Peking, dispatched a group of top aides to negotiate with the Communists, who were on the outskirts of the city. Two of Fu's negotiators returned to the city on January 17, accompanied by T'ao, who was then serving as chief-of-staff of the Peking-Tientsin Front Headquarters. T'ao had been sent into the city to work out the final surrender details—a surrender that was completed on January 31 when the Communist troops marched into their future capital.

To provide for the administration of Peking, the Communists had arranged with the surrendering officials to set up a Joint Administrative Office with three subordinate committees responsible for military, political and cultural, and financial affairs. Headed by PLA veteran Yeh Chien-ying, the Office had six other members—three Communists and three Nationalists. T'ao served on this seven-member body (along with Communists Hsu Ping and Jung Tzu-ho, qq.v.) and was the Communist representative on the military sub-committee.[6] Already the chief-of-staff of the Peking-Tientsin Front Headquarters, he assumed the concurrent post of deputy director of the headquarters' Political Department in March 1949. But when Lin Piao's Fourth Front Army began to push southward in early spring, T'ao was removed from his Peking posts to accompany the troops, an assignment presumably based on his familiarity with both central and south China. He became deputy director under T'an Cheng of the Central China Military Region's Political Department, and when the PLA captured Wuhan in May 1949, he again served under T'an as vice-chairman of the Wuhan Military Control Commission. Then, by the end of the year when T'an Cheng had moved to higher positions, T'ao succeeded him as commission chairman. As the PLA forces moved southward toward Canton the Central China Military Region was redesignated the Central-South Region; T'ao continued to serve as deputy director under T'an Cheng in the Political Department and concurrently as deputy director of the Political Department of Lin Piao's Fourth Field Army, serving here too under T'an. Then in early 1950 he succeeded T'an in both posts, retaining them until 1954–55. In the military sphere, this had the effect of placing T'ao under Lo Jung-huan, Teng Tzu-hui, and T'an Cheng, the first, second, and third political commissars of the PLA forces in central-south China. In fact, however, Lo was occupied for most of this period in Peking, and Teng Tzu-hui devoted most of his time to government administration and economic affairs.

It appears that T'ao was with the PLA troops when they captured Canton in October 1949, because in the following month he was identified as director of the Canton Municipal Government's Staff Office. However, the assignment seems to have been short-lived, for he was back in Wuhan by the turn of the year and remained there until at least May 1950. Wuhan, the key industrial city in central China, became the capital of the Central-South Military and Administrative Committee (CSMAC), which was established in February 1950 to govern six provinces, Hupeh, Hunan, Kiangsi, Honan, Kwangtung, and Kwangsi. The CSMAC was chaired by Lin Piao and included T'ao among its members; he retained his membership from 1953 to 1954, when the CSMAC was known as the Central-South Administrative Committee, and also served from March 1950 to May 1953 as a member of its Finance and Economics Committee. By the summer of 1951 T'ao was serving as acting secretary (in place of Chang Yun-i) of the CCP Committee in Kwangsi, but his assignment there was of relatively short duration, because early in 1952 he was transferred to Kwangtung, where within a brief period he was to become the dominant political figure.

The central-south region was distinguished from the other five regions of China during the early years of the PRC in that it had a special sub-bureau, the South China Sub-bureau, responsible for Kwangtung and Kwangsi, with its capital in Canton. The official title of the sub-bureau (*chung-yang hua-nan fen-chü*) suggests that it was under the direct jurisdiction of the Central Committee in Peking, but it is most probable that it received its direction from the Party's Central-South Bureau, headquartered in Wuhan. This supposition seems borne out by the fact that a number of key officials served in both the bureau and the sub-bureau. T'ao's first position in Kwangtung was as fourth secretary of the South China Sub-bureau (February 1952). His former colleague in Peking, Yeh Chien-ying, was then the first secretary, and Chang Yun-i was the second secretary. Chang, however, spent virtually all his time in neighboring Kwangsi. The third secretary was Fang Fang (q.v.), a veteran south China guerrilla leader, but before the year closed he had run into political difficulties and was dropped to fifth secretary.

When T'ao arrived in Canton, the land reform program, probably the most important political and economic movement during the Communists' consolidation period, was running far behind schedule. In fact, it appears that he was transferred to Kwangtung to speed up the process that seems to have been delayed by Yeh Chien-ying and Fang Fang (qq.v.), both Kwangtung natives. One of T'ao's first actions was to order a survey of the land reform situation, thus bypassing Fang Fang, technically his superior as Sub-bureau third secretary, as well as chairman of the provincial Land Reform Committee. T'ao's arrival in Kwangtung also coincided with the beginning of the "three-anti" movement, a campaign to tighten Party discipline. It fell to T'ao, for example, to announce the expulsion of Tso Hung-t'ao from all of his many positions in Canton and Kwangtung. Tso, another native of Kwangtung, was a veteran of the Communist-led guerrilla campaigns in the province and a close associate of Fang Fang's.

In the view of one Party official who had worked under him, T'ao's growing importance in Kwangtung in that period was due to his extensive knowledge of the Party apparatus and his wide experience regarding agricultural problems. This same official described him as intelligent and tough-minded, with a straightforward and sometimes blunt manner.[7] These qualities and his work in Kwangtung apparently met with the approval of higher authorities. By the fall of 1952, less than a year after T'ao's arrival, Fang Fang had been demoted to fifth secretary of the South China Sub-bureau, the position of third secretary being assumed by T'an Cheng, T'ao Chu's longtime colleague. T'an, however, was primarily active in military affairs; moreover, by the early summer of 1953 T'ao was serving in place of Yeh Chien-ying as acting secretary of the sub-bureau, and immediately previous to this he had also replaced Yeh in the Kwangtung Party Committee by becoming acting secretary. These changes had the effect of making T'ao the top Communist in both Kwangtung and Kwangsi, and he obviously had an important voice in the affairs of the higher-level Central-South Bureau in Wuhan. Though it is evident that T'ao had bypassed Fang Fang in the Party hierarchy, the situation in regard to Yeh Chien-ying, a veteran Communist and already a member of the Party Central Committee, is more complex. It is true that in a June 1952 speech Yeh had admitted to shortcomings, but any suggestion that he might have been in political difficulties must take account of the fact that he was called upon to fill the higher post of acting first secretary in the Party organization for the entire six-province central-south region, in order to replace the ailing Lin Piao.

His place in the Party hierarchy in Kwangtung already established, T'ao was appointed in May 1953 as a provincial vice-governor, and five months later he began to serve as acting governor, again filling the shoes of Governor Yeh Chien-ying. With the establishment of the constitutional government in Peking in 1954, a number of key regional and provincial leaders were permanently transferred to Peking, among them Governor Yeh. Thus, in February 1955 T'ao formally succeeded Yeh as the Kwangtung governor, a post he assumed just a few days after he had been elected (January) as chairman of the Kwangtung Committee of the CPPCC. Not long after these events took place, the South China Party Sub-bureau was abolished (July 1955), and although T'ao then relinquished his top post in the Sub-bureau, he continued to serve as the ranking secretary of the Kwangtung Party Committee, a post he was to hold for another decade.

When the central government and the various "mass" organizations were established in Peking in 1949, T'ao had not received any national post of significance. In fact his only position in a national organization was the rather nominal one of membership on the Preparatory Committee of the All-China Athletic Federation as a representative of the Fourth Field Army. He held this from October 1949 until the Federation was established on a permanent basis in mid-1952. T'ao did not receive another post in Peking until December 1954 when, representing the CCP, he was named to membership on the CPPCC's Second National Committee. He was again elected to represent the Party on the Third Committee (1959–1964). But neither of these assignments took T'ao to Peking very often; rather, he remained in Kwangtung for most of the fifties and early sixties where he continued to be the dominant Party figure. He was constantly reported in the press in those years—attending and frequently presiding over Party meetings and industrial and agricultural conferences, making inspections, and often writing for the Party press, particularly on political and agricultural questions. Initially, most of T'ao's writings were for the Canton *Nan-fang jih-pao* (South China daily), but as he grew in stature his articles appeared more frequently in the national press, particularly those dealing with agriculture. His place in the national hierarchy was fully confirmed at the Party's Eighth National Congress in September 1956. He served on the Congress Presidium (steering committee) and the Credentials Committee, and delivered a lengthy address on agriculture in Kwangtung. At the close of the meetings T'ao was elected to the Party Central Committee; he was one of only 33 men elected to full membership who had been neither a full nor an alternate member of the Seventh Central Committee elected in 1945.

In August 1957 T'ao resigned his Kwangtung governorship on the grounds that he was too fully occupied with his roles as secretary of the Kwangtung Party organization and chairman of the Kwangtung Committee of the CPPCC. He was succeeded as governor by Ch'en Yü (q.v.), a Central Committee member and a Kwangtung native. Although T'ao did not mention the fact, he had just assumed still another significant post (by June 1957) that may have partially accounted for his resignation. The new post was that of political commissar of the Canton Military Region, which controls military affairs in Kwangtung, Kwangsi, and Hunan; he held this post for nearly a decade. These heavy burdens of office may also account for the fact that he was succeeded as chairman of the Kwangtung CPPCC in December 1960 by Miss Ou Meng-chueh (q.v.). Like virtually all leaders of importance, T'ao was active in the "rectification" campaign of 1957–58, heading the special committee established in Kwangtung to carry out the movement. He took on still further responsibilities in early 1958 when he became chairman of a committee to establish an institute in Canton for overseas Chinese, known as Chi-

nan University; in late 1959 he assumed the presidency of the school, continuing in this post until mid-1964.

Although T'ao had written a number of rather well-balanced and fact-laden articles on the national economy in the early and mid-fifties, he was quick to join the chorus of those making extreme claims during the Great Leap Forward. A notable illustration of this appeared in the fifth issue of *Hung-ch'i* (Red flag, August 1, 1958), the Party's most authoritative journal; the title of T'ao's article denoted its exuberant tone: "Refutation of the 'Theory of Limited Increases in Food Production.' " In this piece T'ao made the normal Great Leap claims for increased grain yields—claims that were partially repudiated a year later by the CCP itself. But he has proved himself equally adept in adjusting to the prevalent line of the central leadership, as demonstrated in another *Hung-ch'i* article (February 26, 1964), written in a more sober and conservative period. Although he made some rather extravagant claims in this article for the accomplishments of the communes, he did not indulge in unrealistic claims for high agricultural yields.

Although T'ao had occasionally received important foreign visitors in Canton, his career was almost exclusively oriented toward domestic affairs until about 1960. In the spring of that year he authored an article for a Kwangtung journal, later reprinted in the *JMJP* (August 5, 1960), stressing the importance of Soviet assistance to China. Although this was soon to become virtually a forbidden subject in China, it may have accounted for his selection as a member of Chou En-lai's delegation, sent to Moscow for the 22nd CPSU Congress in October 1961. As it turned out, however, Sino-Soviet differences had already grown so severe that Chou walked out of the conference, leaving T'ao and others in Moscow for another week. T'ao had received this assignment shortly after being identified in a new post, which had catapulted him to a higher level of importance in the CCP. His new position was as first secretary of the Party's Central-South Bureau; the "old" bureau had been abolished in 1954 but was recreated in the wake of the Great Leap Forward difficulties at the Party's Ninth Plenum in January 1961. It is noteworthy that the former bureau had been headquartered in Wuhan, but when it was re-created Canton was made the capital—perhaps because of the apparently strong Party organization that T'ao had built up there. He was first identified in this post in August 1961, but it is probable that he held the post from earlier in the year when the bureau was established. Thus T'ao was placed on the level of some of the most important Party leaders, including the Politburo members who headed the Party organizations in the southwest (Li Ching-ch'üan) and east China (K'o Ch'ing-shih).

In September 1964 T'ao was elected to represent Kwangtung in the Third NPC, and when this legislative body ended its first session in January 1965 he was appointed as a vice-premier of the State Council—his first post in the executive arm of the national government. At this same time he was also elected again to represent the CCP on the Third National Committee of the CPPCC. However, the 1965 issue of the *Jen-min shou-ts'e* (People's handbook) revealed that he had been dropped from the CPPCC, possibly because of his assumption of the far more important post of vice-premier. T'ao now began to take an even more active role in national affairs; in particular, in 1965 he made two keynote speeches in which he insisted that "traditional" Chinese opera must be reformed to reflect a greater "revolutionary" content, a theme that was reiterated in countless articles throughout the year.

In March 1965 T'ao relinquished his first Party secretaryship in Kwangtung to his longtime associate Chao Tzu-yang (q.v.), but he remained in the south until the early summer of 1966. Then, in the early stage of the Cultural Revolution, he was suddenly brought to Peking to assume positions of great importance. By July he had replaced the ousted Lu Ting-i (q.v.) as director of the Central Committee's Propaganda Department, and at the same time he assumed a seat on the small but powerful Central Secretariat. A few weeks later, at the close of the Party's 11th Plenum (August), T'ao was listed fourth among the CCP leadership, ranking after Mao Tse-tung, Lin Piao, and Chou En-lai. He also became a member of the reorganized Politburo and of its Standing Committee. In the two decades after the Seventh Congress in 1945, few CCP leaders had made such a meteoric rise within so short a period. However, T'ao's preeminence was short-lived; he made his last public appearance in the closing days of 1966, and within a short time he was being savagely denounced in both the Red Guard and the official press.

T'ao is married to Tseng Chih, who was born in 1910. Like her husband, she is a Hunanese, coming from I-chang hsien. A Party member since 1933, Tseng worked in the Industry Department of the Central Plains Provisional People's Government (see under Teng Tzu-hui) in 1949, and later in the same department in the CSMAC during the early fifties. She has been a deputy to the NPC since its inauguration in 1954, rising to membership on the Standing Committee in January 1965. Tseng has also worked directly under her husband in the Canton and Kwangtung Party organizations, advancing from deputy secretary (1955) to secretary (1958) of the Canton CCP Committee, and then becoming a deputy secretary of the Kwangtung Committee in 1963. As

of the early 1960's the T'ao's were believed to have two sons, one in his early teens and the other nearing 20.[8]

1. Ezra F. Vogel, *Canton under Communism* (Cambridge, Mass., 1969), p. 116.
2. *SCMP* 3201, p. 13.
3. Ch'en Nung-fei, *Pu-tao te hung-ch'i* (Invincible red flag; Peking, 1959), p. 5.
4. Interview with former Canton government official, Hong Kong, June 1964.
5. Chiang Nan-hsiang et al., *The Roar of a Nation* (Peking, 1963), pp. 152–153.
6. A. Doak Barnett, *China on the Eve of Communist Takeover* (New York, 1964), pp. 332–337.
7. Interview, see note 4.
8. *Ibid.*

T'ao Lu-chia

(1910–   ; Hunan). Vice-chairman, State Economic Commission; alternate member, CCP Central Committee.

T'ao Lu-chia's first known association with the revolutionary movement occurred in mid-1937 immediately after the outbreak of the Sino-Japanese War. At that time a number of young Communist students were fleeing Peking and Tientsin for Communist-held areas in northwest China. Traveling down the Peking-Hankow (Pinghan) Railway in open railway cars, the students had to change at Shih-chia-chuang before proceeding westward to Taiyuan. T'ao helped these students upon their arrival at Shih-chia-chuang; he was described as a "responsible person" of the local National Liberation Vanguards of China (NLVC) chapter.[1] The NLVC had been formed in Peking in early 1936 in the wake of the December Ninth movement, named after demonstrations held on December 9, 1935, by students protesting China's acquiescence to Japanese penetration into north China (see under Li Ch'ang). T'ao's association with the NLVC in 1937 offers strong evidence that he was a college student at that time and belonged either to the CCP or at least to the Communist Youth League.

There was no further reporting about T'ao during the Sino-Japanese War nor during the civil war with the Nationalists. But then in 1949 he emerged as an important Party official in Shansi where he was to remain for the next 16 years. From 1949 to 1952 he headed the provincial Party Propaganda Department and from April 1950 to his transfer to Peking in 1965 he was a member of the Shansi Provincial Government. Under this same government he served as a vice-chairman of the Culture and Education Committee from August 1950 to June 1952. Within the provincial Party structure, he was promoted to a deputy secretaryship by mid-1951. He moved up to first deputy secretary in early

1953 and then took over from Kao K'o-lin (q.v.) as the first secretary by late summer 1953. In the meantime, in 1952, he had become the political commissar of the Shansi Military District. Thus, from the 1952–53 period, T'ao was the dominant figure in Shansi until his 1965 transfer.

T'ao served as a Shansi deputy to the First NPC, which brought the constitutional government into existence at its first session in September 1954. Although he was not named to the Second NPC, whch opened in April 1959, he was elected in a by-election in December 1965 (replacing a deceased colleague) to the Third NPC. In February 1955 he became the chairman of the newly established Shansi chapter of the CPPCC, the quasi-legislative body of only limited importance after the formation of the NPC. He remained as head of the CPPCC in Shansi until his departure from the province in 1965. During his 16-year tenure in Shansi, T'ao seldom left the province. One of the exceptions occurred in September 1956 when he attended the important Eighth National Party Congress, where he submitted a report on industry and agriculture in Shansi. He was again in Peking in May 1958 when the Congress held its second session. On this occasion he was elected an alternate member of the Party Central Committee.

T'ao was very active in internal political affairs in Shansi during his many years there. On a number of occasions he was reported in the company of Politburo members on inspection tours in Shansi; random examples include the visits of P'eng Chen (October 1958), Ch'en I (May–June 1959), and Tung Pi-wu (May 1960). During these years T'ao also contributed several articles for top Party journals and newspapers. These include articles for *Hsueh-hsi* (Study; November 1, 1951), the *JMJP* (May 16, 1958, and June 11, 1960), and *Hung-ch'i* (Red flag; October 16, 1958, March 1, 1959, and May 16, 1963). Most of these articles dealt with economic problems, particularly as they pertained to the situation in Shansi. Possibly it was this experience in economic matters that brought about his transfer in April 1965 to Peking as one of the vice-chairmen of the State Economic Commission. Headed by one of China's top economic specialists, Po I-po, this important commission is in charge of economic planning on an annual basis. T'ao, of course, relinquished his posts in Shansi, being replaced as the first secretary of the Shansi Party Committee by Wei Heng (q.v.), a long-time colleague. Less than a month before his transfer to Peking (April 1965), T'ao had been identified as a secretary of the Party's North China Bureau. In view of the fact that many officials of this bureau hold concurrent posts in Peking, it is possible that T'ao will continue to serve in the bureau as well as State Economic Commission.

---

1. *SCMM* 297, p. 38.

Teng Chung-hsia

(1897–1933; I-chang, Hunan). Early labor leader; member, CCP Central Committee.

Teng Chung-hsia's significance in the history of Chinese communism lies in the leading role he played in the labor movement in the 1920's. A personal friend of Mao Tse-tung, Teng is honored in official history as one of the martyrs of the CCP. He is also remembered as the author of *Chung-kuo chih-kung yun-tung chien-shih* (A short history of the Chinese labor movement).

Teng was born into an impoverished scholar-official family on September 9, 1897. His original name was Teng K'ang and he adopted Chung-hsia (which he often used as a pen name) only after he began his revolutionary career. He was a graduate of the Higher Normal College[1] in Hunan and went to Peking University to study Chinese literature until he abandoned it after the May Fourth Movement. A man of action and wide interests, he was involved in various kinds of extracurricular activities. Like many fellow students, such as Lo Chang-lung, Chang Kuo-t'ao, and Ho Meng-hsiung (qq.v.), three of many who played substantial roles in the Communist Movement, he fell under the influence of Ch'en Tu-hsiu and Li Ta-chao (qq.v.), two Peking University professors who were among the outstanding leaders of the Westernized intelligentsia in China. Under them Teng developed an absorbing interest in Marxism as well as in working among laborers. Thus, in June 1918 he was a founding member (and later, in 1920, a vice-chairman[2]) of the Shao-nien Chung-kuo hsueh-hui (Young China Association), whose leaders included Li Ta-chao. Later in the year Teng established the Chiu-kuo hui (Save the country society) another organization whose activities were promoted by Li Ta-chao.[3] These organizations were used by Li to organize a group for the study of Marxism and socialism, to which Teng also belonged. In March 1919, with Chang Kuo-t'ao, Hsu Te-heng (q.v.), Lo Chia-lun, K'ang Pai-ch'ing, and others, Teng founded the P'ing-min chiao-yü chiang-yen t'uan (Mass education speech corps), which undertook educational activities among the laboring classes in and around Peking.

In the days immediately after the May Fourth Incident, the Peking group stepped up its activities. Li Ta-chao urged members of the Marxist Research society to travel to other cities to spread the movement, and in response to this Teng went to Shanghai where in June he took part in strikes in that city.[4] Returning to Peking, he became one of the major initiators of Communist organizational activities, which began with the arrival of Comintern agent Gregory Voitinsky in the spring of 1920. Mao Tse-tung was in Peking at about this same time, and he and Teng, both Hunanese, renewed their friendship (which dated from at least 1918 during Mao's first trip to Peking). Teng graduated from Peking University in 1920, and in September of that year, with Li Ta-chao, he helped found the Peking branch of the Socialist Youth League, and also with Li he began publishing the *Lao-tung yin* (The workers' voice) in November, a weekly which lasted only a brief time. In the meantime, in collaboration with Chang Kuo-t'ao, Teng organized a night school for the railroad workers and their children at Ch'ang-hsin-tien, a major terminal of the Peking-Hankow Railroad outside Peking. The real objective, however, was to begin a workers' union, which he succeeded in forming by early 1921. It took the name "club" (*chü-lo-pu*) in order not to be confused with the "labor union" (*kung-hui*), an organization of the hated labor contractors. All over China, except Canton, the name *chü-lo-pu* became a popular term for unions of workers; the model workers' club at Ch'ang-hsin-tien was soon imitated by workers at other terminals. With the experience gained here, Teng proceeded to Tientsin, T'ang-shan, and elsewhere to initiate similar railroad workers' organizations.

In July 1921, while the founding congress of the CCP was being held in Shanghai, Teng was attending a conference of the Young China Association in Nanking. With the formation of the CCP, Communist organizational work among laborers began in earnest. Immediately after the inaugural CCP Congress, the Secretariat of the Chinese Labor Unions (Chung-kuo lao-tung chu-ho shu-chi-pu) was formed in Shanghai, with Chang Kuo-t'ao in charge; Teng Chung-hsia became the director of the North China branch, at Peking, where he was assisted by Lo Chang-lung. Teng was one of the editors of the Secretariat's organ *Lao-tung chou-k'an* (Labor weekly). During the summer, with Li Ta-chao, Teng was in Szechwan on a lecture tour, on the invitation of Yun Tai-ying (q.v.). When he returned in the winter, he became secretary of the Peking Municipal Committee of the CCP, of which Lo Chang-lung was also a member.

On May 1, 1922, the Secretariat of the Chinese Labor Unions sponsored the First National Congress of Labor in Canton. In the absence of a national federation of labor, the Congress resolved to make the Labor Secretariat the national coordinating office of Chinese labor organizations. Teng replaced Chang Kuo-t'ao as head of the Secretariat, which he moved from Shanghai to Peking in view of the fact that the center of labor unrest was then in the north China railroad network. Other members of the Secretariat were Chang Kuo-t'ao, Hsiang Ying, and Liu Shao-ch'i (qq.v.); branches were set up in other provinces, with Yuan Ta-shih in charge in Shanghai, Lin Yü-nan (q.v.) in Wuhan, Mao Tse-tung in Changsha, Feng Chü-p'o in Canton, and Wang Chin-mei in Tsinan.

Also in May 1922, immediately after the labor conference, Teng attended the First Congress of the Socialist Youth League in Canton, and he was elected to both the Central Committee and Politburo. He was among the contributors to the League organ *Hsien-ch'ü* (The pioneer), which had been set up prior to the First Congress, and he was also the first editor of the more important journal *Chung-kuo ch'ing-nien* (Chinese youth),[5] which was established in October 1923, but he soon relinquished this post to Yun Tai-ying. In July 1922 Teng was one of the few people who attended the Second Congress of the CCP in Shanghai; he was elected a member of the Central Committee, a position he retained until his death. The CCP was then in the midst of a debate on the wisdom of cooperating with the KMT. The issue was not settled at the Second Congress, but a few weeks later it was again raised at another Party conference. Several of the Peking group of Communists (notably Chang Kuo-t'ao, Ho Meng-hsiung, and Lo Chang-lung) reportedly formed a "radical" faction, which argued that the Party should concentrate its efforts on mobilizing the laboring classes. The opposing faction, the so-called "gradualists," who were led by Teng, held that the time was not ripe for a proletarian class struggle and therefore it was necessary to carry out the national revolution in cooperation with the KMT. With strong backing from the Comintern, those favoring cooperation with the KMT won the debate, and this was then formalized in 1923. Teng played a key role in the talks with the KMT; in early 1923 he was sent by Li Ta-chao to Shanghai to hold talks with Sun Yat-sen on the reorganization of the KMT and the admission of the Communists to Sun's party.[6]

In the meantime, as head of the Labor Secretariat, Teng had faced a period of considerable labor unrest which he did his share to bring about. In August 1922 he led a strike at Ch'ang-hsin-tien, and in October, another at the Kailan mines. The high point of labor unrest was reached when the Secretariat proposed to establish a labor union for all the workers of the Peking-Hankow Railway, then in the domain of the warlord Wu P'ei-fu. In April–May 1922 Wu had defeated Chang Tso-lin in the Fengtien-Chihli War and announced the "protection of labor" as one of his policies to court mass support. Attempting to eliminate whatever influence Chang's ally, the Communications Clique, had over the railroads, Wu was prepared to discuss with Li Ta-chao the use of a secret inspector on each of the six lines which comprised the North China network. Among the young Communists Li recommended were An T'i-ch'eng, Ch'en Wei-jen, Ho Meng-hsiung, and Pao Hui-seng. With about half a year's preparation, by which time workers had been organized at almost every station, a proposal was made to form a union of the Peking-Hankow railroad workers, with the inaugural conference scheduled for February 1, 1923. It was then that Wu felt the Communists had exceeded themselves and he forbade the convocation of the conference. A tense struggle ensued which culminated in the February 7 "massacre" in which Wu's troops, by their brutal execution of more than 40 Communists and labor leaders, compelled the laborers to resume work. With this episode, the tide of labor unrest quickly receded; Teng Chung-hsia was forced to flee to Shanghai, his role in the movement having been discovered.

In June 1923 Teng was in Canton to attend the Third CCP Congress, which endorsed the policy of CCP members joining the KMT as individuals. He then returned to Shanghai, but because the field of labor agitation was temporarily closed, many key Party and Youth League activists congregated at Shanghai University (see under Ch'ü Ch'iu-pai). This short-lived but important school, founded and jointly sponsored in the latter part of 1923 by the CCP and the KMT, trained a significant number of Communist cadres. By virtue of his leadership position in the Youth League, Teng became dean of studies.

Teng was back in Peking in early 1924 and there, on February 7 (the first anniversary of the "massacre") he and a small group of Communists met with the purpose of forming a national railway union.[7] However, the police broke up the meeting, and Teng then returned to Shanghai. Despite the failure in Peking, the year 1924 witnessed the rise of a new tide in the labor movement. Teng resigned from Shanghai University and devoted himself exclusively to the labor movement. In October, in cooperation with Chang Kuo-t'ao, he founded the important weekly *Chung-kuo kung-jen* (The Chinese worker). Early in the next year the labor movement manifested itself in the form of anti-Japanese sentiments. A strike in February against Japanese cotton mills in Shanghai which mobilized some 40,000 workers, began as a "simple economic strike," but the CCP Central Committee sent Teng and Li Li-san (q.v.) to take over its direction. As one commentator has noted, this important strike "marked the end of the long period of inactivity in the Shanghai labor movement and the beginning of the outburst of activity that was to lead to the explosion of May 30"[8] (see below).

While the labor movement was gathering momentum, Teng went to Canton in May 1925 to attend the Second National Congress of Labor at which the All-China Federation of Labor (Chung-hua ch'üan-kuo tsung-kung-hui) was established (and, in effect, replaced the Labor Secretariat). The new federation affiliated to the Red International of Trade Unions (Profintern). Teng was among the 25 members of the Federation's Executive Committee, which included Su Chao-cheng, Li Li-san, Liu Shao-ch'i, and Hsiang Ying

(qq.v.). Moreover, Teng was elected secretary-general of the federation, as well as director of its Propaganda Department.

After the Labor Congress, Teng remained in Canton, by then the revolutionary center of China. Late in May 1925 a storm of labor unrest with an "anti-imperialist" character shook Shanghai (the May 30th Incident) and rapidly spread to other major urban centers. Organized labor in south China responded by starting, on June 19, the famous Hong Kong–Canton strike and boycott, which lasted for a year and a half (see under Su Chao-cheng). A strike committee was formed under the chairmanship of Su Chao-cheng, who had only recently joined the CCP. Teng served as chief adviser of the strike committee, and subordinate to it he was secretary of a Communist fraction which also included Huang P'ing and Ch'en Yen-nien (q.v.).

Teng was deeply occupied in the course of the next year with the Hong Kong–Canton strike, and in this connection he, Su Chao-cheng, Hsiang Ying, and Liu Shao-ch'i went to Hong Kong in March 1926 to attend the inaugural meeting of the Hong Kong Transport Workers' General Union.[9] Two months later, at the Third National Labor Congress held in May 1926, Teng was again elected a member of the Labor Federation's Executive Committee. In addition to his work with the labor movement, Teng also taught at the Peasant Movement Training Institute (see under P'eng P'ai) during its sixth term (May–October 1926) when the Institute was headed by Mao Tse-tung.[10] Teng's activities from the latter part of 1926 (after the Northern Expedition had begun) until mid-1927 are not well documented, but he apparently remained in Canton with the labor movement. In late 1926 he published a study on the strikes in Canton, in which he argued that cooperation with the KMT was still important.[11] However, a half a year later, when the tenuous alliance between the CCP and the Left-KMT came to an end, Teng was among those who took a major role in planning the famous Nanchang Uprising of August 1, 1927 (see under Yeh T'ing).[12] He did not, however, take part in the uprising itself, but a few days later he attended the Party's famous August 7 Emergency Conference, at which Ch'ü Ch'iu-pai (q.v.) replaced Ch'en Tu-hsiu as Party chief.[13] At this time Teng was given the dangerous and difficult task of assuming the secretaryship of the Kiangsu Provincial Committee (headquartered in Shanghai), which was severely strained because its leading members, men such as Ch'en Yen-nien, Chao Shih-yen (q.v.), and Ho Sung-ling, had perished at the hands of the KMT.

In late 1927, just before the Canton Commune (December), Teng led a big strike of some 100,000 textile workers in a factory district in Shanghai. This was quickly suppressed, however, whereupon Teng was assigned to Canton where he replaced the deceased Chang T'ai-lei (q.v.) as secretary of the Kwangtung Provincial Party Committee, while his post in Kiangsu was taken over by Hsiang Ying. His relationship with P'eng P'ai, chief of the Party's East River Special Committee and head of the Hai-lu-feng Soviet, appears to have been strained, and for a while Kwangtung had two centers of Communist authority. However, this situation did not last long, for by April 1928 Teng had gone to Moscow where he attended the Fourth Profintern Congress. He was elected to the Profintern Executive Committee, and in the summer he attended both the Sixth CCP Congress and the Sixth Comintern Congress. For the next two years Teng remained in Moscow as CCP delegate to the Profintern, and with Ch'ü Ch'iu-pai, Huang P'ing, Chang Kuo-t'ao, and Yü Fei, formed the five-man CCP delegation stationed in Moscow. The Chinese delegation led by Ch'ü Ch'iu-pai was soon embroiled in a power struggle with Pavel Mif and his protégés at Sun Yat-sen University. Apart from their intense dislike of Mif, members of the delegation, with their seniority in the CCP and experience in the "Great Revolution," held Mif's young protégés in contempt and worked to block Mif's attempt to foist them on the CCP as instruments of his own domination of the Chinese Communist movement. Teng's involvement in the struggle earned him the intense hatred of Mif's protégés, who soon found the opportunity to retaliate. By the spring of 1930 the delegation had been pushed aside by Mif's machinations, their functions collectively assumed by Chou En-lai, whom Mif sent for from China.

Teng returned to China in the fall of 1930 and was assigned as special delegate of the CCP Central Committee to the West Hunan-Hupeh Soviet area, with the responsibility of the work of the Provincial Committee of the Party. Concurrently, he was political commissar of Ho Lung's (q.v.) military forces. His work in this area met with frustration when the Mif–Ch'en Shao-yü group achieved dominance over the CCP in Shanghai in January 1931 and made a bid to extend its control over the West Hunan-Hupeh Soviet area (see under Hsia Hsi). On November 25, 1931, the Politburo warned the leaders of this soviet area that it was wrong to abandon the Hung-hu Lake base and flee north; the poor advice having originated with Teng, the Politburo ordered the Provincial Committee to censure Teng, which it did in a resolution passed on December 9, 1931, charging him with escapism, pessimism, and the like, and requesting the Politburo to remove him from all work and subject him to Party discipline. The upshot was that Teng left the soviet area and returned to Shanghai in the winter where he was put under Party surveillance for a period.

In Shanghai he was put in charge of the Mutual Aid Headquarters (Hu-chi tsung-hui) with the duties of organizing relief work for Party members in distress. He also took part in mobilizing resistance against the Japanese invasion, and while engaged in the latter activity he was arrested on May 15, 1933, by the French Concession police in Shanghai. He was later turned over to the Nationalists, who took him to Nanking where in mid-October he was executed.

Teng's talent lay mainly in his organizational ability. Most of his writings are in the form of short pieces of an indoctrinating nature and appeared in journals of the Socialist Youth League, the CCP, and workers' organizations. Several of his articles and speeches in connection with the labor movement are conveniently reproduced in *Ti-i-tz'u kuo-nei ko-ming chan-cheng shih-ch'i te kung-jen yun-tung* (The workers' movement during the period of the First Revolutionary Civil War), which was published in Peking in 1963. In the period of KMT-CCP cooperation, Teng also wrote frequently for *Hsin chien-she* (New construction), a KMT journal. But he is best known for the above-mentioned history of the Chinese labor movement covering the period 1919–1926 (*Chung-kuo chih-kung yun-tung chien-shih*). This was written during his stay in Moscow from 1928 to 1930 and was published there in 1930; it was republished in China in 1943 and reissued under the Maoist leadership in 1949 and 1953 with no substantive changes. Despite its overzealous tone, it is a useful source for the early labor movement. Teng's biography, which appears at the end of the volume (and which has been reproduced with only minor changes in several of the Communists' collections of biographies of their "revolutionary martyrs"), forms the basis of this sketch.

Teng was married to Hsia Ming in the 1920's and by the late 1920's they had at least one child. She is the author of a brief essay on Teng's arrest and execution, which was published in 1958.[14] She does not appear to have been politically active in the post-1949 period, but in 1963 the Communist press mentioned that Hsia, described as a "veteran revolutionary," had been occupied in relating revolutionary stories to youngsters.

---

1. *Hung-ch'i p'iao-p'iao* (Red flag fluttering; Peking, 1957), I, 88.

2. *Shao-nien Chung-kuo* (Young China), October 15, 1920, p. 87.

3. Maurice Meisner, *Li Ta-chao and the Origins of Chinese Marxism* (Cambridge, Mass., 1967), p. 71.

4. *Ibid.*, p. 102.

5. Chang Ching-lu, ed., *Chung-kuo hsien-tai ch'u-pan shih-liao* (Historical materials on contemporary Chinese publishing; Peking, 1954), p. 63.

6. Meisner, pp. 219–220.

7. Jean Chesneaux, *The Chinese Labor Movement, 1919–1927* (Stanford, Calif., 1968), p. 221.

8. *Ibid.*, pp. 255–256.

9. *Ibid.*, p. 298.

10. *SCMP* 986, p. 31; Shinkichi Eto, "Hai-lu-feng—The First Chinese Soviet Government," *The China Quarterly*, no. 8:182 (October–December 1961).

11. Chesneaux, p. 536.

12. C. Martin Wilbur, "The Ashes of Defeat," *The China Quarterly*, no. 18:9–10 (April–June 1964).

13. Nym Wales, *The Chinese Labor Movement* (New York, 1945), p. 212.

14. *Hung-ch'i p'iao-p'iao* (Peking, 1958), VIII, 20–23.

Teng Fa

(1906–1946; Yun-fu hsien, Kwangtung). Early Party leader; member, CCP Central Committee.

Teng Fa played an important role in CCP affairs in the thirties and forties. He came from a proletarian background and began to work in the labor movement in the 1920's, then rose to important Party positions in the thirties, and was one of the Party's chief operatives in Sinkiang after 1937. He headed the Central Party School at Yenan in the early forties but had returned to the labor field before the end of the Sino-Japanese War. Teng lost his life in a plane crash in 1946.

Teng's native hsien, Yun-fu in Kwangtung, is on the Pearl River not far west of Canton, an area frequented by the sea-going vessels which could enter the lower parts of the river. He was born into a poor family, but nothing is known about his upbringing. Apparently he had no formal education, because at an early age he went to work as a cabin boy on ships owned by the Butterfield and Swire Company of Britain. Teng had his first taste of labor troubles at age 16, in 1922, when the Chinese Seamen's Union under the leadership of Lin Wei-min and Su Chao-cheng (q.v.) called the seamen's strike that was so disrupting to industries, especially those owned by the British, in many cities of China (see under Su Chao-cheng). Teng was then a foreign-style cook on the river steamers running between Canton and Hong Kong and was said to have been much influenced by the anti-British feelings which the strikers expressed. Three years later, when other and more serious strikes affected the Hong Kong-Canton area (see under Teng Chung-hsia), he had become active in the labor movement and was taking charge of a strike committee. By this time, qualified as a professional labor agitator, Teng had been motivated to teach himself to read and write. In the winter of 1925 he joined the CCP and then entered the Whampoa Military Academy, which had recently been opened by the KMT but which had many young Communists on the staff and among the students.

Also at this time he joined the KMT as did a number of other young members of the CCP.

When the Northern Expedition opened in mid-1926 Teng was put in charge of Youth Corps activities at the Kwangtung KMT Headquarters. Thus he remained in south China while most of his fellow cadets from Whampoa went to Wuhan or Kiangsi with the military forces. By the end of 1927 he was secretary of the CCP branch in the Kwangtung labor union for workers in the vegetable oil industry. In a minor role he participated in the Communists' coup at Canton (December 11–14, 1927), commanding a force of Red guards and assisting one of the Soviet-trained military experts who had been his political instructor at Whampoa. Teng was sufficiently low in rank to be able to remain in the area after the Communists had failed at Canton and many of their better-known agitators were forced to flee. During the year 1928 he held several lesser posts in the Party apparatus in the Canton–Hong Kong organization; he was director of the Organization Department of the Hong Kong Municipal CCP Committee, a south China representative to the All-China Federation of Labor, and he also chaired the Hong Kong Workers' Representatives Conference. Within a brief period he rose to more important positions, becoming secretary of both the Hong Kong and Canton CCP Committees, and head of the Kwangtung Party Committee's Organization Department. At this time also his name began to appear as a contributor to the CCP organ *Hung-ch'i* (Red flag).

Teng Fa left China in 1929 and after visits in Europe went to Moscow. This was his first opportunity for formal study of the theories of Marxism-Leninism; he also learned some Russian. While in Russia he came into close contact with two fellow Chinese Communists whom he impressed very favorably, Wu Yü-chang and Lin Po-ch'ü. Both were 20-odd years Teng's senior but were students in Moscow like himself. He returned to China in time to attend the Third CCP Plenum, held in September 1930. The Plenum was a stormy meeting, at which the policies of Li Li-san (q.v) were reviewed and criticized and the Comintern-led group of Chinese students known as the "28 Bolsheviks" made their opposition to Li felt (see under Ch'in Pang-hsien). There were a number of other groups opposing Li whose presence was also felt at the Plenum, but no single group was strong enough to gain dominance over Li and it is impossible to tell which group placed Teng on the Party Central Committee at this time. However, after this meeting he began to play a role of some importance in Party affairs. Following the Plenum he returned to south China and from there was sent to Hainan Island to contact a local Party leader there, Feng Pai-chü (q.v.), whom he guided in reorganizing a Red military force that Feng had been recruiting for several years. Late in 1930 Teng became secretary of the Kwangtung-Fukien-Kiangsi Border Area Committee and chairman of the Military Committee governing the border area.

By mid-1931 Teng was transferred to the Central Soviet area in Kiangsi where Mao Tse-tung and Chu Te had their headquarters. There he became director of the security apparatus. Ex-Communist Kung Ch'u has written that Teng was selected for this post because of his steadfast loyalty to Mao during the difficult days of the First and Second Nationalist Annihilation Campaigns (1930–31) when Mao's forces experienced some serious internal disloyalties.[1] At the First All-China Congress of Soviets, held in Juichin in November 1931, the Chinese Soviet Republic was established. Teng was elected to the Republic's Central Executive Committee (CEC), and his role as security chief was formalized when he was named chief of the CEC's National Political Security Bureau (Kuo-chia cheng-chih pao-wei chü). One of his top aides in the Bureau was Li K'o-nung (q.v.), another important security official. Teng was re-elected to the CEC at the Second Congress, held in January–February 1934, and at that time he was also named to the newly created CEC Presidium. This 17-member organization, in charge of the day-to-day operations for the larger CEC, was under the chairmanship of Mao Tse-tung, as was the CEC itself. Teng made the Long March with Mao's armies and continued to direct security operations during the march. He was still holding this post when he met American journalist Edgar Snow in the summer of 1936. According to Snow's account it appears that Teng was involved in the intricate negotiations in Sian with dissident KMT generals Yang Hu-ch'eng and Chang Hsueh-liang for closer cooperation with the Communists in north Shensi (an episode described at greater length in the biography of Wang Ping-nan). Snow recounts that when he met Teng in Sian in mid-1936 the latter, disguised as a KMT officer, was living in the residence of Chang Hsueh-liang and that Chiang Kai-shek had put a price on his head of 50,000 silver dollars.[2]

After the start of the Sino-Japanese War and until sometime in the first half of 1942 the Chinese Communists at Yenan opened and developed quite close relations with the autonomous governor of Sinkiang, Sheng Shih-ts'ai (see under Saifudin). Thus in 1937 Teng Fa went to the Sinkiang capital of Tihwa as Yenan's chief representative. Soon he was known to Sheng as chief of the Sinkiang Headquarters of the Communists' Eighth Route Army. While in Sinkiang Teng was sometimes known by his Party name of Fang Lin. Sheng's relations with the Yenan Communists are described in *Sinkiang: Pawn or Pivot?*, which is co-authored by Allen S. Whiting and Sheng Shih-ts'ai. The book also recounts the part played in Sinkiang-CCP affairs by Teng Fa. According to Sheng he applied for CCP membership through Ch'en Shao-yü, K'ang Sheng (qq.v.), and Teng Fa, who were all in Sinkiang at the time, late 1937, but his request was turned down.[3] He continued to have some dealings with Teng over the next year or so until he tired of what he considered to be Teng's intriguing and hence asked Yenan to replace him. Teng was succeeded in 1938 by Ch'en T'an-ch'iu (q.v.) in Sinkiang, but in the meantime Teng had negotiated with Sheng's government an agreement providing for the training of Chinese Communist personnel in the latter's "Sinkiang Flying Corps." According to an article published on the mainland in late 1961, 43 young men, sent from Yenan to Sinkiang in early 1938, were the first Chinese Communists to receive instruction in aviation.[4]

Teng had returned to Yenan by 1939,[5] and in the latter part of the following year he received three positions of considerable importance; he became president of the Central Party School and secretary of the Industrial Workers' Committee (Chih-kung wei-yuan-hui) and the Mass Movement Committee (Min-lien wei-yuan-hui), all three of which were directly subordinate to the Party's Central Committee. In the same year he also took part with Lin Yü-ying (q.v.) in publishing *Chung-kuo kung-jen* (Chinese workers). At the end of 1941 Teng began a reorganization of the Party School, and in the following year, when Mao opened the famous political "rectification" (*cheng-feng*) movement, Teng participated in the program within the school. He left this important institution in 1943, by which time he had already become active again in the labor movement and in the development of local industry that was so vital for the self-sufficiency of the Shensi-Kansu-Ninghsia Border Region.[6] Journalist Israel Epstein, who interviewed Teng in 1944, reported that his "main job" was in connection with the above-mentioned Mass Movement Committee, whose task it was to organize both workers and peasants at the grass-roots levels.[7]

In the summer of 1945 Teng became chairman of the Preparatory Committee of the newly established Liberated Areas Trade Union Federation. In September he left Yenan for Chungking, and from there he went to Paris with Chu Hsueh-fan, the veteran non-Communist labor leader who was then head of the China Association of Labor. In Paris Chu and Teng attended the inaugural congress in September–October of the World Federation of Trade Unions (WFTU), which in a brief time was to become an almost completely Communist-dominated organization. At the meeting Teng was elected to alternate membership on both the General Council and the Executive Committee of the WFTU. A month later Chu and Teng attended the non-Communist 27th International Labor Congress, also held in Paris. Afterwards, over the next few weeks, Teng traveled widely in Western Europe, speaking before overseas Chinese communities and making useful contacts there. He is known to have visited England, Switzerland, and Italy during this period. Teng returned to Chungking in January 1946, having traveled home by way of the Philippines according to Epstein.[8]

Teng was in flight to Yenan to report on the WFTU Congress in Europe when he met his death. He had planned to proceed on from Yenan to Moscow to attend a WFTU meeting. His death occurred on April 8, 1946, in the same plane crash over west Shansi that cost the lives of Wang Jo-fei, Ch'in Pang-hsien, and Yeh T'ing, all prominent CCP leaders also en route to Yenan. His death at age 40 cut short the career of one of the CCP's few leaders whose background was genuinely proletarian and who was becoming a specialist in international labor affairs. Following his death he was succeeded in his most important post, the chairmanship of the Liberated Areas Trade Union Federation's Preparatory Committee, by Liu Ning-i (q.v.).

One perplexing problem remains about Teng's standing in the hierarchy at the time of his death. In view of his membership on the Central Committee as early as 1930, it seems unusual that he was not re-elected at the Party's Seventh National Congress in the spring of 1945. Moreover, immediately after the death of Teng and his three important colleagues in 1946, the CCP published a volume of commemorative articles, and in one of these articles Party veteran Liao Ch'eng-chih asserted that within the "previous 10 years" Teng had been a Politburo member.[9] There is, however, nothing in the available record to confirm Liao's assertion, and the fact that Teng was not even re-elected to the Central Committee in 1945 clearly indicates that he was not still a Politburo member when he died.

Teng Fa married Ch'en Hui-ch'ing in Hong Kong in 1929 while both were working there in the labor movement. Nym Wales (Mrs. Edgar Snow) met Ch'en on her visit to north China in 1937 and described her as a "short, healthy, plain-looking woman," who was very friendly. Then 27 years old, she was one of the small group of women who made the Long March with Mao's army. Ch'en was born in Hong Kong where her father was a machinist, but the family came originally from Canton. At 14 she had to go to work; in 1925 she too participated in the Hong Kong–Canton strikes and then found work in Canton as a member of the KMT Propaganda Department until about the time of the Communist coup in Canton in December 1927. Having already joined the CCP, she participated in the uprising, and then like her husband-to-be, she remained in south China working in the labor movement.[10] It is not known whether she accompanied Teng to the USSR after their marriage, but she must have been with him in Kiangsi in the early thirties, and she was with him in Sinkiang from 1937 to 1939. Ch'en was a contributor to the above-mentioned volume of commemorative essays in 1946 when she was living in Yenan with one of her sons, but nothing further was heard of her until 1962 when she was back in her native province serving as a vice-chairman of the Kwangtung branch of the All-China Federation of Trade Unions.

1. Kung Ch'u, *Wo yü Hung-chün* (The Red Army and I; Hong Kong, 1954), p. 248.
2. Edgar Snow, *Red Star over China* (New York, 1938), pp. 23–24; Edgar Snow, *The Other Side of the River* (London, 1961), p. 264.
3. Allen S. Whiting and Sheng Shih-ts'ai, *Sinkiang: Pawn or Pivot?* (East Lansing, Mich., 1958), p. 201.
4. *Min-tsu t'uan-chieh* (Nationalities unity), no. 12, December 6, 1961, pp. 18–21.
5. *Ibid.*, p. 20.
6. *"Szu-pa" pei-nan lieh-shih chi-nien-ts'e* (In memory of the martyrs who died in the accident of "April Eighth"; Chungking [?], 1946), pp. 343–346; Hua Ying-shen, ed., *Chung-kuo kung-ch'an tang lieh-shih chuan* (Biographies of Chinese Communist Party martyrs; Hong Kong, 1949), pp. 272–275.
7. Israel Epstein, *The Unfinished Revolution in China* (Boston, Mass., 1947), pp. 252–257.
8. *Ibid.*, p. 252.
9. *"Szu-pa" pei-nan lieh-shih chi-nien-ts'e*, p. 223.
10. Nym Wales, *Inside Red China* (New York, 1939), pp. 29–30.

Teng Hsiao-p'ing

(1904–   ; Kuang-an, Szechwan). Member, Politburo Standing Committee, CCP; general secretary, Central Committee, CCP.

Teng Hsiao-p'ing, one of the half-dozen most important political figures in China from the mid-1950's, was among those early Communists trained in France and the Soviet Union during the 1920's. He was a Red Army political officer from the late 1920's through the 1940's, and in the early 1950's he was a top official in the southwest. He rose quickly in the Party hierarchy after his transfer to Peking in 1952. Elected to the Politburo in 1955, Teng became a member of the Politburo Standing Committee in 1956, as well as general secretary of the Party Central Committee. In the decade after the mid-1950's he was deeply involved in CCP relations with foreign Communist parties, and in the 1960's he was one of the major figures in the Sino-Soviet dispute.

Teng was born in Kuang-an, which is on one of the Yangtze River tributaries in Szechwan some 60 miles north of Chungking. He graduated from a middle school in Szechwan and then attended a year-long training program which had been set up in the province to prepare students for study in France on a work-and-study basis. The origins of this scheme are described in the biography of Wu Yü-chang, also a Szechwanese. Teng arrived in France in early 1920; other Szechwanese who went there at approximately the same time and who later gained eminence in the Communist movement include Ch'en I and Nieh Jung-chen (qq.v.). In contrast to Ch'en and Nieh, as well as the important Hunanese group led by Ts'ai Ho-sen (q.v.), relatively little is known about Teng's activities. It appears that he was involved in the celebrated Lyon University movement in 1921 which brought about the expulsion from France of a number of latter-day CCP members (see under Ch'en I). In 1922 he joined the Chinese Socialist Youth League,[1] which had been founded by Wang Jo-fei (q.v.) and others in France. In mid-1922 the league began to publish a mimeographed organ known as *Shao-nien* (Youth), which, in the next year, was renamed *Ch'ih-kuang* (Red glow). This was edited by Ch'en Yen-nien (q.v.), and Teng, placed in charge of the technical work involved, was nicknamed "doctor of mimeographing" by his colleagues.[2] In 1924 Teng joined the CCP. Many years later he told journalist Edgar Snow that he never attended school in France, but that he had been a worker.[3]

By the mid-1920's many of the Communists in France left for home, often by the way of the Soviet Union. Teng went to Moscow in 1926 where he studied for several months.[4] In this same year north China warlord Feng Yü-hsiang was in Moscow seeking further Soviet support for his maneuverings against other north China alliances of warlords. The Russians were quite willing to entertain requests for support as a means of gaining influence with Feng. At the same time, Feng was in contact with top KMT officials and their Communist allies in Canton, both of whom were wooing Feng. This three-sided courtship of Feng had begun in 1925, and by mid-1926 it had become a matter of urgency as the Nationalists, with an active assist from the CCP, launched the Northern Expedition. The reason the Nationalists and Communists were so eager to enlist Feng into the cause of the national revolution was because he controlled the Kuominchün (Nationalist army), one of the most powerful military forces in north China. In August an arrangement was worked out in Canton by Feng's representatives to enlist the Kuominchün into the National Revolutionary Army. Feng then left Moscow for home, and immediately after arriving in China in September he formally swore to an oath to support of the revolutionary cause.

Teng had been in Moscow while these intricate, maneuvers were taking place, but given his youthfulness and relative obscurity in the Communist movement, it is doubtful if he was involved in any direct fashion. It is equally doubtful, as claimed in one Communist account,[5] that he played a significant role in getting Feng to swear his allegiance to the revolutionary cause. Nonetheless, having returned to China at approximately the same time as Feng, he was among the many young CCP members assigned to work with the Kuominchün. Most of them worked in the Kuominchün's Political Department or in the newly established Chung Shan (Sun Yat-sen) Military and Political Academy in Sian. In the words of Feng's biographer, "most of the teachers . . . [at the academy] were Communists," and the "school poured out a stream of political officers."[6] Teng served in the Political Department and he also taught at the school. Among his colleagues were Liu Chih-tan (q.v.) and Liu Po-chien. (The latter, like Teng, studied in both France and Moscow; in the early 1930's he headed an army corps' political department in the First Front Army led by Chu Te, and he continued to be a Red Army political officer until his death in early 1935.) Kao Kang and Hsi Chung-hsun (qq.v.) were among the academy students,[7] and Wei Kung-chih, who later married the important Communist military commander Yeh Chien-ying (q.v.), worked in the Political Department.

Feng Yü-hsiang's willingness to have Communist cadres within his organization came to an abrupt halt in mid-1927 when, like both the right and left wings of the KMT, he purged all Communists from his ranks. As a consequence Teng went to Shanghai where for the next two years he worked in the Party apparatus. By the late 1920's Li Li-san (q.v.) had emerged as the dominant leader of the CCP, and as part of his grand scheme to mobilize Communist units in rural areas, he sent cadres to these areas to gain their allegiance and to assist in strengthening military forces. Teng was sent to Kwangsi in mid-1929 where the Kwangsi Communist Wei Pa-ch'ün had been attempting to develop armed units and soviet bases.

In December 1929 Teng and his colleagues, including Chang Yun-i (q.v.), established the Seventh Red Army and the Yu Chiang (Right River) Soviet in the vicinity of Pai-se.[8] Teng became the army political commissar as well as secretary of the army's front-line committee. (Some sources dispute the Communists' assertion that Teng was the political commissar.) Not long after this, in early 1930, an uprising of KMT troops led to the formation of the Eighth Red Army and the Tso Chiang (Left River) Soviet. However, this soviet was soon crushed, and the remnants from the Eighth Army retreated to the Pai-se area where they were merged into the Seventh Army. In describing these events to Edgar Snow, Teng mentioned that the Communists in Kwangsi "had relations with the Annamite rebels who began the worker-peasant rebellion in 1930" and that French airplanes had bombed areas where Teng was working.[9] These "Annamite rebels" were apparently the members of the Vietnamese Nationalist Party who, in February 1930, sparked an anti-French rebellion, and many of whom, after the revolt was crushed, fled northward into China. These ties with Vietnamese are noteworthy if only because so few Chinese Communist sources make any mention of Vietnam, despite its proximity.

The efforts of the Communists to establish a viable military base in Kwangsi, described at greater length in the biography of Chang Yun-i, were marginal at best. At some time in the early months of 1930 Teng went to Shanghai to report on the situation, and then in the summer he returned to Kwangsi in hopes of moving the troops northward to assist in Li Li-san's plans to assault the Yangtze Valley cities. The march north was begun immediately, but en route the army suffered heavy losses. Moreover, the attacks by the main Red Army units on Changsha and other cities (see under P'eng Te-huai) had already failed before the Seventh Army could reach these areas, and as a consequence the Seventh Army headed for Kiangsi where it was incorporated into forces led by Mao Tse-tung, Chu Te, P'eng Te-huai, and Fang Chih-min. One unit of the Seventh Army, the 21st Division led by Wei Pa-ch'ün, remained in Kwangsi to wage guerrilla warfare; it was ultimately crushed and Wei lost his life in October 1932.

By October 1930 Teng was in Kiangsi where he had been made chief-of-staff in the Third Army Corps of P'eng Te-huai,[10] one of the main elements in the First Front Army. In the early summer of the next year, not long after the Communists had repelled the KMT's Second Annihilation Campaign, Teng was still with P'eng, who was then in command of his corps in the Hsing-kuo hsien area of central Kiangsi.[11] Sometime in the same year Teng was posted to Juichin, the Communist capital, and there he edited a Red Army newspaper. In the early months of 1933 Teng was among those who came under severe attack as supporters of Lo Ming (q.v.).[12] Lo, a Communist official in Fukien, was accused by the Russian-returned student faction led by Ch'in Pang-hsien of fostering defeatist policies in face of the continuing attacks by the Nationalists on the Communist strongholds. Like many others accused of following the so-called Lo Ming line, Teng was soon restored to duty, and in the latter part of 1933 he was lecturing on Party history at the Red Army Academy in Juichin.[13]

Teng was with the Red Army troops which evacuated the Kiangsi base in the fall of 1934 to make the Long March to north Shensi. He probably made the march as director of the Political Department of the First Army Corps, but when Edgar Snow interviewed him in mid-1936 in Kansu, Teng had been elevated to the post of deputy political commissar. The corps was then led by Lin Piao, the commander, and Nieh Jung-chen, the political commissar. When war with Japan broke out in mid-1937, the Communists reorganized their forces into the Eighth Route Army. In the early weeks of the war Teng was in northeast Shansi, which was then the temporary locale of the army headquarters. Journalist Agnes Smedley, who was with the Eighth Route Army for several months early in the war, saw Teng there, identifying him as the assistant to Jen Pi-shih, the director of the General Political Department.[14] Soon afterwards, however, Teng became political commissar of the 129th division, one of the three major components of the Eighth Route Army. The division was led by Liu Po-ch'eng (q.v.), a man with whom Teng would be closely associated for the next decade and a half. The 129th Division operated for much of the war in the T'ai-hang Mountains on the Shansi-Hopeh border, and it was the mainstay force for the Communists' Shansi-Hopeh-Shantung-Honan Border Region. U.S. Military Observer Evans Carlson met Teng, then on an inspection tour, in Nan-kung, south Hopeh, in the spring of 1938. Carlson held lengthy talks with Teng, whom he described as "short, chunky and physically tough," and with a mind "as keen as mustard." The American also wrote that "one afternoon we went over the entire field of international politics, and I was astonished at the extent of his information."[15]

Teng continued throughout the war as political commissar of the 129th Division, the history of which is contained in the biography of Liu Po-ch'eng. Despite Teng's political prominence after 1949, the voluminous Communist accounts of the war years published during the 1950's contain very few references to his work then. During the war he was a fairly frequent contributor to Party and Eighth Route Army publications, such as Chieh-fang (Liberation) in Yenan and Ch'ün-chung (The masses) in Chungking. The latter publication, on January 11, 1944, published a report by Teng on economic conditions in the T'ai-hang region. This report, which stressed the necessity of economic self-sufficiency, appears in an English translation in Stuart Gelder's study of the wartime Communist movement.[16]

The CCP held the Seventh National Congress in Yenan from April to June 1945. Like most of the principal Eighth Route Army and New Fourth Army officers, Teng was elected a member of the Central Committee, very probably in absentia. For about a year after the end of the war, the troops led by Liu Po-ch'eng in the Shansi-Hopeh-Shantung-Honan Border Region saw relatively little action. Rather, this period was characterized by a strengthening of these forces and tactical maneuverings designed to prepare them for the coming battles with the KMT armies. This border area was of vital significance because it was astride key north-south and east-west communications, particularly the rail lines. Throughout this period Teng was constantly with Liu Po-ch'eng, whose biography contains details about the numerous battles fought from mid-1946 through 1949. Other prominent Communist officials who made up the hierarchy of the Shansi-Hopeh-Shantung-Honan Military Region included deputy commanders T'eng Tai-yuan and Wang Hung-k'un (qq.v.) and deputy political commissars Po I-po and Chang Chi-ch'un (qq.v.). Of the many encounters with the Nationalists, none was more important than the Huai–Hai campaign, a series of battles that lasted from November 1948 to January 1949. To coordinate the strategy of the participating Communist armies, the CCP military high command set up a special General Front Committee of five members. Liu and Teng represented their units and Ch'en I, Su Yü, and T'an Chen-lin (qq.v.) represented the East China Field Army. Teng had the distinction of being secretary of the committee.[17] After mauling the Nationalist armies in the Huai–Hai battles, the Liu–Teng columns, now known as the Second Field Army, pushed southward and defeated enemy troops on a wide front along the Yangtze River. After these victories in the spring of 1949, the final conquest of south and southwest China was only a matter of time.

During a lull in the fighting, Liu and Teng went to Peking for the inauguration of the central government in the fall of 1949. At the end of September Teng was appointed a member of the National Committee of the CPPCC, the organization which formally brought the new government into existence on October 1. He was also made a member of two of the highest organs of state, the Central People's Government Council and the People's Revolutionary Military Council, both of which were chaired by Mao Tse-tung until they went out of existence when the central government was reorganized in September 1954. In addition, from October 1949 to December 1954, Teng was a member of the executive board of the Sino-Soviet Friendship Association. Like many of the key regional leaders then in Peking, Teng soon returned to his military units which were poised for the final campaigns against the KMT armies.

In the last two months of 1949, the Second Field Army pushed into Szechwan, Kweichow, Sikang, and Yunnan, in operations coordinated with elements of the First Field Army led by Ho Lung (q.v.). This four-province area formed the new base for the Second Field Army (and the Southwest Military Region), the Party's Southwest Bureau, and the Southwest Military and Administrative Committee (SWMAC). Military and political authority was divided roughly between the three top leaders in this area—Teng, Liu, and Ho. Liu continued to command the Second Field Army and Ho commanded the military region. Teng was political commissar of both the army and the military region, as well as the ranking secretary of the CCP Bureau. The last major step in the consolidation of Communist authority in the southwest took place in July 1950 with the inauguration of the SWMAC. Liu was named chairman, and Teng and Ho were made vice-chairmen. In addition, Teng was given the chairmanship of the SWMAC's Finance and Economics Committee.

The authoritative *Hsin-hua yueh-pao* (issues of April 15, May 15, and October 15, 1950) carried three reports and articles by Teng, which are among the more useful sources of information on conditions in the southwest during the takeover period. The second of these was a report Teng gave in Peking when he returned there for a session of the Central People's Government Council (on April 11). He was back in Peking in February 1951 to give another report on the southwest, but except for these two occasions he appears to have spent most of his time in Chungking from the end of 1949 to mid-1952. In January 1953 the Liu–Teng–Ho threesome was re-elected to their respective posts on the Southwest Administrative Committee (the successor body of the SWMAC), and they continued to hold these positions until the multi-provincial administrations were dissolved in 1954. In fact, however, Liu had already left the area by 1951, and only Ho Lung was in the southwest with any regularity in 1953–54.

In mid-1952 Teng was transferred to Peking, and within the space of a few short years he emerged as one of the towering political figures in China. The first of his many new appointments came in August when he became a vice-premier of Chou En-lai's Government Administration Council (the cabinet). From the establishment of the PRC to the reorganization of the national government in September 1954, Teng was the only vice-premier added to the original four (Ch'en Yun, Tung Pi-wu, Kuo Mo-jo [qq.v.], and Huang Yen-p'ei). In November 1952, in preparation for the inauguration of the First Five-Year Plan (1953–1957), the State Planning Commission was set up under the chairmanship of the ill-fated Kao Kang (q.v.). Teng was appointed one of the 15 members, a post he held until 1954.

Throughout 1953 and the first half of 1954, many of the highest leaders of state were involved in the preparations to convene a national legislative body. This work was carried out by three new committees, one to draft an election law, another to draft a constitution, and a third to supervise nationwide elections. The importance of these committees established in early 1953 can be judged in part from the fact that each was chaired by one of Peking's three most important leaders: Mao Tse-tung, Liu Shao-ch'i, and Chou En-lai. Significantly, only Teng was a member of all three bodies (and he was concurrently secretary-general of the last mentioned). Moreover, he seems to have been the driving force behind the three committees; for example, Teng delivered the explanatory report on the Election Law in February, just three weeks before it was promulgated, and in September 1953 and again in April 1954, he delivered progress reports on the program to hold elections.

In the meantime, Teng was steadily rising in the national hierarchy. Already a member of the CPPCC National Committee, he was elevated to membership on the Standing Committee in February 1953. Dating from approximately this same period, Teng began to make regular public appearances with Mao and the other top Party and government leaders and to deliver reports at national conferences. For example, he spoke before the Second National Supervision Work Conference in February 1953 and the National Communications Conference in August of the same year. He added to his positions in September 1953 when he replaced Po I-po (q.v.) as head of the Finance Ministry and he also became a new vice-chairman of the central government's Finance and Economics Committee. In November 1953, Teng was part of the six-man group headed by Chou En-lai which negotiated a highly important agreement with the North Koreans. This provided for grants to Korea of approximately $340,000,000 to assist in reconstruction work in the wake of the Korean War, which had ended shortly before this. Teng delivered the draft report on the budget for 1954 on June 16, 1954. Three days later he was succeeded by Li Hsien-nien (q.v.) as minister of Finance, and at the same time he was removed as a vice-chairman of the Finance and Economics Committee.

Teng's removal from two important economic posts might have suggested a significant decline in his political fortunes. However, shortly before, in May 1954, he was identified as secretary-general (*pi-shu-chang*) of the CCP Central Committee. Many secondary sources have suggested that Teng replaced Liu Shao-ch'i, but in the absence of specific identifications of this post in the Chinese press it must be assumed that it was a newly activated position. The post is known to have existed from the 1920's (see under K'o Ch'ing-shih and Wang Jo-fei), but it was apparently abandoned sometime in the 1940's. In any case, as of 1954, the Party secretary-general seems to have been in charge of the various organs subordinate to the Central Committee, for example, the Organization and Propaganda Departments.

Liu Shao-ch'i, addressing the Party's Fourth Plenum in February 1954, mentioned "certain high-ranking" but unnamed men who were attempting to carve out "independent kingdoms." It was soon after this, as already noted, that Teng was identified as the Party secretary-general. Then, in March 1955, the CCP convened a national conference. Teng delivered one of the two major reports, a denunciation of an alleged "anti-Party bloc" led by Politburo member Kao Kang and Organization Department director Jao Shu-shih. Teng's report was not published, but the resolution on the "anti-Party bloc" was presumably a summation of his remarks. The purge of Kao and Jao, the most celebrated affair of its kind in the first decade and a half of the PRC, is described in detail in their biographies. The fact that Teng was selected to deliver the denunciatory report suggests that he played a major role in the downfall of Kao and Jao. In any event, a few days later (April 4), Teng was elevated to membership on the Politburo at the Party's Fifth Plenum. (Lin Piao was also elected to the Politburo on this occasion, but there does not seem to be any link between Lin and the Kao–Jao case.)

In the meantime, the plans to hold national elections and to convene a national legislature culminated in September 1954 with the convocation of the First NPC. In the reorganized central government, Teng was reappointed a vice-premier under Chou En-lai, and he was also made one of the 15 vice-chairmen of the National Defense Council. (He was re-elected to both posts in April 1959 and January 1965.) Coinciding with the First NPC meeting, Soviet leader Nikita Khrushchev arrived in China for high-level talks. Teng was a member of the six-man group, headed by Chou En-lai, which negotiated a series of agreements. One of these provided for large amounts of Soviet economic assistance to China, but others—such as the withdrawal of Soviet troops from Port Arthur and the dissolution of Soviet interests in joint-stock companies in Sinkiang—had the broad effect of placing China on par with the Soviet Union in terms of the Sino-Soviet alliance. Not long afterwards, in December 1954, Teng was named a Standing Committee member of the Second CPPCC, a position he held until the Third CPPCC was inaugurated in April 1959.

Until the mid-1950's relatively few foreign Communist party leaders visited Peking. But after this period, presumably as a reflection of the growing Chinese independence from Moscow, more and more foreign Communist party leaders visited China. This situation naturally called for high-level Chinese leaders to participate in talks with these visitors. Within a brief period it became apparent that Teng was among those who took part in these talks most frequently, often in conjunction with Liu Shao-ch'i, Wu Hsiu-ch'üan, and Yang Shang-k'un (qq.v.). In this connection, therefore, Teng was a logical person to attend the historic 20th CPSU Congress when it was held in Moscow in February 1956. Chu Te led the delegation and

Teng was the number two man at the proceedings which heard Khrushchev's famous denunciation of Stalin and the worst trappings of Stalinism. Not long before this, at the CCP's Sixth Plenum in October 1955, Teng had spoken on the question of convening the Eighth National Congress. His plenum speech is not available, but in view of his role at the Congress, convened in September 1956, it appears that he was in charge of the preparations.

Teng's meteoric rise in the CCP hierarchy was reconfirmed on the very day the Party convened its Eighth National Congress in mid-September 1956. He was selected to be one of the 13 members of the congress presidium, as well as secretary-general of the congress secretariat. Liu Shao-ch'i gave the most important speech, the political work report, and Teng was given the task of delivering the second most important address. This dealt with revisions to the Party Constitution, and the importance of collective leadership and Party discipline. It is easily one of the most important documents on the inner workings of the CCP and is frequently cited by analysts of the Communist movement. At the close of the congress Teng was re-elected to the Central Committee. On the next day, at the First Plenum of the new Central Committee, he was re-elected to the Politburo. Under the new constitution, the Standing Committee replaced, in effect, the "old" Secretariat as the highest body in the CCP. Headed by Mao, the Standing Committee included only Liu Shao-ch'i, Chou En-lai, Chu Te, Ch'en Yun, and Teng. He was also elected the ranking secretary of the "new" Secretariat, responsible for the day-to-day implementation of Politburo policies. It is noteworthy that Teng was the only man named to both the Politburo Standing Committee and the Secretariat. Finally, he was also elected general secretary (*tsung shu-chi*) of the Central Committee. (The post of general secretary was apparently a redesignation of Teng's previously held post of secretary-general; in any case, the latter ceased to exist as of this time.)

Teng's speech at the Eighth Party Congress was paralleled in importance by his report to the Third Plenum in September 1957. This report on the "rectification" campaign was delivered only a few months after the CCP had launched "anti-rightist" attacks against those who, during the famous Hundred Flowers movement, had criticized many shortcomings within the CCP. Teng's report was a response to this criticism, but it also outlined in detail a number of steps the Party needed to make to improve its work. For example, he called for the training of "revolutionary experts," who, he said, must be both "red" and "expert." He also stressed the need for retrenchment within the bureaucracy and the decentralization of many functions carried out by the Party and govern-

ment. Six weeks later, in early November, Teng left for Moscow as a member of Mao Tse-tung's delegation to the celebrations marking the 40th anniversary of the Russian Revolution. More important, however, they took part in two Communist "summit" meetings, one consisting of leaders from 12 Communist nations and the other of leaders from 64 Communist parties throughout the world. In May 1958, at the second session of the Eighth Party Congress, Teng delivered a report on these meetings. To judge from the published summary of his report, as well as from accounts in Communist media throughout the world, it appeared then that the Communist world was firmly united. Later, however, when the Sino-Soviet dispute of the 1960's brought forth many disclosures about inter-Communist party relations, it was revealed that the November 1957 meetings represented an important turning point in the deterioration of Sino-Soviet relations.

In May 1958 Teng's stature within the ruling elite was further enhanced when he was cited in the press as one of Mao Tse-tung's "close comrades-in-arms." As of that period this accolade was reserved for the select few; in this instance the only others so designated were Liu Shao-ch'i, Chou En-lai, Chu Te, and Ch'en Yun. A few weeks later Teng was elected a Szechwan deputy to the Second NPC, which opened its inaugural session in April 1959. (In 1964 he was elected to the Third NPC, but this time as a deputy from Peking.) By mid-1958 the movement to set up people's communes throughout China was under way. Presumably to check on the progress of this important campaign, several of Peking's top leaders were dispatched to various locales to make first-hand inspections. Teng spent most of the period from September to November touring Manchuria, north China, and south China. Then, in late November and early December he attended the Party's Sixth Plenum in Wuhan, the meeting which cut back the pace of the commune movement. Teng's name is not linked so closely with the Great Leap Forward and the people's communes as many other top Peking leaders, but he did write a spirited defense of these programs in 1959 when it was already evident that they had run into trouble. This article, written for the October 1, 1959, issue of *Pravda*, was published in the *JMJP* on the following day. It was also reprinted in a collection of articles written to commemorate the 10th anniversary of the PRC.[18]

As noted above, beginning in the mid-fifties Teng spent a considerable amount of time conferring with visiting leaders of foreign Communist parties. This work was occupying even more of his time by the late fifties. For example, from February to April 1959 the majority of press reports of Teng's activities were in connection with the many Communist party leaders who visited China after the 21st CPSU Congress in Moscow. In this same connection, Teng was selected to be deputy leader under Liu Shao-ch'i to attend the celebrations commemorating the 43rd anniversary of the Russian Revolution in November 1960. Once again, as in the case of the 1957 delegation to Moscow led by Mao, the celebrations were secondary in contrast to the convocation of another world Communist "summit" meeting. And, still again, it was not until later years that the outside world learned that the 1960 meetings had been characterized by bitter controversy between the Russians and Chinese regarding international Communist policies—in particular, attitudes toward the sponsorship of wars of "national liberation." Two years later, in a pamphlet published by the French Communist Party, French Communist leader Maurice Thorez (who supported Khrushchev in the dispute) attacked Teng by name for stubbornly espousing a "leftist" and "erroneous" line.[19] Once again it fell to Teng to deliver the report on the "summit" meeting, this time in January 1961 when the CCP held its Ninth Plenum. It is also noteworthy that Teng was the only member of the Politburo Standing Committee who attended both the 1957 and the 1960 meetings.

In July 1961 Teng was one of the Chinese negotiators in the talks with Korean Communist leader Kim Il Sung, which led to the signing of the Sino-Korean Treaty of Friendship, Cooperation, and Mutual Assistance. It appears that this treaty was concluded by the Chinese in an effort to gain the allegiance of the Koreans in the Sino-Soviet dispute, which was now becoming more obvious to the outside world. A few weeks later, in September, Teng led the CCP delegation to the Fourth Congress of the Korean Workers' (Communist) Party. The Chinese delegation emphasized the need for "just wars" of "national liberation" and in general espoused a more bellicose position than the Soviet delegation led by F. R. Kozlov. The Sino-Soviet dispute rose to a new peak of intensity in 1962–63. The Chinese were clearly disturbed with what they regarded as Soviet capitulation to the United States during the famous Cuban missile crisis, as well as by Moscow's failure to support Peking during the brief Sino-Indian border war in the fall of 1962. In the early months of 1963 the most senior Chinese leaders met with the Soviet ambassador in Peking regarding Moscow–Peking disputes. On March 9 Teng informed the ambassador that the Chinese would agree to hold talks "on important questions concerning the international Communist movement." The jockeying continued a few more weeks until Chou En-lai informed the Russians that Teng would visit Moscow for the talks.

On July 5 Teng left Peking for Moscow. From the outset, it was clear that the once vaunted Sino-Soviet alliance was nearing a state of open rupture. Teng had been given an unprecedented send-off—practically every Chinese leader of note in Peking was at the airport to bid him farewell, and his departure was given top billing in the Chinese press. Teng's delegation consisted of P'eng Chen (the deputy leader), K'ang Sheng, Yang Shang-k'un, Liu Ning-i, Wu Hsiu-ch'üan, and P'an Tzu-li (the ambassador in Moscow). As indicated in the biographies of these men, all of them except Ambassador P'an Tzu-li had been involved in bitter verbal exchanges with Soviet party leaders on previous occasions. After two weeks of talks, which were led on the Soviet side by ideologue M. A. Suslov, a brief communiqué was issued. This revealed that neither side had moved from its position and that the dispute would continue, notwithstanding an agreement that the talks had only been recessed until "some" later date.

The welcome given Teng's delegation back in Peking paralleled the send-off two weeks earlier, and it was obviously intended to show the Russians that China stood united in its opposition to the CPSU. Further luster was added to Teng's image in December 1963 when he was designated acting premier in place of Chou En-lai when Chou left for a visit to the Middle East and Africa. Previously, the only man who had been officially named as acting premier was Ch'en Yun (in 1955 and 1956). Apart from Teng's foreign travels and his frequent contacts with foreign Communist leaders, he was reported on countless occasions in the press in connection with domestic events. Many of his appearances were simply matters of protocol, but on numerous occasions he was a featured speaker at conferences held by the Party, the government, the PLA, or the many "mass" organizations. He continued as a member of Peking's inner elite until the Great Proletarian Cultural Revolution was launched in 1966, but soon afterwards he became a frequent target of the Red Guard press, which alleged that he was a "collaborator" of Liu Shao-ch'i.

Teng is married to Cho Lin. She has not been politically active and has confined her public appearances to those ceremonial occasions when her husband met with foreign visitors who had been accompanied by their wives. A former minor PRC official who knew Teng claimed that he had two sons in Peking University in 1961.[20]

1. *Bol'shaya Sovetskaya Entsiklopedya* (Large Soviet encyclopedia; Moscow, 1958), LI, 109–110.

2. Information supplied by Dr. Conrad Brandt.

3. Edgar Snow, *Random Notes on Red China, 1936–1945* (Cambridge, Mass., 1957), p. 137.

4. *Ibid.*

5. Wu Min and Hsiao Feng, *Ts'ung "wu-szu" tao Chung-hua jen-min kung-ho-kuo te tan-sheng* (From "May Fourth" to the birth of the PRC; Peking, 1951), p. 64.

6. James E. Sheridan, *Chinese Warlord: The Career of Feng Yü-hsiang* (Stanford, Calif., 1966), p. 210.

7. Mark Selden, "The Guerrilla Movement in Northwest China," *The China Quarterly*, no. 28:66–67 (October–December 1966).

8. *SCMM* 285, pp. 33–40.

9. Snow, p. 138.

10. *Hung-ch'i p'iao-p'iao* (Red flag fluttering; Peking, 1959), X, 49–52.

11. *Ibid.*

12. Tso-liang Hsiao, *Power Relations within the Chinese Communist Movement, 1930–1934* (Seattle, 1961), p. 240; Harold R. Isaacs, *The Tragedy of the Chinese Revolution* (Stanford, Calif., 2nd rev. ed., 1961), pp. 347–348.

13. *Hung-ch'i p'iao-p'iao* (Peking, 1957), III, 46.

14. Agnes Smedley, *China Fights Back* (London, 1938), p. 85.

15. Evans Fordyce Carlson, *Twin Stars of China* (New York, 1940), pp. 249–252.

16. Stuart Gelder, *The Chinese Communists* (London, 1946), pp. 200–214.

17. *Selected Works of Mao Tse-tung* (Peking, 1961), IV, 339.

18. *Ten Glorious Years* (Peking, 1960), pp. 90–104.

19. *JPRS*, no. 17,772, February 21, 1963.

20. Interview with former PRC official, Hong Kong, June 1963.

Teng Hua

(1910–   ; Kuei-yang hsien, Hunan). Military leader; Korean War veteran; member, CCP Central Committee.

Teng Hua, a career Red Army officer, is a veteran of the Long March, the Sino-Japanese War, and the Korean War. One of the earliest soldiers of the Red Army, he has been a Party Central Committee member since 1956. He was the top PLA commander in Manchuria from 1955 to 1959 but since then has served in a minor political capacity in Szechwan. Teng's political decline was apparently linked with the fall of Politburo member P'eng Te-huai in 1959.

Teng is a native of Kuei-yang hsien in southern Hunan. Born in 1910 into a peasant family, he received only a primary school education. Teng joined the Communist movement in the late 1920's, and although the details are lacking it is evident that he was one of the early members of the Red Army. He may have been with Mao Tse-tung during the Autumn Harvest Uprisings among the Hunanese peasants in 1927 and then followed him to Chingkangshan and Juichin. However, another report states that he

participated in the P'ing-chiang Uprising in northeast Hunan led by P'eng Te-huai (q.v.) in mid-1928, and when P'eng formed his Fifth Red Army the day after the uprising, Teng was made chief-of-staff. By 1931 Teng was a student at a cadres' institute in Juichin, the capital of the central soviet region, and in the same year he was a regimental political commissar in the First Army Corps.

Teng served with the First Army Corps, led by Lin Piao and Nieh Jung-chen, during the Long March (1934–35). The Corps was one of the major components of Mao's First Front Army. By mid-1936 when Edgar Snow visited Communist-held areas in north Shensi, Teng was director of the Political Department of the First Army Corps' Second Division.[1] The division political commissar was then Hsiao Hua and Yang Te-chih was the commander (qq.v.). When the Eighth Route Army was organized in the late summer of 1937, Lin and Nieh were given command of the 115th Division. Teng led one of its units, which moved into the Shansi-Chahar-Hopeh Border Region. For a brief period in 1938 his unit was put under Ho Lung's 120th Division and was combined with forces led by Sung Shih-lun (q.v.). In the "Sung-Teng Detachment," as it is usually described in Communist sources, Sung was the commander and Teng was political commissar. In June they advanced into eastern Hopeh, which was an important communications link to Manchuria for the Japanese. This campaign and the subsequent establishment of the East Hopeh Administrative District are described in the biography of Sung. The main Sung-Teng forces were wiped out in the fall of 1938, but they managed to maintain a small guerrilla base throughout the war, which was particularly useful to the Communists in their struggle against the Nationalists after the war ended in 1945. Little information is available about Teng's wartime record after 1938, but he apparently continued to serve as a political officer with Communist guerrilla units in those portions of Hopeh closest to Manchuria.

When the war ended in the summer of 1945 Lin Piao was sent to Manchuria, where he established the Northeast Democratic Allied Army. Teng accompanied Lin to Manchuria and commanded the Seventh Column. Concurrently, in 1945 he was in command of the Liaohsi (provincial) Military District and was principal of the Liaohsi Military and Political School. In 1948, when the Communists were completing their conquest of Manchuria, Teng assumed command of the 15th Army Corps. He continued in this capacity when Tientsin and Peking fell in January 1949, by which time Lin's forces were known as the Fourth Field Army.

Teng's positions during the next year and a half indicate the course of the Fourth Field Army's drive south. When Nanchang was captured in May 1949 he served briefly as a member of the Nanchang Military Control Commission, and after the fall of Canton in October Teng became commander of the city's garrison force, a post he retained until 1951. He was also made a member of both the Canton Military Control Commission headed by Yeh Chien-ying (q.v.) and the Executive Committee of the Sino-Soviet Friendship Association's Canton branch. At the provincial level he was made first deputy commander of the Kwangtung Military District (again serving under Yeh) and second deputy commander of the South China Military District, which controlled the provinces of Kwangsi and Kwangtung. In 1950 Teng relinquished his post as first deputy commander, but became a member of the Kwangtung Provincial People's Government Council set up on January 1, 1950, under Yeh Chien-ying. In late March he was appointed a member of the Central-South Military and Administrative Committee (CSMAC), the regional administration governing all of south China.

In addition to his administrative posts, Teng continued to command his 15th Army Corps and led the forces that captured Hainan Island in April 1950. This brief and successful campaign was historically important, for it completed the Communist conquest of China—excepting only Tibet, Taiwan, and a few offshore islands. After Hainan fell, Teng became chairman of both the Hainan Military Control Commission and the Hainan Military and Administrative Committee.

In 1951 Teng was transferred from south China to the war in Korea. He was removed from the CSMAC in June 1951 and, although he officially retained his membership on the Kwangtung Provincial People's Government Council until June 1954, he was not active in Kwangtung after 1951. Teng's assignment to Korea probably resulted from the fact that the major units of the "Chinese People's Volunteers" (CPV) in Korea were drawn from the Fourth Field Army, with which he had been associated since its establishment in the winter of 1948–49. Teng was first identified in Korea in July 1951 when he represented the CPV in the initial armistice talks, which began that month. He was replaced in this capacity in October, but by that time he was identified as the CPV deputy commander under Commander P'eng Te-huai. During the next two years Teng commanded elements of the CPV in various battles, and in gratitude for his service the North Korean Government awarded him its highest decoration in February 1953. Teng continued to serve as P'eng's deputy until September 1954 when he replaced him as the CPV commander. However, a month later he relinquished this post to Yang Te-chih (his colleague from the mid-1930's) and returned to Peking.

During his tour of duty in Korea, Teng became a member of both the CPPCC and the NPC. He had been in Korea only a short time when the third session of the CPPCC's First National Committee (October–November 1951) appointed him to fill out part of the First CPPCC term. Teng was not re-elected to the Second CPPCC, which opened in December 1954, but by that date he had already been named to represent the CPV in the more important legislative body, the NPC, which opened in September 1954. He served out his term in the First NPC (1954–1959) but was not re-elected to the Second NPC, which opened in April 1959. He was also made a member of the newly created National Defense Council in September 1954 and was reappointed in April 1959.

After being in Peking for about six months, Teng returned to Manchuria where by May 1955 he became commander of the Shenyang (Mukden) Military Region, which had military jurisdiction over the three Manchurian provinces of Liaoning, Kirin, and Heilungkiang. The same month he was acting chairman of the Chinese military delegation to the Joint Sino-Soviet Commission on the withdrawal of Soviet troops from Port Arthur. In September 1955 Teng attained his present military rank when officer ranks in the PLA were created and Teng was named a colonel general, the equivalent of a U.S. Army lieutenant general. At the same time military awards (the Orders of August First, Independence and Freedom, and Independence) were bestowed; Teng was among those decorated, but it was not indicated which one or ones he received. In September 1956, at the Eighth Party Congress, he was elected a full member of the Central Committee. The next month he led a military delegation to Yugoslavia (October–November 1956) and is thus one of the few PLA officers to have visited that country. When Soviet leader Voroshilov visited Shenyang in April 1957, Teng was on hand to welcome him. Then in October 1958 Teng was reported to have volunteered for service in the ranks in line with a campaign in which PLA officers were supposed to share the common soldier's life and thus learn the point of view of the rank and file.

Teng was last identified as the commander in Shenyang in April 1959 and by November he had been replaced by Ch'en Hsi-lien (q.v.). His activities received no notice from the Chinese press until May 1960 when he was elected a vice-governor of Szechwan—a post of far less significance than his commander's role in Manchuria. Since going to Szechwan Teng has seldom been mentioned in press reports. His fall from effective political power was emphasized by the fact that he was serving under Governor Li Ta-chang, who is only an alternate member of the Central Committee in contrast to Teng's full membership. Moreover, another alternate, Liao

Chih-kao, serves as one of the provincial Party secretaries, a post apparently denied to Teng. Speculation concerning Teng's political stature received another fillip in January 1965 at the close of the first session of the Third NPC when Teng was not re-elected a member of the National Defense Council. The timing of his removal from his military post in Manchuria (1959) coincided with the political demise of P'eng Te-huai, with whom he was associated in Korea. Of course, P'eng was also officially removed from the National Defense Council in January 1965. Teng continues to hold his seat on the Central Committee, but since 1959 this seems to be largely nominal.

1. Edgar Snow, *Red Star over China* (New York, 1938), p. 453.

T'eng Tai-yuan

(1905–　　; Ma-yang, Hunan). Former Red Army political officer; former minister of Railways; member, CCP Central Committee.

A veteran political and staff officer of the Red Army, T'eng Tai-yuan was the minister of Railways for the first 15 years of the PRC. He has been a member of the Party Central Committee since 1945. T'eng was born in Ma-yang (now Chin-ho-chen), a small town in the mountainous and poorly developed part of west Hunan not far from the Kweichow border. He graduated from a provincial normal school in Changsha, the Hunan capital. He is said to have joined the Communist Youth League, which apparently paved the way for his admission into the CCP in 1926. Like so many Communists of that period, T'eng was also a KMT member.[1] In mid-1926 the Northern Expedition was launched from Kwangtung, and by the late summer all of Hunan had been conquered. To prepare the way for this famous expedition, both KMT and CCP organizers had been actively organizing peasant support. T'eng was involved in these endeavors, probably under the direction of Hsia Hsi (q.v.), an important Communist and also a key KMT figure in Hunan at this time. In any case, T'eng was an official in the Hunan Provincial Peasants' Association during the 1926–27 period. The relatively close KMT–CCP cooperation during the early stages of the Northern Expedition soon gave way to rapidly worsening relations, and in Hunan this culminated in the spring of 1927 when Hsia, T'eng, and Mao Tse-tung barely managed to escape arrest in Changsha (see under Hsia Hsi).[2]

The details of T'eng's career in the year after he fled Changsha are not known. However, it appears that he continued his work as a peasant organizer in and around Liu-yang and P'ingchiang in northeast Hunan (not far from Changsha). In any event, he was in the P'ing-chiang area in July 1928 when P'eng Te-huai and Huang Kung-lueh (qq.v.), then serving in the Nationalist Army, mutinied. This defection from the KMT ranks is known in orthodox Maoist accounts as the P'ing-chiang Uprising, which is credited to the work of P'eng, Huang, and T'eng. The rebels established the Fifth Red Army; P'eng was the commander and T'eng was the CCP representative (later redesignated political commissar). After some heavy fighting in the P'ingchiang area, Huang was left there with some 1,000 men, but P'eng and T'eng led most of the Fifth Army southward where late in 1928 they joined forces with Mao Tse-tung and Chu Te at Chingkangshan on the Hunan-Kiangsi border. This association between P'eng and T'eng lasted until about the beginning of the Long March in 1934.

During the next year and a half (from late 1928 to the spring of 1930), P'eng and T'eng campaigned in the Chingkangshan area, then in south Kiangsi, and then again in Chingkangshan. In the spring of 1930 they led the Fifth Red Army northward into south Hupeh.[3] This maneuver was part of the strategy of the then predominant CCP leader, Li Li-san (q.v.). Li's grand design was to capture the major industrial cities in the Yangtze Valley, and in this connection the P'eng-T'eng Fifth Army (augmented by guerrilla units recruited in the Hupeh-Hunan-Kiangsi border area) was redesignated the Third Army Corps. From south Hupeh, the Third Corps turned southward to attack Changsha in Hunan; the city fell in late July 1930 to the Communists, but after a few days they were forced out. A second attack on Changsha in early September, in which the P'eng-T'eng army was joined by troops led by Chu Te and Mao, proved as unsuccessful as the first. The defeated forces then made their way back to southeast Kiangsi.

There are relatively few references to T'eng from the end of 1930 to 1934 when the Communists began the Long March. However, it is clear that he continued to serve with P'eng Te-huai as political commissar of the Third Army Corps. He is known to have taken part in repulsing the Nationalists' First and Second Annihilation Campaigns from the end of 1930 to the spring of 1931 when the Third Corps fought in the Hsingkuo hsien area of central-south Kiangsi. At that time the important Communist Teng Hsiao-p'ing (q.v.) was chief-of-staff of the Third Corps.[4] Moreover, in the late fall of 1933, T'eng Tai-yuan was still the political commissar when the leading officers of the Third Corps were in Chienning hsien in west Fukien.[5] In the meantime, at the First All-China Congress of Soviets, held in Juichin in November 1931, the Chinese Soviet Republic had been established under the chairmanship of Mao Tse-tung. T'eng was elected a member of the Central Executive Committee (CEC), the leading organ of the Republic, and he was re-elected to the CEC at the Second Congress, held in January–February 1934.

T'eng continued to be P'eng Te-huai's chief political officer at least to the outset of the Long March, which began in October 1934. T'eng made the march to north Shensi, but his post with the Third Army Corps had been assumed by Yang Shang-k'un by early 1935, during the early part of the Long March. Soon after arriving in Shensi, T'eng was sent to the Soviet Union where he studied military affairs. He was back in China by 1937. Inferential evidence suggests that he returned home via Sinkiang province, because in the spring of that year he and Ch'en Yun were ordered by the Party Center to contact the remnant forces of the Long March column, originally led by Chang Kuo-t'ao (q.v.), which in a disastrous campaign in late 1936 and early 1937 had moved up the Kansu Corridor toward the Sinkiang border.[6] At the small town of Hsing-hsing-hsia on the Kansu-Sinkiang border, Ch'en and T'eng met these men and accompanied them back to Tihwa, the Sinkiang capital, and later that year made the long journey to Yenan.

After the beginning of the Sino-Japanese War in mid-1937, T'eng was assigned to the staff of the Eighth Route Army, which the Communists activated as soon as hostilities began. Under the army's command structure, Yeh Chien-ying (q.v.) was the chief-of-staff, but because Yeh spent most of the early war years in Nationalist-held areas serving as a liaison officer, his place was often taken by Tso Ch'üan (q.v.), who served as acting chief-of-staff. According to one Communist account,[7] T'eng was identified as chief-of-staff in 1938, but various other accounts mention him as acting chief-of-staff in the early war years. Still other reports suggest that he was chief-of-staff (by 1940) of the Party's Revolutionary Military Council. In any case, it is evident that T'eng was a top staff officer during the war years, part of which were spent in south Shansi where, about 1940, he headed a branch of the Anti-Japanese Military and Political Academy (K'ang-ta).

In view of T'eng's stature as a military officer, there is a surprising lack of information about his work during the later war years. One explanation may be that he spent a portion of this period in Sinkiang where, from the beginning of the war until 1942, the Communists had a mission attached to the headquarters of Sheng Shih-ts'ai, the warlord governor of the province. (The details about this uneasy alliance with Sheng are given in the biographies of Teng Fa and Ch'en T'an-ch'iu.) Among Sheng's papers is a letter dated February 4, 1942, allegedly written to him by Mao Tse-tung, which indicates that T'eng and Chou Hsiao-chou (q.v.) had been on some sort of liaison mission to Sheng's headquarters and had brought back to Mao, in late 1941, a letter from Sheng.[8]

T'eng had advanced to the higher echelons of the Party leadership by the time the CCP held its Seventh National Congress in Yenan from April to June 1945. He was elected to full membership on the Party Central Committee; he continues to hold this position, having been re-elected at the Party's Eighth Congress in 1956. By at least the close of the Sino-Japanese War he was assigned to the 129th Division (commanded by Liu Po-ch'eng) of the Eighth Route Army, the division that controlled the T'ai-yueh and the T'ai-hang mountain area of Shansi and the border area of Shansi, Hopeh, Shantung, and Honan provinces. T'eng's military exploits in September 1945 at a small town near Ch'ang-chih, south Shansi, are described in a volume of Communist reminiscences, which refer to him as the deputy commander of the 129th Division.[9]

In January 1946, under the terms of a cease-fire agreement worked out by U.S. Special Envoy George C. Marshall, an Executive Headquarters was established in Peking. The Americans, Chinese Nationalists, and Chinese Communists each had a delegation assigned to the headquarters. In the early months of 1946 T'eng served as a military adviser to Communist delegation chief Yeh Chien-ying (q.v.). However, it soon became apparent that the cease-fire was going to fail, and thus the Communists withdrew a number of their officers for reassignment elsewhere. T'eng went back to join Liu Po-ch'eng's forces, and by September 1946 he was identified as a deputy commander of the Shansi-Hopeh-Shantung-Honan Military Region.[10] Wang Hung-k'un (q.v.) was the other deputy commander, and both men served under Commander Liu Po-ch'eng and Political Commissar Teng Hsiao-p'ing. Concurrently, T'eng was also a deputy commander of the Shansi-Hopeh-Shantung-Honan PLA, the fighting arm of the Military Region; the exploits of this highly important army are reviewed in the biography of Liu Po-ch'eng.

As the Communist armies were sweeping to new victories in north China the first steps were taken in the spring and summer of 1948 to amalgamate the important political administrations of the border regions in this area, most notably the Shansi-Chahar-Hopeh and the Shansi-Hopeh-Shantung-Honan Border Region governments. This was climaxed in August 1948 when the North China Provisional People's Congress was convened in Hopeh, a congress attended by such important leaders as Nieh Jung-chen, Po I-po, Yang Hsiu-feng, and Sung Shao-wen (qq.v.), as well as T'eng who served on the congress presidium (steering committee). At the close of the congress, the North China People's Government (NCPG) was established under the chairmanship of Tung Pi-wu (q.v.), with T'eng named as one of the members of the government council. He held this post until the NCPG was dissolved in October 1949 when its functions were absorbed by the central PRC government, and during this same period (1948–49) he also assisted Commander Nieh Jung-chen as a deputy commander of the North China Military Region.

T'eng remained with the NCPG when it moved from its capital in Shihchiachuang in Hopeh to Peking in February 1949 shortly after the surrender of Peking by the Nationalists in January. There he took an active part in the preparations for the establishment of the central government as well as for a number of "people's" organizations. The first major step in the process of establishing the new government was the formation in June 1949 of a preparatory committee for the CPPCC, the body that was to bring the central government into existence in the fall of 1949. Because Liu Po-ch'eng was heavily engaged in fighting in central China, T'eng officially represented his erstwhile military chief in the work of the CPPCC preparatory committee, serving on an *ad hoc* committee established to draft the laws of the new government. And, when the First CPPCC was convened in September, T'eng attended as a representative of Liu Po-ch'eng's Second Field Army. T'eng also took part in the formation of the Sino-Soviet Friendship Association (SSFA), one of the most active of the "people's" organizations in the early days of the PRC; he was a member of the preparatory committee set up in July 1949, and when the SSFA was formally established in October he served on the Executive Board (until 1954).

When the new central government was staffed in October 1949, T'eng was appointed as a member of the Government Administration Council (GAC), the cabinet-like organ that originally consisted of Premier Chou En-lai, four vice-premiers, and 15 members. Under the GAC were four major committees; T'eng was named as a member of the Finance and Economics Committee, chaired by top Party economic specialist Ch'en Yun. Yet these appointments to both the central government and "people's" organization were subsidiary to T'eng's work in the reconstruction of China's badly battered railway system. The gargantuan task of rebuilding the rail network underwent a series of steps, the first of which occurred in May 1949 when the Communists formed the PLA Railway Corps, mainly by drawing on the troops and specialists from the railway column of Lin Piao's Fourth Field Army. (The men formerly under Lin's command had had an opportunity to gain extensive experience in railway management and construction work during their days in Manchuria in the late forties.) T'eng was named as the commander of the Railway Corps, a post he was to hold until 1954. His deputy commander was Lü Cheng-ts'ao (q.v.) from Lin's Manchurian army; over the next decade T'eng and Lü worked closely together in railway affairs.

The second major step in the revitalization of the railway network was the organization of the railroad workers into a nationwide union. T'eng attended the provisional congress of the China Railway Workers' Trade Union in July 1949; he spoke on the accomplishments in reconstruction and outlined future tasks. He was also named to the standing committee of the preparatory committee, and when the union was formally organized in February 1950, T'eng was placed on the Standing Committee, a position he may still hold. His predominance in the field of railway work was given its most formal expression in October 1949 when (together with his other appointments in the central government) he was named to head the Ministry of Railways, a post he was to hold for over 15 years.

Unlike many top Party leaders who had a number of diversified duties, T'eng's work in the first decade of the PRC was devoted almost exclusively to the tasks of railway reconstruction. Often in the company of Lü Cheng-ts'ao, his most important assistant, T'eng attended virtually all the many conferences devoted to railway work in the 1950's and in most cases gave the keynote address. To cite two random but typical examples, he spoke at the National Railway Public Security Conference in March 1950 and the first National Railway Model Workers' Congress in September 1951. Similarly, he was often present when new rail lines were opened up or important administrative changes were made in railway administration; an example of the latter occurred in December 1952 when he accompanied Chou En-lai to Harbin to attend the ceremonies marking the transfer to China from the Soviet Union of exclusive rights to administer the important Chinese Changchun Railway (as provided for in a September 1952 agreement with the USSR signed in Moscow). T'eng was also the chief spokesman regarding railway work before governmental organizations, particularly in the early and mid-fifties; from 1950 to 1954, for example, he gave six progress reports on railway construction before meetings of the GAC. He also served the interests of the Ministry of Railways when, in December 1951, he was named as a member of a committee headed by economic specialist Po I-po to enforce a nationwide economic austerity program.

T'eng's work in railroad affairs also extended to travels abroad. From 1953 to 1958 he led four delegations to Communist nations in connection with railway work, and he was also a member of a delegation led by Chu Te to North Korea in August 1955 to participate in the celebrations marking the 10th anniversary of the "liberation" of Korea by the Soviet Union. His first trip was to Moscow in August 1953 to participate in the "All-Union Railwaymen's Day." In the last days of 1955 and early January 1956 he was in Mongolia for the ceremonies held in connection with the opening of the Tsining (Chi-ning)–Ulan Bator Railway, the first direct rail route between China proper and Mongolia. In July 1956 he led a delegation to Poland, where he attended the "Railway Transport Conference of the Socialist Countries," after which he briefly visited East Germany. Two years later (July–August 1958) he led another delegation to Hungary and East Germany.

When the constitutional government was inaugurated at the First NPC in September 1954, T'eng was reappointed as minister of Railways and was also named to membership on the new, but largely impotent, military advisory organ, the National Defense Council. Not long after, when the Second National Committee of the CPPCC was formed (December 1954), T'eng was named to the committee as a representative of the CCP. He was subsequently named again as a Party representative to the Third CPPCC (1959–1964) and to the Fourth National Committee, and at the close of the latter's first session in January 1965 he was elevated to a vice-chairmanship. As already noted, T'eng was elected to the Eighth Central Committee at the Party's Eighth Congress in September 1956. Speaking before the congress on the developments of railways, the picture he painted was largely optimistic, although he admitted that his ministry had been guilty of certain shortcomings due to bureaucracy. T'eng made a few more appearances in the 1957–1959 period; for example, he attended the opening in Wuhan of the Yangtze River Bridge in May 1957 and two months later he spoke at a session of the First NPC. And, as already mentioned, he visited East Europe in mid-1958. After this, however, his appearances became less and less frequent. Between his attendance at an October 1959 conference of "advanced" workers and September 1962 when he received a visiting Korean railway delegation, it appears that he was almost completely inactive. Moreover, during approximately this same period —and extending through 1964—Vice-minister of Railways Lü Cheng-ts'ao served as the acting minister. It may also be significant that the lessening of T'eng's activities coincided with the political fall of Marshal P'eng Te-huai (q.v.) in the early fall of 1959. (As described above P'eng and T'eng had been close associates as early as 1928.) Further light was shed on T'eng's status in the Party when the Third NPC and the Fourth CPPCC both met in December 1964–January 1965. At that time he was reappointed as a member of the rather unimportant National Defense Council and was also made (as already noted) a vice-chairman of the CPPCC. Far more important, however, he was replaced in the Railway Ministry by his long-time assistant, Lü Cheng-ts'ao. The fact that T'eng

made an appearance at at least one session of the CPPCC at this time seems to eliminate the possibility that his political decline was due solely to poor health. The few times that he has been mentioned in the Party press since his removal as minister of Railways have been largely ceremonial—such as his membership on funeral committees. In short, it seems that T'eng Tai-yuan's career as an important Party leader came to a close in the late 1950's and that the positions he retains are largely nominal.

T'eng's speeches and writings form an important body of information on the development of China's rail network. The more useful of these appeared in the following sources: *Hsin-hua yueh-pao* (New China monthly), vol. 1, no. 2, December 15, 1949, pp. 432–433; *JMJP*, February 10, 1950; *People's China*, no. 23, December 1, 1952, pp. 5–8; Hong Kong, *Ta-kung pao*, October 1, 1958.

1. The China Weekly Review, *Who's Who in China* (Shanghai, 1950), p. 195.
2. Jerome Ch'en, *Mao and the Chinese Revolution* (London, 1965), pp. 115–116.
3. Wu Min and Hsiao Feng, *Tsung "wu-szu" tao Chung-hua jen-min kung-ho-kuo te tan-sheng* (From "May Fourth" to the birth of the PRC; Peking, 1951), p. 99.
4. *Hung-ch'i p'iao-p'iao* (Red flag fluttering; Peking, 1959), X, 49–52.
5. *Kuang-ming jih-pao*, January 23, 1959.
6. *Hung-ch'i p'iao-p'iao* (Peking, 1959), X, 106–111.
7. *Ibid.*, (Peking, 1957), V, 245.
8. Allen S. Whiting and Sheng Shih-ts'ai, *Sinkiang: Pawn or Pivot?* (East Lansing, Mich., 1958), p. 231.
9. *The Great Turning Point* (Peking, 1962), p. 42.
10. *Jen-min te chün-tui* (The people's military forces), September 15, 1946 (a newspaper published by the Political Department of the Shansi-Hopeh-Shantung-Honan Military Region).

Teng T'o

(c.1911–   ; Shantung). Managing Director, *Jen-min jih-pao;* alternate secretary, North China Bureau, CCP.

Teng T'o has devoted the major portion of his career in the Chinese Communist movement to the field of journalism. He must have had some journalistic experience prior to 1938, because in that year he was already the editor of the *K'ang-ti pao* (Resistance news), the Party newspaper of the Chin-Ch'a-Chi (Shansi-Chahar-Hopeh) Border Region.[1] The Chin-Ch'a-Chi Border Region (see under Sung Shao-wen) had been formed in early 1938; ostensibly, it was headed by non-Communist Sung Shao-wen, but within the government and Party structure in this region were such stalwart Party leaders as Lin Piao and Nieh Jung-chen. Teng's stature was such that he was a member of the Party Committee for Chin-Ch'a-Chi,[2] although it is not clear how long he held this post. He was known, however, to have been in the Chin-Ch'a-Chi Border Region as late as May 1944, at which time he spoke before a meeting of news workers convened by the Regional Propaganda Department.[3]

Sometime during the latter part of the Sino-Japanese War Teng was transferred from Chin-Ch'a-Chi to Chungking where he worked on the Party paper in that city, the *Hsin-hua jih-pao* (New China daily). When the cease-fire agreement between the KMT and the CCP completely collapsed in early 1947, this newspaper was, of course, closed down and all personnel were evacuated to Yenan or other areas held by the Communists. Although no details are available, it is evident that Teng continued in journalism in the late 1940's, because in July 1949 he was named to the Preparatory Committee of the All-China Journalists' Association (ACJA). Five years later, when the ACJA was organized on a permanent basis (September 1954), Teng replaced Party propagandist Hu Ch'iao-mu (q.v.), who had headed the Preparatory Committee.

Another post that Teng assumed in mid-1949 was membership on the Higher Education Committee of the North China People's Government, the temporary governmental body that ruled the Communist-held portions of north China from its formation in August 1948 until October 1949, when its functions were assumed by the central government. One of the Party founders, Tung Pi-wu, headed this government and he also chaired the Higher Education Committee, which was formed in June 1949. This post in the field of education was the first of several that Teng T'o would hold in the years ahead.

In September 1949, Teng attended the first session of the CPPCC as a representative of the Journalists' Association, although he was not named to the permanent National Committee of the CPPCC. In October 1949 he became a member of the Peking branch of the Sino-Soviet Friendship Association. However, these activities were clearly peripheral to Teng's major assignment as a journalist. By 1950 he was serving as deputy managing director of the *JMJP*, and then in 1952 he assumed the concurrent post of editor-in-chief. Also in 1950 Teng became a regular contributor to *Hsueh-hsi* (Study), the most important Party theoretical journal until it was supplanted by *Hung-ch'i* (Red flag) in 1958. While *Hsueh-hsi* existed—and particularly in the 1950–51 period—Teng was one of the most regular contributors.

He assumed a variety of other positions in the early and mid-1950's. From 1951 to 1953 he served as head of the Propaganda Department of the Peking CCP Committee and was particularly active, while holding this post, in the campaign to promote the ideological "reformation" of intellectuals in Peking and Tientsin. From its formation in May 1952 (to the present), Teng has served on the Standing Committee of the China-India Friendship Association, and in 1953–54 he served as a member of the national committee to implement the Marriage Law. In 1954 he was named to the Board of Directors of the Chinese People's Association for Cultural Relations with Foreign Countries, a position he probably still retains. Also in 1954 Teng was elected as a Shantung deputy to the First NPC (1954–1959); he was re-elected to the Second NPC (1959–1964) but was switched to the Peking constituency for the Third NPC, which held its first session in December 1964–January 1965. When the Academy of Sciences established four specialized departments in May–June 1955, Teng was named to membership in the Department of Philosophy and Social Sciences, headed by academician Kuo Mo-jo. He was also selected for membership on the Central Committee for Popularizing the Common Spoken Language (*p'u-t'ung-hua*), a special committee set up under the chairmanship of Ch'en I in February 1956.

Besides being a member of the China-India Friendship Association, Teng serves on three other similar organizations. When the Sino-Soviet FA held its second conference in December 1954, he was elected to the second Executive Board and was then re-elected to the third Board in April 1959. Similarly, he was elected a Board of Directors member of the China–United Arab Republic FA from its formation in February 1958, and when the China-Poland FA was set up in September of the same year, he was named as a vice-president. He has also served as a Standing Committee member of the rather important China Peace Committee from its reorganization in July 1958.

Teng took his first known trip abroad in January–March 1954 when he led a delegation of journalists to Moscow on a goodwill visit. Two years later (March 1956), he led another group of newsmen abroad, on this occasion to Warsaw for a meeting of the Presidium of the Communist-backed International Organization of Journalists (IOJ). At this time Teng was elected to a vice-chairmanship in the IOJ, holding the post until succeeded by Chin Chung-hua (q.v.) in 1959. As a senior IOJ official, he was one of the main speakers when an executive meeting of this organization was held in Peking in April 1957.

From the winter of 1957–58, Teng's career has had a somewhat different orientation. In November 1957, the Party changed Teng from editor-in-chief of the *JMJP* to managing director, naming another veteran journalist, Wu Leng-hsi (q.v.), to succeed him as editor. Subsequent to this, Teng has been active in more purely political work. Thus, for example, by January 1959 he had become a secretary of the Peking Party Committee (under First Secretary P'eng Chen, a Politburo member), a position he still holds. Even more important was his promotion to the North China Party Bureau, in which he has been an alternate secretary since February 1965, serving in this post under Li Hsueh-feng, a member of the important Party Secretariat.

As in the case of many Party leaders, Teng has made frequent appearances at conferences and commemorative events. He served, for example, on the presidium (steering committee) of a huge conference of "advanced workers" in the cultural and educational fields held in June 1960, and in December 1962 he gave "important instructions" at a congress of the Peking chapter of the Youth League. Among his more ceremonial assignments have been a vice-chairmanship on a special committee to mark the 40th anniversary of the May Fourth movement (April 1959) and membership on the presidium for a meeting commemorating the 80th anniversary of the birth of China's most famous 20th-century writer, Lu Hsun.

Although it is evident that Teng has had a less direct hand in Party journalistic endeavors since the late 1950's, it is equally clear that he has retained an active interest in the general field of culture and education. In addition to his change from the editorship of the *JMJP* to posts on both the Peking Party Committee and the North China Party Bureau, two examples serve to illustrate his continuing work in cultural and educational affairs. For the February 1961 issue of the important journal *Li-shih yen-chiu* (Historical research) Teng wrote an article on the "science of history," presenting what might be considered a standard statement of the Chinese Communist viewpoint. Of particular interest is the fact that this article indicated a rather wide knowledge of Western historiography and Western writings about China. Second, in February 1965 Teng was a major speaker at a large "festival of plays and operas," held in Peking, emphasizing that the "revolutionization" of drama workers was the prerequisite for the revolutionizing of drama work. His speech came amidst a major propaganda drive to replace traditional themes in the operas with more contemporary ideas stressing "class struggle."

---

1. Chalmers A. Johnson, *Peasant Nationalism and Communist Power* (Stanford, Calif., 1962), p. 101.

2. *Ibid.*

3. *Hsin-wen kung-tso chih-nan* (A guide-book to news work; Chang-chia-k'ou, Shansi-Chahar-Hopeh Border Region, 1946), pp. 49–56.

Teng Tzu-hui

(1895– ; Lung-yen, Fukien). Important Party leader in Fukien, 1930's; deputy director Political Department, New Fourth Army, during Sino-Japanese War; specialist in economic affairs; member, CCP Central Committee.

Teng Tzu-hui has been a CCP member since the mid-1920's, when he first became active in his native Fukien. After the Long March began, he remained in Fukien and led guerrilla operations until the beginning of the Sino-Japanese War when he became a top political officer in the New Fourth Army. He became increasingly important in Party affairs after the war and served for a time in the mid-fifties as one of the foremost spokesmen on agricultural policies. Teng has been a CCP Central Committee member since 1945.

Teng comes from Lung-yen hsien in Fukien, a hilly rural area northwest of Amoy where the CCP has been active since the 1920's. Teng's parents were small merchants; they sent him to Amoy where he graduated from middle school. Many young men from Fukien were educated in Japan at that time and Teng himself went there in 1916. After spending a year in Tokyo he returned to China, but his career is undocumented until 1925 when he joined the KMT. The following year he became a CCP member. Between his study in Japan and 1927, when he was teaching in a village school in his native community, Teng may have been associated with the Whampoa Military Academy. Japanese sources assert that he was enrolled there, but this cannot be corroborated in Chinese sources. Moreover, because Teng was about 29 when Whampoa opened in 1924, it seems more likely that he would have been on the administrative staff, rather than a member of the student body. In any case, by 1927 he was engaged in Party work and the peasant movement in Lung-yen (his native hsien), Shang-hang, and Yung-ting, and by the following year he was collaborating with Liu Yung-sheng and Chang Ting-ch'eng in organizing peasant resistance in these areas in southwest Fukien (see under Chang Ting-ch'eng). All three men worked together in Fukien until the Sino-Japanese War began, when they entered the Communists' New Fourth Army.

In 1929, after Mao Tse-tung and Chu retreated from their base on the Hunan-Kiangsi border, they moved across Kiangsi and into west Fukien. Teng, then secretary of the Party organization in west Fukien,[1] participated in the creation of a "revolutionary base" in the area. In the same year he was also the political officer of a detachment of guerrillas operating in Yung-ting hsien, and by about 1930 he had become chairman of a small "soviet" of eight hsien, which was probably subordinate to the larger

West Fukien Soviet headed by Chang Ting-ch'eng.

Representing Communist-held areas in Fukien, Teng attended the First All-China Congress of Soviets, held in Juichin, Kiangsi, in November 1931. The congress established the Chinese Soviet Republic, as well as the Republic's Central Executive Committee (CEC) and a Council of People's Commissars (in effect, the cabinet). Both Teng and his Fukien colleague Chang Ting-ch'eng became members of the CEC, and both were given cabinet-level assignments in the council. Chang was made People's Commissar for Land; Teng was given the portfolio for Finance, and for a period in mid-1932 he served as acting commissar of Land in place of his colleague Chang.[2] However, Teng lost his Finance post during an intense political controversy which concerned various military, political, and economic policies being administered by the acting Party secretary in Fukien, Lo Ming. (Lo Ming's biography contains a discussion of the important "Lo Ming line.") Many years later, Mao Tse-tung termed the charges against Lo and others as a "leftist" error, but in the meantime, in 1933, Teng proved to be one of the major targets of the anti-Lo Ming group. In August 1933, Lin Po-ch'ü (q.v.) replaced Teng as commissar of Finance, although Teng was made the vice-commissar.[3] The principal charges against him concerned the economic sector. Attacked for his "right conservatism" and "wavering" in the face of difficulties, it was claimed that he had failed to mobilize the masses to collect sorely needed funds, and that he was too willing to resort to the printing press as a means of getting funds. It is noteworthy that Teng's "conservatism" in economic policy was demonstrated a quarter of a century later, when he once again found himself in political trouble (see below).

Among others affected by the Lo Ming line were Mao Tse-t'an (a younger brother of Mao Tse-tung), T'an Chen-lin, Teng Hsiao-p'ing, Ch'en T'an-ch'iu, and Hsiao Ching-kuang (qq.v.). Teng Tzu-hui's political difficulties were illustrated anew when the Second All-China Congress of Soviets was convened in January–February 1934 at Juichin. He was demoted from full to alternate membership on the CEC (although it is not known if he lost his post as vice-commissar in the Commissariat of Finance). Yet these political problems became largely academic when, in the fall of 1934, the principal forces evacuated the Kiangsi area to begin the famed Long March to north Shensi. Teng was among those left behind and was placed in charge of a band of local guerrillas, which was forced to move eastward into Fukien. Attached to a battalion under the Independent 24th Division led by Hsiang Ying (q.v.), Teng made his way back to his native area where he merged

his forces with those of Chang Ting-ch'eng and T'an Chen-lin. Other key Communists who also remained behind included Ch'en I and Ch'ü Ch'iu-pai (qq.v.). Teng was with Ch'ü in the Ch'ang-t'ing area in west Fukien in March 1935 when they were apprehended by Nationalist forces. Teng managed to escape, but Ch'ü was taken to Ch'ang-t'ing and soon afterwards executed.

In August 1935, the small band of Communists in southwest Fukien inaugurated the Southwest Fukien Military and Administrative Committee (SWFMAC). Chang Ting-ch'eng became chairman, and T'an Chen-lin and Teng the vice-chairmen. In addition, Teng served as director of the Committee's Finance Department. In the fall of 1936 the SWFMAC divided its forces into two columns; the first, led by Teng, operated in the Lung-yen area. (See also under Chang Ting-ch'eng.) After the outbreak of the Sino-Japanese War in mid-1937, the small Communist forces in the Fukien area were named the Anti-Japanese Volunteers, still under the command of Chang, with T'an and Teng continuing as his principal deputies.

In the latter half of 1937 the Communists held talks with the Nationalists to create the New Fourth Army, which was to operate along the central and lower Yangtze. (The army, drawn mainly from Communist guerrilla units in central-south China and augmented by units dispatched from the Eighth Route Army, is described in the biographies of its two principal commanders, Yeh T'ing and Hsiang Ying.) When the New Fourth Army went into the field in the spring of 1938, Teng was deputy director of the Political Department under Yuan Kuo-p'ing. (Yuan, a veteran political officer, had participated in the Canton Uprising in 1927 and had served in P'eng Te-huai's Third Army Corps as head of the Political Department.) The New Fourth Army, in the early months of its operations, was headquartered south of the Yangtze. In its first year, three of the four detachments were also south of the river, but the Fourth Detachment, commanded at least by 1939 by Chang Yun-i (q.v.), was in northeast Hupeh, from which it moved eastward into north Anhwei. The forces north of the river had steadily increased in number, and therefore, in late 1939, the North Yangtze Command was established under Chang's command. (The South Yangtze Command was headed by Ch'en I.) Teng, who had been north of the river by mid-1939, was appointed director of the northern command's Political Department.[4]

In January 1941 the New Fourth Army headquarters staff was almost totally destroyed as it began to move north of the Yangtze (the New Fourth Army Incident; see under Yeh T'ing). Commander Yeh T'ing was captured by the Nationalists, and both Deputy Commander

Hsiang Ying and Yuan Kuo-p'ing (Teng's former superior) were killed. Because Teng was already north of the river, he was not involved in any of this fighting. The New Fourth Army staff was immediately reorganized; Ch'en I became acting commander, Chang Yun-i was appointed deputy commander, and Liu Shao-ch'i became the political commissar. Teng was placed directly under Liu as director of the Political Department. He held this post until 1946 when the New Fourth Army began to expand its operations. In addition, from 1941 Teng concurrently served as political commissar in P'eng Hsueh-feng's (q.v.) Fourth Division.[5] (P'eng had initially been both commander and political commissar.) Then about 1944, Teng in turn relinquished the post of political commissar to Chang Ai-p'ing (q.v.).

Teng's long career was given recognition when he was elected to the Party Central Committee at the Seventh Congress held in Yenan from April to June 1945. In the postwar period, as a high-ranking political officer, he was one of the principal liaison officials between three important Communist armies: Ch'en I's East China PLA, consisting mainly of troops from the former New Fourth Army, and known later as the Third Field Army; Liu Po-ch'eng's Central Plains PLA, known later as the Second Field Army; and Lin Piao's forces, which had conquered Manchuria and which were later redesignated the Fourth Field Army. The coordinated efforts of these three armies were responsible for the conquest of most of the China mainland by 1949–50; Teng's contributions in those years were in east and central China.

Teng is known to have been in Yenan in the spring of 1946, perhaps to attend conferences related to the forthcoming military campaigns against the Nationalists. He was identified at that time as political commissar of the Central China (Hua-chung) Military Region. Teng had been given this new assignment sometime in the latter part of 1945 or in early 1946 as the Communists readjusted their staff assignments to the newly evolving military situation. Several other key officers in Ch'en I's New Fourth Army were also assigned to the Central China Military Region, most notably Chang Ting-ch'eng, the Region's commander, Su Yü, the deputy commander, and T'an Chen-lin, the deputy political commissar (under Teng). Concurrently with his new political assignment, Teng was also made secretary of the CCP Central China Sub-bureau, then subordinate to the East China Bureau that had its headquarters in the territory under Ch'en I's control in Shantung. According to some reports Teng was a political officer in 1946 in Liu Po-ch'eng's army, which was stationed in the Shansi-Hopeh-Shantung-Honan Border Region. It is not known if Teng went to the border region to assume this role, but it is clear that he

was in close contact with Liu's forces, which, in mid-1947, thrust southward across the Yellow River and moved into the Ta-pieh Mountains northeast of Wuhan (the locale of the old Communist Oyüwan soviet area). Liu turned back north for further campaigning, but he left a number of officers in the Oyüwan region, Teng among them. Later in 1947, those areas in the Oyüwan region under Communist control were merged with another Communist base on the borders of Honan, Anhwei, and Kiangsu provinces. The merger of these two areas, plus some territory in west Honan, became the Central Plains Liberated Area, with Teng as the top official. The Liberated Area was under the general control of Liu Po-ch'eng's army, now called the Central Plains PLA.

When Liu's army had reached the Ta-pieh Mountains, Ch'en I's troops moved eastward from Shantung to fill the gap in southern Hopeh left by Liu's army. Good cooperation on the part of both armies succeeded in severing Nationalist communication lines in the region between the Yellow River and the Yangtze. At the same time both the Lunghai and the Pinghan rail lines were threatened. Kaifeng, taken and lost by the Communists in mid-1948, fell to them for good by the end of the year. During these coordinated efforts on the part of the two armies, Teng was one of the principal liaison officials. Then, following the conquest of Peking in January 1949, Lin Piao's Fourth Field Army also began to move south, capturing Wuhan in May 1949. Here again Teng took part in liaison work, this time between the armies of Lin Piao and Liu Po-ch'eng. By early 1949 he was second political commissar of the Fourth Field Army, serving now directly under Lin's First Political Commissar, Lo Jung-huan (q.v.).

Over the winter of 1948–49 the Communists took the first steps toward the establishment of a governmental apparatus to administer the areas in central China they had conquered. After some three months of preparatory work, the Central Plains Provisional People's Government was established under the chairmanship of Teng at a congress held in Kaifeng (now the Honan capital). Then, in the wake of the advancing Communist armies, the capital was moved to Wuhan (June 1949) where it remained until the government was dissolved in early 1950 (see below).

As the forces of the Fourth Field Army were pushing southward in the latter half of 1949, the Communists' central government was being established in Peking. Although Teng apparently did not attend any of the meetings that established the new government in the fall, he received important appointments in the government and the "mass" organizations. The most important of these was membership on the Central People's Government Council (CPGC);

chaired by Mao Tse-tung, the CPGC was the highest organ of state power and during its existence (1949–1954) passed on virtually all major policies adopted by the central government. He was also named to membership on the government's top military organ, the People's Revolutionary Military Council (also chaired by Mao). In addition, Teng was named as a member of the Finance and Economics Committee (and was promoted to a vice-chairmanship in November 1952) and the Overseas Chinese Affairs Commission; both of these were subordinate to the Government Administration Council (the cabinet). He held all these positions until the constitutional government was inaugurated in September 1954. Moreover, from 1949 to 1954 he was an Executive Board member of the Sino-Soviet Friendship Association, then a very active organization.

In spite of this impressive array of positions in the national government, Teng's tasks in the early years of the PRC were largely confined to the central-south region. His importance there was accentuated by the lingering illness of Lin Piao and the frequent absences of Lo Jung-huan. On paper, Lin held virtually all the critical positions of power in the central-south area from 1949 to 1954 and Lo was initially the second-ranking official. In fact, however, Lo spent most of his time in Peking, where he had important responsibilities with the central government. As the Communists pushed south in 1949, the Central China Military Region evolved into the Central-South Military Region, and, similarly, the CCP's Central China Bureau (formerly a sub-bureau) became the Central-South Bureau. In the military hierarchy Teng became the second political commissar (under Lo Jung-huan) of the Military Region and its Fourth Field Army, and (by 1950) the second-ranking political commissar (again under Lo) of the Central-South Military and Political Academy.[6] In 1952 he was also identified as the deputy commander of the Military Region. However, there is little to suggest that Teng devoted much time to military affairs. Rather, he was deeply involved with Party and government policies, particularly those pertaining to economic problems.

On February 6, 1950, Teng gave a major speech in Wuhan on the work of the Central Plains Provisional People's Government. It was, in fact, a summation report, because on the previous day the Central-South Military and Administrative Committee (CSMAC), also headquartered in Wuhan, was formed as the successor government to the Central Plains Government. The CSMAC was, of course, a much larger organization, covering the six provinces of Honan, Hupeh, Hunan, Kiangsi, Kwangtung, and Kwangsi. Teng became the ranking vice-chairman under Chairman Lin Piao. But, as noted, Lin's prolonged illness had the effect of

making Teng the *de facto* chairman. He was frequently cited as the acting chairman of the CSMAC and he made most of the major reports on its activities. When the CSMAC was reorganized into the Central-South Administrative Committee in January 1953, Teng continued as the senior vice-chairman.

In March 1950, one month after the establishment of the CSMAC, Teng was named to chair its Finance and Economics Committee. In December of the same year he was demoted to vice-chairman of this committee, relinquishing his chairmanship to the politically more important Lin Piao. It appears, however, that Lin's prolonged absence from public duties meant that Teng continued to be the *de facto* chairman of the Finance and Economics Committee. A further indication of Teng's importance in central-south China was revealed in May 1950 when he was named to head a special *ad hoc* organization (*pien-chih*) committee responsible for establishing and staffing the organizations subordinate to the CSMAC. His key role in central-south China during the formative years of the PRC is also illustrated by the large number of his speeches and reports that appeared in the two major Party papers, the Wuhan *Ch'ang-chiang jih-pao* (Yangtze River daily) and the Canton *Nan-fang jih-pao* (Southern daily). His chief responsibilities seem to have been in the field of economics. For example, following the demands made at the third session of the CPPCC (October–November 1951) for greater emphasis on economic problems, the Communists established regional "simplification and austerity" committees. In November 1951 Teng was named to chair the committee for central-south China. He was also appointed director of the Central-South Flood Prevention Headquarters on its formation in April 1952.

Within the Party hierarchy, Teng was third secretary of the Central-South Bureau by 1950 (ranking below Lin Piao and Lo Jung-huan), advancing to second secretary by early 1952, a post he retained until 1954. Over the winter of 1951–52 he was involved in the settlement of a serious case of malfeasance and corruption in Wuhan. Known as the Sung Ying affair, the case involved a number of top Communist officials in Wuhan who had been negligent in investigating the incident and correcting certain injustices. In summing up the case at the meeting in February 1952, Teng noted that he had been convalescing for four months but still admitted that he was "not free from bureaucratism." However, to judge from his later career, it is evident that this did not jeopardize his political standing in the Party. (For more detailed coverage of the Sung Ying case, see under Chang P'ing-hua.) As already suggested, however, Teng's chief responsibilities seem to have been mainly in connection with economic problems and the work of the governmental organ (the CSMAC–CSAC).

In the period from late 1952 through the summer of 1954, a large number of key regional leaders moved to Peking. Some transferred there permanently in 1952, but others (like Teng) made the transfer in gradual phases—in the sense that they shuttled back and forth from the provinces to Peking before transferring permanently in 1954, when the constitutional government was established. As already described, Teng had been made a vice-chairman of the national government's Finance and Economics Committee (headed by Ch'en Yun, q.v.) in November 1952. At this same time he was also appointed as the vice-chairman of the State Planning Commission, newly established to deal with the problems of the First Five-Year Plan, which began in 1953. As originally constituted, the commission had Kao Kang (q.v.) as its chairman, Teng as the only vice-chairman, and 15 members. These were Teng's first two active administrative posts at the national level. Within less than a year he was to receive three others. In January 1953 he was made a member of the committee chaired by Mao Tse-tung to draft the national constitution, and in the following month he was also made a member of a committee (headed by Liu Shao-ch'i) to prepare for the elections (in 1954) to the NPC. Most important, however, was the identification of Teng by July 1953 as head of the Party's Rural Work Department. In spite of the importance of agriculture in China, the department was not identified in Chinese sources until this time. However, the biography of Teng in Moscow's *Bol'shaya Sovetskaya Entsiklopedya* (Large Soviet Encyclopedia; Moscow, 1958, LI, 110) asserts that he held the post from November 1952. In any case, Teng appears to have been the first and, as of the early 1960's, the only director of this highly important body—one that is generally regarded as the chief policy-making organization for agricultural policies within the Communist regime.

Teng's assumption of the direction of the Rural Work Department coincided with the transitional phase between the mutual-aid teams and the agricultural producers' cooperatives. Authorities on Chinese Communist agriculture are generally agreed that Teng favored rather cautious, "go-slow" policies, citing as evidence a number of Teng's major pronouncements, particularly those made at the Party's Eighth National Congress (September 1956) and the Central Committee's Third Plenum (September–October 1957). Among the major policies that he apparently supported were: caution in emulating the policies followed by the Soviet Union in collectivization; the use of purchase quotas as the method to control agriculture (as opposed to the direct planning of agricultural production goals); and the use of material incentives aimed at achieving a balanced, though slower, economic growth.[7] Although it is impossible to say with certainty, the

viewpoints espoused by Teng seem to have prevailed in the mid-fifties. The major turning point in agricultural policies—and in Teng's career—seems to have taken place at the above-mentioned Third Plenum in the fall of 1957. Soon after the Plenum, the Great Leap Forward was inaugurated. For the most part, economic caution was thrown to the winds and, apparently not coincidentally, Teng made fewer and fewer major pronouncements on agricultural policy. Others, most notably Teng's old comrade T'an Chen-lin, began to make the major agricultural policy statements. One authority has persuasively argued that Teng was associated with Ch'en Yun in advocating cautious economic policies—a suggestion that seems borne out by the fact that both Teng and Ch'en have been eclipsed at the policy levels since about 1958.[8] Nonetheless, Teng continued to head the Rural Work Department, although it may have been abolished in the mid-1960's.

In the meantime, during the mid-fifties Teng had received a number of important posts in the national government and the CCP. In 1954 he was elected as a deputy from Wuhan to the First NPC (1954–1959). He was re-elected from Hupeh (which had absorbed the Wuhan constituency in the interim) to the Second NPC (1959–1964) and again to the Third NPC, which opened in December 1964. In September 1954 he was appointed as a vice-premier under Chou En-lai in the State Council, and in the next month he was also named as director of the State Council's Seventh Staff Office. The Staff Office was in charge of coordinating the activities of the ministries and commissions related to agriculture, forestry, and water conservancy. From its inauguration in March 1956 until May 1957, Teng was a member of the State Council's Scientific Planning Commission. At the Party's Eighth National Congress (September 1956) he served on the Congress presidium (steering committee), made the major speech on agricultural policy, and was re-elected to membership on the Central Committee. In July 1957 he assumed still another position (apparently *ad hoc*) when he was named to head the Central Relief Commission; the commission seems to have been established in response to a strong attack in the *JMJP* (July 17) on the inadequacies of disaster relief work.

Teng Tzu-hui clearly reached the peak of his career in the mid-fifties. Then, beginning with the Great Leap Forward in 1958, he began to lose political influence in ways that were more subtle than dramatic. For example, as a top agricultural policy maker, it would not have been surprising if he had been placed on the Party's Politburo at the second session of the Eighth Party Congress in May 1958. However, as described above, in the period before the Congress session, T'an Chen-lin eclipsed Teng as the principal agricultural spokesman—and thus it was T'an rather than Teng who gained a seat on the Politburo.

In September 1959, the State Council's Seventh Staff office (which Teng had headed since 1954) was renamed the Agriculture and Forestry Office. Teng continued as the director, but then in October 1962 he was succeeded by T'an Chen-lin. As a result of this change, T'an heads the top government agricultural body and Teng ostensibly directs the Party's chief agricultural organ. In fact, however, this appears to be an arrangement of conciliation rather than reality—though Teng clearly continues to have a limited role in forming agricultural policy, it is plainly less than in the period prior to the Great Leap Forward.

In October 1962, at the same time he was removed from the Agriculture and Forestry Office, Teng was added as one of six new vice-chairmen of the State Planning Commission. (Of interest is the fact that T'an Chen-lin was also added as a vice-chairman at this time.) Since then, however, Teng has not frequently appeared in public. Moreover, in January 1965, when the new cabinet was appointed at the close of the first session of the Third NPC, he was not reappointed as a vice-premier of the State Council. To some degree this was counterbalanced by his appointment at this same time to the less important position as a vice-chairman of the CPPCC.

Over the years, even after his political decline began about 1958, Teng has contributed quite regularly to the Chinese press, almost always writing about agricultural problems. For example, he contributed an article on agriculture to a collection of essays published to mark the 10th anniversary of the PRC,[9] and for the Party's leading journal, Hung-ch'i (issue of December 12, 1963), he discussed the role of the credit cooperatives, making a strong plea for more effective management. Teng's rather conservative approach to economic problems is well illustrated in an article written for Nung-ts'un kung-tso t'ung-hsun (Rural work correspondence) in 1959, an article that discussed the community mess halls established in the people's communes.[10] His article is more plaintive than dogmatic in tone and suggests that he realized the common dining halls had grave shortcomings.

Had the Chinese Communists followed the economic policies espoused by Teng, it is possible that some of the dislocations resulting from the abortive Great Leap Forward might have been avoided. His opposition to policies ultimately adopted, however, seems to have been sufficiently restrained to allow him to retain a fair degree of political influence. Or, in the words of one writer, Teng apparently formed a part of an "opinion group" but not a "political faction."[11] Nonetheless, as one of the oldest members of the Chinese Communist elite, it is unlikely that he will play a significant role in the future.

1. Bol'shaya Sovetskaya Entsiklopedya (Large Soviet Encyclopedia; Moscow, 1958), LI, 110.

2. Hung-se Chung-hua (Red China; Juichin), August 4, 1932.
3. Tso-liang Hsiao, Power Relations within the Chinese Communist Movement, 1930–1934 (Seattle, Wash., 1961), p. 242.
4. Hsing-huo liao-yuan (A single spark can start a prairie fire; Peking, 1961), VI, 380.
5. Hung-ch'i p'iao-p'iao (Red flag fluttering; Peking, 1957), V, 162.
6. Nan-fang jih-pao (Southern daily), March 26, 1950.
7. Alexander Eckstein, Communist China's Economic Growth and Foreign Trade (New York, 1966), p. 80; Dwight H. Perkins, Market Control and Planning in Communist China (Cambridge, Mass., 1966), pp. 67–68; Franz Schurmann, Ideology and Organization in Communist China (Berkeley, Calif., 1966), pp. 196–204.
8. Schurmann, pp. 196–204.
9. Ten Glorious Years, 1949–1959 (Peking, 1960), pp. 298–327.
10. Translated in ECMM 179, pp. 1–5.
11. Schurmann, p. 56.

Teng Ying-ch'ao

(1903–   ; Hsin-yang, Honan). Vice-chairman, National Women's Federation of China; member, CCP Central Committee.

Teng Ying-ch'ao, the wife of Chou En-lai, is among the most important women in the history of the Chinese Communist movement. Like most women CCP leaders, her political prominence is largely of her own making, rather than the reflection of her marriage to one of Communist China's greatest leaders. Teng's revolutionary career dates back to the May Fourth Movement, and she has taken part in many of the landmark events in Communist history, including the Long March. She spent most of the war years in Chungking as a CCP representative to the Nationalist government. However, most of her career has been devoted to the field of women's affairs, and for many years she has been the second most important woman leader in the CCP, ranking only after Ts'ai Ch'ang. Teng has been a vice-chairman of the women's federation since 1949, and in 1956 she was elected a full member of the Party Central Committee.

Teng, whose original name was Teng Wen-shu, is described as a native of Hsin-yang in southern Honan in most sources, but others use Nanning, Kwangsi or Kuang-shan, Hopeh. Her father, a bankrupt landlord who had been an army officer during the Ch'ing dynasty, died when she was still a child. Her mother supported the family as a schoolteacher and governess, earning enough money to send Teng to study first in Peking and then in Tientsin. Teng was enrolled in the Hopeh First Women's Normal School in Tientsin at the time of the May Fourth Incident in 1919 and it was there that she began her revolutionary career. Before her graduation in 1920 Teng had become deeply involved in the May Fourth Movement.

After the May Fourth Incident, students in the Peking-Tientsin area began to form organizations to agitate for the revitalization of Chinese politics and society. During the 1919–20 period Teng was involved in three of these in Tientsin. Just a few days after the incident Teng helped found the Tientsin Students' Union, and she was also a leading figure in the Tientsin Women's Patriotic Association, which was set up about the same time. In both organizations she headed a "speech-making" corps.[1] Many years later Teng wrote, "We [participants in the May Fourth Movement] . . . had . . . a kind of spontaneous and intuitive realization that to save our country we must carry our activities beyond student circles. We students alone could not save our country. We should 'awaken our fellow citizens.' Consequently we paid much attention to propaganda and organized a number of speech corps."[2] In connection with her work as a student activist, Teng came to know her future husband, Chou En-lai, who was also a student. According to Edgar Snow, they met during the course of a street demonstration.[3]

In September 1919 the Students' Union joined with the women's organization to establish the Chueh-wu she (Awakening society). Chou and Teng were among its most active members.[4] This society was similar to others formed about this time in Peking by Li Ta-chao (q.v.) and his disciples, and it was also spiritually akin to still others which had been formed in Changsha by Mao Tse-tung and in Wuhan by Yun Tai-ying (q.v.). The students' union and the women's organization began to publish *P'ing-min* (The plain people) in 1919; Teng was among the contributors to this short-lived radical journal, which encouraged general strikes and the withholding of taxes in protest against the government. The journal was soon suppressed, but in early 1920 another one called *Chueh-wu* (Awakening), which advocated sweeping social changes, was published by the Awakening Society, with both Teng and Chou as contributors.[5] During this period she was jailed on at least one occasion.[6]

Chou En-lai left for France in 1920 to take part in the work-and-study program (see under Ts'ai Ho-sen), but for the next five years Teng remained in north China where she taught school in both Peking and Tientsin. American journalist Nym Wales, who met Teng in 1937, reports that she once taught at Peking National Normal University, but to judge from Teng's comments about her own career, she apparently taught mainly at the primary school level.[7] In any case, it is clear that she spent most of this period in Tientsin where she continued her political activities. She was a member of the Nü hsing she (Women's star society) and the Nü ch'üan yun-

tung t'ung-meng-hui (Women's rights league), and in 1923 she is known to have contributed articles to newspapers published by the former organization.[8] During this same period, according to an official English-language biographic sketch of Teng, she founded the "Society of Progressive Women" and published a newspaper in Tientsin "dedicated to the welfare of women."[9] Her first formal association with the Communist movement came in 1924 when she joined the Socialist Youth League. The following year she was admitted to the CCP and became head of the Women's Department in the Tientsin CCP organization. Because this was the period of the first united front between the KMT and the CCP, Teng also joined the KMT in 1925.

Toward the end of 1925 Teng went to Canton where she married Chou En-lai. Canton was then the revolutionary center of China, and by the time Teng arrived there (or soon thereafter), a host of other top Communists were in the city, including Mao Tse-tung, P'eng P'ai, Su Chao-cheng, Ts'ai Ch'ang, Lin Po-ch'ü, Wu Yü-chang, Nieh Jung-chen, Hsiao Ch'u-nü, Yun Tai-ying, and Yang Yin (qq.v.). In January 1926 Teng attended the Second KMT Congress. Li Ta-chao, Lin Po-ch'ü, Yun Tai-ying, and Wu Yü-chang were among the Communists elected full members of the KMT Central Executive Committee (CEC), and Teng, Mao Tse-tung, and Hsia Hsi (q.v.) were among the alternates selected from the Communist ranks. Teng had the distinction of being the only woman Communist elected to the CEC. At approximately this time she was working in the KMT's Women's Movement Training Institute under Ho Hsiang-ning, the widow of the prominent left-wing KMT leader Liao Chung-k'ai.[10] Concurrent with these tasks in the KMT hierarchy, Teng also held alternate membership on the CCP Kwangtung-Kwangsi Regional Committee and was secretary of its Women's Activities Committee.

In mid-1926 the Northern Expedition began from Kwangtung. Wuhan was captured in the fall, and over the turn of the year the KMT government was transferred there. Teng went there, where she worked as vice-chairman under Ho Hsiang-ning in the Wuhan government's Women's Department. However, when the tenuous alliance between the CCP and the KMT collapsed in mid-1927, the Communists went underground. From then until 1932 she spent most of her time in the Shanghai underground; the only important exception seems to have been in mid-1928 when she was in Moscow to attend the Sixth CCP Congress. She was named at that time to head the Party's Women's Department.

During the early 1930's, in response to unremitting efforts by the KMT to root out the CCP underground in Shanghai, most of the major Communist leaders there left for the base which Mao Tse-tung and Chu Te had developed on the Kiangsi-Fukien border. By the time Teng arrived (no later than mid-1932) she was clearly one of the most important women in the Communist Party; Hsiang Ching-yü (q.v.), the top woman in the early years of the Communist movement, had been killed in 1928, and thus only Ts'ai Ch'ang was of comparable stature. Teng's arrival at Juichin, the Communist capital, coincided with a period of considerable intra-Party feuding among various factions, particularly the Russian-returned student group headed by Ch'in Pang-hsien and the founders of the base area led by Mao. Teng was immediately involved in some of the doctrinal feuds, as indicated by her key role in denouncing a group of would-be Trotskyites who were allegedly in control of a newly founded theatrical troupe attached to the Red Army. In her capacity as director of the Women's Department of the Central Bureau of the Soviet Areas (see under Hsiang Ying), Teng presided over a "struggle conference," which attacked the theatrical troupe leaders, and her report on these events appeared later in the year in one of the Party's leading organs.[11]

At about the turn of the year 1932–33 Teng was put in charge of a special commission to inquire into the execution of the Central Soviet's labor law. In her report on this investigation, published in early February 1933, she took the position that the "inadequacy of the class struggle was enabling the rich peasants and small landlords to retain their privileged positions."[12] As one writer has noted, this had the effect of placing Teng at odds with views held by Mao.[13] In particular, Teng advocated a greater stress on the trade union movement and argued that "proletarian hegemony" had been ignored except for lip service in Party documents.[14] She even went so far as to advocate "strikes as a means for fostering development of the class struggle and class consciousness."[15]

In January 1934 the CCP held the Fifth Plenum, which Maoist writers have characterized as the peak period of the "third left line" of the Russian-returned student leadership. Teng was reportedly elected an alternate member of the Party Central Committee at that time. Immediately afterwards (January–February), the Second All-China Congress of Soviets was held, and on this occasion Teng was named to membership on the Central Executive Committee, the highest political organ of the Chinese Soviet Republic. In the fall of that year the Communists were forced to abandon the Central Soviet base and begin the Long March, which ended a year later in north Shensi. Teng was one of the few women who made the arduous trek, but because she had contracted tuberculosis, she had to be carried on a stretcher for much of the way.[16]

After her arrival in Shensi in the fall of 1935, Teng was active organizing women. In mid-1936, at Pao-an, Edgar Snow first met her, and a year later in Peking he saw her. immediately after the war began and the Japanese had occupied the city. Teng had gone to Peking in early 1937 for medical treatment, but fearing arrest by the Japanese, she sought out Snow to secure his help in escaping to Shensi. Snow, who said that Teng "possessed one of the most astute political brains" he had "encountered among Chinese women," disguised her as his servant and escorted her to Tientsin where she took a ship for Tsingtao.[17] From there she reached Sian in September where she met Snow's wife, Nym Wales. Miss Wales described her as a "competent-looking matronly woman" who spoke "beautiful clear Mandarin."[18]

Teng's stay in Shensi was brief, because in 1938 she and Chou were sent to Hankow to begin a long tour as Communist representatives to the Nationalist government, which had agreed to a new united front against Japan. Hankow had been the provisional national capital since the previous November (only a few weeks before the fall of Nanking). Teng was one of the seven-member delegation to the First People's Political Council, which had been set up in the spring of 1938 by the KMT as a gesture toward popular representation and the united front. The council held its first meeting in July in Hankow, but before the next session could be convened, the government was evacuated to Chungking. Thereafter, except for a reported trip to Moscow in 1939 for medical treatment, Teng spent most of her time in Chungking until 1943. In the early part of the war the Communists and Nationalists worked in relative harmony, but later a long series of incidents caused a severe deterioration in relations. This culminated in January 1941 with the New Fourth Army Incident (see under Yeh T'ing), when several thousand Communist troops were wiped out by the Nationalists in Anhwei. In a statement later attributed to the pen of Mao Tse-tung, a "spokesman" for the Communists denounced this anti-Communist "plot" and asserted that the Nationalists were planning to close down the Eighth Route Army Liaison Office in Chungking and arrest Chou En-lai, Teng, and others.[19] As this statement indicates, Teng was then an Eighth Route Army representative in Chungking (1940–1943), and although she was not arrested and the liaison office was not closed, the Communists' office in Kweilin was in fact shut down (see under Li K'o-nung). In spite of this situation, Teng continued to be a nominal Communist representative to the Second (1941–42), Third (1942–1945), and Fourth People's Political Councils (1945–46), but she and the other CCP representatives boycotted most of the meetings.

In 1943 Teng returned to Yenan where she remained for the rest of the war. In 1945 she became vice-chairman of the newly established Preparatory Committee for the China Liberated

Areas Women's Federation. This committee, headed by her colleague Ts'ai Ch'ang, was the forerunner of the All-China Federation of Democratic Women established in 1949 (see below). At the CCP's Seventh National Congress, held from April to June 1945, only three women were placed on the Central Committee; Ts'ai Ch'ang was elected a full member, and Teng and Ch'en Shao-min were elected alternates. At this same time, again under Ts'ai Ch'ang, Teng was identified as the deputy secretary of the Party's Women's Committee.

In the days immediately after the end of the war, Mao Tse-tung spent several weeks in Chungking holding talks with Chiang Kai-shek on a number of outstanding issues between the Communists and the Nationalists. Among other things, it was decided to convene a Political Consultative Conference (PCC), which would be attended by all political parties and which would discuss "peaceful national reconstruction" and the convocation of a permanent national assembly. As a consequence, Teng returned to Chungking in December and was present as one of the seven delegates when the PCC was convened there on January 10, 1946, the same day that the two sides declared a cease-fire to be in force on the battlefields. During the three-week-long meetings, Teng co-chaired an *ad hoc* committee responsible for drawing up a resolution for the convocation of a permanent national assembly. Teng and her husband remained in Chungking and then Nanking (to which the national government returned in May), but it quickly became apparent that neither side intended to live up to the cease-fire agreement. Finally, they returned to Yenan in November 1946, and by that time the civil war was in full swing.

A few months after Teng returned to Yenan, it was captured by the Nationalists (March 1947). Many of the Central Committee members remained in north Shensi, but others went to west Hopeh or Manchuria, and still others, of course, were constantly on the move in command of Communist troops. The only information on her activities for the next two years comes from an official 1949 biography, which states simply that in "recent years, she actively participated in the work of land reform." In the meantime, in 1946 Teng was elected a council member of the Communist-dominated Women's International Democratic Federation. Like her colleague Ts'ai Ch'ang, she had been elected as a representative of the above-mentioned Preparatory Committee for the China Liberated Areas Women's Federation. This body, in turn, set up another Preparatory Committee in January 1949 for the purpose of convening a nationwide congress of women; Ts'ai Ch'ang was the chairman, and Teng and Li Te-ch'üan (q.v.) were the two vice-chairmen. This took place in Mukden, but two months later

(by which time Peking was in Communist hands), the First Congress of Women was held (March–April 1949). Teng was one of the featured speakers and was elected a vice-chairman of the All-China Federation of Democratic Women (ACFDW). She continues to hold this position, having been re-elected at congresses held in April 1953 and September 1957. In addition, she was also the ACFDW secretary-general from 1950 until she relinquished the post to Chang Yun (q.v.) in September 1952. (In 1957 the ACFDW was renamed the National Women's Federation of China.)

Like most of the important Communists in Peking immediately after its fall, Teng was deeply involved in preparations for the establishment of the national government and various "people's" and professional organizations. In June 1949 she was one of the members of the Preparatory Committee for the China New Legal Research Society. In the same month, representing the women's federation, she was a member of the Preparatory Committee (chaired by Mao Tse-tung) for the CPPCC, the body which, at its initial session in September, created the PRC government (October 1). At the CPPCC Teng served on the presidium (steering committee) and on an *ad hoc* committee which drafted the Common Program (the equivalent of a constitution), and she delivered a brief address on the role of women in "New China." At the close of the meetings she was elected a member of the Standing Committee of the CPPCC's First National Committee. Immediately afterwards, Teng was made a member of the Political and Legal Affairs Committee, one of the major organs subordinate to her husband's Government Administration Council (the cabinet). And at the same time she was made a member of the First Executive Board of the Sino-Soviet Friendship Association. She held all these posts until 1954.

In December 1949, under the auspices of the Women's International Democratic Federation, the Asian Women's Conference was held in Peking. Attended by 165 delegates from 14 Asian nations (plus 33 "fraternal" delegates from elsewhere around the globe), the week-long meeting was given wide coverage in the Communist press. Teng gave the major address for the Chinese. Entitled "The Struggle of Asian Women," her speech presented a long catalogue of abuses by the "imperialists" in Asia. But its importance lay primarily in her formula by which other "oppressed" peoples could gain their own "liberation": a tightly knit Communist party, an "extensive people's united front," and a strong people's armed force. Although phrased in somewhat less militant tones, Teng's formulation for success was strikingly similar to one presented only a few weeks before by Liu Shao-ch'i. (For the rather hostile reaction in Moscow to Liu's address—and by implication Teng's too

—see under Liu.) A few weeks later the *JMJP* (January 17, 1950) carried Teng's report on the conference which she presented to women cadres working in the central government in early January.

Inferential evidence suggests that during the first part of 1950 Teng was mainly involved in the drafting of the new Marriage Law, which was adopted on May 1. In any event, she was among the principal articulators of the law, and in the years that followed she constantly referred to it in her articles and speeches. It is not surprising, therefore, that when the government established a special committee in January 1953 to "thoroughly implement" the law, Teng was named as one of the vice-chairmen.

Aside from her duties in the government and women's organization, Teng was also involved during the early PRC years with organizations dealing with questions of social welfare and peace. From October 1950 to July 1958 she served on the Standing Committee of the China Peace Committee, and in November 1950 she was a member of Kuo Mo-jo's delegation to the Second World Peace Congress in Warsaw. In November 1951 she became a vice-chairman of the newly established Chinese People's Committee for the Protection of Children, and in December she went to East Berlin for the 11th Council meeting of the Women's International Democratic Federation. In October 1952 Teng was one of the delegates to the Asian and Pacific Regions Peace Conference in Peking (see under Liu Ning-i), and since at least the mid-1950's she has been an honorary chairman of the Chinese Association of Nurses.

In April 1953 Teng delivered the major report before the Second Women's Congress, in which she reviewed the work of the women's federation since its establishment four years earlier. A short time before this she was made a member of the Central Election Committee, and when elections to the First NPC were held in the following year, Teng was elected to represent Honan. At the first session of the First NPC in September 1954, Teng was named a member of the NPC Standing Committee. She was returned from Honan to the Second and Third NPC's, and at the close of their initial sessions (April 1959 and January 1965), she was again named to the Standing Committee. In mid-1953 Teng was the second-ranking alternate member of the Party Central Committee; but on the eve of the Eighth Party Congress in September 1956, she was identified as a full member. (She was apparently promoted at one of the four Central Committee plenums held between February 1954 and September 1956, but no public announcement was made to that effect.) During the Eighth Congress Teng served on both the congress presidium (steering committee) and the credentials committee; the former body was essentially honorific,

but on the 29-member credentials committee Teng and Ts'ai Ch'ang were the only two women. Teng's speech to the congress listed many achievements in women's work, as well as a number of shortcomings (for example, "some departments whose work is suitable for women have flatly refused to engage women workers . . . , or have laid down all sorts of 'commandments and taboos' to restrict their chances of being employed"). To improve the situation, she also made a number of suggestions which, given her position in the CCP hierarchy, could be regarded as policy directives. During the congress Teng was identified as second secretary of the Party's Women's Work Committee; although the nomenclature was slightly different, this is presumably the same post that she has held since 1945, and one she continues to hold.

Teng's address at the Eighth Congress appears to have been her last major speech or article. She has continued to write for the press and speak before a wide variety of conferences; however, most of her articles and speeches since the mid-1950's have been exhortatory in nature (and many of them directed to the youths of China). For example, the September 18, 1960, *JMJP* carried a speech in which she argued that a "revolutionary spirit" was helpful in overcoming diseases, and in a speech to students at Peking University in May 1964 she urged them to delay early marriages on the grounds that personal sacrifices were necessary for the sake of the development of China. Since the mid-1950's Teng has also continued to make a large number of public appearances, many of which were essentially protocol in nature. Similarly, her name has often appeared in connection with landmark events in modern Chinese history, as in 1959 when she was on the preparatory committee for the celebration of the 40th anniversary of the May Fourth Movement, or in 1961 when she was on a similar committee in connection with the 50th anniversary of the 1911 Revolution. Teng's only trip abroad since 1951 took place in March 1961 when she led a delegation to Hanoi to attend the Third National Women's Congress of the Vietnam Democratic Republic.

Teng's various speeches and articles are a rich source of information and policy-level statements on the role of women in China, particularly in the early PRC years. She delivered one of the earliest commentaries on the Marriage Law in May 1950, a speech which was included in a booklet entitled *The Marriage Law of the People's Republic of China* (Peking, 1950). Three years later, in *People's China* (no. 5, March 1, 1953, pp. 8–12) she summarized the situation in regard to the enforcement of this law. Three other articles in *People's China* (no. 6, March 16, 1950, pp. 3–5; no. 5, March 1, 1952, pp. 8–10, 35; no. 23, December 1, 1952, pp. 9–12) provide useful statistics on the number of women working in government organs, industry, and agriculture.

In the above-mentioned 1960 speech, Teng noted that she suffered from a serious case of diabetes in 1953, but she also stated that she had been completely cured and that her earlier tubercular condition had not been a problem for more than 20 years. In political terms, Chou En-lai and Teng are probably the most redoubtable couple in the history of the Chinese Communist movement. The only other couples of roughly comparable stature are Ts'ai Ho-sen and Hsiang Ching-yü, and Li Fu-ch'un and Ts'ai Ch'ang (qq.v.). The Chous are childless.

1. Chow Tse-tsung, *The May Fourth Movement* (Cambridge, Mass., 1960), p. 130.
2. *Ibid.*, p. 354.
3. Edgar Snow, "Red China's Gentleman Hatchet Man," *The Saturday Evening Post,* March 27, 1954, p. 24.
4. Chow, p. 189.
5. Chow Tse-tsung, *Research Guide to the May Fourth Movement* (Cambridge, Mass., 1963), pp. 53, 74–75.
6. Nym Wales, *Inside Red China* (New York, 1939), p. 169.
7. *Ibid.*, p. 296; *SCMP* 3000, pp. 1–12.
8. Chow Tse-tsung, *Guide*, pp. 127–128.
9. *Women in New China* (Peking, 1949), p. 8.
10. C. Martin Wilbur and Julie Lien-ying How, *Documents on Communism, Nationalism, and Soviet Advisers in China, 1918–1927* (New York, 1956), p. 217.
11. Warren Kuo, "The Struggle against the Lo Ming Line in the CCP," *Issues & Studies,* no. 11:37–39 (July 1967).
12. Shanti Swarup, *A Study of the Chinese Communist Movement* (London, 1966), p. 127.
13. *Ibid.*
14. *Ibid.*, p. 155; M. N. Roy, *Revolution and Counter-Revolution in China* (Calcutta, 1946), p. 633.
15. Swarup, p. 160.
16. *SCMP* 2353, p. 19.
17. *Ibid.*; Edgar Snow, *The Battle for Asia* (New York, 1941), pp. 6, 23.
18. Wales, p. 296.
19. *Selected Works of Mao Tse-tung* (Peking, 1965), II, 453.

T'ien Pao, see **Sang-chi-yüeh-hsi**

Ting Ling

(c.1907–   ; Ch'ang-te, Hunan). Purged literary figure.

The most famous woman writer in the Chinese Communist movement, Miss Ting Ling was an important leader of and contributor to the CCP-sponsored literary world until she was purged in the mid-fifties. She was born into what is described by the Communists as a "feudal landlord family."[1] Her father died while she was a small child. Her mother, a militant feminist who is said to have been influenced by the revolutionary ideas of the late Ch'ing period and who joined the CCP in 1927, took the young girl to the city of Ch'ang-te where Ting received her primary schooling. She also attended the Second Provincial Girls' Normal School in T'ao-yuan hsien, Hunan, and then went to Shanghai, where from about 1920 to 1923 she studied at the P'ing-min Girls' School, which had been organized by one of the CCP founders, Ch'en Tu-hsiu (q.v.). Her commitment to Communism probably received its greatest impetus when from about 1923 to 1924 she studied literature at Shanghai University, an institute founded under joint KMT-CCP auspices but which was heavily dominated by the Communists (see under Ch'ü Ch'iu-pai).

In 1924 Ting went to Peking to prepare for the entrance examinations to Peking University, and although it appears that she was not admitted, she attended classes there until 1927. She became acquainted with important Chinese writers like the novelist Shen Ts'ung-wen and writer Hu Yeh-p'in, whom she lived with and ultimately married. During these years Ting began to write short stories and novels, some of this material appearing in *Hsiao-shuo yueh-pao* (Short story monthly). Returning to Shanghai in 1927 with Hu and Shen, they collaborated in editing a short-lived publication known as *Hung-hei yueh-k'an* (Red and black monthly).

Ting was active in the twenties in several leftist and anarchist movements. During these same years she also began to read widely in Western literature, especially Gorky, Tolstoy, Flaubert, and de Maupassant. Her early literary works, discussed at some length in C. T. Hsia's *A History of Modern Chinese Fiction, 1917–1957*, were highly personal, focusing on the emotional crises of youths and students. Most of her heroines were like herself—young girls who rebelled against patriarchal society in order to lead their own lives and to win personal freedom. She articulated the exasperations of youths in a society in transition, and as a consequence Ting had a large audience among China's reading public and acted as a spokesman for the younger generation.

In 1930 in Shanghai Ting joined the CCP, whose members lived a precarious existence resulting from continual suppressive measures taken by the KMT. In the same year she joined the newly formed League of Left-Wing Writers, the most important of the leftist literary organizations of that period. The leftist but non-Communist writer Lu Hsun, the premier literary figure of the time, was the star attraction of the league, but it was dominated organizationally first by Ch'ü Ch'iu-pai and later by Chou Yang (qq.v.), both Communists. In February 1931 Ting's husband Hu Yeh-p'in and four other writers were executed by the Nationalists, an episode treated at length by literary historian T. A. Hsia.[2]

In 1931 Ting began to edit an organ of the League of Left-Wing Writers known as the *Peitou yueh-k'an* (The great dipper), but this was suppressed by the Nationalists in the following year. In 1933 she was apprehended by the KMT in Shanghai's International Settlement and taken to Nanking where she was imprisoned until 1935, after which she was released but kept under surveillance.

Toward the close of 1936 Ting left Nanking for Sian and then made her way in 1937 to the Communist-controlled portions of north Shensi where, in Yenan, she was personally greeted by Mao Tse-tung, whose former wife had been a schoolmate of Ting's. Well known for her work in promoting women's rights, Ting was asked to establish, in cooperation with Teng Ying-ch'ao (Mme. Chou En-lai, q.v.), a women's league in the northwest, which was known as the Women's National Salvation Association. While in Yenan Ting taught at the Anti-Japanese Military and Political Academy (K'ang-ta) and served as a deputy director in a regimental political department. When war with Japan broke out in mid-1937, she led a service corps to the front lines in Shansi where she and her troupe entertained Red Army soldiers. Ting's activities in this period have been chronicled at length in Agnes Smedley's *China Fights Back*. Returning to Yenan, Ting edited the literary page of *Chieh-fang jih-pao* (Liberation daily), the official Party paper that was established in 1941 under the editorship of Ch'in Pang-hsien (q.v.). During these years Ting was one of the leaders in the active cultural life in Yenan, a life that attracted a large number of young, leftist-inclined students to Communist-held territories in those years. She made an outstanding name for herself in Yenan, not so much for her creative work, which fell off considerably, but for her propaganda and organizational activities. Authoress Nym Wales, who met her at this time, described Ting as a person of natural command and leadership.[3]

In the early 1940's the CCP embarked on its first *cheng-feng* (rectification) movement to purge Party cadres and intellectuals of unorthodox ideas and impose a strict ideological line. Initially, the movement was directed as much toward the bureaucratic, dogmatic methods of the cadres as toward the liberal, undisciplined attitudes of the intellectuals. Ting Ling, in the early months of 1942, used the literary page of *Chieh-fang jih-pao* to issue a barrage of criticism against the Party bureaucracy in the same manner as she had criticized KMT officials in an earlier period. She herself published a famous

essay, "Thoughts on March 8," in which she accused Party leaders of failing to carry out the lofty ideals they preached, citing the inequality of women in Yenan as an example.[4]

Even more rebellious were the works published by Ting's close associates. Several of them, like the Manchurian writers Hsiao Chün and Lo Feng, urged the Party to be more tolerant of dissent and demanded the right of criticism. The poet Ai Ch'ing asked the Party to treat writers and intellectuals with more respect. The most controversial article was "The Wild Lily" by translator Wang Shih-wei. In the manner of Djilas' condemnation of the Yugoslav Communist Party some years later, it accused the CCP of creating a new upper class that, like the old regime, headed a bureaucracy with its own system of injustice.

It was in this context and in response to these writers that Mao presented his famous "Talks on Literature and Art," in which he laid the foundation for the Party's control of the intellectuals. Immediately following these "talks," a campaign was launched against Ting Ling and her group. Wang Shih-wei was used as the prime example with which the *cheng-feng* movement was brought to a climax. Though there was little public criticism of Miss Ting, she was removed from her post on the *Chieh-fang jih-pao*, which was taken over by one of her chief accusers, Ai Szu-ch'i (q.v.). For weeks she was forced to attend meetings held expressly to criticize her thought. Then, until 1944, she studied in Party schools and spent some time in factories and villages.

In the postwar period Ting was assigned to Manchuria, where she engaged in propaganda work. Her observations of the land reform work at that time provided the basis for her best and most famous book, *The Sun Shines over Sangkan River*, a work for which she won the Stalin Prize for Literature in 1951, the first Chinese novel so honored. It was the first major work to reflect the complex picture of land reform then going on in the countryside, and as such it stood in contrast to the much-simplified portrayal of agrarian reform presented by the regular CCP propaganda organs. The high standards of the book can be judged from the characters in the novel, who are portrayed in three-dimensional terms. Through her depiction of representative types of landlords, rich peasants, poor peasants, and cadres, Ting described the class relationships in the villages, the peasant struggles against the landlords, and the redistribution of the land. Though this novel was obviously meant to tell the Party the "truth" about land reform, there are episodes where her characters present "truths" other than those of the Party. For example, she has one of the landlords call the CCP a new dynasty and a village teacher describe the cadres as fools who give orders without even knowing how to read. When the landlords lose their authority in the village, she shows them to be as fearful of persecution as their peasant counterparts once were. In fact, she paints this feeling of fear as pervading all classes of the village at the beginning of the land reform movement.

As a member of the delegation led by Ts'ai Ch'ang (q.v.), Ting attended the Second Congress of the Communist-dominated Women's International Democratic Federation (WIDF) in Budapest in December 1948 and was elected to alternate membership on the WIDF Board of Directors. Returning home, she went to Peking (now in Communist hands) and immediately began to take part in preparations for the convocation of the All-China Congress of Literary and Art Workers, held in July 1949 with some 800 delegates in attendance. She served on the Standing Committee of the Presidium (steering committee) and at the close of the Congress was elected to membership on the Standing Committee of the newly established All-China Federation of Literary and Art Circles (ACFLAC). Then, immediately after the Congress adjourned, she was elected a vice-chairman of one of the ACFLAC's subordinate organizations, the All-China Association of Literary Workers (known as the Union of Chinese Writers after 1953), and she was also made director of the ACFLAC Editorial Department. Most important, Ting became editor of *Wen-i pao* (Literary gazette), the journal of the ACFLAC and the principal organ for relaying the Party's cultural policies.

Though Ting's most important work in 1949 was concerned with the literary movement, she was also engaged in other activities. In April she was elected a member of the All-China Federation of Democratic Women's Executive Committee, and in that same month she attended the Communist-dominated World Peace Congress in Prague. In September, representing the ACFLAC, she attended the inaugural session of the CPPCC, and when this organization brought the new government into existence in October, she was appointed a member of the Culture and Education Committee under the Government Administration Council (the cabinet). Also in October she was appointed a member of the Executive Board and the National Committee, respectively, of the Sino-Soviet Friendship Association and the China Peace Committee, two of the most active "mass" organizations in the early PRC years.

In the latter part of October 1949, Ting left Peking for Moscow as head of a delegation sent to the Soviet capital to participate in the October Revolution celebrations, and while in Moscow she also attended a meeting of the WIDF. Toward the end of 1950 she was named to head the Central Literary Research Institute, which was formally established in January 1951 under the Ministry of Culture. A year later, in March 1952, Ting was presented with the above-mentioned Stalin Prize when she was in Moscow as a delegate to the centenary celebrations of Gogol's death. She was back in Moscow in December 1954 as a member of the Chinese writers' delegation to the Second National Congress of Soviet Writers. Earlier that year she was named to Board membership in the Chinese People's Association for the Promotion of Cultural Relations with Foreign Countries (May) and she was also elected as a Shantung deputy to the First NPC, which opened in September.

In the early years of the PRC, competition arose between Miss Ting and Chou Yang for control of the Party's literary organizations and cultural journals. Ting had sided with Lu Hsun in the debate over "literature for national defense" in the thirties (see under Chou Yang) and she had been criticized by Chou Yang in the 1942 *cheng-feng* campaign. Unlike Chou she held a prominent place among China's intellectuals, and like him she was a power in the Party's cultural hierarchy. Both personally and through the pages of the *Wen-i pao* she played a leading role in the campaign against the film "The Story of Wu Hsun" and the literary *cheng-feng* movement of 1951–52. In 1952 she became an editor of *Jen-min wen-hsueh* (People's literature), the journal of the Association of Literary Workers, and at this time relinquished her post on *Wen-i pao* to her close friend Feng Hsueh-feng. Still, despite her activist role and orthodox ideological position, there were certain abiding elements in her thinking that conflicted with the Party's policies and remained beneath the surface. She was concerned with improving professional and literary standards, believing that literary work came from the writer's own feelings and not from a doctrine, such as socialist realism, that is imposed upon him. She represented a more professional, more independent approach to creativity and intellectual activity than Chou Yang's group.

Until 1954 the competition between Ting Ling and Chou Yang persisted. In the early PRC years they had drawn to themselves loyal supporters from the literary and intellectual world. While Chou was almost certainly in closer contact with the top leadership of the Party, Ting and her associates were in charge of two of Communist China's most influential journals. However, in the latter half of 1954, the CCP, with Chou Yang as its spokesman, launched an attack against *Wen-i pao* and its editor, Feng Hsueh-feng, for not conforming with the prevailing Party line. Ting Ling was attacked at this time and also during the Hu Feng (q.v.) campaign of 1955, but she was not criticized in the press and at open meetings. During the relatively liberal Hundred Flowers period in the mid-fifties she said very little in public, but when the "anti-rightist" campaign was launched in 1957 Ting became the chief scapegoat among the left-wing intellectuals.[5] She apparently resisted the campaign against her and publicly denounced her accusers, chief among them Chou Yang and his group. Unable to get an acceptable self-criticism from Ting, the Party began in the latter half of 1957 to remove her from all her posts.

Ting's fall from political grace represents the classic case of the author with high standards of literary excellence pitted against political authorities who allow no place for such an individualistic view. Moreover, the Party was faced with a woman who had a wide audience, especially among the youths of China. Because of this, the Party seemed to feel that the loyalty those youths showed to people like Ting Ling might divert their allegiance to the CCP. Unlike numerous other literary figures who made partial comebacks after the 1957–58 ideological campaign, virtually nothing has been heard of Ting aside from an occasional mention of her name in a pejorative sense. Her last known public appearance occurred in August 1960 when she spoke before the Third Congress of the AC-FLAC, but the text of her speech was not published.

1. *People's China*, no. 8:23 (April 16, 1952).
2. T. A. Hsia, *Enigma of the Five Martyrs* (Berkeley, Calif., 1962), pp. 4–31, 88–99.
3. Nym Wales, *My Yenan Notebook* (Madison, Conn., 1961), p. 156.
4. Merle Goldman, "Writers' Criticisms of the Party in 1942," *The China Quarterly*, no. 17: 205–228 (January–March 1964).
5. Merle Goldman, *Literary Dissent in Communist China* (Cambridge, Mass., 1967), pp. 203–242.

Ting Ying

(1888–1964; Mao-ming hsien, Kwangtung). Agronomist; President, Chinese Academy of Agricultural Sciences.

Ting Ying was probably the most important agronomist in Communist China until his death in 1964. He was born in Mao-ming hsien in southwestern Kwangtung. Ting graduated from the Agricultural College of Tokyo Imperial University in 1924 and returned to Kwangtung in the same year. He spent the next 25 years teaching agronomy in institutes of higher learning in south China, most notably at Kwangtung University in Canton (known after 1926 as Sun Yat-sen University). Much of his time during these years was spent in attempts to improve rice yields, and by 1936 he had developed over 60 improved strains.[1] In the wake of the Japanese invasion in 1937, the staff and students of Sun Yat-sen University (including Ting) moved

out of Canton to Nationalist-held areas. For most of the war the University was located at P'ing-shih in northern Kwangtung.

After the war Ting returned to Canton and remained in the city when the Communists captured it in late 1949. He was immediately named to membership in the Canton chapter of the Sino-Soviet Friendship Association and early in 1950 was placed on the Canton Municipal People's Government Council. However, his first important assignment under the Communists came in mid-1950 when he was named to membership on the national committee of the newly organized All-China Federation of Scientific Societies (ACFSS). When the ACFSS was merged with another scientific organization in September 1958 to form the China Scientific and Technical Association (CSTA), he became one of the vice-chairmen under Chairman Li Szu-kuang (q.v.), a famous geologist. Ting retained this post until his death in 1964. Under the ACFSS (and later the CSTA) a number of local branches were formed; Ting was in charge of the preparatory work for the Kwangtung chapter from 1952, and when it was formally established in November 1961 he was named as the first chairman. Two years later, possibly owing to his advanced age, Ting relinquished the chairmanship to another man, although he continued as the honorary chairman.

In 1952 Ting was appointed president of the newly formed South China Institute of Agricultural Sciences in Canton; he was reappointed to the presidency three years later when this institute was merged with the agricultural colleges of both Sun Yat-sen and Ling-nan universities to form the South China Agricultural College. He continued to hold this position until his death in 1964. He received his first post in the national government when he was elected as a deputy from Kwangtung to the First NPC (1954–1959). He was re-elected to the Second NPC (1959–1964) and again to the Third NPC, his last election coming just one month before his death. When the Department of Biology, Geology, and Geography was formed in May–June 1955 under the Academy of Sciences, Ting was named as a standing committee member. Most important, however, was his appointment to the presidency of the Chinese Academy of Agricultural Sciences. Formed in March 1957, the Academy was assigned the task of coordinating the work of over 200 institutes and experimental stations engaged in agricultural work, as well as the agricultural institutes that had been under the Academy of Sciences and 27 agricultural colleges throughout China. This was his most important assignment in the PRC and the one which occupied much of his time until his death.

In his capacity as an agronomist, Ting made three trips abroad for the PRC. In October 1955 he visited East Germany as a member of an agricultural research delegation and while there was made a corresponding academician of the East German Agricultural Sciences Academy. In Moscow, in January 1958, he negotiated and signed an agreement related to scientific and technical cooperation between the Chinese and Soviet Academies of Agricultural Sciences. Ting was the deputy leader of a delegation to the Sixth Congress of the Communist-dominated World Federation of Scientific Workers, held in Warsaw in September 1959. Before returning home he served as a member of the Chinese delegation, led by science administrator Nieh Jung-chen (q.v.), to celebrations in Germany commemorating the 10th anniversary of the East German government (October). Ting then went to Prague where he negotiated and signed an agreement (December) similar to that signed with the Russians in 1958. He was also given a special citation for his work by the Czech Academy of Agricultural Sciences.

In 1960 Ting moved from Canton to Peking in order to be closer to the work of the Academy of Agricultural Sciences. However, despite his advanced age, he continued to travel widely throughout the country, often to attend provincial agricultural conferences. In January 1963 he was credited with having had a major role in the establishment of experimental stations in Hainan Island, Canton, Kunming, Changsha, Nanking, Tientsin, Urumchi, and Kirin. In addition to contributing to such professional journals as *Chung-kuo Nung-pao* (Agricultural bulletin), he also wrote for the Party press—two of his articles appeared in the Party's most important journal, *Hung-ch'i* (Red flag, issues of July 1, 1961, and October 16, 1962). In collaboration with a team of experts, he also edited a large volume entitled *Chung-kuo shui-tao ts'ai-p'ei-hsueh* (Rice cultivation in China), a work published in 1961 and described as "one of the most significant theoretical works on the subject in recent times."[2]

Together with a number of intellectuals, Ting became a member of the CCP in 1956 at a time when the Party admitted a number of important intellectuals. In view of his advanced age, it is clear that the move had little specific political importance; rather, it can be regarded as one of the Party's continuing efforts to gain the cooperation of the Chinese intelligentsia. Although he was already a Party member, Ting sharply criticized Party agricultural policies during the Hundred Flowers period in the spring of 1957. Speaking before a nationwide conference of the Academy of Sciences in May, he complained of the lack of coordination between agricultural theories and practices and cautioned against grandiose plans to expand agricultural production before the basic research had been completed. Unlike many other Party critics at this time, there are no indications that he was penalized for his criticisms. On the contrary, as suggested above, he continued to be an active contributor to the press. His activities in this connection continued until his death. In fact, his last article, an essay on rice production, appeared in the *JMJP* just a few days after his death.

Ting Ying died in Peking on October 14, 1964, at the age of 76. He was praised for his implementation of Party agricultural policies and was described as having made "important contributions to the theory and practice of the origin and ecology of various types of rice in China, the cultivation of new strains and techniques for high yields." The Communists claim that his studies of the origins of rice in China had taken him into the fields of history, philology, archaeology, paleontology, botany, and geography.[3]

1. *China Reconstructs,* January 1963, p. 13.
2. *Ibid.,* p. 10.
3. *Ibid.,* p. 13.

Ts'ai Ch'ang

(1900–   ; Hsiang-hsiang, Hunan). Chairman, National Women's Federation; member, CCP Central Committee.

Ts'ai Ch'ang, one of the earliest women members of the CCP, is the most important women's leader in the CCP. Trained in both France and the Soviet Union, she has been a member of the Party Central Committee since 1928. Ts'ai was one of the few women to make the Long March. She spent the war years in Yenan and has headed the Women's Federation since its establishment in 1949. Ts'ai is the younger sister of Ts'ai Ho-sen (q.v.), one of the earliest and most important Party leaders, and she is the wife of Li Fu-ch'un (q.v.), a top economic planner.

Ts'ai's father was an official in the Kiangnan Arsenal in Shanghai, which was established by the Ch'ing statesman Tseng Kuo-fan, to whom her mother was distantly related. An official Communist source described her family as "bankrupt small landlords," and as a consequence she could not attend school until the age of 11.[1] She was helped in her efforts to get an education by her mother, a modern-minded woman who took a keen interest in the careers of Ts'ai and her brother, Ts'ai Ho-sen. Ts'ai Ch'ang graduated from the Chou-nan Girls' School in Changsha, where one of her teachers was Hsu T'e-li (q.v.), today one of the "elders" of the Party. At Chou-nan, Ts'ai became close friends with Hsiang Ching-yü (q.v.), who later married Ts'ai Ho-sen. While Ts'ai and her brother were in Changsha their father died, so their mother moved to Changsha and quickly became the mistress of a home which served as a meeting place for her children's politically minded friends, among them Mao Tse-tung.

After graduation from the girls' school, Ts'ai took a job as a school teacher at the primary school which was affiliated to her alma mater. Her first political activity grew out of the establishment by her brother and Mao of a student society, whose members came mainly from the students and faculty at the Hunan First Normal School. This organization, established in the spring of 1918, was called the Hsin-min hsueh-hui (New people's study society), and its principal aims were to work for the interests of China and to train its members to become "new citizens."[2] The society succeeded far beyond the expectations its founding members could have had, because an impressive number of its members later became Communists. Among the 80-odd early members, Hsiang Ching-yü and Ts'ai Ch'ang were the leaders of the women's group.

In 1919 Ts'ai Ho-sen and Mao organized a Hunan group to take part in the work-and-study program in France, which was then attracting many young Chinese intellectuals. In France they hoped to learn more about the challenging new ideas which had struck intellectuals so forcibly when the May Fourth Movement erupted among Chinese students in 1919. The work-and-study scheme had the support of several provincial governments; in the case of Hunan, the government offered relatively good stipends to many of the students. Thus, of the 1,600-odd "worker-students" who went to France in 1919–20, the largest group (roughly a quarter) came from Hunan.[3] In the Changsha area, Ts'ai Ho-sen and Mao were the major organizers among the male students (although Mao himself did not go to France), and Hsiang Ching-yü and Ts'ai Ch'ang served a similar function among the women students at Chou-nan and other schools.[4]

The two women and many of their young colleagues set out for France in the fall of 1919. Many of the Changsha students made their headquarters at the Collège de Montargis, south of Paris, where they organized a branch of the Hsin-min hsueh-hui, which was led by Ts'ai Ho-sen. Among the other members were Li Wei-han (q.v.) and Li Fu-ch'un; the latter was to become Ts'ai's husband in 1923. These same students also established the Kung-hsueh hu-chu she (Work and study cooperative society), and from this nucleus they established a Socialist Youth League and what amounted to a French branch of the CCP. Ts'ai joined the Youth League in 1922 and the CCP in 1923. Many of the Youth League and CCP members were also active in KMT branches in France; for example, Ts'ai's husband Li Fu-ch'un and Chou En-lai held rather important KMT posts in France during the early twenties. Ts'ai is known to have been a KMT member after her return home (see below), and it seems likely that she joined while still in France. During her stay there she worked part-time in a machinery factory, studied politics, and improved her French.

Sometime in 1924 Ts'ai and her husband joined the exodus of Chinese students leaving France for Moscow where they attended the Communist University of the Toilers of the East. Li Fu-ch'un returned to China in late 1924 or early 1925, but Ts'ai remained in Moscow long enough to attend the fifth meeting of the Comintern's Executive Committee (ECCI) in March 1925.[5] Soon afterwards she returned home and was thus in China during the early period of the KMT–CCP alliance. Like many of her colleagues, Ts'ai had joined the KMT by this time.[6] Working initially in Canton, then the revolutionary center of the nation, she immediately plunged into the task of organizing women laborers. When the Communist-supported Canton–Hong Kong strike and boycott began in June 1925, Ts'ai was named to the strike committee. This was headed by Communist labor leader Su Chao-cheng, whose biography describes this important strike in detail. During this period Ts'ai was often associated with Ho Hsiang-ning, the wife of the important Left-KMT leader Liao Chung-k'ai, who was assassinated in August 1925.

When the Northern Expedition was launched from Canton in mid-1926, Ts'ai was one of the few women to serve in the Nationalist Army's General Political Department. Her husband was with the unit which marched through Kiangsi and eventually captured Nanking, but it is not known if Ts'ai was with him at that time. Either before or after the first phase of the Northern Expedition (mid-1926 to early 1927), Ts'ai worked as an organizer of women workers in Nanchang (the Kiangsi capital) and Shanghai. Then, after the complete break in KMT–CCP relations in mid-1927, she worked in the Party underground in the Wuhan area. In the spring of 1928 Ts'ai's girlhood friend and sister-in-law, Hsiang Ching-yü, was captured and executed in Wuhan, and thus Ts'ai assumed the unofficial role of China's leading woman revolutionary.

Because of the increasingly dangerous situation in China for Communist Party members, the CCP held its Sixth National Congress in Moscow in June–July 1928. Many of the Chinese delegates to the congress were studying in Moscow, but others traveled there for the meetings, like Ts'ai and her brother (but not her husband, who remained in China). Ts'ai was elected to the CCP Central Committee, and immediately afterward she was one of the Chinese delegates to the Sixth Comintern Congress (July–September). She remained in the Soviet Union for the next four years, but nothing is known of what she did there. Whatever the nature of her activities, it is clear that she had little trouble in keeping abreast of Party developments in China. During her days in the Russian capital the Chinese had a delegation to the Comintern which included such important men as her brother, Ch'ü Ch'iu-pai, and Chang Kuo-t'ao (qq.v.); older Party leaders like Lin Po-ch'ü and Hsu T'e-li were receiving advanced training at Sun Yat-sen University, and up-and-coming younger leaders like Ch'en Shao-yü and Ch'in Pang-hsien (qq.v.) were at the same school.

Ts'ai returned home in 1932 and immediately proceeded to the Communist base in Kiangsi where her husband was working. In December 1933 she was elected to Executive Committee membership in the Kiangsi Provincial Soviet, one of the constituent bodies of the Chinese Soviet Republic established in Juichin in November 1931. When the Second Congress of the Republic was held in January–February 1934, Ts'ai and her husband were elected members of the Republic's Central Executive Committee, the leading political organ of the Juichin government until the Long March began in the fall of 1934. She was one of the few women who made the year-long trek to the northwest, but because her health was impaired by the rigors of the march she was sent to the Soviet Union for medical treatment. Ts'ai was back in China by the end of the summer of 1936 when journalist Edgar Snow interviewed her and her husband in Kansu. She was then in charge of women's work for the CCP and was also engaged in "white areas work," the term normally denoting efforts by the CCP to gain adherents in areas controlled by the KMT.[7] A year later Snow's wife, Nym Wales, interviewed Ts'ai in Yenan; Miss Wales wrote that Ts'ai had just come to Yenan from Kansu "where she had been in charge of secret organizational work in the White areas." Wales described her as the "dean" of Communist women and, more picturesquely, as "China's Rosa Luxemburg."[8]

During the war years Ts'ai directed women's work for the Shensi-Kansu-Ninghsia Border Region Government, headed the Party's Women's Committee, and worked in the Party Organization Department, in which her husband was a leading official. When the Party held its Seventh Congress in Yenan from April to June 1945, only three women were placed on the Central Committee. Teng Ying-ch'ao (Mme. Chou En-lai) and Ch'en Shao-min (qq.v.) were elected alternates, but only Ts'ai was elected a full member, thus reconfirming her status as the leading woman member of the CCP. She continued to be secretary of the Party's Women's Committee and still holds this post (redesignated first secretary by 1956).

In 1945 Ts'ai became chairman of the newly established Preparatory Committee for the China Liberated Areas Women's Federation, and in this capacity she began to participate in the affairs of the Communist-dominated Women's International Democratic Federation (WIDF).

She was elected a member of the WIDF Council in 1946, and in 1947 she represented the Chinese Women's Federation at a WIDF meeting in Prague. She was promoted to a vice-chairmanship of the WIDF at a meeting in Rome in May 1948, and she was back in Europe to attend the Second WIDF Congress held in Budapest in December 1948; Ts'ai addressed the congress on the development of the women's movement in Asia and Africa, and she was re-elected a WIDF vice-chairman. Earlier that year, at the Sixth Labor Congress, held in Harbin in August 1948, Ts'ai served on the congress presidium (steering committee) and was elected a member of the Sixth Executive Committee of the All-China Federation of Labor (known later as the Federation of Trade Unions). She was also a member of the Seventh Executive Committee from 1953 to 1957.

In January 1949, while Ts'ai was still abroad, she was elected chairman of the Preparatory Committee of the All-China Federation of Democratic Women (ACFDW), which was established in Mukden. Ts'ai's delegation to the Budapest Congress returned home in February 1949, but then in March she was once again in Europe, this time to attend a WIDF Council meeting in Prague. However, she returned home in time to address the inaugural session of the First All-China Women's Congress, held in Peking from March to April. Predictably, Ts'ai was elected chairman (a post she still retains) of the ACFDW, the name of which was changed in 1957 to the National Women's Federation. This organization, one of the largest in China, claimed a membership of 20,000,000 in 1949 and over 75,000,000 only four years later; among its affiliated bodies are the Women's Christian Temperance Union and the YWCA. (Further information on the ACFDW is contained in the biography of Teng Ying-ch'ao, China's second most important woman Communist.)

Like most of the top Communist leaders then in Peking, Ts'ai was busily engaged throughout the spring and summer of 1949 in the preparations for the establishment of the national government and the numerous "people's" organizations which were also set up in this period. In May 1949 she was appointed director of the Women Worker's Department under the Labor Federation, a post she held until the mid-1950's when she was succeeded by Yang Chih-hua, the widow of early Party leader Ch'ü Ch'iu-pai. In June, under the chairmanship of Mao Tse-tung, the Preparatory Committee of the CPPCC was established; Ts'ai was a member of the Standing Committee, and a few weeks later she was named to membership on the Preparatory Committee of the Sino-Soviet Friendship Association. But most important, Ts'ai represented the Women's Federation at the sessions in September of the CPPCC, the organization which brought the national government into existence. She served as a member of the CPPCC presidium (steering committee) and was elected to membership on the permanent CPPCC National Committee. In the new government organs, she became a member of the Central People's Government Council (CPGC), a body which had legislative, executive, and judicial responsibilities and which, in its 34 meetings between 1949 and 1954, passed on virtually all the vital measures adopted in the formative years of the PRC. It consisted of a chairman (Mao), six vice-chairmen, and 56 members. Apart from a few non-Party women (e.g., Mme. Sun Yat-sen), Ts'ai was the only woman member of the CPGC.

Having served on the Sino-Soviet Friendship Association Preparatory Committee, Ts'ai was named to the Executive Board when the organization was formally established in October 1949. Five years later she attended the association's second conference, but she relinquished her position on the Executive Board. Another post which she received in October 1949 was a vice-chairmanship of the China Peace Committee. A year later this committee was reorganized, and from that date until mid-1958 she served on the Standing Committee. In December 1949 the Asian Women's Conference was held in Peking. This was one of the first of many international meetings convened in China during the ensuing years, and as such it symbolized the priority given to the "liberated" women of "new China." Ts'ai chaired the committee in Peking which organized this week-long conference, attended by 165 delegates from 14 Asian countries (see under Teng Ying-ch'ao).

In March 1953 Ts'ai made her last trip abroad when she went to Moscow as a member of Chou En-lai's delegation to Stalin's funeral. She was originally selected to lead the Chinese delegation to the Third World Women's Congress in Copenhagen in June 1953, but for reasons not explained she did not make this trip. Possibly because of her rather frail health, Ts'ai has been less active in the women's and labor movements since the early and middle 1950's. She continues to head the National Women's Federation, but she relinquished her membership on the Trade Union Federation's Executive Committee in late 1957. Moreover, when these two organizations held national congresses in 1953 and 1957, Ts'ai's participation tended to be nominal. For example, at the Third Women's Congress (September 1957), it fell to Chang Yun (q.v.) to deliver the keynote speech. Similarly, after 1958 she ceased to be a regular contributor to Chung-kuo fu-nü (Women of China), the PRC's most important women's magazine.

In early 1953 Ts'ai was named to a special committee to draft the Election Law, and when the elections were held in the following year, she became a deputy from her native Hunan to the First NPC. At the inaugural session of the Congress in September 1954, when the central government was reorganized, Ts'ai was elected to membership on the NPC Standing Committee. She was re-elected to this post at the first sessions of the Second and Third NPC's, held in April 1959 and December 1964–January 1965, respectively. Here again, however, most of the major statements on women's affairs (a frequent topic at the 10 sessions of the NPC between 1954 and 1965) have come from other women leaders. In fact, it appears that Ts'ai's last important, policy-level statement on the role of women was delivered at the Party's Eighth National Congress in September 1956. Her speech dealt with the training and promotion of women cadres. Ts'ai noted that from 1951 to 1955 the number of women cadres had grown from eight to 14.5 per cent of the total number of cadres throughout China, and she urged in strong terms that these figures be increased. Her speech also included an unusually candid statement in support of birth control; she phrased this not in terms of population control, but rather as being beneficial to "women's health, child care, home life and national prosperity." During the congress Ts'ai served on the presidium and the credentials committee, and most important, she was again elected a member of the Party Central Committee.

Since the mid-1950's Ts'ai's name has appeared in connection with scores of ad hoc bodies which clearly take little or none of her time (for example, a preparatory committee to commemorate the 50th anniversary of the 1911 Revolution), and she is frequently mentioned in the press when distinguished visitors are in China. Such patterns are quite normal for many of Peking's major but aging leaders, and it is a pattern which may have evolved in order to allow the elite members of the Party more time to work at policy levels. In any case, unless precluded for reasons of health, Ts'ai was still China's most important woman leader as of the mid-1960's.

1. *Women in New China* (Peking, 1949), pp. 5–7.

2. Jerome Ch'en, *Mao and the Chinese Revolution* (London, 1965), p. 50.

3. Conrad Brandt, *The French-Returned Elite in the Chinese Communist Party,* reprint no. 13, Institute of International Studies, University of California, Berkeley, Calif., 1961, p. 3.

4. Li Jui, *Mao Tse-tung t'ung-chih te ch'u-ch'i ko-ming huo-tung* (Comrade Mao Tse-tung's early revolutionary activities; Peking, 1957), p. 86.

5. *"Szu-pa" pei-nan lieh-shih chi-nien-ts'e* (In memory of the martyrs who died in the "April 8" accident; Chungking [?], 1946), p. 204.

6. Nym Wales, *Inside Red China* (New York, 1939), p. 182.

7. Edgar Snow, *Random Notes on Red China, 1936–1945* (Cambridge, Mass., 1957), p. 138.
8. Wales, pp. 176, 182–185.

Ts'ai Ho-sen

(1890–c.1931; Hsiang-hsiang, Hunan). CCP founder and important early leader; member, CCP Politburo.

Ts'ai Ho-sen was one of the major figures in the early history of the CCP and a close friend of Mao Tse-tung. Ts'ai was never in strong health, nor particularly a man of action, but from his student days in Changsha he displayed a bent for leadership which made him stand out in the group of young Hunanese intellectuals to which Mao also belonged. Intellectually drawn to Marxism and known for his writing skills, Ts'ai was involved in some of the numerous controversies that weakened the Party in the period before the rise of Mao. Nonetheless, he is depicted in orthodox Maoist histories as one of the Party's most respected "martyrs." There is probably no other family which contributed more to the Communist movement; his wife, Hsiang Ching-yü (q.v.), was the most important CCP woman leader of her day, and his sister, Ts'ai Ch'ang (q.v.), assumed a similar role in later years.

Ts'ai, known in his school days as Ts'ai Lin-pin, was born in Hsiang-hsiang, a rural area not far southwest of Changsha, the Hunan capital. He was the eldest of six children. His father was a minor official in the Kiangnan Arsenal in Shanghai which was established by Tseng Kuo-fan, the famous Ch'ing statesman to whom Ts'ai's mother was distantly related. One of Ts'ai's grandfathers served in Tseng Kuo-fan's Hunan Army. Ts'ai's modern-minded mother had a lively interest in her children's careers and opened her home in Changsha to their radical student friends. After entering a primary school for her own education at the age of 50,[1] she accompanied her son and daughter to France where they went as students in 1919 (see below).

Ts'ai went to Changsha in 1913, and enrolled in the tuition-free Hunan First Normal School where he probably first became acquainted with Mao Tse-tung. In 1915 he transferred to the Hunan Higher Normal School. He and Mao became close friends, and Mao often attended the discussion groups of normal school students which were held at the Ts'ai home in Changsha. During one of their summer vacations the two students made a walking trip around the Tung-t'ing Lake region of northern Hunan.[2] They were the leaders of the student society formally established in April 1918. Known as the Hsin-min hsueh-hui (New people's study society), many of its 70-odd members became Communists, among them Hsiang Ching-yü, Ts'ai Ch'ang, Hsia Hsi, and Li Wei-han (qq.v.).

Mao and Ts'ai were instrumental in getting a number of Hunanese students, many of them from the Hsin-min hsueh-hui, to join the student groups then going to France for a program of work and study, while Hsiang Ching-yü and Ts'ai Ch'ang recruited women students in Hunan for the same program. Mao did not accompany them, but Ts'ai and his group left for France in November 1919. Most of the Hunan students went to the Collège de Montargis, south of Paris, where they formed a branch of the Hsin-min hsueh-hui. Remaining in close touch with developments at home, the French group led by Ts'ai was soon drawn to Marxism. Mao took over the leadership of those who remained in Hunan. In connection with this period, one writer has commented that there "is no doubt that Ts'ai's influence on Mao was strong" and that his "passionate revolutionary temperament was very much in tune with Mao's."[3]

Ts'ai and his colleagues established the Kung-hsueh hu-chu she (Work and study cooperative society). This was the nucleus for the establishment in 1921 of the Socialist Youth League in France which in turn led to the formation in mid-1922 of what amounted to a CCP branch in France. But by that time Ts'ai and Hsiang Ching-yü, whom he had married in 1921, had been deported from France (October 1921) for their political activities (see under Ch'en I).

They arrived in Shanghai in the winter of 1921–22 (only a few months after the founding of the CCP) and immediately became active in the Communist movement. During the following decade Ts'ai was frequently involved in the serious ideological and power struggles that were characteristic of the CCP's early growth. There is not sufficient evidence to indicate all the positions which he took as the Party line shifted and turned, but the available evidence suggests a resilience and ability to move from one controlling group to the other.

In July 1922, at the Party's Second Congress, Ts'ai and his wife were both elected to the Central Committee. At the Congress and immediately afterwards, the Party leaders vigorously debated the question of cooperation with the KMT, as well as the issue of whether or not Communists should also join the KMT. In regard to the matter of dual membership, there are conflicting versions about who supported the idea and who opposed it, but it appears that Ts'ai (and, in particular, Party chief Ch'en Tu-hsiu and Chang Kuo-t'ao) opposed the scheme. A month later, a special conference was held at West Lake, Hangchow, to reconsider the question. Comintern representative Maring, who strongly urged acceptance of the proposal, was initially opposed by five delegates, including Ch'en, Chang, and Ts'ai.[4] However, they subsequently changed their views and the conference decided that dual membership would be allowed. Despite his former attitude, Ts'ai was one of the first to join. He was among four men who had done so by 1922, the others being Ch'en Tu-hsiu, Li Ta-chao, and Chang T'ai-lei (qq.v.).[5]

At about this time, Ts'ai was also involved in other intra-Party disputes, among them the controversy regarding the rather novel ideas of one of the Party founders, Li Han-chün. Ts'ai is said to have opposed Li's ideas (described in Li's biography) and in doing so he stood together with Chang Kuo-t'ao. Of interest to the historian is the fact that his collaboration with Chang is mentioned in a biography of Ts'ai published in 1936—before Chang lost his political struggle with Mao Tse-tung and deserted the CCP. However, Chang's name was deleted when this same biography was reprinted in 1952.[6]

Soon after the Second Party Congress, *Hsiang-tao chou-pao* (Guide weekly) was established under Ts'ai's editorship. One of the Party's most influential journals, it was first published in Shanghai in September 1922 (and later in Canton). Ts'ai continued as the editor until the magazine was disbanded in mid-1927, except for a period from late 1925 to early 1927 when he was abroad.[7] Like so many of the Party leaders in Shanghai in the mid-twenties, Ts'ai was on the faculty at Shanghai University, a school that served as a training ground for Communist cadres until it was closed down by the authorities in June 1925 during the early stages of the May 30th Movement. Among his colleagues at the university were Ch'ü Ch'iu-pai, Teng Chung-hsia (q.v.), and Chang T'ai-lei.

When the CCP held its Fourth Congress in Shanghai in January 1925, Ts'ai was once again elected to the Central Committee. During that winter and spring he was one of the chief organizers of trade union activities which culminated in demonstrations known as the May 30th Movement (see under Li Li-san). Ts'ai is said to have favored bold action by the Party to capitalize on the workers' unrest,[8] and with Li Li-san and Ch'ü Ch'iu-pai he was a major figure in the establishment of the Shanghai General Labor Union.[9] In late 1925 the Ts'ai's left for Moscow to attend the Sixth Plenum of the Comintern Executive Committee (ECCI), held in February–March 1926. They remained for a year, returning home in 1927 in time for the Fifth CCP Congress in Hankow (April–May). Ts'ai was elected for the first time to the Politburo and afterwards went to work for the Party's Propaganda Department.

Ts'ai's arrival back in China and the Fifth Congress coincided with the gravest crisis for the CCP since its establishment in 1921. Immediately before the Congress, Chiang Kai-shek and the right-wing KMT had dealt the CCP a stunning defeat in Shanghai that took the lives of scores of important Communist leaders. More-over, the "left" KMT, headquartered in Wuhan, was rapidly growing cool in its relations to the CCP. Ts'ai's reaction to this situation, according to his own version, was to back plans to train Communist armed forces (a strategy opposed by Ch'ü Ch'iu-pai).[10] Because the Red Army did not then exist, this meant, in effect, the fostering of agrarian revolts by Communist-sponsored peasant guerrilla units, or, insurrections from within the ranks of KMT armies. As history was soon to demonstrate, both courses would be futile. In May 1927, the Communists suffered further serious setbacks in Changsha resulting from attacks on their organizations there by military leader Hsu K'o-hsiang, and the abortive counterattacks led by CCP-organized peasant bands from nearby rural areas (mainly from P'ing-chiang and Liu-yang hsien). In the face of the defeats suffered by the ill-equipped peasant forces, Ts'ai offered a "Resolution on Hunan and Hupeh" in June which called for the mobilization of "about 20,000 peasants and 300,000 'KMT masses'" for further attacks on Changsha.[11] No immediate action was taken to implement Ts'ai's plan, but it foreshadowed some of the Party's actions later in the summer.

Following these successive defeats, the CCP underwent an intense internal struggle, during which a new leadership under Ch'ü Ch'iu-pai, Mao, Ts'ai, and others was able to unseat Ch'en Tu-hsiu and lay plans for the far-reaching campaign of peasant insurrections known as the Autumn Harvest Uprisings. The new leadership took control at the famous "Emergency Conference" on August 7, 1927, only one week after the complete KMT-CCP break at the time of the Nanchang Uprising (see under Yeh T'ing). Ch'ü Ch'iu-pai chaired the meeting and Ch'en Tu-hsiu was deposed as the Party chief by a hastily assembled "rump" committee that replaced the Central Committee elected at the Fifth Congress only three months earlier. Despite the fact that Ts'ai and Ch'ü had held differing opinions on important policy issues in the spring of 1927, Ts'ai was named to the "rump" committee and was also appointed secretary of the Party's North China Regional Bureau. In being named to the latter post Ts'ai, in effect, replaced Li Ta-chao (q.v.) who had been executed shortly before by the northern warlords. It is not clear whether Ts'ai went to Peking to assume this post, and if he did, it is evident that he had to operate in an underground capacity. It is known, however, that his wife remained in the Wuhan area, where she was apprehended and executed in the spring of 1928.

In the summer of 1928 Ts'ai was in Moscow again, this time to attend the Sixth CCP Congress. He was re-elected to the Politburo, but on this occasion he opposed Ch'ü Ch'iu-pai. According to Chang Kuo-t'ao, the Party was then divided into two approximately equal factions (see under Ch'ü Ch'iu-pai). Chou En-lai, Li Li-san, and Ch'ü Ch'iu-pai headed the so-called "left" faction, while Ts'ai, Chang Kuo-t'ao, and Hsiang Ying (q.v.) led the "right-wing" group.[12] Over the next few years some of these alignments shifted, but Ts'ai's allegiance seems to have remained unchanged. Following the Congress, Li Li-san took control of the Party, but his political actions were soon to be questioned by the Comintern. Chang Kuo-t'ao has asserted that Ts'ai published an article in June 1929 which was critical of Li Li-san and which was endorsed by the Comintern; this in turn led the Li Li-san leadership to "banish" Ts'ai to Moscow.[13] However, Li Li-san, in his short biography of Ts'ai, stated that Ts'ai had gone to Moscow in early 1929 to be a member of the Chinese delegation, then headed by Ch'ü Ch'iu-pai, to the Comintern.[14] In any event, Ts'ai was in Moscow by mid-1929 and attended the 10th ECCI Plenum in July 1929. (During his stay in the USSR he was briefly confined to a sanitarium on the outskirts of Moscow.) Significantly, he did not return to China until mid-1930 when Li Li-san's power had begun to decline. He may have been accompanied by Ch'ü Ch'iu-pai, who was returning home with Comintern orders to convene the Third Plenum and block Li's ambitions. This critical meeting was convened in late September at Lu-shan in north Kiangsi; Ts'ai attended, and Ch'ü led an unsuccessful attempt to oust Li, presumably aided once more by Ts'ai.

There is some evidence that Ts'ai's attitude toward Ch'ü changed once more during late 1930. A Chinese journal of December 1930 quotes a statement by Ts'ai regarding the situation in the CCP after Li Li-san had been deposed and sent to Moscow in November 1930. Ts'ai declared that an "anti-Comintern move was still going on within the Chinese party leadership," and he charged Ch'ü with being a "factionist" who disrupted the Party. However, the same statement contained Ts'ai's own "confession" of having conducted a "double-faced, unprincipled struggle" against the Party in the past, and promised to correct his previous mistakes. He also expressed the hope that Li Li-san would confide all he might know "about cliques within the CCP" to the Comintern.[15]

In July 1931, by which time the Party was under the control of the so-called "28 Bolshevik" faction (see under Ch'in Pang-hsien), Ts'ai was sent to Hong Kong to direct Party work in Kwangtung. Two months later he was arrested. There are conflicting accounts concerning his death; some suggest he was executed by the British in Hong Kong, but it seems more likely that he was extradited to Canton and executed in the fall of 1931 (or possibly 1932).[16] The Ts'ai's were survived by a son and daughter.

Ts'ai's writings in the 1920's form an impor-

tant contribution to the Party literature of the period. He wrote about the Ch'en Tu-hsiu and Li Li-san controversies, many of his articles appearing in *Hsiang-tao chou-pao*. His long essay, "Chi-hui-chu-i shih" ("A History of Opportunism"), written in 1927 and later published in a Russian version,[17] provides considerable information on Comintern and CCP policies relating to the alliance with the "left" KMT and the progress of peasant insurrections in the spring of 1927. The above-mentioned biographic sketch of Ts'ai by Li Li-san, written while Li himself was "banished" to Moscow, presents a glowing but useful account of the martyred leader and praises him in particular for "opposing the Li Li-san line"![18]

1. Nym Wales, *Inside Red China* (New York, 1939), p. 183.

2. Emi Siao [Hsiao San], *Mao Tse-tung; His Childhood and Youth* (Bombay, 1953), p. 44.

3. Stuart R. Schram, *The Political Thought of Mao Tse-tung* (New York, 1963), p. 25.

4. C. Martin Wilbur and Julie Lien-ying How, eds., *Documents on Communism, Nationalism, and Soviet Advisers in China, 1918–1927* (New York, 1956), p. 84.

5. Conrad Brandt, *Stalin's Failure in China, 1924–1927* (Cambridge, Mass., 1958), p. 157.

6. *Lieh-shih chuan* (Biographies of martyrs; USSR [Moscow?], 1936), pp. 136–137; *Hu-nan ko-ming lieh-shih chuan* (Biographies of Hunan revolutionary martyrs; Changsha, 1952), p. 14.

7. *Hung-ch'i p'iao-p'iao* (Red flag fluttering; Peking, 1957), V, 47.

8. Brandt, p. 52; Jean Chesneaux, *Le Mouvement ouvrier chinois de 1919 à 1927* (Paris, 1962), p. 372.

9. Liu Li-k'ai and Wang Chen, *I-chiu i-chiu chih i-chiu erh-ch'i te Chung-kuo kung-jen yun-tung* (The Chinese workers' movement from 1919 to 1927; Peking, 1954), p. 39.

10. Robert C. North and Xenia J. Eudin, *M. N. Roy's Mission to China* (Berkeley, Calif., 1963), p. 7.

11. Roy Hofheinz, Jr., "The Autumn Harvest Insurrection," *The China Quarterly,* no. 32:40 (October–December 1967).

12. Tso-liang Hsiao, *Power Relations within the Chinese Communist Movement, 1930–1934* (Seattle, Wash., 1961), p. 61.

13. *Ibid.,* p. 27.

14. *Hung-ch'i p'iao-p'iao,* V, 47.

15. Tso-liang Hsiao, p. 85.

16. Siao Yu, *Mao Tse-tung and I Were Beggars* (Syracuse, N.Y., 1959), p. 240; *Hung-ch'i p'iao-p'iao,* V, 49; Ch'en Po-ta, *Notes on Ten Years of Civil War* (Peking, 1954), p. 108.

17. Li Min-hun, ed., *Ch'ih-se tang-an* (Red archives; Peking, 1929); the Russian version is cited in North and Eudin, p. 388.

18. *Hung-ch'i p'iao-p'iao,* V, 46–50.

Ts'ai Shu-fan

(1908–1958; Han-yang hsien, Hupeh). Early revolutionist and labor leader; alternate member, CCP Central Committee.

Ts'ai Shu-fan was active in the labor movement in the early twenties and then received three years of training in Moscow. He was a political officer in the Communist armies during the Kiangsi period, the Long March, the Sino-Japanese War, and the civil war with the Nationalists in the late forties. After the establishment of the PRC in 1949 he worked in the labor field in the southwest. Transferring to Peking in 1954 he specialized in the promotion of athletic activities until his death in an air crash in 1958.

Unlike most of the Chinese Communist elite, Ts'ai came from the working class. He was born into a family of coal miners; both his father and uncle worked in the important mines at Ta-yeh and Han-yang near Hankow. Three days after Ts'ai's birth his family moved to the famous coal mines at An-yuan in western Kiangsi not far from P'ing-hsiang. He attended primary school in An-yuan for only two years before he too became a miner. For three years he served an apprenticeship with the well-known Han-yeh-p'ing Company at P'ing-hsiang, where he engaged in "manual work on the motors, pumps and trams." In 1921 Mao Tse-tung had gone to the Han-yeh-p'ing mines to organize workers. This work was continued by Li Li-san (q.v.), who came to P'ing-hsiang in 1922 where he established a part-time school for workers that Ts'ai attended. In an autobiographical account given to Nym Wales (which provides much of the information for this sketch),[1] Ts'ai claimed that he promoted strikes in the 1923–24 period as a member of the An-yuan Coal Miners' Labor Union. Then only in his middle teens, he joined the Socialist Youth League in 1923. In the next year, when provincial troops were called in to suppress the unions, Ts'ai fled to nearby Changsha. Upon his return to An-yuan he learned that his family had been arrested and was forced to escape again, this time to Nanchang, the Kiangsi capital where he organized workers at an arsenal. In 1926 he was imprisoned for a short time and in 1927, when just 19, he joined the CCP.

In August 1927, shortly after the KMT-CCP split, Ts'ai left for Moscow where he spent the next three years. He enrolled in the Communist University of the Toilers of the East where he studied Chinese and the natural sciences. After completing a six-month term he attended the Sixth Comintern Congress in mid-1928. He subsequently spent six months at Sun Yat-sen University, which had been founded in 1925 and had attracted large numbers of Chinese students in the next few years, only some of whom were Communists. Ts'ai later studied for nine months

at the important Lenin School. While enrolled there he was involved in a minor way in one of the many incidents concerning the Chinese Eastern Railway in Manchuria. The railway was jointly administered by Chinese, Manchurians, and Russians, but on July 10, 1929, Manchurian warlord Chang Hsueh-liang, in conjunction with the Nationalist government, seized the line. After futile diplomatic negotiations the Russians moved troops into western Manchuria and captured a number of Chang's soldiers. According to Ts'ai's account he was temporarily assigned to work with these prisoners. Afterwards he returned to the Lenin School. In 1930 he attended the Fifth International Labor Congress in Moscow and then returned to China. During his long stay in the Soviet Union Ts'ai married a Russian.[2]

Upon his return home Ts'ai worked briefly in the Shanghai labor movement and then, traveling via Hong Kong, made his way on foot to Communist-held areas in Fukien and then to the Kiangsi Soviet area. After working there again briefly in the labor movement, he was assigned to the guerrilla force that Lo Ping-hui (q.v.) had established on the Fukien-Kiangsi border. In 1930 Lo's 12th Army was placed under the First Army Corps, which was one of the major components of the First Front Army led by Chu Te and Mao Tse-tung. Ts'ai fought with this corps during the second and third Annihilation Campaigns conducted in 1931 by the Nationalists against the Communists. He was wounded in 1931 and again in mid-1933 when he lost his left arm. Ts'ai was then serving as political commissar of the Seventh Army Corps, but after he recovered from his injury he was transferred to the same position in Lo Ping-hui's newly organized Ninth Army Corps.

At the Second All-China Congress of Soviets, held in Juichin in January–February 1934, Ts'ai was elected a member of the Central Executive Committee, the governing body of the Chinese Soviet Republic. In the fall of 1934 he was among those who set out on the Long March, and when they reached Kweichow in January 1935 he became a member of the Political Department of the Revolutionary Military Council. After arriving in north Shensi in the fall of 1935, he was made commissioner of the Interior and of Judicial Affairs (posts that were presumably subordinate to the Chinese Soviet Republic). In early 1936 Ts'ai was among those who took part in the thrust from Shensi into Shansi, which ended in defeat for the Communists at the hands of Shansi warlord Yen Hsi-shan (see under Lin Piao). In this endeavor he engaged in organizing partisans for the Communists' 30th Army, led by Yen Hung-yen (q.v.).

When war with Japan broke out in mid-1937 it appears that Ts'ai worked briefly in the Communists' Eighth Route Army liaison office in Sian,[3] but by 1939 he was serving as director of the Political Department of the Army's 129th Division, commanded by Liu Po-ch'eng. Concurrently, Ts'ai was head of the Political Department in the T'ai-hang Military Region in the mountains of southeast Shansi where the 129th Division made its headquarters. However, by the end of the war in 1945 he had been transferred to Nieh Jung-chen's Shansi-Chahar-Hopeh Military Region, where he was deputy director (until 1948) of the Political Department. Then in 1948–49 he was deputy director of the Political Department for the North China Military Region (which included Shansi and Hopeh). Ts'ai returned to Liu Po-ch'eng's forces in 1949 (now known as the Second Field Army) and in this capacity he attended the inaugural session of the CPPCC in Peking in September 1949 when the central government was established. He subsequently participated in the campaigns of the Second Field Army in central and southwest China during the closing months of 1949.

From 1950 to 1954 Ts'ai was a member of the regional government for southwest China, the Southwest Military and Administrative Committee (SWMAC), reorganized into the Southwest Administrative Committee (SWAC) in 1953. He was also a member of the SWMAC–SWAC's Finance and Economics Committee. More important, however, were his posts in the field of labor. From 1950 to 1954 he was director of the Southwest Branch of the All-China Federation of Labor (ACFL), in 1950 he was director of the SWMAC's Labor Department, and in 1952 a vice-chairman of the SWMAC's Labor Employment Committee.

Ts'ai served on the preparatory committee for the Seventh National Labor Congress held in Peking in May 1953. He was made a member of the All-China Federation of Trade Unions' Executive Committee and of the Presidium, which conducts the work of the organization between congresses. In December 1957, at the Eighth Labor Congress, he was re-elected to the Executive Committee but not to the Presidium, because by this time he had become engaged in other fields of work. He returned to Moscow for a second time in April–May 1953 as leader of the Chinese delegation attending the Russian May Day celebrations.

Brought from the southwest to Peking when the First NPC inaugurated the constitutional government in September 1954, Ts'ai represented Chungking in the NPC and continued to do so until his death. With the establishment of the new government, however, he became much less active in labor work and entered into the new field of sports promotion. In October 1954 he was named a vice-chairman under Ho Lung of the State Council's Physical Culture and Sports Commission. By the following fall Ts'ai held two further assignments in the sports field; in November he was named chairman of a committee to organize the 1955 International Friendly Marksmanship Contest, and he was also identified as director of the National Defense Sports Club.

In January 1956 Ts'ai became chairman of a committee to prepare for China's participation in the 16th Olympic Games, held in Melbourne that year, and in October he was made the chief of the 92-member Chinese delegation to the games. However, when it became apparent that the Nationalists would also send a Chinese team to Melbourne, Peking withdrew. In the meantime, in June–July 1955 he led a delegation which included a 159-member gymnastic team to the Czech National Spartakiade in Prague; and from July to August 1956 he headed a group of Chinese athletes on a visit to East Germany. Then in October 1956 Ts'ai was elected to membership on the National Committee of the All-China Athletic Federation.

In September 1956, at the Eighth Party Congress, Ts'ai was elected an alternate member of the Central Committee. In 1958, on the eve of their annual October celebration of Chinese National Day, the PRC established 10 friendship associations for the development of cultural relations with bloc nations; Ts'ai was named to head the China-Hungary Friendship Association. A few days later, while en route to Moscow, he died in an air crash (October 17) that also took the life of the well-known literary figure Cheng Chen-to.

1. Nym Wales, *Red Dust* (Stanford, Calif., 1952), pp. 83–89.
2. Edgar Snow, *Red Star over China* (New York, 1938), p. 367.
3. Nym Wales, *Inside Red China* (New York, 1939), p. 295.

Ts'ao Chü-ju

(c.1904–   ). Financial specialist.

Ts'ao Chü-ju, a finance specialist, was born about 1904.[1] His entire career with the Chinese Communists, which reaches back to the early 1940's, has been devoted to financial affairs, with a particular emphasis on banking. He was engaged in this type of work by 1943, presumably in one of the Communist-held areas. He continued in this field in Manchuria in the late 1940's, serving in 1948–49 as the General Manager of the Northeast (Communist) Bank, presumably under the jurisdiction of the Northeast Administrative Committee. Under this same regional government he was also the secretary-general of the Finance and Economics Committee by 1949.

Ts'ao was brought from Manchuria to Peking in the fall of 1949 when the first staff assignments were being made in the central government. When the national government was established in 1949, the key economic organ under the Government Administration Council (the cabinet) was the Finance and Economics Committee (FEC), headed by China's top economic specialist, Ch'en Yun. Ts'ao was named to membership on the FEC in October 1949, a position he held until the constitutional government was inaugurated in the fall of 1954. The FEC, in turn, had a number of important subordinate bodies, the most important of which was probably the Central Financial and Economic Planning Bureau, in many ways the direct predecessor of the State Planning Commission, which was established in 1952. Ts'ao was named in October 1949 as a deputy director of the Planning Bureau, holding the position until it was abolished in August 1952.

In 1950 Ts'ao received the first two of several appointments in Chinese banking circles. In March 1950 he was named as a member of the Board of Directors of the Bank of China, the institution in charge of banking abroad and subordinate to the People's Bank of China, the main financial institution in China. Two months later he was also named to the Board of the Bank of Communications. In each case he was appointed as a representative of the Bank's "public shares," the other members obstensibly representing "private shares." Ts'ao apparently continues to serve on both boards (see below). He was elevated to the Standing Committee in the Bank of China in November 1954, a position to which he was re-elected in May 1957. However, since that date he has not been directly identified with the activities of this overseas banking organization.

As already described, Ts'ao was a member from 1949 of the Finance and Economics Committee. In April 1951 he was made a deputy secretary-general of the Committee, serving until 1952 under Secretary-General Hsueh Mu-ch'iao and, after August 1952, subordinate to Sung Shao-wen (q.v.), both important economic specialists. More important, in September 1953 he was named as a deputy director of the People's Bank of China, a bank under the direct jurisdiction of the central government. Then, in November 1954, he replaced Nan Han-ch'en (q.v.) as the director, a position he was to hold for over a decade. Under the government reorganization in the fall of 1954, the People's Bank was placed under the State Council at an administrative level one notch below the ministries.

Ts'ao's activities with the People's Bank were wide in range. For example, he was a regular participant in negotiations with foreign banking circles. In May 1954 in Peking he signed three separate agreements with the North Koreans regarding rates of currency and remittances between the People's Bank of China and the Central Bank of Korea. Over the next several years he signed similar agreements with officials from

North Vietnam (November 1955 and June 1959), Rumania (February 1959), and Indonesia (October 1963). In June 1958 he also exchanged letters with the Norwegian ambassador regarding payments between the People's Bank and a Norwegian counterpart. He was also frequently involved in negotiations with visiting economic delegations that went to China in search of aid. An example of this occurred in November–December 1960 when Ernesto Che Guevara, then head of the National Bank of Cuba, went to Peking, a visit resulting in a large-scale loan to Cuba and a commitment to buy large quantities of Cuban sugar. Ts'ao's activities in international finance took him abroad in June 1962, when he led a three-member delegation to Australia (thus becoming one of the extremely few Chinese Communists to have visited that nation). Australian officials described this as a "private" visit to discuss central banking and to return an earlier visit to Peking by the governor of the Commonwealth Bank.[2] It would seem probable that Ts'ao also discussed details in the financing of the huge amount of grain that China was buying from Australia at that time.

Apart from his involvement in international banking matters, Ts'ao has naturally played a major role in domestic fiscal affairs in his capacity as head of the People's Bank. It was he who, on February 17, 1955, gave the official explanations for the issuance of "new people's banknotes" before the State Council. Soon after, he was interviewed by the press on this revaluation of Chinese currency, an interview that was printed in the important Communist annual yearbook.[3] He has also been a rather frequent participant in national conferences related to economics and finance. He spoke, for example, at a national conference in October–November of "advanced workers" in the field of credits and loans, addressing them on the relationship of national economic development and banking activities. Once again, his remarks were reprinted in the annual yearbook.[4] In addition to the publication of these two speeches, Ts'ao is also the author of an article summing up financial developments in the PRC during the first decade of its existence; the article was printed in both the Peking Ta-kung pao (October 12, 1959) and the JMJP (November 1, 1959).

Although the major portion of his career has been devoted to the executive branch of government, Ts'ao served as a Tsinghai deputy to the Second NPC (1959–1964). He was not, however, re-elected to the Third NPC, which opened in December 1964, but at this same time was selected as a "specially invited personage" to sit on the Fourth National Committee of the quasi-legislative CPPCC. And, when the first session of the National Committee closed in January 1965, he was also named to the governing

Standing Committee as a member. In September 1959 Ts'ao received still another post, being named as a member of the Overseas Chinese Affairs Commission under the State Council. This appointment is probably explained by Ts'ao's long ties with the Bank of China, which handles many of the remittances from overseas Chinese, an important source of capital for the PRC.

Ts'ao appeared regularly through 1964 in activities related to the work of the People's Bank of China. But then in February 1965 he was removed from his position as director (no replacement being named). From at least 1957 he had concurrently served as secretary of the Party Committee in the bank, a position that he probably relinquished when he was removed as the bank director. It is also not clear if he retains his seat on the board of the Bank of China (subordinate to the People's Bank) and the Bank of Communications.

1. Interview with a former employee of the PRC Government, Hong Kong, August 1964.
2. *Chinese World* (San Francisco), June 15, 1962.
3. 1956 *Jen-min shou-ts'e* (People's handbook), p. 532.
4. 1957 *Jen-min shou-ts'e*, p. 540.

Ts'ao Meng-chün

(c.1908–   ; Changsha, Hunan). Member of Secretariat, National Women's Federation; member, Standing Committee, NPC.

Miss Ts'ao Meng-chün has had an extremely varied career dating from the mid-1930's. From her college days at the Changsha Provincial Girls' Normal School she seems to have reacted against authority; it is reported that she was expelled from this school because she insisted on bobbing her hair. Later, however, she attended and graduated from Peking University. Sometime in the early 1930's Ts'ao married Tso Kung, a protégé of Sun Fo (the son of Sun Yat-sen), who became a member of the Nationalist Legislative Yuan in the 1940's; later she married Wang K'un-lun, who became a vice-mayor of Peking under the Communists in 1955.

Ts'ao's activities were centered in Nanking in the mid-1930's. There she was involved in such endeavors as the conduct of a nursery as well as the activities of a "Women's Society for the Promotion of Culture" and the better known China National Salvation Association (a nationwide organization that urged cessation of the civil war with the Communists and more active steps to resist Japanese incursions into China). It was in connection with the latter organization that Ts'ao was arrested and briefly imprisoned (1936) by the KMT authorities. The reasons for her arrest were apparently similar to (and perhaps connected with) the arrest of the famous "Seven Gentlemen" (see under Shih Liang), who were held in jails in 1936 and 1937 for their opposition to the government's handling of relations with Japan; they were not released until war broke out with Japan in mid-1937. Ts'ao was apparently released at about this same time. In any event, she was known to have been in Hankow (briefly the capital of China in 1938 after the fall of Nanking), and there (having divorced Tso Kung) she married Wang K'un-lun in 1938. When Hankow fell in late 1938, Ts'ao moved on to Chungking and remained there throughout the war where she established a children's home and took part with Li Te-ch'üan (q.v.) in the formation of the China Women's Association.

After the close of the Sino-Japanese War, Ts'ao went to Shanghai where she engaged in editorial work in the economic research department of the Bank of China and edited a magazine known as *Hsien-tai fu-nü* (Modern women). She also took part in the activities of the China Democratic League, one of the most important of the several non-Communist and non-KMT political organizations. Apparently her work in the League took her to Hong Kong, because she is known to have been a resident of the city in 1948. In November of that year, Ts'ao left for the Communist-controlled areas in Manchuria, and almost immediately after the fall of Peking to the Communists she arrived in the capital (February 25, 1949).

After Ts'ao's arrival in Peking she became occupied in many activities, most of them centering around the women's movement. From her first days in the capital she was active in the preparations for the convocation of the first women's congress (March–April 1949). At the close of the congress she was named to the Executive Committee and the more important Standing Committee of the All-China Federation of Democratic Women (ACFDW). In 1952 she became a deputy secretary-general of the Federation, and when the small and exclusive Secretariat was formed in April 1955, Ts'ao was named as one of the members of the body charged with the daily execution of the affairs of the Federation. She was also in charge of two of the departments subordinate to the ACFDW; for about the first year in the life of the Federation there was a department known as the "KMT-controlled Areas Work Department," which Ts'ao headed—presumably because of her previous connections developed in Chungking, Shanghai, and Hong Kong, where she was acquainted with all shades of Chinese political opinion. The other department Ts'ao headed was the Women's Welfare Department; she held the post from 1949 to a reorganization in 1952.

In the summer and fall of 1949, a number of semi-official "people's" organizations were being established, as well as the government of the

PRC. Ts'ao was busily engaged in these activities, beginning with the Preparatory Committee of the CPPCC, which met in June under the chairmanship of Mao Tse-tung. In September she was present for the first session of the CPPCC, at which time the PRC was established. She attended as a representative of the China National Salvation Association and was subsequently elected as an ACFDW representative to the second and third National Committees of the CPPCC, which existed from 1954 to 1964. She was not, however, re-elected to the Fourth CPPCC, which opened in late 1964. Ts'ao's other activity in 1949 centered about the establishment of three "people's" organizations, each of them formed in October 1949. She was named to the Executive Board of the Sino-Soviet Friendship Association, then one of the most active organizations in China (but after the Sino-Soviet rift became apparent about 1960 it faded into near oblivion). Ts'ao was re-elected to the Executive Committee in 1954 and 1959 and continues to hold this position. In addition, she was a deputy director of the SSFA Organization Department from 1949 to 1954 and in 1953-54 was a deputy director of the International Liaison Department. She was also elected to the National Committee of the China Peace Committee (another post she continues to hold) and was named to the Standing Committee of the Preparatory Committee for the "China New Political Science Research Association." A few years later (April 1953), this was formally organized into the Political Science and Law Association of China, with Ts'ao as one of the members of the National Council. She has been subsequently re-elected to the National Council, most recently in October 1964.

Other assignments received by Ts'ao in the early years of the PRC can be summarized as follows: councillor of the Councillor's Office, Government Administration Council (GAC), 1949–1954; member, Chinese People's Relief Administration, 1950 to date; member, Board of Directors, Red Cross Society of China, 1950 to date; member, National Committee, Chinese People's Committee in Defense of Children, 1951 to date; member, Labor Employment Committee, GAC, 1952–1954; deputy secretary-general, Committee for the Implementation of the Marriage Law, 1953–54.

Writing in 1962, Ts'ao also told of another task she was engaged in during the early 1950's.[1] One of the earliest and most significant of the many Communist programs was the "land reform" movement. As a member of the "20th land reform work corps" of the CPPCC, she took part in the movement from the end of 1951 to the summer of 1952 in Liu-ch'eng hsien in central Kwangsi.

It was also in the early 1950's that Ts'ao made the first of her many trips abroad. Between 1950 and 1964, she went abroad on 18 occasions, visiting 16 different nations in Asia, Europe, and Africa. The majority of these journeys (13 of the 18) have been involved with the Communist-backed international women's movement, led by the Women's International Democratic Federation (WIDF), of which Ts'ao has been a General Council alternate member since 1954. She attended large congresses of the WIDF in Denmark (June 1953), Austria (June 1958), and the USSR (June 1963), as well as meetings of the WIDF Council in Geneva in January 1954 and February 1955; a WIDF-backed "world congress of mothers" held in Lausanne, Switzerland, in July 1955; and celebrations marking the 50th anniversary of "International Women's Day" held in Denmark in April 1960. She has also attended the two Afro-Asian Women's Conferences, one held in Ceylon in February 1958 and the other in Cairo in January 1961. Though these can be considered offshoots of the WIDF, the rift between the Chinese and Russians has made almost all "Afro-Asian" organizations the battleground in struggles for allegiance to either Moscow or Peking. Finally, Ts'ao has been a member or the leader of women's friendship delegations to Korea (for a congress of Korean women in August 1954), France (July 1955), India (December 1956–January 1957), and Africa (where she visited Mali, Ghana, Tanganyika, and Zanzibar from March to June 1964).

Among these trips involving women's activities, the most significant was that to the Soviet Union in June 1963 for the World Congress of Women. It occurred during one of the many peaks in the continuing Sino-Soviet rift and consequently resulted in a disorderly struggle between Moscow and Peking with each side trading insults which were fully reported in the international press (see under Yang Yun-yü). Apart from these activities in the Communist-backed women's international movement, Ts'ao has been abroad on several other occasions worthy of brief notation. In November 1950 she was in Warsaw for the Second World Peace Congress, one of the first major Communist front congresses attended by the Chinese Communists. In March 1953 she was a delegate to the Fifth Congress of the Union of Bulgarian-Soviet Societies in Sofia and in October–December of the same year journeyed to North Korea as a member of a delegation to "comfort" the Chinese troops stationed there. She attended the leftist Asian Countries Conference in New Delhi in April 1955, out of which grew the Afro-Asian Solidarity Conference (see under Yang Shuo), and in July–August 1963 she was in Cuba for the 10th anniversary of the revolutionary movement which brought Fidel Castro to power.

In view of Ts'ao's extensive travels, it is not surprising that she has been a member of one of the main "people's" organizations to foster contact with foreign nations, namely, the Chinese

People's Association for Cultural Relations with Foreign Countries. When this organization was established in May 1954, Ts'ao was named to the Board of Directors and five years later (April 1959) was elevated to the Standing Committee. In a somewhat similar vein, she was named to the Council of the China-Egypt Friendship Association when it was formed in November 1956 (in the wake of the Israeli-Franco-British attack on Egypt), and when the association was merged in February 1958 with a counterpart group for Syria (reflecting the merger of Egypt and Syria), Ts'ao was reappointed as a Council member of the China–United Arab Republic Friendship Association.

In 1954 she was elected as a deputy from her native Hunan to the First NPC, which adopted the PRC Constitution at its first session in September 1954. She was subsequently re-elected to the Second NPC (1959–1964) and to the Third NPC, which held its initial session in December 1964–January 1965. During this latter session she served on the Credentials Committee, and at the close of the meetings in January 1965 she was elevated to membership on the NPC Standing Committee. Although this could presage a greater involvement in domestic affairs, it is clear that Ts'ao's major contribution to the PRC has been in the field of international relations, with a special emphasis on the Communist-backed women's movement. Aside from her numerous journeys outside China, her specialization in foreign affairs is further reflected at home where she very frequently serves as hostess for the ever-increasing number of foreign visitors to China. Random but typical appearances occurred in October 1961 when she was present as Chou En-lai received a Cuban women's delegation and in October 1964 at which time Ts'ao attended a small reception given for the Queen of Burundi by Liu Shao-ch'i.

To judge from the positions and assignments Ts'ao has been given, it would appear that she is a CCP member despite her past affiliation with the China Democratic League and the defunct National Salvation Association. It is even possible that such membership has been kept covert to lend an aura of cooperativeness with the Communist Party by ostensibly non-Party persons. The same, in fact, might be said for her husband since 1938, Wang K'un-lun. Also a graduate of Peking University, Wang has a long record of association with the Kuomintang Revolutionary Committee (one of the eight "democratic" parties) and has been a vice-mayor of Peking since 1955 and a member of the NPC Standing Committee since 1954. Ts'ao was known to have had two daughters by 1954, the elder a student of foreign languages.

1. *JMJP*, March 28, 1962; translated in *SCMP* 2719.

Tseng Ching-ping

(1913–   ; Fukien). Early Fukien guerrilla leader; alternate member, Seventh CCP Central Committee.

Tseng is one of three men who attained rank on the CCP Central Committee at the Seventh National Congress in June 1945 and was not re-elected to the Committee when the Party met for the Eighth National Congress in September 1956. The other two, Li Yü and Liu Tzu-chiu, were dropped about 1950; Tseng's disappearance has never been clearly explained. There have been no reports of his purge from the CCP, and it is assumed that he is still a Party member. Last heard from in 1955, his rather undistinguished career was spent almost entirely in his native Fukien where his activity was first reported in 1931 when he joined the CCP. Together with such well-known leaders as Su Yü and Yeh Fei, Tseng was among those who did not make the Long March, but rather stayed behind to conduct guerrilla operations.[1] In Tseng's case, he was engaged in the 1930's and 1940's in Fukien, and he is known to have been active there leading guerrilla operations as late as 1946. From some time in 1939 he was secretary of the Fukien Party Committee, a position that may have earned him his alternate membership on the national Party Central Committee by the time of the Seventh Party Congress of 1945. He was still holding the Fukien party post in 1948, but in 1949, when the Communists took over the whole of the China mainland, they put Chang Ting-ch'eng, a Party veteran of higher standing, in the Fukien secretary's position.

In 1947 Tseng was identified as commander of the units of the PLA assigned to the Fukien-Chekiang-Kiangsi Border Region, and in May 1949 he was operating in eastern Kiangsi. There his forces were absorbed into the southward moving regular PLA troops (Ch'en I's Third Field Army), which occupied Fukien.

Once Fukien had been occupied by the Communists, it was placed under the jurisdiction of the regional East China Military and Administrative Committee (ECMAC), called the East China Administrative Committee (ECAC) from 1953 to 1954. This was the quasi-military government set up by the occupying army and the civilian personnel it brought with it to effect China's move toward socialism. Tseng was a member of the ECMAC (later ECAC) Land Reform Committee from 1950 to 1954. This position was not particularly important and probably was given to him because of his long service as a resistance leader in Fukien. He must have been somewhat more important as a provincial Party leader in these first years of the Communist occupation, to judge by the positions he held in Fukien. In 1950 he was identified as a secretary-general of the Fukien Party Committee. In

March 1951 he was named chief justice of the People's Court of the Fukien Provincial People's Government. It is not clear how long he held this post, but it was probably no later than the mid-1950's. In 1951 he became a member of the Land Reform Committee of the Fukien Provincial People's Government Council, and in December he was elected to membership on the Fukien Provincial People's Government Council, a position he would hold to at least 1955.

In 1953, probably about December, he became a deputy secretary of the Fukien Party Committee (it is not clear whether at this time he continued to be also the committee's secretary-general). He was identified as deputy secretary of the Fukien Committee several times in the next year. On one such occasion he made a self-criticism of his own work over the preceding few years at a Fukien Party Committee meeting in Foochow in April–May 1954. However, not long after, at the first Fukien Provincial People's Congress (August 1954), Tseng played a prominent role. He served as chairman of the congress presidium (steering committee), gave the major report on the work of the provincial government and its future tasks, and also made the summation at the close of the meetings. Yet the self-criticism in the spring of 1954, seen in retrospect, appears to have been a warning that he was running into serious political trouble. In January 1955 he was elected as chairman of the Fukien CPPCC Committee and in the following month he was reelected a member of the Fukien Provincial People's Government. These were the last occasions that he was reported in the Chinese press. By April 1956 Chiang I-chen (q.v.) had replaced Tseng in the Fukien CPPCC position, and when he failed to be re-elected to the Party Central Committee at the Eighth Party Congress in September 1956, it was clear that he was no longer a political figure of any importance.

1. *Chung-kuo kung-ch'an-tang tsai chung-nan-ti-ch'ü ling-tao ko-ming tou-cheng te li-shih tzu-liao* (Historical materials on the revolutionary struggles led by the Chinese Communist Party in Central-South China; Wuhan, 1951), p. 209.

Tseng Hsi-sheng

(c.1905–   ; Yung-hsing hsien, Hunan). Provincial Party official; member, CCP Central Committee.

Tseng Hsi-sheng was trained at Whampoa and has been a Communist Party member since the mid-1920's. He participated in a number of keynote events of the Communist movement, including the Long March, and served in the New Fourth Army during the Sino-Japanese War. Since the establishment of the PRC in 1949 Tseng has been a provincial Party official, prin-

cipally in Anhwei province. He was elected to the CCP Central Committee in 1956.

Tseng was born about 1905 in Yung-hsing hsien, a hilly region along the Lei River in southern Hunan. Nothing is known of his early life until he attended Whampoa, the well-known Nationalist military academy in Canton. He was in Canton, and probably at Whampoa, in 1925 when he joined the CCP. About the time that the Northern Expedition began in the summer of 1926 Tseng joined the Second Division of the Eighth (Nationalist) Army. The division was commanded by the Hunan military leader Ho Chien, on whose staff Tseng rose to the rank of political instructor at the regimental level. However, he was forced to leave this position in the summer of 1927 when the Nationalists broke relations with the Communists. He then became a Red guerrilla fighter on the Kiangsi-Anhwei border. In this area he very probably made connections with other Red guerrilla forces organized in the late 1920's by Fang Chih-min (q.v.), who was operating along the border of northeast Kiangsi. From northeast Kiangsi Tseng was driven south and eventually he joined the headquarters of Mao Tse-tung and Chu Te at Juichin, south Kiangsi. Here, about 1930, he was identified as a staff member of the Central Revolutionary Military Council. He seems to have been a bureau chief of the Council, possibly concerned with intelligence, because in the following year he was reported to be engaged in intelligence work on the Kiangsi-Hunan border. Tseng took part in the Long March (1934–35), following Mao Tse-tung and his officers across eleven provinces on the march from Kiangsi to the northwest.

Tseng was transferred to east-central China sometime after the Sino-Japanese War opened in the summer of 1937. Early in 1938 the Communists put an army into operation in the Yangtze Valley—the New Fourth Army commanded by General Yeh T'ing. Tseng was reported to be assigned to intelligence with the New Fourth Army soon after its creation. In January 1941 some of its units came into conflict with Nationalist troops that attacked the Communists while the latter were moving north from south Anhwei to cross the Yangtze (the New Fourth Army Incident; see under Yeh T'ing). The survivors of this incident, plus those troops that had successfully established themselves in areas north of the river, were reorganized in February 1941. Because Yeh T'ing had been taken prisoner during the incident, Ch'en I was made the acting commander of the reorganized New Fourth Army. Tseng was given a responsible position as political commissar of the Seventh Division, commanded by Chang Ting-ch'eng (q.v.). The latter had been with the New Fourth Army unit from which the Seventh Division was created; it is possible that some of the experiences described in his biography were shared by Tseng.

From 1941 the Seventh Division operated in the Central Anhwei Military Area, which commanded the banks of the Yangtze as far west as Su-sung in southwest Anhwei. Strategically the area was very important both to the Japanese and the Nationalists who maintained rather strong forces there. Therefore, the Communists were not as strong in this area as in others where the New Fourth Army maintained guerrilla bases; the division's forces numbered only about 5,000 men. In 1945 Tseng was still at the Central Anhwei base, identified as the political commissar there.

In the next four years Tseng apparently did not play a prominent role in the expanding Communist movement and he did not begin to emerge as an important Party leader until 1949 after the Communists had gained control of the mainland. However, he did remain with Ch'en I's army, continuing his work as a political officer. After the end of the war he was identified as the director of the Political Department of the East China Military Region, the military zone in the coastal provinces of Shantung and Kiangsu where the Ch'en I army was in control. He was with this army in 1947 and according to one source was an important officer in the 11th Division of the Seventh Column of Ch'en's East China PLA. The latter, re-named the Third Field Army by early 1949, was one of the best postwar Communist armies.

In 1949, as the Communists were sweeping the mainland, they began to form their politico-military organizations, following for the most part the normal provincial boundaries of China. An exception was made in Anhwei where it was divided into northern and southern regions. Based in the north, with the capital at Hofei, Tseng was the top Communist official in this area from 1949 to 1952. During these years he was the ranking secretary of the North Anhwei Party Committee and the commander of the North Anhwei Military District. Under the civil government structure, known as the North Anhwei People's Administrative Office, he served as a member from 1950 to 1952. Anhwei was subordinate to the multi-provincial organization known as the East China Military and Administrative Committee (ECMAC) from its formal inauguration in January 1950 until it was reorganized into the East China Administrative Committee in December 1952. The ECAC remained in existence until 1954, with Tseng having served as a member of the ECMAC–ECAC during the 1950–1954 period.

In the fall of 1950 the central government in Peking created the Huai River Harnessing Commission, placing it under the national Ministry of Water Conservancy. Devastation from the Huai River flood waters had long been an enormous burden for the peasantry in the Anhwei area. Tseng was named as one of the deputy directors of this commission and was apparently fairly active in the work of the organization in the early 1950's. At a conference of the commission in April–May 1951 (held in Pang-fou, Anhwei) he gave a major report on the work already undertaken to control the river and the plans for 1951. He also wrote an article on the Huai River harnessing project for the September 29, 1951, issue of the Canton *Nan-fang jih-pao*.

In August 1952, North and South Anhwei were merged to form the traditional province of Anhwei. This, of course, required the complete reorganization of the military, governmental, and Party bureaucracies in Anhwei. Tseng received most of the major appointments, and until about 1961 was to remain the dominant figure in Anhwei. He became the provincial governor at the time of the merger, as well as the ranking Party secretary (the designation changing to first secretary in 1956). Within the military structure, he was the political commissar for the provincial military district by early 1953. Finally, although far less important, he was named to the chairmanship of the First Anhwei Committee of the quasi-legislative CPPCC in February 1955 and was then re-elected to the Second Committee in November 1958. In March 1955 he relinquished the governorship of the province to Huang Yen (q.v.), but at this same time he was elected to membership on the Provincial People's Government Council, a post to which he was re-elected in November 1958.

In 1954 Tseng was elected a deputy from Anhwei to the First NPC; he also served from this province in the Second NPC (1959–1964). At the first session of the First NPC (September 1954), when the constitutional government was inaugurated, Tseng served as a member of the Motions Examination Committee under the chairmanship of Hsi Chung-hsun. However, the high point in his career occurred in September 1956 at the Eighth National Party Congress. Tseng spoke before the congress on affairs in Anhwei and at the close of the sessions was elected a full member of the Party Central Committee. Although he was placed 96th on a list of 97 members, his election was nonetheless significant because he was one of only 33 of the 97 members who had not been a member of the Seventh Central Committee elected in 1945.

Back in Anhwei, Tseng was apparently rather active in the provincial activities carried out under the auspices of the nationwide *cheng-feng* (rectification) movement of 1957–58. He became the head of an office for "rectification work" under the Anhwei Party Committee in May 1957, and in the same month gave a speech on the subject before the provincial Party committee. He seemed to be even more active during the Great

Leap Forward, which was inaugurated with the Second Five-Year Plan in 1958. During the period from 1958 to 1960, he authored several articles with the unmistakably ebullient tone of so many pieces written during the Great Leap. Articles by Tseng on water conservancy, the famous "backyard (steel) furnaces," "rightists," and the people's communes appeared in the following important publications: the *JMJP* (March 24, 1958, March 3, 1959, October 21, 1959, June 16, 1960, July 6, 1960) and *Hung-ch'i* (Red flag, June 16, 1958, March 16, 1959, June 16, 1959). During this same period from 1958 to 1960, Tseng served as host to four of China's top leaders who visited Anhwei: Mao Tse-tung, Chou En-lai, Teng Hsiao-p'ing, and Tung Pi-wu. Already the top man in Anhwei, he assumed still another post in 1958 when he became president of Anhwei University, a new school opened in October 1958.

After being reported by the press with great regularity in Anhwei, Tseng was suddenly transferred to Shantung under circumstances that were rather unusual. In mid-1960, the Shantung Party first secretary, Shu T'ung (q.v.), fell out of favor. Then in November of the same year Tseng (in the capacity of Party first secretary for Shantung) appeared at a conference concerning famine relief in Shantung, a rather poor province with a huge population. This period—the winter of 1960–61—witnessed extremely bad conditions all over China in the wake of the disasters brought on by the abortive Great Leap Forward and poor weather. The fall of former First Secretary Shu T'ung from political favor suggests that Tseng was dispatched from Anhwei to neighboring Shantung in a trouble-shooting role. In any event, his tenure there was brief, for by April 1961 he was back in his old position in Anhwei. At the same time that he returned to Anhwei, he was also identified as the second secretary of the East China Party Bureau. The regional bureaus had been re-created in accordance with a decision taken at the Ninth Plenum of the Party Central Committee in January 1961. Tseng's position in the East China Bureau placed him under Politburo member K'o Ch'ing-shih (since deceased) and suggested that he had reached a new plateau in a rising career. However, he made only a few more perfunctory appearances in 1961 and was last reported by the national press in February 1962 serving as a member of the funeral committee for fellow Central Committee member Li K'o-nung. The connection between the two men may be based on the fact that both had had a background in intelligence work. Later in 1962, Li Pao-hua (q.v.) replaced Tseng as the Party first secretary in Anhwei, and by February 1964 he had even replaced Tseng in the rather unimportant post as chairman of the Anhwei Committee of the CPPCC. After serving on both the First and

Second NPC's (1954–1964), Tseng failed to be re-elected to the Third NPC, which opened in late 1964, still another suggestion of political or possibly physical ill-health. The apparent loss of all his posts in Anhwei leaves him as only a member of the Party Central Committee.

Tseng Shan

(c.1904–   ; Hsing-kuo, Kiangsi). Early Party leader; minister of Internal Affairs; member, CCP Central Committee.

Tseng Shan has been an important Party leader since the days of the Kiangsi Soviet in the early 1930's. A member of the Party Central Committee since 1945, he was prominent in east China in the late forties and early fifties as a specialist in economic affairs. Since the mid-fifties he has been active in international liaison work with foreign Communist parties and since 1960 has headed the Ministry of Internal Affairs.

Tseng Shan was born about 1904 into a family deeply involved in revolutionary work in the course of his youth. Tseng's native hsien, Hsing-kuo in central-south Kiangsi, had an important revolutionary history in the late 1920's and early 1930's when the Communists were successfully establishing bases in central China. In the years of the thirties before the Communists embarked upon the Long March (1934), Hsing-kuo was the scene of intense fighting between Communist and Nationalist armies during some of the Annihilation Campaigns waged by the Nationalists in an attempt to stamp out Communism. Tseng's rural hsien is located east of the Kan River, with its capital seat, Hsing-kuo, some 60 miles southeast of the larger river port city of Chi-an (Kian) where for a time Tseng's father, Tseng Ts'ai-ch'in, taught school. Other episodes in the general area of Hsing-kuo which have became famous events in Communist annals include the establishment of a small soviet called the Tung-ku–Hsing-kuo Regional Soviet by the army of Chu Te and Mao Tse-tung in 1929, Chu Te's occupation of Chi-an in October 1930, the occupation of Hsing-kuo by the Nationalists in July 1931 during their Third Annihilation Campaign and its recapture by the Communists in September. Not far northeast of Hsing-kuo are the two small towns of Tung-ku and Fu-t'ien, which figured prominently in the Fu-t'ien Rebellion of December 1930 (see below). Some or all of these events must have involved the Tseng family, who were all said to have joined the Communist Party in the year 1927–28. Later, two of Tseng's brothers and two of his sisters-in-law were captured and died at the hands of the Nationalists.[1] As of 1963 one brother and Tseng's mother were still living and were then in a rural area of China.[2]

Politburo member T'an Chen-lin has written of Tseng that he "did not study in a university or receive any kind of higher education" but began his career as an apprentice to a silk worker.[3] This was very probably the effect of the unsettled revolutionary times in which Tseng grew up, which in turn had their effects upon the Tseng family fortunes. However, he was not lacking in early revolutionary training and experience and by 1930, when in his middle twenties, was serving in the Tung-ku–Hsing-kuo soviet area. He belonged to the military forces led by Mao Tse-tung; some reports speak of him at this time as a personal envoy of Mao. According to one account, Mao dispatched P'eng Te-huai and Tseng to Fu-t'ien in December 1930 to put down an insurrection there, which Mao feared would further endanger the Red armies already endangered by the Annihilation Campaigns of the Nationalists. The Fu-t'ien insurrection was all the more threatening to Mao because it took place among some of the local forces in his own army, causing him to expel a number of officers and men from the Red Army, as well as to reorganize his remaining forces. At the time of the Fu-t'ien rebellion Tseng was chairman of the Kiangsi Provincial Soviet government, which had been established earlier when the Red armies captured Chi-an (Kian), a commercial center on the Kan River west of Fu-t'ien. The circumstances that surround Tseng's assumption of this post are little known but they have been interpreted by one scholar as part of a maneuver sponsored by Mao Tse-tung to get one of his own men into a position of authority in the Kiangsi provincial government.[4] It also appears that Tseng was unpopular with the Fu-t'ien rebels, who were able, at least temporarily, to oust him from that office.[5] However, two years later, in May 1932 when the Communists held the first congress of a re-established Kiangsi Provincial Soviet in central Kiangsi, Tseng was again made chairman of the soviet government with Ch'en Cheng-jen (q.v.) as his vice-chairman. Then there was a second congress of the Kiangsi Provincial Soviet held in December 1933, and at this time Liu Ch'i-yao became chairman, while Tseng was demoted to a vice-chairmanship and Ch'en was dropped. This congress named an Executive Committee of 67 members, which included a number of persons who became prominent in the later Maoist Party leadership. These included: Ch'en I, Ch'en Ch'i-han, Li Fu-ch'un, and Ts'ai Ch'ang (Mme. Li Fu-ch'un).

However, Tseng had strong backers within the CCP and it was not long before he received other and more important posts. Following the meeting of the Fourth CCP Plenum, held in Shanghai in January 1931, the CCP created a nine-member Central Bureau of the Soviet Areas (see under Chou En-lai), which was to have charge of all Party units in the various soviet areas in China, including the Party branches in the Red Army. The bureau was headed by Chou En-lai, had Hsiang Ying as secretary, and its members included Mao Tse-tung, Chu Te, Jen Pi-shih, Yü Fei, and Tseng Shan.[6] It is noteworthy that while Chou, Jen, and some others were in Shanghai at the time the Bureau was created, Mao, Chu, and Tseng were operating in the rural hinterlands of Kiangsi. Hence, though there is very little reporting about Tseng at this period, he was undoubtedly of sufficient stature to be included on such an important committee. In November 1931, when the First All-China Congress of Soviets met at Juichin, south Kiangsi, Tseng became a member of the Central Executive Committee, the governing body for the Chinese Soviet Republic, which the congress brought into being. He was re-elected to the same post at the Second All-China Congress of Soviets in January–February 1934, at which time he was also named Commissar for Internal Affairs, that is, one of the 11 cabinet officials subordinate to the CEC.

Tseng Shan did not make the Long March but remained in central China to work with the local guerrillas when the main forces of the Chu-Mao army left Kiangsi in the fall of 1934. That same year he was operating with the guerrillas on the Kiangsi-Chekiang-Fukien border where Su Yü (q.v.) led the major force. There is very little information about Tseng's activity for the next decade, but from occasional references it appears that he continued to fight in central China till he eventually joined the New Fourth Army, which was activated near Hankow in the spring of 1938. However, according to an unconfirmed report, in 1935 Tseng made his way to Shanghai disguised as a longshoreman and from there went to Moscow where he spent two years. According to this source he returned to China in 1937 with Ch'en Shao-yü, the Chinese representative to the Comintern who had been in the Soviet Union for the previous six years. If this report is true, Tseng must have returned to central China soon after he arrived in Yenan, because in 1938 he is reported to have been a secretary of the Southeast Sub-bureau of the CCP, and during the Sino-Japanese War he conducted Party organizational work with the New Fourth Army. Apparently he continued in this field, for by 1941 to at least 1945 he was the director of the Organization Department of the Party's Central China Bureau, the important organ headed by Liu Shao-ch'i that operated in conjunction with the New Fourth Army. Well known in Party circles by this time, Tseng was made a full member of the Central Committee at the Seventh Party Congress, which met in Yenan from April to June 1945. That same year he was identified as the president of the Central China Reconstruction University. The locale of much of Tseng's wartime activity must have been in northeast and east-central Kiangsu with the headquarters of the New Fourth Army. By 1948

Tseng, along with major forces in the New Fourth Army, had transferred from Kiangsu to Shantung, and when the Shantung provincial capital at Tsinan was captured by the Communists in September 1948, he was named as a vice-chairman of the municipal Military Control Commission. In order to unify the civil administration of those portions of north China held by the Communists, the Shansi-Chahar-Hopeh (Chin-Ch'a-Chi) and the Shansi-Hopeh-Shantung-Honan (Chin-Chi-Lu-Yü) Border Regions were merged in August 1948 to form the North China People's Government. Immediately afterwards Tseng was named as a member of the government's Finance and Economics Committee, an appointment that was a prelude to a number of similar economic administrative tasks he was given in the ensuing years.

In May 1949 Tseng was transferred from Shantung to serve as one of the key civil administrators in Shanghai, which the Communists had just captured. He was immediately named as the ranking vice-mayor under Mayor Ch'en I, the commander of the forces that had captured the city. One of the first acts of the new administration was the establishment of the East China Branch of the People's Bank of China with jurisdiction over banking in Kiangsu, Chekiang, and Anhwei; Tseng was appointed (May 1949) to head the branch and held the post until mid-1950. In September 1949 he received a closely related appointment when he was named to head the newly established East China Finance and Economics Committee (ECFEC). Because the governmental apparatus for east China had not yet been set up, the ECFEC was originally subordinate to Ch'en I's East China Military Region, the civil-military organ that administered east China throughout 1949. Then, over the winter of 1949–50, the Communists established a civil administration known as the East China Military and Administrative Committee (ECMAC). Jao Shu-shih, the top political figure in east China at that time, was appointed as head of the EC-MAC, with Tseng named as one of the vice-chairmen. The ECMAC was formally established in January 1950 with jurisdiction over Kiangsu, Chekiang, Anhwei, Fukien, and Shantung. The Finance and Economics Committee that Tseng had headed from the previous September was placed under the jurisdiction of the ECMAC, with Tseng remaining as the chairman, a post he continued to hold until the abolition of the regional governments in 1954.

Meanwhile, in October 1949, the central government had been formed in Peking. The cabinet, then known as the Government Administration Council (GAC), was composed of Premier Chou En-lai, four vice-premiers and 15 members. Tseng was appointed as one of the members and was also named to membership on one of the four coordinating committees directly subordinate to the GAC, the Finance and Economic Committee headed by top economic administrator Ch'en Yun. Most important, however, he was named to head the Ministry of Textile Industry. Though it is highly unusual for a cabinet minister not to reside in Peking, the explanation in this instance derives from the fact that Shanghai was the center of the textile industry in China. Tseng spent most of the period from 1949 to 1952 in Shanghai, the ECMAC capital, but occasionally he went to Peking to give periodic reports to the GAC. For example, he gave a report before the GAC in February 1950 on steps taken in east China to ameliorate flood and famine conditions.

In the 1950–1952 period, Tseng received further appointments in east China. From October 1950 to November 1952 he served as director of the Huai River Harnessing Commission, an organization subordinate to the central government's Ministry of Water Conservancy. In November 1951 he was named to the council of the East China Branch of the Sino-Soviet Friendship Association, and in the same month he was appointed to head the *ad hoc* East China Committee to Increase Production and Practice Economy. The establishment of the latter committee came as a result of decisions taken at the third session of the First CPPCC (October–November 1951), when major stress was placed upon the need to improve production and to encourage economic austerity. In June of 1952 Tseng became the director of the newly established East China "Old Revolutionary Bases Reconstruction Committee," a reflection of the priority attention the CCP has always given to the former guerrilla areas where Communist cadres and soldiers had worked and fought from the early 1930's.

In August 1952, when the GAC underwent a reorganization, Tseng received new assignments in the national government, relinquishing his post as minister of Textile Industry to Chiang Kuang-nai. At this same time the Ministry of Trade was divided into the Ministries of Foreign Trade and of Commerce. Yeh Chi-chuang (q.v.) assumed the former post and Tseng became the head of the Commerce Ministry. He was also promoted to a vice-chairmanship of the GAC's Finance and Economics Committee. When the ECMAC was reorganized into the East China Administrative Committee (ECAC) in January 1953, he was reappointed as a vice-chairman (still under Jao Shu-shih) and also retained his post as head of the region's Finance and Economics Committee. Even after Tseng was appointed as minister of Commerce in August 1952, he still remained in Shanghai at least for a short time; in the latter part of the same month he gave a major report on economic affairs in east China before a plenary session of the ECMAC. After that, however, he apparently worked mainly in Peking even though he seldom appeared in public. A press item of October 1953 noted that he was absent from a Shanghai meeting of the ECAC because he was working in Peking.

With the abolition of the regional governments in 1954, Tseng was permanently transferred to the capital. In July 1954 he was elected to the national committee of the All-China Federation of Supply and Marketing Cooperatives (AC-FSMC); more important, he was named to head the Federation's Supervisory Committee. The Federation works in close coordination with the Ministry of Commerce (then headed by Tseng) and is charged with the task of stimulating the flow of goods and commodities between the rural and urban sectors of the economy. Although Tseng may continue to be a national committee member of the ACFSMC, he was dropped as the Supervisory Committee chairman in about 1962, a reflection of the fact that by that time he had given up his responsibilities in connection with domestic commerce (see below).

When the constitutional government was inaugurated in the fall of 1954, Tseng was reappointed as head of the Commerce Ministry. The four former coordinating committees under the old GAC were now reorganized into eight staff offices under the State Council, each headed by a top Party figure. Tseng, who had been a vice-chairman of the Finance and Economics Committee, was given a roughly comparable post when he was appointed (October 1954) to be a deputy director of the Fifth Staff Office, the office concerned with finance and trade. In this position Tseng served under Party veteran Li Hsien-nien, the Finance minister. In December 1954 Tseng was made a member of the Second National Committee of the CPPCC, serving as a Party representative. He served in a like capacity on the Third Committee (1959–1964) and was again named as a Party representative to the Fourth National Committee, which opened its first session in December 1964.

At the Party's Eighth National Congress in September 1956, Tseng was re-elected to the Central Committee. During the Congress he presented a written report on the production and distribution of consumer goods in which he reviewed domestic commerce since 1949 and also admitted a number of serious shortcomings in commercial work. Then in mid-November, he was replaced by Ch'en Yun as minister of Commerce. Moreover, over the winter of 1956–57 he was also removed as a deputy director of the important Fifth Staff Office, thus being left without any important government post. In view of the fact that commercial work had been rather sharply criticized shortly before the Eighth Congress, it would seem that Tseng had suffered a political decline. However, other facts suggest that a decision had been made in 1956 to give Tseng a new assignment, namely, an active role as a CCP representative in relations with foreign

Communist parties. His first important assignment in this field took place in May 1956 when he represented the CCP at a congress of the Albanian Labor (Communist) Party. Within the next five years he attended four more Communist congresses in Sweden (December 1957), Albania (February 1961), Norway (March 1961), and Austria (April 1961). With the exception of the February 1961 journey to Albania, when the CCP delegation was led by Li Hsien-nien, Tseng was the ranking Party delegate.

Although Tseng was apparently divorced from domestic tasks from the second half of 1956, he returned to this field by early 1958—a return that coincided with the Great Leap Forward. In January 1958 he was identified as director of the Communications Work Department, an organ directly subordinate to the Party Central Committee. In this capacity he spoke before several nationwide conferences in 1958–59 on the pressing need to integrate China's communications and transport network into the commune system. The most notable of these speeches took place in November 1959 when he gave the closing address before a national conference that dealt with many aspects of the national economy, including communications and transportation work. Since that time, however, he has not been identified in connection with the Party's Communications Work Department.

Tseng was elected in 1958 as a deputy to the Second NPC from Shantung, the province in which he had worked a decade earlier. When the Second NPC held its first session in April 1959, he was elected to the NPC Standing Committee as well as chairman of the NPC Budget Committee. In November 1960 he was named to succeed Miss Ch'ien Ying (q.v.) as minister of Internal Affairs, thus returning to a post similar to the one he had held in 1934 in the Chinese Soviet Republic in Kiangsi. Unlike the situation in many Communist nations, the Internal Affairs Ministry in China is not a euphemism for the secret police; its main tasks are related to veterans' affairs, the census, and emergency relief measures when natural calamities strike. Because the PRC has followed the principle of the separation of powers in the national government, soon after receiving his ministerial post in 1960, Tseng was removed as a member of the NPC Standing Committee. He continued, however, to serve as a deputy to the NPC and to head the NPC's Budget Committee throughout the existence of the Second NPC (1959–1964). Although he was re-elected as a Shantung deputy to the Third NPC, he was replaced by Ku Mu (q.v.) as chairman of the NPC Budget Committee when the Third NPC held its first session in December 1964–January 1965.

Because the Internal Affairs Ministry is not prominently featured in the Communist press,

Tseng is not frequently in the news in connection with his ministerial duties. One of the few instances took place in December 1962 when the press briefly reported that he had spoken before a meeting of the State Council on natural calamities during 1962 and the steps that had been taken to relieve the stricken areas. However, he appears rather often at ceremonies marking various national or Party holidays and, more important, he continues to play a part in maintaining contacts with foreign Communist parties and government leaders from African and Asian nations. For example, in December 1962, he was present when Party General Secretary Teng Hsiao-p'ing held talks with the chairman of the Norwegian Communist Party, and in May 1964 he participated in talks with a prominent political leader from Kenya. Tseng also accompanied Party Propaganda Director Lu Ting-i to East Germany in May 1965 to attend ceremonies marking the 20th anniversary of the end of World War II. While there, Lu and Tseng held talks with representatives of the Socialist Unity (Communist) Party.

In the early years of the PRC, most of the senior Party leaders were engaged in rather diversified tasks. However, after political rule was consolidated in the early 1950's, most of them have tended to work in a single field, such as economics, foreign affairs, or educational work. In this respect, Tseng's career seems to be an exception. His present assignment in the Internal Affairs Ministry bears little relationship to his work as a senior east China economic specialist in the early fifties. Similarly, his continuing contacts with foreign Communist parties seems only vaguely related to his domestic assignments.

Tseng probably reached the peak of his political career in the late forties and early fifties during the crucial takeover period when he was one of the most important Communist officials in east China. The outline of his career since the late fifties suggests that his political importance is now considerably less than that of most of his peers among the Party elite.

1. *SCMP* 2920, p. 7.
2. *Ibid.*
3. *SCMP* 2362, p. 11.
4. Benjamin I. Schwartz, *Chinese Communism and the Rise of Mao* (Cambridge, Mass., 1952), p. 175.
5. Tso-liang Hsiao, *Power Relations within the Chinese Communist Movement, 1930–1934* (Seattle, Wash., 1961), p. 99.
6. *Ibid.*, pp. 150–151.

Tseng Sheng

(c.1910–   ; Hui-yang, Kwangtung). Mayor of Canton; Third Secretary, Canton Party Committee.

Tseng Sheng, whose original name was Tseng Chen-sheng, was born in Hui-yang, a small town in Kwangtung about 75 miles north of Hong Kong. During the Sino-Japanese War he gained a measure of fame by leading the East River (Tung-chiang) guerrilla forces, which in official Communist histories are placed on a par with the Hainan Island guerrilla units as one of the two most important guerrilla forces in south China. During his childhood Tseng studied in Hong Kong, but because his father was a merchant with business interests in Australia, Tseng spent six years of his youth in Sydney where, presumably, he learned English. According to the Communist version, Tseng and his father returned to China (in about 1931) owing to the restrictions imposed on Orientals by the Australian government, after which Tseng studied sociology at Sun Yat-sen (Chung-shan) University in Canton; he reportedly graduated in 1934.

In the mid-1930's in Canton, Tseng was a leading agitator in the movement to resist the persistent Japanese incursions into China. The vigor of his work got him into trouble with the authorities and, fearing arrest, he fled to Hong Kong where he worked in a seamen's union. When the Japanese invaded Kwangtung in the fall of 1938, Tseng was instrumental in the organization of a guerrilla unit of about 1,200 men. Because it was initially composed mainly of Hong Kong seamen, it was known as the "Seamen's Guerrilla Unit," but soon afterward it was renamed the "Hui-Pao People's Anti-Japanese Guerrilla Column" (being named for the area in which it operated, in and around Tseng's native Hui-yang and neighboring Pao-an hsien). In 1939 his guerrillas were ostensibly incorporated into the Chinese Nationalist armies, but because Tseng's forces vied with the Nationalist armies for control in the East River area, an incident in 1940 brought about an eastward retreat by Tseng to the Hai-feng and Lu-feng areas, the former home of the Hailufeng Soviet led by P'eng P'ai (q.v.) in the 1920's. In about 1940, Tseng allied his forces to those of a Communist guerrilla leader named Wang Tso-yao, who had been harassing the Japanese in operations along the Canton-Kowloon Railway not far from Tseng's area of operation. The merger was formalized in 1941 and the combined forces became known as the East River Column. They were probably already under Communist control, but all doubt was removed two years later in December 1943 when they publicly announced their subordination to the Party Central Committee, with Tseng as the commander and Wang Tso-yao as his deputy.[1] The combined force reportedly consisted of about 10,000. When the British lost Hong Kong over the winter of 1941–42, these Communist guerrillas found themselves strategically located astride one of the major escape routes to Nationalist-held areas in the Chinese interior. They were thereby able to facilitate the escape of a number of persons who fled overland, and both British and Nationalist Chinese officials are said to have commended Tseng for his help.

In the summer of 1945 elements of the 359th Brigade (see under Wang En-mao) pushed southward from north China to link up with the East River Column, with the latter ordered to move northward to a rendezvous point in north Kwangtung near Kiangsi. The rendezvous was called off at the last moment when the war suddenly ended and the Red Army Headquarters in Yenan wanted Wang's brigade to return to the north immediately. It is not known if Tseng had any direct role in this abortive venture, but a message reproduced in the *Selected Works of Mao Tse-tung,* dated August 15, 1945, indicates that Mao regarded Tseng's force as an important part of his army. On that date Chu Te "ordered" Japanese General Okamura Yasuji, the Japanese commander-in-chief in China, to send representatives to various Chinese Communist military commanders in order to surrender his troops. Regarding the Japanese troops in Kwangtung, Okamura was instructed to receive orders from General Tseng Sheng of the "Southern China Anti-Japanese Column."[2]

The Nationalists continued to harass Tseng's forces in 1945 and it was not until the nationwide truce of January 1946 that he was able to move the remnants of his forces to the north. The redeployment of his troops was made in mid-1946 to Chefoo, a major port in Shantung then held by the Communists. Tseng and his forces were soon incorporated into units of the Red armies fighting in the area. In August 1947 some of Tseng's units were combined with Kwangtung and Kwangsi officers and men from units of the Nationalists that had surrendered to the Communists or had been captured. This was known as the Kwangtung-Kwangsi Column (Liang-kuang tsung-tui), and with Tseng as the commander it participated in the Communist drive southward, which ultimately brought him back to his native Kwangtung in 1949.

In 1949–50 Tseng assumed posts within the military, government, and Party organizations in South China. In October 1949 he was named to membership on both the Kwangtung Provincial People's Government Council and the Canton Military Control Commission, and in November he became third deputy commander of the Kwangtung Military District. He held all three posts under Yeh Chien-ying, one of the top leaders in south China in the takeover period. By mid-1950 Tseng had also been identified as a member of the South China Sub-bureau of the CCP. However, rather little was heard of him in the first years of the PRC, possibly because so many leaders from central and north China were sent to manage affairs in the south. But by the

mid-1950's, when many of them had been reassigned to other areas of China, Tseng began to receive more prominent attention in the press. In 1954 he was elected a deputy from Kwangtung to the First NPC (1954–1959); he was re-elected to the Second (1959–1964) as well as to the Third, which held its first session in December 1964–January 1965. In 1955 personal military ranks were given to PLA officers and military honors were also awarded. His name was on a composite namelist issued in September 1955, and therefore it is not possible to know which orders he received. His military record suggests, however, that he was granted the Order of Independence and Freedom (for service during the Sino-Japanese War) and the Order of Liberation (for his role in the battles against the Nationalists in the late 1940's). He probably received his military rank at this time, although it was not until 1957 that he was identified with a military rank—as a rear admiral, the equivalent of a two-star admiral in the U.S. Navy. Perhaps Tseng's assignment in the Navy derives from his experience with seamen earlier in his life; the Chinese Communists were hard pressed to find naval talent because they had had little experience with naval warfare. By June 1959 Tseng was identified as the deputy commander of the South China Fleet, although the minuscule Chinese Communist Navy hardly merits so grandiose a designation. In any event, it is clear from Tseng's other activities that he spent only a minimum amount of time with official duties as a naval officer.

In December 1960 Tseng became the mayor of Canton; in May 1961 he was identified as a secretary of the Canton Party Committee, and then by March 1965 he was promoted to the position of third secretary. At the provincial level, Tseng was elected a vice-governor in December 1960 (the same time he became Canton mayor) and was identified as a member of the Kwangtung Party Standing Committee by March 1963. He also holds (or has held) other minor posts. For example, when the Kwangtung government established a special commission to reconstruct the "old revolutionary bases," Tseng was named as one of the vice-chairmen (October 1962); when a nationwide preparatory committee was established in June 1963 for participation in the Indonesian-sponsored "Games of the New Emerging Forces" (see under Jung Kao-t'ang), Tseng was appointed to membership; from at least November 1963 he has been a vice-chairman of the Kwangtung branch of the China Peace Committee; and in January 1965 he was appointed to the preparatory committee for the Second National Sports Meet, scheduled for later in the year.

Working as a senior official in one of China's major cities, Tseng is naturally brought into contact with a large number of foreign visitors. To cite a typical example, he and his wife entertained the Nepalese king and queen when they passed through Canton in September 1961. The semi-annual Canton trade fair is another occasion which brings him into contact with foreigners, as did the inauguration of civil air service with both Pakistan and Cambodia in the spring of 1964. In fact, in April–May 1964 he led a group of Chinese visitors to Pakistan as part of the festivities surrounding the inauguration of the Sino-Pakistani air link, and later in May he led another group to Cambodia for the same purpose. In June 1964 he led a small friendship delegation to Albania, at that time China's staunch ally in East Europe. The Hong Kong non-Communist press reported in early August 1964 that Tseng had arrived in Hong Kong after a brief visit to Cambodia,[3] but information is not available on the purpose of his trip.

Although the total impact of Tseng on the Chinese Communist movement has been relatively minor, he does stand out as one of the more important south China guerrillas who survived great difficulties in the face of hostility from both the Japanese and the Chinese Nationalists and who was cut off from the main Communist forces located hundreds of miles away. The rather minor role he has played even after 1949 in his native Kwangtung may be attributed to policies at the Party center which have tended to slight the men from Kwangtung. This, at any rate, is the feeling of a number of lower-level cadres in Kwangtung who feel that "outsiders" have unfairly usurped most of the key positions from the "natives."

Tseng is married to Juan Ch'ün-ying, but nothing further is known about her.

---

1. *K'ang-jih chan-cheng shih-ch'i chieh-fang-ch'ü kai-k'uang* (A sketch of the liberated areas during the Anti-Japanese War; Peking, 1953), pp. 125–128.

2. *Selected Works of Mao Tse-tung* (Peking, 1961), IV, 39.

3. Hong Kong, *South China Morning Post*, August 7, 1964.

Tseng Yung-ch'üan

(1906–   ; Hunan). Diplomat.

Tseng Yung-chüan, a veteran diplomat, was apparently a military officer during the Sino-Japanese War. In the immediate postwar period he was stationed in the Kalgan area as deputy chief-of-staff of the Shansi-Chahar-Hopeh Military Region, which was commanded by Nieh Jung-chen.[1] Tseng seems to have remained in north China during the civil war, because by 1949 he was second in command of a military academy in Peking. Apart from the universities which the Communists took over when they captured

Peking in January 1949, they established (or transferred from "liberated areas" of north China) three important new universities: North China University (Hua-pei ta-hsueh), North China People's Revolutionary University (Hua-pei jen-min ko-ming ta-hsueh), and the North China Military and Political Academy (Hua-pei chün-cheng ta-hsueh). The last-mentioned was headed by Yeh Chien-ying (concurrently the Peking mayor) and Tseng served as the vice-president.

Tseng was removed from his academic position in 1949 and posted as a diplomat in Moscow; he has remained in diplomatic work since that time. Sino-Soviet relations were established immediately after the Communists officially formed their government in October 1949. Tseng was sent to Moscow as a counsellor of the embassy, and during his three years there he served under ambassadors Wang Chia-hsiang and Chang Wen-t'ien (qq.v.). Tseng was thus in Moscow for the negotiations from December 1949 to February 1950 (conducted by Mao Tse-tung and Chou En-lai), which led to the historic treaty of alliance signed on Febuary 14, 1950. On November 17, 1950, Tseng was promoted to minister-counsellor, and in this capacity served from time to time as chargé d'affaires of the Chinese mission.

In August 1952 Tseng replaced P'eng Ming-chih as ambassador to Poland, presenting his credentials in Warsaw on September 27, 1952. In January 1953 he participated in negotiations in Warsaw which led to the signing of a cultural cooperation agreement for 1953, and 13 months later he took part in the talks which resulted in the signing of the 1954 trade agreement between China and Poland. After two and a half years in Poland, he was transferred in January 1955 to East Germany, replacing Chi P'eng-fei as ambassador. In May of that year he was a member of the delegation led by Defense Minister P'eng Te-huai to the celebrations in Berlin marking the 10th anniversary of the "liberation" of East Germany. In November 1955 he signed a trade and payments agreement for the year 1956, and in the following month accompanied East German Premier Otto Grotewohl to China for a state visit. This important visit led to the signing of several agreements, including the Sino-German Treaty of Friendship and Cooperation. As of that date Peking had signed only one other treaty of friendship (with the Soviet Union).

In May 1956 Tseng was a delegate to the Third Congress of the East German Socialist Unity (Communist) Party and then in the early fall of that year was reported back in China, presumably to attend the Eighth Party Congress (September 1956). Back in Germany, Tseng was in charge of the Chinese delegation to the opening of the annual Leipzig Industrial Fair in March 1957.

In the meantime, while still the ambassador to

Berlin, Tseng was appointed (January 1957) a vice-minister of Foreign Affairs. It was not until June 1957, however, that he was replaced in Germany by Wang Kuo-ch'üan. Over the next years in Peking, it became evident from the visitors he saw and from his negotiations with them that Tseng worked almost exclusively in Sino-Soviet and Sino-East European relations—a logical outgrowth of well over seven years of diplomatic service in those areas. Virtually every Soviet or East European group which visited China after mid-1957 saw Tseng. However, while frequently involved in entertaining such visitors or in negotiations with them, he was a signatory to only one agreement; that was in June 1961 when he signed the exchange of instruments of ratification of the Sino-Czech Consular Treaty. He went back to East Europe once after returning to China, accompanying Ho Lung to Germany for the 12th anniversary of the establishment of the East German government in October 1961. Inevitably, Tseng's work involved him in the Sino-Soviet rift, as was manifested in October 1963 when he "made a clear-cut explanation" to the Soviet ambassador regarding alleged Soviet distortion of the Chinese attitude toward an increase in representation by Asian and African nations on important United Nations organs, in particular the non-permanent seats in the Security Council.

After serving for nine years as a vice-minister, Tseng was removed from this post in January 1966 and was named to succeed Liu Fang as ambassador to Rumania. He presented his credentials in Bucharest on March 17, 1966.

Virtually nothing is known about Tseng's personal life aside from the fact that he is married to Hsu Pei-ju and that he has a limited knowledge of English and Russian.

1. Kalgan, *Chin-Ch'a-Chi jih-pao* (Shansi-Chahar-Hopeh daily), March 1, 1946.

Tso Ch'üan

(1906–1942; Li-ling hsien, Hunan). Important military leader.

Tso Ch'üan was one of the key Red Army staff officers from the early thirties until his death in 1942 when he was deputy chief-of-staff of the Eighth Route Army. He was born in Li-ling hsien, an agricultural community about 50 miles from Changsha, the Hunan capital. Li-ling is the home of a number of important Communists, including Li Li-san. Tso's family of landowners sent him to a provincial middle school, which he attended during the early years of the May Fourth Movement. He went to Kwangtung at age 17 and joined the KMT. That same year, 1923, he entered the Hunan Cadets' School there, one of the several military schools for the different provincial armies supporting the Revolution. In 1924 he transferred to the KMT-

sponsored Whampoa Military Academy, which was headed by Chiang Kai-shek. There Tso became acquainted with Chou En-lai and Nieh Jung-chen (qq.v.), two faculty members who belonged to the CCP. He graduated with a good record from the first class (June 1924–February 1925). Like a number of his classmates, he then joined the forces of Chiang Kai-shek, who recruited many Whampoa cadets into his army to fight the Eastern Expeditions of 1925; they were conducted to drive Ch'en Chiung-ming, Sun Yat-sen's political and military rival, from Kwangtung and to secure the province for Sun and his KMT headquarters. In this same year (1925) he joined the CCP.[1]

In 1926 Tso went to Moscow to attend the Communist University of the Toilers of the East. He spent four years in the Soviet Union, transferring in 1928 to the Red Army Academy (Frunze Military Academy), where one of his classmates was Liu Po-ch'eng (q.v.). Tso was among those who attended the CCP's Sixth National Congress, held in Moscow in mid-1928. He returned to China in 1930 and went to join the Communist armies in Kiangsi. The following year he was operating in Fukien in association with Yang Te-chih (q.v.), also a native of Li-ling hsien. The two men worked closely together for a number of years. In 1931 they were in southern Fukien in Nan-ching hsien, about 50 miles from Amoy. Tso was then political commissar (and by early 1932 also the commander) of the 15th Red Army, a unit initially subordinate to the Fifth Army Corps and later to Lin Piao's First Army Corps. Tso and Yang transferred to the Red Army Academy (Hung-chün ta-hsueh) near Juichin, Kiangsi, when it opened in 1933. Yang enrolled as a student and Tso became a faculty member. Also serving as a lecturer was Liu Po-ch'eng (q.v.), who from 1932 to about 1937 was the chief-of-staff of the Revolutionary Military Committee. At some time prior to the opening of the Long March in the fall of 1934 Tso served as his deputy. His most important military post in this period, however, was as chief-of-staff to Lin Piao from the time that Lin's force was reorganized to form the First Army Corps (see under Lin Piao). Tso held this post from 1932 up to and during the Long March. In the spring of 1935 Tso commanded troops which played an important role in the military maneuvers leading to the successful crossing of the Tatu River in Szechwan (see under Yang Ch'eng-wu), one of the most important episodes of the Long March.[2]

Tso continued to serve in Lin Piao's First Army Corps after the close of the Long March in the fall of 1935. He was still Lin's chief-of-staff as late as the end of 1935,[3] but when Lin became absorbed in the work of re-establishing and enlarging the Red Army Academy, Tso frequently served as acting commander of the Corps. He was identified in this capacity by American author Edgar Snow when he visited north Shensi in 1936.[4] In the late summer of that year Nieh Jung-chen and Tso began to move units under their command to the Hui-ning area of east Kansu to make contact with two other Red Armies that were making their own separate marches to north Shensi. These were the Second Front Army led by Ho Lung (q.v.) and the Fourth Front Army under Chang Kuo-t'ao (q.v.), to which Chu Te had been attached since mid-1935. The rendezvous was accomplished in October 1936. However, according to an account by Liu Po-ch'eng, Nieh and Tso tried in vain to convince Chang Kuo-t'ao to continue his march northward to Shensi rather than to lead his troops westward, a move that led to disastrous results for Chang's troops.[5]

Early in 1937 American journalist Agnes Smedley met Tso near San-yuan, Shensi, not far north of Sian, where the First Army Corps had its headquarters. He was then serving as acting commander of the Corps.[6] When war with Japan broke out in mid-1937 the Communists created the Eighth Route Army and made Tso a ranking staff officer. Once again he frequently assumed the role of his superior, Chief-of-Staff Yeh Chien-ying (q.v.), who spent most of the early war years in Nationalist areas carrying on liaison work for the Communists. During the early months of the war, in his capacity as acting chief-of-staff, Tso was with Commander-in-Chief Chu Te and Political Department Director Jen Pi-shih at the Eighth Route Army's front-line headquarters in Shansi. For a time in the fall of 1938, while his superiors Chu Te and P'eng Te-huai were in Yenan for the Sixth Party Plenum, Tso was actually in charge of Eighth Route Army operations. He was later assigned to Liu Po-ch'eng's 129th Division, which made its headquarters in the T'ai-hang Mountains of eastern Shansi. Tso was there in the spring of 1940 when, concurrently with his post as Eighth Route Army deputy chief-of-staff, he became commander of the Army's Second Column. Units of the Second Column were sent at this time to the Hopeh-Shantung-Honan (Chi-Lu-Yü) Military Region, but Tso was unable to go there himself because of the press of work at the T'ai-hang headquarters. Two years later he was with the Communist units that were driven from central Hopeh by the Japanese and was killed in early June 1942 in the ensuing fighting along the Ch'ing-chang River in southeast Shansi.

When Evans Carlson interviewed Tso in 1937 he spoke of him as having a bearing that "suggested long military training." Agnes Smedley described him as a "suave but reticent intellectual."[7] In the four years he spent in the Soviet Union Tso became sufficiently proficient in Russian to translate a number of Soviet works into Chinese, including a staff manual dealing with combat regulations of the Soviet Red Army. During the war he also wrote several articles on military affairs, especially on the subject of recruiting. Sketches of Tso's life are included in a number of the memorial biographies published by the Communists since 1949.[8] Schools, towns, and even folk songs have been named for him, and amidst considerable ceremony his remains were reburied in Han-tan in south Hopeh on October 20, 1950.[9] On the same day the *JMJP* carried several articles about his career, including one by his long-time colleague Nieh Jung-chen.

1. Edgar Snow, *Random Notes on Red China, 1936–1945* (Cambridge, Mass., 1957), p. 139.
2. *The Long March, Eyewitness Accounts* (Peking, 1963), pp. 74–75.
3. *Ibid.*, p. 184.
4. Edgar Snow, *Red Star over China* (New York, 1938), p. 452.
5. *The Long March, Eyewitness Accounts*, pp. 222–223; Jerome Ch'en, *Mao and the Chinese Revolution* (London, 1965), pp. 196–197.
6. Agnes Smedley, *Battle Hymn of China* (New York, 1945), p. 151.
7. *Ibid.*, p. 154; Evans Fordyce Carlson, *Twin Stars of China* (New York, 1940), p. 67.
8. *Hu-nan ko-ming lieh-shih chuan* (Biographies of Hunan revolutionary martyrs; Changsha, 1952), pp. 26–31; *Hung-ch'i p'iao-p'iao* (Red flag fluttering; Peking, 1957), V, 132–148.
9. *People's China*, no. 17:23 (September 1, 1953); *SCMP* 3049, p. 13.

Tsou Ta-p'eng

(c.1900–   ; Manchuria). A leading intelligence official.

Tsou Ta-p'eng has spent his entire career in intelligence and security work. In view of this fact, only the most fragmentary information is available on the early years of his career. He was reportedly active in Manchuria during the early part of the Sino-Japanese War, probably in intelligence work. However, it is unlikely that Tsou remained for long in Manchuria. CCP work in Manchuria was not very effective during the war and, in addition, other reports from the war period associated Tsou with K'ang Sheng and Li K'o-nung, neither of whom was active in Manchuria. Both K'ang and Li had long careers in intelligence work covering many parts of China, and both were veterans of the "Social Affairs" Department of the Party, the long-used euphemism for intelligence work. Tsou almost certainly spent much of the Sino-Japanese War period working under K'ang or Li in this department.

As World War II was drawing to a close in mid-1945, the Chinese Communists rushed military forces and cadres to Manchuria in a major effort to gain control of this important area. It seems likely that Tsou was among these men sent to Manchuria, if indeed he was not already there. In any event, by 1946 he was serving as a member of the Northeast CCP Bureau and as president of the "High Court," which the Communists had formed in areas under their control in Manchuria. In addition to the Party hierarchy in the Northeast, the Communists also formed a governmental unit known as the Northeast Administrative Committee (NEAC); Tsou was a member of the NEAC from its formation in 1946. For administrative purposes, Changchun (capital of Kirin) was placed under this committee, and when it was captured by the Communists in October 1948, Tsou was named as mayor as well as vice-chairman of the Changchun Military Control Commission, holding both posts until he was transferred to Peking in 1949.

Tsou was among those leaders who met in Peking in September 1949 to form a government. The meetings were held under the auspices of the CPPCC, on which Tsou served as a delegate from the "Northeast Liberated Areas." Although he was not given a position on the permanent CPPCC National Committee, he was appointed (in October) as director of the Information Administration under the Government Administration Council headed by Premier Chou En-lai. Extremely little is known about the Information Administration, an organization at the ministerial level, but it is clear from Tsou's career that it was involved in intelligence work. Apparently the collection of intelligence on foreign countries was one of its chief functions because an organ under its jurisdiction was known as the "External Affairs Investigation and Research Bureau." Possibly in an effort to conceal its intelligence activities, the regime abolished the administration in August 1952.

When Tsou was appointed to the Information Administration in 1949, he was officially identified by the Communists as the "former" secretary-general of the previously mentioned Social Affairs Department of the Party's Central Committee. At this same time, Tsou's former chief, Li K'o-nung, was also described in connection with the Social Affairs Department. Apparently these are the last open references to this intelligence organization by the Communists in the post-1949 period. But over the next few years there were continual references to the department from non-Communist sources, with Tsou almost always mentioned as a senior official.

As already noted, the Information Administration was abolished in August 1952. Not long after Tsou was identified in a new post, this time subordinate to the military hierarchy. He became director of the Liaison Department of the People's Revolutionary Military Council (PRMC), holding the post until the PRMC was abolished with the formation of the constitutional government in 1954. At the time of this governmental reorganization in September 1954, Tsou did not receive any formal government post, but in December of that year he represented the Party on the Second CPPCC (1954–1959), a post to which he was re-elected in April 1959 for the Third CPPCC (1959–1964), and then again for the Fourth CPPCC, which first met in December 1964. On the last occasion, he was elevated to the governing body of the CPPCC, the Standing Committee.

In February 1958, in an effort to handle the increasingly complex field of Chinese foreign relations, Peking established a new commission under the State Council, known as the Commission for Cultural Relations with Foreign Countries. In the following month, Tsou was named a vice-chairman, a post he continues to hold. As is often the case, the Chinese have governmental organizations and "people's" organizations with nearly identical titles. In 1954, a "Chinese People's Association for Cultural Relations with Foreign Countries" had been established; it was reorganized in April 1959, at which time Tsou was added as a Standing Committee member, and then in June 1961 he was elevated to a vice-chairmanship. Presumably Tsou is able to utilize both the governmental and "people's" organizations for intelligence work. The idea that he retains some high-level Party intelligence post was strongly suggested in mid-1963 when he was identified in the Communist press as a "responsible member" of a department directly under the Party Central Committee. There can be little doubt that this referred to some intelligence organization.

In February 1962 Tsou served on the funeral committee for his long-time superior in intelligence work, Li K'o-nung. He also served on funeral committees for trade specialist Chi Ch'ao-ting in August 1963 and Kan Szu-ch'i, a deputy director of the PLA General Political Department, in February 1964. Finally, in October 1964 the Political Science and Law Association of China held its fourth congress; Tsou was elected to the new national council. Aside from official appointments, these are among the extremely few references to Tsou in recent years, clearly a reflection of the secrecy of his work.

Tu Jun-sheng

Secretary-General, Academy of Sciences.

Tu Jun-sheng was one of the key Party officials in central-south China during the early years of the PRC. A specialist in agrarian affairs, he was transferred to Peking where he held important posts in this field during the middle 1950's. By the latter part of the 1950's, however, he began to devote more of his time to the field of science administration, and in 1960 he became secretary-general of the Academy of Sciences.

Tu, who studied at Peking Normal University, became a CCP member prior to the Communist conquest of the mainland in 1949. He must have had a fairly lengthy record within the Party, for by 1950 (and until 1954) he was the secretary-general of the CCP Central-South Bureau, a key post in a bureau responsible for six provinces embracing a huge population. Parallel to the Party Bureau was the Central-South Military and Administrative Committee (CSMAC), renamed the Central-South Administrative Committee in 1953. From 1950 to 1954, when the CSMAC–CSAC was abolished, Tu held several posts within the organization, positions which suggested an emphasis on agricultural affairs. From March 1950 to May 1953 he was a vice-chairman of the Land Reform Committee, serving under Li Hsueh-feng, an important Party leader. From December 1951 to May 1953 he was also a member of the Political and Legal Affairs Committee, and in the fall of 1952 served briefly as a vice-chairman of an *ad hoc* committee established to verify the claims made for farm output.

During his years in the central-south region Tu devoted much of his time to the important problem of land reform. He has been characterized in one study as a leading exponent of a "hard line" in pursuing the land reform goals. This judgment was made on the basis of key speeches made by Tu in November 1950, January 1951, and August 1951.[1] Tu was transferred in the 1953–1954 period to Peking where he continued to specialize in agricultural affairs. He was appointed in October 1954 as a deputy director of the State Council's Seventh Staff Office, the organ charged with coordinating the work of the various government ministries and bureaus involved in agriculture and conservation matters. Within the next year Tu received two more appointments which drew upon his agricultural background. In December 1954 he was named as a representative of peasants to the Second National Committee of the CPPCC, a position he held until the Third Committee was formed in April 1959. More important, by September 1955 Tu was secretary-general of the Rural Work Department of the Party Central Committee, the key organ within the hierarchy that formulates basic agricultural decisions. Based on various speeches made by Tu in the mid-1950's, he appears to have been among those who favored a rapid collectivization of the farmlands. It is not certain when he relinquished this important post, but apparently it was by the late 1950's.

In the interim, Tu received two further posts in semi-official organizations of only moderate significance. In December 1954 he attended the Second National Conference of the Sino-Soviet Friendship Association (SSFA) as a representative of peasants, and at the close of the conference he became a member of the second national SSFA Council; he was re-elected to the third Council in May 1959 and continues in this position. He also served as a deputy secretary-general of the national committee formed in February 1955 to collect signatures in opposition to the use of atomic weapons.

The year 1956 was a major turning point in the development of science in China. It was early in that year, for example, that the ambitious 12-year scientific development plan was announced, and it was about this same time that Tu began to switch his emphasis from agricultural to scientific matters. He participated from 1956 to 1958 in the State Council's Scientific Planning Commission; from its formation in March 1956 to May 1957 he was a deputy secretary-general and thereafter to November 1958 he was a member. In November 1957 he served as a deputy secretary-general of the large scientific delegation led by Kuo Mo-jo to the USSR. Ostensibly this was one of several delegations in Moscow to celebrate the 40th anniversary of the Russian Revolution, but obviously the Chinese scientists and science administrators utilized the occasion to confer with their Soviet counterparts and to inspect Soviet facilities.

In 1958 Tu became affiliated with the Academy of Sciences, and from that time has devoted the major portion of his time to this organization. By February 1958 he was a deputy secretary-general of the academy and by the same month was serving as a secretary of the Party organization within the academy. Then, when an academy vice-president died in 1960, Secretary-General P'ei Li-sheng (q.v.) moved up to a vice-presidency and Tu, in turn, became (by August 1960) the secretary-general, a post in which he continues. A former academy employee has stated that by the early 1960's Tu was considered to be the Party man "who really runs things." This same person, not a Communist, spoke slightingly of Tu's knowledge of science.[2] Tu, in fact, is seldom reported directly in connection with scientific affairs. One of the few such identifications occurred in February 1958 when he delivered a report on Soviet science (after his trip to Moscow in late 1957), and on another occasion he wrote an article reviewing China's progress in the natural sciences for *K'o-hsueh t'ung-pao* (Scientific bulletin; no. 19, 1959). More often, Tu is reported at bureaucratic functions such as the formal signing of scientific agreements with Communists; these identifications suggest that he may oversee for the Party certain aspects of international scientific liaison. Examples of his participation in such ceremonies occurred when scientific agreements were signed with the USSR (October 1961), North Korea (June 1962), Czechoslovakia (September 1962), Bulgaria (June 1963), and Rumania (July 1963).

Tu Jun-sheng is one of the few Communist Party members about whom "inside" knowledge exists. In addition to the above-quoted interview, Soviet scientist Mikhail A. Klochko,[3] a defector, has provided an additional insight into both the inner workings of the Academy and the esteem in which Tu is held by his colleagues. Klochko reported with dismay the amount of time that Chinese scientists devoted to political meetings which detracted from their scientific work. He told of an Academy employee who listened to the above-mentioned report given by Tu after his return from the USSR. His dialogue with the Chinese scientist was as follows: " 'Where are you off to, Su-fen?' I asked her. 'I have to go and listen to Comrade [Tu], the secretary of the Party organization of the Academy. He is reporting on his trip to the Soviet Union. Everyone working for the Academy must go and hear his report,' she said. Shortly after she left, I heard a voice coming over the loudspeakers that were installed in every corridor. I opened the door and saw that the entire passage was cluttered with people, some, like Su-fen, sitting on footstools, others on the floor. It must have been rather hard on them, for Comrade [Tu's] voice poured out at them all day without letup, except during the sacred lunch hour, when he fell silent. 'That fellow dares call himself a Party secretary!' I thought to myself. 'Some Party secretary, wasting the whole day of several thousand workers with his drivel!' I couldn't understand why he had not limited his report to one or even two hours and made it after work, or why he had not simply had the report printed and distributed."

Because Tu has been essentially a behind-the-scenes Party operative, his importance as a science administrator is not easily assessed. In terms of the Party hierarchy, for example, he is far outranked by Politburo member Ch'en Po-ta, one of the Academy of Sciences vice-presidents. Yet it is clear that Ch'en's several policy-level positions in the CCP apparatus must preclude detailed attention to the academy. Thus it appears that many of the major day-to-day responsibilities within the academy rest upon the shoulders of such Party science administrators as Chang Chin-fu, P'ei Li-sheng (qq.v.), and Tu.

---

1. Ezra F. Vogel, *Canton under Communism* (Cambridge, Mass., 1969), pp. 99–114.

2. Interview in Hong Kong, October 1964.

3. Mikhail A. Klochko, *Soviet Scientist in Red China* (New York, 1964), pp. 18–19.

Tuan Chün-i

(c.1912–   ; Shantung). Minister, First Ministry of Machine Building.

Tuan Chün-i, whose original name was Tuan Shang-ch'i, was probably born about 1912 (to judge from the period he was in college). Japanese sources assert that Tuan is a native of Shantung and that he graduated from the school of technology of Tsinan University (Shantung). Tuan was a college student in 1935 when the "December Ninth" student demonstrations took place, first in Peking, and then soon after in many major Chinese cities in protest to Japanese incursions into North China (see under Li Ch'ang). The role that Tuan may have played in the initial demonstrations is unknown, but by mid-1937 he was deeply involved in the movement. Communist sources describe him as of mid-1937 as a "responsible person" of the National Federation of Students and a delegate of the Peiping (Peking) Federation of Students (suggesting that in addition to training in Tsinan, Tuan also studied at a university in Peking).[1]

In the period immediately before and after war broke out with Japan (July 1937) a number of students from Peking and Tientsin went to Nanking (then the national capital and the Kuomintang headquarters) to stimulate the work of the youth movement. Some of these students were Communists or Communist Youth League members. If Tuan was not already a Party member, he probably became one within the next year or two. His whereabouts after mid-1937 when he was in Nanking are unknown. Many of these youths went to Sian and then to Yenan, but still others worked with the National Liberation Vanguard of China (NLVC) in Hankow, temporarily the capital after the fall of Nanking in late 1937. (By this time the NLVC was under the control of the CCP.) Chiang Nan-hsiang, with whom Tuan had been working in Nanking in mid-1937, was known to be in the Hankow area, and the later career of Tuan suggests that he may also have been there.

Assuming that Tuan remained in Hupeh during the Sino-Japanese War it is likely that he had contact with such senior Communists as T'ao Chu and Ch'ien Ying (qq.v.), who were active in guerrilla areas in Hupeh by the late 1930's. In any event, when Tuan received an appointment in mid-1950, he was identified as the former secretary of the Hupeh-Honan District Committee of the CCP, a district in which he may have been active during the late 1930's or 1940's.

As Communist armies were sweeping southward in 1949, functionaries of every description were needed to staff the many new posts. Tuan's history at this juncture is typical of many present-day Communist leaders. Probably owing to his technical education, he received appointments utilizing this background. When Nanking was captured in April 1949, Tuan was named as head of the "Finance and Economics Takeover Committee" under the Nanking Military Control Commission; the commission was then headed by Liu Po-ch'eng, commander of the Communist armies in this area. Liu marched with his forces toward the southwest early in the fall of 1949, and apparently Tuan was among those who accompanied him or followed shortly thereafter. When the Southwest Military and Administrative Committee (SWMAC) was established in July 1950 under Chairman Liu Po-ch'eng, Tuan received three important appointments. He was named a member of the SWMAC, director of its Industry Department, and a vice-chairman of the SWMAC Finance and Economics Committee. Although not formally relieved of one of these positions until 1954, Tuan left the southwest for Peking in 1952 when departments of the Ministry of Heavy Industry were split off from the ministry and placed under two new ministries, the First and Second Ministries of Machine Building. Tuan joined the First Ministry and has remained there to the present. He initially served as a vice-minister under Huang Ching (q.v.), another participant in the student demonstrations of the mid-1930's in Peking. After Huang died in February 1958, Chao Erh-lu succeeded him, but then in September 1960 Tuan replaced Chao as the minister.

The activities of the machine building ministries have been deliberately shrouded in secrecy, so the details of Tuan's work are not well known. It is virtually certain, however, that the First Ministry has (or has had) some role in the manufacture of munitions. Apart from munitions, a clue to other products manufactured by the ministry was provided in December 1959 when Tuan attended the inauguration of a new hydraulic press at the Canton Heavy Machine Tools Plant, and still another clue was given in October 1960 when Tuan was present at the signing in Peking of loan and technical aid agreements with North Korea, accords which called for assistance in the manufacture of rubber tires and radio communications equipment.

In 1954 Tuan was named a deputy from his native Shantung to the First NPC, but he was not re-elected to the Second NPC, which first met in 1959. In August 1955 he was elected to the national committee of the "First Machine Building Trade Union," but his union connections have not been mentioned since that time. Tuan was not often in the news in the late 1950's or early 1960's. Among the few notices of his appearances were in December 1956 when he made an inspection tour of Shantung, in October 1959 when he accompanied Chou En-lai on an inspection of a reservoir near Peking, and in July 1960 when he was in Shenyang for celebra-

tions marking the 40th anniversary of the CCP.

Although not a member of the first three national committees of the CPPCC (1949–1964), Tuan was named as a delegate of the CCP to the Fourth National Committee, which first met in December 1964–January 1965. At the same time that the CPPCC was in session, the Third NPC was holding its first session; Tuan spoke January 2, 1965 in his capacity as the minister of the First Ministry of Building, but details of his speech was not made public. At this same congress session, he was reappointed to his ministerial post.

1. Li Ch'ang *et al., "I-erh-chiu" hui-i-lu* (Reminiscences of "December Ninth"; Peking, 1961), p. 27.

Tung Pi-wu

(1886–   ; Huang-an hsien, Hupeh). Party "elder"; vice-chairman, PRC; secretary, CCP Central Control Commission; member, Politburo.

Party "elder" Tung Pi-wu, also known as Tung Yung-wei, has been a revolutionist since the overthrow of the Manchu dynasty in 1911. One of the Party founders in 1921, he worked for both the CCP and the KMT in Hupeh during the mid-1920's. After the KMT–CCP split in 1927, he studied in Moscow and then returned to become a key official in the Central Soviet in Kiangsi. Tung made the Long March, and then spent most of the war years as a liaison official to the KMT government in Chungking. He was the sole Communist representative at the 1945 conference in San Francisco which organized the United Nations. Tung headed the North China People's Government in the late forties, and since the establishment of the PRC in 1949 he has held a series of top posts in the central government. These include being a vice-premier, chief justice, and a vice-chairman of the PRC. Tung has been a Party Central Committee member since 1934, a Politburo member since 1945, and secretary of the Central Control Commission since 1955. He and his colleagues Lin Po-ch'ü, Wu Yü-chang, Hsu T'e-li, and Hsieh Chueh-tsai are frequently referred to as the "five elders" (*wu-lao*).

Tung was born in Huang-an (now Hung-an) hsien, 50 miles north of Wuhan in the foothills of the Ta-pieh Mountains. Other prominent Communists from Huang-an include Li Hsien-nien and Cheng Wei-san (q.v.). His family has been described as "landless gentry" and "urban petty-bourgeois." The household had 30 persons living under one roof, but the immediate family consisted of only Tung's parents, a brother, and two sisters. His father, a "scholar" (that is, a degree holder), an uncle, and Tung's brother taught for a living, and young Tung studied the classics and became a *Hsiu-ts'ai* degree holder in his 15th year (c. 1901). Yearning for a modern education, he went to Wuchang where he was a middle school student for several years after the turn of the century. There he lived in the dormitory of a reformist and educational society run by a Chinese Christian. Although not yet a revolutionist, he was influenced in those years by this organization and by the writings of Liang Ch'i-ch'ao.

Tung had just begin a middle school teaching career not far from Wuchang when the 1911 Revolution broke out. He immediately returned to Wuchang and enlisted in the "revolutionary army," serving first in logistics work and later in the financial department of the Wuchang military government. In the account of his career given to American journalist Nym Wales in 1937,[1] Tung stated that from the time of the 1911 Revolution "I have been constantly engaged in revolution as a profession." He joined Sun Yat-sen's T'ung-meng hui at the end of 1911 and for the next year and a half he took part in political activities in Hupeh until he was forced to flee to Japan in 1913 when the T'ung-meng hui was suppressed by Yuan Shih-k'ai. In 1914 Tung joined Sun's newly organized Chung-hua ko-ming tang (Chinese revolutionary party), the successor to the T'ung-meng hui, and at the same time he studied law at a college in Tokyo.

At the request of Sun Yat-sen, Tung interrupted his schooling in Japan in 1915 to return to Hupeh to engage in secret work among military forces. He was arrested and imprisoned for half a year. Released in 1916 after Yuan Shih-k'ai's political downfall, Tung returned to Japan and completed his legal studies the following year. In 1917 and 1918, back in China, Tung engaged in propaganda work in the so-called "Defense of the Constitution Army" in west Hupeh near the Szechwan border. In the spring of 1919 he went to Shanghai where he first began his study of Marxism. In this endeavor he was influenced by another Japanese-trained student, Li Han-chün (q.v.), who, like Tung, was to become a founding member of the CCP in 1921. Tung's conversion to Marxism seems to have taken place in the period from mid-1919 to mid-1920. His own description of his thinking then (as related to Nym Wales) is fairly typical of many young intellectuals of the period. "From my own experience, I decided that secret work among the troops [a favorite tactic of Śun Yat-sen] was useless and that it was necessary to lay the foundation for a people's movement. We had always worked with the military leaders, who usually betrayed because they had no revolutionary understanding." He went on to praise the good intentions of many of the 1911 Revolutionists, but "I decided that the revolution had to have a real mass base, and wanted to start a newspaper or school for this purpose." He there-

fore returned to Wuhan where with a handful of other teachers he opened a middle school.

Tung's middle school and a bookstore established by Yun Tai-ying (q.v.) in this same period quickly became gathering places for young Marxist-oriented intellectuals. Among Tung's colleagues or disciples during these years were Ch'en T'an-ch'iu, Yun Tai-ying, Lin Yü-nan, Lin Yü-ying, Hsiao Ch'u-nü, and Li Ch'iu-shih (qq.v.), whose biographies contain further details on the origins of the Communist movement in Hupeh. In the latter half of 1920 and the first half of 1921, Tung spent a good portion of his time establishing the rudiments of a Communist apparatus in Hupeh, and when the CCP held its inaugural congress in 1921 the Hupeh group was clearly one of the two or three most important Communist groups throughout China. Fittingly, therefore, Tung and his colleague Ch'en T'an-ch'iu were the two delegates from Hupeh to the First CCP Congress, held in Shanghai in July 1921. Among the dozen-odd men who attended, only Tung and Mao Tse-tung survived into the middle of the twentieth century as CCP members. (Li Ta and Chang Kuo-t'ao are still alive, but the former left the Party in the 1920's and the latter in the 1930's.) Many years later, in an interview, Tung recalled that the First Congress called for a "struggle against imperialism . . . and warlords." He claimed that he had helped draft the congress documents, which he also noted had been lost.[2]

Returning to Hupeh after the national congress, Tung was a delegate to the First Hupeh CCP Congress in September 1921, and during the next few years he played a key role in developing the Hupeh branch of the Party. However, he had a year-long interlude in Szechwan where he was sent, in his own words, to "revive some of my old tactics of winning over the military forces to revolution." He returned again to Hupeh (about early 1923) where, paralleling the growth of the CCP, a significant labor movement had developed in Wuhan and nearby cities, in which a number of Communists were particularly active (see under Hsiang Ying and Ch'en T'an-ch'iu). The development of the labor movement received a severe blow in February 1923 when warlord Wu P'ei-fu savagely suppressed the railroad workers' union on the Peking-Hankow Railway. The near total collapse of the labor movement in Wuhan, a key industrial city, was among the factors which led the Communists to have a greater interest in cooperation with the KMT. Thus, at the First KMT Congress, held in Canton in January 1924, several Communists were elected to the KMT Central Executive Committee (see under Lin Po-ch'ü), and steps were taken to inaugurate KMT branches in several provinces outside of Kwangtung, then the center of KMT activity. A number of Communists worked in these provincial branches, such as Hsia Hsi (q.v.) in Hunan and Tung in the Hupeh headquarters.

In 1924, together with his Communist colleagues Ch'en T'an-ch'iu and Hsiao Ch'u-nü (q.v.), Tung went to Chin-chai hsien to inaugurate a peasant movement.[3] This was apparently the first effort by either the KMT or the CCP to foster peasant support for the revolutionary cause in this region. Chin-chai is located in west Anhwei close to the Hupeh-Honan borders, and several years later it was one of the areas within the important Oyüwan Soviet (see under Chang Kuo-t'ao). In the period from February to May 1925 Tung claimed to have traveled as far west as Szechwan and as far north as Manchuria and Peking to gain adherents to the revolution. Then in January 1926 he went to Canton to attend the Second KMT Congress. He was elected an alternate member of the Central Executive Committee; other important Communists also elected as alternates were Mao Tse-tung, Hsia Hsi, and Teng Ying-ch'ao. In the months which followed he was one of a small group assigned the task of persuading the important military leader T'ang Sheng-chih, then in Hunan with his army, to join the revolutionary cause. They finally met with success in the late spring of 1926 on the eve of the Northern Expedition, which was launched from Kwangtung against the northern warlords.

When the Northern Expedition began in mid-1926, Tung was in Wuhan. He claims to have taken part in sabotage against enemy troops to help the Northern Expeditionary forces capture the city in the fall of 1926. After the KMT transferred the "national" government to Wuhan during the winter of 1926–27, Tung joined the Hupeh Provincial government as head of the Peasants' and Workers' Bureau. He remained in Wuhan during the turbulent first half of 1927 when the CCP continued its collaboration with the left-wing KMT. In the middle of the year, however, these two factions had an open split; the Communists were expelled from all their posts and were soon forced into hiding. Tung and his former colleague Li Han-chün found a temporary refuge in the Japanese Concession in Wuhan, but Li was captured and executed. Tung escaped to the French Concession, and from there, disguised as a sailor, he made his way to Shanghai and then to Japan. He lived in Kyoto for eight months and then left for Moscow, arriving in September 1928. Three of the other Party "elders"—Lin Po-ch'ü, Wu Yü-chang, and Hsu T'e-li—had taken a similar course of action. There are conflicting reports about which school Tung attended during his three-odd years in Moscow; some say the University of the Toilers of the East, some say Sun Yat-sen University, but Tung himself told Nym Wales that he attended the Lenin School, which was run by the Comintern. He finished his courses in 1931 and returned home the next year.

Tung spent a month in Shanghai and then went to Juichin, the capital of the Central Soviet area which Mao Tse-tung and Chu Te had developed into the Party's chief rural guerrilla base in the early thirties. He claims to have been political director of the Red Academy (presumably the Red Army Academy, established in 1933) and to have organized and served as principal of the Communist Party School. Prior to the Long March in 1934, he also worked in educational affairs under Ch'ü Ch'iu-pai (q.v.). Also in 1934, presumably at the Fifth Plenum in January, he was elected an alternate member of the CCP Central Committee. (At some time before 1945, possibly at the Sixth Plenum in October–November 1938, he was promoted to a full member.) Immediately after the Fifth Plenum, the Communists held the Second All-China Congress of Soviets (January–February 1934). Tung was elected a member of the Central Executive Committee (CEC) of the Chinese Soviet Republic, as well as president of the Supreme Court. He told Nym Wales that he "later" became commissar for Workers' and Peasants' Supervision, one of the cabinet posts under the CEC; if so, he presumably replaced Hsiang Ying (q.v.), who was named to that position at the Second Congress.

Tung set out on the Long March with the main columns which left the Juichin area in October 1934. During the year-long trek to north Shensi he was, in his own words, "commissar of public health," apparently working in collaboration with Fu Lien-chang (q.v.), the leading medical specialist during that period. After the completion of the march, he resumed his post as head of the Party School, first at Wa-yao-pao and then at Pao-an (now known as Chihtan). He apparently continued in this post until the end of 1936 or early 1937.

Tung was one of those who assisted Chou En-lai in his negotiations with Chiang Kai-shek during the famous Sian Incident in December 1936 (see under Chou), and then in September 1937, shortly after the Sino-Japanese War began, he was sent to Sian again. On this occasion he worked with Lin Po-ch'ü. Lin was in charge of the Communists' Eighth Route Army liaison office there, which had been set up during this period of renewed KMT–CCP cooperation. Tung continued as a key liaison official with the KMT for most of the next decade. In the latter part of 1937, not long before Nanking fell to the Japanese, the national capital was moved to Hankow. Tung went there in 1938 as a liaison official with the Nationalist government, and for a period in that year he served as head of the Communists' Yangtze Bureau, apparently replacing Ch'en Shao-yü (q.v.) when Ch'en returned to Yenan in the fall. At one time or another in 1938 an impressive number of top Communists were in Hankow, including Chou En-lai, the head of the CCP group there, and the Communist delegates to the People's Political Council (see below).

In March 1938, in an effort to gain nationwide support from all political factions, the KMT decided to establish the People's Political Council as a consultative body. In June the following seven were "invited" to participate as members: Mao Tse-tung (never more than a nominal member), Lin Po-ch'ü, Wu Yü-chang, Tung, Ch'en Shao-yü, Ch'in Pang-hsien, and Chou En-lai's wife Teng Ying-ch'ao (qq.v.). The inaugural session of the council was held in Hankow in July 1938. Hankow was captured in October, and thus the second council session was held in Chungking, the new capital, in October–November. Tung served as a member of the first through the fourth councils (1938–1947), but because of the ever-increasing tensions between the CCP and the KMT he did not attend any sessions after 1944. His activities in Chungking were, of course, not confined to the rather infrequent meetings of the KMT-dominated People's Political Council. Tung worked closely with Chou En-lai and other important members of the Eighth Route Army liaison office, which served as a focal point for the varied activities of the significant group of CCP members there. Throughout the war years Tung was also a rather frequent contributor to the Communist press, particularly the journal *Ch'ün-chung* (The masses), which was published in Chungking.

In June 1943 Chou En-lai left Chungking for Yenan, and for most of the remaining war period Tung was the chief Communist representative in Chungking. CCP–KMT relations had been steadily deteriorating since the New Fourth Army Incident in January 1941 (see under Yeh T'ing), and they grew no better in September 1943 when Tung walked out of a session of the People's Political Council in response to a denunciation of the Communists by a top Nationalist general.[4] However, partly because of American efforts to reconcile the two sides, Chiang Kai-shek summoned Tung in January 1944 to express an interest in negotiations to resolve various outstanding issues. Tung in turn contacted Yenan for instructions, which brought word that Mao Tse-tung was also willing to negotiate. Two weeks later Tung described to foreign newsmen the aims of the CCP, which included the lifting of the KMT blockade against, and formal recognition of, the Shensi-Kansu-Ninghsia Border Region.[5] Later in the spring the first serious steps toward bilateral negotiations were taken, but at that point Lin Po-ch'ü took over from Tung as the chief Communist negotiator. However, Tung, as well as Wang Jo-fei (q.v.), assisted in the talks which began later that year (see under Lin Po-ch'ü).

Still another activity which occupied Tung's time in Chungking during the war years was a somewhat informal liaison with various "third party" groups (that is, neither Communists nor Nationalists) and political independents who were in general leftist-inclined.[6] Several of the "third party" groups were banded together in October 1944 to form the well-known China Democratic League. With hindsight, it seems that this work eventually accrued to the benefit of the Communists, because in the late 1940's a number of the "third party" leaders joined with the Communists and assumed some rather important posts when the PRC was established in 1949.

In March 1945, Tung was appointed by Chungking as the only Communist on the 10-member delegation headed by T. V. Soong, which the Chinese sent to the conference in San Francisco to establish the United Nations (April–June 1945). The inclusion of Tung in this group resulted from the insistent urgings of Chou En-lai (who initially suggested himself, Tung, and Ch'in Pang-hsien for membership on the delegation); Chou's position was backed by the United States, which saw this as a means of fostering Chinese unity.[7] At almost the same moment that Tung arrived in the United States (April 21), with an entourage including Chang Han-fu and Ch'en Chia-k'ang (qq.v.), Mao Tse-tung was delivering a major address ("On Coalition Government") to the CCP Seventh National Congress. Mao "welcomed" the United Nations Conference, and asserted that Tung had been sent "to express the will of the Chinese people." Predictably, Tung played a minor role at the San Francisco meetings. Afterwards, he toured the United States, and he spoke before overseas Chinese groups, gave interviews to newsmen, and met a few American dignitaries. Tung's visit to the United States is of historical interest for two reasons: he was the first Chinese Communist to attend an important international meeting, and, secondly, he is the only senior Chinese Communist to have visited the United States since the war, except for Wu Hsiu-ch'üan (q.v.), who went to the United Nations in the fall of 1950 in connection with the Korean War.

After his extended stay in the United States, Tung returned home in December 1945. During his absence he had been re-elected to the Central Committee at the Seventh Party Congress, and he was also made a member of the Politburo. Tung immediately plunged into the KMT–CCP mediation efforts, which took a new and important turn with the arrival in China of United States Special Envoy George C. Marshall in December. Tung was a top assistant to Chou En-lai in Chungking, and there, on January 10, 1946, a truce was signed between the Nationalists and Communists. On the same day the new Political Consultative Conference opened to arrange for a coalition government. The seven-member Communist delegation to the conference consisted of Chou, Tung, Wang Jo-fei, Yeh Chien-ying (later replaced by Ch'in Pang-hsien), Wu Yü-chang, Lu Ting-i, and Teng Ying-ch'ao (qq.v.). During the three-week conference several committees were established to deal with various issues; Wu served as the co-convener of one to formulate policies which, in theory, were to be followed by the reorganized government, and he was also a member of another committee to work out arrangements for a national assembly. However, little came of any of these efforts during the ensuing months.

For a little over a year Tung remained in the Nationalist capital (first in Chungking, and then in Nanking when the capital was moved there in May 1946). Working as Chou En-lai's top aide, Tung was in regular contact with both Nationalist officials and the American group headed by General Marshall. By November 1946, despite the truce arrangements, civil war was being waged in various parts of China as the two sides maneuvered for the best strategic position. At this juncture Chou En-lai was ordered back to Yenan. He was replaced as the chief Communist representative by Tung, who was actively assisted by Wang Ping-nan (q.v.). Then, in early March, General Marshall having abandoned his efforts to reconcile the two sides, Tung was evacuated to Yenan.

Apart from Tung's work as an assistant to Chou, he had also been chairman of the Chinese Liberated Areas Relief Association (CLARA) since 1946. This organization had been set up to channel to Communist-held areas relief supplies which had been donated by the United Nations Relief and Rehabilitation Administration, the International Red Cross, and other such agencies. Because of the general political and military turmoil throughout the nation, as well as the remoteness of many Communist areas, there were considerable difficulties in getting supplies to persons living in Communist regions. On numerous occasions from 1946 to 1948, Tung issued appeals for more aid, usually coupling these with charges that the Nationalists were sabotaging efforts to get supplies to Communist areas. On the other hand, a detailed study of the UNRRA efforts in China noted that "local Communist guerilla units and advancing Communist armies periodically ambushed and seized UNRRA equipment, supplies and relief personnel in convoys along disputed borders, and several casualties were suffered at Communist hands."[8] Tung relinquished his CLARA post in April 1950 when this and related organizations were incorporated into the Chinese People's Relief Administration; Tung was elected one of the vice-chairmen, a position he still holds. (Further details on CLARA are found in the biography of Wu Yun-fu, the secretary-general of the organization.)

A few days after Tung returned to Yenan in early March 1947, the city was captured by the Nationalists. His whereabouts for the next year are unknown, although the appeals he issued on behalf of CLARA indicate he was somewhere in the north China hinterlands. The next chapter in Tung's varied career was involved with the establishment of the North China Liberated Area, which in turn rested upon the notable victories won by Communist armies in the Shansi-Chahar-Hopeh and Shansi-Hopeh-Shantung-Honan Border Regions in the latter part of 1947 (see under Nieh Jung-chen and Liu Po-ch'eng). Of particular importance was the capture in November 1947 of Shih-chia-chuang, the vital junction which controlled rail traffic running south from Peking and rail lines from Hopeh into Shansi. Soon after the fall of this city, the two border regions were linked into one contiguous area, and by late March 1948 Mao announced that the merger process was already underway.[9] Two months later the two border regions were amalgamated into the North China Liberated Area. Organizationally, three new bodies were created at this time: the two regional Party organs were merged into the North China Bureau under First Secretary Po I-po and Second Secretary Nieh Jung-chen; the North China Military Region was established, with Nieh as the commander and Po as the political commissar; and a governmental unit known as the North China Joint Administrative Council was set up. These three bodies controlled a population of some 50 million in major parts of Hopeh and Shansi, and portions of Suiyuan, Chahar, Jehol, Honan, and Shantung provinces.

The next step to formalize Communist rule in north China was taken in late June 1948 when the congresses of the two liberated areas decided to convene the North China Provisional People's Congress.[10] Six weeks later, on August 7, the congress opened at Shih-chia-chuang, and was attended by 541 delegates representing a wide variety of groups and interests. Among them were such key Communist figures as Tung Pi-wu, Po I-po, Nieh Jung-chen, Hsieh Chueh-tsai, Yang Hsiu-feng, and Sung Shao-wen (qq.v.). In his inaugural speech Tung described the provisional congress as a prelude to and a miniature version of the national assembly to be held at a later date.[11] At the close of the congress (August 19), the North China People's Government (NCPG) was established, replacing the Joint Administrative Council. Tung was elected chairman, and a month later, when the government's subordinate bodies were staffed, he was made chairman of the Finance and Economics Committee.

Apart from the fact that the Shih-chia-chuang area was the center for the Communists' military, governmental, and Party organs in North China, it took on added importance in May 1948 when Mao Tse-tung arrived in P'ing-shan hsien, only a few miles northwest of the city, just as the North China Liberated Area was being formed. During the next 10 months—until the Central Committee and the PLA Headquarters moved to Peking in March 1949—the Shih-chia-chuang area was in fact the Chinese Communist "capital." One month earlier, Tung's NCPG moved to Peking. The NCPG continued as an active organization throughout the spring and summer of 1949, and in June Tung took on a new assignment as chairman of the government's Higher Education Committee. However, in October, a few weeks after the formal establishment of the PRC, the NCPG was dissolved and its functions were absorbed by the new central government.

Like most of the senior Communists, Tung was busily engaged in mid-1949 in preparations for the establishment of the central government and the numerous "mass" organizations which were to be set up. His many assignments included membership on the preparatory committees for the China New Legal Research Society, the China Social Sciences Workers' Conference, the All-China Educational Workers' Conference, and the Sino-Soviet Friendship Association. He was also a preparatory committee member for the CPPCC, which Mao established in June. When the CPPCC was convened in September to inaugurate the national government, Tung was placed in charge of the *ad hoc* committee to draft the Organic Law of the central government, and he also delivered a speech about the law. Tung attended the CPPCC as a representative of the CCP, and at the close of the proceedings he was elected a member of the CPPCC's First National Committee (to 1954), and from December 1954 to April 1959 he was a vice-chairman of the Second National Committee.

Already a revolutionist for four decades, and then in his mid-sixties, Tung was rewarded with key posts in the new government inaugurated on October 1, 1949. He was made a member of the Central People's Government Council, the highest organ of government (chaired by Mao), and a vice-premier of the Government Administration Council (the cabinet), which was headed by Chou En-lai. Under the cabinet he was also made chairman of the Political and Legal Affairs Committee, one of the four committees which had jurisdiction over several ministries and commissions. In the same month he became a member of the Executive Board of the Sino-Soviet Friendship Association, a post he held until the end of 1954. Also in October 1949 he was appointed to chair the Epidemic Prevention Committee. Because of the ravages of war, disease and pestilence were widespread, and thus in the early PRC years Tung devoted considerable time to these and related problems, such as floods and famines. For example, in October–November 1949 Tung gave reports to top government

bodies on epidemic control work on three occasions; and he was placed in charge of a central relief committee established in February 1950 and a central flood prevention "headquarters" in June 1950. Tung summarized many of these problems in a report given in May 1950, which was published in an authoritative journal.[12]

During the formative years of the PRC, Tung appeared at various public functions on countless occasions, and he also produced a steady flow of reports for various national government organs and conferences. For example, on June 22, 1951, he spoke before the Government Administration Council on provisions for the confiscation of the property of "counterrevolutionary criminals," and a month later, on July 20, he reported on the training of political and legal cadres. Similarly, in April 1953 he spoke at the Second National Judicial Conference, and in March–April 1954 before the Second National Conference on Procurators' Work. In April 1953 he was elected chairman of the newly established Political Science and Law Association; he was re-elected to this post in 1956 and again in 1958, before relinquishing it to Wu Te-feng (q.v.) in 1964. In fact, however, it appears that Tung's position was largely nominal, and that Wu was the main channel through which the CCP exercised control over this organization.

In January 1953 Tung was appointed a member of a committee to draft the national constitution. In the next year he was elected a deputy from his native Hupeh to the First NPC, which, at its inaugural session in September 1954, adopted the constitution. Tung was subsequently returned as a Hupeh deputy to the Second and Third NPC's, which opened their inaugural sessions in April 1959 and December 1964, respectively. At the close of the September 1954 NPC session, he relinquished his post as a vice-premier and was named to succeed Shen Chün-ju as chief justice of the Supreme People's Court. In this capacity Tung spoke on judicial work at the next three sessions of the First NPC (July 22, 1955, June 25, 1956, and July 2, 1957). Although Tung has worked chiefly in domestic affairs since 1949, he was called upon to lead two delegations abroad between 1954 and 1958. In September 1954 he was Peking's representative in Sofia for the 10th anniversary of the celebrations marking the defeat of Nazi Germany in Bulgaria. He was back in Bulgaria on a more important mission in June 1958 when he led the CCP delegation to the Seventh Congress of the Bulgarian Communist Party. From Sofia, Tung took his delegation to Prague for the 11th Congress of the Czech Communist Party, which opened in mid-June, and from there he went to East Berlin for the Fifth Congress of the Socialist Unity (Communist) Party of East Germany in July. After more than two months abroad, he returned home on August 7.

Full details are lacking, but it appears that Tung may have played an important role in the purge of Kao Kang and Jao Shu-shih (qq.v.) in 1954–55. This is suggested by circumstances surrounding the purge, which was publicly announced in early April 1955, immediately after a Party conference in the previous month. It was announced that a new Central Control Commission had been established to prevent a recurrence of a Kao-Jao "anti-Party plot." Tung was placed in charge of the new organization, and he was reconfirmed in this assignment immediately after the Party's historic Eighth Congress in September 1956. Tung chaired the Credentials Committee for the congress and spoke on China's legal system. He was re-elected to the Central Committee, and the day following the congress, at the First Plenum of the new Central Committee, he was re-elected a member of the Politburo and secretary of the Control Commission. In the new 17-man Politburo, four men came from only two hsien: Mao and P'eng Te-huai from Hsiang-t'an in Hunan, and Tung and Li Hsien-nien from Huang-an, Hupeh.

Tung relinquished his post as chief justice to another Party "elder," Hsieh Chueh-tsai, in April 1959 at the inaugural session of the Second NPC. At the same time, however, he and Sung Ch'ing-ling (Mme. Sun Yat-sen) were elected vice-chairmen of the PRC. It was then that Liu Shao-ch'i replaced Mao as PRC chairman. Tung and Sung were again elected vice-chairmen in early 1965 at the Third NPC. This position carries with it numerous ceremonial tasks, and thus Tung has often been on hand to welcome visiting dignitaries and, on occasion, to receive the credentials of diplomats accredited to China. Moreover, because his revolutionary ties reach back half a century, he is normally placed on the *ad hoc* committees to mark historic dates (such as the committee established in September 1961 to commemorate the 1911 Revolution).

For a man who reached his 80th year in the mid-1960's, Tung continues to be surprisingly active, and unlike some of his contemporaries who have been relegated solely to ceremonial tasks, he seems to remain an important political figure. As far back as the mid-1930's Nym Wales found him to be a man of "remarkable physical strength and vitality." Tung has a reading knowledge of both Russian and English; he studied English in middle school and continued his study of the language during his years in Moscow. Tung's family married him to an "old-fashioned wife" in 1910. This union produced one child who died. He reportedly married a Kiangsi woman in 1933, but deserted her during the Long March. He was living with a common-law wife in Yenan in 1937, and about a year later, in Hankow, he married another woman, a marriage which produced three children.

Tung has produced at least two works of interest to historians of the Chinese Communist movement. For the Peking journal *Hsin Kuanch'a* (New observer), no. 13, July 1, 1957, he published an account of the period before and after the Communists' inaugural congress in mid-1921. In the same year he authored a book entitled *"Erh-ch'i" hui-i-lu* (Reminiscences of "February 7th"), which is one of the most detailed Communist studies of the above-mentioned suppression of the Peking-Hankow railway workers' union in 1923, and a useful source of information on the labor movement in Hupeh. Tung wrote both of these works under the pseudonym "Elder Hsi-wu" (Hsi-wu lao-jen).

1. Nym Wales, *Red Dust* (Stanford, Calif., 1952), pp. 35–43.

2. *SCMM* 274, pp. 3–7.

3. *Kung-ch'ing-t'uan, we-te mu-ch'in* (The Communist Youth League, my mother; Peking, 1958), p. 17.

4. *Foreign Relations of the United States: Diplomatic Papers, 1943, China* (Washington, D.C., 1957), pp. 345–346; *Selected Works of Mao Tse-tung* (Peking, 1965), III, 147.

5. *Foreign Relations of the United States: Diplomatic Papers, 1944, China* (Washington, D.C., 1967), VI, 346, 352–353; Gunther Stein, *The Challenge of Red China* (New York, 1945), p. 26.

6. Lyman P. Van Slyke, *Enemies and Friends* (Stanford, Calif., 1967), p. 183.

7. Herbert Feis, *The China Tangle* (Princeton, N.J., 1953), pp. 265–266.

8. J. Franklin Ray, Jr., *UNRRA in China* (New York, 1947), p. 63.

9. *Selected Works of Mao Tse-tung* (Peking, 1961), IV, 221.

10. *China Digest* (Hong Kong), 4.6:10–11 (July 27, 1948).

11. *Ibid.*, 4.9:7 (September 7, 1948).

12. *Hsin-hua yueh-pao* (New China monthly), 2.2:331–333 (June 15, 1950).

Ulanfu

(1906–   ; Tumet Banner, Inner Mongolia). Chairman, Inner Mongolia Autonomous Region; first secretary, Inner Mongolia Autonomous Region CCP Committee; chairman Nationalities Affairs Commission, State Council; alternate member, CCP Politburo.

Ulanfu is the most important non-Han Chinese member of the CCP. Moscow-trained, he has been the dominant CCP figure in Inner Mongolia since the thirties. He was elected an alternate Central Committee member in 1945 and was promoted to alternate membership on the Party Politburo in 1956. Since 1954 he has been a vice-premier and chairman of the central government's Nationalities Affairs Commission.

Ulanfu's name is often transliterated Wu

Lan-fu (the Chinese pronunciation), and he has also been known by the pseudonym of Yun Tse. He comes from a small village in the Tumet Banner of the Bayan Tala League in Inner Mongolia. The area is located west of Kweisui (Huhehot), the one-time capital of Suiyuan province and now the capital of the Inner Mongolia Autonomous Region (IMAR). The Tumet Banner Mongols had become a sedentary and agricultural people living under Chinese administrations, and most of them are Chinese-speaking, having long ago abandoned the use of Mongolian. It is reported that Ulanfu speaks no Mongolian; his education has been Chinese, Russian, and Marxian. He was born in 1906,[1] but nothing is known of his youth. In the summer of 1923 he went to Peking among a group of Mongol students, an event described in an account by Chi Ya-t'ai (q.v.), who tells of the arrival of his fellow Tumet Banner Mongols in Peking and of their immediate enrollment at the Mongolian and Tibetan Institute.[2] This had been established not long before by a Chinese Government intent upon giving a Chinese-oriented education to the youths of the two minorities. Among the Mongol student group was Ulanfu's lifelong associate, K'uei Pi (q.v.), who has been his immediate subordinate in the IMAR for a number of years. Once established at the Mongolian and Tibetan Institute, the Tumet Mongols were soon contacted by Li Ta-chao (q.v.), the leader of the CCP's North China Bureau. In the winter of 1923–24, probably through his efforts, they joined the CCP, then only three years old but already finding a number of sympathetic followers in the fertile university ground which had been prepared by the outbreak of the May Fourth Movement in 1919. In 1925 Ulanfu and others from the Tumet Banner Group at the Peking Institute were active in student demonstrations that followed the May 30th Incident at Shanghai.

Within Inner Mongolia itself it is said that until about 1923 there were "no definitely documented leftist movements." In that year the National Revival Club was organized by a group of "progressive" young Mongols.[3] It is difficult to know who these were, but they must have been influenced by the changes taking place among their compatriots in Outer Mongolia where the Mongols were already working toward autonomy and where the Mongolian People's Republic was established in November 1924. In 1925 Mongol leader Pai Yun-t'i, who later joined the KMT, Ulanfu and some of his Tumet Banner Mongols at the Peking Institute, and others were instrumental in transforming the National Revival Club into the Inner Mongolia People's Party (IMPP). This took place at the first congress of the IMPP held in October 1925 at Kalgan, later the capital of Chahar province. The congress heard a number of views on Mongol aims, because among the delegates sentiments ranged all the way from a desire to join with Outer Mongolia (then dominated by the USSR) to the wish for a Mongol form of government for Inner Mongolia within a federative framework of China. The congress manifesto contained indications that the latter view was more favorably contemplated, though the Mongols did not at all envisage becoming a part of the Chinese provincial system. Ulanfu and his Communist colleagues undoubtedly had influence in the new Mongol Party, but it is unclear what part of the spectrum between the two extreme views they claimed for their own. At any rate, the course of the new party could not be an easy one, depending as it did upon the variables of Chinese politics, as well as upon the different goals sought by the Mongol leadership; these goals in turn were affected by both the Japanese and Russians who tried to further their own aspirations at the expense of the Mongols. In any event, soon after the October 1925 congress in Kalgan, Ulanfu went to the Soviet Union (via Mongolia) where he was to remain for the next five years.

In Moscow Ulanfu enrolled at Sun Yat-sen University; the name of the school was later changed to the Communist University for the Toilers of China. Among his classmates in Moscow was Wang Jo-fei (q.v.), one of the earliest and more important CCP members until his death in an air crash in 1946. Later, in 1931, Wang was Ulanfu's superior in the Party underground in Suiyuan.

Ulanfu returned to China in 1930 and, according to a 1961 Communist account, was engaged in underground work for the CCP in Suiyuan by 1931. In that year he rendezvoused with Wang Jo-fei in Paotow (Pao-t'ou), west of Kweisui. Ulanfu is alleged to have given Wang a report on the Party's "organization in the [Kweisui-Paotow] region, its nationalities work, its military work, etc.," and he also gave Wang a list of aliases used by Communist agents in the area. In October 1931 Wang was arrested, and Ulanfu, unaware of this, narrowly escaped arrest himself at an inn where the two men had intended to rendezvous again.[4] During these happenings Ulanfu was disguised as a merchant, and doubtless was using an alias.

When Ulanfu had returned to China in 1930, he found a very different set of alliances controlling north China from those he had known a few years earlier. A coalition of northern warlord Feng Yü-hsiang and Yen Hsi-shan from Shansi was supported by KMT leader Wang Ching-wei and by Li Tsung-jen from Kwangsi. This group was feuding with the Chiang Kai-shek government in Nanking. In these circumstances, Ulanfu was able, in the early thirties, to find a position as personal secretary to Fu Tso-i, a lieutenant of Yen Hsi-shan. At about this same time he was also a section chief in the Political Department of Fu's Third Cavalry Regiment. In 1931 Fu became chairman of the Suiyuan Provincial Government, Ulanfu following him into the administration there. For the next 10 years he and Fu were associated from time to time both in administering Suiyuan and in fighting the Japanese.

In 1931 the Japanese took over Manchuria, their troops penetrating Jehol in 1932 and moving to the frontier of Chahar in the spring of 1933. That same year Ulanfu was reported to be working with the anti-Japanese Mongol resistance and in 1934 he was reported to be teaching school in his native Tumet Banner. In the next year he was northwest of Kweisui on the outskirts of the small Mongol town of Pai-ling-miao where he took part in a rebellion of Mongol troops against the Japanese. At this point in Ulanfu's career it is necessary to summarize briefly the situation in Inner Mongolia in order to relate his activity to the events there.

In April 1934 a Mongolian Local Autonomous Political Council had been established in the Pai-ling-miao area. Among the group heading the council were the Mongol princes Te Wang and Yun Wang and KMT member Pai Yun-t'i. The first two soon went over to the Japanese but Pai sided with the Nationalists. However, Ulanfu was not one of the two Tumet Banner delegates who attended the Council meeting. Then two years later, in early 1936, by which time the Nationalists had come to fear the growing influence of the Japanese among the Mongols, they placed Shansi warlord Yen Hsi-shan upon the Council as an adviser in hopes that Yen might strengthen the anti-Japanese Mongols in the Mongol coalition. But feuding continued among the leadership for a time until the Council held a policy meeting at Pai-ling-miao in February 1936. At this time the anti-Japanese group split off and in Kweisui they promptly established an opposition Suiyuan-Mongolian Local Autonomous Political Council that had Nationalist backing. The Tumet Banner Mongols now supported the Suiyuan Council, as did northern Chinese warlord Fu Tso-i and another Mongol group among whom Fu had been influential, the Ikechao League in southern Suiyuan that controlled the area south of the Yellow River. The records do not record Ulanfu's connections with this Suiyuan Council, but he must have been at least allied to it. As seen above, in 1935 Ulanfu was in the vicinity of Pai-ling-miao fighting the Japanese forces there. (Mongol forces fighting against the pro-Japanese Mongols in the Pai-ling-miao area in 1935 were said to have been controlled by Fu Tso-i.) In November 1936 he was identified with Fu's troops when the latter supported the Suiyuan Mongols in an attack upon the forces of princes Te and Yun, who had the support of the Japanese. Pai-ling-miao was taken from the Te-Yun Mongols at that time.

In the first half of 1937, after the Sian Incident of December 1936 had brought the KMT and the Communists together to resist the Japanese penetration of China, Ulanfu became a political commissar for the Suiyuan Mongolian Peace Preservation Corps. Presumably the corps was part of the new Suiyuan Council at Kweisui. It was commanded by a Jehol Mongol, Pai Hai-feng, who had formerly studied in Moscow. Prior to 1936 Pai had been in the entourage of Prince Te, but after the split in the Mongol coalition, he had left Te's group and apparently made an alliance with Fu Tso-i. In any event, according to a Communist source, he was then fighting "with garrison troops in Suiyuan." Pai had also once been a member of the CCP, but had withdrawn at an uncertain date, and it is not known whether he still belonged to the Party when he headed the Peace Preservation Corps from 1936 to 1937. At least it is certain that both Mongol Communists Ulanfu and K'uei Pi were connected with Pai's Peace Preservation Corps, and probably both at about this time. Then sometime between 1937 and 1942, Pai's troops were reorganized into an independent brigade of an unknown Mongol banner. Possibly these troops were the ones to which Ulanfu belonged, for in the same period his forces were also reorganized into an independent brigade, a unit of the Ikechao League.

Ulanfu was called to Yenan by 1941 and was there when the Communists' Nationalities Institute opened in September; he was head of the Institute's Education Department.[5] The institute, headed by Kao Kang (q.v.), trained non-Chinese minorities for their future role as cadres and leaders of national minorities under a Communist regime. Among his colleagues on the school's staff was Kao K'o-lin (q.v.), an important Party leader who served with Ulanfu in Suiyuan in the late forties and early fifties. Also in 1941 Ulanfu became chairman of both the Nationalities Affairs Committee of the Shensi-Kansu-Ninghsia Border Region Government and the Mongolian Cultural Association at Yenan. Thus, for the years between 1941 and 1944 when he was transferred away from Yenan, he held important posts dealing with minority problems for the Border Region Government.

Sometime in 1944 Ulanfu was given the task of organizing a Communist base among the Mongols of the Ikechao League, located in southern Suiyuan. The area was apparently a part of the Communists' Shansi-Suiyuan Border Region (see under Chang Su). In a book published in 1946, a Communist journalist described Ulanfu as "one of the leaders" of the Shansi-Suiyuan "liberated area," as well as the chairman of the "Suiyuan-Mongolian Government" which he described as being subordinate to the Shansi-Suiyuan Border Region.[6] In terms of the timing, it appears that Ulanfu's work in the Ikechao League and the "Suiyuan-Mongolian Government" may have been one and the same thing.

Soon after V-J Day the Chinese Communists moved their forces from Jehol into Chahar (portions of both provinces were later absorbed into the IMAR), and for a year Communist troops were in control of Kalgan, the Chahar capital. In November 1945 the CCP inaugurated the Inner Mongolia Autonomous Movement Association with headquarters at Kalgan, thus bringing under the Party's influence the Mongols of the northern segment of Inner Mongolia. Ulanfu became the association's chairman.[7] In March–April 1946 the association met at Ch'eng-te, Jehol, with leaders from a Mongol group based near the small town of Ulanhot (Wang-yeh-miao). The Ulanhot Mongols, who drew their supporters from the Hsing-an Mountains in western Manchuria, had been recognized by the Japanese during the war. Seeking the best possible terms for their own problems, at the end of the war these Mongols had sent emissaries to the Mongolian People's Republic, the Soviet military authorities in Manchuria, the Chinese Nationalists, and to the Chinese Communists. The first two were sympathetic but feared involvement, the Nationalists ignored the Mongols, but the Chinese Communists welcomed them. In exchange for a promise to co-operate with Ulanfu, the CCP encouraged them to establish an autonomous government. Ultimately, however, the Ulanhot Mongols lost their autonomy as a result of the March–April 1946 meetings, under the terms of which they were absorbed into the Ulanfu-led Autonomous Movement Association.

The merger of the two groups gave Ulanfu another advantage after October 1946 when the Nationalists took Kalgan, for it enabled him to have an alternate headquarters for the Autonomous Movement Association when Kalgan fell. Consequently, the Association's headquarters were transferred to Ulanhot where the strong forces of Lin Piao, soon to sweep over Manchuria, could give them protection. On May 1, 1947, the People's Government of the Inner Mongolia Autonomous Region was formally inaugurated at Ulanhot. Ulanfu was made chairman of the new government and commander and political commissar of the Inner Mongolian People's Self-Defense Army. The IMAR controlled initially only the predominantly Mongol areas of western Manchuria, plus the northern portions of Jehol and Chahar, but in 1950, after the Communists controlled the entire mainland, portions of Suiyuan were added and in that same year the IMAR capital was moved to Kalgan.

By the end of the Sino-Japanese War it was evident that Ulanfu was the ranking Mongol in the CCP; indeed, he was probably already the most important non-Han member of the Party. This was made abundantly clear at the Party's Seventh National Congress in Yenan in 1945. Ulanfu was called back from Inner Mongolia to attend the Congress. He spoke before the delegates and at the close of the meetings in June was elected an alternate member of the Central Committee, the only non-Han so honored. Although details on his activities in the late forties are not available, it is probable that he spent most of these years in Inner Mongolia where he was the key leader in the CCP apparatus then being developed there. As already described, from 1947 he was head of both the IMAR Government and the military force in the area. By at least 1949 (and probably from 1947) he was the secretary of the Party's Inner Mongolia Sub-bureau, and although the organizational structure of the Party in Inner Mongolia changed in subsequent years, he has continued as the head of the Party there, a record of longevity unmatched in any other province (or autonomous region) in China.

In 1949 Ulanfu participated in the formation of the new central government in Peking. One of the first major steps leading to the convocation of the CPPCC in September 1949 was the formation of a Preparatory Committee, set up in June under the chairmanship of Mao Tsetung. Ulanfu was named to the Committee's Standing Committee, but because he was occupied in Inner Mongolia, K'uei Pi represented him at the June meetings. However, he was present for the September meetings and played a prominent role. Attending the First Session of the CPPCC as a representative of the IMAR, he served on the Standing Committee of the Presidium (steering committee) as well as the *ad hoc* committee to draft the new government's Organic Law, one of the most important documents adopted at this time. He also spoke to the delegates on developments in Inner Mongolia, and when the meetings closed he was named to Standing Committee membership on the CPPCC's First National Committee, holding the post until the Second CPPCC came into existence in late 1954. Even more important assignments were given to him when the major organs of the new government were established in October 1949. He was appointed a member of the Central People's Government Council (CPGC), the most important organization in the central government. Chaired by Mao Tsetung, the CPGC had six vice-chairmen and 56 members; it was vested with broad legislative, executive, and judicial functions, and at its 34 meetings between 1949 and 1954 it passed on virtually every important measure adopted by the PRC. In addition, under the Government

Administration Council (the cabinet), Ulanfu was made a vice-chairman of the Nationalities Affairs Commission as well as a member of the Political and Legal Affairs Committee. He held all these positions until the constitutional government was inaugurated in 1954. Also in October 1949, he was made a member of the First Executive Board of the Sino-Soviet Friendship Association (SSFA), then one of China's most active "mass" organizations. He was promoted to an SSFA vice-chairmanship in 1954, a post he still holds.

In the latter part of 1949, after the major assignments in the central government had been made, the PRC formalized the structure of the CCP, the government, and the military districts in the provinces and autonomous regions. In Inner Mongolia, for example, the former "People's Self-Defense Army" was transformed into the Inner Mongolia Military District. Ulanfu has dominated this structure just as he has the CCP and government organizations in Inner Mongolia; he has been both commander and political commissar of the district since 1949 (although from 1952 to 1954 it was known as the Suiyuan-Inner Mongolia Military District). In a very unusual arrangement, Ulanfu held key posts not only in Inner Mongolia, but also in neighboring Suiyuan. Here the Communists established in December 1949 the Suiyuan Provincial People's Government, the Suiyuan Military and Administrative Committee, and the Suiyuan Military District. The entire Suiyuan structure was in large measure fictitious and ultimately, in 1954, it was absorbed by the IMAR. The manner in which the CCP placed its Party members in the Suiyuan organizations is illustrated in the following list of key personnel appointed in 1949. (1) Suiyuan Provincial People's Government—governor: Tung Ch'i-wu (a Fu Tso-i follower); vice-governor: K'uei Pi (Ulanfu's CCP colleague); (2) Suiyuan Military and Administrative Committee—chairman: Fu Tso-i; vice-chairmen: Ulanfu; Kao K'o-lin (Ulanfu's Party colleague from the Yenan period); (3) Suiyuan Military District—commander: Fu Tso-i; deputy commander: Ulanfu. The realities of Communist rule in Suiyuan became even more apparent in June 1952 when the central government decreed that Suiyuan province was subordinate to the Government Administration Council and the IMAR, although the province was permitted to continue to settle its ordinary administrative matters. Then, in the following month Ulanfu succeeded Tung Ch'i-wu, the ex-Nationalist, as the Suiyuan governor. At the same time, the CCP organizations in Suiyuan and Inner Mongolia were merged to form the Suiyuan-Inner Mongolia Sub-bureau, with Ulanfu as the secretary. The gradual absorption of Suiyuan into Inner Mongolia was demonstrated in still another way in July 1952 when the capital of the

IMAR was transferred from Kalgan to Kweisui (now known as Huhehot). Kweisui was also the Suiyuan capital, and thus the Communists created the anomalous situation of having one city the capital of two different administrative organizations. The fiction of the Suiyuan organization was finally brought to a close in the first half of 1954 when the province was incorporated into the IMAR.

Unlike many regional leaders, Ulanfu has spent much of his time in Peking, even in the early years of the PRC when the IMAR was still in a state of flux. He attended the majority of the 34 CPGC meetings held in Peking from 1949 to 1954, and from May 1950 to early 1955 he also served as president of the Central Nationalities Institute in Peking, a school that can be regarded as the successor to the Nationalities Institute in Yenan, with which he had been associated in the forties. He was also a member of other organizations that called him to Peking from time to time. Thus, from 1950 to 1958 he was a Standing Committee member of the China Peace Committee (and from 1950 to an uncertain date he was also a member of the Communist-dominated World Peace Council). In addition, he served from the end of 1951 to 1954 as a member of the North China Administrative Committee (NCAC), which was headquartered in Peking and had jurisdiction over the provinces of Suiyuan, Chahar, Hopeh, Shansi, and Pingyuan. He was also in Peking in 1953–54 to attend the meetings of the Committee for Drafting the PRC Constitution, a committee on which he served as a member under the chairmanship of Mao Tse-tung.

Since the establishment of the constitutional government at the NPC in 1954, Ulanfu has been a deputy from the IMAR, serving in the First NPC (1954–1959), the Second (1959–1964), and the Third, which opened in late 1964. At the close of the initial session of the First NPC in September 1954, he was made a vice-premier of the State Council under Chou En-lai and a member of the newly created National Defense Council, a military advisory body of limited authority but considerable prestige. Moreover, he was named as chairman of the State Council's Nationalities Affairs Commission, thereby succeeding Li Wei-han (q.v.). He continues to hold these three positions, but the one with the Nationalities Commission probably occupies more of his time than the others. He is regularly in attendance in Peking for meetings dealing with nationalities problems, as in April–May 1962 when he presided over a five-week-long national conference jointly convened by the Commission and the NPC Nationalities Committee. In September 1955 he was given the Order of Liberation, a PLA decoration awarded for military services in the period from 1945 to 1950, and at the same time he was made a PLA colonel-general (equal to the rank of three-star general in the U.S. Army).

Ulanfu emerged from the Party's Eighth National Congress in September 1956 as one of the CCP's top leaders. While the meetings were in session he served on both the Credentials Committee and the Presidium (steering committee), and he spoke before the delegates on national minority questions. At the close of the Congress he was elevated from alternate to full membership on the Central Committee. More important, at the First Plenum of the new Central Committee (held the day after the Congress closed), he was elected as the ranking alternate member of the Politburo, the CCP's supreme policy organization. Other non-Han Party members were elected to the Central Committee at the Eighth Congress (e.g., Ulanfu's colleague K'uei Pi) but none aside from Ulanfu has reached Politburo membership.

Ulanfu has continued to divide his time about equally between Inner Mongolia and the national capital and has received further appointments in both places, some of them more nominal than real. In 1957, for example, he was named to the Preparatory Committee for Celebrating the 40th Anniversary of the October Revolution, and in the same year he was appointed president of the Inner Mongolia University (although he may no longer hold this post). He regularly travels to Peking for meetings of the NPC or the CCP Central Committee and Politburo, and when there he is frequently mentioned in the press in the company of the highest leaders of state (e.g., Mao, Chou En-lai).

Aside from his domestic duties, Ulanfu has played a rather active role in international relations, particularly those vis-à-vis the Mongolian People's Republic (MPR). In February 1952 he was a member of Nieh Jung-chen's delegation to the funeral of MPR Premier Choibalsan in Ulan Bator. He has returned to the MPR on three occasions, leading CCP delegations to the 12th, 13th, and 14th Congresses of the Mongolian People's Revolutionary (Communist) Party held in November 1954, March 1958, and July 1961, respectively. In May 1955 he led a PRC government to Prague for the 10th anniversary of the defeat of the Nazis, and 11 months later he was in Nepal heading a Chinese delegation to the coronation of the Nepalese king. He accompanied Mao Tse-tung to Moscow in November 1957 as a member of the large delegation to the 40th anniversary of the Russian Revolution, and in May 1961 he and Wu Hsiu-ch'üan left Peking for Paris to attend the 16th Congress of the French Communist Party; however, they were forced to turn back when the French refused them visas. Finally, in October 1964 he led the PRC delegation to Berlin for the 15th anniversary of the East German government, celebrations also attended by Soviet leader Brezhnev.

In the 1960's Ulanfu was given additional assignments in Inner Mongolia. In May 1965 he was elected chairman of the Third Inner Mongolian Committee of the CPPCC. Although the CPPCC has been a relatively unimportant organization since 1954 when the constitutional government was formed, the fact that Ulanfu was named to this post once again illustrates his paramountcy in Inner Mongolia. As of the 1960's no other province or autonomous region had one man serving as the head of the government and CCP organization, commander and political commissar of the military district, and chairman of the CPPCC organization. He was identified in still another key post in mid-1965 when it was revealed that he was second secretary of the Party's North China Bureau. The regional bureaus were re-created in 1961 by the Party Central Committee's Ninth Plenum, apparently in response to the weakening of the Party structure in the provinces in the wake of the difficulties resulting from the Great Leap Forward. In the North China Bureau Ulanfu serves under Li Hsueh-feng (q.v.). Over the years since the establishment of the IMAR in 1947, Ulanfu's responsibilities there have grown as a result of the increase in size and population of the region. Portions of several neighboring provinces in north China and Manchuria were placed under its jurisdiction and the population has grown from 2.4 million in 1952 to 11 million a decade later, only a small portion of whom are Mongols. Although this population is considerably smaller than most Chinese provinces, the area over which Ulanfu presides is exceeded in size only by Sinkiang and Tibet.

Ulanfu has been a regular contributor to the Chinese press, usually writing on subjects related to developments in Inner Mongolia or nationwide questions regarding national minority groups. A number of his more important articles and speeches on the formative years of the IMAR are collected in Current Background no. 190 (July 22, 1952). Later articles include two in the Party's top journal, Hung-ch'i (Red flag, issues of March 1 and October 1, 1959).

----

1. *Peking Review,* no. 19:4 (May 11, 1962).

2. *SCMM* 281, pp. 21–24.

3. Human Relations Area Files (HRAF), *A Regional Handbook on the Inner Mongolia Autonomous Region* (New Haven, Conn., 1956), pp. 49–69.

4. *SCMM* 266, pp. 43–47.

5. *SCMM* 287, p. 30.

6. Mu Hsin, *Chin-sui chieh-fang ch'ü niao-k'an* (A bird's-eye view of the Shansi-Suiyuan Liberated Region; Hsing-hsien, Shansi, 1946) p. 3.

7. *SCMM* 299, p. 10.

Wan I

(c.1904–   ; Hai-ch'eng hsien, Liaoning, Manchuria). Specialist in armaments; alternate member, CCP Central Committee.

Wan I was born about 1904 or soon thereafter in Manchuria, not far from China's important iron-manufacturing center at Anshan, Liaoning. After graduation from the ninth class of the Northeast Military Academy, he joined the Northeast Army of the famous Manchurian warlord Chang Tso-lin, and then of his son, Chang Hsueh-liang. Wan had risen to be commander of the 33rd Regiment of the 11th Division of this army prior to the 1930–1933 period when he is said to have joined the CCP. His record is obscure until the beginning of the Sino-Japanese War in 1937, at which time he was with the Nationalists' 11th Division, then commanded by Ch'ang En-to and stationed on the Shantung-Kiangsu border. In August 1939 he reportedly forced Ch'ang to capitulate to the Communists, after which he brought some 1,500 troops from this army in south Shantung to join them. Wan was subsequently made a deputy division commander in the Communist armies. Later in the war he transferred to the fighting in the Honan-Kiangsu-Anhwei border area, where he was director of the Honan-Kiangsu-Anhwei Administrative Office, a government unit under the general control of the Communist New Fourth Army. Early in 1945 he was identified as director of the Kiangsu-Anhwei Administrative Office.

At the Seventh National Party Congress held in Yenan in April–June 1945 Wan was elected to alternate membership on the Central Committee. After hostilities ended in August 1945, many units of the New Fourth Army were transferred north of the Great Wall into Manchuria, where they joined forces with local resistance groups and eventually formed into the Communist Northeast Democratic Allied Army under the command of Lin Piao. Wan went to his native Manchuria sometime after August 1945 where he became commander of both the Liaopei Military District (1946–47) and the First Column of the Kirin-Liaoning Military Region (1946–1948), both subordinate to the Northeast Democratic Allied Army.

Soon after their arrival in Manchuria, the Communists set up (1946) the Northeast Administrative Committee to govern the territory controlled by their armies. Wan was an original member of this administration, and by 1948 the commander of the First Column of Lin Piao's Northeast Democratic Allied Army. After taking control of Manchuria, the army began to move south into China proper, eventually sweeping across the Yangtze Valley and on to Kwangtung and Hainan (April 1950). Early in 1949 the army was renamed the Fourth Field Army. Wan initially followed Lin's army, but it is not clear where he was stationed. From 1949 to 1951 he was commander of a "special army corps" in the Fourth Field Army and from March 1950 to mid-1951 was a member of the regional government, which the army helped create in central and south China, the Central-South Military and Administrative Committee (CSMAC). From about 1950 until 1952 Wan held another post with the PLA, serving as a deputy commander of the PLA Artillery Force.

In August 1952 he was called to Peking to serve in the newly established Second Ministry of Machine Building, headed by Chao Erh-lu (q.v.). Wan was a vice-minister until September 1954 when the central government was reorganized. He was identified in February 1954 as director of an unspecified organ under the General Staff of the PLA. In September 1954 he was named to membership on the National Defense Council, the newly created and generally unimportant military advisory body. He was reappointed to the Council in April 1959 but was not reappointed at the Third NPC meeting in January 1965. Also in 1954, Wan was elected a deputy from the Shenyang (Mukden) municipality to the First NPC. He served throughout the term of the First NPC but was not reelected to the Second Congress, which opened in 1959.

Wan's only known trip abroad was as an adviser to the Chinese delegation that attended, as observers, the meetings of the Warsaw Pact nations held in Warsaw in May 1955. The delegation, headed by P'eng Te-huai, returned from Poland in June via Moscow. While in the Soviet capital they held talks with Khrushchev.

In September 1955 Wan was among those to receive the PRC's first national military awards and a personal military rank. He received two of the three top awards, the Independence and Freedom Order and the Liberation Order. Subsequent to these awards he was identified as holding the military rank of lieutenant-general, the equivalent of a two-star general in the U.S. Army.

Since 1956 Wan has had three other appointments, each of them related to technical work. From 1957 to 1958 he served as a member of the State Council's Scientific Planning Commission under top science administrator Nieh Jung-chen (q.v.). He held this post until November 1958 when the Commission was merged with another organization to form the Scientific and Technological Commission. In May 1957 and May 1958, Wan was identified as director of a little-known department under the PLA, the Equipment Planning Department. In September 1958, when the China Scientific and Technical Association was formed by merging two mass organizations for the promotion of science,

Wan became a vice-chairman of the new association, a post he continues to hold. The above record, taken in conjunction with his former role in the Second Ministry of Machine Building (then producing munitions), leads to the assumption that Wan must be an important specialist in the armaments field. However, his continued absence from public attention is puzzling. Apparently his last public appearance occurred in March 1956 when he paid his respects at the Polish Embassy in Peking on the death of Polish First Party Secretary Boleslaw Bierut. An assessment of his political stature became even more difficult when, in January 1965, he was not reappointed as a member of the National Defense Council. Wan was one of only nine men not reappointed to the Council, several of whom were in some or total political disfavor.

Wan Li

(Szechwan). Building and construction specialist; Vice-Mayor of Peking.

According to Japanese sources, Wan Li is a native of Szechwan and at one time studied in France. Indirect evidence suggests that Wan may have been a student in Peking during the mid-1930's, a possibility implied by the fact that he was on the funeral committee for two prominent youth leaders of that era, Chang Hsi and P'eng T'ao (both alternate members of the Central Committee at the time of their death), who died in 1959 and 1961, respectively.

Wan first emerged on the national scene in the spring of 1949 as the Communists were sweeping the Nationalist armies from the mainland. These armies reached Nanking, the former Nationalist capital, in late April 1949 where they established politico-military administrations; under the Nanking Military Control Commission Wan became deputy director of the Finance and Economic Takeover Committee and head of the Reconstruction Bureau under the Municipal People's Government.

The armies which had successfully captured Nanking were the same as those which later in 1949 pushed into the southwest. Apparently Wan accompanied these forces, for he was in Chungking by December 1949 serving on the newly formed preparatory committee for the Chungking General Labor Union. In the following year the regional administration for the southwest, known as the Southwest Military and Administrative Committee, was established with Chungking as the headquarters. Wan was named as a member of the Finance and Economics Committee (headed by Teng Hsiao-p'ing) and as deputy director of the Industry Department under Tuan Chün-i, another specialist in building and construction work. He held these posts until November 1952 when he was posted to

Peking (although he was not officially removed from the finance and economics post until September 1954).

As the Chinese economy grew more complex, a number of changes were made in the administrative machinery to handle the new problems. One such change occurred in August 1952 when a Ministry of Building was created, and three months later Wan was transferred from Chungking to become one of the vice-ministers. In the next few years the national press reported only his activity connected with this ministry. A few of the more significant occasions include: a report by Wan before a meeting of the GAC on December 3, 1953, on the work of the ministry; a speech delivered at a conference (February–March 1954) of "model" PLA soldiers working in construction units in Peking; a report given before a planning and construction conference convened by the ministry in February 1955.

In April 1955, Wan received a concurrent post as director of the newly created Urban Construction General Bureau, an organization that stood just below the ministry level in the State Council structure. He held these two posts until a partial State Council reorganization in May 1956, at which time he was removed as a vice-minister of Building (where he had served under Ch'en Cheng-jen and Liu Hsiu-feng). However, at the same time he received a ministerial-level portfolio when the Urban Construction General Bureau was raised to the Ministry of Urban Construction. In the meantime, in October 1955, Wan had led a 10-member delegation of construction experts on an inspection tour of the Soviet Union.

Wan attended the Eighth Party Congress in September 1956 and submitted a written speech on the theme that urban building must be closely linked with industrial construction. Little was heard of him until there was another State Council reorganization in February 1958, at which time Wan's Ministry of Urban Construction was absorbed by the Ministry of Building, leaving Wan without a post in the central government. However, within a month he was identified as a secretary of the Peking Party Committee, a post he continues to hold subordinate to First Secretary P'eng Chen and Second Secretary Liu Jen. Then, in August 1958 he was elected vice-mayor of the Peking Municipal Government, and in October 1959 was named as a vice-chairman of the Peking CPPCC. These three posts in Peking serve as a good illustration of the interlocking directorate which rules China. In the Party structure he serves under P'eng Chen and Liu Jen; in the government organization he is subordinate to P'eng Chen; and, in the CPPCC apparatus he comes under the authority of Liu Jen.

Senior officials in all Chinese cities are obliged

to spend a large amount of time in protocol activities, and quite naturally this is exemplified in the national capital, the site of thousands of official functions each year. Furthermore, since Peking Mayor P'eng Chen is one of the regime's most senior officials, he inevitably becomes involved in policy-level affairs which preclude his participation in many municipal affairs of lesser import. From the numerous appearances Wan has made since 1958, it is clear that he often serves as a proxy for P'eng. Thus in addition to feting numerous foreign visitors, Wan has often been mentioned in connection with anniversary celebrations, meetings of many types, and sports events. For example, he served on the preparatory committee for celebrating the 10th anniversary of the PRC in 1959, on the presidium for a conference of "advanced producers" in October 1959, and was a speaker at a Peking municipal congress of the Young Communist League in December 1962. In the field of sports, Wan served on the preparatory committees for both the first and second national athletic meets, established in September 1958 and January 1965, respectively. He was also a member of the preparatory committee for Chinese participation in the Games of the New Emerging Forces (GANEFO), a body established in June 1963. These games were inaugurated by Indonesian President Sukarno in response to alleged hostility to Indonesia by the International Olympics Committee. The Chinese Communists gave strong support to the Indonesians on this issue and were active participants when the first games were held in 1963.

On a more official level, Wan has served as an NPC deputy from Peking to the Second NPC (1959–1964), and at the second through fourth sessions served as a member of the congress presidium. In 1964 he was re-elected a Peking deputy to the Third NPC, which held its first session in December 1964–January 1965.

Like so many other Chinese leaders, Wan became deeply involved in the Sino-Soviet conflict, which was at a peak in mid-1963. In June 1963, North Korean Supreme People's Assembly President Choi Yong Kun visited China where he received an exceptionally elaborate welcome in an obvious effort to swing the Koreans irrevocably into the Chinese orbit. On June 8, Wan spoke at a rally attended by 100,000 people, where he stressed the necessity for Sino-Korean unity in the face of U.S. "imperialism" and "modern revisionism" (the then current term of opprobrium for the Russians). Three months later, Wan spent two weeks in Korea as a member of a friendship delegation led by Liu Shao-ch'i in another obvious attempt to court the Koreans.

In the meantime, Wan was a featured speaker at an extraordinary rally held in Peking on August 6, 1963. The day before, the United States, the USSR, and Great Britain had signed the famed nuclear test ban treaty in Moscow, a move bitterly opposed by Peking. With Chou En-lai and Ch'en I on the platform, Wan made a number of hostile statements about "some so-called Communists."[1] So strong was the language that Soviet Ambassador Chervonenko walked out and soon after was followed by the representatives of the East European bloc nations—probably the first such occasion since the Communists took power in China.

The Chinese Communists generally do not publicize facts about the personal lives of their leaders. Wan, however, has been an exception to this rule, because in his case the information was related to the political goal of encouraging youths to work willingly in rural areas. In both 1963 and 1964, Wan was cited as a model parent who did not discourage his child from going to the countryside, but rather encouraged it. The son, Wan Po-cha, was reported to be working on a state farm in Honan.[2]

1. Hong Kong *Tiger Standard,* August 7, 1963, quoting Reuter, Peking, August 6, 1963.
2. *SCMM* 397, 404; *SCMP* 3293.

Wang Chao

Specialist in public security work; governor of Tsinghai.

A veteran of public security work, Wang Chao has served in Tsinghai province since 1961 as a Senior Party and government administrator. His antecedents are obscure, but by 1946 he was serving as mayor of Cheng-ting (Hopeh), a city on the important Pinghan (Peking-Hankow) Railway a few miles northeast of Shih-chia-chuang. In 1947 he transferred to Shih-chia-chuang, the junction on the Pinghan line that connects with the rail line running westward to Taiyuan, the capital of Shansi. Shih-chia-chuang was the first important city in north China to be captured by the Communists in the civil war with the Nationalists (November 1947). Wang served there as vice-mayor in 1947–48 under Mayor K'o Ch'ing-shih, later a member of the Party Politburo. In the latter part of 1948 Wang was reported to be working with units of the North China Field Army (led by Nieh Jung-chen), which fought against Fu Tso-i along the Pingsui (Peking-Paotow) Railway.

Sometime about 1949, Wang apparently transferred from the North China Field Army to the First Field Army, which was fighting in the northwest under P'eng Te-huai. In any event, he represented this army at the first session of the First CPPCC, which met in September 1949, at which time the PRC was formally established (October 1). Virtually all the men who attended the First CPPCC received high positions in the central or provincial administrations. Wang was an exception. However, it seems likely (although his activity was not publicly reported) that he was working in some field of security, possibly in the northwest where the First Field Army was headquartered. This assumption is drawn from the fact that Wang was named as a vice-minister of Public Security in October 1954, a post he would be unlikely to receive without having had previous experience in the field. Wang held this position for nearly seven years, serving under Lo Jui-ch'ing, China's top public security specialist until 1959 and thereafter under Hsieh Fu-chih.

The next phase of Wang's career seems out of character for a security official. He has had rather close connections with the large-scale athletic program vigorously supported by Peking since the Communists came to power in 1949, and his two trips abroad have been connected with sports events. The first was in June–July 1955 when he accompanied Hsiao K'o and Ts'ai Shu-fan (qq.v.) to Prague for the First Czech National Spartakiade. The second trip was to East Germany in July–August 1956 as a member of a delegation led by Ts'ai Shu-fan to attend a sports festival. On the latter occasion Wang was identified as the chairman of the Sports Association under the jurisdiction of the Ministry of Public Security. He was also a member of the All-China Athletic Federation from 1956 to 1964 and participated in the year-long preparations for the First National Athletic Meet held in the capital in September 1959. As with most security officials, there is a paucity of information related to his primary work. One of the few times that Wang was mentioned in this regard occurred in April 1956 when he made the opening speech before a national conference of "model people's police." More pertinent to his special field was his appointment in January 1959 to head the Public Security Institute in Peking, a post previously held by the then minister of Public Security, Lo Jui-ch'ing. Rather loosely related to security work was his election in August 1958 to the Third National Council of the Political Science and Law Association of China, a position he held until the Fourth Council was elected in October 1964.

In July 1961, Wang was relieved as a vice-minister of Public Security. This action was soon clarified when he appeared in Tsinghai as the acting first Secretary (by October 1961) of the provincial Party committee. He was sent to Tsinghai to replace First Secretary Kao Feng (q.v.), who had apparently run into political problems. This transfer to the northwest may have been viewed initially as a trouble-shooting role, but it has subsequently developed into a permanent assignment. Wang served as the acting secretary over the 1961–62 winter, but by

April 1962 he was replaced by Yang Chih-lin (q.v.). From that time Wang has been the second secretary of the Tsinghai Party Committee under Yang. In about mid-1962 Wang assumed the acting governorship of the province, serving in place of Yuan Jen-yuan (q.v.) who had been transferred away from the province. He remained as the acting governor until the Tsinghai Provincial People's Council held a session in December 1963, at which time Wang was formally elected as the governor, a post he continues to hold.

Since his transfer to Tsinghai, Wang has been reported in the press with regularity, usually in Sining, the provincial capital. He has most frequently been mentioned in connection with the affairs of the provincial government, often making reports before government organizations on agricultural production and related subjects. In the fall of 1964 he was elected a deputy from Tsinghai to the Third NPC. Wang spoke about the achievements in animal husbandry in Tsinghai before the first session of the Congress (on January 2, 1965). Wang, a Han Chinese, was also appointed at this time to membership on the NPC Nationalities Committee, the important committee dealing with minority affairs. Tsinghai province has one of the largest densities of minority peoples, with over 40 per cent of the population consisting of Tibetans, Mongols, and Kazakhs. The assignment of a veteran security official such as Wang to the Nationalities Committee can be regarded as a watchdog role in view of the persistent resistance by minority nationalities to rule by Han Chinese.

Wang Chen

(1909–   ; Liu-yang hsien, Hunan). Veteran PLA officer; minister of State Farms and Land Reclamation; member, CCP Central Committee.

Wang Chen began his career in the labor movement, but from the late twenties through the 1950's he was an important army commander and political officer. During the middle years of the Sino-Japanese War his troops engaged in productive labor near Yenan, and because of this experience Wang is often cited as the prototype of the officer who is able to lead his men both in combat and in peacetime endeavors. Elected an alternate member of the CCP Central Committee in 1945, he was promoted to full membership in 1956, and since that same year he has headed the Ministry of State Farms and Land Reclamation. Wang has also been known as Wang Chen-lin and as Wang Chen-t'ing.

According to the detailed account of his early life and career which Wang gave to journalist Nym Wales in 1937,[1] he was born in a village in Liu-yang hsien, not far from Changsha, the Hunan capital. Liu-yang produced a significant number of Communists, including Lo Chang-lung, Sung Jen-ch'iung, Wang Shou-tao, Chang Ch'i-lung, and Yang Yung (qq.v.), all of whom were born in the early years of the century. Wang was the oldest of 10 children. His father, a tenant farmer, joined a Communist guerrilla unit in 1930 and was killed fighting in Liu-yang in 1932. After only three years of primary school, Wang went to Changsha about 1922 where he worked as a servant, first in the local army garrison and then in a station master's office of the Canton-Hankow Railway. Within a couple of years he had become a locomotive fireman and in 1924 he joined the Railway Workers' Union.

In 1925 Wang had his first experience in labor organizing when the Railway Union struck in sympathy with unions in Shanghai where there was considerable labor agitation in connection with the May 30th Incident. The strike was led by Kuo Liang, one of the early members of Mao Tse-tung's Hsin-min hsueh-hui (New people's study society) and a key Communist labor leader in Hunan until his death in 1928. The strikers won several economic concessions, a fact that impressed Wang with the "new power of organized labor." In the same year he joined the KMT, which he considered to be "revolutionary" at that time. (The importance of the KMT organization in Hunan and its relationship to the CCP is discussed in the biography of Hsia Hsi). In 1925 Wang was also elected to membership on the Executive Committee of the Changsha branch of the "General Labor Union," apparently a reference to the Hunan Provincial Workers' Federation (ch'üan-sheng kung-t'uan lien-ho-hui), which, after 1923, was headed by Kuo Liang. During 1926 the union engaged in intensive propaganda activities in and around Changsha in preparation for the arrival of the Northern Expedition armies, which captured the city in July of that year.

In January 1927 Wang joined the Communist Youth League and later became a leader of a training class for labor leaders in Changsha, which was held under the auspices of the KMT but was actually directed by the CCP. Wang admits that he could then "barely read and write." During the spring of 1927 tensions increased between the radical leftists in Changsha, who were mainly Communists, and the military units garrisoning the city. These tensions exploded on May 21, 1927, when Ho Chien, commander of the Nationalist 35th Army, revolted against his Left-KMT superior T'ang Sheng-chih and ordered Hsu K'o-hsiang, whose regiment was garrisoning Changsha, to eliminate leftist organizations there. Several hundred peasant militiamen were machine-gunned, leading CCP members were arrested, and the peasant association and provincial labor union were abolished. The final break between the Communists and the Left-KMT took place in mid-1927, and was climaxed on August 1 at the time of the Nanchang Uprising (see under Yeh T'ing).

During the next year Wang remained in the Changsha area where he earned a living as a locomotive inspector and fireman and at the same time continued in covert activities designed to keep the labor movement alive. When Mao Tse-tung staged the Autumn Harvest Uprising in Hunan (September 1927), Wang claims that he and his colleagues tore up the rail tracks to prevent troop trains from going to suppress the insurgents. Later, in November, he took part in an abortive general strike in Changsha, which he described as a "final gesture of retreat" carried out in "desperation and self-defense." In April 1928, scores of CCP and Youth League members in Changsha were arrested, but Wang was able to avoid this because he was then in nearby Yueh-yang. Fearing arrest if he returned to Changsha, Wang decided to go to Hankow in the summer of 1928 where he served briefly in the Kwangsi army of Li Tsung-jen, which was then occupying Hupeh. After working for another month in an iron foundry in Ta-yeh, southeast of Hankow, Wang rejoined Li Tsung-jen's army in late 1928 and retreated with it to the Hupeh-Szechwan border. He organized a Communist branch in the army, but left it in mid-1929 to return to his native Liu-yang and take part in partisan fighting there. He finally reached home in the early fall of 1929, having been sick with typhoid in Hankow for three months. Wang founded local CCP branches and began to organize the peasants in and around Liu-yang and neighboring P'ing-chiang.

In this period the peasant associations were an important source of recruits for bands of Communist-led guerrillas skirmishing with local landlords and Nationalist troops which were in nominal control of the countryside. In the spring of 1930 Wang helped organize a small band of troops known as Red Vanguards. At this juncture the CCP was preparing to implement the Li Li-san policy of capturing major cities in central China. P'eng Te-huai (q.v.) took Changsha in late July 1930, and in support of P'eng, Wang's unit, now known as the First Detachment of Partisans, attacked the Liu-yang hsien capital. His band of 100 men quickly rose to 4,000; it was redesignated the Sixth Army of Red Vanguards and Wang became the political commissar. However, they were too weak to hold Liu-yang, and after being driven out with heavy losses, they joined P'eng Te-huai's troops in Changsha. P'eng was also defeated (early August), after which Wang led his men to a nearby village. A second attack on Changsha was mounted in September 1930. When it was repulsed Wang's forces retreated into east Hunan where it was combined with other partisans to form the Independent First Division commanded by Liu Po-ch'eng (q.v.). Wang became the political commissar of a regiment under the command of "T'an Chia-ssu" (probably T'an Chia-shu). During 1931 Wang's troops were active throughout Hunan, but their main base of operations was in the Hunan-Kiangsi Border Region, which had been founded in 1928–29 and included Mao Tse-tung's old Chingkangshan base. As a delegate from the Border Region, Wang was in Juichin, southeast Kiangsi, in November 1931 when the Chinese Soviet Republic was established by the First All-China Congress of Soviets.

In early 1932, after returning to Hunan, Wang was promoted to Political commissar of the Independent First Division. He served with Li T'ien-chü, who had succeeded Liu Po-ch'eng as division commander in 1931. Li and Wang continued in their posts when the division was elevated to the army level and was put under P'eng Te-huai's Third Army Corps in 1932. Wang was wounded in the summer of 1932 during an attack on Fen-i, west Kiangsi, and was unable to return to duty until the winter when he was made a division-level political commissar in an army now headed by Hsiao K'o (q.v.). Hsiao had only recently been sent to the Hunan-Kiangsi base from Juichin, and then in May 1933 Jen Pi-shih (q.v.) was also dispatched from Juichin to be secretary of the Border Region Party Committee and political commissar of the Military Region. Jen, being a Politburo member, was a much more important figure than Wang Chen. That fall the Nationalists' Fifth Annihilation Campaign was launched. Under the severe attacks that followed, Hsiao's Sixth Army was reduced in size and redesignated the 17th Division. Hsiao K'o continued as its commander and Wang was made director of the Political Department. Wang left the army in late 1933 to attend the Second All-China Congress of Soviets held in Juichin in January–February 1934, and he was elected to the Central Executive Committee of the Chinese Soviet Republic. By the time he rejoined the division it had been driven out of its base and into the Hunan-Hupeh border area (see under Hsiao K'o). Wang then became political commissar of the division. The force became known as the Sixth Red Army Corps sometime before it returned to its Hunan-Kiangsi base.

Unable to maintain its position on the Hunan-Kiangsi border any longer, the Sixth Army Corps began its Long March to the northwest in August 1934, two months before the forces commanded by Chu Te and Mao Tse-tung began their retreat from Kiangsi. In October the Sixth Corps joined Ho Lung's Second Army Corps in northeast Kweichow where the two units were merged to form the Second Front Army with Ho Lung as commander and Jen Pi-shih as political commissar. Hsiao K'o retained command of the Sixth Army Corps, and Wang con-

tinued as its political commissar. The details of the subsequent Long March of 1935–36 are given in the biographies of Hsiao and Ho. Wang Chen was Hsiao's political commissar until they reached north Shensi in late 1936.

With the outbreak of the Sino-Japanese War in mid-1937, Ho Lung became commander of the newly organized 120th Division of the Eighth Route Army. Subordinate to the division were two brigades, the 358th commanded by Hsiao K'o and the 359th led by Wang. During the early years of the war both units were sent to Hopeh; Hsiao operated in areas east of Peking and Wang's 359th Brigade was located west of Peking between the Peking-Hankow Railway and the Shansi border. For the next two years it harassed Japanese units along this important rail line, allegedly tripling its firepower from captured Japanese equipment. The brigade nominally remained under Ho Lung's 120th Division, but for operational purposes it came under the jurisdiction of the 115th Division, which controlled the Shansi-Chahar-Hopeh Border Region (see under Nieh Jung-chen). Relatively little is known of Wang's work in this period, but an article in the November 1965 issue of *China Reconstructs* recounts a battle fought in May 1939, in which Wang directed the forces that defeated a Japanese unit attempting to advance on the Shansi-Chahar-Hopeh headquarters in an area not far southeast of the famous Wu-t'ai Mountain range.

In late 1939 Wang's 359th Brigade was recalled from the Shansi-Chahar-Hopeh area to the Shensi-Kansu-Ninghsia (Shen-Kan-Ning) Border Region to strengthen the defense of the upper reaches of the Yellow River and to protect the Border Region.[2] In December 1941 Wang was elected to represent the town of Mi-chih in north Shensi in the Second Shen-Kan-Ning Border Region Assembly,[3] and at approximately this same time his troops, numbering some 10,000 men, were moved to Nanniwan (Nan-ni-wan), a desolate wasteland located a few miles south of Yenan. Wang's task in Nanniwan, aside from normal garrison duties, was to reclaim the land, to feed his own troops, and, if possible, to produce a surplus for use elsewhere in the Border Region. The timing of this transfer to Nanniwan was significant; the annotators of Mao Tse-tung's *Selected Works* mention that because of continuing Japanese attacks and the KMT blockade, the years 1941 and 1942 were those of the "greatest difficulty for the liberated areas."[4] Wang's units were not the only ones engaged in agriculture but they were the most successful,[5] and the work in Nanniwan quickly came to epitomize the Communist conception of the peasant-soldier—hoe in hand, rifle nearby. A number of Western visitors to the Shen-Kan-Ning Border Region were taken to Nanniwan, and many of them wrote favorable accounts of

Wang and his men.[6] A quarter of a century later the Communists were still harking back to the "spirit of Nanniwan."[7]

In late 1944 Wang's 359th Brigade was sent south to increase the strength of Li Hsien-nien's (q.v.) Fifth Division of the New Fourth Army. During most of the war years Li's men had operated in the Hupeh-Honan-Anhwei borderlands, but toward the end of the war his forces were expanding into the adjacent Hunan-Kiangsi border area. It was into the latter region (Wang Chen's native area) that Wang led his men. In the region around Liu-yang and P'ing-chiang in east Hunan, Wang Chen and his two political officers, Wang Shou-tao and Wang En-mao (qq.v.), established the "Hunan People's Anti-Japanese National Salvation Army." Then, in the summer of 1945, just before the Japanese surrender, Wang Chen's troops again moved south, this time to the Kiangsi-Kwangtung border where they planned to rendezvous with the Communists' East River District guerrilla forces (see under Tseng Sheng). The rendezvous was almost effected when the war ended. Consequently, Wang was ordered to march north again to rejoin Li Hsien-nien in Hupeh.

In the interim, when the CCP held its Seventh National Congress in Yenan from April to June 1945, Wang was elected an alternate member of the new and enlarged Central Committee. He continued to be actively engaged in military affairs in the immediate postwar period. After the Japanese surrender, while the negotiations between the Nationalists and Communists were taking place, Wang was the Communist representative on the field team sent by the Peking Executive Headquarters to supervise the Hankow area. But negotiations soon broke down and hostilities between the Nationalists and Communists were renewed; Wang's troops barely escaped being trapped near Hankow, but he managed to lead his men to the Communist-held Shen-Kan-Ning base in September 1946. From 1946 to 1947 Wang was chief-of-staff of the Shansi-Suiyuan-Shensi-Kansu-Ninghsia Military Headquarters, an area nominally under Ho Lung's command. However, Ho had led his forces eastward, so Wang was left virtually in control. From 1947 to 1948 Wang was commander of the Second Column of P'eng Te-huai's Northwest PLA (later called the First Field Army).

At the very moment the new central government was being formed in Peking in the fall of 1949, Wang's First Army Group was pushing westward into Sinkiang. His difficulties were eased considerably in late September when General T'ao Chih-yueh, the Nationalist garrison commander in Sinkiang, announced his defection to the Communist side. Less than a month later, on October 20, Wang's troops entered Tihwa

(now Urumchi), the Sinkiang capital, and with this victory virtually all of the northwest was in Communist hands. On December 29, T'ao's troops were redesignated the 22nd Army Corps; the former Nationalist officer nominally retained command of this unit, and Wang was named as the political commissar.

The conquests in the northwest had been under the over-all direction of P'eng Te-huai who was made commander and political commissar of the Sinkiang Military District when it was formally established in December 1949. P'eng retained these posts until late 1950, but in fact he was fully occupied in Sian, the PLA headquarters for the northwest, and Wang Chen, his deputy commander, was for practical purposes the top military man in Sinkiang; finally, by 1951, Wang succeeded P'eng as commander and political commissar.

Within a short time after the fall of Sinkiang to the Communists, it became apparent that Wang was to be the dominant Communist leader in the area. In addition to his role in the military establishment, he became the ranking secretary of the Party's Sinkiang Sub-bureau, retaining this post until mid-1952. Moreover, when the Sinkiang Provincial People's Government was established in December 1949, Wang was made a member of the Government Council and chairman of its Finance and Economics Committee, and soon after (March 1950) was also appointed to membership on the Sinkiang Nationalities Affairs Committee. He was also a member of the regional administration, the Northwest Military Administrative Committee (NWMAC), and its successor, the Northwest Administrative Committee, from early 1950 until the regional organizations were abolished in 1954. Wang was also a member of the NWMAC's Finance and Economics Committee from 1950 to early 1953. His only position in a national organization in the early years of the PRC was membership on the National Committee of the All-China Federation of Democratic Youth from 1949 to 1953.

Wang's long-standing experience in the utilization of Red Army troops to assist in productive labor was quickly illustrated in Sinkiang; speaking in January 1950 before a meeting of the Sinkiang Finance and Economics Committee, he outlined the tasks ahead in "production and construction" work by military units in Sinkiang, and he repeated these themes when addressing the third session of the First CPPCC (October–November 1951) in Peking. By the middle of 1952 the Communists began to prepare for the transformation of Sinkiang province into an "autonomous region," and the first step was taken in September when a Preparatory Committee was established with Wang as one of its members. The ultimate establishment of the

Sinkiang-Uighur Autonomous Region is described in the biography of Saifudin. Wang Chen, however, apparently played only a minor role in Sinkiang affairs after August 1952, when his long-time colleague Wang En-mao replaced him as secretary of the Sinkiang Party Sub-bureau. And by the next year he had also succeeded him as political commissar of the Sinkiang Military District. Wang Chen was relieved from these posts to allow him to become a deputy commander of the Northwest Military Region, headquartered in Sian, Shensi. Once again Wang was nominally subordinate to P'eng Te-huai, but as P'eng was then commanding the Chinese forces in Korea, Wang was probably the most important military figure in the northwest until his transfer to Peking in early 1954.

Wang was brought from the northwest to Peking by February 1954 when he was identified as commander and political commissar of the PLA Railway Corps. This assignment probably resulted from the fact that the Railway Corps cooperates more closely with civilian agencies than any other PLA service arm, and few PLA veterans could match Wang's experience in the mobilization of military units for extra-military duties. Aside from its obvious duties during wartime, the Railway Corps has been used extensively in peace-time to repair, improve, and expand rail communications. Wang was elected a PLA deputy to the First NPC, and at the close of the initial session in September 1954, when the constitutional government was created, he was named to membership on the National Defense Council, a position he still holds. In May 1956, during a partial reorganization of the central government, he was appointed minister of State Farms and Land Reclamation, another position he still retains. Once again, Wang almost certainly received this post on the basis of his past experience in opening and developing lands. The head of the Ministry of State Farms and Land Reclamation is probably called upon more than any other minister to inspect outlying and relatively underdeveloped areas of China where much of the work of the ministry is being done. As a consequence, Wang has often been reported in such places as Hainan Island, Sinkiang, and northern Manchuria. He concurrently headed the ministry and the Railway Corps (whose responsibilities are in many respects complementary) until early 1958 when he relinquished the military assignment to another man. Prior to leaving active military service, Wang was made a colonel-general (equivalent to a U.S. Army three-star general) and at the same time (September 1955) he received the three top military decorations covering service from 1927 to 1950: the Orders of August First, Independence and Freedom, and Liberation. His long career with the Communists was given further

recognition one year later when he was promoted to full membership on the Party Central Committee at the Eighth Party Congress.

Presumably because of his increasing experience in northern Manchuria in his ministerial capacity, Wang was named in January 1958 to membership on the newly formed Sungari River Planning Commission, and later in the year he was elected a deputy from Heilungkiang to the Second NPC, which first met in April 1959. He was re-elected from Heilungkiang to the Third NPC, which opened in December 1964. When the State Council formed the Committee to Receive and Resettle Returned Overseas Chinese in February 1960, Wang was appointed as one of the vice-chairmen; the committee had been established to handle the thousands of refugees then returning from Indonesia (see under Liao Ch'eng-chih), many of whom were settled on state farms.

Wang has been abroad on two occasions, the first of which was from October to December 1957 when he led an agro-technical delegation to Japan. He also accompanied P'eng Chen to Hanoi in September–October 1962 as a member of a "friendship" delegation consisting of NPC deputies. His relatively infrequent public appearances are usually in connection with some aspect of agriculture or land reclamation, as in February–March 1964 when he spoke at a national conference on state farms. Similarly, he seldom writes for the press, although he wrote on the subject of state farms for *Hung-ch'i* (no. 7, 1961), and for the *JMJP* of February 1, 1962, he co-authored with Hsu Kuang-ta (q.v.) and Wang Shang-jung an article on early Communist military history (the importance of which is discussed in the biography of Hsia Hsi). Wang's name, however, frequently appears in the press as the living model of the battle-hardened veteran who was willing and able to lead troops in the more mundane work of construction and agricultural production in remote and difficult areas. He is, in short, the living symbol of the "spirit of Nanniwan."

Wang's family life was seriously affected by the chaos that war and revolution brought to China during his younger years. His first marriage, which had been traditionally arranged by his parents, ended in 1927 when his young wife died. He was remarried soon afterwards to a textile worker from Changsha. About two weeks after the marriage, she was killed in the fighting between the leftist forces in Changsha and the troops of Hsu K'o-hsiang (May 1927). Wang's third marriage, about 1934, was to a daughter of a peasant who became a member of the Communist Youth League and a nurse. When Wang made the Long March, she stayed behind. Arrested in 1935, she was imprisoned in Nanchang where presumably she died. When he reached the northwest Wang married, in 1937, for a fourth time. This wife was a native of Manchuria and had studied at Peking University. In 1944 the Wangs had three sons.

1. Nym Wales, *Red Dust* (Stanford, Calif., 1952), pp. 90–101.

2. *SCMP* 2366, pp. 6–9.

3. *Shen-Kan-Ning pien-ch'ü ts'an-i-hui wen-hsien hui-chi* (Collection of documents of the Shensi-Kansu-Ninghsia Border Region Assembly; Peking, 1958), p. 168.

4. *Selected Works of Mao Tse-tung* (Peking, 1965), III, 111.

5. Hsu Yung-ying, *A Survey of the Shensi-Kansu-Ninghsia Border Region* (New York, 1945), pt. II, p. 40.

6. E.g., Harrison Forman, *Report from Red China* (New York, 1945), pp. 39–45.

7. E.g., *CB* 777, pp. 25–29.

Wang Cheng

(c.1909–   ; Kiangsu). Telecommunications specialist; minister, Fourth Ministry of Machine Building.

Wang Cheng has spent virtually his entire career in the Communist movement as a telecommunications specialist, first with the Red armies and later for the civilian government. Born about 1909 in Kiangsu, he attended a middle school in that province where he studied mechanical engineering. In 1928 he entered a school for technicians sponsored by the Nationalist government. Then only about 19, he specialized in telecommunications. After about a year there he was assigned to the Nationalist Army (the 18th Division) and participated in one of the "annihilation" campaigns against the Communists in the Kiangsi-Fukien area. In 1930 he was captured by the Communists in battle and was immediately assigned to his specialized work at the Red Army Headquarters. He was also allowed to join the Communist Party at about this time, possibly because of his special skills, which were sorely needed by the Communists. From 1931 to 1934 he headed the First Signal Communications Branch of the Chinese Workers' and Peasants' Red Army. This grew out of a small unit that Wang was ordered to establish in January 1931 with the principal task to train radio and telecommunications personnel. When originally formed the unit was stationed in Kiangsi near the Juichin headquarters and consisted of only 13 students in addition to the instructors and other personnel.[1] Wang's political commissar in this unit was Feng Wen-pin (q.v.), one of the top youth leaders of a later date who became involved in political difficulties in the 1950's and completely disappeared from the public scene. Wang made the Long March in 1934–35,

and immediately upon his arrival in northern Shensi was named director of the Third Bureau of the People's Revolutionary Military Council, the bureau in charge of communications. Other activities which engaged him in Yenan during the war years included the presidency of a school of telecommunications under the Communist Eighth Route Army and the establishment of the "New China" Broadcasting Station. Nothing is known of Wang's work during the civil war with the Nationalists (1946–1949), but presumably he remained with the Army headquarters plying his valuable trade as a communications expert.

In May 1949 in Peking, Wang was elected to the First National Committee of the newly formed All-China Federation of Democratic Youth; he was not, however, re-elected at the next congress in 1953. In June 1949 he was named to a committee to prepare for a large conference of scientists and science administrators (held in July 1949), which led to the formation in August 1950 of the All-China Federation of Scientific Societies. And in the early fall of 1949 he was one of the representatives from the PLA Headquarters to the first CPPCC, the first session of which brought the PRC into existence. Most significant, however, was the reaffirmation of Wang as the regime's senior telecommunications specialist, both in the military establishment and within the government bureaucracy. In May 1949, the PLA telecommunications system was reorganized into the Telecommunications Bureau under the People's Revolutionary Military Council (PRMC). Wang was named to head this bureau and in this capacity gave a major address before a conference on telecommunications specialists in north China in July 1949. When the first ministerial appointments were made in October 1949, he was named as the only vice-minister of the newly created Ministry of Posts and Telecommunications. Inasmuch as Minister Chu Hsueh-fan (q.v.) was not a Party member, it is evident that Wang, in fact, held the greater political authority within the ministry.

When the PRMC was reorganized in the fall of 1954, Wang was again named to direct the Communications Department, now subordinate to the PLA General Headquarters, a position he apparently still retains. Moreover, from the spring of 1957 he has served concurrently as commander of the PLA Signal Corps, another position he probably still holds. Although he is not often in the news, virtually every appearance is associated with the field of communications. In January–February 1950, for example, he gave the keynote report on tasks and duties for 1950 before a national telecommunications and postal conference. On February 24, 1950, and November 30, 1951, respectively, he reported before the Government Administration

Council (the cabinet) on postal and telecommunications agreements signed with the USSR and East Germany. He received an important assignment in August 1952 when he accompanied Premier Chou En-lai to Moscow as an adviser to negotiate agreements providing for the transfer of the Chinese Changchun Railway to China and for the extension of the joint use of the naval facilities at Port Arthur. Chou returned to Peking in September 1952, but Wang remained in Moscow through the fall, apparently taking part in the highly important economic negotiations led by Li Fu-ch'un, one of Peking's senior economic specialists.

In September 1953, Wang was removed as a vice-minister of Posts and Telecommunications. Apparently this move was made to allow him more time within the military establishment; it was almost three years before he would hold another civilian post. In 1955 military honors and personal military ranks were awarded for past services; the three orders (August First, Independence and Freedom, and Liberation) covered the period from the late 1920's to 1950. Wang received the first and last awards, but rather oddly was not given the award for service during the Sino-Japanese War, even though he unquestionably served in a rather high position with the Eighth Route Army during that period. At about this same time (September 1955), he was also given the rank of Lieutenant General (equivalent to a two-star general in the U.S. Army).

As the 1950's wore on, a number of learned and professional societies were organized to reflect the growing complexities of the Chinese Communist scientific community. One such organization was the China Electronics Society, for which a Preparatory Committee was established in June 1956, with Wang as the chairman. He held this until 1961 when a fellow telecommunications specialist and long-time colleague, Wang Tzu-kang, assumed the position. A year later (May 1957) Wang Cheng was named to membership on the Scientific Planning Commission under the State Council, a post held until this body was completely reorganized in November 1958. It was at approximately the same time, as already noted, that Wang was first identified as the commander of the PLA Signal Corps (April 1957). From 1959 to 1964 he served as a PLA Headquarters deputy to the Second NPC but was changed to the Heilungkiang constituency for the Third NPC, which held its first session in December 1964–January 1965.

In May of 1963, Wang received an important and, by this time, predictable assignment. The State Council created a new ministry with the title Fourth Ministry of Machine Building. Wang was named as minister, and although no information has been released about its functions,

it is clear from the past experience of Wang (as well as of colleagues within the ministry) that it is concerned with the manufacture of electronics equipment. Then, at the close of the first session of the Third NPC in January 1965, he was named to membership on the slightly expanded National Defense Council, a military organization with very limited authority but with considerable prestige. It was in his capacity as minister of the Fourth Ministry of Machine Building that Wang led a government delegation to East Germany in February–March 1965 for the annual Leipzig International Trade Fair at which the Chinese had one of the largest pavilions.

Wang Cheng is one of those exceptional leaders who seem to have been shielded from the heavy protocol duties which consume so much of the time of so many Chinese Communist leaders. Apparently this has been necessitated by the need to exploit his skills. He is one of the very few leaders with both technical training and extensive experience in a highly specialized field. For Wang this situation is all the more burdensome because he is saddled with important responsibilities in both the military establishment and the civilian government. Little is known of his personal life aside from the fact that in 1946 he was the father of a child about two years of age.

1. *Hung-ch'i p'iao-p'iao* (Red flag fluttering; Peking, 1957), III, 9–20.

Wang Chia-hsiang

(1907–   ; Ching-hsien, Anhwei). Specialist in foreign relations and international Communist liaison; member, CCP Central Committee and Central Secretariat.

Wang Chia-hsiang, also known as Wang Chia-ch'iang, joined the Communist Party in 1925. A student in Moscow in the middle and late 1920's, he belonged to the group known as the "28 Bolsheviks," which played a major role in one of the important political controversies within the CCP leadership in the thirties. From 1931 to 1946 he held a responsible position in the Political Department of the Red Army, and for much of that time he was also a member of the Party Politburo. He suffered a notable eclipse at the time of the Seventh Party Congress in 1945, but then rose to be China's first ambassador to the USSR and to hold important Party posts in the postwar period. He was a leading specialist in international Communist work until the early sixties.

Wang was born in Ching-hsien, Anhwei, a rural area about 50 miles south of Wu-hu, the important riverport on the Yangtze. His family, said to be of rural origins, sent Wang to the St. James mission school in Wu-hu for his middle school education. Here he first became involved in political activity via the anti-Christian movement, one of the important political currents of his early youth. The years Wang spent in Wu-hu coincided with the growth of this movement and its focus on the mission schools where students, it was felt, were not being offered a properly Chinese education. When further inflamed by the spread of labor unrest following the May 30th Incident of 1925 in Shanghai, the mounting sentiment against the Christian missions caused the missions to close a number of their schools in the Yangtze basin. Among the schools was Wang's St. James where Wang had been marked as a trouble maker. In 1924, while an upper classman, he had been especially active in getting many of his fellow students to protest the Bible readings and prayer meetings that were a part of the school's curriculum.

Upon leaving Wu-hu and moving to Shanghai Wang became all the more interested in radical student activities. In 1925 he enrolled at Shanghai University, meeting a number of young Communists who were his teachers (see under Ch'ü Ch'iu-pai). He soon joined the Youth League and then the CCP. About 1926 he went to Moscow and in his next few years of study there he became a part of a group of Chinese students who were enrolled at Sun Yat-sen University and who became favorite students of the university chancellor and Comintern official, Pavel Mif. In the next decade these "28 Bolsheviks" came to play an important role in the affairs of the CCP and became embroiled in a political controversy with Mao Tse-tung (see under Ch'in Pang-hsien). Although Wang does not seem to have been so closely associated with Mif and the Comintern as some of the others of his group, in the years in Russia and following, his career was quite similar to theirs. While he was at Sun Yat-sen he was one of four Chinese students selected to attend the "Red Institute for Teachers," an institution offering advanced teaching training along Communist lines. His three colleagues were Ch'en Shao-yü, generally thought to have been the leader of the "28 Bolsheviks" at this time, Ch'in Pang-hsien, and Chang Wen-t'ien (qq.v.). It may have actually been at the Institute that Wang first became closely connected with his three fellow Chinese students.

Wang attended the Sixth CCP Congress held in Moscow in the summer of 1928, although there is no record that he received a Party post at this time. Many of Mif's protégés returned to China with Mif himself in the early summer of 1930, but Wang apparently came back independently, visiting Germany, France, and other West European countries en route. Once in China he became connected with the underground in Shanghai. A Japanese source reports that at this period Wang engaged in laision work with the All-China Federation of Labor and in propaganda work among Shanghai textile workers. By 1930 he had become a member of the Kiangsu Provincial Party Committee[1] (see under Ho Meng-hsiung), which included Shanghai in its territory. But it was not long before he was also drawn into the political maneuvers to oust Li Li-san from power in the Party, one of Mif's prime objects for going to China. These efforts are only imperfectly documented, but apparently they had begun by June 1930 soon after the "28 Bolsheviks" returned. At that time some members of the group tried to get Li to alter certain statements before issuing them in the form of a resolution from the CCP Politburo. The efforts were unsuccessful, and after the resolution containing Li's views had been issued on June 11, 1930, four of the principal opponents to it found themselves under censure. The four, Ch'en, Ch'in, Wang, and Ho Tzu-shu, were all former Mif students. Wang received an official reprimand followed by a term of virtual exile in Hong Kong.[2] However, he was again in Shanghai in January 1931 for the Fourth Party Plenum when the "28 Bolsheviks" were able to remove Li's supporters from the Central Committee and Politburo and replace them by their own men. At this time Wang was among the new Central Committee members; he rose to a place on the Politburo following the execution of Party General Secretary Hsiang Chung-fa (q.v.) in June 1931. The Politburo chief for a brief time after Hsiang's death was Ch'en Shao-yü, who presided over an organization of some seven members. Thus Wang was named to the Party Politburo in an emergency and the election of this group later came under fire from Mao Tse-tung (see under Ch'in Pang-hsien). Wang was probably retained in his Politburo post from 1931 until the Party held its Seventh National Congress in 1945.

During the year 1931, when more and more of the Party leadership was forced to leave Shanghai, Wang joined the exodus to southeast Kiangsi, the headquarters of Mao Tse-tung and Chu Te. He was in Juichin for the opening of the First All-China Congress of Soviets on November 7, 1931. According to the account of an eyewitness, Wang opened the Congress and read a list of the 37 delegates who were chosen to sit on the Presidium (steering committee). Described as "an intellectual" himself, Wang gave a brief biography of each Presidium member as he read the names.[3] He addressed the congress in his capacity of director of the General Political Department of the First Front Army, thus indicating that when the congress opened he already held an important post in the Chu-Mao army, which protected the Kiangsi Communist base. During and immediately following the meetings, he was given two additional military positions of considerable importance. The first was a vice-chairmanship of the Revolutionary Military Council (RMC) headed by Chu Te. This body was directly subordinate to the Central Executive Committee (CEC) of the Chinese Soviet Republic, which had just come into being with the congress. Theoretically the RMC was in charge of the military operations in all the soviets that made up the Chinese Soviet Republic. Wang's second appointment was to the directorship of the RMC's General Political Department. At first this post and that of the directorship of the First Front Army's Political Department must have overlapped, especially as both were at first held by one man, Wang. But in the latter part of 1933 the second post, that with the army, was assumed by Yang Shang-k'un (q.v.), another member of the "28 Bolshevik" group. However, Wang seems to have retained the vice-chairmanship of the RMC and the directorship of its Political Department throughout the Long March and until the outbreak of the Sino-Japanese War in 1937.

The First All-China Congress of Soviets also elected Wang to other government posts; he was named a member of the CEC, and he became the People's Commissar for Foreign Affairs, a post more honorary than important at this time. There were two other prominent members of the "28 Bolshevik" group on the First CEC, Ch'en Shao-yü, who was probably already in Moscow with the Comintern, and Shen Tse-min (q.v.), who was in Oyüwan. Thus Wang was the only member who could have had an active voice in affairs in Kiangsi, and at this time both of his colleagues, Ch'in Pang-hsien and Chang Wen-t'ien, were directing the Party headquarters in Shanghai. They only transferred to Kiangsi in 1933 after the Nationalist police forced the Communists to close the Shanghai headquarters. When the Second All-China Congress of Soviets was held in Juichin in January–February 1934, Chang and Ch'in were both elected to the CEC; Wang was re-elected and was again named People's Commissar for Foreign Affairs. It is significant that at the Second Congress Chang Wen-t'ien took over from Mao the post of People's Commissar for the Soviet Government (the equivalent of the directorship of the cabinet). The Fifth CCP Plenum, about which little is known, was held in Juichin just prior to the Congress, but it must have been presided over by Ch'in, the Party general secretary, and he, Chang, and Wang all retained their Party Politburo and Central Committee posts at the Plenum.

In 1934 Wang was severely wounded by a bomb dropped from a Nationalist plane, possibly while the Communists were on the Long March. The wound caused him such pain that when the March was completed in the fall of 1935 he left north Shensi for the Soviet Union to undergo medical treatment. He returned to China just prior to the outbreak of the Sino-Japanese War. At that time, when American journalist Nym Wales visited Mao's headquarters in north Shensi, she saw Wang and spoke of him as a member of the seven-member Party Politburo and a vice-chairman of the RMC.[4] During the war he continued to hold important political-military positions, although his health was poor and he had to be inactive for long spells, especially in the later war years. At the beginning of the war Jen Pi-shih (q.v.) was put in charge of the Political Department of the Eighth Route Army, the newly named Communist force in north China. But Jen held the post only briefly and by 1938 it was held by Wang, who continued to serve in this capacity until sometime in 1946. For most of his term as Political Department chief, T'an Cheng (q.v.) was his deputy, but because Wang's health was poor, much of the responsibility must have fallen to T'an. Concurrently, in war times Wang was an important administrator at the Communists' Anti-Japanese Military and Political Academy (K'ang-ta), the principal training school for Red Army officers. The Academy was actually headed by Lin Piao, but Lin too suffered poor health and was forced to spend some of the early war years undergoing medical treatment in the Soviet Union. Hence, at this time Wang may have served as acting head. He conducted many officer training classes at K'ang-ta, and he also prepared a training manual for the use of his cadets, which was published in Yenan in 1941. This was entitled *Chung-kuo kung-ch'an tang yü ko-ming chan-cheng* (The Chinese Communist Party and the revolutionary war).

After being wounded in 1934, Wang's health never mended and long hours of overwork did not improve his condition. During the 1940's he contracted tuberculosis and was sent to Vladivostok to receive medical treatment. While hospitalized there he met a Chinese nurse, Chu Hui, whom he later married. She went to Manchuria with the Soviet troops at the end of war and became a superintendent of the Harbin Municipal Hospital, but nothing has been heard of her since that time. In April–June 1945, when the CCP met in Yenan for its Seventh Party Congress, Wang was still in Vladivostok.

In the late 1930's and early 1940's Wang contributed a number of articles on military-political matters to the Communist literature published in Yenan. Thus from 1937 to 1941 he wrote articles for *Chieh-fang* (Liberation) as did Ch'en Shao-yü, Chang Wen-t'ien, and one or two others of the "28 Bolshevik" group. In 1939 he also wrote for the *Pa-lu chün chün-cheng tsa-chih* (Military and political affairs magazine of the Eighth Route Army).[5] The controversy between Mao Tse-tung and the "28 Bolsheviks," which was revealed by Mao when he opened the *cheng-feng* ideological remolding movement in early 1942, is discussed in the biography of Ch'in Pang-hsien. But it is noteworthy that all three of the above leaders, who had been far more frequent contributors to the Communist literature than Wang, ceased publishing significant articles from the beginning of the *cheng-feng* movement,[6] yet Wang continued to write an occasional article from time to time. In fact, he contributed an article to a collection published in Shantung in 1943 commemorating the 22nd anniversary of the CCP's establishment in 1921.[7]

There are reports that Wang had been a member of the Party's Secretariat as early as 1934, a period when he was obviously among the key Party leaders. Information on the Secretariat before 1945 is extremely limited, but it seems to have been a kind of "inner-Politburo." It appears that Wang remained on the Secretariat until the *cheng-feng* movement of the early forties when most members of the "28 Bolshevik" group lost power. It is probably no accident that staunch supporters of Mao Tse-tung came onto the Secretariat at this time; for example, Liu Shao-ch'i became a Secretariat member in 1943 and Jen Pi-shih in 1945. In any event, there is little doubt that Wang had lost much of his political power by the time the Party held its Seventh Party Congress in Yenan from April to June 1945 when he was elected only to alternate membership on the Party Central Committee. Although semi-official sources are conflicting, Wang was apparently promoted to full membership in 1946 (following the death of a full Central Committee member); he was, in any case, definitely a full member by 1949. Wang's activities in the immediate postwar years are not well documented, but it is believed that he spent some of this period in Moscow as a representative of the CCP. In any case, by the late forties he was head of the Propaganda Department of the Party's Northeast Bureau, a post he apparently took over from Lin Feng (q.v.). In addition to Lin Feng, Wang's work in Manchuria put him into contact with some of the CCP's top leaders, including Kao Kang, P'eng Chen, Lin Piao, and Ch'en Yun (qq.v.).

Like many of the leading Communists in Manchuria, Wang was transferred to Peking in 1949 to work in the new central government. He was in Peking in September of that year to participate in the establishment of the national government at the inaugural session of the CPPCC. He attended the meetings as a member of the 16-man CCP delegation headed by Mao Tse-tung and at the close of the sessions

was elected to the CPPCC's First National Committee. In early October he was made a member of the Executive Board of the Sino-Soviet Friendship Association and later in that month was appointed as a vice-minister of Foreign Affairs under Chou En-lai. Chang Han-fu and Li K'o-nung (qq.v.) were also appointed as vice-ministers, but as of 1949 Wang was the only one of the three who held membership on the Party Central Committee. However, his most important assignment at this time was as Peking's ambassador to the Soviet Union (the first ambassadorial appointment made by the PRC). The selection of Wang for this important post was probably based on his seniority in the CCP, his past experience in the Soviet Union, and his knowledge of Russian. He arrived in Moscow at the end of October and presented his credentials on November 3.

Six weeks after Wang assumed his post in Moscow, Mao Tse-tung arrived in the Soviet capital to hold extended negotiations with Stalin. In the latter part of January 1950 Mao was joined by Chou En-lai who brought with him a number of top CCP leaders, including economic specialist Li Fu-ch'un and Trade Minister Yeh Chi-chuang. The talks culminated on February 14 with the signing of the Sino-Soviet Treaty of Friendship, Alliance, and Mutual Assistance. In addition, several other agreements were concluded the same day or during the following weeks. Wang was a leading participant in these negotiations, and following the departure of Mao and Chou in mid-February he signed (March 27) three agreements with the Russians. Under these, two joint stock companies were established in Sinkiang, one for the prospecting and refining of petroleum and coal gas, and another for the exploitation of non-ferrous metals. The third agreement provided for the formation of the Sino-Soviet Civil Aviation Company, which established airline routes between Peking and three Russian cities (Chita, Irkutsk, and Alma Ata).

In July 1950 Wang represented the CCP at the Third Congress of the East Germans' Socialist Unity (Communist) Party in East Berlin. Aside from this mission, the public record suggests that the remainder of his tour in Moscow was largely uneventful. However, it should be noted that during his ambassadorship in Moscow the Korean War broke out (June 1950) and Chinese troops entered into the conflict (October). The exact nature of the involvement of Moscow and Peking in the precipitation of the Korean War remains one of the great unknowns of modern East Asian history. Equally unclear is Wang's connection (if any) with the start of the war or with subsequent Chinese involvement. In any event, not long after the Chinese "volunteers" crossed the Yalu, Wang was withdrawn from Moscow (March 1951) and replaced by Chang Wen-t'ien who, like Wang, was also one of the "28 Bolsheviks." Wang's 16-month tour of duty in Moscow was indeed brief, but a supposition that he was withdrawn because of dissatisfaction by the top Chinese leadership does not seem borne out by his later career.

Upon his return to Peking in early 1951, Wang assumed his post as vice-minister of Foreign Affairs on a full-time basis. From that date to the early sixties he was mainly concerned with relations with other Communist nations and with Communist party leaders in non-Communist nations. In fact, his position in the Foreign Ministry could probably be regarded as a "cover" for an assignment directly subordinate to the Party Central Committee dealing with foreign relations. The U.S. State Department has noted that some sources "have speculated" that Wang heads the Party's "International Liaison Department,"[8] and the facts of Wang's career after 1951 tend to bear out such speculation. It was probably in this capacity that he attended the 19th Soviet Party Congress in October 1952 as a member of a delegation led by Liu Shao-ch'i, which also included such Party stalwarts as Jao Shu-shih, Ch'en I, Li Fu-ch'un, and Liu Ch'ang-sheng. Wang was abroad again in the spring and summer of 1954 when he accompanied Chou En-lai to Switzerland for the historic Geneva Conference, which brought an end to the French efforts to subdue the Communist forces in Indochina. He was a member of an equally important delegation in February 1956, which, under Chu Te's leadership, attended the 20th Congress of the CPSU in Moscow—the congress at which Nikita Khrushchev denounced Stalin in the so-called secret speech.

Wang attended the CCP's Eighth Congress in September 1956, which re-elected him to membership on the Central Committee. At the First Plenum of the new Central Committee (held the day after the Congress closed), he was elected a member (then one of seven) of the Party's Secretariat, the organ headed by Teng Hsiao-p'ing and charged with the day-to-day implementation of Politburo policies. Almost immediately after the Congress, the Hungarian Revolution erupted, imposing severe strains on the solidarity of the Communist bloc. Chou En-lai, Wang, and others were sent to Moscow in early January 1957 on a mission that is commonly described as a Chinese effort to mediate between the Russians and their restive allies in East Europe. After negotiations in Moscow (which included talks with top East German leaders then in the Soviet capital), the Chinese delegation made brief visits to Warsaw and Budapest and then returned to Moscow for

further talks. (Chou En-lai then proceeded to Afghanistan, but Wang returned to Peking in late January.)

Wang was back in Moscow again in November 1957 to attend the celebrations of the 40th anniversary of the Bolshevik Revolution. Led by Mao Tse-tung, the Chinese delegation took part in talks with leaders from all the Communist countries (see under Mao Tse-tung). Wang was the only member of Mao's delegation who did not return to Peking with him on November 21. Though it is possible that Wang remained in Moscow for reasons of health, he may have stayed behind for liaison purposes—a supposition that seems plausible in view of later information that the 1957 negotiations between Communist bloc leaders left a number of key issues unresolved. In any event, he did not appear again in Peking until late April 1958, shortly before the Chinese held the second session of the Eighth Party Congress, at which the 1957 talks in Moscow were a major item for discussion. Wang addressed the Congress, but his speech has never been published.

Wang's importance among the CCP elite was well illustrated in mid-1958 when Khrushchev spent four days in Peking, a visit that was soon followed by the beginning of the "off-shore islands" (Quemoy and Matsu) crisis. Only five Chinese took part in the official talks: Mao, Premier Chou En-lai, Defense Minister P'eng Te-huai, Foreign Minister Ch'en I, and Wang. Continuing his work as a top international liaison official, Wang went abroad again in 1959, accompanying Chu Te to Warsaw in March for the Third Congress of the Polish Communist Party. After the Congress Chu returned to China, but Wang (accompanied by Wu Hsiu-ch'üan, q.v.) went to London for the 26th Congress of the British Communist Party (March–April 1959). He is thus one of the very few high-ranking CCP leaders to have visited Britain since 1949.

Although Wang has not been abroad since his return from England, he continued to participate in negotiations with foreign Communists visiting Peking until the early sixties. In this connection he worked very closely with other specialists in international liaison, including Liu Shao-ch'i, Teng Hsiao-p'ing, P'eng Chen, Liu Ch'ang-sheng, Liu Ning-i, Yang Shang-k'un, and Wu Hsiu-ch'üan (qq.v.). Party liaison was clearly Wang's major assignment after his return from Moscow in 1951, but he also continued to serve in two organizations with which he had been associated since 1949: the CPPCC and the Sino-Soviet Friendship Association (SSFA). As already described, he was a member (representing the CCP) of the CPPCC's First National Committee (1949–1954). In December 1954 he was named to the Second National Committee, this time as a representative of "public bodies for peace and friendship with foreign countries." In addition, he was appointed to the CPPCC's Standing Committee. He has continued to be a CPPCC Standing Committee member on the Third and Fourth National Committees, which first met in April 1959 and December 1964, respectively, both times as a CCP representative. Wang has also continued to serve on the Sino-Soviet Friendship Association's Executive Board, having been reappointed to the second and third boards, established in December 1954 and May 1959, respectively. He was also reappointed as a vice-minister of Foreign Affairs in the fall of 1954 immediately after the constitutional government was inaugurated at the First NPC. However, during a major reshuffle of personnel in September 1959, he was dropped from this post (presumably to allow him to devote more time to Party liaison work). In the following month he published one of the few articles he has written since the PRC came into existence, an article that appeared in the Party's top journal, *Hung-ch'i* (Red flag, October 1, 1959), under the title "The International Significance of the Victory of the Chinese People."

Wang continued to appear in public through the spring of 1962, but since that time he has only been mentioned in connection with the funeral of Lo Jung-huan in December 1963 and his already described affiliation with the CPPCC a year later. Thus, like virtually all of the "28 Bolsheviks," Wang's active political life seems to have come to an end.

1. Modern China Project, Columbia University, New York, Howard L. Boorman, director.
2. Tso-liang Hsiao, *Power Relations within the Chinese Communist Movement, 1930–1934* (Seattle, Wash., 1961), pp. 133–134.
3. Agnes Smedley, *Red Flood over China* (Moscow, 1934), pp. 377, 389.
4. Nym Wales, *Inside Red China* (New York, 1939), pp. 342–343.
5. Chün-tu Hsüeh, *The Chinese Communist Movement, 1937–1949* (Stanford, Calif., 1962), p. 74.
6. Boyd Compton, *Mao's China: Party Reform Documents, 1942–44* (Seattle, Wash., 1942), p. xxxviii.
7. Chün-tu Hsüeh, p. 36.
8. U.S. Department of State, *Biographic Directory,* no. 271, July 20, 1960, p. 6.

Wang Chin-hsiang

(c.1906–   ; I-yang hsien, Kiangsi). Vice-minister of Public Security.

Although little has been heard of public security specialist Wang Chin-hsiang in the 1960's, he was one of the important early leaders of the CCP, particularly in his native Kiangsi. He was born in I-yang hsien, some 50 miles east of P'o-yang Lake in northeast Kiangsi, the native hsien of two other well-known Communists, Fang Chih-min and Shao Shih-p'ing (qq.v.). Although he was seven years younger than Fang and Shao, his early career was closely linked with these men. In 1928, when Wang was 22, he was involved in Communist-inspired peasant uprisings in his native hsien and was doubtless in contact with Fang and Shao, who were at that time actively organizing peasants in and around I-yang hsien (see under Fang Chih-min). By about 1928, an "I-yang hsien Soviet Government" had been formed, and at some point in the late 1920's or early 1930's, Wang was chairman of this government as well as the head of its military department. However, according to a 1962 account by the widow of Fang Chih-min, it is apparent that the I-yang hsien military force consisted (in 1928) of no more than a handful of men and very few arms.[1] In the 1929–30 period the Communists were able to expand their control in Kiangsi, which led to the formation of the Northeast Kiangsi Workers' and Peasants' Democratic Government. Fang Chih-min headed this government from 1930 to 1934, and Wang served as head of the "department of internal affairs" and as president of the court. Also in the early 1930's, the Communists expanded to adjacent areas in Fukien and Chekiang and formed the Fukien-Chekiang-Kiangsi Soviet Government, with Shao Shih-p'ing as chairman and Wang as the vice-chairman. In January–February 1934 the Second All-China Congress of Soviets was held in Juichin, where the Second Central Executive Committee of the Chinese Soviet Republic was elected, theoretically a government organ embracing all the soviet districts then in existence. Wang was elected to the Central Executive Committee at this time, very possibly *in absentia*. Afterwards, he was known to have been a vice-chairman of the Fukien Provincial Soviet Government as well as head of the Security Protection Bureau of this same government. Before Juichin was abandoned in the fall of 1934, Wang was apparently brought to the Party headquarters in Juichin to assume an important post in the Central Committee's Security Bureau. He then completely faded from the published record, possibly a deliberate device owing to the nature of work in Party security.

Wang reappeared not long after the end of World War II. As the war drew to a close in summer of 1945, the Party dispatched a number of top military leaders and cadre (such as Lin Piao) to Manchuria in a bold attempt to win this strategic area. Wang was among these men. When Changchun (present capital of Kirin) was captured by the Communists in

April 1946, Wang was named as a vice-mayor. At this time, however, the Communists did not have much military strength in Manchuria, and a month later the Nationalists drove the Communists from Changchun; it was not to be recaptured by the Communists until October 1948. Although in the 1946 period the Communists' main strength was in the Manchurian countryside, they created a regionwide organization known as the Northeast Administrative Committee. Wang's importance can be gauged in part from the fact that he was named to head the region's Public Security Department.

In September 1949, Wang attended the first session of the CPPCC, which brought the central government into being. He attended as a representative of the "Northeast Liberated Area," and during the course of the session served on the *ad hoc* committee to draft the Organic Law of the Central People's Government, a committee headed by Party veteran Tung Pi-wu. In October 1949, immediately after the CPPCC session, Wang was given an appointment in the central government as a member of the Supreme People's Procuratorate. Also, in October–November 1949, he attended a three-week long national public security conference in Peking, presided over by Public Security Minister Lo Jui-ch'ing and attended by the major security figures in the regime. According to the brief announcement at the close of the conference, it had set up a "uniform pattern" of public security work to be followed in all parts of China.

Wang then returned to Manchuria where he was to remain for the next five years. Coinciding with the establishment of the central government, the regional administration for Manchuria was undergoing changes in the summer and fall of 1949. The Northeast Administrative Committee was renamed the Northeast People's Government in August 1949; Wang was appointed to membership in the government and also retained his post as head of the Public Security Department. Already a member of the central procuratorate in Peking, he was named in addition as Procurator General for the Northeast Branch in April 1950. Also, according to unconfirmed reports in 1950, he was the director of the "Social Affairs Department" of the CCP Northeast Bureau, the euphemistic term long employed by the CCP for intelligence and security work. It was evident, therefore, that by the early 1950's Wang was one of the key security officials in Manchuria.

Wang's stature in Manchuria rose during the 1951–1954 period. He was a member by 1951 of the Northeast Bureau of the Party, then headed by Politburo member Kao Kang, who was to be purged in 1955. When the Northeast People's Government (NEPG) was again reorganized in January 1953, Wang (who had

been only a member of the NEPG) was elevated to a vice-chairmanship of the Northeast Administrative Committee (NEAC) and was named to chair the Political and Legal Affairs Committee. It was the latter post which apparently occupied most of his time in 1953 and 1954. He played a major role in the preparations leading to the selection of candidates for the National People's Congress (ultimately convened in September 1954), and gave a detailed report on his work at a meeting of the NEAC in April 1953. In closely related work, he was named as a vice-chairman of a newly formed committee in April 1954 to discuss the draft constitution, which was subsequently adopted at the First NPC session in September 1954.

In September 1954, just prior to the First NPC meetings, Wang was called to Peking where he was named as a vice-minister of Public Security, the ministry then headed by Lo Jui-ch'ing. In retrospect, it is of interest that Wang was brought to Peking several months after the disappearance of Kao Kang, the former senior Party figure in Manchuria. Kao had disappeared in early 1954 and was then officially purged in March 1955 (at which time it was announced that he had committed suicide). Among many other charges, Kao was accused of attempting to set up a "separate kingdom" in Manchuria. No Party or security officials were publicly cited for having ferreted out Kao's alleged plots, and it is unlikely that the full story of Kao Kang will be known for some time. However, in view of the fact that Wang was one of the top security officials in Manchuria, it seems probable that he was involved in some way in Kao's downfall (as well as the fall of several other leading Party figures—see under Kao Kang).

Soon after Wang went from Manchuria to Peking in 1954 he fell into relative obscurity. He is known, however, to have been involved in Communist China's famous "reform-through-labor" movement, a program which embraces not only ordinary criminals, but also political offenders. His participation in this program was made explicit in April 1957 when he gave a report on the subject before the NPC Standing Committee. However, aside from a few *pro forma* appearances (such as attending a banquet for visiting Cuban military officers in August 1961 or serving on the funeral committee for his long-time colleague Shao Shih-p'ing in March 1965) Wang has not been in the public eye very often. Yet the fact that he retains his position as a vice-minister of Public Security (serving under Hsieh Fu-chih since 1959), suggests that it is the nature of his work in security rather than any political difficulty which shields him from undue publicity.

---

1. Miao Min, *Fang Chih-min: Revolutionary Fighter* (Peking, 1962), p. 71.

Wang En-mao

(Yung-hsin hsien, Kiangsi). First secretary, Sinkiang-Uighur Autonomous Region Party Committee; member CCP Central Committee.

A veteran guerrilla leader from the late twenties and a wartime political officer, Wang En-mao has been the top Party and military leader in Sinkiang since 1952. He is native to Yung-hsin hsien, located in western Kiangsi not far from the Hunan border and to the east of the Chingkang Mountain base where Mao Tse-tung and his followers found refuge in the winter of 1927–28. Mao has written of Yung-hsin in "The Struggle in the Chingkang Mountains," his report to the CCP Central Committee of November 1928. The Party was then having difficulties in its attempts to organize the peasantry there, and although the hsien had seen its share of peasant unrest, Mao asserted that the program to redistribute the land moved slowly because 70 per cent of it belonged to landlords.[1] These attempts to organize the peasants must have been brought home to the peasant family of Wang En-mao, because official accounts state that about 1927 Wang Mei-nan, the father, and his three sons "joined the revolution." The second son, Wang Ping-ho, already a hsien Party secretary, had presumably joined the Party before 1927 and may have been responsible for introducing the other Wangs to Communism. This son was killed by the late twenties in the revolutionary struggles. In 1961 the father was identified as a leader of a commune production brigade in Yung-hsin hsien.

Wang was active in the Hunan-Hupeh-Kiangsi base in the early 1930's and was there in 1933 when Jen Pi-shih arrived to take charge of political affairs. According to a Communist account, Wang and others were "saved from the serious blow of dogmatism" as a result of Jen's leadership (see under Wang Shou-tao). Nothing more is known about Wang until 1941 when he was a political-military leader working closely with Wang Chen (q.v.), then commander of the 359th Brigade. Because the careers of the two Wangs continued to be closely associated for the next 12 years, it is possible that their association antedated 1941 and that the biography of Wang Chen may shed some light on the career of Wang En-mao. The 359th Brigade was subordinate to Ho Lung's 120th division, one of the three divisions of the Communists' Eighth Route Army of north China. In 1942 Ho dispatched this brigade to engage in land reclamation at Nanniwan (Nan-ni-wan), a few miles south of Yenan, and by the following year Wang En-mao was identified as deputy political commissar.[2] As late as the 1960's the Communists have continued to praise the work that was done there as evidence of the willingness of PLA troops to engage in non-military productive labor; for their leadership at Nanniwan, the two Wangs have frequently been cited as exemplary military officers.[3]

Wang En-mao with Wang Chen in 1944 when the 359th Brigade was sent to join Li Hsiennien (q.v.) of the Communists' New Fourth Army in central China. Li was then establishing a large Communist base in the border area of Honan, Hupeh, Hunan, Kiangsi, and Anhwei. After joining Li, Wang En-mao accompanied the 359th Brigade to P'ing-chiang and Liu-yang hsien in eastern Hunan where he and Wang Chen established what the Communists called the "Hunan People's Anti-Japanese National Salvation Army." The force, commanded by Wang Chen, was active in Liu-yang the year before the Sino-Japanese War ended. Wang Shou-tao was the army's political commissar and Wang En-mao was its deputy political commissar.

In the summer of 1945, just prior to the Japanese surrender, the Party decided to establish a base at Wu-ling in the border area of Kwangtung, Kiangsi, and Hunan, a region where the Communists had long been active. Consequently the 359th Brigade was dispatched on an extended march to the south. Led by the three Wangs, it fought its way from Hunan, through Kiangsi, to northern Kwangtung, while at the same time Communist guerrillas from the Kwangtung Tung-chiang (East River) District (see under Tseng Sheng) sent a group north to rendezvous at Wu-ling. The presence of Nationalist troops in areas through which the Kwangtung guerrillas had to pass, and the Japanese surrender in August 1945, kept the two Communist groups from actually meeting. Consequently, after the surrender the 359th Brigade was ordered to return north to rejoin Li Hsiennien, then controlling the so-called "central plains" area of his former Red base. In the ensuing hostilities between the Communists and Nationalists the brigade barely escaped being trapped in an area close to Hankow, but it finally fought its way through Hupeh, Honan, Shensi, and Kansu, and in September 1946 it arrived in the Shensi-Kansu-Ninghsia (Shen-Kan-Ning) Border Region.

In the period from 1946 to 1949 Wang En-mao was political commissar of units led by Wang Chen in and around the Yenan area, the heart of the Shen-Kan-Ning Border Region. Their troops were subordinate to P'eng Te-huai's Northwest PLA, which was designated the First Field Army in early 1949. During the course of that year troops from the First Field Army began to move west. When they arrived in Sinkiang they met little resistance, for both the principal military forces and the key civil officials there had gone over to the Communists (see under Burhan Shahidi) by the time the Communist units reached Tihwa, the capital, on

October 20, 1949. Wang Chen commanded these forces, and Wang En-mao may have been with him at the time. In any event, Wang En-mao pushed onward, moving into Kashgar some 1,000 road miles to the southwest of Tihwa. Aside from the fact that he became chairman of the Kashgar Military Control Commission in 1950, little is known of Wang's work there, but it is reasonable to assume that he was the top Communist official in southwest Sinkiang, where some two thirds of the population live. It is evident that the Party wanted a veteran CCP member—and a Han Chinese—in this inaccessible area, which has witnessed so much political turmoil in recent decades. Wang is known to have remained in southwest Sinkiang until 1952 when he was transferred to Tihwa to take over the duties that Wang Chen had performed until that time. In the meantime he had received other assignments that presumably took him to Tihwa from time to time. By the latter part of 1949 he was a member of the Party's Sinkiang Sub-bureau, and in December of that year he was appointed as a member of the newly established Sinkiang Provincial People's Government Council. In the former position he was subordinate to his long-time colleague Wang Chen, and in the latter he was nominally under Governor Burhan. In July 1950 he was given still another assignment as a member of the Northwest Military and Administrative Committee (NWMAC), a post he continued to hold (1953–54) after the NWMAC was reorganized into the Northwest Administrative Committee.

At approximately the time of Wang Chen's transfer away from Sinkiang in mid-1952, Wang En-mao was brought from Kashgar to Tihwa (renamed Urumchi in February 1954) to replace him as the ranking secretary of the Sinkiang Party Sub-bureau. He was identified in this post in August 1952, and in the next month he was named to a newly established committee to prepare for the transformation of Sinkiang Province into an "autonomous region" to reflect the preponderance of minority groups that make up the Sinkiang population. (According to official Communist statistics, 95 per cent of the Sinkiang population consists of non-Han peoples, with the Uighurs accounting for about 75 per cent of the total provincial population.) It is probable that Wang En-mao also succeeded Wang Chen at this time in the latter's command positions with the Sinkiang Military District. However, it was not until early 1954 that Wang En-mao was identified as acting political commissar; two years later he was identified as both commander and political commissar of the District, positions he still holds. He received still another military post with the establishment in December 1954 of the Sinkiang Production and Construction Corps, whose main tasks are non-military, for example, the building and repair of

railway lines. Ex-Nationalist General T'ao Chih-yueh was appointed as commander and Wang as political commissar, but the latter was seldom mentioned in this post and presumably relinquished it by the late fifties. Somewhat earlier, in September 1954, Wang had attended the inaugural session of the First NPC as a Sinkiang deputy. He continued to represent Sinkiang throughout the term of the First NPC (1954–1959), but he was not re-elected to the Second NPC, which opened in 1959.

On October 1, 1955, the Sinkiang-Uighur Autonomous Region (SUAR) was finally established. Wang had a prominent role in the inaugural ceremonies and was elected to membership on the SUAR Council, a position he still retains. His colleague Saifudin (q.v.) was named as chairman. At this same time the Sinkiang Party Sub-bureau was reorganized into the SUAR Party Committee, with Wang remaining as the first secretary, another position he still retains. In the previous month the PRC presented its army veterans with military awards and gave them personal military ranks. Wang was made a lieutenant general, equivalent to a two-star U.S. Army general, and was given one or more of the military orders. The particular awards were not specified, but in view of his long record it is probable that he received the three standard orders covering military service from 1927 to 1950: the Orders of August First, Independence and Freedom, and Liberation. In mid-October 1955, shortly after the inauguration of the SUAR, Wang led a delegation to the Soviet Union to study animal husbandry. This was his first trip abroad, and he remained in the USSR for 80 days, returning to Urumchi in early January 1956.

In September 1956 Wang took a leading part in the proceedings of the Eighth National CCP Congress, serving on the Credentials Committee for the Congress and presenting a written speech entitled "The Struggle in the Transition to Socialism of the Various Peoples of the SUAR and of the Entire Country." He was elected an alternate member of the Party Central Committee, placing second on the list of alternates after Yang Hsien-chen. Therefore, when full committee members Huang Ching and Lai Jo-yü died, Yang and Wang were promoted to full membership at the Fifth Plenum held immediately following the Second Session of the Eighth Congress (May 1958).

In 1957, when the "rectification" campaign began to curb the spokesmen who had voiced their criticisms during the preceding period of the Hundred Flowers campaign, Wang and Saifudin were made co-heads of an *ad hoc* committee to carry out the more repressive "rectification" measures in Sinkiang. "Rectification" problems were two-edged in Sinkiang, for they concerned not only dissension within the Party but also the objections of minority peoples to the ways in which they were being integrated into Chinese society. The campaign against the dissidents reached a climax when the SUAR Party Committee met from December 1957 to April 1958. During the meetings Wang assured the Committee members that "severe" blows had been dealt to the "rightists" and "regional nationalists" in the SUAR. A number of prominent leaders in Sinkiang were dismissed, including several of the important minority leaders. Wang followed his report to the SUAR CCP Committee by another of mid-1958, which continued to promote the work of the "rectification" campaign. The title of the report denoted its subject: "Struggle to Implement the People's Marxist-Leninist Line for the Solution of the Nationality Question."

Wang received two new posts in the mid-sixties, one in the northwest and the other in the national government. In February 1964 he was identified as one of the secretaries of the Party Northwest Bureau headed by Liu Lan-t'ao. The bureau, established in 1961, is headquartered in Sian, and thus Wang is identified from time to time in that city attending bureau meetings. He received his new post in the national government in January 1965 at the close of the initial session of the Third NPC, when he was elected to membership on the National Defense Council. However, the post carries more prestige than actual authority and it is unlikely that Wang devotes much time to this organization.

Wang En-mao has been the senior Communist leader in Sinkiang since assuming the ranking secretarial post in the Party organization there in 1952. And as of the mid-sixties he is one of the relatively few men to have headed the Party organization in a province (or autonomous region) for well over a decade. The only other Party leader in Sinkiang of roughly comparable stature is native-born Saifudin, chairman of the SUAR and an alternate member of the Party Central Committee. But whereas Saifudin spends much of his time in Peking, Wang seldom leaves Sinkiang. The difficulties in ruling Sinkiang's minority peoples are complicated by the under-developed state of its communications and by its sheer size (one sixth of China's total area). Moreover, since the early sixties the difficulties have been further complicated by the Sino-Soviet rift and the resulting flight into the Soviet Union of thousands of Sinkiang's national minorities, a problem discussed in more detail in the biography of Saifudin.

---

1. *Selected Works of Mao Tse-tung* (London, 1954), I, 87.

2. *CB* 777, p. 27.

3. *CB* 777, pp. 25–29.

Wang Feng

(c.1916–   ; Lan-t'ien hsien, Shensi). First Secretary, Kansu CCP Committee; alternate member, CCP Central Committee.

Wang Feng has spent most of his career in the northwest as a specialist in national minority affairs. He has been an alternate member of the Party Central Committee since 1958 and the Party first secretary in Kansu since 1961. Wang is a native of Lan-t'ien hsien, a few miles southeast of Sian, the Shensi capital. He was one of the youngest men to rise to the level of the Party Central Committee. He graduated from Peking University, presumably in the mid-1930's, and then apparently joined the Communists in his native Shensi. He first came to a degree of prominence in April 1946 when he attended the first session of the Third Assembly of the Shensi-Kansu-Ninghsia (Shen-Kan-Ning) Border Region, held in Yenan. He served as a delegate from Hsin-cheng hsien together with Hsi Chung-hsun (q.v.), an important Party leader who was then an alternate member of the Party Central Committee. Wang presumably remained in the northwest during the late 1940's, for by 1949 he was holding an important post in the Northwest Party Bureau as director of the United Front Work Department. Following the establishment of the central government (October 1949) and the regional governments it created, Wang became chairman of the Nationalities Affairs Committee for the Northwest Military and Administrative Committee (established in January 1950), thus beginning work upon which he has since concentrated. For the four years that the regional Committee existed, he held important positions in the northwest administration, serving as a member of both the Land Reform Committee (1950–1954) and the Political and Legal Affairs Committee (1952–1954). The Communists partially reorganized their regional administrations in 1953, changing the name of the NWMAC to the Northwest Administrative Committee (NWAC). Wang was named to membership on the NWAC and also continued to hold all three of his previous posts there until 1954 when regional governments were abolished.

From the early fifties Wang's career centered on the program to integrate the non-Chinese minorities into the stream of Chinese life. He became president in March 1951 of the Northwest Institute for Nationalities (opened in Lanchow, Kansu, the previous August). He held this post at least until November 1957 and possibly until 1959. In November 1952, Wang was appointed as a vice-chairman of the Nationalities Affairs Commission, a central government organ under the jurisdiction of the Government Administration Council (GAC) until September

1954, when the GAC was renamed as the State Council. He was reappointed to the Commission in October 1954 and September 1959; he served from 1954 under Ulanfu, China's most important national minority leader. In spite of the Peking appointment in 1952, Wang did not move to the capital, but remained for a few more years in the Northwest.

Wang served as a deputy from Tsinghai to the First NPC (1954–1959) but was changed to the Sinkiang constituency for the Second NPC (1959–1964). At the fifth and final session of the First NPC (February 1958), he was elevated to the NPC Standing Committee, the governing body of the Congress when it is not in full session. This appointment became possible owing to the purge of several Standing Committee members, victims of the 1957–58 "rectification" campaign. At the same time that Wang was named to the NPC Standing Committee (February 1958), he made an important speech before the NPC Nationalities Committee on opposing "local nationalism," the usual Communist term for separatist movements among the non-Chinese minorities. The Nationalities Committee of the NPC handles minority affairs for the Congress and is one of its permanent committees. Wang retained his position on the NPC Standing Committee in the Second NPC (1959–1964). At the first session of this Congress (April 1959), he was added to membership on its Nationalities Committee. Thus he served on both the State Council's Nationalities Affairs Commission (the executive branch) and the NPC's Nationalities Committee (the legislative branch), the two most important government bodies concerned with minority affairs. He continues to sit on the State Council's Nationalities Affairs Commission but was not reappointed to the NPC Nationalities Committee at the close of the initial session of the Third NPC (January 1965), possibly because of his transfer away from Peking (see below).

Paralleling his rise in the national government, Wang advanced in the national Party organization (and moved to Peking) by February 1955 when he became a deputy director of the CCP United Front Work Department, a key organ of Party control that handles relations between the CCP and non-Party persons. It also handles some of the Party's work with non-Chinese minorities. In May 1958, at the Second Session of the Eighth National Party Congress, he was elected as an alternate member of the Central Committee.

In April 1956, he was one of the deputy leaders under Vice-premier Ch'en I of the central government delegation sent to Tibet for the inauguration of the preparatory committee by which the Communists were planning to bring the Tibetan Autonomous Region into existence.

By mid-June the group returned to Peking, and in the following month it fell to Wang to give the formal report before the State Council describing the regulations for the new government to be established in Tibet. (The regional government was finally established in September 1965.)

In 1957–58, Wang was active in preparations to bring about the establishment of two other provincial-level "autonomous regions," one for the Chuang minority in Kwangsi and the other for the Huis in Ninghsia. He took part in a March 1957 meeting in Peking, devoted to the establishment of the Kwangsi-Chuang Autonomous Region, and when the region was formally inaugurated in March 1958 he was on hand for the ceremonies in Nanning as a member of a central government delegation led by Politburo member Ho Lung. More important, however, was his participation in the establishment of the Ninghsia-Hui Autonomous Region, an area carved out of a portion of eastern Kansu with the capital at Yin-ch'uan, a center for the Huis (Chinese Muslims) of northwest China. He was present at Lanchow, Kansu, in May 1957 for meetings that dealt with the formation of the Hui region. By July 1958 Wang had become the first secretary of the Party's "work" (i.e., preparatory) committee for the Ninghsia-Hui Autonomous Region, and when the Region was fully established in October 1958, he retained the first secretaryship of the Regional Party Committee. (As constituted in 1958, the region had a population of two million, a third of whom were of Hui origin.)

At the same time that Wang assumed the senior Party position for the Ninghsia-Hui Autonomous Region, Liu Ko-p'ing became chairman of the government apparatus of the region. Liu, a Hui, outranked Wang in the national Party structure owing to the fact that he was a full Central Committee member (from 1956) as opposed to Wang's status as an alternate member (from 1958). Moreover, Wang was serving at that time as a member of the NPC's Nationalities Committee, a committee chaired by Liu. However, on the Party Committee for the Ninghsia-Hui Autonomous Region, Secretary Liu ostensibly served under First Secretary Wang (a Han Chinese).

Although Wang remained as the ranking Party figure in Ninghsia for better than two years, he spent most of this time (1958–1960) elsewhere, mainly in Peking. He appears to have devoted a portion of this time to troubleshooting roles. For example, in June 1959 he accompanied the Panchen Lama from Peking to Lhasa to take part in discussions following on the heels of the violent Tibetan Rebellion that had broken out in March of that year. In January 1961, he again accompanied the Panchen Lama to Tibet, the third such visit there for

Wang. In the meantime, trouble had arisen in the Ninghsia-Hui Autonomous Region. In the late summer of 1960, Regional Chairman Liu Ko-p'ing was accused of "local nationalism" (see under Liu) and was removed, being replaced by Yang Ching-jen (q.v.). Not long after, by early 1961, Yang Ching-jen also assumed the first secretaryship in Ninghsia, thereby succeeding Wang Feng.

In the fall of 1960, soon after the exposure of the political difficulties in Ninghsia, new problems arose in neighboring Kansu, then under the jurisdiction of Party First Secretary Chang Chung-liang, an alternate member of the Party Central Committee. Chang made his last appearance in November 1960 and by January 1961 Wang Feng was identified as the new first secretary for Kansu, a position he continues to hold. Unlike his tenure in Ninghsia (where he seldom remained), Wang has spent most of his time in Lanchow since assuming the senior Kansu Party post in 1961. He is frequently reported in the press in the activities normally associated with a provincial first secretary, such as making reports before Party and Youth League organizations, conducting inspections of industrial and agricultural production, and appearing at rallies marking Communist holidays. He received a significant promotion within the Party structure by February 1964 when he was identified as a secretary of the Northwest Party Bureau, where he serves under First Secretary Liu Lan-t'ao. As already noted, Wang was a deputy from Tsinghai to the First NPC and from Sinkiang to the Second NPC. His constituency was again changed in 1964 when he was elected to the Third NPC from Kansu. However, when the Third NPC held its first session (December 1964–January 1965), he was not re-elected to the NPC Standing Committee nor to the NPC Nationalities Committee, probably because of his transfer from Peking to Kansu.

Although Wang has not written frequently for the Party press, he is the author of a useful summary of Chinese nationalities affairs that appeared in the *JMJP* of September 27, 1959, as part of a series of articles marking the 10th anniversary of the PRC.[1] He also wrote a lengthy article dealing with Party policies regarding minority groups, which appeared in the important journal *Min-tsu t'uan-chieh* (Nationalities unity), combined issue numbers 10–11, November 6, 1961.

1. *CB* 609.

Wang Ho-shou

(c.1908–   ; Hopeh). Alternate member, CCP Central Committee; specialist in heavy industry.

Wang Ho-shou received the first part of his university training at the T'ang-shan College of Civil Engineering in his native .Hopeh (the principal engineering school in north China) before going to Sun Yat-sen University in Moscow for further study. He is reported to have graduated from Sun Yat-sen (presumably in the late 1920's), and at about the same time to have joined the CCP. Almost immediately upon returning to China he must have been sent to work in Manchuria, for in 1929 he was identified as director of the propaganda department of the Manchurian CCP Committee. The extent of his work in Manchuria has not been reported and may not have been particularly effective, for at the time considerable rivalry existed between those Communists in Manchuria who were Manchurian-born Chinese or Koreans (and who were working under the direction of a branch of the Korean Communist Party centering its activity about Harbin) and those members of the CCP sent into Manchuria from China proper. In 1931 Wang was reported to have been working under Liu Shao-ch'i. It is not clear where Wang was working, but it was probably in Shanghai. At least by 1936 Liu was in Peking working among university students, many of whom were becoming aggressively anti-Japanese. Wang was known to have been in underground work in the 1930's and 1940's and to have been arrested three times by the Nationalists. As most of his early career was spent in north China or Manchuria, he must have come into contact with Liu Shao-ch'i at one time or another.

In early 1946 Wang was in Yenan serving as director of the Cadres Section of the Organization Department of the CCP. However, by May of that year he returned to Manchuria where he assumed the post of political commissar of the Heilungkiang Military District (HMD);[1] two years later (1948) he was given the concurrent post of commander of the HMD. It was also in 1948 that he was identified as secretary-general of the Northeast Bureau of the CCP and as an executive committee member of the Northeast Branch of the Sino-Soviet Friendship Association. In addition, during the late forties he served as the Party secretary of Heilungkiang and as a secretary of the Northeast Party Bureau.

The Communists established their provincial and regional governments in Manchuria earlier than in China proper where they did not take over the whole of the mainland until early 1950. Thus they established the Northeast Administrative Committee (NEAC) as a regional administration for Manchuria in 1946, and in August 1949 they reorganized it into the Northeast People's Government (NEPG). During the years 1949 to 1952 Wang served under both administrations where he was director of the Heavy Industry Department, first for the NEAC, and subsequently for the NEPG. (The department name was changed to "Industry Department" in 1950.) During the years from 1949 to 1952 he was concurrently a member of both the Finance and Economics Committee and the Higher Education Committee of the Northeast administration.

During the summer of 1950 Wang was involved in the takeover of economic properties acquired by the Soviets from the Japanese at the end of World War II. The provisions for the takeover procedures had been negotiated in Moscow earlier in 1950 by Mao Tse-tung and Chou En-lai. Under the terms of the agreement, a Sino-Soviet Properties Transfer Commission was established in Manchuria in July 1950, with Wang as a member. The details of the Commission's work are found in the biography of Lin Feng, the top Chinese delegate.

In August 1952 Wang was transferred to Peking to head the Ministry of Heavy Industry. He succeeded Li Fu-ch'un, but when he took over the Ministry it was reorganized and sections of it were transferred to two newly created industrial ministries, the First and Second Ministries of Machine Building. This narrowed the scope of Wang's jursidiction by comparison with the work that Li had directed before him, but at the same time the growing expansion of industry placed greater pressure on the branches of the government dealing with industrial development. Apparently Wang's work in highly industrialized Manchuria (where Li Fu-ch'un had earlier worked) paved the way for the Peking assignment. No sooner had he arrived in Peking than he was selected to be a member of the delegation led by Premier Chou En-lai in August–September 1952 to Moscow, where they negotiated the return of the Chinese Changchun Railway to China and the extension of the joint use of naval facilities at Port Arthur.

As head of the highly important Ministry of Heavy Industry, Wang was called upon to speak before conferences and give periodic reports to government bodies. For example, in November 1952 he spoke before a conference of personnel from factories and mines engaged in heavy industry work, and in June 1953 he delivered a report before the Government Administration Council (the cabinet) on the heavy industry tasks for 1953. In September 1954, at the first session of the First NPC, Wang was reappointed as minister of Heavy Industry, but then in May 1956 the ministry was abolished, with its functions allotted to three new ministries: Building Materials, Chemical Industry, and Metallurgical Industry. Wang was named to the last, a portfolio he was to hold for over eight years. At the same time he replaced Po I-po as chairman of the State Construction Commission, thus receiving two ministerial-level positions, a fairly unusual situation. This lasted nearly two years— until February 1958 when the Commission was

abolished and its functions assumed by the State Planning and State Economic Commissions. At the Eighth National Party Congress in September 1956, Wang addressed the delegates on the development of China's iron and steel industry, and at the close of the congress was elected an alternate member of the Party Central Committee.

In the middle and late 1950's, Wang gave a number of major reports before the annual sessions of the NPC and often took part in entertaining the many foreign visitors to China. He served on the Second National Committee of the CPPCC (1954–1959) as a representative of the CCP and was a deputy from his native Hopeh to the Second NPC, which held its initial session in April 1959. Wang also wrote about the iron and steel industry for major publications. Examples include articles for the *JMJP* of September 26, 1959, and *Hung-ch'i* (Red flag) of May 1, 1960. Not long after publishing the last-mentioned article, Wang began to receive considerably less press attention than earlier. In December 1963 he led a government delegation to North Vietnam to attend the opening ceremonies of a new blast furnace. However, in July 1964 he was replaced as minister of Metallurgical Industry by Lü Tung (q.v.), who had served as his deputy both in Manchuria and in Peking for 15 years. Two months later Wang was elected a deputy from Liaoning to the Third NPC, which held its first session in December 1964–January 1965. (As already noted, he had been a Hopeh deputy to the Second NPC.) Wang's election as a Liaoning deputy to the NPC foreshadowed a new appointment in that province; by July 1965 he was identified as the first secretary of the Anshan Party Committee. Because Anshan is a major steel center, Wang's long experience in the Metallurgical Industry Ministry can probably be put to good use. However, for a man who held a ministerial post and who serves as an alternate Central Committee member, this assignment to a secretaryship at the municipal level appears to be anticlimactic and suggests that in some way he fell into political disfavor in the 1960's.

1. Chou Erh-fu, *Tung-pei heng-tuan-mien* (Northeastern cross section; Hong Kong, 1946), p. 117.

Wang Hung-k'un

(1909–   ; Hupeh). Veteran military leader; deputy commander of the Navy.

Wang Hung-k'un is a career military officer who served in the Red Army until 1950, when he became a deputy commander of the Navy: Nothing is known about Wang before 1930 when he was 21. At that time he was serving as a battalion commander in the Communist guerrilla base in the Hupeh-Honan-Anhwei border area and had probably already joined the CCP. He may have been attracted to the Communist movement by young Communist activists who worked in rural areas, where they capitalized on peasant discontent and organized peasant associations to resist the local authorities. The Hupeh-Honan-Anhwei base was organized from such areas in the three provinces; it became the Oyüwan Soviet in mid-1931 after Chang Kuo-t'ao (q.v.) had arrived from the Shanghai Party headquarters to manage political affairs in the area. Hsu Hsiang-ch'ien (q.v.) was the military leader, and his army, to which Wang belonged, was known from November 1931 as the Fourth Front Army.

By 1931 Wang was commanding the 29th Regiment of the Fourth Red Army in the Oyüwan base.[1] (Later that year the Fourth and 25th Armies became the major components of the above-mentioned Fourth Front Army.) He had advanced by mid-1932 to the command of the Fourth Army's 10th Division, and by May 1934 he was in command of the Fourth Army.[2] These and one other identification in 1937 are the only clues to Wang's career in the years from 1930 to 1937, but a brief sketch of the Fourth Front Army traces the outlines of his career for this period.

Toward the end of 1932 the Fourth Front Army, under the command of Hsu Hsiang-ch'ien and Chang Kuo-t'ao, was forced to retreat from Oyüwan in the face of savage Nationalist attacks. Moving toward Sian, the capital of Shensi, the army was within some 25 miles of the city when it was driven off and forced to turn south into northeast Szechwan. In February 1933 it reached the small town of T'ung-chiang, west of the Ta-pa Mountains on the upper reaches of the Ch'u River. The Communists held the town only briefly, but they returned to it in May and were then able to make it their headquarters for the next two years. There the Red Army established the T'ung-Nan-Pa Soviet (also known as the Szechwan-Shensi Soviet). The term T'ung-Nan-Pa derived from the three principal hsien which the Soviet comprised—T'ung-chiang, Nan-chiang, and Pa-chung. During the remainder of 1933 the Communists expanded over a considerable area in northern Szechwan, moving west to Chao-hua and Ts'ang-ch'i, south to I-lung, Ying-shan, Hsuan-han, and Ta-hsien (Sui-ting), and east to Cheng-kou. By the end of 1933 the Red Army had been pushed back to the original T'ung-Nan-Pa Soviet boundaries, but in the spring of 1934 Hsu Hsiang-ch'ien launched another attack and re-occupied most of the territory he had held the previous year. When Mao Tse-tung and his army from the Kiangsi Soviet reached Tsun-i, Kweichow, in January 1935 on their now historic Long March, Hsu's Fourth Front Army held an area in Szechwan extending

as far south as the line between Lang-chung (Pao-ning) and Ta-hsien.[3]

Chang's Fourth Front Army moved west in the spring of 1934 and met Mao Tse-tung and his armies midway on their Long March when the latter had reached western Szechwan in the summer of 1935. But after the meeting trouble ensued between Mao and Chang Kuo-t'ao, and as a consequence Chang and most of his Fourth Front Army did not go north to Shensi with Mao. Instead they turned west into Sikang province, remaining there for another year before they finally decided to rejoin Mao. They were in Shensi in 1937 when the Sino-Japanese War broke out, after which the Communists organized their forces in north China into the Eighth Route Army. The 129th Division of the Army, led by Liu Po-ch'eng, absorbed most of Hsu and Chang's Fourth Front Army. Hsu became a deputy commander of the 129th Division and commander of its 385th Brigade. Wang Hung-k'un was also assigned to the 129th Division and may have commanded the 385th Brigade briefly.

In 1939 Wang was identified as part of Hsu Hsiang-ch'ien's command; in August 1938 Hsu's brigade had been sent into southern Hopeh to establish the South Hopeh Military District, which was under Liu Po-ch'eng's 129th Division. In 1939 Wang was the political commissar in the South Hopeh Military District (described in the biography of Yang Hsiu-feng, who headed the local resistance in the area). In April 1939 Hsu was sent east into Shantung to take charge of guerrilla operations there, and again Wang followed him, being identified as commander of the West Shantung Military District. Hsu was called back to Yenan in 1942, and soon afterwards his troops in Shantung were transferred from the command of the Eighth Route Army in north China and placed under Ch'en I's New Fourth Army in east China. Wang presumably remained with this army for the duration of the war.

In the early postwar period elements of the New Fourth Army in Shantung were transferred back to Liu Po-ch'eng's command, and by the late summer of 1946 Wang was a deputy commander of Liu's Shansi-Hopeh-Shantung-Honan (Chin-Chi-Lu-Yü) Military Region.[4] Wang was with Liu's armies which expanded southward into the Yangtze basin. Reaching the old Oyüwan territory in the Ta-pieh Mountains on the boundaries of Hupeh, Honan, and Anhwei provinces in mid-1947, the Communists established the Central Plains Liberated Area. Wang was then in command of the Sixth Column of Liu's Central Plains Liberation Army. Liu's army, known as the Second Field Army from early 1949, captured the Wuhan cities in the spring of 1949 in cooperation with Lin Piao's Fourth Field Army. At approximately this time Wang was again transferred, this time to Lin Piao's forces, assuming command in 1949 of the 17th Army Corps of the Fourth Field Army. Wang concurrently became deputy commander of the Hupeh Military District under Commander Li Hsien-nien, with whom he had previously been associated in Oyüwan and the Fourth Front Army.

In 1950, when provincial and regional government administrations were established in central-south China, Wang was named to membership on the Hupeh Provincial People's Government Council and the Central-South Military and Administrative Committee (CSMAC), which had jurisdiction over several provinces, including Hupeh. He remained a nominal member of the CSMAC until 1951 and of the Hupeh government until 1954; however, by October 1950 he had already been transferred to Peking to become a deputy commander of the Chinese Navy under Commander Hsiao Ching-kuang (q.v.). Of the several men who have been Navy deputy commanders, only Wang has served continuously from 1950 to the mid-1960's.

Wang was a deputy from the East China Military Region to the First NPC, which met initially in September 1954 to inaugurate the constitutional government. He was appointed at that time to membership on the National Defense Council, a position he still retains. He was elected to the Second NPC (1959–1964) and to the Third NPC, which opened in December 1964. In the last two congresses Wang represented the Navy. He became an admiral in 1955 when personal military ranks were created. His rank is the second highest in the Chinese Navy. That same year military decorations were also given for the first time; Wang received all three top awards—the Orders of August First, Independence and Freedom, and Liberation—covering military service from 1927 to 1950.

Since his transfer to Peking in 1950 Wang's public appearances have been confined almost exclusively to military affairs (e.g., receptions for visiting military leaders). His only trip abroad was to Yugoslavia, a country seldom visited by Chinese leaders. He spent a month there in October–November 1956 as a member of a military delegation led by General Teng Hua (q.v.).

---

1. *Hung-ch'i p'iao-p'iao* (Red flag fluttering; Peking, 1957), III, 70–81.

2. Norman Hanwell, "The Chinese Red Army," *Asia,* May 1936, p. 319.

3. Anthony Garavente, "The Long March," *The China Quarterly,* no. 22:109–112 (April–June 1965).

4. *Jen-min te chün-tui* (The people's military forces), September 15, 1946 (a newspaper published by the Chin-Chi-Lu-Yü Military Region).

Wang Jen-chung

(c.1906–   ; Hopeh). Former first secretary, Hupeh Party Committee; alternate member, CCP Central Committee.

Wang Jen-chung, a longtime Party leader in Hupeh, has been associated with the Communists since the days of the Kiangsi Soviet in the early thirties. He made the Long March, after which he studied at and graduated from the North Shensi Public School (Shen-pei kunghsueh), one of the most important of the Communist-run schools in the Yenan area.

After the Sino-Japanese War broke out, Wang was assigned as a political officer to the guerrilla forces of Li Hsien-nien (q.v.), which were located in the Hupeh-Honan region north of Wuhan. Wang's service with Li was apparently rather brief, because by 1938 he was transferred northward to his native Hopeh. Communist military forces led by Hsu Hsiang-ch'ien (of the 129th Division) had pushed into southern Hopeh in mid-1938 and had established the South Hopeh Military District. Simultaneously, a civil organ known as the South Hopeh Administrative Office was set up under the chairmanship of Yang Hsiu-feng (q.v.), a Peking professor who joined the Communist guerrillas when the war broke out. Paralleling the South Hopeh Administrative Office (SHAO) was the South Hopeh Party Committee. Sometime during the war (and until the late 1940's) Wang was chairman of the SHAO. He apparently succeeded Yang Hsiu-feng, possibly when Yang was promoted to the chairmanship of the Chin-Chi-Lu-Yü (Shansi-Hopeh-Shantung-Honan) Border Region Government, which was formed in July 1941. During the war, Wang was also director of the South Hopeh Party Committee's Propaganda Department. The other wartime post that Wang was known to have held was membership on the above-described Chin-Chi-Lu-Yü Government Council.

Following the capture by the Communists of Tsinan, the Shantung capital, in September 1948, Wang was assigned to head the governmental organ for that city—known as the Tsinan Administrative Office. However, in the first part of 1949 he was apparently assigned to the forces led by his former superior, Li Hsien-nien, who was then commanding troops in Hupeh. In any event, he was with Li in the spring when the Communists captured Wuhan, the Hupeh capital. Li was appointed as the provincial governor, with Wang as one of the vice-governors. He received another appointment in the Hupeh government in September 1950 when he was named a vice-chairman of the Hupeh Finance and Economics Committee, also chaired by Li Hsien-nien. In the interim, in early 1950, the Communists established a governmental organ known as the Central-South Military and Administrative Committee (CSMAC), with jurisdiction over six provinces, including Hupeh. Under the CSMAC, Wang was a member of the CSMAC's Finance and Economics Committee, retaining this position until shortly after the CSMAC was reorganized, in January 1953, into the Central-South Administrative Committee (CSAC). Following this reorganization, he was a member of the CSAC until its dissolution in 1954.

In early 1952, in the midst of the "three-anti" campaign being waged against corruption, waste, and bureaucracy, Wang was involved (though not adversely) in a major scandal that rocked the Party in Wuhan. Known as the "Sung Ying case" (see under Chang P'ing-hua), it involved the corrupt behavior of two Party members, Miss Sung Ying, the deputy director of the Wuhan Public Health Bureau, and Chou Chi-fang, a Wuhan vice-mayor. In the ensuing investigations, a number of local officials were dismissed from their jobs, expelled from the Party, or in several cases given prison sentences. Among those affected were Wuhan Mayor Wu Te-feng and the ranking municipal Party secretary, Chang P'ing-hua, both of whom were temporarily dismissed from their positions. In the ensuing reshuffle of personnel, Wang was transferred (February 1952) from his provincial vice-governorship to become a vice-mayor of Wuhan—once again serving under Li Hsien-nien, who was named at the same time as the mayor.

Further evidence of Wang's increasingly important role in Hupeh and Wuhan affairs comes from the fact that he received other new assignments in early 1952, just as the Sung Ying case was reaching its climax. By January 1952 he was a member of the Standing Committee of the Hupeh Party Committee, and in February he was named to chair the Wuhan "anti-corruption check-up committee"—presumably to prevent another major scandal. Finally, in the following month, he was named a member of the Central-South Anti-Epidemic Committee. At the time of the Sung Ying case, Li Hsien-nien had assumed the post of ranking secretary of the Wuhan Party Committee (in addition to being the new mayor). However, by early 1953 Wang was serving as both the acting mayor and as the ranking secretary. In late 1954 and early 1955, Wang relinquished both of these posts to other men. However, the transfer to Peking in mid-1954 of Li Hsien-nien, the most important political official in Hupeh, opened the way for more important tasks for Wang Jen-chung. By the fall of 1954 he had become the Hupeh Party first secretary. Soon after, in February 1955, he was elected to membership on the Hupeh Provincial People's Council (to which he was re-elected in September 1964) and as chairman of

the Hupeh Committee of the quasi-legislative CPPCC. He was re-elected to the latter post in June 1959 and September 1964.

In 1954 Wang received his first assignment at the national level when he was elected a deputy from Wuhan to the First NPC (1954–1959), and at the first two sessions of the NPC (1954 and 1955) he served on the *ad hoc* Motions Examination Committee. However, he was not re-elected to the Second NPC, which opened in April 1959. It was also in the mid-1950's that Wang began his rise to national prominence in Party affairs. At the Eighth Party Congress in September 1956 he spoke on Party leadership in industry, with particular reference to Hupeh. Wang's speech centered on a problem that had troubled Chinese industrial management in the mid-1950's, namely, the role of the Party committee within industrial enterprises. Following the Soviet model, the Chinese had been using a system of management which, Wang argued, had diluted the authority of the Party committee. He claimed that the "erroneous" policies in the latter half of 1953 had caused "serious losses" in industrial enterprises in Hupeh. By 1955, however, the Party had again gained control of the industrial system. Wang urged Party cadres to continue this control: "The Party committee must not relax its political leadership and turn itself into an administrative organ. The leading comrades of the Party committee must never confine themselves in the sea of administration." (A further discussion of Party control in industry is contained in the biography of Li Hsueh-feng, who also spoke on the subject at the Eighth Congress.) Less than two years later, at the second session of the Eighth Party Congress in May 1958, Wank was elected an alternate member of the Party Central Committee.

Wang was quite active in Hupeh during the "anti-rightist" campaign of 1957–58 and was a vigorous supporter of the Great Leap Forward from its beginnings in 1958. In the late 1950's and early 1960's in particular, he was often reported in the company of Mao Tse-tung when Mao made frequent visits to Wuhan. Because of the city's singular importance as a railway hub, a river port, and central China's leading industrial center, it has been visited with regularity by top Chinese officials and countless foreign guests. As a consequence, Wang received considerable press attention in connection with these visits. In addition, as Hupeh's senior Party official, he participated in the many *ad hoc* committees established to inspect agricultural and industrial production in the province; he was, for example, chairman of such a committee set up in February 1959. His work in Hupeh was given recognition in 1961 when the Party established the Central-South Bureau under First

Secretary T'ao Chu (q.v.); by November of that year Wang was identified as the second secretary. The bureau headquarters are located in Canton (where T'ao worked until 1966), and thus Wang was the senior bureau official in Wuhan. Two years later, in 1963, he became the political commissar of the Wuhan Military Region, which has jurisdiction over PLA forces in Hupeh and Honan.

Wang's work in Hupeh centered around Party affairs, but like many other top provincial leaders throughout China, he was also given a number of other titles (most of them presumably honorific). For example, from 1953 to 1955 he was chairman of the provincial chapter of the Sino-Soviet Friendship Association, and in mid-1954 he was made the head of a special headquarters to prevent flood damage in the Wuhan area. Similarly, in 1958 he was named to membership in the Wuhan chapter of the Union of Chinese Writers, and in the same year he was reported as a guest lecturer on political affairs at Wuhan University.

Wang was a more frequent contributor to the Party press than most provincial leaders, particularly in the period beginning in the late fifties. In the early stages of the famous Great Leap Forward, for example, he wrote an article for the *JMJP* (February 15, 1958), extolling the virtues of the new movement. For the June 1, 1958, issue of *Hung-ch'i* (Red flag), Wang wrote on the inevitability of "relying on the masses." This article was of no particular intrinsic significance, but because it was the inaugural issue of the Party's most important journal, it was symbolically important in terms of Wang's career. (Only a few days earlier, as noted above, he had been elected an alternate member of the Central Committee.) He also wrote on Party leadership and economic affairs for later issues of *Hung-ch'i* (January 1, 1961, and August 31, 1964).

Wang remained in Hupeh until 1966, and as of that date he was one of the relatively few important provincial officials who had remained in the same province since the establishment of the PRC in 1949. Then, in July 1966, during the earliest days of the Great Proletarian Cultural Revolution, he was brought to Peking and made a deputy head of the Cultural Revolution Group subordinate to the CCP Central Committee. A few weeks later (although he was still in Peking), he was further identified as the First Secretary of the Party's Central-South Bureau. This sudden rise to positions of great importance —all the more notable because he was only an alternate member of the Central Committee— gave way to an equally sudden fall in the closing days of the year. Wang's five-month long political rise and fall coincided almost exactly with the political fortunes of T'ao Chu. Therefore,

it was not surprising that the denunciations of Wang stressed his close ties with T'ao.

Wang Jo-fei

(1896–1946; An-shun hsien, Kweichow). Early member of CCP; member, CCP Central Committee.

Wang Jo-fei was one of the first members of the CCP and was among the influential group that took part in the work-and-study program in France during the early twenties. After further training in Moscow he returned to China to become a major figure in the stormy events that took place in Shanghai in the mid-twenties. He spent the years from 1928 to 1931 as a CCP delegate to the Comintern and soon after his return home was imprisoned in north China for more than five years. During the Sino-Japanese War Wang held key posts in Yenan and was also one of the Party's top negotiators with the Nationalists in the later war years and during the immediate postwar period. A member of the Fifth and Seventh Central Committees, Wang was killed in an air crash in 1946.

Wang was born in 1896 into a landlord family in An-shun hsien some 50 miles southwest of Kweiyang in Kweichow province. From his early boyhood Wang was reared by his uncle, Huang Ch'i-sheng, a man who was to influence Wang throughout his career and who died with him in the same air crash in 1946. Moving to Kweiyang, Wang enrolled in the Ta-te Primary School, which his uncle had founded. He got his first taste of revolutionary activity when he joined a students' guard unit during the 1911 Revolution, and a few years later he played a minor role in the actions taken by local military figures who were resisting Yuan Shih-k'ai's attempts to become the new emperor of China. Afterwards, Wang returned to the Ta-te school where he taught for a brief time. Then, having won a government scholarship to study in Japan, Wang left for Tokyo late in 1917. He spent about a year and a half there, but according to his own testimony he spent most of his time teaching himself even though he was nominally a student at Waseda University.

Like so many students of his generation, Wang claims to have been deeply influenced by the October Revolution in Russia and the May Fourth Movement in China. Therefore, immediately after the latter event erupted in May 1919 he returned home, going first to Kweichow. From there he went to Shansi in the company of his uncle, who was leading an "inspection mission" to Yen Hsi-shan's famed "model province," and then to Kiangsu to visit a model hsien. Wang then learned that he might take part in the work-and-study program in France, which was sponsored by Ts'ai Yuan-p'ei and other progressive national leaders. Having borrowed money, he left Shanghai in the fall of 1919 for France. Although he did not know them at the time, Wang sailed on the same ship that took such famous latter-day Communists to France as Ts'ai Ho-sen, his sister Ts'ai Ch'ang, and Hsiang Ching-yü (qq.v.).

Wang spent over three years in France (and a brief time in Belgium), but only three months of this time were devoted to formal studies. He spent the remainder of the period as a factory worker and political organizer together with Ts'ai Ho-sen, Chou En-lai, Chao Shih-yen, Ch'en Yen-nien, Li Li-san, Ch'en I (qq.v.), and a host of other student-workers. Few if any of them were more active than Wang in organizing political activities, including protests against the French government and Chinese diplomats stationed in France. For example, Chou En-lai and Wang were the leaders of a demonstration held in Paris in February 1921 to protest the termination of financial aid to the Chinese students. And later in the same year he was among the leaders of the so-called Lyons University demonstrations (see under Ch'en I). Wang was also one of the founders of the Socialist Youth League in the winter of 1921–22, a group that was reorganized into the European branch of the CCP in mid-1922. Also in 1922, Wang joined the French Communist Party (a fact ignored in most Chinese Communist accounts of Wang's life, but one mentioned by Wang himself), and in the same year he also became a member of the CCP. Under the organizational auspices of the Youth League (and later the European CCP branch), Wang and his worker-student colleagues founded *Shao-nien* (Youth) in Paris in August 1922. This important journal propagated communistic ideas and attacked other doctrines, such as anarchism, that were espoused by a number of the students in France.[1]

In late 1922 and early 1923 a number of Chinese students in France (many of them not Communists) journeyed to Moscow to study at the Communist University of the Toilers of the East. Wang was a member of a group of 12 students who went to the Soviet Union in the spring of 1923. He remained there for two years and was still in Moscow in March 1925 when the Comintern convened its Fifth Enlarged Plenum, a session that Wang appears to have attended. Within two months, however, he was back in China where he attended the Second National Congress of Labor in Canton, which established the All-China Federation of Labor and affiliated it with the Red International of Trade Unions (Profintern). From Canton he proceeded to north China where he became, by mid-1925, secretary of the Party's Honan-Shensi Regional Committee, a post that was presumably subordinate to Li Ta-chao's North China Regional Committee. The north China political situation at this time was extremely complex and was dominated by the intrigues of the feuding warlords, among them Feng Yü-hsiang, who was beginning to develop ties with both Soviet and Chinese Communists.[2] A number of Chinese Communists were then cooperating to some degree with Feng's Kuominchün (Nationalist Army), just as they were with the KMT in southern China. Wang is reported to have engaged in labor agitation at this time among the workers on the important Peking-Hankow and Lunghai Railways.[3]

Wang's tenure in north China was short-lived; by the latter part of 1925 he was transferred to Shanghai to become the Party's first secretary-general (*pi-shu-chang*), serving under Party General Secretary Ch'en Tu-hsiu (q.v.). Wang's fall from the Central Committee in 1928 (see below) may have been related to the alleged fact that he was on close terms with Ch'en Tu-hsiu. Wang is credited in Communist sources with a major role in the organization and leadership of strikes and insurrections in Shanghai in preparation for the arrival in that city of the National Revolutionary Army, which was advancing on the city during the course of the Northern Expedition (see under Chao Shih-yen). He remained there as secretary-general until April 1927 when the forces under Chiang Kai-shek suppressed the insurrections in Shanghai and executed a number of top Communists. At this juncture Wang made his way to Wuhan to attend the CCP's Fifth Congress, which elected him a member of the Central Committee. Immediately after the meetings adjourned in May, he was sent back to Shanghai where he directed propaganda activities for the Party's Kiangsu Provincial Committee. Then, following the Nanchang Uprising (see under Yeh T'ing) of August 1, 1927, which brought about the final break between the CCP and the KMT, Wang was among those who attended the important and controversial August 7 Emergency Conference (probably held in Hankow), which deposed Ch'en Tu-hsiu and elevated Ch'ü Ch'iu-pai to head the CCP. In the meantime, Kiangsu Provincial Secretary Ch'en Yen-nien, Wang's colleague in France, was apprehended and executed by the Nationalists. Wang was then dispatched to Shanghai again, this time to serve as a member of the Standing Committee of the Kiangsu CCP Committee, now headed by Teng Chung-hsia (q.v.). Like most Communist operatives in Shanghai during these dangerous days, Wang's activities over the following months are not well documented, but he is credited in Communist accounts with having organized peasant uprisings in the area around Wusih (Wu-hsi) and in northern Kiangsu at approximately the same time that Mao Tse-tung was a leader of the Autumn Harvest Uprisings in central China.

In the wake of the numerous disasters which beset the CCP throughout 1927, the Party underwent a period of self-examination that culminated in November when the Provisional Politburo (elected at the above-mentioned August 7 Emergency Conference) issued a resolution on Party discipline. The resolution reviewed the various "mistakes" that had been made in Shanghai and other cities, as well as the abortive Party-backed peasant uprisings. Moreover, the Politburo removed a number of Communist leaders (among them Mao Tse-tung) from various key posts and reprimanded others. Wang was among those reprimanded for his "mistakes in leadership."[4] This action against Wang also may have been related to his close ties with the now officially discredited Ch'en Tu-hsiu. In any event, he was under a political cloud in the summer of 1928 when he was in Moscow to attend the CCP's Sixth Congress. Wang failed to gain re-election to the Party's Central Committee, which soon came to be dominated by Li Li-san. Official Communist accounts of his career pointedly note that he was elected to the Fifth and Seventh Central Committees, but no mention is made of the Sixth; however, Chang Kuo-t'ao has claimed that Wang was elected an alternate member at this time.

Wang remained in Moscow for the next three years as a CCP delegate to the Comintern. As he prepared to return to China in 1931, Wang could look back upon a life that had kept him abroad for 10 of his 35 years and two thirds of his adult life, a career pattern that was quite unusual among the more important Chinese Communist leaders. During these many years abroad Wang had learned Japanese, French, and Russian, and another Communist who was imprisoned with Wang in the thirties (see below) recalled that though he knew very little English he studied the language while in prison.

Wang returned to China in mid-1931, going first to Kiangsi where Mao Tse-tung and others were establishing a rural base, and then to Inner Mongolia to "carry out armed struggles" in Shensi, Kansu, Ninghsia, and Suiyuan provinces, areas where the Communist movement was underdeveloped in contrast to the more revolutionary south. He was in Inner Mongolia only a few months when, disguised as a merchant and using the alias of Huang Ching-chai, he was arrested in Paotow shortly after having made contact with Ulanfu (q.v.), a top CCP operative in the area. This took place in October 1931, and for the next five and a half years Wang remained in prison, first in Paotow, then in Kweisui, and fianlly in Taiyuan. It was not until the late spring of 1937 that he was released from prison and placed under a kind of house arrest, in part through the efforts of Po I-po and K'o Ch'ing-shih (qq.v.). According to the Communist version of Wang's release, Shansi Governor Yen

Hsi-shan wanted him to remain in Shansi and work for him.[5] Wang refused, however, and then when war with Japan broke out a few weeks later, he was allowed to leave Taiyuan and under orders from Liu Shao-ch'i proceeded to Yenan. Over the remaining years of his life Wang held a number of important posts, the first of which was as director of the Propaganda Department for the Party's Shensi-Kansu-Ninghsia Regional Committee. In the period after 1939 he served successively as deputy chief-of-staff of the Communists' Eighth Route Army, secretary-general (pi-shu-chang) of the Central Committee's North China-Central China (hua-pei hua-chung) Work Committee, Central Committee secretary-general, and director of the Party's Research Office (Tang-wu yen-chiu shih). As these positions suggest, Wang's wartime activities were quite varied. In addition to research and writing on questions of guerrilla warfare and agrarian policies in the "liberated" areas, he made occasional trips from Yenan to other Communist bases, as in the fall of 1942 when he traveled to the Shansi-Suiyuan region. In the spring of 1945, at the Seventh Party Congress, Wang was once again elected to the Central Committee.

In the middle years of the war period Wang also began to make periodic visits to the liaison mission that Chou En-lai headed in Chungking, the Nationalist capital, and after the spring of 1944 he spent most of his time there in negotiations with both the Nationalists and American diplomats. At times (in the absence of Chou En-lai), he was the ranking Communist official in Chungking, as in June 1945 when he called on American Ambassador Patrick Hurley to discuss the possibilities for KMT–CCP cooperation. The famous China "White Paper" reveals the following paraphrase of Wang's remarks to Hurley: "General Wang stated frankly that real communism in China under present conditions was impossible. The General stated, however, with perfect candor that the Party now supported democratic principles but only as a stepping stone to a future communistic state."[6]

In August 1945 Wang accompanied Mao Tse-tung and Chou En-lai to Chungking to hold talks with Chiang Kai-shek, and in January 1946 he was a Communist delegate to the Political Consultative Conference, which was also held in Chungking. He remained there until April 8, 1946, when, on a flight from Chungking to Yenan, he was killed in a crash in Shansi that took the lives of Ch'in Pang-hsien, Yeh T'ing, Teng Fa (qq.v.), as well as Wang's uncle, Huang Ch'i-sheng.

Wang was survived by a seven-year-old son and by his wife, Li P'ei-chih, whom he had married in Honan in the fall of 1925. In the early thirties, when Wang was in prison, his wife worked with the Communists in Fukien.

Since 1949 she has held a number of fairly important posts in the CCP, the PRC national government, and the "mass" organizations. A member of the Executive Committee of the All-China Federation of Democratic Women since 1949, she was a member of the Supreme People's Court from 1949 to 1954 and has been a deputy from her native Hopeh since the latter year. In the early fifties Li was deputy director of studies at Chinese People's University in Peking and has been a vice-president of the school since April 1959. She received her most important post when the CCP expanded the size of its Central Control Commission at the 10th Plenum in September 1962 and appointed her as an alternate member.

The most valuable source material on Wang's career is found in a commemorative volume published by the Communist delegation in Chungking, of which he had been a member. Entitled *"Szu-pa" pei-nan lieh-shih chi-nien-ts'e* (In memory of the martyrs who died in the accident of April 8), it contains an official obituary, a brief autobiographical essay by Wang, and a number of useful sketches by former colleagues on various phases of his career. Wang's years of imprisonment are covered in considerable detail in *Wang Jo-fei tsai yü chung* (Wang Jo-fei in prison), written by Yang Chih-lin and Ch'iao Ming-fu and published in 1961; those sections contributed by Yang were published in English in 1962 under the title *Iron Bars but Not a Cage*.

1. Chow Tse-tsung, *Research Guide to the May Fourth Movement* (Cambridge, Mass., 1963), p. 113.

2. *Chinese Warlord, The Career of Feng Yü-hsiang* (Stanford, Calif., 1966), pp. 164ff.

3. C. Martin Wilbur and Julie Lien-ying How, eds., *Documents on Communism, Nationalism, and Soviet Advisers in China, 1918–1927* (New York, 1956), pp. 323–324.

4. Karl A. Wittfogel, "The Legend of 'Maoism,' " *The China Quarterly*, no. 2:16–34 (April–June 1960); Warren Kuo, *Analytical History of [the] Chinese Communist Party* (Taipei, Taiwan, 1966), pp. 476–479.

5. *JMJP*, August 14, 1962.

6. *United States Relations With China, With Special Reference to the Period 1944–1949* (Washington, D.C., 1949), pp. 103–104.

Wang Kuang-wei

Vice-chairman, State Planning Commission.

Wang Kuang-wei, one of Communist China's more important economic planners, has held senior posts in the State Planning Commission since its establishment in 1952. He first emerged as an administrator in the postwar period in Manchuria, serving in those portions of Nun-chiang province under Communist control. From 1946 to 1947 he was secretary-general of the Nunchiang Provincial Government as well as director of the government's Civil Affairs Department. Until abolished as a province by the Communists in late 1948, Nunchiang was subordinate to the multi-provincial government organ known as the Northeast Administrative Committee (NEAC). In 1949 Wang was serving as a deputy secretary-general of the NEAC, and when it was reorganized into the Northeast People's Government (NEPG) in August 1949 he retained this position. In September 1951 Wang assumed another NEPG administrative post, becoming director of its Staff Office. Concurrent with his work for the regionwide NEPG was Wang's post as secretary-general of the Kirin Provincial People's Government in 1951; in the same year he was secretary-general of the United Front Work Department of the CCP's Northeast Bureau.

Aside from an article for the *JMJP* of January 22, 1951, on one of China's first agricultural producer cooperatives and his leadership of a team to inspect spring plowing in the northeast in 1952, little information is available on Wang's work in Manchuria. In late 1952, in anticipation of the First Five-Year Plan which began in 1953, the Communists formed the State Planning Commission. By October 1953 Wang had been brought to Peking from the northeast to work in the commission as a deputy secretary-general. His rise in this important organization, the one charged with long-range economic planning, has been steady since he first joined it in 1953. When the commission was completely reorganized in September–October 1954 (during a general government reorganization), Wang was named as a commission member and by the following May was promoted to secretary-general. Then, in January 1956, Wang was again promoted, this time to a vice-chairmanship under Chairman Li Fu-ch'un, one of Peking's top economic specialists. Although there have been numerous changes within the commission, Wang has retained his vice-chairmanship and as of 1965 had been a vice-chairman longer than any other man. (He is, however, politically outranked as a vice-chairman by several top Party figures, including Politburo members Li Hsien-nien and T'an Chen-lin.)

In 1959 and 1960, Wang went abroad on two economic missions. In August–September 1959 he accompanied Party leader Hsi Chung-hsun to the USSR to attend an exhibition of economic achievements and from there journeyed to Brno, Czechoslovakia, for an international fair. In May 1960 Wang joined Chou En-lai in North Vietnam for official talks with Vietnamese leaders; no agreements were announced, but Wang's presence in Hanoi suggested that economic cooperation had been a major point for discussion. Wang's participation in international affairs seems to have centered on Vietnam because in January 1961 he again participated in talks with the Vietnamese. On this occasion in Peking the talks led to the conclusion of agreements regarding Chinese loans and the supply of various commodities by China to North Vietnam. Just prior to this agreement, Wang received another important assignment in the State Council when he was named (December 1960) as a deputy director of the Agricultural and Forestry Office, the organization which oversees the work of several ministries and bureaus. He continues to hold this position. Even before Wang received this appointment in agricultural affairs, it was already evident that he was specializing in this field of work. The evidence derives from his rather copious writings on agricultural matters for important journals. His more significant articles include: "How to Organize Agricultural Labor," *Chi-hua ching-chi* (Planned economy), August 9, 1957 (translated in *ECMM* 100); "Some of the Ways to Agricultural Development," *Hsueh-hsi* (Study), September 3, 1957; "Develop Agriculture to Speed Up Our Socialist Industrialization," Peking, *Ta-kung pao*, November 10, 1957; "On the Modernization of China's Agriculture," *Hsueh-hsi,* January 3, 1958; "Strengthen the Aid Given by Industry to Agriculture," *Hung-ch'i* (Red flag), August 16, 1959 (translated in *JPRS* 989-D; the same article also appeared in *JMJP,* August 17, 1959); "The Big Leap in China's Economy," *World Marxist Review* (Prague), June 1960. (The Sino-Soviet dispute was beginning to emerge at this time, and thus this was one of the last Chinese contributions to this international Communist magazine, generally regarded as the most important single journal of the Communist bloc.) "Actively and Steadily Carry Out the Technical Transformation of Agriculture," *Ching-chi yen-chiu* (Economic research), March 17, 1963. (This article was singled out for praise in the December 17, 1963, issue of the same journal.)

In September 1964 Wang was elected as a deputy from Shantung to the Third NPC, which held its first session in December 1964–January 1965. In March and April 1965 he spent a month in Africa as a member of an NPC delegation led by Liu Ning-i, an NPC Vice-Chairman and a Party Central Committee member. Wang was the only member of the delegation specializing in economic work. The group visited Guinea, Mali, the Central African Republic, the Congo (Brazzaville), and Ghana. Although Wang is infrequently mentioned in the press, his stature can be gauged in part from the importance of the positions he holds in the government hierarchy and from the frequency of his contributions to important newspapers and journals.

Wang Kuo-ch'üan

(Honan). Former Party official; diplomat.

Wang Kuo-ch'üan, a native of Honan, was an important Party official in the 1950's until his transfer to the diplomatic service in 1957. He was not identified until 1949 when he attended the first session of the CPPCC, the organization that brought the PRC into existence in September. Wang attended this session as a representative of "peasant organizations" from one of the "liberated areas"; therefore he had probably been engaged in Party work in rural areas. By early 1950 he was serving as the ranking Party secretary for Jehol province, a position he was to hold for six years. In December 1955 Jehol was abolished, with its territory being incorporated into Inner Mongolia, Hopeh, and Liaoning. But before it was dissolved, Wang held almost all positions of importance in the province. He was named in June 1951 to the Jehol Provincial People's Government and two months later was named to chair the provincial Economic Planning Committee. He relinquished the latter post in January 1953, but then in February 1955 he succeeded to the provincial governorship. In the same month he was also elected chairman of the First Jehol Committee of the quasi-legislative CPPCC. Finally, he was elected as a Jehol deputy to the First NPC (1954–1959).

Little is known about Wang's work in Jehol. However, he did contribute an article about the provincial "struggle against bureaucratism," which appeared in the June 13, 1953, issue of the Shenyang (Mukden) *Tung-pei jih-pao* (Northeast daily) and a major report on provincial affairs delivered at the congress session in February 1955, at which time he became the Jehol governor. Wang surrendered all his positions in Jehol, of course, when the province was abolished in December 1955, although apparently the deputies from Jehol (Wang among them) were allowed to sit in the NPC even after the province was dissolved.

In June 1957 Wang was named to succeed Tseng Yung-ch'üan (q.v.) as ambassador to East Germany, a position he formally assumed in August of that year and one in which he would remain for six and a half years. His tour there was largely uneventful, the published record revealing mainly the normal negotiations of agreements and attendance at various protocol functions. The agreements or protocols signed by Wang included one related to public health (December 1957), a trade protocol (March 1960), and a cultural cooperation agreement (August 1962), each of these being signed in Germany. He also participated in talks in Peking held with East German Prime Minister Otto Grotewohl in January 1959, negotiations that culminated in a consular convention and a long-term trade agreement. On five occasions

(1958, 1959, 1960, 1962, 1963) he was an official PRC representative to the important annual Leipzig spring trade fair.

During his tenure in Berlin, several top Chinese Communist officials visited there. For example, Tung Pi-wu was in Berlin in July 1958 for the Fifth Congress of the East German Socialist Unity (Communist) Party, and Nieh Jung-chen and Ho Lung led PRC delegations to the 10th and 12th anniversary celebrations of the "German Democratic Republic" in 1959 and 1961, respectively. Yet it is almost certain that the major highlight of his stay in Berlin occurred in January 1963 when Wu Hsiu-ch'üan was in Germany for the Sixth Congress of the Socialist Unity Party. This was the last of four congresses in East Europe attended by Wu, each of which featured violent verbal battles between the Chinese and Soviet delegates as part of the Sino-Soviet rift (see under Wu Hsiu-ch'üan). Chinese–East German government-to-government relations ostensibly remained the same after this congress (where the Germans had openly sided with the Russians), but in fact relations deteriorated during Wang's last year in Berlin. The deterioration was perhaps best illustrated by a rather bizarre occurrence in December 1963, just a month before Wang left for home. According to a Western news source, Wang had the locks in the Chinese embassy changed by locksmiths called in from West Germany.[1]

Early in 1964 Wang and his wife left Berlin for home; he was formally replaced in February by Chang Hai-feng. Just two months later he was named to succeed Wang Ping-nan (q.v.) as ambassador to Poland. He presented his credentials in Warsaw in July 1964. The assignment in Poland has been of peculiar significance since 1955 because from that year the Chinese ambassador in Warsaw has been the negotiator for the Chinese side in the Sino-American "ambassadorial-level" talks (see under Wang Ping-nan). By the time of Wang Kuo-ch'üan's arrival in 1964 these talks had assumed added significance in view of the intensification of the war in Vietnam. Wang held his first talk with his American counterpart, Ambassador John Cabot, on July 29, 1964; it was the 123rd such session held between the two sides. If the assignment of Wang to these talks is not an attestation of his abilities, it is at least an affirmation by the Peking hierarchy of their trust in his loyalty. A reporter for the London *Observer* (September 19, 1965) described Ambassador Wang as a "neatly attired" six-footer in his fifties, who had once been a political commissar in the Chinese Red Army.

As a general practice men stationed abroad do not serve in the NPC. An exception seems to have been made in the case of Wang, who, as already noted, was a Jehol deputy to the First NPC (1954–1959). While in Germany he was named to the Second NPC (1959–1964) as a deputy from Hopeh (one of the provinces that absorbed a portion of Jehol). And soon after his arrival in Warsaw he was named as a deputy from his native Honan to the Third NPC, which opened in December 1964.

1. *Hong Kong Tiger-Standard,* December 21, 1963.

Wang Ming, see **Ch'en Shao-yü**

Wang Pi-ch'eng

(Hunan). Deputy-commander, Nanking Military Region.

Wang Pi-ch'eng is a native of Hunan where his family were said to have been poor peasants. Nothing is known of his early history until the time of the Sino-Japanese War when he belonged to the Communist New Fourth Army and served as a commander in the First Division commanded by Su Yü (q.v.). This must have happened following the New Fourth Army Incident of January 1941 when the top command of the New Fourth Army was reorganized and Su Yü was put in charge of the First Division, which operated in the Central Kiangsu Military District between Huai-an and the Yangtze. The area lies east of the Grand Canal. Later in the war Su expanded his territory to include the Kiangsu-Chekiang border region, and from 1944 to 1945 Su was the commander of the Kiangsu-Chekiang Military District. Wang served on Su's staff for the remaining years of the war and for some five years after the war ended continued to be associated with his wartime chief. From 1941 Wang headed the Second Brigade of Su Yü's First Division and successively commanded the Second and then the Third Military Sub-districts of the Kiangsu-Chekiang Military District.

After these earlier war years nothing further was heard of Wang's activity until 1947 when he was identified as the commander of the Sixth Division belonging to the New Fourth Army forces, which became the East China PLA in 1947 and the Third Field Army early in 1949 (see under Ch'en I). For about five years after hostilities ended in August 1945, Wang remained in the Kiangsu-Chekiang Military Area; he was the commander of the Sixth Column of the East China PLA in 1948, probably an extension of the military command he held in 1947. He was in charge of troops stationed about Hangchow early in 1949 when he was identified as the commander of the Seventh Army Group belonging to the Third Field Army; T'an Chen-lin (q.v.), with whom Wang was to continue to be associated for several years, was the army group political commissar. Concurrent

with Wang's post as Seventh Army Group commander was his position of commander in the
24th Army, which belonged to the Seventh Army
Group. Also from 1949 and possibly until 1953,
Wang was the deputy commander of the
Chekiang Military District, an area that was also
under the jurisdiction of the Third Field Army.
By April 1949 Wang Chien-an took over the
command of the Seventh Army Group from
Wang Pi-ch'eng. Wang Chien-an had formerly
commanded East China PLA forces in the Central Shantung Military District. In 1951, another
former New Fourth Army officer, Chang Ai-
p'ing (q.v.), became the commander of the
Chekiang Military District. Wang was active in
the Nanking area in 1950 when he was put in
charge of the Eighth Army Group of the Third
Field Army, the force which had been operating around Nanking at least from the time
that the Communists took over that city in
April 1949. His name was mentioned in connection with the Eighth Group only in 1950,
so he probably did not hold this command for
long.

After a career that seems to have been devoted exclusively to military affairs, Wang received his first civil position in February 1951
when he was appointed a member of the
Chekiang Provincial People's Government, a
post that placed him under his former military
comrade-in-arms, Governor T'an Chen-lin.
Then, for a long period, Wang's activities went
unreported in the Communist press. He re-
emerged in September–October 1954 when he
led a 72-member delegation of the Communist
forces in Korea (known as the "Chinese People's Volunteers") to China to attend the
elaborate festivities staged to commemorate the
fifth anniversary of the PRC. His long absence
from the scene in China suggests that he may
have commanded troops during the Korean War.

By the latter part of 1955 Wang had permanently returned to China, once again being assigned to work in east China. By December
1955 he was identified as the Shanghai Garrison
commander, a post he held until early 1961.
Shortly before this identification, the PRC had
given personal military ranks to its officer corps,
and by early 1956 Wang was identified as a
lieutenant-general (the equivalent of a two-star
general in the U.S. Army). During his years in
Shanghai, Wang was frequently mentioned in
the press, particularly in connection with visiting military delegations. For example, he was
among those welcoming units of a visiting Soviet
naval fleet in June 1956. In January 1957 he
was named to membership on the Shanghai
Municipal People's Council; he was re-elected
in November 1958 but relinquished the position
in 1961 when he was transferred to Nanking
(see below). During his tour of duty in Shanghai, he also held membership on the Council of

the Shanghai chapter of the Sino-Soviet Friendship Association (from December 1959).

As in the case of most officers of his rank,
Wang frequently spoke before conferences held
by the Party or other organizations. Thus, in
May 1957, he spoke at a Party Congress of the
Shanghai Garrison Command on the traditions
of the PLA and the need for physical fitness,
and in March 1960 he spoke before a conference of the people's militia in Shanghai. From
time to time he also wrote for the Party press,
an example of which appeared in the September
23, 1959, issue of the Shanghai *Chieh-fang jih-
pao* (Liberation daily), where Wang stressed
the dual role of the PLA in defending the "people" and in participating in construction proj-
ects. After more than five years in Shanghai,
Wang was transferred to Nanking in the spring
of 1961.

When Wang was first identified in Nanking
at a May Day (1961) rally, he was simply
described as "a commanding officer" of the
Nanking Military Region (NMR), responsible
for the provinces of Kiangsu (including Shanghai), Chekiang, and Anhwei. By early 1964 his
position was clarified as that of a deputy commander of the NMR; in fact, however, he was
probably holding this post from the time of his
transfer to Nanking in 1961. In Nanking, Wang
serves under Commander Hsu Shih-yu (q.v.),
an alternate member of the Party Central Committee. The NMR is one of the most important
of the military commands because, in addition
to controlling two key communication points
(Shanghai and Nanking), Nanking is the locale
of some of the important PLA military academies. Wang received his first assignment in
the national government when he was elected
as a deputy from the PLA to the Third NPC,
the first session of which met in December
1964–January 1965.

Wang P'ing

(c.1911–   ; Juichin, Kiangsi). Veteran political officer; political commissar, Nanking Military Region.

A Red Army officer from the early thirties,
Wang P'ing made the Long March and took
part in the Sino-Japanese War as a political
officer and Party official in the Shansi-Chahar-
Hopeh area. He served in north China during
the early years of the PRC and then spent five
years in Korea with the Chinese People's Volunteers before returning home to become political
commissar of the Nanking Military Region.
Wang was born in Juichin, the capital of the
Soviet base that Mao Tse-tung and Chu Te
held until the Long March began in the fall of
1934. Wang would have been in his late teens
when the Chu-Mao forces were established in
and around his native Juichin, and it was prob-

ably there that he joined the Communists. He was, in any event, with the Red Army on the Long March, serving as head of the Political Department of the Third Army Corps, a major component of the Long March forces led by P'eng Te-huai. In mid-1935, as Wang's unit was moving north through Szechwan, he negotiated an agreement with the Yi peoples (a national minority group) to allow the Long Marchers safe passage through the area.[1]

Japanese sources report that Wang graduated from the first class of the Red Army Academy (Hung-chün ta-hsueh); this may refer to the academy established in 1933 on the outskirts of Juichin, but it more probably refers to the school of the same name that the Communists re-established in north Shensi in mid-1936. When war with Japan broke out in mid-1937, Wang was assigned to Lin Piao's 115th Division, one of the three major units in the Communists' Eighth Route Army. In the fall he participated in the battle at P'ing-hsing Pass in northern Shansi, a much-celebrated battle in Communist annals and one of the few won by Chinese forces during the war (see under Lin Piao). After this, Wang was sent into the Fou-p'ing area in western Hopeh where he became chairman of a "mobilization committee" that was established to organize the peasantry into self-defense units. Not long after these events, U.S. Naval Observer Evans Carlson interviewed a colleague of Wang's who told him: "Wang P'ing went around to the various villages and counties organizing mobilization committees and propaganda groups. The old civil administration had broken down because most of the officials had fled before the invaders. It was necessary to restore order and convince the people that by cooperating they would resist successfully."[2] At approximately this time Wang became a political commissar in the forces led by Lü Cheng-ts'ao (q.v.), a Manchurian military leader who had joined the Communists soon after the war began and whose units were placed under the jurisdiction of the 115th Division. To consolidate their position in the area, the Communists established the Shansi-Chahar-Hopeh (Chin-Ch'a-Chi) Border Region in January 1938 at Fou-p'ing. In addition to the Border Region Government (see under Sung Shao-wen, the chairman), they set up a Party Committee for the area. Wang was made a committee member, thus being placed in the company of such top Communists as Lin Piao, Ho Lung, Nieh Jung-chen, and P'eng Chen.[3] Nothing further was reported about his wartime activities, but he probably remained in the Chin-Ch'a-Chi area as a political officer and Party organizer.

With the assistance of U.S. Special Envoy George C. Marshall, a cease-fire agreement was signed in January 1946 to bring a halt to the fighting between Communist and Nationalist forces, and to enforce the agreement field teams were posted in various parts of China, each of which had an American, a Chinese Nationalist, and a Chinese Communist representative. Holding the simulated rank of lieutenant colonel, Wang served briefly in 1946 as the Chinese Communist delegate to the field team stationed in Hai-lung hsien, located about 125 miles northeast of Mukden. But when the truce broke down completely over the 1946–47 winter he was transferred to Lin Piao's forces in Manchuria where he commanded a regiment and later a division. Lin's armies pushed from Manchuria into China proper in the closing days of 1948; most of his units pushed directly southward, but Wang was assigned to Chahar, an area with which he was familiar from his previous service. From 1949 to an unknown date he was chairman of the Military Control Commission in Ta-t'ung, Chahar, an important rail junction on the line between Kalgan and Taiyuan, the Shansi capital. Concurrently, from 1949 to 1952 he was commander of the Chahar Military District. In addition to these military posts, Wang received his first civil assignment in July 1950 when he was appointed as a vice-governor of Chahar, serving here under Chang Su (q.v.), another political-military veteran with extensive experience in north China. Less than two months later he became director of the Chahar Government's Public Security Office. In July 1951 Wang was removed from the security post and the vice-governorship, and then very little was heard of his activities until March 1953 when he was identified as director of the Cadres' (personnel) Department under the North China Military Region (NCMR). In effect, this was a transfer within the same overall military organization, for until Chahar province was abolished in November 1952 the provincial military district had come under the NCMR. Wang worked in the NCMR under his old superior from the Chin-Ch'a-Chi Border Region days, Nieh Jung-chen. However, he did not long remain in Peking, the headquarters of the NCMR, because in the latter part of 1953, not long after the Korean War had ended (July), Wang was transferred to North Korea to serve with the Chinese People's Volunteers (CPV), as the PLA forces in Korea were known.

Wang remained in Korea for five years, a tour of duty matched by few other senior officers in the PLA. During the first years he was there relatively little was reported in the Chinese press about his activities, one of the few occasions being in October 1954 when he led a delegation from the CPV headquarters to celebrations in Pyongyang marking the fourth anniversary of China's entry into the Korean War. It was not until August 1957 that he was identified as the

CPV political commissar, a position he assumed from Li Chih-min (q.v.). In the meantime, when the PRC presented its Red Army veterans with military honors and personal ranks in September 1955, Wang received the Orders of Independence and Freedom and of Liberation, awards covering Red Army service from 1937 to 1950, and he was made a colonel general (equivalent to a three-star U.S. Army general).

In the latter part of February 1958 an important delegation led by Chou En-lai went to Korea to arrange for the withdrawal of the CPV, negotiations in which Wang doubtless played a leading role. Until this time the Chinese press had been relatively quiet about the activities of the CPV, but after the withdrawal agreement was reached, the Chinese newspapers gave extensive coverage to the staged departure of Chinese troops over the next half year. The motivation for this obviously derived in part from a desire to show that Chinese forces were being transferred home while U.S. forces continued to "occupy" South Korea. Wang himself was mentioned on numerous occasions (e.g., attending a round of farewell banquets), and on the eve of his departure in October 1958 he was given the Korean government's highest award, the Korean National Flag Order. He and other top CPV commanders were feted in Peking in the days immediately following their return home, and Wang wrote a highly propagandistic article for the *JMJP* (November 4, 1958) entitled "The Volunteers—Witnesses of the Paper Tiger."

Shortly before Wang returned to China he had been elected to the Second NPC as a deputy from the CPV. Such representation, of course, became largely nominal when in early 1959 he was assigned to the Nanking Military Region (NMR) as the political commissar, a position he still retains. Responsible for military affairs in Kiangsu, Chekiang, Anhwei, and Shanghai, the NMR is one of the most important military regions; it is also the locale of a number of top military academies and training schools. In the same month that he took up his new assignment (April 1959), Wang was elected to membership on the PRC's National Defense Council, an organization of nominal power and authority, but one of considerable prestige. He was reappointed to the Council in January 1965 and continues to hold the post. Wang was first identified in April 1962 as political commissar of the PLA Military Academy (Chün-shih hsueh-yuan) in Nanking, one of the Communists' top training institutes and the approximate counterpart of a Western command and staff school. He succeeded Chung Ch'i-kuang (q.v.) in this post and apparently still holds it. There is much uncertainty about military institutes in China; Li Chih-min, for example, was identified as political commissar of

the "Military Academy" (also Chün-shih hsueh-yuan) in 1963, but Li clearly works in Peking. Consequently, Wang seems to be the senior political officer of the Military Academy "at Nanking," whereas Li is political commissar of the Academy "at Peking." In any event, the Chinese press continues to associate Wang with the Nanking Academy, although in generic language, that is, ". . . of the Academy." Wang had also assumed a civil post by September 1964 when he was identified as a Nanking vice-mayor; at this same time he was re-elected to the Third NPC, which opened in December 1964, on this occasion as a PLA deputy from the NMR. Presumably for reasons of security, the Chinese press is extremely guarded in its coverage of the PLA officers corps (ceremonial occasions excepted), and as a consequence, Wang's activities in Nanking are infrequently reported. But it is clear that he spends most of his time there, only occasionally going to Peking.

Since returning from Korea in 1958, Wang P'ing has been abroad three times, twice returning to Korea and once traveling to Africa. His first return trip to Korea was as a member of Ho Lung's military "goodwill" mission of October–November 1960. He was there again in April–May 1963 when Politburo member P'eng Chen led a 10-man NPC delegation to Pyongyang. Wang was in Africa from March to April 1965 as deputy leader under Liu Ning-i (q.v.) of another parliamentary group that visited Guinea, Mali, the Central African Republic, the Congo (Brazzaville), and Ghana.

1. Chang Ai-p'ing, *Ts'ung Tsun-i tao Ta-tu Ho* (From Tsun-i to the Ta-tu River; Hong Kong, 1960), p. 35.
2. Evans Fordyce Carlson, *Twin Stars of China* (New York, 1940), p. 236.
3. Chalmers A. Johnson, *Peasant Nationalism and Communist Power* (Stanford, Calif., 1962), p. 101.

Wang Ping-chang

(c.1908–   ; Hunan). Air Force officer; minister, Seventh Ministry of Machine Building.

There is some confusion about the identification of Wang Ping-chang, for there appear to be two men by this name born only a few years apart. Japanese sources list a Wang Ping-chang born in Hunan about 1908 who later attended a Red Army academy in Moscow. A Wang Ping-chang is listed in the student directory of the well-known Whampoa Military Academy at Canton; this Wang, a native of Inner Mongolia, was born in 1902.[1] Allowing for discrepancies in reporting birth dates, both reports could refer to the same man. This, however, seems unlikely. As a graduate of Whampoa, from which many cadets entered the CCP in the middle 1920's, a man would probably have been eligible for all three top national military honors (initially awarded in 1955), each of these awards being for service during a distinct period in the years between 1927 and 1950. In 1955 Wang Ping-chang won only the Liberation Order, that given for service from 1945 to 1950. This would seem more appropriate for the man whose career is given here, who it is assumed did not attend Whampoa.

Although the Chinese Air Force existed chiefly on paper in 1949, Wang was already associated with it in some capacity. It was as a representative of the Air Force that he was named to the preparatory committee of the All-China Athletic Federation (ACAF) when it was formed in October 1949. Wang was not heard of again until the ACAF was established on a permanent basis in June 1952, at which time he was named to its National Committee. (He was not re-elected, however, at the next congress in October 1956.) It was also in mid-1952 that Wang was identified as a deputy commander of the Air Force in the Central-South Military Region. However, he was soon in Peking attending a national sports meet sponsored by the PLA in commemoration of the 25th anniversary of the Red Army (a holiday falling on August 1); Wang has been in Peking continuously since that time.

His first assignment in Peking (noted by September 1952) was as chief-of-staff of the Air Force. Massive Soviet assistance following the Chinese entry into the Korean War (October 1950) had brought about such a rapid growth of the Chinese Air Force that, by the end of the war in mid-1953, it was one of the world's largest. By the following March (1953), Wang was promoted to be one of the deputy commanders of the Air Force under Liu Ya-lou, the father of the modern Chinese Air Force and its only commander until his death in 1965. This identification of Wang in early 1953 occurred when he was named to Chou En-lai's delegation to the funeral of Stalin in Moscow. Chou returned to Peking quickly, but Wang remained in Moscow for a few weeks longer, and in April 1953 he accompanied Minister of Foreign Trade Yeh Chi-chuang, then negotiating in Moscow, to Hungary for celebrations marking the eighth anniversary of the victory over Germany.

Wang's work in the Air Force was rewarded in 1954 and 1955 with an appointment and a military award. In September 1954 he was named to membership on the newly formed National Defense Council, a military advisory body with little power but considerable prestige. He was subsequently renamed to the council in April 1959 and January 1965. The military award was the above-mentioned Order of Liberation, given for distinguished military service

during the years 1945 to 1950. Personal military ranks were also created at this time; Wang was made a lieutenant general of the Air Force (equivalent to a two-star general in the U.S. Air Force).

In the mid-1950's Wang was mentioned in the national press regularly in the performance of such activities as entertaining foreign visitors, negotiating agreements, or attending conferences. For example, he attended a party for visiting Burmese Premier U Nu in December 1954 and later that month welcomed a Soviet delegation that had arrived to negotiate a civil air agreement. Wang presumably took part in these negotiations, which led to the signing of a civil air service agreement in late December 1954. In March 1955 he gave the opening address before the first congress of Air Force "heroes and models." Wang took his second trip abroad in October–November 1956 when he was a member of a military delegation led by General Teng Hua (q.v.) to Yugoslavia. Following this, very little was heard of him for several years, although he was reappointed to the National Defense Council in 1959. He began to reappear at public functions again in 1961, and in 1964 was elected as an Air Force deputy to the Third NPC, which held its first session in December 1964–January 1965. At the close of this session, Wang was named to head the newly created Seventh Ministry of Machine Building, a ministry probably engaged in the production of aeronautical equipment. It is not clear if Wang has retained his post as deputy commander of the Air Force.

1. *Huang-p'u t'ung-hsueh tsung-ming-ts'e* (Whampoa student directory; n.p., 1933), p. 130.

Wang Ping-nan

(1906–   ; San-yuan hsien, Shensi). Veteran diplomat; vice-minister, Ministry of Foreign Affairs.

One of the PRC's best-known diplomats, Wang Ping-nan has worked closely with Chou En-lai since the mid-thirties. He has been with the Foreign Ministry since the establishment of the PRC in 1949, and from 1955 to 1964 he was concurrently ambassador to Poland and the senior Chinese representative to the Sino-American ambassadorial-level negotiations held in Geneva and then Warsaw to discuss outstanding issues between the United States and the PRC.

Wang was born into a rich landlord family in San-yuan hsien, a few miles north of Sian, the Shensi provincial capital. His father, Wang Pao-shan, was an intimate friend of the powerful Shensi warlord Yang Hu-ch'eng, an association that was to be beneficial to young Wang.[1] He is also said to have known Yü Yu-jen, another native of San-yuan who was an important

T'ung-meng hui and KMT leader. Yü, a man of progressive ideas, was prominent in educational circles in Shensi from about 1918 to 1922 when Wang was in his teens. Wang graduated from a military academy in Loyang, Honan, and then studied in Japan from 1929 to 1930, after which he reportedly worked as a secretary to Yang Hu-ch'eng for a brief time. According to his former wife's account, Wang was by this time a Communist Party member, having joined, presumably in secret, in 1925.[2]

In 1931 Wang went to Germany where he studied sociology at the University of Berlin until 1935, and as a consequence of his training he is fluent in German and has a halting knowledge of English. He was active in Berlin as a leader of Chinese youths studying there and as a member of the Berlin branch of the Communist Third International, better known as the Comintern. During his years in Berlin he came to know a German girl, Anna von Kleist, an accomplished linguist whose name has frequently been associated with the Comintern. They were married while on a visit to London in 1935,[3] and in the late thirties and early forties Mme. Wang was well known to Westerners in China in her capacity as a secretary to Mme. Sun Yat-sen.

The Wangs left Berlin for China in February 1936, stopping over in Moscow where, according to American journalist Edgar Snow, Wang Ping-nan conferred with Ch'en Shao-yü, the CCP representative to the Comintern, about the political situation in northwest China.[4] Wang agreed that he would attempt to persuade Yang Hu-ch'eng, then the Nationalists' "pacification commissioner" of the northwest, to join the united front that had been basic Comintern policy since 1935. Wang arrived in Peking in March 1936 and quickly went to Sian to contact Yang. He apparently succeeded in his assignment with little difficulty, probably because Yang, though nominally subordinate to Chiang Kai-shek, had little interest in implementing Chiang's orders to crush Mao Tse-tung's Communists in north Shensi, preferring to cooperate with the Red forces to resist Japanese encroachments in north China. Under the previous arrangements made in Moscow with Ch'en Shao-yü, Wang notified Ch'en of the success of his talks with Yang Hu-ch'eng. A Comintern agent was then supposed to have contacted Yang, but when Ch'en Shao-yü failed to respond to the repeated communications from Wang Ping-nan, Yang made his contacts directly with the Communists in north Shensi. In any case, by mid-1936 Wang was serving under Yang as his "chief Communist liaison" man and in this capacity was an important link in helping Edgar Snow reach the Communist-held areas of Shensi where he was to get the material for his classic *Red Star over China*. Wang was probably taking orders from Teng Fa

(q.v.), a veteran of the Communist intelligence and underground network who was then working in Sian.[5]

As an associate of Yang Hu-ch'eng's, though under CCP direction, Wang was involved in the famous Sian Incident when Chiang Kai-shek was kidnapped in December 1936 by Yang Hu-ch'eng and warlord Chang Hsueh-liang (see under Chou En-lai). Not long after the outbreak of the Sino-Japanese War in mid-1937, Wang was sent to Chungking, and because his CCP membership was still not publicly known, he was able to hold minor posts in the KMT and to serve (in 1939) as a secretary of the People's Foreign Relations Association, an organization initially formed in Hankow in 1938, which engaged in foreign policy research and published materials in both Chinese and English. He also served as a liaison man for the Communists' Eighth Route Army and by 1942, his Party membership now made public, he became a secretary and spokesman for Chou En-lai, the Communists' senior representative in Chungking during the war years.

Except for a time in mid-1945 when he was briefly in India with his wife engaging in Communist activities (the details of which are unknown), Wang remained with Chou En-lai as a top assistant throughout the war and postwar period, thereby becoming a member of Chou's coterie, a group that includes such prominent foreign affairs specialists as Chang Han-fu, Ch'iao Kuan-hua, and Ch'en Chia-k'ang (qq.v.). Wang was in frequent contact with Westerners in Chungking, Nanking, and Shanghai, and particularly with Americans during the period of the Marshall Mission from the end of 1945 to early 1947.[6] Finally, when the January 1946 cease-fire agreement worked out under the auspices of U.S. Special Envoy George C. Marshall collapsed, Wang was among those evacuated to Yenan in late February 1947.

Wang's activities in the late forties are not documented in detail, but it is known that he was the deputy director of the Foreign Affairs Section of the CCP Central Committee. By no later than the summer of 1949 he was in Peking where he participated in various conferences to establish "mass" organizations under the Communist regime. Thus, in June he became a Preparatory Committee member of the China New Legal Research Society and in September a Standing Committee member of the China New Political Science Association's Preparatory Committee. He was also a Preparatory Committee member of the Sino-Soviet Friendship Association (SSFA) from July to October when he was named to the SSFA's First Executive Board, holding this post until December 1954. Soon after the central government was inaugurated in October 1949, he was appointed director of the Foreign Ministry's Staff Office, the position that was to occupy most of his time over the next five years. The exact nature of his duties in this post are not known, but he apparently served as Foreign Minister Chou En-lai's administrative chief. He was frequently mentioned in the press in connection with visits to China by foreign dignitaries, as when Mongolian Premier Tsedenbal visited China in the fall of 1952, or when Indian Prime Minister Nehru was in China two years later. Concurrent with his Foreign Ministry responsibilities was Wang's Board membership of the Chinese People's Institute of Foreign Affairs from its formation in December 1949 to 1955 (see under Chang Hsi-jo, the president).

From April to July 1954 Wang was secretary-general of Chou En-lai's delegation to the Geneva Conference, which brought an end to fighting between the French and the Communist forces of Ho Chi-minh in Indochina. In October of the same year he was appointed an assistant-minister of Foreign Affairs (one rank below a vice-minister). He retained his Foreign Ministry Staff Office directorship, but then in January 1955 he was relieved of both posts and appointed ambassador to Poland, replacing Tseng Yung-ch'üan (q.v.). Wang presented his credentials in Warsaw in March, remaining there for nine years, the longest continuous tour in a single country by any PRC ambassador. Less than two months after his arrival, he attended the first meeting of the Warsaw Pact as a member of Defense Minister P'eng Te-huai's delegation. Because the PRC is not a member of the Pact, the Chinese attended as observers (see under P'eng Te-huai). In July 1955 Wang was a member of Ho Lung's delegation brought from China to attend the celebrations in Warsaw marking the 10th anniversary of the Polish People's Republic, and in March 1959 he attended the Third Congress of the Polish United Workers' (Communist) Party as a member of Chu Te's delegation.

In July 1955 Wang was named as China's representative to the so-called ambassadorial-level talks between the United States and the PRC. Three months earlier, at the close of the Bandung Conference, Chou En-lai had announced Peking's willingness to undertake these talks, which were designed to settle outstanding issues between the United States and China. The negotiations began on August 1, 1955, in Geneva, with American Representative U. Alexis Johnson commuting from his ambassadorial post in Prague, and Wang traveling from Warsaw. The talks began on a promising note when each side agreed to release the nationals of the other side held in its country. (Most of the Americans in China were being held in prison, but the Chinese in the United States were merely forbidden to leave the country.) Although both sides had agreed to hold their talks in private, it soon became apparent that little progress was being made on other issues—principally the problem of the status of Taiwan, a question on which both nations remained adamant.

The talks dragged on until December 1957 when Ambassador Johnson was transferred. The Chinese protested that the new American delegate was not of "ambassadorial" rank (which, technically, was correct), and broke off the talks. The negotiations remained suspended until mid-1958 when the so-called "off-shore islands" crisis (involving the shelling of Matsu and Quemoy Islands by the Communists) had the effect of bringing both sides together again. The meetings were now transferred to Warsaw where Wang began talks with the new American envoy, Jacob Beam, on September 15, 1958. Beam, in turn, was replaced by Ambassador John Cabot, who first negotiated with Wang on March 1, 1962; the talks were still continuing when Wang was recalled to Peking two years later. In all, Wang took part in 120 meetings during his nine-year tour as the Chinese representative.

The importance of the Geneva-Warsaw talks is best measured by noting that they have been the only direct and regular diplomatic channel between the United States and Communist China since the establishment of the PRC in 1949. Non-Communist diplomats who have been stationed in Peking have frequently commented in private conversations that the United States probably has better and more direct contacts with the Chinese through the ambassadorial talks than most non-Communist diplomats in Peking who have been isolated in many respects from top PRC officials. However, because of the aforementioned privacy of the talks, little is known in detail about the negotiations. The best account of the talks is probably that written by veteran American diplomat Kenneth T. Young, who concluded that they are of genuine value, having already served to lessen tensions in situations that might otherwise have grown into serious crises.[7]

Apart from his role in the Sino-American talks, Wang was also one of Peking's senior diplomats in Europe during a period that witnessed historic events and saw the evolution of Eastern Europe away from the total Soviet domination of the early fifties. Poland was particularly restive in the mid-fifties, especially in the fall of 1956 during the Hungarian Rebellion, and it is generally believed that the PRC supported the East Europeans in their desires to lessen their subordination to Moscow. It is not konwn what role Wang may have played in these events, but he did participate in talks with top Polish leaders in January 1957, when Chou En-lai visited Warsaw, seemingly as a mediator between the Poles and the Russians. Like all diplomats, much of Wang's time was devoted to the negotiation of trade and other agreements, as well as to protocol functions, such as hosting banquets marking China's National Day. He also used his visits to Geneva for the Sino-American talks to contact other diplomats, as in the early fall of 1955 when he held informal talks with Italian officials regarding increased Sino-Italian trade and the possibility of establishing formal diplomatic relations.

Wang returned home on at least three occasions during his tour in Warsaw. The first of these took place in April 1957 when he accompanied Polish Premier Cyrankiewicz on a state visit to China, and he was again in Peking in mid-1958 just prior to the resumption of the Sino-American talks. Although not officially named as a member of Ch'en I's delegation to the Geneva Conference on Laos, he was present with Ch'en in Geneva from May to July 1961, participating in the negotiations. Wang was back in Peking again in mid-1962, presumably to assist in formulating Chinese policies for the closing phase of the Geneva Conference, and then he was in Geneva with Ch'en I for the last days of the proceedings (July 1962), this time as an official member of the Chinese delegation.

Wang was replaced in Warsaw by Wang Kuoch'üan (q.v.) in April 1964, returning home to become a vice-minister in the Foreign Ministry, a position he still retains. Although diplomats stationed abroad do not normally serve in the NPC, Wang was a nominal deputy from Liaoning to the Second NPC, which lasted from 1959 to 1964. Not long after his return to China he was elected to the Third NPC, which opened in December 1964, this time from his native Shensi.

Wang is said to have bourgeois tastes, particularly enjoying good food and drink. One Western diplomat in Peking during the early fifties gained the impression that Wang was pleased that his assignment to Warsaw would take him away from the drabness of life in Peking.[8] Wang divorced his German wife in the late forties and has since married a Chinese woman who has borne him two children. He is frequently confused with a Chinese of the same name, a man who graduated from Tsinghua University in 1927 and who received a doctorate from the University of Pennsylvania in 1933. This Wang, an economist, is a specialist in transportation problems and has been a member of the Maritime Arbitration Commission since January 1959 (see under Sun Ta-kuang).

1. Edgar Snow, *The Other Side of the River* (London, 1963), p. 264; Edgar Snow, *Random Notes on China, 1936–1945* (Cambridge, Mass., 1957), p. 4.
2. Anna Wang, *Ich kämpfte für Mao* (I fought for Mao; Hamburg, Germany, 1964), p. 23.
3. *Ibid.*, p. 22.
4. *Ibid.*, p. 23; Snow, *Random Notes*, p. 4.
5. Snow, *The Other Side of the River*, pp. 262–264.
6. U.S. Department of State, *United States Relations with China* (Washington, D.C., 1949), pp. 109, 111, 230–231, 657, 664–668.
7. Kenneth T. Young, "American Dealings with Peking," *Foreign Affairs*, 45:77–87 (October 1966).
8. Interview with Western diplomat, San Francisco, June 1961.

Wang Shang-jung

(c.1906–   ; Hopeh). Military leader; alternate member, CCP Central Committee.

Wang Shang-jung has been an officer in the Red Army since its founding in 1927. He was born about 1906 in Hopeh and studied in Moscow, probably in the 1920's, at either a military academy or Sun Yat-sen University. Wang joined the Communist Party at the time of the Nanchang Uprising (August 1927), and when it failed he joined the military forces led by Hsiao K'o (q.v.). Hsiao, then only 18, had joined the Party several months prior to the uprising in which he also participated. When the Communist coup failed, he organized a small independent band of disaffected youths and led them to join the guerrilla forces of Mao Tse-tung and Chu Te, who had established their headquarters at Chingkangshan on the Kiangsi-Hunan border. With Hsiao's guerrillas, Wang became a commander of a regiment and then of a brigade. Having arrived at Chingkangshan, Hsiao's forces were integrated into Chu Te's Fourth Army.

By the mid-1930's Wang was participating in the military campaigns in the Hunan-Hupeh-Szechwan-Kweichow Soviet, led by Ho Lung's Second Front Army.[1] Wang presumably made the Long March with Ho's forces, which arrived in north Shensi in 1936, about one year after Mao had arrived there.

In the autumn of 1937, Wang became a deputy commander of the 359th Brigade of Ho Lung's 120th Division, one of the three divisions of the Communists' Eighth Route Army. He was later a deputy commander of the 120th Division. By 1940, he had become commander of the Second Independent Brigade of the 120th Division and concurrently commander of the Fourth Military Sub-district of the Northwest Shansi Military District. Guerrilla units of the Eighth Route Army held most of Shansi during the Sino-Japanese War. By 1946, Wang had transferred to the Fifth Military Sub-district in the Shansi-Suiyuan Military Region, where he led the First Independent Brigade in Chang Tsung-hsun's (q.v.) 358th Brigade.

In 1949 Wang was an army deputy commander under P'eng Te-huai's First Field Army, which had jurisdiction over Tsinghai, Sinkiang, and Kansu provinces. In January 1950, when the Communists established their provincial administration for Tsinghai, Wang became a member of the Tsinghai Provincial People's Government, and from August 1950 to March 1953 he was a vice-chairman of its Finance and Economics Committee.

In the latter half of 1952 Wang was transferred to Peking to assume new responsibilities. By August 1952 he was a deputy director of the Operations Department of the PLA, then under the jurisdiction of the People's Revolutionary Military Council (PRMC). The PRMC was abolished in the fall of 1954 at which time the entire military establishment underwent many organizational changes. Wang, however, retained his position, only now subordinate to the PLA General Staff. By May 1959 he was director of the Operations Department, a position he apparently still holds.

When personal military ranks were established in 1955, Wang was made a lieutenant-general. Simultaneously, he was awarded two of the three highest military honors, the Order of August First for service in the period 1927 to 1937, and the Order of Liberation for the 1945–1950 period. It is not clear why he failed to receive the award for service during the Sino-Japanese War, especially since he is known to have been active during that period.

Wang was elected an alternate member of the Party Central Committee in May 1958 at the second session of the Eighth National Congress. A year later he accompanied the Panchen Lama on the latter's visit to the Ministry of Defense and the PLA Headquarters. During the visit Wang gave an account of how the PLA had quickly ended the Tibetan rebellion. In July 1960 he was in Chengtu, the Szechwan capital, attending a memorial service for a former colleague in Tsinghai, General Ho Ping-yen. This report, placing Wang in southwest China, coupled with the paucity of information on him since 1959 suggests that he may have some special military assignment in connection with Tibet and the Sino-Indian border.

1. *JMJP,* February 1, 1962.

Wang Shih-t'ai

(c.1908–   ; Lo-ch'uan hsien, Shensi). Secretary, Kansu CCP Committee; alternate member, CCP Central Committee.

One of the earliest members of the CCP in Shensi province, Wang Shih-t'ai has spent most of his career as a military and political leader in the northwest. He was elected an alternate member of the Party Central Committee in 1956 and has been a secretary of the Kansu CCP Committee since 1961. Wang was born about 1908 in Lo-ch'uan hsien, located 50 miles south of Yenan in Shensi. After graduating from the Number Six Middle School in Yenan he joined the Communist guerrillas in north Shensi. The guerrillas were organized in 1928 by Liu Chih-tan (q.v.), a Whampoa graduate who returned to his native Shensi after the mid-1927 split between the Communists and Nationalists.

According to a 1957 Communist account, in 1932 "Liu Chih-tan and Wang Shih-t'ai organized three guerrilla forces, known as the North Shensi, Kuan-chung, and Shensi-Kansu guerrillas. Guerrilla warfare was inaugurated, land reform was developed, soviet government authority was established, and the Shensi-Kansu Border Soviet District was formed."[1] This account, postdating the 1955 purge of Kao Kang (q.v.), artificially inflates Wang's role in these activities. Although Wang was in fact an important participant in these events, Kao Kang was then clearly next in importance to Liu Chih-tan. In the ensuing years, Liu, Kao Kang, and Wang developed their forces into two units, known as the 26th and 27th Armies. In July 1933 Wang was in command of the crack Second Regiment of the 26th Red Army's 42nd Division when it was decimated by a superior KMT force at Wei-hua near Sian. As a consequence of this defeat the center of guerrilla activity moved north closer to Pao-an. Wang Shih-t'ai led his surviving troops there in late 1933. In June 1934 some of the guerrilla forces were reorganized and the North Shensi Revolutionary Area centered in An-ting was established. Wang became a regimental commander of the new force.[2]

In the meantime, Wang had been elected a member of the Central Executive Committee (CEC) of the Chinese Soviet Republic. This occurred in January–February 1934 at the Second All-China Congress of Soviets held in Juichin, the capital of the republic in Kiangsi. The CEC was presided over by Mao Tse-tung. Wang's election, almost certainly *in absentia,* was rather unusual in that there is no evidence that more senior Shensi leaders like Liu Chih-tan and Kao Kang were also elected. In any event, Wang's major contributions to the Communist movement continued to be in the northwest. He held a series of significant posts in the Shensi-Kansu-Ninghsia (Shen-Kan-Ning) Border Region, which was formed following the outbreak of the war with Japan in mid-1937. He is said to have been commander of the San-pien Military Sub-district, covering the northwestern section of the Shen-Kan-Ning region. Another report placed him as the garrison commander of the Kuan-chung Sub-district in the southern part of the region. By 1941 he had transferred to the Border Region capital at Yenan, where he served as the acting commander of the Shansi-Suiyuan-Shensi-Kansu-Ninghsia Joint Defense Headquarters. (By the

1942–43 period Ho Lung was commander of this headquarters.) Toward the end of the war Wang was the garrison commander and political commissar of the Shen-Kan-Ning Border Region. In 1946 he was in command of the Peace Preservation Headquarters (*pao-an szu-ling-pu*), presumably a redesignation of the previous commands he had held in Yenan.

Aside from his military duties Wang also held posts in the legislative and executive organs of the Shen-Kan-Ning Border Region Government. He was a deputy from Ch'ü-hsien in Kansu to the Second Assembly of the Border Region (1941–1946), attending the Assembly sessions held in Yenan in November 1941 and December 1944. In the Third Assembly (1946–1949) Wang was again named as a deputy, this time representing the military establishment. At the close of the initial session of the Third Assembly (April 1946), he was elected a member of the Shen-Kan-Ning Government Council, the executive branch under Chairman Lin Po-ch'ü (q.v.).

With the end of hostilities against Japan, the forces under Wang's command began to be absorbed into the main Communist armies, which were beginning to emerge in preparation for the conquest of the mainland. First identified as the commanding officer of the Third Column of P'eng Te-huai's Northwest PLA, by 1947 Wang was transferred to command the Fourth Column of the Northwest PLA. These units were apparently integrated into P'eng's First Field Army by early 1949 when field armies were created; Wang's forces were then called the Fourth Army and were subordinate to the First Field Army's Second Corps. From 1949 to 1951 Wang was political commissar of the Second Corps, which was commanded by Hsu Kuang-ta (q.v.). During 1949 the First Field Army conquered the northwest, including Yenan, the former Communist capital, ultimately expanding in the latter part of the year to conduct mopping up operations in Ninghsia, Kansu, Tsinghai, and Sinkiang.

Just prior to the final military thrusts into the northwest in late 1949, Wang returned to Peking briefly to take part (as a representative of the First Field Army) in the meetings of the CPPCC, the organization that brought the PRC into existence on October 1, 1949. During these sessions, held in late September, he served on the *ad hoc* committee that drafted the Organic Law of the Central People's Government, one of the principal documents adopted then. Wang did not receive any appointments in the central government but was immediately sent back to the northwest. There he assumed several posts in the Kansu Provincial People's Government (formally established in January 1950), as well as in the regional government with jurisdiction over Kansu, the Northwest Military and Administrative Committee (NWMAC). The NWMAC was headed by Wang's long-time military superior, P'eng Te-huai. Wang was a member of the NWMAC from its formation in January 1950, serving also from March 1950 as a member of its Finance and Economics Committee. From late 1951 he was further identified as a member of the Northwest Party Bureau. Within the Kansu Provincial Government he was a vice-governor and initially (from March 1950) chairman of the government's Finance and Economics Committee. However, he was demoted to the vice-chairmanship of this committee in July 1950, being replaced by Chang Te-sheng (q.v.), a former colleague from the Shen-Kan-Ning Government.

Wang was not frequently reported in the press during the early 1950's; however, he did give "instructions" to the newly established Kansu Nationalities Affairs Committee in May 1950, and he was among those who attended the fourth meeting of the NWMAC in Sian in November 1951. During this same period, as already described, he retained his position in the military establishment as political commissar of the Second Corps under P'eng Te-huai's First Field Army. In July 1951 he received a new post closely related to his military role when he was named as director and political commissar of the Northwest Railway Construction Bureau. The post was an important one, for the development of railways in the northwest has been a major concern of the Communist government. Wang remained in this post for 13 months, gaining experience for the vice-ministership in the Ministry of Railways, which he assumed in Peking in August 1952. In this ministry he served under T'eng Tai-yuan (q.v.), a long-time colleague of P'eng Te-huai. He remained in the post until the constitutional government was inaugurated at the first session of the First NPC in September 1954. At this time Wang, a deputy from Kiangsu to the NPC, was made a member of the military advisory organ, the National Defense Council, a post he still retains. With the reorganization of the central government at this same time, Wang transferred (October 1954) from the Railway Ministry to a comparable position as a vice-chairman of the newly established State Construction Commission, serving here under Po I-po, one of China's top economic specialists.

For the next three and a half years Wang's activities centered around the Construction Commission. In November 1954 he was deputy head of a construction engineering delegation that toured the USSR. Immediately after his return home he served as deputy to Lü Cheng-ts'ao (q.v.) in negotiations that led to the signing on December 24, 1954, of agreements and protocols to assist North Vietnam in the restoration of its communication facilities. In October 1955

Wang was again in the USSR as head of another construction engineering delegation. Two years later, in October 1957, he went to Wuhan to officially "accept" for the central government the famed Yangtze River Bridge, which provided a rail link across the Yangtze (joining the Peking-Hankow and the Hankow-Canton Railways). In the meantime, at the Eighth Party Congress in September 1956, his long Party career received official recognition when he was elected as an alternate member of the Central Committee.

In February 1958, during a partial government reorganization, Wang's State Construction Commission was abolished, and its functions were taken over by the State Planning Commission, the State Economic Commission, and the Ministry of Building. Nothing was heard about Wang for over a year, but then it was revealed that he had been transferred back to his native northwest. In April 1959 he was identified in Lanchow, Kansu, as a vice-chairman of the "Northwest Economic Coordinating Region," a unit possibly under the control of one of the major commissions in Peking (such as the State Planning Commission). Another lengthy period passed before Wang was again identified (August 1961), this time as a secretary of the Kansu Party Committee. This new position, which Wang still retains, was assumed at approximately the same time that Wang Feng (q.v.) became the Party first secretary in Kansu, replacing Chang Chung-liang (q.v.), who was presumably removed for political reasons.

Although relatively little was heard about Wang's activities in the ensuing years, his position as a leader of significance was reaffirmed in 1964–65. As already described, Wang had served from 1954 to 1959 as a deputy from Kiangsu to the First NPC. He was not re-elected to the Second NPC (1959–1964). But then in 1964 he was elected from Kansu to the Third NPC, and at its initial session, which closed in January 1965, he was elected a member of the NPC Standing Committee.

1. *Hung-ch'i p'iao-p'iao* (Red flag fluttering; Peking, 1957), V, 115.
2. Mark Selden, "The Guerrilla Movement in Northwest China: The Origins of the Shensi-Kansu-Ninghsia Border Region," *The China Quarterly,* no. 29:65–69 (January–March 1967).

Wang Shih-ying

Member, CCP Control Commission.

Wang Shih-ying was a CCP member by 1944 when he was identified as a department director in Yenan under the famed Eighth Route Army of the Communist forces. By the following year he was deputy chief-of-staff of the Eighth Route Army Headquarters in Yenan.

In January 1946 a cease-fire arrangement was agreed upon by the Nationalists and Communists, an agreement brought about by American General George C. Marshall. To implement this, an Executive Headquarters was established in Peking, with representatives from the Nationalists, the Communists, and the Americans. In addition, field teams were established in many Chinese cities to deal with local problems in keeping the peace. Wang was the Communist member of the team stationed in Hsu-chou (Suchow) in northwestern Kiangsu. When the truce collapsed in early 1947, these teams were, of course, disbanded.

Wang was not reported again until January 1949 when Communist forces captured Tientsin. There he served as a member of the quasi-military organization which governed the city, the Tientsin Military Control Commission. In addition, from May 1949 he served as deputy commander (under Yang Ch'eng-wu, q.v.) of the Tientsin Garrison. But before the year was out he had been transferred to the northwest, the area in which he had first achieved prominence with the Communists in the mid-1940's.

Wang was in Shansi by the early fall of 1949 where he served as a vice-governor under governors Ch'eng Tzu-hua, Lai Jo-yü, and P'ei Li-sheng. Within the next few years he assumed a host of other positions in the government and Party organizations in Shansi. In governmental work he became a member of the Finance and Economics Committee in August 1950 and chairman of the Political and Legal Affairs Committee in June 1952. Then in April 1956 he succeeded P'ei Li-sheng as governor, P'ei having been transferred to the Academy of Sciences in Peking. In the Shansi Party structure, Wang was by 1951 deputy director of the Propaganda Department; he was a member of the Standing Committee of the Shansi Party by 1953, and was then promoted to deputy secretary by May 1955 and secretary by July 1959 (under First Secretary T'ao Lu-chia). Wang was also prominent in Shansi in the local organization of the CPPCC, the principal legislative arm of the regime until the establishment of the NPC in 1954. Wang represented Shansi when he attended the important second and third sessions of the CPPCC held in Peking in June 1950 and October–November 1951, respectively; at the former the important Land Reform Law was adopted, and at the latter major decisions were taken to promote economic austerity in order to bolster the war effort in Korea. With this background in CPPCC work in Shansi and Peking, it was natural that he should have been elected a vice-chairman of the First Shansi CPPCC when it was formed in February 1955, a position he was to hold until the second provincial committee of the Shansi CPPCC was formed in August 1959.

Wang was also active in Shansi in one of the more important of the "people's" organizations, the China Peace Committee, of which he was chairman by November 1950. In 1953 election committees were formed in all provinces in preparation for the 1954 elections to the NPC. Wang chaired the Shansi Election Committee, established in May 1953, and when the 1954 elections were held he was elected a Shansi deputy to the First NPC (1954–1959). He was re-elected from Shansi to the Second NPC (1959–1964), but apparently because of his transfer to Peking he was not elected to the Third NPC, which first met in late 1964. During the 1953–54 period Wang served on two "comfort" delegations which visited PLA units; he accompanied Ho Lung to Korea in October–November 1953 to entertain and inspect Chinese troops there, and in February 1954 visited troops in north China and Inner Mongolia.

Relatively little was heard of Wang in the late 1950's and early 1960's. In fact, Wei Heng served as acting governor of Shansi from late 1956 until December 1958, at which time he replaced Wang as the governor. Wang did, however, submit a written statement before the fourth session of the NPC in July 1957 on the necessity to struggle against nature to insure good harvests, and in May 1958 he served on the funeral committee for Central Committee member Lai Jo-yü, a former superior in Shansi in the early 1950's.

In April 1959, Wang was named to the Third National Committee of the CPPCC as a "specially invited personage" and at the close of the session was selected for membership on the Standing Committee, the organ charged with the management of the CPPCC when the National Committee is not in session. At this same time he was also appointed a vice-chairman of the Literary and Historical Source Materials Research Committee under the CPPCC, a committee headed by Party Central Committee alternate Fan Wen-lan, the most important Party historian in China. This last appointment suggested a transfer from Shansi to Peking, for after August 1959 Wang was no longer reported in Shansi. In fact, he did not appear again in public until July 1963, when he was on hand to welcome back Teng Hsiao-p'ing to Peking following the unsuccessful meetings held with Soviet leaders in Moscow to resolve Sino-Soviet conflicts. Other facts, however, suggest that Wang was working behind the scenes in disciplinary and inspection work. In September 1962, the 10th Party Plenum adopted the decision to expand the important Central Control Commission, the watchdog organization of the Central Committee. Wang was among those appointed to the expanded Control Commission.

Information on Wang continues to be minimal. Aside from the welcome for Teng Hsiao-

p'ing and membership on funeral committees for two men of marginal importance, the only other mention of Wang in the press came at the first session of the Fourth CPPCC National Committee. The session was held in December 1964–January 1965, with Wang again a "specially invited personage." And when the session closed he was re-elected to the Standing Committee. He was not, however, reappointed to a vice-chairmanship of the CPPCC's Literary and Historical Source Materials Research Committee. It may be that his main assignment under the Party's Control Commission is to provide guidance to the members of the CPPCC, many of whom are non-Communists cooperating with the regime.

Wang Shou-tao

(1907–   ; Liu-yang, Hunan). Communications specialist; a secretary, Central-South Bureau, CCP; member, CCP Central Committee.

A veteran of guerrilla fighting in central China and the Shanghai underground in the twenties and thirties, Wang Shou-tao was a political officer during the Long March and the Sino-Japanese War. He became an alternate member of the Party Central Committee in 1945 and then served in Manchuria during the late forties. In the early years of the PRC he was a top Party official in Hunan and then in the 12-year period from 1952 to 1964 he was one of the central government's leading specialists in communications and transport work, heading the Communications Ministry for five of these years. Elected a full member of the Party Central Committee in 1956, Wang has been a secretary of the Party's Central-South Bureau since 1964.

Wang was born in Liu-yang hsien, Hunan, an important center of revolutionary activities in the twenties. Liu-yang has probably produced more important Communists than any other hsien in China; the impressive roster includes Sung Jen-ch'iung, Lo Chang-lung, Chang Ch'i-lung, Yang Yung, and Wang Chen (qq.v.), all of whom were born in the first decade of the century. The details of Wang Shou-tao's early career are drawn from interviews given to American journalists in 1936–37 and from an autobiographical account by Wang written in 1963 (sources that are somewhat conflicting).[1] Born into a poor peasant family, as a youth Wang sold firewood and tended the family's only ox. He told Edgar Snow that because firewood was available only on places owned by landlords, he and his brother were forced to steal it. One day they were caught and his brother was imprisoned by the landlord, an act that embittered Wang. He did not attend primary school until the age of nine or ten, but poverty soon forced him to leave. Wang was then apprenticed to a maker of firecrackers by an uncle who had become his guardian when his family had "moved to a distant place." After half a year in this work, his uncle put him back in school, this time under an "old-style Chinese teacher," with whom he studied for a year. This same teacher helped Wang enter a higher primary school. Although still a young teenager, Wang claimed that under the influence of the May Fourth Movement (beginning in 1919) he agitated for education for the masses and resistance to Japanese aggression in China. At this juncture, Wang's father returned to Liu-yang and insisted that the young Wang prepare for a wedding that his father had arranged years earlier. Wang refused and quarreled with his father, and eventually the match was broken off. Then, with help from a teacher and relatives, Wang enrolled (1922) in a middle school in Changsha, the Hunan capital and a center of revolutionary thought in the twenties. Wang has written that "progressive" periodicals "awakened in me a strong desire to help to save the motherland." Still later, he entered a state agricultural school in Changsha and while there became a member of the Socialist Youth League (1924).

Wang was expelled from school for writing a manifesto attacking school and government authorities, after which he returned to his native Liu-yang. Influenced by articles in *Chung-kuo ch'ing-nien* (China youth), one of the most important journals of that period, Wang set about organizing peasant groups in Hunan. According to his account, by then he "understood the nature of the class struggle." Fearing arrest for his activities, he fled to Canton, traveling via Shanghai where he was briefly detained by British police for passing a counterfeit silver dollar. Once in Canton (1925), he enrolled in the Peasant Movement Training Institute and in the same year joined the CCP. (In Wang's own account, he asserts that he went to Canton in 1926 and studied at the Institute from May to September, but this appears to be a falsification designed to place him at the school when Mao Tse-tung was the director; in any case, it differs from the accounts he gave to Edgar Snow ten years after he had been there.) While at the Institute, Wang studied under such top Communists as P'eng P'ai, Mao, Chou En-lai, Wu Yüchang, Ch'ü Ch'iu-pai, Teng Chung-hsia, and Yun Tai-ying (qq.v.). Prior to graduation, Wang's class spent two weeks under P'eng P'ai's direction in Hai-feng, Kwangtung, gaining practical experience in the peasant movement in the area where P'eng's Communist leadership had been quite successful.

Wang returned to Hunan in 1926 to engage in revolutionary work, going first to Changsha where leftist activities were strong. Already a CCP member, he joined the KMT in order to participate in the preparations for the Northern Expedition, which began in the summer of 1926 and was led by the KMT. At this period the CCP and the KMT were working in some cooperation and dual party membership was allowable. By the end of 1926 he was organizing peasants in Ch'i-yang, southwest of Heng-yang, a rail and riverport center of southern Hunan. According to Wang peasant associations such as he organized in Ch'i-yang played a major role in the success of the Northern Expedition.

Until the spring of 1927 the Communists had cooperated with the KMT during the course of the Northern Expedition, but then in the late spring and early summer the KMT carried out a number of anti-Communist actions. As a consequence, Wang was forced to flee southward from Ch'i-yang to find refuge. He remained in hiding for nearly half a year, during which he first read the *Communist Manifesto* and a condensation of Marx's *Das Kapital*. Toward the end of 1927 he returned to his native Liu-yang to help organize peasant uprisings. A short period before this Mao Tse-tung had conducted similar operations during the famous Autumn Harvest Uprisings, only to be driven away a short time later. Wang, however, in his capacity as secretary of the CCP Liu-yang hsien Committee, remained in this area where, in mid-1928, P'eng Te-huai and Huang Kung-lueh (qq.v.) staged the P'ing-chiang Uprising (not far north of Liu-yang) and established the Fifth Red Army. P'eng was soon forced to move most of his troops southward, but Huang Kung-lueh remained in the area which was soon designated by the Communists as the Hunan-Hupeh-Kiangsi Border Region. In 1928 Wang became secretary of the CCP organization in the area, known as the Hunan-Hupeh-Kiangsi Special Committee, and in the next year, when a "soviet government" was formed there, he was made a member of the government committee.

In mid-1930, under the direction of the Li Li-san leadership, the Communists made their ill-fated attempts to capture key central China cities. Wang, who had been operating in areas not far from Changsha, the Hunan capital, was assigned to the forces led by P'eng Te-huai, which assaulted Changsha at the end of July and held it for a few days. With the capture of Changsha, Li Li-san was made chairman of the so-called Hunan Provincial Soviet Government. However, because Li never arrived, Wang substituted for him as the chairman. When the Communists were driven from the city, Wang's wife, who had accompanied him to Changsha to work among the textile workers, was arrested and executed. Her husband narrowly escaped and fled to Shanghai where he worked in the CCP underground; this probably brought him into close contact with Party leaders Li K'onung, Ch'en Keng, and K'o Ch'ing-shih (qq.v.), all of whom were then active in the underground. During his time in Shanghai Wang claims that he attended a CCP-organized "secret training class" where Party leader Jen Pi-shih (q.v.) gave lectures on Party organizational methods.[2]

Wang had gone to Shanghai just about the time Li Li-san was censured by the Party and was removed from office, his influence in the CCP being vigorously opposed by the group of Russian-returned students who returned to China from Moscow in the spring of 1930 to unseat him (see under Ch'en Shao-yü). By January 1931 this group had got control of the Party and proceeded to send its representatives into the rural areas where the Party had been operating to take over the direction of political affairs wherever possible. In 1932 Wang was sent to the Hunan-Kiangsi border region where he worked as secretary of the Party Committee. Other Communists active in the area about the time Wang arrived there included Hsiao K'o, Chang P'ing-hua, Wang En-mao, and Chang Ch'i-lung (qq.v.). Then in May 1933, Jen Pi-shih was assigned to the Hunan-Kiangsi border region as secretary of the border area Party Committee (apparently replacing Wang Shou-tao) and as political commissar for the military area there, which was controlled by Hsiao K'o and his Sixth Red Army Corps. According to an article written by Wang in 1951 (an orthodox Maoist account), after Jen's arrival "the grave situation resulting from the incorrect line of leftist dogmatism [that is, the Russian-returned student leadership] was eased up," and some of the border area leaders were "saved" from following the line of "dogmatism."[3] In addition to Wang Shou-tao, those who escaped this "fate" included Chang Ch'i-lung, Chang P'ing-hua, and Wang En-mao. The 1951 account does not unravel the obscure record of just what happened after Jen's arrival in 1933, but at least Wang's subsequent career exculpated him of the Maoist charge of "dogmatism," with which much of the Russian-returned student leadership has been accused.

Wang went to Juichin to attend the Second All-China Congress of Soviets held in January–February 1934; he apparently remained with the Chu-Mao troops in Kiangsi, because he made the Long March as a member of the Red Army Political Department in 1934–35. In early 1936, soon after the arrival of the Long March forces in north Shensi, the Communists undertook a brief campaign into neighboring Shansi. This foray into Shansi (described at further length in the biography of Liu Chih-tan) gained for the Communists new recruits for their military forces and badly needed supplies. At this time Wang was appointed director of the Political Department of the 15th Red Army, which was commanded by Hsu Hai-tung (q.v.). After the westward withdrawal from Shansi in the spring of 1936, the 15th Corps maintained its head-

quarters in Yü-wang, then in Kansu, but now in Ninghsia. Wang was in Yü-wang when he was interviewed in mid-1936 by Edgar Snow.

At about the time of the outbreak of war in 1937, Wang went to Yenan to be secretary-general to Chang Wen-t'ien, then general secretary of the CCP Central Committee. Apparently this assignment was of short duration, for beginning in 1938 he taught at three of the major Party schools in Yenan—the Marx-Lenin Institute, the Central Party School, and the Central Research Institute. According to one source (allegedly quoting an official document), Wang was praised for his activities during these years: "Particularly during the literary purge [of 1942], Wang . . . contributed much to the struggle against Wang Shih-wei."[4] The latter, a Moscow-trained CCP member and author-translator, was one of the major victims during the Mao-led *cheng-feng* (rectification) movement of 1942.[5] Wang himself has written that during the period from 1941 to the fall of 1944 he worked directly under his old colleague Jen Pi-shih in the Party Center.[6]

After several years of non-military duties, Wang returned to the fighting front in late 1944 or early 1945 when he was assigned to the 359th Brigade, headed by his colleague Wang Chen. The 359th was given the task of moving south, passing through Hunan, and rendezvous-ing with elements of the Tung-chiang (East River) Column, a Communist unit that had been operating for many years in Kwangtung. Wang Chen commanded this operation; Wang Shou-tao was his political commissar and Wang En-mao was the deputy political commissar. (For a longer description of this mission, see under Wang En-mao.) When the rendezvous was cancelled by higher Communist authorities just after the Japanese surrender in August 1945, the unit turned back to the north and, after about a year of fighting against Nationalist units, returned to north Shensi via a circuitous path that took the forces through Hunan, Hupeh, Honan, and Kansu.

Because of his command responsibilities in central-south China, Wang probably did not attend the Party's Seventh Congress in Yenan, April–June 1945. But he was elected an alternate member of the new Central Committee, placing fifth on the list of alternates. In January 1946 the CCP and the KMT agreed to a cease-fire agreement worked out by U.S. mediator George C. Marshall, under the terms of which local truce supervision teams were established. Wang was assigned as the CCP representative in Mukden (Shenyang) and remained in Manchuria until the entire region was conquered by Lin Piao's forces in late 1948. Presumably because of his familiarity with Mukden, Wang was made a member of the Municipal Military Control Commission when the Communists captured the city in November 1948. At about this time he also became director of the Industry Department under the Northeast Administrative Committee, which had been established under Lin Feng (q.v.) in 1946 to govern those portions of Manchuria controlled by the Communists.

Wang presumably accompanied Lin Piao's forces as they pushed southward into China proper over the winter of 1948–49, first taking Tientsin and Peking and then moving into the Yangtze Valley area. He remained with these forces until they "peacefully liberated" Hunan in August 1949. For the next three years Wang worked in Hunan and its capital city, Changsha, where he was one of the top leaders. He became a vice-chairman of the Changsha Military Control Commission in August 1949 under Hsiao Ching-kuang (q.v.) who, like Wang, was also a Central Committee alternate. By the end of 1949 Wang was identified as the first deputy secretary of the Hunan CCP Committee. Here he served under Huang K'o-ch'eng (q.v.), still another alternate member of the Party Central Committee. During Huang's absences in 1950 and 1951, Wang served on occasion as the acting Hunan secretary. He was also prominent in the Hunan government structure, serving as governor from March 1950 until early 1952 when he was transferred to Peking (see below). In addition to the gubernatorial post, he headed the Hunan Finance and Economics Committee briefly in mid-1950 but was then demoted to a vice-chairmanship to give way to the more politically senior Huang K'o-ch'eng, who assumed the chairmanship in September 1950. In addition, Wang also chaired the Hunan government's Nationalities Affairs Committee from November 1951 to March 1952. Like most officials of his stature, Wang was affiliated with the regional Central-South Military and Administrative Committee (CSMAC), chaired by Lin Piao, headquartered in Wuhan, and responsible for the six provinces of Honan, Hupeh, Hunan, Kiangsi, Kwangtung, and Kwangsi. Wang was a member of the CSMAC from its inauguration in February 1950.

Wang spent most of the early years of the PRC in Hunan but went on occasion to Wuhan for meetings of the CSMAC or to Peking to deliver reports before the national government. In June 1950, for example, he spoke before the second session of the CPPCC in Peking on conditions in Hunan. Similarly, he published articles on Hunan in the regional and provincial press, for example, in *Ch'ang-chiang jih-pao* (Yangtze River daily), April 30, 1951. Drawing on his extensive experience in Hunan, Wang also wrote a long and historically useful article that covered 30 years (1921–1951) of "heroic struggles" in the province.[7]

In early 1952 Wang was transferred to Peking, relinquishing the Hunan governorship to non-Communist Ch'eng Ch'ien, a former high-ranking KMT official. (Wang did hold the post of Hunan vice-governor from February 1952 to February 1955, but in view of his transfer this was obviously only a nominal post.) His new assignment in Peking, assumed in April 1952, was a vice-ministership of Communications. Here he ostensibly served under non-Communist Chang Po-chün, but in view of Wang's position in the CCP, it is apparent that he was the most powerful official in the ministry. The main responsibility of the ministry is waterway communications, one of the most important types in China. (Railways and telecommunications are subordinate to two other ministries.) From July 1952 until 1954 he was also a member of the central government's Labor Employment Committee, created to deal with the problem of unemployment.

From 1952 to 1954, Wang spoke before several communications conferences, as in August 1953 when he addressed a nationwide meeting. He also led a scientific and technical delegation abroad from July to September 1954; in July he signed a scientific and technical cooperation agreement with the Poles and then spent a month in the USSR, presumably inspecting Soviet communications facilities. In September–October 1954 the central government was reorganized; Wang lost his post in the Communications Ministry, but immediately afterwards (October) he was appointed to head the newly created Sixth Staff Office of the State Council. In effect, this was a promotion, for the Staff Office was responsible for coordinating the work of all central government agencies concerned with rail, highway, and water communications. He remained in this assignment for almost five years until, during another reorganization, the Sixth Staff Office was merged with two others into the Industry and Communications Office (September 1959) and placed under the directorship of economic specialist Li Fu-ch'un (q.v.).

From December 1954 to April 1959, Wang was a CCP representative on the CPPCC's Second National Committee (as well as a Standing Committee member), but the post was largely nominal and most of his efforts continued to be directed toward technical and industrial matters. Having already negotiated with the Poles over technical questions in 1954, Wang headed the Chinese side in talks held in Peking in May 1955 by the Joint Commission for Sino-Polish Scientific and Technical Cooperation, and then from March 1956 to May 1957 he was a member of Ch'en I's Scientific Planning Commission, established to implement a 12-year scientific program launched in early 1956.

Owing to the death of several full Party Central Committee members, by the eve of the Party's Eighth Congress in September 1956 Wang was the ranking alternate member (and there is, in fact, inferential evidence that he had already been promoted to full membership prior to the Congress). In any case, he was elected to full membership at the Congress and also addressed the delegates on the subject of transport and telecommunications. In May of the following year he was sent by the CCP to attend the 11th Congress of the Finnish Communist Party, the first and only assignment of this sort that Wang has had.

Although Wang had not been elected to the First NPC when it was established in 1954, he had spoken before the legislature in his capacity as a government administrator, as in June 1956 when he addressed the NPC on the subject of transport and telecommunications. But then, to replace a deceased NPC deputy, he was named to represent Shensi in time for the third session of the NPC in June–July 1957. He subsequently served as a deputy from Shantung to the Second NPC (1959–1964) and from Kwangtung to the Third NPC, which opened in December 1964. In July 1957 he was also named as a member of the Central Relief Committee, formed in response to charges in the national press that famine relief had been mismanaged.

In early 1958 Communications Minister Chang Po-chün fell victim to the nationwide "rectification" campaign, being singled out as one of the leading "rightists." Wang, who had been in the ministry earlier, was brought in to replace Chang (February). Three months later he was named to chair a special committee to restore and expand the Grand Canal. By this time the Great Leap Forward had been launched (early 1958), and to judge from his writings, Wang was among the more ardent backers of this ultimately abortive attempt to modernize and industrialize China in record-breaking time. In addition to several articles on communications for the *JMJP* (e.g., issues of September 23, 1959, and February 19, 1960), he also wrote an article on the same subject for the Party's top journal, *Hung-ch'i* (Red flag, January 16, 1959). As China's top man in communications, Wang was on occasion involved in the international aspects of this field, as in March 1959 when he signed a Sino-Ceylonese Air Transport Agreement (although the civil air link has never been brought to fruition). In July of the same year he also led a water transport delegation to Moscow. Similarly, he was usually among the Chinese negotiators when a foreign transport or communications group visited China.

After more than five years in the post, Wang turned over the Communications Ministry portfolio to Sun Ta-kuang (q.v.), one of his deputies, in July 1964. The reason for his removal was revealed a few days later when he was identified as a secretary of the Party's Central-South Bureau in Canton. Familiar with the area

from his service there in the early fifties, Wang worked under First Secretary T'ao Chu (q.v.). By the mid-sixties, the Central-South Bureau seemed to be staffed with more senior Party leaders than any of the five other regional bureaus. Among these are Central Committee members Ch'en Yü and Wu Chih-p'u and alternates Wang Jen-chung and Huang Yung-sheng. It is possible, though undocumented, that Wang was sent to this region as a communications specialist, in view of the intensification of the nearby Vietnam war.

Although Wang's responsibilities are mainly in the south, he holds two positions in the national administration (apart from his Party Central Committee membership). As already described, he was elected as a Kwangtung deputy to the Third NPC, which held its first session in December 1964–January 1965. He was also named as a representative of CCP to the Fourth National Committee of the CPPCC, which held its initial session concurrently with the NPC meetings. At the close of the CPPCC meetings in January 1965, he was named as a member of its Standing Committee.

1. Nym Wales, *Red Dust* (Stanford, Calif., 1952), pp. 77–79; Edgar Snow, *Random Notes on Red China, 1936–1945* (Cambridge, Mass., 1957), pp. 140–142; Wang Shou-tao, "The Peasant's Role in China's Revolution," *China Reconstructs*, 12:24–27 (October 1963).
2. *SCMP* 216, p. 20.
3. *Ibid.*
4. Biographical Service no. 25, Union Research Institute (Hong Kong), September 25, 1956.
5. Merle Goldman, "Writers' Criticism of the Party in 1942," *The China Quarterly*, no. 17:210–213 (January–March 1964).
6. *SCMP* 216, pp. 20–21.
7. *Chung-kuo Kung-ch'an-tang tsai chung-nan ti-ch'ü ling-tao ko-ming tou-cheng te li-shih tzu-liao* (Historical materials on the revolutionary struggles led by the Chinese Communist Party in central-south China; Wuhan, 1951), I, 9–18.

Wang Shu-sheng

(Hsiao-kan hsien, Hupeh). Military leader; vice-minister of National Defense; member, CCP Central Committee.

Wang Shu-sheng is a career military officer who has been a Communist Party member since the mid-twenties. A veteran of the Oyüwan Soviet and the Long March, Wang commanded troops for the New Fourth Army in the Honan-Hupeh area during the Sino-Japanese War and the civil war with the Nationalists in the late forties. In the early years of the PRC he was the senior military officer in Hupeh and since

1954 he has been a vice-minister of National Defense. Wang was elected to the Party Central Committee in 1956.

Wang was born in Hsiao-kan hsien, northwest of Wuhan in Hupeh province. The son of a landlord and a graduate of a higher primary school, Wang was a CCP member by 1927 when he and Cheng Wei-san (q.v.) were among the leading Party activists working in the vicinity of Huang-an and Ma-ch'eng hsien in the Ta-pieh mountain area some 100 miles northeast of Wuhan.[1] Wang may also have been associated with Hsu Hai-tung (q.v.), who was then in this area. Wang and Cheng Wei-sen engaged in guerrilla warfare during the ensuing years, and then in the early 1930's their units were incorporated into the Communists' Oyüwan Soviet under the leadership of Chang Kuo-t'ao and Hsu Hsiang-ch'ien (qq.v.). In late 1932, unable to withstand attacks by the Nationalists, Chang and Hsu led their forces westward to an inaccessible rural area along the upper reaches of the Ch'u River in northwest Szechwan. In May 1933 the Communists organized the T'ung-Nan-Pa Soviet (named for the three principal hsien in the area). The Communists' military forces, by now known as the Fourth Front Army, were commanded by Hsu Hsiang-ch'ien, with Wang as the deputy commander.[2]

In early 1935 the Fourth Front Army began to move westward to the western border of Szechwan to meet Mao Tse-tung's Long Marchers, who had evacuated Kiangsi in late 1934. Wang was with Hsu Hsiang-ch'ien's forces when they left the T'ung-Nan-Pa Soviet and in May 1935 he took part in an engagement fought against Nationalist units.[3] In the next month the Fourth Front Army met the First Front Army, led by Chu Te and Mao at Mao-kung in western Szechwan. From the few references to Wang Shu-sheng in the next two years it is evident that he remained with the part of Chang Kuo-t'ao's army that did not follow Mao to Shensi but instead turned westward to spend the winter of 1935–36 in Kan-tzu, Sikang (see under Chang Kuo-t'ao). In the late spring of 1936 the Second Front Army, led by Ho Lung (q.v.), arrived in Kan-tzu. The combined forces began to march northward, but upon reaching eastern Kansu in the fall of 1936, three major units of the Fourth Front Army (the Fifth, Ninth, and 30th Armies) were ordered to march westward toward Sinkiang. Orthodox Maoist histories claim that this was ordered by Chang Kuo-t'ao. As these units began their advance up the Kansu Corridor they suffered serious losses in the winter of 1936–37 at the hands of Generals Hu Tsung-nan and Ma Pu-fang, the Moslem warlord. The survivors managed to flee westward into the Ch'i-lien Mountains in Tsinghai where in March 1937 they were divided into two units, one known as the Left Detachment and the other as the Right Detachment. Wang was placed in charge of the latter, which consisted of some 300 foot soldiers from the former Ninth Army, plus about 100 cavalrymen.[4]

There are reports that Wang led his men all the way to Tihwa, the Sinkiang capital, in 1937. But this seems unlikely in view of the great distance from the Ch'i-lien Mountains to Tihua. In any event, by the latter part of 1937, after war with Japan had begun, Wang was serving as a member of the Central Plains Party Committee in an area that encompassed the former Oyüwan base. At this time he also assumed the command of the West Honan Military District, a position he seems to have held until 1946. The district was part of the Communists' Honan-Hupeh Border Region, occupied by a column of guerrillas led by Li Hsien-nien (q.v.), who had been associated with Wang in the T'ung-Nan-Pa Soviet and on the Long March. In the early years of the war these guerrillas occupied an extensive area on both sides of the Peking-Hankow Railway running between Hsin-yang, Honan, and Ying-shan, Hupeh. Early in 1941 Li's guerrillas were incorporated into the New Fourth Army in east-central China. At the close of the war the central China area around Wuhan (including the former Oyüwan base) was known as the Central Plains Liberated Region, with Li Hsien-nien as its military commander.

Wang remained in the Honan-Hupeh area in the immediate postwar period. In the latter part of 1945 the units in Hunan and Hupeh, led by Li Hsien-nien and Wang, were badly beaten by Nationalist forces. This defeat was cited by Mao Tse-tung in a November 1945 essay designed to show that the Nationalists had every intention of crushing the Communists by force.[5] In June of the next year Li Hsien-nien and Wang, who was then commanding the First Column of the Central Plains Military Region, were ordered to break through the Nationalist encirclement and proceed to the Shensi-Kansu-Ninghsia Border Region.[6] Two years later, in 1948, he accompanied Li to the Ta-pieh Mountains and became commander of the Honan-Hupeh Military Region. In mid-1949, when the Communists captured all of Hupeh, Wang became deputy commander of the provincial military district, and in 1950 he succeeded Li Hsien-nien as the commander. He remained as the Hupeh commander until 1954, and in addition he held the following posts: member, Central-South Military and Administrative Committee, 1950–1953; member, Hupeh Provincial People's Government Council, 1950–1955; deputy director, Ching-chiang (Chingkiang) Flood Harnessing Committee, 1952; third deputy commander, Central-South Military Region, 1954.

In the latter part of 1954 Wang was transferred to Peking where he has become one of the most important military leaders in China.

He served as a Hupeh deputy to the First NPC (1954–1959), and at the inaugural meeting of the NPC in September 1954 he was elected to the National Defense Council, the military advisory arm of the PRC. In the following month he was appointed a vice-minister of the newly created Ministry of National Defense. He continues to hold both positions, serving in the ministry under P'eng Te-huai until September 1959 and thereafter under Lin Piao. In September 1955 the Communists established officer ranks in the PLA and national military honors. Wang was made one of the very few senior (four-star) generals and given the three top military awards—the Orders of August First, Independence and Freedom, and Liberation. Exactly a year later he was elected a member of the Central Committee at the Party's Eighth National Congress. He was one of 33 men elected to full membership who had been neither a full nor an alternate member of the Seventh Central Committee elected at the Seventh Congress in 1945.

In 1956 Wang also became director of the PLA General Ordnance Department and in this capacity gave the opening address to the First Conference of PLA Advanced Ordnance Workers in May 1957. (The Ordnance Department was later absorbed by the Rear Services Department at an unknown date, and it appears that Wang relinquished this assignment in the late fifties.) He made his first trip abroad in 1959 as a member of P'eng Te-huai's 12-man military delegation to East Europe and Mongolia. Leaving China in late April, the group spent about a week in each of the following countries: Poland, East Germany, Czechoslovakia, Hungary, Rumania, Bulgaria, Albania, and Mongolia. It returned to China in mid-June.

In the years since his transfer to Peking, Wang has been frequently reported at official social functions as well as a number of military conferences. For example, in the spring of 1960 he attended a national militia conference and a PLA conference of cultural and educational "activists," and in September 1961 he was among those who received U.K. Field Marshal Montgomery on his visit to China. Wang's stature in the PLA hierarchy is perhaps best gauged by his tenure in the Ministry of Defense. Since it was established in 1954, 12 men have been viceministers, but only three of them have served continuously from that date to the mid-1960's: Hsiao Ching-kuang, Liao Han-sheng (qq.v.), and Wang.

---

1. Nym Wales, *Red Dust* (Stanford, Calif., 1952), p. 153; *Chung-kuo Kung-ch'an-tang tsai chung-nan-ti-ch'ü ling-tao ko-ming tou-cheng te li-shih tzu-liao* (Historical materials on the revolutionary struggles led by the CCP in central and South China; Wuhan, 1951), p. 275.

2. Norman Hanwell, "The Chinese Red Army," *Asia* (New York), 36:319 (May 1936).
3. *Hsing-huo liao-yuan* (A single spark can start a prairie fire; Hong Kong, 1960), p. 366.
4. *Hung-ch'i p'iao-p'iao* (Red flag fluttering; Peking, 1959), X, 98.
5. *Selected Works of Mao Tse-tung* (Peking, 1961), IV, 66.
6. *Chieh-fang chan-cheng hui-i-lu* (Recollections of the liberation war; Peking, 1961), p. 57.

Wang Tao-han

Specialist in scientific and technological affairs; vice-minister, First Ministry of Machine Building.

Wang Tao-han was for many years a senior technician in East China and, after 1952, in Peking. By 1945, when first identified by Japanese sources, he was already a deputy director of the "Huai-nan-su-wan" Border Region Administrative Office. A 1947 Communist handbook lists 19 "liberated areas," among which were "Huai-nan" (south of the Huai River) and "Su-wan" (Kiangsu and Anhwei). Apparently the Japanese data refer to these two areas, which may have been linked for administrative purposes. In any event, by 1946 Wang was known to be the deputy director of the Kiangsu-Anhwei Border Region Financial Department.

Sometime toward the end of the civil war with the Nationalists Wang moved southward into Chekiang and was named as vice-chairman of the Hangchow Military Control Commission after the city fell to the Communists on May 3, 1949. In this same year he also assumed two important posts in the Chekiang governmental structure, as director of both the Finance and Commerce Departments. Prior to the formal establishment in January 1950 of the East China Military and Administrative Committee (EC-MAC), the Communists had set up various *ad hoc* organs under the East China Military Region. One such organ was the East China Finance and Economics Committee, subordinate to which was an Industry Department headed by Wang. Then, with the formation of the ECMAC in January 1950, the Industry Department was placed under the jurisdiction of the ECMAC, with Wang retaining his directorship. In addition, he was named as a member of the ECMAC's Finance and Economics Committee. He was officially appointed to both these posts in February 1950 and held both to November 1952.

Wang was transferred from Chekiang to Shanghai by 1951, and in that year he was named a member of the Shanghai Finance and Economics Committee. The only other press reports about Wang during this period both occurred in November 1951 when he attended the fourth ECMAC meeting and spoke on increasing production at a meeting of the ECMAC Industry Department, of which he was the head.

In August 1952 several new ministries were formed under the national government, one of them the First Ministry of Machine Building, a ministry created from sections of the Ministry of Heavy Industry. Wang was named as a vice-minister, and although this ministry has subsequently undergone a series of reorganizations he has remained in his post. Wang made his first trip abroad as a member of the important group led by Chou En-lai to Moscow for the negotiations of August–September 1952, which led to the return of the Chinese Changchun (Manchuria) Railway to China and the extension of the term of joint use of Port Arthur as a naval base.

Beginning in 1953, Peking established joint committees with each of the other bloc nations to facilitate scientific liaison. For example, the "Sino-Czech Joint Committee for Scientific and Technical Cooperation" was formed in 1953. These committees have met approximately every six months, with the site alternating between Peking and the other capitals in the bloc. Wang has been the key Chinese official ("chairman of the Chinese side") on the joint committees for Sino-Czech and Sino-East German liaison. In this role he has signed agreements, which typically provide for such things as the exchange of blueprints or personnel, in the following years and cities. June 1953: Peking-Czechoslovakia; October 1953: Berlin-East Germany; June 1954: Peking-East Germany; July 1958: Berlin-East Germany; August 1958: Prague-Czechoslovakia; May 1959: Peking-Czechoslovakia; April 1960: Peking-East Germany; February 1961: Prague-Czechoslovakia; July 1962: Peking-Czechoslovakia and Prague-Czechoslovakia.

Aside from working on these formalized committees, Wang signed a very important agreement in Moscow in August 1958 providing for Soviet assistance in the building of 47 metallurgical, chemical, engineering, timber-processing, construction materials plants, coal mines, and power stations. In retrospect, this was probably one of the last Sino-Soviet agreements of significance to be signed prior to the rift between Peking and Moscow.

In addition to his negotiations with foreign technical specialists, Wang assumed other posts and engaged in other important activities dating from the mid-1950's. He served from November 1953 as a member of the Standing Committee of the First Executive Committee of the All-China Federation of Industry and Commerce (ACFIC), an organization established to foster greater participation from the men who were China's foremost industrialists and merchants in the pre-1949 period. In all such organizations the CCP has placed its own men; the selection of Wang for such a post probably rested on his technical background. Nonetheless, when the

Second Executive Committee of the ACFIC was formed in December 1956 he was dropped from membership. From 1954 Wang has also been a senior official of the China Mechanical Engineering Society; he was named as a vice-chairman at the society's second congress in August 1954 and was then promoted to chairman in 1962, a post he continues to hold. This is one of a number of learned societies subordinate to the China Scientific and Technical Association, of which Wang has been a member of the National Committee since its reorganization in September 1958.

Wang was also reported from time to time in the mid-1950's to be working with trade unions and "advanced" workers. For example, he attended the First National Congress of the First Machine Building Trade Union in August 1955 and gave a report before the National Conference of Outstanding Workers in the Machine Building Industry the following April.

Already well established in scientific and technical affairs, it was natural that he should be appointed in May 1957 to the reorganized and much expanded Scientific Planning Commission (SPC) under the State Council; he held this post until still another reorganization of the SPC in November 1958. In November 1957, Mao Tse-tung led a delegation to Moscow for the 40th anniversary celebrations of the Bolshevik Revolution. A number of technical delegations accompanied Mao, one of them a scientific group led by Academy of Sciences President Kuo Mo-jo. Wang was a member of this delegation, probably the largest group of scientists to leave China at one time since 1949.

In response to China's growing interest in foreign trade and aid, a Bureau for Economic Relations with Foreign Countries was formed in 1960 under the State Council. Four years later this was raised to a commission, and not long after Wang was named (October 1964) as a vice-chairman under Fang I, a Central Committee alternate and specialist in aid and trade matters. If this commission parallels a similar one in the Soviet Union it will concentrate on aid programs as opposed to trade which is handled by the Ministry of Foreign Trade. Still another indication of Wang's increasing ties with affairs abroad came in December 1964 when he was named as a member of the Fourth National Committee of the CPPCC as a representative of "peace and friendship associations with foreign countries."

Wang Ts'ung-wu

(c.1901–   ; Nei-huang hsien, Honan). Specialist in Party organization work; deputy secretary, CCP Control Commission; member, CCP Central Committee.

Wang Ts'ung-wu is a veteran specialist in Party organizational and control work. A member of the Party since the mid-twenties, Wang spent most of his early Party career in north China. Elected an alternate member of the Party Central Committee in 1945, he was promoted to full membership in 1956. He has also been a deputy secretary of the Party's Central Control Commission since 1956.

Wang was born in the village of Hou-hua, Nei-huang hsien. Nei-huang is a rural community in northeast Honan, located some 25 miles southeast of the industrial city of An-yang and not far from the borders of Hopeh and Shantung. His family was so poor that they had to send him to beg along with his mother and sister. In the early twenties he came into contact with the Communist movement through a local organization known as the Society of Poor People, supported by the CCP and working to bring relief to the needy. His sister, Wang Hsien-jung, now acclaimed by the Communists as a "revolutionary mother," joined the society, and presumably Wang did too. A CCP member by 1925, he was occupied from that year to 1927 organizing Party branches among peasants and salt workers in towns and villages just to the east of his native Nei-huang.[1] By 1929 Wang was head of the Party underground in Nei-huang.

Between 1929 and 1949 there is a gap in detailed information about Wang's career, and the scattered references to his activities do not mention specific dates. At some time after 1929 he went to the Soviet Union where he graduated from the University of the Toilers of China, the successor to Sun Yat-sen University. After returning home, Wang served with the Red Army as a political officer, rising from political commissar at the division level, to the army, and finally to the army corps level. During the middle years of the Sino-Japanese War he worked in Yenan under Wang Jo-fei (q.v.) in an investigation of land policies; this led to the adoption in early 1942 of a new agrarian program, the significance of which is discussed in the biography of Liu Hsiu-feng. Later, he became director of the Organization Department of the Party's Central Plains Bureau, responsible for the area centering around the territory of the old Oyüwan Soviet, which was located on the borders of Hupeh, Honan, and Anhwei. During the war he was also secretary of a Party district committee in the Hopeh-Shantung-Honan Border Region (located to the north of the Central Plains area), as well as a CCP official in the larger Shansi-Hopeh-Shantung-Honan (Chin-Chi-Lu-Yü) Border Region (see under Yang Hsiu-feng).

Wang's work as a Party organizer and underground worker was given recognition at the Party's Seventh National Congress, held in Yenan in April-June 1945, when he was elected an alternate member of the Central Committee. By March 1946 he was director of the Organiza-

tion Department of the Chin-Chi-Lu-Yü Party Committee; he was identified in this post when he attended a session of the Chin-Chi-Lu-Yü Assembly, held in Han-tan, southwest Hopeh.[2] By the late forties he had been promoted to director of the Organization Department of the Party's North China Bureau, a post he held until the Bureau was dissolved in 1954. He received his first governmental post in December 1951 when he was named to membership on the newly created North China Administrative Committee (NCAC). Responsible for the provinces of Hopeh, Pingyuan, Suiyuan, Shansi, and Chahar, the NCAC was chaired by Liu Lan-t'ao, another veteran of Party work in north China. In 1953–54 Wang also chaired the NCAC's People's Supervision Committee, a body that carried out in the government some of the supervisory tasks performed for and within the Party by the Organization Department. He held these posts in the NCAC until August 1954, just before the creation of the constitutional government, which absorbed the NCAC into the national bureaucracy.

Wang's work with the NCAC was clearly less important than his activities on behalf of the Party's North China Bureau. As already noted, he headed the Bureau's Organization Department. In addition, from 1951 to 1954 he was head of both the Rural Work Department and the Discipline Inspection Committee. The 1945 Party Constitution had provided for the establishment of both central and local Control Commissions, but these were not set up at the time, and instead less authoritative Discipline Inspections Committees were formed, such as the one headed by Wang. The latter were abolished in 1955 when Control Commissions were finally instituted in the wake of the Kao Kang (q.v.) purge. Wang rose to a still higher position in the North China Bureau by 1953 when he was identified as second deputy secretary, and in the following month he became first deputy secretary, a post that placed him under three more senior secretaries, Po I-po, Nieh Jung-chen, and Liu Lan-t'ao (qq.v.).

Possibly in connection with his Discipline Inspection Committee Work, Wang made a number of trips in the early fifties on so-called comfort missions, essentially entertainment and inspection missions sent out to a given area or battle front. In August 1951 he was a deputy leader of one such mission to the old "liberated areas" in the former Chin-Chi-Lu-Yü region. In the same capacity in January 1953 he visited units of the "Chinese People's Volunteers," the Chinese forces then fighting in Korea. In both February and July 1954 he performed the same function in visiting PLA units stationed in China.

Wang has represented the CCP in the CPPCC since the Second National Committee was formed in December 1954. He has been both a National Committee and Standing Committee member of the Second CPPCC (1954–1959), the Third CPPCC (1959–1964), and was re-elected to the Fourth CPPCC, which held its initial session in December 1964–January 1965. In April–May 1956 he made a second trip to North Korea, this time as a member of Nieh Jung-chen's delegation, which attended the Third Congress of the Korean Workers' (Communist) Party. He was abroad again in November–December 1959 as a member of T'an Chen-lin's delegation to the Seventh Congress of the Hungarian Socialist Workers' (Communist) Party.

When the CCP met for its Eighth National Congress in September 1956, Wang was promoted to full membership on the Central Committee. The day after the Congress closed, at the First Plenum of the new Central Committee, he was elected a member and one of the five deputy secretaries of the Party Control Commission, headed by Tung Pi-wu. In 1958 Wang made two of his relatively few public appearances, both in connection with control and supervision work; he spoke at the Seventh National Supervision Work Conference sponsored by the Ministry of Supervision (February–March) and at the Party's Third National Control Conference (March). He received a new assignment by September 1961 when he was identified as president of the Party's Higher Party School, the principal institute for the training of high-ranking Party members. He held this position until the fall of 1962 or possibly the spring of 1963. Wang's predecessor was Yang Hsien-chen (q.v.), who was last identified in the post in the spring of 1959; the change in the presidency may have resulted from Yang's political difficulties, which were made public in 1964. It may be noteworthy that though Yang had had long years of theoretical training (mainly in the Soviet Union), Wang had a very different background, his training having been almost entirely in Party organization and control work. After a little over a year as president, Wang was in turn replaced by the politically more important Lin Feng (q.v.); Wang was last identified in the presidency in October 1962, and by at least May 1963 Lin had assumed the position.

Since relinquishing the presidency of the Party School, Wang has apparently concentrated on international Party liaison work. Virtually every appearance he has made in recent years has been associated with foreign Communist Party leaders, as in March 1964 when I. G. Maurer, a member of the Rumanian Politburo, visited China. Wang has not been a frequent contributor to the Party press, although he did write an article entitled "The Solidarity and Discipline of the Party" for the December 16, 1959, issue of *Hung-ch'i* (Red flag), the Party's leading journal.

1. Ch'i Wu, *I-ko ko-ming ken-chü te ch'eng-chang; k'ang-Jih chan-cheng ho chieh-fang chan-cheng shih-ch'i te Chin-Chi-Lu-Yü pien-ch'ü kai-k'uang* (The establishment and growth of a revolutionary base: A general account of the Shansi-Hopeh-Shantung-Honan Border Region during the anti-Japanese war and the war of liberation; Peking, 1958), p. 18.
2. Yenan, *Chieh-fang jih-pao* (Liberation daily), March 30, 1946.

Wang Wei

Chairman, All-China Youth Federation.

Wang Wei, whose antecedents are unknown, is a rapidly rising youth leader who heads one of the two most important youth organizations, the All-China Youth Federation. He first came to prominence in May 1953 when he was appointed to membership on the People's Supervision Committee of the governmental organization known as the Central-South Administrative Committee (CSAC), then governing Honan, Hupeh, Hunan, Kiangsi, Kwangtung, and Kwangsi. The work of the Supervision Committee, with broad investigative powers, came to an end in 1954 when the regional government administrations were abolished. It was also in 1953 that Wang received his first known assignment in youth affairs, serving from 1953 to 1954 as a deputy secretary of the Central-South Work Committee of the New Democratic Youth League (known after mid-1957 as the Communist Youth League). Since that time his rise in the Youth League has been steady. He served on the presidium (steering committee) for the Youth League Congress held in June–July 1953, at which time he was elected to both the Central Committee and its Standing Committee. He was re-elected to these posts at the subsequent youth congresses held in May 1957 and June 1964. In addition, he served as the head of the Organization Department (1955–1957), always an important organ of power in Communist organizations, and from 1957 has also been a member of the most important organ within the league, that is, the Secretariat, the unit in charge of the day-to-day work of the league. Since the June 1964 Congress, he has been officially listed as the third-ranking secretary, under First Secretary Hu Yao-pang and Secretary Hu K'o-shih (qq.v.). Wang is almost certainly younger than Hu Yao-pang and Hu K'o-shih, but by the mid-1960's he could be regarded as immediately junior in rank to these two men. He is clearly a prime example of a rising functionary who has made his name exclusively in the post-war era.

Wang received his initial appointment in the national government in 1954 when the NPC first met, thereby ushering in the constitutional government (September 1954). He was a Honan deputy to the First NPC (1954–1959), but was changed to the Hopeh constituency for the Second NPC (1959–1964). He was again elected from Hopeh for the Third NPC, which held its first session in December 1964–January 1965, with Wang serving as a member of the Congress presidium during this session. He spoke on youth affairs before the sessions of the NPC held in February 1958 and April 1959. Apart from this work in the national legislature, however, his activities have centered almost exclusively on youth work. More particularly, he appears to be a specialist in international activities of the Chinese youth movement. Between 1955 and 1963, he led six youth delegations abroad to attend congresses of other Communist youth organizations or to make "youth friendship" visits. Five of these trips took him to Communist nations (Czechoslovakia, February 1955 and August 1960; North Vietnam, October 1956; Hungary and Poland, September–October 1958; and North Korea, November 1963). His visit to Czechoslovakia in 1960 was for the purpose of attending meetings of the Communist-dominated International Union of Students, as was another trip (to Iraq in September–October 1960). Wang made still another visit to a Communist nation in February 1960 when he accompanied Liu Ch'ang-sheng to Moscow for the celebrations marking the 10th anniversary of the Sino-Soviet Treaty of Friendship, Alliance, and Mutual Assistance, the cornerstone of Chinese Communist foreign policy during the first decade of the PRC. The association with Liu Ch'ang-sheng (q.v.), a Central Committee member, suggests that Wang is beginning to play an increasingly important part in international liaison work. Liu has long been one of the key Party officials engaged in international liaison between the CCP and other Communist parties and Communist-front organizations. Wang was scheduled to have made still another trip in January 1963 when he left Peking leading a youth group destined for the Eighth Congress of the Democratic Youth League of Japan. However, the Chinese youth group was denied entry into Japan by the Japanese authorities.

Although Wang made a late entry into the ranks of the All-China Youth Federation, by January 1965 he was heading the organization, second only to the Youth League in importance. From 1958 to 1962 he served as a member of the Federation's National Committee but was dropped from the organization when the Fourth National Committee was formed in April 1962. Perhaps there were plans that did not eventuate to reassign Wang to other work at this time. However, when the higher echelons of the Federation were restaffed in January 1965, he was brought back into the organization to replace Liu Hsi-yuan (q.v.) as the Federation chairman.

Although Wang's specialty seems to be international youth affairs, he has also been involved in some of the domestic activities of Chinese youths. For example, he served as a member of the presidium for two national conferences of "youth activists in building socialism" (September 1955 and November–December 1958) and in May 1964 he took part in celebrations marking the 45th anniversary of the May Fourth Movement. He has been an occasional contributor to the Communist press; an example appeared in the June 5, 1960, issue of the *JMJP*, an article dealing with the education of Young Pioneers in Communist schools.

Wang Wei-chou

(1887–1970; K'ai-hsien, Szechwan). Standing Committee member, CCP Control Commission, member, CCP Central Committee.

One of the oldest of the Chinese Communist leaders, Wang Wei-chou joined the CCP in the late twenties after a long career in revolutionary activity in Szechwan that began during the 1911 Revolution. He served as a garrison commander and civil administrator in Kansu and Shensi during the Sino-Japanese War and then as a government official in the southwest during the early years of the PRC. Wang was elected an alternate member of the Party Central Committee in 1945; he was promoted to full membership in 1956, at which time he was also named to the Party's Central Control Commission.

Wang was born in 1887, into a landlord family in K'ai-hsien in northern Szechwan. Little is known of his early life, but by the 1911 Revolution he was serving in the army as garrison commander in Ta-hsien, 50 miles west of K'ai-hsien. In association with Liu Po-ch'eng and Wu Yü-chang (qq.v.), both natives of Szechwan, he is said to have taken part in the revolution that overturned the Manchu Dynasty. As indicated below, Wang's ties with Wu over the next four decades were particularly close, and it was allegedly Wu and Liu who brought Wang into the CCP. He was still in the military in 1915–16 when, apparently in association with Liu Po-ch'eng and Chu Te, he participated in revolts that swept southwest China (particularly Szechwan) in opposition to Yuan Shih-k'ai's attempts to enthrone himself as the new emperor of China. At some time in the late teens Wang left the army and, like many Chinese of this period, went to Japan. He is known to have gone from Japan to Korea in 1919 where he was associated with Communist groups. Wang's presence in Korea is noteworthy if only because so few Chinese Communist leaders had been there prior to 1945 (principally, of course, because Korea was under complete Japanese domination). Moreover, the year that he was in

Korea—1919—coincided with the initial steps in the establishment of the Korean Communist Party (albeit outside Korea proper).[1] Possibly through connections with Korean Communists, Wang made his way to the Soviet Union in 1919. According to an account written by Wu Yü-chang,[2] Wang returned to Peking in August 1920 after a year of "work and study" in Russia. Wang gave Wu a "rather detailed account" of conditions in the Soviet Union, then in the throes of "war Communism." The two men then convened a meeting of students in Peking and solicited funds to be sent to Russia. Wu's account also claims that Wang later collected funds in Shanghai.

Little is known about Wang's activities in the early twenties, but at some time in that period he returned to Szechwan where he opened a school in Hsuan-han, not far from his native K'ai-hsien in the northern part of the province. After the failure of the Nanchang Uprising in August 1927 (see under Yeh T'ing), Wang helped to stage local Communist-led revolts in Kuang-han hsien, Szechwan, a few miles north of Chengtu. When these failed he turned to underground work. In the following year (1928), through the introduction of Liu Po-ch'eng and Wu Yü-chang, Wang was admitted to the CCP.

Wang's activities in north Szechwan from 1928 to 1932 are not well documented, but he apparently remained in command of troops variously described as "bandits" or "Communists." In any event, he was still in the area in late 1932 when Hsu Hsiang-ch'ien (q.v.) led his Fourth Front Army from the old Communist Oyüwan base to north Szechwan. By the first half of 1933 the Communists had established the T'ung-Nan-Pa Soviet, named for the principal hsien in northeast Szechwan, which the Soviet occupied. This area (also known as the Szechwan-Shensi Soviet) is described in the biography of Wang Hung-k'un. Wang Wei-chou associated himself with the Soviet and placed his troops under the command of the Fourth Front Army. When the Second All-China Congress of Soviets was held in Juichin in January–February 1934, he was elected to the governing Central Executive Committee, almost certainly *in absentia*. Hsu Hsiang-ch'ien's forces were then composed of five armies; there is conflicting evidence, but apparently Wang commanded the 33rd Army as of 1934. A Western journalist who visited the Soviet areas in the mid-thirties (shortly after the Communists departed) commented that the 33rd Army was newly organized and poorly equipped.[3]

In the first part of 1935 the forces led by Hsu and Chang Kuo-t'ao (q.v.) left Szechwan; the complex route taken on their portion of the Long March is described in Hsu Hsiang-ch'ien's biography. When the Sino-Japanese War broke out in mid-1937, Hsu's troops were absorbed

into the 129th Division under Liu Po-ch'eng's command. One of this Division's subordinate elements was the 385th Brigade. This brigade was apparently commanded by Wang Hung-k'un (q.v.) during the early stages of the war, but whereas Wang Hung-k'un operated in Hopeh and Shantung, Wang Wei-chou apparently remained in the eastern Kansu area. In any event, from about 1940 to the close of the war he seems to have commanded the 385th Brigade, or at least elements of it. He was identified as a brigade commander in Ch'ing-yang hsien, southeast Kansu, in 1939 and during the war was also commissioner of what the Communists called the East Kansu Administrative District. In November 1941 Wang attended the Second Assembly of the Shensi-Kansu-Ninghsia (Shen-Kan-Ning) Border Region, originally established in 1937 with its capital at Yenan.[4]

By 1943 Wang had been transferred from Ch'ing-yang in Kansu to Kuan-chung, one of the major sub-divisions of the larger Shen-Kan-Ning Border Region. Kuan-chung was located in Shensi, its southernmost boundary only about 50 miles north of Sian. Like many Eighth Route Army units on garrison duty, during the latter stages of the war Wang's troops were mainly occupied in agricultural work.[5] Work of this sort received great praise from the top Party leaders, who regarded it as a means for the Red Army to stay close to the "masses." At the Party's Seventh National Congress, held in Yenan from April to June 1945, Wang was elected an alternate member of the Central Committee. Then about 58, he was one of the oldest men elected.

In 1945 Wang accompanied Chou En-lai to Chungking where the Communists had a liaison mission. This assignment may have been made because of Wang's familiarity with his native province. Following the cease-fire agreement worked out by U.S. Special Envoy George C. Marshall in January 1946, the Communists were able to operate as an open political party. As a consequence, at an April 30 press conference in Chungking, Chou En-lai revealed that Wu Yü-chang was the secretary of the Szechwan CCP Committee and that Wang was his deputy. Wu has candidly explained the situation, noting that because the capital was then being transferred from Chungking to Nanking, it was necessary to bring the Szechwan CCP Committee into the open in order to carry on "united front work and the struggle against the Kuomintang."[6] Wu and Wang immediately set about to "gain real recognition" for the status of the CCP in Chungking. In short order the relations between the CCP and the KMT in Chungking worsened. According to Wu's version, the Communist office was under constant KMT surveillance and "the Kuomintang newspapers fabricated rumours every day: either saying Comrade Wang Wei-chou had already arrived in northern Szechwan [Wang's native area] to organize an armed uprising, or that we wanted to start riots in Chungking, scheming to use these rumours as a pretext to do mischief to us."

By the early summer of 1946 the CCP apparently believed that Wang's position in Chungking had become untenable and that he "should be sent away." According to the Communist version, the KMT initially blocked Wang's departure by refusing to issue him an airline ticket but finally did so upon Wu Yü-chang's intervention with Chang Ch'ün, then head of the KMT provisional headquarters in Chungking. When Chang agreed to Wang's departure in the summer of 1946 he is alleged to have said to Wu: " 'Wang handles military affairs, and if he doesn't leave, everybody will be uneasy.' " Wang then proceeded to Nanking to join Chou En-lai, but in November 1946 Chou broke off the talks and returned to Yenan, presumably taking Wang with him.

Once back in the northwest, Wang resumed his duties in the military establishment. By 1948 he was a deputy commander under Ho Lung of the Shensi-Kansu-Ninghsia-Shansi-Suiyuan Joint Defense Headquarters, and when this evolved into the Northwest Military Region in 1949 he continued to serve under Ho. When Sian fell to the Communists in May 1949, Ho became head of the Municipal Military Control Commission and Wang was named to head the Sian Defense Force (presumably a garrison command post). He remained there throughout the summer and then in September 1949 he went to Peking as a representative of the "Northwest Liberated Areas" to attend the CPPCC meetings which brought the new central government into existence (October 1). Wang may have returned to the northwest after the meetings in Peking, but if so he was only there briefly, for by the first half of 1950 he was transferred to the southwest (as was his superior, Ho Lung). With this transfer, Wang's active career in military affairs was brought to an end. Already in his mid-sixties, he has since concentrated mainly on political matters.

To administer the four provinces of Szechwan, Yunnan, Sikang, and Kweichow, the Communists established the Southwest Military and Administrative Committee (SWMAC) in July 1950 under the chairmanship of Liu Po-ch'eng, Wang's former colleague. Among the vice-chairmen were imporant Party leaders Ho Lung and Teng Hsiao-p'ing, as well as Wang. Concurrently, Wang was named to head the SWMAC's Nationalities Affairs Committee. The selection of Wang for this assignment may have derived from the fact that his native area in north Szechwan is heavily populated by minority peoples. He received a closely related post in April 1951 when he became president of the Southwest Nationalities Institute in Chengtu, Szechwan; the newly organized school formally opened in June 1951. Then, in November of the same year, Wang was identified as director of the Southwest Party Bureau's United Front Work Department. United Front work is principally concerned with gaining the allegiance of non-Communist intellectuals, but in areas where appropriate (as in southwest China) united front specialists are also responsible for gaining the allegiance of the non-Han minority peoples. Wang's other assignment under the SWMAC was as head of the Political and Legal Affairs Committee (late November 1951 to mid-1953). When the SWMAC was reorganized into the Southwest Administrative Committee in February 1953, he retained his vice-chairmanship, still under Liu Po-ch'eng. From October to November of that year he accompanied his colleague Ho Lung to North Korea as a deputy leader of a large delegation sent to "comfort" the Chinese troops who remained there after the Korean War.

When the regional governments were disbanded in mid-1954, Wang was transferred to Peking where he assumed posts in the constitutional government, inaugurated at the opening session of the First NPC (September). Unlike many important Party leaders who hold only nominal positions in the NPC, Wang has been fairly active in this legislative organ. He has been a Szechwan deputy to the First, Second, and Third NPC's, which opened their first sessions in September 1954, April 1959, and December 1964, respectively. More important, he has been a member of the NPC Standing Committee since 1954, as well as a member of the NPC Credentials Committee (and since mid-1956, a vice-chairman of the Credentials Committee). At the Party's Eighth Congress in September 1956, Wang was elevated from alternate to full membership on the Party Central Committee. On the day after the Congress, at the First Plenum of the new Central Committee, he was elected a member of the Party's Central Control Commission, in charge of internal Party discipline. Five years later a Standing Committee was established within the Control Commission, and Wang was named as one of the members, a post he still retains. Because of the security that surrounds the work of the Control Commission, virtually nothing is known of his work in this capacity.

Wang has spent most of his time in Peking since 1954, but on occasion has made tours in the provinces, as in May 1956 when he inspected Inner Mongolia and in October of the same year when he led a large delegation to visit national minority peoples in Szechwan and Yunnan. He also represented the PRC abroad on three occasions between 1959 and 1961. In his capacity as a council member of the China-

Poland Friendship Association he led a group to Warsaw in July–August 1959 for the 15th anniversary of Polish National Day, and in October of the same year he led a demobilized servicemen's delegation to Moscow. He was in Ulan Bator in June–July 1961 as a member of Ulanfu's delegation sent to attend the 14th Congress of the Mongolian People's Revolutionary (Communist) Party and to participate in celebrations marking the 40th anniversary of the Mongolian "revolution." Apart from these activities, Wang's name is mentioned in the press most frequently in connection with protocol functions; for example, as a NPC Standing Committee member he often participates in serving as a host to foreign parliamentary delegations visiting China.

[Wang died in Peking on January 10, 1970, at the age of 83.]

1. Robert A. Scalapino and Chong-sik Lee, "The Origins of the Korean Communist Movement (I)," *The Journal of Asian Studies,* 20:12 (November 1960).

2. *ECMM* 173, p. 6.

3. Norman Hanwell, "The Chinese Red Army," *Asia,* May 1936, p. 319.

4. *Shen-Kan-Ning pien-ch'u ts'an-i-hui wen-hsien hui-chi* (Collection of documents of the Shensi-Kansu-Ninghsia Border Region Assembly; Peking, 1958), p. 168.

5. Hsu Yung-ying, *A Survey of Shensi-Kansu-Ninghsia Border Region* (New York, 1945), pt. II, p. 40.

6. Wu Yü-chang, "The Bankruptcy of the U.S.–Chiang Kai-shek Peace Plot," *The Great Turning Point* (Peking, 1962), pp. 16–19.

Wang Yu-p'ing

(1910–   ; Shantung). Diplomat.

Diplomat Wang Yu-p'ing is a university graduate and reportedly knows Russian. According to a Cuban Communist source, he joined the Communist Party in 1931,[1] and in the same year he is known to have joined the Communist armed forces. The Cuban source asserts that he participated in the Long March (1934–35). No record of Wang's activity during the Sino-Japanese War is available, and only fragmentary details exist regarding his career during the civil war against the Nationalists (1946–1949). The Cuban source provides information that during this period he was an engineer in the Red armies; he apparently also served as a political officer and at one point in the late 1940's he was director of the Political Department of a group army.

When the PRC was established on October 1, 1949, the other Communist nations immediately accorded it recognition. However, it was some months before Peking dispatched ambassadors to most of these nations. Thus, although Sino-Rumanian relations were established in October 1949, it was not until June 1950 that Wang (officially described as a general) was appointed; in August he presented his credentials in Bucharest. During his four years in Bucharest he negotiated and then signed on June 9, 1953, the 1953 plan for the implementation of the Sino-Rumanian Cultural Cooperation Agreement, and on April 19, 1954, also in Bucharest, he signed the annual trade pact covering the year 1954. He also witnessed the signing of various agreements in Bucharest and Peking and presumably played some role in the negotiations. For example, he was present in October 1953 when a visiting Chinese official signed a protocol on scientific and technical cooperation, and back in Peking, he witnessed the signing of a cultural pact between the two nations in May 1954.

On November 20, 1954, Wang was replaced by K'o Pai-nien in Rumania, but on the same day was reassigned to become Peking's first ambassador to Norway. Oslo and Peking had recognized each other as early as January 1950, but it was not until October 1954 that the two nations agreed to the establishment of formal diplomatic ties. Wang arrived in Oslo on June 1, 1955, and presented his credentials a few days later to King Haakon VII. The record of Sino-Norwegian ties is generally sparse, as is illustrated by the fact that no government-to-government pact was signed between the two nations until mid-1958 (after Wang's departure), and therefore Wang was seldom in the news. The very few times he was mentioned publicly were usually in connection with receptions given by the embassy in Oslo in commemoration of a Chinese Communist holiday. After less than three years in Norway, Wang was replaced in April 1958 by Hsu I-hsin and then returned home for another assignment.

In July 1958 China and Cambodia agreed to the establishment of diplomatic relations. A month later Wang was named as the first ambassador (thereby becoming the first Chinese ambassador to open three embassies). Before leaving for Phnom Penh he took part in the elaborate festivities for Cambodian Premier Norodom Sihanouk who visited Peking in August 1958. In the following month he went to Cambodia and on September 25th presented his credentials. In contrast to his previous assignments in Bucharest and Oslo, Wang's life was an intensively busy one in Phnom Penh. During his three and a half years there Sino-Cambodian relations grew increasingly close. It is difficult to say how large a role Wang played in this situation; certainly the intensification of the war in Vietnam and the political and military instability in neighboring Laos helped to bring Cambodia closer to its huge neighbor to the north.

In a more specific sense, Wang was constantly

in the news in connection with a heavy flow of Chinese delegations of every type to Phnom Penh, as well as with an equally large number of Cambodian groups that visited China. During his tenure as envoy to Cambodia, he returned to China at least twice. His return in December 1960 in the company of Cambodian Prince Norodom Sihanouk was particularly important, because during this visit Sihanouk signed the Sino-Cambodian Treaty of Friendship and Mutual Non-aggression. A little over a year later, on the eve of his departure, Wang was decorated with a medal signifying his "friendly cooperation." A few days later, on February 9, 1962, he left for home, having been replaced by Ch'en Shu-liang.

Following his return to China Wang was not apparently given a specific assignment, but he did remain within the Foreign Ministry as a counsellor. In this capacity he accompanied Liu Shao-ch'i on a friendship visit to Cambodia in May 1963. (Prior to this leg of his trip, Liu had been in Indonesia and Burma, and after his visit to Cambodia he went to North Vietnam. Wang, however, only accompanied Liu during the Cambodian portion of the trip.) Aside from this one trip, nothing else was heard of Wang from his February 1962 departure from Cambodia until December 1963 when a Cuban newspaper announced that he had been named to succeed Shen Chien as the ambassador to Cuba; therefore Wang was one of the very few Chinese diplomats to have served in four different nations. His appointment was made official in January 1964 and he arrived in Havana in May 1964, presenting his credentials on May 21. Sino-Cuban relations have been rather active during his stay in that country, and thus Wang receives considerable coverage in the national press. Aside from the normal receptions and other diplomatic functions, he was reported as the signatory on August 11, 1964, of a protocol on economic cooperation. His assignment in Havana must be considered an appointment of more than average significance. Cuba is the only nation in the Western Hemisphere with which Peking maintains diplomatic relations. Furthermore, the Castro regime is probably considered a key prize in the contest for allegiance being waged by the Chinese and Soviet Communists in their ideological dispute, and doubtless one of Wang's assignments is to win the Cubans for the Chinese "camp."

In September 1964 Wang was elected as a deputy from his native Shantung to the Third NPC, which held its first session in December 1964–January 1965. This must be regarded as an exception, because the general practice has been that those who serve abroad do not also serve in the Congress.

---

1. *Hoy,* December 6, 1963.

Wei Heng

First secretary, Shansi CCP Committee.

Wei Heng, whose antecedents are unknown, apparently began his rise in the Party hierarchy through Party organizational channels. By mid-1952 he was already the director of the Organization Department of the Shansi Party Committee; at this time (June 1952) he was given an appointment in the provincial government (broadly parallel to his functions within the Party) as chairman of the People's Supervision Committee of the Shansi Provincial Government. In the following May (1953) Wei was named to membership on the Shansi Electoral Committee, the committee responsible for the management of provincial elections in preparation for the First NPC in 1954. In both 1953 and 1954 he also undertook investigations in Shansi on the progress of Party work and leadership. Apparently Wei's activities were favorably recognized, for by November 1954 he was elevated from his Organization Department post in Shansi to become a member of the Shansi Party Standing Committee under First Secretary T'ao Lu-chia (q.v.).

By January 1955 Wei had risen to second deputy secretary of the Shansi Party Committee and two years later (February 1957) was a secretary (still under First Secretary T'ao Lu-chia). In the interim he was also moving up the hierarchical ladder in the Shansi government channels. In April 1956 he was elected as a vice-governor; by October of the same year he was acting governor in place of Governor Wang Shih-ying (q.v.); he continued to serve as acting governor until he finally replaced Wang as governor in elections of December 1958. Thus by the late 1950's Wei was probably the second-ranking official in the province after First Party Secretary T'ao Lu-chia (an alternate member of the Party Central Committee). Wei has been reported in the press with the frequency generally accorded an official of his stature; thus he has received press attention in connection with inspections in Shansi, celebrations normally attended by senior provincial leaders, and meetings over which he presided. Of interest is the fact that he accompanied three Politburo members (Chu Te, Ch'en I, and Tung Pi-wu) on inspections made in Shansi in September 1958, May–June 1959, and May 1960, respectively.

One of the rare occasions when Wei left Shansi was in June–July 1960 when he led a delegation to the 29th Poznan International Fair in Poland, a somewhat unusual assignment for a provincial official. Another assignment which has presumably brought him to Peking from time to time has been as a Shansi deputy to the NPC. He served as a deputy for the Second NPC (1959–1964) and was then re-elected in October 1964 for the Third NPC, which held its first session in December 1964–January 1965. At the meeting in October 1964, Wei was re-elected as the Shansi governor.

In the spring of 1965 Shansi First Secretary T'ao Lu-chia was transferred to Peking to assume an important position in the field of economic planning. Not long after, in July 1965, Wei was identified as the successor to T'ao in the post of the provincial Party first secretary. Probably because of this new assignment in the Shansi Party hierarchy, Wei relinquished the provincial governorship to Wang Ch'ien in December 1965. At the same time, however, he was elected a member of the Shansi Provincial People's Council and chairman (replacing T'ao Lu-chia) of the Third Shansi Committee of the CPPCC.

Wei Kuo-ch'ing

(c.1914–   ; Tung-lan hsien, Kwangsi). Chairman, Kwangsi-Chuang Autonomous Region; alternate member, CCP Central Committee.

Wei Kuo-ch'ing was born about 1914, although one source uses the year 1908. He is one of the very few members of a national minority group to have risen to the Party Central Committee. Wei belongs to the Chuang minority, the largest ethnic minority in China, most of whom live in Kwangsi. It is possible that Wei was first attracted to the Communist Party through the efforts of Wei Pa-ch'ün (1894–1932), who was also a Chuang from Tung-lan hsien. Wei Pa-ch'ün founded a peasant training institute in the Tung-lan area in the mid-1920's and later formed the Tung-lan Revolutionary Committee. This became the nucleus of the Communists' Seventh Red Army (see under Chang Yun-i). In 1930 this army moved from Kwangsi to the Kiangsi Soviet area where many of its units were merged with other Communist armies. In the same year, Wei Kuo-ch'ing was identified as a member of the First Army Corps, formed in mid-1930 under the leadership of Chu Te and Mao Tse-tung. Two years later, Wei was a regimental commander in P'eng Te-huai's Third Army Corps, one of the major components of the Chu-Mao forces (known by then as the First Front Army).

Wei was not heard of again until 1938, by which time he was a troop commander in the Communist New Fourth Army in east-central China. This assignment suggests that he did not make the Long March to the northwest, because the New Fourth Army, activated in 1938, was recruited largely from military forces that remained in central-south China when the Chu-Mao armies left Kiangsi in 1934. However, after the start of the Sino-Japanese War, two units from the Eighth Route Army were sent from Shansi to join the New Fourth Army; these were recruited from troops which had made the

Long March. Because Wei had connections with both of these units in the 1940's, it is possible that he made the Long March before joining the New Fourth Army. One of the Eighth Route Army units, under the command of P'eng Hsueh-feng (q.v.), left Shansi in the fall of 1938 and was incorporated into the New Fourth Army in June 1939. In August 1940, when P'eng's unit (then called the Sixth Detachment) was at Ko-yang in north Anhwei, it was joined by a second and larger unit sent from the Eighth Route Army. This second force became the Third Division under Huang K'o-ch'eng after the New Fourth Army Incident of January 1941 (see under Yeh T'ing). In 1941 Wei was a commander in the division's Eighth Brigade, and in that same year the division moved eastward and made its headquarters in Fou-ning, in northeast Kiangsu east of the Grand Canal. Three years later, however, Wei was identified as a commander of the New Fourth Army's Fourth Division, which was operating north of the Huai River. The Fourth Division was commanded by P'eng Hsueh-feng (q.v.) until 1944. By the following year Wei was deputy commander of the Fourth Division.

In the immediate postwar period Wei remained in the area north of the Huai River. In early 1946, under the terms of the cease-fire agreement worked out by U.S. Special Envoy George C. Marshall, special field teams were stationed in many cities to supervise the truce. Holding the simulated rank of major-general, Wei was the Communist representative to the field team at Hsu-chou, an important rail center in northwest Kiangsu. However, in the latter half of 1946, as the truce began to collapse, many of the Communist representatives to the various field teams returned to their military units. Wei now took command of the Second Column under the East China PLA, and in this capacity he took part in the victorious Huai-Hai Campaign fought in the closing weeks of 1948 and early 1949 in and around Hsu-chou. At approximately this time Wei became deputy political commissar of the 10th Army Group, one of the major components of Ch'en I's Third Field Army (the new name for the East China PLA).

After the decisive Huai-Hai Campaign, Ch'en I's men began their southward advance along the coastal provinces. When Soochow (Su-chou), west of Shanghai, fell in late April 1949, Wei became chairman of the city's Military Control Commission. In August he was replaced in Soochow by Hui Yü-yü; at the same time Wei was promoted to political commissar of Yeh Fei's (q.v.) 10th Army Group, and in this capacity he moved south to Foochow, the Fukien capital, to assume new and important posts. Foochow was captured in mid-August 1949; Wei became mayor of the city, chairman of the Foochow Military Control Commission, and both deputy political commissar and director of the Political Department of the Fukien Military District. In the early years of the PRC, Chang Ting-ch'eng was the leading Communist official in Fukien, and Yeh Fei and Wei were two of his top aides.

Wei continued to be the Foochow mayor until the spring of 1951 and apparently held his other posts in Fukien until the mid-1950's. However, he received very little attention in the press in the early 1950's, perhaps because he held a particularly sensitive post; in sending a message of condolence at the time of Stalin's funeral in March 1953, Wei was identified as "a commander" of Public Security forces. There is rather little information on the Public Security troops, but it is known that their functions include the protection of vital installations, particularly in borderland or coastal regions. And, because of its proximity to Taiwan, the Fukien coast has been a sensitive area to the Communists since they conquered the province in 1949.

In 1954 Wei was elected a deputy from his native Kwangsi to the First NPC. He was re-elected to the Second NPC (1959–1964) and again to the Third NPC, which held its first session in December 1964–January 1965. At the close of the initial session of the First NPC in September 1954, Wei was elected to membership on the Standing Committee, which is responsible for the affairs of the congress between the annual sessions. At the same time, he was made a member of the National Defense Council, the military advisory organ with little authority but considerable prestige. He has twice been re-named to the Council (1959 and 1965). In the following month (October 1954), when assignments under the reorganized government were made, Wei was appointed a vice-chairman of the State Council's Nationalities Affairs Commission. His appointment obviously related to his Chuang nationality, just as Ulanfu's Mongol origins accounted for his being made the commission chairman. Wei assumed still another position in 1954 when he was selected for membership on the Second Executive Committee of the Sino-Soviet Friendship Association (SSFA), then a very active organization. He was named to the Third Committee in May 1959, but after the early 1960's, the SSFA became relatively inactive in the wake of the Sino-Soviet rift.

Two more national honors came to Wei in 1955 and 1956. In 1955 military orders were awarded for service in the Red Army from 1927 to 1950. Because his name was on a composite list, it is not certain that Wei received all three major orders, but in view of his lengthy military career it is likely that he did. More important, he was elected an alternate member of the Party Central Committee at the Eighth Party Congress held in September 1956.

In the interim, Wei had been transferred back to his native Kwangsi. Chang Yun-i, the Kwangsi governor, had been transferred to Peking in the fall of 1954 when the central government was reorganized. Wei was sent to Kwangsi to replace him and was formally elected governor in February 1955. There he shared power with Party First Secretaries Ch'en Man-yuan and Liu Chien-hsun (qq.v.). By January 1957 Wei was identified as a Party secretary in Kwangsi; he was promoted to second secretary by March 1961 and finally succeeded Liu Chien-hsun as first secretary in October 1961 (Liu having been transferred to Honan). In April 1957, possibly to relieve him of responsibilities normally exercised in Peking, Wei was removed as a vice-chairman of the Nationalities Affairs Commission, and at about the same time also lost his post as a member of the NPC Standing Committee. In September of the same year, the first steps were taken to transform Kwangsi from a province to an "autonomous region" for the Chuang minorities. Wei was named to chair the preparatory committee (September 1957) and played a major role in the formal inauguration in March 1958 of the Kwangsi-Chuang Autonomous Region (KCAR). At the initial congress of the KCAR he made the keynote speech on the work of the region and was then elected KCAR chairman, a position he still retains.

By October 1961, as already noted, Wei was both chairman of the governmental apparatus for Kwangsi and the Party first secretary. Between 1962 and 1965 he received three further appointments, which gave him the dominant role within the KCAR. In December 1962 he was elected to the chairmanship of the Kwangsi Committee of the CPPCC. In February 1964 he became first political commissar of the Kwangsi Military District, and just one year later he was also identified as the first secretary of the Military District's Party Committee. In the early 1950's it was normal practice for one provincial official to hold several key concurrent positions within the Party, the government, and the army. However, by the late 1950's the increasing complexities of the society brought about a greater division of labor, with relatively few provincial officials holding important concurrent posts. Wei's multiplicity of positions, therefore, must be viewed as an exception, and presumably as a tribute to his abilities.

As a key official in Kwangsi, Wei has been frequently occupied with the tasks normally given to a man of his political stature—making inspections, attending conferences, and hosting the numerous foreign visitors to Nanning, the regional capital. Because Nanning is a transportation center for travel to Southeast Asia, he is often mentioned by the press in connection with visits abroad of important Chinese leaders. For example, he was present in December 1961 for the departure to Vietnam of Marshal Yeh Chien-ying.

Wei was selected to be a representative of the national minorities on the Fourth National Committee of the CPPCC, which opened in December 1964, and when the meetings closed in January 1965 he was elected a vice-chairman of the CPPCC. He has occasionally written for major publications, one of the more significant being the article "Struggle for the Acceleration of the Economic Construction of Kwangsi," which appeared in *Min-tsu t'uan-chieh* (Nationalities unity, no. 4, April 1963), the most important journal devoted to the affairs of China's minority groups. The July 16, 1963, issue of *Chung-kuo ch'ing-nien pao* (China youth news) carried a speech by Wei urging youths to choose agriculture as a lifetime career, an address he had given in Kwangsi before a meeting of "activists" in rural areas.

Wei is married to Hsu Ch'i-ch'ien; nothing further is known about her.

Wu Chih-p'u

(c.1906–   ; Ch'i-hsien, Honan). Provincial Party leader; member, CCP Central Committee.

Wu Chih-p'u, who has also been known as Wu T'ien-hsiang, was a political officer with the New Fourth Army during the Sino-Japanese War. After the Communists took power in 1949 he was governor of Honan for the next 12 years, and since 1962 he has been a secretary of the Party's Central-South Bureau. Wu was elected a member of the CCP Central Committee in 1956.

Wu is a native of Ch'i-hsien, located some 30 miles southeast of Kaifeng in Honan province. Aside from the report that he was once an elementary school teacher, nothing is known of his early career. In the spring of 1938, not long after the Sino-Japanese War began, Wu was leading a detachment of Communist guerrilla troops in eastern Honan (his native region).[1] Later that year the important Communist military officer P'eng Hsueh-feng (q.v.) was sent from Shansi to east Honan at the head of another detachment. Although there is no documentation, it appears that Wu's guerrillas were merged with those led by P'eng. During the course of the next year, 1939, P'eng's troops moved eastward into Anhwei province and were designated the Sixth Detachment of the Communists' New Fourth Army. Immediately following the New Fourth Army Incident in January 1941 (see under Yeh T'ing), the army was reorganized. The Sixth Detachment was reorganized into the Fourth Division under P'eng's command. Some time during the remaining years of the war, Wu became director of the division's Political Department. The Fourth Division controlled an area the Communists called the North Huai Military

District. It was bounded on the south by the Huai River, on the west by the Tientsin-Pukow Railway, on the north by a line running from the Grand Canal to Hsu-chou (Kiangsu), and on the east by the Grand Canal. Wu was with P'eng when the latter was killed in 1944, and several years later he co-authored a brief sketch of P'eng's career, which appeared in one of the better known collections of biographies of Chinese Communist "martyrs."[2]

Wu apparently remained in the region north of the Huai River in the immediate postwar period. During the first year of the civil war, Communist guerrilla units in this area were hard pressed by the Nationalists, but in mid-1947 the Communists took to the offensive when Liu Po-ch'eng's (q.v.) armies crossed the Yellow River in a southward thrust which carried to the Ta-pieh Mountains on the Hupeh-Honan-Anhwei border. In the course of this offensive the Central Plains Liberated Area was set up; this area, in turn, was subdivided into three sections, one of which was the Honan-Anhwei-Kiangsu (HAK) Border Region. The executive arm of the Border Region was known as the HAK Administrative Office; Wu was made the director and retained the post until 1949 when this part of China was conquered by the PLA. In the meantime, northern Honan was the scene of numerous battles, many of them in the region around Kaifeng on the important Lunghai Railway. The city fell to the Communists in June 1948; it was retaken by the Nationalists, but was finally captured by the PLA in October 1948. In 1948–49 Wu was the Kaifeng mayor, and it was there in March 1949 that the Communists, having conquered the entire area, established the Central Plains Provisional People's Government under the chairmanship of Teng Tzu-hui (q.v.). Wu was made one of the two vice-chairmen.

At the second conference of the Central Plains Government, held in Kaifeng in May 1949, Wu was appointed the first Communist governor of Honan, China's third most populous province. In the wake of the southward advance of the PLA, the Central Plains capital was moved to Wuhan in June 1949; Wu retained his vice-chairmanship with this short-lived government, but he remained in Honan to carry out his duties as governor, a post he was to hold for 12 more years. (Kaifeng was the Honan capital until October 1954, after which it was transferred to Chengchow.) He was also president of Honan University (located in Kaifeng) from 1949 to about the end of 1950. In September 1949 Wu was in Peking where, as a representative of the Central China Liberated Area, he attended the inaugural session of the CPPCC, the body that established the national government on October 1. A few days later, he was elected a member of the First Executive Board of the Sino-Soviet Friendship Association (to 1954).

In early February 1950 the Central-South Military and Administrative Committee (CSMAC) was established in Wuhan as the successor to the Central Plains Government. Wu was a member of the CSMAC, which had jurisdiction over Honan, Hupeh, Hunan, Kiangsi, Kwangtung, and Kwangsi provinces, and he retained his membership in 1953–54, when the CSMAC was redesignated the Central-South Administrative Committee. Later in 1950 he received two national-level posts. The first of these was membership on the Board of Directors of the newly established All-China Federation of Cooperatives (see under Ch'eng Tzu-hua) from mid-1950 to mid-1954. Secondly, he was made a deputy director under Tseng Shan (q.v.) of the Huai River Harnessing Commission when it was established in October 1950 as a subordinate body of the Ministry of Water Conservancy in Peking. The work of the commission presumably received priority attention, because earlier in 1950 Mao Tse-tung pledged, in a widely publicized statement, that the taming of the Huai was to be one of the major tasks in central China. Because of serious water control problems in Honan caused by both the Huai and Yellow Rivers, Wu was frequently involved during the 1950's in related tasks. Thus, in mid-1952, mid-1953, and again in May 1957, he was put in charge of hastily created Yellow River "flood prevention headquarters" necessitated by heavy rainfall. Similarly, he was among the dignitaries who spoke in April 1957 when work commenced on the huge and highly important Sanmen Gorge Dam, astride the Yellow River on the Honan-Shansi border.

Most leading provincial officials in the early PRC years held concurrent posts in the CCP, government, and military hierarchies, but Wu's activities seem to have been confined mainly to the governmental apparatus. (The leading Party and military official in those years was Chang Hsi, q.v., and, after 1953, P'an Fu-sheng, q.v.) However, Wu was identified as second secretary of the CCP Honan Committee in February–March 1954 when he gave a report to his Honan colleagues on the decisions taken at the Party Central Committee's Fourth Plenum, which had laid the groundwork for the purge of Kao Kang and Jao Shu-shih (qq.v.). Not long afterwards, he was elected a Honan deputy to the First NPC, and at its first session in September 1954 he was named a member of the NPC Credentials Committee. He was returned from Honan to the Second NPC (1959–1964) and once again served on the Credentials Committee.

In February 1955 and again in December 1958, Wu was re-elected governor of Honan, and from the mid-fifties to the early sixties he was regularly reported in the provincial press in connection with his varied duties as the governor. At the Eighth National Party Congress in September 1956, Wu was a member of the *ad hoc* credentials committee, and he also submitted a report on the income of members of the agricultural producer cooperatives. At the close of the congress he was one of only 33 men elected a full member of the Party Central Committee who had never previously been an alternate member. In terms of the CCP hierarchy in Honan, this created a rather unusual situation, because First Secretary P'an Fu-sheng, Wu's immediate superior, was only elected to alternate Central Committee membership at the congress. However, a year and a half later the Honan Party apparatus underwent a major shakeup at the second session of the Eighth National Party Congress (May 1958). P'an Fu-sheng was "exposed" as a "right opportunist" and was described as the "former" first secretary in Honan. The details were soon forthcoming; in early June, with Wu in the chair as the new Honan first secretary, a session of the CCP Honan Committee was convened. Among the numerous charges against P'an (described at length in his biography) was his opposition to the rapid pace of agricultural collectivization in Honan.

Wu came into the spotlight of the national press in mid-1958 in connection with the campaign to replace cooperatives with the famous people's communes. The reasons for Wu's sudden prominence were twofold. First, the commune movement was launched in Honan with the establishment of the much publicized "Sputnik" Commune, and second, Mao Tse-tung made a personal inspection trip to Honan in August 1958. As reported in the press, Wu exuded confidence about the commune program; Mao agreed: "Correct. If there is a commune [like the one he had just visited], then there can be many of them!"[3] One writer has observed that Wu's advance in power in Honan may have been because of his "precociousness" in anticipating the commune movement.[4] In the days that followed, a spate of articles extolling the new campaign were published by many national and provincial leaders. Wu was among them, writing an article entitled "From Agricultural Producer Cooperatives to People's Communes" for the September 16, 1958, issue of *Hung-ch'i* (Red flag; no. 8), the top Party journal. This article was among those selected for republication in an English-language pamphlet entitled *People's Communes in China* (Peking, 1958).

By 1959 Wu had assumed two new positions in Honan, both of which had been held by the now deposed P'an Fu-sheng until the previous spring. First, in February 1959 Wu was elected chairman of the Honan Provincial Committee of the CPPCC, and three months later he was identified as political commissar of the Honan

Military District. Thus, with the assumption of the latter post, Wu headed the Honan government and CCP hierarchies, and he was also the top provincial PLA political officer. A year later, in April 1960, he led the CCP delegation to the 12th Congress of the Finnish Communist Party. This was a somewhat unusual assignment in view of the fact that most such missions have been led by Party leaders working in Peking.

Beginning in the latter part of 1958 the Communists began a slow but steady retreat from the more extreme forms of the communes. This was reflected in another *Hung-ch'i* article by Wu (no. 1, January 1, 1960) in which he emphasized the need to "stabilize" the movement. And later in the year, writing for the same journal (no. 18, September 16), he was among the earliest Party leaders to emphasize a newly emerging line, namely, that "agriculture should be the foundation" of the national economy. This general theme was to be repeated thousands of times in the next few years as the Communists attempted to recover from the dire effects of the Great Leap Forward, which had been launched in 1958. For reasons that are not clear, Wu was succeeded in mid-1961 by Liu Chien-hsun (q.v.) as the CCP Honan first secretary, and Wu, in turn, was demoted to second secretary. In the Party hierarchy the situation that had previously existed between Wu and P'an Fu-sheng now existed between Wu and Liu, that is, a full Central Committee member serving under an alternate.

Wu was only reported in Honan for a brief period after his demotion, and then in the fall of 1961 he disappeared from the news. He re-emerged in October 1962 with a new assignment as a secretary of the Party's Central-South Bureau, headquartered in Canton, where he served under First Secretary T'ao Chu (q.v.). It is clear that the Party's regional bureaus are at a higher level than the provincial committees, but because Wu is merely one of several secretaries in the regional bureau (as opposed to having been first and second secretary at the provincial level), it is difficult to know if his new job represents a promotion, a demotion, or simply a lateral transfer. In any case, he was reported in the press with regularity through the mid-1960's.

Because Wu was a rather frequent contributor to the press during the Great Leap Forward 'and its immediate aftermath, his articles represent a useful body of information for the study of the views of a leading provincial official during that period. Aside from those already cited, the following sources contain his more important writings: *Chung-kuo ch'ing-nien pao* (China youth newspaper), September 16, 1958 (translated in *CB* 524); *JMJP*, June 14, 1960; *Chung-kuo ch'ing-nien* (no. 11, October 1, 1960; translated in *SCMM* 233); and, *Chung-kuo*

ch'ing-nien (no. 20, October 16, 1960; translated in *SCMM* 241).

1. *K'ang-Jih chan-cheng shih-ch'i te Chung-kuo Jen-min Chieh-fang Chün* (The Chinese People's Liberation Army during the Anti-Japanese War; Peking, 1953), p. 95.
2. Hua Ying-shen, ed., *Chung-kuo kung-ch'an tang lieh-shih chuan* (Biographies of Chinese Communist Party martyrs; Hong Kong, 1949), pp. 183–187.
3. Franz Schurmann, *Ideology and Organization in Communist China* (Berkeley, Calif., 1966), p. 475.
4. Roy Hofheinz, "Rural Administration in Communist China," *The China Quarterly,* no. 11:155 (July–September 1962).

Wu Heng

(c.1915–   ). Vice-chairman, Scientific and Technological Commission, State Council.

Wu Heng, one of Communist China's more important science administrators, was a student in the mid-thirties when large numbers of students participated in activities opposing continuing Japanese incursions into China. Anti-Japanese developments reached a peak in late 1935 when students staged large demonstrations in Peking. Because the demonstrations broke out on December 9, 1935, this event came to be known as the December Ninth Movement (see under Li Ch'ang). Early in 1936 the more left-wing elements among the students formed the National Liberation Vanguard of China (NLVC) and by the spring of 1936 this organization was largely under Communist control. Li Ch'ang, a top student official in the NLVC, has written that Wu was working in Hsu-chou (Su-chow) in northwest Kiangsu where he and others "rallied a number of students" from Peking and Tientsin who, "together with the local youths, actively carried out" work to arouse the Chinese populace to resist the Japanese. From the context of Li Ch'ang's article,[1] it is not possible to know the exact period he was referring to, but apparently he meant the days immediately following the start of the Sino-Japanese War in July 1937 when hundreds of NLVC members fled from metropolitan areas in east and north China. In any event, later references to Wu Heng as a geologist suggest that he was a geology student in one of the major Chinese cities some time between late 1935 and 1937.

Nothing further is known of Wu's career until 1949 when he was working in Heilungkiang province as head of the Department of Industry. Four more years passed before he was again identified, this time as a member of a delegation of Chinese scientists that visited the Soviet Union to inspect the state of Soviet science. The group, led by Ch'ien San-ch'iang (q.v.), one of China's greatest scientists (a nuclear physicist), remained in the Soviet Union from February to May 1953. In the following year the Chinese Academy of Sciences initiated the first steps in the establishment of four specialized departments. Wu was named (April 1954) as a deputy director of a preparatory body charged with the task of establishing the academy's Department of Technology. However, when the departments were fully organized in May–June 1955, Wu was transferred from the Technology Department to the Department of Biology, Geology, and Geography where he became a member of the Department's Standing Committee, a more logical assignment in view of his background as a geologist. (In subsequent years, this department has undergone a number of changes, and since 1961 has been known as the Department of Earth Sciences.)

In the interim, Wu had become a deputy secretary-general of the Academy of Sciences by mid-1954 and in this capacity gave a report before a July 1954 forum of the Academy on the "exchange of experiences" in the study of Soviet sciences. He received his first appointment in the national government in March 1956 when he was named as a deputy secretary-general of the newly established Scientific Planning Commission. The commission was headed by Vice-premier Ch'en I until May 1957 and thereafter by science administrator Nieh Jung-chen. In November 1958 this commission was merged with the National Technological Commission to form the Scientific and Technological Commission; Nieh Jung-chen was named as chairman, and Wu was one of his vice-chairmen; Wu still retains the position and it occupies most of his time. While the Scientific Planning Commission still existed, Wu participated in two important scientific meetings; at a March 1958 meeting of the commission he reported on research work in 1957 and the plans for 1958, and in November 1958 he presided over another conference dealing with the availability of scientific materials and information.

Beginning in 1959 Wu began to devote a large amount of time to foreign liaison concerning scientific and technical cooperation. With exceptions, most of this work has been with other Communist nations and has frequently taken him abroad. In the five and a half year period from late 1959 to mid-1965, Wu negotiated and signed no less than 21 scientific and technical cooperation agreements. Six of these were signed with the USSR (February 1960, June 1961, October 1961, June 1962, June 1963, and June 1965) and five with North Vietnam (December 1959, November 1960, July 1961, July 1962, and July 1963). Among the other Communist countries, one each was signed with the Mongolians (June 1962), the Poles (June 1964), the Rumanians (July 1964), and the East Germans

(July 1964). The remaining six were signed with Indonesia (May 1964 and March 1965), the United Arab Republic (August 1964 and January 1965), Algeria (December 1964), and Cambodia (March 1965). About half of these negotiations took place abroad, and thus Wu is among the more experienced of Peking's scientific administrators in terms of first-hand contact with foreign scientific achievements. To negotiate these agreements, he visited Moscow (1960, 1961, 1962), Hanoi (1961, 1963), Warsaw (1964), Bucharest (1964), East Berlin (1964), Algiers (1964), Cairo (1965), Jakarta (1965), and Phnom Penh (1965).

Although Wu's major contribution to the PRC after 1959 has been in the field of international scientific and technical liaison, he has continued to play a limited role in domestic scientific affairs. In November 1959 Wu spoke at the first conference on stratigraphy (a branch of geology dealing with the life of past ages as recorded by fossil animals and plants) and was elected as a vice-chairman of the National Stratigraphic Committee. In October 1963 he gave a report before another conference, this one dealing with the publication of books on chemical engineering. Also, in the same month, he spoke at a conference on the exchange of materials among various ministries and scientific research institutions of higher learning in north China. In the latter part of 1963 the Communists referred to an exhibition of scientific and technical information that was sponsored by the "China Scientific and Technological Information Research Institute." Wu was named as the director of the preparatory committee for this institute, a fact revealed in the semi-official 1964 yearbook.[2] In the meantime, presumably owing to his heavy work schedule for the State Council's Scientific and Technological Commission, he was removed (c.1962) as a deputy secretary-general of the Academy of Sciences.

Wu is the author of an article for the authoritative *Hung-ch'i* (Red flag, issue of December 1, 1959) dealing with the effective use of natural resources "to serve the cause of socialist construction." As a leading scientific bureaucrat, he is probably in close touch with fellow science administrators like Nieh Jung-chen, Fan Ch'ang-chiang, P'ei Li-sheng, and Tu Jun-sheng (qq.v.), each of whom, like Wu, is a veteran member of the CCP.

1. *SCMM* 297, p. 37.
2. 1964 *Jen-min shou-ts'e* (People's handbook), p. 285.

Wu Hsiu-ch'üan

(c.1908–   ; Wuchang, Hupeh). Specialist in international Communist party activities; member, CCP Central Committee.

A veteran Red Army officer, Wu Hsiu-ch'üan worked in the Foreign Ministry before becoming Peking's first ambassador to Yugoslavia. Since the mid-fifties he has devoted his time almost exclusively to the international Communist movement, and from 1960 has been in the forefront of the ideological dispute with the Soviet Union.

Wu was born about 1908 in Wuchang, the important port on the Yangtze River. In 1923, while still in his teens, he is said to have joined the revolutionary movement as a student organizer. Wu graduated from a middle school in Wuhan and then went to the Soviet Union for further study, remaining there from 1926 to 1931. Chang Kuo-t'ao (q.v.), who was in Russia at the same time and saw Wu frequently, characterizes him as a "man with ability and ambition," a dedicated and disciplined Communist.[1] Within a year of his arrival in Moscow Wu joined the CCP. While in the USSR he attended Sun Yat-sen (Chung-shan) University, a school that attracted a large number of Chinese youths in the mid-twenties, and also studied at a Red Army artillery school. At the latter he acted as an interpreter for Chinese colleagues whose Russian was not as fluent as his. (Wu is also said to have a limited command of English.) It is probable that Wu attended the Sixth National Congress of the CCP, which was held in Moscow in mid-1928 because of repression of the CCP in China following the 1927 split with the KMT.

When Wu returned to China in 1931 he taught briefly at Futan University in Shanghai and then made his way to the Kiangsi base where the Chinese Soviet Republic headed by Mao Tse-tung was established in November of that year. Wu was assigned to the army, serving successively as a battalion and regimental commander. In 1932 he was chief-of-staff of the Red Army Headquarters in Kiangsi, and when the Communists opened the Red Army Military Academy near Juichin in 1933, Wu served as an instructor. At the same time he was able to put his Russian to use by acting as a translator in the office of the Comintern, which had a representative in the Chinese Soviet area. Toward the end of the Kiangsi Soviet period Wu became a member of P'eng Te-huai's Third Army Corps, and as chief-of-staff of his force he made the Long March (1934–35).

P'eng's force was an important element in the First Front Army, commanded by Chu Te and Mao Tse-tung, which led the Long March from Kiangsi to the northwest. In mid-1935, when the First Front Army rendezvoused in western Szechwan with Chang Kuo-t'ao's Fourth Front Army, which had come from its base in Szechwan, a disagreement arose between Mao and Chang. Consequently, the two leaders separated; Chu Te remained with Chang while Mao and his forces, including P'eng's Third Army

Corps, continued north to Shensi. Wu remained Third Corps chief-of-staff (although some reports state that he was deputy chief-of-staff). After arriving in north Shensi he is reported to have been briefly assigned to the 15th Army Corps (see under Hsu Hai-tung), which was already operating in north Shensi when Mao's army arrived there in the fall of 1935. In December 1936 the Communists moved their north Shensi capital to Yenan and Wu was put in charge of a reception center which was subordinate to the Party's United Front Work Department. In 1936 Wu also became the director of the Party's Foreign Affairs Department, although it is not known how long he held this position.

From 1938 to 1939 Wu was secretary-general of the Shensi-Kansu-Ninghsia (Shen-Kan-Ning) Border Region Government. In this capacity he served under Lin Po-ch'ü, the chairman of the government. At some time in 1939 Wu was transferred to Lanchow, the Kansu capital, where he became director of the Communists' Eighth Route Army Office which was maintained for liaison with the KMT. He is reported to have returned to Yenan in 1940, but nothing further was heard of his activity until the end of the Sino-Japanese War.

At about the time that hostilities ended in the summer of 1945 Wu was transferred to Manchuria along with such top leaders as Lin Piao, Kao Kang, and Ch'en Yun. By 1946 he was chief-of-staff of Lin Piao's Northeast Democratic Allied Army, formed by a merger of forces sent from China proper with local resistance units that had been operating in Manchuria for many years. Wu was sent to Peking for a brief time in 1946 to serve under Yeh Chien-ying (q.v.) as the chief-of-staff of the Communist delegation to the Peking Executive Headquarters, the organization established to supervise the cease-fire agreement worked out between the Nationalists and the Communists by United States Special Envoy George C. Marshall. In addition to the headquarters in Peking, a number of local teams were established to supervise the truce; by the latter part of 1946 Wu was also the chief-of-staff of the so-called Changchun (Manchuria) Advance Headquarters set up by the main headquarters in Peking. When full-scale civil war broke out over the winter of 1946–47, Wu returned to his post as chief-of-staff of the Northeast Democratic Allied Army.

The Communists captured Mukden (Shenyang) in early November 1948, thereby breaking the back of Nationalist resistance in Manchuria. Wu was appointed as a vice-chairman of the Mukden Military Control Commission and commander of the city's garrison force. Following the conquest of Mukden, Lin Piao's forces moved southward from Manchuria in the winter of 1948–49 in preparation for the assaults on Peking and Tientsin. The forces that remained behind were now placed under the command of the Northeast Military Region (NEMR). Kao Kang, the most important political figure in Manchuria after the departure of Lin Piao and others in late 1948, was named as the NEMR commander; Wu was his chief-of-staff. Wu held this position until his transfer to Peking in the latter part of 1949. Still another post he held in the late 1940's was as commandant of the Northeast Military and Political Academy in Tsitsihar.

The Northeast People's Government (NEPG) was formed in Mukden (Shenyang) in August 1949 under Kao Kang, just one month prior to the establishment of the central government in Peking. Wu was among those originally elected to membership on the NEPG Council, but almost immediately afterwards he was transferred to Peking to work in the Foreign Ministry, where he was to remain for the next several years. Probably because of his experience in the Soviet Union and his knowledge of Russian, Wu was assigned (December 1949) to head the Foreign Ministry's Soviet Union and East European Affairs Department, which, during the first years of the PRC, was by far the most active of the ministry's foreign desks. From this time onward, Wu has devoted himself almost exclusively to the field of international relations. His first important assignment came in January 1950 when he accompanied Chou En-lai to Moscow to join Mao Tse-tung (who had arrived a month earlier) for the negotiations that led to the signing by Chou on February 14, 1950, of the Sino-Soviet Treaty of Friendship, Alliance, and Mutual Assistance, the cornerstone of Sino-Soviet relations for the next decade. Wu went in the company of other such important Communists as Li Fu-ch'un and Yeh Chi-chuang (qq.v.). Mao, Chou and most of the delegation left for home in mid-February, but Wu remained behind to take part in further negotiations led by Minister of Trade Yeh Chi-chuang. These talks finally led to the signing of still further agreements in April, after which Yeh and Wu returned home.

Wu was the leader of a landmark delegation in the history of the PRC, when, in November 1950, he led a group to New York to present the Chinese case before the United Nations regarding the outbreak of the Korean War and the entry of Chinese troops into that conflict (which occurred just one month before he arrived in New York). Wu made a long and vitriolic attack on the United States, demanding that the Security Council condemn the United States and further demanding the withdrawal of the United States from both Korea and Taiwan. Although no actions were taken on Wu's demands, the delegation is unique in that it is the only Chinese Communist group to have gone to the United States in the history of the PRC. Wu returned

to Peking via London, Prague, and Moscow, arriving home on December 30, 1950, just four days after he had officially been appointed as a vice-minister of Foreign Affairs. At the same time, he continued to head the Soviet Union and East European Affairs Department until July 1952. In April 1951, not long after his return, he was named to the second board of directors of the Chinese People's Institute of Foreign Affairs, holding this post until July 1955 when the third board was formed (at which time Wu was abroad—see below).

Throughout the remainder of the early fifties, Wu continued to be mainly concerned with bloc affairs, frequently participating in negotiations with other Communist countries and serving as a host for visiting bloc delegations in China. He also made two more trips abroad, serving as a member of Nieh Jung-chen's delegation that attended the funeral of Mongolian Party leader Choibalsan in February 1952, and also as a member of Chou En-lai's delegation to the funeral ceremonies for Stalin in March 1953. In 1954 he was elected as a Szechwan deputy to the First NPC; this was one of Wu's few assignments not directly related to foreign affairs, but even this became largely nominal when he was sent abroad in the spring of 1955. In December 1954, he attended the second national conference of the Sino-Soviet Friendship Association as a representative of the CCP, but he was not elected to a permanent post and does not seem to have been active in the organization.

Following the lead of the Russians in their efforts to improve relations with the Yugoslavs, the Chinese and Yugoslav ambassadors in Moscow began negotiations in late 1954 to establish formal diplomatic relations. (In October 1949 the Chinese had ignored the offer by the Yugoslavs to establish diplomatic ties.) Then, on January 10, 1955, the PRC and Yugoslavia agreed to establish relations at the ambassadorial level. In March Wu was removed as a vice-minister of Foreign Affairs and named as Peking's first (and only) ambassador to Belgrade. He arrived in the Yugoslav capital in May 1955 at almost the same moment that Soviet leaders Khrushchev and Bulganin arrived there in an attempt to secure a *rapprochement* with Tito.

During Wu's three years in Belgrade, Sino-Yugoslav relations were fairly friendly, but never really intimate. A number of important Yugoslav delegations visited Peking during this period, and the Chinese reciprocated by sending trade, military, and cultural delegations to Belgrade, led by such important personalities as K'ung Yuan, Lu Hsu-chang, Teng Hua, and Ch'en Chung-ching (qq.v.). Then, in the spring of 1958, the Chinese charged the Yugoslavs with following "revisionistic" policies. Relations quickly slipped from a state of bare toleration to outright hostility. Finally, Wu left for home in June 1958 (shortly after which the Yugoslavs retaliated by withdrawing their ambassador in Peking). Wu was officially removed in September 1958, and since that date the embassy in Belgrade has been in the care of a chargé d'affaires (paralleled by an identical situation in the Yugoslav embassy in Peking).

During Wu's tour of duty in Belgrade, he made at least two trips home, one of them coinciding with the convocation of the Eighth Party Congress in September 1956. Wu was elected at the Congress to membership on the Party Central Committee, one of the 33 persons elected to full membership who had been neither a full nor an alternate member of the Seventh Central Committee elected in 1945. Since his return to China in 1958, he has devoted himself almost exclusively to relations between the CCP and other Communist parties throughout the world. In this connection, he is known to hold a top-level post in one of the departments directly subordinate to the Party Central Committee. Because of the air of secrecy that surrounds many Party departments, his exact assignment is not known; a Polish news agency in March 1959 described Wu as "head of the Foreign Section," but in late 1964 the English-language *Peking Review* described him as a deputy director of "a department" under the Central Committee. Whatever his exact position may be, Wu's work in international Party affairs brings him into regular contact with such top Party operatives as Liu Shao-ch'i, Teng Hsiao-p'ing, P'eng Chen, K'ang Sheng, Wang Chia-hsiang, Liu Lan-t'ao, and Liu Ning-i.

Wu's activities as one of Peking's top international Communist Party experts is well-illustrated by his activity in the six-year period from 1959 to 1964 when he led or was a member of delegations to 11 different countries (including three trips to Moscow and two to Pyongyang). All but one of the important visits were to the Communist bloc, the one exception occurring in March–April 1959 when he accompanied Wang Chia-hsiang to London for the 26th Congress of the British Communist Party, immediately after he had accompanied Marshal Chu Te to the Third Congress of the Polish Communist Party in Warsaw (March 1959). He was a member of two historic delegations in 1960, the first led by Politburo alternate K'ang Sheng to meetings of the Warsaw Treaty Political Consultative Committee in Moscow (February) and the second led by Politburo member P'eng Chen to the Third Rumanian Workers' (Communist) Party Congress in Bucharest (June). At the former, the Sino-Soviet rift came partially into the open, and then in Bucharest P'eng Chen and Nikita Khrushchev openly traded hostile remarks as the ideological conflict moved into high gear (see under K'ang Sheng and P'eng Chen). In August 1960, a few weeks

before Castro recognized the Peking government (and while a Chinese Nationalist embassy still existed in Havana), Wu led a CCP delegation to the Eighth Congress of the Cuban People's Socialist Party; as of that time, he was one of the very few Chinese Communist leaders who had visited Castro's Cuba.

Wu's next venture abroad proved to be abortive; accompanying Ulanfu (q.v.), he left Peking in early May 1961 for the 16th Congress of the French Communist Party. However, the French government refused visas to the two Chinese. In September of that year, Wu accompanied Teng Hsiao-p'ing to the Fourth Congress of the Korean Workers' (Communist) Party, a visit that coincided with a determined and seemingly successful effort of the Chinese to woo the Koreans into their orbit. All these trips, however, were mere preliminaries (in terms of Wu's career) to the difficult assignment he was given over the winter of 1962–63. Although the Sino-Soviet dispute was plainly evident at this time, the polemics had been governed by some degree of restraint. Now, however, restraint was flung aside. From early November to mid-December 1962 Wu attended three Party congresses in East Europe (Bulgaria, Hungary, and Czechoslovakia); at each of these meetings the Chinese were subjected to a torrent of abuse from the Russians and their allies in East Europe. Wu replied in kind and often in highly sarcastic terms; he defended China and Albania (China's only ideological ally in East Europe) and claimed that the "unilateral" attacks by the Soviets had "undermined the international solidarity of the proletariat."

Wu returned to Peking from Europe in mid-December 1962 where, apparently, he received a full vote of confidence from his superiors. Thus, when the next round in the polemics began at the Party congress in Berlin (January 1963), the CCP once again sent Wu as head of the Chinese delegation. Khrushchev was present at these meetings, as was a Yugoslav delegation —the first Party congress attended by the Yugoslavs since the Moscow-Belgrade split in 1948.[2] According to a Reuter's dispatch, during Wu's speech on January 18, "whistles, boos, shouts and feet stamping completely drowned the voice of . . . Wu." When he spoke of "socialist unity," he drew "sarcastic laughter"; nor was he accorded the normal ovation at the close of his remarks. After Wu's oft-interrupted speech, one of his aides reportedly commented: "We will not be intimidated by this cheap invective."[3]

To resolve their differences, the Chinese and Russians agreed to one more high-level meeting between the CCP and the CPSU. The preliminary negotiations, in which Wu participated, took place in the first half of 1963. Finally, in July 1963 Teng Hsiao-p'ing led a top-level group, including Wu, to Moscow for the talks, which took two weeks. From the outset, it was clear that the talks would fail—as indeed they did. Not long after, in September 1963, Wu spent two weeks in Korea as a member of Liu Shao-ch'i's "friendship" delegation in what appeared to be still another attempt by the Chinese to retain the allegiance of the Korean Communists. In 1964, Wu made two more trips to bloc nations; he accompanied Chou En-lai to Moscow for the celebrations marking the 47th anniversary of the Russian Revolution (November), and then he went with Politburo member Li Hsien-nien to Albania for the 20th anniversary of the liberation of the Albanians from the Nazi armies (November–December).

Between these many trips abroad and directly in connection with them, Wu was reported with great regularity in Peking where he was a participant in the talks with nearly every foreign Communist party delegation to visit Peking. Particularly in the post-1960 period, as the Russians and Chinese jockeyed for supremacy in the Communist world, the number of such Communist party delegations visiting both Moscow and Peking grew to large proportions. Apart from his post in the Party center, the only other position that Wu is known to hold is with the quasi-legislative and largely impotent CPPCC. As a Party representative, Wu was named to the Third National Committee of the CPPCC, and at the close of the first session (April 1959) he was named to the Standing Committee. He was renamed to both posts in the CPPCC's Fourth National Committee, the first session of which closed in January 1965.

Wu's role as a senior international Party liaison official serves as a useful barometer for gauging Chinese Communist policies. Thus, in the earliest days of the PRC, Wu was spokesman at the United Nations for Peking's unyielding posture. In the mid-fifties, during the relatively "soft" period of Chinese Communist foreign policy, it was Wu who represented Peking in the *rapprochement* with the Yugoslavs. And, when the pendulum swung to a tougher and more strident foreign policy, Wu was among those in the forefront as a major CCP spokesman.

1. Modern China Project, Columbia University, New York, Howard L. Boorman, director.
2. *New York Times* (international edition), January 14, 1963.
3. Hong Kong, *South China Morning Post,* January 19, 1963.

Wu Hsueh-ch'ien

Former youth leader; specialist in Afro-Asian relations.

Wu Hsueh-ch'ien, formerly a youth leader, has devoted his attention to Afro-Asian affairs since about 1960. He first emerged in 1950

as a delegate to a youth congress in Czechoslovakia and spent the next decade engaged in similar endeavors in international liaison work. By the late 1950's, he was one of the most widely traveled of the younger Chinese Communist leaders. The pattern of his travels helps illustrate the development of his rising career and also suggests a means employed by the Communists to train young leaders in the field of international relations. Between 1950 and 1958, Wu made 17 trips to 14 different countries. With one minor exception, he led (or was a member of) delegations concerned with youth affairs. These included such important events as the fifth and sixth Communist-sponsored World Youth Festivals held, respectively, in Warsaw (July–August 1955) and Moscow (July–August 1957). Then in about 1958 Wu dropped out of international youth affairs; he subsequently reappeared in a new and more significant role which, among other things, brought him into contact with higher-level CCP leaders.

Because of seven post-1960 trips abroad, Wu might now be described as an Afro-Asian specialist. Among these trips were those to two extremely important conferences, the second and third Afro-Asian People's Solidarity Conferences (see under Yang Shuo) held in Guinea in April 1960 and Tanganyika in January 1963 and led by Central Committee members Liao Ch'eng-chih and Liu Ning-i, respectively. Wu was also one of the observers at the Third All-African People's Conference held in Cairo in March 1961. He has also been a participant in the Communist-sponsored peace movement; he attended a "general disarmament and peace" conference in Moscow in July 1962 and the 10th "World Conference against Atomic and Hydrogen Bombs" in Japan in July–August 1964. Like many Chinese Communist travelers during the early 1960's, Wu attended conferences at which his colleagues openly clashed with Soviet delegates. Two examples include the above-mentioned conferences in Tanganyika and Japan (see under Liu Ning-i).

Wu's travels are chronicled as follows. 1950: Czechoslovakia, June; Hungary, June; 1951: India, February–June; 1952: Indonesia, November–December; 1953: Rumania, July–September; 1954: Austria, December; 1955: Poland, July–August; Belgium, November–December; Czechoslovakia, December 1955–January 1956; 1956: France, January; 1957: Japan, March–April; USSR, July–August; India, November; Burma, November; 1958: UAR, March; USSR, April; Iraq, June; 1960: Guinea, April; 1961: UAR, January; UAR, March; 1962: USSR, July; 1963: Tanganyika, January; Kenya, December; 1964: Japan, July–August.

Wu's main organizational affiliation through the 1950's was with the two leading youth organizations, the New Democratic Youth League

(NDYL, known as the Communist Youth League after 1957) and the All-China Federation of Democratic Youth (ACFDY, renamed the All-China Youth Federation in 1958). In the NDYL, the training ground for CCP members, Wu served as the deputy director of the International Liaison Department from 1950 to 1953 when he was promoted to director, holding this post until at least 1957. And in the ACFDY he served as director of its International Liaison Department from 1953 to 1958, thus being placed in control of international youth liaison work (in the two key youth organizations) for most of the mid-1950's. Within the Youth League he was also a Central Committee member from the congress held in 1953 to that held in 1964, and from 1957 to 1964 was a member of the Standing Committee of the Central Committee. Similarly, in the ACFDY he was a member of the National Committee from 1953 to 1962, of the Standing Committee from 1958 to 1962 and was one of the vice-chairmen from 1958 to 1962. Although these affiliations carry into 1962 and 1964 (when youth congresses were held), he had virtually nothing to do with youth work by 1960.

From 1954, Wu began to participate in the "people's" organizations which unofficially manage a large and increasingly important segment of Chinese foreign affairs. In May 1954 he became a member of the board of directors of the newly formed Chinese People's Association for Cultural Relations with Foreign Countries, a post he presumably continues to hold. When an *ad hoc* preparatory committee was formed in January 1956 to participate in the 16th Olympic Games (held in Melbourne), Wu was named as a member, although the effort proved to be in vain because the Chinese Communists did not take part in the games. He was a member of another *ad hoc* committee in 1956, this one formed in November, to "support Egypt's resistance to aggression" by Israel, England, and France over the Suez Canal. In April 1960 he was named to the council of the newly established China-Africa People's Friendship Association. This was formed just a few days after Wu left with Central Committee member Liao Ch'eng-chih to attend the second Afro-Asian People's Solidarity Conference in Guinea. Less than a year later, in January 1961, he was added as a member of the Afro-Asian People's Solidarity Committee of China, that is, of the national chapter of the international Afro-Asian People's Solidarity Council in which he had already been participating.

Finally, in December 1964 he was added to one more "people's" association dealing with external relations, the Chinese People's Institute of Foreign Affairs; Wu was elected to the Standing Committee of the National Council at the Institute's fourth congress.

Wu's career reached a new plateau by January 1964 when he was identified as a "leading functionary" of a department under the Party Central Committee. This phrase is used for a number of fairly senior Party officials who work in fields which the Chinese apparently wish to conceal. From the outlines of Wu's career, however, it is probable that he works in a Party international liaison office, perhaps with an emphasis on African affairs. It seems significant that the first two times he was identified in this post it was in connection with a visiting Algerian official. In fact, it is probable that he already held this post in December 1963 when he accompanied Foreign Minister Ch'en I to Kenya for its independence celebrations.

In late 1964, Wu received two more appointments, one official and one more in a semi-official "people's" organization. In September he was elected a deputy from Anhwei to the Third NPC, which opened its first session in December 1964, and in October he was named to the Board of Directors of the Political Science and Law Association of China.

Wu Kai-chih

(c.1907–   ). Member, CCP Central Control Commission.

A specialist in Party control and supervisory work, Wu Kai-chih was a deputy chief justice of the Supreme People's Court from 1949 to 1954 and since 1956 he has served on the Party's Central Control Commission. Wu's earliest known association with the CCP was in 1927 when he participated in the Autumn Harvest Uprisings,[1] instigated by Mao Tse-tung and others in central China in September 1927. It is probable though undocumented that Wu was already a Communist Party member by this time. Another reference to Wu's early activities places him with Ho Lung's forces at P'u-ning, near Swatow, in the early fall of 1927.[2] This apparently refers to the military operations led by Ho Lung and others as they were making their way south toward Swatow after their failure to hold Nanchang (see under Ho Lung).

There are no further accounts of Wu's activities until October 1949 when the PRC was established and he was appointed a deputy chief justice of the Supreme People's Court in the new central government. Wu was identified at that time as a Party member and the "former" director of the Military Legal Section (*chün-fa ch'u*) under the PLA General Headquarters. When established in 1949, the Supreme Court was headed by Shen Chün-ju, a well-known leader of the China Democratic League. The only other deputy chief justice, Chang Chih-jang (q.v.), is also a non-Communist, and thus Wu was the only senior court official who belonged to the CCP. One of Wu's few public appearances as deputy chief justice occurred in July–August 1950 when he spoke at the First National Legal Conference on the subject of trials by people's courts. From 1949 to 1954 he was also a member of the Political and Legal Affairs Committee (chaired by Tung Pi-wu), one of the most important subordinate organs of the Government Administration Council (the cabinet). Wu attended the third session of the First CPPCC in October–November 1951. A major topic discussed at this meeting was the necessity to economize in view of the strains placed upon the economy by the Korean War. Soon afterwards, in December 1951, the Central Austerity Examination Committee was established under the chairmanship of economic specialist Po I-po (q.v.). Wu was named to membership on this committee, which was quite active in late 1951 and the first half of 1952.

In September 1954, at the initial session of the First NPC, the Supreme Court was reorganized and Wu was dropped as a deputy chief justice. He attended the First NPC (1954–1959) as a deputy from Shantung but was not re-elected to the Second NPC, which first met in April 1959. In December 1954 he became a member of the Second National Committee of the CPPCC as a representative of the CCP. He was again a Party representative to the Third CPPCC National Committee (1959–1964), but on the Fourth National Committee, which opened its first session in December 1964 he attended as a "specially invited person" rather than as a Party representative. In addition, for the second through the fourth CPPCC terms he has served on the Standing Committee, the governing body when the National Committee is not in session. From 1957 to 1959 Wu was also a member of the CPPCC's Local Work Committee, which investigates the activities of the provincial and municipal branches of the CPPCC.

Wu received his first important Party post in 1956. At the first plenary session of the Eighth Central Committee (held September 28, the day after the Eighth Party Congress closed), he was named to membership on the Party's Central Control Commission, which is headed by one of his former superiors, Tung Pi-wu. Five years later, in 1961, he was identified as a member of the Commission's Standing Committee, thus being placed among the principal officers of this important organization, which is responsible for Party supervision and discipline. Since then Wu's activities have seldom been reported in the Chinese press, probably because of the element of security that surrounds the work of the Control Commission.

---

1. *SCMP* 3013, p. 18.
2. *Kiangsi jih-pao* (Kiangsi daily), August 7, 1957.

Wu Leng-hsi

(c.1915–   ; Hsin-hui hsien, Kwangtung). Editor-in-chief, *JMJP;* director, New China News Agency.

Wu Leng-hsi has risen to a position of great prominence in the Chinese Communist world of journalism and propaganda, heading both the *JMJP* and the chief news service, New China News Agency. Wu's journalistic career apparently began in Yenan, where he worked during the Sino-Japanese War as a staff member of both the New China News Agency (NCNA) and the *Chieh-fang jih-pao* (Liberation daily), the latter being the approximate equivalent of the present-day *JMJP*.

One of the first mass organizations which the Communists established was the All-China Journalists' Association (ACJA). Preparations for this began in July 1949 in Peking, with Wu named as a member of the preparatory committee. When the Association was organized on a permanent basis in September 1954, he was named as one of the four vice-chairmen under Teng T'o (q.v.). By the fall of 1959 Wu was serving as acting chairman, and at the second national conference of the ACJA in March 1960, he succeeded Teng T'o as chairman.

Wu's rise in the Journalists' Association was paralleled by his climb up the hierarchical ladder in the NCNA, the official news agency subordinate to the Government Administration Council (the cabinet, known as the State Council after 1954). By the latter part of 1949 he was serving as editor-in-chief of the NCNA, and then in December 1950 he was promoted to the post of deputy director. Two years later (December 1952) he was elevated to the directorship, a post he continues to hold.

Beginning in 1952 Wu made several trips abroad for the PRC. In December 1952 he was a member of a large delegation led by Sung Ch'ing-ling (Mme. Sun Yat-sen) to the World Peace Congress in Vienna, and in April 1953 he led a cultural delegation to Poland. But his first significant trip did not occur until April 1954 when he accompanied Premier Chou En-lai to the Geneva Conference, which brought about the French withdrawal from Indochina. Wu's position was that of "adviser" to Chou. Seven years later, in May 1961, Wu was again in Geneva—on this occasion as a member of Foreign Minister Ch'en I's delegation to the conference to settle the conflict in Laos. (Although the conference lasted for over a year, Ch'en returned to Peking in July, taking Wu with him.) While he was in Geneva in 1961, Wu served as the ranking spokesman for the delegation, giving several press conferences to the huge gathering of newsmen. Wu's two other trips abroad took place in 1963 and 1964; in October–November 1963 he was in North Korea as head of a *JMJP* delegation and in February 1964 he led a similar group to North Vietnam.

During the period from the mid-1950's to the early 1960's, Wu received several new governmental and semi-official positions, as well as highly important posts within the CCP. In May 1954 he was named to membership on the Board of Directors of the mass organization known as the Chinese People's Association for Cultural Relations with Foreign Countries, a position he probably still retains. When a governmental counterpart (the Commission for Cultural Relations with Foreign Countries) was established four years later, Wu was named to membership there also (March 1958). He was elected a Tientsin deputy to the First NPC (1954–1959) but was switched to representation from Kwangtung for the Second NPC (1959–1964) and for the Third NPC, which held its first session in December 1964–January 1965; at the close of this session he was elevated to membership on the NPC Standing Committee. Five other posts of minor importance which Wu probably still retains are: member, Board of Directors, Chinese People's Institute of Foreign Affairs, July 1955; member, Committee for the Popularization of Standard Spoken Chinese (*p'u-t'ung-hua*), February 1956; member, Standing Committee, China Peace Committee, July 1958; president, "Institute of Journalism for Training Red and Expert Personnel," October 1958 (a school begun at the peak of the Great Leap Forward); and vice-president, China-Latin America Friendship Association, March 1960. These posts were peripheral to two important new assignments: editor-in-chief of the *JMJP* and a deputy director of the Party Propaganda Department. He was named to the editorship of the *JMJP* in November 1957, replacing Teng T'o, who was transferred to the post of Managing Director of the *JMJP;* thus Wu was placed in charge of the daily operations of China's leading newspaper and its leading news agency. He was first identified in the Party propaganda post in September 1964.

As one of China's most senior Party journalists, Wu is very frequently on hand to entertain foreign journalists and propagandists who visit China. Perhaps the most significant of these occasions occurred when the Communist-backed International Organization of Journalists held a conference in Peking in April 1957, a meeting at which Wu served as one of the Chinese delegates. The prestige of Wu's name and offices has also been used in forming a number of *ad hoc* committees to mark significant occasions. For example, he served on the presidium for a meeting in September 1959 to celebrate the 10th anniversary of the PRC; he also served the presidium in September 1961 for festivities commemorating the 80th birthday of Lu Hsun, modern China's greatest writer. Similarly, he makes frequent appearances at nationwide conferences which involve journalistic interests; he served on the preparatory committee, for example, for a national conference of "advanced cultural and educational workers" held in June 1960.

Wu's prominence in Party journalistic circles doubtless brings him into close contact with high Party leaders. Indeed, as editor of the Party's daily organ (the *JMJP*) it would seem mandatory that he have rather intimate ties with and ready access to such people as Lu Ting-i, head of the Propaganda Department and an alternate Politburo member.

Wu Po

(c.1913–   ; Anhwei). Specialist in tax affairs; vice-minister, Ministry of Finance.

Wu Po, one of Peking's most experienced financial specialists, is a normal school graduate. At some time in the 1930's or 1940's he joined the CCP, working in the underground while at the same time earning a living as a merchant and a schoolteacher. Wu had probably gone to Communist-held areas by 1948, when he joined the North China People's Government (NCPG) in 1948. This was formed in August 1948 as the Communists were conquering north China, and it was eventually absorbed by the central government in October 1949, shortly after the establishment of the latter in Peking. Wu served in the NCPG as deputy director of the Finance Department under Jung Tzu-ho (q.v.), another long-time finance specialist.

With the formation of the central government in the fall of 1949, Wu was assigned to the Ministry of Finance and has remained in the ministry ever since, except for a one-year gap in 1960–61. He has thus served under ministers Po I-po, Teng Hsiao-p'ing, and Li Hsien-nien, three of the most senior members of the Party hierarchy. Wu's first assignment was as director of the ministry's Staff Office, a post he held from December 1949 until he was promoted to vice-minister in 1952. As such, he presented a report at a December 15, 1950, meeting of the Government Administration Council on a series of tax regulations, which were subsequently adopted. Wu was also a participant in the famous "three-anti" movement of the early 1950's to root out the three "evils" of corruption, waste, and bureaucratism. A New China News Agency report of February 1, 1952, stated that he had represented the Ministry of Finance in a major corruption case which came before the Supreme People's Court.

In August 1952 Wu was promoted from head of the Finance Ministry's Staff Office to the post of vice-minister. Since then Wu has made numerous reports before top governmental bodies, and without exception they have dealt with tax matters. Five important reports serve as examples: (1) amendments to the tax system and measures governing the circulation tax on merchandise, delivered at the 164th GAC meeting on December 26, 1952; (2) regulations governing taxes on cultural events, at the 25th State Council meeting on March 9, 1956; (3) regulations concerning the 1958 national construction bonds, to the 83rd meeting of the NPC Standing Committee on November 6, 1957; (4) report on agricultural taxes, before the 96th NPC Standing Committee meeting on June 3, 1958; and (5) reports on rules for financial administration in national autonomous (minority) areas, on the improvement of the administration of revenue receipts, and on the cessation of the issuance of national economic construction bonds from 1959, delivered to the 97th NPC Standing Committee meeting on June 5, 1958. Wu also attended a national conference of directors of tax bureaus where he delivered the summary speech at the close of the two-week meeting on May 31, 1959.

Though Wu has specialized in domestic financial matters, he has also played a role in international financial negotiations, particularly with the North Koreans. He participated in the negotiations which led to the signing on May 20, 1954, of two agreements: the Sino-Korean Agreement on the Rate of Exchange between the National Currencies, and the Sino-Korean Protocol on Currency Exchange along the Border between the Two Countries. In addition, Wu was named in May 1957 to the Board of Supervisors of the Bank of China, a post he presumably continues to hold. The Bank of China is the institution which manages the foreign business of the People's Bank of China and is subordinate to the People's Bank in the government structure.

In September 1960, Wu was identified as a deputy director of the People's Bank of China. However, it was not until three months later that he was officially appointed to the post, at which time he was also removed as vice-minister of Finance. He remained with the bank for just one year, and then in December 1961 he reassumed his old position in the Finance Ministry. There are no obvious reasons for this one-year transfer, but it is noteworthy that it coincided with the worst economic difficulties in the wake of the disastrous Great Leap Forward movement.

A former employee of the Finance Ministry in the 1950's has attested to Wu's importance in the ministry.[1] Described as a quiet man who is diligent in his work, Wu was regarded as the most important man in the day-to-day management of the ministry, excepting only his colleague, Jung Tzu-ho. Minister Li Hsien-nien was (and is) a far more important political figure than either Wu or Jung, but because of his numerous other policy-level positions, Li has been forced to spend much of his time away from the Finance Ministry. The former ministry employee also asserted that Wu is a member of the ministry's CCP Committee and that in the middle 1950's he played a leading role in tax reforms which were adopted then.

Although not a deputy to the First or Second NPC, Wu was elected to the Third as a deputy from Anhwei, and when the first session was held in December 1964–January 1965, he was named to the Motions Examination Committee, the *ad hoc* body which passes preliminary judgment on legislation before the Congress.

At least two articles by Wu have appeared in the national press and periodicals: "Explanations for the Draft Regulations for Agricultural Taxes of the People's Republic of China," *JMJP*, June 5, 1958; and "Explanations on the Draft Regulations of the People's Republic of China Governing the Consolidated Industrial and Commercial Tax," *Jen-min Shui-wu* (People's taxation), September 19, 1958.

1. Interview held in Hong Kong, August 1964.

Wu Te

(c.1910–   ; Hopeh). Party administrator; alternate member, CCP Central Committee.

Wu Te has been a political officer and Party administrator in north and northeast China during most of his career. A native of Hopeh province, he was born in either Feng-jun (a small town near T'ang-shan) or Paoting. He has spent a considerable part of his life in the vicinity of the important Hopeh cities of T'ang-shan, Tientsin, Paoting, and Peking. He reportedly studied at Peking National University, presumably in the late twenties or early thirties. Before the Sino-Japanese War, Wu worked as a labor organizer in the mines of eastern Hopeh. During the war he entered the Communist-supported labor movement and worked in the border area between the provinces of Hopeh, Chahar, Jehol, and Liaoning. Subsequently, he apparently made contact with the troops of a Manchurian military leader, Lü Cheng-ts'ao (q.v.), whose troops had been decimated while fighting the Japanese along the Peking-Hankow Railroad in 1937. In the winter of 1937–38 Lü and his guerrillas began to cooperate with the Communists, and Communist political officers were sent to Lü's base to help organize the central Hopeh plains (see under Lü Cheng-ts'ao). Sometime prior to 1940 Wu was reported to be serving as a regimental political commissar with Lü's army. Later he was identified as the secretary of the Political Department of the Shansi-Chahar-Hopeh (Chin-Ch'a-Chi) Border Region, to which the central Hopeh base belonged. Described as the "leading cadre responsible for Party work in eastern Hopeh," Wu went to Yenan in the early fall of 1940 to report on his work to Mao Tse-tung.[1]

There is no further mention of Wu's activity until 1948 when he was a leader of the labor movement in the Hopeh-Chahar-Jehol-Liaoning area; he was identified in this capacity when he became a member of the Preparatory Committee for the Sixth National Congress of the All-China Labor Federation (ACFL), which met in Harbin in August 1948. At this same time he was also identified as a "former" member of the North China Staff Office of the Federation of Labor. The Congress elected him to the ACFL Executive Committee where he served until the federation held its Seventh Congress in May 1953.

Four months after the Harbin labor congress, T'ang-shan in east Hopeh fell to the advancing Communist armies (December 1948). Wu became the secretary of its municipal Party Committee. When the central government was established in October 1949 he relinquished this post for a national government portfolio as a vice-minister of the Ministry of Fuel Industry, headed by Ch'en Yü. Wu held the post for less than a year, because by mid-1950 he had already assumed important responsibilities in local administration that took him away from Peking.

As of mid-1950 he was serving as the ranking secretary of the Pingyuan Provincial Party Committee, a member of the Pingyuan Provincial People's Government, and a vice-chairman of the Government's Finance and Economics Committee. Pingyuan was created by the Communists in August 1949 out of territories in the wartime Shansi-Honan-Hopeh Border Region plus a large segment of Shantung. It was dissolved in November 1952, at which time the old provincial boundaries were approximately restored. However, by August 1952, Wu had been transferred to Tientsin where he remained for the next four years. During this time he apparently made a reputation for himself, taking an active part in many phases of Tientsin's political life as the following assignments indicate. 1952–c.1956: deputy secretary, Tientsin Party Committee, by August 1952, presumably until his transfer to Kirin early in 1956; 1952–1953: vice-mayor, Tientsin, August 1952 to May 1953; 1953–1955: mayor, Tientsin, May 1953, replacing Huang Ching; replaced by Huang Huo-ch'ing, January 1955; 1952–1957: president, Tientsin University, October 1952; replaced by Chang Kuo-fan, April 1957; 1953: director, Tientsin Committee for the Implementation of the Marriage Law, January; 1953: deputy director, Finance and Economics Committee, Tientsin government, spring; member, Tientsin Election Committee, established in May; director, Tientsin Committee to Sell Government Bonds, December; 1954: member, Tientsin Committee for the Discussion of the Draft Constitution, June.

During the 1953–54 period Wu was also a member of the North China Administrative Committee, the regional government for north China, and from 1954 to 1959 he represented Tientsin in the First NPC. However, he was not re-elected to the Second NPC, which opened in April 1959.

In April 1956 Wu was identified in the Manchurian province of Kirin as first secretary of the Provincial Party Committee. From that time his principal posts in Kirin were as follows. 1958–1966: political commissar, Kirin Military District, by November; 1958–?: vice-chairman, Sungari River Valley Planning Commission, established January; 1958–?: part-time professor, Northeast People's University, Changchun, July.

In September 1956 Wu was elected an alternate member of the Party Central Committee at the CCP's Eighth National Congress. He submitted a written speech to the Congress entitled "A Manifestation of Contradictions with Industrial Construction." One of the few other reports or articles by Wu appeared in the *JMJP* (May 24, 1958) under the title "Liberation of Thought in Preparation for the Technological Revolution."

After arriving in Kirin, in his capacity as the chief Party representative there, Wu was host to a number of important foreign visitors, especially Koreans. He has also frequently taken such leading Party officials as Chou En-lai, Tung Pi-wu, and Lin Feng on tours to inspect the province. Wu's only known trip abroad took place in October–November 1963 when he was a member of a Party delegation to North Korea, led by the first secretary of the Party's Northeast Bureau, Sung Jen-ch'iung. The purpose of this visit was not revealed in the official releases. In this same month (October 1963) Wu was first identified as one of the secretaries of the CCP Northeast Bureau.

Wu remained in Kirin until mid-1966 when, in the early stages of the Great Proletarian Cultural Revolution, he was transferred to Peking to become second secretary of the Peking CCP Committee and acting mayor of the city, thereby replacing Liu Jen (q.v.) in the former post and P'eng Chen (q.v.) in the latter.

---

1. Wang Huo, *Chieh Chen-kuo, Guerrilla Hero* (Peking, 1961), p. 119.

Wu Te-feng

(c.1900–   ; Hupeh). Vice-president, Supreme People's Court; member, CCP Central Control Commission.

Wu Te-feng is a specialist in intelligence and legal affairs. Born of well-to-do parents, he graduated from both the First Hupeh Provincial Normal School and the Wuchang Higher Normal College and then taught at a middle school for a brief time. Sometime in the mid-1920's, Wu joined the CCP, and like so many Communists of that period he also joined the KMT, serving in about 1926–27 as an Executive Committee member of the KMT Hupeh Provincial Headquarters. Concurrently, he was a member of the Wuhan Municipal Government Council, then dominated by the left-KMT, which was headquartered in that city. In 1927 he established and was principal of the Chung Shih Middle School in Hankow, and in the same year he also founded in Hankow a Communist newspaper called *Ch'ün-chung pao* (Masses daily).

In the spring of 1927 all CCP ties with Chiang Kai-shek's right-KMT were severed, and by the middle of the year the Communists' uneasy alliance with the left-KMT was shattered. Driven underground, the CCP immediately began to plan a series of peasant uprisings in central China—the famous Autumn Harvest Uprisings, which began in early September 1927. In his capacity as secretary of the Party's South Hupeh Special Committee, Wu took part in the planning for an attack on Hsien-ning (due south of Wuhan), although he took the position that the attack should be abandoned because of the "panicky" state of the peasantry in that area.[1] Nonetheless, attacks were made on communication facilities near Hsien-ning. Then, in the face of superior military force, the attack on Hsien-ning was abandoned and the Special Committee (and presumably Wu) fled southward to an area near the Kiangsi border.

Wu's whereabouts over the ensuing months are not known, but by 1928 he had made his way to the Communist base in Kiangsi. From his arrival there until the Long March of the mid-1930's, he apparently divided his time between Kiangsi, Hunan, and Shanghai; he was engaged in intelligence and security work, thus setting the pattern for his career over the next 35 years. In 1932–33 he was serving as head of the Party's Political Security Bureau for Kiangsi and then in 1933 became director of the Political Security Bureau for the Sixth Red Army. In January–February 1934, at the Second All-China Congress of Soviets in Juichin, the capital of the Chinese Soviet Republic, Wu was elected a member of the Republic's Central Executive Committee. He was possibly elected *in absentia,* because the Sixth Red Army to which he was attached was then maneuvering along the Hunan-Kiangsi border. In any event, the Chinese Soviet Republic came to an undeclared end in the latter part of 1934 when the central base was abandoned and the Red Army embarked on the Long March. Wu began the March

as head of the Political Security Bureau of the Sixth Red Army, continuing in this position when this army was absorbed by the Second Front Army (headed by Ho Lung) during the long trek to the northwest.

From his arrival in Shensi in 1936 until the close of the Sino-Japanese War in 1945, Wu's activities are shrouded in secrecy and therefore only a bare outline of his work can be constructed. He was known to have worked in Sian, the Shensi capital, in about 1936 serving as head of the Communist "special services" in that city. In the mid-1930's Sian was a city steeped in intrigue—with the actors including the pro-Chiang Kai-shek forces, those favoring dissident generals (notably Chang Hsueh-liang and Yang Hu-ch'eng), and, of course, the Communists. In addition to his work in Sian, Wu was also known to have been (in the period just prior to the outbreak of the war) a member of the Party's Social Affairs Department and the founder (probably in Yenan) of an intelligence school. The "Social Affairs" Department was the Communist euphemism of that period for the intelligence section of the Party.

When the war broke out against the Japanese in mid-1937, the Communists organized their military forces in the Yenan area into three divisions, one of them the 120th Division led by Ho Lung. Wu joined this division at some point during the war, presumably serving as an intelligence or political officer. However, there are no facts available about his career until the end of the war when he was working in Jehol and Liaoning, once again in intelligence; specifically, he was the director of Communist intelligence activities in this area—a crucial sector because it was the gateway to Manchuria. At about this same time Wu had another assignment closely related to intelligence as director of the Organization Department of the Jehol Party Committee. Once again the record fades on Wu until the Communists conquered the mainland in 1949; in the interim it seems safe to conclude that he was in intelligence or security work, probably in north China or Manchuria.

Wu apparently accompanied the Red armies south, because when the capital of his native Hupeh was captured in May 1949 he was appointed mayor of Wuhan and a member of the Wuhan Military Control Commission. In July 1950 he was named as chairman of the Wuhan Finance and Economics Committee, but just two months later Chang P'ing-hua replaced him as chairman, with Wu remaining on the committee as a vice-chairman. Within the Party structure for Wuhan he was a first deputy secretary by 1950 and the secretary of the Party Committee within the Wuhan government. In the interim, over the winter of 1949–50, the multi-provincial governmental unit which included Hupeh was formed under the name of the

Central-South Military and Administrative Committee (CSMAC); in December 1949 Wu was named as one of the members.

As mayor of central China's most important city, Wu was regularly reported in the press in the early 1950's. For example, he gave a major report on municipal affairs at a "people's representative conference" in June 1951, and in December of that year he spoke before a Wuhan Party conference on the necessity of increasing production and practicing austerity. Wu was further identified in 1951 in two additional positions; in February 1951 he was serving as chairman of the Wuhan Committee against Corruption and in June as president of a Wuhan "administrative academy," apparently one of the numerous schools in China in the early 1950's for the training of cadres.

Wu's career was suddenly placed in jeopardy in early 1952 when a major scandal broke in Wuhan. Known as the Sung Ying case (see under Chang P'ing-hua), it was one of a number of episodes of the san-fan (three-anti) movement designed to reduce corruption, waste, and bureaucratism. More specifically, the case involved the misuse of public funds, the arrest of an innocent person, and attempts by Party officials to cover up their mistakes. A number of senior officials in central China were involved, and among these, Wu was one of the more severely punished. He was explicitly criticized for "protecting the oppression of democracy and violating rights." He was then removed from all of his government (and presumably Party) posts. Wu was replaced as the Wuhan mayor by Li Hsien-nien, who later rose to be a Politburo member.

Although Wu's career seemed finished in early 1952, he was restored to political favor with surprising quickness. In September 1952, less than seven months after his demotions, he was named as secretary-general of the Political and Legal Affairs Committee of the Central-South Military and Administrative Committee, retaining this position when the CSMAC was reorganized into the Central-South Administrative Committee in January 1953. He remained in central-south China until the inauguration of the constitutional government in September 1954, at which time he was permanently transferred to Peking.

By 1953 the period of "reconstruction" of Communist China had ended; this was true in the legal field as well as many others. It was in this year, for example, that the first major steps were taken toward the drafting of a constitution and the preparations for elections which were to be held in 1954. Within the fields of political science and law, the formalization of these professions and studies was given organizational expression in April 1953 with the founding of the Political Science and Law Association of China (PSLAC). Wu's position within the PSLAC was relatively modest to judge by the

elections of the inaugural congress of April 1953; he was elected only as a member of the council. However, at the subsequent three congresses (March 1956, August 1958, and October 1964), Wu rose to the top position within this organization. At the March 1956 congress he was named a vice-chairman and concurrently secretary-general. Because the aging Tung Pi-wu was the chairman during those years (and also because Tung, as a Politburo member, was probably more concerned with policy matters at a higher level), the fact that Wu was secretary-general strongly suggests that by 1956 he was the de facto head of the organization. The PSLAC was structurally changed at the third congress in August 1958; Wu was once again named as a vice-chairman, but instead of continuing as the secretary-general (now defunct), he became the first secretary of the newly formed Secretariat. Finally, at the October 1964 congress, Wu replaced Tung Pi-wu as chairman (Tung being made an honorary chairman) and continued as first secretary.

As a major figure in the field of public administration and law, Wu was a natural candidate for a major role in the NPC from its formation in 1954. He served on the First NPC (1954–1959) as a deputy from his native Hupeh but then was elected from Shantung to the Second NPC (1959–1964) and to the Third NPC, which held its first session in December 1964–January 1965.

At the close of the first session of the NPC in September 1954, the central government was reorganized. One newly created organ was the First Staff Office of the State Council, of which Lo Jui-ch'ing, the Public Security minister, was the director. This office stood between the premier and the various ministries and bureaus dealing with public security and law and was thus a coordinating body. Wu was named as deputy director. During another reorganization in September 1959 this office was redesignated as the Political and Legal Affairs Office, now led by the new Public Security Minister (Hsieh Fu-chih); Wu was reappointed as the only deputy director. For reasons which are not clear, the office was abolished in 1960 or 1961.

From May 1957 until November 1958 Wu served as a member of the State Council's Scientific Planning Commission. However, there is no indication that he played a significant role in this organization, probably because this period coincided almost exactly with the "rectification" movement, during which the legal field came under severe attack. Wu was one of the advocates for the Party viewpoint, as was well illustrated by an article he wrote in January 1958 and a new position he assumed the following month. The article was for Cheng-fa yen-chiu (Political and legal research), no. 1, 1958, the organ of the Political Science and Law Association. Entitled "Struggle to Defend Socialist Legality," it urged that counsel for the defense should act in the interest of the state rather than of the accused. The new post symbolizing Wu's position within the legal profession was gained in February 1958 during the fifth session of the First NPC when he was named to the NPC Bills Committee. Throughout the summer and fall of 1957 a number of political scientists and lawyers were accused of various offenses against the state and the "people." These charges culminated in a number of dismissals at the NPC session. Specifically, several men were purged from the Bills Committee of the NPC, the body charged with drafting legislation. Wu was named to fill one of the vacancies created by the dismissal of a colleague. He was again named to the Bills Committee for the term of the Second NPC (1959–1964) and was once more selected for membership at the close of the first session of the Third NPC (January 1965).

In April 1959, Wu was named to the Third National Committee of the CPPCC as a representative of social science associations. He was also named to the Standing Committee of the CPPCC, the organ charged with the management of the CPPCC when the national committee is not in session. However, when the Fourth CPPCC was inaugurated in December 1964, Wu was not re-elected.

Wu was appointed a vice-president of the Supreme People's Court in April 1961, a position he continues to hold. Nothing is known of the part he may play in the actual work of the court, but in at least one respect it has proved a useful position: it has served as a title of considerable prestige when he meets with foreign visitors. Among the Party leaders in Peking, Wu ranks high in the group that has contact with foreigners. He sees many of the members of the legal and political science delegations that visit Peking, and he has also served as semi-official spokesman when meeting with foreign visitors intent upon writing about China's legal system.[2]

Although it is seldom mentioned in the press, Wu received what may well be his most important assignment in 1962 when he was named to the Party's Central Control Commission. The decision to expand the size of the Control Commission was taken at the 10th plenum of the Party Central Committee in September 1962; the official communiqué of the plenum noted cryptically that this expansion was to "strengthen the work of the Party Control Commissions at all levels." At the time Wu received this appointment it placed him in three organizations headed by Tung Pi-wu (the Political Science and Law Association, the Supreme Court, and the Control Commission). At about the time Wu received this new post, he was also named (December 1962) to the Standing Committee of the newly established China-Cuba Friendship Association.

Although Wu Te-feng is not a member of the Party Central Committee, he appears to be the most important Party figure in the field of law and political science. Little is known of his personal life or characteristics, but one foreign visitor has described Wu as "vigorous, with a bristly mustache."[3]

1. Roy Hofheinz, Jr., "The Autumn Harvest Insurrection," *The China Quarterly,* no. 32:51–55 (October–December 1967).
2. For example, see Julio Alvarez del Vayo, *China Triumphs* (New York, 1964), pp. 145–149.
3. Felix Greene, *Awakened China* (New York, 1961), p. 191.

Wu Yü-chang

(1878–1966; Jung-hsien, Szechwan). Early T'ung-meng hui and KMT member; president, Chinese People's University; specialist in language reform; member, CCP Central Committee.

Wu Yü-chang, also known as Wu Yung-shan, was an active revolutionist from the turn of the century and an early member of both the T'ung-meng hui and the KMT. Educated in Japan, and later in France and the Soviet Union, he participated in the 1911 Revolution and then helped set up the work-and-study scheme for students in France. He was particularly active in both the KMT and the CCP during the period of their collaboration in the mid-twenties. He spent most of the period from 1927 to 1938 in the USSR, but for a brief period he edited a newspaper in France. During the Sino-Japanese War he was one of the key educators in Yenan, a role in which he continued after the establishment of the PRC in 1949. He was the major figure in the program to reform the Chinese written language. Wu was elected to the CCP Central Committee in 1938, and re-elected in 1945 and 1956. He and his colleagues Lin Po-ch'ü, Tung Pi-wu, Hsu T'e-li, and Hsieh Chueh-tsai are often referred to as the "five elders" (*wu-lao*).

Wu was born into a large landlord family in Jung-hsien, located in southern Szechwan 25 miles west of Tzu-kung. In 1892 he went to Chengtu with his older brother Wu Yung-k'un to study there, but returned home a few months later when their mother died. Wu records being influenced during this period by the reformers K'ang Yu-wei and Liang Ch'i-ch'ao, and during the famed "hundred days reform" of 1898, when he was studying at the Hsu-ch'uan Shu-yuan (Hsuchuan Academy) in Tzu-kung, he claims to have led a reform movement. Around the turn of the century Wu was tutoring the children of a landlord. In 1902 he went back to his studies, and in the same year took and failed the examinations which would have won him a place, under the imperial system, in the government bureaucracy.

At the end of 1902 Wu and his brother Yung-k'un decided to continue their studies in Japan. Leaving his wife and two infant children at home, Wu arrived in Tokyo in March 1903. Beginning that year, Japan trained more Chinese students than any other country; there were already 1,300 students there in 1904, and within two years the figure reached no less than 15,000. A great number of the participants in the 1911 Revolution were schooled in Japan, but Wu is one of the relatively few latter-day CCP members who studied there—and he was there for a good deal longer than most of them.

Wu's arrival in Japan coincided with an active "resist-Russia" campaign among Chinese students, a movement resulting from Russian penetration into Manchuria in the 1902–03 period. Two important organizations grew out of this movement, the Volunteer Corps to Oppose Russia (Chü-o i-yung-tui) and the related Society for the Education of a Militant People (Chün-kuo-min chiao-yü hui). Wu claims to have joined both organizations soon after his arrival. During his first two and a half years in Japan, he studied at a school which offered a special course for Chinese students, but his brother returned home in early 1904. During these years he was influenced by the writings of Kōtoku Shūsui, a well-known Japanese journalist who was a leading social democrat and later an anarchist. Wu joined the T'ung-meng hui upon its founding by Sun Yat-sen and Huang Hsing in 1905, and in the same year he was an executive secretary of the Association of Chinese Students studying in Japan.

Wu completed his initial schooling in 1906, and then went to the city of Okayama where he studied electrical engineering in the technology department of the Japanese government-sponsored Number Six Higher School, a preparatory school for college. In 1907 he and some Szechwanese colleagues founded Szu-ch'uan tsa-chih (Szechwan magazine), a weekly edited by Wu which had a more radical orientation than Min Pao, the famous organ of the T'ung-meng hui. Because of these new responsibilities he took a year's leave of absence from his school in Okayama. At this juncture, Wu was joined in Japan by his eldest brother, Wu Yung-hsun, who was a member in Szechwan of the Ko-lao-hui (Elder brother society), one of the most famous secret societies in China. Wu sponsored his brother for membership in the T'ung-meng hui. Wu claims to have played an important part, in the latter half of 1907, in establishing the Kung-chin-hui (Progressive association). This society, one of the subsidiary organizations of the T'ung-meng hui, was formed by merging several secret societies. A number of its leaders, including Sun Wu, later played key roles in the 1911 Revolution.

The publication efforts of the Szechwan students came to a halt in 1908 when a Manchu government official arranged to have their journal suppressed. Wu himself was fined and given a half-year suspended sentence. He returned to school in Okayama that fall (and graduated in 1911). Wu claims to have taken part in assassination attempts against Manchu officials (then a favorite tactic of the T'ung-meng hui), although he himself did not return to China. In fact, Wu has written of his role in Wang Ching-wei's famous and abortive effort to assassinate the Manchu prince regent in 1910. Wu returned to China in mid-1910, and for the next year he was involved in various anti-Manchu intrigues, including a mission back to Japan to buy munitions. He was back in his native hsien when the Manchus were overthrown during the 1911 Revolution. He took part in the revolution, purportedly together with two famous latter-day Communists, Liu Po-ch'eng and Wang Wei-chou (qq.v.). Soon afterwards he went to Nanking to participate in the provisional government of the Republic of China, which was set up on January 1, 1912. He worked for a short time under Sun Yat-sen in the secretariat of the president's office.

In 1912–13 Wu was involved in the complex maneuverings between Sun and Yuan Shih-k'ai, and for a brief period was in the latter's employ. Then, after the failure of the "second revolution" (against Yuan) in 1913, Yuan ordered Wu's arrest. Hearing of this, Wu's elder brother Yung-k'un, then blind and ill, committed suicide. In late 1913 Wu left China for his second sojourn abroad.

Wu arrived in France in early 1914 and several months later enrolled in the Law University of Paris where he studied politics and economics. In 1912, previous to his departure for France, he had worked in Szechwan for the Society for Frugal Study in France, organized that year in China by several prominent Chinese, including anarchist Li Shih-tseng and educator Ts'ai Yuan-p'ei. The organization attempted to get financial help for students and established special schools to prepare them for their study in France. Yuan Shih-k'ai soon forced the dissolution of the society, but Li, Wu, and other society leaders persisted in their efforts and enlarged the program to include workers as well as students. This led to the famous work-and-study scheme, and to the formation in Paris in 1915 of the Society for Frugal Study by Means of Labor.[1] The alumni of the work-study plan in France produced some of the most famous names in Chinese Communist history, including Chou En-lai, Ts'ai Ho-sen, Li Fu-ch'un, Chao Shih-yen, Li Li-san, and Ts'ai Ch'ang (qq.v.). Insofar as the Chinese Communist movement is concerned, Wu can be regarded as the "father" of this program, even though the work-study plan also trained a significant number of latter-day KMT members—a fact generally ignored by CCP historians.

In the latter part of 1916 Wu left for home. He traveled through Russia with Ts'ai Yuan-p'ei and arrived in Peking in February 1917. There, continuing his efforts to encourage students to study in France, he set up a preparatory school for that purpose. One of the students, Chao Shih-yen (q.v.), was instrumental in persuading Wu to join the CCP several years later. With the rapidly changing political fortunes so character-istic of that period, Wu found it expedient to flee Peking in mid-1917, and by late in the year he was back in Szechwan. The province was then controlled by Hsiung K'o-wu, with whom Wu was well acquainted from the 1911 Revolution period. During the next two years, apart from his continuing efforts to promote the work-and-study scheme, Wu worked in a liaison capacity between Hsiung and Sun Yat-sen and was in-volved in the endless maneuvers among the shift-ing warlord alliances. These tasks took him to several places in China, but after 1919 he spent most of his time in his native Szechwan.

The origins of Marxism and a Communist ap-paratus in Szechwan have not been studied in detail, and although Wu was one of the earlier Party members there, he was not the first. That distinction may belong to Li Shih-hsun, whom Wu memorialized in a poem published many years later.[2] While still a teenager, Li organized chapters of the Socialist Youth League in the First Middle School and the Higher Normal In-stitute in Chengtu in 1921. He later attended Communist-dominated Shanghai University, took part in the Northern Expedition as a political officer under Chou Shih-ti (q.v.), and partici-pated in the Nanchang Uprising. After the CCP became an underground organization in 1927, he held top posts in Kiangsu, Chekiang, and Kwangtung. He was captured and executed on Hainan Island in 1931. By the time Wu Yü-chang arrived in Szechwan in late 1919, he claims to have been deeply impressed by the Russian Revolution (as well as by John Reed's classic *Ten Days That Shook the World*) and the May Fourth Movement. Wu has also described his active participation in, and subsequent disillu-sionment with, political activities aimed toward provincial self-government. This took place in 1920–21. In the meantime, in mid-1920, he assumed the presidency of the Chengtu Higher Normal Institute. The school, in Wu's account, soon became a center for progressive ideas, which were gaining adherents in many urban centers in China during that period.

In a revealing statement about his background, Wu has written that apart from his duties at the institute, "I exploited my past relations with the upper social strata of Szechwan" to give refuge to revolutionists. Thus, in 1922, when he learned that the important Youth League leader

Yun Tai-ying (q.v.) had been arrested, Wu was able to gain his release. Yun then accepted Wu's invitation to teach at the institute, and while he was there "Marxist propaganda activities were pushed forward to a new stage." Wu wanted to join the Youth League, which the above-men-tioned Li Shih-hsun had already set up in 1921 at the institute, but because he was then in his mid-forties he was unable to do so. Therefore, in 1923 he, a colleague named Yang An-kung, and some 20 others secretly founded the China Young Communist Party (Chung-kuo ch'ing-nien kung-ch'an-tang). "Because Szechwan was far away," to use his own words, Wu was still unaware that the CCP had been established two years earlier. In January 1924 warlord Yang Sen captured Chengtu. Wu lost his post, and a few months later, fearing arrest by the Yang administration, he left Szechwan with Liu Po-ch'eng for Shanghai, and from there to Canton. In Canton Wu renewed his ties with Sun Yat-sen and became one of Sun's secretaries.

In early 1925 Wu went to Peking to see Sun Yat-sen. Sun was then fatally ill and died in March, but Wu did see his former pupil, Chao Shih-yen, by then an important CCP leader. After holding talks with Chao, Wu decided to join the CCP, and then arranged to have the China Young Communist Party in Szechwan amalgamated into the CCP. In August he went to Szechwan to head the KMT branch there, a not uncommon occurrence during this period of KMT–CCP cooperation. Moreover, in Septem-ber, using KMT funds, he established the Sino-French Institute (Chung-Fa hsueh-hsiao) to train revolutionary cadres. The school reportedly had over 200 students. Two months later, in No-vember 1925, Wu and Yang An-kung were among the Szechwan delegates elected to the Second KMT Congress, which convened in Can-ton in January 1926. Wu served as secretary-general of the congress, and he was one of eight Communists elected to the 36-member Central Executive Committee (CEC). The Communists at this juncture had gained an impressive num-ber of positions within the KMT hierarchy, the details of which are discussed in the biography of Lin Po-ch'ü.

After the Second KMT Congress, Wu re-turned to Szechwan because, in the words of his biographer Ho Ch'i-fang, he wanted to resume direction of the KMT branch, which he had so recently established. However, illness forced him to seek hospitalization in Chungking. In July 1926, just as the Northern Expedition be-gan, Wu returned to Canton. It was apparently at that time that he was among the many CCP members who lectured to the Peasant Movement Training Institute, then headed by Mao Tse-tung.[3] In the middle of the fall in Canton, and again at the end of the year in Wuhan, he was deeply involved in meetings concerning the transfer of the capital from Canton to Wuhan and the subsequent steps to form the new government in the latter city.[4] By the early part of 1927 tension had greatly increased between Chiang Kai-shek on the one hand and the left-wing KMT and their Communist allies in Wuhan on the other hand (see under Lin Po-ch'ü). The convocation in March of the Third KMT Plenum in Wuhan marked the height of left-KMT and CCP collaboration, and from this meeting Wu emerged with impressive new posts as: member of the CEC's Standing Committee; member of the Political Council; acting head of the KMT Organization Department pending the return to China of left-KMT leader Wang Ching-wei on April 1; and member of the National Government Council.

But the left-KMT, with one eye on the growing power of Chiang (who on April 12 staged his famous anti-Communist coup in Shanghai), soon became disenchanted with the CCP. The break came in mid-July 1927, and this in turn led to the Communist revolt known as the Nanchang Uprising. Wu and several top Communists left Wuhan for Nanchang in the last two weeks of July, and there, on August 1, the revolt took place (see under Yeh T'ing). A 25-member Revolutionary Committee was immediately established; Wu was made one of the members, as well as secretary-general of the Secretariat. When Nanchang was lost within a few days, the Communists marched south to Kwangtung where they captured Swatow. But this victory was equally short-lived, and Wu and his colleagues fled to the countryside, and then to Hong Kong. Wu was now to begin his third and longest stay abroad. He arrived in Moscow toward the end of the year with his fellow Szechwanese Liu Po-ch'eng.

Although undocumented, it is probable that Wu attended the Sixth CCP Congress, held in Moscow in mid-1928. From that same year until his graduation in 1930, Wu and his fellow "elder" Lin Po-ch'ü attended Sun Yat-sen University, which was later renamed the Communist University of the Toilers of China. In an article written in 1960, Wu stated that in early 1929, after "progressing in the study of Leninism," he and Lin were enrolled in a special class within the school. He further claimed, without elaboration, that they took part in the "practical struggle" against the Trotsky and Bukharin "elements."[5] Upon graduation, Wu and Lin went to Vladivostok where Wu taught language courses in the Far Eastern Industrial University, later known as the Far Eastern Normal University.[6] (Another source calls this the Far Eastern Workers' Leninist School.[7]) Both men had a keen interest in language reform, and Wu taught his students about this, including a plan to Latinize Chinese characters. In September 1931 Wu and Lin attended the First Conference on the Latin-

ization of Chinese in Vladivostok. (See also under Lin Po-ch'ü.)

A second conference on Latinization was held in 1932, but appears that Wu had by then returned to Moscow. Nothing further is known of his activities until July–August 1935 when he attended the Seventh Comintern Congress in Moscow (see under Ch'en Shao-yü). This famous meeting called for a united front in the "struggle against fascism," directed in the west against Hitler and in the east against the Japanese militarists. Accordingly, Wu was sent to Paris where he set up the *Chiu-kuo shih-pao* (National salvation times), with the explicit purpose of propagating the "anti-Japanese people's united front." The *Chiu-kuo shih-pao* concentrated on news about the ever-increasing number of anti-Japanese activities in China. It frequently reprinted speeches and articles by Ch'en Shao-yü (q.v.), the CCP delegate to the Comintern; and it also carried the speeches of top leaders in Yenan, such as Mao Tse-tung's report in May 1937 at a CCP conference.

Sometime toward the end of 1936 Wu returned to Moscow where he taught at the Communist University of the Toilers of the East (not to be confused with the school Wu attended a few years earlier). He continued his research on language reform and published a few works on this subject. Then in November 1937, a few months after the Sino-Japanese War broke out, he returned to Paris. He was purportedly in rather close touch with Chinese Nationalist diplomats in an effort to stimulate propaganda against the Japanese, and he was also in contact with various peace groups, which were then proliferating in Western Europe in the wake of the growing menace of Hitler. In February 1938 Wu was in London for the International Peace Conference (called the World Anti-Aggression Congress in Chinese Communist sources), a meeting attended by 800 delegates from 21 nations, including key Chinese Nationalist diplomats posted in West Europe. Wu left for home the next month. Traveling by way of Saigon where he spoke to overseas Chinese groups about the war effort against Japan, Wu arrived in Wuhan in April. Then in his 60th year, Wu had spent a third of his life abroad—a record unmatched by any other senior member of the Chinese Communist elite.

In Wuhan, then the temporary national capital, Wu immediately plunged into united front work, and in June 1938 a publishing house there brought out a collection of his writings and speeches on the "war of resistance." At this same time he was selected as one of the seven CCP delegates to the newly established People's Political Council, a consultative organ set up by the national government. He attended the sessions through 1939, first in Wuhan and then in Chungking, but in November 1939 he went to

Yenan because of illness, and by the middle of the war official Chinese Nationalist sources no longer listed him as a Council member. In the meantime, at the Sixth Plenum of the CCP, held in Yenan in October–November 1938, Wu and his old colleague Lin Po-ch'ü were both elected members of the Party Central Committee.

In Yenan Wu assumed the presidency of the famous Lu Hsun Art Academy (c.1939), a school which attracted many young students who went to the Communist capital during the war. Later, in 1941, the academy, plus the North Shensi Public School, the Yenan Chinese Women's University, the Mao Tse-tung Youth Cadres Institute, the Foreign Languages Institute, the Natural Sciences Institute, and the Administrative Institute were all amalgamated into Yenan University. Wu became the president, but by 1944 he was replaced by Chou Yang (q.v.). Wu's obituary reveals that at some point during these years he served as director of the Cultural Committee under the Shensi-Kansu-Ninghsia Border Region Government, which was headed by Lin Po-ch'ü, and he was also chairman of the Yenan Association for the Promotion of Constitutional Government from its founding in February 1940. Wu continued his interests in language reform, and when the Sin Wenz (lit. "new writing") Society was formed in November 1940, he was one of the sponsors. An authoritative study on language reform paraphrases remarks by Wu at the founding conference to the effect that "only by means of the New Writing would it be possible to build a state on the foundations of the New Democracy."[8]

Wu was one of the speakers at the Seventh National Party Congress, which met in Yenan from April to June 1945, and he was also re-elected to the Central Committee. Immediately after the war ended in August, Mao flew to Chungking for discussions with Chiang Kai-shek on a number of outstanding issues. From these talks came an agreement to convene the Political Consultative Conference in Chungking. Wu was a member of the top-level delegation of seven, led by Chou En-lai, sent to Chungking in mid-December 1945. A few weeks later, when the conference was convened (January 10, the same day a cease-fire agreement took effect between Nationalist and Communist armies), Wu was named to the special committee to draft the new national constitution. The conference had little substantive effect, and within a few months civil war was renewed throughout much of China. There remained, however, the facade of continuing negotiations, principally through the efforts of United States Envoy George C. Marshall, and thus Wu was able to remain in Nationalist-held China for more than a year. When the national capital was moved back to Nanking in the spring of 1946, Chou En-lai went there, but Wu remained in

Chungking. By this time Wu was the secretary of the CCP Szechwan Provincial Committee, and he was assisted by his fellow Szechwanese Wang Wei-chou (q.v.).

After Chou's departure, the situation became increasingly difficult for the CCP in Chungking, and by the end of 1946 and the early days of 1947 Wu and his colleagues were in a virtual state of house arrest. Finally, the negotiations collapsed, and all Communist representatives in Nationalist-held areas were ordered to leave. Wu flew back to Yenan on March 8, 1947, less than two weeks before it fell to Nationalist armies. Some years later Wu wrote a detailed account of this period, which was published in Peking in 1961 as part of a collection of articles entitled *Chien-fang chan-tou hui-i-lu* (Reminiscences of the Liberation War); in the next year Wu's essay was translated and published in a collection entitled *The Great Turning Point.*

By the spring of 1948 Wu had gone to southeast Shansi, long a Communist stronghold in the heart of the Shansi-Hopeh-Shantung-Honan Border Region. At this juncture, the region was amalgamated with the Shansi-Chahar-Hopeh Border Region to form the North China Liberated Area (see under Tung Pi-wu). Accordingly, the two major Communist universities in the two regions, the Northern University and the North China Associated University, were merged to form the North China University (Hua-pei ta-hsueh). Wu became the president, and three of his top assistants were Fan Wen-lan, Ch'ien Chün-jui and Ai Szu-ch'i (qq.v.). Wu apparently remained in Shansi until 1949 when Peking was surrendered to the Communists. In June he was appointed a member of the Higher Education Committee of the North China People's Government, and throughout the rest of the summer he was active in preparations leading to the establishment of the central government and various "mass" and professional organizations. In July he attended three major conferences, which elected him to preparatory organs for the Sino-Soviet Friendship Association, the All-China Congress of Natural Science Workers, and the All-China Educational Workers' Conference. At the same time he became vice-chairman of the Preparatory Committee of the China New History Research Association, and later, when the Chinese History Association was founded in July 1951, he and Fan Wen-lan became the two vice-chairmen under Chairman Kuo Mo-jo (q.v.).

As a representative of the CCP, Wu attended the meetings of the CPPCC in September 1949. In the new central government, established on October 1, he became a member of the important Central People's Government Council, which was chaired by Mao. He was also made a member of the Political and Legal Affairs

Committee under Chou En-lai's Government Administration Council (the cabinet). Wu held both posts until the government was reorganized in the fall of 1954. In October he was elected a vice-chairman of the Sino-Soviet Friendship Association, a post he retained to his death.

In December 1949 the government approved the establishment of the Chinese People's University, one of the most important in China. The university traces its origins back to the schools in Shensi and Shansi with which Wu had long been associated. It began operations in early 1950 and was formally inaugurated in September; Wu was the first and only president until his death. At least in its formative years, emphasis was placed on enrolling students who had been industrial "model" workers and "revolutionary cadres," many of them of peasant origin with a few years of "practical revolutionary experience." Nearly a decade later it was claimed that more than 3,000 teachers had been trained in Marxist-Leninist theories, and another 12,000 in financial, economic, political, and legal fields. By then the university had an enrollment of 7,000 regular and 7,200 correspondence students, and a faculty and staff of 2,000.

In August 1950 Wu was elected chairman of the China Educational Trade Union, and from 1953 he was an Executive Committee member of the parent organization, the All-China Federation of Trade Unions. He continued in both positions until his death. Also in August 1950, Wu chaired a nationwide conference of scientists, and from this came the establishment of two scientific organizations. One, the All-China Federation of Scientific Societies, was the parent body for professional societies (for example, chemistry and physics). The other, the All-China Association for the Dissemination of Scientific and Technical Knowledge, was set up to spread rather elementary technological information on a wide-scale basis. (See under Li Szu-kuang and Liang Hsi, the respective chairmen.) Wu was named honorary chairman of both organizations and continued to be so until September 1958 when they were merged to form the China Scientific and Technical Association.

In July 1951 Wu was named to the Administrative Committee of the newly founded Central Political and Legal Cadres Academy (see under P'eng Chen). He was selected in early 1953 to serve on a committee to draft the election law, one of the first steps in preparation for the convocation of the NPC in 1954. Wu was elected from his native Szechwan to the First NPC, which held its inaugural session in September 1954. He was elected a member of the NPC Standing Committee and was re-elected in April 1959 and January 1965 to the Second and Third NPC Standing Committees.

One of Wu's major concerns in the post-1949 period was in connection with language reform. In October 1949, just a few days after the PRC was established, he became chairman of the newly organized Association for Reforming the Chinese Written Language, and he also assumed the chairmanship of the organization's Examination and Research Committee. In February 1952 the activities of the association were placed under the Research Committee for Reforming the Chinese Written Language. This committee, of which the well-known educator Ma Hsu-lun was the chairman and Wu the vice-chairman, was subordinate to the Government Administration Council's Culture and Education Committee. Over the next two and a half years the language committee conducted intensive research on various schemes (for example, simplified characters) to reform the language. In November 1954, shortly after the central government was reorganized, the Language Research Committee (its title slightly altered to Committee for Reforming the Chinese Written Language) was placed directly under Chou En-lai's State Council. Wu now assumed the chairmanship, and with the possible exception of his responsibilities with the Chinese People's University, the language reform committee consumed most of his time until his death 12 years later.

The language reform program moved into high gear in the mid-1950's. In January 1955 Wu's committee published a draft plan for simplifying Chinese characters. In October the National Language Reform Conference, the first one held in the post-1949 period, was convened. Fittingly, Wu chaired the meeting, and he gave the opening address, which dealt with the simplification of characters, the popularization of the "common language" (p'u-t'ung-hua), and principles of language reform. His report was subsequently published in the 1956 edition of the authoritative Jen-min shou-ts'e. On the heels of this conference, the national press began to use some 230 simplified characters, a figure which increased several fold within the next few years. The press also began to print in horizontal rather than the age-old vertical fashion in order to facilitate the use of a phonetic script using Latin letters.

Further decisions regarding the language program were taken in early 1956. After hearing explanations by Wu, the State Council in late January adopted a decision on the publication of the plan for using simplified characters and a directive on the promotion of the "common speech." A few days later, on February 10, Wu was appointed one of the vice-chairmen of a committee to popularize the "common speech," and in the next month he was also made a vice-chairman of the National Association for the Elimination of Illiteracy, an organization initially placed directly under the

State Council. Several weeks later, in May, Wu spoke before the State Council on problems regarding the Latinization of the language. After further experimentation, in November 1957 the State Council ratified the plan to phoneticize Chinese with the Latin alphabet. In all of these schemes, the total eradication of the ideographs was treated as something for the distant future; rather, the speeches by Wu and others emphasized that the various plans were intended to facilitate the learning of Chinese, which in turn would hasten the elimination of illiteracy. In this connection, for the December 11, 1957, issue of the *JMJP*, Wu co-authored an informative article on more than six decades of work to phoneticize the language.

Wu also spoke on the language reform program at the Eighth National Party Congress in September 1956, and in February 1958, at the fifth session of the First NPC, he delivered a particulary informative talk on the subject. This was published later in the year, together with other documents and speeches, in a pamphlet entitled *Reform of the Chinese Written Language*. In June 1960, speaking at a national conference of "advanced" workers in culture and education, Wu summarized some of the results of the various plans which by then had been in operation for a few years. He claimed that since the fall of 1958 the new alphabetic script and "common speech" had been taught in the majority of primary, middle, and normal schools, and that over 500 simplified characters had been introduced in books, newspapers, and magazines.

In the meantime, Wu had received some new appointments. From the end of 1954 to April 1959, as a representative of the CCP, he was a member of the Second National Committee of the CPPCC. In May 1955 he was made a member of the newly established Department of Philosophy and Social Sciences under the Academy of Sciences, and in October he was made a member of the Academy's Science Awards Committee. As already noted, Wu was among the speakers at the Eighth Party Congress in September 1956; at the close of the congress he was again re-elected a member of the CCP Central Committee. Exactly a year later he was appointed president of the Institute of Socialism, which formally opened in October 1956. This school was established to train high-ranking officials from the various "democratic" (that is, non-Communist) political parties. The institute offered a one-year course in Marxism-Leninism, which featured classes in dialectical materialism, political economics, and China's revolutionary history. A good percentage of the "students" were middle-aged men.

In spite of his very advanced age, Wu continued to be quite active in public life through the mid-1960's. As might be expected, his name regularly appeared on the many *ad hoc* committees set up to celebrate historic occasions in modern Chinese history (for example, he was a vice-chairman of the committee to commemorate the 50th anniversary of the 1911 Revolution). To his final years he continued to display an active interest in the language program, and in this regard he wrote a long and informative article for the *JMJP* of February 17, 1964 (translated in *SCMP* 3174), and in August of that year he traveled to Sian to deliver the opening speech at the fourth national conference on the results of teaching the "common speech."

Wu died in Peking on December 12, 1966, in his 88th year. He was given the press coverage and memorial services befitting his long revolutionary career. He was apparently survived by a daughter and son, both of whom were born around the turn of the century. His son, an electrical engineer, studied in France and worked in a Nationalist factory during the Sino-Japanese War.

An important source on Wu's career through 1945 is *Wu Yü-chang T'ung-chih ko-ming ku-shih* (The revolutionary story of Comrade Wu Yü-chang; Hong Kong, 1949), written by Ho Ch'i-fang, a Szechwanese colleague and a man of letters. This is richly supplemented by several of Wu's own writings. The most important is *Hsin-hai ko-ming* (The Hsin-hai Revolution), published in 1961, and translated with only minor changes the next year under the title *The Revolution of 1911*. This is part history and part autobiography, and it contains a lengthy section on his years in Japan. Another important item, which deals with Wu's conversion to Communism, is his long essay which appeared in *Chung-kuo ch'ing-nien* (China youth), no. 9, May 1, 1959.

1. Chow Tse-tsung, *The May Fourth Movement* (Cambridge, Mass., 1960) pp. 36–37.

2. *JMJP*, August 3, 1962.

3. *SCMP* 986, p. 31.

4. C. Martin Wilbur and Julie Lien-ying How, *Documents on Communism, Nationalism, and Soviet Advisers in China, 1918–1927* (New York, 1956), pp. 371, 381; Li Yun-han, *Tsung jung kung tao ch'ing tang* (From the admission of the Communists to the purification of the [Nationalist] Party; Taipei, 1966), p. 531.

5. *Chung-kuo ch'ing-nien* (China youth), no. 12:13–15 (June 16, 1960).

6. *Hung-ch'i p'iao-p'iao* (Red flag fluttering; Peking, 1957), IV, 164–170.

7. Ho Ch'i-fang, *Wu Yü-chang T'ung-chih ko-ming ku-shih* (The revolutionary story of Comrade Wu Yü-chang; Hong Kong, 1949), p. 33.

8. John De Francis, *Nationalism and Language Reform in China* (Princeton, N.J., 1950), pp. 129–131.

Wu Yun-fu

(c.1906–   ; Chekiang). Member, Control Commission, CCP; vice-president, Chinese Red Cross Society.

Few Chinese Communist leaders have had such varied careers as Wu Yun-fu, who has been a telecommunications expert, a specialist in relief and rehabilitation work, and a senior figure in Party discipline and inspection work. Wu graduated from a middle school and then became active in the Communist movement by 1930 when he studied at a secret Party school in the French concession in Shanghai.[1] Among his fellow students at the school was Li Ch'iang (q.v.), presently a vice-minister of Foreign Trade. After this training, Wu, already a Party member, was sent to the Kiangsi Soviet area where he became the political director of the Red Army Central Radio Station. He almost certainly made the Long March of 1934–35, because by the mid-1930's he was stationed with Red Army units in northern Shensi.

During the Sino-Japanese War the Communist Eighth Route Army had a Liaison Office in Sian, capital of Shensi. Wu worked in this office where he served under one of the ranking Communists of the period, Lin Po-ch'ü (q.v.), who for a period headed this office. One of Wu's principal tasks in this job was to arrange for supplies to be sent to Communist forces in north Shensi, where the headquarters of the Eighth Route Army was located. Japanese government reports also claim that he served during the war as a liaison officer for the New Fourth Army stationed in east-central China. At some time before the war ended he was also in Yenan where his knowledge of communications was again utilized; he was reported to have been in charge of Communist radio activities in the Communist capital.

In July 1945 a decision was taken in Yenan to establish relief organizations for the Communist-held areas, and by January 1946 such organizations had been established on a preparatory basis in eight of the Communist "liberated areas." In April 1946 in Peking the China Liberated Areas Relief Association (CLARA) was formally established; the Communists were able to take these organizational steps in the city of Peking by virtue of the cease-fire agreement that had been worked out between Communists and Nationalists in January 1946 by U.S. General George C. Marshall. In the meantime, the United Nations Relief and Rehabilitation Administration (UNRRA) had already begun operations in China during the final stages of the war in cooperation with the China National Relief and Rehabilitation Administration (CNRRA), which was sponsored by the Chinese Nationalist Government. With the formation of the Communist-backed CLARA in April 1946, Wu was named as the CLARA secretary-general and when the CLARA gained permission to open an office in Shanghai (July 1946), Wu was made the head of this office, a position which presumably brought him into regular contact with UNRRA officials.

Under the terms of the above-mentioned truce agreement, the Peking Executive Headquarters was established, and under this Headquarters were a number of specialized organs, one of which was the Relief Liaison Group. Concurrently with his CLARA tasks in Shanghai, Wu was also named as the Communist representative on the Relief Liaison Group, holding the simulated rank of major general. CCP–KMT relations had, by 1947, deteriorated into full-scale civil war and although the Peking Executive Headquarters was dissolved early in 1947, Wu and other CLARA officials were allowed to remain in Shanghai. Finally, however, they were expelled in December 1947 and sent to Communist-held areas. Yenan, the Communist capital, had been captured in early 1947, but in November 1947 (just one month prior to Wu's expulsion from Shanghai) the Communists had captured the important city of Shihchiachuang in southwest Hopeh. Wu's men from Shanghai and other CLARA officials who had been in Yenan were united in Shihchiachuang where they were to remain until September 1949 when they moved to Peking, then in Communist hands. (In that same month Wu attended the first session of the CPPCC in Peking, at which time the PRC was established. He attended as a "specially invited delegate.")

At the close of 1949 the *raison d'être* of relief in "liberated areas" was rapidly coming to an end with the complete conquest of the mainland. Plans were laid, therefore, to dissolve CLARA and to establish a new nationwide organization. These plans were carried out in April 1950 when the Communists held a large "Chinese People's Relief Conference." Wu, then still secretary-general of the CLARA, served on the conference presidium (steering committee). He made one of the major reports, a report which serves as the basis for much of the information above on relief work in Communist areas in the postwar period.[2] At the close of the conference he was elected as a member of the Executive Committee and as secretary-general of the Chinese People's Relief Administration (CPRA), a position he still retains under President Sung Ch'ing-ling (Mme. Sun Yat-sen). Although less well known than such persons as Mme. Sun, Tung Pi-wu, and Hsieh Chueh-tsai—each of whom has played an important role in relief work in recent years—it is probable that Wu has, in fact, had a greater impact on the actual day-to-day relief operations than any other person since the late 1940's.

In 1950 the Communists were making a

serious bid for membership in the United Nations, and during that year a number of appointments (all in vain) were made to the UN and its subordinate organizations. One such appointment was made in August 1950 when Wu was appointed as Peking's representative-designate to the International Children's Emergency Fund. In the same month he was named to the Standing Committee of the Chinese Red Cross Society. In October 1961 he was elevated to a vice-presidency, but in view of the fact that Miss Li Te-ch'üan, who was of little political power, was president of the society until 1965, it is apparent that Wu was and is one of the most important officials within this organization.

It was in October 1950 that Wu took the first of six trips abroad, each directly or closely related to the Red Cross Society. He led a Chinese government delegation to the 21st Council meeting of the International Red Cross (IRC) in Monaco (Li Te-ch'üan led the Chinese Red Cross Society delegation). He was a member of another delegation to an IRC meeting in Toronto in July–August 1952 (thereby becoming one of the few Chinese Communists to have visited North America) and led a group to Geneva in December 1952 for still another Red Cross meeting. In October–November 1954 he visited Japan as a member of Li Te-ch'üan's Red Cross Society delegation; he led another Red Cross group to Yugoslavia in September 1957; and finally, in November–December 1961, he headed a group to Japan for talks with survivors of the atomic bombing of Hiroshima and to tour areas hit by a typhoon. This last trip was made as an official of the Chinese People's Relief Administration.

Wu received a long series of other appointments in the early and mid-1950's. One of the numerous Chinese gestures of hostility toward the United States was the creation of a "Central People's Government Committee for the Disposal of American-subsidized Relief Organizations." By 1951 Wu was serving as secretary-general of this committee, and in the same year he was named to the Chinese People's Committee in Defense of Children. From 1953 to 1959 Wu served as a vice-chairman of the China Association for the Welfare of the Blind, and from 1956 to 1959 he also chaired the Committee of the China Welfare Institute for the Deaf and Dumb. When the mass organization known as the Chinese People's Association for Cultural Relations with Foreign Countries was established in May 1954, he was named to the Board of Directors (a position he probably still holds), and when a governmental counterpart was created in 1958 under the name of the Commission for Cultural Relations with Foreign Relations, he was also named to membership (March 1958). Another appointment he received in 1954 was as a deputy from Kiangsu to the First NPC (1954–1959); he was not, however, re-elected to the Second NPC.

In October 1956, Wu was appointed as a vice-minister of Public Health; the minister at the time was Miss Li Te-ch'üan, under whom he was also serving in the Red Cross Society. When the State Council underwent a major reshuffle of personnel in September 1959, he was not reappointed. However, shortly afterwards he was again named as a vice-minister (January 1960). Although he held this government position during the late 1950's and early 1960's, most of his time was apparently devoted to his quasi-official positions in the mass organizations and, further, he received still more such positions during this period. He was named, in July 1958, to National Committee membership on the China Peace Committee and to Standing Committee membership in March 1960 within the China–Latin America Friendship Association. He was also often in attendance when foreign visitors were in China, particularly if some aspect of relief and rehabilitation work was involved. Since 1959 Wu has also served on the CPPCC National Committee. CPPCC membership is by either political parties or by functional groups; logically, Wu has been a representative of relief and welfare organizations, serving on the Third National Committee (1959–1964) and then re-elected to the Fourth Committee, which first met in late 1964.

In September 1962, at the 10th Party Plenum, it was decided to "strengthen the work of the Party Control Commissions at all levels" and to expand the size of the Central Control Commission headed by Politburo member Tung Pi-wu, one of the Party founders. Membership on the commission is governed in part by functional categories (i.e., military men, Party propagandists, women leaders). Wu was named to the commission at this time (as well as to alternate Standing Committee membership), so that he probably has major responsibilities for discipline and inspection in the many relief and welfare organizations in China. Not long afterwards (April 1963) he was removed as a vice-minister of Public Health, but his prior appointment to the Control Commission suggests that he was being relieved of administrative tasks in favor of the more important work on the Control Commission. As in the case of many members of this sensitive commission, he has not made many public appearances since his appointment.

Wu married Miss Hsiung Yuan-ching in 1938, but nothing further is known about this woman.

---

1. *Wu-ling feng-yun* (The gathering clouds on the Wuling Mountains; Hong Kong, 1961), pp. 55–57.

2. *Hsin-hua yueh-pao* (New China monthly; Peking, June 15, 1950), p. 334.

Yang Ch'eng-wu

(c.1912–　　　; Ch'ang-t'ing, Fukien). Veteran Red Army officer; acting chief-of-staff, PLA; alternate member, CCP Central Committee.

A veteran political and staff officer since the early thirties, Yang Ch'eng-wu is one of the most battle-tested of the many Red Army leaders. He fought in several critical battles on the Long March and then led Communist troops against the Japanese in Shansi and Hopeh during the Sino-Japanese War. He also played a prominent part in the struggle in north China against the Nationalists in the late forties. Since the PRC was established in 1949 he has been an important staff officer, first in Tientsin and then in Peking, and he may also have participated in the Korean War. Yang advanced to deputy chief-of-staff of the PLA in 1959, and seven years later to acting chief-of-staff.

Yang is native to Ch'ang-t'ing, a town in western Fukien in which Communist sympathizers in the late twenties were in frequent communication with the well-known Red base at Juichin, not far across the Kiangsi border. Ultimately, by the early thirties, Ch'ang-t'ing became a part of this base and was the medical center for the Red armies (see under Fu Lien-chang). Yang is said to have come from a family of rich peasants who gave him a middle school education before he became a Communist.[1] According to his own account, Yang took part in a peasant revolt in west Fukien in 1929 with Liu Ya-lou (q.v.), also a Fukienese. In 1930 both young men were "drafted" into the Fourth Red Army commanded by Chu Te.[2] By 1932 Yang had risen to be political commissar of the Fourth Regiment of the Second Division. This division was a part of the First Army Corps, the designation given to Chu Te's forces in mid-1930. When it had merged with P'eng Te-huai's (q.v.) Third Army Corps later in 1930, Chu's force became known as the First Front Army, a unit that fought in western Fukien and eastern Kiangsi until it began the Long March in the fall of 1934.

During the Long March Yang continued as political commissar of the Fourth Regiment, a unit that took part in the capture of Tsun-i in Kweichow from the Nationalists in January 1935. Tsun-i was the site of an important conference held by the Communists during the March, a conference from which Maoist historians now claim that Mao Tse-tung emerged as the CCP's dominant leader. By May 1935 the marchers had made their way into eastern Sikang where they had another savage encounter with the Nationalists as they tried to cross the Ta-tu River at An-shun-ch'ang. The crossing of the river after capturing the famous Lu-ting chain bridge is described by Edgar Snow as "the most critical incident of the Long March." Spanning a narrow gorge between high mountains and a swift and deep river, the bridge was the "last possible crossing of the Tatu east of Tibet."[3] The successful crossing enabled Mao's forces to proceed north into Szechwan for their rendezvous with Chang Kuo-t'ao's Fourth Front Army, which was coming from north Szechwan (see under Chang Kuo-t'ao). Yang has written a firsthand account of the crossing, because it was his Fourth Regiment that was ordered by Lin Piao to take the bridge and capture the town of Lu-ting to the north. Pushing north from Szechwan with Mao's forces, Yang's regiment captured a strategic pass in southwestern Kansu in September 1935.[4]

According to Yang's memorial account of Liu Ya-lou, Liu was his commanding officer throughout the Long March. In this same account Yang has written that after the Communists had reached north Shensi both he and Liu took part in a Communist thrust eastward into Shansi. The attacks on Yen Hsi-shan's forces in Shansi in early 1936 were initially successful, but when the Nationalist government reinforced Yen's troops, the Communists were repulsed and forced to retreat into northern Shensi. Back in Shensi the two men studied at the Red Army Academy (Hung-chün ta-hsüeh), which had branches both at Wa-yao-pao and Pao-an, the towns where Mao Tse-tung made his headquarters before establishing them at Yenan.[5]

When the Sino-Japanese War broke out in July 1937, Liu Ya-lou remained at the military academy, but Yang followed his commander Lin Piao to the battlefields of north Shansi. As commander of an independent regiment in Lin's 115th Division of the Eighth Route Army, Yang and his forces crossed the Yellow River in September 1937 and advanced to the vicinity of Wu-t'ai Mountain in northeast Shansi. Here Lin's 115th Division made its headquarters and then moved north to engage the Japanese at P'ing-hsing-kuan, where they encircled and destroyed a major portion of the Japanese Fifth Division, commanded by Lieutenant General Itagaki Seishirō, a battle the Communists claim as one of their major victories of the war. After this encounter Lin Piao did not himself engage much in front-line warfare, but left the fighting to his deputy, Nieh Jung-chen (q.v.), a man with whom Yang Ch'eng-wu has long been associated. Yang participated with Nieh in guerrilla activities along the borders of Shansi, Hopeh, and Chahar provinces. In the area controlled by Nieh's Wu-t'ai Mountain base, the Communists soon established the Shansi-Chahar-Hopeh (Chin-Ch'a-Chi) Border Region Government. The government was set up in January 1938 and, in the prevailing atmosphere of cooperation to resist the Japanese, it was immediately accorded official recognition by the Nationalist government. The political and strategic importance of the Chin-Ch'a-Chi area is described in the biographies of Nieh Jung-chen and Sung Shao-wen. In particular, the area was situated between four important Japanese-controlled rail lines, which were the object of many harassing guerrilla attacks in which Nieh and Yang's forces took part, and by the end of the war the Communists were cutting the lines at will.

Yang's first move eastward took place in October 1937 when he led his independent regiment from Shansi into western Hopeh where he began recruiting among the peasantry to build up his forces. At this time and later in the war, he was in charge of one of the four administrative sub-divisions of the Wu-t'ai base area, the I-hsin and Man-ch'eng hsien base in western Hopeh where, according to a Japanese study of 1940, his forces—now enlarged to the division level—numbered some 7,000 men.[6] In 1941 he was identified by other titles that refer in general to the same area in west and central Hopeh; the first was as commander of the Shansi-Hopeh Military Sub-district and the second as commander of the Fifth Sub-district of the West Hopeh Military District. By the end of the war, at which time Yang's forces were designated the Second Column of Nieh Jung-chen's Chin-Ch'a-Chi Command, the column had a reported strength of 30,000 men. At this same time he was in command of the Central Hopeh Military District. Yang has written a rather detailed account of his operations against the Japanese in the period after December 1941.[7]

Soon after V-J Day in 1945, Yang participated in the capture of Kalgan (Chang-chia-k'ou), the capital of Chahar. The city was held until October 1946 when Nationalist forces under Fu Tso-i occupied it. A year later, identified as commander of the First Independent Division, Yang and his forces combined with the troops led by Yang Te-chih (q.v.) to capture Shih-chia-chuang, the important rail junction in western Hopeh. The city fell on November 12, 1947, and has been described in official Communist sources as the "first important city in north China to be liberated." Yang continued to fight for the cities of north China and has been cited in Mao Tse-tung's *Selected Works* for his contributions to the Liaohsi-Shenyang campaign, described by the Communists as the first of the "three greatest campaigns of decisive significance" in the civil war against the Nationalists. In a directive of September 1948, Mao ordered his top field commanders in Manchuria, Lin Piao and Lo Jung-huan, to coordinate their attacks with the armies commanded by Lo Jui-ch'ing (q.v.) and Yang to wipe out 35 Nationalist brigades and to capture all the cities along the four major rail lines leading into Peking—excepting only Peking itself, Tientsin, and Mukden (Shenyang).[8] When the successful completion of these operations led to the fall of these

cities by January 1949, Yang moved westward and, in coordination with units led by Lo Jui-ch'ing and Yang Te-chih, captured Taiyuan, the Shansi capital, in April 1949.

Soon after the fall of Taiyuan, Yang was reassigned to Tientsin where in June 1949 he assumed command of the Tientsin garrison, a position he was to hold until at least the spring of 1953.[9] At approximately the same time as these events, Yang received his first national post when he was elected to membership on the National Committee of the All-China Federation of Democratic Youth at its first congress in May 1949. Then about 37 years of age, Yang held this position until the next youth congress in mid-1953. With the fighting in north China now at an end, he was free to engage in other non-military activities. Thus, as a representative of PLA Headquarters, in September 1949 he attended the first session of the CPPCC, the body that brought the new central government into existence (October 1). While the meetings were in session, Yang served on a special committee to draft the Common Program, the Communists' equivalent of a constitution until one was formally adopted in 1954 at the First NPC.

After the meetings in Peking, Yang returned to Tientsin where, in January 1950, he was appointed a member of the Tientsin Municipal People's Government Council. He was identified at this time as commander of the Seventh Corps of the North China Military Region, whose commander was Nieh Jung-chen.[10] He retained the Tientsin government post until at least mid-1953, but it is not certain how long he commanded the Seventh Corps. Another post Yang held from 1950 was as a deputy commander of the joint Peking-Tientsin Garrison Command, here again serving under Nieh. There is an unconfirmed report that Yang led the 66th, 67th, and 68th Armies into the Korean War in 1951; if true, he was apparently there a relatively short time, for in December of that year he was appointed a member of the North China Administrative Committee (NCAC; see under Liu Lan-t'ao, the chairman), at which time he was once again identified as commander of the Tientsin garrison. He retained his membership on the NCAC until it was abolished in 1954.

By the early fall of 1952 Yang was permanently transferred to Peking, although he nominally retained his posts in nearby Tientsin until the following year. He now assumed the new post of chief-of-staff of the North China Military Region, and by the spring of 1954 he was concurrently a deputy commander. This region was abolished about 1954–55, but Yang continued to receive new military assignments in Peking during the mid-fifties. By early 1955 he had assumed from Nieh Jung-chen the command of the Peking-Tientsin garrison, continuing in the post until 1956, and from the latter year until

1957 he was commander of the PLA Air Defense (anti-aircraft) Force. In 1957–58 he was also identified as commander of PLA units in Peking, a generic identification used by the Communists that could refer to either the Peking Garrison Command or the larger Peking Military Region. The latter, in effect, was in large measure a successor to the North China Military Region, although it only covers the provinces of Hopeh and Shansi in contrast to the larger area embraced by the North China Region.

In the meantime, Yang had received other new assignments in the government and the CCP. He attended the First NPC (1954–1959) as a deputy from Tientsin, and at the close of its initial session in September 1954 he was named to membership on the newly created National Defense Council. He has since been reappointed to this military advisory body in April 1959 and January 1965. In 1955, when military ranks and honors were first awarded, he was made a colonel-general (equal to a three-star general in the U.S. Army) and was given the Orders of Independence and Freedom and of Liberation, awards covering his service during the Sino-Japanese War and the civil war with the Nationalists in the late forties. Despite his notable contributions on the Long March, Yang was not initially given the August First Order, which covered military service in the decade from 1927 to 1937. However, two years later he was given this order in a ceremony in Peking. More important, at the Party's Eighth National Congress in September 1956, he was elected an alternate member of the Central Committee.

Since 1955 Yang has made three trips abroad, each in connection with military affairs. In July 1955 he attended Soviet Air Force Day ceremonies in Moscow with his colleague Liu Ya-lou. He led a military goodwill delegation to Indonesia (traveling via Burma) in April–May 1959, and in December 1961 he spent two weeks in North Vietnam as a member of a group headed by military veteran Yeh Chien-ying to attend celebrations marking the 17th anniversary of the North Vietnamese army. Since the mid-fifties Yang has appeared in public in Peking with considerable frequency; virtually all these appearances have been related to military affairs. In addition to such protocol functions as welcoming foreign military delegations, he has also appeared at many military meetings, as in the spring of 1961 when he co-chaired a conference on PLA communications and cryptography.

Yang reached a new level of importance by March 1959 when he was identified as a deputy chief-of-staff of the PLA, a post that placed him under Huang K'o-ch'eng (q.v.) until September 1959 and thereafter under Lo Jui-ch'ing, a former colleague. Then, during the "great proletarian cultural revolution" of mid-1966, Lo fell from power along with such top Communists as P'eng Chen, Lu Ting-i (both on the Politburo), and Chou Yang (qq.v.), an alternate member of the Central Committee. Lo's disappearance from the public scene had first been noted when he failed to appear at an important PLA political conference (a conference at which Yang spoke) in December 1965–January 1966. Lo's political demise was confirmed on August 1, 1966, when Yang was identified as the acting chief-of-staff. In the history of the PRC, he is the first alternate member of the Party Central Committee to hold this critical position, all of his predecessors having been full members. And aside from PLA Political Department Director Hsiao Hua, he is the first man born after the first decade of the century to have assumed a top PLA post.

Yang has been an occasional contributor to the press; apart from the military reminiscences already cited, he contributed an article on military affairs for the Party's leading journal, *Hung-ch'i* (Red flag, issue of February 16, 1959). He is married to Chao Chih-chen, but nothing is known of her background.

---

1. Chalmers A. Johnson, *Peasant Nationalism and Communist Power* (Stanford, Calif., 1962), p. 221.
2. *SCMP* 3463, p. 13.
3. Edgar Snow, *Red Star over China* (New York, 1938), pp. 182, 185.
4. *Stories of the Long March* (Peking, 1958), pp. 61–76; *China Reconstructs,* 14:32–37 (July 1965).
5. *SCMP* 3463, p. 13.
6. Johnson, p. 102.
7. *Peking Review,* no. 47:15–19 (November 19, 1965); *ibid.,* no. 49:16–21 (December 3, 1965).
8. *Selected Works of Mao Tse-tung* (Peking, 1961), IV, 261–262.
9. *JMJP,* June 30, 1949.
10. Shanghai, *Chieh-fang jih-pao* (Liberation daily), January 19, 1950.

Yang Ch'i-ch'ing

(Hunan). Vice-minister of Public Security.

Yang Ch'i-ch'ing, a specialist in public security work, first came to national attention when the North China People's Government was formed by the Communists in August 1948. He was named as the deputy director of the Public Security Department, serving under another veteran specialist in security matters, Hsu Chien-kuo (q.v.). This temporary government was dissolved in October 1949 when its functions were assumed by the newly formed central government in Peking. Yang participated in the formation of this central government as a delegate to the first CPPCC meeting in September 1949, which established the central governmental apparatus. He was listed at the CPPCC as a delegate representing the PLA Headquarters, but it is impossible to surmise exactly what tasks he may have performed in the military headquarters. In view of his background he was probably involved in some aspect of military security work.

When the government was formally organized in the fall of 1949, Yang was given four posts, each dealing with some phase of discipline or control activity. He was named as a member of both the Supreme People's Procuratorate and the Political and Legal Affairs Committee of the cabinet, then known as the Government Administration Council. Most important, however, he was appointed the only vice-minister of Public Security under Lo Jui-ch'ing, China's top security official for the next decade. Aside from a trouble-shooting mission in central-south China during the 1952–1954 period (see below), Yang has served continuously as a vice-minister and is thus the only person at the ministerial or vice-ministerial level to have such a long connection with this important ministry. Concurrently with his vice-ministership, Yang served for a year (December 1949–November 1950) as director of the ministry's Political Security Bureau; as might be expected, there is no information about this obviously sensitive bureau.

In 1951–52, the Party was engaged in a major campaign known as the *san-fan* (three anti) movement, which sought to eradicate from Chinese society the three vices of corruption, waste, and bureaucratism. One of the most celebrated cases of the campaign was the Sung Ying episode, named for a senior public health official who was involved in thefts at a Wuhan hospital (see under Chang P'ing-hua). Among those implicated in the case was Pu Sheng-kuang, who was vice-chairman of the Political and Legal Affairs Committee of the Central-South Military and Administrative Committee (CSMAC), director of Public Security for the CSMAC, and Procurator-General for the central-south branch of the Supreme People's Procuratorate. Pu was charged with "depraved" living and the "obstruction of the anti-corruption movement" and was removed from these posts. Yang was named to fill all of them in February 1952. The importance of the case can be judged in part by the fact that a Public Security vice-minister (Yang) was brought from Peking to Wuhan, presumably to tighten the security in central-south China.

In addition to his supervisory activities in the central-south China region, Yang also engaged in other activities. In March 1952 he was named a member of the Central-South Anti-Epidemic Committee, and in the following month was appointed as a vice-chairman of a special "opium and narcotics suppression committee" under the CSMAC. When the CSMAC was reorganized and renamed the Central-South Administrative Committee in January 1953, Yang was also named to membership on this important regional organization. The other position of importance held by Yang in his two and a half years in the central-south region was as commander of the Wuhan Garrison Headquarters of the PLA in 1953–54.

Having apparently improved the security situation in central-south China, Yang was brought back to Peking in September 1954 and was reappointed to his old post as a vice-minister of Public Security, a position he continues to hold. Like most security figures, he does not receive much attention from the press. Yet the rare instances when he is cited are usually of obvious significance. For example, he was a Hupeh delegate to the Eighth Party Congress in September 1956. In April 1958 he gave instructions at an Anhwei provincial conference on security work, and in June 1964 he accompanied Mao Tse-tung and several other Politburo members when they met with delegates to various conferences then being held in Peking, including representatives to a conference of the Public Security Forces. He is also mentioned on occasion as among those welcoming foreign visitors to China or Chinese delegations returning to Peking. More important, Yang was sent abroad three times in recent years. In April 1955 he accompanied Chou En-lai to the famous Afro-Asian Conference (better known as the Bandung Conference) in Indonesia. Yang was listed as an adviser, but it seems more likely that he in fact accompanied the delegation (which included several top political figures apart from Chou En-lai) as a security aide. And in August 1957 and July 1962 he took delegations to Mongolia for the 35th anniversary of the Mongolian military forces and the 40th anniversary of the Mongolian Ministry of Public Security, respectively.

As already mentioned, Yang was a PLA representative to the First CPPCC in 1949. He was not, however, associated with the Second CPPCC (1954–1959). But then in April 1959 he returned to activity in this "united front" organization; on this occasion Yang served as Party representative on the Third National Committee and was also named to the Standing Committee, charged with handling the work of the CPPCC when the National Committee is not in session. When the Fourth CPPCC held its first meeting in December 1964–January 1965, Yang was again selected as a Party delegate and was once more named to the Standing Committee.

Yang Ching-jen

(Kansu). Chairman, Ninghsia-Hui Autonomous Region; First Secretary, Ninghsia-Hui Party Committee.

Yang Ching-jen has spent much of his career working in the northwest where so many of his fellow Hui live. A high imam (prayer leader) among the Hui (Muslim) peoples, Yang is often mentioned in the Chinese press with his Muslim name, Ibrahim, before his Sinicized name. He joined the Communist Party during the Sino-Japanese War and by 1941 was serving in an "Islamic Cavalry Brigade" as the chief-of-staff. During this same period he also held civil posts in Yenan, serving as head of the Minority Nationalities Section of the Party's Northwest Bureau as well as holding membership on the Nationalities Affairs Committee under the civil administration in the northwest, known as the Shensi-Kansu-Ninghsia Border Region Government. Yang also was chief of the Staff Office, generally an important office in Chinese Communist organizations and one concerned with day-to-day management and administrative problems. These positions dealing with national minorities were the first of many that Yang would hold in the years ahead.

Yang was active in the spring of 1949 in the formation of the two important youth organizations, the New Democratic Youth League (NDYL) and the All-China Federation of Democratic Youth (ACFDY). He was a Central Committee member of the former from April 1949 to the next NDYL congress in mid-1953 and also served as a National Committee member in the ACFDY from April 1949 to June 1953, at which time he was transferred out of this organization. When youth organization officials are removed, it is usually because of age or because their experience is needed elsewhere, and generally they have no further direct relations with the organization in question. For reasons which are not evident, an exception was made in Yang's case, and he was brought back to the federation (renamed the All-China Youth Federation in 1958) to serve as a vice-chairman from April 1958 to April 1962.

In June 1949 the preparatory committee for the CPPCC was set up under Mao Tse-tung; Yang was named as a member, and when the CPPCC held its first session in September 1949 to form the central government, he attended as a representative of the national minorities and served on the important Credentials Committee for the CPPCC session. When the central government was staffed in the following weeks, Yang received assignments within the Nationalities Affairs Commission of the Government Administration Council (the cabinet). He was named to membership on the commission under chairman Li Wei-han, a veteran Party leader; in addition, Yang was named to head the commission's Staff Office, a post he held until about 1953. In other words, Yang was given the identical positions under the central government which he had held under the Shensi-Kansu-Ninghsia Government during and immediately after the Sino-Japanese War.

Although Yang spent most of the first decade of the PRC in the national capital, he received nominal appointments under the regional politico-military administration for the northwest, known as the Northwest Military and Administrative Committee from its formation in January 1950 and as the Northwest Administrative Committee from its reorganization in January 1953 to its dissolution in November 1954. From March 1950 until 1954 he was also a member of the Northwest Nationalities Affairs Committee.

Yang's next major assignment began in 1952 when the first steps were taken to form the China Islamic Association. In addition to religious personages, a number of Party-affiliated men of Hui nationality were needed (in accordance with normal Communist practice) to organize this society. Yang was thus named to a vice-chairmanship on the preparatory committee (1952–53), and when the first national conference was held in May 1953, he was elected as one of the vice-chairmen. Because Chairman Burhan (q.v.) was a relative newcomer to the Communist Party, it may be that Yang was in fact the most significant Party figure in the association. At the next national conference (December 1956) he was one of the principal speakers and at the close of the meeting was re-elected as a vice-chairman. However, at the third conference held in October–November 1963, Yang was dropped from membership, probably because of his transfer in 1962 to very responsible positions in Ninghsia.

In 1954, Yang was elected from his native Kansu to the First NPC (1954–1959); he was re-elected to the Second NPC (1959–1964), but by the time that elections were held for the Third NPC (1964 to date) Yang was working in Ninghsia and was therefore elected from that Autonomous Region. He also served as a member of the Credentials Committee under all three Congresses, and for most of the individual sessions of the Congress has served on the Motions Examination Committee, a committee newly formed for each session. Soon after the constitutional government was established in the fall of 1954 at the First NPC session, Yang was named (October 1954) as a vice-chairman of the Nationalities Affairs Commission; in effect, this was a promotion because he had previously only been a member. However, because of his 1960 transfer out of Peking he was dropped in December 1960 as a vice-chairman (but still retains membership on the commission).

Like many national minority leaders, Yang is often involved in events symbolizing the Communist treatment of non-Han Chinese. For example, he was among the members of a central government delegation that journeyed to Inner Mongolia in April–May 1957 for the 10th anniversary of the establishment of that Autonomous

Region. Similarly, he took part in the inauguration ceremonies of the Ninghsia-Hui Autonomous Region (NHAR) in October 1958. The latter event was a foretaste of future events in Yang's career. In mid-1960 the chairman of the NHAR (Liu Ko-p'ing, a leading Hui) was accused of "local nationalism" and was removed from his post in September 1960. Yang was immediately transferred from Peking to replace Liu and has been there since in this capacity. Not long afterwards (by February 1961), Yang had also assumed the senior Party post when he succeeded Wang Feng as the First Secretary of the Ninghsia-Hui Party Committee. While such concurrency of posts within one province was a frequent situation in the early 1950's, it had become a relatively rare occurrence by the 1960's. Thus it seems to suggest a rather unusual trust in Yang (not even a Central Committee member) when he became (by March 1964) the political commissar of the Ninghsia Military District. Furthermore, he was given still another significant post by March 1965 when he was identified as a secretary of the Northwest Party Bureau under First Secretary Liu Lan-t'ao.

Aside from these major positions, Yang has held a host of lesser posts, in many cases obviously because he belongs to one of China's minority nationalities. From October 1949 to about 1952 he was a board member of the Association for the Reform of the Chinese Written Language. In the spring and summer of 1950 he took part in the preparatory work which led to the formation of the China Educational Trade Union, and from 1950 to 1961 he served on the board of the Chinese Red Cross Society. In May 1956 he was named to the board of the newly formed China-Pakistan Friendship Association, and when a similar organization involving Egypt was established in November 1956 he was also named to that board of directors. In September 1957 the China-Syria Friendship Association was founded, with Yang as one of the vice-presidents. Following the merger of Egypt and Syria into the United Arab Republic (UAR) in February 1958, the Chinese merged the two organizations into a China–UAR Friendship and named Yang to a vice-presidency. In July 1958 he was selected for national committee membership on the reorganized China Peace Committee, and in April 1960 he became a board member of the China-Africa People's Friendship Association. Except where noted, Yang retains his positions in all these organizations.

Yang's writings include an article for the *JMJP* of March 4, 1951, on the affairs of the national minorities, and for a joint number (10-11) of *Min-tsu t'uan-chieh* (Nationalities unity) in 1963 he wrote an article commemorating the fifth anniversary of the Ninghsia-Hui Autonomous Region, in which he reviewed the accomplishments of the region.

Yang Hsien-chen

(c.1899–   ; Hupeh). Marxist philosopher; former president, Higher Party School; member, CCP Central Committee.

Yang Hsien-chen was an important Party philosopher and ideologue until the early 1960's when he was removed from the presidency of the Higher Party School and denounced. He was born about 1899 (or possibly a few years earlier). Nothing is known of his earlier years, but in the early 1920's or shortly before, he studied at the Russian Language Institute (O-wen chuan-k'o hsueh-yuan) and Peking Normal University, apparently graduating from the latter. The Russian Language Institute had been established by the Peiyang military clique to train diplomatic personnel and the language specialists necessary to deal with the Russians in the administration of the Chinese Eastern Railway in Manchuria. In terms of the Chinese Communist Movement, the most notable student at the language school was Ch'ü Ch'iu-pai (q.v.), whose interest in Communism was stimulated by his study there. It is probable that Yang was acquainted with Ch'ü at the institute or else in the Soviet Union a short time later.

Sometime in the early twenties Yang left China for Europe, but there is a good deal of uncertainty about his activities over the next two decades owing to a number of conflicting reports. He apparently studied philosophy in Germany before going to Moscow where he attended the Communist University of the Toilers of the East, an institute attended by such leading CCP members as Jen Pi-shih, Wang Jo-fei, and Hsiao Ching-kuang (qq.v.). After graduating he became head of the Publications Department of the Comintern's Far East Bureau. He reportedly returned to China during the early thirties and visited the Kiangsi Soviet where Mao Tse-tung and Chu Te had built a rural Soviet base of considerable size and importance. Because Yang's views were said to have been too close to those of Mao's, he was "required to return to Moscow" by Ch'en Shao-yü (q.v.), who was then contending with Mao for control of the CCP.[1]

Yang was next identified in 1936 as head of the China Department of the Soviet Union's Foreign Language Press, where he was in charge of translating Soviet ideological works into Chinese. In the accusations made against Yang in the sixties (see below), it was noted that he was writing articles for Communist newspapers in north China as early as August 1941, suggesting that he returned home at least by that date (although some sources claim that it was not for another year or two). He is also reported to have replaced Ch'en Shao-yü as head of the "Party Histories Committee" at some time during the latter stages of the Sino-Japanese War and to have made another visit to the Soviet Union during the year 1946–47.[2]

By mid-1949 Yang was in Peking where he participated in two large conferences to mobilize the talents of China's social scientists, many of them non-Communists. One of these meetings led to the establishment of the China Philosophy Association (see under Ai Szu-ch'i), while the other, more comprehensive in nature, laid the groundwork for the establishment of several social science organizations, among them the Political Science and Law Association, an organization in which Yang was to be involved in later years. He received no posts in the central government established in the fall of 1949, but the November issue of *Hsueh-hsi* (Study), then the Party's top journal, revealed that Yang had delivered a lecture on the question of the "mass line" in Chinese Communist ideology before a cadre training class sponsored by the Peking Party Committee in October 1949. Then, rather curiously, nothing was heard of his work until April 1953 when the above-mentioned Political Science and Law Association of China (PSLAC) was established under the chairmanship of Politburo member Tung Pi-wu. Yang was elected to the First National Council and in subsequent years he was re-elected to the Second and Third National Councils (1956 and 1958).

When Yang was named to the PSLAC Council in April 1953 there was little to distinguish him from scores of other Party ideologues, but in little more than three years he rose to impressive heights in the Party hierarchy and as a Party ideologue. In May 1953 he addressed the Seventh All-China Trade Union Congress on the "role of Marxism-Leninism in the emancipation of the Chinese workers," delivering his talk on the 135th anniversary of Marx's birth. He was identified at this time as vice-president of the Party Central Committee's Marx-Lenin Institute, a theoretical training school for leading Party cadres. Less than two years later (April 1955), Yang was identified as the president, soon after which the institute was renamed the Higher Party School.

Throughout the 1950's Yang seems to have been engaged principally in writing and lecturing on Marxism. For example, in May 1953 he was appointed as a lecturer for a training class of teachers who had been directed to make an intensive study of *The History of the Communist Party of the Soviet Union (B)*, one of the most important works during the Stalinist period. Similarly, in March 1955 and again in May 1956 he lectured before forums sponsored by the All-China Federation of Literary and Art Circles. Yang's most important article in these years, "Collective Leadership Is the Highest Principle of Party Leadership," appeared in *Hsueh-hsi* (no. 3, March 2, 1954). The mid-fifties also witnessed a series of new appointments for Yang. In May 1954 he was identified as deputy-director of the Party Propaganda Department's Theoretical Education Division, and a short time later he was elected from his native Hupeh to the First NPC, the legislative body that brought the constitutional government into existence at its initial session in September 1954. He served throughout the term of the First NPC and was then re-elected to the Second NPC (1959–1964). In December 1954 Yang was appointed a member of the Preparatory Committee of the Academy of Sciences' Research Institute of Philosophy, which was established in 1955 (see under Hu Sheng). And when the academy established a Department of Philosophy and Social Sciences in May–June 1955, Yang was appointed as a member. He received still another academy appointment in October of that year when he was named to membership on its Science Awards Committee.

In February 1956, Yang attended the second session of the CPPCC's Second National Committee as an observer, and when the Third CPPCC was convened in April 1959, he was elected a member of the National Committee as a representative of social science organizations. On this occasion he was also named to Standing Committee membership. More important, at the Party's Eighth National Congress in September 1956, Yang was elected first among 73 alternate members of the Central Committee. His election to the Party's highest organ came as something of a surprise, for he was less well known than virtually all the men who ranked below him, not to mention scores of Party leaders who were not even elected to the Central Committee. Less than two years later, following the death of a full Central Committee member, Yang was elevated to Central Committee membership at the Party Central Committee's Fifth Plenum, held in late May 1958 immediately after the important Second Session of the Eighth Party Congress.

In May 1959 Yang attended three academic forums sponsored by the China Philosophy Association, where problems in logic and philosophy were discussed. Four years passed before he was again mentioned in the national press— and then only in a *pro forma* appearance to welcome back Teng Hsiao-p'ing from Moscow. In December 1963 he paid his last respects to Marshal Lo Jung-huan and in February 1964 he performed a similar ritual in connection with the death of General Kan Szu-ch'i. This was Yang's last public appearance before he was engulfed in a wave of Party-directed attacks that began in July 1964 and were still continuing two years later. Yang, it was charged, had for many years opposed Mao Tse-tung's position that everything contains "contradictions" and that these can only be resolved by endless struggles in which the contradictory elements tend to assume the nature of each other, until at last a new unity emerges. In Maoist terms, the key to this methodology is to "divide one into two," thus bringing the issues (or "contradictions") into the open and allowing the struggle to take place. Yang, in essence, agreed with this method of analysis, but rather than stressing the contradictory aspects of a problem (e.g., capitalism versus communism), he allegedly argued that the differences or contradictions should be set aside and then it would be possible to reunite the common aspects into the whole. This he defined as the process of "two combining into one."[3] Such a position was held by Party theorists to be an "intolerable distortion" of Marxist theory and a denial of the need for "struggle." In more contemporary Communist parlance, Yang's theories were labeled as a form of "revisionism" (the term of opprobrium for the Soviet Union). One Western writer, quoting in part from the accusations against Yang, summed up the charges as follows: "Yang's lectures in the Higher Party School on his theory were an 'intentional and systematic attempt to counterattack the proletarian world outlook with the reactionary world outlook.' He and his henchmen were 'intentionally . . . helping the modern revisionists to publicize class peace and cooperation,' providing the bourgeois and feudal remnants in China with theoretical weapons to oppose the Socialist Education Movement at the very time Chairman Mao and the Central Committee were stressing class struggle to arm the masses against these dangers."[4]

It is common Party practice that, once under fire, the accused's "offenses" are dated back many years. In Yang's case they were carried back to 1941 when, it is alleged, he had written an article for a Party newspaper, which argued the position that the "new democratic revolution" in China "was none other than the capitalist road."[5] However, it is significant that the Party press has continued to refer to Yang as "comrade," the standard indication that he remains a Party member and may one day return to political favor.

Yang, of course, was removed as president of the Higher Party School, but the date of his removal remains in doubt. From the context of the above-mentioned April 1959 forums, it appears that he then still retained the presidency. However, in September 1961 Wang Ts'ung-wu (q.v.), an important member of the Party's security and control apparatus, was identified as the president. In the charges against Yang it was revealed that he had been lecturing at the School as late as April 1964; earlier, in 1961, he was also identified as director of the School's Philosophical Education Research Bureau, but it is probable that he was also removed from this post after the attacks began in mid-1964. Yang was not re-elected to the Third NPC in the elections held in the fall of 1964, nor in October of that year was he re-elected to the National Council of the Political Science and Law Association. Yet two months later he was re-elected to represent social science organizations on the Fourth National Committee of the CPPCC, which held its first session in December 1964–January 1965. In a gesture that was obviously deliberate, however, he was not re-elected to the CPPCC Standing Committee.

In view of Yang's rather advanced age, it is most unlikely that he will again figure prominently in the Chinese Communist Movement. This seems all the more likely as long as the Sino-Soviet dispute continues to be unresolved. Although Yang was not directly linked with the Soviet Union, the context of many articles in the Communist press suggests that the Party elite felt that he had been corrupted by Khrushchevite doctrines. In this connection it is worth emphasizing that few CCP leaders have spent as much time in the Soviet Union as Yang Hsien-chen.

---

1. Adam Oliver, "Rectification of Mainland China Intellectuals, 1964–65," *Asian Survey,* 5:475–490 (October 1965).
2. *Ibid.*
3. A. C. Miller, "The Divisive Heresy," *Far Eastern Economic Review,* 46:411–412 (November 19, 1964).
4. Oliver, p. 480.
5. *SCMP* 3347, p. 6.

Yang Hsien-tung

(1905–   ; Hopeh). Agronomist; vice-minister of Agriculture.

Yang Hsien-tung, a non-Communist, is one of Communist China's leading agricultural experts and is a well-trained and highly experienced specialist in the production of cotton. He stands as a prime example of the utilization by the Communists of a person with special skills, which have a high priority in China.

Although Yang's father was a farmer, he was presumably wealthy enough to send his son to Nanking University where he spent the years from 1923 to 1927. Yang then worked as an experimental cotton grower for an experimental station in Hupeh (1928–29), then served during the period from 1930 to 1934 as technical director of the Hupeh Cotton Improvement Commission and, concurrently, as a member of the Cotton Industry Committee of China. Following this he went to the United States where he received a master's degree at Cornell in 1935 and a doctorate in 1937. He immediately returned to China, where he assumed the directorship of the Hupeh Cotton Improvement Station (1937–

1939). Presumably because of the wartime situation, Yang went to southwest China in 1939 where the Nationalist government had its provisional capital and assumed the position of director of the Department of Agricultural Economics of the Szechwan Provincial Agricultural Institute. He held this post until 1942 and then by 1943 was a research fellow and director of the Division of Marketing and Extension of the Wood Oil Research Institute, an organization subordinate to the Foreign Trade Commission in Chungking, the Nationalist capital. Also by 1943 he was a member of the China Cotton Improvement Association, an official of the Cotton Statistical Association, and a member of the Agricultural Association of China.

At the end of the war Yang returned to Hupeh where he became the deputy director of the Hupeh Regional Office of the China National Relief and Rehabilitation Administration (1945–1948). Then, when the Communists conquered the mainland in 1949, he remained in Hupeh and offered his services to the new government. Prior to the establishment of the central Communist government in the early fall of 1949, Yang remained in Hupeh where he served as the dean of the College of Agriculture of Wuhan University. However, he took part in the formation of the national government in the latter half of 1949 and since that time has remained in Peking. He attended the initial meetings of the CPPCC in September 1949 as a representative of the "Central China Liberated Area," and when the central government was staffed in the next month, he was made a vice-minister of Agriculture. As of the mid-1960's, Yang was the only person at the ministerial or vice-ministerial level who had served continuously in the Ministry of Agriculture since the establishment of the central government in 1949. Yang is one of the exceedingly few men who have served at this level in any ministry for this length of time, presumably because of his reliability and competence.

In his capacity as a veteran agronomist, Yang has attended a large number of conferences related to the production of cotton, China's most important industrial crop. He spoke, for example, on ways to improve cotton-growing techniques at a conference in March 1954, and in August 1956 he headed the Chinese delegation at the eighth International Plant Quarantine and Protection Conference held in Peking. Similar instances occurred in February 1961 when he journeyed to Wuchang, Hupeh, to address another conference dealing with the improvement of agricultural production, and in December 1961 when he spoke in Changsha, Hunan, at the first National Conference of the China Crops Society.

Yang has also been an especially prominent figure in several of the learned societies devoted to agriculture. From about 1953 to 1956 he headed the preparatory committee of the important China Society of Agronomy, and when this organization was established on a permanent basis in March 1956, he was named as the president, a position he still retains. Like most learned societies, the Society of Agronomy was subordinate to the All-China Federation of Scientific Societies (ACFSS). In the central organization of the ACFSS, Yang served from 1953 to 1958 as a deputy director of the Organization Department. And when the ACFSS was merged with another organization to form the China Scientific and Technical Association (September 1958), Yang was elected to its National Committee, another position he continues to hold. He was also a speaker at the inaugural meeting in February 1956 of the preparatory committee of the China Agricultural Mechanization Association, although he has not held any senior position in the national headquarters of this body. In an apparent attempt to coordinate all phases of agricultural research, the Communists established the Academy of Agricultural Sciences in March 1957 under the presidency of the late Ting Ying (q.v.), one of China's top rice-growing experts. Yang was named at this time to the advisory Academic Committee of the newly founded Academy.

Although he has been an active participant in the affairs of the academic community, Yang's major assignments have centered around his work as a government official. In addition to his post as a vice-minister of Agriculture, he received two additional assignments in the midfifties—one in the executive branch of government and the other in the legislative branch. In the period from May 1957 to November 1958 he served as a member of the State Council's Scientific Planning Commission, headed by science administrator and Vice-premier Nieh Jung-chen. His legislative post has been as a deputy from Honan, a cotton-growing province, to the First NPC (1954–1959), to the Second NPC (1959–1964), as well as to the Third NPC, which opened in December 1964. Yang has been a more active participant than most in the annual sessions of the NPC, having served as a member of the Motions Examination Committee, which is convened on an *ad hoc* basis during each session of the NPC. He has also been a speaker before the full Congress sessions; for example, at a session of the Second NPC in April 1959, Yang addressed the Congress, claiming that in 1958 China had surpassed the United States in cotton production.

Yang's work for the national government has also extended to the field of international scientific liaison. His first venture into this field was more propagandistic than scientific—as an agricultural scientist, he was an obvious choice for membership in a group led by the minister of

Public Health (Li Te-ch'üan) in 1952 to North Korea to "investigate the American imperialist crimes of bacteriological warfare," a major facet of one of Peking's most extensive propaganda campaigns conducted during the Korean War. In September of 1953 Yang was a member of China's delegation to Budapest for the third conference of the Communist-backed World Federation of Scientific Workers (to which the Chinese were affiliated through the above-mentioned All-China Federation of Scientific Societies). He accompanied Vice-premier Li Hsien-nien to Albania in November–December 1954 to take part in celebrations marking the 10th anniversary of the "liberation" of Albania from Nazi Germany. While there he signed a protocol with Albanian officials covering technical co-operation during the year 1955. Before Li Hsien-nien took this group to Tirana, Sino-Albanian relations were virtually non-existent. After that time, however, and particularly during the 1960's, Sino-Albanian relations grew apace. Yang Hsien-tung has been one of the more active Chinese officials who has had continuing contacts with Albanian officials. In June 1958 in Peking, he headed the Chinese side in negotiations with an Albanian delegation that led to the signing of another agreement on scientific and technical cooperation. Similarly, in March 1964 in Peking, Yang signed still another technical agreement with the Albanians, this one relating to cooperation in agricultural endeavors. Logically, therefore, Yang also serves as a council member of the China-Albania Friendship Association, a position in which he was identified as early as September 1963 when welcoming a group of Albanian visitors to China.

Yang's work in international affairs has extended to other nations besides Albania. In April 1955 he accompanied Vice-premier Teng Tzu-hui (another one of Peking's top Party agricultural specialists) to Hungary to take part in celebrations commemorating the 10th anniversary of the "liberation" of Hungary, and in October 1957 he led a group to Moscow for a scientific conference dealing with cotton production. He remained in Moscow through November, serving as a member of the scientific delegation led by Academy of Sciences President Kuo Mo-jo, who was in Moscow to participate in celebrations marking the 40th anniversary of the Russian Revolution. In July 1958 Yang led an agricultural delegation to East Germany and Czechoslovakia; back in Peking, he headed the Chinese side in negotiations with Bulgarian officials that culminated in the signing on November 13, 1958, of a Sino-Bulgarian protocol on scientific and technical cooperation. He was also an official member of the Chinese delegation to the largest international scientific conference ever sponsored by the Chinese Communist Government; known as the Peking Scientific Symposium, the 11-day conference was held in August 1964 with over 350 delegates from 44 countries in attendance. The conference, attended mainly by persons from Asian, African, or Latin American nations, had a political significance in that it was not sponsored by the World Federation of Scientific Workers (WFSW). In the 1950's, both the Chinese and the Russians had been active participants in the WFSW activities (Yang included). However, as a part of the continuing Sino-Soviet ideological dispute, the Chinese had little to do with the WFSW after the early 1960's. The Peking Symposium of 1964, therefore, can be regarded as Peking's answer to the activities of the Moscow-dominated WFSW.

Like many Chinese officials, Yang has lent his name to "people's" organizations devoted to one or another aspect of foreign affairs. From its formation in February 1956, he served as a member of the Asian Solidarity Committee of China (known as the Afro-Asian Solidarity Committee since May 1958), and when the China Peace Committee was reorganized in July 1958, Yang was added as a member of the National Committee. However, he was dropped from these organizations when they were both reorganized in June 1965. Yang has written on occasion for the Chinese press; notable examples appeared in the English-language *People's China* (February 16, 1954) and the June 1963 issue of *Chung-kuo nung-pao* (Chinese agricultural bulletin). The former dealt with problems related to growing cotton and the latter with the topic of plant protection.

In private life, Yang married Viola H. C. Tang in 1940. Nothing further is known about this marriage apart from the fact that they had one child by 1943.

Yang Hsiu-feng

(1898– ; Ch'ien-an, Hopeh). President, Supreme People's Court; member, CCP Central Committee.

Yang Hsiu-feng is one of the few academics to have reached the level of the Party Central Committee. He was a college professor of some prominence in Peking when, in the mid-thirties, he became politically active in the movement to resist the steady Japanese encroachments into north China. After war broke out in 1937 he fled from Peking and began to organize a resistance movement in south Hopeh. From 1938 to 1948 Yang was head of the Communists' South Hopeh Administrative Office and then the Shansi-Hopeh-Shantung-Honan Border Region Government. He was the first Communist governor of Hopeh (1949–1952), and from 1952 to 1965 he was one of the PRC's senior educational administrators. In January 1965 Yang was appointed president of the Supreme People's Court. He did not join the CCP until 1939, when he was over 40, and was elected a member of the Party Central Committee in 1956.

Yang Hsiu-feng (also known as Yang Hsiu-lin) was born in 1898 in Ch'ien-an on the Luan River in eastern Hopeh. He is a graduate of the Department of History and Geography at the National Peking Normal University. In 1929 he enrolled at the University of Paris, and on returning to Peking he lectured on history at Hopeh Teachers' College for Women. He then became commissioner of education in the provincial government of Hopeh and at about the same time was a professor at the Hopeh Provincial College of Law and Commerce in Tientsin. From 1933 to 1937 Yang was a professor at his alma mater and was teaching there in the winter of 1935–36 when the December Ninth student movement erupted in protest against Japanese penetration into north China. The National Liberation Vanguard, a militant student organization founded in 1936, which soon came under Communist domination (see under Li Ch'ang), grew out of the movement. The National Salvation Association, a liberal organization founded in May 1936, had a wider popular base and cooperated with the students. Yang belonged to the association and was also associated with the Liberation Vanguard, which a number of his students joined. He talked to students at the summer camps held by the Liberation Vanguard just prior to the outbreak of war, trying to alert them to the dangers of Japanese aggression. Communist sources describe him as a "progressive" professor at that time.[1]

When war broke out, Yang, his wife, and a number of his students escaped to southern Hopeh to join the local resistance and help organize the peasants as guerrillas. Although he initially planned to fight for the Nationalist Government, conflicts soon arose between Yang's group and some of the local leaders and their Nationalist allies. Yang's men then made overtures to the Communist guerrillas, who had established an Eighth Route Army headquarters in 1937 at Ch'in-chou in the nearby T'ai-hang Mountains of southeastern Shansi.[2] According to a wartime account Yang gave American journalist Jack Belden, he went to this headquarters (commanded by Po I-po) because he hoped to enlist the help of a number of his former students there against the Nationalist-oriented guerrillas and the Japanese. Belden wrote that he was small, wizened, and hard of hearing and noted that he spoke with a clear Peking accent.[3]

It is reported that at the invitation of Yang's guerrillas the Eighth Route Army sent Hsu Hsiang-ch'ien (q.v.) in the summer of 1938 into southern Hopeh where he organized the South Hopeh Military District, which incorporated Yang's guerrillas.[4] At a meeting of delegates from about 50 hsien held at Nan-kung in August 1938,

the South Hopeh Administrative Office was established, with Yang as chairman and Sung Jen-ch'iung (q.v.) as vice-chairman.[5] This office was the political organization that coincided with Hsu Hsiang-ch'ien's South Hopeh Military District. Sung and Hsu were both Party members, but Yang was not. Yang's appointment conformed to the wartime united front policy under which the Communists cooperated with non-Communist elements in the local population to help run the Red guerrilla bases. The Nationalists objected to the establishment of the South Hopeh Office and ordered its abolition in the fall of 1938. The KMT took another step in mid-1939 when they sent Lu Chung-lin, a prominent military leader, to Hopeh to become the provincial governor and to unite all the local guerrilla units who opposed the Japanese. For a while there were parallel administrations, but the situation was resolved when some of Lu's troops defected to the Japanese and his government, in effect, collapsed.[6]

In 1939 Yang finally joined the CCP, and in the following year a liaison office was established to coordinate his South Hopeh Administrative Office with areas to the west known as the T'ai-hang and the T'ai-yueh bases. At a meeting held in July 1941 these three areas were linked with other Communist bases on the Hopeh-Shantung-Honan border to form the Shansi-Hopeh-Shantung-Honan (Chih-Chi-Lu-Yü) Border Region Government. Yang was named as the chairman, a position he held until 1948, while the vice-chairmen were Po I-po and Jung Tzu-ho (qq.v.).

In the postwar period the Communist-held areas throughout China were gradually expanded and merged with territories in adjoining "liberated areas." In north China, the Chin-Chi-Lu-Yü Border Region was extended north until in November 1947 it was linked to the Shansi-Chahar-Hopeh Border Region. The areas were merged officially in May 1948 and the merger was formalized in August at the North China Provisional People's Congress. Yang was the principal speaker for his border region and Sung Shao-wen (q.v.) was the spokesman for the Shansi-Chahar-Hopeh Border Region. Yang also served as a member of the Congress' Presidium and Credentials Committee. At the close of the meetings the short-lived North China People's Government (NCPG) was established. It was headquartered in the Shih-chia-chuang area of western Hopeh until it moved to Peking in February 1949 shortly after that city fell to the Communists. The NCPG functioned as a rough approximation of the central government until it was abolished immediately after the inauguration of the PRC in October 1949. Tung Pi-wu (q.v.) was the NCPG chairman and Po I-po was the first vice-chairman. Lan Kung-wu, a prominent non-Communist cultural and educational leader, was the second vice-chairman and Yang Hsiu-feng the third. In addition Yang served in the government as chairman of the People's Supervision Committee and as a member of the Finance and Economics and Higher Education Committees.

Representing the North China "liberated area," in September 1949 Yang attended the inaugural session of the CPPCC, the organization that brought the new central government into existence on October 1. While the meetings were in session, he served on the *ad hoc* committee that drafted the Organic Law of the CPPCC, one of the key documents adopted at that time. Finally, from this time until 1954 he was a member of the CPPCC Standing Committee, which was responsible for the affairs of the CPPCC when the National Committee was not in session. However, in the early years of the PRC his primary responsibilities were at the regional, provincial, and municipal levels. Already in August 1949, two months before the establishment of the national government, Yang had become governor of Hopeh province, a position he retained until November 1952 when he was replaced by the province's leading Party official, Lin T'ieh (q.v.).

During the three years that Yang was the Hopeh governor, the provincial capital was located at Paoting. However, it appears that he spent at least part of his time in Tientsin where he served after March 1950 as vice-chairman of the municipal government's Finance and Economics Committee. In the 1951–52 period he held a similar post in the Hopeh Provincial Government. In December 1951 the Communists established a north China regional government (to replace the Ministry of North China Affairs), which was known as the North China Administrative Committee. Yang was a member of this new governmental apparatus until it was reorganized in February 1953, by which time he had already assumed a new post in Peking.

In November 1952 Yang transferred to Peking where he assumed his first high post in the national bureaucracy as vice-minister of Higher Education. In this position he was ostensibly subordinate to Ma Hsu-lun, a prominent non-Communist educator who is chairman of the China Association for Promoting Democracy (one of the political parties that is nominally on par with the CCP). Less than two years later, when the constitutional government was established at the first session of the First NPC in September 1954, Yang succeeded Ma in the Higher Education Ministry. In February 1958 the ministry was merged with the Ministry of Education to form a new Ministry of Education, with Yang retaining the portfolio. This arrangement continued until July 1964 when the Communists re-created the former Education and Higher Education ministries. Yang again headed the latter, but shortly thereafter, in January

1965, he relinquished the post to Chiang Nan-hsiang (q.v.); Yang in turn replaced Hsieh Chueh-tsai (q.v.) as president of the Supreme People's Court. At an even higher administrative level within the State Council, Yang became deputy director in January 1957 of the Second Staff Office, which is responsible for directing and coordinating the work of the State Council's various commissions, ministries, and bureaus that deal with education and culture. The Staff Office was redesignated the Culture and Education Office in 1959. Yang was finally removed as a deputy director in mid-1965, half a year after he had assumed the presidency of the Supreme Court. During his nearly 13 years as one of the PRC's leading educational administrators, Yang made frequent public appearances and addressed many different conferences and government bodies (e.g., the annual NPC sessions) on educational affairs. Several of his speeches and reports are conveniently collected in Stewart Fraser's *Chinese Communist Education.*[7]

In addition to his work in the educational bureaucracy Yang has also held other government posts. From 1954 to 1959 he represented his native Hopeh as a deputy to the First NPC; he was re-elected to the Second NPC (1959–1964) but not to the Third. In the executive arm of the government he was made a member of the State Council's Scientific Planning Committee when it was formed in March 1956, serving as a vice-chairman from May 1957 until November 1958 when the Committee was reorganized into the Scientific and Technological Commission.

In September 1956, at the CCP's Eighth National Congress, Yang was a member of the presidium (steering committee), and at the conclusion of the Congress he was elected a member of the Central Committee.

Yang has had considerable experience in foreign relations. In late 1955 and early 1956 he helped negotiate a Sino-Polish Cultural Agreement with a Polish delegation, and in November 1957 he signed the Sino-Polish Educational Cooperation agreement for the year 1958. In February–March 1958 he led a delegation of educational experts to Poland, East Germany, and the Soviet Union. Yang became chairman of the newly inaugurated China-Vietnam Friendship Association in September 1958 and has twice visited North Vietnam in this connection. In September–October 1959 he led a small delegation there to commemorate the 10th anniversary of the PRC's establishment. Three years later, in August–September 1962, he again visited Hanoi, this time to celebrate the 17th anniversary of the founding of the North Vietnamese Government. In September–October 1963 Yang led an education delegation to Albania. Perhaps his most important trip abroad took place from April to May 1964 when the educational group he led visited the United Arab Republic (UAR), Algeria, Mali, Zanzibar, and Guinea. In the UAR, Mali, and Guinea he signed cultural cooperation agreements.

Yang's wife Sun Wen-shu studied in Japan. She fled Peking with Yang when the Sino-Japanese War broke out in mid-1937, working with him in the resistance in south Hopeh, and presumably also in the Chin-Chi-Lu-Yü Border Region. From 1949 to 1953 Sun was an alternate member of the First Executive Committee of the All-China Federation of Democratic Women (ACFDW). She became a full member at the Second ACFDW Congress in 1953 and was re-elected at the Third Congress in 1957. From January 1955 to June 1959 she was assistant minister of Education, and since 1959 she has been a member of the National Committee of the CPPCC.

1. Chiang Nan-hsiang et al., The Roar of a Nation (Peking, 1963), pp. 32–33.
2. Chalmers A. Johnson, Peasant Nationalism and Communist Power (Stanford, Calif., 1962), p. 222.
3. Jack Belden, China Shakes the World (New York, 1949), pp. 71–83.
4. Johnson, p. 108.
5. K'ang-Jih chan-cheng shih-ch'i chieh-fang-ch'ü kai-k'uang (A sketch of the liberated areas during the anti-Japanese war; Peking, 1953), pp. 50–51.
6. Johnson, p. 225; Boyd Compton, Mao's China (Seattle, Wash., 1952), p. xviii.
7. Stewart Fraser, ed., Chinese Communist Education (New York, 1965), pp. 215–221, 246–251, 301–307, 322–340, 365–375.

Yang I-ch'en

(c.1910–   ; Honan). Vice-governor of Hopeh; alternate member, CCP Central Committee.

By 1947 Yang I-ch'en was working in the Shantung Military District, although the nature of his duties is unknown. A large number of the men fighting in this area were later assigned to the forces that drove into south China in late 1949. Yang was apparently among them because by the end of 1949 he was serving in the South China Sub-bureau (having jurisdiction over Kwangtung and Kwangsi). But then in the first half of 1950 he was transferred north to serve in Honan province. There he became a member of the Honan Party Committee, as well as director of the Committee's Organization Department. In July of 1950 he was also named to membership on the Honan Provincial People's Government. In the following January he was appointed to chair the provincial government's People's Supervision Committee, a logical appointment for one already involved with the provincial Party Organization Department.

By January 1952 Yang had risen to become second secretary of the Honan Party Committee but soon afterward was transferred back to south China. His first known assignment was in Canton where in March 1952 he was named to head the municipal "five-anti" movement committee, an assignment probably based on his experience in Honan in organization and supervision work. The "five-anti" campaign was one of the major drives of the early 1950's, a movement directed against the businessmen. Specifically, the five "evils" of business were bribery, tax evasion, fraud, theft of government property, and theft of state economic secrets. By mid-1952 Yang was identified as the second secretary of the Canton Party Committee, a position he held for less than a year.

Yang's work at the municipal level was rewarded in 1952–53 with promotions to the more important South China Sub-bureau (with its headquarters in Canton), in which he had briefly served in 1949. By September 1952 he was the Organization Department director for the sub-bureau, a post he held until 1953. In 1953 he was identified as director of the Urban Work Department; from 1953 to 1954 he was head of the Industry Department; and from 1953 to 1955 he also headed the Workers' Committee. This extensive Party experience led to his appointment in 1954 as the second deputy secretary, a post he held until the sub-bureau was abolished in July 1955.

Apart from his work for the South China Party Sub-bureau, Yang had assignments within the Kwangtung government structure and with mass organizations in that province. In April 1953 he was elected to the Executive Committee of the Kwangtung Trade Union Council, and in December of the same year, in his capacity as chairman of the provincial committee to "overhaul local industry," he spoke before the second Kwangtung Provincial Conference on Local Industry. In August 1954 he was elected as a Kwangtung deputy to the First NPC (1954–1959), and in February 1955 he was named to membership on the Kwangtung Provincial People's Council.

Yang's work in south China was rewarded with an important promotion in July 1955 when he was transferred to Peking to head the newly organized Ministry for the Purchase of Agricultural Supplies. This ministry was abolished in November 1956, but at that same time Yang was named to head the Ministry of Urban Services which absorbed the functions of the defunct Ministry for the Purchase of Agricultural Supplies. Yang's new ministry underwent a change of name in February 1958, being known thereafter as the Second Ministry of Commerce, with Yang maintaining his portfolio. The ministry underwent still another change in September 1958 when the First and Second Ministries of

Commerce were merged to form the Ministry of Commerce, with Ch'eng Tzu-hua as the minister. Not long before this last change, Yang had been elected an alternate member of the Party Central Committee at the second session of the Eighth Party Congress in May 1958.

Soon after the merger of the two ministries of Commerce—with the resulting loss of a portfolio for Yang—he was relegated to an insignificant position in Tsinghai, one of China's most remote and least populous provinces. In April 1959 he was named as a vice-chairman of a committee to stimulate production in Tsinghai, and two months later he was also identified as the director of the Tsinghai government's Department of Commerce. He was mentioned in the Tsinghai press again in the spring of 1960 but then fell from public attention. About three years passed before there was any further news of Yang; then, sometime in late 1962 or early 1963, he became a vice-governor of Hopeh. Normally the Communists announce the election of provincial vice-governors, but in this instance the information was revealed in the 1963 edition of the semi-official *Jen-min shou-ts'e* (People's handbook). Little has been heard about Yang since this transfer to Hopeh, although he was re-elected to the post in October 1964 and in February 1965 he was reported accompanying Politburo member Tung Pi-wu on an inspection of Paoting.

Yang I-ch'en has apparently not been a major contributor to the Party press, but he did write an article for the June 15, 1958, issue of *Hung-ch'i* (Red flag), the most important Party journal. It was entitled "Seek Out Resources and Unearth Potentials in order to Do a Better Job of Rural Purchasing Work."

Yang Li-san

(1900–1954; Changsha hsien, Hunan). Veteran military logistics expert.

Yang Li-san was one of the CCP's leading military logistics experts. At the time of his death he had belonged for 27 years to the Party, joining it not long before he became a platoon commander in the Wuhan garrison force, which mutinied at the time of the Nanchang Uprising on August 1, 1927, and subsequently went to the aid of Mao Tse-tung, fighting with the peasants in the Autumn Harvest Uprisings in the fall of 1927. Through the Kiangsi Soviet period and during the Long March he belonged to Mao's military headquarters.

Yang was born into a family of tenant farmers in Changsha hsien, where the provincial capital is located. Nothing is known about his education aside from the statement in his obituary that it was "only through long periods of half-farming and half-study that he acquired his cultural knowledge." He is said to have come under the influence of Communism in 1921, the year the CCP was founded. In 1925 Yang is reported to have organized a peasant association in Changsha hsien, and in January 1927 he joined the CCP. He belonged to an independent military unit at Wuhan by the summer of 1927, and just prior to the uprising at Nanchang on August 1, 1927, the uprising that signaled the break in relations between the CCP and the KMT, his unit joined the Wuhan garrison force commanded by Lu Te-ming. The garrison force also revolted in sympathy with the Communists on the day after the uprising at Nanchang, following which it set out by boat for Kiukiang (Chiuchang) on the Yangtze north of Nanchang, with the aim of joining the Nanchang insurgents. The Communists were quickly defeated at Nanchang and the Wuhan garrison arrived too late to make connections with the routed troops. Therefore, it moved to the Hunan–north Kiangsi area where it soon merged with local peasant forces there under the supervision of the Communists. In September Mao staged the first of the Autumn Uprisings in Hunan, and the Wuhan garrison was on the spot to join forces with his peasant-staffed army. When they were defeated soon thereafter, Mao led the survivors, Yang among them, to the mountains of Chingkang on the Hunan-Kiangsi border where he proceeded to establish a permanent guerrilla base.

From this time Yang remained with the headquarters of Mao's Red Army. He was made chief aide-de-camp and director of the General Affairs Department of the First Front Army in Kiangsi (commanded by Chu Te and Mao) in October 1930. When this army made its march on Fukien in 1932 Yang was put in charge of the Staff Office belonging to the Rear Services (logistics) Department of the Revolutionary Military Council, the chief military directorate of the Communists in the Kiangsi Soviet. When the Kiangsi Communists made the Long March from 1934 to 1935, Yang continued in logistics work. During the Sino-Japanese War he doubled in the role of political commissar and head of the military depot at Yenan. He was made deputy chief-of-staff of the general headquarters at the front in the autumn of 1943, but he was mostly occupied with the post of chief of the Rear Services Department, to which he was concurrently assigned. Though he had belonged to the CCP since 1927 he held few Party positions during his career; however, in 1945 he became a member of the Standing Committee and director of the Economic Department of the Central Bureau of the CCP organization in the Shansi-Hopeh-Shantung-Honan Border Region. Possibly, therefore, beginning in 1943 when he was assigned to the fighting front, he may have begun to be concerned with the border area. It was an area of considerable strategic importance because it commanded the communications route by which the Red forces could move from the Yenan base into Shantung. Liu Po-ch'eng and his 129th Division were in charge of military operations there, while Yang Hsiu-feng (q.v.) was in charge of the political administration.

After the end of the Sino-Japanese War Yang became the director of the Joint Office of General Affairs of the four-province border area, and at the same time deputy chief of the North China Office of Finance and Economics, the latter a rather uncertain title taken from Communist sources, which probably refers to an office in the North China People's Government, established in August 1948. At the same time that he held the latter posts he was chief of the Rear Services of the Revolutionary Military Council and commander of Rear Services for the North China Military Region. He was a representative of the Second Field Army (commanded by Liu Po-ch'eng) to the First CPPCC, which opened in September 1949 to inaugurate the PRC government on October 1. During this session he served as a member of the Committee to Draft the Organic Law of the CPPCC, one of the most important documents of the new government. With the inauguration of the PRC he served briefly in a ministerial post, holding the portfolio of the Ministry of Food Industry from its creation until it was abolished a year later. From 1949 until 1954 he also served as a member of the important Finance and Economics Committee under the Government Administration Council (the cabinet). Apart from these posts in the central government, Yang continued to hold important positions in the military establishment. In the same month that he became minister of Food Industry (October 1949), he was also appointed to head the Rear Services Department under the People's Revolutionary Military Council, the highest military organ under the central government. He continued as director of rear services until replaced just before his death by Huang K'o-ch'eng (q.v.). Concurrently, Yang was the director of the PLA Finance Department from 1953 until his death.

Yang died on November 28, 1954, in the Kremlin hospital in Moscow where he had gone for a treatment of a brain tumor, for which he had been under treatment for some time. The facts of his career are drawn mainly from the official obituary published in the Peking *JMJP* of December 8, 1954, and from a commemorative article written by Nieh Jung-chen (*JMJP,* December 6, 1954).

Yang Ming-chai

(Shantung). Comintern official.

Yang Ming-chai was of some significance in Chinese Communism during its very first two or three years as a channel of Russian influence by virtue of his bilingualism. He came from a poor family in Shantung, which appears to have migrated to Siberia. During tsarist times, Yang journeyed through Siberia to Moscow where he spent more than 10 years working and studying. After the October Revolution he joined the Soviet Communist Party, and in April 1920 he appeared in Peking accompanying a delegation of Comintern agents, whom he served as guide and interpreter. Members of the Comintern delegation were Gregory Voitinsky, I. K. Mamaev, and their wives. (Mamaev had some knowledge of Chinese; he was in charge of Chinese affairs at the Far Eastern Secretariat at Irkutsk; he returned to China in the fall of 1924 as political adviser at the Whampoa Military Academy and served during the Northern Expedition as adviser to Li Tsung-jen's Seventh Corps of the National Revolutionary Army.) The Voitinsky group had been sent to China to investigate the May Fourth Movement and to mobilize sentiment in China in ways that would be favorable to the Soviet Union. The delegation got in touch with Sergei A. Polevoy, a faculty member of the Russian Department of Peking University who sympathized with the new Soviet regime; Polevoy introduced them to his colleague, Li Ta-chao, who had organized a society for the study of Marxist theory and a society for the study of Soviet Russia only the month before, in March 1920. Li Ta-chao in turn directed them to Ch'en Tu-hsiu in Shanghai, who was then editing the *Hsin ch'ing-nien* (New youth).

In May 1920 Ch'en Tu-hsiu assembled a number of individuals (Li Han-chün, Shen Hsuan-lu, Li Ta, Yü Hsiu-sung, and Shih Ts'un-t'ung) to secure their agreement to form a provisional central committee and draft the statutes of the projected Communist Party. The committee elected Ch'en as secretary and proposed to set up similar cells in other cities. In the same month, also in Shanghai, Yang assisted in the formation of the first Communist cell (which was led by a provisional committee with Ch'en as secretary) and, in August, the first nucleus of the Socialist Youth League. He was also placed in charge of the Sino-Russian News Agency, a cover organization for Voitinsky's activities, and of the Foreign Language School, also a cover for Communist organizational activities. Its proposed French and English classes were never held, but one was given for Russian; Yang Ming-chai and Mrs. Voitinsky tutored a fluctuating group of 10 to 20 students and prepared them for further study at the Communist University of the Toilers of the East, the important cadres' school in Moscow. The first batch of students left for the Soviet Union in the winter of 1920–21; the group included Liu Shao-ch'i, Jen Pi-shih (qq.v.), P'eng Shu-chih, Lo I-nung, Pu Shih-ch'i, Yuan Ta-shih, Pao P'u, and Liao Hua-p'ing.

Late in 1920 the pace of Communist activity slowed down somewhat as Ch'en left for Canton to serve as provincial educational commissioner in Ch'en Chiung-ming's government, and Voitinsky too departed for the Soviet Union. Also, much dissension among anarchists and communists was evident at this time. Other members departed from Shanghai, Shen Hsuan-lu going to Canton, Shih Ts'un-t'ung to Japan. About this time, an Educational Commission (Chiao-yü wei-yuan-hui) was organized with Tung Pi-wu (q.v.) and Yang Ming-chai in charge, the primary objective being to screen the Socialist Youth League elements to send them to the Soviet Union for training.

At about the time of the formation of the CCP in mid-1921, Yang switched his membership from the CPSU to the CCP. Then in September 1921, he was arrested by the Shanghai Settlement authorities along with Ch'en Tu-hsiu and his wife, K'o Ch'ing-shih (q.v.), and Pao Hui-seng. Bolshevik gold proved most useful at this juncture, when Comintern agent Maring hired a French lawyer and had Ch'en Tu-hsiu bailed out after a day and a half at a cost of 50,000 yuan; Yang and the rest remained in jail for a few more days until they were released after being convicted and fined 5,000 yuan (also on Comintern expense) for propagating bolshevism in the *Hsin ch'ing-nien.* Nothing more is known about Yang's connections with the Chinese Communists. According to Chang Kuo-t'ao, he broke with them sometime in 1923–24.

It is known that Yang published in 1922 a Chinese version of Tolstoy's short story, *The Forged Coupon,* and a commentary on the controversy on Eastern and Western civilizations.[1]

---

1. Chow Tse-tsung, *The May Fourth Movement* (Cambridge, Mass., 1960), pp. 243–244.

Yang Shang-k'uei

(Hsing-kuo hsien, Kiangsi). First Secretary, Kiangsi CCP Committee.

Yang Shang-k'uei, a Communist since the early thirties, was among those left behind in the Kiangsi area when the main Communist forces embarked on the Long March in 1934. He returned to Kiangsi in 1949 and since then has been one of the key provincial Party officials. Yang was born in Hsing-kuo hsien in central-south Kiangsi, probably in the early years of the century. When the Long Marchers left the area in the fall of 1934 he was assigned to the Kiangsi-Kwangtung Border Region, where he participated in guerrilla operations under the general direction of Hsiang Ying and Ch'en I (qq.v.) for the next few years. He was then deputy secretary of the Party organization in the Kiangsi-Kwangtung base. By early 1935 the Nationalist armies had reduced the Communist

forces there to 200–300 men, and in the following years they were beset by hunger, illness, and defections to the Nationalists. The most notable defector of this period was Kung Ch'u, the chief-of-staff of the South Kiangsi Military District, who two decades later published his well-known *Wo yü hung-chün* (The Red Army and I) in Hong Kong. The fortunes of the Communists dwindled to the point where many of them had to engage in menial tasks to survive; Yang has recorded, for example, that he made and peddled bamboo baskets. Although they maintained sporadic contacts with neighboring bands of Communist guerrillas, in effect they operated independently of the Party Center in Yenan. In Yang's account of these years he states that as of the latter part of 1936 "We had been out of contact with the Central Committee for more than two years, and had never been able to make connection even by our numerous and round-about attempts."[1]

The extreme difficulties of maintaining a viable Communist movement on the Kiangsi-Kwangtung border persisted until the outbreak of the Sino-Japanese War in mid-1937. During the period of cooperation with the KMT which existed in the early stages of the war, many of the guerrilla units moved northward to fight in the Communists' New Fourth Army (see under Ch'en I). Yang, however, remained behind in Kiangsi and until 1939 he worked in the "liaison offices" established by the New Fourth Army in Chi-an (Kian) and Kan-hsien. He was the senior Communist in the area when Chiang Ching-kuo, the son of Chiang Kai-shek, was appointed the supervisory officer of an 11-hsien area in southern Kiangsi which included the Communist base areas. Chiang appears to have been a moderately successful administrator, but the Communist accounts predictably describe his rule as tyrannical.

In late 1939 Yang was ordered to Yenan to attend a Party meeting, and from his own account it is clear that he did not return to Kiangsi until it was conquered by Liu Po-ch'eng's (q.v.) armies in 1949. It is probable, though undocumented, that he was assigned to Liu's 129th Division after he went to Yenan in 1939. In any event, he was with Liu's units in May 1949 when they captured Nanchang, the Kiangsi capital. The Nanchang Military Control Commission was established in early June under the direction of Ch'en Cheng-jen, Ch'en Ch'i-han, and Shao Shih-p'ing (qq.v.), all of whom, like Yang, were natives of Kiangsi. Yang was made a commission member and became second deputy secretary under Ch'en Cheng-jen in the provincial Party Committee. In the governmental apparatus he became a member of the Kiangsi Provincial People's Government in March 1950, a post he still retains. In this capacity he served under Governor Shao Shih-p'ing. For a time in 1951 Yang chaired the Southwest Kiangsi People's Administrative District, an area with which he was intimately familiar from his guerrilla days.

Yang's rise in the Kiangsi hierarchy coincided with Ch'en Cheng-jen's transfer to Peking in late 1952. By early 1953 Yang was the ranking Party secretary, a post that was redesignated first secretary in 1956 and one that he still holds. Moreover, by the latter part of 1953 Yang succeeded to Ch'en's other key Kiangsi post when he was identified as political commissar of the provincial military district. He retained this post to at least the end of 1959, but he was not identified in it in later years. After the transfer from Kiangsi of Ch'en Ch'i-han in 1954, Yang and Governor Shao Shih-p'ing were the two top Kiangsi leaders (until Shao's death in 1965). Yang received still another provincial post in January 1955 when he became chairman of the Kiangsi Committee of the CPPCC, another position he continues to hold. In December of that year the Kiangsi Provincial Planning Committee was established under Yang's direction, but there has been no further information about his work in connection with this assignment.

In September 1956 Yang attended the Party's Eighth Congress in Peking and presented a report on how to improve conditions in the "old revolutionary bases." He was not, however, elected to the Central Committee, nor was he elected at the second session of the Congress in May 1958. As of the latter date only three provincial first secretaries were not on the Central Committee: Chou Lin in Kweichow, Kao Feng (qq.v.) in Tsinghai, and Yang in Kiangsi. There were no indications then nor in later years that Yang was denied this seat for any political reason. In fact, his activities throughout the fifties and early sixties were typical of provincial officials of his stature throughout China. He was frequently reported in the press addressing Party and government bodies, making inspection trips, and welcoming visitors to the province. Yang also received a number of lesser posts, as in mid-1958 when he was appointed president of the newly established Kiangsi University. Many of these positions were *ad hoc,* as in September 1957 when he chaired a committee to prepare for the celebrations in Kiangsi marking the 40th anniversary of the Russian Revolution or in late 1958 when he led a group that reviewed the accomplishments of the "people's communes" in Kiangsi. He received his first regional post in early 1965 when he became a secretary of the Party's East China Bureau.

Yang is the chief chronicler of the Communists' experience in the Kiangsi-Kwangtung area during the post-Long March years. For the third and 10th volumes of a series of revolutionary reminiscences entitled *Hung-ch'i p'iao-p'iao* (Peking, dated 1957 and 1959, respectively), he wrote brief essays on this period. He also contributed a piece to the November 1960 issue of the English-language monthly *China Reconstructs* entitled "Difficult Years." Far more useful is *The Red Kiangsi-Kwangtung Border Region* which was published by the Foreign Languages Press in 1961. (A condensed version of this book is in volume of essays entitled *The Unquenchable Spark;* Peking, 1963.) These accounts contain the normal Communist rhetoric, but they are revealing for their insights into Communist strategy, tactics, and mass mobilization.

1. Yang Shang-k'uei, *The Red Kiangsi-Kwangtung Border Region* (Peking, 1961), pp. 132–133.

Yang Shang-k'un

(c.1905–   ; Szechwan). Alternate member, CCP Secretariat; member, CCP Central Committee.

Yang Shang-k'un, a member of the Russian-returned student group, has been a key figure in the internal operations of the CCP for many years. Since 1956 he has been a member of the Party Central Committee and an alternate member of the CCP's powerful Central Secretariat. He was born into a wealthy landlord family, and his father, who married twice, had about 20 children. Yang attended middle school in Chengtu and joined the Communist Youth League in 1925. In the next year he was a student in Chungking at the Sino-French Institute (Chung-Fa hsueh-hsiao). This school had been set up in September 1925 by Wu Yü-chang (q.v.), who was later to become an important Communist but whose major position then was as head of the KMT organization in Szechwan. The purpose of the institute was to train revolutionary cadres for the KMT, which was then working quite closely with the CCP.

In early 1927, by which time Yang had probably joined the CCP, he was in Shanghai, where he worked briefly as a labor organizer under the direction of Chou En-lai. The Communists in Shanghai were then attempting to set off insurrectionary strikes designed to deliver the city to the Northern Expeditionary forces, which arrived there in March (see under Chao Shih-yen). However, on April 12, only three weeks after Chiang Kai-shek's armies entered Shanghai, Chiang engineered an anti-Communist coup during which scores of Communists and leftists were killed, and those who survived went underground or fled the city. At some time in 1927 after these events, Yang went to Moscow and enrolled at Sun Yat-sen University, which, during his years there, was renamed the Communist University of the Toilers of China. The school was headed by Pavel Mif, who was later to play a key role in CCP history.

When Yang went to Moscow he had already studied English and French, and during his three years there he learned enough Russian to act as interpreter and translator of classroom lectures for some of his Chinese colleagues who were less well equipped. Among his schoolmates was Li Po-chao, a fellow Szechwanese whom he married in 1930. Both belonged to the group of favorite students of Chancellor Mif, the group which came to be known as the "28 Bolsheviks" or the Russian-returned student faction. In the spring of 1930 Mif, then in his capacity as a Comintern representative, was sent to China at a time when the CCP under Li Li-san's leadership was moving counter to the wishes of the Comintern. Mif and his student protégés who accompanied him succeeded in the following months in replacing Li and placing a number of the "28 Bolsheviks" in high positions within the CCP (see under Ch'en Shao-yü and Ch'in Pang-hsien, two of the most important leaders of the student faction). Yang was assigned to the Party headquarters in Shanghai, and for the next two years he worked in the underground until the constant surveillance of the Nationalists became so formidable that many Party officials, Yang among them, left Shanghai for Kiangsi where Chu Te and Mao Tse-tung had built up a sizable armed force and base area.

Yang entered the Communist Soviet area in 1932 and according to some reports became the head of the Party School in Juichin. However, according to other and apparently more reliable sources, Tung Pi-wu established and was the first president of the school. In early 1933, writing for a leading Party journal in Kiangsi, Yang was among the returned-student group members who heaped invective on certain military and Party leaders charged with undue pessimism, defeatism, and "opportunism" in the conduct of the struggle to repel the continuing attacks from Nationalist armies.[1] This important campaign against the "Lo Ming line," which proved to be a serious setback for the supporters of Mao Tse-tung, is described in the biography of Lo Ming.

By no later than November 1933, Yang was director of the Political Department of the First Front Army, serving directly under Chou En-lai, the Army's political commissar.[2] Not long afterward, when the Chinese Soviet Republic convened the Second All-China Congress of Soviets in Juichin (January–February 1934), Yang was elected a member of the Republic's Central Executive Committee. In the fall of the same year the Communist forces moved out of Kiangsi on the Long March. At approximately that time, it appears that Yang relinquished his First Front Army political post to Ch'in Pang-hsien (q.v.), another Russian-returned student, and was assigned to P'eng Te-huai's Third Army Corps,

one of the major components of the First Front Army, led on the Long March by Chu Te and Mao Tse-tung. By no later than the spring of 1935, when the Communist columns were about halfway to their ultimate destination in north Shensi, Yang was serving as political commissar of P'eng's Third Army Corps.[3] He is reported to have been concurrently the deputy director of the Political Department of the Revolutionary Military Council, the top military body under the CEC. The Political Department was then headed by Wang Chia-hsiang (q.v.), still another of the Russian-returned students.

During or soon after the Long March ended in the fall of 1935, Yang reassumed from Ch'in Pang-hsien the directorship of the Political Department of the First Front Army. Yang was holding this post in the early months of 1936 when the Communists crossed the Yellow River into Shansi.[4] During this partially successful thrust into Shansi, the Red Army was able to get badly needed supplies and to recruit young men for army service (see under Liu Chih-tan). However, by the spring of 1936 the Communists were driven out of Shansi and turned back into the Shensi-Kansu-Ninghsia border areas. Soon after this, Yang was interviewed by Edgar Snow; he provided the American journalist with considerable information about the composition of the Red Army (e.g., age, class composition, Party and Youth League membership).[5] Of interest is the fact that the information supplied by Yang coincided closely with statistics published in Peking many years later about the early history of the Red Army.[6] Yang continued in his political post with the First Front Army, then commanded by P'eng Te-huai, until approximately the outbreak of the Sino-Japanese War in mid-1937 when the Communist military forces were reorganized into the Eighth Route Army. In 1937, with the possibility of war on the horizon, Yang was sent to the Peking-Tientsin area to plan for the evacuation of Communist Party members to Communist-held areas in case of war. He was then attached to the North China Party Bureau and probably worked under the direction of Liu Shao-ch'i and P'eng Chen. After the outbreak of war, the personnel of the North China Bureau, including Liu and Yang, withdrew to Shansi; the Bureau headquarters were located in Lin-fen, southwest of Taiyuan, from late 1937 until Lin-fen also fell to the Japanese in early 1938. While in Lin-fen Yang worked with members of the National Liberation Vanguards of China (NLVC), a youth organization established in north China in early 1936 (see under Li Ch'ang) that had come under CCP control. During the brief period that the NLVC and the CCP North China Bureau were located in Lin-fen, the NLVC had established a small newspaper to which Yang contributed editorials. He also lectured NLVC members on methods of organizing youths and the masses in the Shansi hinterlands.[7]

Yang spent most of the war years in Yenan where, from 1940 to about 1946, he was the secretary-general of the Eighth Route Army Headquarters. Japanese sources claim that he was serving as secretary of the North China Bureau in 1943, as well as head of that Bureau's United Front Department, positions that suggest he may have left Yenan occasionally to work in Japanese-occupied areas of north China. He is known to have attended the Seventh National Congress of the Party in Yenan (April–June 1945) where he was one of the speakers.[8] Yang's activities in the postwar period are obscure, but he was known to have had connections with the China Liberated Areas Relief Administration (CLARA) in 1947. As its name suggests, CLARA served as the channel for shipping relief supplies to Communist-held areas, many of these supplies coming from the United Nations Relief and Rehabilitation Administration (UNRRA). This connection with CLARA may have taken Yang to Peking and Shanghai where CLARA had offices. (A discussion of both CLARA and UNRRA is found in the biography of Wu Yun-fu.)

Unlike virtually all important Communist leaders, Yang was given no post in the PRC government when it was established in the fall of 1949. In Yang's case, however, his importance in the Party hierarchy probably accounted for the fact that he was not given a government post. By at least the time the central government was formed, Yang was working as the director of the Staff Office of the Party's Central Committee—in effect, the top administrator of the affairs of the Central Committee on a day-to-day basis. Internal Party affairs are seldom discussed in the news media, but inferential evidence suggests that he has had a key role in Party personnel policies. For example, Yang frequently makes inspection tours of the provinces and has been a member of the funeral committee for nearly every CCP leader of significance who has died in the 1950's and 1960's, a fact suggestive of his importance in protocol-conscious Communist China. Closely related to the Staff Office directorship, Yang also served as a deputy secretary-general to Secretary-General Teng Hsiao-p'ing in the brief period when this post existed in the mid-fifties. And, when the new Secretariat was created in 1956 (see below), Yang was named as an alternate secretary, once again serving under Teng Hsiao-p'ing.

The one new position that Yang did receive in 1949 was as a member of the then active Sino-Soviet Friendship Association's Executive Board, a logical reflection of his training in Moscow years earlier. He served in the SSFA from its establishment in October 1949 until a new Executive Board was organized in December 1954. Also in December 1954 he was named as a representative of the CCP to the Second National Committee of the CPPCC; he was also named to the Standing Committee and was then re-elected to both posts in the Third CPPCC (1959–1964). But Yang was transferred, in effect, to the more important NPC in 1964–1965; he was elected from his native Szechwan in late 1964, and when the Third NPC held its first session in December 1964–January 1965 he was named as a vice-chairman of the NPC Standing Committee.

Yang's activities at the historic Eighth Party Congress in September 1956 once again typified his role as a key internal Party operative. He served on the Congress Secretariat (under the direction of Teng Hsiao-p'ing) as well as the credentials committee. Yang submitted a written report to the congress on the need to strengthen work in the old Communist revolutionary bases and at the close of the meetings was elected a full member of the Party Central Committee—thus becoming one of 33 persons elected to full Central Committee membership who had been neither full nor alternate members of the Central Committee elected at the previous Congress in 1945. More important, at the first plenum of the new Central Committee (held the day after the Congress closed), Yang was named an alternate member of the reorganized Party Secretariat, the organ charged with carrying out the policies of the Politburo. Here again Yang serves under Teng Hsiao-p'ing, the ranking secretary of the Secretariat. By the following April, he was also identified as the secretary of the Committee for Organs Directly Subordinate to the Central Committee (e.g., the Organization and Propaganda Departments). Holding this cluster of posts in the Party Center obviously places Yang in a position to have a detailed knowledge of virtually all aspects of Party work.

Although Yang's prime responsibilities appear to be in connection with domestic Party affairs, by 1955 he began to assume an important role in negotiations with foreign Communist parties, particularly the Soviet Party. His role in this field is best illustrated by his participation in three of the most important delegations to Moscow in the history of Sino-Soviet relations and of world Communism—delegations led by Mao Tse-tung (November 1957), Liu Shao-ch'i (November–December 1960), and Teng Hsiao-p'ing (July 1963). The first two groups attended summit meetings of Communist leaders from many countries, whereas the 1963 trip involved only the Chinese and Soviet Communist Parties. The Sino-Soviet polemics of the early sixties have revealed that the 1957 and 1960 meetings were characterized by sharp and bitter disagreements about global Communist strategy, with the Chinese Communists arguing for foreign policies stridently oriented toward the spread of world revolution—by violence if necessary. The 1963 negotiations in Moscow came amidst the polemics and were clearly foredoomed to failure in the sense that they held open virtually no hope of resolving Sino-Soviet ideological differences. Teng Hsiao-p'ing and Yang are the only Chinese Communist leaders who attended all three of these meetings, a unique distinction among the CCP leadership.

Yang has been married to Li Po-chao since 1930. Born in 1911, Li is also a native of Szechwan (Chungking) where her father was a hsien magistrate. In an account of her life given to Miss Nym Wales in 1937,[9] Li claimed that she first became interested in the revolution at the time of the May 30th Movement in 1925 when she was 14, but even earlier, while attending a girls' normal school in Szechwan, she had been much influenced by one of her teachers, a prominent young Communist leader named Yun Tai-ying (q.v.). Li joined the Communist Youth League in 1926 and went to work in Shanghai where her future husband, Yang Shang-k'un, came the following year to work with the Party. Li worked for a year with the CCP in Shanghai, and then, probably about the time that the Nationalists took over the city she, like Yang and others, fled to Moscow. Li also enrolled at Sun Yat-sen University and like Yang returned to China in 1930, the year they were married. After a year in Shanghai with her husband, Li went briefly to the Communist-held area in Fukien where she engaged in political work. From there, in 1932, she went to Juichin, the capital of the Chinese Soviet Republic, where she was an editor for *Hung-se Chung-hua* (Red China), the organ of the government of the Republic, which was set up in December 1931 under the editorship of Chou I-li. In 1934 she took part in the establishment of a school of dramatics, the Gorky Drama School, which was her initiation into work which she has continued to the present. Li was one of the few women who made the Long March, which she embarked upon with the army of Mao Tse-tung, as did her husband. However, when Mao's forces met Chang Kuo-t'ao's Fourth Front Army in west Szechwan in mid-1935, Li separated from Mao's army (and her husband) and joined the Fourth Front Army, which moved to Sikang to spend the winter of 1935–36. This group did not join Mao's forces in Shensi until late 1936 (see under Chang Kuo-t'ao).

Since 1949 Li has been a member of the National Committee of the All-China Federation of Literary and Art Circles (ACFLAC). She has also been affiliated with two of the organizations subordinate to the ACFLAC, the All-China Association of Drama Workers and the Union of Chinese Writers; she has been on the Standing Committee of the former since 1949 and a member of the Executive Committee of the latter since 1953. Her main activities have probably centered around the Central Theatrical Institute where she has served as a vice-president since 1952 and secretary of the Party committee by 1965. Li has also been a deputy from her native Szechwan since the NPC was established in 1954.

1. Tso-liang Hsiao, *Power Relations within the Chinese Communist Movement, 1930–1934* (Seattle, Wash., 1961), pp. 238–239.
2. *Kuang-ming jih-pao,* January 23, 1959.
3. *Hsing-huo liao-yuan* (A single spark can start a prairie fire; Hong Kong, 1960), p. 71.
4. *Shan-hsi ko-ming tou-cheng hui-i-lu* (Reminiscences of revolutionary struggles in Shansi; Taiyuan [?], preface dated 1961), p. 31.
5. Edgar Snow, *Red Star over China* (New York, 1938), pp. 256–258.
6. *Ti-erh-tz'u kuo-nei ko-ming chan-cheng shih-ch'i shih-shih lun-ts'ung* (Accounts of the second revolutionary civil war; Peking, 1956), pp. 63–64.
7. SCMM 297, pp. 38–39.
8. Conrad Brandt, Benjamin Schwartz, and John K. Fairbank, *A Documentary History of Chinese Communism* (Cambridge, Mass., 1952), p. 293.
9. Nym Wales, *Inside Red China* (New York, 1939), pp. 27–29.

Yang Shuo

(1913–   ; Shantung). Secretary-general of the China Committee for Liaison with the Permanent Bureau of Afro-Asian Writers.

Yang Shuo was born in the small town of P'eng-lai on the coast of Pohai (the Gulf of Chihli) in Shantung.[1] He went to Harbin as a teenager to study English, and while there was deeply influenced by Western literature. Later he entered the Harbin University of Law and Political Science, and at the same time studied classical Chinese literature and wrote poetry in the traditional style. This interlude in Harbin was interrupted in 1931 with the Japanese takeover of Manchuria. Like many other intellectuals, Yang, then about 18, fled to Shanghai. Again like many of the intelligentsia, he went from Shanghai to Yenan after the outbreak of the Sino-Japanese War in mid-1937. After this time, according to the Communist account, he "began his creative efforts," his first work being *The Spur of the Pamirs,* a novel about the resistance to the Japanese. One of his short stories of this period, "Purge by Fire," with a setting in his native Shantung, appeared in an anthology of Chinese short stories published in the United States in 1947.[2]

In the fall of 1939 Yang joined the Eighth Route Army, serving in Shansi and Hopeh as a cultural worker and propagandist. In 1943, at the age of 30, he was sent back to Yenan, where he spent the next three years studying at the

Central Party School, the very important institute devoted to training higher Party cadres. During the civil war of the late 1940's, Yang was a war correspondent and continued writing novels and short stories based on his personal experiences. He was in Peking after the fall of the city to the Communists in 1949, and in July of that year attended the All-China Congress of Literary and Art Workers. During the life of the congress he served on two *ad hoc* bodies; he headed the News Section and was a member of a "Novel Committee" (apparently a committee to suggest work to novelists attending the congress). Out of this huge and important congress grew the All-China Federation of Literary and Art Circles, plus a number of affiliated organizations created immediately after the congress closed. One of these was the All-China Association of Literary Workers, to which Yang was elected as an alternate member of the Executive Committee. Four years later, when another congress was held, the name was changed to the Union of Chinese Writers (October 1953) and Yang was elevated to full membership on the Executive Committee.

Yang spent the 1949–50 period working on a novel describing the exploits of the PLA Railway Engineering Corps. Then, immediately after the entry of the "Chinese People's Volunteers" into the Korean War (October 1950), he went to North Korea, serving there as a cultural and propaganda worker, as well as continuing his work as a novelist. He apparently spent most of the war in Korea, and out of this experience came what is probably his most famous novel, *A Thousand Miles of Lovely Land*. Yang was back in Peking by mid-1953, and in late July, identified as a "popular writer," he left for Bucharest to attend the Communist-dominated Fourth World Youth Festival of Youth and Students (August–September).

Since his return from Korea to China in 1953, Yang has devoted almost all his time to the promotion of Chinese ties with the Afro-Asian world. One of the first major efforts of the Chinese in this field began in 1955 when the Chinese were leading participants in the "Asian Countries Conference" held in New Delhi in April 1955 just prior to the more famous Afro-Asian (Bandung) Conference in Indonesia. Among other things, the conference decided to set up permanent "liaison machinery" and urged each of the 17 attending nations to form national committees. In February 1956 the Chinese established the Asian Solidarity Committee of China. Although Yang served on the preparatory committee for this new organization, he was not named to the permanent Committee. However, in retrospect, it is clear that he was operating behind the scenes. In December 1957–January 1958, the first Afro-Asian Solidarity Conference was held in Cairo,

and one of the decisions taken was to establish a Permanent Secretariat there. In April 1958, Yang was designated as the first Chinese delegate to the Secretariat and for the next year or so spent most of his time in Cairo. He was succeeded by Chu Tzu-ch'i (q.v.) by September 1959. In the meantime, the Asian Solidarity Committee of China, reflecting the rapid emergence of African nations, was renamed the Afro-Asian Solidarity Committee of China in May 1958 and two months later was reorganized and expanded. Yang was added to the committee and was also named as one of the deputy secretaries-general, positions he retains.

In the meantime, Yang was also becoming deeply involved in another facet of Afro-Asian cooperation: liaison with other writers in Africa and Asia. This was first given organizational expression in July 1956 when he went to New Delhi for the preparatory meetings for the first Asian Writers' Conference. In December of that year the then minister of Culture, Shen Yen-ping (Mao Tun), led a Chinese delegation to the first Asian Writers' Conference in New Delhi, accompanied by Yang, who served as secretary-general of the group (often, in Chinese delegations, the key man). Yang did not return with the delegation to Peking but remained briefly in India and then in late January 1957 accompanied an Indian writer on a good-will mission to Egypt. The next Writers' Conference was held in Tashkent, the USSR, in October 1958, renamed from "Asian" to "Afro-Asian Writers' Conference." Yang attended the meeting, traveling from Cairo where he was then stationed. One of the decisions taken at this large-scale meeting was to establish a Permanent Bureau of Afro-Asian Writers in Colombo, Ceylon. In pursuance of this decision, the Chinese formed (April 1959) a China Committee for Liaison with the Permanent Bureau, naming Yang to the really effective post: the secretary-generalship, another post he continues to hold. Since assuming this position, he has taken five trips directly in connection with the bureau. He attended a January 1961 meeting of the bureau in Colombo, an "emergency meeting" of the organization in Tokyo in March–April 1961, and the second Afro-Asian Writers' Conference (AAWC) in Cairo in February 1962. In July 1963 he led a writers' delegation to meetings of the Permanent Bureau and to the Executive Committee of the AAWC in Indonesia, and in April 1964 he was reported in Ghana as a member of a Permanent Bureau delegation touring Africa. (The group subsequently toured Brazzaville, the Congo, Zanzibar, Tanganyika, and the United Arab Republic, but it is not known if Yang remained with the delegation.) This work in international liaison among writers derives from his role within the Union of Chinese Writers. Among the various sub-committees of the union is the Foreign Literature Committee, of which Yang was a vice-chairman from February 1955 and chairman by September 1960.

In addition to the long sojourns in both North Korea and Cairo, plus the several trips already described above, between 1958 and 1963 Yang took eight additional trips abroad. July 1958: Sweden, Congress on Disarmament and International Cooperation; December 1958: Ghana, All-African People's Conference; November–December 1959: Albania, 15th anniversary of "liberation" of Albania; April 1960: Guinea, Second Afro-Asian People's Solidarity Conference; October 1960: Ceylon, Celebrations for China's National Day (October 1); January 1961: United Arab Republic, Extraordinary Session, Afro-Asian Solidarity Council; May 1962: Guinea, Meeting of Preparatory Committee, Afro-Asian Lawyers' Conference; July 1962: USSR, World Congress for General Disarmament and Peace; February 1963: Tanganyika, Third Afro-Asian People's Solidarity Conference.

In addition to the positions already described above, Yang is known to hold at least another seven; predictably, all are in the field of fostering closer relations with foreign countries. When the China Peace Committee was reorganized in July 1958, he was added to the National Conference. In February 1958, at the time of the formation of the China-United Arab Republic Friendship Association, he was named to the Council of this organization. He became a Standing Committee member of both the China-Latin America Friendship Association and the China-Africa People's Friendship Association from the dates of their formation (March 1960 and April 1960, respectively) and was also named to the Council of the China-Japan Friendship Association when it was formed in October 1963. In November 1964, he was identified as a vice-president of the Peking chapter of the Sino-Soviet Friendship Association. From 1959 he has served in the CPPCC, holding membership on the Third National Committee (April 1959–December 1964) and on the Fourth National Committee, which first met in December 1964–January 1965; he has served in the CPPCC as a representative of "organizations for peaceful and friendly relations with foreign countries."

Yang has made frequent appearances in Peking in the 1960's as Peking's relations with the Afro-Asian world have increased. In particular, he almost always makes an appearance when writers from Africa or Asia visit China. Also, being a writer, he is a frequent contributor to the national press, often writing an article following one of his many trips abroad. A typical example is found in the April 7, 1963, issue of the *JMJP*, in which he wrote a brief sketch of Tanganyika following his trip to that country two months earlier. Yang is apparently

held in high regard by the ruling elite. He was singled out for praise in 1953 by Chou Yang, generally considered the "literary czar" of Communist China, and in 1962 Stalin Prize winner Chou Li-po praised Yang for the profuseness of his writings. During the Hu Feng (q.v.) controversy in 1955, Yang's works were described by one advocate for Hu as being "unbearable,"[3] but in view of the fact that Hu was labeled a "counterrevolutionary," this may be taken in Party circles to be a flattering comment.

1. All information on Yang prior to 1949 is derived from a biographical sketch published at the end of one of his novelettes, *Snowflakes* (Peking, 1961).

2. Chi-chen Wang, ed., *Stories of China at War* (New York, 1947), pp. 66–75.

3. *JMJP,* June 10, 1955.

Yang Te-chih

(1910–   ; Li-ling hsien, Hunan). Commander, Tsinan Military Region; alternate member, CCP Central Committee.

A military leader throughout his career, Yang Te-chih has served in the Red Army since 1927. He made the Long March and was an active combat commander during the Sino-Japanese War and the ensuing civil war with the Nationalists in the late forties. One of the principal officers with the Chinese forces who took part in the Korean War, Yang was elected an alternate member of the Party Central Committee in 1956 and has commanded the Tsinan (Shantung) Military Region since 1958.

Yang was born into a peasant family.[1] Known originally as Yang Shao-ch'i, he comes from Li-ling hsien, located some 50 miles southeast of Changsha, the Hunan capital. A number of early Communist leaders are native to Li-ling, among them Li Li-san. In the 1920's Mao Tse-tung and others began to organize the peasants of Li-ling, one of the five hsien visited by Mao in early 1927 before he wrote his famous report on conditions among the Hunan peasantry. Yang joined the Red Army in 1927, and in the following year he was a soldier in a special service battalion of the Fourth Red Army, the name given to the combined units of Mao and Chu Te after they joined forces at Chingkang-shan in the spring of 1928. In June of that year Yang was transferred to the Ninth Company of the Third Battalion, a unit under the 28th Regiment of the Chu-Mao forces.

By 1931 Yang had been transferred again, this time to Fukien where he served with Tso Ch'üan (q.v.), also a native of Li-ling hsien. Yang was in Tso's 15th Red Army, a unit initially under the Fifth Army Corps and later Lin Piao's First Army Corps. In 1931 they were stationed in Nan-ching hsien, Fukien, about 50 miles from Amoy. Yang has written about these and later experiences with Tso for a series of revolutionary reminiscences published in 1957.[2]

After serving in Fukien, Yang enrolled at the Red Army Academy (Hung-chün ta-hsueh) in Kiangsi,[3] an institution founded in 1933. In that same year he became commander of the First Regiment of Lin Piao's First Army Corps and in this capacity fought against the Nationalists during the Fifth Annihilation Campaign of 1934. During the Long March, which began later that year, Yang's First Regiment formed part of the marchers' vanguard. In May 1935 his unit took part in the difficult and critical crossing of the Ta-tu River in western Szechwan, a much-heralded event (described in the biography of Yang Ch'eng-wu).[4] On the way north to Shensi, as the troops crossed Kansu, Yang's First Regiment engaged in battles with troops led by the Ma family, independent northwestern militarists who controlled the area.

In the early part of 1936, soon after the Long Marchers arrived in north Shensi, Yang took part in a Communist thrust into Shansi, an important but short-lived campaign (described in the biography of Liu Chih-tan). The attacks on Shansi Governor Yen Hsi-shan's forces were initially successful, but the tide was turned when the Nationalist government reinforced Yen's troops, causing the Communists to retreat to their base in Shensi. By approximately this time Yang was commanding the Second Division, with Hsiao Hua (q.v.) serving as division political commissar. The Second Division was subordinate to Lin Piao's First Army Corps, although in this period Yang's old colleague Tso Ch'üan frequently served as acting commander. In the middle or latter part of 1936 Yang re-enrolled and spent seven months studying at the Red Army Academy, which had been transferred to north Shensi from Kiangsi. In 1937 its name was changed to the Anti-Japanese Military and Political Academy, often known by its abbreviated name, K'ang-ta. Among his fellow students were Yang Yung and Su Chen-hua (qq.v.), both of whom were associates of Yang Te-chih in future years.

Following his graduation in 1937 Yang returned to Lin Piao's forces. Soon after the war with Japan began in mid-1937, Yang's Second Division was reorganized into the 685th Regiment and placed under Lin Piao's 115th Division, one of the three divisions comprised by the Communists' Eighth Route Army.[5] The 685th Regiment belonged to the 343rd Brigade commanded by Ch'en Kuang. At the beginning of the war there were three brigades in Lin Piao's 115th Division—the 340th (see under Su Chen-hua), the 343rd, and the 344th. In September 1937 these units participated in the battle for P'ing-hsing Pass in northeast Shansi, a widely heralded engagement that gave the Communists their first major victory over the Japanese. Fol-

lowing this success Lin Piao led the 343rd and 344th Brigades south to the mountains on the Shansi-Hopeh-Honan border, where he left them to fight independently for a time. Some of these forces later joined the 129th Division, commanded by Liu Po-ch'eng (q.v.). Liu's troops were expanded into the Shansi-Hopeh-Honan-Shantung border area in the year 1938–39. At the same time certain units remained with the 115th Division and ultimately fought in Shantung; still others transferred to the New Fourth Army (see under Hsu Hai-tung). Some of the troops of the 343rd Brigade crossed through Hopeh into Shantung as early as May 1938 (see under Yang Yung), but Yang Te-chih's moves are uncertain until the spring of 1939, when he led special forces into the Hopeh-Shantung-Honan border region. In 1939 Yang (who was earlier identified as the 685th Regiment commander) was now identified as deputy commander of the 344th Brigade and commander of the Second Column of the Eighth Route Army. Apparently the column was still for a time a part of the 115th Division, although it later became a unit of the 129th Division, which controlled the Shansi-Hopeh-Shantung-Honan (Chin-Chi-Lu-Yü) Border Region. Leading the Second Column with Su Chen-hua and Ts'ui T'ien-min (political commissar of the PLA Railway Corps since 1957), Yang advanced eastward into Shantung in March 1939 and by the middle of that year had established a Communist military base in the three-province border known as the Hopeh-Shantung-Honan (Chi-Lu-Yü) Military Region.[6] The formation of the base area was accomplished through the combined efforts of Yang Te-chih, Yang Yung, Su Chen-hua, all initially commanders on the staff of Lin Piao's 115th Division.

In 1941 the Chi-Lu-Yü military base became part of the larger Shansi-Hopeh-Shantung-Honan Border Region (see under Yang Hsiu-feng), the border government that was in the territory controlled on the military side by Liu Po-ch'eng. In 1941 Yang Te-chih became commander of the Chi-Lu-Yü Military Region, probably when the larger Chin-Chi-Lu-Yü Region was inaugurated. His military command now included the military base in west Shantung, initially established by Hsiao Hua (q.v.) in the late thirties; but at about the time that Yang Te-chih assumed the Chi-Lu-Yü command, Yang Yung became commander of the West Shantung Military District. For the remainder of the war Yang Te-chih held the Chi-Lu-Yü post and was particularly active in that portion of his territory bordering on the Yellow River. Throughout this period he worked in close cooperation with Yang Yung, Ts'ui T'ien-min, and Su Chen-hua, the last-mentioned in charge of political work at Yang Te-chih's military base.

Toward the end of the Sino-Japanese War,

Yang Te-chih was separated from his wartime base and, in association with Su Chen-hua, led some 20,000 troops which were dispatched northward, first to the outskirts of Tientsin, then east to the Hsi-feng Pass, and later into Jehol where they went in November 1945. In Jehol Yang was given command of a division belonging to the Jehol-Liaoning Military Region. Soon after V-J Day the Communists had moved their forces from Jehol into Chahar where they captured Kalgan (Chang-chia-k'ou), the Chahar provincial capital. In the fall of 1945 Yang's forces were ordered to the aid of the Communist troops in Kalgan, but en route they were intercepted by Nationalist forces, which inflicted heavy losses on Yang's units. In 1947 he was commander of the First Column of the Shansi-Chahar-Hopeh Military Region and participated in the successful battles for Ch'ing-feng-tien and Shih-chia-chuang in the fall. By 1948 he was in command of the Second Army Group of the North China PLA, led by Nieh Jung-chen. In December of that year he was coordinating the actions of his forces with those led by Commanders Lo Jui-ch'ing and Keng Piao (qq.v.) as the Communist units of the North China PLA began their encirclement of Peking and other major north China cities.[7]

After the successful completion of these operations, Yang moved his units to the northwest where P'eng Te-huai's army, known as the First Field Army after January 1949, was battling with the Nationalists. Yang took part in the capture of Yin-ch'uan, the Ninghsia capital, in September 1949. He was then in command of the 19th Corps of the conquering army and had Li Chih-min (q.v.) as his political commissar. Yang and Li were later to be associated together in Korea during the war there in the early fifties (see below). Yang's units took up garrison duties in Yin-ch'uan, and Yang himself became chairman of the municipal Military Control Commission, which was immediately established. Six weeks later, in early November, he was named as commander of the newly established Ninghsia Military District (which included Yin-ch'uan), with P'an Tzu-li (q.v.) as his political commissar.[8]

Over the winter of 1949–50 the Communists established provincial and regional governmental units to administer their newly conquered territories. At this time Yang was transferred from Ninghsia to neighboring Shensi, and when the Shensi Provincial People's Government was formed in January 1950 he became a member of the Government Council. In the same month the Northwest Military and Administrative Committee (NWMAC) was formed under the chairmanship of P'eng Te-huai to govern Shensi, Ninghsia, Tsinghai, Kansu, and Sinkiang. Yang was named to NWMAC membership and nominally held this and the Shensi government posts

until early 1953. However, before the year 1950 ended Yang was transferred to North Korea, leading the 63rd, 64th, and 65th armies of the "Chinese People's Volunteers" (CPV) into the war, following the decision of the Chinese to enter the war in October 1950. From 1951 to mid-1953, when replaced by Li Ta (q.v.), he was CPV chief-of-staff. Concurrently, in late 1952 he became a deputy commander of the CPV under P'eng Te-huai, his former superior in the northwest. He had assumed still another post in 1954 when he became deputy director of the Political Department, serving under his colleague Li Chih-min. For his services in the war, Yang was given the highest Korean decoration in February 1953, the Order of the National Flag. Then, in October 1954, when the fighting had already been over for 15 months, he succeeded Teng Hua (q.v.) as the CPV commander. Finally, after more than four years in Korea, Yang was replaced by his former colleague Yang Yung in March 1955.

While Yang Te-chih was in Korea, the constitutional government in Peking was established at the first session of the First NPC in September 1954. Under the new government a military advisory body known as the National Defense Council was established. Yang was named to council membership in 1954 and was reappointed in April 1959 and January 1965, but as it seldom meets, it obviously has not occupied much of his time. Upon his return to China in 1955 Yang had been sent to the Nanking Military Academy to study military tactics, graduating from the staff college in early 1958. In the year of his entry into the school, national military honors and personal military ranks were created. Yang was made a colonel-general (equivalent to a three-star U.S. Army general), and he was also given one or more of the three orders covering military service from the birth of the Red Army in 1927 until 1950. His long career as a military officer was given more important recognition in September 1956 when he was elected an alternate member of the Party's Central Committee at the Eighth National Congress. Yang was placed third on the list of alternates, and since the first two alternates were promoted to full membership in 1958 (replacing two deceased members), Yang has been the top-ranking alternate.

Upon graduation in early 1958 from the Nanking Military Academy, Yang replaced Wang Hsin-t'ing as commander of the Tsinan Military Region, a command that includes the whole of Shantung province. Here he has worked in cooperation with Shu T'ung, Tseng Hsi-sheng, and T'an Ch'i-lung (qq.v.), the three men who have been the first secretaries of the CCP Shantung Committee since Yang's arrival in the province. Soon after assuming his command, he was identified in the concurrent position of second secretary of the Military Region's CCP Committee. In November 1958 he was elected a member of the Shantung Provincial People's Government Council, and at the same time he was also elected a Shantung deputy to the Second NPC, which first met in April 1959. He was subsequently elected again from Shantung to the Third NPC, which held its first session in December 1964–January 1965. Yang retains all of these posts in Shantung, although it is evident that his governmental posts are peripheral to his military duties.

Aside from his tour of duty in Korea, Yang's only trip outside China took place in 1959 when he was a member of P'eng Te-huai's military "goodwill" delegation to the USSR and East Europe. From April to June the group visited the Soviet Union, East Germany, Czechoslovakia, Hungary, Rumania, Bulgaria, and Albania, returning home via Mongolia. While in Albania Yang was awarded the "guerrilla" medal by the Albanian government.

1. Edgar Snow, *Random Notes on Red China, 1936–1945* (Cambridge, Mass., 1957), p. 143.
2. *Hung-ch'i p'iao-p'iao* (Red flag fluttering; Peking, 1957), V, 132–137.
3. Edgar Snow, p. 143.
4. *Stories of the Long March* (Peking 1959), pp. 51–60; *Hung-ch'i p'iao-p'iao* (Peking, 1957), II, 6–13.
5. *Shan-hsi ko-ming tou-cheng hui-i-lu* (Reminiscences of revolutionary struggles in Shansi; Taiyuan [?], preface dated 1961), pp. 40–49.
6. *K'ang-jih chan-cheng shih-ch'i chieh-fang-ch'ü kai-k'uang* (A sketch of the liberated areas during the anti-Japanese war; Peking, 1953), p. 50.
7. *Selected Works of Mao Tse-tung* (Peking, 1961), IV, 290–291.
8. Hong Kong, *Ta-kung pao,* November 3, 1949.

Yang Yin

(?–1929; Chung-shan hsien, Kwangtung). Early CCP labor leader; alternate member, CCP Politburo.

Yang Yin was an important CCP labor leader in south China during the early 1920's. He participated in the Hong Kong seamen's strike of 1922 and the Canton–Hong Kong strike of 1925–26. Yang played a leading role in the Canton Commune of December 1927, and in the following year he was elected an alternate member of the CCP Politburo. He was arrested and executed by the Nationalists in 1929.

Yang was born in Chung-shan (then Hsiang-shan) hsien, a coastal district in Kwangtung south of Canton where Sun Yat-sen was born. The area produced many of the seamen who worked in the south China coastal cities, among them Su Chao-cheng (q.v.), whose career was closely linked to Yang's. Prior to the 1911 Revolution both men were members of Sun Yat-sen's T'ung-meng hui, the precursor of the KMT. Yang engaged in liaison work for the T'ung-meng hui with the south China secret societies. Nothing is known of his family background, but his early connections with the Salt Administration suggest that he received some education.[1]

In early 1921 Lin Wei-min (a protégé of Sun Yat-sen) and Su organized the Chinese Seamen's Union, with its headquarters in Hong Kong. They then organized the first strike among Chinese seamen, which began in January 1922 (see under Su Chao-cheng). The strike, in which Yang participated, was his first known connection with the labor movement. He joined the CCP the following year in Canton where he had been sent to organize workers on the Canton-Hankow Railway. In 1924 Yang was in Shanghai to assist in the strike at the Nanyang Tobacco Company organized by Hsiang Ching-yü (q.v.) and others. In 1925–26 he was very active in the Canton–Hong Kong strike and boycott, which was directed especially against British interests in those cities. The strike, which began in June 1925 in response to the May 30th Incident in Shanghai, is described in the biography of Su Chao-cheng who was then chairman of the All-China Federation of Labor. In mid-1926, while the strike was still in progress, the Northern Expedition began. Many of the Communists in Canton accompanied the Nationalist armies to Wuhan, but Yang remained in Canton and when the strike ended in the fall he became a member of the CCP Kwangtung Provincial Committee. In this capacity he traveled extensively throughout the province supervising Party activities, and in the latter part of 1927 he spent a brief time in Hainan Island on a similar mission.[2]

In the meantime the uneasy KMT–CCP alliance had been completely broken by mid-1927. The Communists were suppressed in many places, under what they term the "white terror," but they moved aggressively to gain control of the labor movement and to capture major industrial centers. Unsuccessful attempts were made to capture Nanchang and Swatow (see under Yeh T'ing) in August and September. In early December another attempt was made, this time in Canton. Yeh T'ing, Yeh Chien-ying, and others led the Red military forces in the Canton coup, while Chang T'ai-lei, the secretary of the Kwangtung CCP Committee, had been instructed to prepare for the coup within the city. Yang Yin was one of the activists who assisted him, serving on the Communists' hastily established Revolutionary Military Committee. The Communists entered the city on December 11, 1927, and organized the Canton Commune. Yang's colleague Su Chao-cheng was made commune chairman, but because he never got to Canton Chang T'ai-lei served as acting chairman. A "People's Committee" was established to govern the city; subordinate to this committee, Yang, who had led some of the street fighting, was made People's Commissar for the Suppression of Counter-revolutionaries (*hsiao-ch'ing fan-ko-ming wei-yuan*).

The Communists were only able to hold Canton until December 13. They suffered great losses among their supporters and workers and also in the military regiment that captured the city. Chang T'ai-lei lost his life, but Yang was among those who escaped. With the survivors of the Red troops he fled to the Communist-controlled Hai-lu-feng Soviet in the East River District of Kwangtung between Canton and Swatow, which P'eng P'ai (q.v.) had established prior to the abortive Canton coup. Yang assisted P'eng in building up the Hai-lu-feng guerrilla units, and he served under P'eng as vice-chairman of the Hai-lu-feng Soviet Government. This was a short-lived assignment, for in February 1928 the Nationalists suppressed the Soviet, with the Communists again sustaining heavy losses. Yang and P'eng fled to Shanghai where they remained for the rest of their lives. In June–July 1928 the CCP held its Sixth Congress in Moscow, and though it appears that neither Yang nor P'eng attended it, both were elected to the Central Committee; Yang was made an alternate and P'eng a full member of the Politburo. Yang and P'eng continued their work for the Party underground until August 24, 1929, when they and some of their associates were betrayed by Pai Hsin, a former colleague in Hai-lu-feng.[4] They were arrested by the International Concession police, turned over to the Nationalists, and executed outside Shanghai on August 31. Yang and P'eng are celebrated in Communist histories as revolutionary "martyrs," and to honor them a military institute known as the P'eng-Yang Infantry School was established in the central soviet region where Mao Tse-tung and Chu Te had their headquarters in the early thirties.[5]

Yang was apparently married twice. His first wife is said to have died before he became a Communist in 1923.[6] In early 1963 the Communist press mentioned that P'an P'ei-chen, described as the "wife of martyr Yang Yin," had attended a meeting of representatives of old revolutionary bases in Kwangtung.[7] Yang P'ao-an, one of the eight Communists elected to the KMT Central Executive Committee at the Second KMT Congress in January 1926, was said to have been his uncle.[8]

1. Nym Wales, *The Chinese Labor Movement* (New York, 1945), p. 211.

2. Modern China Project, Columbia University, New York, Howard L. Boorman, director.

3. *Ti-erh-tz'u kuo-nei ko-ming chan-cheng shih-ch'i shih-shih lun-ts'ung* (Accounts of the second revolutionary civil war; Peking, 1956), p. 29.

4. Shinkichi Eto, "Hai-lu-feng—The First Chinese Soviet Government," *The China Quarterly*, no. 9:180 (January–March 1962); *Hung-ch'i p'iao-p'iao* (Red flag fluttering; Peking, 1957), V, 45.

5. *Ti-erh-tz'u kuo-nei ko-ming chan-cheng shih-ch'i shih-shih lun-ts'ung*, p. 60.

6. Modern China Project.

7. *Nan-fang jih-pao* (Southern daily; Canton), January 22, 1963.

8. Modern China Project.

Yang Yun-yü

Liaison official to international Communist women's movement.

When the PRC was established in 1949, Yang Yun-yü was an obscure woman leader, but by the 1960's she had risen to be the leading Chinese contact with the international Communist women's movement. She first came to notice in the spring of 1949 when elected a member of the Executive Committee of the All-China Federation of Democratic Women (ACFDW). Four years later, at the next women's congress (April 1953), she was re-elected to the Executive Committee. At the next congress (September 1957) she was again re-elected to the Executive Committee, but more important she was made one of the secretaries of the small Secretariat, the small inner group charged with the day-to-day management of the National Women's Federation (as the ACFDW was renamed in 1957).

Yang's activities in the early 1950's are rather obscure, although it is evident that she was working in Peking. She was known to be a vice-chairman of the Peking chapter of the Women's Federation in 1952–53, and in March 1952 she was appointed a judge on the Peking Municipal People's Court, a clue that she may have received some academic training in law. She also journeyed abroad in these years, attending May Day celebrations in Moscow in 1951 as a member of a Sino-Soviet Friendship Association delegation.

Yang's career took a significant turn in 1953. At the Third World Women's Congress in Copenhagen in June 1953, she was elected an alternate member of the General Council of the Women's International Democratic Federation (WIDF), as well as a secretary of the WIDF Secretariat. As a consequence of the latter position, she was posted to WIDF Headquarters in East Berlin for a portion of the mid-1950's (approximately 1953–1955). During this period she was a delegate to a WIDF meeting in Geneva in January 1954 and attended the WIDF-sponsored "Congress of World Mothers" in Lausanne, Switzerland, in July 1955. She was also a member of a delegation to the first Afro-Asian Women's Conference held in Ceylon in February 1958. During these same years of the mid-1950's, Yang received new appointments in organizations in China, both official and quasi-official. She was elected as a Honan deputy to the First NPC (1954–1959); she was transferred to the Shantung constituency for the Second NPC (1959–1964) and for the Third, which held its first session in December 1964–January 1965. In September 1957 she was named to the council of the newly formed China-Syria Friendship Association (CSFA) and when the CSFA was merged with the counterpart for Egypt in February 1958 (coinciding with the merger of Egypt and Syria), she was reappointed to the council for the China-United Arab Republic Friendship Association. Five months later, in July 1958, she was named to membership on the National Committee of the China Peace Committee, another position that she continues to hold.

Until 1960, Yang had never been the leader of a delegation abroad. An indication of her rising stature lies in the fact that between 1960 and 1964 she led no less than 12 delegations abroad—all involving women's affairs (mainly the WIDF). She headed groups to the following WIDF meetings: Indonesia, January–February 1960; Poland, November 1960; Rumania, October 1961; Mali, January–February 1962; Czechoslovakia, May–June 1962; the USSR, June 1963; East Germany, December 1963; Bulgaria, October 1964. In addition, she also attended a WIDF meeting in November–December 1962 in East Berlin. Her other trips were as: leader of a delegation to the Afro-Asian Women's Conference in Cairo, January 1961; leader of a delegation to the Fifth Congress of the Women's Union of Albania, October 1961; leader of a group to the World Rally of Women for Disarmament in Vienna in March 1962; leader of a women's friendship delegation to Japan in June 1964; and member of a delegation led by Liu Ning-i to Hanoi in November–December 1964 for a large conference to promote "solidarity" with the Vietnamese.

The journey to Moscow in June 1963 for the World Women's Congress was clearly a high point in Yang's career. The congress was attended by about 1,300 delegates and soon turned into a platform for a thorough airing of the Sino-Soviet dispute, then at a peak. In a bitter speech, Yang denounced the management of the congress, the "slanderers" of China, and refused to endorse a general resolution backed by almost all the other delegates. She remained in Moscow long enough to welcome Teng Hsiao-p'ing (July 5, 1963) when the latter arrived for the historic talks with the CPSU leaders, which led only to a stalemate in the Sino-Soviet dispute. Two weeks later, back in Peking, Yang delivered the main address before a mass rally, called to welcome her group back to China. In this remarkable speech,[1] she catalogued a lengthy list of China's grievances, going as far

as to register an acid complaint about allegedly inadequate hotel accommodations for her delegation.

In spite of the adverse treatment supposedly meted out to the Chinese, it appears that Yang was elevated from a secretaryship in the WIDF to a vice-presidency; she has been identified in this post by non-Chinese sources in the period after the rowdy Moscow meeting in mid-1963. Moreover, as the already mentioned travels indicate, she continues to take part in WIDF affairs. At the same time, there are some indications that she may have begun to take a larger part in domestic affairs, possibly with an emphasis on sports. She was named to membership on the State Council's Physical Culture and Sports Commission in September 1959 and when the All-China Athletic Federation held its fourth congress in January–February 1964, she was elected to the National Committee. In August 1964, the regime formed a permanent National Committee to participate in the Indonesian-backed "Games of the New Emerging Forces" (GANEFO; see under Jung Kao-t'ang); Yang was selected for National Committee membership. Still another assignment involving athletics occurred in January 1965 when Yang was named to the preparatory committee for the second national sports meet scheduled for later in 1965. An additional indication of Yang's rise took place at the first session of the Third NPC in December 1964–January 1965. For the first time she was made a member of the NPC Standing Committee, the permanent organization of the Congress, which meets with regularity and is in charge of the affairs of the Congress between the annual sessions.

1. The full text is in *Peking Review*, July 26, 1963.

Yang Yung

(1906–   ; Liu-yang hsien, Hunan). Deputy chief-of-staff, PLA; alternate member, CCP Central Committee.

Yang Yung is a veteran Red Army officer whose career has been devoted almost exclusively to military service. He made the Long March and was one of the most active army officers during the Sino-Japanese War and the civil war against the Nationalists in the late forties. Yang served with the Chinese People's Volunteers in North Korea between 1954 and 1958 and has been an alternate member of the Party Central Committee since 1956. He became a deputy chief-of-staff of the PLA General Staff in 1961.

Yang was born in Liu-yang hsien, Hunan, a hsien which has produced an exceptionally large number of important Communists, including Central Committee members Lo Chang-lung,

Sung Jen-ch'iung, Wang Shou-tao, and Wang Chen (qq.v.). Situated to the east of Changsha, Liu-yang was an area of considerable peasant unrest and one where Mao Tse-tung and others had organized the peasantry in the 1920's. In the early months of 1927 armed peasant bands were organized in Liu-yang. Then, not long after the Nanchang Uprising of August 1 (see under Yeh T'ing), these peasant forces in Liu-yang and nearby hsien were one of the major elements in the Autumn Harvest Uprisings, which began in September. Yang was a member of a Liu-yang guerrilla band at that time, and it appears that he was among those who retreated southward with Mao to the Chingkang Mountain base on the Hunan-Kiangsi border.

Yang joined the CCP sometime between the late 1920's and 1933 when he was enrolled at the Red Army Academy in Juichin, the headquarters of the Red Army in southeast Kiangsi. By the summer of 1934 he was political commissar of the 10th Regiment under the Fourth Division of P'eng Te-huai's Third Army Corps.[1] He took part in a battle at that time in the vicinity of Kuang-ch'ang (east Kiangsi) in which Fourth Division Commander Hung Ch'ao was killed. A short time after this Yang made the Long March to north Shensi (1934–35), after which he continued his studies in the Red Army Academy, which had been re-established in Shensi.

Soon after the Sino-Japanese War began in mid-1937, Yang was assigned to Lin Piao's 115th Division, one of the three divisions in the Eighth Route Army. He became political commissar and deputy commander (under Li T'ien-yu) of the 686th Regiment, which was under the 115th Division's 343rd Brigade. In this capacity he was one of the battle-field commanders in the much-heralded victory over the Japanese at P'ing-hsing-kuan in northeast Shansi in the fall of 1937. During the course of this battle Yang was wounded.[2] In the spring of 1938 major elements of Lin's division moved eastward into Hopeh and Shantung, where they were under the operational control of Hsu Hsiang-ch'ien (q.v.). Hsu was a top commander in Liu Po-ch'eng's 129th Division, the second of the three divisions of the Eighth Route Army. With his own forces now designated the First Brigade, Yang was fighting in south Hopeh by May 1938. That same month at least a part of Yang's former 686th Regiment was fighting in southeast Hopeh and across the border into Shantung, but it is not clear whether Yang was also with these troops. However, by 1939 he was definitely in Shantung, and his First Brigade was by then redesignated the Third Brigade. Yang also became deputy commander under Hsiao Hua (q.v.) of the West Shantung Military District. Later in 1939 Yang's forces were merged with those led by Yang Te-chih (who

had also been an original brigade-level officer under Lin Piao). These two men, in addition to Su Chen-hua (qq.v.), proceeded to establish the Hopeh-Shantung-Honan (Chi-Lu-Yü) Military Region. Yang Te-chih was the region's commander, with Yang Yung as deputy commander and Su Chen-hua as political commissar. The Chi-Lu-Yü area was later incorporated into the larger Shansi-Hopeh-Shantung-Honan (Chin-Chi-Lu-Yü) Border Region, which was established in mid-1941 (see under Yang Hsiu-feng). Also in 1941, Yang Yung assumed command of the West Shantung Military District, a part of the Chi-Lu-Yü Military Region.

The triumvirate of Yang Yung, Yang Te-chih, and Su Chen-hua continued to work together for the remaining years of the Sino-Japanese War and the civil war against the Nationalists, and Yang Yung and Su were together until the early 1950's. Among the many campaigns in which they fought, perhaps the most famous was the Hundred Regiments' Offensive launched in August 1940 in five provinces of north China. It continued for four months, provoking savage retaliation by the Japanese and equally savage counterattacks from the Communists. In the later years of the war, when the Communists turned more to economic warfare to deny food and other necessities to the Japanese and to interrupt their lines of communications, there is no reporting of Yang's activities, but inferential evidence suggests that he remained in the Chi-Lu-Yü area. After the war his forces were enlarged and redesignated the First Column of the Central Plains Liberation Army, which was commanded by Liu Po-ch'eng. American correspondent Jack Belden has written that two assassination attempts were made on Yang's life by KMT agents when he was stationed in Tsining (Chi-ning) in west Shantung about 1947.[3]

Yang's First Column was reorganized into the Fifth Army Group by the time the Communists fought and won the critical Huai-Hai Campaign in Kiangsu and Anhwei in late 1948 and early 1949. Yang's army was then still subordinate to Liu Po-ch'eng, whose army was known by this time as the Second Field Army. Liu's troops crossed the Yangtze in the spring of 1949 and then moved into the southwest, taking Szechwan, Sikang, Kweichow, and Yunnan. On November 15, 1949, Liu's army entered Kweiyang, the capital of Kweichow. Liu and his staff established the Kweiyang Military Control Commission (KMCC) immediately after the city's capture, leaving Yang Yung and Su Chen-hua in charge of affairs in Kweichow while the army pushed farther west. Yang was named a member of the KMCC, and at the same time given command of the Kweichow Military District. In December 1949 he became governor of Kweichow, and in June 1950 chairman of the provincial Finance and Economics Committee. In July 1950 the Communists established the multi-provincial Southwest Military and Administrative Committee (SWMAC) under the chairmanship of Liu Po-ch'eng to govern Szechwan, Sikang, Yunnan, and Kweichow. Yang was a member of the SWMAC from its formation until it was reorganized in early 1953. He nominally retained the governorship of Kweichow until he was succeeded by Chou Lin (q.v.) in early 1955, but by that time Yang was already in North Korea (see below).

Various non-Communist sources identified Yang as commander of the Air Force of the Southwest Military Region in 1952, but there is no confirmation of this appointment, nor are his whereabouts known at that time. He turned up in Korea in the spring of 1954 as a deputy commander of the Chinese People's Volunteers (CPV), but because his whereabouts during the last year of the Korean War are not known, it is possible that he spent at least some of that time in Korea. By the time Yang was publicly identified in 1954, his wartime colleague Yang Te-chih was also a CPV deputy commander, both men serving under Commander Teng Hua (q.v.). Yang Te-chih became the commander in October 1954, and then in March 1955 Yang Yung succeeded to this post.

While Yang was in Korea the Chinese Communists reorganized the national government in September 1954 at the inaugural session of the First NPC. He was named to membership on the newly established National Defense Council, the military advisory organ of the central government, and was reappointed to this post in April 1959 and January 1965. When personal military ranks were first given to PLA officers in 1955, Yang became a colonel-general, equivalent to a three-star general in the U.S. Army. In September 1956, at the CCP's Eighth Congress, he was elected an alternate member of the Central Committee, as were his longtime associates Yang Te-chih and Su Chen-hua.

Yang Yung remained in Korea until the CPV was officially withdrawn in 1958. He was present to welcome Premier Chou En-lai when the latter came to Korea to complete the negotiations for the withdrawal of the Chinese military forces; Yang probably had a hand in the negotiations (February 14–21), which led to the signing of a joint agreement for the withdrawal. On February 25 Yang signed a joint order with the chief of the Korean General Staff arranging for Korea's assumption of the defense work that had previously been assumed by the CPV, and at the same time he became chief of the CPV committee formed to hand over the defense work to the Koreans. The Chinese press had remained relatively quiet about the activities of the CPV in Korea until the agreement for the withdrawal had been signed. Yang's activities, therefore, received little attention from 1954 to 1958, but once the agreement was signed he was given considerable press coverage. On October 24, the eve of his departure, he was awarded the Order of the National Flag by the Koreans.

Soon after his return to China, Yang reported on the CPV to the Standing Committees of the NPC and the CPPCC at one of their joint meetings. By June 1959 he was identified as commander of the Peking Military Region (with jurisdiction over Hopeh and Shansi), apparently assuming the post from Yang Ch'eng-wu. In October of that year he was also identified as commander of the Peking-Tientsin Garrison. He held the latter post only until the spring of 1960 when the two cities were given separate garrison commands. He received an even more important post by mid-1961 when he was identified as a deputy chief-of-staff of the PLA, another position that he still retains. As a top PLA staff officer and commander of the Peking Military Region, Yang is frequently on hand for official functions, especially those of a protocol nature having to do with Korea. He has also lent his name to various *ad hoc* bodies, as in September 1959 when he was a member of a preparatory committee for celebrating the 10th anniversary of the PRC. Yang has been a regular contributor to the press since 1959, but most of his writings are routine articles, usually commemorating some aspect of Chinese assistance to Korea during the Korean War.

Yang has been abroad twice since returning from Korea in 1958. In October–November 1960 he was a member of Ho Lung's "goodwill" mission to North Korea for a three-week visit, which coincided with the 10th anniversary of the entry of the CPV into the Korean War. In October–November 1964 Yang accompanied Foreign Minister Ch'en I to Algeria as deputy leader of a delegation sent to participate in the 10th anniversary of the Algerian Revolution; concurrently, Yang headed a military delegation to the celebrations, and he remained with this group in Algeria for two weeks after Ch'en I had left for China.

1. *Hung-ch'i p'iao-p'iao* (Red flag fluttering; Peking, 1957), III, 114.
2. *Saga of Resistance to Japanese Invasion* (Peking, 1959), p. 11; *Peking Review,* no. 39: 24–27 (September 24, 1965).
3. Jack Belden, *China Shakes the World* (New York, 1949), p. 192.

Yao Chung-ming

(1914– ; Ch'i-hsia, Shantung). Guerrilla leader in Sino-Japanese War; diplomat.

Yao Chung-ming graduated from National Peking University (Peita) in the mid-1930's where he participated in student strikes in 1935–36, presumably those strikes carried out in protest to Japanese incursions into north China and usually known under the name of the December Ninth movement (see under Li Ch'ang). Perhaps it was at Peking University that he learned a bit of Japanese and English. Yao's later career suggests that he may have studied law or international relations.

Yao was reportedly arrested in 1937 for his anti-Japanese activities and imprisoned in Tsinan, Shantung. However, he was released when the Sino-Japanese War began that year. He took part in organizing a band of peasants and students in Shantung, and late in 1937 this group made its way to the Communist capital at Yenan where he doubtless met many of his former Peking University classmates, who had reached Yenan by similarly circuitous paths. Little is known of his life in Yenan during the war except for the fact that he joined the CCP there and attended a Party school, probably the Central Party School.

It may have been during his study at the Party school that he co-authored a play, published in 1945, entitled "Comrades, You've Taken the Wrong Path!" This play, according to an official Communist description, tells of the "struggle against rightist opportunism in the revolutionary ranks" during the Sino-Japanese War, and 19 years after it was written it was still being staged by a repertory company in Peking.[1] A New China News Agency report of December 1962 also mentioned a play by Yao entitled "Fresh in the Memory of the Chinese People," but aside from the comment that it dealt with "revolutionary history," there was no specific indication of its date or place of publication.

In the latter part of the Sino-Japanese War, Yao was serving as Chief-of-Staff of the 359th Brigade in the Shansi-Suiyuan-Shensi-Kansu-Ninghsia Command under Ho Lung (q.v.). At the close of the war and into 1946 he was leading Communist guerrilla forces in his native Shantung, operating mainly around the city of Lin-i, not far from the Kiangsu border. In 1946, Yao was named as a Communist liaison official with the United Nations Relief and Rehabilitation Administration (UNRRA) Office in Tsingtao, an important coastal city in Shantung. During this same period, the Nationalists, Communists, and Americans established the Peking Executive Headquarters in an attempt to halt the civil war. Yao served as a representative on the Field Truce Team at Tsingtao and so was in regular contact with both Chinese Nationalists and Americans.

When the truce talks collapsed and the civil war was renewed in early 1947, Yao left Tsingtao for Communist-controlled Chefoo (Yen-t'ai), the important port city in northeastern Shantung, where he became mayor. At this stage in the war, the Communists controlled very few coastal and industrial cities and were therefore anxious not to alienate the local businessmen and industrialists. The Communist policy was illustrated by Yao when he spoke before a conference of industrialists and merchants in 1947; after surveying general improvements, he conceded that many of these businessmen had been worried about "revisions" in the enforcement of Communist land reform policies in the rural areas near Chefoo. However, he promised them that no such "revisions" would apply to industry and trade. He closed by stating: "I want you to rest assured that there will be no 'reforms' and no 'revision' in industry and commerce. There is only one course, i.e. development."[2]

In 1948 Yao was transferred to Wei-fang (also known as Wei-hsien) in northern Shantung, where he became the mayor, a post he held until 1949. In September 1948 the Shantung capital, Tsinan, was captured by the Communists, and in the following year Yao was transferred to this city to assume the concurrent positions of deputy commander of the garrison and vice-mayor. Later in 1949 he was promoted to mayor of Tsinan, a post he held until his appointment abroad in mid-1950. During this same period he was also a member of the Shantung Provincial People's Government.

In December 1949, Burma became the first non-Communist nation to recognize Communist China. Formal diplomatic relations were agreed upon in June 1950, at which time Yao was appointed as ambassador. When he presented his credentials in Rangoon on September 5, 1950, he was the second Chinese ambassador accredited to a non-Communist nation, being preceded abroad only by Wang Jen-shu in Indonesia. Inasmuch as Sino-Burmese relations were quite active during Yao's seven and a half-year tour, he was often reported in the press holding receptions for the many Burmese going to or returning from China, or for the large number of Chinese missions that visited Burma in those years. Yao also signed several agreements with the Burmese, including a three-year trade agreement signed on April 22, 1954, the first government-to-government pact concluded between Communist China and Burma.

In the course of his lengthy tenure in Burma, Yao returned to China several times. The most important of these concerned visits by Premier U Nu to China, occurring in December 1954, October–November 1956, and March–April 1957. Perhaps the highlight of Yao's stay in Burma took place in June 1954 when Chou En-lai visited there en route home from the Geneva Conference, where a settlement to the Indochina problem was being worked out. During this brief stay by Chou he reaffirmed the famed "five principles of peaceful coexistence," which received so much attention in the mid-1950's.

When Yao was recalled from Burma in February 1958 he had served the longest single tour abroad of any Chinese ambassador. For the next three and a half years he continued to be deeply involved in Chinese foreign and political affairs. When the third national council of the Political Science and Law Association of China was formed in August 1958, Yao was named to the council and was also named as one of the four secretaries under First Secretary Wu Te-feng (q.v.). In October 1964 a new council was elected, with Yao as a member; however, because of a new assignment abroad, he was not renamed a secretary. In January 1959 he was selected for membership on the newly formed Maritime Arbitration Commission under the China Council for the Promotion of International Trade.

In January 1960 Yao became director of the Treaty and Law Department of the Ministry of Foreign Affairs, a post he held until assigned to Indonesia in mid-1961. Because he held this position and because of his long stay in Burma, it was natural that he be appointed as chief Chinese representative for the Sino-Burmese Boundary Joint Committee, which held its first meeting in June 1960. Between that date and May 1961, Yao led the Chinese negotiators in six meetings, with the sites alternating between Burma and China. Because of his role in these talks he was in Burma in early January 1961 when Chou En-lai visited there to exchange the instruments of ratification for the boundary treaty which Yao had worked out. It was during this same visit that the Burmese president decorated Yao with the "heroic honor" medal for his work in the negotiations. In the meantime, in April 1960, he was named to the Standing Committee of the newly formed China-Africa People's Friendship Association.

Yao was appointed as ambassador to Indonesia in July 1961, replacing Huang Chen. He arrived in Jakarta with his wife in early August and presented his credentials to President Sukarno on August 14. Judged from his first four years there, Yao's work in Indonesia must be described as successful from the Chinese Communist viewpoint. During his tour Sino-Indonesian relations grew increasingly close, and American-Indonesian relations cooled noticeably. Because several top Indonesian leaders visited Peking in the early 1960's, Yao was often back in China. The most important Chinese visitor to Indonesia during Yao's tour was obviously Liu Shao-ch'i, who came in April 1963. For reasons which were never clarified, serious rioting broke out in Indonesia shortly after Liu departed, with overseas Chinese the chief target. Yao made official representations to the Indonesian authorities about these disturbances. Because this was embarrassing, par-

ticularly in the wake of Liu Shao-ch'i's visit, the Chinese blamed the riots on "imperialists and counterrevolutionists." In June 1963, Yao punctuated Chinese displeasure over events in Indonesia by making a large donation to Indonesian and Chinese nationals who suffered in the "counterrevolutionary disturbances." Not long after that, outspoken Indonesian President Sukarno described Yao as being "too serious," with the additional comment that he liked ambassadors to be "informal and gay."[3] However, Yao's effectiveness in Indonesia did not appear to be impaired in the period after the president's rather caustic remark.

In 1963, the Indonesians decided to hold the "Games of the New Emerging Forces" (GANEFO) in response to what they felt was hostile treatment toward Indonesia by the International Olympics Committee. The Chinese Communists enthusiastically endorsed this plan (being themselves excluded from the Olympics). As a consequence, Yao was often involved in GANEFO affairs in 1963 and went to Jakarta with Politburo member Ho Lung, Peking's delegate to the first games in November 1963. Yao was also on hand in Jakarta in April 1964 as an official member of the delegation led by Foreign Minister Ch'en I to the preparatory meeting for the Second Afro-Asian Conference, scheduled for 1965 on or about the 10th anniversary of the first conference, better known to the world as the Bandung Conference. Another development which occupied Yao's time after mid-1963 was the formation of the Malaysian Federation, which merged Malaya, Singapore, and former British territories in Borneo. The Indonesians bitterly opposed this merger and the Chinese Communists gave Jakarta strong diplomatic support for its position. As a consequence, Yao was often in conference with Indonesian leaders over this matter. While still abroad, it was announced (December 1962) that Yao had won membership in the Union of Chinese Writers because of the merits of the previously mentioned plays authored many years earlier.

1. *Chinese Literature*, no. 1, 1964, p. 103.

2. *The Second Congress of Chefoo General Trade Union Federation* (Chefoo, n.d.), pp. 31–32.

3. Hong Kong *Tiger Standard*, August 29, 1963.

Yao I-lin

(c.1915–   ; Anhwei). Former youth leader; minister of Commerce; director, Finance and Trade Political Department, CCP Central Committee; alternate member, CCP Central Committee.

Yao I-lin is one of Communist China's top economic officials, specializing in financial and trade affairs. He was born about 1915 in Anhwei Province[1] into a prominent and presumably well-to-do family. His father, who died in Yao's infancy, had been a supporter of Yuan Shih-k'ai and a prominent official in Peking during the latter years of the Ch'ing Dynasty.[2] Yao's real name was Yao K'o-kuang, a name he was still using through his college days in the mid-thirties. In his youth he studied at a Christian school. He then regarded himself as a Christian,[3] and it was probably during these years that he gained his fluency in English. Yao attended a middle school attached to Kuang-hua University in Shanghai in the early thirties where, according to a former schoolmate, he was one of the top students and known for his articulateness.[4] In 1934 he enrolled in Tsinghua University in Peking where he majored in history, and at this time or soon thereafter became a member of the CCP.

Yao was one of the participants in the "December Ninth" movement that broke out on December 9, 1935 when students at the major Peking universities demonstrated against KMT policies they regarded as impotent in the face of steady encroachments by the Japanese on Chinese sovereignty in north China. It is not clear if Yao took part in the initial phases of the movement, but by early 1936 he was already deeply involved. According to an account by Li Ch'ang, in whose biography the movement is described in greater detail, Yao was briefly arrested on the Tsinghua campus on February 29, 1936, but he was able to escape immediately. Li describes Yao as then engaging in Party work in Peking.[5] Yao remained at Tsinghua for another year before he was expelled, presumably for his political activities.

During Yao's college days he was a close colleague of Huang Ching (q.v.),[6] one of the leading participants in the "December Ninth" movement, and it is also likely that he was close to P'eng T'ao (q.v.), another student leader. All three men were to rise to Party Central Committee stature in the 1950's, and when Huang died in 1958 and P'eng in 1961, Yao was a member of the funeral committee for both men. It is also probable that he was taking orders in the thirties from P'eng Chen (q.v.) who seems to have been the leading CCP figure in Peking soon after the movement began.

There is little reporting on Yao's activities in the war and postwar years, but it is apparent that he, like many of his fellow students in Peking, went to the Communist-held areas of north or northwest China when war erupted against Japan in mid-1937. According to the few available reports, he served during the war as secretary-general of the Northern Sub-bureau that was subordinate to the Party's North China Bureau, here again probably under P'eng Chen, and on December 13, 1945 he wrote an article commemorating the 10th anniversary of the "December Ninth" movement for the leading Communist newspaper in north China, the Yenan *Chieh-fang jih-pao* (Liberation daily).[7] By 1946 he was serving as a political commissar with the Communist forces in the Chin-Ch'a-Chi (Shansi-Chahar-Hopeh) Border Region (see under Nieh Jung-chen). This appears to be Yao's only association with the Red armies, a career pattern that is typical of many students of the mid-thirties, most of whom were engaged during the war years in youth or propaganda work and who later, after the Communist government was established in 1949, moved into fields that required a rather sophisticated educational background. Other contemporaries of Yao's of whom this can be said include Li Ch'ang and Chiang Nan-hsiang (q.v.).

In the late forties Yao remained in the Chin-Ch'a-Chi area, the government of which was merged with the Chin-Chi-Lu-Yü (Shansi-Hopeh-Shantung-Honan) Border Region Government to form the North China People's Government (NCPG) in August 1948. The NCPG moved from Shih-chia-chuang, Hopeh to Peking in early 1949, remaining in existence until its functions were absorbed by the new central government in October 1949. Yao's duties within the NCPG were a precursor to what has come to be his special field of competence—finance and economics. Under the NCPG Yao headed the Industry and Commerce Department and also served as a member of its Finance and Economics Committee. He received a similar assignment in October 1949 under the Government Administration Council (the cabinet) when he was appointed a vice-minister of Trade under veteran Communist Yeh Chi-chuang (q.v.).

The Ministry of Trade was responsible for both domestic commerce and foreign trade, and it is evident that Yao was involved in both fields. On the domestic side he became in 1950 a member of two organizations whose functions were closely related to the Trade Ministry. The first of these, the All-China Federation of Cooperatives (ACFC), has major responsibilities for coordinating the exchange of commodities between the rural and urban areas. Yao became a member of the Federation's provisional Board of Directors in July 1950, and in November of that year was elected to the Board's Standing Committee. When the ACFC was established on a permanent basis in July 1952, Yao continued as a Standing Committee member, and he has been a member of the National Committee since mid-1954 when the Federation was reorganized and renamed the All-China Federation of Supply and Marketing Cooperatives. The other organization particularly related to domestic commerce to which Yao belongs is the China Democratic National Construction Association (CD-

NCA) which, though nominally a political party, is more akin to a chamber of commerce and is composed mainly of industrialists and businessmen, most of them non-Communists. Yao was a member of the CDNCA Standing Committee from 1950 to 1952, and since 1955 has been a member of its Central Committee. He also took a prominent part in the numerous movements in the early fifties to economize and increase production, serving in 1951–1952, for example, as a member of the central government's "austerity examination committee" that was chaired by top economic specialist Po I-po.

Yao was equally active in the field of foreign trade in the early fifties, particularly with other Communist nations. In early 1951 he signed trade agreements with Hungarian and Polish officials in Peking, and from March to June of the same year he was in Moscow negotiating a trade agreement with the Soviet Union. Immediately after returning home he signed another trade agreement with Polish representatives (July 1951). He ceased to have much involvement in foreign trade after August 1952 when the Ministry of Trade was divided into the Ministries of Foreign Trade and Commerce, with Yao assigned as a vice-minister of the latter, serving under Minister Tseng Shan.

Yao was reappointed to his vice-ministership immediately after the close of the initial session of the First NPC in September 1954, the legislative body that brought the constitutional government into existence. He served throughout the term of the First NPC (1954–1959) as a deputy from Kiangsi, and was also a member of the NPC's permanent Budget Committee as well as of the *ad hoc* Motions Examinations Committee for the second through the fifth NPC sessions held from mid-1955 to early 1958. Speaking in June 1956 before the third NPC session, Yao admitted to criticisms that had been directed to the Ministry of Commerce, addressing himself in particular to the problems of the shoddy quality of goods as well as the insufficiency of certain commodities produced under the direction of the Ministry. There is little to indicate, however, that these admissions adversely affected his career. In fact, he spoke soon after at the Party's Eighth Congress, held in September 1956, and when the Congress was convened again for a second session in May 1958, he was elected an alternate member of the Party's Central Committee.

In February 1958, during a partial reorganization of the State Council, the Ministry of Commerce was renamed the First Ministry of Commerce and the Ministry of Urban Services was retitled the Second Ministry of Commerce. Yao continued as a vice-minister in the First Ministry, thereby continuing to serve under Ch'en Yun, then China's top economic expert, who had succeeded Tseng Shan in November

1956. Then, in still another reorganization of September 1958, the two ministries were recombined under the previous name, the Ministry of Commerce. Yao remained a vice-minister, now serving under Ch'eng Tzu-hua (q.v.), a leading figure in the Cooperatives Federation who had succeeded Ch'en Yun, then falling into political decline, presumably because of opposition to the policies of the Great Leap Forward inaugurated earlier in the year. Yao advanced to an even more important post in the economic bureaucracy in September 1959 when he was appointed a deputy director of the Finance and Trade Office, responsible for coordinating the activities of the State Council's commissions, ministries, and bureaus concerned with financial and trade matters. He still retains this post, working under Director Li Hsien-nien, Peking's leading financial specialist since the mid-fifties. A few days after receiving the State Council appointment, in writing an article on commercial work in the first decade of the PRC (*JMJP,* September 28, 1959), he was identified as a deputy director of the Party Central Committee's Finance and Trade Work Department, the Party's counterpart to the government Finance and Trade Office. In this position Yao came under Director Ma Ming-fang (q.v.), but when Ma was transferred to Manchuria in 1961 it appears that Yao succeeded him as the *de facto* director. Yao rose to his highest Party position by June 1964 when he was identified as director of the Central Committee's Finance and Trade Political Department; this "political" department was a reorganization of the former "work" department and reflected a movement begun in the early part of 1964 to inject greater political control into virtually all aspects of the Chinese economy. In the meantime, in February 1960, Yao had succeeded Ch'eng Tzu-hua as head of the Ministry of Commerce, another post he retains. As a consequence, Yao directs the Party's top finance and trade department and the Ministry of Commerce, and is the number two man under Li Hsien-nien in the State Council's Finance and Trade Office, a combination of positions that places him among the PRC's key economic officials.

Unlike many important Party leaders, Yao has seldom been called upon to participate in extracurricular activities (e.g., ideological campaigns). Virtually all his appearances have been in direct connection with his major field of work: financial and trade affairs. He has spoken on these subjects before a number of nationwide conferences, including NPC sessions, as in April 1960 when he addressed the second session of the Second NPC on the tasks of commercial departments in organizing urban "people's communes." In March–April 1964 he was in Hanoi leading a commercial delegation to North Vietnam, presumably working out details for Chinese assistance to the Vietnamese in the war that was then rapidly escalating in the southern sector of Vietnam. Apart from his finance and trade positions, Yao has represented the CCP in the CPPCC since the Third National Committee was established in 1959. He was also a CPPCC Standing Committee member during the term of the Third CPPCC (1959–1964), but when the Fourth Committee was formed in December 1964–January 1965, he was only elected to the National Committee.

Yao's concentration on finance and trade work is reflected in his writings for the Chinese press. Two of his articles, written in 1952 and 1953, provide useful surveys of the efforts to revive and develop industry and commerce in the early years of the PRC.[8] A more polemical account appeared in the Party's top journal, *Hung-ch'i* (Red flag, November 16, 1962), under the title "Hold high the banner of Mao Tse-tung's thought and make a greater success of socialist commerce."

1. Interview with former Kuang-hua University student in Cambridge, Mass., August, 1966.
2. Nym Wales, *Notes on the Chinese Student Movement, 1935–1936* (Madison, Conn., 1959), p. 135.
3. *Ibid.*
4. Interview, August 1966.
5. *SCMM* 296, p. 31.
6. Nym Wales, *My Yenan Notebooks* (Madison, Conn., 1961), p. 178.
7. John Israel, "The December 9th Movement: A Case Study in Chinese Communist Historiography," *The China Quarterly,* no. 23:145 (July–September 1965).
8. *New China's Economic Achievements, 1949–1952* (Peking, 1952), pp. 219–235; *People's China,* no. 4:5–7 (February 16, 1953).

Yeh Chi-chuang

(1893–1967; Hsin-hsing hsien, Kwangtung). Former minister of Foreign Trade; member, CCP Central Committee.

Yeh Chi-chuang was the Red Army's foremost logistics specialist from the early thirties until the Communist conquest of the mainland in 1949, after which he was the PRC's leading expert in foreign trade. He was born in Hsin-hsing hsien, located about 50 miles west of Canton in Kwangtung province. Because his father was a prosperous businessman connected with firms in Canton and Hong Kong,[1] Yeh probably spent little time in his native hsien. He studied law and then practiced for a brief interval, probably in Hong Kong.[2] Communist sources mention neither his bourgeois background nor his educational training. In 1925 he joined the CCP and in the same year he partic-

ipated in the famous Canton–Hong Kong strike, which began in June (see under Su Chao-cheng). Yeh was working at this time as an editor of a leftist newspaper in Hong Kong. When his pro-labor sympathies came to the attention of the British authorities, they ordered his arrest. Yeh fled to the mainland[3] and made his way to the rural hinterlands where the Communists had military forces. In the next few years he engaged in political work for the CCP, serving as an inspector of a Party provincial committee, then as a secretary of a hsien committee, and finally as a secretary of a Party committee at the district level.

By late 1929 Yeh was operating in west Kwangsi as chief of supplies in the Seventh Red Army commanded by Chang Yun-i (q.v.).[4] The origins of the Seventh Red Army and of the small soviet it supported on the Yu River near Pai-se are described in the biography of Chang Yun-i, who had been sent to Kwangsi after the Communists' defeats at Nanchang and Swatow in 1927. Evidently Yeh, like Chang, was one of the Party activists sent to infiltrate the army of Li Ming-jui, the local warlord who held west Kwangsi. The Seventh Army was created in December 1929 from some of Li's forces, but several months later it was ordered to move out of the province by Li Li-san (q.v.), leader of the Party headquarters in Shanghai (see under Teng Hsiao-p'ing). Li Li-san needed the Seventh Army to reinforce his armies, which were being sent to the Yangtze valley to attack the leading industrial cities. Yeh, director of the Seventh Army's Political Department in 1931, was probably connected with these moves, although the part he played in them has not been recorded. Possibly he followed his chief, Chang Yun-i, to Juichin, the headquarters of Mao Tse-tung in southeast Kiangsi, because he was there in November 1931 when the Chinese Soviet Republic's government was established under Mao. Yeh was named people's commissar of trade for the new government and at approximately the same time he became director and political commissar of the General Supply Department (*tsung-kung pu*) of the First Front Army, led by Chu Te and Mao.

These logistic tasks were carried out on the crude level of enforced procurement, which often amounted to commandeering food and supplies from the local peasants. The experience gained in supplying a fighting guerrilla army proved good training for Yeh who continued to work in trade and finance until his death. During the Long March Yeh continued to direct the Supply Department for the First Front Army, one of the principal armies making the march. He served concurrently as a deputy political commissar. He remained in these posts from the time the army reached north Shensi in the fall of 1935 until the opening of the Sino-Japanese

War when the Communists reorganized their military forces.

When the Eighth Route Army was created in August 1937, Yeh was named to head the Rear Services Department (*hou-ch'in pu*), his major wartime task. It appears, however, that he relinquished this post to Yang Li-san (q.v.) in 1943. Yeh also served in the Second Assembly of the Shensi-Kansu-Ninghsia (Shen-Kan-Ning) Border Region Government as a deputy from Yen-ch'uan, a region in Shensi not far to the northeast of Yenan. In this capacity he attended the meetings of the first session of the Second Assembly in November 1941, and of the second session in December 1944. Because the Communists in Yenan controlled far more territory and maintained larger military forces than they had in Kiangsi before the Long March, the question of supplies became increasingly important, especially after the early 1940's, when the KMT enforced an economic blockade of the Communist areas. Barter, exchange, and trade geared to war times were conducted largely within the Communist-held territory; Yeh must have taken part in the controlled exchange, for by 1945 he was manager of the official trading company for the Shen-Kan-Ning Border Region. He also served during the war years as director of the Border Region's Bureau of Supplies (*wu-tzu chü*).

Now established as an expert in economic affairs, Yeh accompanied the Red military forces that moved into Manchuria at the close of hostilities in August 1945. The military forces were led by Lin Piao, who was accompanied by such high-ranking Party leaders as Ch'en Yun, Kao Kang, Li Fu-ch'un, and Lin Feng. Lin's Northeast Democratic Allied Army (NEDAA) came into being early in 1946. For a time in 1946 Yeh was a deputy chief-of-staff of Lin's army, and when the NEDAA was redesignated the Northeast PLA in 1948, he became head of its Rear Services Department. Earlier, in the spring of 1946 the Communists created their first government in Manchuria, the Northeast Administrative Committee (NEAC), with the capital at Harbin. The NEAC was headed by Lin Feng; Ch'en Yun headed the Finance and Economics Committee, to which Yeh, along with Li Fu-ch'un, was assigned. By 1948 he was serving concurrently as director of the NEAC's Finance and Commerce Department.

In May 1949 Yeh was made a vice-chairman of the NEAC's Finance and Economics Committee, holding the higher post for only four months because the government in Manchuria was reorganized in August 1949 on the eve of the establishment of the central government at Peking. When the Northeast People's Government (NEPG) came into being in August 1949 the capital was moved to Shenyang. At this time Kao Kang replaced Lin Feng as head of the government. Kao also took over the responsibilities of the Finance and Economics Committee from Ch'en Yun; Yeh continued to serve as a vice-chairman of this committee, now under Kao. Yeh also became director of the Foreign Trade Department and was named a member of the NEPG Council.

Yeh relinquished all his posts in Manchuria when the Central People's Government was formed in October 1949. At that time he was transferred to Peking and named to membership on the Finance and Economics Committee under the Government Administration Council (the cabinet). In this capacity Yeh served under Committee Chairman Ch'en Yun, his former superior in the northeast. More important was his appointment as minister of Trade, then responsible for both domestic commerce and foreign trade. Three years later, during the government reorganization of August 1952, the responsibilities for domestic commerce were transferred to the new Ministry of Commerce headed by Tseng Shan (q.v.). Yeh's ministry was renamed the Ministry of Foreign Trade, with Yeh as head of the reorganized portfolio. As of January 1965, when he was reappointed as the minister, Yeh was one of only three men to have held a ministerial post continuously from the establishment of the PRC in 1949—the other two being Chu Hsueh-fan (Posts and Telecommunications) and Fu Tso-i (Water Conservancy), both non-Communists.

One of Yeh's first important assignments came in January 1950 when he was sent to Moscow in the company of such important Communist leaders as Chou En-lai, Li Fu-ch'un, and Wu Hsiu-ch'üan (qq.v.). The delegation went to Moscow to continue the negotiations with the Russians which Mao Tse-tung had begun a month earlier. The talks eventually led to the signing on February 14, 1950, of the Sino-Soviet Treaty of Friendship, Alliance, and Mutual Assistance, the cornerstone of Sino-Soviet relations for the next decade. Mao, Chou, and most of the others left for home in mid-February, but Yeh remained behind as head of a trade delegation to engage in further negotiations. When these talks were finally concluded in April, Yeh returned to Peking. This trip to Moscow was a prelude to many similar visits abroad. There are few officials in the PRC, in fact, who have traveled as widely as Yeh. From his Moscow visit in 1950 to the end of 1964, he was in the following 13 nations: The USSR (five times), Hungary, Indonesia, Poland (twice), East Germany, Czechoslovakia, Egypt, the Sudan, Ceylon, North Korea (three times), Mongolia, North Vietnam, and Burma. In almost all instances he headed trade delegations and signed the official trade agreements or protocols. The only notable exception concerned his visit to Indonesia; this took place in April 1955 when he accompanied Chou En-lai as a member of the Chinese delegation to the Afro-Asian ("Bandung") Conference.

During this same 1950–1964 period, Yeh was also constantly engaged in trade negotiations in Peking. He is known to have signed well over 50 trade agreements or protocols in China with representatives from at least 24 different nations. As a reflection of the political orientation of the PRC during the first years of its existence, most of Yeh's negotiations took place with Communist countries. After the mid-fifties, however, he was also engaged in talks with officials from non-Communist nations, particularly the Afro-Asian countries. In addition to the scores of agreements to which Yeh was China's official signatory, he participated in negotiations with many other nations which led to agreements signed by other Chinese Communist leaders.

Although Yeh was the most important PRC official in the conduct of foreign trade until his death, he also devoted a portion of his time to other activities related to domestic commercial affairs. In July 1950 he became the director of the Board of Supervisors of the newly formed All-China Federation of Cooperatives, an organization whose main task is to stimulate the flow of goods and commodities between the rural and urban sectors of the economy. This assignment was particularly appropriate until 1952 when Yeh's Ministry of Trade was in charge of domestic as well as foreign trade. He continued to hold this post until mid-1954 when he was replaced by Tseng Shan, the same man who in August 1952 had taken over the portfolio for domestic commerce. In his capacity as the Trade minister, Yeh was also involved in the establishment of the All-China Federation of Industry and Commerce (ACFIC). The first steps in this process took place in the fall of 1951 when an 18-member group, including Yeh, was given the task of convening a conference to form a national organization made up principally of private businessmen and industrialists. Subsequently, a large preparatory conference was held in June 1952, at the close of which Yeh was named to the Standing Committee of the Preparatory Committee. However, when the ACFIC was finally established as a permanent organization in November 1953, Yeh dropped his affiliation, probably because he had been removed from his responsibilities regarding domestic commerce in August 1952.

As already described, when the Finance and Economics Committee (FEC) was established in October 1949, Yeh was named as a member. By May 1951 he was also serving as chairman of the FEC's Tariff Commission, and then in

August 1952 he was promoted to be a vice-chairman of the FEC, a post he continued to hold until the FEC was dissolved at the inauguration of the constitutional government in September 1954. As its title suggests, the FEC was charged with coordinating the activities of several ministries and commissions. Under the structure of the reorganized government (September 1954), a new set of "staff offices" was created with coordinating responsibilities. In October Yeh was named as a deputy-director of the Fifth Staff Office, with specific responsibilities in the fields of finance and trade. It was headed by Finance Minister Li Hsien-nien (q.v.), one of Peking's most prominent economic specialists. Under still another reorganization, in September 1959, the numbered staff offices were redesignated; the Fifth Office became known as the Finance and Trade Office, with Li continuing as the director and Yeh as one of the deputy directors. He continued to hold this important position as well as his Foreign Trade portfolio until his death in 1967.

When the Second National Committee of the quasi-legislative CPPCC was formed in December 1954, Yeh served as a member representing the CCP. He was not re-elected in April 1959 when the Third CPPCC was established, but was at the same time transferred to the more important NPC. Yeh was elected to the Second NPC (1959–1964) as a deputy from his native Kwangtung and was re-elected to the Third NPC, the first session of which was held in December 1964–January 1965. More important, Yeh was elected to membership on the Party Central Committee at the Eighth National Congress in September 1956. He was one of 33 men elected directly to full membership who had been neither a full nor an alternate member of the Party's Seventh Central Committee elected in 1945 in Yenan. By the end of 1957 he was also identified as a vice-chairman of the Central Committee's Finance and Economics Committee; however, this organization seems to have been abolished by 1958.

From the earliest days of the PRC, Yeh was a frequent speaker before meetings of the legislative and executive organs of the central government. In virtually every instance he gave reports on the state of China's foreign trade, as, for example, when he presented a written report before the historic Eighth Party Congress in 1956. Unlike most important Chinese Communist leaders, Yeh was not required to devote much attention to extracurricular activities—such as the time-consuming work involved in domestic ideological campaigns or the international Communist "peace" movement. Rather, Yeh's career exemplified the life of a technocrat who was allowed to give almost single-minded attention to the complex problem of managing

China's foreign trade. He was quite active until early 1965, when Lin Hai-yan (q.v.) became acting minister of Foreign Trade, apparently because of Yeh's ill health. On June 27, 1967, Yeh died in Peking at the age of 74.

1. Gunther Stein, *The Challenge of Red China* (New York, 1945), p. 182.
2. *Ibid.*
3. *Ibid.*
4. *SCMM* 295, p. 39.

Yeh Chien-ying

(1898–   ; Mei-hsien, Kwangtung). Veteran Red Army staff officer; member, Central Secretariat and Politburo, CCP.

Already an experienced military officer when he joined the CCP in 1927, Yeh Chien-ying participated in many of the landmark events of the Communist movement in the twenties and thirties, including the Long March from Kiangsi to Shensi. During the Sino-Japanese War he was among the Communists' top liaison officials with the Nationalists, serving also as chief-of-staff of the Eighth Route Army. He headed the Communist mission at the Peking Executive Headquarters in 1946–47, and in the early years of the PRC he was among the key officials in central-south China. Since the mid-fifties he has been a top PLA staff officer in Peking. Known to have been a Party Central Committee member since 1945, he rose to membership on the CCP Central Secretariat in 1966.

Yeh, a Hakka, was born in a village in Mei-hsien in eastern Kwangtung, some 70 miles north of Swatow. This hsien was the scene of considerable guerrilla warfare from the twenties through the forties. Reared in a merchant's family, Yeh studied in a Cantonese primary school and graduated in 1919 from the 12th class of the well-known Yunnan Military Academy, an institute attended by Chu Te several years earlier. From Yunnan Yeh went to Fukien where he joined the army of Ch'en Chiung-ming, a prominent military leader and one of Sun Yat-sen's opponents. However, not long afterwards, Yeh left Ch'en and went to Canton to work with Sun and the KMT. In an interview with American author Edgar Snow in 1936, Yeh claimed that after the Sun-Joffe agreement (January 1923) he joined the CCP,[1] but this conflicts with an official biography of Yeh issued in 1955, which dates his Party membership from 1927.[2] In any event, with the opening of Whampoa Military Academy in 1924 under the presidency of Chiang Kai-shek, Yeh became an instructor there. The importance the CCP attaches to Yeh's work at Whampoa is evident from an authoritative Communist-published history (1958), which states: "Chou En-lai, Yeh Chien-ying and other Communists held leading posts in the academy."[3]

This seems to be no exaggeration; Yeh told Snow that he worked under Galen (Blücher), a Soviet general who trained Chinese at Whampoa, and according to other reports he also served for a time as an assistant to KMT General Ho Ying-ch'in, the dean of Whampoa. In the 1925–26 period he served first as chief-of-staff of the 21st Division of Ho's First National Revolutionary Army and then as division commander. During this same period he also took part, as commander of a Whampoa cadets' training regiment, in campaigns against Ch'en Chiung-ming.

During the year 1926 Yeh joined the Nationalist Fourth Army, which was commanded first by Li Chi-shen and then by Chang Fa-k'uei. It was Chang who led this major Nationalist force in the Northern Expedition. Yeh served as chief-of-staff of the Army's 12th Division, and as the Northern Expedition got underway in mid-1926 he took charge of the Cadet's Special Training Regiment from Whampoa, which was incorporated within it. When the army captured Wuchang in October 1926 the important industrial Wuhan area fell to the Nationalists and the seat of their government was soon moved there from Canton. At Wuhan the Nationalists also established a branch of their Whampoa Military Academy (see under Yun Tai-ying). The Fourth Army was redesignated the Second Front Army by the time it had taken over Wuhan, and an important unit of this Nationalist force, the 24th Division, was under the command of Communist Yeh T'ing (q.v.), who had the trust of his superior, Chang Fa-k'uei. Yeh Chien-ying was chief-of-staff of the 24th Division and may also have been chief-of-staff of the entire Fourth (and later the Second) Front Army, as some reports assert.

In the summer of 1927, as relations between the Communists and the KMT were deteriorating, Chang Fa-k'uei moved his military headquarters to Kiukiang (Chiu-chiang) in Kiangsi not far north of the provincial capital at Nanchang, where Chu Te's Special Training Regiment acted as a garrison force. Thus, the 24th Division was moved to the outskirts of Nanchang about the end of July. Previously, on July 18, Yeh Chien-ying had attended a secret meeting of Communist leaders and sympathizers, held at a small village near the capital.[4] According to Chu Te, who was also there, this was the initial planning meeting for the Nanchang Uprising on August 1. At the secret July meeting Yeh Chien-ying was among those chosen for membership on the Front-line Committee that was to make final plans for the uprising,[5] and he seems to have been with the troops of his 24th Division when they participated in the coup.[6]

Information about the next phase of Yeh's career is drawn largely from the account Ch'eng Tzu-hua (q.v.) gave journalist Nym Wales in

1937. Ch'eng and another Communist, Hsu Hsiang-ch'ien (q.v.), belonged to the Wuhan Whampoa Special Cadet's Training Regiment, which went over to the Communists after the Nanchang Uprising. The regiment was not able to join the Communist insurgents at Nanchang; it was moved to Kiukiang on August 4, and Chang Fa-k'uei, who now became suspicious of the Communist sympathizers in his Second Front Army, disarmed it. However, the unit managed to hold together and fight other battles for the Communists. Although documentation is lacking, it is possible that the regiment managed to survive under the leadership of Yeh Chien-ying, who did not accompany the major Communist forces, which escaped from Nanchang and made their way south to Swatow (see under Yeh T'ing). After the Communist defeat at Swatow in late September (the month in which the official biography of Yeh Chien-ying states that he joined the CCP), Yeh T'ing accompanied Chou En-lai to Hong Kong. According to the Agnes Smedley biography of Chu Te, Chou and Yeh T'ing were accompanied from Swatow to Hong Kong by Yeh Chien-ying, but this must be viewed with caution as Chu Te's report was based on hearsay.[7] It would appear more likely that Yeh Chien-ying remained with the Training Regiment that spearheaded the Communist insurrection at Canton in December, where it finally joined forces with the other Red military units that had escaped from Nanchang. In any event, Yeh participated in the Canton insurrection as head of the Training Regiment[8] and he was also one of the planners for this uprising, as he had been at Nanchang. In the brief interval that the Communists held the city he was deputy commander of the Red military force created by the short-lived Communist government for Canton. Then, when the Communists were driven out by Chang Fa-k'uei and other Nationalist military leaders, Yeh fled to Hong Kong where he arrived about mid-December.

Yeh later made his way to Shanghai, where he worked briefly in the CCP organization, and then went to Moscow, arriving in time to attend the CCP's Sixth Congress,[9] held in the Soviet capital in mid-1928 to escape KMT surveillance and probable suppression. Yeh told Snow that he spent two years studying in the Soviet Union;[10] he is reported to have attended either the Red Army Academy or the Communist University of the Toilers of the East. He also spent some time traveling in Germany. Yeh's experiences in Europe probably account for his rudimentary knowledge of Russian, German, and English. One source has speculated that while in Europe Yeh was elected to the Party Central Committee at its Third Plenum (September 1930),[11] but this remains uncorroborated. He returned to China in 1931, going first to Shanghai; however, presumably because

Shanghai was rapidly becoming untenable for CCP operations, he soon made his way to the Kiangsi area (1932) where Chu Te and Mao Tse-tung had built up a formidable rural base. Yeh was not in Juichin when the First All-China Congress of Soviets was held (November 1931), but although he was not elected to the Central Executive Committee (CEC) he was appointed in the following month to membership on the CEC's Central Revolutionary Military Council,[12] then chaired by Chu Te. By the following year he was also serving as chief-of-staff of the Military Council. It appears that he held this post only a short time and was replaced by Liu Po-ch'eng, although some sources suggest that Yeh and Liu alternated in the post from 1932 to 1937, that is, before and during the Long March and until the outbreak of the Sino-Japanese War. In approximately the 1932–33 period Yeh was president of the Red Army School (Hung-chün hsueh-hsiao; not to be confused with the more important Red Army Academy, Hung-chün ta-hsueh).

In theory the Military Council supervised the activities of the many and scattered Red Army units in central-south China, and even those as far distant as Szechwan. Therefore, the staff position with the Council was largely nominal. But by late 1933 Yeh was holding a position of more immediate relevance, that is, as chief-of-staff of Chu Te's First Front Army,[13] the backbone force of the Kiangsi area. Here he served with his Whampoa colleague Chou En-lai, who was the Army's political commissar.

At the Second All-China Congress of Soviets, held in January–February 1934 in Juichin, Yeh was elected a member of the Chinese Soviet Republic's CEC. Then in October of that year he set out on the Long March; according to one account he was Chu Te's chief-of-staff and also a commander of a regiment drawn from the Red Army Academy.[14] If, in fact, the chief-of-staff position refers to the First Front Army, then Yeh soon relinquished it to Liu Po-ch'eng, who held the post by the end of the year. Yeh apparently played a role of some significance in the dispute between Mao Tse-tung and Chang Kuo-t'ao over the ultimate destination of the Long Marchers (see under Chang Kuo-t'ao). This was specifically mentioned in an authoritative (and Maoist) sketch of Yeh's career in 1955 when he was made a PLA marshal (see below). Although he had already made a reputation as a skilled strategist, his decision to side with Mao was undoubtedly valuable in advancing his career in later years.

In mid-1936, several months after the Mao Tse-tung forces arrived in north Shensi, Edgar Snow interviewed Yeh at Pao-an, then the Communist capital. Snow described him as chief of the general staff of the Eastern Front and still a Revolutionary Military Council member.

Throughout the early months of 1936, troops commanded by KMT Generals Chang Hsueh-liang and Yang Hu-ch'eng had frequently clashed with Communist elements in Shensi, but neither of these generals had much stomach for such harassments, preferring instead to unite all Chinese forces to resist the steady Japanese encroachments on Chinese sovereignty. Contacts were made between the Communists and Chang and Yang, and clashes soon gave way to increasingly friendly contacts. As a respected strategist, Yeh was even invited by Chang Hsueh-liang to Sian to discuss means of improving the fighting qualities of his troops.[15] It was presumably Yeh's familiarity with Chang that led to the former's selection as one of the Communist negotiators sent to Sian in December 1936 immediately after the arrest by generals Chang and Yang of Chiang Kai-shek (the Sian Incident). Yeh took part in these talks together with such top Communists as Chou En-lai, Ch'in Pang-hsien, and Li K'o-nung (qq.v.).

When war with Japan broke out in July 1937, Yeh was sent once again to Sian to head the Communist liaison office there, but later in the same year he was assigned to Nanking to direct a similar office. Still later, after the fall of Nanking (October 1937), Yeh was dispatched to Hankow to serve as a liaison official. U.S. Naval Observer Evans Carlson, who saw Yeh in Hankow, has written that he was "frequently consulted by the Generalissimo or his staff on military matters." Carlson has also supplied a brief description of Yeh: "a hearty, explosive individual, invariably good natured, of medium height and stocky," and an "indefatigable worker."[16] When Hankow was lost to the Japanese in late 1938, Yeh became dean of the Nationalists' Guerrilla Warfare Training Center, a move in keeping with the spirit of cooperation that existed between the KMT and the CCP in the early days of the war and also one designed to take advantage of the knowledge of guerrilla warfare in which Communist officers were more skilled than their Nationalist counterparts.

By mid-1939 Yeh was working with Chou En-lai in the Communist liaison mission at Chungking, the wartime capital. Jurisdictional disputes and armed clashes between Communist and Nationalist forces had by this time grown to rather serious proportions. Accordingly, as Chiang Kai-shek has written, he "sent for" Chou and Yeh to "caution" them and warn them that they "must obey" Nationalist government orders. But the disputes continued and then in July 1940 the Chungking authorities worked out an arrangement with Chou and Yeh to avoid further clashes.[17] These events, according to Chiang Kai-shek, were a prelude to the far more serious New Fourth Army Incident of January 1941 (see under Yeh T'ing). By this time Yeh had, it seems, returned to Yenan

where he resumed his post as chief-of-staff of the Eighth Route Army, a position he had nominally held during the early war years. Because he was engaged in staff work, rather little was reported about his activities for the balance of the war. However, during this period he wrote a useful summary of the Communist military operations and in June 1944 he presented an even more useful military summary in a briefing given to foreign and Chinese correspondents in Yenan.[18] Commenting on Yeh's wartime liaison duties, Edgar Snow has noted that he became acquainted with many foreign journalists and diplomats, and because Chou En-lai "was basically a political general," he "relied heavily on Yeh's military knowledge and ability to analyze military situations. He was highly regarded for his sound strategic concepts by both Mao and Chou."[19]

Yeh was among the speakers at the Party's Seventh National Congress, held in Yenan from April to June 1945, and at the close of the meetings he was elected to the Seventh Central Committee. Toward the end of the year the Communists sent a top-level team to Chungking as delegates to the Political Consultative Conference, which was convened in January 1946. The seven-member group included Chou En-lai and his wife Teng Ying-ch'ao, Tung Pi-wu, Wang Jo-fei, Wu Yü-chang, Lu Ting-i (qq.v.), and Yeh. At the same time that the conference opened, the Nationalists and Communists signed a cease-fire agreement worked out through the mediation efforts of U.S. Special Envoy George C. Marshall. To implement it an Executive Headquarters was established in Peking under a tripartite arrangement; Walter S. Robertson represented the Americans, Lieutenant General Cheng K'ai-min the Nationalists, and Yeh (with the simulated rank of lieutenant general) the Communists. The Executive Headquarters began to function on January 14, 1946, but it soon became apparent that CCP-KMT differences were too fundamental to be settled through this arrangement. Within a few months serious clashes were taking place, and by November Chou En-lai, who had signed the cease-fire agreement for the Communists, left Nanking for Yenan. The train of events now moved quickly. In late January 1947 the United States announced the termination of its efforts to bring about peace. One month later Yeh and his subordinates in Peking were evacuated by American military aircraft to Yenan, and within days of his arrival the Nationalists assaulted and captured Yenan, the Communists' capital for a decade. The civil war would now be fought to a finish. Yeh once again returned to his familiar role as a staff officer, serving as deputy chief-of-staff of the PLA units, which fought for two more years in north China before they would capture Peking.

In January 1949, as the PLA stood poised on the outskirts of Peking, the Communists formed their governmental organs, which were to begin functioning on the last day of the month, when KMT General Fu Tso-i finally surrendered. Yeh was given three important posts: the chairmanship of the Peking Military Control Commission, the city's mayoralty, and the chairmanship of a special body known as the Peking Joint Administrative Office (see under T'ao Chu). Yeh was among the most logical choices for these assignments, because his familiarity with the city and with a number of the holdover KMT officials there was probably unmatched in the Communist ranks. Similarly, his familiarity with many leading KMT leaders probably accounted for his selection as one of the Communist delegates in the negotiations held in Peking with representatives of Acting Nationalist President Li Tsung-jen in April, talks that were foredoomed, from the Nationalist viewpoint, owing to the speed with which the Communist armies were advancing southward. The negotiations quickly ended when the Communists' proposals, which were tantamount to surrender terms, were turned down by the Nationalists.

For a brief time in 1949 Yeh also headed the newly established North China Military and Political Academy (Hua-pei chün-cheng ta-hsueh), but then in early September he turned over his key posts in Peking to Nieh Jung-chen (q.v.) and went south to join the PLA forces, which had by now reached Kwangtung and would soon enter its capital, Canton. In the military sphere he became commander and political commissar of both the Kwangtung Military District and the high-level South China Military Region (responsible for both Kwangtung and Kwangsi), posts he held until 1952. In the civil administration he became mayor of Canton, chairman of the city's Military Control Commission, and the Kwangtung governor. Completing his domination of virtually all the key jobs in Kwangtung and south China, Yeh also assumed the ranking secretarial posts in the Party's South China Sub-bureau and the Canton Committee, and he even became chairman of the Canton branch of the Sino-Soviet Friendship Association. The choice of Yeh as the top Communist official in Kwangtung clearly resulted from the facts that he was one of the very few top-level CCP members native to the area (although he had not worked in Kwangtung for over 20 years) and that he could speak both Cantonese and the Hakka dialect. Moreover, from the point of view of the "local" (i.e., Kwangtung) cadres, he was a good selection; he was highly regarded by these "local" cadres, who formed the backbone of the leadership in Kwangtung in the early days of PRC rule there.[20]

Apart from his Kwangtung-south China posts, Yeh was also made a vice-chairman of the Communists' Central-South Military and Administrative Committee (CSMAC), established in Wuhan in February 1950 to rule over Honan, Hupeh, Hunan, Kiangsi, Kwangtung, and Kwangsi. Here he served under Lin Piao, and when the CSMAC was reorganized in January 1953 into the Central-South Administrative Committee he was again made a vice-chairman, remaining so until regional administrations were abolished in 1954. In the meantime, just as Yeh was leaving Peking for the south, the new central government was being organized at the initial session of the CPPCC in September 1949. (Yeh was a PLA delegate to the CPPCC, but he did not attend the first CPPCC session.) In October 1949 he was named to membership on two of the national government's most important organs, the Central People's Government Council (CPGC) and the People's Revolutionary Military Council, both of which were headed by Mao Tse-tung; he also became a member of the government's Overseas Chinese Affairs Commission. Yeh held all three of these positions until the government was reorganized in the fall of 1954.

To a large degree Yeh's posts in Peking were largely nominal, because he remained in south China for most of the early years of the PRC. For example, the CPGC held 34 meetings between 1949 and 1954, but Yeh is known to have attended only four of them. His most important report to the central authorities seems to have been one made at the third session of the CPPCC in October 1951, when he reviewed the achievements in land reform and the suppression of "counterrevolutionaries" in south China. In the years from 1949 to about mid-1952, Yeh was almost invariably the keynote speaker at the innumerable meetings of the CCP and governmental organs that ruled Kwangtung and south China. He also assumed new assignments. In 1950 he became president of Nan-fang (South China) University in Canton and chairman of the Kwangtung Government's Finance and Economic Committee, and in 1951 he assumed the presidency of the Canton branch of the PLA's Central-South Military and Political Academy (Chung-nan chün-cheng ta-hsueh). Also, in the latter part of 1951 he became secretary of the newly established Kwangtung CCP Committee. However, with the exception of the last-named post, these new positions were probably peripheral to his many other responsibilities.

In 1952 T'ao Chu (q.v.) was brought into Kwangtung to hasten the progress of the land reform program, which had faltered badly there. Yeh seems to have been blamed in part for these developments (as suggested by a mildly worded "confession" he made in the spring of 1953), but most of the onus fell on his ranking deputy, Fang Fang (q.v.), the third secretary of the South China Party Sub-bureau and chairman of the Kwangtung Land Reform Committee. Within a year Yeh had relinquished most of his responsibilities in Canton, Kwangtung, and south China to others, principally T'ao Chu. Whatever the merits of the case that Yeh's record in Kwangtung was unsatisfactory, they must be balanced against the fact that in 1952–53 he was promoted to even more important posts that the ailing Lin Piao was unable to perform. In the latter half of 1952 Yeh became acting commander of the Central-South Military Region and in the next year he also assumed Lin's top post in the Central-South Party Bureau (initially as acting secretary and then in 1954 as full secretary). Because both the Military Region and the Party Bureau were headquartered in Wuhan, Yeh spent most of these years there, only occasionally returning to Canton where, in name at least, he remained the top official until 1954.

Yeh was among the many regional leaders brought to Peking in 1954 when virtually all the organs of power in China were being reorganized. In June 1954 he was promoted to a vice-chairmanship on the People's Revolutionary Military Council (PRMC), but he held this only until September when the Council was abolished. In mid-1954 he was elected a Kwangtung deputy to the First NPC, and since that time he has been one of the more active participants in the legislative body. At the close of the inaugural NPC session in September 1954, he was selected for membership on the permanent NPC Standing Committee. (Yeh represented the PLA on the Second and Third NPC's, which opened in April 1959 and December 1964, respectively.) He was also named in September 1954 as a vice-chairman of the National Defense Council, the successor to the PRMC, although a less important organization. He continues to hold his seat on both the NPC Standing Committee and the Defense Council.

Soon after the government was reorganized, the central organs within the PLA were also reorganized and their personnel reshuffled. Yeh now became (November 1954) director of the Armed Forces Supervision Department, the approximate equivalent of an inspector-general in Western military establishments. The department is seldom mentioned in the Chinese press, and therefore it is not certain that Yeh still presides over it. Less than a year later (September 1955), Yeh's impressive career as a military leader was given full recognition when he was made a PLA marshal and awarded the Orders of August First, Independence and Freedom, and Liberation, decorations covering the period from 1927 to 1950. Although a large number of men received the three orders, only nine others were made marshals, the top rank in the PLA. Then, when the CCP held its Eighth National Congress in September 1956, he was re-elected a member of the Central Committee.

Since transferring to Peking in 1954, Yeh has

frequently spoken on national military policies —policies that were changing in the mid-fifties as the Communists were readjusting their tactical and strategic concepts, theretofore mainly oriented toward guerrilla warfare. Though it is difficult to discern the attitudes of Chinese military leaders from their public utterances (which tend to shift with the Party line), Yeh appears to be a rather strong advocate of the need to utilize modern weaponry, including, if necessary, the purchase of sophisticated weapons from abroad. He has, however, also criticized those who indiscriminately attempt to incorporate foreign experience into Chinese military doctrine. He was perhaps most explicit in urging the utilization of science to advance Chinese military strength in an address made at the inauguration of the Academy of Military Sciences in Peking.[21] Yeh has served as academy president and political commissar since its establishment in March 1958.

A distinguishing characteristic of Yeh's career is that during the post-1949 period he has been abroad more often than any other prominent military leader except Ho Lung. (Marshal Ch'en I has traveled more frequently, but most of his trips have been in the capacity of foreign minister.) Yeh has led military delegations to the following countries: Burma, December 1956–January 1957; India, January–March 1958; Poland, October–November 1958; and North Vietnam, December 1961. He was also the deputy leader under P'eng Te-huai of the military delegation sent to Moscow in November–December 1957 for the 40th anniversary of the Russian Revolution. Further, he served on two other delegations which, though not officially military missions, doubtless provided him opportunities to inspect foreign military establishments; the first was in August–September 1960 when he accompanied Politburo member Li Fu-ch'un to Hanoi to attend a Party congress, and the other took place in September 1963 when he was a member of Liu Shao-ch'i's "friendship" delegation to North Korea.

By at least 1961 Yeh was serving as a Standing Committee member of the Military Affairs Committee (MAC) the Party's top military body. In this same year he was also identified as chairman of the MAC's Regulations Examination Subcommittee. Although he did not serve on the Second or Third CPPCC, Yeh was selected as a CCP representative on the Fourth National Committee and in January 1965, at the close of its first session, he was elected as a CPPCC vice-chairman, a position he still retains. Far more important, however, was his dramatic advance in the Party hierarchy in the early stages of the "great proletarian cultural revolution" in mid-1966. Yeh was elevated to membership on the Central Secretariat, most probably as the replacement for the purged PLA Chief-of-Staff, Lo Jui-ch'ing. Yeh is the only active military man on the Secretariat, the organ that implements Politburo policies. Shortly after he took up this new post, the CCP held its 11th Plenum (August 1966); no official announcements were made about changes in personnel, but by January 1967 Yeh was identified as a Politburo member.

In 1936 Yeh married Wei Kung-chih, one of the few women who survived the Long March. A CCP member since 1927, she studied in France and then received special training in Moscow in dramatics. After her return home she helped organize dramatic groups and the Gorky Drama School in Kiangsi. After the Long March she continued in this line of work as head of the "Anti-Japanese Dramatics Society" in Yenan, but nothing is known of her career after that. As of 1947 the Yeh's had two sons and two daughters. Yeh is also said to have been married to Tseng Hsien-chih, who was trained in Japan and who has been active in the National Women's Federation since 1949. There have been many reports from the non-Communist press in Hong Kong that Yeh has close family connections with persons living in Hong Kong and Macao, but none of these has been verified.

1. Edgar Snow, *Random Notes on Red China, 1936–1945* (Cambridge, Mass., 1957), p. 144.
2. *SCMP* 1139, p. 16.
3. *An Outline History of China* (Peking, 1958), p. 327.
4. Agnes Smedley, *The Great Road* (New York, 1956), p. 199.
5. *Ibid.*, p. 201.
6. J. Guillermaz, "The Nanchang Uprising," *The China Quarterly*, no. 11:165 (July–September 1962).
7. Smedley, p. 209.
8. Jerome Ch'en, *Mao and the Chinese Revolution* (London, 1965), p. 136.
9. Conrad Brandt, Benjamin Schwartz, and John K. Fairbank, *A Documentary History of Chinese Communism* (Cambridge, Mass., 1952), p. 124.
10. Snow, p. 144.
11. John E. Rue, *Mao Tse-tung in Opposition, 1927–1935* (Stanford, Calif., 1966), p. 240.
12. *Hung-se Chung-hua* (Red China), no. 2:4 (December 18, 1931).
13. *Kuang-ming jih-pao*, January 23, 1959.
14. Smedley, p. 310.
15. Ch'en, pp. 202–203.
16. Evans Fordyce Carlson, *Twin Stars of China* (New York, 1940), p. 279.
17. Chiang Kai-shek, *Soviet Russia in China* (New York, 1957), pp. 92–93.
18. Stuart Gelder, *The Chinese Communists* (London, 1946), pp. 73–102.
19. Snow, p. 144.
20. Ezra F. Vogel, *Canton under Communism* (Cambridge, Mass., 1969), pp. 52, 54–55.
21. Ellis Joffe, *Party and Army: Professionalism and Political Control in the Chinese Officer Corps, 1949–1964* (Cambridge, Mass. 1965), pp. 23–24.

Yeh Fei

(1909–   ; Fu-an hsien, Fukien). First secretary, Fukien CCP Committee; political commissar, Foochow Military Region; alternate member, CCP Central Committee.

A Communist guerrilla leader since the 1920's, Yeh Fei was among the more important commanders with the Communists' New Fourth Army during the Sino-Japanese War. He has spent the entire period since the PRC was established in his native Fukien, and since 1954 has been the Party's top official there. He was elected an alternate member of the Party Central Committee in 1956 and since 1958 has been political commissar of the Foochow Military Region. Yeh was born in Fu-an hsien, located in northeast Fukien near the coast and a little to the south of the Chekiang border. He began his career as a revolutionist in his late teens when he joined a band of guerrillas operating in the eastern sector of Fukien. In 1926 he helped organize a guerrilla base in eastern Fukien and he joined the CCP in the following year. In the early 1930's Yeh was connected with the Communists' Chinese Soviet Republic in Kiangsi where he graduated from a Red Army training center.

There are no further records of Yeh's career until 1937 when he was back in east Fukien as a guerrilla fighter. The scattered bands of Communist guerrillas that were active in east and central China prior to the outbreak of the Sino-Japanese War were all brought together in the fall of 1937 and organized into the Communists' New Fourth Army (see under Yeh T'ing, the commander). Officially created in September 1937, the army actually came into being in January 1938 when Yeh T'ing established his headquarters at Nanchang, the capital of Kiangsi. Previous to the organization of the army and as of about mid-1937 Yeh Fei was in command of a small unit of the "East Fukien Independent Division," a guerrilla force operating along the Fukien coast.[1] When the so-called division was incorporated into the New Fourth Army it became the core of the Sixth Regiment. By 1939 the regiment belonged to the First Detachment of the New Fourth Army, a unit then fighting in southwest Kiangsu not far south of Nanking in an area extending from Tan-yang on the Grand Canal to Li-shui above Shih-chiu Lake. The detachment was under the command of Ch'en I (q.v.), with Liu Yen as the political commissar. Rapidly growing in strength, the New Fourth Army, which had initially been composed of four detachments, was enlarged to six by November 1939 when its troops were divided into two major commands, the North and South Yangtze Commands based north and south of the river. When it was first organized Ch'en I headed the South Yangtze Command, which was composed of three detachments. These were based just south of the Yangtze in an area extending for some 100 miles between Tan-yang, Kiangsu, to Fan-ch'ang in Anhwei, southwest of the river city of Wuhu.[2] In the next year most of these troops and Ch'en I himself moved north of the river, leaving Yeh T'ing and Hsiang Ying (q.v.), his deputy, with the force attached to the headquarters staff based in south Anhwei at Ching-hsien. When late in 1940 these troops received orders from the Nationalists to move across the Yangtze and confine the operations of the New Fourth Army to those portions of the Third War Zone north of the river, the Communists and Nationalists came into conflict. The defeat suffered by the headquarters staff in early January 1941, known as the New Fourth Army Incident, saw the death of Hsiang Ying and the capture of Yeh T'ing.

This defeat brought about an extensive reorganization of the New Fourth Army, with Ch'en I becoming acting commander and Liu Shao-ch'i the political commissar. At this time (February 1941) the First Detachment, to which Yeh Fei belonged, became the First Division; the division was commanded by Su Yü (q.v.), with Yeh Fei serving as one of his deputy commanders. Concurrently, Yeh was commander and political commissar of the First Brigade of the First Division. From 1941 to 1946 Yeh served as Su's deputy, even taking over briefly as the division's acting commander in 1941. Ultimately, by early 1946, he succeeded Su Yü as the division commander.[3] During the war years the division was active in central Kiangsu (Su-chung) in an area bounded by the Yangtze on the south, the Grand Canal on the west, by a line between Huai-an and the coast on the north, and by the Pacific on the east.[4]

In the immediate postwar period Yeh's First Division was incorporated into the East China PLA, which changed its name to the East China Field Army in 1948 and to the Third Field Army (under Ch'en I) about January 1949. As it advanced southward along the coast, the Third Field Army took possession of all the coastal provinces except Kwangtung; the titles of Yeh's positions mark a part of the army's progress as it moved south. Thus, in April 1949 he became a member of the Soochow (Kiangsu) Military Control Commission. In August he held the same post on the Control Commission for Foochow, Fukien, and finally in October 1949, after the Third Field Army had occupied Amoy, he became chairman of the Amoy Military Control Commission. During these operations Yeh commanded the Third Field Army's 10th Army Group; some of his units fought their way into Kwangtung, but Yeh apparently remained in his native Fukien where he has since remained as a top military-political figure. By this time he had also assumed command of the Fukien Military District, a post he held until about 1954, and in August 1949 he was given his first major civil post, becoming a vice-governor of Fukien under Governor Chang Ting-ch'eng (q.v.). Chang, already a Party Central Committee member and Yeh's senior by some 10 years, was the top leader in Fukien in the early years of the PRC, but it soon became evident that Yeh was being groomed to succeed him. In 1949 he was identified as a member of the Fukien Party Committee, and by the spring of 1953 he was serving in place of Chang Ting-ch'eng as the acting secretary. Then, when Chang was transferred to Peking in the autumn of 1954 to become chief procurator in the national government, Yeh replaced him as the ranking secretary. He also succeeded Chang as the provincial governor in February 1955, retaining this post until he in turn was replaced by Chiang I-chen (q.v.) in February 1959. When Yeh relinquished the Fukien governorship he was elected as a member of the Fukien Provincial People's Government Council, another post he still holds.

Yeh has worked principally in Fukien since 1949, but he has also held posts at the regional and national levels. Early in 1950 the East China Military and Administrative Committee (ECMAC) was established to govern the provinces of Shantung, Kiangsu, Anhwei, Chekiang, and Fukien. Yeh was an ECMAC member from 1950 to 1953, continuing as a member in 1953–54 when the ECMAC was reorganized into the East China Administrative Committee. In the national government he was a member of the Overseas Chinese Affairs Commission under the Government Administration Council (the cabinet) from the establishment of the central government in 1949 until 1954. Then in September 1954, when the constitutional government came into being, Yeh was named to membership on the newly established National Defense Council, a position to which he was reappointed in April 1959 and January 1965. The new government had been brought into existence by the First NPC. Yeh was not then a deputy to the NPC, but following the death of a Fukien representative, he was named to replace him and assumed his seat in the legislative body for its third session in mid-1956. He served out the term of the First NPC but was not elected to the Second Congress, which opened in April 1959. In February 1960 he was named to the State Council's ad hoc Committee for Receiving and Resettling Returned Overseas Chinese Committee, established in response to the needs of Chinese returning from Indonesia in the winter of 1959–60, many of whom were resettled in Yeh's province.

Like most major provincial leaders, Yeh has engaged in extracurricular activities in addition to his more important assignments in Fukien. In 1951, for example, he was head of the Fukien branch of the East China Military and Political College. In the same year he was identified as a member of the Fukien chapter of the Sino-Soviet Friendship Association, and by 1958 he had become the chairman. He is also frequently reported making inspection tours in the province, as in early 1959 when he visited a number of the "people's communes" in Fukien. Moreover, he was chairman of the Fukien Committee of the CPPCC from February 1959 until late 1965. He has been a colonel-general (equivalent to a three-star U.S. Army general) since ranks were first given to PLA officers in 1955, and in the same year he was given one or more of the military decorations awarded for service in the Red armies from 1927 to 1950. He gained his highest post in the CCP in September 1956 when he was elected an alternate member of the Party Central Committee at the Eighth Party Congress in Peking. Yeh presented a written report before the Congress on the development of industry and agriculture in Fukien.

In the mid-fifties China's multi-provincial military regions were reorganized; Fukien and Kiangsi provinces were placed under the Foochow Military Region. By mid-1958 Yeh was identified as both commander and political commissar of the region, and although he relinquished the command role in 1960 to Han Hsien-ch'u (q.v.), he remains as the chief political officer. The military posts in Fukien are of particular importance, situated as they are across from the Nationalist-held islands of Matsu and Quemoy. The area, often referred to by the Communists as the "Fukien Front," came into international prominence in mid-1958 during the so-called "offshore islands crisis," when the Communists began to shell the Matsu Island group. In spite of his continuing responsibilities with the military forces in Fukien, Yeh's primary responsibilities seem to rest with the Fukien Provincial Party Committee where he continues as the first secretary. He received an additional Party assignment by October 1963 when he was identified as a secretary of the CCP's East China Bureau. His responsibilities to the bureau presumably require his presence on occasion in Shanghai where its headquarters are located. Yeh has been an occasional contributor to the national and provincial press. Two of his articles, both dealing with the Great Leap Forward, which was inaugurated in 1958, have appeared in the *JMJP* (May 22, 1958, and February 8, 1960).

---

1. *The Unquenchable Spark* (Peking, 1963), p. 122.
2. Chalmers A. Johnson, *Peasant Nationalism and Communist Power* (Stanford, Calif., 1962), pp. 124–125.

3. Chang-chia-k'ou, *Chin-Ch'a-Chi jih-pao* (Shansi-Chahar-Hopeh daily), March 4, 1946.
4. Johnson, p. 145.

Yeh T'ing

(1897–1946; Hui-yang, Kwangtung). Early Communist military leader; commander, New Fourth Army, 1937–1941.

One of the outstanding military leaders in modern Chinese revolutionary history, Yeh T'ing joined the CCP in 1925 and in the following year commanded a vanguard unit on the Northern Expedition. In mid-1927 he was one of the key figures in the Nanchang Uprising, which marked the birth of the Red Army, and at the end of the year he was commander-in-chief of Communist units during the abortive Canton Commune. Yeh left the CCP and spent the next several years abroad, but when the Sino-Japanese War began he was made commander of the New Fourth Army, the Communists' major force in east-central China. He was captured during the New Fourth Army Incident of January 1941 and was imprisoned by the Nationalists for the next five years. Immediately after his release in 1946 he died in an air crash while en route to Yenan. Throughout his career his military reputation far outweighed his importance as a Communist Party member.

Yeh, also known as Yeh Hsi-P'ing, is often referred to in Party documents by his *tzu*, Hsi-i. His family, native to Hui-yang (Hui-chou), a small town about 60 miles north of Hong Kong, were said to be of peasant origin. Nothing is known of Yeh's early upbringing, but his education suggests a family of some means. In his 16th year (c.1913) he entered a military primary school at Whampoa on the outskirts of Canton, and he then studied at the famous Paoting Military Academy. Yeh graduated with the sixth class of cadets in 1919. A number of his schoolmates, including Chang Yun-i (q.v.), Teng Yen-ta, and Hsueh Yueh, were destined to play key roles in public affairs and Yeh was to be in rather close association with them at one time or another. Soon after graduation, Yeh went to Chang-chou in south Fukien where he served in the forces commanded by Ch'en Chiung-ming, best known as the reformer governor of Kwangtung and commander of the powerful Kwangtung Army, who first assisted and then opposed Sun Yat-sen in the early 1920's. Yeh took part in Ch'en's military campaign which enabled the latter to return to Canton in 1920 and which in turn enabled Sun to return there to establish his "national government." It was also Ch'en Chiung-ming who invited the Marxist Ch'en Tu-hsiu (q.v.) to Kwangtung to direct provincial education the year before he came the first head of the CCP when it was established in mid-1921. Thus Yeh entered into China's revolutionary heartland when he returned to Kwangtung with Ch'en Chiung-ming, then the provincial governor. As a company commander in Ch'en's Kwangtung Army, Yeh was witness to the complex political and military maneuverings of Ch'en and Sun Yat-sen as the two men grew to be rivals. Before long the power struggle had spread to the Kwangtung Army, a part of which went over to Sun. One of the units supporting Sun was the First Division, in which Yeh's schoolmate Teng Yen-ta was an officer. In 1922 Teng became commander of a guards regiment in the First Division, a regiment formed to protect Sun's headquarters. In the same year Yeh became a battalion commander in this regiment, and he also joined Sun's KMT.

In becoming an officer in the guards regiment Yeh joined the group of active young political and military men who were then working closely with Sun Yat-sen. Chang Fa-k'uei and Hsueh Yueh were among his fellow officers, and he was a friend of Liao Chung-k'ai, the important leftist KMT leader who was a close adviser to Sun. It was the guards regiment which protected Sun during the time of dangerous intrigues carried on against him by Ch'en Chiung-ming, and when the latter's troops forced Sun and his wife (Sung Ch'ing-ling, q.v.) to flee from Canton in the summer of 1922, the regiment conducted them to a gunboat which took them to safety. Yeh's own reward was to be made chief-of-staff of the special Kwangtung Gendarmerie (of Sun's forces), which, in conjunction with Li Chi-shen's units and armies from Yunnan and Kwangsi, defeated Ch'en Chiung-ming's troops in Canton and thereby allowed Sun Yat-sen to return there.

In 1923, at the urging of Sun Yat-sen's Russian advisers, plans were set in motion to establish a modern military school, Whampoa, in which Chiang Kai-shek was to become the commandant and Liao Chung-k'ai the KMT representative. In connection with the general military training program, Yeh was sent to Moscow in 1924 to join the young Communist Chang T'ai-lei (q.v.) who had gone there the previous year with Chiang Kai-shek to investigate Russian military schools in preparation for the opening of the Whampoa Academy. Yeh joined Chang at the Communist University of the Toilers of the East in 1924, and then spent 10 months at the Red Army Military Academy. One of Yeh's academy classmates, and later a military colleague, was Nieh Jung-chen (q.v.), who had gone to Moscow after joining the CCP while a student in France and Belgium. In 1925 Yeh became a member of the Moscow branch of the CCP. He left for home that year, traveling by way of Berlin where he became acquainted with Chu Te (q.v.), then a student in Germany and also a CCP member.

Yeh's return home in the latter part of 1925 coincided approximately with the final elimination by Chiang Kai-shek and Li Chi-shen of Ch'en Chiung-ming's power in Kwangtung, and this in turn made it possible for the KMT to prepare for expanded military operations against the northern warlords. Yeh served briefly as chief of the Staff Office in Li Chi-shen's Fourth Army, and then in November 1925 he was appointed to command and train a regiment under Chang Fa-k'uei's 12th Division (which in turn was subordinate to the Fourth Army). Yeh's unit, initially known as the 34th Regiment, was soon redesignated the Independent Regiment.

Yeh's regiment, of which Communist Chou Shih-ti (q.v.) was chief-of-staff, became a focus of Communist interests, and in late March 1926 the CCP made plans to transfer a number of its members to his command from other units in the Fourth Army. Communist sources claim that about half of all cadres at the company level and above were CCP or Youth League members. As the regiment was readied to move north, the important Party official Chang Kuo-t'ao (q.v.) called a secret meeting of the Communists in the regiment and instructed them to seek further recruits as the regiment made its way into unconquered territory. In May 1926, before the Northern Expedition was formally launched, Yeh's Independent Regiment advanced into Hunan to assist Hunanese military leader T'ang Sheng-chih, whose forces were under attack by northern warlord Wu P'ei-fu. The strategy was to wrest from Wu P'ei-fu the key central China province of Hupeh, which contained the vital tricity complex of Wuhan where the Nationalist government was to center its authority. Yeh's highly successful campaigns during the earliest phase of the Northern Expedition gained for him a reputation as a skilled military strategist. Assisted by KMT and CCP activists already working in the Changsha area (see under Hsia Hsi), Yeh's men entered the Hunan capital in July 1926. The Northern Expedition Army then moved northward; Hanyang and Hankow were successfully assaulted in early September, and Wuchang, the third of the Wuhan cities, was besieged until October 10 when it surrendered. Chou Shih-ti, Yeh's chief-of-staff, wrote a detailed account of these events many years later, but the account suffers from the scant attention given to forces other than those led by Yeh.[1]

The Fourth Army was reorganized not long after the fall of Wuhan; Yeh was then promoted to command the 24th Division in Chang Fa-k'uei's 11th Army. Concurrently, he served as the Wuchang garrison commander. His forces were still well staffed with CCP members, several of whom were to become important Communist commanders in the years ahead. Among them was Lin Piao (q.v.), then a junior officer. In the early spring of 1927 other elements of the Northern Expedition captured Nanking, while still others (led by Chiang Kai-shek) took Shanghai. A few weeks later, in mid-April, Chiang established the "national capital" at Nanking, which, in effect, was a rival capital to that established a few months before by the Left-KMT in Wuhan. Shortly thereafter, in May, Yeh played the major role in the suppression of a revolt led by Hsia Tou-yin, a division commander in forces which were supposed to be supporting the Wuhan government. In mid-May, Hsia, in an action sometimes attributed to the machinations of Chiang Kai-shek, moved his troops from west Hupeh to within 25 miles of Wuhan where he was stopped by Yeh T'ing's hastily assembled forces, which were partially composed of Whampoa cadets.[2] In this endeavor he was assisted by Yun Tai-ying (q.v.), then a leading official at the Wuhan branch of the Whampoa Academy.

In the early summer of 1927 the military forces under the Left-KMT in Wuhan were again reorganized. Chang Fa-k'uei, one of the mainstays of the Wuhan government, was transferred to the Nanchang region of Kiangsi, his forces now designated the Second Front Army and headquartered to the north of Nanchang at Chiu-chiang (Kiukiang). In this area his troops were not defending the government at Wuhan from the northern warlords as much as they were protecting it against possible inroads from the headquarters of Chiang Kai-shek at Nanking. Yeh's 24th Division was then deployed near the north bank of the Yangtze in Hupeh, just to the north of Kiukiang on the south side of the river.

The redeployment of Yeh's troops coincided with the marked deterioration in relations between the CCP and the Left-KMT in Wuhan, a process which reached a crisis point in mid-July 1927 when Communists were dismissed from the Wuhan government. In response to this situation, the Communists began to prepare quickly for a coup, which, though engineered by the CCP, was carried out under the banner of the KMT. The coup on August 1 is known in Communist history as the Nanchang Uprising, and it is the date celebrated as the birth of the Red Army. The relatively abundant source materials[3] on the Uprising and its aftermath differ in minor details, but the basic outline is clear enough. Communist accounts written long after the event frequently credit it to the foursome of Chu Te, Chou En-lai, Ho Lung (not yet a Communist), and Yeh T'ing. The role of the last three is well established, but Chu Te's contributions were clearly less important, if only in contrast to Chou, Ho, and Yeh. Others on the scene included Chang Kuo-t'ao, Li Li-san, Nieh Jung-chen, Liu Po-ch'eng, Chou Shih-ti, Chou I-ch'ün (qq.v.), and T'an P'ing-shan. As this partial list of Communist notables suggests, the cream of the CCP

elite was then in the Nanchang-Kiukiang area, or not far away in other central China cities.

Yeh had a major hand in the planning for the uprising, which his division, in collaboration with Ho Lung's 20th Army and troops led by Chu Te in Nanchang, carried out on August 1. The city quickly came under Communist control, immediately after which a 25-member Revolutionary Committee was established. The committee members included Yeh, prominent members of the Left-KMT such as Mme. Sun Yat-sen and Ho Hsiang-ning (Mme. Liao Chung-k'ai), and Second Front Army Commander Chang Fa-k'uei (who of course did not sanction his inclusion and who a few days later drove the Communists from the city). Subordinate to the Revolutionary Committee, Yeh was a member of the Military Directorate (ts'an-mou-t'uan). The reorganized troops, who usurped the designation Second Front Army, were led by Ho Lung, the general commander (tsung-chih-hui), and by Yeh, the front-line general commander (ch'ien-ti tsung-chih-hui).

The number of troops which Ho, Yeh, and their colleagues were able to muster is a matter of dispute. The figure used by Communist historians, 30,000, is clearly too high; the total was probably closer to 20,000, and a figure which would include only effective, armed soldiers was probably even lower. In any case, the Communists were driven from Nanchang on August 4–5 with few casualties. The order of battle was as follows: Ho Lung's 20th Army had three divisions, and Yeh's troops, now known as the 11th Army, also consisted of three divisions. Chu Te's forces, though designated the Ninth Army, consisted of only one regiment. Nieh Jung-chen was the Party representative in Yeh's army; one of his divisions, the 25th, was commanded by Chou Shih-ti, but another, the 10th, defected to the opposition just as the main body of troops were moving southward from Nanchang. During the next six weeks they moved south through Kiangsi and Fukien, and finally, on September 23, they captured Swatow on the Kwangtung coast. Swatow was held for a week, during the course of which Yeh was wounded. The combination of defections, illness, and battle deaths on the march south and the subsequent defeat at Swatow had reduced the Communist troops by about 90 per cent. Yeh escaped with some 700 men to the countryside. Chou Shih-ti's 25th Division, which had been fighting a rearguard action north of Swatow, now became separated from Yeh and joined forces with Chu Te to retreat into Fukien, but Yeh merged his men with those led by Ho Lung and withdrew to Lu-feng on the Kwangtung coast where P'eng P'ai (q.v.) was organizing a small Communist soviet.

After a very brief stay in the Lu-feng area, Yeh went with Nieh Jung-chen and Chou En-lai to Hong Kong, and from there he was smuggled back to Canton just in time to take charge of the Communist military forces at the coup there on December 11, 1927. Yeh arrived only six hours before the coup began,[4] but he played a key role in the operation, which had been initially organized by Chang T'ai-lei (q.v.) and others. The famed Canton Commune was then established, and when Chang was killed on the 12th, Yeh emerged as the major figure on the scene.[5] On the next day the Communists were defeated and driven to the countryside after sustaining losses of over 2,000 men inflicted by Chang Fa-k'uei's army, which had come south from Kiangsi after the Nanchang Uprising. Some of the remnant Communist troops made their way to the Hailufeng Soviet where P'eng P'ai (q.v.) was in charge (see under Hsu Hsiang-ch'ien), but Yeh T'ing soon went abroad.

In the latter part of 1927 and early 1928, the CCP underwent a self-examination of the policies and tactics which had led to the string of disasters from the Nanchang Uprising to the collapse of the Canton Commune. Like virtually all the participants in these events, Yeh was the object of some criticism from the Party Center, then led by Ch'ü Ch'iu-pai. In terms of the Nanchang Uprising, and the subsequent march south to Kwangtung, it was suggested that he had been too conciliatory toward Chang Fa-k'uei, that his troops had not carried out enough political work among the peasantry as they moved through Kiangsi and Fukien, and that he had chosen the less strategic route for the latter part of the southward march. Yeh, in turn, was critical of the Party leadership, especially in regard to the Canton uprising. In his report on the coup, he charged that it had been badly organized, poorly supported, and that the Communists' military forces had been outnumbered and under-equipped. The masses "took no part in the uprising," nor did the peasants "help us by destroying the [rail] tracks." Finally, according to Yeh, the workers in Hong Kong "did not display the least sympathy for the insurrection."[6]

Agnes Smedley, who had close contacts with many key members of the CCP elite, claims that Yeh resigned from the CCP after the collapse of the Canton Commune. He is known to have gone to the USSR in 1928, and veteran Communist leader Wu Yü-chang (q.v.) has written that in the same year he and Yeh vacationed together on the Black Sea.[7] In 1929 he went to west Europe where he apparently remained for the next five years. There is little reporting on him during those years, but it is known that he and his wife spent some time in Paris, Berlin, and Vienna where Yeh is said to have studied science. In Yeh's official obituary there is a vaguely worded statement that he was in Fukien after the collapse of the insurrectionary Fukien People's Government (see under K'ai Feng), which existed from November 1933 to January 1934.

Not long after the outbreak of the Sino-Japanese War in mid-1937, negotiations began between the KMT and the CCP to activate a Communist army—ultimately designated the New Fourth Army—in the lower Yangtze Valley (see under Ch'in Pang-hsien and Hsiang Ying). In this region there had been no unified Communist military force to compare with the units Mao Tse-tung had assembled in north Shensi after the Long March. Rather, in the Yangtze area and to the south there were a number of Communist-controlled guerrilla bands which had been left behind when the Long March forces left Kiangsi in October 1934. These semi-independent units were widely scattered in small pockets in Chekiang, Fukien, Kwangtung, Kiangsi, Hunan, Hupeh, Anhwei, and Honan. Leadership of these bands was under Hsiang Ying, Ch'en I, Teng Tzu-hui, Su Yü, T'an Chen-lin, Chang Ting-ch'eng (qq.v.), and others. These men had been fighting for survival (see under Ch'en I), and had been largely out of touch with Mao's headquarters for three years. It is not clear how Yeh came into the picture as the nominee to head an army that would bring together these scattered forces. All the above-mentioned leaders were long-time CCP members and all had extensive guerrilla warfare experience, which Yeh lacked almost entirely. However, Yeh had been a Party member in the twenties when he was well known to the CCP leadership. He also enjoyed a good reputation as a military commander, made during the Kwangtung campaigns of the twenties and on the Northern Expedition when he was associated with a number of KMT officers. For example, his Paoting classmate Hsueh Yueh was an important commander in the Third War Zone where the New Fourth Army was to operate. Edgar Snow, in discussing Yeh's appointment, suggests that it may have been "in the nature of a face-saving arrangement" for Chiang Kai-shek, who, by accepting Yeh, "avoided completely sanctioning" Hsiang Ying,[8] the veteran Communist who became deputy commander and political commissar of the New Fourth Army and who also headed the CCP apparatus in the areas where the army operated. In brief, Yeh seems to have been a candidate acceptable to both sides.

Yeh was appointed New Fourth Army commander in October 1937, but the army did not come into being until January 1938 when he established his headquarters in Nanchang. In early March he arrived in Yenan for conferences with the CCP hierarchy, but he was soon back to his troops, which went into operation in April. The army initially had four detachments, the Fourth operating north of the Yangtze, first in north Hupeh and then in central Anhwei (see under Chang Yun-i). The other three detachments operated in Anhwei and Kiangsu south of the Yangtze along important communications lines close to Wuhu and Nanking. Brief descriptions of these detachments are found in the biographies of Ch'en I, Chang Ting-ch'eng, and T'an Chen-lin, the respective commanders of the First, Second, and Third Detachments. When the army was first activated it consisted of about 12,000 men, the largest contingent of which had previously been in the old Communist Oyüwan base (see under Chang Kuo-t'ao).[9] Early in its history Yeh moved his headquarters to Ching-hsien, some 50 miles south of Wuhu.

Communist descriptions of the New Fourth Army make no mention of any discord in the Yeh-Hsiang team. However, Agnes Smedley published a revealing account based on a visit to the army's area of operations in the latter part of 1938. According to her, Yeh "had left the Army and had asked . . . Chiang Kai-shek to relieve him of his command." The reason, in her words, was that the Nationalist government "held him responsible for the Army, yet rejected his requests for funds and equipment to enable it to meet the ever-growing Japanese offensive against it. On the other hand," she continued, "the Communist leaders, particularly [Deputy Commander] Hsiang Ying, conducted intrigues which prevented Yeh from exercising any control over the Army."[10] However, the difficulties between Yeh and Hsiang (described in further detail in the latter's biography) were apparently soon patched up.

Miss Smedley is also the source for a strikingly unusual event that involved Yeh in 1939. Early in the war Kao Chün-t'ing, the commander of the above-mentioned Fourth Detachment (the only important unit north of the Yangtze) developed into a "local militarist." According to this account, Kao, previously a key official in the old Oyüwan Soviet, was guilty of a wide range of corrupt practices. In late 1938 Chang Yun-i (q.v.) was sent to investigate Kao's activities. Chang was unable to rectify the situation, but then in the spring of 1939 Yeh himself went to Kao's headquarters. He placed Kao under arrest and brought him to trial before his own soldiers, who voted for a death sentence. In June 1939 Yeh ordered the sentence carried out. This case appears to have been unique, because no other senior commander in the Communist military establishment is known to have been executed during the course of the Sino-Japanese War.

Even more serious troubles than the Kao affair arose for the New Fourth Army in 1939 as KMT-CCP cooperation in the early war period gave way to a serious deterioration in relations. This political rivalry led to an incident in June 1939 in P'ing-chiang hsien in the Communists' old Hunan-Hupeh-Kiangsi base; T'u Cheng-k'un, the secretary of the CCP Hunan-Hupeh-Kiangsi Special Committee and concurrently head of the New Fourth Army's P'ing-chiang Liaison Office, was killed together with several of his colleagues.[11] Other incidents continued to strain relations for the next year. Alarmed at the growing strength of the New Fourth Army, in the fall of 1940 Nationalist authorities ordered Yeh to move his troops north of the river. The first deadline for the move was November 1940, but this was extended to mid-December. The New Fourth Army was then divided into commands north and south of the Yangtze headed by Chang Yun-i and Ch'en I, respectively, but by September most of the Army's forces had moved north of the river and were operating in various districts of Hupeh, Anhwei, Kiangsu, and Chekiang, extending beyond the bounds of Ku Chu-t'ung's Third War Zone into the Fifth War Zone commanded by Li Tsung-jen. Thus, only Yeh's headquarters force remained south of the Yangtze. The route by which the Communists were to cross the river is in dispute, the Communists claiming that the Nationalists were forcing them to cross the river in places where they were most in danger of attack from the Japanese. In December, as they were preparing for the move, Yen visited the headquarters of the Third War Zone to fix the final route. His troops finally started to move by early January 1941, with Yeh himself leading three regiments and a training detachment. When his men ran into Nationalist opposition, Yeh left his troops on invitation from Nationalist General Shangkuan Yun-hsiang, then the acting Third War Zone commander, who asked him to visit his headquarters for the final arrangements. Yeh was at the Nationalist headquarters when he was apprehended and put under arrest.[12] Thus he was not with his troops when they were ambushed and many of them, including Hsiang Ying and Yuan Kuo-p'ing, director of the Political Department, were killed. The event, known as the New Fourth Army (or South Anhwei) Incident, aroused a storm of protest from both sides, and the conflicting charges by the KMT and the CCP have largely obscured the reasons that triggered the Nationalist attack. In support of one of their claims, however, it should be noted that the Communists, when ambushed, were not actually heading north from Ching-hsien. Rather, they were encircled at Mao-lin, a few miles southwest of their original base at Ching-hsien.

The KMT case against the Communists is conveniently contained in a handbook published in New York in 1943 under the auspices of the Nationalist government. This source also reproduces extracts from a speech made by Chiang Kai-shek a few days after the incident.[13] The Generalissimo stated: "I have often compared the army to a family wherein I look upon the soldiers under me as a father regards his children. If his children behave well the father feels they reflect honor upon him; if badly, they disgrace him." The Communist reply (later attributed to Mao) is markedly different: the New

Fourth Army had been "treacherously attacked by the pro-Japanese clique [of the KMT hierarchy]."[14] At the time of the incident, the New Fourth Army numbered about 100,000 men, 9,000 of whom were killed, wounded, or captured during the incident. Predictably, Chiang Kai-shek immediately ordered the army disbanded, and for the remaining war years it was, in Nationalist eyes, an illegal military unit. Equally predictable, the Communist leadership in Yenan immediately reorganized the high command for the New Fourth Army. Ch'en I, whose biography contains a history of the army in the ensuing years, was made acting commander, and Liu Shao-ch'i became political commissar. Yeh T'ing was court-martialed for insubordination and a "plot to stage a revolt." He was first imprisoned by the Nationalists at Shang-jao, Kiangsi, next in En-shih, Hupeh, and then in Kweilin, Kwangsi. Immediately after the war he was sent to a prison in Chungking. In the KMT-CCP negotiations following the Japanese surrender, the Communists made repeated demands for his release. He was finally set free on March 4, 1946. The next day Yeh requested that the Party Center "restore" (hui-fu) his CCP membership. The request was immediately granted, but a month later (April 8), while en route to Yenan with Wang Jo-fei, Ch'in Pang-hsien, and Teng Fa (qq.v.), he was killed in an air crash in northwest Shansi.

Chang Kuo-t'ao has described Yeh as a very able man with a great interest in military affairs, but one who was bored by staff work which he preferred to delegate to subordinates. He further described Yeh's character in terms of pride, independence, and arrogance.[15] Chang Fa-k'uei, under whom Yeh served before the Nanchang Uprising, had a high regard for Yeh, depicting him as being "alert, intelligent, and a good commander." Chang further commented that he considered Yeh to be loyal to the Nationalists at the time of the Nanchang Uprising, even though he knew Yeh was a CCP member.[16] The treatment accorded Yeh by Communist historians after his death stands in contrast to that given Hsiang Ying, who died in the New Fourth Army Incident. In fact, Maoist historians have placed much of the blame for the debacle upon Hsiang (see under Hsiang). On the other hand, Yeh died a hero in the eyes of the Communist press. His career is reviewed by friends, relatives, and colleagues in a volume published soon after the 1946 air accident, a source which also covers the lives of the three other leading Communists who died with him.[17]

Yeh's wife, Li Hsiu-wen, the daughter of a well-to-do gentry family from Nan-hai, Kwangtung, was a graduate of a women's normal college in Canton. She married Yeh in 1926 when he was training the Independent Regiment for the Northern Expedition. She was with her husband in Europe during the early thirties, and during the war years she lived in Macao and Kweilin. She rejoined her husband immediately after his release from prison in Chungking in 1946, but a month later, in her 40th year, she was killed in the airplane accident which took her husband's life. The Yeh's had nine children; one of them died as a youth and two others died in the air crash. Yeh had a brother who at the time of the New Fourth Army Incident was captured and interned. He later escaped and when met by an American Office of War Information official in the 1940's, he was badly crippled from his prison experiences.[18] Nothing further is known about him.

1. "Szu-pa" pei-nan lieh-shih chi-nien-ts'e (In memory of the martyrs who died in the accident of "April 8"; Chungking, 1946), pp. 333–340.

2. Robert C. North and Xenia J. Eudin, M. N. Roy's Mission to China (Berkeley, Calif., 1963), pp. 98–99.

3. J. Guillermaz, "The Nanchang Uprising," The China Quarterly, no. 11:161–168 (July–September 1962); C. Martin Wilbur, "The Ashes of Defeat," ibid., no. 18:3–54 (April–June 1964); Wei Hung-yun, ed., "Pa-i" ch'i-i (The "August First" uprising; Wuhan, 1957) pp. 8–25; Ti-erh-tz'u kuo-nei ko-ming chan-cheng shih-ch'i shih-shih lun-ts'ung (Accounts of the second revolutionary civil war; Peking, 1956), pp. 1–11.

4. Harold R. Isaacs, The Tragedy of the Chinese Revolution, 2nd rev. ed. (Stanford, Calif., 1961), p. 287.

5. Hsiao Tso-liang, "Chinese Communism and the Canton Soviet of 1927," The China Quarterly, no. 30:49–78 (April–June 1967).

6. Isaacs, pp. 283, 287–288.

7. "Szu-pa" pei-nan lieh-shih chi-nien-ts'e, p. 191.

8. Edgar Snow, The Battle for Asia (New York, 1941), p. 134.

9. Lyman P. Van Slyke, ed., The Chinese Communist Movement: A Report of the United States War Department, July 1945 (Stanford, Calif., 1968), p. 83; Israel Epstein, The People's War (London, 1939), p. 261.

10. Agnes Smedley, Battle Hymn of China (New York, 1943), pp. 257–259.

11. Chalmers A. Johnson, Peasant Nationalism and Communist Power (Stanford, Calif., 1962), p. 129; Selected Works of Mao Tse-tung (Peking, 1965), II, 257–261; Hu-nan ko-ming lieh-shih chuan (Biographies of Hunan revolutionary martyrs; Changsha, 1952), pp. 87–88.

12. Israel Epstein, The Unfinished Revolution in China (Boston, 1947), pp. 190–191.

13. The Chinese Ministry of Information, comp., China Handbook, 1937–1943 (New York, 1943), pp. 327–332.

14. *Selected Works of Mao Tse-tung* (Peking, 1965), II, 451–458.

15. Modern China Project, Columbia University, New York, Howard L. Boorman, director.

16. Letter from Chang Fa-k'uei to General Samuel B. Griffith, made available to the authors, 1966.

17. *"Szu-pa" pei-nan lieh-shih chi-nien-ts'e*, pp. 8–10, *passim*.

18. Agnes Smedley, *The Great Road* (New York, 1956), p. 378.

Yen Hung-yen

(c.1908–   ; Shensi). First secretary, Yunnan Party Committee; alternate member, CCP Central Committee.

A veteran of Communist-led guerrilla warfare in Shensi from the mid-1920's, Yen Hung-yen remained in this area until the postwar period when he was a political officer with troops that won important victories in north-central and southwest China in the late forties. He served as a senior Communist political and military official in Szechwan during the first decade of Communist rule, and since 1959 he has been a top official in Yunnan. Yen was elected an alternate member of the Party Central Committee in 1956.

In 1924, while still a teenager, Yen entered the army of a local warlord in north Shensi, and he joined the Party a year later while still with this army. In the fall of 1927, following the break between the Communists and the Nationalists, Yen began organizing local units of Shensi peasant guerrillas into a Red Army unit. Fighting in the Shensi-Shansi border area, in the years after 1927 he organized a small band of fighters known as the "west Shansi guerrilla band." Late in 1931 he led his men across the border to join forces in Shensi with Communist guerrilla units led by Liu Chih-tan (q.v.). Liu, a graduate of the Whampoa Military Academy, had joined the Party in 1925 and returned to his native Shensi to work with the peasant guerrillas in 1928. A brief history of Liu's army is contained in his biography; the army was active in north Shensi by the time Mao Tse-tung's Long Marchers arrived there in the fall of 1935 and united with Liu's troops. Yen probably also became a member of the merged army, for by 1936 he was identified as a commander of the 30th Red Army. The 30th Army initially belonged to the forces under Chang Kuo-t'ao and Hsu Hsiang-ch'ien, which moved out of the Oyüwan Soviet in the fall of 1932 and reached north Shensi in 1936.

Yen's wartime record is not well documented, but he apparently remained for most of this period in his native Shensi. He was a deputy from Fu-hsien, Shensi, to the Second Assembly of the Shensi-Kansu-Ninghsia Border Region Government, which first met in Yenan in November 1941. (Fu-hsien is located on the Lo River 40 miles south of Yenan.) Yen also attended the second session of the Second Assembly in December 1944. In the postwar period he was assigned to the Shansi-Hopeh-Shantung-Honan Field Army, serving by 1947 as director of the Political Department of Army's Third Column. The Third Column, under the command of Ch'en Hsi-lien (q.v.), took part in the successful Huai-Hai Campaign in north-central Anhwei in late 1948 and early 1949. By this time Yen was deputy political commissar of the Third Column, and when the column was designated the Third Army Corps in 1949 (subordinate to Liu Po-ch'eng's Second Field Army), Yen was appointed director of the Corps' Political Department. Liu's Field Army won a number of key victories in central China during the spring of 1949, and in the latter part of the year and early 1950, it was largely responsible for the conquest of southwest China.

Yen was with the Second Field Army when it moved into Szechwan in late 1949. He remained in Szechwan, China's most populous province, for a decade, fulfilling the triple functions of military, Party, and government administrator. Unlike any other province, the Communists divided Szechwan into four geographic units until the traditional boundaries were restored in August 1952. From early 1950 until August 1952, the government organ where Yen operated was known as the East Szechwan People's Administrative Office. Under this office, Yen held the ranking administrative and judicial posts, serving as chairman of the office and as chief justice of the People's Court. In the military field he was deputy political commissar of the East Szechwan Military District from 1950 to 1952, and under the Party Committee for East Szechwan he was first deputy secretary by late 1951. Although a very important official in East Szechwan, Yen was subordinate to Hsieh Fu-chih (q.v.), who was secretary of the East Szechwan Party Committee and the political commissar of the Military District.

Although Yen's major contributions in the early 1950's were in East Szechwan, he was also a member of the Southwest Military and Administrative Committee (SWMAC), the organ that governed Szechwan, Kweichow, Yunnan, and Sikang. Like the East Szechwan Administrative Office, the headquarters of the SWMAC was located in Chungking. When the SWMAC was reorganized into the Southwest Administrative Committee in February 1953, Yen continued to serve with the new organization until it was abolished in November 1954. In August 1952 the four separate units that had governed Szechwan were combined into a single unit, with Yen assuming important posts, mainly subordinate to Li Ching-ch'üan (q.v.), the top leader in Szechwan after 1952 and a Politburo member after 1958. Yen's principal posts were: vice-governor of Szechwan, 1952–1959; first deputy political commissar of the Szechwan Military District (under Political Commissar Li Ching-ch'üan), 1952–?; secretary of the Szechwan Party Committee (under First Secretary Li Ching-ch'üan), by late 1956–1959; deputy political commissar of the Chengtu Military Region (responsible for Szechwan), 1957–1959. Yen was also a deputy from Szechwan to the First and Second NPC's (1954–1964), the legislative council that brought the constitutional government into being at its initial session in September 1954. However, after his transfer in 1959 to Yunnan (see below), he was elected as a Yunnan deputy to the Third NPC, which opened its first session in December 1964.

Yen's lengthy military record received official recognition in 1954 and 1955. When the National Defense Council was created in September 1954, Yen was named as a member. He was reappointed to this military advisory body in April 1959 and January 1965. In September 1955, when national military honors were first awarded, he received all three of the top awards (the Orders of August First, Independence and Freedom, and Liberation) for service from 1927 to 1950. Personal military ranks were also created in 1955, although it was not until September 1957 that Yen was identified as a colonel-general, equivalent to a three-star general in the U.S. Army.

Yen was elected an alternate member of the Party Central Committee at the Eighth CCP Congress in September 1956. Three years later (September 1959), after nearly a decade in Szechwan, he was transferred to neighboring Yunnan to assume the first secretaryship of the Party Committee. Yen replaced his former superior, Hsieh Fu-chih, who was made the new minister of Public Security in Peking. In Szechwan, Yen had spread his activities rather evenly among the various duties involving military, governmental, and Party affairs. His work in Yunnan has apparently centered more narrowly on Party activities, but by the spring of 1964 he was identified as a "responsible official" of the Kunming Military region.

Although Szechwan and Yunnan are situated in rather remote parts of China, Yen has had a limited involvement in foreign affairs. While still in Szechwan he had participated in a large delegation drawn from all parts of China, which visited North Korea to "comfort" Chinese troops stationed there. The delegation visited Korea in October–December 1953 under the general leadership of Ho Lung; Yen was a deputy leader of one of the sub-delegations. In 1960 and 1963, Yen was a vice-chairman of two closely related

ad hoc committees that had been set up to receive and resettle returning overseas Chinese. The first of these, established in February 1960, was charged with the task of resettling the thousands of Chinese returning from Indonesia, where they allegedly had been mistreated by the Indonesians. In similar circumstances, a special committee to resettle Chinese from India was formed in April 1963, not long after the border conflict between India and China in late 1962. In addition to such short-term ventures, Yen has been in contact regularly with foreign visitors because Kunming, the Yunnan capital, is frequently visited by foreigners from Southeast Asia as well as Chinese leaders en route abroad.

Yü Ch'iu-li

(Szechwan?). Minister of Petroleum Industry.

Yü Ch'iu-li, a veteran army officer and government administrator, apparently began his career about 1934 when he was a personal guard (*ching-wei-yuan*) for Jen Pi-shih (q.v.), the chief Party official in the Communists' Hunan-Kiangsi base.[1] The Communist army there, known as the Sixth Army Corps, was commanded by Hsiao K'o (q.v.). In the fall of 1934 the Sixth Corps moved from the Hunan-Kiangsi base to northeast Kweichow where it joined forces with Ho Lung's Second Army Corps, and in the subsequent months the joint force established the Hunan-Hupeh-Szechwan-Kweichow base. This locale, added to the fact that Yü was later a Szechwan deputy to the NPC, suggests that he may be a native of Szechwan. He was probably no more than a teenager and of no particular importance in this period, because when the Communists created national military honors in 1955 (covering service from 1927 to 1950), Yü's award was only for the final period (1945–1950), an indication that he had not achieved a very significant position before that date.

Although documentation is lacking, it is probable that Yü made the Long March with Jen and then worked with the Red Armies in northwest China. In any event, he was in the northwest at the close of the civil war with the Nationalists, because when the Tsinghai Military District was formally established on October 1, 1949, Yü was named as deputy political commissar under Commissar Liao Han-sheng (q.v.). Sometime in the early 1950's Yü was transferred from northwest to southwest China and by July 1952 was director of the Rear Services (logistics) Department of the Southwest Military Region. He remained in this position until at least early 1954.

In 1955 the Communists created personal military ranks and awarded national military honors for past performances in the Red Armies. Yü was given a first class Order of Liberation (September 1955), implying a significant role in the civil war against the Nationalists in the late 1940's. At about this same time he was also made a lieutenant-general in the PLA, equivalent to a two-star general in the U.S. Army. Less than a year later, in August 1956, Yü was appointed as director of the Finance Department of the PLA. However, he only held the post until November 1957 when he was named as political commissar of the General Rear Services Department of the PLA. Shortly afterwards, Yü changed jobs with Li Chü-k'uei, succeeding Li as minister of the Petroleum Industry in February 1958 during a general governmental reorganization. In the following month Li replaced Yü as political commissar in the Rear Services post. Thus by the winter of 1957–58 Yü had given up his active posts in the PLA and turned to a purely civilian career.

Although the head of one of the most vital ministries, Yü has been infrequently reported in the national press. Interestingly, when he has been mentioned it has often been when he was away from Peking. For example, he was reported in Szechwan in April 1958, in the Harbin (Manchuria) area in March 1960, and again in Szechwan in July 1960. Yü's importance in the hierarchy was also suggested in November 1960 when he was in Wuhan—virtually assuring that he attended the important Sixth Party Plenum, at which time the Party decided to slow down the pace and the severity of the communalization of China.

Yü was elected a deputy from Szechwan to the Second NPC (1959–1964) and was re-elected from the same province to the Third NPC. At the first session of the Third NPC (December 1964–January 1965), Yü spoke before the Congress on the achievements of the petroleum industry in the previous years. Like so many other ranking government officials, he attends nationwide conferences, serves on funeral committees for colleagues, and authors articles for the Communist press and publications. For example, he was a member of the preparatory committee for a national conference of "advanced producers," and when the conference was held in October 1959 served on the presidium. He was a funeral committee member for two veteran political officers, Chu Ming and Kan Szu-ch'i, who died, respectively, in January 1964 and February 1964. And he was also on the funeral committee for P'eng T'ao (the Minister of Chemical Industry) with whom Yü had served at the cabinet level.

Significant articles authored by Yü include: "The Petroleum Industry Made a Great Leap Forward," Hong Kong *Ta-kung pao*, October 1, 1958; "Look at the Overall Trends and the Main Trends, Distinguish the Direction of the Wind, and Mobilize the Active Elements," *Hung-ch'i* (Red flag), November 1, 1959; "Accelerate the Tempo of Development in the Petroleum Industry" *JMJP*, November 18, 1959.

---

1. *Hung-ch'i p'iao-p'iao* (Red flag fluttering; Peking, 1957), V, 257.

Yü I-ch'uan

(c.1924–   ; Yunnan). Former Party and government administrator in Yunnan; secretary, Chekiang Party Control Commission.

A native of Yunnan, Yü I-ch'uan is one of the youngest of the Chinese Communist leaders. According to Japanese sources, he graduated from a Communist Party school; details are not available, but to judge from his age the schooling must have taken place in Yenan during the Sino-Japanese War.

In 1949 the Second Field Army under the command of Liu Po-ch'eng and Teng Hsiao-p'ing fought its way against the Nationalists through central China and into the southwest. Yü was serving as a deputy director of the political department of the Fourth Group Army within the field army. His native Yunnan was captured in December 1949, and he was assigned as director of the Political Department for the Yunnan Military District.

As in the case of many PLA officers—and especially political officers—Yü soon gave up his military assignments in favor of positions within the governmental and Party hierarchies. He served briefly in 1950 as a member of the Yunnan Provincial People's Government, but his main work in the early 1950's was with the Party. In 1951–52 he headed the Yunnan Party Committee's Propaganda Department; another post he assumed in 1951 was as a deputy secretary of the Party Committee. Over the next few years Yü climbed the hierarchical ladder—by early 1955 he advanced to second secretary and then in mid-1956 became a secretary, serving under First Secretaries Hsieh Fu-chih and (from 1959) under Yen Hung-yen, the former a full member of the Party Central Committee and the latter an alternate member.

From February 1955 to July 1959, Yü was a vice-chairman of the First Yunnan Committee of the CPPCC, another post he held under Hsieh Fu-chih. The reason Yü was not re-elected to this position in 1959 was probably because he had assumed a much more important post in the interim; in mid-1957, Yunnan Governor Kuo Ying-ch'iu was attacked for incompetence by the Yunnan Party press. When the next provincial elections were held (March 1958), Yü was named to succeed Kuo. In 1959, Yü was elected as a deputy from Yunnan to the Second NPC (1959–1964) and was then re-elected in 1964 to the Third NPC, which held its first session in December 1964–January 1965.

It was apparent that by the late 1950's Yü, who was both governor and second ranking secretary of the provincial Party Committee, was the most important official in Yunnan with the exception of First Party Secretary Yen Hung-yen. As an official of this stature, Yü was mentioned in the provincial press with considerable frequency; he was reported making inspection trips within the province, attending meetings of the Party or government, or attending functions in celebration of Communist holidays. Furthermore, because the Yunnan capital (Kunming) is a major point of entry into or exit from south China, he was often in the company of distinguished visitors from abroad (such as Burmese leader Ne Win in March 1961) or high-level Chinese Party leaders en route abroad (like P'eng Chen who passed through Kunming in September 1962 en route to Vietnam).

Until mid-1963 the press reported Yü's activities in Yunnan with regularity; then, early in 1964, Yunnan Vice-governor Liu Ming-hui was identified as the acting governor. In May 1964 Yü made one last appearance as the governor and in September of that year was re-elected from Yunnan to the Third NPC. However, in the following month (October 1964) he was suddenly transferred to Chekiang where he assumed a new position as the head of the Chekiang Party Control Commission, the organization charged with the task of maintaining intra-Party discipline and supervision. Not long after, in February 1965, Yü was formally replaced as the Yunnan governor by Chou Hsing, a veteran Party official who has specialized in public security work.

In private life Yü is married to Wang Ching, who has been a member of the Executive Committee of the National Women's Federation since the third national congress of the Federation in September 1957.

Yü I-fu

(c.1902–   ; T'ai-an, Liaoning). Party official, Kirin Province.

Yü I-fu was born in T'ai-an, near the city of Mukden (Shenyang) in Liaoning province. He graduated from Nan-k'ai Middle School in Tientsin and later from Yenching in Peking. American Communist journalist Anna Louise Strong has provided an account of Yü's early career, based on an interview with him in 1946. Following the Mukden Incident in 1931, at which time Yü was serving as the principal of a high school in Tsitsihar, he abandoned his career as an educator to join the forces of Manchurian warlord Chang Hsueh-liang.[1] By the mid-1930's he took a prominent part in a number of the organizations that were trying to awaken China to the realities of Japanese incursions into China. The most famous and significant of these organizations was the National Salvation Association. Also sometime in the mid-1930's Yü became a Party member, after which he served as the chief editor of the central China branch of the Communist New China News Agency. From this work he became connected with the Communist New Fourth Army in east-central China, serving during the war as head of the "Liaison Department."

It was also during the war period that Yü spent some time in Hong Kong. Chow Ching-wen, a prominent member of the China Democratic League who left Communist China in the mid-1950's, has described his contact with Yü in Hong Kong in 1941. Chow and Yü were fellow Manchurians and, according to Chow, old friends. Presumably on the basis of this friendship, Yü approached Chow in Hong Kong for contributions to the work of the "Anti-Japanese United Front," which Chow Ching-wen interpreted to be a request from the Communists.[2]

At the end of the war against Japan, Yü was assigned to his native Manchuria. There, from 1946, he served as governor of those portions of Nunchiang under Communist control. Nunchiang was one of the provinces in Manchuria created by the Nationalists after the war but never really occupied by them. The capital was located at Tsitsihar (Lung-chiang). He remained in this post until the winter of 1948–49 when Nunkinag was incorporated into Heilungkiang province, with Yü continuing as the governor of the reorganized province. Although already a Communist Party member, Yü was the leader in 1947 of the Tsitsihar branch of the China Democratic League, ostensibly a political party devoid of control by the CCP. From 1946 to 1949 he also served as a member of the Northeast Administrative Committee (NEAC), the governmental apparatus in charge of all Manchuria, the chairman of which was Party administrator Lin Feng (q.v.). When the NEAC was reorganized into the Northeast People's Government in August 1949 (by which time Manchuria was completely in Communist hands), Yü continued to serve as a member. In the following month, he traveled to Peking to take part in the first session of the First CPPCC, the conference that brought the PRC into existence; Yü attended as a delegate from the "Northeast Liberated Areas." Although he was not selected for membership on the permanent National Committee of the CPPCC, he apparently was associated with the CPPCC branch in Heilungkiang. This assumption is made on the basis of the fact that he attended the third session of the CPPCC (October–November 1951) as a representative of local branches of the national organization.

Like many of his colleagues, Yü was active in the Sino-Soviet Friendship Association (SSFA) in the early days of the PRC. When the organization was founded in Peking in October 1949, he was named to membership on the first Executive Board, but he has not had any apparent connection with the organization since December 1954 when he attended its second national conference. Earlier, during the period from 1949 to 1952, Japanese sources identified him as a "responsible official" of the SSFA in Manchuria. His other extracurricular activities in Manchuria in the early 1950's included work with the peace movement. He was the chairman of the Heilungkiang Branch of the China Peace Committee as well as a member of the Northeast Work Committee of the same organization.

In November 1952, he was succeeded as the governor of Heilungkiang by Chao Te-tsun, who was subsequently purged (1955) as an accomplice of Politburo member Kao Kang (q.v.). Yü was reassigned to Peking where, by the spring of 1953, he was serving under Li Wei-han as a deputy director of the Party Central Committee's United Front Department. Yü's extensive contacts with the educational field made him a logical choice for this department, whose principal activity is to gain the cooperation of China's non-Communists, especially the intellectuals. For the next several years he was reported in Peking with considerable regularity as a united front specialist, often attending forums held for the guidance and direction of the non-Party intellectuals. He was given a closely related position in March 1956 when a Study (*Hsueh-hsi*) Committee was established under the auspices of the National Committee of the CPPCC. As in the case of the United Front Department, Yü served here directly under Li Wei-han. The chief purpose of the Study Committee was to offer forums and short-term classes where the non-CCP intellectuals heard lectures and discussed Party policies.

Apart from his post in the United Front Department, Yü served in the mid-1950's in the national legislative body, the First NPC. He was a deputy from Harbin to the First NPC (1954–1959) but was not re-elected to the Second NPC, which first convened in April 1959. Yü was transferred back to Manchuria by March 1960 at which time he was elected as a secretary of the Kirin Provincial Party Committee, a position subordinate to First Secretary Wu Te, an alternate member of the Central Committee. Yü continues to hold this post. He received a government post in the Kirin Provincial People's Council in August 1962 when he was elected as a member of the government Council. Yü once again received an assignment at the national level in late 1964, being named a "specially invited personage" to the Fourth National Committee of the CPPCC and, in addition, at the close of the first session of the National Committee in January 1965 he was selected to serve on the permanent Standing Committee.

Yü is the author of a 22-page pamphlet that was published in 1946 while he was serving as governor of the Communist-controlled portions of Nunchiang province. It was entitled *Which Path Should the People of the Northeast Follow?*[3] and it exhorted Manchurian youths to follow the path of "new democracy" as opposed (in Yü's words) to the "fascist path" of the KMT. Since the founding of the PRC, he has also contributed articles to the Party press. The *Hei-lung-chiang jih-pao* (Heilungkiang daily) of March 25, 1951, carried a summary by Yü of the work of the provincial government in 1950 and plans for 1951. And for the *JMJP* of September 21, 1960, and January 20, 1962, he wrote on problems of leadership at the hsien level and on the necessity to carry on the traditions of the Party.

1. Anna Louise Strong, *Tomorrow's China* (New York, 1948), p. 100.
2. Chow Ching-wen, *Ten Years of Storm* (New York, 1960), p. 32.
3. *Tung-pei jen-min ying-kai tsou shen-mo tao-lu* (Nunchiang, Manchuria, 1946).

Yü Kuang-yuan

(c.1915–   ; Hupeh?). Former youth leader; social and natural sciences administrator; vice-chairman, Scientific and Technological Commission, State Council.

Yü Kuang-yuan is among China's more important Party intellectuals, specializing in the administration of the social and natural sciences in the CCP, the central government, and the Academy of Sciences. A prolific writer, he is the author of articles on such varied topics as economics, ideology, administration, and agriculture. Inferential evidence suggests that Yü is native to Hupeh. Nothing is known of his youth until 1935 when he was a student in Peking, probably at Tsinghua University. On December 9 of that year a student demonstration was staged in opposition to KMT policies, which were regarded as ineffectual in resisting the steady Japanese incursions into north China. From these demonstrations there arose a nationwide campaign, known as the December Ninth Movement (see under Li Ch'ang), which involved thousands of students. To carry their views to the peasantry, several student propaganda teams set out in early January 1936 for the rural areas to the south of Peking. Yü joined a group that was led by Tsinghua students and included Li Ch'ang, one of the major youth leaders of the period.[1] After returning to Peking, the students formed the National Liberation Vanguards of China (NLVC), an organization that within the year was to come under Communist control. Yü joined the NLVC, and then in July 1937, following the outbreak of the Sino-Japanese War, he fled Peking for Paoting and went from there to Taiyuan in Shansi, where the NLVC made its headquarters until the city fell to the Japanese in November 1937. By 1938 he was in Wuhan where he headed the branch office of the NLVC, working in cooperation with Li Ch'ang, Chiang Nan-hsiang, and Huang Hua (qq.v.), all of whom later became important CCP members. Yü and the others worked in Wuhan under the direction of the Party's Yangtze Bureau.[2]

Yü's wartime career is not documented, but it is probable that he, like many of the "December Ninth" students, was engaged principally in youth and propaganda work. His later career suggests that he might also have studied at one of the Party schools in north or northwest China. In 1948 he was working in Shih-chia-chuang, Hopeh, an important city that had fallen to the Communists in the previous November and that served as the Communists capital until they moved into Peking in early 1949. While in Shih-chia-chuang, Yü was engaged in the translation of Marxian works into Chinese;[3] he then went to Peking, where in July 1949 he participated in two large conferences, one of philosophers and the other of social science "workers." In the ensuing years Yü was to spend much of his time working with social scientists, but in addition he has also worked closely with natural scientists. In this regard Yü is distinguished from a number of Party leaders who can be rather distinctly separated into two categories: the social scientist administrators (e.g., Ch'en Po-ta) and the natural science administrators (e.g., Nieh Jung-chen). In general, Yü has worked in both fields.

In 1949 Yü published a small book entitled *Tiao-ch'a yen-chiu* (Investigation [and] research), and by 1951 a fourth revised edition had been published in Peking under the title *Tsen-yang tso tiao-ch'a yen-chiu ho t'ung-chi* (How to undertake investigation, research, and statistical [work]). During this same period he became a frequent contributor to *Chung-kuo ch'ing-nien* (China youth), the official organ of the New Democratic Youth League (later known as the Communist Youth League). During the year 1950, for example, Yü contributed no less than 12 articles to the youth fortnightly publication, on topics ranging from interpretations of Engels to articles on "revolutionary heroism" and "new patriotism." It appears that this outpouring of material attracted the attention of the Party hierarchy, because toward the end of 1950 Yü began to write regularly for *Hsueh-hsi* (Study), the CCP's major political and theoretical journal from its establishment in 1949 until it was superseded by *Hung-ch'i* (Red flag) in 1958. Together with Hu Sheng (q.v.) and Wang Hui-te, he published in *Hsueh-hsi* one of the longest series of articles that has ever appeared in a Chinese Communist publication. Under the general title "Lectures on the Fundamental Knowledge of the Social Sciences," the series ran in 29 issues from late 1950 to early 1952, covering such subjects as "class struggle" and the "strategy and tactics of the Communist Party." Many of these articles concerned Party policies toward private enterprise and the "national bourgeoisie." (This series and its political ramifications are discussed at greater length in the biography of Hu Sheng.)

By 1952 Yü was one of the editors of *Hsueh-hsi*.[4] It is clear that in the early years of the PRC his time was devoted principally to pedagogical and ideological work for *Chung-kuo ch'ing-nien* and *Hsueh-hsi,* but by the mid-fifties Yü had become more involved in social and natural science administrative work. Thus, in February 1955 he was named to a committee to organize popular lectures on atomic energy, and in May–June 1955, when the Academy of Sciences established four major academic departments, Yü was appointed to Standing Committee membership in the Department of Philosophy and Social Sciences, a position he still holds. These two appointments—one in the natural and the other in the social sciences—illustrate the manner in which he has worked in both fields. Early in 1956 the PRC embarked on a large-scale 12-year program to improve science in China, and to implement the plan the government established the Scientific Planning Commission in March 1956. Yü served as one of the deputy secretaries-general, a post he held until the commission was merged with the State Technological Commission in November 1958 to form the Scientific and Technological Commission (STC). He was appointed an STC vice-chairman and works under Nieh Jung-chen, China's top science administrator. In addition to these posts in the executive branch of government, Yü also serves in the legislature, having been elected a Hupeh deputy to the Third NPC, which opened in December 1964.

Yü was newly identified in a post subordinate to the CCP Central Committee at the Party's Eighth Congress in September 1956 when he spoke on scientific achievements and problems before the Congress in his capacity as director of the Propaganda Department's Science Division.[5] He stressed the priorities that had been given to the development of science, urged better working conditions for scientists, and advocated greater study of Soviet science and experience. He may still be Science Division director, but he has not been identified as such since mid-1958. In October 1956 he was appointed a deputy director of the State Council's Bureau of Experts, an organ apparently responsible for the placement of high-level scientific and technical personnel; Yü retained this post until the bureau was abolished in June 1959 and its functions were placed under the above-mentioned Scientific and Technological Commission.

In December 1956 he became a member of the Academic Committee of the Academy of Science's newly established Institute of Psychology, and in November of the following year he was a member of Kuo Mo-jo's academy delegation sent to the Soviet Union to attend the celebrations commemorating the 40th anniversary of the Russian Revolution and to negotiate scientific cooperation agreements with Soviet officials and scientists.

Prior to his 1957 trip to Moscow Yü had concerned himself almost exclusively with domestic affairs, but since then he has been increasingly involved in international relations. In April 1960 he went to Prague to attend a forum on the economic role of countries under the socialist system, which was co-sponsored by the Czech Academy of Sciences and the journal *Problems of Peace and Socialism.* This important monthly, entitled *World Marxist Review* in its English edition, was begun in September 1958 and was designed to consolidate a common ideological-political line for the Communist bloc nations.[6] Yü's article for the August 1960 issue of the *World Marxist Review,* entitled "The Role of Politics in Speeding up the Development of Socialist Economy," is one of the relatively few written for this journal by a Chinese.

Yü was back in Europe in October 1960 for meetings in Budapest of the Communist-dominated World Federation of Scientific Workers, and in November–December he and physicist Chou P'ei-yuan (q.v.) were in Moscow to attend one of the "Pugwash Conferences," a name derived from the village in Canada where the first conference was held in 1957, under the auspices of American industrialist Cyrus Eaton. These conferences, which have brought together distinguished scientists from both Communist and non-Communist nations (including the United States), are among the very few in which both Chinese and Americans have participated, but they have been boycotted by Peking since 1960 as a result of the Sino-Soviet rift. Yü was abroad again in October 1964 when he accompanied Ulanfu (q.v.) to Berlin for the 15th anniversary of the East German government. Two months before this he had been one of the deputy leaders of the Chinese delegation to the 1964 Peking Symposium, an important conference attended by 367 social and natural scientists from 44 nations, most of them in Asia, Africa, or Latin America (see under delegation leader Chou P'ei-yuan).

There are few Communists in the post-1949 period who have written as frequently and on such varied topics as Yü. Apart from those articles already mentioned, he co-authored a two-volume series of political articles published in 1950 under the title *Chung-kuo ko-ming tu-pen* (Chinese revolutionary reader; Hong Kong, Canton, and Shanghai), and he has been an editorial committee member and contributor to *Ching-chi yen-chiu* (Economic research), a leading economic journal. Important articles by Yü have also appeared in the *JMJP* (September 4, 1957, October 22, 1957, and August 13, 1959), as well as in the Party's top journal, *Hung-ch'i* (July 16, 1958, June 1, 1959, and February 1, 1960).

1. *SCMM* 296, p. 28.
2. *SCMM* 297, pp. 36–40.
3. Chang Ching-lu, ed., *Chung-kuo ch'u-pan shih liao pu-pien* (Supplementary historical materials on Chinese publishing; Peking, 1957), p. 451.
4. *CB* 166, p. 3.
5. John M. H. Lindbeck, "The Organisation and Development of Science," *The China Quarterly,* no. 6:98–132 (April–June 1961).
6. Zbigniew K. Brzezinski, *The Soviet Bloc, Unity and Conflict,* rev. ed. (New York, 1961), pp. 464–465.

Yuan Jen-yuan

(Liu-yang, Hunan). Veteran Party and Government administrator; member, Control Commission, Central Committee, CCP.

Yuan Jen-yuan is a native of Liu-yang in northeast Hunan, the hsien which produced such Party veterans as Sung Jen-ch'iung, Yang Yung, and Chang Ch'i-lung (qq.v.). Although many Communist leaders have frequently changed the locale of their work, few can match Yuan's peripatetic record. In an autobiographic account[1] he briefly outlined his career from the mid-1920's to the mid-1930's. In June 1926 the Hunan Party Committee sent a number of men (presumably including Yuan) to western Hunan; the following year he was sent to northwest Hunan where he worked for about two years in the region in and around Tz'u-li and Shih-men hsien, areas then under the control of Ho Lung (q.v.), the prominent Communist military leader and, at this period, the head of the West Hunan-Hupeh soviet district.

In 1928 or 1929 Yuan went from Hunan to Shanghai, and from there the Party sent him, in August 1929, to Kwangsi to take part in the development of the Red Seventh Army (see under Chang Yun-i). Yuan went with this army to the soviet area in southern Kiangsi in 1930. Subsequently he must have been transferred to the western part of the province, for in 1934 he set out on the Long March with the Sixth Army Corps (see under Hsiao K'o). Unlike the forces led by Mao Tse-tung, which concluded the Long March in October 1935, those with whom Yuan was involved did not complete the march until the latter part of 1936.

In 1936–37, Yuan served as a political commissar with the forces led by Ho Lung. In 1937, after the outbreak of the Sino-Japanese War in mid-year, Ho's forces were organized into the 120th Division, one of the three divisions under the Eighth Route Army, the principal Communist military force in north and northwest China. The 120th Division had as one of its major components the 359th Brigade, led by Wang Chen (q.v.), a man with whom Yuan had been associated on the Long March. In the early stages of the war Yuan was head of the Political Department in Wang's brigade, and fought with Wang in campaigns in Shansi, Shantung, and northern Hopeh. Toward the latter part of the war he is known to have been back in Shensi; he commanded troops under Wang in Nanniwan (south of Yenan), a place made famous as an area reclaimed by the Red armies and one in which these armies lived off the land tilled by the soldiers. Into the 1960's the Communists were still citing the "spirit of Nanniwan" as being synonymous with self-reliance in agricultural production. The other post held by Yuan toward the end of the war was that of commissioner of the Sui-te district, one of the major sub-divisions of the Shensi-Kansu-Ninghsia Border Region government. This was apparently the first of the many non-military posts Yuan was to hold in the years ahead. He is known to have taken part in the combat against Nationalist General Hu Tsung-nan during the civil war (1946–1949) with the Nationalists. However, by 1948 he had been transferred to Manchuria where he was serving as a vice-governor of those portions of Kirin province then controlled by the Communists; the Kirin governor at that time was the veteran Manchurian guerrilla leader Chou Pao-chung.

Toward the end of the civil war with the Nationalists, Yuan was assigned to the Fourth Field Army led by Lin Piao, which swept out of Manchuria, captured Peking and Tientsin in early 1949, and then continued its conquest of central and south China through that year. Yuan accompanied these forces as far as his native Hunan, which Lin Piao's forces reached by August 1949; there he remained as a major civil official for the next four years. The Communists' governmental structure for Hunan was somewhat more complex than in most other areas. Aside from a military control commission in the capital (Changsha) of which Yuan was a member in 1949, there was also the Hunan People's Military and Administrative Committee (HP-MAC) and the Hunan Provisional Government (HPG). The Communists at first made use of the two Nationalists leaders, Ch'eng Ch'ien and Ch'en Ming-jen, who had surrendered Hunan without a fight. The former was named as the ostensible head of the HPMAC, but it was no doubt led by the deputy director, Huang K'o-ch'eng, a veteran CCP leader. (Yuan was

named as a member of this politico-military organization.) In similar fashion, Ch'en Ming-shu, the other Nationalist leader, was named to head the provisional government, but with a veteran Communist (in this instance Yuan) as the vice-governor. This structure of military and governmental control was erected in the closing days of August and early September 1949, but in March–April 1950 the provisional government was dissolved in favor of the permanent Hunan Provincial People's Government. At this time Yuan was reappointed as a vice-governor, serving now under Governor Wang Shou-tao, then an alternate member of the Party's Seventh Central Committee. In addition, in July 1950, Yuan was appointed to the Hunan Finance and Economics Committee, and in November 1951 was named as chairman of the government's Political and Legal Affairs Committee. By 1953 he was identified as a member of the Hunan Party Committee, although it is likely that he had been deeply involved in the Hunanese Party affairs from his arrival there in 1949. In any event, in 1953 Yuan was removed and assigned to Peking (December 1953) as a vice-minister of Internal Affairs, a position he held until still another transfer in 1958.

Relatively little was heard about Yuan during the four and a half years that he was a vice-minister of Internal Affairs. This ministry is engaged in various relief programs, census taking, and veterans' welfare work. Thus Yuan made two reports in January 1956 before the State Council on the work of a school for disabled servicemen and on the activities of a home for disabled veterans. In July 1957, during the nationwide rectification campaign, relief work by the central government came under attack. The government replied to these charges, but in an apparent attempt to improve work in calamity areas the State Council established on July 26, 1957, the Central Relief Committee; Yuan was named as one of the members. A persistent problem in the control of the populace, one of the partial responsibilities of the Ministry of Internal Affairs, has been the steady influx of people from rural areas into the cities, a phenomenon described by the Communists as the "blind outflow" of the rural populace to the cities. Yuan was apparently involved in measures to prevent this, because in December 1957 he made a report before the State Council on a joint State Council–Party Central Committee directive regarding this matter.

In the late spring of 1958 Yuan was removed as a vice-minister in Peking and suddenly transferred to Tsinghai province in the northwest. In retrospect, this seems to have been a troubleshooting mission. Early in 1958 the Tsinghai governor, Sun Tso-pin (q.v.), was charged with being a "rightist." By June 1958 Yuan was identified as the acting governor, and then at a Tsinghai congress which ended in July he was formally elected as the governor. At the same time as these events were transpiring, Yuan also was identified (June 1958) as one of the secretaries of the Tsinghai provincial Party committee under First Secretary Kao Feng. At the session when Yuan was elected governor, he was also elected a Tsinghai deputy to the Second NPC (1959–1964), but because of a transfer away from Tsinghai in 1962, he was not re-elected to the Third NPC in 1964.

During Yuan's tenure in Tsinghai he was reported with the frequency that can be expected of a senior provincial authority—attending many meetings of the government organizations, making inspections of industrial and agricultural enterprises, greeting visitors to the province from Peking, and participating in anniversary celebrations (such as May Day). In May 1959 he was elected as president of the Tsinghai chapter of the China Peace Committee, but he probably relinquished the post after his transfer in 1962. He wrote an article on the need to exploit the resources of the pastoral areas of Tsinghai for the *JMJP* of April 20, 1959. Also, as an NPC deputy from the province, Yuan spoke in Peking at the second session of the Second NPC in April 1960 on large-scale reclamation work in Tsinghai.

Then, after Yuan's final appearance in Tsinghai in July 1962, Wang Chao became the acting governor of the province, and Yuan's whereabouts have not been reported since that time. However, two subsequent appointments virtually assure that he is again working in Peking. His first appointment came at (or soon after) the 10th plenum of the Party Central Committee in September 1962. It was decided at that meeting to expand the Control Commission, the Party organ charged with discipline and inspection functions. Yuan was named as a member of the commission and was also named to the commission's standing committee; because the latter is the organ which manages the commission when all the members are not in session, it seems likely that these men are stationed in Peking. Two years later Yuan was named as a representative of CCP to the Fourth National Committee of the CPPCC, which held its first session in December 1964–January 1965. At this session he was elected to the permanent body of the CPPCC, the Standing Committee. Because one of the chief functions of the CPPCC is to organize the work and channel the activities of the many non-Communists working for the regime, it is logical that Yuan, a Control Commission member, should be associated with the CPPCC.

---

1. *Chung-kuo kung-ch'an-tang tsai chung-nan-ti-ch'ü ling-tao ko-ming tou-cheng te li-shih* *tzu-liao* (Historical materials on the revolutionary struggles led by the Chinese Communist Party in Central and South China; Wuhan, 1951), I, 229–232.

Yuan Pao-hua

Minister for the Allocation of Materials.

Although Yuan Pao-hua did not emerge into the limelight until 1957, he had risen by 1964 to a ministerial position in the central government. When first identified in January 1957, he was named as an assistant minister of Metallurgical Industry where he served under Minister Wang Ho-shou, an alternate member of the Party Central Committee and a veteran specialist in industrial management. Yuan was promoted from assistant minister to vice-minister in September 1959. It was during his time with the Metallurgical Industry Ministry that he made two of his rare appearances; in June 1959 he spoke at ceremonies marking the completion of a new large blast furnace on the outskirts of Peking, and in November of the same year he addressed a conference designed to improve cooperation between several key ministries, including his own Metallurgical Industry Ministry.

In the fall of 1960, Yuan was removed as a vice-minister of Metallurgical Industry, but shortly before this he was appointed (September 1960) as a vice-chairman of the State Economic Commission headed by Politburo alternate member Po I-po, one of China's top specialists in economic affairs. Yuan continues to hold this position in the Economic Commission, the organization charged with handling economic planning on an annual basis (as opposed to the State Planning Commission, which deals with long-range planning). Virtually nothing more was heard about Yuan until September 1963 when he was appointed as the director of the State Administrative Bureau of Supplies under the State Council, a bureau that had been created four months earlier but had gone unstaffed until Yuan was appointed. The bureau had been established in the wake of a spate of articles and editorials over the winter of 1962–63, which had pointed to serious deficiencies in the distribution of materials and supplies to industry and agriculture. There had also been complaints that complex administrative links and roundabout transportation methods had caused unnecessary losses in both time and money. The new bureau, apparently, was designed to remove these difficulties in China's increasingly complex economic affairs. In view of the fact that Yuan and his five deputy directors (all appointed at the same time) had served in the State Economic Commission, the new bureau must have been closely linked to this important planning organization. Yuan's bureau gained in stature and presumably importance in November 1964 when it was elevated to the ministerial level under the title Ministry for the Allocation of Materials. Yuan was named to head the ministry and continues to hold the position. It was also in the fall of 1964 that he was elected as a Honan deputy to the Third NPC, which held its first session in December 1964–January 1965.

Yuan's brief career in the higher echelons of the Chinese Communist movement is exceedingly unusual. Few men in contemporary China have come to the public scene so late and yet risen to a ministerial post in such a short period.

Yun Tai-ying

(1895–1931; Wuchang, Hupeh). Early CCP and Youth League leader; member, CCP Central Committee.

Yun Tai-Ying, a leading intellectual and activist in the first decade of CCP history, was particularly effective with students and young intellectuals, who knew him through his voluminous writings, his great skill as a public speaker, and his organizational work in the youth movement. Often using the pen names Tai-ying or Tan-i, he was a frequent contributor to Party journals, and for a period in the mid-twenties he edited the Youth League's *Chungkuo ch'ing-nien* (China youth). In 1926 he was one of the few Communists elected to the KMT Central Executive Committee, and in the same year he was the chief political instructor at the Whampoa Military Academy. In 1927 Yun was elected to the CCP Central Committee, and in the latter half of that year he played a key role in the Nanchang Uprising and the Canton Commune. After the CCP became an underground organization, Yun worked mainly in Shanghai. He was arrested there in 1930, and in the following year he was executed.

Yun was born in Wuchang, Hupeh; his family were scholar-officials who came originally from Ch'ang-chou (Wu-chin) in southern Kiangsu. He was a student at Chung-hua University in Wuchang in 1915 when the notorious Japanese "Twenty-one Demands" aroused strong anti-Japanese reactions throughout China. Yun is said to have taken part in demonstrations in Wuchang aimed at stimulating a boycott against Japanese goods. Within a short time he became more deeply involved in political activism and began to contribute (by 1917) to several magazines that propagated the "new thought" and "new literature" movements. Probably the most important of these was the *Hsin ch'ing-nien* (New youth), the intellectual journal edited by Ch'en Tu-hsiu (q.v.), which first appeared in 1915 and came to be so closely connected with the aims of the May Fourth Movement.

In 1919 Yun graduated from Chung-hua University and took a job as director of the middle school attached to the university. His graduation coincided with the nationwide upsurge of intellectual and political activity which began with the May Fourth Movement, and his new post enabled him to remain in close contact with the student movement. He was then a member of the Young China Association (Shaonien Chung-kuo hsueh-hui), which included such important national and local intellectuals as Li Ta-chao, Teng Chung-hsia, and Mao Tse-tung.[1] Like much of the young intelligentsia of this period, Yun was constantly modifying his political ideas. His translation of Karl Kautsky's *Class Struggle* in 1919[2] suggests an attraction to the theories of the European social democrats. And as late as 1920 he retained a strong attachment to anarchism, a doctrine which interested a number of latter-day Communists, including Mao Tse-tung. Yun's final conversion to Marxism seems to have taken place in the first half of 1921, on the eve of the establishment of the CCP.

The industrialized Wuhan area, a key center of political agitation, witnessed a rapid growth of political and intellectual organizations, many of which sponsored magazines that propagated a wide variety of reforms in government and society. In the period from 1919 to 1921 Yun participated in the establishment and leadership in Wuhan of the Social Welfare Society (Shehui fu-li hui). Years later Mao Tse-tung mentioned the society to Edgar Snow, comparing it to the New People's Study Society, which he and Ts'ai Ho-sen had established in Hunan in 1917–18. Mao also noted that Lin Piao (q.v.), then a young teenager, had been a member of Yun's organization.[3]

In late 1919 Yun and his associates also established the Social Benefit Book Store (Li-ch'ün shu-she), which dealt in May Fourth and Marxian literature and which was frequented by students in Wuhan. The store had business dealings with a similar one in Changsha established by Mao Tse-tung in 1920, as well as with schools in Hunan, Anhwei, Szechwan, and Honan. Another enterprise was a small textile factory intended to demonstrate the half-work, half-study program then being advocated by many progressive intellectuals.[4] In 1921 Yun and others also set up a part-time school for workers in Wuhan and another one for peasants in a rural area in nearby Huang-kang hsien. In these various endeavors Yun worked closely with Lin Yü-nan, Hsiao Ch'u-nü, Li Ch'iu-shih (qq.v.), and other modern-minded intellectuals who ultimately became Communists. It is also probable that he was in contact with Tung Pi-wu and Ch'en T'an-ch'iu (qq.v.), who in late 1920 established a provisional Communist branch in Wuhan and who attended the founding congress of the CCP in mid-1921 in Shanghai. In this same period (1920), Yun took part in organizing the Socialist Youth League, an organization in which he would later become a top official.

In the early summer of 1921, Yun was present at a meeting at Huang-kang attended by young peasants, workers, and students, who had been influenced by the Social Welfare Society. Also attended by representatives of Mao's Wen-hua Book Store in Changsha, the assembled group apparently could not agree on the future aims of the youth movement. Yun is said to have opposed the nationalistic tendencies of the delegates and to have led the way to the establishment of a new organization, the Mutual Preservation Society (Kung-ts'un she). Its constitution advocated the dictatorship of the proletariat and "supported Bolshevism" and the Soviet Union. The Mutual Preservation Society apparently took over control of the Social Benefit Book Store, but the Society was dissolved in the first half of 1922, by which time most of its key members had joined the CCP.

Yun himself joined the Party in 1921, and in the late summer of that year he and his colleague Li Ch'iu-shih went to Lu-chou in southern Szechwan where they established the Lu-chou Associated Normal School, with Yun as the director. Within a short time they established Socialist Youth League and CCP branches in the school.[5] Yun also arranged for Li Ta-chao and Teng Chung-hsia (fellow members of the Young China Association) to come to Szechwan for a lecture tour. In 1922 Yun was arrested in Lu-chou by gendarmes in the employ of a Szechwanese military leader. He was released through the intervention of Wu Yü-chang (q.v.), who was a rather prominent KMT member before joining the CCP in 1925. After Yun's release he went to Chengtu where, at the invitation of Wu Yü-chang, he taught at the Chengtu Higher Normal Institute, of which Wu was the president.[6] A popular lecturer and already well-known to students through his prolific writings, Yun apparently also taught for a brief time in the early twenties at Mao Tse-tung's alma mater, the Hunan First Normal School in Changsha.[7]

Yun returned to Wuhan in 1922 where he resumed his post as director of the Chung-hua middle school. He continued his work in the student movement and through one of his students he met his wife-to-be at this time. When Socialist Youth League leader Chang T'ai-lei (q.v.) went to Moscow in the summer of 1923, Yun was ordered to Shanghai to work with the League. At its Second Congress in Nanking in August 1923 he was elected to the Executive Committee of the League's Central Committee and placed in charge of the Propaganda Department. He also became affiliated with the League's official journal, *Chung-kuo ch'ing-nien* (China youth), which began publication in October 1923. Teng Chung-hsia was the first editor, but after a brief time he was succeeded by Yun and Hsiao Ch'u-nü, who co-edited the journal, and then finally by Yun alone in 1924.[8] He was well suited to the task. Although best known in the Yangtze Valley area, his political essays had appeared in youth and student publications in many other Chinese cities.[9]

Concurrent with these duties, Yun held an instructorship at the radical Shanghai University, which, though nominally under KMT direction, was dominated by such key CCP members as Ch'ü Ch'iu-pai and Teng Chung-hsia. Like many prominent Youth League and CCP members in the period after the Communists began their collaboration with the KMT (1923), Yun joined the KMT and became secretary of the Workers' and Peasants' Department of the Shanghai KMT Headquarters.

Yun was re-elected to the League's Central Committee at the Third Congress held in Shanghai in January 1925 when the name of the organization was changed to the Communist Youth League. He was among the many Communists who helped organize the strikes in Shanghai in May 1925 (the "May 30th Movement"), which caused considerable disruption there and rapidly spread to other urban areas (see under Li Li-san.) A number of Yun's writings were published in this period by the Shanghai Book Store (Shang-hai shu-tien), which had been established by the CCP in November 1923. In 1925 it published a four-volume text, which Yun edited for use in evening classes run by the Party for Shanghai workers.[10]

From Shanghai Yun went to Canton where in January 1926 he was elected a member of the KMT Central Executive Committee at the Second KMT Congress. Other prominent Communists elected to the CEC at this time of rather close KMT-CCP collaboration included Li Ta-chao, Wu Yü-chang, and Lin Po-ch'ü; Mao Tse-tung was among the Communists elected an alternate CEC member. In March of that year Yun became chief political instructor at the Whampoa Military Academy. Apart from his teaching responsibilities at Whampoa, he also taught at the KMT Peasant Movement Training Institute, which came under increasing Communist domination (see under P'eng P'ai). During its sixth class, when Mao headed the Institute (May–October 1926), Yun lectured on Chinese history.[11]

In mid-1926 the Nationalists, with support from the Communists, launched the Northern Expedition. The Wuhan cities were in the hands of the National Revolutionary Army by October, and soon afterwards Yun went there. In early 1927 he became a member of the Hupeh Provincial Government Council, but his most important work was with the newly opened Central Military and Political Academy (in effect, a branch of the famous Whampoa Academy); the left-wing KMT had opened the academy in Wuhan soon after establishing the seat of the Nationalist Government there during the winter of 1926–27. Teng Yen-ta was commandant of the academy, but because he was so fully occupied with his numerous other posts in the left-wing KMT government in Wuhan, Yun was the *de facto* head of the school. When the CCP held its Fifth Congress in Wuhan from late April to early May 1927, Yun was elected a member of the Central Committee. Shortly before the congress, the right-wing KMT under Chiang Kai-shek had staged its dramatic anti-Communist coup in Shanghai. And in the weeks that followed, the CCP alliance with the left-wing KMT in Wuhan was growing increasingly precarious. Nonetheless, when KMT officer Hsia Tou-yin rebelled and marched toward Wuhan to overthrow the left-wing KMT government, he was met and defeated some 25 miles from Wuhan in the latter part of May by Yeh T'ing (q.v.), the Wuchang Garrison commander and a CCP member. Yun assisted in this operation by assembling several hundred cadets from his military academy who took part in the successful battle against Hsia.

By July 1927 CCP relations with the left-KMT had all but ended, and when a warrant was issued for Yun's arrest he took refuge with relatives in a nearby village. However, within a few days he was in Chiu-chiang (Kiukiang) and then in Nanchang where he played a major role in planning and executing the Nanchang Uprising on August 1, the date now used by the Communists as the birth of the Red Army (see under Yeh T'ing).[12] In particular, he seems to have had an important part in persuading Ho Lung (q.v.) to bring his 20th KMT Army over to the Communist side.[13] Immediately after staging the revolt, the Communists established a 25-member Revolutionary Committee, as well as its seven-member Presidium. Yun was named to both bodies, and he was also appointed acting commissar for Propaganda (in place of Kuo Mo-jo).[14] The Communists were routed from Nanchang within a few days, after which they marched south to Kwangtung. Yun made the march south to Swatow, which was held for a few days in late September. When they were again defeated, Yun fled to the nearby Communist stronghold at Lu-feng, and from there he made his way to Hong Kong.

Yun remained in Hong Kong for a few weeks, and then he went to Canton where the Communists made still another attempt to capture a major city. After the uprising there on December 11, 1927, Yun was made secretary-general of the short-lived Canton Commune, which was headed by Chang T'ai-lei (q.v.), who lost his life there.[15] Within less than three days the Communists were totally defeated, and the survivors fled in various directions. Yun went to Hong Kong again where he edited a Communist newspaper and worked in the Party underground.

In the summer of 1928 Yun went to Shanghai where he became secretary-general of the Party's Propaganda Department and contributed to leading Communist journals such as *Pu-erh-sai-wei-k'o* (Bolshevik). With the CCP now outlawed, its cadres carried on their activities underground; conditions were precarious and the Nationalist police were constantly on the alert for "dangerous agitators." Under these circumstances the CCP held its Sixth Congress in Moscow. Convened in mid-1928, the Congress elected Yun *in absentia* to the new Central Committee. The new central organs of the CCP soon came to be dominated by Li Li-san (q.v.). Yun's opposition to Li's headstrong leadership was reflected in the numerous articles he wrote in 1928 and 1929, and by the latter year Yun's authority in the CCP had sharply diminished. In the fall of 1929 Li's Central Committee, possibly to get Yun out of the way, sent him from Shanghai to the west Fukien area to investigate the difficulties that a small group of Communist guerrillas were experiencing. When he returned to Shanghai in early 1930 he was given the modest position of committee secretary in the well-known Chapei district of Shanghai and later in the eastern section of the city. Work there was especially dangerous and Yun did not long survive police vigilance. In April 1930, after attending a union meeting, he was caught and jailed in nearby Soochow. When first imprisoned he concealed his real identity; he was subsequently sentenced to five years in prison, still under an assumed name. When Ch'ü Ch'iu-pai and Chou En-lai returned to China from Moscow in mid-1930 they sought to arrange for Yun's escape. Their efforts failed, however, because Yun's identity as an important Communist was revealed by a CCP defector, Ku Shun-chang. Yun, by then imprisoned in Nanking, was executed by the Nationalists on April 29, 1931. Speaking before the Eighth Party Congress many years later (1956), Li Li-san mentioned Yun's death in the course of an effusive confession of past "mistakes." Li asserted that the excesses of his past leadership in the 1928–1930 period had caused the death of some "splendid cadres." Yun was the only one of those he mentioned.

Yun was married for a second time in late 1926 or early 1927 to Shen Pao-ying. They had a son born in 1928. Shen worked in the Shanghai underground with Yun after 1928 and took part in the futile attempt to arrange for her husband's escape from prison. Nothing is known about her subsequent career, but in 1957 she wrote a sketch about Yun's career for *Chung-kuo ch'ing-nien* (China youth, no. 6, March 16, 1957). Yun's younger brother, Yun Tzu-ch'iang (1899–1963), was a prominent scientist, who remained on the mainland after 1949. A CCP member, he was identified at the time of his death as a vice-chairman of the China Chemistry and Chemical Engineering Society and a vice-chairman of the Physics, Mathematics, and Chemistry Department of the Academy of Sciences.

The standard Communist biography of Yun appears in Hua Ying-shen, ed., *Chung-kuo Kung-ch'an-tang lieh-shih chuan* (Biographies of Chinese Communist Party martyrs; Hong Kong, 1949). This is supplemented by the above-mentioned sketch of Yun's career by his wife, which was reprinted in *Kung-ch'ing-t'uan, wo-te mu-ch'in* (The Communist Youth League, my mother; Peking, 1958); this book also contains another essay on Yun by a former colleague. *Li-shih yen-chiu* (Historical research; vol. V, no. 11, 1958) published a detailed diary which Yun had kept at the time of the May Fourth Incident in 1919.

---

1. Chow Tse-tsung, *The May Fourth Movement* (Cambridge, Mass., 1960), p. 252.

2. Maurice Meisner, *Li Ta-chao and the Origins of Chinese Marxism* (Cambridge, Mass., 1967), p. 115.

3. Edgar Snow, *Red Star over China* (New York, 1938), p. 132.

4. Chang Ching-lu, ed., *Chung-kuo hsien-tai ch'u-pan shih-liao* (Historical materials on contemporary Chinese publishing; Peking, 1954), p. 44.

5. *Kung-ch'ing-t'uan, wo-te mu-ch'in* (The Communist Youth League, my mother; Peking, 1958), p. 278.

6. *ECMM* 173, p. 12.

7. Chow Tse-tsung, p. 349.

8. Chang Ching-lu, p. 63; Chungking, *Hsin-hua jih-pao* (New China daily), June 29, 1940.

9. Chow Tse-tsung, *Research Guide to the May Fourth Movement* (Cambridge, Mass., 1963), pp. 29, 37, 45, 89, 101, 111, 122.

10. Chang Ching-lu, pp. 61–67.

11. *Ibid.*, p. 77.

12. C. Martin Wilbur, "The Ashes of Defeat," *The China Quarterly*, no. 18:3–54, (April–June 1964).

13. Ibid., p. 25.

14. *Ti-erh-tz'u kuo-nei ko-ming chan-cheng shih-ch'i shih-shih lun-ts'ung* (Accounts of the second revolutionary civil war; Peking, 1956), p. 3.

15. Ibid., p. 29.

Selected Bibliography

The bibliography does not contain the many handbooks and yearbooks published in Peking and Taipei, nor the various personnel directories published by the United States and Japanese governments. Periodicals, both in Chinese and English, have also been omitted. Exhaustive listings of handbooks, directories, and periodicals can be found in guides and bibliographies by Chow Tse-tsung, Chün-tu Hsüeh, and Peter Berton and Eugene Wu, all of which are cited below.

The Agrarian Reform Law of the People's Republic of China and other Relevant Documents. Peking, 1950.

Band, Claire and William. *Two Years with the Chinese Communists.* New Haven, Conn.: Yale University Press, 1948.

Barendsen, Robert. *Half-Work Half-Study Schools in Communist China.* Washington, D. C.: U.S. Department of Health, Education, and Welfare, 1964.

Barnett, A. Doak. *Communist China and Asia: Challenge to American Policy.* New York: Random House, 1960.

────── *China on the Eve of Communist Takeover.* New York: Praeger, 1961.

──────, ed. *Communist Strategies in Asia.* New York: Praeger, 1963.

────── *Communist China: The Early Years, 1949–1955.* New York: Praeger, 1964.

Belden, Jack. *China Shakes the World.* New York: Harper, 1949.

Berton, Peter, and Eugene Wu. *Contemporary China: A Research Guide.* Stanford, Calif.: Hoover Institution, 1967.

Bodde, Derk. *Peking Diary: 1948–1949.* New York: Abelard-Schuman, 1950.

Boorman, Howard L., ed. *Biographical Dictionary of Republican China.* New York: Columbia University Press, vol. I, 1967; vol. II, 1968.

──────, Alexander Eckstein, Philip E. Mosely, and Benjamin Schwartz. *Moscow-Peking Axis: Strengths and Strains.* New York: Harper, 1957.

Borg, Dorothy. *The United States and the Far Eastern Crisis of 1933–1938.* Cambridge, Mass.: Harvard University Press, 1964.

Brandt, Conrad. *Stalin's Failure in China, 1924–1927.* Cambridge, Mass.: Harvard University Press, 1958.

──────, Benjamin Schwartz, and John K. Fairbank. *A Documentary History of Chinese Communism.* Cambridge, Mass.: Harvard University Press, 1952.

Briere, O. *Fifty Years of Chinese Philosophy, 1898–1948.* London: Allen and Unwin, 1956.

Bueschel, Richard M. *Communist Chinese Air Power.* New York: Praeger, 1968.

Builders of the Ming Tombs Reservoir. Peking, 1958.

Carlson, Evans Fordyce. *Twin Stars of China.* New York: Dodd and Mead, 1940.

Chang Ai-p'ing. *Ts'ung Tsun-i tao Ta-tu-ho* (From Tsun-i to the Tatu River). Hong Kong, 1960.

Chang Chih-i. *Chung-kuo ko-ming te min-tsu wen-t'i ho min-tsu cheng-ts'e chiang-hua* (The nationalities question in the Chinese revolution and discussions of nationalities policies). Peking, 1956.

Chang Ching-lu, ed. *Chung-kuo hsien-tai ch'u-pan shih-liao* (Historical materials on contemporary Chinese publishing). Peking, 1954.

──────, ed. *Chung-kuo ch'u-pan shih-liao pu-pien* (Supplementary historical materials on Chinese publishing). Peking, 1957.

Chang Chün-ying. *Ko-ming yü fan-ko-ming te chueh-chan: Chung-kuo jen-min chieh-fang chan-cheng chien-shih* (The decisive battle between revolution and counter-revolution: A brief history of the Chinese people's liberation war). Peking, 1961.

Chao Kuo-chün. *The Mass Organizations in Communist China.* Cambridge, Mass.: Harvard University Press, 1953.

────── *Agrarian Policies of Mainland China: A Documentary Study, 1949–1956.* Cambridge, Mass.: Harvard University Press, 1957.

────── *Economic Planning and Organization in Mainland China: A Documentary Study, 1949–1957.* Vol. I. Cambridge, Mass.: Harvard University Press, 1963.

Chao Tsu. *Before the Dawn.* Peking, 1958.

Chassin, Lionel Max. *The Communist Conquest of China: A History of the Civil War, 1945–1949.* Cambridge, Mass.: Harvard University Press, 1965.

Chen Chang-feng. *On the Long March with Chairman Mao.* Peking, 1959.

Ch'ên, Jerome. *Mao and the Chinese Revolution.* London: Oxford University Press, 1965.

Ch'en Kung-po. *The Communist Movement in China*. Ed. and intro. by C. Martin Wilbur. East Asian Institute, Columbia University, New York, 1960.

Ch'en Po-ta. *Mao Tse-tung on the Chinese Revolution*. Peking, 1953.

―――― *Speech Before the Study Group of Research Members of Academia Sinica*. Peking, 1953.

―――― *Notes on Mao Tse-tung's "Report of an Investigation into the Peasant Movement in Hunan"*. Peking, 1954.

―――― *Notes on Ten Years of Civil War, 1927–1936*. Peking, 1954.

―――― *A Study of Land Rent in Pre-Liberation China*. Peking, 1958.

Cheng Chu-yuan. *Scientific and Engineering Manpower in Communist China, 1949–1963*. Washington, D.C.: National Science Foundation, 1965.

Cheng-feng wen-hsien (Rectification documents). Hong Kong, 1949.

Cheng, J. Chester, ed. *The Politics of the Chinese Red Army*. Stanford, Calif.: Hoover Institution, 1966.

Chesneaux, Jean. *Le Mouvement ouvrier chinois de 1919 à 1927*. Paris: Mouton, 1962.

―――― *The Chinese Labor Movement, 1919–1927*. Stanford, Calif.: Stanford University Press, 1968.

Ch'i Wu. *I-ko ko-ming ken-chü te ch'eng-chang; k'ang-Jih chan-cheng shih-ch'i te Chin-Chi-Lu-Yü pien-ch'ü kai-k'uang* (The establishment and growth of a revolutionary base: A general account of the Shansi-Hopeh-Shantung-Honan Border Region during the anti-Japanese war and the war of liberation). Peking, 1958.

Chiang Kai-shek. *Soviet Russia in China*. New York: Farrar, Straus and Cudahy, 1957.

Chiang Nan-hsiang et al. *The Roar of a Nation: Reminiscences of the December 9th Student Movement*. Peking, 1963.

Ch'ien Chün-jui et al. *Chiu-wang shou-ts'e* (The salvation handbook). Shanghai, 1938.

Ch'ien-li-yueh chin-tu Ju-ho (The thousand mile leap across the Ju River). Hong Kong, 1961.

Ch'ien Tuan-sheng. *The Government and Politics of China*. Cambridge, Mass.: Harvard University Press, 1950.

Chin Fan. *Tsai hung-chün ch'ang-cheng te tao-lu shang* (On the road of the Red Army's Long March). Peking, 1957.

China in Transition: Selected Articles 1952–1956 by Writers for China Reconstructs. Peking, 1957.

China's Revolutionary Wars. Peking, 1951.

Chinese Workers March Towards Socialism. Peking, 1956.

Chou Erh-fu. *Tung-pei heng-tuan-mien* (Northeastern cross section).

―――― *Pai Ch'iu-en tai-fu* (Dr. Bethune). Peking, 1962.

Chou, Eric. *A Man Must Choose: The Dilemma of a Chinese Patriot*. London: Longmans, 1963.

Chou Shih-chao. *Wo-men te shih-piao* (Our model teacher). Peking, 1958.

Chow Ching-wen. *Ten Years of Storm: The True Story of the Communist Regime in China*. New York: Holt, Rinehart and Winston, 1960.

Chow Tse-tsung. *The May Fourth Movement: Intellectual Revolution in Modern China*. Cambridge, Mass.: Harvard University Press, 1960.

―――― *Research Guide to the May Fourth Movement: Intellectual Revolution in Modern China, 1915–1924*. Cambridge, Mass.: Harvard University Press, 1963.

A Chronicle of the Principal Events Relating to the Indo-China Question, 1940–1954. Peking, 1954.

A Chronicle of the Principal Events Relating to the Korean Question, 1945–1954. Peking, 1954.

Chu Teh. *On the Battlefronts of the Liberated Areas*. Peking, 1952.

Chung-hua ch'üan-kuo wen-hsueh i-shu kung-tso-che tai-piao ta-hui chi-nien wen-chi (Commemorative articles of the All-China Congress of Literary and Art Workers). Peking, 1950.

Chung I-mou, ed. *Hai-lu-feng nung-min yün-tung* (The Hai-lu-feng peasant movement). Canton, 1957.

Chung-kuo hsin min-chu-chu-i ch'ing-nien-t'uan (China New Democratic Youth League). Hong Kong, 1949.

Chung-kuo kung-ch'an-tang tsai chung-nan-ti-ch'ü ling-tao ko-ming tou-cheng te li-shih tzu-liao (Historical materials on the revolutionary struggles led by the CCP in central-south China). Vol. I. Wuhan, 1951.

Clegg, Arthur. *The Birth of New China*. London: Lawrence and Wishart, 1943.

Clubb, O. Edmund. *Twentieth Century China*. New York: Columbia University Press, 1964.

―――― *Communism in China: As Reported from Hankow in 1932*. New York: Columbia University Press, 1968.

Cohen, Arthur A. *The Communism of Mao Tse-tung*. Chicago, Ill.: University of Chicago Press, 1964.

The Common Program and Other Documents of the First Plenary Session of the Chinese People's Political Consultative Conference. Peking, 1950.

Communist China, 1955–1959: Policy Documents with Analysis. Foreword by Robert R. Bowie and John K. Fairbank.

Cambridge, Mass.: Harvard University Press, 1962.

Compton, Boyd, trans. *Mao's China: Party Reform Documents, 1942–44.* Seattle, Wash.: University of Washington Press, 1952.

Cooley, John K. *East Wind over Africa: Red China's African Offensive.* New York: Walker, 1965.

Culture, Education and Health in New China. Peking, 1952.

Dalai Lama. *My Land and My People.* New York: McGraw-Hill, 1962.

Dallin, David J. *The Rise of Russia in Asia.* New Haven, Conn.: Yale University Press, 1949.

De Francis, John. *Nationalism and Language Reform in China.* Princeton, N.J.: Princeton University Press, 1950.

Degras, Jane. *The Communist International 1919–1943: Documents.* London: Oxford University Press, vol. I, 1956; vol. II, 1960; vol. III, 1965.

Doolin, Dennis J. *Territorial Claims in the Sino-Soviet Conflict.* Stanford, Calif.: Hoover Institution, 1965.

Dutt, Vidya Prakash. *China and the World.* New York: Praeger, 1964.

Eckstein, Alexander. *Communist China's Economic Growth and Foreign Trade: Implications for U.S. Policy.* New York: McGraw-Hill, 1966.

Eighth National Congress of the Communist Party of China. 3 vols. Peking, 1956.

The Electoral Law of the People's Republic of China for the All-China People's Congress and Local People's Congresses of All Levels. Peking, 1953.

Elegant, Robert S. *China's Red Masters: Political Biographies of the Chinese Communist Leaders.* New York: Twayne, 1951.

Epstein, Israel. *The People's War.* London: Victor Gollancz, 1939.

—— *The Unfinished Revolution.* Boston, Mass.: Little, Brown and Co., 1947.

Eudin, Xenia Joukoff, and Robert C. North. *Soviet Russia and the East, 1920–1927: A Documentary Survey.* Stanford, Calif.: Stanford University Press, 1957.

Fairbank, John K., Edwin O. Reischauer, and Albert M. Craig. *East Asia: The Modern Transformation.* Boston, Mass.: Houghton Mifflin, 1965.

Faure, Edgar. *The Serpent and the Tortoise: Problems of the New China.* New York: St. Martin's, 1958.

Feis, Herbert. *The China Tangle.* Princeton, N.J.: Princeton University Press, 1953.

Feng Hsueh-feng. *Hui-i Lu Hsun* (Reminiscences of Lu Hsun). Peking, 1957.

Feng Yü-hsiang chiang-chün chi-nien ts'e (Commemorative accounts of General Feng Yü-hsiang). Hong Kong, n.d.

Feuerwerker, Albert, and S. Cheng. *Chinese Communist Studies of Modern Chinese History.* Cambridge, Mass.: East Asian Research Center, Harvard University, 1961.

First Five-Year Plan for Development of the National Economy of the People's Republic of China in 1953–1957. Peking, 1956.

Flame on High Mountain. Peking, 1959.

Forman, Harrison. *Report from Red China.* New York: Henry Holt, 1945.

Fraser, Stuart, comp. and ed. *Chinese Communist Education: Records of the First Decade.* New York: Wiley, 1965.

Gelder, Stuart. *The Chinese Communists.* London: Victor Gollancz, 1946.

George, Alexander L. *The Chinese Communist Army in Action: The Korean War and its Aftermath.* New York: Columbia University Press, 1967.

Gillin, Donald G. *Warlord Yen Hsi-shan in Shansi Province, 1911–1949.* Princeton, N.J.: Princeton University Press, 1967.

Gittings, John. *The Role of the Chinese Army.* London: Oxford University Press, 1967.

Goldman, Merle. *Literary Dissent in Communist China.* Cambridge, Mass.: Harvard University Press, 1967.

Gologo, Mamadou. *China: A Great People, A Great Destiny.* Peking, 1965.

Gould, Sidney H., ed. *Sciences in Communist China.* Washington, D.C.: American Association for the Advancement of Science, 1961.

The Great Turning Point. Peking, 1962.

Griffith, Samuel B., II. *The Chinese People's Liberation Army.* New York: McGraw-Hill, 1967.

Guillain, Robert. *When China Wakes.* New York: Walker, 1966.

Halperin, Morton H. *China and the Bomb.* New York: Praeger, 1965.

Halpern, A. M. *Policies Toward China: Views From Six Continents.* New York: McGraw-Hill, 1965.

Hanrahan, Gene Z. *Chinese Communist Guerrilla Tactics.* New York, 1952.

Hanson, Haldore. *"Humane Endeavour".* New York: Farrar and Rinehart, 1939.

Hinton, Harold C. *Communist China in World Politics.* Boston, Mass.: Houghton Mifflin, 1966.

Ho Hsiang-ning. *Hui-i Chung-shan ho Liao Chung-k'ai* (Reminiscences about Sun Yat-sen and Liao Chung-k'ai). Peking, 1957.

Ho Kan-chih. *A History of the Modern Chinese Revolution.* Peking, 1960.

Ho Ping-ti and Tang Tsou. *China in Crisis.* 3 vols. Chicago, Ill.: University of Chicago Press, 1968.

Hofheinz, Roy Mark, "The Peasant Movement and Rural Revolution: Chinese Communists in the Countryside (1923–7)." Ph.D. diss., Harvard University, 1966.

Hogg, George. *I See a New China.* Boston, Mass.: Little, Brown and Co., 1944.

Hou Feng, ed. *P'eng P'ai lieh-shih chuan-lüeh* (A biographical sketch of martyr P'eng P'ai). Canton, 1959.

Hsi-wu lao-jen [Elder Hsi-wu]. *"Erh-ch'i" hui-i-lu* (Reminiscences of "February Seventh"). Peking, 1957.

Hsia, C. T. *A History of Modern Chinese Fiction, 1917–1957.* New Haven, Conn.: Yale University Press, 1961.

Hsia, Tsi-an. *The Gate of Darkness.* Seattle, Wash.: University of Washington Press, 1968.

Hsiao Tso-liang. *Power Relations within the Chinese Communist Movement, 1930–1934.* Seattle, Wash.: University of Washington Press, 1961.

Hsieh, Alice Langley. *Communist China's Strategy in the Nuclear Era.* Englewood Cliffs, N.J.: Prentice-Hall, 1962.

Hsing-huo Liao-yuan (A single spark can start a prairie fire). Hong Kong, 1960.

Hsiung Fu et al. *Shih-yüeh ko-ming te tao-lu* (The road of the October Revolution). Peking, 1958.

Hsiung-shih tu Ch'ang-chiang (Heroic forces cross the Yangtze River). Hong Kong, 1961.

Hsu Kai-yu. *Chou En-lai.* New York: Doubleday, 1968.

Hsu Kuang-p'ing. *Lu Hsun hui-i-lu* (Reminiscences about Lu Hsun). Peking, 1961.

Hsu Yung Ying. *A Survey of the Shensi-Kansu-Ninghsia Border Region.* New York: Institute of Pacific Relations, 1945.

Hsüeh Chün-tu. *The Chinese Communist Movement, 1921–1937.* Stanford, Calif.: Hoover Institution, 1960.

—— *The Chinese Communist Movement, 1937–1949.* Stanford, Calif.: Hoover Institution, 1962.

Hsueh ho lei te hui-i (Memories of blood and tears). Peking, 1963.

Hsueh Mu-chiao, Su Hsing, and Lin Tse-li. *The Socialist Transformation of the National Economy in China.* Peking, 1960.

Hu Chang-tu. *China: Its People, Its Society, Its Culture.* New Haven, Conn.: Human Relations Area Files, Inc., 1960.

Hu Chiao-mu. *Thirty Years of the Communist Party of China.* Peking, 1952.

Hu Chung-ch'ih. *K'ang-Mei yuan-Chao yun-tung shih-hua* (A brief history of the Resist-America Aid-Korea Movement). Peking, 1956.

Hu Hua, ed. *Chung-kuo hsin min-chu-chu-i ko-ming shih* (A history of China's new democratic revolution). Hong Kong, 1950.

—— *Chung-kuo hsin min-chu-chu-i ko-ming shih ts'an-k'ao tzu-liao* (Reference materials on the history of China's new democratic revolution). Peking, 1951.

Hu-k'ou pa-ya (Pulling the tiger's teeth). Hong Kong, 1960.

Hu-nan ko-ming lieh-shih chuan (Biographies of Hunan revolutionary martyrs). Changsha, 1952.

Hua Ying-shen, ed. *Chung-kuo kung-ch'an-tang lieh-shih chuan* (Biographies of Chinese Communist martyrs). Hong Kong, 1949.

Hudson, G. F., Richard Lowenthal, and Roderick MacFarquhar. *The Sino-Soviet Dispute.* New York: Praeger, 1961.

Hung-ch'i p'iao-p'iao (Red flag fluttering). Vols. I–X. Peking, 1957–1959.

I-erh-chiu yun-tung (The December Ninth movement). Peking, 1954.

Important Documents Concerning the Question of Taiwan. Peking, 1955.

Iriye Akira. *After Imperialism: The Search for a New Order in the Far East, 1921–1931.* Cambridge, Mass.: Harvard University Press, 1965.

Isaacs, Harold R. *The Tragedy of the Chinese Revolution.* 2nd rev. ed. Stanford, Calif.: Stanford University Press, 1961.

Israel, John. *Student Nationalism in China, 1927–1937.* Stanford, Calif.: Stanford University Press, 1966.

Joffe, Ellis. *Party and Army: Professionalism and Political Control in the Chinese Officer Corps, 1949–1964.* Cambridge, Mass.: East Asian Research Center, Harvard University, 1965.

Johnson, Chalmers A. *Peasant Nationalism and Communist Power.* Stanford, Calif.: Stanford University Press, 1962.

Johnston, Douglas M., and Chiu Hungdah, eds. *Agreements of the People's Republic of China, 1949–1967: A Calendar.* Cambridge, Mass.: Harvard University Press, 1968.

Kahin, George McTurnan. *The Asian-African Conference.* Ithaca, N.Y.: Cornell University Press, 1956.

K'ang-Jih chan-cheng shih-ch'i chieh-fang-ch'ü kai-k'uang (A sketch of the liberated areas during the Anti-Japanese War). Peking, 1953.

Kirby, Stuart, ed. *Contemporary China.* Vol. VI (1962–1964). Hong Kong: Hong Kong University Press, 1968.

Kuan Ta-tung. *The Socialist Transformation of Capitalist Industry and Commerce in China.* Peking, 1960.

Kublin, Hyman. *Asian Revolutionary.* Princeton, N.J.: Princeton University Press, 1964.

Kun, Bela. Introduction to *Fundamental Laws of the Chinese Soviet Republic*. New York: International Publishers, 1934.

Kung-ch'ing-t'uan, wo te mu-ch'in (The Communist Youth League, my mother). Peking, 1958.

Kung Ch'u. *Wo yü hung-chün* (The Red Army and I). Hong Kong, 1954.

Kuo, Warren. *Analytical History of [the] Chinese Communist Party*. Taipei, Institute of International Relations, book one, 1966; book two, 1968.

Kwok, D. W. Y. *Scientism in Chinese Thought, 1900–1950*. New Haven, Conn.: Yale University Press, 1965.

Lall, Arthur. *How Communist China Negotiates*. New York: Columbia University Press, 1968.

Lattimore, Owen. *Pivot of Asia: Sinkiang and the Inner Asian Frontiers of China and Russia*. Boston, Mass.: Little, Brown and Co., 1950.

Leng Shao Chuan and Norman D. Palmer. *Sun Yat-sen and Communism*. New York: Praeger, 1960.

Lewis, John Wilson. *Leadership in Communist China*. Ithaca, N.Y.: Cornell University Press, 1963.

Li Ch'ang et al. *"I-erh-chiu" hui-i-lu* (Reminiscences of "December Ninth"). Peking, 1961.

Li Choh-ming. *The Statistical System of Communist China*. Berkeley, Calif.: University of California Press, 1962.

Li Jui. *Mao Tse-tung t'ung-chih te ch'u-ch'i ko-ming huo-tung* (Comrade Mao Tse-tung's early revolutionary activities). Peking, 1957.

Li Ming et al. *Chung-kung liu lieh-shih hsiao-chuan* (Short biographies of six Chinese Communist martyrs). Hong Kong, 1949.

Li Po-chao. *Nü kung-ch'an-tang yuan* (Women of the Communist Party). Peking, 1963.

Li Yu-chih, ed. *Chung-kuo hsien-tai ko-ming yun-tung ku-shih* (Episodes from China's modern revolutionary movement). Vol. II. Nanking, 1957.

Li Yun-han. *Tsung jung kung tao ch'ing tang* (From the admission of the Communists to the purification of the [Nationalist] Party). Taipei, 1966.

Liao Chung-k'ai chi (Collected writings of Liao Chung-k'ai). Peking, 1963.

Liao Kai-lung. *Hsin Chung-kuo shih tsen-yang tan-sheng te* (How New China was born). Shanghai, 1951.

——— *Chung-kuo jen-min chieh-fang chan-cheng chien-shih* (A brief history of the Chinese people's war of liberation). Shanghai, 1952.

——— *From Yenan to Peking*. Peking, 1954.

Lieh-shih chuan (Biographies of martyrs). Vol. I. Moscow (?), 1936.

Lieh-shih Hsiang Ching-yü (Martyr Hsiang Ching-yü). Peking, 1958.

Lindsay, Michael. *Notes on Educational Problems in Communist China, 1941–47*. New York: Institute of Pacific Relations, 1950.

Ling Nai-min. *Tibetan Sourcebook*. Hong Kong: Union Research Institute, 1964.

Liu, Alan P. L. *The Press and Journals in Communist China*. Cambridge, Mass.: Center for International Studies, Massachusetts Institute of Technology, 1966.

Liu, F. F. *A Military History of Modern China, 1924–1949*. Princeton, N.J.: Princeton University Press, 1956.

Liu Li-k'ai and Wang Chen. *I-chiu-i-chiu chih i-chiu-erh-ch'i te Chung-kuo kung-jen yun-tung* (The Chinese workers' movement from 1919 to 1927). Peking, 1954.

Liu Pai-yü. *Huan-hsing tung-pei* (Traveling in the Northeast). Shanghai, 1946.

Liu Shao-ch'i. *On Inner-Party Struggle*. Peking, 1952.

——— *On the Party*. Peking, 1952.

——— *Internationalism and Nationalism*. Peking, 1954.

——— *How to be a Good Communist*. Peking, 1964.

The Long March: Eyewitness Accounts. Peking, 1963.

Lü Chien, ed. *Li Ta-chao ho Ch'ü Ch'iu-pai* (Li Ta-chao and Ch'ü Ch'iu-pai). Shanghai, 1951.

MacFarquhar, Roderick. *The Hundred Flowers Campaign and the Chinese Intellectuals*. New York: Praeger, 1960.

Mao Tse-tung et al. *China: The March Toward Unity*. New York: Workers Library Publishers, 1937.

McLane, Charles B. *Soviet Policy and the Chinese Communists, 1931–1946*. New York: Columbia University Press, 1958.

Meisner, Maurice. *Li Ta-chao and the Origins of Chinese Marxism*. Cambridge, Mass.: Harvard University Press, 1967.

Miao Min. *Fang Chih-min*. Peking, 1962.

Miff, P. *Heroic China: Fifteen Years of the Communist Party of China*. New York: Workers Library Publishers, 1937.

Mu Fu-sheng. *The Wilting of the Hundred Flowers: The Chinese Intelligentsia under Mao*. New York: Praeger, 1962.

Neuhauser, Charles. *Third World Politics: China and the Afro-Asian People's Solidarity Organization, 1957–1967*. Cambridge, Mass.: East Asian Research Center, Harvard University, 1968.

Nollau, Gunther. *International Communism and World Revolution*. New York: Praeger, 1961.

North, Robert C. *Kuomintang and Chinese Communist Elites*. Stanford, Calif.: Stanford University Press, 1952.

―――― *Moscow and Chinese Communists*. Stanford, Calif.: Stanford University Press, 1953.

―――― and Xenia J. Eudin. *M. N. Roy's Mission to China*. Berkeley, Calif.: University of California Press, 1963.

Orleans, Leo A. *Professional Manpower and Education in Communist China*. Washington, D.C.: National Science Foundation, 1960.

An Outline History of China. Peking, 1958.

Panikkar, K. M. *In Two Chinas: Memoirs of a Diplomat*. London: Allen and Unwin, 1955.

Payne, Robert. *Mao Tse-tung*. New York: Henry Schuman, 1962.

Peck, Graham. *Two Kinds of Time*. 2nd ed., rev. and abridged. Boston, Mass.: Houghton Mifflin, 1967.

Perkins, Dwight H. *Market Control and Planning in Communist China*. Cambridge, Mass.: Harvard University Press, 1966.

Policy Towards Nationalities of the People's Republic of China. Peking, 1953.

Reform of the Chinese Written Language. Peking, 1958.

A Regional Handbook on the Inner Mongolia Autonomous Region. Seattle, Wash.: Human Relations Area Files, 1956.

Revolutionary China Today. New York: Workers Library Publishers, 1934.

Rhoads, Edward J. M. *The Chinese Red Army, 1927–1963: An Annotated Bibliography*. Cambridge, Mass.: East Asian Research Center, Harvard University, 1964.

Rigg, Robert B. *Red China's Fighting Hordes*. Harrisburg, Pa.: Military Service Publishing Co., 1951.

Rinden, Robert, and Roxane Witke. *The Red Flag Waves: A Guide to the "Hung-ch'i p'iao-p'iao" Collection*. Berkeley, Calif.: Center for Chinese Studies, University of California, 1968.

Roy, M. N. *My Experiences in China*. Calcutta: Renaissance Publishers, 1945.

―――― *Revolution and Counter-Revolution in China*. Calcutta: Renaissance Publishers, 1946.

Rue, John E. *Mao Tse-tung in Opposition, 1927–1935*. Stanford, Calif.: Stanford University Press, 1966.

Saga of Resistance to Japanese Invasion. Peking, 1959.

Scalapino, Robert A., and George T. Yu. *The Chinese Anarchist Movement*. Berkeley, Calif.: Center for Chinese Studies, University of California, 1961.

Schram, Stuart R. *The Political Thought of Mao Tse-tung*. New York: Praeger, 1963.

―――― *Mao Tse-tung*. New York: Simon and Schuster, 1966.

Schurmann, Franz. *Ideology and Organization in Communist China*. Berkeley, Calif.: University of California Press, 1966.

―――― and Orville Schell. *The China Reader: Republican China*. New York: Random House, 1967.

―――― *The China Reader: Communist China*. New York: Random House, 1967.

Schwartz, Benjamin I. *Chinese Communism and the Rise of Mao*. Cambridge, Mass.: Harvard University Press, 1951.

Scott, A. C. *Literature and the Arts in Twentieth Century China*. New York: Doubleday, 1963.

Selden, Mark. "Yenan Communism: Revolution in the Shensi-Kansu-Ninghsia Border Region, 1927–1945." Ph.D. diss., Yale University, New Haven, Conn., 1967.

Selected Works of Mao Tse-tung. Peking, vol. I, 1964; vols. II and III, 1965; vol. IV, 1961.

Seton-Watson, Hugh. *From Lenin to Malenkov: The History of World Communism*. New York: Praeger, 1955.

Shabad, Theodore. *China's Changing Map: A Political and Economic Geography of the Chinese People's Republic*. New York: Praeger, 1956.

Shan-hsi ko-ming tou-cheng hui-i-lu (Reminiscences of revolutionary struggles in Shansi). Taiyuan (?), preface 1961.

Sheridan, James E. *Chinese Warlord: The Career of Feng Yü-hsiang*. Stanford, Calif.: Stanford University Press, 1966.

Smedley, Agnes. *China's Red Army Marches*. New York: Vanguard Press, 1934.

―――― *Red Flood over China*. Moscow, 1934.

―――― *China Fights Back*. London: Victor-Gollancz, 1938.

―――― *Battle Hymn of China*. New York: Knopf, 1943.

―――― *The Great Road: The Life and Times of Chu Te*. New York: Monthly Review Press, 1956.

Snow, Edgar. *Red Star over China*. New York: Random House, 1938.

―――― *The Battle for Asia*. Cleveland, Ohio: World Publishing Company, 1941.

―――― *Random Notes on Red China, 1936–1945*. Cambridge, Mass., 1957.

―――― *Journey to the Beginning*. London: Victor Gollancz, 1960.

―――― *The Other Side of the River*. London: Victor Gollancz, 1963.

Socialist Upsurge in China's Countryside. Peking, 1957.

Soong Ching Ling. *The Struggle for New China*. Peking, 1953.

Stein, Gunther. *The Challenge of Red China*. New York: McGraw-Hill, 1945.

Stories of the Long March. Peking, 1958.

Strong, Anna Louise. *Tomorrow's China.* New York: Committee for a Democratic Far Eastern Policy, 1948.

——— *The Chinese Conquer China.* New York: Doubleday, 1949.

——— *The Rise of the Chinese People's Communes.* Peking, 1959.

——— *When Serfs Stood Up in Tibet.* Peking, 1960.

——— *The Rise of the Chinese People's Communes—And Six Years After.* Peking, 1964.

——— *China's Millions: Revolution in Central China, 1927.* Peking, 1965.

Suh Dae-sook. *The Korean Communist Movement, 1918–1948.* Princeton, N.J.: Princeton University Press, 1967.

Sung Chih-te. *Yen-che hung-chün chan-shih te chiao-yin* (Following in the footsteps of the soldiers of the Red Army). Peking, 1956.

Swarup, Shanti. *A Study of the Chinese Communist Movement.* London: Oxford University Press, 1966.

Szu Ma-lu. *Ch'ü Ch'iu-pai chuan* (The Ch'ü Ch'iu-pai story). Hong Kong, 1962.

"Szu-pa" pei-nan lieh-shih chi-nien-ts'e (In memory of the martyrs who died in the accident of "April 8th"). Chungking, 1946.

Tagore, Amitendranath. *Literary Debates in Modern China, 1918–1937.* Tokyo: Centre for East Asian Cultural Studies, 1967.

T'ang Leang-li, ed. *Suppressing Communist-Banditry in China.* Shanghai: China United Press, 1934.

Taylor, George E. *The Struggle for North China.* New York: Institute of Pacific Relations, 1940.

Ten Glorious Years. Peking, 1960.

Teng Chung-hsia. *Chung-kuo chih-kung yun-tung chien-shih* (A short history of the Chinese labor movement). N.p., 1949.

Teng Hung. *Ti-i-ko feng-lang* (The first storm). Hong Kong, 1962.

Teng Tse-hui [Teng Tzu-hui]. *The Outstanding Success of the Agrarian Reform Movement in China.* Peking, 1954.

Thomas, S. B. *Recent Political and Economic Developments in China.* New York: Institute of Pacific Relations, 1950.

——— *Government and Administration in Communist China.* New York: Institute of Pacific Relations, 1953.

Ti-liu-tz'u ch'üan-kuo lao-tung ta-hui (The Sixth All-China Labor Congress). Hong Kong, 1948.

Ti-erh-tz'u kuo-nei ko-ming chan-cheng shih-ch'i shih-shih lun-ts'ung (Accounts of the second revolutionary civil war). Peking, 1956.

Ti-i-tz'u kuo-nei ko-ming chan-cheng shih-ch'i te kung-jen yun-tung (The worker's movement during the period of the first revolutionary civil war). Peking, 1963.

Ti-san-tz'u kuo-nei ko-ming chan-tou ta-shih yueh-piao (Monthly summary of major events during the third revolutionary civil war). Peking, 1961.

Ti-szu-chün chi-shih (A history of the Fourth Army). Canton, 1949.

Townsend, James R. *Political Participation in Communist China.* Berkeley, Calif.: University of California Press, 1967.

Treadgold, Donald W., ed., *Soviet and Chinese Communism: Similarities and Differences.* Seattle, Wash.: University of Washington Press, 1967.

Tsou Tang. *America's Failure in China, 1941–1950.* Chicago, Ill.: University of Chicago Press, 1963.

Tung Chün-lun. *Liu Chih-tan te ku-shih* (The story of Liu Chih-tan). Peking, 1956.

Tzu Fang. *Chi i-erh-chiu* (Remember December Ninth). Peking, 1955.

United States Department of Commerce. *The Size, Composition, and Growth of the Population of Mainland China.* Washington, D.C., 1961.

United States Department of State. *Papers Relating to the Foreign Relations of the United States, 1930.* Vol. II. Washington, D.C.: Government Printing Office, 1945.

——— *United States Relations with China: With Special Reference to the Period 1944–1949.* Washington, D.C.: Government Printing Office, 1949.

——— *Foreign Relations of the United States: Diplomatic Papers, 1943, China.* Washington, D.C.: Government Printing Office, 1957.

——— *Foreign Relations of the United States: Diplomatic Papers, 1944, China.* Vol. VI. Washington, D.C.: Government Printing Office, 1967.

The Unquenchable Spark. Peking, 1963.

Van Slyke, Lyman P. *Enemies and Friends: The United Front in Chinese Communist History.* Stanford, Calif.: Stanford University Press, 1967.

———, ed. *The Chinese Communist Movement: A Report of the United States War Department, July 1945.* Stanford, Calif.: Stanford University Press, 1968.

Vogel, Ezra F. *Canton under Communism: Programs and Politics in a Provincial Capital, 1949–1968.* Cambridge, Mass.: Harvard University Press, 1969.

Wales, Nym. *Inside Red China.* New York: Doubleday, Doran, 1939.

——— *The Chinese Labor Movement.* New York: John Day, 1945.

—— *Red Dust.* Stanford, Calif.: Stanford University Press, 1952.

—— *Notes on the Chinese Student Movement, 1935–1936.* Madison, Conn. Privately published, 1959.

—— *My Yenan Notebooks.* Madison, Conn. Privately published, 1961.

Walker, Kenneth R. *Planning in Chinese Agriculture: Socialisation and the Private Sector, 1956–1962.* London: Frank Cass, 1965.

Wang Chi. *Mainland China Organizations of Higher Learning in Science and Technology and Their Publications: A Selected Guide.* Washington, D.C.: Library of Congress, 1961.

Wang Chien-min. *Chung-kuo kung-ch'an-tang shih-kao* (Draft history of the CCP). 3 vols. Taipei, 1965.

Wang Chun-heng. *A Simple Geography of China.* Peking, 1958.

Wang Shih et al. *Chung-kuo kung-ch'an-tang li-shih chien-pien* (A brief history of the CCP). Shanghai, 1958; *JPRS* translation no. 8756, August 16, 1961.

Wang Shu-jen. *Min-hsi jen-min chien-ch'ih tou-cheng erh-shih-nien* (The West Fukien people's hard 20-year struggle). Shanghai, 1951.

Wang, Y. C. *Chinese Intellectuals and the West, 1872–1949.* Chapel Hill, N.C.: University of North Carolina Press, 1966.

Wei ch'un-chieh tang te tsu-chih erh tou-cheng (Struggle to purify the Party organization). Hong Kong, 1948.

Wei, Henry. *China and Soviet Russia.* Princeton, N.J.: Van Nostrand, 1956.

Wei Hung-yun, ed. *"Pa-i" ch'i-i* (The "August First" uprising). Wuhan, 1957.

White, Theodore H., and Annalee Jacoby. *Thunder Out of China.* New York: William Sloane, 1946.

Whiting, Allen S. *China Crosses the Yalu: The Decision to Enter the Korean War.* New York: Macmillan, 1960.

—— *Soviet Policies in China 1917–1924.* Stanford, Calif.: Stanford University Press, 1968.

—— and Sheng Shih-ts'ai. *Sinkiang: Pawn or Pivot?* East Lansing, Mich.: Michigan State University Press, 1958.

Wilbur, C. Martin, ed. *Chinese Sources on the History of the Chinese Communist Movement.* New York: East Asian Institute, Columbia University, 1950.

—— and Julie Lien-ying How, eds. *Documents on Communism, Nationalism, and Soviet Advisers in China, 1918–1927.* New York: Columbia University Press, 1956.

Wu, Eugene. *Leaders of Twentieth-Century China.* Stanford, Calif.: Stanford University Press, 1956.

Wu Hsiang-hsiang, ed. *Chung-kuo kung-ch'an-tang chih t'ou-shih* (Revelations of the CCP). Taipei, 1962.

Wu-ling feng-yün (The gathering clouds on the Wuling Mountains). Hong Kong, 1961.

Wu Min and Hsiao Feng. *Ts'ung "wu-szu" tao Chung-hua jen-min kung-ho-kuo te tan-sheng* (From "May Fourth" to the birth of the PRC). Peking, 1951.

Wu Yü-chang. *Hsin-hai ko-ming* (The revolution of 1911). Peking, 1961.

—— *The Revolution of 1911: A Great Democratic Revolution of China.* Peking, 1962.

Wu Yuan-li. *The Economy of Communist China.* New York: Praeger, 1965.

Yang Chih-lin. *Iron Bars But Not a Cage: Wang Jo-fei's Days in Prison.* Peking, 1962.

—— and Ch'iao Ming-fu. *Wang Jo-fei tsai yü chung* (Wang Jo-fei in prison). Hong Kong, 1961.

Yang Shang-kuei. *The Red Kiangsi-Kwangtung Border Region.* Peking, 1961.

Yen, Maria. *The Umbrella Garden.* Hong Kong: Union Press, 1957.

Young, Arthur N. *China's Wartime Finance and Inflation, 1937–1945.* Cambridge, Mass.: Harvard University Press, 1965.

Yu, Frederick T. C. *Mass Persuasion in Communist China.* New York: Praeger, 1964.

Zagoria, Donald S. *The Sino-Soviet Conflict 1956–1961.* Princeton, N.J.: Princeton University Press, 1962.

Appendices

Unless otherwise noted, all information is current to 1965. The symbol (†) indicates that the individual is not one of the 433 biographic entries.

Contents of Appendices

Part I. Personal Data

1. Date of Birth

Pre-1880

Ch'en Tu-hsiu	Hsu T'e-li	Ta P'u-sheng	Wu Yü-chang
Ho Shu-heng			

1880–1885

Hsieh Chueh-tsai	Liang Hsi	Shirob Jaltso	Su Chao-cheng
Li Chu-ch'en			

1886–1890

Chang Hsi-jo	Hsiang Chung-fa	Lin Po-ch'ü	Ts'ai Ho-sen
Chou Chien-jen	Li Szu-kuang	Sung Ch'ing-ling	Tung Pi-wu
Chu Te	Li Ta-chao	Ting Ying	Wang Wei-chou

1891–1895

Chang Chih-jang	Fan Wen-lan	Kuo Mo-jo	Nan Han-ch'en
Chang Yun-i	Fu Lien-chang	Liu Po-ch'eng	Teng Tzu-hui
Chao Shou-shan	Hsiang Ching-yü	Mao Tse-min	Yeh Chi-chuang
Ch'en Kung-po	Hsiao Ch'u-nü	Mao Tse-tung	Yun Tai-ying
Chi Fang	Hsu Te-heng		

1896–1900

Burhan Shahidi	Chou I-ch'ün	Huang Kung-lueh	P'eng P'ai
Chang Ch'i-lung	Ch'ü Ch'iu-pai	K'ang Sheng	P'eng Te-huai
Chang Chia-fu	Ch'u T'u-nan	Ku Ta-ts'un	Shao Shih-p'ing
Chang Kuo-t'ao	Fang Chih-min	Li Fu-ch'un	Shen Tse-min
Chang T'ai-lei	Ho Ch'ang-kung	Li K'o-nung	Shen Yen-ping
Chang Ting-ch'eng	Ho Lung	Li Li-san	Teng Chung-hsia
Chang Tsung-hsun	Hsia Hsi	Li Te-ch'üan	Ts'ai Ch'ang
Chang Wen-t'ien	Hsiang Ying	Li Wei-han	Tsou Ta-p'eng
Chang Yu-yü	Hsieh Fu-chih	Lin Yü-ying	Wang Jo-fei
Ch'en Ch'i-han	Hsu Chih-chen	Liu Shao-ch'i	Wu Te-feng
Ch'en Shao-min	Hsu Hai-tung	Lo Ping-hui	Yang Hsien-chen
Ch'en T'an-ch'iu	Hsu Ping	Ma Hsi-wu	Yang Hsiu-feng
Ch'en Yen-nien	Hsu Ti-hsin	Nieh Jung-chen	Yang Li-san
Ch'en Yun	Hu Yü-chih	P'an Tzu-li	Yeh Chien-ying
Chou En-lai	Huang Huo-ch'ing	P'ei Li-sheng	Yeh T'ing

1901–1905

An Tzu-wen
Chang Chi-ch'un
Chang Ch'in-ch'iu
Chang Ching-wu
Chang Han-fu
Chang P'ing-hua
Chao Erh-lu
Chao I-min
Chao Shih-yen
Ch'en Cheng-jen
Ch'en I
Ch'en Keng
Ch'en Po-ta
Ch'en Shao-yü
Ch'en Yü
Ch'eng Tzu-hua
Cheng Wei-san
Chi Ch'ao-ting
Chia T'o-fu
Chin Chung-hua
Chin Ming

Chou Huan
Chou Pao-chung
Chou P'ei-yuan
Chou Shih-ti
Chung Fu-hsiang
Fang Fang
Feng Pai-chü
Ho Meng-hsiung
Hsi Chung-hsun
Hsiao Ching-kuang
Hsu Hsiang-ch'ien
Hsu Kuang-ta
Hsueh Mu-ch'iao
Hu Feng
Huang K'o-ch'eng
Huang Yung-sheng
Jao Shu-shih
Jen Pi-shih
Kan Szu-ch'i
Kao Kang
K'o Ch'ing-shih

K'o Pai-nien
Kuan Hsiang-ying
K'uei Pi
Li Ch'iu-shih
Li I-mang
Li Ta
Li Yü
Li Yu-wen
Lin T'ieh
Liu Ch'ang-sheng
Liu Chih-tan
Liu Lan-t'ao
Liu Tzu-chiu
Lo Chang-lung
Lo I-nung
Lo Jung-huan
Lo Teng-hsien
Lü Cheng-ts'ao
Lu Ting-i
Ma Ming-fang

Ou Meng-chueh
P'an Fu-sheng
P'eng Chen
P'eng Hsueh-feng
Sha Ch'ien-li
Sung Jen-ch'iung
Sung Shih-lun
T'an Chen-lin
T'an Cheng
Teng Hsiao-p'ing
T'eng Tai-yuan
Teng Ying-ch'ao
Ts'ao Chü-ju
Tseng Hsi-sheng
Tseng Shan
Wan I
Wang Ts'ung-wu
Yang Hsien-tung
Yang Shang-k'un
Yü I-fu

1906–1910

Ai Szu-ch'i
Chang Ai-p'ing
Chang Su
Chang Te-sheng
Chao Chien-min
Chao Po-p'ing
Chao P'u-ch'u
Ch'en Ch'ang-hao
Ch'en Man-yuan
Ch'en Shih-ch'ü
Cheng Sen-yü
Chi Ya-t'ai
Ch'i Yen-ming
Ch'ien Chün-jui
Ch'in Pang-hsien
Chou Yang
Chu Te-hai
Chung Ch'i-kuang
Fan Ch'ang-chiang
Fang Ch'iang
Fang I
Han Hsien-ch'u
Han Nien-lung
Ho Ch'eng-hsiang
Ho Wei
Ho Ying
Hsiao Fang-chou
Hsiao K'o
Hsu Shih-yu
Hsu Yun-pei

Huang Chen
Huang Hua
Huang Ou-tung
Hui Yü-yü
Hung Hsueh-chih
Jung Kao-t'ang
Jung Tzu-ho
K'ai Feng
Keng Piao
Ku Cho-hsin
K'ung Yuan
Lai Ch'uan-chu
Lai Jo-yü
Li Che-jen
Li Chieh-po
Li Chien-chen
Li Chih-min
Li Ching-ch'üan
Li Chü-k'uei
Li Hsien-nien
Li Hsueh-feng
Li Pao-hua
Li Ta-chang
Li T'ao
Liao Ch'eng-chih
Liao Chih-kao
Liao Han-sheng
Liao Lu-yen
Lin Feng
Lin Piao

Liu Chen
Liu Chien-hsun
Liu Hsiao
Liu Jen
Liu Lan-po
Liu Ning-i
Liu Ting
Liu Tzu-hou
Liu Ya-lou
Lo Jui-ch'ing
Lu P'ing
Ma Wen-jui
Mei I
Meng Yung-ch'ien
Ouyang Ch'in
P'eng Shao-hui
Po I-po
Shih Liang
Shu T'ung
Shuai Meng-ch'i
Su Chen-hua
Su Yü
Sung Shao-wen
T'ang Liang
T'ao Chu
T'ao Lu-chia
Teng Fa
Teng Hua
Ting Ling

Ts'ai Shu-fan
Ts'ao Meng-chün
Tseng Sheng
Tseng Yung-ch'üan
Tso Ch'üan
Ulanfu
Wang Chen
Wang Cheng
Wang Chia-hsiang
Wang Chin-hsiang
Wang Ho-shou
Wang Hung-k'un
Wang Jen-chung
Wang Ping-chang
Wang Ping-nan
Wang Shang-jung
Wang Shih-t'ai
Wang Shou-tao
Wang Yu-p'ing
Wu Chih-p'u
Wu Hsiu-ch'üan
Wu Kai-chih
Wu Te
Wu Yun-fu
Yang I-ch'en
Yang Te-chih
Yang Yung
Yeh Fei
Yen Hung-yen

1911–1915

Chang Chih-hsiang
Chang Chung-liang
Chang Hsi
Chang Kuo-chien
Chang Ta-chih
Chao An-po
Ch'en Chia-k'ang
Ch'en Chung-ching
Ch'en Hsi-lien
Ch'en P'ei-hsien
Chiang Nan-hsiang
Ch'iao Kuan-hua
Ch'ien Hsin-chung

Ch'ien San-ch'iang
Ch'iu Ch'uang-ch'eng
Chou Hsiao-chou
Chu Tzu-ch'i
Feng Wen-pin
Han Kuang
Hsiao Hua
Hu Ch'iao-mu
Hu Sheng
Hu Yao-pang
Huang Ching
K'ang Yung-ho
Ko Pao-ch'üan

Lei Jen-min
Li Ch'ang
Lin Hai-yun
Liu Ko-p'ing
Liu Pai-yü
Lo Kuei-po
Lu Hsu-chang
P'eng T'ao
Saifudin
Sun Chih-yuan
T'an Ch'i-lung
Teng T'o

Tseng Ching-ping
Tuan Chün-i
Wang P'ing
Wei Kuo-ch'ing
Wu Heng
Wu Leng-hsi
Wu Po
Yang Ch'eng-wu
Yang Shuo
Yao Chung-ming
Yao I-lin
Yü Kuang-yuan

1916–1920

Ch'en Yü
Hsiung Fu

Huang Yen
Liu Tao-sheng

Ma Yü-huai
Sang-chi-yueh-hsi

Wang Feng

post-1920

Hu Ch'i-li

Yü I-ch'uan

Date Unknown

Chang Chih-i
Chang Chin-fu
Chang Hsiu-chu
Chang Kuo-hua
Chang Lien-hua
Chang Lin-chih
Chang T'i-hsueh
Chang Tzu-i
Chang Yen
Chang Yun
Chao Tzu-yang
Chiang Hua
Chiang I-chen
Chiang Ming
Chiang Wei-ch'ing
Ch'ien Li-jen
Ch'ien Ying
Chou Jung-hsin
Chou Lin

Fang Ming
Han Che-i
Hsu Chien-kuo
Hsu Li-ch'ün
Hsu Tzu-jung
Hu K'o-shih
Kao Feng
Kao K'o-lin
Kao Yang
Ku Mu
Kung Tzu-jung
Lai Chi-fa
Li Ch'iang
Li Ch'u-li
Li Fan-wu
Li Han-chün
Li Shih-ying
Lin Yü-nan
Liu Hsi-wu

Liu Hsi-yuan
Liu Hsiu-feng
Liu Ming-fu
Liu Yü-min
Lo Ch'iung
Lo Ming
Lü Tung
Ou T'ang-liang
Pai Ju-ping
P'ing Chieh-san
Sha Wen-han
Shen Hung
Sun Ta-kuang
Sun Tso-pin
Tu Jun-sheng
Wan Li
Wang Chao
Wang En-mao

Wang Kuang-wei
Wang Kuo-ch'üan
Wang Pi-ch'eng
Wang Shih-ying
Wang Shu-sheng
Wang Tao-han
Wang Wei
Wei Heng
Wu Hsueh-ch'ien
Yang Ch'i-ch'ing
Yang Ching-jen
Yang Ming-chai
Yang Shang-k'uei
Yang Yin
Yang Yun-yü
Yü Ch'iu-li
Yuan Jen-yuan
Yuan Pao-hua

2. Biographees Who Have Died

Note: Of the 433 biographees in this volume, 80 (18 percent) had died by 1970. However, only 42 (10 percent) had died when the Communists established the PRC in 1949.

Ai Szu-ch'i	c.1910–1966	Li Ch'iu-shih	1903–1931
Chang Hsi	1912–1959	Li Han-chün	?–1927
Chang Kuo-chien	1912–1962	Li K'o-nung	1898–1962
Chang T'ai-lei	1898–1927	Li Ta-chao	1889–1927
Chang Te-sheng	1909–1965	Liang Hsi	1883–1958
Chao Erh-lu	c.1905–1967	Lin Po-ch'ü	1886–1960
Chao Shih-yen	1901–1927	Lin Yü-nan	?–1931
Chao Shou-shan	c.1893–1965	Lin Yü-ying	1896–1942
Ch'en Keng	1904–1961	Liu Ch'ang-sheng	1904–1967
Ch'en Kung-po	1892–1946	Liu Chih-tan	1902–1936
Ch'en T'an-ch'iu	1896–1943	Liu Ya-lou	1910–1965
Ch'en Tu-hsiu	1879–1942	Lo Chang-lung	1901–?1949
Ch'en Yen-nien	1898–1927	Lo I-nung	1901–1928
Chi Ch'ao-ting	1903–1963	Lo Jung-huan	1902–1963
Ch'in Pang-hsien	1907–1946	Lo Ping-hui	1897–1946
Chou I-ch'ün	c.1898–1931	Lo Teng-hsien	1904–1933
Chou Pao-chung	1902–1964	Ma Hsi-wu	1898–1962
Ch'ü Ch'iu-pai	1899–1935	Mao Tse-min	1895–1943
Fan Wen-lan	1893–1969	P'eng Hsueh-feng	1905–1944
Fang Chih-min	1899–1935	P'eng P'ai	1896–1929
Ho Meng-hsiung	1903–1931	P'eng T'ao	1913–1961
Ho Shu-heng	1874–1935	Shao Shih-p'ing	1899–1965
Hsia Hsi	c.1900–c.1935	Shen Tse-min	1898–1934
Hsiang Ching-yü	1895–1928	Su Chao-cheng	1885–1929
Hsiang Chung-fa	c.1888–1931	Sun Chih-yuan	c.1911–1966
Hsiang Ying	1898–1941	Ta P'u-sheng	1874–1965
Hsiao Ch'u-nü	1894–1927	Teng Chung-hsia	1897–1933
Hsu Chih-chen	1898–1964	Teng Fa	1906–1946
Hsu T'e-li	1877–1968	Ting Ying	1888–1964
Huang Ching	1911–1958	Ts'ai Ho-sen	1890–c.1931
Huang Kung-lueh	1898–1931	Ts'ai Shu-fan	1908–1958
Jen Pi-shih	1904–1950	Tso Ch'üan	1906–1942
K'ai Feng	1907–1955	Wang Jo-fei	1896–1946
Kan Szu-ch'i	1904–1964	Wang Wei-chou	1887–1970
Kao Kang	c.1902–c.1954	Wu Yü-chang	1878–1966
K'o Ch'ing-shih	1902–1965	Yang Li-san	1900–1954
Ku Ta-ts'un	1897–1966	Yang Yin	?–1929
Kuan Hsiang-ying	1902–1946	Yeh Chi-chuang	1893–1967
Lai Ch'uan-chu	1910–1965	Yeh T'ing	1897–1946
Lai Jo-yü	1910–1958	Yun Tai-ying	1895–1931

3. Women

Chang Ch'in-ch'iu
Chang Yun
Ch'en Shao-min
Ch'ien Ying
Hsiang Ching-yü (Mme. Ts'ai Ho-sen)
Li Chien-chen
Li Te-ch'üan (Mme. Feng Yü-hsiang)
Lo Ch'iung
Ou Meng-chueh

Ou T'ang-liang
Shih Liang
Shuai Meng-ch'i
Sung Ch'ing-ling (Mme. Sun Yat-sen)
Teng Ying-ch'ao (Mme. Chou En-lai)
Ting Ling
Ts'ai Ch'ang (Mme. Li Fu-ch'un)
Ts'ao Meng-chün

4. National Minorities

Hakka

Ch'en Kung-po   Yeh Chien-ying

Hui

Liu Ko-p'ing   Ma Yü-huai   Ta P'u-sheng   Yang Ching-jen
Ma Hsi-wu

Mongolian

Chi Ya-t'ai   K'uei Pi   Ulanfu

Tibetan

Sang-chi-yueh-hsi   Shirob Jaltso

Uighur

Burhan Shahidi   Saifudin

Other

Chou Pao-chung   Chu Te-hai (Korean)   Kuan Hsiang-ying   Wei Kuo-ch'ing
  (Min-chia)   (Manchu)   (Chuang)

5. Native Province

Anhwei

			Other
An-ch'ing hsien,	*Ching-hsien*	*Liu-an hsien*	Chang Yun ?
see *Huai-ning hsien*	Wang Chia-hsiang	Ch'en Shao-yü	Chao P'u-ch'u
Ch'ao-hsien	*Huai-ning*	Huang Yen	K'o Ch'ing-shih
Li K'o-nung	Ch'en Tu-hsiu	*T'ung-ch'eng hsien*	Wu Po
	Ch'en Yen-nien	Huang Chen	Yao I-lin

Chekiang

			Other
Chia-hsing hsien	*Shao-hsing hsien*	*T'ung-hsiang hsien*	Chang Ch'in-ch'iu
Chin Chung-hua	Ch'ien San-ch'iang	Shen Tse-min	Chang Chin-fu
Chu-chi hsien	Chou Chien-jen	Shen Yen-ping	Chao An-po
Feng Wen-pin	Fan Wen-lan	*Wu-hsing hsien*	Cheng Sen-yü
Shang-yü hsien	Huang Ching	Liang Hsi	Wu Yun-fu
Hu Yü-chih			

Fukien

			Other
Ch'ang-t'ing hsien	*Fu-an hsien*	*T'ing-chou,*	Chang Kuo-chien
Fu Lien-chang	Yeh Fei	see *Ch'ang-t'ing hsien*	Su Yü
Yang Ch'eng-wu	*Hui-an hsien*	*Wu-p'ing hsien*	Tseng Ching-ping
Foochow	Ch'en Po-ta	Liu Ya-lou	
Ch'en P'ei-hsien	*Lung-yen hsien*	*Yung-ting hsien*	
Fang I	Teng Tzu-hui	Chang Ting-ch'eng	

Honan

		Other	
Ch'i-hsien	*Nan-yang hsien*	Ho Wei	Wang Kuo-ch'üan
Wu Chih-p'u	P'eng Hsueh-feng	Li Shih-ying	Yang I-ch'en
Hsin-yang	*Nei-huang hsien*		
Teng Ying-ch'ao	Wang Ts'ung-wu		

Hopeh

Ch'ien-an hsien
Yang Hsiu-feng
Feng-jun hsien
Li Chieh-po
Jen-ch'iu hsien
Ma Yü-huai
Lo-t'ing hsien
Li Pao-hua
Li Ta-chao
Man-ch'eng hsien
Liu Ning-i

Nan-kung hsien
Hsu Ping
P'ing-hsiang hsien
Chang Hsi
T'ung-hsien
Li Te-ch'üan
Wan-hsien
Liu Hsiu-feng
Wan-p'ing hsien
Ch'i Yen-ming

Wei-hsien
(formerly Chahar
Province)
Chang Su
Other
Chang Lin-chih
Chao I-min
Hsu Yun-pei
Huang Hua ?
Liu Chien-hsun

Liu Ko-p'ing
Liu Tzu-hou
Lu P'ing ?
P'ing Chieh-san
Sun Chih-yuan
Wang Ho-shou
Wang Jen-chung
Wang Shang-jung
Wu Te
Yang Hsien-tung

Hunan

Changsha
Chou Hsiao-chou
Hsiao Ching-kuang
Hsu Kuang-ta
Hsu T'e-li
(born near Changsha)
Ts'ao Meng-chün
Yang Li-san
Ch'ang-te
Ting Ling
Chia-ho hsien
Hsiao K'o
Han-shou hsien
Hsu Chih-chen
Heng-shan hsien
Lo Jung-huan
Hsiang-hsiang hsien
Ch'en Keng
Ts'ai Ch'ang
Ts'ai Ho-sen
Hsiang-t'an hsien
Ho Meng-hsiung
Huang Kung-lueh
Lo I-nung
Mao Tse-min
Mao Tse-tung
P'eng Te-huai

Hsiang-yin hsien
Jen Pi-shih
Hsu-p'u hsien
Hsiang Ching-yü
Hua-jung hsien
Ho Ch'ang-kung
I-chang hsien
Li T'ao
Teng Chung-hsia
I-yang hsien
Chou Yang
Hsia Hsi
Kuei-yang hsien
Teng Hua
Li-ling hsien
Chang Chi-ch'un
Keng Piao
Li Li-san
Li Wei-han
Liao Han-sheng
Tso Ch'üan
Yang Te-chih
Lin-li hsien
Chang Ching-wu
Ling-ling hsien
Lin Po-ch'ü

Liu-yang hsien
Chang Ch'i-lung
Lo Chang-lung
Sung Jen-ch'iung
T'an Cheng
(probably)
Wang Chen
Wang Shou-tao
Yang Yung
Yuan Jen-yuan
Ma-yang hsien
T'eng Tai-yuan
Ning-hsiang hsien
Hsieh Chueh-tsai
Ho Shu-heng
Liu Shao-ch'i
Ouyang Ch'in ?
Sang-chih hsien
Ho Lung
Yu-hsien
T'an Chen-lin
Yung-chou,
see *Ling-ling hsien.*
Yung-hsing hsien
Huang K'o-ch'eng
Tseng Hsi-sheng

Yung-shun hsien
Li Chu-ch'en
Other
Chang P'ing-hua
Chang Tzu-i
Fang Ch'iang
Han Hsien-ch'u
Hu Yao-pang
K'ai Feng
Kan Szu-ch'i
Li Chih-min
Li Chü-k'uei
Li Fu-ch'un
Liu Hsiao
P'eng Shao-hui
Shuai Meng-ch'i
Su Chen-hua
Sung Shih-lun
T'ang Liang
T'ao Chu
T'ao Lu-chia
Tseng Yung-ch'üan
Wang Pi-ch'eng
Wang Ping-chang
Yang Ch'i-ch'ing

Hupeh

Chin-k'ou hsien
Li Ch'iu-shih
Ching-men hsien
Ch'en Shih-ch'ü
Han-yang hsien
Ts'ai Shu-fan
Hsiao-kan hsien
Wang Shu-sheng
Huang-an hsien
Cheng Wei-san
Li Hsien-nien
Tung Pi-wu

Huang-kang hsien
Li Szu-kuang
Lin Piao
Huang-p'i hsien
Hsu Hai-tung
I-tu hsien
Hu Feng
Kuang-chi hsien
Ch'en Chia-k'ang
Wuhan
Chang Chih-i
Hsiang Ying

(Wuchang)
Wu Hsiu-ch'üan
(Wuchang)
Yun Tai-ying
(Wuchang)
Other
Ch'en Ch'ang-hao
Ch'en Hsi-lien
Ch'en T'an-ch'iu
Chiang Hua
Hsiang Chung-fa
Hsiao Ch'u-nü

Hsieh Fu-chih
Hsu Chien-kuo
Hsu Shih-yu
Huang Huo-ch'ing
Li Han-chün
Lin Yü-nan
Lin Yü-ying
Liu Chen
Wang Hung-k'un
Wu Te-feng
Yang Hsien-chen
Yü Kuang-yuan ?

Inner Mongolia

Tumet Banner
Chi Ya-t'ai   K'uei Pi   Ulanfu

Kansu

Sun Tso-pin ?   Yang Ching-jen

Kiangsi

Chi-shui hsien
Chang Kuo-t'ao
Chiu-chiang hsien,
see *Kiukiang hsien*
Hsing-kuo hsien
Hsiao Hua
Tseng Shan
Yang Shang-k'uei
Hui-ch'ang hsien
Li Ching-ch'üan

I-yang hsien
Fang Chih-min
Shao Shih-p'ing
Wang Chin-hsiang
Juichin
Ch'iu Ch'uang-ch'eng
Wang P'ing
Kiukiang hsien
(Chiu-chiang hsien)
Hsu Te-heng

Lin-ch'uan hsien
Jao Shu-shih
P'ing-hsiang hsien
K'ung Yuan
P'o-yang hsien
P'eng T'ao
Tung-hsiang hsien
Shu T'ung
Yung-feng hsien
Huang Yung-sheng

Yung-hsin hsien
Wang En-mao
Other
Chang Kuo-hua
Ch'en Cheng-jen
Ch'en Ch'i-han
Huang Ou-tung
Hung Hsueh-chih
Lai Ch'uan-chu
T'an Ch'i-lung

Kiangsu

Ch'ang-chou
Chang Han-fu
Chang T'ai-lei
Ch'ü Ch'iu-pai
Shih Liang
Ching-p'u hsien
Ch'en Yun
Hai-men hsien
Chi Fang
Huai-an hsien
Chou En-lai

I-hsing hsien
Chou P'ei-yuan
Liu-ho hsien
Ta P'u-sheng
Nan-hui hsien
Chang Wen-t'ien
Su-chou hsien
Hu Sheng
Sha Ch'ien-li
Tung-t'ai hsien
Ko Pao-ch'üan

Wu-chin,
see *Ch'ang-chou.*
Wu-hsi hsien
(Wusih hsien)
Ch'ien Chün-jui
Ch'in Pang-hsien
Lu Ting-i
Wu-sung city
(Woosung)
Ch'ien Hsin-chung

Yen-ch'eng hsien
Ch'iao Kuan-hua
Hu Ch'iao-mu
Other
Chang Chih-jang
Ch'en Chung-ching
Chiang Wei-ch'ing
Liao Lu-yen
Wang Cheng

Kwangsi

Meng-shan hsien
Ch'en Man-yuan

Tung-lan hsien
Wei Kuo-ch'ing

Other
Chung Fu-hsiang

Kwangtung

Canton
Ch'en Kung-po
Chieh-yang hsien
Hsu Ti-hsin
Chung-shan (Shekki)
hsien
Yang Yin
Feng-shun hsien
Li Chien-chen
Hai-feng hsien
P'eng P'ai

Hainan Island
Ch'iung-shan hsien
Feng Pai-chü
Wen-ch'ang hsien
Chang Yun-i
Other
Chou Shih-ti
Ho Ying
Hsiang-shan hsien
Su Chao-cheng
Hsin-hsing hsien
Yeh Chi-chuang

Hsin-hui hsien
Wu Leng-hsi
Hui-yang hsien
Tseng Sheng
Yeh T'ing
Mao-ming hsien
Ting Ying
Mei-hsien
Chung Ch'i-kuang
Yeh Chien-ying
Pao-an hsien
Ch'en Yü

P'u-ning hsien
Fang Fang
Swatow
Mei I
Wu-hua hsien
Ku Ta-ts'un
Yun-fu hsien
Teng Fa
Other
Lo Kuei-po ?
Lo Teng-hsien
Ou Meng-chueh

Kweichow

An-shun hsien
Wang Jo-fei

Jen-huai hsien
Han Nien-lung

Other
Chou Lin

Manchuria (*Heilungkiang*)

Mu-ling hsien
  Li Fan-wu

Wang-k'uei hsien
  Lin Feng

Other
  Tsou Ta-p'eng

Manchuria (*Kirin*)

Han Kuang

Manchuria (*Liaoning*)

Feng-ch'eng hsien
  Liu Lan-po
Hai-ch'eng hsien
  Lü Cheng-ts'ao
  Wan I

I-hsien
  Ku Cho-hsin
Liao-yang hsien
  Li Yu-wen

T'ai-an hsien
  Yü I-fu

Other
  Chou Huan
  Kao Yang
  Kuan Hsiang-ying

Peking

Liu Pai-yü

Meng Yung-ch'ien ?

Shanghai

Lu Hsu-chang

Shen Hung

Sung Ch'ing-ling

Shansi

Chao-ch'eng hsien
  Nan Han-ch'en
Ch'ü-wu hsien
  P'eng Chen
Fen-yang hsien
  Chi Ch'ao-ting
Hsia-hsien
  Ch'eng Tzu-hua

Ling-ch'iu hsien
  Jung Tzu-ho
Ling-shih hsien
  Chang Yu-yü
Ting-hsiang hsien
  Po I-po
T'un-liu hsien
  Sung Shao-wen

Wu-t'ai hsien
  Hsu Hsiang-ch'ien
  Lai Jo-yü
Yuan-p'ing hsien
  Chao Erh-lu
Yung-chi hsien
  Li Hsueh-feng

Other
  Ho Ch'eng-hsiang ?
  K'ang Yung-ho ?
  Lei Jen-min
  Li Yü ?
  P'ei Li-sheng

Shantung

Ch'i-hsia hsien
  Yao Chung-ming
Chiu-hai-yang hsien,
  see *Hai-yang hsien.*
Chu-ch'eng hsien
  K'ang Sheng

Hai-yang hsien
  Liu Ch'ang-sheng
P'eng-lai hsien
  Yang Shuo
Shou-kuang hsien
  Ch'en Shao-min

Wen-teng hsien
  P'an Fu-sheng
Other
  Chao Chien-min
  Chin Ming
  Han Che-i

Liu Tzu-chiu ?
Teng T'o
Tuan Chün-i
Wang Yu-p'ing
Yang Ming-chai

Shensi

Ch'ao-i
  Chang Hsi-jo
Feng-hsiang hsien
  Chang Ta-chih
Fu-p'ing hsien
  Chang Chung-liang
  Hsi Chung-hsun
Heng-shan hsien
  Kao Kang
Hu-hsien
  Chao Shou-shan

Lan-t'ien hsien
  Wang Feng
Lo-ch'uan hsien
  Wang Shih-t'ai
Mi-chih hsien
  Liu Lan-t'ao
  Ma Ming-fang
Pao-an hsien
  Liu Chih-tan
  Ma Hsi-wu

San-yuan hsien
  Wang Ping-nan
Shen-mu hsien
  Chia T'o-fu
Sui-te hsien
  Ma Wen-jui
Wei-nan hsien
  Chang Tsung-hsun
Yü-lin hsien
  Chang Te-sheng

Other
  An Tzu-wen ?
  Chao Po-p'ing
  Hui Yü-yü
  Jung Kao-t'ang ?
  Kao K'o-lin
  Li Ta
  Pai Ju-ping
  P'an Tzu-li
  Yen Hung-yen

Sinkiang

Aksu
Burhan Shahidi ?

Artush (A-t'u-shih)
Saifudin

Szechwan

Chia-ting hsien
 (now Lo-shan hsien)
 Kuo Mo-jo
 Li I-mang
Chiang-ching hsien
 Nieh Jung-chen
Ch'ien-ning hsien
 Liao Chih-kao
I-lung hsien
 Chu Te

Jung-hsien
 Wu Yü-chang
K'ai-hsien
 Liu Po-ch'eng
 Wang Wei-chou
Kuang-an hsien
 Teng Hsiao-p'ing
Lo-chih hsien
 Ch'en I

Lo-chan hsien,
 see *Chia-ting hsien.*
Nan-ch'ung hsien
 Lo Jui-ch'ing
Nei-chiang hsien
 Fan Ch'ang-chiang
Tang-pa hsien
 Sang-chi-yueh-hsi
Yu-yang hsien
 Chao Shih-yen

Other
 Chang Ai-p'ing
 Hsiung Fu
 Lai Chi-fa
 Li Ta-chang
 Lin T'ieh
 Liu Jen
 Wan Li
 Yang Shang-k'un
 Yü Ch'iu-li ?

Tsinghai

Hsun-hua hsien
 Shirob Jaltso

Other
 Kao Feng

Yunnan

I-liang hsien
 Lo Ping-hui
Ta-li hsien
 Chou Pao-chung

T'eng-ch'ung hsien
 Ai Szu-ch'i

Wen-shan hsien
 Ch'u T'u-nan

Other
 Yü I-ch'uan

Abroad

Korea
 Chu Te-hai

Japan
 Liao Ch'eng-chih

No Information

Chang Chia-fu	Chou Jung-hsin	Li Ch'iang	Sun Ta-kuang
Chang Chih-hsiang	Chu Tzu-ch'i	Li Ch'u-li	Ts'ao Chü-ju
Chang Hsiu-chu	Fang Ming	Lin Hai-yun	Tu Jun-sheng
Chang Lien-hua	Hsiao Fang-chou	Liu Hsi-wu	Wang Chao
Chang T'i-hsueh	Hsu Li-ch'ün	Liu Hsi-yuan	Wang Kuang-wei
Chang Yen	Hsu Tzu-jung	Liu Ming-fu	Wang Shih-ying
Chao Tzu-yang	Hsueh Mu-ch'iao	Liu Tao-sheng	Wang Tao-han
Ch'en Yü	Hu Ch'i-li	Liu Ting	Wang Wei
Chiang I-chen	Hu K'o-shih	Liu Yü-min	Wei Heng
Chiang Ming	K'o Pai-nien	Lo Ch'iung	Wu Heng
Chiang Nan-hsiang	Ku Mu	Lo Ming	Wu Hsueh-ch'ien
Ch'ien Li-jen	Kung Tzu-jung	Lü Tung	Wu Kai-chih
Ch'ien Ying	Li Ch'ang	Ou T'ang-liang	Yang Yun-yü
Chou I-ch'ün	Li Che-jen	Sha Wen-han	Yuan Pao-hua

6. Class Origin

Note: The material in this appendix should be treated with caution. From the scanty information published by the Chinese Communists, it is clear that there is a tendency to emphasize humble origins and to ignore or distort class origin if the person in question came from a well-to-do family. Some persons are listed in more than one category.

Proletariat

Ch'en Yü	Hsiang Ying	Li Chien-chen	T'an Chen-lin
Feng Pai-chü	Hsu Hai-tung	Lo Teng-hsien	T'ang Liang
Fu Lien-chang	Hu Feng	Shen Hung	Teng Fa
Hsiang Chung-fa	Kuan Hsiang-ying		

Poor and Middle Peasant

Chang Ting-ch'eng	Ho Lung	Liu Shao-ch'i	Su Chao-cheng
Chang Wen-t'ien	Hsiao Hua	Lo I-nung	T'an Ch'i-lung
Chang Yu-yü	Hsu Shih-yu	Lo Ping-hui	Wang Chen
Chao Shou-shan	Hsu T'e-li	Lü Cheng-ts'ao	Wang En-mao
Ch'en Hsi-lien	Huang Chen	Ma Hsi-wu	Wang Pi-ch'eng
Ch'en Po-ta	Kan Szu-ch'i	Nan Han-ch'en	Wang Shou-tao
Ch'en Shao-min	Ku Ta-ts'un	P'eng Chen	Yang Ch'eng-wu
Ch'en Shao-yü	Li Ta-chao	P'eng Hsueh-feng	Yang Te-chih
Ch'eng Tzu-hua	Liu Ch'ang-sheng	P'eng Te-huai	Yeh T'ing
Chu Te ?	Liu Chih-tan		

Rich Peasant, Well-to-do, and Landlord

Chang Kuo-t'ao	Hsu Kuang-ta	Liu Hsiao	Teng Ying-ch'ao
Chao Chien-min	Hsu Ping	Lo Chang-lung	Ting Ling
Ch'en Keng	Hu Ch'iao-mu	Lo Jui-ch'ing	Tso Ch'üan
Chou Chien-jen	Huang Ching	Lu Ting-i	Wang Jo-fei
Chou En-lai	Huang Kung-lueh	Mao Tse-min	Wang Ping-nan
Chou P'ei-yuan	Jen Pi-shih	Mao Tse-tung	Wang Shu-sheng
Chou Yang	K'ang Sheng	Nieh Jung-chen	Wang Wei-chou
Fan Ch'ang-chiang	Kao Kang	P'eng P'ai	Wu Te-feng
Ho Wei	K'o Ch'ing-shih	Shen Tse-min	Wu Yü-chang
Hsiao K'o	Kuo Mo-jo	Shen Yen-ping	Yang Shang-k'un
Hsieh Chueh-tsai	Li Han-chün	Sung Ch'ing-ling	Yao I-lin
Hsu Hsiang-ch'ien	Lin Po-ch'ü		

Official and Intellectual

Ch'en Cheng-jen	Chou Chien-jen	Ko Pao-ch'üan	Lin Po-ch'ü
Ch'en I	Fan Ch'ang-chiang	Li Ch'iu-shih	Teng Chung-hsia
Ch'en Tu-hsiu	Hsiao Ching-kuang	Li Fu-ch'un	Ts'ai Ch'ang
Ch'en Yen-nien	Hsu Hsiang-ch'ien	Li Li-san	Ts'ai Ho-sen
Chi Ch'ao-ting	Huang Kung-lueh	Li Wei-han	Yun Tai-ying
Ch'in Pang-hsien	Jen Pi-shih	Liao Ch'eng-chih	

Business

Chang T'ai-lei	Kuo Mo-jo	Lu Ting-i	Yeh Chi-chuang
Ch'en Shih-ch'ü	Lin Piao	Saifudin	Yeh Chien-ying
Fang Fang	Lo Jung-huan	Teng Tzu-hui	

7. Higher Education in China

Note: This category applies to education beyond the middle-school level. An asterisk indicates an instructor; two asterisks indicates a student who was later an instructor.

Peking University

Chang Kuo-t'ao	Ho Meng-hsiung	Lin Feng	Teng Chung-hsia
Chang Yu-yü	Hsu Te-heng	Liu Lan-t'ao	Ting Ling
Ch'en Chung-ching	Hu Ch'i-li	Liu Tzu-hou ?	Ts'ao Meng-chün
Ch'en Kung-po	Hu Sheng	Lo Chang-lung	Wang Feng
*Ch'en Tu-hsiu	Huang Ching	Nan Han-ch'en	Wu Te
Ch'ü Ch'iu-pai	*Li Ta-chao	Po I-po	Yang Hsiu-feng
Fan Ch'ang-chiang	Li Yu-wen	Sung Shao-wen	Yao Chung-ming
**Fan Wen-lan			

Peking Normal College

An Tzu-wen	Chao Shih-yen ?	Shao Shih-p'ing	Tu Jun-sheng
Chang Su	Ch'u T'u-nan	Sun Chih-yuan ?	Yang Hsien-chen

Tsinghua University (*Peking*)

Chang Han-fu	Ch'ien San-ch'iang	Hu Ch'iao-mu	Yao I-lin
Chi Ch'ao-ting	**Chou P'ei-yuan	Li Ch'ang	Yü Kuang-yuan
Ch'iao Kuan-hua	Hsueh Mu-ch'iao	Liao Chih-kao	

Yenching University (*Peking*)

Ch'i Yen-ming	K'o Pai-nien ?	Yü I-fu
Huang Hua	Li Te-ch'üan	

Other Schools in the Peking Area

Chang T'ai-lei	Ch'ü Ch'iu-pai	Liu Ning-i	Ulanfu
Chao Shih-yen	K'uei Pi	P'eng T'ao	Wang Ho-shou
*Ch'en Po-ta	Li Fan-wu	*Tseng Yung-ch'üan	Yang Hsien-chen
Chi Ya-t'ai			

Schools in Shansi

Hsu Hsiang-ch'ien	Lei Jen-min	Po I-po
Jung Tzu-ho	Nan Han-ch'en	

Shanghai University

Chang Ch'in-ch'iu	*Ch'ü Ch'iu-pai	K'ang Sheng	Ting Ling
*Chang T'ai-lei	Fang Chih-min ?	Li I-mang	Wang Chia-hsiang
Ch'en Po-ta ?	*Hsiao Ch'u-nü	*Shen Yen-ping	Yang Shang-k'un
Ch'en Shao-yü	Jao Shu-shih	*Teng Chung-hsia	*Yun Tai-ying
Ch'in Pang-hsien			

Other Schools in the Shanghai Area

Chang Chih-jang	Feng Pai-chü	*Kuo Mo-jo	Sha Ch'ien-li
Chang T'ai-lei	Hsu T'e-li	Liu Shao-ch'i	Shen Tse-min
Chang Yun	Hsu Ti-hsin	Lo I-nung	Shih Liang
Chao P'u-ch'u	Huang Chen	Lu Hsu-chang	*Wu Hsiu-ch'üan
Ch'in Pang-hsien	Jen Pi-shih	Lu Ting-i	Yang Ming-chai
Chou Yang	K'o Pai-nien ?		

Nanking Schools

Chang Wen-t'ien	Shen Tse-min	Yang Hsien-tung
K'o Ch'ing-shih	Shen Yen-ping	

Sun Yat-sen University (Canton)

Hsu Ti-hsin	*Li Ch'iu-shih	Ou Meng-chueh
*Kuo Mo-jo	Lo Jung-huan	Tseng Sheng

Other Schools in the Canton Area

Ch'en Kung-po	*Hsiao Ch'u-nü	Hsu Ti-hsin	Lin T'ieh

Schools in the Wuhan Area

Ch'en Chia-k'ang	Ho Wei	*Li Han-chün	Wu Te-feng
*Ch'en T'an-ch'iu	Hsiao Ch'u-nü	*Shao Shih-p'ing	Yun Tai-ying
Ch'ü Ch'iu-pai	Li Ch'iu-shih		

Schools in the Changsha Area

Chang Ch'i-lung	Hsiao Ching-kuang	Lo Chang-lung	Ts'ai Ch'ang
Ch'en Chung-ching	**Hsu T'e-li	Lo Jung-huan	Ts'ai Ho-sen
Han Hsien-ch'u	Kan Szu-ch'i	Mao Tse-min	Ts'ao Meng-chün
Ho Ch'ang-kung	Li Fu-ch'un	Mao Tse-tung	Wang Chen
*Ho Shu-heng	Li Li-san	T'an Cheng ?	Wang Shou-tao
Hsia Hsi	**Li Wei-han	Teng Chung-hsia	*Yun Tai-ying
Hsiang Ching-yü	Liu Shao-ch'i	T'eng Tai-yuan	

Other Schools

*Ai Szu-ch'i	Ch'ien Hsin-chung	Hsu T'e-li	Ma Ming-fang
An Tzu-wen	Chin Chung-hua	Hsu Ti-hsin	Po I-po
*Chang Ch'in-ch'iu	Ch'in Pang-hsien	Hu Ch'iao-mu	Saifudin
Chang Hsi	Chou En-lai	Hu Yü-chih	Shao Shih-p'ing
*Chang Kuo-chien	Chou Lin	Huang Ching	*Shirob Jaltso
Chang T'ai-lei	*Chou Yang	K'uei Pi	Teng Ying-ch'ao
Chao P'u-ch'u	Ch'ü Ch'iu-pai	Li Chieh-po	Tuan Chün-i
Ch'en Chung-ching	Chu Te	*Li Ch'iu-shih	Tung Pi-wu
Ch'en I	*Fan Wen-lan	Li Chu-ch'en	Ulanfu
Ch'en Po-ta	Fang Chih-min	Li Fan-wu	Wang Ho-shou
*Ch'en T'an-ch'iu	Fang Fang	Li Li-san	*Wu Hsiu-ch'üan
Ch'en Tu-hsiu	Fu Lien-chang	Li Ta-chao	Wu Yü-chang
Cheng Wei-san	Ho Shu-heng	Lin Po-ch'ü	Yang Shang-k'un
Chia T'o-fu	Hsieh Chueh-tsai	Liu Ning-i	Yang Shuo
Ch'ien Chün-jui			

8. Military Education in China

Note: An asterisk indicates instructors. Two asterisks indicate students who were later instructors.

Whampoa Military Academy

Chang Chi-ch'un	*Chou Pao-chung	*Li Fu-ch'un	Sung Shih-lun
Chang Tsung-hsun	Chou Shih-ti	Lin Piao	T'ao Chu ?
Ch'en Ch'i-han	*Ch'ü Ch'iu-pai	Liu Chih-tan	Teng Fa
*Ch'en I	Hsiao Ching-kuang	Lo Jui-ch'ing	*Teng Tzu-hui ?
Ch'en Keng	*Hsiao Ch'u-nü	*Nieh Jung-chen	Tseng Hsi-sheng
Ch'eng Tzu-hua	**Hsu Hsiang-ch'ien	Ouyang Ch'in	Tso Ch'üan
*Chi Fang	Hsu Kuang-ta	P'an Tzu-li	*Yeh Chien-ying
*Chou En-lai	Huang K'o-ch'eng	Sung Jen-ch'iung	*Yun Tai-ying
Chou I-ch'ün	Huang Kung-lueh		

Chung Shan Military and Political Academy, Sian

Hsi Chung-hsun	Kao Kang	*Liu Chih-tan	*Teng Hsiao-p'ing

Red Army School (Hung-chün hsueh-hsiao)
and Red Army Academy (Hung-chün ta-hsueh), Juichin

Chang Ai-p'ing ?	Ch'iu Ch'uang-ch'eng	Liu Tao-sheng	*Teng Hsiao-p'ing
Chang Tsung-hsun	*Chou Shih-ti	*Lo Kuei-po	*Tso Ch'üan
Chao Erh-lu	*Ho Ch'ang-kung	*Ouyang Ch'in	*Tung Pi-wu
*Ch'en Keng	Huang Yung-sheng	*P'eng Hsueh-feng	*Wu Hsiu-ch'üan
Ch'en Man-yuan	Li Chien-chen	Sung Jen-ch'iung	Yang Te-chih
Ch'eng Tzu-hua	Liu Po-ch'eng	Sung Shih-lun	Yang Yung
*Chiang I-chen			

Red Army Academy and Anti-Japanese Military
and Political Academy (K'ang-ta), Shensi

Note: The Red Army Academy was renamed K'ang-ta in early 1937.

*Ai Szu-ch'i	Ho Wei	Li Hsien-nien	*P'eng Shao-hui
*Chang Ai-p'ing	Hsieh Fu-chih ?	Li T'ao	*Shao Shih-p'ing
*Chang Chi-ch'un	*Hsu Hsiang-ch'ien	*Lin Piao	Su Chen-hua
Chang Chung-liang	Hsu Kuang-ta	Liu Chen ?	*T'eng Tai-yuan
Chang Ta-chih	Hsu Shih-yu	*Liu Ting	*Ting Ling
*Chang Wen-t'ien	*Hsueh Mu-ch'iao	**Liu Ya-lou	*Wang Chia-hsiang
Chao Erh-lu	Hu Yao-pang	*Lo Jui-ch'ing	Wang P'ing
Ch'en Hsi-lien	Huang Yung-sheng	*Lo Jung-huan	*Wang Shu-sheng
Ch'en Shih-ch'ü	**Keng Piao	*Mao Tse-tung	Yang Ch'eng-wu
*Feng Wen-pin	*Lai Ch'uan-chu	*Nieh Jung-chen	Yang Te-chih
Han Hsien-ch'u	**Li Ching-ch'üan	P'eng Hsueh-feng	Yang Yung
*Ho Ch'ang-kung			

Other Military Schools

*Chang Yun	Chou Pao-chung	P'eng Te-huai	Wang Ping-nan
Chang Yun-i	**Chu Te	Tso Ch'üan	*Yeh Chien-ying
Chi Fang	*Lü Cheng-ts'ao	Wan I	Yeh T'ing
*Ch'iu Ch'uang-ch'eng	*P'eng Hsueh-feng		

9. Education Abroad

Note: Education abroad is defined very loosely. The man who went abroad and graduated from college after four years is the exception rather than the rule.

France

Chao Shih-yen	Hsiang Ching-yü	Li Wei-han	Wan Li ?
Ch'en I	Hsu Te-heng	Nieh Jung-chen	Wang Jo-fei
Ch'en Yen-nien	Hsu T'e-li	Teng Hsiao-p'ing ?	Wu Yü-chang
Ch'ien San-ch'iang	Hu Yü-chih	Ts'ai Ch'ang	Yang Hsiu-feng
Chou En-lai	Li Fu-ch'un	Ts'ai Ho-sen	Yeh T'ing
Ho Ch'ang-kung	Li Li-san		

Germany

Burhan Shahidi	Chu Te	Liang Hsi	Yang Hsien-chen
Ch'iao Kuan-hua	Hsu Ping	Wang Ping-nan	Yeh T'ing

Japan

Ch'en Tu-hsiu	Li Szu-kuang	Lin Po-ch'ü	Wang Jo-fei
Chou En-lai	Liang Hsi	P'eng P'ai	Wang Ping-nan
Chou Yang	Liao Ch'eng-chih	Ting Ying	Wang Wei-chou
Li Chu-ch'en	Lin Feng	Tung Pi-wu	Wu Yü-chang
Li Han-chün			

United Kingdom

Chang Han-fu ?	Chang Hsi-jo	Hsu Te-heng	Li Szu-kuang

United States

Chang Chih-jang	Ch'en Chung-ching	Chou P'ei-yuan	Yang Hsien-tung
Chang Han-fu	Ch'en Kung-po	Sung Ch'ing-ling	
Chang Hsi-jo	Chi Ch'ao-ting		

USSR

Communist University of the Toilers of the East

Chang T'ai-lei	Hsiao Ching-kuang	Li Fu-ch'un	Ts'ai Ch'ang
Ch'en Yen-nien	Hsu Chih-chen	Lin Feng	Tso Ch'üan
Ch'ü Ch'iu-pai	Jen Pi-shih	Liu Shao-ch'i	Wang Jo-fei
Chu Te	Kuan Hsiang-ying	Lo I-nung	Yang Hsien-chen
Hsiang Ching-yü	Li Ch'iu-shih	Nieh Jung-chen	Yeh T'ing

Sun Yat-sen University

(*later: Communist University of the Toilers of China*)

Chang Ch'in-ch'iu	Ch'in Pang-hsien	Kan Szu-ch'i	Wang Chia-hsiang
Chang Kuo-t'ao	Ho Shu-heng	Lin Po-ch'ü	Wang Ho-shou
Chang Wen-t'ien	Hsia Hsi	Lu Ting-i ?	Wang Ts'ung-wu
Ch'en Ch'ang-hao	Hsu Ping	Shen Tse-min	Wu Hsiu-ch'üan
Ch'en Po-ta	Hsu T'e-li	Ts'ai Shu-fan	Wu Yü-chang
Ch'en Shao-yü	K'ai Feng	Ulanfu	Yang Shang-k'un

Moscow University

Han Kuang   Li Yu-wen ?   P'ei Li-sheng ?
Li Chü-k'uei ?   Liu Jen

Red Army (Frunze) Military Academy

Fang Ch'iang   Liu Ya-lou   Tso Ch'üan   Wu Hsiu-ch'üan ?
Li Ta   Nieh Jung-chen   Wang Ping-chang   Yeh T'ing
Liu Po-ch'eng

Other Institutions

An Tzu-wen ?   Ch'iu Ch'uang-ch'eng   Huang Kung-lueh   Teng Hsiao-p'ing
Chang Chi-ch'un   Chou Pao-chung ?   K'ang Sheng   T'eng Tai-yuan
Chang Ch'in-ch'iu ?   Hsiang Chung-fa   K'ung Yuan   Ts'ai Ho-sen
Chao Shih-yen ?   Hsiao Ching-kuang   Li Li-san   Ts'ai Shu-fan
Ch'en Ch'ang-hao ?   Hsu Kuang-ta ?   Liu Chen   Tung Pi-wu
Ch'en Keng ?   Hsu Ping   Saifudin   Wang Chia-hsiang
Ch'ien Hsin-chung   Hsueh Mu-ch'iao ?   Teng Fa ?   Wang Wei-chou
Ch'in Pang-hsien   Huang Huo-ch'ing

Other Countries

Ho Ch'ang-kung   Ta P'u-sheng   Yang Hsien-chen   Yeh T'ing
Nieh Jung-chen

10. Membership in "Democratic" (non-Communist) Political Parties

Note: "Democratic" political party members who are concurrently CCP members are indicated by an asterisk.

China Democratic League

*Chi Fang   Ch'u T'u-nan   Sha Ch'ien-li   *Ts'ao Meng-chün
 Chou Chien-jen[1]   *Hu Yü-chih   Shih Liang   *Yü I-fu

Kuomintang Revolutionary Committee

*Li Te-ch'üan

Chinese Peasants' and Workers' Democratic Party

*Chi Fang

Chiu San Society

*Chou P'ei-yuan   Hsu Te-heng   Liang Hsi

[1] Until the Ninth CCP Congress in 1969 Chou was thought not to be a Communist Party member. See Appendix 50.

China Democratic National Construction Association

*Hsu Ti-hsin	Li Chu-ch'en	*Nan Han-ch'en	Sha Ch'ien-li

China Association for Promoting Democracy

*Chao P'u-ch'u	Chou Chien-jen	*Fang Ming

11. Non-Party Democratic Personages

Note: The term "non-Party democratic personage" (*wu-tang-p'ai min-chu jen-shih*) is Communist usage and indicates membership in neither the CCP nor one of the "democratic" political parties.

Chang Chih-jang	Hu Feng	Shirob Jaltso	Ta P'u-sheng
Chang Hsi-jo	Liang Hsi	Sung Ch'ing-ling	Yang Hsien-tung
Ch'ien San-ch'iang[1]	Shen Yen-ping		

[1] Until the Ninth CCP Congress in 1969 Ch'ien was thought not to be a Communist Party member. See Appendix 50.

Part II. Early CCP Activities and Organizations

12. Date of Joining the CCP

Note: The reader is cautioned that there is much uncertainty in many dates of admission to the CCP. Some entries are little more than calculated guesses; this is particularly true regarding the 10-year categories.

1921–1925

Chang Ch'i-lung
Chang Ch'in-ch'iu
Chang Kuo-t'ao
Chang T'ai-lei
Chang Wen-t'ien
Chang Yun
Chao Shih-yen
Ch'en Ch'ang-hao
Ch'en I
Ch'en Keng
Ch'en Kung-po
Ch'en Shao-yü
Ch'en T'an-ch'iu
Ch'en Tu-hsiu
Ch'en Yen-nien
Ch'en Yü
Cheng Wei-san
Chi Ya-t'ai
Ch'in Pang-hsien
Chou En-lai
Chou Shih-ti
Ch'ü Ch'iu-pai
Chu Te

Fang Chih-min
Ho Ch'ang-kung
Ho Meng-hsiung
Ho Shu-heng
Hsia Hsi
Hsiang Ching-yü
Hsiang Chung-fa
Hsiang Ying
Hsiao Ching-kuang
Hsiao Ch'u-nü
Hsieh Chueh-tsai
Hsu Chih-chen
Hsu Ti-hsin
Jao Shu-shih
Jen Pi-shih
K'ang Sheng
K'o Ch'ing-shih
Ku Ta-ts'un
Kuan Hsiang-ying
K'uei Pi
Li Ch'iu-shih
Li Fu-ch'un
Li Han-chün

Li I-mang
Li Li-san
Li Ta-chao
Li Wei-han
Lin Piao
Lin Po-ch'ü
Lin Yü-nan
Lin Yü-ying
Liu Chih-tan
Liu Ning-i
Liu Shao-ch'i
Lo Chang-lung
Lo I-nung
Lo Teng-hsien
Lu Ting-i
Ma Ming-fang
Mao Tse-min
Mao Tse-tung
Nieh Jung-chen
P'an Tzu-li
P'eng Chen
P'eng P'ai
Shao Shih-p'ing

Su Chao-cheng
T'ao Chu
Teng Chung-hsia
Teng Fa
Teng Hsiao-p'ing
Teng Ying-ch'ao
Ts'ai Ch'ang
Ts'ai Ho-sen
Tseng Hsi-sheng
Tso Ch'üan
Tung Pi-wu
Ulanfu
Wang Chen
Wang Chia-hsiang
Wang Jo-fei
Wang Ping-nan
Wang Shou-tao
Wu Yü-chang
Yang Ming-chai
Yang Yin
Yeh T'ing
Yen Hung-yen
Yun Tai-ying

1926–1930

Chang Ai-p'ing
Chang Chi-ch'un
Chang Ching-wu
Chang Chung-liang
Chang Kuo-chien
Chang Lien-hua
Chang Su
Chang Te-sheng
Chang Ting-ch'eng
Chang Yun-i
Chao Erh-lu
Ch'en Cheng-jen
Ch'en Hsi-lien
Ch'en Po-ta
Ch'en Shao-min
Ch'en Shih-ch'ü
Ch'en Yun
Ch'eng Tzu-hua

Chi Ch'ao-ting
Chia T'o-fu
Ch'ien Chün-jui
Ch'iu Ch'uang-ch'eng
Chou I-ch'ün
Chou Pao-chung
Fang Fang
Feng Pai-chü
Feng Wen-pin
Ho Lung
Hsi Chung-hsun
Hsiao Hua
Hsiao K'o
Hsu Hai-tung
Hsu Hsiang-ch'ien
Hsu Kuang-ta
Hsu T'e-li
Huang Huo-ch'ing

Huang K'o-ch'eng
Huang Kung-lueh
Huang Yung-sheng
Jung Tzu-ho
K'ai Feng
Kan Szu-ch'i
Kao Kang
Keng Piao
K'o Pai-nien
K'ung Yuan
Kuo Mo-jo[1]
Lai Ch'uan-chu
Lai Jo-yü
Lei Jen-min
Li Ch'iang
Li Chien-chen
Li Chih-min
Li Ching-ch'üan

Li Hsien-nien
Li K'o-nung
Li Pao-hua
Li Ta
Li T'ao
Li Yü
Liao Ch'eng-chih
Liao Han-sheng
Lin Feng
Liu Ch'ang-sheng
Liu Hsiao
Liu Hsiu-feng
Liu Lan-t'ao
Liu Ming-fu
Liu Po-ch'eng
Liu Tzu-chiu
Liu Ya-lou
Lo Jui-ch'ing

[1] Kuo joined the CCP in 1927; his membership apparently lapsed and then he was admitted again in 1958.

Lo Jung-huan
Lo Kuei-po
Lo Ping-hui
Nan Han-ch'en
Ou Meng-chueh
P'eng Hsueh-feng
P'eng Te-huai
Po I-po
Shen Tse-min
Shu T'ung
Su Chen-hua

Su Yü
Sun Chih-yuan
Sung Jen-ch'iung
Sung Shih-lun
T'an Chen-lin
T'an Cheng
Teng Hua
T'eng Tai-yuan
Teng Tzu-hui
Ting Ling
Ts'ai Shu-fan

Tseng Shan
Wang Cheng
Wang En-mao
Wang Ho-shou
Wang Hung-k'un
Wang Shang-jung
Wang Shih-t'ai
Wang Ts'ung-wu
Wang Wei-chou
Wu Hsiu-ch'üan
Wu Kai-chih

Wu Yun-fu
Yang Ch'eng-wu
Yang Li-san
Yang Shang-k'un
Yang Shuo
Yang Yung
Yeh Chi-chuang
Yeh Chien-ying
Yeh Fei
Yuan Jen-yuan

1920's

An Tzu-wen
Chang Ta-chih
Chang Tsung-hsun
Chang Tzu-i

Ch'en Man-yuan
Fang Ch'iang
Han Hsien-ch'u
Hsu Ping

Hu Yü-chih
Lo Ming
P'eng Shao-hui

Wang Shu-sheng
Wei Kuo-ch'ing
Wu Te-feng

1931–1935

Ai Szu-ch'i
Chang Hsi
Chang Kuo-hua
Chang Lin-chih
Chang P'ing-hua
Ch'en Ch'i-han
Ch'en Chia-k'ang
Ch'en P'ei-hsien
Chiang I-chen
Ch'ien Hsin-chung
Ch'ien Ying
Chou Hsiao-chou
Chou Yang

Chu Te-hai
Chung Fu-hsiang
Fan Wen-lan
Han Kuang
Han Nien-lung
Ho Ch'eng-hsiang
Ho Wei
Hsieh Fu-chih
Hsu Shih-yu
Hu Yao-pang
Huang Chen
Huang Ching
Huang Hua

Ko Pao-ch'üan
Ku Cho-hsin
Li Fan-wu
Li Shih-ying
Liu Chen
Liu Hsi-wu
Liu Ko-p'ing
Ma Hsi-wu
Ma Wen-jui
Ma Yü-huai
Pai Ju-ping
P'eng T'ao
Shuai Meng-ch'i

Sun Tso-pin
T'ang Liang
Tseng Ching-ping
Tsou Ta-p'eng
Tuan Chün-i
Wan I
Wang Chin-hsiang
Wang P'ing
Wang Yu-p'ing
Yang Shang-k'uei
Yang Te-chih
Yao I-lin

1936–1940

Chang Chih-i
Chang Han-fu
Chang Yen
Chang Yu-yü
Chao Chien-min
Ch'en Chung-ching
Cheng Sen-yü
Chiang Hua
Chiang Nan-hsiang
Ch'iao Kuan-hua

Fan Ch'ang-chiang
Fang I
Hu Sheng
K'ang Yung-ho
Li Ch'ang
Li Che-jen
Li Ta-chang
Li Yu-wen
Liao Lu-yen
Liu Jen

Liu Ting
Liu Tzu-hou
Lü Cheng-ts'ao
Lu P'ing
Mei I
Sang-chi-yueh-hsi
T'an Ch'i-lung
T'ao Lu-chia
Teng T'o
Ts'ao Meng-chün

Wang Feng
Wang Jen-chung
Wu Chih-p'u
Wu Heng
Wu Leng-hsi
Wu Te
Yang Ching-jen
Yang Hsiu-feng
Yao Chung-ming
Yü Kuang-yuan

1930's

Chang Chia-fu
Chao I-min
Ch'i Yen-ming
Chou Huan
Hsu Chien-kuo
Hsu Tzu-jung

Hsueh Mu-ch'iao
Hu Ch'iao-mu
Hung Hsueh-chih
Jung Kao-t'ang
Li Chieh-po

Li Hsueh-feng
Liu Chien-hsun
Liu Lan-po
Liu Tao-sheng
Ouyang Ch'in

Sha Wen-han
Tseng Sheng
Wang Pi-ch'eng
Wu Po
Yü I-fu

1941–1945

Chang Chin-fu	Chiang Ming	Hui Yü-yü	P'ei Li-sheng
Chang T'i-hsueh	Chin Chung-hua	Lu Hsu-chang	Wang Shih-ying
Chao Shou-shan			

1946–1950

Burhan Shahidi	Chung Ch'i-kuang	Saifudin	Tseng Yung-ch'üan

1940's

Chang Chih-hsiang	Chou Lin	Huang Yen	Lin T'ieh
Chao An-po	Han Che-i	Kao Feng	Meng Yung-ch'ien
Chao Po-p'ing	Ho Ying	Kao K'o-lin	P'an Fu-sheng
Chao Tzu-yang	Hsiung Fu	Kao Yang	Tu Jun-sheng
Chiang Wei-ch'ing	Hsu Li-ch'ün	Ku Mu	Yang Ch'i-ch'ing
Chin Ming	Hsu Yun-pei	Li Ch'u-li	Yang I-ch'en
Chou Jung-hsin	Huang Ou-tung	Liao Chih-kao	Yü I-ch'uan

Post–1950

Chou P'ei-yuan	Li Szu-kuang	Li Te-ch'üan	Ting Ying
Kuo Mo-jo[2]			

 [2] Kuo had been a CCP member earlier. See note 1 above.

Date Unknown

Chang Hsiu-chu	Hu K'o-shih	Ou T'ang-liang	Wang Ping-chang
Chao P'u-ch'u	Kung Tzu-jung	P'ing Chieh-san	Wang Tao-han
Ch'en Yü	Lai Chi-fa	Shen Hung	Wang Wei
Chi Fang	Li Chü-k'uei	Sun Ta-kuang	Wei Heng
Ch'ien Li-jen	Lin Hai-yun	Sung Shao-wen	Wu Hsueh-ch'ien
Chu Tzu-ch'i	Liu Hsi-yuan	Ts'ao Chü-ju	Yang Hsien-chen
Fang Ming	Liu Pai-yü	Wan Li	Yang Yun-yü
Fu Lien-chang	Liu Yü-min	Wang Chao	Yü Ch'iu-li
Hsiao Fang-chou	Lo Ch'iung	Wang Kuang-wei	Yuan Pao-hua
Hu Ch'i-li	Lü Tung	Wang Kuo-ch'üan	

13. Attendance at CCP Congresses (1921–1945)

Note: There is considerable uncertainty about who attended the congresses of the CCP prior to 1949. The following lists deal only with those men treated in this volume and must be regarded as a rough guide.

First Congress

Shanghai, July 1921
Number attending: about 12

Chang Kuo-t'ao	Ch'en T'an-ch'iu	Li Han-chün	Tung Pi-wu
Ch'en Kung-po	Ho Shu-heng	Mao Tse-tung	

Second Congress

Shanghai, July 1922
Number attending: 12–20

Chang Kuo-t'ao	Ch'en Tu-hsiu	Li Ta-chao	Ts'ai Ho-sen
Chang T'ai-lei	Ho Meng-hsiung	Lo Chang-lung	
Ch'en T'an-ch'iu	Hsiang Ching-yü	Teng Chung-hsia	

Third Congress

Canton, June 1923
Number attending: 20–30

Chang Kuo-t'ao	Ch'en Tu-hsiu	Li Li-san ?	Teng Chung-hsia
Chang T'ai-lei	Ch'ü Ch'iu-pai	Li Ta-chao	Ts'ai Ho-sen
Ch'en T'an-ch'iu	Ho Meng-hsiung	Mao Tse-tung	

Fourth Congress

Shanghai, January 1925
Number attending: about 20

Chang T'ai-lei	Ch'en Tu-hsiu	Ho Ch'ang-kung ?	Ts'ai Ho-sen
Ch'en T'an-ch'iu			

Fifth Congress

Wuhan, April-May 1927
Number attending: about 100

Chang Kuo-t'ao	Chou En-lai	Li Wei-han	P'eng P'ai
Chang T'ai-lei	Ch'ü Ch'iu-pai	Liu Shao-ch'i	Su Chao-cheng
Ch'en Shao-yü	Hsiang Ching-yü	Lo I-nung	Ts'ai Ho-sen
Ch'en T'an-ch'iu	Hsiang Chung-fa ?	Mao Tse-tung	Wang Jo-fei
Ch'en Tu-hsiu	Jen Pi-shih	Ou Meng-chueh ?	Yun Tai-ying
Ch'en Yen-nien	Li Li-san ?		

Sixth Congress

Moscow, June-July 1928
Number attending: 84–119

Chang Kuo-t'ao	Hsiang Chung-fa	Lo Teng-hsien ?	Ts'ai Ho-sen
Ch'en Shao-yü	Hsiang Ying	Lu Ting-i	Tso Ch'üan
Ch'en T'an-ch'iu	K'ai Feng	Ma Ming-fang	Wang Chia-hsiang
Ch'en Yü ?	Kuan Hsiang-ying	Shen Tse-min	Wang Jo-fei
Ch'in Pang-hsien	Li Li-san	Su Chao-cheng	Wu Hsiu-ch'üan
Chou En-lai	Lin Po-ch'ü	Teng Chung-hsia	Wu Yü-chang ?
Ch'ü Ch'iu-pai	Liu Po-ch'eng ?	Teng Ying-ch'ao	Yeh Chien-ying
Ho Meng-hsiung ?	Liu Shao-ch'i	Ts'ai Ch'ang	
Hsiang Ching-yü	Lo Chang-lung		

Seventh Congress

Yenan, April-June 1945
Number attending: 752

Chang Ting-ch'eng
Chang Wen-t'ien
Ch'en I
Ch'en Po-ta
Ch'en Shao-yü ?
Ch'en Yü ?
Ch'en Yun
Ch'in Pang-hsien
Chou En-lai
Chu Te

Ho Lung
Hsu Hsiang-ch'ien
Hsu T'e-li
Jen Pi-shih
K'ang Sheng
Kao Kang
Ku Ta-ts'un
Li Fu-ch'un
Lin Piao
Lin Po-ch'ü

Liu Lan-po
Liu Po-ch'eng
Liu Shao-ch'i
Lo Jui-ch'ing ?
Lo Jung-huan ?
Lü Cheng-ts'ao
Lu Ting-i
Mao Tse-tung
Nieh Jung-chen
P'eng Chen

P'eng Te-huai
Shao Shih-p'ing
Teng Ying-ch'ao ?
Ulanfu
Wang Chen ?
Wang Jo-fei
Wu Yü-chang
Yang Shang-k'un
Yeh Chien-ying

14. Association with Comintern and Profintern

Note: Almost all major CCP leaders had some contact with Comintern or Profintern (Trade Union International) representatives in China. However, the following men had a more specific association in the sense of attending Comintern or Profintern congresses or a plenum of the Comintern's Executive Committee in Moscow. The dates of Comintern Congresses in which CCP members participated are: Third Congress, June-July 1921; Fourth, November 1922; Fifth, June-July 1924; Sixth, July-September 1928; Seventh, July-August 1935.

Chang Kuo-t'ao
Chang T'ai-lei
Chao Shih-yen
Ch'en Tu-hsiu
Ch'en Shao-yü
Ch'en Yun
Chi Ch'ao-ting

Ch'in Pang-hsien
Chou En-lai
Ch'ü Ch'iu-pai
Hsiang Ching-yü
K'ang Sheng
Kuan Hsiang-ying
Li Li-san

Li Ta-chao
Lin Yü-ying
Liu Ming-fu
Liu Shao-ch'i
Mao Tse-tung
Su Chao-cheng
Teng Chung-hsia

Ts'ai Ho-sen
Wang Jo-fei
Wang Ping-nan
Wu Yü-chang
Yang Hsien-chen
Yang Ming-chai

15. Politburo Membership (1920's to 1955)

Chang T'ai-lei
Chang Kuo-t'ao
Chang Wen-t'ien
Ch'en Shao-yü
Ch'en Yü
Ch'en Yun
Ch'in Pang-hsien
Chou En-lai
Ch'ü Ch'iu-pai

Chu Te
Hsiang Chung-fa
Hsiang Ying
Jen Pi-shih
K'ai Feng ?
Kao Kang
Li Li-san
Li Wei-han
Lin Piao

Lin Po-ch'ü
Lin Yü-ying
Liu Shao-ch'i
Lo I-nung
Lo Teng-hsien
Mao Tse-tung
P'eng Chen
P'eng P'ai

P'eng Te-huai
Su Chao-cheng
Teng Chung-hsia
Teng Fa
Ts'ai Ho-sen
Tung Pi-wu
Wang Chia-hsiang
Yang Yin (alternate)

16. Central Committee Membership (to 1945)

Chang Kuo-t'ao
Chang T'ai-lei
Chang Wen-t'ien
Chao Shih-yen
Ch'en Shao-yü
Ch'en T'an-ch'iu
Ch'en Tu-hsiu
Ch'en Yen-nien

Ch'en Yü
Ch'en Yun
Ch'in Pang-hsien
Chou En-lai
Ch'ü Ch'iu-pai
Chu Te
Ho Ch'ang-kung
Ho Lung

Ho Meng-hsiung
Hsia Hsi
Hsiang Ching-yü
Hsiang Chung-fa
Hsiang Ying
Jen Pi-shih
K'ai Feng ?
K'ang Sheng

K'o Ch'ing-shih
Kuan Hsiang-ying
Li Ch'iu-shih
Li Fu-ch'un
Li Li-san
Li Ta-chao
Li Wei-han
Lin Po-ch'ü

Lin Yü-ying
Liu Shao-ch'i
Lo Chang-lung
Lo I-nung
Mao Tse-tung
P'eng P'ai

P'eng Te-huai
Shen Tse-min
Su Chao-cheng
Teng Chung-hsia
Teng Fa

Teng Ying-ch'ao
  (alternate)
Ts'ai Ch'ang
Ts'ai Ho-sen
Tung Pi-wu

Wang Chia-hsiang
Wang Jo-fei
Wu Yü-chang
Yang Yin
Yeh Chien-ying
Yun Tai-ying

17. Central Secretariat Membership (to 1956)

Note: Despite the importance of the Secretariat, very little is known about its composition.

Ch'en Shao-yü
Ch'en Tu-hsiu
Ch'en Yun
Chou En-lai

Ch'ü Ch'iu-pai
Chu Te
Hsiang Chung-fa
Jen Pi-shih

Li Wei-han
Liu Shao-ch'i
Lo Teng-hsien

Mao Tse-tung
P'eng Chen
Wang Chia-hsiang

18. Revolutionary Military Council (to 1949)

Note: The Revolutionary Military Council dates to the Kiangsi period. It was technically a government organ of the Chinese Soviet Republic, but from the Long March it was subordinate to the Party.

Chang Ching-wu
Chang Kuo-t'ao
Chang Yun-i
Ch'en Yun
Chou En-lai
Chu Te
Ho Lung

Hsiang Ying
Hsu Hai-tung
Hsu Hsiang-ch'ien
Kuan Hsiang-ying
Lin Piao
Liu Shao-ch'i
Lü Cheng-ts'ao

Mao Tse-tung
P'eng Te-huai
Shao Shih-p'ing
T'an Chen-lin
T'eng Tai-yuan
Ts'ai Shu-fan

Tseng Hsi-sheng
Wang Cheng
Wang Chia-hsiang
Yang Li-san
Yang Shang-k'un
Yeh Chien-ying

19. Central Committee Organs (post-Long March to 1949)

Organization Department

An Tzu-wen
Ch'en Yun

Ch'in Pang-hsien
Li Fu-ch'un

Li Wei-han
Liu Shao-ch'i

P'eng Chen
Ts'ai Ch'ang

United Front Work Department

Ch'en Shao-yü
Han Kuang

Ho Ch'eng-hsiang
K'o Ch'ing-shih

Li Wei-han

Nan Han-ch'en

Propaganda Department

Ch'en Po-ta

Ch'in Pang-hsien

Hsu T'e-li

K'ai Feng

Finance and Economics Department

Ch'en Yun

Hsueh Mu-ch'iao

Li Fu-ch'un

Other Departments

Ai Szu-ch'i
Ch'en Shao-yü
Fan Wen-lan
Jen Pi-shih

Li K'o-nung
Liu Hsiu-feng
Teng Fa
Teng Ying-ch'ao

Ts'ai Ch'ang
Wang Jo-fei

Wang Ping-nan
Wu Hsiu-ch'üan

Part III. Participation in Important Events

20. 1911 Revolution

Chang Hsi-jo
Chang Yun-i
Ch'en T'an-ch'iu
Ch'en Tu-hsiu

Chu Te
Hsu T'e-li
Li Szu-kuang
Li Ta-chao

Lin Po-ch'ü
Liu Po-ch'eng
Su Chao-cheng
Tung Pi-wu

Wang Jo-fei
Wang Wei-chou
Wu Yü-chang

21. May Fourth Movement (1919)

Chang Kuo-t'ao
Chang T'ai-lei
Chang Wen-t'ien
Chang Yun
Chao Shih-yen
Ch'en Kung-po
Ch'en Tu-hsiu
Ch'eng Tzu-hua
Chou En-lai
Ch'ü Ch'iu-pai

Ch'u T'u-nan
Fang Chih-min
Fang Fang
Ho Ch'ang-kung
Ho Meng-hsiung
Ho Shu-heng
Hsiang Ching-yü
Hsiao Ch'u-nü
Hsu Chih-chen
Hsu Te-heng

Li Ch'iu-shih
Li Fu-ch'un
Li Han-chün
Li K'o-nung
Li Ta-chao
Li Wei-han
Lo Chang-lung
Lo I-nung
Lu Ting-i
Mao Tse-tung

Shen Tse-min
Shen Yen-ping
Teng Chung-hsia
Teng Ying-ch'ao
Tung Pi-wu
Wang Jo-fei
Wang Shou-tao
Yun Tai-ying

22. Peasant Movement Training Institute, 1924–1926

Note: The institute, located in Canton, was under KMT jurisdiction, but was dominated by the CCP. The heads of the institute and the instructors are marked with an asterisk.

*Chang T'ai-lei
Chang Ting-ch'eng
*Chou En-lai
*Ch'ü Ch'iu-pai
Fang Fang

Feng Wen-pin
*Hsiao Ch'u-nü
*Kuo Mo-jo
Li Ching-ch'üan
*Li Li-san

*Lin Po-ch'ü
Mao Tse-min
*Mao Tse-tung
*P'eng P'ai

*Teng Chung-hsia
Wang Shou-tao
*Wu Yü-chang
*Yun Tai-ying

23. May 30th Incident (1925)

Chang Ch'in-ch'iu
Chang T'ai-lei
Chao Shih-yen
Ch'en Yen-nien
Ch'en Yü
Ch'en Yun
Ch'ü Ch'iu-pai

Feng Pai-chü ?
Hsiang Ying
Hu Feng
Kan Szu-ch'i
Kuo Mo-jo
Li Li-san
Lin Piao

Liu Ning-i
Liu Shao-ch'i
Lo Teng-hsien
P'eng Hsueh-feng
Su Chao-cheng
Teng Chung-hsia

Ts'ai Ho-sen
Ulanfu
Wang Chen
Yang Yin
Yun Tai-ying

24. Northern Expedition (1926–1927)

Chang Yun-i
Ch'en Ch'i-han
Ch'en I
Ch'en Po-ta
Chi Fang
Chou En-lai
Chou I-ch'ün
Chou Shih-ti
Chu Te
Ho Lung
Hsiao Ching-kuang

Hsiao K'o
Hsu Hai-tung
Hsu Te-heng
Huang Kung-lueh
Kuo Mo-jo
Li Hsien-nien
Li I-mang
Li Fu-ch'un
Lin Piao
Lin Po-ch'ü
Liu Chih-tan

Liu Po-ch'eng
Lo I-nung
Lo Ping-hui
Nieh Jung-chen
P'eng Te-huai
Shen Yen-ping
Shih Liang
Sung Shih-lun ?
T'an Cheng
T'ao Chu ?

Teng Hsiao-p'ing
Ts'ai Ch'ang
Tseng Hsi-sheng
Tung Pi-wu
Wang Chen
Wang Shou-tao
Yeh Chien-ying
Yeh T'ing
Yun Tai-ying

25. Nanchang Uprising (1927)

Chang Kuo-t'ao
Chang T'ai-lei
Ch'en Ch'i-han
Ch'en I
Ch'en Keng
Chou En-lai
Chou I-ch'ün
Chou Shih-ti
Chu Te
Fang Ch'iang

Ho Lung
Hsia Hsi
Hsiao K'o
Hsu Kuang-ta
Hsu T'e-li
Kuo Mo-jo
Li I-mang
Li Li-san
Li Wei-han
Lin Piao

Lin Po-ch'ü
Liu Po-ch'eng
Lo I-nung
Lo Jui-ch'ing
Lo Jung-huan
Nieh Jung-chen
P'eng P'ai
Shu T'ung
Su Chao-cheng
Su Yü

T'an Cheng
Teng Chung-hsia
Wang Shang-jung
Wu Te-feng
Wu Yü-chang
Yang Li-san
Yang Yung
Yeh Chien-ying
Yeh T'ing
Yun Tai-ying

26. Autumn Harvest Uprisings (1927)

Chang Chi-ch'un
Chang Tsung-hsun
Ch'en Shih-ch'ü
Cheng Wei-san
Ho Ch'ang-kung

Huang K'o-ch'eng
Huang Yung-sheng
Lo I-nung
Lo Jung-huan
Mao Tse-tung

P'eng P'ai
Shao Shih-p'ing
T'an Chen-lin
Teng Hua ?

Wu Kai-chih
Wu Te-feng
Yang Li-san
Yang Yung

27. Chingkangshan (1927–1928)

Chang Chi-ch'un
Chang Tsung-hsun
Chao Erh-lu
Ch'en I
Ch'en Shih-ch'ü
Chu Te
Fu Lien-chang
Ho Ch'ang-kung

Hsiao Hua
Huang K'o-ch'eng
Huang Yung-sheng
Li Chih-min
Li Chü-k'uei
Li T'ao
Lin Piao
Lo Jui-ch'ing

Lo Jung-huan
Mao Tse-min
Mao Tse-tung
P'eng Te-huai
Su Chen-hua
Su Yü
T'an Chen-lin

T'an Cheng
Teng Hua
T'eng Tai-yuan
Wang Shang-jung
Wang Shu-sheng
Yang Li-san
Yang Yung ?

28. Canton Commune (1927)

Chang T'ai-lei	Li Han-chün ?	Su Chao-cheng	Yang Yin
Ch'en Yü	Lo Teng-hsien	(*in absentia*)	Yeh Chien-ying
Hsu Hsiang-ch'ien	P'eng P'ai	T'ao Chu	Yeh T'ing
Li Ch'iu-shih	(*in absentia*)	Teng Fa	Yun Tai-ying

29. P'ing-chiang Uprising (1928)

Chang Ai-p'ing	Huang Kung-lueh	P'eng Te-huai	T'eng Tai-yuan
Ch'en Shih-ch'ü	Li Chü-k'uei	Teng Hua ?	
Feng Wen-pin	P'eng Shao-hui		

30. Fu-t'ien Incident (1930)

Chang Ai-p'ing	Chu Te	Mao Tse-tung	P'eng Te-huai
Ch'en I	Huang Kung-leh	Sung Shih-lun	Tseng Shan

31. The Long March (1934–1936)

Chang Ai-p'ing	Feng Wen-pin	Li Hsien-nien	T'ao Chu
Chang Chi-ch'un	Fu Lien-chang	Li I-mang	Teng Fa
Chang Ch'i-lung	Han Hsien-ch'u	Li K'o-nung	Teng Hsiao-p'ing
Chang Ch'in-ch'iu	Han Nien-lung ?	Li Ta	Teng Hua
Chang Ching-wu	Ho Ch'ang-kung	Li T'ao	T'eng Tai-yuan
Chang Kuo-chien	Ho Lung	Li Wei-han	Teng Ying-ch'ao
Chang Kuo-hua ?	Hsi Chung-hsun	Liao Ch'eng-chih	Ts'ai Ch'ang
Chang Kuo-t'ao	Hsia Hsi	Liao Han-sheng	Ts'ai Shu-fan
Chang Tsung-hsun	Hsiao Ching-kuang	Lin Piao	Tseng Hsi-sheng
Chang Tzu-i	Hsiao Hua	Lin Po-ch'ü	Tso Ch'üan
Chang Wen-t'ien	Hsiao K'o	Liu Chen	Tung Pi-wu
Chang Yun-i	Hsieh Chueh-tsai	Liu Hsiao	Wang Chen
Chao Erh-lu	Hsieh Fu-chih ?	Liu Po-ch'eng	Wang Cheng
Ch'en Ch'ang-hao	Hsu Hai-tung	Liu Shao-ch'i	Wang Chia-hsiang
Ch'en Cheng-jen	Hsu Hsiang-ch'ien	Liu Ya-Lou	Wang Hung-k'un ?
Ch'en Ch'i-han	Hsu Kuang-ta	Lo Jui-ch'ing	Wang Jen-chung
Ch'en Hsi-lien	Hsu Shih-yu	Lo Jung-huan	Wang P'ing
Ch'en Keng	Hsu T'e-li	Lo Kuei-po	Wang Shang-jung
Ch'en Man-yuan	Hsu Yun-pei	Lo Ping-hui	Wang Shou-tao
Ch'en Shao-min	Hu Yao-pang ?	Lu Ting-i	Wang Shu-sheng
Ch'en Shih-ch'ü	Huang Chen	Mao Tse-min	Wang Wei-chou
Ch'en Yun	Huang Huo-ch'ing	Mao Tse-tung	Wang Yu-p'ing
Ch'eng Tzu-hua	Huang K'o-ch'eng	Nieh Jung-chen	Wei Kuo-ch'ing
Cheng Wei-san	Huang Yung-sheng	Ouyang Ch'in	Wu Hsiu-ch'üan
Chia T'o-fu	Jen Pi-shih	P'an Tzu-li	Wu Te-feng
Chiang I-chen	K'ai Feng ?	P'eng Hsueh-feng	Wu Yun-fu
Ch'ien Hsin-chung ?	Kan Szu-ch'i	P'eng Shao-hui	Yang Ch'eng-wu
Ch'in Pang-hsien	Keng Piao	P'eng Te-huai	Yang Li-san
Chou En-lai	Kuan Hsiang-ying	Sang-chi-yueh-hsi	Yang Shang-k'un
Chou Hsiao-chou	Lai Ch'uan-chu	Shao Shih-p'ing	Yang Te-chih
Chou Huan	Li Chien-chen	Shu T'ung	Yang Yung
Chou Shih-ti	Li Chih-min	Su Chen-hua	Yeh Chi-chuang
Chu Te	Li Ching-ch'üan	Sung Jen-ch'iung	Yeh Chien-ying
Chung Fu-hsiang	Li Chü-k'uei	Sung Shih-lun	Yü Ch'iu-li
Fang Ch'iang	Li Fu-ch'un	T'an Cheng	Yuan Jen-yuan

32. Sinkiang Group (late 1930's to early 1940's)

Note: Sinkiang Group applies to those men involved in the complex relations concerning the administration of Sinkiang province by General Sheng Shih-ts'ai during the early and middle years of the Sino-Japanese War.

Burhan Shahidi	Ch'en Yun	K'ang Sheng	Shen Yen-ping
Ch'en Shao-yü	Chou Hsiao-chou	Ma Ming-fang	Teng Fa
Ch'en T'an-ch'iu	Jen Pi-shih	Mao Tse-min	

33. December Ninth Movement (1935)

Ch'en Chung-ching	Hsu Te-heng	Lin Feng ?	Tuan Chün-i
Ch'en Po-ta	Huang Ching	Liu Shao-ch'i	Wu Heng
Ch'i Yen-ming	Huang Hua	Lu P'ing	Yao Chung-ming
Chiang Ming	Jung Kao-t'ang	P'eng Chen	Yao I-lin
Chiang Nan-hsiang	Li Ch'ang	P'eng T'ao	Yü Kuang-yuan
Ho Wei	Li Che-jen		

34. Sian Incident (1936)

Chao Shou-shan	Li K'o-nung	Teng Fa	P'eng Te-huai
Ch'in Pang-hsien	Li T'ao	Tung Pi-wu	Yeh Chien-ying
Chou En-lai	Lin Po-ch'ü	Wang Ping-nan	

35. New Fourth Army Incident (1941)

Ch'en I	Hsiang Ying	Liu Shao-ch'i	Yeh T'ing

36. Marshall Mission (1945–1947)

Chang Ching-wu	Huang Hua	Liao Ch'eng-chih	Tung Pi-wu
Chao Erh-lu	Jao Shu-shih	Liu Chien-hsun	Wang Ping-nan
Ch'en Keng	Jung Kao-t'ang	Lo Jui-ch'ing	Wang Shou-tao
Ch'ien Chün-jui	Keng Piao	Lu Ting-i	Wei Kuo-ch'ing
Chou En-lai	K'o Pai-nien	Shu T'ung	Wu Hsiu-ch'üan
Fang Fang	Lei Jen-min	Sun Chih-yuan	Wu Yü-chang
Han Nien-lung	Li Ch'u-li	Sung Shih-lun	Wu Yun-fu
Hsu Kuang-ta	Li K'o-nung	T'an Cheng	Yao Chung-ming
Huang Chen	Li Li-san	T'eng Tai-yuan	Yeh Chien-ying

37. Manchuria (pre-1945)

Note: Despite the importance of Manchuria, it was outside the mainstream of the Chinese Communist movement until the end of the Sino-Japanese War. The few persons who were involved there are listed below.

Chou Pao-chung	Jao Shu-shih	Liu Shao-ch'i	Lü Cheng-ts'ao
Chu Te-hai	Li Chieh-po	Liu Lan-po	Tsou Ta-p'eng
Han Kuang	Li Fan-wu	Lo Teng-hsien	Wang Ho-shou
Ho Ch'eng-hsiang	Li Yu-wen		

38. Manchuria (post-1945)

Note: Immediately after the war a large number of important military and political leaders were sent to Manchuria. Most of them were assigned to other parts of China after the conquest of Manchuria in late 1948.

An Tzu-wen
Chang Ch'i-lung
Chang Ching-wu
Chang Wen-t'ien
Ch'en Yü
Ch'en Yun
Chiang Nan-hsiang
Ch'iu Ch'uang-ch'eng
Chou Huan
Chou Pao-chung
Fang Ch'iang
Ho Ch'eng-kung
Hsiao Ching-kuang
Hsiao K'o
Huang Huo-ch'ing

Huang K'o-ch'eng
Huang Ou-tung
Huang Yung-sheng
Hung Hsueh-chih
Kao Kang
Ku Cho-hsin
Ku Ta-ts'un
Lai Ch'uan-chu
Li Chieh-po
Li Chü-k'uei
Li Fu-ch'un
Li I-mang
Li Li-san
Li Ta-chang
Li T'ao

Li Yu-wen
Lin Feng
Lin Piao
Liu Chen
Liu Hsi-wu
Liu Ming-fu
Liu Ya-lou
Lo Jung-huan
Lü Cheng-ts'ao
Ouyang Ch'in
P'eng Chen
Sha Ch'ien-li
Shao Shih-p'ing
Sung Jen-ch'iung
T'an Cheng

T'ao Chu
Teng Hua
Ting Ling
Ts'ao Chü-ju
Tsou Ta-p'eng
Wan I
Wang Chia-hsiang
Wang Chin-hsiang
Wang Ho-shou
Wang Kuang-wei
Wang Kuo-ch'üan
Wang Shou-tao
Wu Hsiu-ch'üan
Yeh Chi-chuang
Yü I-fu

Part IV. Chinese Communist Armies

39. Pre-Yenan: First Front Army

Chang Ai-p'ing
Chang Chi-ch'un
Chang Tsung-hsun
Chao Erh-lu
Ch'en I
Chia T'o-fu
Ch'in Pang-hsien
Chou En-lai
Chou Huan
Chu Te
Hsiao Ching-kuang
Hsiao Hua
Huang Chen
Huang Kung-lueh

Huang Yung-sheng
Keng Piao
Lai Ch'uan-chu
Li Ching-ch'üan
Li Fu-ch'un
Li I-mang
Li K'o-nung
Li T'ao
Liao Ch'eng-chih
Lin Piao
Liu Hsiao
Liu Po-ch'eng
Liu Ya-lou
Lo Jui-ch'ing

Lo Jung-huan
Lo Ping-hui
Lu Ting-i
Mao Tse-min
Mao Tse-tung
Nieh Jung-chen
Ouyang Ch'in
P'eng Hsueh-feng
P'eng Te-huai
Shao Shih-p'ing
Shu T'ung
Sung Shih-lun
Teng Fa
Teng Hsiao-p'ing

Teng Hua
T'eng Tai-yuan
Tso Ch'üan
Wang Chia-hsiang
Wang Shou-tao
Wei Kuo-ch'ing
Wu Hsiu-ch'üan
Yang Ch'eng-wu
Yang Li-san
Yang Shang-k'un
Yang Te-chih
Yang Yung
Yeh Chi-chuang
Yeh Chien-ying

40. Pre-Yenan: Second Front Army

Ho Lung
Hsia Hsi
Hsiao K'o
Hsu Kuang-ta

Jen Pi-shih
Kan Szu-ch'i
Kuan Hsiang-ying
Li Ching-ch'üan

Liao Han-sheng
Teng Chung-hsia
Wang Chen

Wu Te-feng
Yü Ch'iu-li
Yuan Jen-yuan

41. Pre-Yenan: Fourth Front Army

Chang Ch'in-ch'iu
Chang Kuo-chien
Chang Kuo-t'ao
Chang Tsung-hsun
Chao Erh-lu
Ch'en Ch'ang-hao

Ch'en Hsi-lien
Ch'en Man-yuan
Ch'eng Tzu-hua
Cheng Wei-san
Ch'ien Hsin-chung
Han Hsien-ch'u

Hsu Hsiang-ch'ien
Hsu Shih-yu
Huang Huo-ch'ing
Li Hsien-nien
Liao Ch'eng-chih
Liu Chen

P'an Tzu-li
Sang-chi-yueh-hsi
Wang Hung-k'un
Wang Shu-sheng
Wang Wei-chou
Yen Hung-yen

42. Eighth Route Army

Headquarters (or unidentified by specific division)

Chang Chung-liang
Chao Chien-min
Chao Erh-lu
Chiang Hua
Ch'iu Ch'uang-ch'eng ?
Chou Huan
Chu Te
Huang Hua
Jen Pi-shih

Keng Piao
Li K'o-nung
Li T'ao
Liao Ch'eng-chih
Lin Po-ch'ü
Lo Jui-ch'ing
Lu Ting-i
P'eng Hsueh-feng
P'eng Te-huai

Sun Chih-yuan
T'an Cheng
Teng Hsiao-p'ing
T'eng Tai-yuan
Tso Ch'üan
Wang Chen
Wang Cheng
Wang Chia-hsiang

Wang Jo-fei
Wang Shih-ying
Wang Shou-tao
Wu Hsiu-ch'üan
Wu Yun-fu
Yang Shang-k'un
Yang Shuo
Yeh Chien-ying

115th Division

(Shansi-Chahar-Hopeh area)

Chang Kuo-hua	Hsu Hai-tung	Liu Chen	Teng Hua
Chao Erh-lu	Huang K'o-ch'eng	Lo Jung-huan	Wang Chen
Ch'en Ch'i-han	Huang Yung-sheng	Lü Cheng-ts'ao	Wang P'ing
Ch'en Man-yuan	Keng Piao	Nieh Jung-chen	Yang Ch'eng-wu
Ch'en Shih-ch'ü	Li Li-san	P'eng Chen	Yang Te-chih
Ch'eng Tzu-hua	Li Shih-ying	Sung Shih-lun	Yang Yung
Hsiao Hua	Lin Piao		

120th Division

(Shansi-Suiyuan and Shensi-Kansu-Ninghsia areas)

Chang Ching-wu	Hsiao K'o	Lin Feng	Wang En-mao
Chang P'ing-hua	Hsu Kuang-ta	Lü Cheng-ts'ao	Wang Shang-jung
Chang Tsung-hsun	Kan Szu-ch'i	Lo Kuei-po	Wang Shou-tao
Chou Shih-ti	Kuan Hsiang-ying	Pai Ju-ping	Yao Chung-ming
Ho Lung	Lei Jen-min	P'eng Shao-hui	Yuan Jen-yuan
Hsi Chung-hsun	Li Ching-ch'üan	Wang Chen	
Hsiao Ching-kuang	Liao Han-sheng		

129th Division

(Shansi-Hopeh-Shantung-Honan area)

Chang Ching-wu	Hsu Kuang-ta	Li Yü	Teng Hsiao-p'ing
Chang Kuo-hua	Hsu Shih-yu	Liu Po-ch'eng	T'eng Tai-yuan
Ch'en Hsi-lien	Huang Chen	P'eng T'ao	Ts'ai Shu-fan
Ch'en Keng	Jung Tzu-ho	Sang-chi-yueh-hsi	Tso Ch'üan
Han Hsien-ch'u	Lai Jo-yü	Su Chen-hua	Wang Hung-k'un
Hsieh Fu-chih	Li Chü-k'uei	Sung Jen-ch'iung	Wang Wei-chou
Hsu Hsiang-ch'ien	Li Ta	T'ang Liang	Yang Shang-k'uei

43. New Fourth Army

New Fourth Army (to 1941)

Chang Ai-p'ing	Fang I	Lo Ping-hui	Tseng Shan
Chang Ting-ch'eng	Hsiang Ying	P'eng Hsueh-feng	Wei Kuo-ch'ing
Chang Yen	Jao Shu-shih	Su Yü	Wu Chih-p'u
Chang Yun-i	Lai Ch'uan-chu	T'an Chen-lin	Yeh Fei
Ch'en I	Li Hsien-nien	Teng Tzu-hui	Yeh T'ing
Chi Fang	Li I-mang	Tseng Hsi-sheng	
Chiang Hua	Liu Shao-ch'i		

New Fourth Army (post-1941)

Headquarters (or unidentified by specific division)

Chang Yun-i	Ch'ien Chün-jui	Liu Shao-ch'i	Tseng Shan
Ch'en I	Fang I	Liu Tzu-chiu	Wan I
Ch'en P'ei-hsien	Jao Shu-shih	Sha Wen-han ?	Wang Hung-k'un
Ch'en Shih-ch'ü	Lai Ch'uan-chu	Shu T'ung	Yü I-fu
Chi Fang	Li Yü	Teng Tzu-hui	

First Division

| Chung Ch'i-kuang | Su Yü | Wang Pi-ch'eng | Yeh Fei |

Second Division

| Chang Chin-fu
Chang Yun-i | Cheng Wei-san | Huang Yen | Lo Ping-hui |

Third Division

| Chang Ai-p'ing
Chin Ming | Huang K'o-cheng | Hung Hsueh-chih | Wei Kuo-ch'ing |

Fourth Division

| Chang Ai-p'ing
Liu Chen | P'eng Hsueh-feng
Teng Tzu-hui | Wei Kuo-ch'ing | Wu Chih-p'u |

Fifth Division

| Chang Chih-i
Chang T'i-hsueh | Cheng Wei-san
Hsu Tzu-jung | Li Hsien-nien
T'ao Chu | Wang Chen |

Sixth Division

| Chiang Wei-ch'ing | Liu Ch'ang-sheng | T'an Chen-lin |

Seventh Division

| Chang Ting-ch'eng | Tseng Hsi-sheng |

Eighth Division

T'an Ch'i-lung

44. Recipients of Military Orders (1955)

Note: In 1955 the PRC awarded military orders to its Red Army veterans. Three categories of awards were given: Order of August First, for service between August 1, 1927, and July 6, 1937 (that is, from the birth of the Red Army through the Long March); Order of Independence and Freedom, July 7, 1937, to September 2, 1945 (the Sino-Japanese War); and Order of Liberation, September 3, 1945, to June 30, 1950 (the civil war against the Nationalists). Each category is divided into three classes; the following table includes only recipients of first-class awards. No special awards have been created for participants in the Korean War, but a list of Korean War participants is found in Appendix 45.

Recipient	Order of August First	Order of Independence and Freedom	Order of Liberation	Order Unspecified
Chang Ai-p'ing	x	x	x	
Chang Ching-wu	x	x	x	
Chang Kuo-hua		x	x	
Chang Ta-chih				x
Chang Tsung-hsun	x	x	x	
Chang Yun-i	x	x	x	
Chao Erh-lu	x	x	x	
Chao Shou-shan				x
Ch'en Ch'i-han				x
Ch'en Hsi-lien				x
Ch'en I	x	x	x	
Ch'en Keng	x	x	x	
Ch'en Shih-ch'ü		x	x	
Ch'iu Ch'uang-ch'eng			x	
Chou Huan				x
Chou Pao-chung	x	x	x	
Chou Shih-ti	x	x	x	
Chu Te	x	x	x	
Chung Ch'i-kuang				x
Feng Pai-chü	x	x	x	
Fu Lien-chang			x	
Han Hsien-ch'u				x
Ho Lung	x	x	x	
Hsiao Ching-kuang	x	x	x	
Hsiao Hua	x	x	x	
Hsiao K'o	x	x	x	
Hsieh Fu-chih	x	x	x	
Hsu Hai-tung				x
Hsu Hsiang-ch'ien	x	x	x	
Hsu Kuang-ta	x	x	x	
Hsu Shih-yu				x
Huang K'o-ch'eng	x	x	x	
Huang Yung-sheng		x		x
Hung Hsueh-chih	x	x	x	
Kan Szu-ch'i	x	x	x	
Lai Ch'uan-chu	x	x	x	
Li K'o-nung	x	x	x	
Li Ta	x	x	x	
Li T'ao	x	x	x	
Liao Han-sheng				x
Lin Piao	x	x	x	
Liu Hsi-yuan			x	
Liu Po-ch'eng	x	x	x	
Liu Tao-sheng	x	x	x	
Liu Ya-lou	x	x	x	
Lo Jui-ch'ing	x	x	x	
Lo Jung-huan	x	x	x	
Lü Cheng-ts'ao		x	x	
Nieh Jung-chen	x	x	x	
P'eng Shao-hui	x	x	x	
P'eng Te-huai	x	x	x	
Saifudin				x
Su Chen-hua		x	x	
Su Yü	x	x	x	
Sung Jen-ch'iung	x	x	x	

Recipient	Order of August First	Order of Independence and Freedom	Order of Liberation	Order Unspecified
Sung Shih-lun				x
T'an Cheng	x	x	x	
T'ang Liang				x
Teng Hua				x
Tseng Sheng				x
Ulanfu			x	
Wan I		x	x	
Wang Chen	x	x	x	
Wang Cheng	x		x	
Wang En-mao				x
Wang Hung-k'un	x	x	x	
Wang P'ing		x	x	
Wang Ping-chang			x	
Wang Shang-jung	x		x	
Wang Shu-sheng	x	x	x	
Wei Kuo-ch'ing				x
Yang Ch'eng-wu	x	x	x	
Yang Te-chih				x
Yeh Chien-ying	x	x	x	
Yeh Fei				x
Yen Hung-yen	x	x	x	
Yü Ch'iu-li			x	

45. Korean War Participants

Chao Chien-min	Kan Szu-ch'i	P'eng Te-huai	Wang P'ing
Ch'en Keng	Li Chih-min	Sung Shih-lun	Yang Ch'eng-wu ?
Han Hsien-ch'u	Li Ta	Teng Hua	Yang Te-chih
Hsu Shih-yu ?	Liu Chen	Wang Pi-ch'eng	Yang Yung
Hung Hsueh-chih	Lo Jung-huan ?		

Part V. Participation in Soviets (1927–1937)

46. Central Executive Committee, Chinese Soviet Republic

Note: Following is a cumulative list of members of the First and Second Central Executive Committees (CEC), the highest political organ of the Chinese Soviet Republic in Juichin, Kiangsi. The First CEC was elected in November 1931 at the First All-China Congress of Soviets, and the Second CEC was elected at the second congress in January-February 1934. The letter *x* signifies full membership and *a* indicates alternate membership. There were no alternates on the First CEC.

Member	First CEC 1931	Second CEC 1934	Member	First CEC 1931	Second CEC 1934
†Chan I-chin		x	Chou En-lai	x	x
Chang Ai-p'ing		a	†Chou I-k'ai		x
†Chang Chi-chih		x	†Chou I-li	x	
Chang Ch'in-ch'iu		x	†Chou Kuang-k'un		x
†Chang Chin-lou		x	†Chou Kuei-hsiang		a
†Chang Ch'un-ch'ing		x	†Chou K'un		x
†Chang Hua-hsien	x		†Chou Shao-wen		x
†Chang Jan-ho		x	†Chou Yueh-lin		x
†Chang Kuan-i		x	†Chu Chao-hsiang		x
Chang Kuo-t'ao	x	x	†Chu Ch'i		x
†Chang Ta-ho		x	Ch'ü Ch'iu-pai	x	x
†Chang Te-san		x	†Chu Jui		x
Chang Ting-ch'eng	x	x	†Chu Jung-sheng		x
Chang Wen-t'ien		x	Chu Te	x	x
†Chang Yun-hsien		x	†Ch'ü Teng-kao	x	
Chang Yun-i	x		†Chu Ti-yuan		x
†Ch'en A-chin		x	†Chu Wei-yuan		x
Ch'en Ch'ang-hao		x	†Chung Ch'ang-t'ao		x
Ch'en Cheng-jen	x		†Chung Hsun-jen		x
†Ch'en Fu-yuan	x		†Chung I-chin		a
†Ch'en Hsiang-sheng		x	†Chung Kuei-hsin		x
†Ch'en Hung-shih		x	†Chung Pao-yuan		x
Ch'en I	x	x	†Chung Shih-pin		x
†Ch'en Kuang		x	†Fan Le-ch'un	x	x
Ch'en Shao-yü	x	x	†Fang Chen-hua		a
†Chen Shou-ch'ang		x	Fang Chih-min	x	x
Ch'en T'an-ch'iu		x	†Fang Ching-ho		a
†Ch'en Tzu-ch'ien		x	†Feng Hsueh-feng		a
Ch'en Yü	x		†Fu Ts'ai-hsiu		x
Ch'en Yun		x	†Ho Ch'ang		x
†Cheng Chen-fen		x	Ho Ch'ang-kung		x
†Ch'eng Fang-wu		x	†Ho Chen-wu		x
Cheng Wei-san		x	Ho Lung	x	x
†Chia Yuan		a	Ho Shu-heng	x	x
†Chiang A-san		x	†Ho Wei		x
Ch'in Pang-hsien		x	Hsia Hsi	x	x
†Chin Wei-ying		x	Hsiang Ying	x	x
†Ch'iu Hsien-ying		x	†Hsiao Heng-t'ai	x	
†Ch'iu Shih-feng		a	Hsiao K'o		x
†Chou Chien-p'ing		x	†Hsiao Shih-pang		x

Member	First CEC 1931	Second CEC 1934
†Hsieh Chen-fu		a
†Hsieh Hsien-szu		x
†Hsieh Ming-jen		x
†Hsieh Ping-huang		a
†Hsieh Yü-ch'in		x
†Hsiung Hsien-pi		x
†Hsiung Kuo-ping		x
†Hsu Hsi-ken	x	
Hsu Hsiang-ch'ien		x
†Hsu Ming-fu		a
†Hsu Shun-yuan		a
†Hsu Ta-chih		x
Hsu T'e-li	x	x
†Hsu Yen-kang		x
†Hsun Huai-chou		x
†Hu Chün-ho	x	
†Hu Hai	x	x
Hua Hsin-hsiang		a
†Huang Ch'ang-chiao		x
†Huang Chia-kao		x
†Huang Fa-kuei		x
†Huang Fu-wu		a
†Huang I-chang		x
†Huang Kuang-pao		x
†Huang P'ing	x	
†Huang Su	x	x
†Huang Tao		x
†Huang Wan-sheng		x
†Hung Shui		x
†Hung Tzu-ch'ing	x	
Jen Pi-shih	x	x
†Juan Hsiao-hsien	x	x
K'ai Feng		x
†K'ang K'o-ch'ing		a
K'ang Sheng		x
†Kao Chün-t'ing		x
†Kao Tzu-li		x
†Ko Yao-shan	x	
Ku Ta-ts'un	x	x
†Ku Tso-lin		x
†Kuan Ch'un-hsiang		x
Kuan Hsiang-ying		x
†Kuan Ying		x
†Kuang Chu-ch'üan		a
†K'uang Piao		x
†K'ung Ho-ch'ung	x	x
†K'ung Shu-an		x
†Kuo Shu-shen		x
†Lai Mei-yü		x
†Li Ch'eng-chia		x
†Li Chien-chen		x
†Li Cho-jan		x
Li Fu-ch'un		x
Li Hsien-nien		x
Li I-mang		a
Li K'o-nung		a
†Li Mei-ch'ün		a
†Li Tsung-po	x	
†Li Tz'u-fan		a
†Li Wei-hai		x
Li Wei-han		x
†Liang Po-t'ai		x
†Liao Han-hua		a
†Lin Kuo-sung		x
Lin Piao	x	x
Lin Po-ch'ü		x
†Liu Ch'i-yao		x
†Liu Chien-chung	x	
†Liu Ch'ou-hsi		x
†Liu Ch'ün-hsien		x
Liu Hsiao		x
†Liu I		a
†Liu Kuang-ch'en		x
†Liu Kuang-wan	x	
†Liu Kuo-chu		x
†Liu Ming-hui		x
Liu Po-ch'eng		x
Liu Po-chien		x
Liu Shao-ch'i	x	x
†Liu Sheng-yuan	x	
†Liu Shih-chieh		x
†Liu Ta-ch'ao	x	
†Liu Yen-yü		a
Lo Jui-ch'ing		x
Lo Jung-huan		a
Lo Ping-hui	x	x
Lo Teng-hsien	x	
†Lo Tzu-ming		x
†Lou Meng-hsia		x
†Lu Fu-t'an	x	
†Lu Te-kuang	x	
†Lung Ch'un-shan		a
Mao Tse-tung	x	x
†Nieh Hung-chün		x
Nieh Jung-chen		x
†P'an Han-nien		x
†P'an Shih-chung		x
†P'eng Jen-ch'ang		x
†P'eng Kuei	x	
P'eng Te-huai	x	x
†Pi Shih-t'i		x
Shao Shih-p'ing	x	x
Shen Tse-min	x	
†Sung Pai-min		x
T'an Chen-lin	x	
†T'an Yü-pao		x
†Teng Chen-hsun		x
Teng Fa	x	x
†Teng P'ing		a
T'eng Tai-yuan	x	x

Member	First CEC 1931	Second CEC 1934	Member	First CEC 1931	Second CEC 1934
Teng Tzu-hui	x	a	†Wang Sheng-jung		x
†Teng Yao-sheng		a	Wang Shih-t'ai		x
Teng Ying-ch'ao		x	Wang Wei-chou		x
Ts'ai Ch'ang		x	†Wang Yung-sheng	x	
†Ts'ai Kan		x	†Wei Pa-ch'ün	x	
Ts'ai Shu-fan		x	†Wu Chih-min	x	
†Tseng Hung-i		x	†Wu Lan-fu		x
†Tseng Kuang-lan		x	†Wu Liang-p'ing		x
Tseng Shan	x	x	†Wu Pi-hsien		x
†Tsou Chung-ts'ai		a	Wu Te-feng		x
†Tsou Tun-hou		a	†Wu Tzu-yuan		x
†Ts'ui Ch'i	x		Wu Yü-chang		x
†T'u Chen-nung		x	†Yang Ch'i-hsin		x
†Tuan Te-ch'ang	x		†Yang Ping-lung		a
†Tung Ch'ang-sheng		a	Yang Shang-k'un		x
†Tung Chen-t'ang		x	†Yang Shih-chu		x
Tung Pi-wu		x	Yeh Chien-ying		x
†Wan Yung-ch'eng		x	†Yeh Te-kuei		a
Wang Chen		x	†Yen Li-chi		a
Wang Chia-hsiang	x	x	†Yin Jen-kuei		a
Wang Chin-hsiang		x	†Yü Han-ch'ao	x	x
†Wang Feng-ming		x	†Yü Hung-wen		x
†Wang Hsien-hsuan		x	†Yü Hung-yuan		x
†Wang Hsiu-chang		x	†Yuan Kuo-p'ing		x
†Wang Ju-ch'ih		x	†Yuan Te-sheng	x	
			†Yueh Shao-hua		x

†Indicates that the individual is not one of the 433 biographic entries.

47. Officials of the Central Executive Committee, Chinese Soviet Republic

Note: The officials of the Central Executive Committee were elected at the close of the First and Second All-China Congresses of Soviets in Juichin, Kiangsi, held in November 1931 and January-February 1934, respectively. † indicates that the individual is not one of the 433 biographic entries.

	1931	1934
Chairman, Central Executive Committee	Mao Tse-tung	Mao Tse-tung
Vice-Chairmen, Central Executive Committee	Hsiang Ying	Hsiang Ying
	Chang Kuo-t'ao	Chang Kuo-t'ao

Council of People's Commissars

	1931	1934
Chairman	Mao Tse-tung	Chang Wen-t'ien
People's Commissar for Foreign Affairs	Wang Chia-hsiang	Wang Chia-hsiang
People's Commissar for Military Affairs	Chu Te	Chu Te
People's Commissar for Labor	Hsiang Ying	†Teng Chen-hsun
People's Commissar for Finance	Teng Tzu-hui	Lin Po-ch'ü
People's Commissar for Land	Chang Ting-ch'eng	†Kao Tzu-li
People's Commissar for Judicial Affairs	Chang Kuo-t'ao	†Liang Po-t'ai
People's Commissar for Internal Affairs	†Chou I-li	Tseng Shan
People's Commissar for Education	Ch'ü Ch'iu-pai	Ch'ü Ch'iu-pai
People's Commissar for Workers' and Peasants' Investigation	Ho Shu-heng	Hsiang Ying
Chief, National Political Security Bureau	Teng Fa	
People's Commissar for National Economy		†Wu Liang-p'ing
People's Commissar for Food		Ch'en T'an-ch'iu

48. Presence in Soviets (1927–1937)

Hai-lu-feng, Kwangtung

Ch'eng Tzu-hua	Ku Ta-ts'un	P'eng P'ai	Yang Yin
Hsu Hsiang-ch'ien			

Kiangsi

Chang Ai-p'ing	Feng Wen-pin	Li T'ao	Tseng Shan
Chang Kuo-chien	Fu Lien-chang	Li Wei-han	Tso Ch'üan
Chang Kuo-hua	Ho Ch'ang-kung	Lin Piao	Tung Pi-wu
Chang Tzu-i	Ho Ch'eng-hsiang	Lin Po-ch'ü	Wang Chia-hsiang
Chang Wen-t'ien	Ho Shu-heng	Liu Shao-ch'i	Wang Jen-chung
Chang Yun-i	Hsiang Ying	Liu Tao-sheng	Wang Jo-fei
Ch'en I	Hsieh Chueh-tsai	Liu Ya-lou	Wang Shou-tao
Ch'en Man-yuan	Hsu T'e-li	Lo Jung-huan	Wu Hsiu-ch'üan
Ch'en P'ei-hsien	Hu Yao-pang	Mao Tse-min	Wu Yun-fu
Ch'en Shih-ch'ü	Huang Kung-lueh	Mao Tse-tung	Yang Ch'eng-wu
Ch'en T'an-ch'iu	Huang Yung-sheng	Ouyang Ch'in	Yang Hsien-chen
Ch'en Yun	Jen Pi-shih	P'eng Te-huai	Yang Li-san
Chia T'o-fu	K'ai Feng	Shu T'ung	Yang Shang-k'un
Chiang I-chen	Kan Szu-ch'i	T'an Cheng	Yang Yung
Ch'in Pang-hsien	Keng Piao	Teng Fa	Yeh Chi-chuang
Ch'iu Ch'uang-ch'eng	Li Chien-chen	Teng Hsiao-p'ing	Yeh Chien-ying
Chou En-lai	Li Ching-ch'üan	Teng Ying-ch'ao	Yuan Jen-yuan
Chou Shih-ti	Li Fu-ch'un	Ts'ai Ch'ang	
Ch'ü Ch'iu-pai	Li I-mang	Ts'ai Shu-fan	
Chu Te	Li Ta	Tseng Hsi-sheng	

Oyüwan

Chang Ch'in-ch'iu	Ch'en Hsi-lien	Hsu Hai-tung	Liu Chen
Chang Ching-wu	Ch'en Keng	Hsu Hsiang-ch'ien	Shen Tse-min
Chang Kuo-t'ao	Ch'eng Tzu-hua	Huang Huo-ch'ing	Wang Hung-k'un
Chang Ta-chih	Cheng Wei-san	Huang Yen	Wang Shu-sheng
Ch'en Ch'ang-hao	Ch'ien Hsin-chung	Li Hsien-nien	

Shensi

Cheng Wei-san	Liu Chih-tan	Ma Ming-fang	Wang Shih-t'ai
Chia T'o-fu	Liu Lan-t'ao	Ma Wen-jui	Yen Hung-yen
Kao Kang	Ma Hsi-wu		

Other

Chang Ch'i-lung	Hsu Hsiang-ch'ien	Mao Tse-min	Wang Chen
Chang P'ing-hua	Hsu Kuang-ta	Sang-chi-yueh-hsi	Wang Chin-hsiang
Chang Ting-ch'eng	Huang Kung-lueh	Shao Shih-p'ing	Wang En-mao
Ch'en Cheng-jen	Ku Ta-ts'un	Su Yü	Wang Jo-fei
Ch'en T'an-ch'iu	Kuan Hsiang-ying	T'an Chen-lin	Wang Shou-tao
Fang Chih-min	Li Chien-chen	T'ao Chu	Wang Shu-sheng
Fang Fang	Li Hsien-nien	Teng Chung-hsia	Yang Shang-k'uei
Ho Ch'ang-kung	Lin Piao	Teng Fa	Yang Te-chih
Ho Lung	Liu Chih-tan	Teng Hsiao-p'ing	Yeh Fei
Hsiao Ching-kuang	Liu Hsiao	Teng Tzu-hui	Yun Tai-ying
Hsiao K'o	Liu Tao-sheng	Tso Ch'üan	
Hsieh Chueh-tsai	Lo Ming	Ulanfu	

Part VI. Participation in Border Regions (1937–1949)

49. Participation in Border Regions and Liberated Areas (1937–1949)

Shensi-Kansu-Ninghsia (*Shen-Kan-Ning*)

Ai Szu-ch'i
Chang Ch'in-ch'iu
Chang Chung-liang
Chang Kuo-t'ao
Chang Te-sheng
Chang Wen-t'ien
Chao Po-p'ing
Ch'en I
Ch'en Po-ta
Ch'en Shao-yü
Ch'en Yü
Ch'en Yun
Chia T'o-fu
Chiang Nan-hsiang
Ch'in Pang-hsien
Ch'iu Ch'uang-ch'eng
Chou En-lai
Chou Yang
Chu Te
Fan Wen-lan
Fang Fang
Ho Ch'ang-kung
Ho Lung
Hsi Chung-hsun

Hsiao Ching-kuang
Hsieh Chueh-tsai
Hsu Kuang-ta
Hsu Hsiang-ch'ien
Hsu T'e-li
Hsueh Mu-ch'iao
Hu Ch'iao-mu
Huang Hua
Jen Pi-shih
K'ai Feng
Kao Feng
Kao Kang
K'o Ch'ing-shih
K'o Pai-nien
Ku Ta-ts'un
Kuan Hsiang-ying
K'uei Pi
Li Chieh-po
Li Fu-ch'un
Li I-mang
Li T'ao
Li Wei-han
Li Yu-wen
Liao Ch'eng-chih

Lin Piao
Lin Po-ch'ü
Lin Yü-ying
Liu Ch'ang-sheng
Liu Hsiu-feng
Liu Ning-i
Liu Pai-yü
Liu Shao-ch'i
Liu Ya-lou
Lo Ch'iung
Lo Jui-ch'ing
Lo Jung-huan
Lu Ting-i
Ma Hsi-wu
Ma Ming-fang
Ma Wen-jui
Mao Tse-min
Mao Tse-tung
Nan Han-ch'en
P'an Tzu-li
P'eng Chen
P'eng Te-huai
Po I-po
Sang-chi-yueh-hsi

Shao Shih-p'ing
Shen Hung
Sun Tso-pin
T'an Cheng
Teng Ying-ch'ao
Ting Ling
Ts'ai Ch'ang
Tso Ch'üan
Tung Pi-wu
Ulanfu
Wang Chen
Wang En-mao
Wang Jo-fei
Wang Ping-nan
Wang Shih-t'ai
Wang Wei-chou
Wu Hsiu-ch'üan
Wu Yü-chang
Yang Ching-jen
Yang Shang-k'uei
Yeh Chi-chuang
Yeh Chien-ying
Yen Hung-yen

Shansi-Chahar-Hopeh (*Chin-Ch'a-Chi*)

Chang Kuo-chien
Chang Su
Chao Erh-lu
Ch'en Man-yuan
Ch'eng Tzu-hua
Chiang I-chen
Chou Yang
Hsu Chien-kuo
Huang Ching
Huang Yung-sheng
Jung Tzu-ho

Keng Piao
K'o Ch'ing-shih
Lai Jo-yü
Li Fan-wu
Li Hsueh-feng
Li Pao-hua
Li Ta-chang
Liu Hsiu-feng
Liu Lan-t'ao
Liu Tao-sheng
Lo Jung-huan

Lü Cheng-ts'ao
Ma Yü-huai
Nan Han-ch'en
Nieh Jung-chen
Shao Shih-p'ing
Shen Hung
Shu T'ung
Sun Chih-yuan
Sung Shao-wen
Sung Shih-lun
Teng Hua

Teng T'o
Tseng Yung-ch'üan
Wang Chen
Wang P'ing
Wu Te
Wu Yü-chang
Yang Ch'eng-wu
Yang Te-chih
Yao I-lin

Shansi-Hopeh-Shantung-Honan (*Chin-Chi-Lu-Yü*)

Ai Szu-ch'i
An Tzu-wen
Chang Chi-ch'un
Chang Kuo-hua
Chang Lin-chih
Chang Yu-yü
Fan Wen-lan
Hsieh Fu-chih

Hsu Hsiang-ch'ien
Huang Chen
Jung Tzu-ho
Ku Cho-hsin
Lai Jo-yü
Li Ch'u-li
Li Hsueh-feng
Lin T'ieh

Liu Chien-hsun
Liu Po-ch'eng
Po I-po
Su Chen-hua
Sung Jen-ch'iung
Teng Hsiao-p'ing
T'eng Tai-yuan
Tso Ch'üan

Wang Hung-k'un
Wang Jen-chung
Wang Ts'ung-wu
Yang Hsiu-feng
Yang Li-san
Yang Te-chih

Shansi-Suiyuan (Chin-Sui)

Chang P'ing-hua	Hsu Kuang-ta	Lo Kuei-po	Sun Chih-yuan
Chang Tsung-hsun	Kuan Hsiang-ying	Lü Cheng-ts'ao	Ulanfu
Chang Yu-yü	Li Ching-ch'üan	Pai Ju-ping	Wang Chen
Chou Shih-ti	Li Ta	P'eng Shao-hui	Wang Shang-jung
Ho Lung	Lin Feng		

Other Border Regions and Liberated Areas

Chang T'i-hsueh	Fang Fang	Li I-mang	T'ao Chu
Ch'en I	Feng Pai-chü	Liu Shao-ch'i	Teng Hua
Cheng Wei-san	Jao Shu-shih	Liu Tao-sheng	Wu Chih-p'u
Fan Ch'ang-chiang	K'uei Pi	Lo Jui-ch'ing	Yang Shang-k'uei
Fang I	Li Hsien-nien		

Part VII. Later CCP Organizations

50. Seventh, Eighth, and Ninth Central Committees (1945–   )

Note: Following is a composite of the full and alternate members of the Central Committee elected at the Seventh, Eighth, and Ninth Party Congresses, held in April-June 1945, September 1956, and April 1969, respectively. In addition, the Eighth Congress convened a second session in May 1958; those persons elected then are indicated by the year in parentheses. The letter *a* indicates alternate members; all others are full members. For Central Committee members elected before 1945, see Appendix 16.

Seventh, Eighth, and Ninth CCP Central Committees

Member	Seventh 1945	Eighth 1956–58	Ninth 1969
An Tzu-wen		8	
Chang Ai-p'ing		8a (1958)	
Chang Chi-ch'un	7a	8	
†Chang Chi-hui			9a
Chang Ch'i-lung		8a	
†Chang Chiang-lin			9a
†Chang Ch'ih-ming			9
Chang Chin-fu		8a (1958)	
Chang Ching-wu		8a	
†Chang Ch'un-ch'iao			9
Chang Chung-liang		8a (1958)	
†Chang Fu-heng			9
†Chang Fu-kuei			9
Chang Han-fu		8a	
†Chang Heng-yun			9
Chang Hsi		8a (died 1959)	
†Chang Hsi-t'ing			9a
†Chang Hsiu-ch'uan			9a
†Chang I-hsiang			9
†Chang Jih-ch'ing			9a
Chang Kuo-hua			9
Chang Lin-chih		8a	
†Chang Ling-pin			9a
Chang P'ing-hua		8a (1958)	
†Chang Shih-chung			9a
Chang Su		8a (1958)	
†Chang Szu-chou			9a
Chang Ta-chih		8a	9
Chang Te-sheng		8a (died 1965)	
Chang T'i-hsueh			9
†Chang T'ien-yun			9
Chang Ting-ch'eng	7	8	9
†Chang Ts'ai-ch'ien			9
Chang Tsung-hsun	7a	8a	
Chang Wen-t'ien	7	8	

Seventh, Eighth, and Ninth CCP Central Committees (cont'd)

Member	Seventh 1945	Eighth 1956–58	Ninth 1969
†Chang Yen-ch'eng			9a
†Chang Ying-ts'ai			9a
Chang Yun		8a	
Chang Yun-i	7	8	9
†Chao Ch'i-min			9a
Chao Chien-min		8a	
Chao Erh-lu		8 (died 1967)	
†Chao Feng			9a
†Chao Hsing-yuan			9a
Chao I-min		8a (1958)	
Chao Po-p'ing		8a (1958)	
Ch'en Cheng-jen		8a	
Ch'en Ch'i-han		8a	9
†Ch'en Ho-fa			9a
Ch'en Hsi-lien		8a	9
†Ch'en Hsien-jui			9
†Ch'en Hua-t'ang			9a
Ch'en I	7	8	9
†Ch'en Jen-ch'i			9a
†Ch'en Kan-feng			9a
†Ch'en K'ang			9
Ch'en Keng	7a	8 (died 1961)	
†Ch'en Li-yun			9a
Ch'en Man-yuan		8a	
Ch'en P'ei-hsien		8a	
Ch'en Po-ta	7a	8	9
Ch'en Shao-min	7a	8	
Ch'en Shao-yü	7	8	
Ch'en Shih-ch'ü			9
Ch'en T'an-ch'iu	7 (died 1943)		
Ch'en Yü	7a	8	9
Ch'en Yun	7	8	9
†Ch'en Yung-kuei			9
†Cheng San-sheng			9a
†Ch'eng Shih-ch'ing			9
Ch'eng Tzu-hua	7a	8	
Cheng Wei-san	7	8	
†Cheng Wei-shan			9
†Ch'i-lin-wang-tan			9a
†Chi Teng-k'uei			9
Chia T'o-fu		8	
†Chiang Ch'ing			9
†Chiang Hsieh-yuan			9
Chiang Hua		8a	
†Chiang Li-yin			9
Chiang Nan-hsiang		8a	
†Chiang Pao-ti			9a
Chiang Wei-ch'ing		8a	
†Chiang Yung-hui			9
†Chiao Lin-i			9a
†Ch'ien Chih-kuang			9
Ch'ien Chün-jui		8a	
†Ch'ien Hsueh-sen			9a
Ch'ien Ying		8	
Ch'in Pang-hsien	7 (died 1946)		

Seventh, Eighth, and Ninth CCP Central Committees (cont'd)

Member	Seventh 1945	Eighth 1956–58	Ninth 1969
†Chin Tsu-min			9a
Ch'iu Ch'uang-ch'eng			9
†Ch'iu Hui-tso			9
†Ch'iu Kuo-kuang			9
Chou Chien-jen			9
†Chou Ch'ih-p'ing			9
Chou En-lai	7	8	9
Chou Hsiao-chou		8a (1958)	
†Chou Hsing			9
Chou Huan		8a	
Chou Pao-chung		8a (died 1964)	
Chou Yang		8a	
†Chu Kuang-ya			9a
Chu Te	7	8	9
Chu Te-hai		8a	
Chung Ch'i-kuang		8a	
†Fan Hsiao-chü			9a
†Fan Te-ling			9a
Fan Wen-lan		8a	9 (died 1969)
Fang I		8a (1958)	9a
†Fang Ming			9a
†Feng Chan-wu			9a
Feng Pai-chü		8a	
†Fu Ch'uan-tso			9a
Han Hsien-ch'u		8a (1958)	9
Han Kuang		8a	
†Han Ying			9a
Ho Lung	7	8	
Hsi Chung-hsun	7a	8	
†Hsia Pang-yin			9
Hsiao Ching-kuang	7a	8	9
Hsiao Hua		8	
Hsiao K'o		8	
†Hsieh Chia-hsiang			9
†Hsieh Chia-t'ang			9a
Hsieh Chueh-tsai		8a	
Hsieh Fu-chih		8	9
†Hsieh Hsueh-kung			9
†Hsieh Wang-ch'un			9a
†Hsien Heng-han			9
†Hsu Ch'ih			9a
†Hsu Ching-hsien			9
Hsu Hai-tung		8	9
Hsu Hsiang-ch'ien	7	8	9
Hsu Kuang-ta		8	
Hsu Ping		8a	
Hsu Shih-yu		8a	9
Hsu T'e-li	7	8 (died 1968)	
Hsu Tzu-jung		8a	
†Hu Chi-tsung			9
Hu Ch'iao-mu		8	
†Hu Liang-ts'ai			9a
†Hu Wei			9a
Hu Yao-pang		8	
†Hua Kuo-feng			9

Seventh, Eighth, and Ninth CCP Central Committees (cont'd)

Member	Seventh 1945	Eighth 1956–58	Ninth 1969
†Hua Lin-sen			9a
Huang Chen			9
†Huang Ch'eng-lien			9a
†Huang Chih-yung			9a
Huang Ching		8 (died 1958)	
Huang Huo-ch'ing		8a	
†Huang Jung-hai			9a
Huang K'o-ch'eng	7a	8	
Huang Ou-tung		8a	
†Huang Tso-chen			9a
†Huang Wen-ming			9a
Huang Yung-sheng		8a	9
Hung Hsueh-chih		8a	
†I Yao-ts'ai			9a
†Jao Hsing-li			9
Jao Shu-shih	7		
Jen Pi-shih	7 (died 1950)		
Jen Szu-chung			9
†Jou-tzu-t'u-erh-ti			9a
†Juan Po-sheng			9a
Kan Szu-ch'i		8a (died 1964)	
†K'ang Chien-min			9a
†K'ang Lin			9a
K'ang Sheng	7	8	9
Kao Kang	7 (died 1955?)		
Kao K'o-lin		8a	
†Kao Wei-sung			9
†Keng Ch'i-ch'ang			9a
Keng Piao			9
K'o Ch'ing-shih		8 (died 1965)	
Ku Ta-ts'un	7a	8a (died 1966)	
Kuan Hsiang-ying	7 (died 1946)		
†Kuang Jen-nung			9
K'uei Pi		8a	
†K'ung Shih-ch'üan			9
K'ung Yuan		8a (1958)	
†Kuo Hung-chieh			9a
Kuo Mo-jo			9
†Kuo Yü-feng			9a
Lai Chi-fa			9
Lai Jo-yü		8 (died 1958)	
†Lan I-nung			9a
†Lan Jung-yü			9a
Li Ch'ang		8a	
†Li Chen			9
Li Ch'iang			9
Li Chieh-po		8a (1958)	
Li Chien-chen		8a	
Li Chih-min		8a	
Li Ching-ch'üan		8	
Li Fu-ch'un	7	8	9
Li Hsien-nien	7	8	9
Li Hsueh-feng		8	9
†Li Hua-min			9a
†Li Jui-shan			9

Seventh, Eighth, and Ninth CCP Central Committees (cont'd)

Member	Seventh 1945	Eighth 1956–58	Ninth 1969
Li K'o-nung		8 (died 1962)	
†Li Li			9a
Li Li-san	7	8	
Li Pao-hua	7a	8	
†Li Shou-lin			9a
†Li Shu-mao			9a
†Li Shui-ch'ing			9
†Li Shun-ta			9
†Li Su-wen			9
Li Szu-kuang			9
Li Ta-chang		8a	9
Li T'ao		8a	
†Li Te-sheng			9
†Li T'ien-yu			9
†Li Ting-shan			9a
†Li Tsai-han			9a
†Li Tso-p'eng			9
Li Wei-han		8	
Li Yü	7a		
†Li Yuan			9a
†Li Yueh-sung			9a
†Liang Chin-t'ang			9a
†Liang Hsing-ch'u			9
Liao Ch'eng-chih	7a	8	
Liao Chih-kao		8a (1958)	
Liao Han-sheng		8a	
Liao Lu-yen		8a	
Lin Feng	7	8	
Lin Piao	7	8	9
Lin Po-ch'ü	7	8 (died 1960)	
Lin T'ieh		8	
Liu Ch'ang-sheng	7a	8 (died 1967)	
Liu Chen		8a (1958)	
†Liu Chen-hua			9a
†Liu Chieh-t'ing			9
Liu Chien-hsun		8a (1958)	9
†Liu Ch'un-ch'iao			9a
†Liu Chün-i			9
†Liu Feng			9
†Liu Hao-t'ien			9a
†Liu Hsi-ch'ang			9
†Liu Hsi-yao			9a
Liu Hsiao	7a	8	
†Liu Hsien-ch'üan			9
†Liu Hsing-yuan			9
Liu Jen		8a	
Liu Ko-p'ing		8	9
Liu Lan-po		8a	
Liu Lan-t'ao	7a	8	
Liu Ning-i		8	
Liu Po-ch'eng	7	8	9
Liu Shao-ch'i	7	8	
†Liu Sheng-t'ien			9
Liu Tzu-chiu	7a		
Liu Tzu-hou		8a (1958)	9

Seventh, Eighth, and Ninth CCP Central Committees (cont'd)

Member	Seventh 1945	Eighth 1956–58	Ninth 1969
†Liu Wei			9
Liu Ya-lou		8 (died 1965)	
†Lo Ch'un-ti			9a
†Lo Hsi-k'ang			9a
Lo Jui-ch'ing	7a	8	
Lo Jung-huan	7	8 (died 1963)	
Lo Kuei-po		8a	
†Lo Yuan-fa			9a
Lü Cheng-ts'ao	7a	8	
†Lü Ho			9a
†Lu Jui-lin			9
†Lu Ta-tung			9a
†Lu T'ien-chi			9
Lu Ting-i	7	8	
†Lü Ts'un-chieh			9a
†Lü Yü-lan			9
†Lung Kuang-ch'ien			9a
†Lung Shu-chin			9
†Ma Fu-ch'üan			9
Ma Ming-fang	7a	8	
†Ma T'ien-shui			9a
Ma Wen-jui		8a	
Mao Tse-tung	7	8	9
†Mo Hsien-yao			9
†Nan P'ing			9
†Ni Chih-fu			9
Nieh Jung-chen	7	8	9
†Nieh Yuan-tsu			9a
†Nien Chi-jung			9
Ou Meng-chueh		8a	
Ouyang Ch'in		8	
P'an Fu-sheng		8a	9
†P'an Mei-ying			9a
†P'an Shih-kao			9
P'an Tzu-li		8a	
†Pao-jih-lo-tai			9
†P'ei Chou-yü			9a
P'eng Chen	7	8	
†P'eng Ch'ung			9a
†P'eng Kuei-ho			9a
P'eng Shao-hui			9
P'eng T'ao		8a (1958; died 1961)	
P'eng Te-huai	7	8	
†P'i Ting-chün			9
Po I-po	7	8	
Saifudin		**8a**	9
Sang-chi-yueh-hsi [T'ien Pao]		8a	9
Shao Shih-p'ing		8a (died 1965)	
†Shen Mao-kung			9
†Shih Shao-hua			9a
†Shu Chi-ch'eng			9a
Shu T'ung		8	
Shuai Meng-ch'i		8a	
Su Chen-hua		8a	
†Su Ching			9

Seventh, Eighth, and Ninth CCP Central Committees (cont'd)

Member	Seventh 1945	Eighth 1956–58	Ninth 1969
Su Yü	7a	8	9
Sun Chih-yuan		8a (1958; died 1966)	
Sung Jen-ch'iung	7a	8	
†Sung Shuang-lai			9a
Sung Shih-lun		8a	
†Ta Lo			9a
T'an Chen-lin	7	8	
T'an Cheng	7a	8	
T'an Ch'i-lung		8a	9a
†T'an Fu-jen			9
†T'ang Ch'i-shan			9
†T'ang Chung-fu			9
T'ang Liang		8a (1958)	9a
T'ao Chu		8	
T'ao Lu-chia		8a (1958)	
†T'eng Hai-ch'ing			9
Teng Hsiao-p'ing	7	8	
Teng Hua		8	9a
T'eng Tai-yuan	7	8	9
Teng Tzu-hui	7	8	9
Teng Ying-ch'ao	7a	8	9
†T'ien Hua-kuei			9
†Ting Sheng			9
Ts'ai Ch'ang	7	8	9
†Ts'ai Hsieh-pin			9
Ts'ai Shu-fan		8a (died 1958)	
†Ts'ai Shu-mei			9
†Ts'ao I-ou			9
†Ts'ao Li-huai			9
†Ts'en Kuo-jung			9a
Tseng Ching-ping	7a		
Tseng Hsi-sheng		8	
†Tseng Kuo-hua			9
Tseng Shan	7	8	9
†Tseng Shao-shan			9
†Tseng Szu-yü			9
†Tseng Yung-ya			9a
†Ts'ui Hai-lung			9a
†Ts'ui Hsiu-fan			9a
†Tsung Hsi-yun			9
†Tu P'ing			9
†Tung Ming-hui			9
Tung Pi-wu	7	8	9
Ulanfu	7a	8	
Wan I	7a	8a	
†Wang Chao-chu			9
Wang Chen	7a	8	9
Wang Chia-hsiang	7a	8	
†Wang Chia-tao			9a
†Wang Chih-ch'iang			9a
†Wang Chin-hsi			9
Wang En-mao		8a*	9a
Wang Feng		8a (1958)	
Wang Ho-shou		8a	
†Wang Hsiao-yü			9

Seventh, Eighth, and Ninth CCP Central Committees (cont'd)

Member	Seventh 1945	Eighth 1956–58	Ninth 1969
†Wang Hsin			9a
†Wang Hsin-t'ing			9
†Wang Hsiu-chen			9
†Wang Huai-hsiang			9
†Wang Hui-ch'iu			9
Wang Hung-k'un			9
†Wang Hung-wen			9
Wang Jen-chung		8a (1958)	
Wang Jo-fei	7 (died 1946)		
†Wang Kuang-lin			9a
†Wang Kuo-fan			9
†Wang Liu-sheng			9a
†Wang Pai-tan			9
Wang Ping-chang			9
Wang Shang-jung		8a (1958)	
Wang Shih-t'ai		8a	
Wang Shou-tao	7a	8	9
Wang Shu-sheng		8	9
†Wang T'i			9a
Wang Ts'ung-wu	7a	8	
†Wang Tung-hsing			9
Wang Wei-chou	7a	8	
†Wang Wei-kuo			9a
†Wei Feng-ying			9
Wei Kuo-ch'ing		8a	9
†Wei Ping-k'uei			9
†Wei Tsu-chen			9a
†Wen Hsiang-lan			9a
†Wen Yü-ch'eng			9
Wu Chih-p'u		8	
†Wu Chin-ch'üan			9a
†Wu Ch'un-jen			9a
†Wu Chung			9a
†Wu Fa-hsien			9
Wu Hsiu-ch'üan		8	
†Wu Jui-lin			9
†Wu Kuei-hsien			9
†Wu Ta-sheng			9
†Wu T'ao			9
Wu Te		8a	9
Wu Yü-chang	7	8 (died 1966)	
Yang Ch'eng-wu		8a	
†Yang Ch'un-fu			9
†Yang Chün-sheng			9a
†Yang Fu-chen			9
Yang Hsien-chen		8a*	
Yang Hsiu-feng		8	
†Yang Huan-min			9a
Yang I-ch'en		8a (1958)	
Yang Shang-k'un		8	
Yang Te-chih		8a	9
†Yang Tsung			9a
Yang Yung		8a	
Yao I-lin		8a (1958)	
†Yao Lien-wei			9a

Seventh, Eighth, and Ninth CCP Central Committees (cont'd)

Member	Seventh 1945	Eighth 1956–58	Ninth 1969
†Yao Wen-yuan			9
Yeh Chi-chuang		8 (died 1967)	
Yeh Chien-ying	7	8	9
†Yeh Ch'ün			9
Yeh Fei		8a	
†Yen Chung-ch'uan			9a
Yen Hung-yen		8a	
Yü Ch'iu-li			9
†Yü Sang			9
†Yu T'ai-chung			9a
†Yuan Sheng-p'ing			9

*Promoted to full member in 1958.
†Indicates that the individual is not one of the 433 biographic entries.

51. Selected Materials from the Ninth Party Congress (1969)

Note: This appendix and Appendix 50 are the only materials in this volume dealing with the Ninth Party Congress of April 1969 and the Central Committee Plenum held immediately thereafter. The reader can use this appendix to see which of the major biographees alive in 1969 were dropped from the Central Committee or, conversely, were elected to the Central Committee for the first time. A cursory glance at the list of those *not* re-elected provides a dramatic view of the effects of the Cultural Revolution. † indicates that the individual is not one of the 433 biographic entries.

Politburo (1969–   )

Note: The following officials were elected at the First Plenum of the Ninth Central Committee on April 28, 1969. Mao Tse-tung and Lin Piao are listed in rank order, but following the procedure used by the Chinese in publishing the list of Politburo members, all other names are arranged alphabetically.

Standing Committee

Mao Tse-tung   Ch'en Po-ta   Chou En-lai   K'ang Sheng
Lin Piao

Members

Mao Tse-tung	†Ch'iu Hui-tso	K'ang Sheng	†Wu Fa-hsien
Lin Piao	Chou En-lai	Li Hsien-nien	†Yao Wen-yuan
†Chang Ch'un-ch'iao	Chu Te	†Li Tso-p'eng	Yeh Chien-ying
Ch'en Hsi-lien	Hsieh Fu-chih	Liu Po-ch'eng	†Yeh Ch'ün
Ch'en Po-ta	Hsu Shih-yu	Tung Pi-wu	
†Chiang Ch'ing	Huang Yung-sheng		

Alternate Members

†Chi Teng-k'uei   Li Hsueh-feng   †Li Te-sheng   †Wang Tung-hsing

Major Biographees First Elected to the Central Committee at the Ninth Congress

Chang Kuo-hua	Chou Chien-jen	Lai Chi-fa	Wang Hung-k'un
Chang T'i-hsueh	Huang Chen	Li Ch'iang	Wang Ping-chang
Ch'en Shih-ch'ü	Keng Piao	Li Szu-kuang	Yü Ch'iu-li
Ch'iu Ch'uang-ch'eng	Kuo Mo-jo	P'eng Shao-hui	

Major Biographees Not Re-Elected to the Ninth Central Committee

Note: This list *excludes* all persons who died prior to the Ninth Party Congress in April 1969.

An Tzu-wen	Chou Huan	Li Wei-han	T'an Chen-lin
Chang Ai-p'ing	Chou Yang	Liao Ch'eng-chih	T'an Cheng
Chang Chi-ch'un	Chu Te-hai	Liao Chih-kao	T'ao Chu
Chang Ch'i-lung	Chung Ch'i-kuang	Liao Han-sheng	T'ao Lu-chia
Chang Chin-fu	Feng Pai-chü	Liao Lu-yen	Teng Hsiao-p'ing
Chang Ching-wu	Han Kuang	Lin Feng	Tseng Hsi-sheng
Chang Chung-liang	Ho Lung	Lin T'ieh	Ulanfu
Chang Han-fu	Hsi Chung-hsun	Liu Chen	Wan I
Chang Lin-chih	Hsiao Hua	Liu Hsiao	Wang Chia-hsiang
Chang P'ing-hua	Hsiao K'o	Liu Jen	Wang Feng
Chang Su	Hsieh Chueh-tsai	Liu Lan-po	Wang Ho-shou
Chang Tsung-hsun	Hsu Kuang-ta	Liu Lan-t'ao	Wang Jen-chung
Chang Wen-t'ien	Hsu Ping	Liu Ning-i	Wang Shang-jung
Chang Yun	Hsu Tzu-jung	Liu Shao-ch'i	Wang Shih-t'ai
Chao Chien-min	Hu Ch'iao-mu	Lo Jui-ch'ing	Wang Ts'ung-wu
Chao I-min	Hu Yao-pang	Lo Kuei-po	Wang Wei-chou
Chao Po-p'ing	Huang Huo-ch'ing	Lü Cheng-ts'ao	Wu Chih-p'u
Ch'en Cheng-jen	Huang K'o-ch'eng	Lu Ting-i	Wu Hsiu-ch'üan
Ch'en Man-yuan	Huang Ou-tung	Ma Ming-fang	Yang Ch'eng-wu
Ch'en P'ei-hsien	Hung Hsueh-chih	Ma Wen-jui	Yang Hsien-chen
Ch'en Shao-min	Kao K'o-lin	Ou Meng-chueh	Yang Hsiu-feng
Ch'en Shao-yü	K'uei Pi	Ouyang Ch'in	Yang I-ch'en
Ch'eng Tzu-hua	K'ung Yuan	P'an Tzu-li	Yang Shang-k'un
Cheng Wei-san	Li Ch'ang	P'eng Chen	Yang Yung
Chia T'o-fu	Li Chieh-po	P'eng Te-huai	Yao I-lin
Chiang Hua	Li Chien-chen	Po I-po	Yeh Fei
Chiang Nan-hsiang	Li Chih-min	Shu T'ung	Yen Hung-yen
Chiang Wei-ch'ing	Li Ching-ch'üan	Shuai Meng-ch'i	
Ch'ien Chün-jui	Li Li-san	Su Chen-hua	
Ch'ien Ying	Li Pao-hua	Sung Jen-ch'iung	
Chou Hsiao-chou	Li T'ao	Sung Shih-lun	

52. Politburo (1956–   )

Note: The following officials were elected at either the First or Fifth Plenums of the Eighth Central Committee, held on September 28, 1956, and May 25, 1958, respectively. The chairman and vice-chairmen of the Central Committee, as well as the general secretary of the Central Committee, are also members of the Politburo Standing Committee. For an earlier list of Politburo members, see Appendix 15; for the new Politburo elected in 1969, see Appendix 51.

Chairman		*Vice-Chairmen*	
Mao Tse-tung	1956–	Liu Shao-ch'i	1956–
		Chou En-lai	1956–
General Secretary		Chu Te	1956–
		Ch'en Yun	1956–
Teng Hsiao-p'ing	1956–	Lin Piao	1958–

Politburo Members (*in rank order*)

Mao Tse-tung	1956–		Lo Jung-huan	1956–1963
Liu Shao-ch'i	1956–		Ch'en I	1956–
Chou En-lai	1956–		Li Fu-ch'un	1956–
Chu Te	1956–		P'eng Te-huai	1956–
Ch'en Yun	1956–		Liu Po-ch'eng	1956–
Teng Hsiao-p'ing	1956–		Ho Lung	1956–
Lin Piao	1956–		Li Hsien-nien	1956–
Lin Po-ch'ü	1956–1960		K'o Ch'ing-shih	1958–1965
Tung Pi-wu	1956–		Li Ching-ch'üan	1958–
P'eng Chen	1956–		T'an Chen-lin	1958–

Alternates

Ulanfu	1956–		Ch'en Po-ta	1956–
Chang Wen-t'ien	1956–		K'ang Sheng	1956–
Lu Ting-i	1956–		Po I-po	1956–

53. Central Secretariat (1956–   )

Note: This body is to be distinguished from the "old" Secretariat listed in Appendix 17. The "new" Secretariat, the executive arm of the Politburo, is less important than the former body. The first personnel were elected at the First Plenum of the Eighth Central Committee, held the day after the Eighth Party Congress in September 1956. Names are in rank order.

Secretaries

Teng Hsiao-p'ing	1956–		Li Hsueh-feng	1956–
P'eng Chen	1956–		Li Fu-ch'un	1958–
Wang Chia-hsiang	1956–		Li Hsien-nien	1958–
T'an Chen-lin	1956–		Lu Ting-i	1962–
T'an Cheng	1956–1962		K'ang Sheng	1962–
Huang K'o-ch'eng	1956–1962		Lo Jui-ch'ing	1962–

Alternate Secretaries

Liu Lan-t'ao	1956–		Hu Ch'iao-mu	1956–
Yang Shang-k'un	1956–			

54. Central Control Commission (1955–   )

Note: The Central Control Commission was established by the Fifth Plenum, April 1955. Only the appointment of Tung Pi-wu was announced then. The other officials were appointed in September 1956 at the First Plenum of the Eighth Central Committee. Names are in rank order.

Secretary

Tung Pi-wu	1955–

Deputy Secretaries

Liu Lan-t'ao	1956–1962		Wang Ts'ung-wu	1956–
Chang Yun-i	1962–		Ch'ien Ying	1956–
Hsiao Hua	1956–		Liu Hsi-wu	1956–

55. Central Committee Departments (1949–   )

Note: Unless otherwise noted, the organizations listed below are presumed to have existed before 1949. Pre-1949 organs are listed in Appendix 19. A few of the Central Committee departments are mentioned regularly in the press, but most of them are not. As a consequence, there are many uncertainties about dates; the biographies should be consulted for details.

Communications Work Department

Note: Established about 1957 as a result of a division of the Industrial and Communications Work Department. The Communications Work Department was apparently dissolved and its functions placed under the Industrial and Communications Political Department in the mid-1960's—see below.

Director: Tseng Shan

Industrial and Communications Work Department

Note: Established in late 1950's; name altered to Finance and Trade Political Department about 1964.

Directors: Ma Ming-fang   Yao I-lin

Industrial and Communications Work Department

Note: Established about 1956, but about a year later some of its functions were assumed by the Communications Work Department. In approximately 1964 the two departments were merged and the title was altered to the Industrial and Communications Political Department.

Directors: Li Hsueh-feng   Ku Mu

International Liaison Department

Note: Neither this department nor the director listed below was confirmed in Chinese press media, but the existence of the department and Wu's directorship were mentioned by a Polish news agency in 1959.

Director: Wu Hsiu-ch'üan

Military Affairs Committee

Note: Little was known about this committee until the 1960's, although P'eng Te-huai spoke on behalf of it at the Eighth Party Congress in 1956. Mao Tse-tung is probably the chairman, but P'eng Te-huai and then Lin Piao have apparently been the *de facto* heads.

Chairman	*Vice-Chairmen*		
Mao Tse-tung ?	Lin Piao	Ho Lung	Nieh Jung-chen

Standing Committee Members

Ho Lung	Hsu Hsiang-ch'ien	Liu Po-ch'eng	Nieh Jung-chen
Hsiao Hua	Lin Piao	Lo Jung-huan	Yeh Chien-ying

Organization Department

Directors: P'eng Chen　　　Jao Shu-shih　　　An Tzu-wen

Propaganda Department

Directors: Lu Ting-i　　　Hsi Chung-hsun　　　Lu Ting-i

Rural Work Department

Note: Established about 1952–53 and possibly abolished in the 1960's.

Director: Teng Tzu-hui

Social Affairs Department

Note: Commonly regarded as an intelligence organization, the department has not been mentioned in the press since the early 1950's.

Director: Li K'o-nung

Staff Office

Director: Yang Shang-k'un

United Front Work Department

Directors: Li Wei-han　　　Hsu Ping

Women's Work Committee

First Secretary: Ts'ai Ch'ang

56. Regional Party Bureaus (1949–55; 1961–　　)

Note: The CCP had a regional structure for many years before 1949, and by the time the PRC was established in October 1949 there were already bureaus in north, northeast, and northwest China. By the end of that year, following the conquest of the mainland, the bureaus for central-south, east, and southwest China had been established. The following compilation deals only with the post-1949 period. The dates for the abolition of the bureaus in the 1954–55 period are: Central-South, November 1954; South China Sub-bureau, July 1955; East China, July 1955; North China, August 1954; Northeast, May 1955; Northwest, June 1955; Southwest, May 1955.

In the 1949–1954 period, several of the top secretaries left their areas long before the bureaus were abolished, and their subordinate secretaries often acted on their behalf. Biographies should be consulted for details about dates and changing posts.

The South China Sub-bureau is listed here because of its regional title; for the Shantung, Sinkiang, and Suiyuan-Inner Mongolia sub-bureaus, see Appendix 57.

Several of the provinces listed under the various bureaus were dissolved in the 1950's; details are found in Appendix 66.

All the regional bureaus were abolished by mid-1955, but they were formally re-created in accordance with the decision of the Central Committee's Ninth Plenum in January 1961.

Central-South

(Honan, Hunan, Hupeh, Kiangsi,[1] Kwangsi, Kwangtung)

1949–1954		*1961–*	
First secretary	Lin Piao Yeh Chien-ying	*First secretary*	T'ao Chu
		Second secretary	Wang Jen-chung
Other senior secretaries	Lo Jung-huan Teng Tzu-hui T'an Cheng Li Hsueh-feng Li Hsien-nien	*Third secretary*	Ch'en Yü

South China Sub-Bureau

(Kwangsi, Kwangtung)

1949–1955

First secretary	Yeh Chien-ying
Acting first secretary	T'ao Chu
Other senior secretaries	Chang Yun-i Fang Fang T'an Cheng

[1] Kiangsi was subordinate to this bureau during the 1949–1955 period, but it was shifted to the jurisdiction of the East China Bureau in 1961.

East China

(Anhwei, Chekiang, Fukien, Kiangsi,[2] Kiangsu, Shantung)

1949–1955		*1961–*	
First secretary	Jao Shu-shih T'an Chen-lin	*First secretary*	K'o Ch'ing-shih
		Second secretary	Tseng Hsi-sheng
Other senior secretaries	Ch'en I Chang Ting-ch'eng	*Third Secretary*	Li Pao-hua

[2] Kiangi was shifted from the jurisdiction of the Central-South Bureau to this bureau in 1961.

North China

(Chahar, Hopeh, Pingyuan, Shansi, Suiyuan)

1949–1954   *1961–*

First secretary	Po I-po	*First secretary*	Li Hsueh-feng
Other senior secretaries	Nieh Jung-chen	*Second secretary*	Ulanfu
	Chou Jung-hsin		
	Liu Lan-t'ao	*Thrd secretary*	Lin T'ieh
	Wang Ts'ung-wu		
	Chang Su		
	Liu Hsiu-feng		

Northeast Bureau

(Heilungkiang, Jehol, Kirin, Liaohsi, Liaotung, Sungkiang)

1949–1955   *1961–*

First secretary	Kao Kang	*First secretary*	Sung Jen-ch'iung
Other senior secretaries	Li Fu-ch'un	*Second secretary*	Ouyang Ch'in
	Lin Feng	*Third secretary*	Ma Ming-fang

Northwest Bureau

(Kansu, Ninghsia, Shensi, Sinkiang, Tsinghai)

1949–1955   *1961–*

First secretary	Hsi Chung-hsun	*First secretary*	Liu Lan-t'ao
Other senior secretaries	Ma Ming-fang	*Second secretary*	Chang Te-sheng
	Ma Wen jui	*Third secretary*	Hu Yao-pang

Southwest Bureau

(Kweichow, Sikang, Szechwan, Yunnan)

1949–1955   *1961–*

First secretary	Teng Hsiao-p'ing	*First secretary*	Li Ching-ch'üan
	Ho Lung		
Other senior secretaries	Liu Po-ch'eng		
	Sung Jen-ch'iung		
	Chang Chi-ch'un		

57. Provincial Party Committees (1949–   )

Note: Following is a list of the senior Party secretaries in provinces, autonomous regions, and the cities of Peking and Shanghai. In the early PRC years these men were known simply as "secretaries," but in the 1953–1955 period the ranking secretarial post was redesignated "first secretary." For the many mergers and divisions of provinces, see Appendix 66. † indicates that the individual is not one of the 433 biographic entries.

Anhwei

Tseng Hsi-sheng	1952–1960	Li Pao-hua	1962–
Tseng Hsi-sheng	1961–1962		

Anhwei, North

Tseng Hsi-sheng	1949–1952

Anhwei, South

†Ma T'ien-shui	c.1950–?

Antung

Liu Lan-po	1946–1949

Chahar

Liu Tao-sheng	1946–?	†Yang Keng-t'ien	c.1950–1952

Chekiang

T'an Chen-lin	1949–1952	Chiang Hua	1955–
T'an Ch'i-lung	1952–1955		

Fukien

Chang Ting-ch'eng	1949–1954	Yeh Fei	1954–

Heilungkiang

Chang Ch'i-lung	?–1950	Ouyang Ch'in	1954–
†Chao Te-tsun	1950–1954		

Hokiang

(no information)

Honan

Chang Hsi	1949–1952	Wu Chih-p'u	1958–1961
P'an Fu-sheng	1953–1958	Liu Chien-hsun	1961–

Hopeh

Lin T'ieh	1949–

Hsingan

(no information)

Hunan

Huang K'o-ch'eng	1949–1952	Chou Hsiao-chou	1953–1959
Chin Ming	1952–1953	Chang P'ing-hua	1959–

Hupeh

Li Hsien-nien	1949–1954	Wang Jen-chung	1954–

Inner Mongolia

Note: Inner Mongolia was a sub-bureau under the Party Central Committee until 1952 when it was merged with the Suiyuan Party apparatus and became known as the Suiyuan–Inner Mongolia Sub-bureau. It reverted to the Inner Mongolia Sub-bureau in 1954–1955, but since 1955 it has been known as the Inner Mongolian Autonomous Region Committee.

Ulanfu	1949–

Jehol

†Li Yun-ch'ang	c.1949–1949	Wang Kuo-ch'üan	1950–1955

Kansu

Chang Te-sheng	1949–1954	Wang Feng	1961–
Chang Chung-liang	1954–1961		

Kiangsi

Ch'en Cheng-jen	1949–1952	Yang Shang-k'uei	1953–

Kiangsu

K'o Ch'ing-shih	1952–1955	Chiang Wei-ch'ing	1955–

Kiangsu, North

†Hsiao Wang-tung	1949–1952

Kiangsu, South

Ch'en P'ei-hsien	1949–1952

Kirin

Liu Hsi-wu	1950–1952	Wu Te	1956–
†Li Meng-ling	1952–?		

Kwangsi

Chang Yun-i	1949–1955	Liu Chien-hsun	1957–1961
Ch'en Man-yuan	1955–1957	Wei Kuo-ch'ing	1961–

Kwangtung

Yeh Chien-ying	1951–1955	Chao Tzu-yang	1965–
T'ao Chu	1955–1965		

Kweichow

Su Chen-hua	1949–1954	Li Ta-chang	1965–1965
Chou Lin	c.1954–1965	†Chia Ch'i-yun	1965–

Liaohsi

†Kuo Feng	1950–1954

Liaoning

Huang Ou-tung	1954–1958	Huang Huo-ch'ing	1958–

Liaopei

(no information)

Liaotung

Chang Wen-t'ien	c.1949–1950	Chang Ch'i-lung	1950–1953
Liu Lan-po	1950–1950	Kao Yang	1953–1954

Ninghsia

P'an Tzu-li	1949–1951	Wang Feng	1958–1961
†Chu Min	c.1953–?	Yang Ching-jen	1961–

Nunkiang

(no information)

Peking

P'eng Chen	1949–

Pingyuan

Wu Te	1950–1952

Shanghai

Jao Shu-shih	1949–1952	K'o Ch'ing-shih	1955–1965
Ch'en I	1952–1954	Ch'en P'ei-hsien	1965–

Shansi

Ch'eng Tzu-hua	1949–1951		T'ao Lu-chia	1953–1965
Lai Jo-yü	1951–1951		Wei Heng	1965–
Kao K'o-lin	1952–1953			

Shantung

Note: Shangtung was a sub-bureau under the Party Central Committee until October 1955.

K'ang Sheng	1949–1955		Tseng Hsi-sheng	1960–1961
Shu T'ung	1955–1960		T'an Ch'i-lung	1961–

Shensi

Ma Ming-fang	c.1949–1952		Hu Yao-pang (acting)	1965–1965
P'an Tzu-li	1952–1954		†Huo Shih-lien	1965–
Chang Te-sheng	1955–1965			

Sikang

Liao Chih-kao	1950–1955

Sinkiang

Note: Sinkiang was a sub-bureau under the Party Central Committee until October 1955.

Wang Chen	1949–1952		Wang En-mao	1952–

Suiyuan

(See also *Inner Mongolia.*)

Kao K'o-lin	1949–1952

Sungkiang

†Chang Ts'e	c.1949–1951		†Li Ch'ang-ch'ing	c.1953–1954
†Jao Pin	1951–c.1952			

Szechwan

Li Ching-ch'üan	1952–1965		Liao Chih-kao	1965–

Szechwan, East

Hsieh Fu-chih	1950–1952

Szechwan, North

(no information)

Szechwan, South

(no information)

Szechwan, West

   (no information)

Tibet

   Note: The Party apparatus in Tibet was known as work committee until 1965.

   Chang Ching-wu   c.1956–1965   Chang Kuo-hua   1965–

Tsinghai

   Chang Chung-liang   1949–1954   Wang Chao (acting)   1961–1962
   Kao Feng   1954–1960   †Yang Chih-lin   1962–

Yunnan

   Sung Jen-ch'iung   1951–1953   Yen Hung-yen   1959–
   Hsieh Fu-chih   1953–1959

Part VIII. The PRC: Government Organs

Note: † indicates that the individual is not one of the 433 biographic entries.

58. Central People's Government Council (1949–1954)

Note: The council was the most important government organ from 1949 to 1954. It was officially defined as the "highest executive body," but it also exercised broad legislative and judicial powers. Except for the death of a few members, the composition was unchanged until the council was abolished in September 1954. Summaries of the 10th through the 34th (and last) meetings are found in *CB* no. 276, January 20, 1954, and no. 300, October 30, 1954. The Government Administration Council (the cabinet), the People's Revolutionary Military Council, the Supreme People's Court, the Supreme People's Procuratorate, and (from 1952 to 1954) the State Planning Commission were all subordinate to the Central People's Government Council.

Chairman

Mao Tse-tung

Vice Chairmen

†Chang Lan	Kao Kang	Liu Shao-ch'i	Sung Ch'ing-ling
Chu Te	†Li Chi-shen		

Members (56)

†Chang Chih-chung	†Ho Hsiang-ning	Lin Feng	Po I-po
Chang Hsi-jo	Ho Lung	Lin Piao	Saifudin
†Chang Nan-hsien	Hsi Chung-hsun	Lin Po-ch'ü	†Shen Chün-ju
†Chang Po-chün	Hsu Hsiang-ch'ien	Liu Ko-p'ing	Shen Yen-ping
†Chang Tung-sun	Hsu T'e-li	Liu Po-ch'eng	†Szut'u Mei-t'ang
Chang Yun-i	†Huang Yen-p'ei	†Liu Ya-tzu	†T'an P'ing-shan
†Ch'en Chia-keng	Jao Shu-shih	Lo Jung-huan	Teng Hsiao-p'ing
Ch'en I	K'ang Sheng	†Lung Yun	Teng Tzu-hui
†Ch'en Ming-shu	†Kao Ch'ung-min	Ma Hsu-lun	Ts'ai Ch'ang
†Ch'en Shu-t'ung	Kuo Mo-jo	†Ma Yin-ch'u	†Ts'ai T'ing-k'ai
Ch'en Yun	†Li Chang-ta	Nieh Jung-chen	Tung Pi-wu
†Ch'eng Ch'ien	Li Chu-ch'en	P'eng Chen	Ulanfu
Chou En-lai	†Li Hsi-chiu	P'eng Te-huai	Wu Yü-chang
†Fu Tso-i	Li Li-san	†P'eng Tse-min	Yeh Chien-ying

Secretary General

Lin Po-ch'ü

59. Government Administration Council—State Council (cabinet)

Note: The cabinet of the PRC was known as the Government Administration Council from 1949 to 1954, and as the State Council thereafter.

Premier

Chou En-lai	1949–

Vice-Premiers

Ch'en I	1954–		Lo Jui-ch'ing	1959–
Ch'en Yun	1949–		Lu Ting-i	1959–
Ho Lung	1954–		Nieh Jung-chen	1956–
Hsi Chung-hsun	1959–1965		P'eng Te-huai	1954–1965
Hsieh Fu-chih	1965–		Po I-po	1956–
Huang Yen-p'ei	1949–1954		T'an Chen-lin	1959–
K'o Ch'ing-shih	1965–1965		T'ao Chu	1965–
Kuo Mo-jo	1949–1954		Teng Hsiao-p'ing	1952–
Li Fu-ch'un	1954–		Teng Tzu-hui	1954–1965
Li Hsien-nien	1954–		Tung Pi-wu	1949–1954
Lin Piao	1954–		Ulanfu	1954–

Secretaries-General

Li Wei-han	1949–1953		Chou Jung-hsin	1965–
Hsi Chung-hsun	1953-1965			

Committees, Numbered Staff Offices, and Staff Offices

Note: Since 1949 the GAC/State Council has had an administrative hierarchy between the premier and the various ministries. These were known as committees from 1949 to 1954, as numbered staff offices between 1954 and 1959, and as staff offices since 1959. The heads of these bodies are listed below.

1949–1954

Culture and Education Committee	Kuo Mo-jo	October 1949–September 1954
Finance and Economics Committee	Ch'en Yun	October 1949–September 1954
People's Supervision Committee	†T'an P'ing-shan	October 1949–September 1954
Political and Legal Affairs Committee	Tung Pi-wu	October 1949–September 1954
State Planning Committee	Kao Kang	November 1952–September 1954

1954–1959

First Staff Office (public security, internal affairs, justice, supervision, labor)	Lo Jui-ch'ing	September 1954–September 1959
Second Staff Office (culture, education, science)	Lin Feng	September 1954–September 1959
Third Staff Office (heavy industry, construction, planning)	Po I-po	September 1954–September 1959
Fourth Staff Office (light industry)	Chia T'o-fu	September 1954–September 1959
Fifth Staff Office (finance, trade, food)	Li Hsien-nien	September 1954–September 1959
Sixth Staff Office (transport, communications)	Wang Shou-tao	September 1954–September 1959
Seventh Staff Office (agriculture, forestry, conservation)	Teng Tzu-hui	September 1954–September 1959
Eighth Staff Office (united front)	Li Wei-han	September 1954–September 1959

1959–

Agriculture and Forestry	Teng Tzu-hui	September 1959–October 1962
Staff Office	T'an Chen-lin	October 1962–
Culture and Education	Chang Chi-ch'un	September 1959–
Staff Office		
Finance and Trade	Li Hsien-nien	September 1959–
Staff Office		
Foreign Affairs	Ch'en I	March 1958–
Staff Office		

Note: This office was created in February 1958 when all other such offices had numbers. It is placed here for convenience.

Industry and Communications	Li Fu-ch'un	September 1959–April 1961
Staff Office	Po I-po	April 1961–

Internal Affairs Staff Office, *see* Political and Legal Affairs Staff Office.

Political and Legal Affairs	Hsieh Fu-chih	September 1959–c.1961
Staff Office	Hsieh Fu-chih	May 1963–

Note: This office was omitted from the 1961 *Jen-min shou-ts'e* (People's Handbook), so perhaps it was abolished in that year. In May 1963 it was re-established under the name Internal Affairs Staff Office.

Ministries and Commissions

Note: All organizations listed below are ministries unless otherwise indicated. The initial date listed after the name of the first minister is also the date the ministry or commission was established unless otherwise noted.

Agriculture

†Li Shu-ch'eng	October 1949–September 1954
Liao Lu-yen	September 1954–

In December 1950 this ministry and the Ministry of Light Industry absorbed some of the functions of the Ministry of Food Industry.

Agricultural Machinery

Ch'en Cheng-jen	August 1959–January 1965

In January 1965 this ministry was renamed the Eighth Ministry of Machine Building.

Agricultural Supplies, Purchase of

Yang I-ch'en	July 1955–November 1956

In November 1956 this ministry was absorbed by the Ministry of Urban Services.

Allocation of Materials

Yuan Pao-hua	November 1964–

Aquatic Products

Hsu Te-heng	May 1956–

Building

vacant	August 1952–November 1952
Ch'en Cheng-jen	November 1952–September 1954
Liu Hsiu-feng	September 1954–November 1964
†Li Jen-chün	November 1964–March 1965
Liu Yü-min	March 1965–

(*Chien-chu kung-ch'eng pu;* sometimes translated "Building Construction." Not to be confused with the Ministry of Building Materials Industry [*Chien-chu ts'ai-liao kung-yeh pu*] which it absorbed in February 1958.) Also in February 1958 it absorbed the Ministry of Urban Construction and, along with the State Planning Commission and the National Economic Commission, absorbed some functions of the National Construction Commission. In March 1965 it was divided, one part retaining the title Ministry of Building and the other being designated Ministry of Building Materials Industry.

Building Materials Industry

Lai Chi-fa	May 1956–February 1958
Lai Chi-fa	March 1965–

(*Chien-chu ts'ai-liao kung-yeh pu.* Not to be confused with the Ministry of Building [*Chien-chu kung-ch'eng pu*] by which it was absorbed in February 1958.) Along with the Ministries of Metallurgical Industry and Chemical Industry, it had been established in May 1956 when the Ministry of Heavy Industry was divided. In March 1965 it was re-created by the division of the Ministry of Building into this ministry and the portion retaining the title Ministry of Building.

Capital Construction Commission, State see *State Capital Construction Commission.*

Chemical Industry

P'eng T'ao	May 1956–November 1961
vacant	November 1961–July 1962
Kao Yang	July 1962–

This ministry, along with the Ministries of Building Materials Industry and Metallurgical Industry, was formed through the division of the Ministry of Heavy Industry in May 1956.

City Construction, see *Urban Construction.*

City Services, see *Urban Services.*

Coal Industry

Ch'en Yü	July 1955–September 1957
Chang Lin-chih	September 1957–

This ministry, along with the Ministries of Petroleum Industry and Electric Power Industry, was formed through the division of the Ministry of Fuel Industry in July 1955.

Codification Commission, State, see *State Codification Commission.*

Commerce

Tseng Shan	August 1952–November 1956
Ch'en Yun	November 1956–February 1958
Ch'en Yun	February 1958–September 1958 (name changed—see note below)
Ch'eng Tzu-hua	September 1958–February 1960
Yao I-lin	February 1960–

This ministry, along with the Ministry of Foreign Trade, was formed through the division of the Ministry of Trade in August 1952. It was renamed the First Ministry of Commerce in February 1958 at which time the Urban Services Ministry was redesignated the Second Ministry of Commerce. Then, in September 1958, the First and Second Ministries were merged and adopted the name Ministry of Commerce.

Commerce, First see *Commerce.*

Commerce, Second, see *Ministry of Urban Services.*

Commodity Price Commission, National, see *National Commodity Price Commission.*

Communications

†Chang Po-chün	October 1949–Feburary 1958
Wang Shou-tao	February 1958–July 1964
Sun Ta-kuang	July 1964–

Construction Commission, State, see *State Construction Commission.*

Cultural Relations with Foreign Countries, Commission for

Chang Hsi-jo	February 1958–

In February 1958 this was raised from a bureau of the same name.

Culture

Shen Yen-ping	October 1949–January 1965
Lu Ting-i	January 1965–

Defense, National, see *National Defense.*

Economic Commission, State, see *State Economic Commission.*

Economic Relations with Foreign Countries, Commission for

Fang I	June 1964–

In June 1964 this was raised from a bureau of the same name.

Education

†Ma Hsu-lun	October 1949–November 1952
Chang Hsi-jo	November 1952–February 1958
Yang Hsiu-feng	February 1958–July 1964
Ho Wei	July 1964–

In November 1952 the Ministry of Higher Education was formed to supplement the work of this ministry. In February 1958 the two were merged, retaining the title Ministry of Education. Then in June 1964 they were redivided.

Education, Higher

†Ma Hsu-lun	November 1952–September 1954
Yang Hsiu-feng	September 1954–February 1958
vacant	June 1964–July 1964
Yang Hsiu-feng	July 1964–January 1965
Chiang Nan-hsiang	January 1965–

Originally formed in November 1952 to supplement the work of the Ministry of Education, it merged with the Ministry of Education in February 1958, taking the title of the latter. In June 1964 it was re-created by the division of the Ministry of Education.

Electric Power Industry

| Liu Lan-po | July 1955–February 1958 |

(*Tien-li kung-yeh pu*. Not to be confused with the Ministry of Power Equipment Industry [*Tien-chi chih-tsao kung-yeh pu*], which existed from May 1956 to February 1958.) Along with the Ministries of Coal Industry and Petroleum Industry, it was formed through a division of the Ministry of Fuel Industry in July 1955. In February 1958 it merged with the Ministry of Water Conservancy and the new body took the title of Ministry of Water Conservancy and Electric Power.

Finance

Po I-po	October 1949–September 1953
Teng Hsiao-p'ing	September 1953–June 1954
Li Hsien-nien	June 1954–

Food

| †Chang Nai-ch'i | August 1952–February 1958 |
| Sha Ch'ien-li | February 1958– |

(*Liang-shih pu*. Not to be confused with the Ministry of Food Industry [*Shih-p'in kung-yeh pu*].)

Food Industry

| Yang Li-san | October 1949–December 1950 |
| Li Chu-ch'en | May 1956–February 1958 |

(*Shih-p'in kung-yeh pu*. Not to be confused with the Ministry of Food [*Liang-shih pu*], which was established in August 1952.) In December 1950 its functions were taken over by the Ministries of Light Industry and Agriculture, but it was re-created upon the abolition of the Ministry of Local Industry in May 1956. In February 1958 it was absorbed by the Ministry of Light Industry.

Foreign Affairs

| Chou En-lai | October 1949–February 1958 |
| Ch'en I | February 1958– |

Foreign Trade, see *Trade, Foreign.*

Forestry

Liang Hsi	October 1949–December 1958
vacant	December 1958–April 1959
†Liu Wen-hui	April 1959–

(*Lin-yeh pu.* It was originally named Forestry and Land Reclamation [*Lin k'en pu*], but the name was changed when responsibility for reclamation work was transferred to the Ministry of Agriculture in November 1951.) In February 1958, the Ministry absorbed the Ministry of Timber Industry.

Fuel Industry

Ch'en Yü	October 1949–July 1955

In July 1955 this ministry was dissolved to form the ministries of Electric Power Industry, Coal Industry, and Petroleum.

Geology

Li Szu-kuang	August 1952–

Health, see *Public Health.*

Heavy Industry

Ch'en Yun	October 1949–April 1950
Li Fu-ch'un	April 1950–August 1952
Wang Ho-shou	August 1952–May 1956

Some of this ministry's functions were transferred to the First and Second Ministries of Machine Building in August 1952. In May 1956 it was abolished and its functions taken over by the Ministries of Building Materials Industry, Metallurgical Industry, and Chemical Industry.

Higher Education, see *Education, Higher.*

Illiteracy, Commission for Eliminating

Ch'u T'u-nan	November 1952–September 1954
Chen I	March 1956–?

When this body was re-created in 1956 it was entitled "Association" (*hsieh-hui*) rather than commission. It was listed in the 1957 and 1958 editions of the *Jen-min shou-ts'e* (People's handbook), but not in later editions.

Interior (Internal Affairs)

Hsieh Chueh-tsai	October 1949–April 1959
Ch'ien Ying	April 1959–November 1960
Tseng Shan	November 1960–

Justice

Shih Liang	October 1949–April 1959

In April 1959 the ministry's functions were taken over by the Supreme People's Court.

Labor

Li Li-san	October 1949–September 1954
Ma Wen-jui	September 1954–

Law Commission

Ch'en Shao-yü	October 1949–September 1954
Hsu Te-heng (acting)	1951–September 1954

In September 1954 this commission was abolished and a Bureau of Legal Affairs was established which presumably took over some or all of the commission's functions.

Light Industry

†Huang Yen-p'ei	October 1949–September 1954
Chia T'o-fu	September 1954–May 1956
Sha Ch'ien-li	May 1956–February 1958
Li Chu-ch'en	February 1958–

In December 1950 this ministry and the Ministry of Agriculture absorbed some of the functions of the Ministry of Food Industry. In February 1958 it completely absorbed the Ministry of Food Industry. In February 1965 it was divided into the First and Second Ministries of Light Industry, with this ministry taking the title First Ministry of Light Industry.

Light Industry, First, see Light Industry.

Light Industry, Second

Hsu Yun-pei	February 1965–

Established upon the division of the Ministry of Light Industry.

Local Industry

Sha Ch'ien-li	September 1954–May 1956

In May 1956, when this ministry was abolished, at least some of its functions were taken over by the Ministry of Food Industry.

Machine Building, First

Huang Ching	August 1952–February 1958
Chao Erh-lu	February 1958–September 1960
Tuan Chün-i	September 1960–

Established from portions of the Ministry of Heavy Industry. In February 1958, it absorbed what was then the Second Ministry of Machine Building and the Ministry of Power Equipment Industry.

Machine Building, Second

Chao Erh-lu	August 1952–February 1958

Established from portions of the Ministry of Heavy Industry. In February 1958 this ministry was absorbed by the First Ministry of Machine Building.

Machine Building, Second

　　Sung Jen-ch'iung　　　　February 1958–September 1960
　　†Liu Chieh　　　　　　　September 1960–

Not to be confused with the above ministry of the same name. This ministry was, in effect, what had been known as the Third Ministry of Machine Building until the merger of the First and Second Ministries of Machine Building in February 1958, when the Third Ministry was renumbered the Second Ministry of Machine Building. (See below.)

Machine Building, Third

　　Chang Lin-chih　　　　　April 1955–May 1956
　　Sung Jen-ch'iung　　　　November 1956–February 1958

This ministry was abolished for a six-month period in mid-1956, but was re-created. Then, with the February 1958 merger of the First and Second Ministries of Machine Building, this ministry was re-numbered the Second Ministry of Machine Building. (See above.)

Machine Building, Third

　　†Chang Lien-k'uei　　　　September 1960–January 1961
　　Sun Chih-yuan　　　　　January 1961–

Not to be confused with the above ministry of the same name. This was a completely new Third Ministry of Machine Building, created in September 1960.

Machine Building, Fourth

　　Wang Cheng　　　　　　May 1963–

Machine Building, Fifth

　　Ch'iu Ch'uang-ch'eng　　September 1963–

Machine Building, Sixth

　　Fang Ch'iang　　　　　　September 1963–

Machine Building, Seventh

　　Wang Ping-chang　　　　January 1965–

Machine Building, Eighth

　　Ch'en Cheng-jen　　　　　January 1965–

This ministry had formerly been titled the Ministry of Agricultural Machinery.

Marine Products, see *Aquatic Products.*

Metallurgical Industry

　　Wang Ho-shou　　　　　May 1956–July 1964
　　Lü Tung　　　　　　　　July 1964–

This ministry and the Ministries of Building Materials Industry and Chemical Industry were formed through a division of the Ministry of Heavy Industry in May 1956.

National Commodity Price Commission

vacant   May 1963–September 1963
Hsueh Mu-ch'iao   September 1963–

National Defense

P'eng Te-huai   September 1954–September 1959
Lin Piao   September 1959–

Nationalities Affairs Commission

Li Wei-han   October 1949–September 1954
Ulanfu   September 1954–

North China Affairs

Liu Lan-t'ao   September 1950–January 1953

This was known as a ministry from its establishment until December 1951 when it was renamed the North China Administrative Committee. It continued to be subordinate to the Government Administration Council until January 1953 when it became a separate regional government (see Appendix 65).

Overseas Chinese Affairs Commission

†Ho Hsiang-ning   October 1949–April 1959
Liao Ch'eng-chih   April 1959–

Personnel

An Tzu-wen   September 1950–September 1954

In September 1954, upon the abolition of this ministry, a Personnel Bureau was established; presumably this took over some or all of the ministry's functions.

Petroleum Industry

Li Chü-k'uei   July 1955–February 1958
Yü Ch'iu-li   February 1958–

This ministry and the Ministries of Coal Industry and Electric Power Industry were formed by the division of the Ministry of Fuel Industry in July 1955.

Phoneticization of the Chinese Language, Commission for

Kuo Mo-jo   October 1956–?

This commission was listed in the 1957 and 1958 editions of the *Jen-min shou-ts'e* (People's handbook), but not in later editions.

Phoneticization of Standard Spoken Chinese, Commission for

Ch'en I   February 1956–?

This commission was listed in the 1957 and 1958 editions of the *Jen-min shou-ts'e* (People's handbook), but not in later editions.

Physical Culture and Sports Commission

    Ho Lung   November 1952–

Planning Commission, State, see *State Planning Commission.*

Posts and Telecommunications

    †Chu Hsueh-fan   October 1949–

Power Equipment Industry

    Chang Lin-chih   May 1956–February 1958

(*Tien-chi chih-tsao kung-yeh pu.* Not to be confused with the Ministry of Electric Power Industry [*Tien-li kung-yeh pu*] which existed from July 1955 to February 1958.) This ministry and the Second Ministry of Machine Building were absorbed by the First Ministry of Machine Building in February 1958.

Public Health

    Li Te-ch'üan   October 1949–January 1965
    Ch'ien Hsin-chung   January 1965–

Public Security

    Lo Jui-ch'ing   October 1949–September 1959
    Hsieh Fu-chih   September 1959–

Purchase of Agricultural Supplies, Ministry for, see *Agricultural Supplies, Purchase of.*

Railways

    T'eng Tai-yuan   October 1949–January 1965
    Lü Cheng-ts'ao   August 1960–January 1965
      (acting)
    Lü Cheng-ts'ao   January 1965–

Scientific and Technological Commission

    Nieh Jung-chen   November 1958–

Formed through a merger of the Scientific Planning Commission and the National Technological Commission.

Scientific Planning Commission

    Ch'en I   March 1956–May 1957
    Nieh Jung-chen   May 1957–November 1958

In November 1958 this commission merged with the National Technological Commission to form the Scientific and Technological Commission.

State Capital Construction Commission

Ch'en Yün   October 1958–January 1961
Ku Mu   March 1965–

Established in September 1958. When abolished in January 1961, its functions were taken over by the State Planning Commission. It was re-created in March 1965.

State Codification Commission

Chou Jung-hsin   November 1963–

Established in September 1963.

State Construction Commission

Po I-po   September 1954–May 1956
Wang Ho-shou   May 1956–February 1958

In February 1958 the commission was abolished, and its functions were taken over by the State Planning Commission, the National Economic Commission, and the Ministry of Building.

State Economic Commission

Po I-po   May 1956–

This commission, the State Planning Commission, and the Ministry of Building took over the functions of the National Construction Commission when the latter was abolished in February 1958.

State Farms and Land Reclamation

Wang Chen   May 1956–

State Planning Commission

Kao Kang   November 1952–September 1954
Li Fu-ch'un   September 1954–

From November 1952 to September 1954 this commission was formally subordinate to the Central Peoples' Government Council (see Appendix 58) and thus not technically at the ministry-commission level. It is included here for convenience. This commission, the Ministry of Building, and the State Economic Commission each absorbed some of the functions of the National Construction Commission when the latter was abolished in February 1958. The State Planning Commission also took over the functions of the State Capital Construction Commission when it was abolished in January 1961.

State Technological Commission

Huang Ching   May 1956–February 1958
Han Kuang   February 1958–November 1958
(acting)

In November 1958 this commission merged with the Scientific Planning Commission to form the Scientific and Technological Commission.

Supervision

Ch'ien Ying   September 1954–April 1959

This ministry was formed from the People's Supervision Committee, which existed from 1949 to 1954. It was abolished at the same time as the Ministry of Justice; although it was noted that the functions of the latter had been taken over by the Supreme People's Court, no mention was made of the functions of the Ministry of Supervision.

Technological Commission, State, see *State Technological Commission.*

Textile Industry

Tseng Shan   October 1949–August 1952
†Chiang Kuang-nai   August 1952–

Timber Industry

†Lo Lung-chi   May 1956–February 1958

Not to be confused with the Ministry of Forestry, by which this ministry was absorbed in February 1958.

Trade

Yeh Chi-chuang   October 1949–August 1952

In August 1952 this ministry was divided into the Ministries of Foreign Trade and Commerce.

Trade, Foreign

Yeh Chi-chuang   August 1952–

This ministry and the Ministry of Commerce were formed through a division of the Ministry of Trade in August 1952.

Urban Construction

Wan Li   May 1956–February 1958

In February 1958 this was absorbed by the Ministry of Building.

Urban Services

vacant   May 1956–November 1956
Yang I-ch'en   November 1956–February 1958
Yang I-ch'en   February 1958–September 1958

The post of minister remained vacant after the establishment of this ministry until the abolition of the Ministry for the Purchase of Agricultural Supplies in November 1956, when the latter's functions were taken over by the Ministry of Urban Service. Then, in February 1958, this ministry was renamed the Second Ministry of Commerce. The latter, in turn, merged with the First Ministry of Commerce in September 1958 to form the Ministry of Commerce.

Water Conservancy

†Fu Tso-i   October 1949–February 1958

In February 1958 this ministry merged with the Ministry of Electric Power Industry to form the Ministry of Water Conservancy and Electric Power.

Water Conservancy and Electric Power

†Fu Tso-i   February 1958–

Formed in February 1958 by the merger of the Ministries of Water Conservancy and Electric Power Industry.

60. Supreme People's Court

Chief Justices

†Shen Chün-ju	1949–1954	Hsieh Chueh-tsai	1959–1965
Tung Pi-wu	1954–1959	Yang Hsiu-feng	1965–

Deputy Chief Justices

Chang Chih-jang	1949–	Ma Hsi-wu	1954–1962
Wu Kai-chih	1949–1954	Ch'en Ch'i-han	1957–
Chang Su	1954–1954	†Wang Wei-kang	1959–
Kao K'o-lin	1954–c.1961	Wu Te-feng	1961–

61. Supreme People's Procuratorate

Procurators General

Lo Jung-huan	1949–1954	Chang Ting-ch'eng	1954–

Deputy Procurators General

†Lan Kung-wu	1949–1957	Li Shih-ying	1955–1962
†Li Liu-ju	1949–	†Huang Huo-hsing	1955–
Kao K'o-lin	1953–1954	†Chou Hsing	1958–c.1961
†T'an Cheng-wen	1954–1961	Chang Su	1962–
†Liang Kuo-pin	1954–1958		

62. People's Revolutionary Military Council

Note: The Military Council existed from 1949 to 1954 as an organ directly subordinate to the Central People's Government Council.

Chairman   Mao Tse-tung

Vice-Chairmen

Ch'en I	1954–1954	Lin Piao	1951–1954
†Ch'eng Ch'ien	1949–1954	Liu Po-ch'eng	1954–1954
Chou En-lai	1949–1954	Liu Shao-ch'i	1949–1954
Chu Te	1949–1954	Lo Jung-huan	1954–1954
Ho Lung	1954–1954	Nieh Jung-chen	1954–1954
Hsu Hsiang-ch'ien	1954–1954	P'eng Te-huai	1949–1954
Kao Kang	1951–1954	Yeh Chien-ying	1954–1954

Members

†Chang Chih-chung	1949–1954		†Liu Fei	1949–1954
Chang Yun-i	1949–1954		Liu Po-ch'eng	1949–1954
Ch'en I	1949–1954		Lo Jui-ch'ing	1949–1954
†Fu Tso-i	1949–1954		†Lung Yun	1949–1954
Ho Lung	1949–1954		Nieh Jung-chen	1949–1954
Hsi Chung-hsun	1949–1954		†Sa Chen-ping	1949–1952
Hsu Hai-tung	1954–1954		Su Yü	1949–1954
Hsu Hsiang-ch'ien	1949–1954		Teng Hsiao-p'ing	1949–1954
Jao Shu-shih	1949–1954		Teng Tzu-hui	1949–1954
Kao Kang	1949–1951		†Ts'ai T'ing-k'ai	1949–1954
Li Hsien-nien	1949–1954		Yeh Chien-ying	1949–1954
Lin Piao	1949–1951			

63. NPC Standing Committee

Chairmen

Liu Shao-ch'i	1954–1959		Chu Te	1959–

Vice-Chairmen

†A-p'ei A-wang-chin-mei			Li Ching-ch'üan	1965–
(Ngapo Ngawang			Li Hsueh-feng	1965–
Jigme)	1965–		Li Wei-han	1954–1965
†Chang Chih-chung	1965–		Lin Feng	1959–
†Chang Lan	1954–1955		Lin Po-ch'ü	1954–1960
†Ch'en Shu-t'ung	1954–1966		Liu Ning-i	1965–
†Ch'eng Ch'ien	1959–1968		Liu Po-ch'eng	1959–
Chou Chien-jen	1965–		Lo Jung-huan	1954–1963
†Dalai Lama	1954–1965		†Panchen Lama	1959–1965
†Ho Hsiang-ning	1959–		P'eng Chen	1954–
Hsu Hsiang-ch'ien	1965–		Saifudin	1954–
†Huang Yen-p'ei	1954–1965		†Shen Chün-ju	1954–1963
K'ang Sheng	1965–		Sung Ch'ing-ling	1954–1959
Kuo Mo-jo	1954–		†Yang Ming-hsien	1965–1967
†Li Chi-shen	1954–1959			

Secretaries-General

P'eng Chen	1954–1965		Liu Ning-i	1965–

64. National Defense Council

Chairmen

Mao Tse-tung	1954–1959		Liu Shao-ch'i	1959–

Vice-Chairmen

†Chang Chih-chung	1954–		Lo Jui-ch'ing	1965–
Ch'en I	1954–		Lo Jung-huan	1954–1963
†Ch'eng Ch'ien	1954–1968		†Lung Yun	1954–1958
Chu Te	1954–1959		Nieh Jung-chen	1954–
†Fu Tso-i	1954–		P'eng Te-huai	1954–1965
Ho Lung	1954–		Teng Hsiao-p'ing	1954–
Hsu Hsiang-ch'ien	1954–		†Ts'ai T'ing-k'ai	1962–1968
Lin Piao	1954–		†Wei Li-huang	1959–1960
Liu Po-ch'eng	1954–		Yeh Chien-ying	1954–

65. Regional Governments

Note: From 1949 to 1954 regional governments existed at an administrative level between the central government and the provinces. These were known as Military and Administrative Committees (MAC) to the turn of the year 1952–53 and as Administrative Committees (AC) thereafter. Modifications to this general practice are described in the lists below. It should also be noted that some of the formal appointment dates were made slightly before or after the MAC's or AC's came into existence; the dates used below correspond to the inauguration dates of the committees. The capital seat of the committees is inserted after the name of the MAC/AC, followed by the provinces under their jurisdiction.

Central-South MAC/AC

(Wuhan, Hupeh, Hunan, Honan, Kiangsi, Kwangtung, Kwangsi)

CSMAC established February 5, 1950; abolished January 21, 1953.
CSAC established January 21, 1953; abolished November 7, 1954.

Chairman

Lin Piao	1950–1954

Vice-Chairmen

†Chang Nan-hsien	1950–1954	Li Hsien-nien	1952–1954
Chang Yun-i	1953–1954	Li Hsueh-feng	1952–1954
†Ch'en Ming-shu	1953–1954	Teng Tzu-hui	1950–1954
†Ch'eng Ch'ien	1950–1954	Yeh Chien-ying	1950–1954

East China MAC/AC

(Shanghai, Shantung, Kiangsi, Anhwei, Chekiang, Fukien)

ECMAC established January 27, 1950; abolished December 2, 1952.
ECAC established December 2, 1952; abolished August 29, 1954.

Chairman

Jao Shu-shih	1950–1954

Vice-Chairmen

Chang Ting-ch'eng	1952–1954	Su Yü	1950–1954
†Ch'en Chia-keng	1952–1954	T'an Chen-lin	1952–1954
†Liu Ya-tzu	1952–1954	Tseng Shan	1950–1954
†Ma Yin-ch'u	1950–1954	†Yen Hui-ch'ing	1950–1950
†Sheng P'ei-hua	1952–1954		

North China People's Government

Note: This government was established on August 19, 1948 at Shih-chia-chuang while the civil war was still being waged, and then moved to Peking in February 1949. It was abolished on October 31, 1949.

Chairman

Tung Pi-wu	1948–1949

Vice-Chairmen

†Lan Kung-wu	1948–1949	Yang Hsiu-feng	1948–1949
Po I-po	1948–1949		

Ministry of North China Affairs

Note: This ministry was subordinate to the Government Administration Council and thus not technically a regional government; it is reproduced here for the sake of continuity. Established September 5, 1950; abolished December 28, 1951.

Minister

Liu Lan-t'ao	1950–1951

Vice-Minister

†Tao Hsi-chin	1950–1951

North China AC

(Peking, Hopeh, Shansi, Chahar, Pingyuan, Suiyuan)

Note: Like the ministry above, the North China AC was under the Government Administration Council from its establishment on December 28, 1951. It was reorganized as a regional government on February 9, 1953 and abolished August 15, 1954.

Chairman

Liu Lan-t'ao	1951–1954

Vice-Chairmen

Chang Su	1951–1954	Liu Hsiu-feng	1951–1954
Li Chu-ch'en	1953–1954		

Northeast AC

Established 1946; abolished 1949.

Chairman

Lin Feng	1946–1949

Vice-Chairmen

†Chang Hsueh-szu	1946–1949	†Kao Ch'ung-min	1946–1949

Northeast People's Government

(Mukden, Sungkiang, Kirin, Heilungkiang, Liaotung, Liaohsi, Jehol)

Established August 27, 1949; abolished January 23, 1953.

Chairman

Kao Kang   1949–1953

Vice Chairmen

| †Kao Ch'ung-min | 1949–1953 | Lin Feng | 1949–1953 |
| Li Fu-ch'un | 1949–1953 | | |

Northeast AC

(Mukden, Sungkiang, Kirin, Heilungkiang, Liaotung, Liaohsi, Jehol)

Established January 23, 1953; abolished August 15, 1954.

Chairman

Kao Kang   1953–1954

Vice-Chairmen

†Chang Ming-yuan	1953–1954	†Li Cho-jan	1953–1954
†Kao Ch'ung-min	1953–1954	Lin Feng	1953–1954
Ku Cho-hsin	1953–1954	Wang Chin-hsiang	1953–1954

Northwest MAC/AC

(Sian, Shensi, Kansu, Ninghsia, Tsinghai, Sinkiang)

NWMAC established January 19, 1950; abolished January 27, 1953.
NWAC established January 27, 1953; abolished November 8, 1954.

Chairman

P'eng Te-huai   1950–1954

Vice-Chairmen

†Chang Chih-chung	1950–1954	Ma Ming-fang	1952–1954
Hsi Chung-hsun	1950–1954	Saifudin	1953–1954
†Huang Cheng-ch'ing	1953–1954	†Yang Ming-hsien	1953–1954
†Ma Hung-pin	1953–1954		

Southwest MAC/AC

(Chungking, Szechwan, Kweichow, Yunnan, Sikang)

SWMAC established July 26, 1950; abolished February 28, 1953.
SWAC established February 28, 1953; abolished November 1, 1954.

Chairman

   Liu Po-ch'eng   1950–1954

Vice Chairmen

Ho Lung	1950–1954	Sung Jen-ch'iung	1952–1954
†Hsiung K'o-wu	1950–1954	†Teng Hsi-hou	1953–1954
†Liu Wen-hui	1950–1954	Teng Hsiao-p'ing	1950–1954
†Lu Han	1952–1954	Wang Wei-chou	1950–1954
†Lung Yun	1950–1954		

66. Provincial Governments

Note: Following is a list of governors of provinces, chairmen of autonomous regions, and the mayors of Peking and Shanghai (the two cities which have been continuously subordinate to the central government since 1949).

The most complex geographic situation exists in Manchuria. After the war ended in 1945, the Nationalists divided the three traditional Manchurian provinces of Liaoning, Kirin, and Heilungkiang into the following nine: Liaoning, Liaopei, Antung, Kirin, Hokiang, Sungkiang, Heilungkiang, Nunkiang, and Hsingan. When the Communists gained control of portions of these provinces during the civil war, they established their own governments and used the same nine provinces as units of authority. Then, when all Manchuria fell to the Communists they redivided the region (in 1949) into the following five provinces: Liaotung, Liaohsi, Kirin, Heilungkiang, and Sungkiang. These five provinces, plus Jehol, constituted the northeast region of China when the PRC was established in October 1949. Moreover, Anhwei and Kiangsu provinces were divided into provincial-level north and south "administrative offices" before October 1949, and when Szechwan was conquered at the end of the year it was divided into north, east, south, and west "administrative offices." All three provinces returned to their traditional boundaries in 1952. Finally, in August 1949, Pingyuan province was carved out of the Communists' wartime Shansi-Hopeh-Shangtung-Honan Border Region. Other post-1949 changes are described below. Information is inclusive through 1965.

Anhwei

(Formed from merger of North and South Anhwei Administrative Offices in August 1952)

Tseng Hsi-sheng	1952–1955	Huang Yen	1955–

Anhwei, North

†Sung Jih-ch'ang	1949–1950	Huang Yen	1950–1952

Anhwei, South

†Wei Ming	1949–1952

Antung

†Kao Ch'ung-min   c.1946–1949

Chahar

(Dissolved November 1952 and incorporated into Shansi and Hopeh)

Chang Su	1945–1951	†Yang Keng-t'ien	1951–1952

Chekiang

T'an Chen-lin	1949–1952	Sha Wen-han	1955–1957
T'an Ch'i-lung	1952–1955	Chou Chien-jen	1958–

Fukien

Chang Ting-ch'eng	1949–1955	Chiang I-chen	1959–1962
Yeh Fei	1955–1959	†Wei Chin-shui	1962–

Heilungkiang

†Ch'en Ta-fan	?–1949	Han Kuang	1954–1956
Yü I-fu	1949–1952	Ouyang Ch'in	1956–1958
†Chao Te-tsun	1952–1953	Li Fan-wu	1958–
†Ch'en Lei	1953–1954		

Hokiang

†Li Yen-lu   1946–1949

Honan

Wu Chih-p'u	1949–c.1961	†Wen Min-sheng	1962–

Hopeh

Yang Hsiu-feng	1949–1952	Liu Tzu-hou	1958–
Lin T'ieh	1952–1958		

Hsingan

†T'e-mu-erh-pa-ken   c.1947–?

Hunan

†Ch'en Ming-jen	1949–1950	†Ch'eng Ch'ien	1952–
Wang Shou-tao	1950–1952		

Hupeh

Li Hsien-nien	1949–1954	Chang T'i-hsueh	1956–
Liu Tzu-hou	1954–1956		

Inner Mongolia

    Ulanfu   1947–

Jehol

(Dissolved December 1955 and incorporated into Hopeh, Liaoning, and Inner Mongolia)

†Li Yun-ch'ang	1945–c.1949	†Shen Yueh	1953–1955
†Li Tzu-kuang	c.1949–1949	Wang Kuo-ch'üan	1955–1955
†Lo Ch'eng-te	1949–1953		

Kansu

    †Teng Pao-shan   1949–

Kiangsi

    Shao Shih-p'ing   1949–1965   †Fang Chih-ch'un   1965–

Kiangsu

(Formed from merger of North and South Kiangsu Administrative Offices in November 1952)

    T'an Chen-lin   1952–1955   Hui Yü-yü   1955–

Kiangsu, North

    †Ho Hsi-ming   1949–1950   Hui Yü-yü   1950–1952

Kiangsu, South

    †Kuan Wen-wei   1949–1952

Kirin

| Chou Pao-chung | c.1947–1949 | Li Yu-wen | 1952– |
| †Chou Ch'ih-heng | 1949–1952 | | |

Kwangsi

(Changed from Kwangsi Province to Kwangsi-Chuang Autonomous Region in March 1958)

    Chang Yun-i   1949–1955   Wei Kuo-ch'ing   1955–

Kwangtung

| Yeh Chien-ying | 1949–1955 | Ch'en Yü | 1957– |
| T'ao Chu | 1955–1957 | | |

Kweichow

| Yang Yung | 1949–1955 | †Li Li | 1965– |
| Chou Lin | 1955–1965 | | |

Liaohsi

(Merged with Liaotung in August 1954 to form Liaoning)

†Lo Ch'eng-te	?–1949	†Yang I-ch'en	1949–1954

Liaoning

(Formed from merger of Liaohsi and Liaotung in August 1954)

†Tu Che-heng	1954–1958	Huang Ou-tung	1958–

Liaopei

Li Yu-wen	1946–1947	†Yen Pao-hang	1947–1949

Liaotung

(Merged with Liaohsi in August 1954 to form Liaoning)

Liu Lan-po	1949–1950	†Li T'ao	1952–1954
Kao Yang	1950–1952		

Ninghsia

(Ninghsia was dissolved in September 1954 and incorporated into Kansu. In March 1958 it was re-activated as Ninghsia-Hui Autonomous Region)

P'an Tzu-li	1949–1951	Liu Ko-p'ing	1958–1960
†Hsing Chao-t'ang	1951–1954	Yang Ching-jen	1960–

Nunkiang

Yü I-fu	1946–1949

Peking

Yeh Chien-ying	1949–1949	P'eng Chen	1951–
Nieh Jung-chen	1949–1951		

Pingyuan

(Dissolved in November 1952 and incorporated into Honan and Shantung)

†Ch'ao Che-fu	1949–1952

Shanghai

Ch'en I	1949–1958	†Ts'ao Ti-ch'iu	1965–
K'o Ch'ing-shih	1958–1965		

Shansi

Ch'eng Tzu-hua	1949–1951	Wang Shih-ying	1956–1958
Lai Jo-yü	1951–1951	Wei Heng	1958–1965
P'ei Li-sheng	1951–1956	Wang Ch'ien	1965–

Shantung

Li Yü	1945–1949	T'an Ch'i-lung	1958–1963
K'ang Sheng	1949–1955	Pai Ju-ping	1963–
Chao Chien-min	1955–1958		

Shensi

Ma Ming-fang	1949–1952	Chao Po-p'ing	1959–1963
Chao Shou-shan	1952–1959	†Li Ch'i-ming	1963–

Sikang

(Dissolved in October 1955 and incorporated into Szechwan)

Liao Chih-kao	1950–1955

Sinkiang

(Changed from Sinkiang Province to Sinkiang-Uighur Autonomous Region in October 1955)

Burhan Shahidi	1949–1955	Saifudin	1955–

Suiyuan

(Dissolved in March 1954 and incorporated into Inner Mongolia)

†Yang Chih-lin	1949–1949	Ulanfu	1952–1954
†Tung Ch'i-wu	1949–1952		

Sungkiang

(Dissolved in August 1954 and incorporated into Heilungkiang)

†Feng Chung-yun	1946–1952	†Ch'iang Hsiao-ch'u	1952–1954

Szechwan

(Formed from merger of East, North, South and West Szechwan Administrative Offices in August 1952)

Li Ching-ch'üan	1952–1955	Li Ta-chang	1955–

Szechwan, East, see *Szechwan*

Yen Hung-yen	1950–1952

Szechwan, North, see *Szechwan.*

Hu Yao-pang	1950–1952

Szechwan, South, see *Szechwan.*

Li Ta-chang	1950–1952

Szechwan, West, see *Szechwan.*

    Li Ching-ch'üan   1950–1952

Tibet

(A "Tibet Local Government" existed when the Communists took control of Tibet in 1951. In April 1956 the Preparatory Committee of the Tibet Autonomous Region was established, and in September 1965 Tibet became a full-fledged autonomous region.)

†Dalai Lama	1951–1959	†A-p'ei A-wang-chin-mei	
†Panchen Lama (acting)	1959–1965		1965–

Tsinghai

Chao Shou-shan	1949–1952	Yuan Jen-yuan	1958–1963
Chang Chung-liang	1952–1954	Wang Chao	1963–
Sun Tso-pin	1954–1958		

Yunnan

Ch'en Keng	1950–1955	Yü I-ch'uan	1958–1965
†Kuo Ying-ch'iu	1955–1958	†Chou Hsing	1965–

Part IX: The Post–1949 Military Establishment

67. PLA Headquarters and Service Arms

Note: † indicates that the individual is not one of the 433 biographic entries.

General Staff Department

Chief of Staff

Hsu Hsiang-ch'ien	1949–1954	Su Yü	1954–1958
Nieh Jung-chen		Huang K'o-ch'eng	1958–1959
(acting)	1949–1954	Lo Jui-ch'ing	1959–

General Political Department

Director

Lo Jung-huan	1950–1956	Lo Jung-huan (de facto)	
T'an Cheng	1956–1964		c.1960–1963
		Hsiao Hua	1964–

Rear Services Department (Logistics)

Director

Yang Li-san	1949–1954	Hung Hsueh-chih	1956–1959
Huang K'o-ch'eng	1954–1956	†Ch'iu Hui-tso	1959–

General Cadres Department

Director

Lo Jung-huan	1950–1956	Hsiao Hua	1956–?1959

General Ordnance Department

Director

Wang Shu-sheng	1956–?

People's Armed Forces Department (Militia)

Director

Chang Ching-wu	c.1950–1951	Chou Shih-ti	c.1953–?

Armed Forces Supervision Department

Director

Yeh Chien-ying	1954–?

General Training Department

Director

Hsiao K'o	c.1951–1954	Hsiao K'o	1957–c.1959
Liu Po-ch'eng	1954–1957		

Air Defense Force

Commander

Chou Shih-ti	1951–1956	Yang Ch'eng-wu	1956–1957

Political Commissar

†T'ang T'ien-chi	1953–?

Air Force

Commander

Liu Ya-lou	1949–1965	†Wu Fa-hsien	1965–

Political Commissar

†Wu Fa-hsien	1957–1965	†Yü Li-chin	1965–?

Armored Force

Commander

Hsu Kuang-ta	1951–

Political Commissar

†Hsiang Chung-hua	c.1958–1965	†Huang Chih-yung	1965–

Artillery Force

Commander

Ch'en Hsi-lien	1951–1959	†Wu K'o-hua	c.1965–
Ch'iu Ch'uang-ch'eng	?1959–?1963		

Political Commissar

Ch'iu Ch'uang-ch'eng	1956–c.1961	†Ch'en Jen-ch'i	c.1961–?

Engineer Corps

Commander

Ch'en Shih-ch'ü	1952–

Political Commissar

†Huang Chih-yung	c.1958–1965

Navy

   Commander

   Hsiao Ching-kuang   1950–

   Political Commissar
   Su Chen-hua   c.1957–

Public Security Force

   Commander

   Lo Jui-ch'ing   c.1950–c.1959   Hsieh Fu-chih   c.1960–

   Political Commissar

   Lo Jui-ch'ing   1953–c.1959   Hsieh Fu-chih   c.1960–

Railway Corps

   Commander

   T'eng Tai-yuan   1949–1954   †Li Shou-hsuan   1958–?
   Wang Chen   1954–1958

   Political Commissar

   Wang Chen   1954–1958   †Ts'ui T'ien-min   c.1958–?

Signal Corps

   Commander

   Wang Cheng   1957–

   Political Commissar

   †Chu Ming   c.1959–?

68. Military Regions

Note: The materials below are arranged to show the continuity between the military regions in the pre- and post-1954 periods. It should be noted that Kiangsi is the one province which does not fit this pattern of geographical continuity — see under the Central–South Region for 1949–1954 and under the Foochow Region for 1954–   .

In the 1949–1954 period, many of the posts were held only nominally; the individual biographies should be consulted for details. In the post-1954 period there are many uncertainties about exact posts because of the Chinese practice of referring to senior officers in generic language, for example, "a commanding officer."

† indicates that the individual is not one of the 433 biographic entries.

1949–1954	*1954–*

Central-South Military Region
(Honan, Hunan, Hupeh, Kiangsi, Kwangtung, Kwangsi)

(*Fourth Field Army*)

Commander	Lin Piao
Commander (acting)	Yeh Chien-ying
Political Commissar	Lo Jung-huan

East China Military Region
(Anhwei, Chekiang, Fukien, Kiangsu, Shantung)

(*Third Field Army*)

Commander	Ch'en I
Political Commissar	Jao Shu-shih

North China Military Region
(Chahar, Hopeh, Pingyuan, Shansi, Suiyuan)

Commander	Nieh Jung-chen
Political Commissar	Po I-po

Canton Military Region
(Hunan, Kwangsi, Kwangtung)

Commander	Huang Yung-sheng
	†Li T'ien-yu
	Huang Yung-sheng
Political Commissar	T'ao Chu
	†Li T'ien-yu

Wuhan Military Region
(Honan, Hupeh)

Commander	†Ch'en Tsai-tao
Political Commissar	†Li Ch'eng-fang
	Wang Jen-chung

Foochow Military Region
(Fukien, Kiangsi)

Commander	Yeh Fei
	Han Hsien-ch'u
Political Commissar	Yeh Fei

Nanking Military Region
(Anhwei, Chekiang, Kiangsu)

Commander	Hsu Shih-yu
Political Commissar	T'ang Liang
	K'o Ch'ing-shih

Tsinan Military Region
(Shantung)

Commander	†Wang Hsin-t'ing
	Yang Te-chih
Political Commissar	Shu T'ung
	†Wang Hsin-t'ing
	T'an Ch'i-lung

Peking Military Region
(Hopeh, Shansi)

Commander	Yang Ch'eng-wu
	Yang Yung
Political Commissar	†Chu Liang-ts'ai

Northeast Military Region
(Heilungkiang, Jehol, Kirin, Liaohsi,
Liaotung, Sungkiang)

Commander	Kao Kang
Political Commissar	Kao Kang

Shenyang Military Region
(Heilungkiang, Kirin, Liaoning)

Commander	Teng Hua
	Ch'en Hsi-lien
Political Commissar	Chou Huan
	Lai Ch'uan-chu
	Sung Jen-ch'iung

Northwest Military Region
(Kansu, Ninghsia, Shensi, Sinkiang,
Tsinghai)

(*First Field Army*)

Commander	P'eng Te-huai
Political Commissar	Hsi Chung-hsun

Lanchow Military Region
(Kansu, Ninghsia, Shensi, Tsinghai)

Commander	Chang Ta-chih
Political Commissar	†Hsien Heng-han
	Liu Lan-t'ao

Sinkiang Military Region

Commander	P'eng Te-huai
	Wang Chen
	Wang En-mao
Political Commissar	P'eng Te-huai
	Wang Chen
	Wang En-mao

Southwest Military Region
(Kweichow, Sikang, Szechwan, Yunnan)

(*Second Field Army*)

Commander	Ho Lung
Political Commissar	Teng Hsiao-p'ing

Chengtu Military Region
(Szechwan)

Commander	†Ho Ping-yen
	†Huang Hsin-t'ing
Political Commissar	†Kuo Lin-hsiang
	Li Ching-ch'üan

Kunming Military Region
(Kweichow, Yunnan)

Commander	Hsieh Fu-chih
	†Ch'en K'ang ?
	†Ch'in Chi-wei ?
Political Commissar	Hsieh Fu-chih
	Yen Hung-yen

Note: The following two regions were not subordinate to any of the six military regions in the 1949–1954 period.

Inner Mongolia Military Region

Commander	Ulanfu
Political Commissar	Ulanfu

Tibet Military Region

Commander	Chang Kuo-hua
Political Commissar	†T'an Kuan-san

Part X: Mass Organizations

69. Mass Organizations (selected list)

Note: Following is a list of "mass" or "people's" organizations, several of which in Western terminology would more properly be described as professional organizations. In most instances, the heads of the organizations are entitled chairman (although many secondary sources use president or director). † Indicates that the individual is not one of the 433 biographic entries.

Afro-Asian Solidarity Committee of China

Kuo Mo-jo	1956–1958	Liao Ch'eng-chih	1958–

All-China Athletic Federation

†Ma Yueh-han	1952–

All-China Federation of Supply and Marketing Cooperatives

Ch'eng Tzu-hua	1954–1957	P'an Fu-sheng	
Chang Ch'i-lung	1957–1962	(acting)	1962–1963
		P'an Fu-sheng	1963–

Chinese People's Association for Cultural Relations with Foreign Countries

Ch'u T'u-nan	1954–

Chinese People's Institute of Foreign Affairs

Chang Hsi-jo	1949–

All-China Federation of Industry and Commerce

†Ch'en Shu-t'ung	1953–

China Committee for the Promotion of International Trade

Nan Han-ch'en	1952–

All-China Journalists' Association

Teng T'o	1954–1960	Wu Leng-hsi	1960–

All-China Federation of Labor

Ch'en Yun	1948–1953	Liu Ning-i	1958–
Lai Jo-yü	1953–1958		

All-China Federation of Literary and Art Circles

Kuo Mo-jo	1949–

China Peace Committee

Kuo Mo-jo	1949–

Political Science and Law Association of China

Tung Pi-wu	1953–1964	Wu Te-feng	1964–

China Scientific and Technical Association

Li Szu-kuang	1958–

Sino-Soviet Friendship Association

Liu Shao-ch'i	1949–1954	Sung Ch'ing-ling	1954–

All-China Federation of Students

†Hsieh Pang-ting	1949–1951	Hu Ch'i-li	1956–1965
†T'ien Te-min	1951–1956	†Wu Shao-tsu	1965–

All-China Federation of Democratic Women

Ts'ai Ch'ang	1949–

All-China Federation of Democratic Youth

Liao Ch'eng-chih	1949–1958	Wang Wei	1965–
Liu Hsi-yuan	1958–1965		

New Democratic Youth League[1]

Feng Wen-pin	1949–1952	Hu Yao-pang	1952–

---

[1] The Youth League has a dual subordination. It is an arm of the CCP, but it is also one of the affiliates of the All-China Federation of Democratic Youth.

Part XI: Travel Abroad

Note: These appendices are geared to the post-1949 period. Appendix 71 does indicate pre-1949 experience in particular countries, but for further information on pre-1949 foreign travel see the appendices dealing with education abroad, attendance at CCP Congresses, and association with the Comintern and Profintern (9, 13, and 14, respectively). For information about Korean War participation see Appendix 45.

70. Foreign Travel: By Purpose

Note: This appendix is divided by categories indicating the purpose and year of trips abroad. The categories are:

Agriculture, Forestry, Fisheries
Asian Countries Conference and
   Afro-Asian Solidarity Conferences
Bandung Conference
Culture
Diplomacy
Economics, Trade, Aid
Education
Foreign Communist Party Meetings
Geneva Conferences on Indochina
   (1954) and Laos (1961–1962)
Goodwill and Ceremonial Visits
Health

Journalism
Labor
Law
Military
NPC Delegations
Peace Movement
Religion
Science and
   Technology
Sports
Women
Youth

If the man in question remained in the region for more than a year, or over the turn of a year, only the initial year is listed. Also, if he visited the same region more than once in the same year, or visited more than one country, the year is only listed once.

Agriculture, Forestry, Fisheries

USSR
Hsu Te-heng   57
Liao Lu-yen   57
Wang En-mao   55

East Europe
Liao Lu-yen   57
Meng Yung-ch'ien   54
Ting Ying   55
Yang Hsien-tung   58

West Europe
Hsiao Fang-chou   53

Asian Communist States
Hsu Te-heng   59
Liao Lu-yen   59

Japan
Wang Chen   57

1132

Asian Countries Conference and Afro-Asian Solidarity Conferences

Note: This category includes other trips to meetings or organizations set up under these auspices.

West Europe
Chu Tzu-ch'i   63

Asian Communist States
Kuo Mo-jo   64

South and Southeast Asia
Chi Ch'ao-ting   59, 61
Chin Chung-hua   59
Ch'u T'u-nan   55
Chu Tzu-ch'i   55, 61
Kuo Mo-jo   55
Li I-mang   55
Liao Ch'eng-chih   55, 59
Liu Ning-i   55, 61
Meng Yung-ch'ien   55
Nan Han-ch'en   63
Saifudin   55
Ts'ao Meng-chün   55

Japan
Chao An-po   64

Egypt and the Middle East
Burhan Shahidi   57, 61
Chao P'u-ch'u   57
Cheng Sen-yü   57
Chi Ch'ao-ting   57, 58, 60, 62
Chin Chung-hua   57
Ch'u T'u-nan   57
Chu Tzu-ch'i   57, 59
Kuo Mo-jo   57
Liao Ch'eng-chih   61
Nan Han-ch'en   58, 59, 60
Ta P'u-sheng   55
Wu Hsueh-ch'ien   61
Yang Shuo   58, 61
Yang Yun-yü   61

Africa (excluding Egypt)
Burhan Shahidi   60
Chi Ch'ao-ting   60, 63
Ch'ien Li-jen   65
Chin Chung-hua   65
Chu Tzu-ch'i   60, 61, 63, 64
Fang Ming   64
Liao Ch'eng-chih   60, 65
Liu Ning-i   57, 60, 61, 63
Yang Shuo   60, 62, 63

Bandung Conference

Note: This category includes anniversary celebrations of the first Bandung Conference and discussions of holding a second one.

West Europe
Fang I   64

South and Southeast Asia
Chang Han-fu   55, 65
Ch'en Chia-k'ang   55
Ch'en I   55, 64
Cheng Sen-yü   55
Ch'iao Kuan-hua   55, 65
Chin Chung-hua   55
Chou En-lai   55
Huang Chen   65

Huang Hua   55
Liao Ch'eng-chih   55
Ta P'u-sheng   55
Yang Ch'i-ch'ing   55
Yeh Chi-chuang   55

Africa (excluding Egypt)
Chang Han-fu   65
Ch'en I   63
Meng Yung-ch'ien   60
Wu Hsueh-ch'ien   60, 63

Culture

USSR
Ch'ien Chün-jui   56, 59
Chou Yang   54, 58
Ch'u T'u-nan   55
Ko Pao-ch'üan   58

Liu Pai-yü   50, 58
Mei I   57
Shen Yen-ping   57, 58, 59
Ting Ling   54
Yang Shuo   58

East Europe
Chang Chih-hsiang   55, 59
Ch'en Chung-ching   58
Ch'ien Chün-jui   53
Chung Fu-hsiang   55
Fan Ch'ang-chiang   53
Hu Yü-chih   64
Ko Pao-ch'üan   50
Li Ch'ang   65
Li I-mang   52
Liu Pai-yü   56
Shen Yen-ping   53, 60
Wu Leng-hsi   53

West Europe
Chang Chih-hsiang   55, 60
Ch'en Chung-ching   60
Chin Chung-hua   64
Chou P'ei-yuan   58
Ch'u T'u-nan   55
Hsu Ti-hsin   58

Asian Communist States
Chang Chih-hsiang   57, 62
Ch'u T'u-nan   59
Liu Pai-yü   62

South and Southeast Asia
Chang Chih-hsiang   60
Ch'en I   61

Chou Yang   56
Ch'u T'u-nan   57, 60, 63
Li I-mang   51
Liu Pai-yü   51, 61
Shen Yen-ping   56
Yang Shuo   56, 61, 63

Japan
Liu Pai-yü   61
Yang Shuo   61

Egypt and the Middle East
Burhan Shahidi   56, 59
Ch'en Chung-ching   59
Ma Yü-huai   56
Shen Yen-ping   62
Yang Hsiu-feng   64

Africa (*excluding Egypt*)
Burhan Shahidi   56
Ma Yü-huai   56
Yang Hsiu-feng   64
Yang Shuo   64

North and South America
Chao I-min   54
Ch'en Chung-ching   60
Chou Yang   62
Ch'u T'u-nan   56
Li I-mang   53

Diplomacy

Note: This category includes negotiations of major treaties and high-level political talks. For negotiations among Communist Parties see "Foreign Communist Party Meetings."

USSR
Chang Wen-t'ien   51
Ch'en Chia-k'ang   52
Ch'en Po-ta   49, 57
Ch'en Yü   52
Ch'en Yun   52
Ch'iu Ch'uang-ch'eng   52
Chou En-lai   50, 52, 54, 57, 64
Chu Te   56
Ho Lung   57, 64
Hu Ch'iao-mu   57
Ko Pao-ch'üan   49
Li Fu-ch'un   50, 52
Li Hsien-nien   57
Liu Ch'ang-sheng   56, 60
Liu Hsiao   55
Liu Ning-i   57
Liu Tzu-chiu   52
Liu Ya-lou   52
Lü Tung   50
Mao Tse-tung   49, 57

Ouyang Ch'in   50
P'an Tzu-li   62
P'eng Chen   60
P'eng Te-huai   55, 59
Shen Hung   50
Sung Shao-wen   52
Tseng Yung-ch'üan   49
Ulanfu   57
Wang Cheng   52
Wang Chia-hsiang   49, 57
Wang Ho-shou   52
Wang Tao-han   52
Wu Hsiu-ch'üan   50, 63
Yang Shang-k'un   63

East Europe
Ch'en I   54
Chou En-lai   54, 57, 64
Chu Te   56
Ho Lung   57
Hsu Chien-kuo   59, 64

Huang Chen   50
K'o Pai-nien   55
Li K'o-nung   54
Tseng Yung-ch'üan   52
Wang Chia-hsiang   57
Wang Kuo-ch'üan   57
Wang Ping-nan   55
Wang Yu-p'ing   50
Wu Hsiu-ch'üan   55

West Europe

Han Nien-lung   56
Huang Chen   64
Keng Piao   50
K'o Pai-nien   63
Lu Hsu-chang   63
Wang Ping-nan   55
Wang Yu-p'ing   55

Asian Communist States

Chang Han-fu   60
Chang Yen   61
Chi Ya-t'ai   52
Ch'iao Kuan-hua   60
Chou En-lai   54, 56, 58, 60
Chu Te   56
Han Nien-lung   60
Ho Lung   56
Ho Wei   58
Ho Ying   54
Huang Hua   53
Huang Huo-ch'ing   63
Lin Feng   63
Liu Shao-ch'i   63
Lo Kuei-po   54
P'an Tzu-li   54
P'eng Chen   62
P'eng Te-huai   59
Su Yü   58
Wang Kuang-wei   60

South and Southeast Asia

Chang Han-fu   60, 64
Chang Wen-t'ien   57
Chang Yen   56, 60
Ch'en I   61, 64
Ch'iao Kuan-hua   60
Chou En-lai   54, 56, 57, 60, 61, 64
Han Nien-lung   51, 65
Ho Lung   56
Ho Wei   61
Ho Ying   51
Huang Chen   54, 62
Keng Piao   56, 63
Li Hsueh-feng   65
Li I-mang   58
Liu Shao-ch'i   63
P'an Tzu-li   56
Wang Yu-p'ing   58
Yao Chung-ming   50, 61

Egypt and the Middle East

Ch'en Chia-k'ang   56, 57, 64
Chou En-lai   63
Huang Chen   62
Huang Hua   66

Africa (excluding Egypt)

Chou En-lai   64
Ho Ying   62, 63, 64
Huang Chen   62
Huang Hua   60, 64
Lei Jen-min   58
Liu Ch'ang-sheng   61

North and South America

Ch'en Chung-ching   50
Ch'iao Kuan-hua   50
Chou P'ei-yuan   57, 58
Wang Yu-p'ing   64
Wu Hsiu-ch'üan   50

Economics, Trade, Aid

Note: In addition to economic, trade, and aid missions, this category includes trade fairs, transportation, and industry.

USSR

Chang Ch'i-lung   57
Chang Ch'in-ch'iu   53
Ch'en Yun   58
Ch'eng Tzu-hua   54
Chi Ch'ao-ting   52
Chiang Ming   53
Hsi Chung-hsun   59
Lei Jen-min   52
Li Che-jen   55, 57, 59
Li Ch'iang   52, 61, 62, 63
Li Chu-ch'en   52

Li Fu-ch'un   58
Liu Hsiu-feng   55
Lü Cheng-ts'ao   64
Lu Hsu-chang   52
Meng Yung-ch'ien   52
Nan Han-ch'en   52
Saifudin   50
Sha Ch'ien-li   51
Wan Li   55
Wang Kuang-wei   59
Wang Shih-t'ai   54, 55
Wang Shou-tao   59

Education

Foreign Communist Party Meetings

Note: This category includes a few trips to meet with other Communist Party leaders, but the overwhelming majority are delegations to Communist Party Congresses.

USSR
Ch'en I   52
Chou En-lai   59, 61
Chu Te   56
Hu Ch'iao-mu   57, 60
Jao Shu-shih   52
K'ang Sheng   59, 61, 63
Li Ching-ch'üan   60
Li Fu-ch'un   52
Li Hsueh-feng   59
Liao Ch'eng-chih   60
Liu Ch'ang-sheng   52
Liu Ning-i   59, 60, 63
Liu Shao-ch'i   52, 60
Lu Ting-i   60
Mao Tse-tung   57
P'eng Chen   60, 61, 63
T'an Chen-lin   56
T'ao Chu   61
Teng Hsiao-p'ing   56, 57, 60, 63
Wang Chia-hsiang   52, 56
Wu Hsiu-ch'üan   63
Yang Shang-k'un   57, 60

East Europe
An Tzu-wen   58
Chang P'ing-hua   63
Chao I-min   58
Ch'eng Tzu-hua   57
Chiang Nan-hsiang   61
Ch'ien Chün-jui   49
Chu Te   55, 59
Hsiung Fu   62, 63
K'ang Sheng   56, 60
K'ang Yung-ho   62
Li Hsien-nien   61
Liu Ch'ang-sheng   54
Liu Lan-t'ao   55
Nieh Jung-chen   55
P'eng Chen   60
Po I-po   60

T'an Chen-lin   59
Ts'ao Meng-chün   53
Tseng Shan   56, 61
Tung Pi-wu   58
Wang Chia-hsiang   50, 59
Wang Ts'ung-wu   59
Wu Hsiu-ch'üan   59, 60, 62, 63

West Europe
Chang Chi-ch'un   61
Chao I-min   61, 62
Ch'en Yü   60
Lin T'ieh   60
Liu Ch'ang-sheng   56, 60
Liu Lan-t'ao   58
Liu Ning-i   57, 63
P'eng Chen   56
T'an Chen-lin   55
Tseng Shan   61
Wang Chia-hsiang   59
Wang Shou-tao   57
Wu Chih-p'u   60
Wu Hsiu-ch'üan   59

Asian Communist States
K'ang Sheng   61
Li Fu-ch'un   60
Liao Ch'eng-chih   60
Liao Lu-yen   54
Ma Ming-fang   58
Nieh Jung-chen   56
Teng Hsiao-p'ing   61
Ulanfu   54, 58, 61
Wang Ts'ung-wu   56
Wang Wei-chou   61
Wu Hsiu-ch'üan   61
Yeh Chien-ying   60

North and South America
Wu Hsiu-ch'üan   60

Geneva Conference on Indochina (1954) and Laos (1961–62)

West Europe
Chang Han-fu   61
Chang Wen-t'ien   54
Ch'en Chia-k'ang   54
Ch'en I   61, 62
Ch'iao Kuan-hua   54, 61
Chou En-lai   54
Hsiung Fu   61
Huang Hua   54

K'o Pai-nien   54
Lei Jen-min   54
Li K'o-nung   54
Liu Hsiao   61
Lo Kuei-po   54
Wang Chia-hsiang   54
Wang Ping-nan   54, 61
Wu Leng-hsi   54, 61

Goodwill and Ceremonial Visits

USSR

Burhan Shahidi   58
Chang Hsiu-chu   61
Chang Tsung-hsun   53
Chao Shou-shan   58
Ch'ien Chün-jui   53, 57
Ch'ien San-ch'iang   53
Ch'ien Ying   59
Chin Chung-hua   60
Chou En-lai   53
Chou P'ei-yuan   55
Ho Wei   65
Hsu Chih-chen   49
Hsu Kuang-ta   60, 65
Hu Yü-chih   56
K'ang Sheng   60, 64
K'ang Yung-ho   61
Ko Pao-ch'üan   56
Kuo Mo-jo   53, 57
Li Ch'ang   65
Li Chu-ch'en   60
Li Te-ch'üan   53
Liao Ch'eng-chih   53, 60
Lin Feng   65
Lin Po-ch'ü   51
Liu Ch'ang-sheng   53, 57, 60
Liu Hsiao   64
Liu Lan-t'ao   58
Liu Ning-i   60
Liu Tzu-chiu   52
Liu Ya-lou   56
Lo Jui-ch'ing   53
P'eng Chen   60
Saifudin   57
Sung Ch'ing-ling   53, 57
Teng T'o   54
Ting Ling   49, 52
Ts'ai Ch'ang   53
Ts'ai Shu-fan   53
Wang Ping-chang   53
Wang Wei   60
Wu Hsiu-ch'üan   53, 64
Yang Yun-yü   51
Yeh Chi-chuang   52

East Europe

Burhan Shahidi   58
Chang Hsiu-chu   57
Chang Tsung-hsun   58
Chao I-min   65
Chao Shou-shan   59
Ch'en I   54
Chiang Nan-hsiang   61
Chou En-lai   53
Chou P'ei-yuan   64
Chu Te   56, 59
Ho Lung   55, 61
Hsi Chung-hsun   59, 60
Hsu Li-ch'ün   50

Hu Yao-pang   62
Kao K'o-lin   59
Kuo Mo-jo   53, 58
Lai Chi-fa   55
Li Ch'iang   64
Li Chu-ch'en   59
Li Fu-ch'un   53
Li Hsien-nien   54, 57, 64
Liu Hsiao   56, 58
Liu Lan-t'ao   55, 56
Liu Ning-i   50
Liu Ya-lou   64
Mei I   64
Nieh Jung-chen   56, 59
Ou T'ang-liang   56
P'eng Te-huai   55
Saifudin   57, 60
Sha Ch'ien-li   55
Ting Ying   59
Tseng Shan   65
Tseng Yung-ch'üan   61
Tung Pi-wu   54
Ulanfu   55, 64
Wang Ping-chang   53
Wang Wei-chou   59
Wu Hsiu-ch'üan   64
Yang Hsien-tung   54, 55
Yang Shuo   59
Yeh Chi-chuang   53
Yü Kuang-yuan   64

West Europe

Chang Yun   54
Chao I-min   60
Chou P'ei-yuan   50
Li I-mang   53
Li Te-ch'üan   50
Liu Ning-i   50

Asian Communist States

Chang Chi-ch'un   63, 64
Chang Chih-hsiang   61
Chang Hsiu-chu   52
Chang Su   59, 62, 64
Chang Yen   56
Chao Shou-shan   52
Ch'en Hsi-lien   60
Ch'en I   60, 63
Chi Ya-t'ai   60
Chiang Ming   56
Ch'iao Kuan-hua   63
Chin Chung-hua   53
Chu Te   55
Fang I   63, 64
Ho Lung   53
Hsu Chien-kuo   53
Hsu Chih-chen   59
Hsu Kuang-ta   61
Hsu Ping   53

Hsu Te-heng   50, 58
Huang Chen   63, 64
Kan Szu-ch'i   58
K'ang Yung-ho   64
Kuo Mo-jo   50, 58
Li Chieh-po   51, 60
Li Chih-min   56
Li Chu-ch'en   62
Li Fu-ch'un   60
Li Hsien-nien   56
Li Hsueh-feng   52
Li Li-san   50
Li Te-ch'üan   60
Liao Ch'eng-chih   60
Lin Po-ch'ü   59
Liu Ya-lou   60
Nieh Jung-chen   52
P'ing Chieh-san   53
Sha Ch'ien-li   52
Shao Shih-p'ing   53
T'eng Tai-yuan   53
Ts'ao Meng-chün   54
Ulanfu   52
Wan Li   63
Wang Chen   62
Wang Pi-ch'eng   54
Wang P'ing   60
Wang Shih-ying   53
Wang Ts'ung-wu   53
Wang Wei-chou   53
Wu Hsiu-ch'üan   52, 63
Yang Ch'eng-wu   61
Yang Ch'i-ch'ing   57, 62
Yang Hsiu-feng   59, 62
Yang Yun-yü   64
Yang Yung   58
Yeh Chien-ying   63
Yen Hung-yen   53

South and Southeast Asia

Chang Ai-p'ing   58, 60
Chang Han-fu   64
Chang Su   56
Ch'en I   60, 61, 63, 64
Ch'iao Kuan-hua   54
Ho Lung   56
Hsieh Fu-chih   57
Hu Yü-chih   64
Huang Chen   63, 64
K'ung Yuan   60, 64
Lei Jen-min   61
Li Chu-ch'en   61
Liao Ch'eng-chih   55
Liu Shao-ch'i   63
Liu Tzu-chiu   55
Lo Jui-ch'ing   60
Ma Yü-huai   56, 64
Sung Ch'ing-ling   55, 56, 64
Ta P'u-sheng   56

Health

Journalism

Labor

Law

Military

Wang Wei-chou   59
Wu Hsiu-ch'üan   60
Yang Ch'eng-wu   55
Yang Te-chih   59
Yeh Chien-ying   57

East Europe
Chang Wen-t'ien   59
Lai Ch'uan-chu   58
Nieh Jung-chen   56
P'eng Te-huai   55, 59
Wan I   55
Wang Hung-k'un   56
Wang Ping-chang   56
Wang Shu-sheng   59
Yang Te-chih   59
Yeh Chien-ying   58

West Europe
P'eng Shao-hui   63

Asian Communist States
Chang Tsung-hsun   59
Chang Wen-t'ien   58
Chang Yen   58
Ch'en I   58

Ho Lung   60
Huang Yung-sheng   61
Liu Ning-i   64
Liu Ya-lou   61
Lo Jui-ch'ing   59
Wang Shu-sheng   59
Yang Shuo   50
Yang Te-chih   59
Yeh Chien-ying   61

South and Southeast Asia
Fang Ch'iang   58
Liu Ya-lou   64
Yang Ch'eng-wu   59
Yeh Chien-ying   56, 58

Egypt and the Middle East
Sung Shih-lun   62

Africa (excluding Egypt)
Li Chih-min   63
Yang Yung   64

North and South America
Liu Ya-lou   63

National People's Congress Delegations

USSR
Chang Yu-yü   56
Liang Hsi   56
P'eng Chen   56

East Europe
Chang Yu-yü   56
Liang Hsi   56
P'eng Chen   56

West Europe
Saifudin   57

Asian Communist States
Hu Yü-chih   61

K'uei Pi   59
Liu Ch'ang-sheng   61
P'eng Chen   62
Po I-po   62
Wang P'ing   63

South and Southeast Asia
Burhan Shahidi   61
Chang Yu-yü   61
Kuo Mo-jo   61

Africa (excluding Egypt)
Wang Kuang-wei   64
Wang P'ing   65

Peace Movement

USSR
Burhan Shahidi   59
Cheng Sen-yü   59
Ch'ien Chün-jui   49
Chin Chung-hua   62
Chu Tzu-ch'i   59, 62
K'ang Yung-ho   62

Kuo Mo-jo   51, 52, 59
Liao Ch'eng-chih   59
Ou T'ang-liang   59, 62
Shen Yen-ping   62
Wu Hsueh-ch'ien   62
Yang Shuo   62

Religion

Science and Technology

Note: This category includes delegations of the World Federation of Scientific Workers and of the Academy of Sciences. Because the Academy includes the social sciences as well as the natural sciences, a few of the following people may have been discussing social, rather than natural sciences on their trips.

USSR
Chang Yu-yü　61
Ch'en Po-ta　49
Ch'ien Hsin-chung　57
Ch'ien San-ch'iang　53, 56, 57
Chou Jung-hsin　57
Chou P'ei-yuan　57, 60, 62
Fan Ch'ang-chiang　57
Hsueh Mu-ch'iao　54
Kuo Mo-jo　49, 57, 58
Li Ch'iang　56
Liu Lan-po　55
P'ei Li-sheng　60
Ting Ying　58
Tu Jun-sheng　57
Wang Tao-han　57
Wu Heng　60, 62
Yang Hsien-tung　57
Yü Kuang-yuan　57, 60

East Europe
Chang Lin-chih　52, 54
Ch'ien San-ch'iang　52
Chou P'ei-yuan　53, 55, 59, 60, 61, 62
Kuo Mo-jo　50
Li Szu-kuang　51
Liang Hsi　51
Liu Lan-po　54
Shen Hung　63
Ting Ying　59

Wu Heng　64
Yang Hsien-tung　53
Yü Kuang-yuan　60

West Europe
Chou P'ei-yuan　56, 57, 61, 63
Sun Ta-kuang　55

Asian Communist States
Chang Chin-fu　63
Wu Heng　61, 63

South and Southeast Asia
Chou P'ei-yuan　60
Han Nien-lung　65
Wu Heng　65

Japan
Hsiung Fu　55
Kuo Mo-jo　55

Egypt and the Middle East
Wu Heng　65

Africa (excluding Egypt)
Wu Heng　64

North and South America
Lu Hsu-chang　60

Sports

USSR
Chang Lien-hua　61
Ho Lung　54
Jung Kao-t'ang　54
Li Ta　61

East Europe
Chang Lien-hua　61
Jung Kao-t'ang　64, 65
Li Ta　60, 63
Liu Tao-sheng　51
Ts'ai Shu-fan　55, 56
Wang Chao　55, 56

West Europe
Chang Lien-hua　55, 56, 58

Jung Kao-t'ang　52, 55

Asian Communist States
Li Ta　64

South and Southeast Asia
Chang Lien-hua　62, 64
Ho Lung　63
Jung Kao-t'ang　63

Japan
Jung Kao-t'ang　56, 62

North and South America
Jung Kao-t'ang　64

Women

USSR
Chang Yun   57
Ou T'ang-liang   63
Ts'ao Meng-chün   63
Yang Yun-yü   63

East Europe
Chang Yun   58
Li Te-ch'üan   51, 56, 57
Shih Liang   56
Teng Ying-ch'ao   51
Ts'ai Ch'ang   49
Yang Yun-yü   53, 55, 60, 61, 62, 63, 64

West Europe
Chang Yun   53
Li Te-ch'üan   53, 55, 56, 60
Lo Ch'iung   55
Shih Liang   49
Ts'ao Meng-chün   53, 54, 55, 58, 60
Yang Yun-yü   53, 54, 55, 62

Asian Communist States
Shuai Meng-ch'i   56
Teng Ying-ch'ao   61

South and Southeast Asia
Li Te-ch'üan   55
Shih Liang   56, 58
Ts'ao Meng-chün   58
Yang Yun-yü   58, 60

Japan
Yang Yun-yü   64

Egypt and the Middle East
Ts'ao Meng-chün   61
Yang Yun-yü   61

Africa (excluding Egypt)
Yang Yun-yü   62

Youth

USSR
Ch'ien Li-jen   57, 61
Feng Wen-pin   50
Hsiao Hua   49
Hu Ch'i-li   61
Hu K'o-shih   55, 57, 58
Hu Yao-pang   57
Li Ch'ang   51
Wu Hsueh-ch'ien   57, 58

East Europe
Ch'ien Li-jen   53, 57
Ch'ien San-ch'iang   50
Feng Wen-pin   51
Hsiao Hua   49
Hsu Li-ch'ün   50
Hu Ch'i-li   56
Hu K'o-shih   59
Hu Yao-pang   53
Liao Ch'eng-chih   49, 50, 51
Liu Hsi-yuan   56, 59
Ou T'ang-liang   53, 55
Wang Wei   55, 58, 60
Wu Hsueh-ch'ien   50, 53, 54, 55
Yang Shuo   53

West Europe
Ch'ien Li-jen   54, 59, 61, 62
Liu Hsi-yuan   59
Wu Hsueh-ch'ien   55, 56

Asian Communist States
Hu Ch'i-li   54
Hu K'o-shih   54, 61
Wang Wei   56, 63

South and Southeast Asia
Ch'ien Li-jen   56
Liu Hsi-yuan   57
Wu Hsueh-ch'ien   51, 52, 57

Japan
Liu Hsi-yuan   57
Wu Hsueh-ch'ien   64

Egypt and the Middle East
Hu Ch'i-li   58
Liu Hsi-yuan   59
Wang Wei   60
Wu Hsueh-ch'ien   58

Africa (excluding Egypt)
Ch'ien Li-jen   63
Hu Ch'i-li   60

North and South America
Ch'ien Li-jen   60
Hu Ch'i-li   62, 63

71. Foreign Travel: By Area

Note: This appendix is divided by the areas and countries. The areas are as follows:

Asian Communist States
Soviet Union
East Europe
West Europe (including Australia and
  New Zealand)

South and Southeast Asia
Japan
Egypt and the Middle East
Africa
North and South America

Travel to Asian Communist States

Note: x indicates pre-1949 experience in the country. *?* indicates uncertainty about a trip.

Name	Mongolia	North Vietnam	North Korea	Name	Mongolia	North Vietnam	North Korea
Chang Chi-ch'un		1	1	Kan Szu-ch'i			1
Chang Chih-hsiang	2	1	1	K'ang Sheng			1
Chang Chin-fu			1	K'ang Yung-ho	1	1	
Chang Han-fu		1		K'o Pai-nien			1
Chang Hsiu-chu			1	K'uei Pi	1		
Chang Su	1		2	Kuo Mo-jo		1	2
Chang Ting-ch'eng		1		Li Che-jen	1		
Chang Tsung-hsun	1			Li Ch'iang	1	1	2
Chang Wen-t'ien			1	Li Chieh-po			2
Chang Yen		2	1	Li Chu-ch'en			1
Chao Shou-shan			1	Li Fu-ch'un		1	
Ch'en Hsi-lien			1	Li Hsien-nien	1		
Ch'en I	1	2	1	Li Hsueh-feng			1
Ch'en Yü		1		Li Li-san			x 1
Chi Ya-t'ai	2			Li Ta		1	
Chiang Ming	3			Li Te-ch'üan	x 1		2
Ch'iao Kuan-hua	1	3	1	Liao Ch'eng-chih		1	2
Ch'ien Hsin-chung			1	Liao Lu-yen	2		1
Chin Chung-hua			1	Lin Feng			1
Chou Chien-jen			1	Lin Hai-yun		1	
Chou En-lai	2	3	1	Lin Po-ch'ü	1		
Chu Te	1		1	Liu Ch'ang-sheng		1	1
Ch'u T'u-nan			1	Liu Ming-fu	1		
Fang I		2	1	Liu Ning-i		1	
Han Nien-lung	1			Liu Pai-yü			2
Ho Lung		1	2	Liu Shao-ch'i		1	1
Ho Wei		1		Liu Ya-lou		1	1
Ho Ying	1			Liu Yü-min			1
Hsu Chien-kuo			1	Lo Jui-ch'ing			1
Hsu Chih-chen		2		Lo Kuei-po		1	
Hsu Hai-tung	x			Lü Cheng-ts'ao		1	?2
Hsu Kuang-ta	1			Lu Hsu-chang	1		
Hsu Ping			1	Ma Ming-fang	1		
Hsu Te-heng		1	2	Mei I		1	1
Hu Ch'i-li			1	Nan Han-ch'en			1
Hu K'o-shih		1	1	Nieh Jung-chen	1		1
Huang Chen		1		Ouyang Ch'in			1
Huang Hua			1	P'an Tzu-li			1
Huang Huo-ch'ing			1	P'eng Chen		1	1
Huang Yung-sheng		1		P'eng Te-huai	1		

Name	Mongolia	North Vietnam	North Korea
P'ing Chieh-san			1
Po I-po		1	
Saifudin		1	
Sha Ch'ien-li			1
Shao Shih-p'ing			1
Shuai Meng-ch'i		1	
Su Yü			1
Sung Jen-ch'iung			1
Teng Hsiao-p'ing			1
T'eng Tai-yuan	1		1
Teng Ying-ch'ao		1	
Ts'ao Meng-chün			2
Ulanfu	4		
Wan Li			1
Wang Chen		1	
Wang Ho-shou			1
Wang Kuang-wei		1	
Wang Pi-ch'eng			1
Wang P'ing			2
Wang Shih-ying			1
Wang Shu-sheng	1		
Wang Ts'ung-wu			2

Name	Mongolia	North Vietnam	North Korea
Wang Wei		1	1
Wang Wei-chou	1		x 1
Wu Heng		2	
Wu Hsiu-ch'üan	1		2
Wu Leng-hsi		1	1
Wu Te			1
Yang Ch'eng-wu		1	
Yang Ch'i-ch'ing	2		
Yang Hsien-tung			1
Yang Hsiu-feng		2	
Yang Shuo			1
Yang Te-chih	1		
Yang Yun-yü		1	
Yang Yung			1
Yao I-lin		1	
Yeh Chi-chuang	1	1	2
Yeh Chien-ying		2	1
Yen Hung-yen			1
Country totals	43	58	92
(post-1949)			
Total trips: 193			

Travel to the Soviet Union

Name	Pre-1949	Number of post-1949 trips	Name	Pre-1949	Number of post-1949 trips
An Tzu-wen	x	0	Ch'en Yen-nien	x	0
Burhan Shahidi	x	3	Ch'en Yü		2
Chang Chi-ch'un	x	0	Ch'en Yun	x	3
Chang Ch'i-lung		1	Cheng Sen-yü		1
Chang Ch'in-ch'iu	x	1	Ch'eng Tzu-hua		1
Chang Hsiu-chu		2	Chi Ch'ao-ting	x	1
Chang Kuo-t'ao	x	0	Chiang Ming		1
Chang Lien-hua		1	Ch'iao Kuan-hua		1
Chang T'ai-lei	x	0	Ch'ien Chün-jui		5
Chang Tsung-hsun		1	Ch'ien Hsin-chung		3
Chang Wen-t'ien	x	1	Ch'ien Li-jen		2
Chang Yu-yü		2	Ch'ien San-ch'iang		4
Chang Yun		1	Ch'ien Ying		1
Chao Shih-yen	x	0	Chin Chung-hua		2
Chao Shou-shan		1	Ch'in Pang-hsien	x	0
Ch'en Ch'ang-hao	x	0	Ch'iu Ch'uang-ch'eng	x	1
Ch'en Chia-k'ang		1	Chou En-lai	x	8
Ch'en Hsi-lien		1	Chou Jung-hsin		1
Ch'en I		1	Chou Pao-chung	x	0
Ch'en Keng	x	0	Chou P'ei-yuan		4
Ch'en Po-ta		3	Chou Yang		2
Ch'en Shao-min		1	Ch'ü Ch'iu-pai	x	0
Ch'en Shao-yü	x	1	Chu Te	x	2
Ch'en T'an-ch'iu	x	0	Ch'u T'u-nan		1
Ch'en Tu-hsiu	x	0	Chu Tzu-ch'i		3

Name	Pre-1949	Number of post-1949 trips	Name	Pre-1949	Number of post-1949 trips
Fan Ch'ang-chiang		1	Li Li-san	x	0
Fang Ch'iang	x	0	Li Ta	x	1
Fang Ming		1	Li Ta-chao	x	0
Feng Wen-pin		1	Li Te-ch'üan	x	4
Han Kuang	x	0	Li Yu-wen	?x	0
Ho Ch'eng-hsiang		1	Liang Hsi		1
Ho Lung		3	Liao Ch'eng-chih	x	3
Ho Meng-hsiung	?x	0	Liao Lu-yen		1
Ho Shu-heng	x	0	Lin Feng	x	1
Ho Wei		1	Lin Piao	x	0
Hsi Chung-hsun		2	Lin Po-ch'ü	x	1
Hsia Hsi	x	0	Lin Yü-ying	x	0
Hsiang Ching-yü	x	0	Liu Ch'ang-sheng		7
Hsiang Chung-fa	x	0	Liu Chen	x	1
Hsiang Ying	x	0	Liu Hsiao		2
Hsiao Ching-kuang	x	0	Liu Hsiu-feng		1
Hsiao Hua		1	Liu Jen	x	0
Hsiung Fu		?1	Liu Lan-po		1
Hsu Chih-chen	x	1	Liu Lan-t'ao		2
Hsu Hsiang-ch'ien	x	0	Liu Ning-i	x	5
Hsu Kuang-ta	x	3	Liu Pai-yü		2
Hsu Ping	x	0	Liu Po-ch'eng	x	0
Hsu Te-heng		1	Liu Shao-ch'i	x	2
Hsu T'e-li	x	0	Liu Tzu-chiu		2
Hsueh Mu-ch'iao		1	Liu Ya-lou	x	3
Hu Ch'i-li		1	Lo I-nung	x	0
Hu Ch'iao-mu		2	Lo Jui-ch'ing	x	1
Hu K'o-shih		3	Lo Teng-hsien	?x	0
Hu Yao-pang		1	Lü Cheng-ts'ao		1
Hu Yü-chih	x	1	Lu Hsu-chang		1
Huang Huo-ch'ing	x	0	Lu Ting-i		1
Hung Hsueh-chih		1	Lü Tung		1
Jao Shu-shih	?x	1	Ma Ming-fang	x	0
Jen Pi-shih	x	1	Ma Wen-jui		1
Jung Kao-t'ang		1	Mao Tse-min	x	0
K'ang Sheng	x	6	Mao Tse-tung		2
K'ang Yung-ho		5	Mei I		1
Kao Kang	x	0	Meng Yung-ch'ien		2
Ko Pao-ch'üan	x	4	Nan Han-ch'en	x	1
Kuan Hsiang-ying	x	0	Nieh Jung-chen	x	2
K'ung Yuan	x	0	Ou T'ang-liang		4
Kuo Mo-jo	x	9	Ouyang Ch'in		1
Lai Jo-yü		2	P'an Tzu-li		1
Lei Jen-min		2	P'ei Li-sheng	?x	1
Li Che-jen		4	P'eng Chen		4
Li Ch'ang		2	P'eng T'ao		1
Li Ch'iang	x	6	P'eng Te-huai		3
Li Ching-ch'üan		1	Saifudin	x	3
Li Ch'iu-shih	x	0	Sha Ch'ien-li		1
Li Chu-ch'en		2	Shen Hung		1
Li Chü-k'uei	?x	0	Shen Tse-min	x	0
Li Fu-ch'un	x	3	Shen Yen-ping		4
Li Hsien-nien		1	Shih Liang		1
Li Hsueh-feng		1	Su Chao-cheng	x	0
Li K'o-nung		1	Su Yü		1

Name	Pre-1949	Number of post-1949 trips	Name	Pre-1949	Number of post-1949 trips
Sung Ch'ing-ling	x	2	Wang Jo-fei	x	0
Sung Shao-wen		1	Wang Kuang-wei		1
T'an Chen-lin		1	Wang Ping-chang	x	1
T'an Cheng		1	Wang Shih-t'ai		2
T'ao Chu		1	Wang Shou-tao		1
Teng Chung-hsia	x	0	Wang Tao-han		3
Teng Fa	x	0	Wang Ts'ung-wu	x	0
Teng Hsiao-p'ing	x	4	Wang Wei		1
T'eng Tai-yuan	x	1	Wang Wei-chou		1
Teng T'o		1	Wu Heng		3
Teng Ying-ch'ao	x	0	Wu Hsiu-ch'üan	x	6
Ting Ling		3	Wu Hsueh-ch'ien		3
Ting Ying		1	Yang Ch'eng-wu		1
Ts'ai Ch'ang	x	1	Yang Hsien-chen	x	0
Ts'ai Ho-sen	x	0	Yang Hsien-tung		1
Ts'ai Shu-fan	x	1	Yang Li-san		1
Ts'ao Meng-chün		1	Yang Ming-chai	x	0
Tseng Yung-ch'üan		2	Yang Shang-k'un	x	3
Tso Ch'üan	x	0	Yang Shuo		2
Tu Jun-sheng		1	Yang Te-chih		1
Tung Pi-wu	x	0	Yang Yun-yü		2
Ulanfu	x	1	Yao I-lin		1
Wan I		1	Yeh Chi-chuang		5
Wan Li		1	Yeh Chien-ying	x	1
Wang Cheng		1	Yeh T'ing	x	0
Wang Chia-hsiang	x	5	Yü Kuang-yuan		2
Wang En-mao		1		──	──
Wang Ho-shou	x	1		100	305

Travel to East Europe

Note: x indicates pre-1949 experience in the country. ? indicates uncertainty about a trip. References to Austria are for the pre-1955 period.

Name	Albania	Austria	Bulgaria	Czechoslovakia	Germany	Hungary	Poland	Rumania	Yugoslavia
An Tzu-wen			1	1		1			
Burhan Shahidi					1		1	1	
Chang Ch'i-lung						1			
Chang Chih-hsiang			1	1		1			1
Chang Ch'in-ch'iu						x			
Chang Hsi-jo				1					
Chang Hsiu-chu						1	1		1
Chang Lien-hua	1								
Chang Lin-chih				2					
Chang P'ing-hua					1				

Name	Albania	Austria	Bulgaria	Czechoslovakia	Germany	Hungary	Poland	Rumania	Yugoslavia
Chang Tsung-hsun	1		1	1	1	1	1	1	
Chang Wen-t'ien					1		2		
Chang Yu-yü	1		2	1				1	1
Chang Yun				1			1		
Chao I-min	1		1	1	1			1	
Chao Shou-shan					1				
Ch'en Chia-k'ang				x					
Ch'en Chung-ching			1			1		1	1
Ch'en I	1				1		1		
Ch'en Shao-min					1				
Ch'en Yü		2	1		2				
Cheng Sen-yü		3		1	1	2		1	
Ch'eng Tzu-hua					1				
Chiang Ming							1	1	
Chiang Nan-hsiang	1								
Ch'iao Kuan-hua	1				1		1		
Ch'ien Chün-jui			1	1	1	1	1	1	
Ch'ien Li-jen				1				1	
Ch'ien San-ch'iang		3					1		
Chin Chung-hua		2	1	1	1	1	1	1	
Chou En-lai	1			1	1	1	2		
Chou P'ei-yuan	1		1		1	1	3	1	
Chu Te				1	1	2	3	1	
Chung Fu-hsiang			1	1					
Fan Ch'ang-chiang		1			1				
Fang I	1								
Fang Ming		2	2				1		
Feng Wen-pin					1				
Ho Ch'eng-hsiang				1	1	1			
Ho Lung					1	1	2		
Hsi Chung-hsun				1	2	1			
Hsiao Fang-chou					1				1
Hsiao Hua			1	1		1	1		
Hsiung Fu			1	1	1	1	1		
Hsu Chien-kuo	1							1	
Hsu Chih-chen					1		?1	?1	
Hsu Li-chün				1	1	1			
Hsu Te-heng				1					
Hu Ch'i-li				3					
Hu K'o-shih					1				
Hu Yao-pang	1							1	
Hu Yü-chih								1	
Huang Chen	1					1			
Jung Kao-t'ang	1								1
K'ang Sheng					1			1	
K'ang Yung-ho			2		3	1	1		
Kao K'o-lin					1				
K'o Pai-nien		2	1	1	1			1	
Ko Pao-ch'üan				1			1		
K'uei Pi		1							

Name	Albania	Austria	Bulgaria	Czechoslovakia	Germany	Hungary	Poland	Rumania	Yugoslavia
K'ung Yuan	1			2		1			2
Kuo Mo-jo		4		2	3	3	1	1	
Lai Chi-fa					1				
Lai Ch'uan-chu							1		
Lei Jen-min					1				
Li Che-jen							1		
Li Ch'ang								1	
Li Ch'iang				1	1		1	1	
Li Chieh-po		1			1		1	1	
Li Chu-ch'en		1			2				
Li Fu-ch'un				1					
Li Hsien-nien	3			1					
Li I-mang		4	1	2	4	2		1	
Li K'o-nung				1					
Li Pao-hua							1		
Li Szu-kuang				1					
Li Ta	1			1					
Li Te-ch'üan	1		2	2	1	1	2	1	1
Liang Hsi	1		1	2				1	1
Liao Ch'eng-chih		3		2	2	2	2		
Liao Lu-yen			1						1
Lin Hai-yun			1	1	1			1	
Liu Ch'ang-sheng	2	2	1	3	2	2	1	1	2
Liu Hsi-yuan	1			1	1				
Liu Hsiao			1				1		
Liu Hsiu-feng							1		
Liu Lan-po				1					
Liu Lan-t'ao				1	1	1	1	1	
Liu Ning-i		5		x4	1	x3	4	3	x1
Liu Pai-yü									1
Liu Tao-sheng				1					
Liu Tzu-chiu				1					
Liu Ya-lou								1	
Lo Ch'iung		1							
Lü Cheng-ts'ao					1	1	1		
Lu Hsu-chang	1				1				1
Ma Wen-jui							1		
Mei I	1			1		1	1		
Meng Yung-ch'ien		2				1			
Nan Han-ch'en				1	2	1	1		
Nieh Jung-chen				2	2	1	1	2	
Ou Meng-chueh						x			
Ou T'ang-liang	1	1	1	2			1	2	1
P'eng Chen	1		1	1				2	1
P'eng Te-huai	1		1	1	2	1	2	1	
Po I-po							1		
Saifudin				1	1				
Sha Ch'ien-li					1				
Shen Hung						1			
Shen Yen-ping		3			1	1	3		

Name	Albania	Austria	Bulgaria	Czechoslovakia	Germany	Hungary	Poland	Rumania	Yugoslavia
Shih Liang		1		1					
Sun Ta-kuang	1								
Sung Ch'ing-ling		1							
Ta P'u-sheng		1							
T'an Chen-lin						1			
T'eng Tai-yuan					2	1	1		
Teng T'o							1		
Teng Ying-ch'ao					1		2		
Ting Ling				1		x			
Ting Ying				1	2		1		
Ts'ai Ch'ang				1		x			
Ts'ai Shu-fan				1	1				
Ts'ao Meng-chün			1				1		
Tseng Shan	2				1				
Tseng Yung-ch'üan					3		1		
Tung Pi-wu			2	1	1				
Ulanfu				1	1				
Wan I							1		
Wang Chao				1	1				
Wang Cheng					1				
Wang Chia-hsiang					1	1	2		
Wang Hung-k'un									1
Wang Kuang-wei				1					
Wang Kuo-ch'üan					1		1		
Wang Ping-chang						1			1
Wang Ping-nan							1		
Wang Shu-sheng	1		1	1	1	1	1	1	
Wang Tao-han				3	2				
Wang Ts'ung-wu						1			
Wang Wei				2		1	1		
Wang Wei-chou							1		
Wang Yu-p'ing								1	
Wei Heng							1		
Wu Heng					1		1	1	
Wu Hsiu-ch'üan	1		1	2	1	1	1	1	1
Wu Hsueh-ch'ien		1		2		1	1	1	
Wu Leng-hsi		1					1		
Wu Yun-fu									1
Yang Hsien-tung	1			1	1	2			
Yang Hsiu-feng	1								
Yang Shuo	1							1	
Yang Te-chih	1		1	1	1	1		1	
Yang Yun-yü	1		1	1	2		1	1	
Yeh Chi-chuang				1	1	1	2		
Yeh Chien-ying							1		
Yü Kuang-yuan				1	1	1			
Country totals (post-1949)	39	48	37	91	97	57	82	47	22

Total trips: 520

Travel to West Europe

Note: x indicates pre-1949 experience in the country. *?* indicates uncertainty about a trip. Austria refers to post-1955. Country totals include only post-1949 travel. This chart includes Australia and New Zealand.

Name	Austria	Belgium	Denmark	England	Finland	France	Germany	Italy	Netherlands	Norway	Sweden	Switzerland
Burhan Shahidi				1			x				4	
Chang Chi-ch'un											1	
Chang Chih-hsiang[a]		1		1		1		1	1		2	1
Chang Chih-jang		1										
Chang Han-fu				?x								1
Chang Hsi-jo				x								
Chang Lien-hua[b]						1		1			1	
Chang Wen-t'ien												1
Chang Yen												1
Chang Yun			1			1						
Chao I-min				2				2			1	
Chao P'u-ch'u											2	
Chao Shih-yen						x						
Ch'en Chia-k'ang			x	x	x	x		x		x	x	1
Ch'en Chung-ching												1
Ch'en I						x						2
Ch'en Tu-hsiu						x						
Ch'en Yen-nien						x						
Ch'en Yü[c]						?x						
Cheng Sen-yü	2					2					4	
Chi Ch'ao-ting[d]	x4	x1		1		1	x1	1			3	3
Ch'iao Kuan-hua						x	x					2
Ch'ien Li-jen	1					2					2	
Ch'ien San-ch'iang						x					1	
Chin Chung-hua	2	1			1	1	1	1	1		3	1
Chou En-lai		x		x		x	x					1
Chou P'ei-yuan		1		x2	1			1				2
Ch'ü Ch'iu-pai						x	x					
Chu Te						x	x					
Ch'u T'u-nan[e]			1			2					3	
Chu Tzu-ch'i[f]	1					1					3	
Fang I												1
Fang Ming				1								
Han Nien-lung											1	
Ho Ch'ang-kung		x				x						
Hsiang Ching-yü						x						
Hsiao Fang-chou			1									
Hsiung Fu												1
Hsu Ping							x					
Hsu Te-heng				x		x					1	
Hsu T'e-li						x	x					
Hsu Ti-hsin				1				1				1
Hu Yü-chih						x						
Huang Chen						x					3	
Huang Hua						1						1

Name	Austria	Belgium	Denmark	England	Finland	France	Germany	Italy	Netherlands	Norway	Sweden	Switzerland
Jao Shu-shih						x						
Jung Kao-t'ang					1	1						
K'ang Yung-ho	1											
Keng Piao			1		1						1	
K'o Pai-nien			1									1
Ko Pao-ch'üan												1
Kuo Mo-jo					1					1	5	
Lei Jen-min			1		2			1		1	1	1
Li Chu-ch'en											1	
Li Fu-ch'un						x	x					
Li I-mang					2	1					4	
Li K'o-nung												1
Li Li-san						x						
Li Szu-kuang				x								
Li Te-ch'üan[g]			3	3				1		1	3	4
Li Wei-han						x						
Liang Hsi							x					
Liao Ch'eng-chih		x			1	x	x	1	x		5	
Lin Hai-yun					1							
Lin T'ieh		1										
Liu Ch'ang-sheng[h]	1	1			1	2		2				
Liu Hsi-yuan	1											
Liu Hsiao												1
Liu Lan-t'ao			1									
Liu Ning-i[i]		1		?2	3	x1		x1			4	
Liu Yü-min				1						1	1	
Lo Ch'iung												1
Lo Kuei-po												1
Lu Hsu-chang				1	1				1		1	1
Mei I					1							
Meng Yung-ch'ien											1	
Nieh Jung-chen		x				x						1
Ou T'ang-liang	1					x					2	
P'eng Chen								1				
P'eng Shao-hui											1	
Saifudin					1							
Shen Yen-ping			1		1					1	2	
Shih Liang						1						
Shirob Jaltso											1	
Sun Ta-kuang									1			
Sung Ch'ing-ling[j]							x					
T'an Chen-lin								1				
Teng Fa[k]						x						
Teng Hsiao-p'ing						x						
Ts'ai Ch'ang						x		x				
Ts'ai Ho-sen						x						
Ts'ao Chü-ju[l]												
Ts'ao Meng-chün	1		2			1						?3
Tseng Shan	1									1		
Wan Li						?x						

Name	Austria	Belgium	Denmark	England	Finland	France	Germany	Italy	Netherlands	Norway	Sweden	Switzerland
Wang Chia-hsiang				1		x	x					1
Wang Jo-fei		x				x						
Wang Ping-nan				x	x		x					3
Wang Shou-tao					1							
Wang Yu-p'ing										1		
Wu Chih-p'u					1							
Wu Hsiu-ch'üan				2								
Wu Hsueh-ch'ien		1				1						
Wu Leng-hsi												2
Wu Yü-chang				x		x						
Wu Yun-fu[m]												1
Yang Hsien-chen							x					
Yang Hsiu-feng						x						
Yang Shuo											1	
Yang Yun-yü	1		1									2
Yeh Chien-ying							x					
Yeh T'ing	x					x	x					
Country totals (post-1949)	17	9	14	19	28	14	2	16	4	7	69	46

Total trips: 257

a Chang Chih-hsiang also made a trip to Greece.
b Chang Lien-hua also made a trip to Portugal.
c Ch'en Yü also made a trip to Australia and New Zealand.
d Chi Ch'ao-ting also made a pre-1949 trip to Australia.
e Ch'u T'u-nan also made a trip to Iceland.
f Chu Tzu-ch'i also made a trip to Cyprus.
g Li Te-ch'üan also made a trip to Monaco.
h Liu Ch'ang-sheng also made a trip to Australia.
i Liu Ning-i also made a trip to Cyprus and one to New Zealand.
j Sung Ch'ing-ling also traveled in other unspecified parts of Europe in the pre-1949 period.
k Teng Fa also traveled in other unspecified parts of Europe in the pre-1949 period.
l Ts'ao Chü-ju made one trip to Australia.
m Wu Yun-fu also made a trip to Monaco.

Travel to South and Southeast Asia

Note: x indicates pre-1949 experience in the country.

Name	Afghanistan	Burma	Cambodia	Ceylon	India	Indonesia	Nepal	Pakistan
Burhan Shahidi	1	1		1	2	1		
Chang Ai-p'ing		1			1			
Chang Chih-hsiang		1						
Chang Chih-jang					1			
Chang Han-fu		1	2		2	2	1	2

Name	Afghanistan	Burma	Cambodia	Ceylon	India	Indonesia	Nepal	Pakistan
Chang Hsiu-chu						1		
Chang Lien-hua						2		
Chang Su						1		
Chang Wen-t'ien						1		1
Chang Yen		2	2		2		1	1
Chang Yu-yü		1				1		
Chao I-min		1						1
Chao P'u-ch'u		4	1	2	3	1	1	
Ch'en Chia-k'ang						1		
Ch'en I	1	6	3	1	1	5	1	1
Ch'en Yü						1		
Cheng Sen-yü				1	4			
Chi Ch'ao-ting		1		1	x2	1		
Ch'iao Kuan-hua		5	2	1	3	3	1	2
Ch'ien Hsin-chung								1
Ch'ien Li-jen						1		
Chin Chung-hua					3			
Chou En-lai	1	6	1	2	4	1	2	2
Chou P'ei-yuan					2			
Chou Yang					1			
Ch'u T'u-nan		2			1		1	1
Chu Tzu-ch'i				1	1	1		
Fang Ch'iang					1			
Fang Ming					1	1		
Han Nien-lung	1						1	2
Ho Lung	1	1	1	1	4	1	1	2
Ho Wei[a]								
Ho Ying						1		
Hsieh Fu-chih		1						
Hu Yü-chih		1				x1	2	
Huang Chen		3	1	2		4		1
Huang Hua						1		
Jung Kao-t'ang						1		
K'ang Yung-ho						1		
Keng Piao		1						1
K'ung Yuan	1	1		1	1	1		1
Kuo Mo-jo		1		1	1	1		
Lei Jen-min		3		2				
Li Che-jen					1			
Li Chieh-po				2	1	1		
Li Chu-ch'en		2				1		
Li Hsien-nien								1
Li Hsueh-feng						1		
Li I-mang		2			2			
Li Te-ch'üan					2			1
Liao Ch'eng-chih		1		1	4	1		1
Lin Hai-yun		1						1
Liu Ch'ang-sheng		2				1		
Liu Hsi-yuan		1			1			
Liu Ning-i		1		1	3	1		1

Name	Afghanistan	Burma	Cambodia	Ceylon	India	Indonesia	Nepal	Pakistan
Liu Pai-yü		1		1	1			
Liu Shao-ch'i		1	1			1		
Liu Tzu-chiu		1						
Liu Ya-lou								1
Lo Jui-ch'ing		1						
Ma Yü-huai				1		3		1
Mei I						1		
Meng Yung-ch'ien					2			
Nan Han-ch'en					1			1
Ou T'ang-liang					1			
P'an Tzu-li					1		1	
Saifudin	x				1			
Shih Liang				1	1			
Shirob Jaltso		2	1	1			1	
Shen Yen-ping					1			
Sung Ch'ing-ling		2		1	1	1		1
Ta P'u-sheng	1				1	3		1
Ts'ao Meng-chün				1	2			
Tseng Sheng			1					1
Ulanfu							1	
Wang Ping-nan					x			
Wang Yu-p'ing			2					
Wu Heng			1			1		
Wu Hsueh-ch'ien		1			2	1		
Wu Yü-chang[b]								
Yang Ch'eng-wu						1		
Yang Ch'i-ch'ing						1		
Yang Shuo				2	2	1		
Yang Yun-yü				1		1		
Yao Chung-ming		1				1		
Yeh Chi-chuang		1		1		1		
Yeh Chien-ying		1			1			
Country totals (post-1949)	7	66	19	31	73	60	15	30

Total trips: 302

[a] Ho Wei visited Laos.
[b] Wu Yü-chang visited South Vietnam in 1938.

Travel to Japan

Name	Pre-1949	Post-1949	Name	Pre-1949	Post-1949
Chang Chih-jang		1	Li Szu-kuang	x	0
Chang T'ai-lei	x	0	Li Ta-chao	x	0
Chang Wen-t'ien	x	0	Li Te-ch'üan		2
Chao An-po		5	Liang Hsi	x	0
Chao P'u-ch'u		6	Liao Ch'eng-chih	x	2
Ch'en Tu-hsiu	x	0	Lin Feng	x	0
Ch'en Yü		2	Lin Po-ch'ü	x	0
Cheng Sen-yü		6	Liu Hsi-yuan		1
Ch'iao Kuan-hua	x	0	Liu Ning-i		5
Chin Chung-hua		1	Liu Pai-yü		1
Chou En-lai	x	0	Lu Hsu-chang		1
Chou P'ei-yuan		1	Nan Han-ch'en	x	2
Chou Shih-ti	x	0	P'eng P'ai	x	0
Chou Yang	x	0	Shen Yen-ping	x	0
Ch'u T'u-nan		1	Sung Ch'ing-ling	x	0
Chu Tzu-ch'i		3	Ting Ying	x	0
Fang Ming		1	Tung Pi-wu	x	0
Hsiung Fu		1	Wang Chen		1
Hsu T'e-li	x	0	Wang Jo-fei	x	0
Hu Feng	x	0	Wang Ping-nan	x	0
Jung Kao-t'ang		2	Wang Wei-chou	x	0
K'ang Yung-ho		2	Wu Hsueh-ch'ien		2
K'o Pai-nien		1	Wu Yü-chang	x	0
Kuo Mo-jo	x	1	Wu Yun-fu		2
Lei Jen-min		1	Yang Shuo		1
Li Chieh-po		2	Yang Yun-yü		1
Li Chu-ch'en	x	1		—	—
Li Han-chün	x	0	Total	28	59

Travel to Egypt and the Middle East

Note: x indicates pre-1949 experience in the country.

Name	UAR (Egypt)	Syria	Lebanon	Saudi Arabia	Iraq
Burhan Shahidi[a]	5	2	2	1	1
Chang Han-fu	1				1
Chao I-min	1				
Chao P'u-ch'u	1				
Ch'en Chia-k'ang[b]	1				
Ch'en Chung-ching					1
Ch'en I	1				
Cheng Sen-yü	1				
Chi Ch'ao-ting	5		1		1
Chiang Ming	1	1	1	1	
Ch'iao Kuan-hua	1				
Ch'ien Hsin-chung	1				
Chin Chung-hua	1				1
Chou En-lai	1				
Ch'u T'u-nan	1				

Name	UAR (Egypt)	Syria	Lebanon	Saudi Arabia	Iraq
Chu Tzu-ch'i	2		1		
Fang Ming	1				
Hu Ch'i-li	1				
Huang Chen	2				
Huang Hua	1				
K'ang Yung-ho	1				
K'ung Yuan	1				
Kuo Mo-jo	1				
Li Te-ch'üan			1		
Liao Ch'eng-chih	1				
Liu Ch'ang-sheng					1
Liu Hsi-yuan	1				
Liu Ning-i	2				
Lo Kuei-po					1
Lu Hsu-chang	2				1
Ma Yü-huai	1	1	1	1	
Nan Han-ch'en[c]	3				
Shen Yen-ping	1				
Shih Liang		1			
Sun Ta-kuang	1				
Sung Shih-lun					1
Ta P'u-sheng	x2			1	
Ts'ao Meng-chün	1				
Wang Wei					1
Wu Heng	1				
Wu Hsueh-ch'ien	3				1
Yang Hsiu-feng	1				
Yang Shuo	3				
Yang Yun-yü	1				
Yeh Chi-chuang	1				
Country totals (post-1949)	57	5	7	4	11
Total trips: 87					

[a] Burhan Shahidi also made a trip to Jordan.
[b] Ch'en Chia-k'ang also made a trip to Yemen.
[c] Nan also visited Kuwait.

Travel to Africa

Note: All these trips occurred in the post-1949 period. There was no travel to the region before 1949.

Name	Algeria	Kenya	Guinea	Congo (Brazzaville)	Mali	Ghana	Tanganyika	Somalia	Tunisia	Morocco	Sudan	Ethiopia
Burhan Shahidi[a]			1						1		1	1
Chang Han-fu[b]	1											
Chang Yu-yü			1									
Chao I-min	2											
Ch'en Chia-k'ang												1

Name	Algeria	Kenya	Guinea	Congo (Brazzaville)	Mali	Ghana	Tanganyika	Somalia	Tunisia	Morocco	Sudan	Ethiopia
Ch'en I	2	1	1		1	1		1	1	1	1	1
Ch'en Yü	1			1								
Chi Ch'ao-ting			1				1					
Ch'iao Kuan-hua	1		1		1	1		1	1	1	1	1
Ch'ien Li-jen[c]		1			1	1	1	1				
Chin Chung-hua			1									
Chou En-lai	1		1		1	1		1	1	1	1	1
Chu Tzu-ch'i	1		4				1		1			
Fang I	1		1		1							
Fang Ming	1		1		1							
Ho Wei				1								
Ho Ying[d]		1					1					
Hsiao Fang-chou	1											
Hsu Kuang-ta	1											
Hu Ch'i-li									1	1		
Huang Chen	1		2		1	2		1	1	1	1	1
Huang Hua[e]				1		1	1					
K'ung Yuan	1		1		1	1		1	1	1	1	1
Lei Jen-min									1	1		
Li Chih-min	1											
Liao Ch'eng-chih			1			1						
Liu Ch'ang-sheng[f]			1		1	1						
Liu Ning-i[g]			2	1	1	1	1					
Lu Hsu-chang[h]		1	1	1	2	1				1		
Ma Yü-huai											1	1
Meng Yung-ch'ien			1									
Nan Han-ch'en	1				1							
Nieh Jung-chen						1						
Ts'ao Meng-chün[i]					1	1	1					
Wang Kuang-wei[j]			1	1	1	1						
Wang P'ing[k]			1	1	1	1						
Wu Heng	1											
Wu Hsueh-ch'ien		1	1				1					
Yang Hsiu-feng[l]	1		1		1							
Yang Shuo			2			2	1					
Yang Yun-yü					1							
Yang Yung	1	1										
Yeh Chi-chuang											1	
Country totals	20	6	28	7	18	18	9	6	9	8	8	8

Total trips: 173

a Burhan Shahidi also visited Libya.
b Chang Han-fu also visited Tanzania.
c Ch'ien Li-jen also visited Senegal.
d Ho Ying also visited Zanzibar, Burundi (twice), Uganda (twice), Zambia, and Nyasaland.
e Huang Hua also visited Dahomey.
f Liu Ch'ang-sheng also visited Niger, Upper Volta, Senegal, Togo, and Dahomey.
g Liu Ning-i also visited the Central African Republic.
h Lu Hsu-chang also visited Nigeria (twice), Sierra Leone, Niger, Dahomey, Cameroun, and the Central African Republic.
i Ts'ao Meng-chün also visited Zanzibar.
j Wang Kuang-wei also visited the Central African Republic.
k Wang P'ing also visited the Central African Republic.
l Yang Hsiu-feng also visited Zanzibar.

Travel to North and South America

Note: x indicates pre-1949 experience in the country. *?* indicates uncertainty about a trip. There were no trips to Cuba before 1960. Country totals include only post-1949 travel.

Name	Brazil	Canada	Chile	Cuba	U. S.
Chang Chih-hsiang				1	
Chang Chih-jang					x
Chang Han-fu					x
Chang Hsi-jo					x
Chang Wen-t'ien					x
Chao I-min			1		
Ch'en Chia-k'ang					x
Ch'en Chung-ching		1		1	x1
Ch'en Kung-po					x
Cheng Sen-yü				1	
Chi Ch'ao-ting[a]	1				x
Ch'iao Kuan-hua					1
Ch'ien Li-jen			1	1	
Chin Chung-hua				1	
Chou P'ei-yuan		2			x
Chou Yang				1	
Ch'u T'u-nan[b]	1		1	1	
Fang Ming	1				
Hu Ch'i-li	1			1	
Hu Yü-chih					x
Jao Shu-shih		?x			?x
Jung Kao-t'ang				1	
K'ang Yung-ho				1	
Kuo Mo-jo				1	
Li Ch'ang				1	
Li I-mang			1		
Li Te-ch'üan		1		1	x
Lin Hai-yun				1	
Liu Ch'ang-sheng			1		
Liu Ya-lou				1	
Lu Hsu-chang				1	
Lu Ting-i					x
Mei I[c]	1		1	1	
Nan Han-ch'en[d]	1		1	1	
Sung Ch'ing-ling					x
Ts'ao Meng-chün				1	
Tung Pi-wu					x
Wang Yu-p'ing				1	
Wu Hsiu-ch'üan				1	1
Wu Yun-fu	1				
Yang Hsien-tung					x
Country totals (post-1949)	7	4	7	21	3
Total trips: 47					

[a] Chi Ch'ao-ting also visited Mexico.
[b] Ch'u T'u-nan also visited Uruguay and Argentina.
[c] Mei I also visited Ecuador.
[d] Nan Han-ch'en also visited Argentina.

Part XII: Fields of Work

72. Agriculture, Forestry, Land Reclamation

Chang Hsiu-chu
Chao Tzu-yang
Ch'en Cheng-jen
Ch'en Man-yuan
Chiang I-chen
Hsiao K'o

Li Fan-wu
Li Pao-hua
Li Yü
Liang Hsi
Liao Lu-yen
Liu Lan-po

Shen Hung
T'an Chen-lin
T'ao Chu
Teng Tzu-hui
Ting Ying

Tu Jun-sheng
Wang Chen
Wang Kuang-wei
Yang Hsien-tung
Yang I-ch'en

73. Athletics

Chang Lien-hua
Ho Lung

Jung Kao-t'ang
Li Ta

Liu Tao-sheng
Ts'ai Shu-fan

Wang Chao

74. Commerce (domestic)

Ch'en Yun
Ch'eng Tzu-hua
Hsu Ti-hsin

Li Chu-ch'en
Li Hsien-nien
Sha Ch'ien-li

Tseng Shan
Yang I-ch'en

Yao I-lin
Yeh Chi-chuang

75. Cooperatives

Chang Ch'i-lung
Ch'eng Tzu-hua

Chin Chung-hua
Lo Ch'iung

Meng Yung-ch'ien
Pai Ju-ping

P'an Fu-sheng
Po I-po

76. Economics and Finance (including banking)

Chang Ch'i-lung
Chang Hsi
Chang Kuo-chien
Chao Erh-lu
Ch'en Po-ta
Ch'en Yü
Ch'en Yun
Ch'eng Tzu-hua
Chi Ch'ao-ting
Chia T'o-fu
Chin Ming

Fang I
Han Che-i
Hsueh Mu-ch'iao
Jung Tzu-ho
Kao Kang
Ku Cho-hsin
Ku Mu
Li Che-jen
Li Fu-ch'un
Li Hsien-nien
Li Li-san

Li Wei-han
Liu Ming-fu
Mao Tse-min
Nan Han-ch'en
Pai Ju-ping
P'eng T'ao
Po I-po
Sun Chih-yuan
Sung Shao-wen
T'an Chen-lin
T'ao Lu-chia

Teng Hsiao-p'ing
Teng Tzu-hui
Ts'ao Chü-ju
Tseng Shan
Wang Kuang-wei
Wang Shih-t'ai
Wu Po
Yao I-lin
Yeh Chi-chuang
Yü Ch'iu-li
Yuan Pao-hua

77. Education, Culture, Language Reform

Chang Chi-ch'un
Chang Chia-fu
Chang Chih-hsiang
Chang Ch'in-ch'iu
Chang Hsi-jo
Ch'en I
Ch'en Po-ta
Chiang Nan-hsiang
Ch'ien Chün-jui

Chin Chung-hua
Chou Jung-hsin
Ch'ü Ch'iu-pai
Ch'u T'u-nan
Fan Ch'ang-chiang
Fan Wen-lan
Fang Ming
Ho Ch'eng-hsiang
Ho Shu-heng

Ho Wei
Hsi Chung-hsun
Hsu T'e-li
Hu Ch'iao-mu
Kuo Mo-jo
Li Ch'ang
Li Chieh-po
Lin Feng

Lin Po-ch'ü
Lu P'ing
Lu Ting-i
Sha Wen-han
Shen Yen-ping
Wu Yü-chang
Yang Hsien-chen
Yang Hsiu-feng

78. Foreign Aid, Trade, and Scientific Cooperation

Chang Han-fu
Chang Lin-chih
Chang Su
Chang Wen-t'ien
Chi Ch'ao-ting
Chiang Ming
Chou En-lai
Fan Ch'ang-chiang
Fang I
Han Kuang
Han Nien-lung
Ho Wei
Ho Ying

Hsiao Fang-chou
Hsu Chien-kuo
Hsu Ti-hsin
Huang Chen
K'ung Yuan
Lei Jen-min
Li Che-jen
Li Ch'iang
Li I-mang
Liao Lu-yen
Lin Hai-yun
Liu Lan-po
Liu Ming-fu

Lü Cheng-ts'ao
Lu Hsu-chang
Lü Tung
Nan Han-ch'en
P'an Tzu-li
P'ei Li-sheng
Po I-po
Sun Ta-kuang
Ting Ying
Ts'ao Chü-ju
Tseng Yung-ch'üan
Tu Jun-sheng
Tuan Chün-i

Wang Cheng
Wang Chia-hsiang
Wang Kuang-wei
Wang Kuo-ch'üan
Wang Shih-t'ai
Wang Tao-han
Wang Yu-p'ing
Wu Heng
Wu Hsiu-ch'üan
Yao Chung-ming
Yao I-lin
Yeh Chi-chuang

79. Government and Party Control (Supervision) Work (see also Public Security)

An Tzu-wen
Chang Chia-fu
Chang P'ing-hua
Chang Ting-ch'eng
Chang Tzu-i
Chang Yun-i
Ch'en Ch'i-han
Ch'en Shao-min
Chi Ya-t'ai
Ch'ien Ying

Chou Shih-ti
Hsiao Hua
Hsieh Fu-chih
Hsu Li-ch'ün
Hsu Te-heng
Kao K'o-lin
Kao Yang
Kung Tzu-jung
Li Chien-chen

Li Ch'u-li
Li Shih-ying
Li Wei-han
Liu Hsi-wu
Liu Lan-t'ao
Ma Ming-fang
Ou Meng-chueh
Shuai Meng-ch'i
Tung Pi-wu

Wang Shih-ying
Wang Ts'ung-wu
Wang Wei-chou
Wu Kai-chih
Wu Te-feng
Wu Yun-fu
Yü I-ch'uan
Yuan Jen-yuan

80. Industry

Chang Ch'in-ch'iu
Chang Lin-chih
Chao Erh-lu
Ch'en Cheng-jen
Ch'en Yü
Ch'en Yun
Ch'eng Tzu-hua
Chia T'o-fu
Chiang Ming
Ch'iu Ch'uang-ch'eng
Fang Ch'iang
Hsu Yun-pei

Ho Ch'ang-kung
Hsu Te-heng
Hsu Yun-pei
Huang Ching
Kao Yang
Ku Mu
Lai Chi-fa
Li Chu-ch'en
Li Chü-k'uei
Li Fu-ch'un
Li Pao-hua
Li Yü

Liu Hsiu-feng
Liu Lan-po
Liu Ting
Liu Yü-min
Lü Tung
P'eng T'ao
Po I-po
Sha Ch'ien-li
Shen Hung
Sun Chih-yuan
Sung Jen-ch'iung

Sung Shao-wen
Tseng Shan
Tuan Chün-i
Wan Li
Wang Cheng
Wang Ho-shou
Wang Ping-chang
Wang Shih-t'ai
Wang Tao-han
Yang Li-san
Yü Ch'iu-li

81. Intelligence

Chang Kuo-chien   Li K'o-nung   Tsou Ta-p'eng   Wang Shou-tao
K'ang Sheng   Li T'ao

82. International Affairs

Note: This appendix is divided into three parts. First is a list of personnel in the Foreign Ministry and the Office of Foreign Affairs, except for ambassadors who are listed in the second part. The third part consists of a list of international organizations in which the Communists have been active. See also Appendix 70, which contains a section dealing with those men who have been abroad to attend foreign Communist Party Congresses. † indicates that the individual is not one of the 433 biographic entries.

Foreign Ministry and Office of Foreign Affairs

Chang Han-fu   Ch'en I   Fang I   Liao Ch'eng-chih
Chang Yen   Ch'iao Kuan-hua   K'ung Yuan   Liu Ning-i
Ch'en Chung-ching Chou En-lai   Li K'o-nung

Ambassadors

Note: The PRC maintains embassies in the following countries, with the exception of the Netherlands and the United Kingdom. In those two cases the Chinese have an office of the chargé d'affaires, and the senior diplomat is known as the chargé d'affaires. The dates are the official dates of appointment and removal. Information is current through 1965.

Afghanistan
†Ting Kuo-yü   1955–1958
†Hao T'ing   1958–1965
†Ch'en Feng   1965–

Albania
†Hsu I-hsin   1954–1957
†Lo Shih-kao   1957–1964
 Hsu Chien-kuo   1964–

Algeria
†Tseng T'ao   1962–

Britain, see *United Kingdom.*

Bulgaria
†Ts'ao Hsiang-jen   1950–1954
†Chou Chu-an   1954–1957
†Chu Ch'i-wen   1957–1962
†Hsieh Pang-chih   1962–

Burma
 Yao Chung-ming   1950–1958
 Li I-mang   1958–1963
 Keng Piao   1963–

Burundi[1]
†Liu Yü-feng   1964–1965

Cambodia
 Wang Yu-p'ing   1958–1962
†Ch'en Shu-liang   1962–

Central African Republic
†Meng Ying   1964–

Ceylon
†Chang Ts'an-ming   1957–1962
†Hsieh K'o-hsi   1962–

Congo (Brazzaville)
†Chou Ch'iu-yeh   1964–

Cuba
†Shen Chien   1960–1964
 Wang Yu-p'ing   1964–

Czechoslovakia
†T'an Hsi-lin   1950–1954
†Ts'ao Ying   1954–1961
†Chung Hsi-tung   1961–

Appendices 1164

Dahomey
†Li Yun-ch'uan — 1965–

Denmark
Keng Piao (minister) — 1950–1955
†Ch'ai Ch'eng-wen (minister) — 1955–1956
†Cheng Wei-chih — 1956–1961
†Wang Sen — 1961–1963
K'o Pai-nien — 1963–

Finland
Keng Piao (minister) — 1950–1954
†Ch'en Hsin-jen — 1954–1959
†Kan Yeh-t'ao — 1959–1962
†Chang Po-ch'uan — 1962–1965
†Yueh Hsin — 1965–

France
Huang Chen — 1964–

Germany (East)
†Chi P'eng-fei[2] — 1950–1955
Tseng Yung-ch'üan — 1955–1957
Wang Kuo-ch'üan — 1957–1964
†Chang Hai-feng — 1964–

Ghana
Huang Hua — 1960–

Guinea
†K'o Hua — 1960–1964
†Ch'ai Tse-min — 1964–

Hungary
Huang Chen — 1950–1954
†Hao Te-ch'ing — 1954–1961
†Ch'ai Tse-min — 1961–1964
†Han K'o-hua — 1964–

India[3]
†Yuan Chung-hsien — 1950–1956
P'an Tzu-li — 1956–1962

Indonesia
†Wang Jen-shu — 1950–1954
Huang Chen — 1954–1961
Yao Chung-ming — 1961–

Iraq
†Ch'en Chih-fang — 1958–1960
†Chang Wei-lieh — 1960–

Kenya
†Wang Yü-t'ien — 1964–

Korea (North)
†Ni Chih-liang — 1950–1954
P'an Tzu-li — 1954–1956
†Ch'iao Hsiao-kuang — 1956–1961
Hao Te-ch'ing — 1961–1965
†Chiao Jo-yü — 1965–

Laos
†Liu Ch'un — 1962–

Mali
†Lai Ya-li — 1961–1965
†Ma Tzu-ch'ing — 1965–

Mauritania
†Lü Chih-hsien — 1965–

Mongolia
Chi Ya-t'ai — 1950–1954
Ho Ying — 1954–1958
†Hsieh Fu-sheng — 1958–1963
†Chang Ts'an-ming — 1963–

Morocco
†Pai Jen — 1959–1961
†Yang Ch'i-liang — 1961–

Nepal
†Yuan Chung-hsien — 1955–1956
P'an Tzu-li — 1956–1960
†Chang Shih-chieh — 1960–

Netherlands
†Hsieh Li — 1955–1963
†Li En-ch'iu — 1963–

Norway
Wang Yu-p'ing — 1954–1958
†Hsu I-hsin — 1958–1962
†Ch'in Li-chen — 1962–1965
†Feng Yü-chiu — 1965–

Pakistan
Han Nien-lung — 1951–1956
Keng Piao — 1956–1959
†Ting Kuo-yü — 1959–

Poland
†P'eng Ming-chih — 1950–1952
Tseng Yung-ch'üan — 1952–1955
Wang Ping-nan — 1955–1964
Wang Kuo-ch'üan — 1964–

Rumania
Wang Yu-p'ing — 1950–1954
K'o Pai-nien — 1954–1959
Hsu Chien-kuo — 1959–1964
†Liu Fang — 1964–

Somalia			UAR (formerly Egypt)	
†Chang Yueh	1961–1964		Ch'en Chia-k'ang	1956–
†Yang Shou-cheng	1964–			
			United Kingdom	
Sudan			†Huan Hsiang	1954–1962
†Wang Yü-t'ien	1959–1962		†Hsiung Hsiang-hui	1962–
†Ku Hsiao-po	1962–			
			USSR	
Sweden			Wang Chia-hsiang	1949–1951
Keng Piao	1950–1956		Chang Wen-t'ien	1951–1955
Han Nien-lung	1956–1958		Liu Hsiao	1955–1962
†Tung Yueh-ch'ien	1958–1964		P'an Tzu-li	1962–
†Yang Po-chen	1964–			
			Vietnam (North)	
Switzerland			Lo Kuei-po	1954–1957
†Feng Hsuan[4]	1950–1959		Ho Wei	1957–1962
†Li Ch'ing-ch'üan	1959–		†Chu Ch'i-wen	1962–
Syria[5]			Yemen	
†Ch'en Chih-fang	1956–1958		Ch'en Chia-k'ang[6]	1957–1964
†Hsu I-hsin	1962–		†Wang Jo-chieh	1964–
Tanzania (formerly Tanganyika)			Yugoslavia[7]	
Ho Ying	1962–		Wu Hsiu-ch'üan	1955–1958
Tunisia			Zambia	
†Yao Nien	1964–		†Ch'in Li-chen	1965–
Uganda			Zanzibar[8]	
Ho Ying	1963–1964		†Meng Ying	1964–1964
†Ch'en Chih-fang	1964–			

[1] Diplomatic relations with Burundi were suspended in January 1965.

[2] Chi was chief of the "diplomatic mission" from 1950 to 1954 and ambassador thereafter.

[3] Because of the serious deterioration of Sino-Indian relations, no ambassador was named to replace P'an Tzu-li. However, the PRC still maintains an embassy in New Delhi.

[4] Feng was minister to 1956 and ambassador thereafter.

[5] Syria was part of the UAR from 1958 to 1961.

[6] Ch'en was minister to 1963 and ambassador thereafter.

[7] Because of the deterioration of Sino-Yugoslav relations, no ambassador was named to replace Wu Hsiu-ch'üan.

[8] Zanzibar and Tanganyika merged in 1964 to form Tanzania.

Participants in Selected International Organizations

Afro-Asian Solidarity Organization

(See Appendix 70)

International Broadcasting Organization

Mei I

International Organization of Journalists

Chin Chung-hua   Hu Ch'iao-mu   Teng T'o   Wu Leng-hsi

International Association of Democratic Lawyers

Chang Chih-jang   Chang Yu-yü   K'o Pai-nien

World Peace Council

   (See Appendix 70)

World Federation of Scientific Workers

Chou P'ei-yuan   Li Szu-kuang   Yang Hsien-tung   Yü Kuang-yuan
Fan Ch'ang-chiang   Liang Hsi

International Union of Students

Liao Ch'eng-chih   Wang Wei

World Federation of Trade Unions

Ch'en Yü   K'ang Yung-ho   Liu Ch'ang-sheng   Liu Shao-ch'i
Fang Ming   Li Chieh-po   Liu Ning-i

Women's International Democratic Federation

Chang Ch'in-ch'iu   Shih Liang   Ting Ling   Ts'ao Meng-chün
Li Te-ch'üan   Teng Ying-ch'ao   Ts'ai Ch'ang   Yang Yun-yü

World Federation of Democratic Youth

Ch'ien Li-jen   Liao Ch'eng-chih   Liu Hsi-yuan   Ou T'ang-liang
Hu Yao-pang

83. Journalism, Propaganda, Ideology

Ai Szu-ch'i
Chang Chi-ch'un
Chang Han-fu
Chang Wen-t'ien
Chang Yu-yü
Chao Shih-yen
Ch'en Ch'ang-hao
Ch'en Po-ta
Ch'en Shao-yü
Ch'en Tu-hsiu
Ch'en Yun
Chiang Nan-hsiang
Ch'iao Kuan-hua
Ch'ien Chün-jui
Chin Chung-hua
Ch'in Pang-hsien
Chou Yang
Ch'ü Ch'iu-pai
Chu Tzu-ch'i
Fan Ch'ang-chiang
Fan Wen-lan
Fang Chih-min
Ho Shu-heng
Hsi Chung-hsun
Hsiao Ch'u-nü
Hsiung Fu
Hsu Li-ch'ün
Hsu T'e-li
Hsu Ti-hsin
Hu Ch'iao-mu
Hu K'o-shih
Hu Sheng
Hu Yü-chih
K'ai Feng
K'o Ch'ing-shih
K'o Pai-nien
Ko Pao-ch'üan
Kuo Mo-jo
Li Ch'iu-shih
Li Fu-ch'un
Li Han-chün
Li Li-san
Li Ta-chao
Liao Ch'eng-chih
Liu Pai-yü
Liu Shao-ch'i
Lu Ting-i
Mao Tse-min
Mao Tse-tung
Mei I
Sha Wen-han
Shen Yen-ping
T'ao Lu-chia
Teng Chung-hsia
Teng T'o
Ting Ling
Ts'ai Ho-sen
Ts'ao Meng-chün
Wang Jo-fei
Wu Leng-hsi
Yang Hsien-chen
Yü Kuang-yuan
Yun Tai-ying

84. Labor Unions

Chang Ch'in-ch'iu
Chang Hsiu-chu
Chang Kuo-t'ao
Chang Tzu-i
Chao Shih-yen
Ch'en Kung-po
Ch'en Shao-min
Ch'en Yü
Ch'en Yü
Ch'en Yun
Ch'in Pang-hsien
Fang Ming

Ho Meng-hsiung
Hsiang Ching-yü
Hsiang Chung-fa
Hsiang Ying
Hsu Chih-chen
Jao Shu-shih
K'ang Yung-ho
Kuan Hsiang-ying
Lai Jo-yü
Li Chieh-po
Li Ch'iu-shih

Li Han-chün
Li Li-san
Lin Yü-nan
Lin Yü-ying
Liu Ch'ang-sheng
Liu Ning-i
Liu Shao-ch'i
Liu Tzu-chiu
Lo Chang-lung
Lo Teng-hsien
Ma Wen-jui

Mao Tse-min
Mao Tse-tung
Su Chao-cheng
Teng Chung-hsia
Teng Fa
Ts'ai Ch'ang
Ts'ai Shu-fan
Wang Chen
Wang Jo-fei
Wu Yü-chang
Yang Yin

85. Law and Political Science

Chang Chih-jang
Chang Hsi-jo
Chang Su
Chang Ting-ch'eng
Chang Yu-yü

Ch'en Ch'i-han
Ch'en Shao-yü
Hsieh Chueh-tsai
Hsieh Fu-chih
Hsu Te-heng

Li Shih-ying
Lo Jui-ch'ing
Ma Hsi-wu
P'eng Chen

Shih Liang
Tung Pi-wu
Wu Te-feng
Yang Hsiu-feng

86. Literature and Art

Chang Wen-t'ien
Chou Yang
Ch'ü Ch'iu-pai
Hu Feng

Ko Pao-ch'üan
Kuo Mo-jo
Li I-mang

Liu Pai-yü
Shen Tse-min
Shen Yen-ping

Ting Ling
Yang Shuo
Yao Chung-ming

87. Medicine and Public Health

Ch'ien Hsin-chung

Fu Lien-chang

Hsu Yun-pei

Li Te-ch'üan

88. Overseas Chinese

Chin Chung-hua

Fang Fang

Liao Ch'eng-chih

Sun Ta-kuang

89. Public Security

Chang Ta-chih
Hsieh Fu-chih
Hsu Chien-kuo

Hsu Tzu-jung
Kan Szu-ch'i
Li Shih-ying

Lo Jui-ch'ing
Wang Chao

Wang Chin-hsiang
Yang Ch'i-ch'ing

90. Religion

Burhan Shahidi
Chang Chih-i

Chao P'u-ch'u
Ho Ch'eng-hsiang

Shirob Jaltso

Ta P'u-sheng

91. Science and Science Administration

Chang Chin-fu
Ch'en I
Ch'en Po-ta
Ch'ien San-ch'iang
Chou Chien-jen

Chou P'ei-yuan
Fan Ch'ang-chiang
Han Kuang
Huang Ching
Kuo Mo-jo

Li Szu-kuang
Liang Hsi
Lin Feng
Nieh Jung-chen
P'ei Li-sheng

Tu Jun-sheng
Wu Heng
Yang Hsiu-feng
Yü Kuang-yuan

92. Social Relief and Welfare

Chao P'u-ch'u
Ch'ien Ying
Hsieh Chueh-tsai

Hsu Tzu-jung
Li Te-ch'üan
Ou T'ang-liang

Sung Ch'ing-ling
Ts'ao Meng-chün
Tseng Hsi-sheng

Tseng Shan
Wu Yun-fu
Yuan Jen-yuan

93. Transportation and Telecommunications

Chang Kuo-chien
Chao Chien-min
Chung Fu-hsiang
Li Ch'iang

Li Fu-ch'un
Lü Cheng-ts'ao
Lu P'ing
Pai Ju-ping

Po I-po
Sun Ta-kuang
T'eng Tai-yuan

Wang Cheng
Wang Shih-t'ai
Wang Shou-tao

94. United Front Work

Note: This appendix applies to the post-1949 period, and includes those individuals engaged in liaison with or supervision over non-Communist intellectuals; non-Communist industrialists and businessmen; religious groups; overseas Chinese; national minority groups; and the "democratic" (non-Communist) political parties. Because so many of those listed below have specialized in nationalities affairs, they are listed separately. See also Appendices 88 and 90.

General

Chang Chih-i
Chao P'u-ch'u
Ch'i Yen-ming
Fang Fang
Ho Ch'eng-hsiang

Hsu Ping
Hsu Ti-hsin
Li Wei-han
Liao Ch'eng-chih
Liu Ko-p'ing

Ou Meng-chueh
P'ing Chieh-san
Sun Tso-pin
Wang Chao

Wang En-mao
Wang Feng
Wang Wei-chou
Yü I-fu

Nationalities Affairs

Chang Chih-i
Chi Ya-t'ai
Chou Lin
Chou Pao-chung
Chu Te-hai

K'uei Pi
Li Wei-han
Liao Chih-kao
Liu Ko-p'ing
Ma Yü-huai

P'ing Chieh-san
Saifudin
Sang-chi-yueh-hsi
Shirob Jaltso
Ulanfu

Wang Chao
Wang Feng
Wei Kuo-ch'ing
Yang Ching-jen

95. Women's Work

Chang Ch'in-ch'iu
Chang Yun
Ch'en Shao-min
Ch'ien Ying
Hsiang Ching-yü

Li Chien-chen
Li Te-ch'üan
Lo Ch'iung
Ma Wen-jui
Ou Meng-chueh

Ou T'ang-liang
Shih Liang
Shuai Meng-ch'i
Sung Ch'ing-ling

Teng Ying-ch'ao
Ts'ai Ch'ang
Ts'ao Meng-chün
Yang Yun-yü

96. Youth Work

Chang T'ai-lei
Ch'en Ch'ang-hao
Ch'en Chia-k'ang
Ch'en Chung-ching
Ch'en Kung-po
Ch'en P'ei-hsien
Chiang Nan-hsiang
Ch'ien Chün-jui
Ch'ien Li-jen
Ch'ien San-ch'iang
Ch'in Pang-hsien

Feng Wen-pin
Hsiao Ch'u-nü
Hsiao Hua
Hsu Li-ch'ün
Hu Ch'i-li
Hu Ch'iao-mu
Hu K'o-shih
Hu Yao-pang
Huang Ching
Huang Hua
Jen Pi-shih

Jung Kao-t'ang
K'ai Feng
Kuan Hsiang-ying
Li Ch'ang
Li Ch'iu-shih
Liao Ch'eng-chih
Liu Chih-tan
Liu Hsi-yuan
Lu P'ing
Lu Ting-i
Mao Tse-min

Ou T'ang-liang
P'eng T'ao
Teng Chung-hsia
Teng Fa
Ts'ai Ho-sen
Wang Jo-fei
Wang Wei
Wu Hsueh-ch'ien
Yang Ching-jen
Yun Tai-ying

Glossary-Name Index

The Glossary–Name Index contains approximately 1,750 names.

The names of the 433 biographies are set in italics.

See is a cross-reference to the biography or appendix in which a person is mentioned.

Alt. (alternate name for) is used to indicate pseudonyms, aliases, or any other name by which the individual in question is known.

Special note should be made of the fact that the only appendix following major entries is Appendix 51, which deals with the elections to the Central Committee at the Ninth Party Congress in April 1969. No information about the congress is contained in the biographies of the major entries.

A few familiar Chinese personalities, usually from the Republican period, and non-Oriental language names, have been omitted from the Glossary–Name Index. Notable examples include Roosevelt, Yuan Shih-k'ai, Sun Yat-sen, and Chiang Kai-shek.

The glossary does not list organizations or special terms, but the biographies have romanizations where it seemed appropriate. The overwhelming majority of special terms and organizations mentioned in the text are listed in one of the following easily available books:

Mary Clabaugh Wright, ed., *China in Revolution: The First Phase, 1900–1913* (New Haven, Conn., 1968), pp. 477–488.

Chow Tse-tsung, *Research Guide to the May Fourth Movement: Intellectual Revolution in Modern China, 1915–1924* (Cambridge, Mass., 1963).

C. Martin Wilbur and Julie Lien-ying How, eds., *Documents on Communism, Nationalism, and Soviet Advisers in China, 1918–1927* (New York, 1956), pp. 537–547.

Conrad Brandt, Benjamin Schwartz, and John K. Fairbank, *A Documentary History of Chinese Communism* (Cambridge, Mass., 1952), pp. 515–540.

Tso-liang Hsiao, *Power Relations within the Chinese Communist Movement, 1930–1934* (Seattle, Wash., 1961), pp. 313–352.

Franz Schurman, *Ideology and Organization in Communist China* (2nd ed., Berkeley, Calif., 1968), pp. xvii–xxiii.

There is no standard work containing a glossary for organizations in China since 1949. The annual editions of the *Jen-min shou-ts'e* list hundreds of organizations, but these do not provide an English rendering.

A Chin	阿 金	See Li Wei-han
A-i-mu	阿衣木	See Saifudin
A-p'ei	阿沛	See Chang Kuo-hua,
A-wang-chin-mei	阿旺晋美	apps. 63, 66
Ah [Ch'ing] Hsiang		Alt. A Chin
Ah Ying	阿 英	Alt. Ch'ien Hsing-ts'un
Ahyimu		Alt. A-i-mu
Ai Ch'ing	艾 青	See Chou Yang,

		Ting Ling
Ai Szu-ch'i	艾思奇	
Akhmedjan Kasimi		See Saifudin
An T'i-ch'eng	安體誠	See Li Ta-chao, Teng Chung-hsia
An Tzu-wen	安子文	See app. 51
Batochir		Alt. Li Yü-chih
Burhan Shahidi	鮑爾漢	
Ch'ai Ch'eng-wen	柴成文	See app. 82

Chao Te-tsun	趙德尊	hua See Chang Ch'i-lung, Han Kuang, Kao Kang, Li Ch'ang, Ouyang Ch'in, Yü I-fu, apps. 57, 66
Chao Tzu-hsuan	趙自選	See Chang T'ai-lei
Chao Tzu-yang	趙紫阳	
Chao Ying	趙 瑛	See Li K'o-nung
Chao Yun	趙 雲	Alt. K'ang Sheng
Ch'en A-chin	陳阿金	See app. 46
Ch'en Ch'ang	陳 昌	Alt. Ch'en Chang-fu
Ch'en Chang-fu	陳章甫	See Mao Tse-tung
Ch'en Ch'ang-hao	陳昌浩	
Ch'en Ch'eng	陳 誠	See Chou En-lai, Kuo Mo-jo
Ch'en Cheng-jen	陳正人	See app. 51
Ch'en Ch'i-han	陳奇涵	
Ch'en Ch'i-hsia	陳企霞	See Chou Yang
Ch'en Chia-k'ang	陳家康	
Ch'en Chia-keng	陳嘉庚	See Ch'en Po-ta, Fang Fang, Hu Yü-chih, apps. 58, 65
Ch'en Ch'iao-nien	陳喬年	See Ch'en Tu-hsiu, Ch'en Yen-nien
Ch'en Chih-fang	陳志方	See app. 82
Ch'en Chih-mei	陳志梅	Alt. Ch'en Po-ta
Ch'en Chiung-ming	陳炯明	See Ch'en Keng, Ch'en Kung-po, Ch'en Tu-hsiu, Chou En-lai, Chou Shih-ti, Fang Fang, Hsu Hsiang-ch'ien, Lo Ping-hui, P'eng P'ai, Tso Ch'üan, Yeh Chien-ying, Yeh T'ing
Ch'en Chung-ching	陳忠經	
Ch'en, Eugene		Alt. Ch'en Yu-jen
Ch'en Feng	陳 楓	See app. 82
Ch'en Fu-yuan	陳福元	See app. 46
Ch'en Hai-sung	陳海松	See Li Hsien-nien
Ch'en Ho-fa	陳和發	See app. 50
Ch'en Hsi-lien	陳錫聯	
Ch'en Hsiang-sheng	陳祥生	See app. 46
Ch'en Hsien-jui	陳先瑞	See app. 50
Ch'en Hsin-jen	陳辛仁	See app. 82
Ch'en Hsiu-liang	陳修良	See Sha Wen-han
Ch'en Hua-t'ang	陳華堂	See app. 50

Ch'en Hui-ch'ing	陳慧清	See Teng Fa
Ch'en Hung-shih	陳洪時	See app. 46
Ch'en I	陳 毅	
Ch'en Jen-ch'i	陳仁麒	See apps. 50, 67
Chen, K. P.		Alt. Ch'en Kuang-fu
Ch'en K'ai-ch'u	陳開初	Alt. Ch'en Hsi-lien
Ch'en Kan-feng	陳敢峰	See app. 50
Ch'en K'ang	陳 康	See apps. 50, 68
Ch'en K'ang-pai	陳康白	See Li Ch'ang
Ch'en Keng	陳 賡	
Ch'en K'o-han	陳克寒	See Hu Ch'iao-mu
Ch'en Kuang	陳 光	See Hsiao Hua, Lo Jung-huan, Yang Te-chih, app. 46
Ch'en Kuang-fu	陳光甫	See Chi Ch'ao-ting
Ch'en Kung-po	陳公博	
Ch'en Kuo-fu	陳果夫	See Ch'en Po-ta
Ch'en Lei	陳 雷	See app. 66
Ch'en Li-fu	陳立夫	See Ch'en Po-ta, Shirob Jaltso
Ch'en Li-yun	陳励耘	See app. 50
Ch'en Lu	陳 簏	See Li Li-san
Ch'en Man-yuan	陳漫遠	See app. 51
Ch'en Ming	陳 明	See Huang Chen
Ch'en Ming-jen	陳明仁	See Huang K'o-ch'eng, Lin Piao, Yuan Jen-yuan, app. 66
Ch'en Ming-shu	陳銘樞	See Chang Yun-i, K'ai Feng, Liu Ko-p'ing, P'eng Te-huai, Yuan Jen-yuan, apps. 58, 65
Chen Pan-tsu		Alt. Ch'en T'an-ch'iu
Ch'en P'ei-hsien	陳丕顯	See app. 51
Ch'en P'i-hsien		Alt. Ch'en P'ei-hsien
Ch'en Ping-sheng	陳炳生	See Su Chao-cheng
Ch'en Po-ta	陳伯達	
Ch'en Po-ts'un	陳伯村	See Kao Kang, Lin Feng
Ch'en Shao-min	陳少敏	See app. 51
Ch'en Shao-yü	陳紹禹	See app. 51
Ch'en Shih-ch'ü	陳士榘	See app. 51
Ch'en Shou-ch'ang	陳壽昌	See app. 46
Ch'en Shu-liang	陳叔亮	See Wang Yu-p'ing, app. 82
Ch'en Shu-t'ung	陳叔通	See Hsu Ti-hsin, Li Wei-han, apps. 58, 63, 69
Ch'en Sung-nien	陳松年	See Ch'en Tu-hsiu
Ch'en Ta-fan	陳大凡	See app. 66

Ku Ching	顧　静	See Hui Yü-yü
Ku Cho-hsin	顧卓新	
Ku Chu-t'ung	顧祝同	See Ch'en I, Su Yü, T'an Chen-lin, Yeh T'ing
Ku Hsiao-po	谷小波	See app. 82
Ku Hsiung-i	谷雄一	See Po I-po
Ku Mu	谷　牧	
Ku Shun-chang	顧順章	See Ch'en Keng, Ch'in Pang-hsien, Chou En-lai, Hsiang Chung-fa, Li K'o-nung, Li Wei-han, Yun Tai-ying
Ku Ta-ch'uan	顧大川	See Li Ch'ang
Ku Ta-ts'un	古大存	
Ku Tso-lin	顧作霖	See Shao Shih-p'ing, app. 46
Kuan Ch'un-hsiang	關春香	See app. 46
Kuan Hsiang-ying	關向應	
Kuan Wen-wei	管文蔚	See Ch'en I, Chi Fang, Chung Ch'i-kuang, Lo Ping-hui, app. 66
Kuan Ying	關　英	See app. 46
Kuang Chi-hsun	鄺繼勛	See Ho Lung, Hsu Hsiang-ch'ien
Kuang Chu-ch'üan	廣朱權	See app. 46
Kuang Jen-nung	鄺任農	See app. 50
K'uang Piao	曠　彪	See app. 46
K'uei Pi	奎　璧	See app. 51
Kung Ch'u	龔　楚	See Ch'en I, Teng Fa, Yang Shang-k'uei
K'ung, H. H.		Alt. K'ung Hsiang-hsi
K'ung Ho-ch'ung	孔荷寵	See Fang Chih-min, Lo Ping-hui, app. 46
K'ung Hsiang-hsi	孔祥熙	See Ch'en Po-ta, Chi Ch'ao-ting, Meng Yung-ch'ien, Sung Ch'ing-ling
Kung P'eng	龔　澎	See Chang Han-fu, Ch'iao Kuan-hua
Kung P'u-sheng	龔普生	See Chang Han-fu, Ch'iao Kuan-hua
K'ung Shih-ch'üan	孔石泉	See app. 50
K'ung Shu-an	孔書安	See app. 46
K'ung Te-chih	孔德祉	See Shen Yen-ping
Kung Tzu-jung	龔子榮	
Kung Wei-hang	龔維航	See Ch'iao Kuan-hua

K'ung Yuan	孔　原	See app. 51
Kuo Ch'un-t'ao	郭春濤	See Liao Lu-yen
Kuo Feng	郭　峯	See Kao Kang, app. 57
Kuo Hung-chieh	郭宏杰	See app. 50
Kuo K'ai-chen	郭開貞	Alt. Kuo Mo-jo
Kuo Liang	郭　亮	See Ho Lung, Hsia Hsi, Mao Tse-tung, Wang Chen
Kuo Lin-hsiang	郭林祥	See app. 68
Kuo Ming-ch'iu	郭明秋	See Lin Feng, P'eng T'ao
Kuo Mo-jo	郭沫若	See app. 51
Kuo Ping-sheng	郭炳生	See P'eng Hsueh-feng
Kuo Po	郭　博	See Kuo Mo-jo
Kuo Po-ho	郭伯和	See Ch'en T'an-ch'iu
Kuo Shu-shen	郭述申	See app. 46
Kuo T'ien-min	郭天民	See Li Hsien-nien
Kuo Ying-ch'iu	郭影秋	See Yü I-ch'uan, app. 66
Kuo Yü-feng	郭玉峰	See app. 50
La-hsi-ta	拉希达	See Burhan Shahidi
Lai Chi-fa	賴際發	See app. 51
Lai Ch'uan-chu	賴傳珠	
Lai Jo-yü	賴若愚	
Lai Mei-yü	賴美玉	See app. 46
Lai Ya-li	賴亞力	See app. 82
Lan I-nung	藍亦農	See app. 50
Lan Jung-yü	藍榮玉	See app. 50
Lan Kung-wu	藍公武	See Yang Hsiu-feng, apps. 61, 65
Lan P'ing	藍　蘋	Alt. Chiang Ch'ing
Lee, J. S.		Alt. Li Szu-kuang
Lee, Jonguei Su-kuang		Alt. Li Szu-kuang
Lei Ching-t'ien	雷經天	See Chang Yun-i
Lei Jen-min	雷任民	
Li Ang	李　昂	See Chou I-ch'ün
Li Ch'ang	李　昌	See app. 51
Li Ch'ang-ch'ing	李常青	See app. 57
Li Chang-ta	李章達	See app. 58
Li Che-jen	李哲人	
Li Chen	李　震	See app. 50
Li Chen	李　貞	See Kan Szu-ch'i
Li Ch'eng-chia	李成甲	See app. 46
Li Ch'eng-fang	李成芳	See app. 68
Li Ch'i-ming	李啓明	See Chao Po-p'ing, app. 66
Li Chi-po		Alt. Li Chieh-po
Li Chi-shen	李濟琛	See Chang T'ai-lei, Chang Wen-t'ien, Chang Yun-i, Chi Fang, Chou Shih-

Shen Chün-ju	沈鈞儒	See Fan Ch'ang-chiang, Sha Ch'ien-li, Shih Liang, Wu Kai-chih, apps. 58, 60, 63
Shen Hsuan-lu	沈玄盧	See Yang Ming-chai
Shen Hung	沈鴻	
Shen Mao-kung	申茂功	See app. 50
Shen Pao-ying	潘葆英	See Yun Tai-ying
Shen P'u	沈譜	See Fan Ch'ang-chiang
Shen Ting-i	沈定一	See Chang T'ai-lei, Ch'en Tu-hsiu, Ch'ü Ch'iu-pai, Lin Po-ch'ü
Shen Tse-min	沈澤民	
Shen Ts'ung-wen	沈從文	See Ting Ling
Shen Tuan-hsien	沈端先	Alt. Hsia Yen
Shen Tzu-chiu	沈茲九	See Chin Chung-hua, Hu Yü-chih
Shen Yen-ping	沈雁冰	
Shen Yueh	沈越	See app. 66
Sheng P'ei-hua	盛丕華	See app. 65
Sheng Shih-ts'ai	盛世才	See Burhan Shahidi, Chang Chih-i, Chang Tzu-i, Ch'en Shao-yü, Ch'en T'an-ch'iu, Ch'en Yun, Chou Hsiao-chou, Ch'ü Ch'iu-pai, Han Kuang, K'ang Sheng, Ma Ming-fang, Mao Tse-min, Saifudin, Shen Yen-ping, Su Chao-cheng, Teng Fa, T'eng Tai-yuan
Shih Hsun-ch'uan	史訓川	See Li Ch'iu-shih
Shih Liang	史良	
Shih Min	史敏	See Hsu Te-heng
Shih Shao-hua	石少華	See app. 50
Shih Ts'un-t'ung	施存統	See Ch'ü Ch'iu-pai, Yang Ming-chai
Shih Yang	施洋	Alt. Chao Shih-yen
Shih Yang	施洋	See Hsiang Chung-fa
Shih Ying	石英	Alt. Chao Shih-yen
Shirob Jaltso	喜饒嘉措	
Shu Chi-ch'eng	舒積成	See app. 50
Shu T'ung	舒同	See app. 51
Shuai Meng-ch'i	帥孟奇	See app. 51
Siao, Emi		Alt. Hsiao San

Songgi Ish		Alt. Sang-chi-yueh-hsi
Soong, Charles Jones		See Sung Ch'ing-ling
Soong Ching Ling		Alt. Sung Ch'ing-ling
Soong, T. V.		Alt. Sung Tzu-wen
Strakhov		Alt. Ch'ü Ch'iu-pai
Su Chao-cheng	蘇兆徵	
Su Chen-hua	蘇振華	See app. 51
Su Ching	蘇静	See app. 50
Su Ching-kuan	蘇井觀	See Chang Ch'in-ch'iu
Su Hui	蘇惠	See Fang Fang
Su Man-ju	蘇曼殊	See Li K'o-nung
Su Wen	蘇汶	See Ch'ü Ch'iu-pai
Su Yü	粟裕	
Sun Ch'i-meng	孫起孟	See Hsu Ping
Sun Chih-yuan	孫志遠	
Sun Ch'uan-fang	孫傳芳	See Chao Shih-yen, Chou En-lai, Lo I-nung
Sun Fo	孫科	See Ts'ao Meng-chün
Sun Hsiao-shan	孫小山	See Li Li-san
Sun Hsiao-ts'un	孫曉村	See Ch'ien Chün-jui
Sun Liang-ch'eng	孫良誠	See Hsu Ping
Sun Ping-wen	孫炳文	See Chu Te
Sun Ta-kuang	孫大光	
Sun Tso-pin	孫作賓	
Sun Wen-shu	孫文淑	See Yang Hsiu-feng
Sun Wu	孫武	See Wu Yü-chang
Sun Yat-sen, Mme.		Alt. Sung Ch'ing-ling
Sung Ai-ling	宋藹齡	See Sung Ch'ing-ling
Sung Che-yuan	宋哲元	See Chang Yu-yü, Li Ch'ang
Sung Ch'iao-sheng	宋喬生	See T'an Chen-lin
Sung Ch'ing-ling	宋慶齡	
Sung Hsi-lien	宋希濂	See Burhan Shahidi
Sung I-p'ing	宋一平	See Chiang Nan-hsiang, Li Ch'ang
Sung Jen-ch'iung	宋仁窮	See app. 51
Sung Jih-ch'ang	宋日昌	See app. 66
Sung Mei-ling	宋美齡	See Sung Ch'ing-ling
Sung Pai-min	宋白民	See app. 46
Sung Shao-wen	宋劭文	
Sung Shih-lun	宋時輪	See app. 51
Sung Shuang-lai	宋双來	See app. 50
Sung Tzu-an	宋子安	See Sung Ch'ing-ling
Sung Tzu-liang	宋子良	See Sung Ch'ing-ling
Sung Tzu-wen	宋子文	See Ch'en Po-ta,

Harvard East Asian Series